An Introduction to Modern Philosophy

Examining the Human Condition

Sixth Edition

the late **Alburey Castell**
Donald M. Borchert
Arthur Zucker
Ohio University

Macmillan College Publishing Company
New York
Maxwell Macmillan Canada
Toronto
Maxwell Macmillan International
New York   Oxford   Singapore   Sydney

Editor: Maggie Barbieri
Production Editor: Sharon Lee
Production Manager: Paul Smolenski
Art Coordinator: Vincent A. Smith
Cover Designer: Hothouse Designs, Inc.
Cover art: Reginald Wickham
Artist: Jane Lopez
Electronic Text Management: Ben Ko, Marilyn Wilson Phelps, Matthew Williams

This book was set in Zapf Calligraphic 801 by Macmillan College Publishing Company and was printed and bound by Book Press, Inc. The cover was printed by Phoenix Color Corp.

Macmillan College Publishing Company
866 Third Avenue
New York, NY 10022

Macmillan College Publishing Company is part of the
Maxwell Communication Group of Companies.

Maxwell Macmillan Canada, Inc.
1200 Eglinton Avenue East, Suite 200
Don Mills, Ontario M3C 3N1

Library of Congress Cataloging-in-Publication Data

Castell, Alburey, 1904–1987
    An introduction to modern philosophy : examining the human
condition / Alburey Castell, Donald M. Borchert, and Arthur Zucker.
    —6th ed.
        p.   cm.
    Includes bibliographical references and index.
    ISBN 0-02-320092-8
    1. Philosophy, Modern. 2. Philosophy—Introductions.
I. Borchert, Donald M., 1934–   / II. Zucker, Arthur, 1942–
III. Title. IV. Title: Modern philosophy.
B791.C3   1993
190—dc20   93-6964
                                                  CIP

Printing: 1 2 3 4 5 6 7 8 9   Year: 4 5 6 7.

Acknowledgments

Alfred A. Knopf. ALBERT CAMUS, *The Plague*, Stuart Gilbert, trans., 1972. Copyright © 1948 by Stuart Gilbert. Reprinted by permission of Alfred A. Knopf, Inc.

American Society for Aesthetics. MORRIS WEITZ, "The Role of Theory in Aesthetics," in *The Journal of Aesthetics and Art Criticism* XV, No. 1 (September 1956). Reprinted by permission.

Atheneum. HENRY CLARKE WARREN, trans., "Introduction to the *Jakata* (i.58.81) and the *Mahavagga* (i.21.1)," in *Buddhism in Translation*, 1987.

Bantam Doubleday Dell Publishing Group, Inc. RAYMOND A. MOODY, JR., *The Light Beyond*, copyright © 1988 by Raymond A. Moody, Jr. Used by permission of Bantam Doubleday Dell Publishing Group, Inc.

Beacon Press. VIKTOR E. FRANKL, from *Man's Search for Meaning: An Introduction to Logotherapy*, copyright © 1959, 1962, 1984, 1992 by Viktor E. Frankl. Reprinted by permission of Beacon Press.

Benziger Publishing Company. SAINT THOMAS AQUINAS, *Summa Theologica*, Laurence Shapcote, trans., 1911. Excerpts reprinted by permission.

Brown University. BRAND BLANSHARD, "The New Subjectivism in Ethics," in *Philosophy and Phenomenological Research* 9, No. 3 (March 1949). Reprinted by permission.

Cambridge University Press. NED BLOCK, "What Intuitions About Homunculi Don't Show," in *Behavioral and Brain Sciences*, Vol. 3 (1980). Reprinted with the permission of Cambridge University Press.

Cambridge University Press. BRUCE BRIDGEMAN, "Brains + Progress = Minds," in *Behavioral and Brain Sciences*, Vol. 3 (1980). Reprinted with the permission of Cambridge University Press.

Cambridge University Press. JOHN SEARLE, "Minds, Brains and Programs," in *Behavioral and Brain Sciences*, Vol. 3 (1980). Reprinted with the permission of Cambridge University Press.

Dover Publications, Inc. A. J. AYER, *Language, Truth and Logic*, 2nd ed., 1946. Reprinted by permission.

Frederick Ungar Publishing Co. CORLISS LAMONT, *The Illusion of Immortality*, rev. ed., 1965. Reprinted by permission of the author.

HarperCollins, Publishers, Inc. ANTONY FLEW, *The Presumption of Atheism*, 1976. Reprinted by permission of HarperCollins, Publisher, Inc.

HarperCollins, Publishers, Inc. GILBERT RYLE, *The Concept of Mind*, approximately 20 pages. Copyright © 1949 by Gilbert Ryle. Reprinted by permission of HarperCollins, Publishers, Inc.

HarperCollins, Publishers, Inc. WALTER STACE, *Religion and the Modern Mind*, selected excerpt. Copyright © 1952 by W. T. Stace. Reprinted by permission of HarperCollins, Publishers, Inc.

Harvard University Press. ALVIN I. GOLDMAN, *Epistemology and Cognition*, 1986. Reprinted by permission of the publishers, Cambridge, Mass.: Harvard University Press, copyright © 1986 by the President and Fellows of Harvard College.

Johns Hopkins University Press. HERBERT FEIGL, "The Scientific Outlook: Naturalism and Humanism," in *American Quarterly* 1 (1949). Reprinted by permission.

Macmillan Publishing Company. H. GENE BLOCKER, *Philosophy of Art*, 1979. Reprinted with the permission of Charles Scribner's Sons, an imprint of Macmillan Publishing Company. Copyright © 1979 Gene Blocker.

The New York Times Company. JOHN MARKOFF, "Can Machines Think? Humans Match Wits," *The New York Times*, November 9, 1991. Copyright © 1991 by the New York Times Company.

Oxford University Press. From *The New English Bible*. Copyright © the Delegates of the Oxford University Press and the Syndics of the Cambridge University Press, 1961, 1970, 1989. Reprinted by permission.

Oxford University Press. A. J. AYER, "Demonstration of the Impossibility of Metaphysics," in *Mind* XLIII (1934).

Oxford University Press. RICHARD M. HARE, *The Language of Morals*, 1952. Reprinted by permission of Oxford University Press.

Oxford University Press. A. M. TURING, "Computing Machinery and Intelligence," in *Mind* 59, (1950). Reprinted by permission of Oxford University Press.

Philosophical Library. JEAN-PAUL SARTRE, *Existentialism Is a Humanism*, copyright © 1946. Reprinted by permission.

Prentice Hall. NORMAN MALCOLM, *Knowledge and Certainty*, copyright © 1963 by Norman Malcolm.

Princeton University Press. S. RADHAKRISHNAN AND CHARLES A. MOORE, eds., "Samyutta Nikayo, 5.420," cited in *A Source Book in Indian Philosophy*, 1957. Reprinted by permission.

Princeton University Press. RICHARD RORTY, *Philosophy and the Mirror of Nature*, 1979. Reprinted by permission.

Routledge, Chapman and Hall, Inc. PAUL FEYERABEND, "Introduction" from his *Against Method*, rev. ed., 1988, by permission of the publisher, Routledge, Chapman and Hall, Inc.

Routledge, Chapman and Hall, Inc. ALISON JAGGAR, "Love and Knowledge: Emotion in Feminist Epistemology." Reprinted from *Women, Knowledge and*

Reality, Ann Garry and Marilyn Pearsall, eds., 1989, by permission of the publisher, Routledge, Chapman and Hall, Inc.

Routledge & Kegan Paul Ltd. PETER GEACH, "Immortality," in *God and the Soul*, 1969.

Rowman & Littlefield Publishers. ROBERT ALMEDER, *Death and Personal Survival: The Evidence for Life After Death*, copyright © 1992 by Rowman & Littlefield Publishers. Reprinted by permission.

St. Martin's Press, Inc. DOROTHY EMMET, from *The Moral Prism*, 1979. Reprinted with permission of St. Martin's Press, Incorporated.

SCM Press Ltd. ANTONY FLEW, "Theology and Falsification," in *New Essays in Philosophical Theology*, Antony Flew and Alasdair MacIntyre, eds., 1955, pp. 90-96. Reprinted by permission.

Scientific American, Inc. JERRY FODOR, *The Mind-Body Problem* (January 1981). Reprinted with permission. Copyright © 1981 by Scientific American, Inc. All rights reserved.

Springer-Verlag. JOHN ECCLES, *The Self and Its Brain*, copyright © 1976. Reprinted by permission.

Springer-Verlag. KARL POPPER, *The Self and Its Brain*, copyright © 1976. Reprinted by permission.

Theology Today. JOHN HICK, "Theology and Verification," in *Theology Today* 17 (1960). Reprinted by permission.

University of California Press. C. J. DUCASSE, *Is Life After Death Possible?*, Foerster Lecture Series 2, copyright © 1948 by the Regents of the University of California.

University of California Press. LARRY LAUDEN, *Science and Values: An Essay on the Aims of Science and Their Role in Scientific Debate*, excerpts from Chapter 4, copyright © 1984 The Regents of the University of California.

University of Chicago Press. THOMAS KUHN, "The Structure of Scientific Revolutions," originally published in *International Encyclopedia of Unified Science*, Vol. 2, No. 2, 1962.

University Press of America. ALBERT SCHEVEN, comp., *Swahili Proverbs*, 1985. Reprinted by permission.

Westview Press. KEITH LEHRER, *Theory of Knowledge*, 1990. Reprinted by permission of Westview Press, Boulder, Colorado.

Writers House, Inc. MARTIN LUTHER KING, JR., "Letter from Birmingham Jail, April 16, 1963," from *Why We Can't Wait*. Reprinted by arrangement with The Heirs to the Estate of Martin Luther King, Jr., c/o Joan Daves Agency as agent for the proprietor. Copyright © 1963 by Martin Luther King, Jr., copyright renewed 1991 by Coretta Scott King.

Yale University Press. WILLIAM KELLY SIMPSON, ed., "Wisdom of Ptahhotpe," in *The Literature of Ancient Egypt*, 1972. Excerpts reprinted by permission.

Yale University Press. C. L. STEVENSON, *Ethics and Language*, 1944. Excerpts reprinted by permission.

A Note on the Sixth Edition

This text continues to be aimed at introducing students to the wonder and rigor of philosophical analysis. We have tried for a balance between making things plain to the novice and being true to the rigorous demands of philosophy. This is the justification for our editorial comments breaking up the original sources and for occasional contemporary renderings of older works. Sometimes the material is just too difficult or too long for beginning students, who often need to be reassured that they have actually understood a passage before they are ready to go on.

Each chapter reflects answers to the enduring questions of philosophy. Two new sections have been added to this edition: Chapter 11, *What Is Science: Positivism to Postmodernism,* and an epilogue, *Making Sense Out of Life.* To make room for these and other additions, the chapter on the philosophy of history has been omitted from this edition. The following chapters have been considerably expanded by adding more points of view as represented by contemporary readings: Chapter 2, *Am I a Body and a Mind?*; Chapter 3, *Am I Free or Determined?*; Chapter 4, *Can I Survive Death?*; Chapter 6, *On What Principles Do I Judge Things Right or Wrong?*; and Chapter 10, *When Can I Say "I Know"?*

The text now covers identity theory as well as the cognitive science approach to the mind-body problem, including articles by Jerry Fodor, A. M. Turing, John Searle, and two replies to Searle; also included is Norman Malcolm on other minds and an attempt at a neurophysiological defense of dualism by Sir John Eccles. On the free-will issue, John Bender offers a strong contemporary defense of compatibilism; Karl Popper gives a spirited critique of scientifically based determinism. In the section on immortality, new data on the existence of an afterlife is presented, along with an analysis by Peter Geach of what immortality ought to mean. Bernard Gert and Dorothy Emmet on ethics; Alvin Goldman and Keith Lehrer on epistemology; and Thomas Kuhn, Larry Laudan, Allison Jaggar, Paul Feyerabend, and Richard Rorty on science and the relativism of knowledge round out the additions.

The epilogue shows how a philosophical mind would try to make sense of the question "What is the meaning of life?" We take up non-Western answers in this section so that students can see a broad approach to answers. Given that philosophical questions asked in the Socratic tradition aim at an answer to "What is the good life—a life with meaning?" we see this epilogue as an appropriate end to the book.

We are convinced that these additions and especially the epilogue would be pleasing to Alburey Castell, who edited the first edition in 1943 and continued to be senior editor until his death in 1987.

We would like to thank the Macmillan editor of Philosophy and Religion, Maggie Barbieri, for her enthusiastic support of this revised edition. Our thanks also go to Sharon Lee, the production editor for this book at Macmillan. We were also helped with the permissions by Gina McCormack and Ami Johnston and with copy editing by Peg Gluntz. Chris Delasandry assisted with the compiling of the index. And as always, Alice Donohoe, the Philosophy Department secretary, made everything work.

Naturally, our wives, Mary Ellen and Laurie, have to be thanked, for if anyone suffered through the pains of producing this book, they did.

Donald M. Borchert
Arthur Zucker
Ohio University
Athens, Ohio
August 1993

Contents

What Is Philosophy?

This book is an introduction to philosophy. It is written with the beginning student of philosophy in mind. We must, therefore, try to get clear from the outset what "philosophy" is.

People use the word "philosophy" in a number of contexts. Perhaps you have heard breweries advertise their philosophy of beer making, and innkeepers proclaim their philosophy of innkeeping, and coaches debate their philosophies of football or basketball. When people speak of "philosophy" in these settings they usually take the word to mean "a point of view," or "a personal outlook," or "a personal way or technique for doing something." And while these people use the term "philosophy" quite unhesitatingly, most of them would probably be somewhat reluctant to call themselves philosophers. Indeed, would we not find it rather strange if we heard one of them say, "As a philosopher, I think a hotel should be managed to ensure that every unit turns a profit"?

This hesitancy of people to call themselves "philosophers" at the same time that they find themselves expounding on their "philosophies" of this or that suggests that they sense that the philosophy of the philosopher is something other than a personal point of view or a certain technique for doing something.

What, then, does philosophy mean for the philosopher?

The term "philosophy" is derived from two Greek words: *philein* meaning "to love" and *sophia* meaning "wisdom." *Philosophy*, then, is "the love of wisdom," and a *philosopher* is a "lover of wisdom." According to an ancient tradition, the first person to call himself a "philosopher" was the sixth century B.C. Greek thinker, Pythagoras.

But what does it mean to call oneself a lover of wisdom? And what is this "wisdom" that the philosopher loves, seeks, and pursues? Clearly, what we are looking for is a definition of philosophy. An engaging and instructive way to formulate one is to observe a philosopher in action and then to single out those characteristics of the philosopher which seem to make that person a philosopher. Let us try such an approach, and let us consider as our model philosopher Socrates whose status as a philosopher is eminent and secure. The material we have selected to represent Socrates is basically the account of his trial recorded by one of his most celebrated students, Plato. As you read Plato's account of Socrates defending himself before a citizen jury in Athens almost 2,500 years ago, try to figure out what it is about Socrates that has led people to regard him as a notable philosopher.

SOCRATES

THE EXAMINED LIFE

Socrates was born about 470 B.C.—shortly after the Persian invasions of Greece had been repulsed and just before a golden age of Athenian culture flourished under the leadership of Pericles. From 460 B.C. until his death in 430 B.C., Pericles was the political leader of an increasingly democratic and culturally creative Athens. The flowering of Athenian culture at this time was magnificently symbolized by Pericles' reconstruction of the Acropolis with its new majestic Parthenon—a temple dedicated to the goddess Athena whose colossal statue, carved in gold and ivory by Phidias and set within the Parthenon, reminded the Athenians that their success over the Persians and the glories of their expanding empire were gifts of the gods.

As democracy developed in Athens a key factor in a politician's success became the ability to influence the citizenry through eloquent speeches. Accordingly, when various itinerant scholars called the Sophists—who tried to popularize knowledge and who offered lessons in rhetoric—appeared in Athens during the fifth century B.C., they were sought out by young Athenians with political ambitions. These Sophists concentrated on the techniques of persuasion and refutation. They taught their clientele how to defend and oppose various conflicting opinions with the consequence that serious questions were raised whether or not there was any abiding truth to which all humans could assent. In such an intellectual climate it is not surprising that belief in the traditional gods came to be questioned. Nor is it surprising that the conservative and traditional sectors of Athenian society viewed the teachings of the Sophists with great alarm. Indeed when one of Pericles' friends among the Sophists was prosecuted for his alleged pernicious religious ideas, not even the intervention of Pericles himself could save the Sophist from condemnation.

As Athens entered its protracted struggle with Sparta, the Athenian democracy became the victim of incompetent leadership, treachery, and fickle public opinion, all of which contributed to the humiliating defeat of Athens in 404 B.C. No clearer evidence of the weakness of Athenian democracy can be found than the situation that prevailed in the courts. Citizen juries, which had been introduced by Solon in the sixth century as a court of appeal, were enlarged until they comprised some six thousand jurors. These jurors were subdivided into smaller juries, each of which contained five hundred and one jurors. To enable even the poorest of citizens to leave their work to participate in juries, the Athenians legislated payment for jury service. This truly noble idea, however, was corrupted when the state treasury became exhausted and juries found it convenient to lay heavy fines on accused citizens, irrespective of their guilt or innocence, in order to insure that the funds would be available for their salaries. In this environment, the additional decadent practice developed whereby wealthy citizens would be accused of fictitious crimes to entice them to settle out of court with their accusers rather than face the greed of a citizen jury. It was before such a jury that Socrates was hauled in 399 B.C. to respond to charges that he was corrupting the youth of Athens with his teachings. And it is to Socrates' defense on that occasion that we wish to direct our attention to view a philosopher in action.

Bear in mind that Athenian society was far from stable. In the aftermath of Sparta's victory over Athens, the nobles were struggling with the democratic masses for control of the state; and the ideas of the Sophists were vying with the traditional beliefs for the intellectual commitment of the citizenry. It was not an enviable time to stand before a citizen's jury in Athens. Yet the seventy-year-old Socrates presents a courageous and noble defense.

Socrates begins with a plea that he be allowed to speak in his accustomed manner, the power of which resides not in the force of eloquence but in the force of truth.

How you, O Athenians, have been affected by my accusers, I cannot tell; but I know that they almost made me forget who I was—so persuasively did they speak; and yet they have hardly uttered a word of truth. But of the many falsehoods told by them, there was one which quite amazed me—I mean when they said that you should be upon your guard and not allow yourselves to be deceived by the force of my eloquence. To say this, when they were certain to be detected as soon as I opened my lips and proved myself to be anything but a great speaker, did indeed appear to me most shameless—unless by the force of eloquence they mean the force of truth; for if such is their meaning, I admit that I am eloquent. But in how different a way from theirs! Well, as I was saying, they have scarcely spoken the truth at all; but from me you shall hear the whole truth; not, however, delivered after their manner in a set oration duly ornamented with words and phrases. No, by heaven! but I shall use the words and arguments which occur to me at the moment; for I am confident in the justice of my cause; at my time of life I ought not to be appearing before you, O men of Athens, in the character of a juvenile orator—let no one expect it of me. And I must beg of you to grant me a favor—if I defend myself in my accustomed manner and you hear me using the words which I have been in the habit of using in the agora, at the tables of the money-changers, or anywhere else, I would ask you not to be surprised, and not to interrupt me on this account. For I am more than seventy years of age, and appearing now for the first time in a court of law, I am quite a stranger to the language of the place; and therefore I would have you regard me as if I were really a stranger, whom you would excuse if he spoke in his native tongue and after the fashion of his country—Am I making an unfair request of you? Never mind the manner, which may or may not be good; but think only of the truth of my words, and give heed to that; let the speaker speak truly and the judge decide justly.

Socrates proceeds to identify the charges leveled against him. It is alleged that he is a student of the physical world, with the implication that such studies are incompatible with traditional religious belief. After all, if you demythologize heavenly bodies by saying the sun is rock and the moon is earth, have you not discarded the notion that the sun and the moon are divine beings? Furthermore, it is alleged that Socrates has traditional values all mixed up when he debates with people. That is to say, what most people would regard as "good," he considered to be "evil," and vice versa. And furthermore, he accepts money from people to teach them these problematic doctrines. These accusations had been associated with Socrates for many years and were reinforced publicly in the play, *Clouds*, by Aristophanes, who made Socrates appear as a shiftless, ridiculous wizard with words.

Well, then, I must make my defence, and endeavor to clear away in a short time, a slander which has lasted a long time. May I succeed, if to succeed be for my good and yours, or likely to avail me in my cause! The task is not an easy one; I quite understand the nature of it. And so leaving the event with God, in obedience to the law, I will now make my defence.

I will begin at the beginning, and ask what is the accusation which has given rise to the slander of me, and in fact has encouraged Meletus to prefer this charge against me. Well, what do the slanderers say? They shall be my prosecutors, and I will sum up their words in an affidavit: "Socrates is an evil-doer, and a curious person, who searches into things under the earth and in heaven, and he makes the worse appear the better cause; and he teaches the aforesaid doctrines to others." Such is the nature of the accusation; it is just what you have yourselves seen in the comedy of Aristophanes, who has introduced a man whom he calls Socrates, going about and saying that he walks in air, and talking a deal of nonsense concerning matters of which I do not pretend to know either much or little—not that I mean to speak disparagingly of any one who is a student of natural philosophy. I should be very sorry if Meletus could bring so grave a charge against me. But the simple truth is, O Athenians, that I have nothing to do with physical speculations. Very many of those here present are witnesses to the truth of this, and to them I appeal. Speak then, you who have heard me, and tell your neighbors whether any of you have ever known me hold forth in few words or in many upon such matters. . . . You hear the answer. And from what they say of this part of the charge you will be able to judge of the truth of the rest.

As little foundation is there for the report that I am a teacher, and take money; this accusation has no more truth in it than the other. Although, if a man were really able to instruct mankind, to receive money for giving instruction would, in my opinion, be an honor to him. There is Gorgias of Leontium, and Prodicus of Ceos, and Hippias of Elis, who go the round of the cities, and are able to persuade the young men to leave their own citizens by whom they might be taught for nothing, and come to them whom they not only pay, but are thankful if they may be allowed to pay them.

I dare say, Athenians, that some one among you will reply, 'Yes, Socrates, but what is the origin of these accusations which are brought against you; there must have been something strange which you have been doing? All these rumors and this talk about you would never have arisen if you had been like other men; tell us, then, what is the cause of them, for we should be sorry to judge hastily of you.' Now I regard this as a fair challenge, and I will endeavor to explain to you the reason why I am called wise and have such an evil fame. Please to attend then. And although some of you may think that I am joking, I declare that I will tell you the entire truth. Men of Athens, this reputation of mine has come of a certain sort of wisdom which I possess. If you ask me what kind of wisdom, I reply, wisdom such as may perhaps be attained by man, for to that extent I am inclined to believe that I am wise; whereas the persons of whom I was speaking have a superhuman wisdom, which I may fail to describe, because I have it not myself; and he who says that I have, speaks falsely, and is taking away my character. And here, O men of Athens, I must beg you not to interrupt me, even, if I seem to say something extravagant. For the word which I will speak is not mine. I will refer you to a witness who is worthy of credit; that witness shall be the God of Delphi—he will tell you about my wisdom, if I have any, and of what sort it is. You must have known Chaerephon; he was early a friend of mine, and also a friend of yours, for he shared in the recent exile of the people, and returned with you. Well, Chaerephon, as you know, was very impetuous in all his doings, and he went to Delphi and boldly asked the oracle to tell him whether—as I was saying, I must beg you not to interrupt—he asked the oracle to tell him whether any one was wiser than I was, and the Pythian prophetess answered, that there was no man wiser. Chaerephon is dead himself; but his brother, who is in court, will confirm the truth of what I am saying.

Why do I mention this? Because I am going to explain to you why I have such an evil name. When I heard the answer, I said to myself, What can the god mean? and what is the interpretation of his riddle? for I know that I have no wisdom, small or great. What then can he mean when he says that I am the wisest of men? And yet he is a god, and cannot lie; that would be against his nature. After long consideration, I thought of a method of trying the question. I reflect that if I could only find a man wiser than myself, then I might go to the god with a refutation in my hand. I should say to him, 'Here is a man who is wiser than I am; but you said that I was the wisest.' Accordingly I went to one who had the reputation of wisdom, and observed him— his name I need not mention; he was a politician whom I selected for examination— and the result was as follows: When I began to talk with him, I could not help thinking that he was not really wise, although he was thought wise by many, and still wiser by himself; and thereupon I tried to explain to him that he thought himself wise, but was not really wise; and the consequence was that he hated me, and his enmity was shared by several who were present and heard me. So I left him, saying to myself, as I went away: Well, although I do not suppose that either of us knows anything really beautiful and good, I am better off than he is,—for he knows nothing, and thinks that he knows; I neither know nor think that I know. In this latter particular, then, I seem to have slightly the advantage of him. Then I went to another who had still higher pretensions to wisdom, and my conclusion was exactly the same. Whereupon I made another enemy of him, and of many others besides him.

Then I went to one man after another, being not unconscious of the enmity which I provoked, and I lamented and feared this: But necessity was laid upon me,— the word of God, I thought, ought to be considered first. And I said to myself, Go I must to all who appear to know, and find out the meaning of the oracle. And I swear to you, Athenians, by the dog I swear—for I must tell you the truth—the result of my mission was just this: I found that the men most in repute were all but the most fool- ish; and that others less esteemed were really wiser and better.

This inquisition had led to my having many enemies of the worst and most dangerous kind, and has given occasion also to many calumnies. And I am called wise, for my hearers always imagine that I myself possess the wisdom which I find wanting in others; but the truth is, O men of Athens, that God only is wise; and by his answer he intends to show that the wisdom of men is worth little or nothing; he is not speaking of Socrates, he is only using my name by way of illustration, as if he said, He, O men, is the wisest, who, like Socrates, knows that his wisdom is in truth worth nothing. And so I go about the world, obedient to the god, and search and make enquiry into the wisdom of any one, whether citizen or stranger, who appears to be wise; and if he is not wise, then in vindication of the oracle I show him that he is not wise; and my occupation quite absorbs me, and I have no time to give either to any public matter of interest or to any concern of my own, but I am in utter poverty by reason of my devotion to the god.

There is another thing—young men of the richer classes, who have not much to do, come about me of their own accord; they like to hear the pretenders examined, and they often imitate me, and proceed to examine others; there are plenty of persons, as they quickly discover, who think that they know something but really know little or nothing; and then those who are examined by them instead of being angry with themselves are angry with me: This confounded Socrates, they say; this villainous misleader of youth!—and if somebody asks them, Why, what evil does he practise or teach? they do not know, and cannot tell; but in order that they may not appear to be at a loss, they repeat the ready-made charges which are used against all philosophers about teaching things up in the clouds and under the earth, and having no gods, making the worse appear the better cause; for they do not like to confess that their pretence of knowledge has been detected—which is the truth; and as they are numerous and ambitious and energetic, and are drawn up in battle array and have persuasive tongues, they have filled your ears with their loud and inveterate calumnies. And this is the reason why my three accusers, Meletus and Anytus and Lycon, have set upon me; Meletus, who has a quarrel with me on behalf of the poets; Anytus, on behalf of the craftsmen and politicians; Lycon, on behalf of the rhetoricians; and as I said at the beginning, I cannot expect to get rid of such a mass of calumny all in a moment. And this, O men of Athens, is the truth and the whole truth; I have concealed nothing, I have dissembled nothing. And yet, I know that my plainness of speech makes them hate me, and what is their hatred but a proof that I am speaking the truth?—Hence has arisen the prejudice against me; and this is the reason of it, as you will find out either in this or in any future enquiry.

In brief, Socrates explains that the evil opinion about himself held by many is the result of his effort to understand what an oracle had said. In the ancient city of Delphi there was a shrine to which the Greeks would sometimes go in quest of prophetic answers to their questions. The human attendants at the shrine, speaking for the god Apollo, had declared that no one was wiser than Socrates. To challenge that saying of the oracle, Socrates sought out allegedly wise people in order to find someone wiser than himself. With his penetrating questions, however, he exposed their pretensions to wisdom and thereby generated hostility in those he had questioned.

For example, a short time before he appeared in court, Socrates encountered his friend Euthyphro and discovered that he, like Socrates, was involved in litigation. After describing the charges that Meletus was bringing against him, Socrates asked Euthyphro to explain his suit. Much to Socrates' amazement, Euthyphro declared that he was prosecuting his own father for "murder" because of the way he let a slave die. Euthyphro firmly believed that, in prosecuting his father, he was exhibiting a high level of piety even though, according to the conventional wisdom of the time, disloyalty to one's father seemed to be an enormously impious act. Euthyphro describes the alleged murder:

> Now the man who is dead was a poor dependant of mine who worked for us as a field labourer on our farm in Naxos, and one day in a fit of drunken passion he got into a quarrel with one of our domestic servants and slew him. My father bound him hand and foot and threw him into a ditch, and then sent to Athens to ask of a diviner what he should do with him. Meanwhile he never attended to him and took no care about him, for he regarded him as a murderer; and thought that no great harm would be done even if he did die. Now this was just what happened. For such was the effect of cold and hunger and chains upon him, that before the messenger returned from the diviner, he was dead. And my father and family are angry with me for taking the part of the murderer and prosecuting my father. They say that he did not kill him, and that if he did, the dead man was a murderer, and I ought not to take any notice, for that a son is impious who prosecutes a father. Which shows, Socrates, how little they know what the gods think about piety and impiety.

Euthyphro goes on to claim that he, more than any other person, has exact knowledge about piety and impiety, and it is this knowledge that gives him the confidence that he is being most pious in prosecuting his father. Here, then, is one of those people who claims to have unusual wisdom, and from whom Socrates is prepared to learn. Alas, however, the incisive questions of Socrates reveal that Euthyphro's purported theological wisdom is confused and internally inconsistent. Here is part of the dialogue.

> *Soc.* And what is piety, and what is impiety?
>
> *Euth.* Piety is doing as I am doing; that is to say, prosecuting any one who is guilty of murder, sacrilege, or of any similar crime—whether he be your father or mother, or whoever he may be—that makes no difference; and not to prosecute them is impiety. And please to consider, Socrates, what a notable proof I will give you of the truth of my words, a proof which I have already given to others:—of the principle, I mean, that the impious, whoever he may be, ought not to go unpunished. For do not men regard Zeus as the best and most righteous of the gods?—and yet they admit that he bound his father (Cronos) because he wickedly devoured his sons, and that he too had punished his own father (Uranus) for a similar reason, in a nameless manner. And yet when I proceed against my father, they are angry with me. So inconsistent are they in their way of talking when the gods are concerned, and when I am concerned.
>
> *Soc.* And do you really believe that the gods fought with one another, and had dire quarrels, battles, and the like, as the poets say, and as you may see represented in the world of the great artists? Are all these tales of the gods true, Euthyphro?
>
> *Euth.* Yes, Socrates; and, as I was saying, I can tell you, if you would like to hear them, many other things about the gods which would quite amaze you.

Soc. I dare say; and you shall tell me them at some other time when I have leisure. But just at present I would rather hear from you a more precise answer, which you have not as yet given, my friend, to the question, What is "piety"? When asked, you only replied, Doing as you do, charging your father with murder.

Euth. And what I said was true, Socrates.

Soc. No doubt, Euthyphro; but you would admit that there are many other pious acts?

Euth. There are.

Soc. Remember that I did not ask you to give me two or three examples of piety, but to explain the general idea which makes all pious things to be pious.

Euth. I remember.

Soc. Tell me what is the nature of this idea, and then I shall have a standard to which I may look, and by which I may measure actions, whether yours or those of any one else, and then I shall be able to say that such and such an action is pious, such another impious.

Euth. I will tell you, if you like.

Soc. I should very much like.

Euth. Piety, then, is that which is dear to the gods, and impiety is that which is not dear to them.

Soc. Very good, Euthyphro; you have now given me the sort of answer which I wanted. But whether what you say is true or not I cannot as yet tell, although I make no doubt that you will prove the truth of your words.

Euth. Of course.

Soc. Come, then, and let us examine what we are saying. That thing or person which is dear to the gods is pious, and that thing or person which is hateful to the gods is impious, these two being the extreme opposites of one another. Was not that said?

Euth. It was.

Soc. And well said?

Euth. Yes, Socrates, I thought so; it was certainly said.

Soc. And further, Euthyphro, the gods were admitted to have enmities and hatreds and differences?

Euth. Yes, that was also said.

Soc. And what sort of difference creates enmity and anger? Suppose for example that you and I, my good friend, differ about a number; do differences of this sort make us enemies and set us at variance with one another? Do we not go at once to arithmetic, and put an end to them by a sum?

Euth. True.

Soc. Or suppose that we differ about magnitudes, do we not quickly mend the differences by measuring?

Euth. Very true.

Soc. And we end a controversy about heavy and light by resorting to a weighing machine?

Euth. To be sure.

Soc. But what differences are there which cannot be thus decided, and which therefore make us angry and set us at enmity with one another? I dare say the answer does not occur to you at the moment, and therefore I will suggest that these enmities arise when the matters of differences are just and unjust, good and evil, honorable and dishonorable. Are not these the points about which men differ, and about which when we are unable satisfactorily to decide our differences, you and I and all of us quarrel, when we do quarrel?

Euth. Yes, Socrates, the nature of the differences about which we quarrel is such as you describe.

Soc. And the quarrels of the gods, noble Euthyphro, when they occur, are of a like nature.

Euth. Certainly they are.

Soc. They have differences of opinion, as you say, about good and evil, just and unjust, honorable and dishonorable; there would have been no quarrels among them, if there had been no such differences—would there now?

Euth. You are quite right.

Soc. Does not every man love that which he deems noble and just and good, and hate the opposite of them?

Euth. Very true.

Soc. But, as you say, people regard the same things, some as just and others as unjust, about these they dispute; and so there arise wars and fightings among them.

Euth. Very true.

Soc. Then the same things are hated by the gods and loved by the gods, and are both hateful and dear to them?

Euth. True.

Soc. And upon this view the same things, Euthyphro, will be pious and also impious?

Euth. So I should suppose.

Soc. Then, my friend, I remark with surprise that you have not answered the question which I asked. For I certainly did not ask you to tell me what action is both pious and impious; but now it would seem that what is loved by the gods is also hated by them. And therefore, Euthyphro, in thus chastising your father you may very likely be doing what is agreeable to Zeus but disagreeable to Cronos or Uranus, and what is acceptable to Hephaestus but unacceptable to Here, and there may be other gods who have similar differences of opinion.

The dialogue continues as Euthyphro adjusts and readjusts his definitions of piety and impiety in response to the pressing questions of Socrates. The discussion closes with Euthyphro being driven to admit that either his claims at the beginning of the dialogue are false or his claims at the end of the dialogue are false. Both cannot be true.

Soc. Then either we were wrong in our former assertion; or, if we were right then, we are wrong now.

Euth.   One of the two must be true.

Soc.   Then we must begin again and ask, What is piety? That is an enquiry which I shall never be weary of pursuing as far as in me lies; and I entreat you not to scorn me, but to apply your mind to the utmost, and tell me the truth. For, if any man knows, you are he; and therefore I must detain you, like Proteus, until you tell. If you had not certainly known the nature of piety and impiety, I am confident that you would never, on behalf of a serf, have charged your aged father with murder. You would not have run such a risk of doing wrong in the sight of the gods, and you would have had too much respect for the opinions of men. I am sure, therefore, that you know the nature of piety and impiety. Speak out then, my dear Euthyphro, and do not hide your knowledge.

Euth.   Another time, Socrates, for I am in a hurry, and must go now.

Soc.   Alas! my companion, and will you leave me in despair? I was hoping that you would instruct me in the nature of piety and impiety. . . .

Did Euthyphro depart as a friend or as a new foe? Clearly, the wisdom of Socrates—a wisdom rooted in the recognition of how little he knew—is set in sharp contrast to the wisdom of his contemporaries, such as Euthyphro, who pretended to know so much but were unaware of their own ignorance. Made aware of their ignorance, these "wise" persons were probably pleased to see the one who had put their ideas on trial now himself on trial for his life.

Returning now to the trial, Socrates responds to the allegation that he is an evil-doer who corrupts the youth, who does not believe in the gods of the state, but who believes in novel deities. With his characteristically incisive questions, Socrates exposes the inconsistent, self-contradictory, and ill-founded nature of these charges championed by Meletus.

He says that I am a doer of evil, and corrupt the youth; but I say, O men of Athens that Meletus is a doer of evil, in that he pretends to be in earnest when he is only in jest, and is so eager to bring men to trial from a pretended zeal and interest about matters in which he really never had the smallest interest. And the truth of this I will endeavor to prove to you.

Come hither, Meletus, and let me ask a question of you. You think a great deal about the improvement of youth?

Yes, I do.

Tell the judges, then, who is their improver; for you must know, as you have taken the pains to discover their corrupter, and are citing and accusing me before them. Speak, then, and tell the judges who their improver is—Observe, Meletus, that you are silent, and have nothing to say. But is not this rather disgraceful, and a very considerable proof of what I was saying, that you have no interest in the matter? Speak up, friend, and tell us who their improver is.

The laws.

But that, my good sir, is not my meaning. I want to know who the person is, who, in the first place, knows the laws.

The judges, Socrates, who are present in court.

What, do you mean to say, Meletus, that they are able to instruct and improve youth?

Certainly they are.

What, all of them, or some only and not others?

All of them.

By the goddess Here, that is good news! There are plenty of improvers, then. And what do you say of the audience,—do they improve them?

Yes, they do.

And the senators?

Yes, the senators improve them.

But perhaps the members of the assembly corrupt them?—or do they too improve them?

They improve them.

Then every Athenian improves and elevates them; all with the exception of myself; and I alone am their corrupter? Is that what you affirm?

That is what I stoutly affirm.

I am very unfortunate if you are right. But suppose I ask you a question: How about horses? Does one man do them harm and all the world good? Is not the exact opposite the truth? One man is able to do them good, or at least not many;—the trainer of horses, that is to say, does them good, and others who have to do with them rather injure them? Is not that true, Meletus, of horses, or of any other animals? Most assuredly it is; whether you and Anytus say yes or no. Happy indeed would be the condition of youth if they had one corrupter only, and all the rest of the world were their improvers. But you, Meletus, have sufficiently shown that you never had a thought about the young; your carelessness is seen in your not caring about the very things which you bring against me.

And now, Meletus, I will ask you another question—by Zeus I will: Which is better, to live among bad citizens, or among good ones? Answer, friend, I say; the question is one which may be easily answered. Do not the good do their neighbors good, and the bad do them evil?

Certainly.

And is there any one who would rather be injured than benefited by those who live with him? Answer, my good friend, the law requires you to answer—does any one like to be injured?

Certainly not.

And when you accuse me of corrupting and deteriorating the youth, do you allege that I corrupt them intentionally or unintentionally?

Intentionally, I say.

But you have just admitted that the good do their neighbors good, and evil do them evil. Now, is that a truth which your superior wisdom has recognized thus early in life, and am I, at my age, in such darkness and ignorance as not to know that if a man with whom I have to live is corrupted by me, I am very likely to be harmed by him; and yet I corrupt him, and intentionally, too—so you say, although neither I nor any other human being is ever likely to be convinced by you. But either I do not corrupt them, or I corrupt them unintentionally; and on either view of the case you lie. If my offence is unintentional, the law has no cognizance of unintentional offences; you ought to have taken me privately, and warned and admonished me; for if I had been better advised, I should have left off doing what I only did unintentionally—no doubt I should; but you would have nothing to say to me and refused to teach me. And now you bring me up in this court, which is a place not of instruction, but of punishment.

It will be very clear to you, Athenians, as I was saying, that Meletus has no care at all, great or small, about the matter. But still I should like to know, Meletus, in what

I am affirmed to corrupt the young. I suppose you mean, as I infer from your indictment, that I teach them not to acknowledge the gods which the state acknowledges, but some other new divinities or spiritual agencies in their stead. These are the lessons by which I corrupt the youth, as you say.

Yes, that I say emphatically.

Then, by the gods, Meletus, of whom we are speaking, tell me and the court in somewhat plainer terms, what you mean! For I do not as yet understand whether you affirm that I teach other men to acknowledge some gods, and therefore that I do believe in gods, and am not an entire atheist—this you do not lay to my charge,—but only you say that they are not the same gods which the city recognizes—the charge is that they are different gods. Or, do you mean that I am an atheist simply, and a teacher of atheism?

I mean the latter—that you are a complete atheist.

What an extraordinary statement! Why do you think so, Meletus? Do you mean that I do not believe in the godhead of the sun or moon, like other men?

I assure you, judges, that he does not; for he says that the sun is stone, and the moon earth.

Friend Meletus, you think that you are accusing Anaxagoras; and you have but a bad opinion of the judges, if you fancy them illiterate to such a degree as not to know that these doctrines are found in the books of Anaxagoras the Clazomenian, which are full of them. And so, forsooth, the youth are said to be taught them by Socrates, when there are not unfrequently exhibitions of them at the theater (price of admission one drachma at the most); and they might pay their money, and laugh at Socrates if he pretends to father these extraordinary views. And so, Meletus, you really think that I do not believe in any god?

I swear by Zeus that you believe absolutely in none at all.

Nobody will believe you, Meletus, and I am pretty sure that you do not believe yourself. I cannot help thinking, men of Athens, that Meletus is reckless and impudent, and that he has written this indictment in a spirit of mere wantonness and youthful bravado. Has he not compounded a riddle, thinking to try me? He said to himself:—I shall see whether the wise Socrates will discover my facetious contradiction, or whether I shall be able to deceive him and the rest of them. For he certainly does appear to me to contradict himself in the indictment as much as if he said that Socrates is guilty of not believing in the gods, and yet of believing in them—but this is not like a person who is in earnest.

I should like you, O men of Athens, to join me in examining what I conceive to be his inconsistency; and do you, Meletus, answer. And I must remind the audience of my request that they would not make a disturbance if I speak in my accustomed manner.

Did ever man, Meletus, believe in the existence of human things, and not of human beings? . . . I wish, men of Athens, that he would answer, and not be always trying to get up an interruption. Did ever any man believe in horsemanship, and not in horses? or in flute-playing, and not in flute-players? No, my friend; I will answer to you and to the court, as you refuse to answer for yourself. There is no man who ever did. But now please to answer the next question: Can a man believe in spiritual and divine agencies, and not in spirits or demigods?

He cannot.

How lucky I am to have extracted that answer, by the assistance of the court! But then you swear in the indictment that I teach and believe in divine or spiritual agencies (new or old, no matter for that); at any rate, I believe in spiritual agencies,—so you say and swear in the affidavit; and yet if I believe in divine beings, how can I help believing in spirits and demigods;—must I not? To be sure I must; and therefore I may assume that your silence gives consent. Now what are spirits or demigods? are they not either gods or the sons of gods?

Certainly they are.

But this is what I call the facetious riddle invented by you: the demigods or spirits are gods, and you say first that I do not believe in gods, and then again that I do believe in gods; that is, if I believe in demigods. For if the demigods are the illegitimate sons of gods, whether by the nymphs or by any other mothers, of whom they are said to be the sons—what human being will ever believe that there are no gods if they are the sons of gods? You might as well affirm the existence of mules, and deny that of horses and asses. Such nonsense, Meletus, could only have been tended by you to make trial of me. You have put this into the indictment because you had nothing real of which to accuse me. But no one who has a particle of understanding will ever be convinced by you that the same men can believe in divine and superhuman things, and yet not believe there are gods and demigods and heroes.

I have said enough to answer to the charge of Meletus; any elaborate defence is unnecessary; but I know only too well how many are the enmities which I have incurred; and this is what will be my destruction if I am destroyed;—not Meletus, nor yet Anytus, but the envy and detraction of the world, which has been the death of many good men, and will probably be the death of many more; there is no danger of my being the last of them.

Can one believe Meletus that every Athenian except Socrates promotes the well-being of the youth? Can one believe Meletus that Socrates would intentionally do harm to his neighbors when Socrates was aware that such injury would backfire on himself? Can one believe Meletus that Socrates is an atheist when in fact he believes in divine agencies? Such queries certainly erode the strength of Meletus' allegations. Yet it is not the truth or falsity of these charges that will determine his fate, but rather the intensity of the hostility which Socrates' probing questions have engendered in the populace. Judgment based on incited passions rather than on reasoned assessment is what one would expect from a jury of five hundred and one members.

The death penalty hangs over Socrates' head. Is he prepared to change his ways in order to subdue the hostility of the citizenry? Is he willing to stop exposing the pretense of wisdom among his fellow Athenians to save his life? Is he willing to give up philosophizing in order to avoid death? His response is unequivocal.

Men of Athens, I honor and love you; but I shall obey God rather than you, and while I have life and strength I shall never cease from the practice and teaching of philosophy, exhorting any one whom I meet and saying to him after my manner: You, my friend—a citizen of the great and mighty and wise city of Athens,—are you not ashamed of heaping up the greatest amount of money and honor and reputation, and caring so little about wisdom and truth and the greatest improvement of the soul, which you never regard or heed at all? And if the person with whom I am arguing, says: Yes, but I do care; then I do not leave him or let him go at once; but I proceed to interrogate and examine and cross-examine him, and if I think that he has no virtue in him, but only says that he has, I reproach him with undervaluing the greater, and overvaluing the less. And I shall repeat the same words to every one whom I meet, young and old, citizen and alien, but especially to the citizens, inasmuch as they are my brethren. For know that this is the command of God; and I believe that no greater good has ever happened in the state than my service to the God. For I do nothing but go about persuading you all, old and young alike, not to take thought for your persons or your properties, but first and chiefly to care about the greatest improvement of the soul. I tell you that virtue is not given by money, but that from virtue comes money and every other good of man, public as well as private. This is my teaching, and if this is the doctrine which corrupts the youth, I am a mischievous person. But if any one says that this is not my teaching, he is speaking an untruth. Wherefore, O men of Athens, I say to you, do as Anytus bids or not as Anytus bids, and either acquit me or not; but whichever you do, understand that I shall never alter my ways, not even if I have to die many times.

The vote is taken, and it is close. Socrates is found guilty, but thirty additional votes (out of 501) being cast in his favor would have resulted in his acquittal. His accusers call for the death penalty, and Socrates is offered the opportunity to argue for a lesser penalty. Instead, with a touch of irony, Socrates suggests that he should be rewarded in a fashion similar to the treatment accorded to victorious Olympian athletes because of the benefit that his philosophizing has brought to Athens. Unwilling to admit that he has wronged anyone, Socrates refuses to acknowledge that he deserves any punishment whatsoever. We rejoin the dialogue at the point where Socrates is examining the suggestion that he propose "exile" as the court's penalty.

Some one will say: Yes, Socrates, but cannot you hold your tongue, and then you may go into a foreign city, and no one will interfere with you? Now I have great difficulty in making you understand my answer to this. For if I tell you that to do as you say would be a disobedience to the God, and therefore that I cannot hold my tongue, you will not believe that I am serious; and if I say again that daily to discourse about virtue, and of those other things about which you hear me examining myself and others, is the greatest good of man, and that the unexamined life is not worth living, you are still less likely to believe me. Yet I say what is true, although a thing of which it is hard for me to persuade you. Also, I have never been accustomed to think that I deserve to suffer any harm. Had I money I might have estimated the offence at what I was able to pay, and not have been much the worse. But I have none, and therefore I must ask you to proportion the fine to my means. Well, perhaps I could afford a mina, and therefore I propose that penalty: Plato, Crito, Critobulus, and Apollodorus, my friends here, bid me say thirty minae, and they will be the sureties. Let thirty minae be the penalty; for which sum they will be ample security to you.

Another vote is taken. Socrates is condemned to death. In his concluding statement, he addresses his accusers and charges that they are guilty of unrighteousness.

You think that I was convicted because I had no words of the sort which would have procured my acquittal—I mean, if I had thought fit to leave nothing undone or unsaid. Not so; the deficiency which led to my conviction was not of words—certainly not. But I had not the boldness or impudence or inclination to address you as you would have liked me to do, weeping and wailing and lamenting, and saying and doing many things which you have been accustomed to hear from others, and which, as I maintain, are unworthy of me. I thought at the time that I ought not to do anything common or mean when in danger; nor do I now repent of the style of my defence; I would rather die having spoken after my manner, than speak in your manner and live. For neither in war nor yet at law ought I or any man to use every way of escaping death. Often in battle there can be no doubt that if a man will throw away his arms, and fall on his knees before his pursuers, he may escape death; and in other dangers there are other ways of escaping death, if a man is willing to say and do anything. The difficulty, my friends, is not to avoid death, but to avoid unrighteousness; for that runs faster than death. I am old and move slowly, and the slower runner has overtaken me, and my accusers are keen and quick, and the faster runner, who is unrighteousness, has overtaken them. And now I depart hence condemned by you to suffer the penalty of death,—they too go their ways condemned by the truth to suffer the penalty of villainy and wrong; and I must abide by my award—let them abide by theirs. I suppose that these things may be regarded as fated,—and I think that they are well.

Socrates also has some parting words for his friends among the jurors who are distressed by the apparently evil outcome of the trial. To encourage them, Socrates suggests that death is either going to sleep or going on a journey, and that neither of those possibilities would occasion any evil for him.

Friends, who would have acquitted me, I would also like to talk with you about the thing which has come to pass, while the magistrates are busy, and before I go to the place at which I must die. Stay then a little, for we may as well talk with one another while there is time. . . .

Let us reflect . . . and we shall see that there is great reason to hope that death is a good; for one of two things—either death is a state of nothingness and utter unconsciousness, or, as men say, there is a change and migration of the soul from this world to another. Now if you suppose that there is no consciousness, but a sleep like the sleep of him who is undisturbed even by dreams, death will be an unspeakable gain. For if a person were to select the night in which his sleep was undisturbed even by dreams, and were to compare with this the other days and nights of his life, and then were to tell us how many days and nights he had passed in the course of his life better and more pleasantly than this one, I think that any man, I will not say a private man, but even the great king will not find many such days or nights, when compared with the others. Now if death be of such a nature, I say that to die is gain; for eternity is then only a single night. But if death is the journey to another place, and there, as men say, all the dead abide, what good, O my friends and judges, can be greater than this? If indeed when the pilgrim arrives in the world below, he is delivered from the professors of justice in this world, and finds the true judges who are said to give judgment there, Minos and Rhadamanthus and Aeacus and Triptolemus, and other sons of God who were righteous in their own life, that pilgrimage will be worth making. What would not a man give if he might converse with Orpheus and Musaeus and Hesiod and Homer? Nay, if this be true, let me die again and again. I myself, too, shall have a wonderful interest in there meeting and conversing with Palamedes, and

Ajax the son of Telamon, and any other ancient hero who has suffered death through an unjust judgment; and there will be no small pleasure, as I think, in comparing my own sufferings with theirs. Above all, I shall then be able to continue my search into true and false knowledge; as in this world, so also in the next; and I shall find out who is wise, and who pretends to be wise, and is not. What would not a man give, O judges, to be able to examine the leader of the great Trojan expedition; or Odysseus or Sisyphus, or numberless others, men and women too! What infinite delight would there be in conversing with them and asking them questions! In another world they do not put a man to death for asking questions; assuredly not. For besides being happier than we are, they will be immortal, if what is said is true.

Wherefore, O judges, be of good cheer about death, and know of a certainty, that no evil can happen to a good man, either in life or after death. He and his are not neglected by the gods . . .

I have a favor to ask . . When my sons are grown up, I would ask you, O my friends, to punish them; And I would have you trouble them, as I have troubled you, if they seem to care about riches, or anything, more than about virtue; or if they pretend to be something when they are really nothing,—then reprove them, as I have reproved you, for not caring about that for which they ought to care, and thinking that they are something when they are really nothing. And if you do this, both I and my sons will have received justice at your hands.

The hour of departure has arrived, and we go our ways—I to die, and you to live. Which is better God only knows.

Having viewed Socrates the philosopher in action, are you now able to say what philosophy is? If you are having some difficulty, take heart because contemporary professional philosophers are by no means in agreement about how philosophy should be defined. Indeed, one could view the current philosophical scene as a debate between two different views of philosophy. On the one hand, there is the modern analytic tradition which has roots in eighteenth century British empiricism, modern science, and twentieth century logical positivism. It emphasizes the analysis of language in order to achieve both clarity and also the resolution of verbal disputes. Would not the modern analytic philosopher who focuses on the clarification of the meaning of words be following the example of Socrates as he challenged Euthyphro to clarify his concept of "piety"? On the other hand, there is the more speculative tradition of philosophy (as exemplified by metaphysicians such as Descartes, Spinoza, Leibniz, and Hegel) which tries to formulate answers to such questions as the nature of human existence, the purpose of human life, the prospect of life after death, the existence of God, the nature of ultimate reality, the features necessary for the good life, and so forth. Could not such philosophers also claim to be following the example of Socrates when he summoned his contemporaries to pursue virtue and as he speculated about whether death was going to sleep on going on a journey?

If both of these traditions can legitimately appeal to Socrates in support of their views, does it not seem likely that philosophy in the Socratic tradition involves both views, that it embraces concern for clarifying the words of human discourse and also formulating responses to perennial human questions? The presence of these two emphases in the Socratic tradition can be seen if we consider the Socratic *goal* and *method* of philosophizing.

The Socratic Goal.   What did Socrates want to accomplish? Some might say that Socrates wished primarily to make himself appear wise by making others look foolish. If so, Socrates was a clever and arrogant man. Others might say that his major goal was to promote social change by teaching young people how to question and discredit the authorities of society. If so, Socrates was something of a revolutionary. Still others might say that Socrates wished to nourish the examined life. Let us consider this latter alternative in more detail.

You will recall that Socrates declared that "the unexamined life is not worth living." Why is it not worth living? The unexamined life does not ponder questions like this: Who am I? What ought I to do? What may I hope? The unexamined life does not evaluate alternative futures. It lives with the flow. The unexamined life hears no evil and sees no evil. It is devoid of critical self-assessment. It stifles the breath of reason. It violates a distinctive human capacity. In contrast, the examined life allows human reason to breathe, live, and grow strong. The examined life seeks not simply to satisfy curiosity, but rather strives for human virtue. Remember how concerned Socrates was about virtue. Recall that he asked his friends to punish his sons when they are grown if they cared about anything more than virtue. The examined life and the pursuit of virtue were dear to Socrates and they were linked together in the philosophical task. Through the examined life, one could pursue answers to fundamental human questions, discover what it means to be a human being, and learn what human virtue is. Does not the philosophic quest in the Socratic tradition, then, seem to include the pursuit of the examined life in order to make virtue abound?

The Socratic Method.   How did Socrates pursue this goal? At least two features of Socrates' method stand out. First, he sought conceptual clarification. Even as he challenged Euthyphro over the meaning of piety, no doubt he would require us to be clear about the meaning of virtue. He might ask us, for example, if virtue stands for the personal qualities that a particular culture at a specific time finds attractive. If so, would not the meaning of virtue vary according to time and place? Or is virtue transcultural? If so, would not human beings who pursued virtue have a common goal? If so, what would be the human characteristics that these people from diverse cultures would consider to be at the heart of virtue? Notice how the philosophic goal inspires one question after another.

Second, the Socratic method involved a critical examination of received opinions and accepted beliefs. In the wake of the declaration of the Oracle of Apollo at Delphi, Socrates went about testing the knowledge claims of his contemporaries. Suppose you said "I believe that there is a God who cares for humankind." Socrates would probably ask you, "On what basis do you hold that belief?" Clearly, Socrates would be asking you to justify your belief. What do you think Socrates would accept as justification for your belief? Would quoting from sacred scriptures do the job? Would citing a personal, private religious experience count as evidence to justify your belief? How about summoning the testimony of the leaders of society who also believe in God? Would their testimony satisfy Socrates? What about the so-called proofs for the existence of God offered by Aristotle, Thomas Aquinas, Rene Descartes, William Paley, and others? Finding evidence to justify one's belief in God is not easy, as we will discover in the chapter on God's existence. Indeed, finding evidence to justify a good number of our beliefs is no easy matter.

If we are able to produce evidence that justifies our belief that God exists, then we could say that we have *knowledge* that God exists. But in whose eyes does the evidence for our belief have to be convincing? Do all rational persons have to agree that our evidence is sufficient before we can claim that our belief is justified? Or would the concurrence of the majority of rational persons be sufficient? Or should we be willing to settle for something less than a majority? And would it be permissible to speak of degrees of justification depending upon the quantity and quality of the evidence we are able to cite in support of our belief? What if we are unable to produce evidence that justifies our belief that God exists? Must we then abandon that belief? Indeed, is it ever permissible to hold a belief that is unjustified? Furthermore, what really counts as evidence? These are the kinds of questions that give rise to a theory of knowledge, and to that subject we will be devoting a full chapter later in this book.

Philosophers, in the Socratic tradition, pursue the examined life in order to generate virtue; and the virtue that Socrates and his disciples had in mind is multifaceted. It involves the fulfillment of all the distinctively human potentialities, the harmonious blending of human appetites, emotions, and thinking. In other words, to pursue virtue is to seek human flourishing. The method philosophers use in this pursuit involves both conceptual clarification and the critical examination of accepted beliefs. Unrelentingly, philosophers ask us, "What do you mean by that?" and "What evidence do you have to support that belief?"

If we agree with Socrates that the unexamined life is not worth living, and decide to pursue the examined life, then we must subject the beliefs of humankind to rigorous scrutiny. But where should we begin? Let us return to the life of Socrates for a suggestion. The ancient oracle of Apollo at Delphi, where the divine declaration had been made that no one was wiser than Socrates, has some advice for us. At the entrance to that shrine these words were carved in stone: "Know Thyself." Those words suggest an intriguing point of departure for us. Perhaps the examined life should begin with an attempt to understand who or what *we* are. The pursuit of such self-knowledge would, in due course, prompt us to raise additional questions, which would cease only when we have examined the whole human condition. In this book we have adopted the oracle's advice.

The questions we have explored include the following:

Am I a body and a mind?
Am I determined or free?
Am I mortal or immortal?
Am I a creature of God?

On what basis shall I judge things morally?
On what basis shall I judge things artistically?
On what basis shall I judge the law?
On what basis shall I claim to have knowledge?
What shall I say about ultimate reality?
Does my life have any meaning?
What does science tell me about the world?

All of these are perennial questions, which generation after generation of Socrates' disciples have encountered as they have pursued the examined life. We have selected passages from the writings of modern philosophers who will often propose conflicting answers to these questions. The debate between these philosophers will at times be heated, and, we hope, at all times engaging. As we ourselves try to fashion responses to these questions (and respond to them we must), occasionally we will achieve some strongly warranted answers to our questions. Frequently, however, our questioning will result in uncertainties. Indeed, we will find ourselves in what Bertrand Russell referred to as the "no man's land" between the knowledge of science and the dogma of theology. Yet those uncertainties can be celebrated as the high cost of being human, of being rational, of being open to the future, of being able to ask questions that we are perhaps unable to answer completely.

NOTE ON SOURCES.   The material in this section is quoted from Plato, "Euthyphro" and "Apology," trans. B. Jowett in *The Dialogues of Plato*, 4th ed. (Oxford, England: Oxford University Press, 1953).

Am I a Body and a Mind?

THE QUESTION POSED

I am free; I am immortal; I am a creature of God. Each of these is an answer to the question, "What am I?" We shall discuss these answers in Chapters 3–5. In this chapter, we focus on three different kinds of answers: I am just a mind, I am just a body, I am some mix of the two. These answers show the influence of the philosopher-mathematician, René Descartes. He began by asking "What can I know with certainty?" His answer set the stage for western philosophy's discussion of the mind, and how it can affect the body, and whether or not we can know if there are minds other than our own.

Descartes wrote during the period often called the rise of the new science. The new science basically embraced materialism, a view which held that matter is the primary feature of reality and relegates mind or spirit either to a secondary, dependent status or to no status at all. Promulgated by sixth- and fifth-century B.C. Greek philosophers like Leucippus and Democritus, materialism was overshadowed for centuries by the doctrines of Plato, Aristotle, and Christian theologians who accorded mind (or spirit) a more prominent and independent position in the landscape of reality.

Materialism, however, garnered a formidable ally in modern science. Medieval scientists had busied themselves with the task of discovering how one class of being is logically related to another class of beings. Modern science was born when scientists expanded their concerns beyond the issue of group relatedness to include both the quest for generalizations based on empirical data (note the work of Francis Bacon [1561–1626] in this development) and also the use of mathematical reasoning. Now the method of mathematical reasoning involves the quantification of the observed facts, the expression of those quantities in formulae, the synthesis of those formulae into explanatory systems, the prediction of the behavior of phenomena through those systems, and the testing of those predictions against empirical data. It was particularly in astronomy that this new mathematical method developed, especially through the work of Copernicus (1473–1543), Kepler (1571–1630), Brahe (1546–1601), and Galileo (1564–1642).

The view of reality that emerged from this new science seemed to support materialism. According to the new science, physical reality was depicted as matter in motion. Matter objectively possessed position, shape, size, mass, and velocity. All these characteristics were definable, so their relations to one another could be reasoned out, as in geometry. In contrast, smells, sounds, colors, and tastes could be identified only by putting a person in a situation where the person will have the experience we have in mind and saying, "There, that is what I mean." These latter characteristics that do not lend themselves to deductions and reasoning were considered to be not objectively real. They were rather "appearances" that arise in us when our sense organs are stimulated by objectively real matter with its geometrical characteristics. Objective reality, accordingly, came to be viewed as basically a world of material objects moving in a mechanistic fashion. That view of reality left precious little room, if any, for an immaterial mind, for human freedom, for immortality, and for a spiritual being called God—all of which had been prominent in medieval thought. Materialism, then, seemed to have gained an ally in the new science; and that new science's impressive explanatory power and its capacity to aid humans in the manipulation of their environment made it a formidable ally indeed!

Writing during this time, but not entirely from within the tradition, Descartes developed an impressive philosophical system in which the human was interpreted as being both a mind (*res cogitans*) and a body (*res extensa*).

The twentieth-century philosopher Gilbert Ryle, our second author, contends that Descartes made a serious mistake in logic, called the category-mistake. Next, we read excerpts from J. J. C. Smart and Jerry Fodor, who agree with Ryle that Descartes has made serious errors but are not convinced that Ryle's answer to the mind-body problem is acceptable. Smart and Fodor appeal to contemporary advances in science to support their view. Smart appeals to neurophysiology, whereas Fodor uses advances in computer science. Our fifth author, Allen Turing, takes computer technology just about as far as it will go when he claims that we will probably be forced to admit that very advanced computers can be said to think. John Searle, the next author in this section, thinks that those who appeal to computer science to bolster the view that thinking is nothing more than what computers do have made a serious mistake—one just as serious as the category-mistake apparently made by Descartes. Finally, after a digression into the question, "Are there other minds?" we return to a modern statement of Cartesian dualism from Nobel prize–winning neurophysiologist, John Eccles.

RENÉ DESCARTES

I AM A MIND (*RES COGITANS*) AND A BODY (*RES EXTENSA*)

Philosophical interest in the nature of the human being begins for many persons with the writings by René Descartes in the middle of the seventeenth century. As a French Catholic, Descartes was raised to believe that a person, a referent of personal pronouns, is a created spiritual substance, obscurely related to a body and the world of matter, rational, active, free, and immortal. Such a conception of man is far removed from the claim that he is simply a part of nature.

Descartes' reasoning takes off from his realization that an increasing number and range of his beliefs were either doubtful or false. This triggered the question whether *any* of his beliefs were neither doubtful nor false. To settle this he asked whether any of his beliefs were indubitable, not doubtable. *Not doubtable* is a stronger term than *not doubtful*. If a claim is not doubtable, then there are no possible circumstances that could make it doubtful.

Well, if, like Descartes, you are harassed by doubts and denials, and if doubting and denying are modes of thinking, then there is no doubt that, there is no doubting that, it is not doubtable that, you do think. There is, under the conditions of such harassment, no such question as, "Do you perform the activity that is normally called *thinking*?" You cannot cast reasonable doubt on the claim that you think that you are, as Descartes says of himself, a *res cogitans*, a thinking thing. And further, if to think, you must exist, then the indubitable character of "I think" carries over to "I am." As he says, "I think, therefore I am; *cogito, ergo sum*." Granted that he is, indubitably, a *res cogitans*, and therefore an existing thing, are there any other claims he can make about himself? He is a *res cogitans*. Is he anything else? That is one line along which he worked.

A second and related line took off from the question, "What is it to think?" "What is the nature, the defining character, of the activity which a thinker, a rational animal, typically performs?" Hence such titles as *Rules for the Direction of the Understanding*, and *Discourse on the Method of Rightly Conducting One's Reason and Seeking Truth in the Sciences*. A third line took off from the contrast between an activity and passivity. This concern centers on the contrast between what I *do* and what *happens* to me. What sort of event happens to me because I am a rational animal, a *res cogitans*, which does not happen to a stone or a plant? Descartes' treatise on these matters, published in 1649, the year before he died, is called *The Passions of the Soul*, meaning the modes of passivity to which the souls, the psyches, of rational animals are liable. It dealt with sensations and emotions and related modes of passivity.

In respect to modern interest in the nature of the human being, Descartes is something of a *Caput Nili*, a source of the Nile. When he is working at the question of the nature of the *I* in *I think*, the outcome is a contribution to metaphysics. When he is working at the question of the nature of the thinking activity performed by the *I*, the outcome is a contribution to logic and epistemology. When he is working at the question of the nature of the conscious (or, later, subconscious) processes that occur in or to the psyches of rational animals, the outcome is a contribution to philosophical psychology. Like Plato among the ancients, Descartes among the moderns is an excellent introduction to the philosophical study of the nature of man.

BIOGRAPHICAL NOTE. Descartes was born in France in 1596 and died in Sweden in 1650 at the age of fifty-four. His formal education from eight to sixteen was received at the Jesuit college of La Flêche. Here he acquired the essentials of a "gentleman's education," which he subsequently devoted much time to erasing. Before he had turned seventeen he put aside his books and after a few lessons in fencing and horsemanship went to "the great world of Paris." Here he remained for about five years, living at first the usual life of gaiety and gambling, but retiring after a while to the quiet and seclusion of an obscure lodging house. His thoughtful temper reasserted itself. Habits of reflection acquired at La Fleche, and roused once more by a Catholic friend, Father Mersenne, took possession of him again.

In 1618 Descartes left Paris, determined to see the world. He became a soldier, serving in three different European armies, in the Netherlands, in Bavaria, and in Hungary. It was a life that gave him much time for thought during months of idleness in winter quarters. He stuck to soldiering for three or four years, then resolved "no longer to carry a musket." Army days over, he continued his travels for five or six years more, visiting Switzerland and Italy, until in 1628, he decided that he had read enough in the "great book of the world."

In 1629, his mind crowded with ideas demanding to be written down, he settled in Holland. He was seeking quiet and seclusion once more. His European retirement, as he called it, lasted twenty years. These were years of fruitful production. Book followed book. His reputation spread. He had the intellectuals of his generation for his readers, and its rulers for his patrons and friends. In rapid succession he wrote *Quest for Truth, Rules for the Direction of the Mind, Discourse on Method, Meditations on First Philosophy, Principles of Philosophy, Treatise on the Passions*, and many other volumes that soon became stock-in-trade for the philosophically minded of his day. In 1649 he was invited by Queen Christina of Sweden to visit her at Stockholm and expound the principles of the "new philosophy." After much hesitation, and against the advice of his friends, he agreed to go. It cost him his life, for he caught a cold in his lungs that brought about his death.

THE ARGUMENT OF THE PASSAGES. Most of the following passages are quoted, abridged, or paraphrased from Descartes' *Meditations on First Philosophy*. The thought in this small book might be paraphrased as follows: I was given the usual gentlemen's education in my youth. Presently I became skeptical of most of what had been taught me. Accordingly, I determined to abandon all my learning and begin again with a clean slate upon which no one but myself should write, and upon which nothing should be written that was not clear and distinct. I needed, as a starting point, something that could stand against skepticism, something not doubtable. To that end I set about the cultivation of my doubt. My doubts were brought to an end by the fact of my own existence. The fact that I was doubting entailed necessarily my own existence as a doubter. From this *indubitandum* my reconstruction must proceed. Could I use the undoubtability of my own existence to prove the existence of anything else? Two great steps were in order: to demonstrate the existence of God and the existence of the material world. The steps by which I moved from doubts about things taught me at school, to the demonstrated existence of myself, God, and the external world, constitute the theme of these *Meditations*.

The first passages supply some autobiographical facts:

I had been nourished on letters since my childhood, and since I was given to believe that by their means a clear and certain knowledge could be obtained of all that is useful in life, I had an extreme desire to acquire instruction.

But as soon as I had achieved the entire course of study at the close of which one is usually received into the ranks of the learned, I entirely changed my opinion. I found myself embarrassed with so many doubts and errors that it seemed to me that the effort to instruct myself had no effect other than the increasing discovery of my own ignorance. And yet I was studying at one of the most celebrated schools in Europe, where I thought there must be men of learning if such were to be found anywhere in the world.

I learned there all that others had learned. Moreover, not being satisfied with the sciences that we were taught, I even read through all books which fell into my hands, treating of what is considered most curious and rare. Along with this, I knew the judgments which others had formed of me, and I did not feel that I was esteemed inferior to my fellow students. And finally, our century seemed to me as flourishing, and as fertile in great minds, as any which had preceded it.

These reflections combined to make me take the liberty of judging all others by myself, and of coming to the conclusion that there was no learning in the world such as I had formerly believed it to be.

That is why, as soon as age permitted me to emerge from the control of my tutors, I entirely quitted the study of letters. I resolved to seek no other knowledge than that which could be found in myself, or at least in the great book of the world. I employed the rest of my youth in travel, in seeing courts and armies, in intercourse with men of diverse temperaments and conditions, in collecting varied experiences, in testing myself in the various predicaments in which I was placed by fortune. In all circumstances I sought to bring my mind to bear on the things that came before it so that I might derive some profit from my experience.

For nine years I did nothing but roam hither and thither, trying to be a spectator rather than an actor in all the comedies which the world displays. Especially did I ask myself, in each matter that came before me, whether anything could make it subject to suspicion or doubt.

I considered the manners and customs of other men, and found nothing to give me settled convictions. I remarked in them almost as much diversity as I had formerly seen in the opinions of philosophers. So much was this so, that I learned to believe nothing too certainly of which I had been convinced only by example and custom.

I thus concluded that it is much more custom and example that persuade us than any certain knowledge. And this despite the fact that the voice of the majority affords no proof of any value in matters a little difficult to discover. Such truths are like to have been discovered by one man, more than by a nation. But I could not, however, put my finger on a single person whose opinions seemed preferable to those of others.

I found I was constrained, so to speak, to undertake the direction of my own inquiries.

As regards all the opinions which, up to that time, I had embraced, I thought I could not do better than try once for all to sweep them completely away. Later on they might be replaced, either by others which were better, or by the same when I had made them conform to the uniformity of a rational scheme. I firmly believed that by this means I should succeed much better than if I had built on foundations and principles of which I had allowed myself to be persuaded in youth without having inquired into their truth. My design has never extended beyond trying to reform my own opinions and to build on a foundation which is entirely my own.

I was not seeking to imitate the skeptics, who only doubt for the sake of doubting and pretend always to be uncertain. On the contrary, my design was only to provide myself with good ground for assurance, to reject the quicksand and the mud in order to find the rock or clay.

These remarks give us the terms of this self-imposed task; on the one hand, to work himself free from the opinions he had accepted as part of a normal education, on the other, to avoid mere skepticism. The execution of this design called for a definite procedure. This Descartes outlines:

Like one who walks alone and in the twilight, I resolved to go slowly, to use so much circumspection that even if my advance was very small at least I guarded myself from falling. I did not wish to reject any opinion finally until I had planned out the task I had undertaken, and until I had sought out the true method of arriving at a knowledge of the things of which my mind was capable.

In my younger days I had studied logic and geometry and algebra—three sciences which, it seemed, ought to contribute something to the design I had in view.

But, in examining them, I observed in respect to logic, that syllogisms and the rest served better to explain those things which one already knows than to learn something new. As to geometry and algebra, they embrace only the most abstract matters, such as appear to have no actual use. This made me feel that some other method must be found exempt from their fault. So, in place of the many precepts of which logic is composed, and the many rules and formulae of which mathematics is composed, I settled on four rules for the direction of the understanding.

My first rule was to accept nothing as true which I did not clearly recognize to be so; to accept nothing more than what was presented to my mind so clearly and distinctly that I could have no occasion to doubt it. The second rule was to divide each problem or difficulty into as many parts as possible. The third rule was to commence my reflections with objects which were the simplest and easiest to understand, and rise thence, little by little, to knowledge of the most complex. The fourth rule was to make enumerations so complete, and reviews so general, that I should be certain to have omitted nothing.

Those long chains of reasoning which geometricians make had caused me to imagine that all parts of human knowledge might be mutually related in the same fashion; and that, provided we abstain from receiving anything as true which is not so, and always deduce one conclusion from some other, there can be nothing so remote that we cannot reach it, nor so recondite that we cannot discover it.

But what pleased me most, in this method which I was determined to follow, was that I was certain by its means to exercise my reason in all things; if not perfectly, at least as well as was in my power. I felt that, in making use of it, my mind would gradually accustom itself to think about its objects more accurately and distinctly.

The first of the above rules is perhaps the important one: to accept nothing as true that he did not clearly recognize to be so.'It is one thing to lay this rule down. It is another to abide by it. The difficulty is in knowing where to start searching for one indubitable fact. But the search is under way.

. . . it is necessary for me to reject as false everything as to which I can imagine the least ground of doubt, in order to see if anything remains that is entirely certain. So I set myself seriously and freely to the general upheaval of all my former opinions.

To that end it is not requisite that I examine each opinion in particular. That would be an endless undertaking. Owing, however, to the fact that the destruction of the foundations brings with it the downfall of the rest of the edifice, I shall only attack those principles upon which all my former opinions rested.

All that up to the present time I have accepted as most true and certain I have learned either from the senses or through the senses. But it is sometimes proved to me that these senses are deceptive. And it is wiser not to trust entirely to anything by which we have once been deceived.

But it may be objected that, although the senses sometimes deceive us concerning things which are hardly perceptible or are very far away, there are yet many things as to which we cannot reasonably have any doubt although we recognize them by their means. For example, there is the fact that I am here, seated by the fire, attired in a dressing gown, having this paper in my hand. And how could I deny that these hands and this body are mine?

At the same time I must remember that I am in the habit of sleeping, and in my dreams representing to myself the same things. How often has it happened that I dreamt I was in this particular place, dressed and seated near the fire, while in reality I was lying undressed in bed. On many occasions I have in sleep been deceived by similar illusions. In thinking carefully about this fact, I see that there are manifestly no certain indications by which we may clearly distinguish wakefulness from sleep.

Suppose we assume, then, that we are asleep; that all these particulars, e.g., opening our eyes, shaking our head, extending our hand, are but false delusions; that possibly neither our hands nor our body are such as they appear to us to be.

There is a point, however, which we must not overlook. We must admit that the things which are represented to us in sleep are like painted representations which can only have been formed as the counterparts of something real and true, i.e., not illusory. It would follow from this admission that those general things at least, i.e., eyes, head, hands, body, are not imaginary things but things really existent.

We are bound, at the same time, to confess that there are some objects yet more simple and universal than eyes, a head, a body, etc., namely, colors, shapes, size, number, etc., which are real and true. For, whether I am awake or asleep, red is not blue, two and three make five, squares have only four sides, and so on. It does not seem possible that truths so clear can be suspected of any falsity.

Nevertheless, I have long had fixed in my mind the belief that an all-powerful God existed by whom I have been created such as I am. But how do I know that He has not brought it to pass that there is no earth, no heaven, no extended body, no magnitude, no place; and that, nonetheless, I possess perceptions of all these things which seem to me to exist just exactly as I now see them?

It might be urged against this suggestion that God has not desired that I should be thus deceived. For is He not said to be supremely good? However, if it is contrary to His goodness to have made me such that I am constantly deceived, it would also seem to be contrary to His goodness to permit me to be sometimes deceived; and yet it cannot be denied that He does permit this.

There may indeed be those who, rather than believe that all other things are uncertain, would prefer to deny the existence of a God so powerful. Let us not oppose them. Let us suppose, then, not that God (who is supremely good and the fountain of truth) but some evil genius not less powerful than deceitful, has employed his whole energies in deceiving me.

I shall suppose, then, that some evil genius not less powerful than deceitful is employing His whole energies to deceive me. I shall consider that the heavens, the earth, colors, shapes, sounds, and all other external things, are nothing but illusions and dreams by which this evil genius has laid traps for my credulity. I shall consider myself as having no hands, no eyes, no flesh, no blood, nor any senses; yet falsely believing myself to possess all these things. I shall remain obstinately attached to this idea. If, by this means, it is not in my power to arrive at the knowledge of any truth, I may at least do what is in my power, namely, suspend judgment, and thus avoid belief in anything false and avoid being imposed upon by this arch deceiver, however powerful and deceptive he may be.

Determined to "doubt everything," until doubt becomes impossible of being pushed further, Descartes has had recourse to heroic measures. The senses have been discredited, and with them the credibility of the external world revealed by the senses. This, one might have thought, would have sufficed. But assurance must be made doubly sure. Hence the hypothesis of a malignant genius who deceives him. At this point the eagerly sought *indubitandum* begins to appear:

I suppose, then, that all the things that I see are false. I persuade myself that nothing has ever existed of all that my fallacious memory represents to me. I consider that I possess no senses. I imagine that body, figure, extension, motion, and place are but the fictions of my mind. What, then, can be esteemed as true? Perhaps nothing at all, unless that there is nothing in the world that is certain.

But immediately I notice that while I wish to think all things false, it is nonetheless absolutely essential that I, who wish to think this, should truly exist. There is a powerful and cunning deceiver who employs his ingenuity in misleading me? Let it be granted. It follows the more that I exist, if he deceives me. If I did not exist, he could not deceive me. This truth, "I think, therefore I am; *cogito, ergo sum*," is so certain, so assured, that all the most extravagant skepticism is incapable of shaking it. This truth, "I am. I exist," I can receive without scruple as the first principle of the philosophy for which I am seeking.

Descartes has used doubt to defeat doubt. He has found his *indubitandum*. He has discovered that which is undoubtable. Clearly and distinctly he has recognized that his thinking presupposes the "I" doing the thinking, and that his being deceived by the malignant genius (if such be the case) presupposes the "I" in order for this deception to occur. That this "I" exists he can be completely certain.

He then proceeds to ponder what the nature of this "I," this *res cogitans*, this thinking thing is.

> I think, therefore, I am. But what am I? I do not yet know; and hence I must be careful less I imprudently take some other object in place of myself and thus go astray in respect of this knowledge which I hold to be the most certain of all that I formerly believed.
>
> What then did I formerly believe myself to be? I considered myself as having a face, hands, arms, and all that system of members which I designate by the name of body. In addition to this, I considered that I was nourished, that I walked, that I felt, and that I thought.
>
> But what am I, now that I assume that there is an evil and malicious genius who employs all his powers to deceive me? Can I affirm, with as much certainty as I can affirm my existence, that I possess any of the least of all those things which I have just now ascribed to myself? I pause to consider. I resolve all these things in my mind. I find none of the bodily attributes which I can ascribe to myself.
>
> What of thinking? I find that thought alone is an attribute which cannot be separated from me. I am, I exist; that is certain. But this certainty reposes on the "I think" which preceded. I am trying here not to admit anything which is not necessarily true. To speak thus strictly, I am nothing more than a thing which thinks, that is, to say, a mind, an understanding. I am a real thing. I really exist. But what am I? I have answered: a thing which thinks.
>
> I am a thing which thinks. And what more? What is a thing which thinks? It is a thing which doubts, understands, conceives, affirms, denies, wills, refuses, imagines, feels. Certainly it is no small matter if all these things pertain to my nature.
>
> But why should they not so pertain? Am I not that being who now doubts nearly everything, who nevertheless understands certain things, who affirms that only one thing is true, who denies all other things, who desires to know more, who is averse from being deceived, who imagines many things, who perceives many things? Is there, in all this, anything which is less certain than that I exist? Indeed, it is so evident that it is I who doubt, who understand, who desire, and so on, that there is no reason here to add anything to explain it. From this time I begin to know what I am with a little more clearness and distinctness than before.

Doubt has been explored and exploited. The existence of the "I" has been shown to be undoubtable. Because the existence of that which thinks (*res cogitans*) can be proven without having proven the existence of the body (*res extensa*), the mind must be logically distinct from the body. Can the certainty of the existence of the mind be used as a stepping-stone to other certainties? For example, the existence of the body? But what about the malignant genius? Can Descartes be certain of anything else at all as long as that evil deceiver lurks in the background? To dispose of the evil deceiver, then, must be the next item on Descartes' agenda.

> I shall now close my eyes; I shall stop my ears. I shall call away all my senses. I shall efface from my thoughts all images of material things—or, since that is hardly possible—I shall esteem them as vain and false. Thus holding converse only with my self, and considering my own nature, I shall try to reach a better knowledge of what I am.
>
> I am a thing which thinks; that is to say, that doubts, affirms, denies, knows, is ignorant, wills, desires, imagines, perceives. For, as I remarked before, although the

things which I perceive and imagine are perhaps nothing apart from me, yet the perceptions and imaginings certainly reside in me. And in the little that I have just said, I think I have summed up all that I really know or was hitherto aware that I knew. To extend my knowledge further, I shall look around more carefully and see whether I cannot still discover in myself some other things which I have not hitherto perceived.

I am certain that I am a thing which thinks. But if I am indeed certain of this I must know what is requisite to render me certain of anything. I must possess a standard of certainty. In this first knowledge which I have gained, what is there that assures me of its truth? Nothing except the clear and distinct perception of what I state. This, indeed, would not suffice to assure me that what I state is true if it could ever happen that I should clearly and distinctly perceive to be true something which was in fact false. Accordingly, I can establish as a general rule that all things which I perceive very clearly and very distinctly are true.

All things which I perceive very clearly and very distinctly, are true. If I have heretofore judged that such matters could be doubted, it was because it came into my mind that perhaps a God might have endowed me with such a nature that I might have been deceived even concerning things which seemed to me most manifest. I see no reason to believe that there is a God who is a deceiver; however, as yet I have not satisfied myself that there is a God at all.

I must inquire whether there is a God. And, if I find that there is a God, I must also inquire whether He may be a deceiver. For, without a knowledge of these two truths, I do not see that I can ever be certain of anything.

Now, it is obvious that there must be at least as much reality in any cause as in its effect. For whence could the effect derive its reality, if not from its cause? From this it follows that something cannot proceed from nothing; and that the more or the greater cannot proceed from the less.

The longer and more carefully I investigate these matters, the more clearly and distinctly do I perceive their truth. But what may I conclude from it all, finally? It is this: If I have any idea which I myself cannot be the cause of, it follows of necessity that I am not alone in the world, that there is some other being which exists as the cause of this idea. Have I any such idea?

There is the idea of God. Is this idea something that could have originated in, been caused by, me? By the name *God* I understand a being that is infinite, eternal, immutable, independent, all-knowing, all-powerful, by which I myself and everything else (if anything else does exist) have been created.

Now, all these qualities are such that the more diligently I attend to them, the less do they appear capable of originating in me alone. Hence, from what was premised above, we must conclude that God necessarily exists as the origin of this idea I have of Him. For, to consider but one point, the idea of a being or a substance is within me owing to the fact that I am myself a being or substance; nevertheless, I would not have the idea of an infinite being, since I am myself finite, unless it had proceeded from some being who was infinite.

I see nothing in all that I have just said which, by the light of nature, is not manifest to anyone who desires to think attentively on the subject. It only remains to examine into the manner in which I have acquired this idea from God.

I have not received it through the senses; nor is it a fiction of my mind, for it is not in my power to take from or add to it. The only alternative is that it is innate in me, just as the idea of myself is innate in me.

It is not strange that God, in creating me, placed this idea within me to be like the mark of the workman imprinted on his work. For, from the fact that God created me it is most probable that He has placed His image and similitude upon me. The whole strength of the argument which I have here used to prove the existence of God consists in this: it is not possible that my nature should be what it is, and that I should have in myself the idea of a God, if God did not exist. God, whose idea is in me, possesses all those supreme perfections of which our mind may have some idea but without understanding them all; is liable to no errors or defects, and has none of those marks which denote imperfection. From this it is manifest that He cannot be a deceiver, since fraud and deception proceed from some defect.

Before I pass on to the consideration of other truths which may be derived from this one, it seems to me right to pause for a while to contemplate God Himself, to ponder at leisure His marvelous attributes, to consider and to admire and to adore the beauty of His light. Faith teaches us that supreme felicity of the life to come consists in this contemplation of the Divine Majesty. Even so we continue to learn by experience that a similar meditation, though less perfect, causes us to enjoy the greatest satisfaction of which we are capable in this life.

Disillusionment. Systematic doubt. Existence of self as a thinking thing. Existence of God, no longer the deceiving genius of the early part of the argument. There remains only the external world, revealed by the senses. Can this be reinstated? Can its existence be shown to be part of the network, inextricably bound up with his own and Deity's nature and existence?

And so I see that the certainty and truth of all knowledge depends alone upon the knowledge of the true God. Before I knew Him, I could not have a perfect knowledge of any other thing. Now that I know Him I have the means of acquiring a perfect knowledge of any infinitude of things.

Nothing further now remains but to inquire whether material things exist. And first of all I shall recall those matters which I hitherto held to be true, as having perceived them through the senses; in the next place I shall examine the reasons which have since obliged me to place them in doubt; and in the last place I shall consider which of them I must now believe.

First of all, I perceived that I had a head, hands, feet, and all other members of which this body is composed. Further, I was sensible that this body was placed amid many others. In them, in addition to extension, figure, and motion, I remarked hardness, heat, light, color, scents, sounds, and so forth.

Considering the ideas of all these qualities which presented themselves to my mind, it was not without reason that I believed my self to perceive objects quite different from my thought, to wit, bodies from which those ideas proceeded. For I found by experience that these ideas of all these qualities presented themselves to me without my consent being needed. Thus, I could not perceive any object unless it were present to the organs of sense; nor could I help but perceive it, when it was present.

Furthermore, because these ideas which I received through my senses were clearer, more lively, more distinct, than any ideas I could myself frame in meditation or find in memory, it appeared as though they could not have proceeded from my mind. So, therefore, I concluded that they must have been produced in me by some other things. And, since I had no knowledge of these objects except the knowledge which the ideas themselves gave me, nothing was more likely to occur to my mind than that the objects themselves were similar to the ideas which were caused.

But afterwards many experiences destroyed, little by little, all the faith which I had rested in my senses. For example, I observed that towers, which from afar appeared to me to be round, seemed square when more closely observed; that colossal statues seemed quite tiny when viewed from a distance; that persons whose legs or arms had been cut off seemed to feel pain in the part which had been amputated; that my dreams, which could not be caused by outside objects, closely resembled my waking moments; and so on.

Now, however, that I begin to know myself better ("I am a thing which thinks") and to discover more clearly the author of my being, I do not think I should rashly admit all the things which the senses seem to teach me, nor do I think that I should doubt them all universally.

This much is certain, i.e., clear and distinct: There is in me the capacity to receive and recognize the ideas of sensible things. The active cause of these ideas which I passively receive cannot be in me, since those ideas are often produced in me without my contributing in any way to the same, often even against my will. It follows that the power which produces these ideas resides in some substance different from me. This substance is either a material object of God or some other creature.

But, I have argued already, God is no deceiver. He has given me a very great inclination to believe that my ideas of sensible objects are sent or conveyed to me by external material objects. I do not see how He could be defended from the accusation of deceit if these ideas were produced in me by any cause other than material objects. Hence we must allow that material objects exist.

We have examined a brief summary of Descartes' thought. In response to our question, "Am I a body and a mind?" Descartes would say, "I am both." Notice that he has supported that claim in the following way. He has established the existence of his mind (*res cogitans*) on the certainty of his own thinking. Then from the certainty of the imperfection of his own thinking he has demonstrated the existence of the standard of perfection, namely God. Finally, from the certainty of God's perfection he has shown that external bodies (*res extensa*) such as his own, do in fact exist.

NOTE ON SOURCES.   The material in this section is quoted, abridged, or paraphrased from René Descartes, *The Philosophical Works of Descartes*, translated by E. Haldane and G. R. T. Ross (New York: Dover Publications, Inc., 1955) I. The autobiographical account and the statement of the rules is from the *Discourse on Methods*, Parts I, II, III. The rest is from *Meditations* I, II, III, and VI.

2   GILBERT RYLE

DESCARTES WAS CONFUSED

FROM DESCARTES TO RYLE.   The mind–body problem basically involves three issues: Can a valid distinction between mind and body be made? If so, are there any existing things that correspond to those two terms? If that is so, what is the relation between mind and body? Although philosophers as far back as Plato dealt with some of these issues, Descartes was really the first to develop a systematic theory about the natures and interrelationships of mind and body. For him, body was a thing extended in space and unthinking, whereas mind was a thinking thing unextended in space. For him both body and mind were substances of different sorts so intimately united in the human being that mental events can affect physical events, and vice versa.

Descartes' position has been called dualism because of its affirmation of *two* substances. A good number of philosophers have followed Descartes in adopting dualism, although they may differ with him on how mind and body interact. Other philosophers, aware of the perplexing problems associated with dualism, have rejected dualism in favor of monism, which affirms *one* substance—either mind or body, but not both. Ryle mounts an attack on dualism in general and on Descartes in particular; an attack which every dualist committed to the examined life must take seriously.

BIOGRAPHICAL NOTE.   Gilbert Ryle was born in 1900. His academic education was received at Oxford where he taught until his retirement. He succeeded R. G. Collingwood as Waynflete professor of metaphysical philosophy at the University of Oxford at the end of World War II. He succeeded G. E. Moore as editor of the distinguished philosophical journal *Mind* in 1947. He published his most important and influential book, *The Concept of Mind*, in 1949. For the years 1945–1960, he was one of the most widely read and influential philosophers in the Anglo-American academic world. The reasons for this are to be found in the volumes of *Mind*, in his *Concept of Mind* (1949), his *Dilemmas* (1954), his *Plato's Progress* (1966), and his two volumes of *Collected Papers* (1971). He died in 1976.

THE ARGUMENT OF THE PASSAGES.   The following selection is Chapter One of Gilbert Ryle's *Concept of Mind*. In this chapter, titled *Descartes' Myth*, Ryle sets the problem for his book: How should we conceive of the nature of a mind and its relation to a body? The answer that most persons in the Western world, especially since Descartes' lifetime, have given to that question, Ryle calls the "official doctrine" and believes that it bristles with theoretical difficulties.

The chapter is divided into three sections and a brief terminal historical note. Section One, The Official Doctrine, is a vivid and deflationary account of how many, indeed most, people conceive of a person in terms of a mind–body dualism. Every person, the doctrine declares, has a mind and a body, or *is* a combination, a union of a mind and a body. Bodies are located in space and are subject to mechanical laws. In contrast, minds are not located in space, have no spatial dimensions, no spatial size or shape, and are not subject to mechanical laws. Frequently, the terms *external* and *internal, outer* and *inner*, used in a metaphorical sense, are applied to bodies and minds, respectively. Bodies have surfaces, can meet and collide and jolt; minds have no surfaces, cannot meet "head on." How these spatial bodies are related to nonspatial minds is obscure. How they can influence each other, "interact," is a difficult theoretical question. Events in one body can directly cause events in another body. But do events in one mind cause events in another mind? And do events in a mind cause events in the body which that mind presumably "inhabits"? If not, minds are shut out from their bodies and shut off from each other.

Additional difficulties with the "official doctrine" arise. Bodily processes can be observed by second-party observers: I can observe that your body is blanching and sweating and trembling. But I cannot thus observe workings in your mind. They are not witnessable by me. They are "private" to you. I can observe your body wince. I cannot feel your pain. Each of us has direct and unchallengeable knowledge of at least some events in our own minds, but no such knowledge of events in each other's minds. I can observe what happens to or goes on in your body. I may infer from that to what happens or goes on in your mind, but I have no way of confirming that inference by any observation. The question then arises: Does any person have any good reason for believing in the existence of other minds? Other bodies, yes; other minds, how so? The "official doctrine," then, leads us to the notion that each person has two "histories": a history of one's bodily events and a history of one's mental events. But, says Ryle, the relation between these two "histories" is not at all clear.

(1) THE OFFICIAL DOCTRINE

There is a doctrine about the nature and place of minds which is so prevalent among theorists and even among laymen that it deserves to be described as the official theory. Most philosophers, psychologists and religious teachers subscribe, with minor reservations, to its main articles and, although they admit certain theoretical difficulties in it, they tend to assume that these can be overcome without serious modifications being made to the architecture of the theory. It will be argued here that the central principles of the doctrine are unsound and conflict with the whole body of what we know about minds when we are not speculating about them.

The official doctrine, which hails chiefly from Descartes, is something like this. With the doubtful exceptions of idiots and infants in arms every human being has both a body and a mind. Some would prefer to say that every human being is both a body and a mind. His body and his mind are ordinarily harnessed together, but after the death of the body his mind may continue to exist and function.

Human bodies are in space and are subject to the mechanical laws which govern all other bodies in space. Bodily processes and states can be inspected by external observers. So a man's bodily life is as much a public affair as are the lives of animals and reptiles and even as the careers of trees, crystals and planets.

But minds are not in space, nor are their operations subject to mechanical laws. The workings of one mind are not witnessable by other observers; its career is private. Only I can take direct cognisance of the states and processes of my own mind. A person therefore lives through two collateral histories, one consisting of what happens in and to his body, the other consisting of what happens in and to his mind. The first is public, the second private. The events in the first history are events in the physical world, those in the second are events in the mental world.

It has been disputed whether a person does or can directly monitor all or only some of the episodes of his own private history; but, according to the official doctrine, of at least some of these episodes he has direct and unchallengeable cognisance. In consciousness, self-consciousness and introspection he is directly and authentically apprised of the present states and operations of his mind. He may have great or small uncertainties about concurrent and adjacent episodes in the physical world, but he can have none about at least part of what is momentarily occupying his mind.

It is customary to express this bifurcation of his two lives and of his two worlds by saying that the things and events which belong to the physical world, including his own body, are external, while the workings of his own mind are internal. This antithesis of outer and inner is of course meant to be construed as a metaphor, since minds, not being in space, could not be described as being spatially inside anything else, or as having things going on spatially inside themselves. But relapses from this good intention are common and theorists are found speculating how stimuli, the physical sources of which are yards or miles outside a person's skin, can generate mental responses inside his skull, or how decisions framed inside his cranium can set going movements of his extremities.

Even when "inner" and "outer" are construed as metaphors, the problem how a person's mind and body influence one another is notoriously charged with theoretical difficulties. What the mind wills, the legs, arms, and tongue execute; what affects the ear and the eye has something to do with what the mind perceives; grimaces and smiles betray the mind's moods and bodily castigations lead, it is hoped, to moral improvement. But the actual transactions between the episodes of the private history and those of the public history remain mysterious, since by definition they can belong to neither series. They could not be reported among the happenings described in a person's autobiography of his inner life, nor could they be reported among those described in someone else's biography of that person's overt career. They can be inspected neither by introspection nor by laboratory experiment. They are theoretical shuttlecocks which are forever being bandied from the physiologist back to the psychologist and from the psychologist back to the physiologist.

Underlying this partly metaphorical representation of the bifurcation of a person's two lives there is a seemingly more profound and philosophical assumption. It is assumed that there are two different kinds of existence or status. What exists or happens may have the status of physical existence, or it may have the status of mental existence. Somewhat as the faces of coins are either heads of tails, or somewhat as living creatures are either male or female, so, it is supposed, some existing is physical existing, other existing is mental existing. It is a necessary feature of what has physical existence that it is in space and time; it is a necessary feature of what has mental existence that it is in time but not in space. What has physical existence is composed of matter, or else is a function of matter; what has mental existence consists of consciousness, or else is a function of consciousness.

There is thus a polar opposition between mind and matter, an opposition which is often brought out as follows. Material objects are situated in a common field, known as "space," and what happens to one body in one part of space is mechanically connected with what happens to other bodies in other parts of space. But mental happenings occur in insulated fields, known as "minds," and there is, apart maybe from telepathy, no direct causal connection between what happens in one mind and what happens in another. Only through the medium of the public physical world can the mind of one person make a difference to the mind of another. The mind is its own place and in his inner life each of us lives the life of a ghostly Robinson Crusoe. People can see, hear and jolt one another's bodies, but they are irremediably blind and deaf to the workings of one another's minds and inoperative upon them.

What sort of knowledge can be secured of the workings of a mind? On the one side, according to the official theory, a person has direct knowledge of the best imaginable kind of the workings of his own mind. Mental states and processes are (or are normally) conscious states and processes, and the consciousness which irradiates them can engender no illusions and leaves the door open for no doubts. A person's present thinkings, feelings and willings, his perceivings, rememberings and imaginings are intrinsically "phosphorescent"; their existence and their nature are inevitably betrayed to the owner. The inner life is a stream of consciousness of such a sort that it would be absurd to suggest that the mind whose life is that stream might be unaware of what is passing down it.

True, the evidence adduced recently by Freud seemed to show that there exist channels tributary to this stream, which run hidden from their owner. People are actuated by impulses the existence of which they vigorously disavow; some of their thoughts differ from the thoughts which they acknowledge; and some of the actions which they think they will to perform they do not really will. They are thoroughly gulled by some of their own hypocrisies and they successfully ignore facts about their mental lives which on the official theory ought to be patent to them. Holders of the official theory tend, however, to maintain that anyhow in normal circumstances a person must be directly and authentically seized of the present state and workings of his own mind.

Besides being currently supplied with these alleged immediate data of consciousness, a person is also generally supposed to be able to exercise from time to time a special kind of perception, namely inner perception, or introspection. He can take a (non-optical) "look" at what is passing in his mind. Not only can he view and scrutinize a flower through his sense of sight and listen to and discriminate the notes of a bell through his sense of hearing; he can also reflectively or introspectively watch, without any bodily organ of sense, the current episodes of his inner life. This self-observation is also commonly supposed to be immune from illusion, confusion, or doubt. A mind's reports of its own affairs have a certainty superior to the best that is possessed by its reports of matters in the physical world. Sense-perceptions can, but consciousness and introspection cannot, be mistaken or confused.

On the other side, one person has no direct access of any sort to the events of the inner life of another. He cannot do better than make problematic inferences from the observed behavior of the other person's body to the states of mind, which by analogy from his own conduct, he supposes to be signalized by that behavior. Direct access to the workings of a mind is the privilege of that mind itself; in default of such privileged access, the workings of one mind are inevitably occult to everyone else. For the supposed arguments from bodily movements similar to their own to mental workings similar to their own would lack any possibility of observational corroboration. Not unnaturally, therefore, an adherent of the official theory finds it difficult to resist this consequence of his premises, that he has no good reason to believe that there do exist minds other than his own. Even if he prefers to believe that to other human bodies there are harnessed minds not unlike his own, he cannot claim to be able to discover their individual characteristics, or the particular things that they undergo and do. Absolute solitude is on this showing the ineluctable destiny of the soul. Only our bodies can meet.

As a necessary corollary of this general scheme there is implicitly prescribed a special way of construing our ordinary concepts of mental powers and operations. The verbs, nouns, and adjectives, with which in ordinary life we describe the wits, characteristics, and higher grade performances of the people with whom we have to do, are required to be construed as signifying special episodes in their secret histories, or else as signifying tendencies for such episodes to occur. When someone is described as knowing, believing, or guessing something, as hoping, dreading, intending, or shirking something, as designing this or being amused at that, these verbs are supposed to denote the occurrence or specific modifications in his (to us) occult stream of consciousness. Only his own privileged access to this stream in direct awareness and introspection could provide authentic testimony that these mental-conduct verbs are correctly or incorrectly applied. The onlooker, be he teacher, critic, biographer, or friend, can never assure himself that his comments have any vestige of truth. Yet it was just because we do in fact know how to make such comments, make them with general correctness and correct them when they turn out to be confused or mistaken, that philosophers found it necessary to construct their theories of the nature and place of minds. Finding mental-conduct concepts being regularly and effectively used, they properly sought to fix their logical geography. But the logical geography officially recommended would entail that there could be no regular or effective use of these mental-conduct concepts in our descriptions of, and prescriptions for, other people's minds.

Ryle's claim, then, is that the "official" doctrine is that a person's body is a "machine" intimately but obscurely related to his mind, which "inhabits" or "animates" his body machine. He refers to this traditional body-mind dualism as the doctrine of the "ghost in the machine," and claims that those who hold it are thereby involved in a number of theoretical absurdities, all of which express in one way or another a gross and flagrant "category-mistake." He gives examples of category-mistakes, none of which is the particular category-mistake present in the untenable notion of a person as a "ghost in a machine." A person who, having seen the colleges that make up Oxford University, asked, "Where, now, is the university?" would be guilty of a category-mistake, imagining that the university itself existed in the same way that the colleges did. Similarly, with a person who, having witnessed the marching of the battalions that make up a division, should then ask to see the division, ignoring the fact that a division does not exist in the way that its battalions do. His other examples are to the same effect. A more blatantly nonsensical example of category-mistake would be made by a person who should say, "She came in a taxi and left in a rage," and then go on to ask questions about the rage that presupposed that it had the same order of existence as the taxi; for example, "How fast did it travel?" "What fuel did it use?" and so on. To such a person we would say, "Your questions do not arise, a rage belongs in a radically different category from a taxi." In this second section of Chapter 1, Ryle is more concerned to illustrate the notion of a category-mistake, and how it could give rise to completely pointless and misleading questions, than to spell out the particular category-mistake that gives rise to the "impossible" "ghost-in-the-machine" notion of a person as a body united with a mind. It takes the rest of the book to spell out *that* category-mistake and to suggest some other way of conceiving of the body–mind relation.

(2) THE ABSURDITY OF THE OFFICIAL DOCTRINE

Such in outline is the official theory. I shall often speak of it, with deliberate abusiveness, as "the dogma of the Ghost in the Machine." I hope to prove that it is entirely false, and false not in detail but in principle. It is not merely an assemblage of particular mistakes. It is one big mistake and a mistake of a special kind. It is namely, a category-mistake. It represents the facts of mental life as if they belonged to one logical type or category (or range of types or categories), when they actually belong to another. The dogma is, therefore, a philosopher's myth. In attempting to explode the myth I shall probably be taken to be denying well-known facts about the mental life of human beings, and my plea that I aim at doing nothing more than rectify the logic of mental-conduct concepts will probably be disallowed as mere subterfuge.

I must first indicate what is meant by the phrase "category-mistake." This I do in a series of illustrations.

A foreigner visiting Oxford or Cambridge for the first time is shown a number of colleges, libraries, playing fields, museums, scientific departments, and administrative officers. He then asks, "But where is the University? I have seen where the members of the College live, where the Registrar works, where the scientists experiment and the rest. But I have not yet seen the University in which reside and work the members of your University." It has then to be explained to him that the University is not another collateral institution, some ulterior counterpart to the colleges, laboratories and offices which he has seen. The University is just the way in which all that he has already seen is organized. When they are seen and when their coordination is understood, the University has been seen. His mistake lay in his innocent assumption that it was correct to speak of Christ Church, the Bodleian Library, the Ashmolean Museum, *and* the University, to speak, that is, as if "the University" stood for an extra member of the class of which these other units are members. He was mistakenly allocating the University to the same category as that to which the other institutions belong.

The same mistake would be made by a child witnessing the march-past of a division, who, having pointed out to him such and such battalions, batteries, squadrons, etc., asked when the division was going to appear. He would be supposing that a division was a counterpart to the units already seen, partly similar to them and partly unlike them. He would be shown his mistake by being told that in watching the battalions, batteries, and squadrons marching past he had been watching the division marching past. The march-past was not a parade of battalions, batteries, squadrons, *and* a division; it was a parade of battalions, batteries, and squadrons *of* a division.

One more illustration. A foreigner watching his first game of cricket learns what are the functions of the bowlers, the batsmen, the fielders, the umpires, and the scorers. He then says, "But there is no one left on the field to contribute the famous element of team-spirit. I see who does the bowling, the batting, and the wicketkeeping; but I do not see whose role it is to exercise *esprit de corps.*" Once more, it would have to be explained that he was looking for the wrong type of thing. Team-spirit is not another cricketing-operation supplementary to all of the other special tasks. It is roughly, the keenness with which each of the special tasks is performed, and performing a task keenly is not performing two tasks. Certainly exhibiting team-spirit is not the same thing as bowling or catching, but nor is it a third thing such that we can say that the bowler first bowls *and* then exhibits team-spirit or that a fielder is at a given moment *either* catching *or* displaying *esprit de corps.*

These illustrations of category-mistakes have a common feature which must be noted. The mistakes were made by people who did not know how to wield the concepts *University, division* and *team-spirit.* Their puzzles arose from inability to use certain items in the English vocabulary.

The theoretically interesting category-mistakes are those made by people who are perfectly competent to apply concepts, at least in the situations with which they are familiar, but are still liable in their abstract thinking to allocate those concepts to logical types to which they do not belong. An instance of a mistake of this sort would be the following story. A student of politics has learned the main differences between the British, the French and the American Constitutions, and has learned also the differences and connections between the Cabinet, Parliament, the various Ministries, the Judicature and the Church of England. But he still becomes embarrassed when asked questions about the connections between the Church of England, the Home Office, and the British Constitution. For while the Church and the Home Office are institutions, the British Constitution is not another institution in the same sense of that noun. So inter-institutional relations which can be asserted or denied to hold between the Church and the Home Office cannot be asserted or denied to hold between either of them and the British Constitution. "The British Constitution" is not a term of the same logical type as "the Home Office" and "the Church of England." In a partially similar way, John Doe may be a relative, a friend, an enemy or a stranger to Richard Roe; but he cannot be any of these things to the Average Taxpayer. He knows how to talk sense in certain sorts of discussions about the Average Taxpayer, but he is baffled to say why he could not come across him in the street as he can come across Richard Roe.

It is pertinent to our main subject to notice that, so long as the student of politics continues to think of the British Constitution as a counterpart to the other institutions, he will tend to describe it as a mysteriously occult institution; and so long as John Doe continues to think of the Average Taxpayer as a fellow-citizen, he will tend to think of him as an elusive insubstantial man, a ghost who is everywhere yet nowhere.

My destructive purpose is to show that a family of radical category-mistakes is the source of the double-life theory. The representation of a person as a ghost mysteriously ensconced in a machine derives from this argument. Because, as is true, a person's thinking, feeling and purposive doing cannot be described solely in the idioms of physics, chemistry and physiology, therefore they must be described in counterpart idioms. As the human body is a complex organized unit, so the human mind must be another complex organized unit, though one made of a different sort of stuff and a different sort of structure. Or, again, as the human body, like any other parcel of matter, is a field of causes and effects, so the mind must be another field of causes and effects, though not (Heaven be praised) mechanical causes and effects.

In the upcoming third section Ryle asks how this body–mind category-mistake ever came to be made anyway. To use his own words to frame this question, we could ask, "What was the intellectual origin of what I have yet to prove to be the Cartesian category-mistake?" His answer is along this line: Finding that the mechanistic model of modern science made good sense of processes that go on in the physical world, Descartes saw that if that model were applied to the human being as a complete and sufficient explanation of human activity, then dire consequences would result in the religious and ethical domains. For example, if the human is only a complex physical machine, what becomes of the soul, freedom, immortality, and moral accountability? Unwilling, therefore, to reduce humans to the status of mere complex clockworks, Descartes and his philosophical followers suggested that whereas such sciences as physics, chemistry, and physiology made good sense of the mechanical processes that go on in the body, another science, say, psychology, would investigate the nonmechanical processes that go on in the mind. This of course, presupposed the "existence" of bodies *and* minds, bodily substances and processes, *and* mental substances and processes. The more the scheme "worked," the more it "confirmed" this body–mind dualism. Once the dualism was thoroughly installed, there arose all the tangle of cross-category questions and puzzles that have made a theoretical shambles of our notion of a person and of our notion of the relation of physics to psychology.

(3) THE ORIGIN OF THE CATEGORY-MISTAKE

One of the chief intellectual origins of what I have yet to prove to be the Cartesian category-mistake seems to be this. When Galileo showed that his methods of scientific discovery were competent to provide a mechanical theory which should cover every occupant of space, Descartes found in himself two conflicting motives. As a man of scientific genius he could not but endorse the claims of mechanics, yet as a religious and moral man he could not accept, as Hobbes accepted, the discouraging rider to those claims, namely that human nature differs only in degree of complexity from clockwork. The mental could not be just a variety of the mechanical.

He and subsequent philosophers naturally but erroneously availed themselves of the following escape-route. Since mental-conduct words are not to be construed as signifying the occurrence of mechanical processes, they must be construed as signifying the occurrence of nonmechanical processes; since mechanical laws explain movements in space as the effects of other movements in space, other laws must explain some of the non-spatial workings of minds as the effects of other non-spatial workings of minds. The difference between the human behaviors which we describe as intelligent and those which we describe as unintelligent must be a difference in their causation; so, while some movements of human tongues and limbs are the effects of mechanical causes, others must be the effects of non-mechanical causes i.e., some issue from movements of particles of matter, others from workings of the mind.

The differences between the physical and the mental were thus represented as differences inside the common framework of the categories of "thing," "stuff," "attribute," "state," "process," "change," "cause," and "effect." Minds are things, but different sort of things from bodies; mental processes are causes and effects, but different sorts of causes and effects from bodily movements. And so on. Somewhat as the foreigner expected the University to be an extra edifice, rather like a college but also considerably different, so the repudiators of mechanism represented minds as extra centers of causal processes, rather like machines but also considerably different from them. Their theory was a para-mechanical hypothesis.

That this assumption was at the heart of the doctrine is shown by the fact that there was from the beginning felt to be a major theoretical difficulty in explaining how minds can influence and be influenced by bodies. How can a mental process, such as willing, cause spatial movements like the movements of the tongue? How can a physical change in the optic nerve have among its effects a mind's perception of a flash of light? This notorious crux by itself shows the logical mould into which Descartes pressed his theory of the mind. It was the self-same mould into which he and Galileo set their mechanics. Still unwittingly adhering to the grammar of mechanics he tried to avert disaster by describing minds in what was merely an obverse vocabulary. The workings of minds had to be described by the mere negatives of the specific descriptions given to bodies; they are not in space, they are not motions, they are not modification of matter, they are not accessible to public observation. Minds are not bits of clockwork, they are just bits of not-clockwork.

As thus represented, minds are not merely ghosts harnessed to machines, they are themselves just spectral machines. Though the human body is an engine, it is not quite an ordinary engine, since some of its workings are governed by another engine inside it—this interior governor-engine being one of a very special sort. It is invisible, inaudible and it has no size or weight. It cannot be taken to bits and the laws it obeys are not those known to ordinary engineers. Nothing is known of how it governs the bodily engine.

A second major crux points the same moral. Since, according to the doctrine, minds belong to the same category as bodies and since bodies are rigidly governed by mechanical laws, it seemed to many theorists to follow that minds must be similarly governed by rigid non-mechanical laws. The physical world is a deterministic system, so the mental world must be a deterministic system. Bodies cannot help the modifications that they undergo, so minds cannot help pursuing the careers fixed for them. *Responsibility, choice, merit* and *demerit* are therefore inapplicable concepts—unless the compromise solution is adopted of saying that the laws governing mental processes, unlike those governing physical processes, have the congenial attribute of being only rather rigid. The problem of the Freedom of the Will was the problem how to reconcile the hypothesis that minds are to be described in terms drawn from the categories of mechanics with the knowledge that higher-grade human conduct is not a piece with the behaviour of machines.

It is an historical curiosity that it was not noticed that the entire argument was broken-backed. Theorists correctly assumed that any sane man could already recognise the differences between, say, rational and non-rational utterances or between purposive and automatic behavior. Else there would have been nothing requiring to be salved from mechanism. Yet the explanation given presupposed that one person could in principle never recognise the difference between the rational and irrational utterances issuing from other human bodies, since he could never get access to the postulated immaterial causes of some of their utterances. Save for the doubtful exception of himself, he could never tell the difference between a man and a Robot. It would have to be conceded, for example, that, for all that we can tell, the inner lives of persons who are classed as idiots or lunatics are as rational as those of anyone else. Perhaps only their overt behaviour is disappointing; that is to say, perhaps "idiots" are not really idiotic, or "lunatics" lunatic. Perhaps, too, some of those who are classed as sane are really idiots. According to the theory, external observers could never know how the overt behaviour of others is correlated with their mental powers and processes and so they could never know or even plausibly conjecture whether their applications of mental-conduct concepts to these other people were correct or incorrect. It would then be hazardous or impossible for a man to claim sanity or logical consistency even for himself, since he would be debarred from comparing his own performances with those of others. In short, our characteristics of persons and their performances as intelligent, prudent and virtuous or as stupid, hypocritical and cowardly could never have been made, so the problem of providing a special causal hypothesis to serve as the basis of such diagnoses would never have arisen. The question, "How do persons differ from machines?" arose just because everyone already knew how to apply mental-conduct concepts before the new causal hypothesis was introduced. This hypothesis could not therefore be the source of the criteria used in those applications. Nor, of course, has the causal hypothesis in any degree improved our handling of those criteria. We still distinguish good from bad arithmetic, polite from impolite conduct and fertile from infertile imaginations in the ways in which

Descartes himself distinguished them before and after he speculated how the applicability of these criteria was compatible with the principle of mechanical causation.

He had mistaken the logic of his problem. Instead of asking by what criteria intelligent behaviour is actually distinguished from non-intelligent behaviour, he asked "Given that the principle of mechanical causation does not tell us the difference, what other causal principle will tell us?" He realized that the problem was not one of the mechanics and assumed that it must therefore be one of some counterpart to mechanics. Not unnaturally psychology is often cast for just this role.

When two terms belong to the same category, it is proper to construct conjunctive propositions embodying them. Thus a purchaser may say that he bought a left-hand glove and a right-hand glove, but not that he brought a left-hand glove, a right-hand glove and a pair of gloves. "She came home in a flood of tears and a sedan-chair" is a well-known joke based on the absurdity of conjoining terms of different types. It would have been equally ridiculous to construct the disjunction "She came home either in a flood of tears or else in a sedan-chair." Now the dogma of the Ghost in the Machine does just this. It maintains that there exist both bodies and minds; that there occur physical processes and mental processes; that there are mechanical causes of corporeal movements and mental causes of corporeal movements. I shall argue that these and other analogous conjunctions are absurd; but, it must be noticed, the argument will not show that either of the illegitimately conjoined propositions is absurd in itself. I am not, for example, denying that there occur mental processes. Doing long division is a mental process and so is making a joke. But I am saying that the phrase "there occur mental processes" does not mean the same sort of thing as "there occur physical processes," and, therefore, that it makes no sense to conjoin or disjoin the two.

If my argument is successful, there will follow some interesting consequences. First, the hallowed contrast between Mind and Matter will be dissipated, but dissipated not by either of the equally hallowed absorptions of Mind by Matter or of Matter by Mind, but in quite a different way. For the seeming contrast of the two will be shown to be as illegitimate as would be the contrast of "she came home in a flood of tears" and "she came home in a sedan-chair." The belief that there is a polar opposition between Mind and Matter is the belief that they are terms of the same logical type.

It will also follow that both Idealism and Materialism are answers to an improper question. The "reduction" of mental states and processes to physical states and processes, presupposes the legitimacy of the disjunction "Either there exist minds or there exist bodies (but not both)." It would be like saying, "Either she bought a left-hand and a right-hand glove or she bought a pair of gloves (but not both)."

It is perfectly proper to say, in one logical tone of voice, that there exist minds and to say, in another logical tone of voice, that there exist bodies. But these expressions do not indicate two different species of existence, for "existence" is not a generic word like "coloured" or "sexed." They indicate two different senses of "exist," somewhat as "rising" has different senses in the "the tide is rising," "hopes are rising," and "the average age of death is rising." A man would be thought to be making a poor joke who said that three things are now rising, namely the tide, hopes and the average age of death. It would be just as good or bad a joke to say that there exist prime numbers and Wednesdays and public opinions and navies; or that there exist both minds and bodies. In the succeeding chapters I try to prove that the official theory does rest on a batch of category-mistakes by showing that logically absurd corollaries follow from it. The exhibition of these absurdities will have the constructive effect of bringing out part of the correct logic of mental-conduct concepts.

HISTORICAL NOTES

It would not be true to say that the official theory derives solely from Descartes' theories, or even from a more widespread anxiety about the implications of seventeenth century mechanics. Scholastic and Reformation theology had schooled the intellects of the scientists as well as of the laymen, philosophers and clerics of that age. Stoic–Augustinian theories of the will were embedded in the Calvinist doctrines of sin and grace; Platonic and Aristotelian theories of the intellect shaped the orthodox doctrines of the immortality of the soul in the new syntax of Galileo. The theologian's privacy of conscience became the philosopher's privacy of consciousness, and what had been the bogy of Predestination reappeared as the bogy of Determinism.

It would also not be true to say that the two-worlds myth did no theoretical good. Myths often do a lot of theoretical good, while they are still new. One benefit bestowed by the para-mechanical myth was that it partly superannuated the then prevalent para-political myth. Minds and their Faculties had previously been described by analogies with political superiors and political subordinates. The idioms used were those of ruling, obeying, collaborating and rebelling. They survived and still survive in many ethical and some epistemological discussions. As, in physics, the new myth of occult Forces was a scientific improvement on the old myth of Final Causes, so, in anthropological and psychological theory, the new myth of hidden operations, impulses and agencies was an improvement on the old myth of dictations, differences, and disobediences.

According to Ryle, then, at the heart of Descartes' mind–body dualism is a serious category-mistake. That mistake involves the assumption that mind and body exist in the *same sort of way*. It is permissible, says Ryle, to speak of minds and mental processes as existing. For example, we might say that "Socrates had a keen mind" and then go on to discuss what we mean by his "keen mind." Such a conversation would be legitimate provided we did not assume that Socrates' "keen mind" existed in the same sort of way as a "purple robe" in the statement "Socrates had a purple robe." "Keen minds" do not exist in the same sort of way that "purple robes" exist. "Minds" involve mental processes. "Robes" involve physical processes; and so do "bodies." The whole mind–body problem assumes that mind and body, mental processes, and physical processes exist in the same sort of way. "Not so!" says Ryle.

We are misled, argues Ryle, when we assume that terms such as happy, sad, angry, bewildered, intelligent—mentalistic terms as they are often called by philosophers—are properties like tall, short, and red-haired. These latter properties are readily determined properties of people. It takes only a glance to see that Wilt Chamberlain is tall, that Mickey Rooney is short, and that Little Orphan Annie has orange-red hair. Mentalistic terms are, however, different. They are dispositions to behave in certain ways. For example, to call a person intelligent is to say that the person is very likely to be able to do certain things; e.g., score well on SAT tests and calculus exams. But it is important to remember that a person can be intelligent and do stupid things now and then. This is what makes "being intelligent" a dispositional property. Just as glass is fragile even when it is not shattering, so an intelligent person is intelligent even when doing poorly on one quiz. But a tall person cannot also be short (unless one is playing with words and contexts).

A somewhat extended example will help. Most sugar cubes are white. We can tell this by looking at the cube. Most sugar cubes are also soluble in hot water. This we cannot tell just by looking at the sugar cube itself. Saying that the sugar cube is soluble means that when it is placed in hot water, the sugar cube will dissolve. Solubility is a dispositional property. White is not a dispositional property.

Descartes did not make the distinction between dispositional and nondispositional properties. Ryle imagines that someone says to Descartes "I see the sugar and its whiteness, but where is its solubility?" Or, more to our point, suppose someone said, "I hear Sam screaming and see that Sam is red in the face and breathing hard, but where is the anger?" The insight that mentalistic properties are really dispositional properties, determinable, but not readily determined, leads to rejecting the question, "Where is the anger?" as misguided—based on the incorrect assumption that all properties are nondispositional.

Often, Ryle's position is referred to as logical behaviorism. "Behaviorism" is meant to call attention to the need to focus on behavior, whereas "logical" is meant to remind us that Ryle is talking about the logic of the concepts; i.e., the meanings, and relationships between the meanings, of the words we use to talk about pain, anger, love, hate, fear, anxiety, etc.

Remember that Descartes was trying to understand how the mental world, which he insisted had to be nonextended, could interact with the physical world, which was extended. This was a problem because the model for causality at the time was a push or a pull. How could a nonextended thing push or pull anything? This problem of how the mind interacts with the body is called the mind–body problem.

It is by no means clear whether Ryle is correct in thinking that he has dissolved the mind–body problem. As Jerry Fodor points out, in an article which we shall soon read, Ryle does a commendable job criticizing Descartes, but, for all his cleverness, leaves us wondering about whether the mind–body problem has really been dissolved. Thus, it is worth looking at some other answers to the mind–body problem.

1. Everything is really mental. The physical is only an aspect of the mental. That is, the physical can be fully understood in terms of the mental. This view is called idealism or absolute idealism. G. W. F. Hegel held a version of idealism known as objective idealism. George Berkeley held a version of idealism which has come to be called subjective idealism.
2. Everything is just physical. The mental is only an aspect of the physical. That is, the mental can be fully understood solely and only in terms of the physical. Contemporary philosophers J. J. C. Smart and David M.

Armstrong hold variations of this position, which is known as The Identity Theory. Herbert Feigl, who will be cited in the selection from Smart that we will read, also believed that the mental was an aspect of the physical.

Answers (1) and (2) are forms of Monism—the view that there is only one kind of thing; and that what appear to be other kinds of things can be understood in terms of this one basic kind of thing because, when properly understood, there is only one kind of basic thing.

3. The mental and the physical are two aspects of yet another kind of thing. This position is called the dual aspect view. Seventeenth century philosopher Benedict (Baruch) Spinoza held this view.
4. The mental and the physical are parallel. They do not really interact. The interaction is only apparent. It is due to their being set up in a series so that it looks as if there is interaction. This position is called parallelism. Spinoza's contemporary, Leibniz, held this position.
5. Every mental thing is related to a physical thing in the way that oil gauge readings in an automobile are related to oil pressure. It is the pressure that causes the reading. The reading itself usually has no causal effect on the pressure or anything else. This view is called epiphenomenalism, a name which picturesquely suggests the mental hanging from the physical as an epiphyte (such as an orchid or a fern) hangs from a tree. American philosopher William James held this view.
6. The mental is the ability to make complex computations. If this ability is restricted to brains, then this is just a refined version of Identity Theory. When it is assumed that it does not matter what kind of thing actually does the complex computation, the view is called functionalism. Functionalism is an answer to the mind–body problem that is related to the growth of the field known as cognitive science, a mix of philosophy, mathematics, linguistics, computer science, and psychology. Jerry Fodor is a firm proponent of this view.

The mind–body problem was not the only problem Descartes had. Once he had determined that certainty could be found only with the *cogito* as the starting point, how could he ever be sure that there were other minds, other things with thoughts. Perception is not only untrustworthy it also fails to let us see the thoughts of others. (Notice that in Descartes' view, the word *other* can mean only "other thing that looks and acts just as I do.") This problem is called (not unsurprisingly) the problem of other minds.

In the next readings, we will see some contemporary attempts to answer both the mind–body problem as well as the problem of other minds.

NOTE ON SOURCES.   The material in this section is quoted from Gilbert Ryle, *Concept of Mind* (New York: Harper & Row, 1949), Chapter 1.

J. J. C. SMART

THE IDENTITY THEORY

FROM RYLE TO SMART.   The Identity Theory is a famous attempt to solve the mind–body problem. Very simply, the Identity Theory asserts that mental states are nothing more than neurophysiological states; the mental is just a lot of bio-chemistry. Because of this, we say that the Identity Theory reduces the mental to the physical. It is sometimes referred to as physicalistic reductionism, because the mental has been reduced to the physical. In Smart's version of the Identity Theory, the mental as a category should drop out of existence, just as we are now sure that there are no, and never were, mermaids. This kind of reductionism is called eliminative reductionism. As we will see, Smart does not want to be committed to the view that we do not have experiences, or the view that different experiences are experienced differently. As some philosophers say, Smart does not deny the existence of raw feels. (See his reply to Objection 3.)

What is a raw feel? We have no problem telling the difference between the smell of a rose and the smell of a garlic clove. The experiences are not just quantitatively different, that is, occurring at different times or in different places. We tell them apart as two experiences because they are also qualitatively different; that is, they smell different. We have even less trouble distinguishing between the experiences of touching a rose and smelling a rose. In both cases, a rose is subjected to our senses, but we have no trouble distinguishing the experiences. Philosophers use the expression "raw feel" to characterize the basic experienced difference that allows us to distinguish these experiences. We might sum it all up by saying of these experiences, "they just feel different." It is these differences that are crucial to the way we experience our lives. How could any reasonable theory of the mental and physical deny that these experiences are real?

BIOGRAPHICAL NOTE.   Smart was born in Cambridge, England in 1920. He was educated at the University of Glasgow and Oxford, where he received his D.Phil. degree. He has taught at the University of Adelaide, where he was the Hughes Professor of Philosophy. Dr. Smart is presently professor emeritus at the Institute of Advanced Studies at the Australian National University in Canberra. Besides his many publications in philosophy of science and philosophy of mind, Smart has also published many works on ethics, especially the philosophy of Utilitarianism.

THE ARGUMENT OF THE PASSAGES.   Some examples of the sort of identity Smart has in mind will help.

"The morning star" and "the evening star" both refer to the same thing—the planet Venus. "Superman" and "Clark Kent" are both the same person. "Lake Victoria" and "the source of the Nile" refer to the same body of water. "Lightning" and "an electrical discharge" are not two different things. There is just one thing. In each of these cases, the identity had to be discovered.

Both Australia and the planet Pluto were discovered. It took only the correct way of looking, with a ship and with a telescope. Once we know the rules for taking square roots, the identity of 3 and $\sqrt{9}$ follows logically. But this identity is not discovered in the same way that islands and planets are discovered. Knowing how to build ships and sail them would not lead to discovering Australia unless there actually were a very large island (small continent) to be found. The identity between mind and body is a matter of scientifically discoverable fact. This is opposed to logical identities as in definitions, e.g., trigonometric identities ($\tan \theta = \text{sine } \theta / \cos \theta$.)

Once Smart convinces us that this sort of identity is feasible he gives general reasons for accepting the Identity Theory. The progress of science seems to indicate that mental states will be discovered to be brain states. "Nomological danglers" should be avoided. A nomological dangler is something that by definition cannot be fit into the laws of science. ("Nomological" means in accord with a law. Dangler is just a colorful way of referring to something's not fitting in with science.) Of all scientific and philosophical accounts, Smart claims the brain process theory (the mental is identical to a brain process) makes the most sense. As a theory, it is simple, fecund (leads to many other important ideas), and coheres (fits) with other things that we believe.

> It seems to me that science is increasingly giving us a viewpoint whereby organisms are able to be seen as physicochemical mechanisms; it seems that even the behavior of man himself will one day be explicable in mechanistic terms. There does seem to be, so far as science is concerned, nothing in the world but increasingly complex arrangements of physical constituents. All except for one place: in consciousness. That is, for a full description of what is going on in a man you would have to mention not only the physical processes in his tissues, glands, nervous system, and so forth, but also his states of consciousness: his visual, auditory, and tactual sensations, his aches and pains. That these should be *correlated* with brain processes does not help, for to say that they are *correlated* is to say that they are something "over and above." So sensations, states of consciousness, do seem to be the one sort of thing left outside the physicalist picture, and for various reasons I just cannot believe that this can be so. That everything should be explicable in terms of physics (together of course with descriptions of the ways in which the parts are put together—roughly, biology is to physics as radio-engineering is to electromagnetism) except the occurrence of sensations seems to me to be frankly unbelievable. Such sensations would be "nomological danglers," to use Feigl's expression. It is not often realized how odd would be the laws whereby these nomological danglers would dangle. It is sometimes asked, "Why can't there be psychophysical laws which are of a novel sort, just as the laws of electricity and magnetism were novelties from the standpoint of Newtonian mechanics?" Certainly we are pretty sure in the future to come across new ultimate laws of a novel type, but I expect them to relate simple constituents: for example, whatever ultimate particles are then in vogue. I cannot believe that *ultimate* laws of nature could relate simple constituents to configurations consisting of perhaps billions of neurons (and goodness knows how many billion billions of ultimate particles) all put together for all the world as though their main purpose in life was to be a negative feedback mechanism of a complicated sort. Such ultimate laws would be like nothing so far known in science. They have a queer "smell" to them. I am just unable to believe in the nomological danglers themselves or in the laws whereby they would dangle. If any philosophical arguments

seemed to compel us to believe in such things, I would suspect a catch in the argument. In any case it is the object of this paper to show that there are no philosophical arguments which compel us to be dualists. . . .

For on my view there are, in a sense, no sensations. A man is a vast arrangement of physical particles, but there are not, over and above this, sensations or states of consciousness. There are just behavioral factors about this vast mechanism. . . .

Saying "I love you" is just part of the behavior which is the exercise of the disposition of loving someone. Though I am very receptive to the above "expressive" account of sensation statements, I do not feel that it will quite do the trick. Maybe this is because I have not thought it out sufficiently, but it does seem to me as though, when a person says "I have an after-image," he *is* making a genuine report, and that when he says "I have a pain," he *is* doing more than "replace pain-behavior," and that "this more" is not just to say that he is in distress. I am not so sure, however, that to admit this is to admit that there are nonphysical correlates of brain processes. Why should not sensations just be brain processes of a certain sort? There are, of course, well-known (as well as lesser-known) philosophical objections to the view that reports of sensations are reports of brain-processes, but I shall try to argue that these arguments are by no means as cogent as is commonly thought to be the case.

Let me first try to state more accurately the thesis that sensations are brain-processes. It is not the thesis that, for example, "after-image" or "ache" means the same as "brain process of sort X" (where "X" is replaced by a description of a certain sort of brain process). It is that, in so far as "after-image" or "ache" is a report of a process, it is a report of a process that *happens to be* a brain process. It follows that the thesis does not claim that sensation statements can be *translated* into statements about brain processes. All it claims is that in so far as a sensation statement is a report of something, that something is in fact a brain process. Sensations are nothing over and above brain processes. Nations are nothing "over and above" citizens.

REMARKS ON IDENTITY

When I say that a sensation is a brain process or that lightning is an electric discharge, I am using "is" in the sense of strict identity. When I say that sensation is a brain process or that lightning is an electric discharge I do not mean just that the sensation is somehow spatially or temporally continuous with the brain process or that that lightning is just spatially or temporally continuous with discharge. When on the other hand I say that the successful general is the same person as the small boy who stole the apples I mean only that the successful general I see before me is a time slice of the same four-dimensional object of which the small boy stealing apples is an earlier time slice. However, the four-dimensional object which has the general-I-see-before-me for its late time slice is identical in the strict sense with the four-dimensional object which has the small-boy-stealing-apples for an early time slice. I distinguish these two senses of "is identical with" because I wish to make it clear that the brain-process doctrine asserts identity in the *strict* sense.

Now with the Identity Theory stated, Smart lists, and tries to answer, typical objections to his version of the Identity Theory.

Objection 1. Any illiterate peasant can talk perfectly well about his after-images, how things look or feel to him, or about his aches and pains, and yet he may known nothing whatever about neurophysiology. A man may, like Aristotle, believe that the brain is an organ for cooling the body without any impairment of his ability to make true statements about his sensations. Hence the things we are talking about when we describe our sensations cannot be processes in the brain.

Reply.   You might as well say that a nation of slugabeds, who never saw the Morning Star or knew of its existence, or who had never thought of the expression "the Morning Star," but who used the expression "the Evening Star" perfectly well, could not use this expression to refer to the same entity as we refer to (and describe as) "the Morning Star."

You may object that the Morning Star is in a sense not the very same thing as the Evening Star, but only something spatiotemporally continuous with it. That is, you may say that the Morning Star is not the Evening Star in the strict sense of "identity" that I distinguished earlier.

There is, however, a more plausible example. Consider lightning. Modern physical science tells us that lightning is a certain kind of electrical discharge due to ionization of clouds of water vapor in the atmosphere. This, it is now believed, is what the true nature of lightning is. Note that there are not two things: a flash of lightning and an electrical discharge. There is one thing, a flash of lightning, which is described scientifically as an electrical discharge to the earth from a cloud of ionized water molecules. The case is not at all like that of explaining a footprint by reference to a burglar. We say that what lightning really is, what its true nature as revealed by science is, is an electrical discharge. (It is not the true nature of a footprint to be a burglar.)

Objection 2.   It is only a contingent fact (if it is a fact) that when we have a certain kind of sensation there is a certain kind of process in our brain. Indeed it is possible, though perhaps in the highest degree unlikely, that our present physiological theories will be as out of date as the ancient theory connecting mental processes with goings on in the heart. It follows that when we report a sensation we are not reporting a brain process.

Reply.   The objection certainly proves that when we say "I have an after-image" we cannot *mean* something of the form "I have such and such a brain process." But this does not show that what we report (having an after-image) is not *in fact* a brain process. "I see lightning" does not *mean* I see an electrical discharge." Indeed, it is logically possible (though highly unlikely) that the electrical discharge account of lightning might one day be given up. Again, "I see the Evening Star" does not *mean* the same as "I see the Morning Star," and yet "The Evening Star and the Morning Star are one and the same thing" is a contingent proposition. Possibly Objection 2 derives some of its apparent strength from a "Fido"–Fido theory of meaning. If the meaning of an expression were what the expression named, then of course it *would* follow from the fact that "sensation" and "brain process" have different meanings that they cannot name one and the same thing.

Objection 3.   Even if Objections 1 and 2 do not prove that sensations are something over and above brain processes, they do prove that the qualities of sensations are something over and above the qualities of brain processes.

This objection points out that our experiences have properties. The way that seeing a rose "feels" is what distinguishes the experience from smelling a rose.

How can our mental experiences be identical to brain states? Sometimes the criticism is put this way. For two things to be identical, they must have all their properties in common. But brain states are just chemical reactions and chemical reactions have no "feels." So brain states cannot be identical to our mental experiences.

In reply, Smart proposes the following. Brain states, as processes in the brain, have certain properties. Seeing a red rose is identical to certain brain processes. The raw feeling of seeing a red rose is identical to the properties of the brain processes—not identical to the brain process itself.

Smart comments that he is less confident of this answer than he is of any of the others. This is a telling comment, for his answer is, in effect, nothing more than a restatement of the Identity Theory.

As a scientific hypothesis the Identity Theory sounds plausible. But think back to Objection 3. Does the idea that our being conscious is identical to properties of biochemical states in the brain seem at all reasonable? Can being conscious be nothing more than just the properties of chemicals? Science may suggest a yes answer. But even Identity theorists admit that common sense yields a strong No.

NOTE ON SOURCES.   The material in this section is from J. J. C. Smart, "Sensations and Brain Processes" in *The Philosophy of Mind*, edited by V. C. Chappell (Englewood Cliffs, New Jersey: Prentice-Hall, 1962).

4 JERRY FODOR

FUNCTIONALISM AS A CRITIQUE OF IDENTITY THEORY AND LOGICAL BEHAVIORISM

FROM SMART TO FODOR.   Using a computer as a model for understanding the brain and mind has seemed reasonable, given all the advances made by computer scientists in the last few decades. Fodor is an expert in linguistics as well as computers. He is one of the original driving forces behind the cognitive science movement, which suggests that by combining computer science, linguistics, mathematics, psychology, and philosophy, we will finally come to understand the human mind.

BIOGRAPHICAL NOTE.   Jerry Fodor was born in New York City in 1935. He received a Ph.D. in Philosophy from Princeton University in 1960. Fodor has taught at the Massachusetts Institute of Technology and Graduate School and University Center of the City University of New York. He is currently a member of the philosophy department at Rutgers, the State University of New Jersey in New Brunswick, New Jersey. Fodor is well known for his work on the structure of language and for his contributions to the development of cognitive science.

THE ARGUMENT OF THE PASSAGES.   As already mentioned, functionalism is the view that the mental life (seen as the ability to compute) of anything is the result of how that thing is put together; i.e., its program. What the thing is made of is irrelevant. The emphasis is on how the thing functions; how its parts work by interrelating. Therefore, in this view, people (made basically of carbon and water), computers (made of plastic and metals), creatures made of silicon and, according to Fodor, even ghosts (with no bodies) can have mental lives.

The (Central State) Identity Theory, Fodor points out, has the advantage of being consistent with the aims of contemporary psychology and neurophysiology. In this, he is in agreement with Smart. But Fodor argues that the Identity Theory is too restrictive in its claim that mental states are brain states or states of the central nervous system. After all, claims Fodor, the main feature of the mental is the ability to process information. Why restrict this feature only to carbon- and water-based units?

Fodor offers a functionalist analysis of "headache": it is the sort of mental state associated with taking aspirin in those people who also know about aspirin, believe that it works, and desire to get rid of their headache.

In what has become a famous example, Fodor uses a Coke machine to show the difference between a functionalist machine and a purely stimulus–response machine, the sort that would not have mental states. With the stimulus–response machine, we put in a dime (Fodor points out that this is an old example) and out comes a Coke. If anything else goes in, the machine just "sits there." The machine is completely describable, according to Fodor, by the external states, dime-in, Coke-out, machine "sits there." No internal states are needed to describe the machine. To use a word we used in discussing Ryle, this is a determinate machine.

With the functionalistic machine, we can use nickels or quarters as well as dimes. If we put in a quarter, we get: Coke-out and fifteen cents out. If we put in a dime, we get Coke-out. When we put in a nickel, we get what could be described as "machine just sitting there" unless we add another nickel, in which case we get a Coke-out. Thus, the better description for the state after putting in the first nickel is "waiting,"—and this is an internal state of the machine, the analogue to a mental state. The internal state is dispositional (not fully behavioral), since it does not have an output. Notice the similarities and differences between Fodor and Ryle. Also note that Coke machines can be made out of many materials. The software description of the machine does not mention what the machine must be made of. That is an open question. In regard to this question, Fodor briefly describes Turing machines, which are generalized computers. (For a fuller discussion of Turing machines, see the introduction to the next reading.)

Fodor discusses a problem faced by both identity theories and functionalistic theories. Both are stymied by the existence of raw feels. How can simple chemicals—what else is a brain state—be a raw feel? That is, it seems as though the Identity Theory rules out the existence of raw feels and, therefore, consciousness. He concludes by suggesting that the best way to understand the nature of consciousness (and perhaps come to grips with the problems presented by raw feels) is to use the powers of cognitive science—a suggestion that we will see subjected to sharp scrutiny by John Searle in reading 6.

THE MIND–BODY PROBLEM

Could calculating machines have pains, Martians have expectations and disembodied spirits have thoughts? The modern functionalist approach to psychology raises the logical possibility that they could.

Modern philosophy of science has been devoted largely to the formal and systematic description of the successful practices of working scientists. The philosopher does not try to dictate how scientific inquiry and argument ought to be conducted. Instead he tries to enumerate the principles and practices that have contributed to good science. The philosopher has devoted the most attention to analyzing the methodological peculiarities of the physical sciences. The analysis has helped to clarify the nature of confirmation, the logical structure of scientific theories, the formal properties of statements that express laws, and the question of whether theoretical entities actually exist.

It is only rather recently that philosophers have become seriously interested in the methodological tenets of psychology. Psychological explanations of behavior refer liberally to the mind and to states, operations and processes of the mind. The philosophical difficulty comes in stating in unambiguous language what such references imply.

Traditional philosophies of mind can be divided into two broad categories: dualist theories and materialist theories. In the dualist approach the mind is a nonphysical substance. In materialist theories the mental is not distinct from the physical; indeed, all mental states, properties, processes and operations are in principle identical with physical states, properties, processes and operations. Some materialists, known as behaviorists, maintain that all talk of mental causes can be eliminated from the language of psychology in favor of talk of environmental stimuli and behavioral responses. Other materialists, the identity theorists, contend that there are mental causes and that they are identical with neurophysiological events in the brain.

In the past 15 years a philosophy of mind called functionalism that is neither dualist nor materialist has emerged from philosophical reflection on developments in artificial intelligence, computational theory, linguistics, cybernetics and psychology. All these fields, which are collectively known as the cognitive sciences, have in common a certain level of abstraction and a concern with systems that process information. Functionalism, which seeks to provide a philosophical account of this level of abstraction, recognizes the possibility that systems as diverse as human beings, calculating machines and disembodied spirits could all have mental states. In the functionalist view the psychology of a system depends not on the stuff it is made of (living cells, metal or spiritual energy) but on how the stuff is put together. Functionalism is a difficult concept, and one way of coming to grips with it is to review the deficiencies of the dualist and materialist philosophies of mind it aims to displace.

The chief drawback of dualism is its failure to account adequately for mental causation. If the mind is nonphysical, it has no position in physical space. How, then, can a mental cause give rise to a behavioral effect that has a position in space? To put it another way, how can the nonphysical give rise to the physical without violating the laws of the conservation of mass, of energy and of momentum?

The dualist might respond that the problem of how an immaterial substance can cause physical events is not much obscurer than the problem of how one physical event can cause another. Yet there is an important difference: there are many clear cases of physical causation but not one clear case of nonphysical causation. Physical interaction is something philosophers, like all other people, have to live with. Nonphysical interaction, however, may be no more than an artifact of the immaterialist construal of the mental. Most philosophers now agree that no argument has successfully demonstrated why mind–body causation should not be regarded as a species of physical causation.

Dualism is also incompatible with the practices of working psychologists. The psychologist frequently applies the experimental methods of the physical sciences to the study of the mind. If mental processes were different in kind from physical processes, there would be no reason to expect these methods to work in the realm of the mental. In order to justify their experimental methods many psychologists urgently sought an alternative to dualism.

In the 1920s John B. Watson of Johns Hopkins University made the radical suggestion that behavior does not have mental causes. He regarded the behavior of an organism as its observable responses to stimuli, which he took to be the causes of its behavior. Over the next 30 years psychologists such as B. F. Skinner of Harvard University developed Watson's ideas into an elaborate world view in which the role of psychology was to catalogue the laws that determine causal relations between stimuli and responses. In this "radical behaviorist" view the problem of explaining the nature of the mind-body interaction vanishes; there is no such interaction.

Radical behaviorism has always worn an air of paradox. For better or worse, the idea of mental causation is deeply ingrained in our everyday language and in our ways of understanding our fellow men and ourselves. For example, people commonly attribute behavior to beliefs, to knowledge and to expectations. Brown puts gas in his tank because he believes the car will not run without it. Jones writes not "acheive" but "achieve" because he knows the rule about putting *i* before *e*. Even when a behavioral response is closely tied to an environmental stimulus, mental processes often intervene. Smith carries an umbrella because the sky is cloudy, but the weather is only part of the story. There are apparently also mental links in the causal chain: observation and expectation. The clouds affect Smith's behavior only because he observes them and because they induce in him an expectation of rain.

The radical behaviorist is unmoved by appeals to such cases. He is prepared to dismiss references to mental causes, however plausible they may seem, as the residue of outworn creeds. The radical behaviorist predicts that as psychologists come to understand more about the relations between stimuli and responses they will find it increasingly possible to explain behavior without postulating mental causes.

The strongest argument against behaviorism is that psychology has not turned out this way; the opposite has happened. As psychology has matured, the framework of mental states and processes that is apparently needed to account for experimental observations has grown all the more elaborate. Particularly in the case of human behavior psychological theories satisfying the methodological tenets of radical behaviorism have proved largely sterile, as would be expected if the postulated mental processes are real and causally effective.

Nevertheless, many philosophers were initially drawn to radical behaviorism because, paradoxes and all, it seemed better than dualism. Since a psychology committed to immaterial substances was unacceptable, philosophers turned to radical behaviorism because it seemed to be the only alternative materialist philosophy of mind. The choice, as they saw it, was between radical behaviorism and ghosts.

By the early 1960s philosophers began to have doubts that dualism and radical behaviorism exhausted the possible approaches to the philosophy of mind. Since the two theories seemed unattractive, the right strategy might be to develop a materialist philosophy of mind that nonetheless allowed for mental causes. Two such philosophies emerged, one called logical behaviorism and the other called the central-state identity theory.

Logical behaviorism is a semantic theory about what mental terms mean. The basic idea is that attributing a mental state (say thirst) to an organism is the same as saying that the organism is disposed to behave in a particular way (for example to drink if there is water available). On this view every mental ascription is equivalent in meaning to an if–then statement (called a behavioral hypothetical) that expresses a behavioral disposition. For example, "Smith is thirsty" might be taken to be equivalent to the dispositional statement "If there were water available, then Smith would drink some." By definition a behavioral hypothetical includes no mental terms. The if-clause of the hypothetical speaks only of stimuli and the then-clause speaks only of behavioral responses. Since stimuli and responses are physical events, logical behaviorism is a species of materialism.

The strength of logical behaviorism is that by translating mental language into the language of stimuli and responses it provides an interpretation of psychological explanations in which behavioral effects are attributed to mental causes. Mental causation is simply the manifestation of a behavioral disposition. More precisely, mental causation is what happens when an organism has a behavioral disposition and the if-clause of the behavioral hypothetical expressing the disposition happens to be true. For example, the causal statement "Smith drank some water because he was thirsty" might be taken to mean "if there were water available, then Smith would drink some, and there was water available."

I have somewhat oversimplified logical behaviorism by assuming that each mental ascription can be translated by a unique behavioral hypothetical. Actually the logical behaviorist often maintains that it takes an open-ended set (perhaps an infinite set) of behavioral hypotheticals to spell out the behavioral disposition expressed by a mental term. The mental ascription "Smith is thirsty" might also be satisfied by the hypothetical "If there were orange juice available, then Smith would drink some" and by a host of other hypotheticals. In any event the logical behaviorist does not usually maintain he can actually enumerate all the hypotheticals that correspond to a behavioral disposition expressing a given mental term. He only insists that in principle the meaning of any mental term can be conveyed by behavioral hypotheticals.

The way the logical behaviorist has interpreted a mental term such as thirsty is modeled after the way many philosophers have interpreted a physical disposition such as fragility. The physical disposition "The glass is fragile" is often taken to mean something like "If the glass were struck, then it would break." By the same token the logical behaviorist's analysis of mental causation is similar to the received analysis of one kind of physical causation. The causal statement "The glass broke because it was fragile" is taken to mean something like "If the glass were struck, then it would break, and the glass was struck."

By equating mental terms with behavioral dispositions the logical behaviorist has put mental terms on a par with the nonbehavioral dispositions of the physical sciences. That is a promising move, because the analysis of nonbehavioral dispositions is on relatively solid philosophical ground. An explanation attributing the breaking of a glass to its fragility is surely something even the staunchest materialist can accept. By arguing that mental terms are synonymous with dispositional terms, the logical behaviorist has provided something the radical behaviorist could not: a materialist account of mental causation.

Nevertheless, the analogy between mental causation as construed by the logical behaviorist and physical causation goes only so far. The logical behaviorist treats the manifestation of a disposition as the sole form of mental causation, whereas the physical sciences recognize additional kinds of causation. There is the kind of causation where one physical event causes another, as when the breaking of a glass is attributed to its having been struck. In fact, explanations that involve event-event causation are presumably more basic than dispositional explanations, because the manifestation of a disposition (the breaking of a fragile glass) always involves event-event causation and not vice versa. In the realm of the mental many examples of event-event causation involve one mental state's causing another, and for this kind of causation logical behaviorism provides no analysis. As a result the logical behaviorist is committed to the tacit and implausible assumption that psychology requires a less robust notion of causation than the physical sciences require.

Event-event causation actually seems to be quite common in the realm of the mental. Mental causes typically give rise to behavioral effects by virtue of their interaction with other mental causes. For example, having a headache causes a disposition to take aspirin only if one also has the desire to get rid of the headache, the belief that aspirin exists, the belief that taking aspirin reduces headaches and so on. Since mental states interact in generating behavior, it will be necessary to find a construal of psychological explanations that posits mental processes: causal sequences of mental events. It is this construal that logical behaviorism fails to provide.

Such considerations bring out a fundamental way in which logical behaviorism is quite similar to radical behaviorism. It is true that the logical behaviorist, unlike the radical behaviorist, acknowledges the existence of mental states. Yet since the underlying tenet of logical behaviorism is that references to mental states can be translated out of psychological explanations by employing behavioral hypotheticals, all talk of mental states and processes is in a sense heuristic. The only facts to which the behaviorist is actually committed are facts about relations between stimuli and responses. In this respect logical behaviorism is just radical behaviorism in a semantic form. Although the former theory offers a construal of mental causation, the construal is Pickwickian.* What does not really exist cannot cause anything, and the logical behaviorist, like the radical behaviorist, believes deep down that mental causes do not exist.

An alternative materialist theory of the mind to logical behaviorism is the central-state identity theory. According to this theory, mental events, states and processes are identical with neurophysiological events in the brain, and the property of being in a certain mental state (such as having a headache or believing it will rain) is identical with the property of being in a certain neurophysiological state. On this basis it is easy to make sense of the idea that a behavioral effect might sometimes have a chain of mental causes; that will be the case whenever a behavioral effect is contingent on the appropriate sequence of neurophysiological events.

The central-state identity theory acknowledges that it is possible for mental causes to interact causally without ever giving rise to any behavioral effect, as when a

---

* [Eccentric. –Ed.]

person thinks for a while about what he ought to do and then decides to do nothing. If mental processes are neurophysiological, they must have the causal properties of neurophysiological processes. Since neurophysiological processes are presumably physical processes, the central-state identity theory ensures that the concept of mental causation is as rich as the concept of physical causation.

The central-state identity theory provides a satisfactory account of what the mental terms in psychological explanations refer to, and so it is favored by psychologists who are dissatisfied with behaviorism. The behaviorist maintains that mental terms refer to nothing or that they refer to the parameters of stimulus-response relations. Either way the existence of mental entities is only illusory. The identity theorist, on the other hand, argues that mental terms refer to neurophysiological states. Thus he can take seriously the project of explaining behavior by appealing to its mental causes.

The chief advantage of the identity theory is that it takes the explanatory constructs of psychology at face value, which is surely something a philosophy of mind ought to do if it can. The identity theory shows how the mentalistic explanations of psychology could be not mere heuristics but literal accounts of the causal history of behavior. Moreover, since the identity theory is not a semantic thesis, it is immune to many arguments that cast in doubt logical behaviorism. A drawback of logical behaviorism is that the observation "John has a headache" does not seem to mean the same thing as a statement of the form "John is disposed to behave in such and such a way." The identity theorist, however, can live with the fact that "John has a headache" and "John is in such and such a brain state" are not synonymous. The assertion of the identity theorist is not that these sentences mean the same thing but only that they are rendered true (or false) by the same neurophysiological phenomena.

The identity theory can be held either as a doctrine about mental particulars (John's current pain or Bill's fear of animals) or as a doctrine about mental universals, or properties (having a pain or being afraid of animals). The two doctrines, called respectively token physicalism and type physicalism, differ in strength and plausibility. Token physicalism maintains only that all the mental particulars that happen to exist are neurophysiological, whereas type physicalism makes the more sweeping assertion that all the mental particulars there could possibly be are neurophysiological. Token physicalism does not rule out the logical possibility of machines and disembodied spirits having mental properties. Type physicalism dismisses this possibility because neither machines or disembodied spirits have neurons.

Type physicalism is not a plausible doctrine about mental properties even if token physicalism is right about mental particulars. The problem with type physicalism is that the psychological constitution of a system seems to depend not on its hardware, or physical composition, but on its software, or program. Why should the philosopher dismiss the possibility that silicon-based Martians have pains, assuming that the silicon is properly organized? And why should the philosopher rule out the possibility of machines having beliefs, assuming that the machines are correctly programmed? If it is logically possible that Martians and machines could have mental properties, then mental properties and neurophysiological processes cannot be identical, however much they prove to be coextensive.

What it all comes down to is that there seems to be a level of abstraction at which the generalizations of psychology are most naturally pitched. This level of abstraction cuts across differences in the physical composition of the systems to which psychological generalizations apply. In the cognitive sciences, at least, the natural domain for psychological theorizing seems to be all systems that process information. The problem with type physicalism is that there are possible information-processing systems with the same psychological constitution as human beings but not the same physical organization. In principle all kinds of physically different things could have human software.

This situation calls for a relational account of mental properties that abstracts them from the physical structure of their bearers. In spite of the objections to logical behaviorism that I presented above, logical behaviorism was at least on the right track in offering a relational interpretation of mental properties: to have a headache is to be disposed to exhibit a certain pattern of relations between the stimuli one encounters and the responses one exhibits. If that is what having a headache is, however, there is no reason in principle why only heads that are physically similar to ours can ache. Indeed, according to logical behaviorism, it is a necessary truth that any system that has our stimulus-response contingencies also has our headaches.

All of this emerged 10 or 15 years ago as a nasty dilemma for the materialist program in the philosophy of mind. On the one hand the identity theorist (and not the logical behaviorist) had got right the causal character of the interactions of mind and body. On the other the logical behaviorist (and not the identity theorist) had got right the relational character of mental properties. Functionalism has apparently been able to resolve the dilemma. By stressing the distinction computer science draws between hardware and software the functionalist can make sense of both the causal and the relational character of the mental.

The intuition underlying functionalism is that what determines the psychological type to which a mental particular belongs is the causal role of the particular in the mental life of the organism. Functional individuation is differentiation with respect to causal role. A headache, for example, is identified with the type of mental state that among other things causes a disposition for taking aspirin in people who believe aspirin relieves a headache, causes a desire to rid oneself of the pain one is feeling, often causes someone who speaks English to say such things as "I have a headache" and is brought on by overwork, eyestrain and tension. This list is presumably not complete. More will be known about the nature of a headache as psychological and physiological research discovers more about its causal role.

Functionalism construes the concept of causal role in such a way that a mental state can be defined by its causal relations to other mental states. In this respect functionalism is completely different from logical behaviorism. Another major difference is that functionalism is not a reductionist thesis. It does not foresee, even in principle, the elimination of mentalistic concepts from the explanatory apparatus of psychological theories.

The difference between functionalism and logical behaviorism is brought out by the fact that functionalism is fully compatible with token physicalism. The functionalist would not be disturbed if brain events turn out to be the only things with the functional properties that define mental states. Indeed, most functionalists fully expect it will turn out that way.

Since functionalism recognizes that mental particulars may be physical, it is compatible with the idea that mental causation is a species of physical causation. In other words, functionalism tolerates the materialist solution to the mind-body problem provided by the central-state identity theory. It is possible for the functionalist to assert both that mental properties are typically defined in terms of their relations and that interactions of mind and body are typically causal in however robust a notion of causality is required by psychological explanations. The logical behaviorist can endorse only the first assertion and the type physicalist only the second. As a result functionalism seems to capture the best features of the materialist alternatives to dualism. It is no wonder that functionalism has become increasingly popular.

Machines provide good examples of two concepts that are central to functionalism: the concept that mental states are interdefined and the concept that they can be realized by many systems. The illustration [Figure 2-1] contrasts a behavioristic Coke machine with a mentalistic one. Both machines dispense a Coke for 10 cents. (The price has not been affected by inflation.) The states of the machines are defined by reference to their causal roles, but only the machine on the left would satisfy the behaviorist. Its single state (*S0*) is completely specified in terms of stimuli and responses. *S0* is the state a machine is in if, and only if, given a dime as the input, it dispenses a Coke as the output.

The machine on the right in the illustration has interdefined states (*S1* and *S2*), which are characteristic of functionalism. *S1* is the state of a machine is in if, and only if, (1) given a nickel, it dispenses nothing and proceeds to *S2*, and (2) given a dime, it dispenses a Coke and stays in *S1*. *S2* is the state a machine is in if, and only if, (1) given a nickel, it dispenses a Coke and proceeds to *S1*, and (2) given a dime, it dispenses a Coke and a nickel and proceeds to *S1*. What *S1* and *S2* jointly amount to is the machine's dispensing a Coke if it is given a dime, dispensing a Coke and a nickel if it is given a dime and a nickel and waiting to be given a second nickel if it has been given a first one.

Since *S1* and *S2* are each defined by hypothetical statements, they can be viewed as dispositions. Nevertheless, they are not behavioral dispositions because the consequences an input has for a machine in *S1* or *S2* are not specified solely in terms of the output of the machine. Rather, the consequences also involve the machine's internal states.

Nothing about the way I have described the behavioristic and mentalistic Coke machines puts constraints on what they could be made of. Any system whose states bore the proper relations to inputs, outputs and other states could be one of these machines. No doubt it is reasonable to expect such a system to be constructed out of such things as wheels, levers and diodes (token physicalism for Coke machines). Similarly, it is reasonable to expect that our minds may prove to be neurophysiological (token physicalism for human beings).

Nevertheless, the software description of a Coke machine does not logically require wheels, levers and diodes for its concrete realization. By the same token, the software description of the mind does not logically require neurons. As far as functionalism is concerned a Coke machine with states *S1* and *S2* could be made of ectoplasm, if there is such stuff and if its states have the right causal properties. Functionalism allows for the possibility of disembodied Coke machines in exactly the same way and to the same extent that it allows for the possibility of disembodied minds.

To say that *S1* and *S2* are interdefined and realizable by different kinds of hardware is not, of course, to say that a Coke machine has a mind. Although interdefinition and functional specification are typical features of mental states, they are clearly not sufficient for mentality. What more is required is a question to which I shall return below.

	STATE S0
DIME INPUT	DISPENSES A COKE

	STATE S1	STATE S2
NICKEL INPUT	GIVES NO OUTPUT AND GOES TO S2	DISPENSES A COKE AND GOES TO S1
DIME INPUT	DISPENSES A COKE AND STAYS IN S1	DISPENSES A COKE AND A NICKEL AND GOES TO S1

Figure 2.1. *Two Coke machines bring out the difference between behaviorism (the doctrine that there are no mental causes) and mentalism (the doctrine that there are mental causes). Both machines dispense a Coke for 10 cents and have states that are defined by reference to their causal role. The machine at the left is a behavioristic one: its single state (S0) is defined solely in terms of the input and the output. The machine at the right is a mentalistic one: its two states (S1, S2) must be defined not only in terms of the input and the output but also in terms of each other. To put it another way, the output of the Coke machine depends on the state the machine is in as well as on the input. The functionalist philosopher maintains that mental states are interdefined, like the internal states of the mentalistic Coke machine.*

Some philosophers are suspicious of functionalism because it seems too easy. Since functionalism licenses the individuation of states by reference to their causal role, it appears to allow a trivial explanation of any observed event *E*, that is, it appears to postulate an *E*-causer. For example, what makes the valves in a machine open? Why, the operation of a valve opener. And what is a valve opener? Why, anything that has the functionally defined property of causing valves to open.

In psychology this kind of question-begging often takes the form of theories that in effect postulate homunculi with the selfsame intellectual capacities the theorist set out to explain. Such is the case when visual perception is explained by simply postulating psychological mechanisms that process visual information. The behaviorist has often charged the mentalist, sometimes justifiably, of mongering this kind of question-begging pseudo explanation. The charge will have to be met if functionally defined mental states are to have a serious role in psychological theories.

The burden of the accusation is not untruth but triviality. There can be no doubt that it is a valve opener that opens valves, and it is likely that visual perception is mediated by the processing of visual information. The charge is that such putative functional explanations are mere platitudes. The functionalist can meet this objection by allowing functionally defined theoretical constructs only where mechanisms exist that can carry out the function and only where he has some notion of what such mechanisms might be like. One way of imposing this requirement is to identify the mental processes that psychology postulates with the operations of the restricted class of possible computers called Turing machines.

A Turing machine can be informally characterized as a mechanism with a finite number of program states. The inputs and outputs of the machine are written on a tape that is divided into squares each of which includes a symbol from a finite alphabet. The machine scans the tape one square at a time. It can erase the symbol on a scanned square and print a new one in its place. The machine can execute only the elementary mechanical operations of scanning, erasing, printing, moving the tape and changing state.

The program states of the Turing machine are defined solely in terms of the input symbols on the tape, the output symbols on the tape, the elementary operations and the other states of the program. Each program state is therefore functionally defined by the part it plays in the overall operation of the machine. Since the functional role of a state depends on the relation of the state to other states as well as to inputs and outputs, the relational character of the mental state is captured by the Turing-machine version of functionalism. Since the definition of a program state never refers to the physical structure of the system running the program, the Turing-machine version of functionalism also captures the ideas that the character of a mental state is independent of its physical realization. A human being, a roomful of people, a computer and a disembodied spirit would all be a Turing machine if they operated according to a Turing-machine program.

The proposal is to restrict the functional definition of psychological states to those that can be expressed in terms of the program states of Turing machines. If this restriction can be enforced, it provides a guarantee that psychological theories will be compatible with the demands of mechanisms. Since Turing machines are very simple devices, they are in principle quite easy to build. Consequently by formulating a psychological explanation as a Turing-machine program the psychologist ensures that the explanation is mechanistic, even though the hardware realizing the mechanism is left open.

There are many kinds of computational mechanisms other than Turing machines, and so the formulation of a functionalist psychological theory in Turing-machine notation provides only a sufficient condition for the theory's being mechanically realizable. What makes the condition interesting, however, is that the simple Turing machine can perform many complex tasks. Although the elementary operations of the Turing machine are restricted, iterations of the operations enable the machine to carry out any well-defined computation on discrete symbols.

An important tendency in the cognitive sciences is to treat the mind chiefly as a device that manipulates symbols. If a mental process can be functionally defined as an operation on symbols, there is a Turing machine capable of carrying out the computation and a variety of mechanisms for realizing the Turing machine. Where the manipulation of symbols is important the Turing machine provides a connection between functional explanation and mechanistic explanation.

The reduction of a psychological theory to a program for a Turing machine is a way of exorcising the homunculi. The reduction ensures that no operations have been postulated except those that could be performed by a familiar mechanism. Of course, the working psychologist usually cannot specify the reduction for each functionally individuated process in every theory he is prepared to take seriously. In practice the argument usually goes in the opposite direction; if the postulation of a mental operation is essential to some cherished psychological explanation, the theorist tends to assume that there must be a program for a Turing machine that will carry out that operation.

The "black boxes" that are common in flow charts drawn by psychologists often serve to indicate postulated mental processes for which Turing reductions are wanting. Even so, the possibility in principle of such reductions serves as a methodological constraint on psychological theorizing by determining what functional definitions are to be allowed and what it would be like to know that everything has been explained that could possibly need explanation.

Such is the origin, the provenance and the promise of contemporary functionalism. How much has it actually paid off? This question is not easy to answer because much of what is now happening in the philosophy of mind and the cognitive sciences is directed at exploring the scope and limits of the functionalist explanations of behavior. I shall, however, give a brief overview.

An obvious objection to functionalism as a theory of the mind is that the functionalist definition is not limited to mental states and processes. Catalysts, Coke machines, valve openers, pencil sharpeners, mousetraps and ministers of finance are all in one way or another concepts that are functionally defined, but none is a mental concept such as pain, belief and desire. What, then, characterizes the mental? And can it be captured in a functionalist framework?

The traditional view in the philosophy of mind has it that mental states are distinguished by their having what are called either qualitative content or intentional content. I shall discuss qualitative content first.

It is not easy to say what qualitative content is; indeed, according to some theories, it is not even possible to say what it is because it can be known not by description but only by direct experience. I shall nonetheless attempt to describe it. Try to imagine looking at a blank wall through a red filter. Now change the filter to a green one and leave everything else exactly the way it was. Something about the character of your experience changes when the filter does, and it is this kind of thing that philosophers call qualitative content. I am not entirely comfortable about introducing qualitative content in this way, but it is a subject with which many philosophers are not comfortable.

The reason qualitative content is a problem for functionalism is straightforward. Functionalism is committed to defining mental states in terms of their causes and effects. It seems, however, as if two mental states could have all the same causal relations and yet could differ in their qualitative content. Let me illustrate this with the classic puzzle of the inverted spectrum.

It seems possible to imagine two observers who are alike in all relevant psychological respects except that experiences having the qualitative content of red for one observer would have the qualitative content of green for the other. Nothing about their behavior need reveal the difference because both of them see ripe tomatoes and flaming sunsets as being similar in color and both of them call that color "red." Moreover, the causal connection between their (qualitatively distinct) experiences and their other mental states could also be identical. Perhaps they both think of Little Red Riding Hood when they see ripe tomatoes, feel depressed when they see the color green and so on. It seems as if anything that could be packed into the notion of the causal role of their experiences could be shared by them, and yet the qualitative content of the experiences could be as different as you like. If this is possible, then the functionalist account does not work for mental states that have qualitative content. If one person is having a green experience while another person is having a red one, then surely they must be in different mental states.

The example of the inverted spectrum is more than a verbal puzzle. Having qualitative content is supposed to be a chief factor in what makes a mental state conscious. Many psychologists who are inclined to accept the functionalist framework are nonetheless worried about the failure of functionalism to reveal much about the nature of consciousness. Functionalists have made a few ingenious attempts to talk themselves and their colleagues out of this worry, but they have not, in my view, done so with much success. (For example, perhaps one is wrong in thinking one can imagine what an inverted spectrum would be like.) As matters stand, the problem of qualitative content poses a serious threat to the assertion that functionalism can provide a general theory of the mental.

Functionalism has fared much better with the intentional content of mental states. Indeed, it is here that the major achievements of recent cognitive science are found. To say that a mental state has intentional content is to say that it has certain semantic properties. For example, for Enrico to believe Galileo was Italian apparently involves a three-way relation between Enrico, a belief and a proposition that is the content of the belief (namely the proposition that Galileo was Italian). In particular it is an essential property of Enrico's belief that it is about Galileo (and not about, say, Newton) and that it is true if, and only if, Galileo was indeed Italian. Philosophers are divided on how these considerations fit together, but it is widely agreed that beliefs involve semantic properties such as expressing a proposition, being true or false and being about one thing rather than another.

It is important to understand the semantic properties of beliefs because theories in the cognitive sciences are largely about the beliefs organisms have. Theories of learning and perception, for example, are chiefly accounts of how the host of beliefs an organism has are determined by the character of its experiences and its genetic endowment. The functionalist account of mental states does not by itself provide the required insights. Mousetraps are functionally defined, yet mousetraps do not express propositions, and they are not true or false.

There is at least one kind of thing other than a mental state that has intentional content: a symbol. Like thoughts, symbols seem to be about things. If someone says, "Galileo was Italian," his utterance, like Enrico's belief, expresses a proposition about

Galileo that is true or false depending on Galileo's homeland. This parallel between the symbolic and the mental underlies the traditional quest for a unified treatment of language and mind. Cognitive science is now trying to provide such a treatment.

The basic concept is simple but striking. Assume that there are such things as mental symbols (mental representations) and that mental symbols have semantic properties. On this view having a belief involves being related to a mental symbol, and the belief inherits its semantic properties from the mental symbol that figures in the relation. Mental processes (thinking, perceiving, learning and so on) involve causal interactions among relational states such as having a belief. The semantic properties of the words and sentences we utter are in turn inherited from the semantic properties of the mental states that language expresses.

Associating semantic properties of mental states with those of mental symbols is fully compatible with the computer metaphor, because it is natural to think of the computer as a mechanism that manipulates symbols. A computation is a causal chain of computer states, and the links in the chain are operations on semantically interpreted formulas in a machine code. To think of a system (such as the nervous system) as a computer is to raise questions about the nature of the code in which it computes and the semantic properties of the symbols in the code. In fact, the analogy between minds and computers actually implies the postulation of mental symbols. There is no computation without representation.

The representational account of the mind, however, predates considerably the invention of the computing machine. It is a throwback to classical epistemology, which is a tradition that includes philosophers as diverse as John Locke, David Hume, George Berkeley, René Descartes, Immanuel Kant, John Stuart Mill and William James.

Hume, for one, developed a representational theory of the mind that included five points. First, there exist "Ideas," which are a species of mental symbol. Second, having a belief involves entertaining an Idea. Third, mental processes are causal associations of Ideas. Fourth, Ideas are like pictures. And fifth, Ideas have their semantic properties by virtue of what they resemble: the Idea of John is about John because it looks like him.

Contemporary cognitive psychologists do not accept the details of Hume's theory, although they endorse much of its spirit. Theories of computation provide a far richer account of mental processes than the mere association of Ideas. And only a few psychologists still think that imagery is the chief vehicle of mental representation. Nevertheless, the most significant break with Hume's theory lies in the abandoning of resemblance as an explanation of the semantic properties of mental representations.

Many philosophers, starting with Berkeley, have argued that there is something seriously wrong with the suggestion that the semantic relation between a thought and what the thought is about could be one of resemblance. Consider the thought that John is tall. Clearly the thought is true only of the state of affairs consisting of John's being tall. A theory of the semantic properties of a thought should therefore explain how this particular thought is related to this particular state of affairs. According to the resemblance theory, entertaining the thought involves having a mental image that shows John to be tall. To put it another way, the relation between the thought that John is tall and his being tall is like the relation between a tall man and his portrait.

The difficulty with the resemblance theory is that any portrait showing John to be tall must also show him to be many other things: clothed or naked, lying, standing or sitting, having a head or not having one, and so on. A portrait of a tall man who is sitting down resembles a man's being seated as much as it resembles a man's being tall. On the resemblance theory it is not clear what distinguishes thoughts about John's height from thoughts about his posture.

The resemblance theory turns out to encounter paradoxes at every turn. The possibility of construing beliefs as involving relations to semantically interpreted mental representations clearly depends on having an acceptable account of where the semantic properties of the mental representations come from. If resemblance will not provide this account, what will?

The current idea is that the semantic properties of a mental representation are determined by aspects of its functional role. In other words, a sufficient condition for having semantic properties can be specified in causal terms. This is the connection between functionalism and the representational theory of the mind. Modern cognitive psychology rests largely on the hope that these two doctrines can be made to support each other.

No philosopher is now prepared to say exactly how the functional role of a mental representation determines its semantic properties. Nevertheless, the functionalist recognizes three types of causal relation among psychological states involving mental representations, and they might serve to fix the semantic properties of mental representations. The three types are causal relations among mental states and stimuli, mental states and responses and some mental states and other ones.

Consider the belief that John is tall. Presumably the following facts, which correspond respectively to the three types of causal relation, are relevant to determining the semantic properties of the mental representation involved in the belief. First, the belief is a normal effect of certain stimulations, such as seeing John in circumstances that reveal his height. Second, the belief is the normal cause of certain behavioral effects, such as uttering "John is tall." Third, the belief is a normal cause of certain other beliefs and a normal effect of certain other beliefs. For example, anyone who believes John is tall is very likely also to believe someone is tall. Having the first belief is normally causally sufficient for having the second belief. And anyone who believes everyone in the room is tall and also believes John is in the room will very likely believe John is tall. The third belief is a normal effect of the first two. In short, the functionalist maintains that the proposition expressed by a given mental representation depends on the causal properties of the mental states in which that mental representation figures.

The concept that the semantic properties of mental representations are determined by aspects of their functional role is at the center of current work in the cognitive sciences. Nevertheless, the concept may not be true. Many philosophers who are unsympathetic to the cognitive turn in modern psychology doubt its truth, and many psychologists would probably reject it in the bald and unelaborated way that I have sketched it. Yet even in its skeletal form, there is this much to be said in its favor: it legitimizes the notion of mental representation, which has become increasingly important to theorizing in every branch of the cognitive sciences. Recent advances in formulating and testing hypotheses about the character of mental representations in fields ranging from phonetics to computer vision suggest that the concept of mental representation is fundamental to empirical theories of the mind.

The behaviorist has rejected the appeal to mental representation because it runs counter to his view of the explanatory mechanisms that can figure in psychological theories. Nevertheless, the science of mental representation is now flourishing. The history of science reveals that when a successful theory comes into conflict with a methodological scruple, it is generally the scruple that gives way. Accordingly the functionalist has relaxed the behaviorist constraints on psychological explanations. There is probably no better way to decide what is methodologically permissible in science than by investigating what successful science requires.

NOTE ON SOURCES.   Jerry Fodor, "The Mind–Body Problem," *The Scientific American*, Vol. 244, No. 1 (January, 1981), pp. 114–123.

5   A. M. TURING

MACHINES CAN THINK

FROM FODOR TO TURING.   Functionalism must show that software is enough to do mental-like things. Put another way, Functionalism, if it is to be an important and interesting philosophical view, must answer "yes" to the question, "Can computers think?"

To understand these questions in the manner of cognitive scientists, we will start with a look at the concept of model and then go on to describe a Turing machine. The following are four senses of the word *model*.

    a. How will this dress look on real women?
       Try it on a model.

Most fashion models are idealized people. Fashion models are chosen because they best "show off" the clothes. Very few of us look like fashion models.

    b. Will this plane survive a wind storm?
       Try a scale model in a wind tunnel.

A scale model is just like what it models except for size. We assume that the scale model will act just like what it models. This assumption is usually borne out.

    c. How will this drug act in humans?
       Try it on beagles and bunnies, both of which have physiologies like humans.

Obviously beagles and bunnies are not too much like people except perhaps in some of their anatomy and their physiology. They are known to be and are called good animal models for studying the effects of drugs in humans.

    d. How will this gas act if we heat it to 150 degrees centigrade?
       The answer is that it will expand according to the ideal gas law, which is
       based on assumptions about the actions of molecules that make up a gas.
       The ideal gas law assumes that gas molecules are perfectly elastic, randomly
       moving points with no mass or diameter. Despite these incorrect assump-
       tions, the ideal gas law yields excellent predictions under most circum-
       stances. The ideal gas law can be considered to be a mathematical model.

In the list above, we have seen different sorts of models. They are all departures from reality that help us to understand reality. To understand a Turing machine, we have to focus on the sense of model given in (d). There is no ideal gas because there is no molecule that is perfectly elastic, with no mass or diameter. That there is no such gas and cannot be is why we say that it is an ideal gas.

A Turing machine is an ideal computer. It is a model for any digital computer. It is a mathematical abstraction used to highlight what is important in a digital computer. The Turing machine works by scanning a finite (but potentially infinite) tape that is divided into squares. The symbols scanned are: 1, 0, or empty square. The machine can do the following things: move right, move left, stay centered, erase, erase and print one of the allowed symbols. That is all the machine is allowed to do. It turns out that this is a very powerful computing machine. Indeed, whatever we can decide effectively can be computed on a Turing machine. This is called the Church-Turing hypothesis.* What exactly does this mean? "To decide effectively" means that there is an algorithm. To have an algorithm (from al-Khuwarizmi, an Arab mathematician of the ninth century) is to have a mechanical procedure that will give a definite yes or no answer to a question in a finite number of steps. The word "mechanical" is used to stress that no insight is needed to get the answer.

The following questions have algorithms: What is the shortest distance between two cities? Given the present board in a chess game, can white win? The first question would probably require a relatively short algorithm. The second would require a much longer algorithm.

The following questions have no algorithmic solutions: Is there a Loch Ness monster? Is the *Mona Lisa* more beautiful than *Guernica*?

Since any problem for which there is an algorithm can be done on a Turing machine, and since a Turing machine is just a mathematical abstraction in the way that an ideal gas is an abstraction, we get the result Fodor wanted: only the program counts—not the material from which a computer might be built. Put another way, *any* material that can be used to build a computer might function well enough to be said to think.

BIOGRAPHICAL NOTE.   Alan Turing was born in 1912 in London, England. He received a Ph.D. in mathematics from Princeton in 1938 for work he completed under mathematician-logician Alonzo Church. Turing returned to England, where after completing a fellowship at King's College, he took up work for the government as a code-breaker. Turing was instrumental in creating the Enigma Machine, the device that the British used to decode German messages during World War II. In 1948, Turing took over what was then the computer with the largest memory in the world. His work laid the foundation for what has come to be called "artificial intelligence." Turing became the victim of British antihomosexual programs. He was found to be a homosexual and brought up on charges of soliciting sex. Turing

---

*   Alonzo Church is a famous American logician-mathematician.

was given the choice of a prison term or undergoing a drug treatment meant to cure him of his "problem." He chose the latter. Unfortunately, it seems to have led to psychological problems, and in 1954 Turing committed suicide.

THE ARGUMENT OF THE PASSAGES.   Alan Turing proposed that if a person could not tell the difference between another person and a computer imitating a person thinking, then we should be convinced that it is acceptable to say that computers can think.

THE IMITATION GAME

I propose to consider the question "Can machines think?" This should begin with definitions of the meaning of the terms "machine" and "think." The definitions might be framed so as to reflect so far as possible the normal use of the words, but this attitude is dangerous. If the meaning of the words "machine" and "think" are to be found by examining how they are commonly used it is difficult to escape the conclusion that the meaning and the answer to the question, "Can machines think?" is to be sought in a statistical survey such as a Gallup poll. But this is absurd. Instead of attempting such a definition I shall replace the question by another, which is closely related to it and is expressed in relatively unambiguous words.

The new form of the problem can be described in terms of a game which we call the "imitation game." It is played with three people, a man (A), a woman (B), and an interrogator (C) who may be of either sex. The interrogator stays in a room apart from the other two. The object of the game for the interrogator is to determine which of the other two is the man and which is the woman. He knows them by labels X and Y, and at the end of the game he says either "X is A and Y is B" or "X is B and Y is A." The interrogator is allowed to put questions to A and B thus:

C: Will X please tell me the length of his or her hair?

Now suppose X is actually A, then A must answer. It is A's object in the game to try to cause C to make the wrong identification. His answer might therefore be

"My hair is shingled, and the longest strands are about nine inches long."

In order that tones of voice may not help the interrogator the answers should be written, or better still, typewritten. The ideal arrangement is to have a teleprinter communicating between the two rooms. Alternatively the question and answers can be repeated by an intermediary. The object of the game for the third player (B) is to help the interrogator. The best strategy for her is probably to give truthful answers. She can add such things as "I am the woman, don't listen to him!" to her answers, but it will avail nothing as the man can make similar remarks.

We now ask the question, "What will happen when a machine takes the part of A in this game?" Will the interrogator decide wrongly as often when the game is played like this as he does when the game is played between a man and a woman? These questions replace our original, "Can machines think?"

CRITIQUE OF THE NEW PROBLEM

As well as asking, "What is the answer to this new form of the question," one may ask, "Is this new question a worthy one to investigate?" This latter question we investigate without further ado, thereby cutting short an infinite regress.

The new problem has the advantage of drawing a fairly sharp line between the physical and the intellectual capacities of a man. No engineer or chemist claims to be able to produce a material which is indistinguishable from the human skin. It is possible that at some time this might be done, but even supposing this invention available we should feel there was little point in trying to make a "thinking machine" more human by dressing it up in such artificial flesh. The form in which we have set the problem reflects this fact in the condition which prevents the interrogator from seeing or touching the other competitors, or hearing their voices. Some other advantages of the proposed criterion may be shown up by specimen questions and answers. Thus:

Q: Please write me a sonnet on the subject of the Forth Bridge.

A: Count me out on this one. I never could write poetry.

Q: Add 34957 to 70764.

A: (Pause about 30 seconds and then give as answer) 105621.

Q: Do you play chess?

A: Yes.

Q: I have K at my K1, and no other pieces. You have only K at K6 and R at R1. It is your move. What do you play?

A: (After a pause of 15 seconds) R-R8 mate.

The question and answer method seems to be suitable for introducing almost any one of the fields of human endeavor that we wish to include. We do not wish to penalize the machine for its inability to shine in the beauty competition, nor to penalize a man for losing in a race against an airplane. The conditions of our game make these disabilities irrelevant. The "witnesses" can brag, if they consider it advisable, as much as they please about their charms, strength or heroism, but the interrogator cannot demand practical demonstrations.

The game may perhaps be criticized on the ground that the odds are weighted too heavily against the machine. If the man were to try and pretend to be the machine he would clearly make a very poor showing. He would be given away at once by slowness and inaccuracy in arithmetic. May not machines carry out something which ought to be described as thinking but which is very different from what a man does? This objection is a very strong one, but at least we can say that if, nevertheless, a machine can be constructed to play the imitation game satisfactorily, we need not be troubled by this objection.

It might be urged that when playing the "imitation game" the best strategy for the machine may possibly be something other than imitation of the behavior of a man. This may be, but I think it is unlikely that there is any great effect of this kind. In any case there is no intention to investigate here the theory of the game, and it will be assumed that the best strategy is to try to provide answers that would naturally be given by a man.

CONTRARY VIEWS ON THE MAIN QUESTION

We may now consider the ground to have been cleared and we are ready to proceed to the debate on our question, "Can machines think?" and the variant of it quoted at the end of the last section. We cannot altogether abandon the original form of the problem, for opinions will differ as to the appropriateness of the substitution and we must at least listen to what has to be said in this connection.

It will simplify matters for the reader if I explain first my own beliefs in the matter. Consider first the more accurate form of the question. I believe that in about fifty years' time it will be possible to program computers, with a storage capacity of about 10^9, to make them play the imitation game so well that an average interrogator will not have more than 70 per cent chance of making the right identification after five minutes of questioning. The original question, "Can machines think?" I believe to be too meaningless to deserve discussion. Nevertheless I believe that at the end of the century the use of words and general educated opinion will have altered so much that one will be able to speak of machines thinking without expecting to be contradicted. I believe further that no useful purpose is served by concealing these beliefs. The popular view that scientists proceed inexorably from well-established fact to well-established fact, never being influenced by any unproved conjecture, is quite mistaken. Provided it is made clear which are proved facts and which are conjectures, no harm can result. Conjectures are of great importance since they suggest useful lines of research.

Turing's Game sets up a situation where according to Turing, it is easily conceivable that a computer could "fool" us. If we cannot make the distinction between a computer and another person, then we can begin to see that machines probably can give answers so similar to a person's that perhaps it makes sense to say that machines think. Turing of course has assumed that the question "Can machines think?" has as a reasonable translation "Can a machine trick us into identifying it as a person thinking as opposed to a machine carrying out an algorithm?" Are these questions equivalent?

If you think that Turing's approach is preposterous and that no one could really be fooled by a computer, you might find this article from the *New York Times* very interesting.

CAN MACHINES THINK? HUMANS MATCH WITS

By John Markoff
Special to the New York Times

A group of human judges chosen to represent the Boston man-in-the-street engaged in a three-hour battle of wits with a handful of computer programs today. The idea was to answer what many scientists and philosophers believe will become the central question of the information age: Can machines think?

It was hard to tell—harder than one might have, pardon the expression, thought.

The judges typed questions into computer terminals and tried to decide from the responses whether they were communicating with a man or a machine. One program proved convincing enough to fool 5 of the 10 judges. Two other programs fooled some of the people for some of the time. But the humans had, uh, second thoughts and realized that what they had thought were human thoughts were actually coming from diskettes, hard drives, monitors and electricity.

CUTTING THROUGH A DEBATE

The tournament was the first attempt to run a Turing Test, the experiment first proposed by the British mathematician Alan M. Turing 41 years ago as a simple way of cutting through the philosophical debate about whether a machine could ever be built to mimic the human mind. If a person communicating with such a machine could not tell whether it was a computer or humans, Mr. Turing reasoned, the question would be resolved.

Throughout the afternoon, while the typed conversations between programs and judges flickered on large screens in an auditorium at the Boston Computer Museum, a group of scientists and philosophers grappled with the meaning of the event.

"If a computer were to pass an unrestricted Turing Test," said Daniel Dennett, a professor of cognitive studies at Tufts University, "it will raise a number of deep civil rights questions. For example, it would be a crime to unplug such a machine because it would be a person in a legal sense. Turing should be thought of as a pioneer in machine rights."

And the conversations were intriguing. First prize went to a commercial software program called PC Therapist III, which was designed to engage its questioner in a whimsical conversation about nothing in particular. The program was written by Joseph Weintraub, the president of Thinking Software, Inc., a small artificial intelligence software company in Woodside, Queens.

At one point Mr. Weintraub's program suggested to a judge: "Perhaps you're not getting enough affection from your partner in the relationship."

"What are the key elements that are important in relationships in order to prevent conflict or problems?" the judge responded.

"I think you don't think I think," answered the terminal.

"What kind of a response to a question is that?" asked the judge. "Next question: Do you think romantic relationships are unrealistic, doomed from the start?"

"I do tend to walk around with my head in the clouds," the terminal echoed.

"Are you a romantic?" the judge queried.

"I take in whatever you ask," came the reply.

"Have you experienced problems in romantic relationships?" came another query.

"I try to be agreeable," responded the terminal.

Many of the watching experts, including scientists, philosophers and psychologists who assembled here, said they were surprised by the outcome. Computer experts said they could easily tell the human from the computer respondents. Unlike the untrained observers, the experts spotted the "common sense" mistakes that were an immediate giveaway.

PRIZE FOR "MOST HUMAN"

There were several other confusing results from the contests. One of the human confederates, Cynthia Clay, who was judged "most human of all contestants," was nevertheless judged to be a computer by two judges.

But the deeper question of whether computers will ever be able to convincingly mimic human beings and what it will mean for the human spirit if they can, remained tantalizingly distant.

The significance of the interim test was hotly debated by the contest's sponsors after the conclusion of today's event.

"These were real judges," said Oliver Strimpel, the executive director of the Boston Computer Museum, one of the sponsors of the test. "Maybe the Turing Test isn't as difficult as we first thought."

HARD TO TELL DIFFERENCE

Mr. Turing believed that by the end of the century it would be possible to program computers to make them play an "imitation game" well enough so that an average human judge would not be able to determine if a conversation typed at a computer terminal was a human "confederate" or a computer.

That assumption has become the subject of a bitter debate between scientists and philosophers who have taken sides on the question over whether the human mind will ever be reduced to a set of computer programs.

The first modern version of the Turing Test, made possible by the establishment of a $100,000 prize by philanthropist Hugh Loebner and with the support of the National Science Foundation and the Alfred P. Sloane Foundation, was not the true test that Mr. Turing envisioned. Because of limitations in the programs' capabilities, each was confined to discussing a narrow topic, such as women's clothing, romantic relationships, or Burgundy wine. For winning the first limited contest, Mr. Weintraub was awarded a prize of $1,500.

The contest organizers said they believed it was a valuable exercise that would focus public interest on questions that have until now remained the realm of philosophers and artificial intelligence researchers.

"We're witnessing history today," said Keay Dewdney, a computer scientist at the University of Western Ontario and the author of the Computer Recreations section in Scientific American. Mr. Dewdney provided expert commentary while strolling back and forth in front of the different screens. "This is the first Turing Test," he said, "however restricted."

AT THE START: OOPS!

Still, like many of the mythical confrontations between human and computer in science fiction literature and cinema, the first interim Turing test involved a technique glitch.

The start of the contest was delayed almost 45 minutes while technicians scrambled to sort out a telephone problem that kept telephone lines connecting two of the human confederates to the contest busy. When it did start, the number of terminals and screens was reduced from the original ten to eight.

Several members of the Loebner Prize committee said they thought that the glitch had make the task more difficult for the judges.

Joseph Weizenbaum, a Massachusetts Institute of Technology computer scientist, said that he was struck by how similar PC Therapist was to a program that he had written several decades ago called Eliza. Eliza became widely popular for engaging questioners in an simple nonsensical conversation. He said that such programs were very difficult to trick because it was difficult for humans to assess the nonsensical replies from the program.

After the contest, Mr. Dewdney said he had quickly decided that there were six programs and two humans behind the terminals. But he was surprised when he heard that people in the audience were changing their minds about several of the programs late in the contest.

A SHAKESPEARE CURVE

In particular, at a terminal which was discussing Shakespeare's plays, a great deal of confusion was inspired because the terminal kept changing its answer to the question, "What is your favorite play?"

"That really threw a lot of people for a loop," Mr. Dewdney said.

One of the human judges, Lou-Anne Kroutil, a student and part-time auto mechanic, said she had been fooled by PC Therapist when it responded with a nonsense answer.

"It typed something that I thought was trite, and when I responded it interacted with me in a very convincing fashion," she said.

Mr. Weintraub's program held a number of the audience spellbound and many were still scratching their heads after watching several hours of conversation. One conversation with it went as follows:

Terminal: A whim is a sudden capricious and often peculiar behavior. A bit of sunlight in a grim grey world!

Judge: Something like a hunch?

Terminal: Everybody sets out to do something and everybody does something, but no one does what he sets out to do.

Judge: Well anyway I would imagine whimsical conversation is like a series of knight's moves in chess—sort of zig-zag rather than following any particular line.

Terminal: A whimsical person is subject to erratic behavior and unpredictable thoughts. . . . How nice to be unpredictable.

Judge: Are you kidding? Sure, total predictability would make the world a dull place, but unpredictability is hardly a virtue!

After the contest was over Dr. Loebner pronounced himself satisfied with the results and said that he felt that the Turing Test would now have a life of its own. Dr. Loebner is president of Crowne Industries, an equipment supply firm in Orange, N.J.

He said that he had thought of sponsoring a Turing Test seven years ago as a way of sparking interest in the idea of designing artificially intelligent programs.

Describing himself as a "dyed-in-the-wool" utopian, he said that in both literature and science there has been a long and noble tradition by those who have attempted to build machines with human qualities.

Frankensteins and Golems are both a possibility, he said, "But I think it's a noble undertaking for a species to attempt to invent a superior intelligence."

The New York City philanthropist also revealed another, possibly more personal motivation in sponsoring the contest that bears his name: "I'm in favor of 100 percent unemployment. I've always wanted computers to do all the work."

NOTE ON SOURCES. The material in this section is from A. M. Turing, "Computing Machinery and Intelligence," *Mind*, Vol. 59 No. 236 (1950), pp. 433–460; J. Markoff; "Can Machines Think? Humans Match Wits," *The New York Times*, November 9, 1991.

6 JOHN SEARLE

COMPUTERS CANNOT THINK

FROM TURING TO SEARLE. Despite advances made in computer science and the related fields of cognitive science and artificial intelligence, not all philosophers are agreed that this approach holds the key to unraveling the mysteries of the mind–body problem. Just as Ryle pointed out that we were misled by a picture of the mind, so these philosophers think that cognitive scientists may be misleading themselves by using computers as the model of minds.

BIOGRAPHICAL NOTE.   John Searle was born in Denver, Colorado in 1932. He received his D.Phil. from Oxford (England) in 1959. He teaches at the University of California at Berkeley. Searle is especially well known for his work in philosophy of language. His Chinese Room Argument has generated much discussion among researchers in cognitive science.

THE ARGUMENT OF THE PASSAGES.   John Searle disagrees with much of the approach of the cognitive scientists as they try to understand the mind. He asks: How good is computer simulation of thinking? His answer is: Not good at all. He uses an example to make his general point that artificial intelligence is not really human intelligence. First, he distinguishes two versions of artificial intelligence.

> What psychological and philosophical significance should we attach to recent efforts at computer simulations of human cognitive capacities? In answering this question, I find it useful to distinguish what I will call "strong" AI from "weak" or "cautious" AI (artificial intelligence). According to weak AI, the principal value of the computer in the study of the mind is that it gives us a very powerful tool. For example, it enables us to formulate and test hypotheses in a more rigorous and precise fashion. But according to strong AI, the computer is not merely a tool in the study of the mind; rather, the appropriately programmed computer really *is* a mind, in the sense that computers given the right programs can be literally said to *understand* and have other cognitive states. In strong AI, because the programmed computer has cognitive states, the programs are not mere tools that enable us to test psychological explanations; rather, the programs are themselves the explanations.
>
> I have no objection to the claims of weak AI, at least as far as this article is concerned. My discussion here will be directed at the claims I have defined as those of strong AI, specifically the claim that the appropriately programmed computer literally has cognitive states and that the programs thereby explain human cognition. When I hereafter refer to AI, I have in mind the strong version, as expressed by these two claims.
>
> I will consider the work of Roger Schank and his colleagues at Yale (Schank and Abelson 1977), because I am more familiar with it than I am with any other similar claims, and because it provides a very clear example of the sort of work I wish to examine. But nothing that follows depends upon the details of Schank's programs. The same arguments would apply to Winograd's SHRDLU (Winograd 1973), Weizenbaum's ELIZA (Weizenbaum 1965), and indeed any Turing machine simulation of human mental phenomena. . . .
>
> Very briefly, and leaving out the various details, one can describe Schank's program as follows: The aim of the program is to simulate the human ability to understand stories. It is characteristic of human beings' story-understanding capacity that they can answer questions about the story even though the information that they give was never explicitly stated in the story. Thus, for example, suppose you are given the following story: "A man went into a restaurant and ordered a hamburger. When the hamburger arrived it was burned to a crisp, and the man stormed out of the restaurant angrily, without paying for the burger or leaving a tip." Now, if you are asked, "Did the man eat the hamburger?" you will presumably answer, "No, he did not." Similarly, if you are given the following story: "A man went into a restaurant and ordered a hamburger; when the hamburger came he was very pleased with

it; and as he left the restaurant he gave the waitress a large tip before paying his bill," and you are asked the question, "Did the man eat the hamburger?" you will presumably answer, "Yes, he ate the hamburger." Now Schank's machines can similarly answer questions about restaurants in this fashion. To do this, they have a "representation" of the sort of information that human beings have about restaurants, which enables them to answer such questions as those above, given these sorts of stories. When the machine is given the story and then asked the question, the machine will print out answers of the sort that we would expect human beings to give if told similar stories. Partisans of strong AI claim that in this question and answer sequence the machine is not only simulating a human ability but also (1) that the machine can literally be said to *understand* the story and provide the answers to questions, and (2) that what the machine and its program do *explains* the human ability to understand the story and answer questions about it.

Both claims seem to me to be totally unsupported by Schank's work, as I will attempt to show in what follows.

Weak AI helps in our understanding of thinking, whereas strong AI claims that a computer is (or has) a mind. Strong AI claims that the computer has cognitive states and its program is the explanation for human understanding.

Proponents of strong AI point out that to understand a story is to be able to read the story and give answers to questions not specifically mentioned in the story itself. There are machines that can do this. Thus, the strong AI claim is that the machines really do understand the stories and that programs are the explanation for understanding.

Searle uses an example to show us that the claims of strong AI are wrong. He asks us to imagine the following situation, which has come to be called the Chinese Room.

Suppose that I'm locked in a room and given a large batch of Chinese writing. Suppose furthermore (as is indeed the case) that I know no Chinese, either written or spoken, and that I'm not even confident that I could recognize Chinese writing as Chinese writing distinct from, say, Japanese writing or meaningless squiggles. To me, Chinese writing is just so many meaningless squiggles. Now suppose further that after this first batch of Chinese writing I am given a second batch of Chinese script together with a set of rules for correlating the second batch with the first batch. The rules are in English, and I understand these rules as well as any other native speaker of English. They enable me to correlate one set of formal symbols with another set of formal symbols, and all that "formal" means here is that I can identify the symbols entirely by their shapes. Now suppose also that I am given a third batch of Chinese symbols together with some instructions, again in English, that enable me to correlate elements of this third batch with the first two batches, and these rules instruct me how to give back certain Chinese symbols with certain sorts of shapes in response to certain sorts of shapes given me in the third batch. Unknown to me, the people who are giving me all of these symbols called the first batch a "script," they call the second batch a "story," and they call the third batch "questions." Furthermore, they call the symbols I give them back in response to the third batch "answers to the questions," and the set of rules in English that they gave me, they call the "program." Now just to complicate the story a little, imagine that these people also give me stories in English, which I understand, and they then ask me questions in English about these stories, and I give them back answers in English. Suppose also that after a while I got so good at following the instructions for manipulating the Chinese symbols and the programmers get so good at writing the programs that from the external point of view—that is, from the point of view of somebody outside the room in which I am locked—my answers to the questions are absolutely indistinguishable from those of native Chinese speakers. Nobody just looking at my answers can tell that I don't speak a word of Chinese. Let us also suppose that my answer to the English questions are, as they no doubt would be, indistinguishable from those of other native English speakers, for the simple reason that I am a native English speaker. From the external point of view—from the point of view of someone reading my "answers"—the answers to the Chinese questions and the English questions are equally good. But in the Chinese case, unlike the English case, I produce the answers by manipulating uninterpreted formal symbols. As far as the Chinese is concerned, I simply behave like a computer. I perform computational operations on formally specified elements. For the purposes of the Chinese, I am simply an instantiation of the computer program.

Now the claims made by strong AI are that the programmed computer understands the stories and that the program in some sense explains human understanding. But we are now in a position to examine these claims in light of our thought experiment.

1. As regards the first claim, it seems to me quite obvious in the example that I do not understand a word of Chinese stories. I have inputs and outputs that are indistinguishable from those of the native Chinese speaker, and I can have any formal program you like, but I still understand nothing. For the same reasons, Schank's computer understands nothing of any stories, whether in Chinese, English, or whatever, since in the Chinese case the computer is me, and in the cases where the computer is not me, the computer has nothing more than I have in the case where I understand nothing.

2. As regards the second claim, that the program explains human understanding, we can see that the computer and its program do not provide sufficient conditions of understanding since the computer and the program are functioning, and there is no understanding. But does it even provide a necessary condition or a significant contribution to understanding? One of the claims made by the supporters of strong AI is that when I understand a story in English, what I am doing is exactly the same—or perhaps more of the same—as what I was doing in manipulating the Chinese symbols. It is simply more formal symbol manipulation that distinguishes the case in English, where I do understand, from the case in Chinese where I don't. I have not demonstrated that this claim is false, but it would certainly appear an incredible claim in the example. Such plausibility as the claim has derives from the supposition that we can construct a program that will have the same inputs and outputs as native speakers, and in addition we assume that speakers have some level of description where they are also instantiations of a program. On the basis of these two assumptions we assume that even if Schank's program isn't the whole story about understanding, it may be part of the story. Well, I suppose that is an empirical possibility, but not the slightest reason has so far been given to believe that it is true, since what is suggested—though certainly not demonstrated—by the example is that the computer program is simply irrelevant to my understanding of the story. In the Chinese case I have everything that artificial intelligence can put into me by way of a program, and I understand nothing;

in the English case I understand everything, and there is so far no reason at all to suppose that my understanding has anything to do with computer programs, that is, with computational operations on purely formally specified elements. As long as the program is defined in terms of computational operations on purely formally defined elements, what the example suggests is that these by themselves have no interesting connection with understanding. They are certainly not sufficient conditions, and not the slightest reason has been given to suppose that they are necessary conditions or even that they make a significant contribution to understanding. Notice that the force of the argument is not simply that different machines can have the same input and output while operating on different formal principles—that is not the point at all. Rather, whatever purely formal principles you put into the computer, they will not be sufficient for understanding, since a human will be able to follow the formal principles without understanding anything. No reason whatever has been offered to suppose that such principles are necessary or even contributory, since no reason has been given to suppose that when I understand English I am operating with any formal program at all.

Well, then, what is it that I have in the case of the English sentences that I do not have in the case of the Chinese sentences? The obvious answer is that I know what the former mean, while I haven't the faintest idea what the latter mean.

Strong AI has to say that I understand Chinese. But it is clear that I do not—I am only manipulating symbols. Because of this, the computer can't be a model for human understanding. When I understand, something else beyond manipulating symbols has taken place. Understanding, according to Searle, requires more than just inputs and outputs. Searle concludes that computers literally understand nothing.

NOTE ON SOURCES. The material in this section is from John Searle, "Minds, Brains and Programs," *The Behavioral and Brain Sciences*, Vol. III, No. 3, pp. 417–424.

7   BRUCE BRIDGEMAN AND NED BLOCK

SEARLE IS MISTAKEN

FROM SEARLE TO BRIDGEMAN AND BLOCK   Of course, not all philosophers or cognitive scientists agree with Searle. Both Bruce Bridgeman and Ned Block find what they take to be flaws in Searle's approach.

BIOGRAPHICAL NOTES.   Bruce Bridgeman was born in 1944 in Bloomfield, New Jersey. His specialty is physiological psychology and physiology of vision. He currently teaches at the University of California at Santa Cruz.

Ned Block was born in Chicago, Illinois in 1942. He received his Ph.D. in philosophy from Harvard in 1971. He has worked in the fields of psycholinguistics and cognitive science. Block currently teaches at M.I.T.

ARGUMENT OF THE PASSAGES. Bridgeman argues that the computer Searle imagines is too weak. To understand, a computer needs more input and more feedback relations with the outside world. Searle stresses the need for having content in our experiences (intentionality) in order to show that computers cannot have true mental states. But Bridgeman insists that we do many things by rote with no awareness of any content; e.g., many mathematical problems, riding bicycles, reading, choosing which shirt to wear, matching socks, etc.

... the existing information stored in the brain, both that given in genetic development and that added by experience.... came without intentionality of the sort that Searle seems to require, the genetic information being received from long strings of DNA base sequences (clearly there was no intentionality here), and previous inputs being made up of the same streams of 0.1–volt signals that constitute the present input. Now it is clear that no neuron receiving any of these signals or similar signals generated inside the brain has any idea of what is going on. The neuron is only a humble machine which receives inputs and generates outputs as a function of the temporal and spatial relations of the inputs, and its own structural properties. To assert any further properties of brains is the worst sort of dualism.

Searle grants that humans have intentionality, and toward the end of his article he also admits that many animals might have intentionality also. But how far down the phylogenetic scale is he willing to go (see "Cognition and Consciousness in Nonhuman Species," *BBS* 1(4) 1978)? Does a single-celled animal have intentionality? Clearly not, for it is only a simple machine which receives physically identifiable inputs and "automatically" generates reflex outputs. The hydra with a few dozen neurons might be explained in the same way, a simple nerve network with inputs and outputs that are restricted, relatively easy to understand, and processed according to fixed patterns. Now what about the mollusc with a few hundred neurons, the insect with a few thousand, the amphibian with a few million, or the mammal with billions? To make his argument convincing, Searle needs a criterion for a dividing line in his implicit dualism.

We are left with a human brain that has an intention-free, genetically determined structure, on which are superimposed the results of storms of tiny nerve signals. From this we somehow introspect an intentionality that cannot be assigned to machines. Searle uses the example of arithmetic manipulations to show how humans "understand" something that machines don't. I submit that neither humans nor machines understand numbers in the sense Searle intends. The understanding of numbers greater than about five is always an illusion, for humans can deal with larger numbers only by using memorized tricks rather than true understanding. If I want to add 27 to 54, I don't use some direct numerical understanding or even a spatial or electrical analogue in my brain. Instead, I apply rules that I memorized in elementary school without really knowing what they meant, and combine these rules with memorized facts of addition of one-digit numbers to arrive at an answer without understanding the numbers themselves. Though I have the feeling that I am performing operations on numbers, in terms of the algorithms I use there is nothing numerical about it. In the same way I can add numbers in the billions, although neither I nor anyone else has any concept of what these numbers mean in terms of perceptually meaningful quantities. Any further understanding of the number system that I possess is irrelevant, for it is not used in performing simple computations.

The illusion of having a consciousness of numbers is similar to the illusion of having a full-color, well focused visual field; such a concept exists in our consciousness, but the physiological reality falls far short of the introspection. High-quality color information is available only in about the central thirty degrees of the visual field, and the best spatial information in only one or two degrees. I suggest that the feeling of intentionality is a cognitive illusion similar to the feeling of the high-quality visual image. Consciousness is a neurological system like any other, with functions such as the long-term direction of behavior (intentionality?), access to long-term memories, and several other characteristics that make it a powerful, though limited-capacity, processor of biologically useful information.

All of Searle's replies to his *Gedankenexperiment* are variations on the theme that I have described here, that an adequately designed machine could include intentionality as an emergent quality even though individual parts (transistors, neurons, or whatever) have none. All of the replies have an element of truth, and their shortcomings are more in their failure to communicate the similarity of brains and machines to Searle than in any internal weaknesses. Perhaps the most important difference between brains and machines lies not in their instantiation but in their history, for humans have evolved to perform a variety of poorly understood functions including reproduction and survival in a complex social and ecological context. Programs, being designed without extensive evolution, have more restricted goals and motivations.

Searle's accusation of dualism in AI falls wide of the mark because the mechanist does not insist on a particular mechanism in the organism, but only that "mental" processes be represented in a physical system when the system is functioning. A program lying on a tape spool in a corner is no more conscious than a brain preserved in a glass jar, and insisting that the program if read into an appropriate computer would function with intentionality asserts only that the adequate machine consists of an organization imposed on a physical substrate. The organization is no more mentalistic than the substrate itself. Artificial intelligence is about programs rather than machines only because the process of organizing information and inputs and outputs into an information system has been largely solved by digital computers. Therefore, the program is the only step in the process left to worry about.

Searle may well be right that present programs (as in Schank & Abelson 1977) do not instantiate intentionality according to his definition. The issue is not whether present programs do this but whether it is possible in principle to build machines that make plans and achieve goals. Searle has given us no evidence that this is not possible.

Ned Block says that Searle is right—at this stage of the game. But at some point, evidence may overtake our intuitions. When we change some of our everyday concepts because of advances in science, we often are jarred and don't want to give in. Block's point is that while our intuitions now are the intuitions of Searle, those intuitions may themselves be changed by advances in computer science. Block has something like this in mind. Dolphins originally looked like any other fish. We treated them the way we treated other fish. If someone had said to us three hundred years ago that dolphins have a language, our intuitions would have been to reject the claim. Now, we know better, in large part because of advances in science.

First, we are willing, and rightly so, to accept counterintuitive consequences of claims for which we have substantial evidence. It once seemed intuitively absurd to assert that the earth was whirling through space at breakneck speed, but in the face of the evidence for the Copernican view, such an intuition should be (and eventually was) rejected as irrelevant to the truth of the matter. More relevantly, a grapefruit-sized head-enclosed blob of gray protoplasm seems, at least at first blush, a most implausible seat of mentality. But if your intuitions still balk at brains as seats of mentality, you should ignore your intuitions as irrelevant to the truth of the matter, given the remarkable evidence for the role of the brain in our mental life. Searle presents some alleged counterintuitive consequences of the view of cognition as formal symbol manipulation. But his argument does not even have the right *form*, for in order to know whether we should reject the doctrine because of its alleged counterintuitive consequences, we must know what sort of evidence there is *in favor* of the doctrine. If the evidence for the doctrine is overwhelming, then incompatible intuitions should be ignored, just as should intuitions that the brain couldn't be the seat of mentality. So Searle's argument has a missing premise to the effect that the evidence *isn't* sufficient to overrule the intuitions.

Well, is such a missing premise *true*? I think that anyone who takes a good undergraduate cognitive psychology course would see enough evidence to justify *tentatively* disregarding intuitions of the sort that Searle appeals to. Many theories in the tradition of thinking as formal symbol manipulation have a moderate (though admittedly not overwhelming) degree of empirical support.

A second point against Searle has to do with another aspect of the logic of appeals to intuition. At best, intuition reveals facts about our *concepts* (at worst, facts about a motley of factors such as our prejudices, ignorance, and, still worse, our lack of imagination—as when people accepted the deliverance of intuition that two straight lines cannot cross twice). So even if we were to accept Searle's appeal to intuitions as showing that homunculus heads that formally manipulate symbols do not think, what this would show is that our formal symbol-manipulation theories do not provide a sufficient condition for the application of our ordinary intentional concepts. The more interesting issue, however, is whether the homunculus head's formal symbol manipulation falls in the same scientific natural kind (see Putnam 1975a) as our intentional processes. If so, then the homunculus head does think in a reasonable scientific sense of the term—and so much the worse for the ordinary concept. Moreover, if we are very concerned with ordinary intentional concepts, we can give sufficient conditions for their application by building in ad hoc conditions designed to rule out the putative counterexamples. A first stab (inadequate, but improvable—see Putnam 1975b, p. 435; Block 1978, p. 292) would be to add the condition that in order to think, realizations of the symbol-manipulating system must not have operations mediated by entities that themselves have symbol manipulation typical of intentional systems. The ad hocness of such a condition is not an objection to it, given that what we are trying to do is "reconstruct" an everyday concept out of a scientific one; we can expect the everyday concept to be scientifically characterizable only in an unnatural way. (See Fodor's commentary on Searle, this issue.) Finally, there is good reason for thinking that the Putnam-Kripke account of the semantics of "thought" and other intentional terms is correct. If so, and if the formal symbol manipulation of the homunculus head falls in the same natural kind as our cognitive processes, then the homunculus head *does* think, in the ordinary sense as well as in the scientific sense of the term.

The upshot of both these points is that the real crux of the debate rests on a matter that Searle does not so much as mention: what the *evidence* is for the formal symbol-manipulation point of view.

NOTE ON SOURCES.   The material in this section is from Bruce Bridgeman, "Brains and Programs-Minds," *The Behavioral and Brain Sciences*, Vol. III, No. 3 (1980), pp. 427–428; and Ned Block, "What Intuitions About Homunculi Don't Show," *The Behavioral and Brain Sciences*, Vol. III, No. 3 (1980), pp. 417–424.

8 NORMAN MALCOLM

THE ARGUMENT FROM ANALOGY FOR OTHER MINDS IS BASED ON A MISCONCEPTION

FROM DESCARTES TO MALCOLM.   We have said that Descartes created two important problems for philosophers who followed his ideas. One was the mind–body problem. We have just completed a look at that problem. Now we turn to the other problem, the problem of other minds. That is, how can we justify our belief that there are other minds; that each of us is not alone in thought in the universe?

For Descartes, the existence of other minds was insured by the existence of a good and all powerful God; a God who could not be a deceiver. Once Descartes proves the existence of this kind of God from the Cogito (see Chapter 5 for proofs for the existence of God), the idea that there are other minds is too well entrenched to be false. It could only be false if God were a deceiver.

Another approach to proving the existence of other minds relies on the use of analogies, i.e., likenesses. One sort of argument is this. In similar circumstances, e.g., when we are stuck by pins, we both cry "Ouch!" Since you are like me in all other respects, you must also be like me in this respect: that when you are stuck with a pin, you feel pain just as I do. Arguments like this one are called arguments from analogy for the existence of other minds.

BIOGRAPHICAL NOTE.   Norman Malcolm was born in Kansas in 1911. He received a Ph.D. in philosophy from Harvard in 1940. After studying at Cambridge (England) from 1938–1940, Malcolm taught at Princeton and then at Cornell, beginning in 1946 until his retirement. Malcolm studied with the influential but enigmatic philosopher Ludwig Wittgenstein while at Cambridge. The two became close friends. Thus, Malcolm became a respected interpreter of the views of Wittgenstein. Malcolm wrote in many areas related to the philosophy of mind, including a book on dreaming and one on memory. He died in 1990.

THE ARGUMENT OF THE PASSAGES.   Malcolm begins by criticizing J. S. Mill's argument from analogy for the existence of other minds. Mill's argument is easy to follow and sounds so reasonable that we are taken aback that anyone should find fault with it. How else can we argue to the minds of others except on the basis of similarities to ourselves? Against this, Malcolm makes a simple point. When I say "I have a pain" and mean by it that I am in a certain mental state, then when I say of you that you are in pain, "pain" cannot refer to my mental state. Can it refer to your mental state? Malcolm insists that there is no evidence for this, since there is no way for me to know that your mental state when you are in pain is just like mine when I am in pain. It must then refer only to your behavior. Therefore, the argument from analogy never provides the conclusion that there are other mental states. At most, it might show that other things that look like me behave the way I do in similar circumstances.

I believe that the argument from analogy for the existence of other minds still enjoys more credit than it deserves, and my first aim will be to show that it leads nowhere. J. S. Mill is one of the many who have accepted the argument and I take his statement of it as representative. He puts to himself the question, "By what evidence do I know, or by what considerations am I led to believe, that there exist other sentient creatures; that the walking and speaking figures which I see and hear, have sensations and thoughts, or in other words, possess Minds?" His answer is the following:

> I conclude that other human beings have feelings like me, because, first they have bodies like me, which I know, in my own case, to be the antecedent condition of feelings; and because, secondly, they exhibit the acts, and other outward signs, which in my own case I know by experience to be caused by feelings. I am conscious in myself of a series of facts connected by an uniform sequence, of which the beginning is modifications of my body, the middle is feelings, and the end is outward demeanor. In the case of other human beings I have the evidence of my senses for the first and last links of the series, but not for the intermediate link. I find, however, that the sequence between the first and last is as regular and constant in those other cases as it is in mine. In my own case I know that the first link produces the last through the intermediate link, and could not produce it without. Experience, therefore, obliges me to conclude that there must be an intermediate link; which must either be the same in others as in myself, or a different one: I must either believe them to be alive, or to be automations; and by believing them to be alive, that is, by supposing the link to be of the same nature as in the case of which I have experience, and which is in all other respects similar, I bring other human beings, as phenomena, under the same generalizations which I know by experience to be the true theory of my own existence.

I shall pass by the possible objection that this would be very *weak* inductive reasoning, based as it is on the observation of a single instance. More interesting is the following point: Suppose this reasoning could yield a conclusion of the sort "It is probable that that human figure" (pointing at some person other than oneself) "has thoughts and feelings." Then there is a question as to whether this conclusion can *mean* anything to the philosopher who draws it, because there is a question as whether the sentence "That human figure has thoughts and feelings" can mean anything to him. Why should this be a question? Because the assumption from which Mill starts is that he has *no criterion* for determining whether another "walking and speaking figure" does or does not have thoughts and feelings. If he had a criterion he could apply it, establishing with certainty that this or that human figure does or does not have feelings (for the only plausible criterion would lie in behavior and circumstances that are open to view), and there would be no call to resort to tenuous analogical reasoning that yields at best a probability. If Mill has no criterion for the existence of feelings other than his own then in that sense he does not understand the sentence "That human figure has feelings" and therefore does not understand the sentence "It is *probable* that that human figure has feelings."

There is a familiar inclination to make the following reply: "Although I have no criterion of verification still I *understand*, for example, the sentence 'He has a pain.' For I understand the meaning of 'I have a pain.' and 'He has a pain' means that he has the *same* thing I have when I have a pain." But this is a fruitless maneuver. If I do not know how to establish that someone has a pain then I do not know how to establish that he has the *same* as I have when I have a pain. You cannot improve my under-standing of "he has a pain" by this recourse to the notion of "the same." unless you give me a criterion for saying that someone *has* the same as I have. If you can do this you will have no use for the argument from analogy: and if you cannot then you do not understand the supposed conclusion of that argument. A philosopher who pur-ports to rely on the analogical argument cannot, I think, escape this dilemma.

Malcolm insists that it takes more than correct answers to questions to estab-lish that there is true understanding. But unlike Searle, who looks for the appro-priate inner mental state of understanding, Malcolm focuses on the proper behavior from the right sorts of things; so for Malcolm, computers cannot think.

I wish to argue that no amount of intelligible sounds coming from an oak tree or a kitchen table could create any probability that it has sensations and thoughts. The question to be asked is: What would show that a tree or table *understands* the sounds that come from it? We can imagine that useful warnings, true descriptions and pre-dictions, even "replies" to questions, should emanate from a tree, so that it came to be of enormous value to its owner. How should we establish that it understood those sentences? Should we "question" it? Suppose that the tree "said" that there was a vixen in the neighborhood, and we "asked" it "What is a vixen?," and it "replied," "A vixen is a female fox." It might go on to do as well for "female" and "fox." This perfor-mance might incline us to say that the tree understood the words, in contrast to the possible case in which it answered "I don't know" or did not answer at all. But would it show that the tree understood the words in the same sense that a person could understand them? With a person such a performance would create a presumption that he could make correct *applications* of the word in question; but not so with a tree. To see this point think of the normal teaching of words (e.g., "spoon," "dog," "red") to a child and how one decides whether he understands them. At a primitive stage of teaching one does not require or expect definitions, but rather that the child should *pick out* reds from blues, dogs from cats, spoons from forks. This involves his looking, pointing, reaching for and going to the right things and not the wrong ones. That a child says "red" when a red thing and "blue" when a blue thing is put before him is indicative of a mastery of those words *only* in conjunction with the other activities of looking, pointing, trying to get, fetching, and carrying. Try to suppose that he says the right words but looks at and reaches for the wrong things. Should we be tempted to say that he has mastered the use of those words? No, indeed. The disparity between words and behavior would make us say that he does not understand the words. In the case of a tree there could be no disparity between its words and its "behavior" because it is logically incapable of behavior of the relevant kind.

Since it has nothing like the human face and body it makes no sense to say of a tree, or an electronic computer, that it is looking or pointing at or fetching something. (Of course one can always *invent* in a sense for these expressions.) Therefore it would make no sense to say that it did or did not understand the above words. Trees and computers cannot either pass or fail the tests that a child is put through. They cannot take them. That an object was a source of intelligible sounds or other signs (no matter how sequential) would not be enough by itself to establish that it had thoughts or sensations. How informative sentences and valuable predictions could emanate from a gorse-bush might be a grave scientific problem, but the explanation could never be that the gorse-bush has a mind. Better no explanation than nonsense!

In closing his attack on the argument from analogy, Malcolm focuses on one of its presuppositions; namely, that we learn from observing ourselves when to say things like, "I am in pain" or "I just had a thought." He suggests following the philosopher, Ludwig Wittgenstein, that "I have a toothache" should be likened to holding one's cheek, groaning and wincing when biting on a peanut. Once we see that the question, "How does one know when it is appropriate to say 'I have a toothache,'" is nonsensical, we can see that we do not learn by observing ourselves whether we are in pain or have a thought. And, once we admit this, we cannot generate the problem of other minds simply by pointing out that while I know when to say "I have a pain" by monitoring my pain-states, I cannot monitor your pain states in the same way and therefore can never know when I can say "You have a pain."

The destruction of the argument from analogy also destroys the *problem* for which it was supposed to provide a solution. A philosopher feels himself in a difficulty about other minds because he assumes that first of all he is acquainted with mental phenomena "from his own case." What troubles him is how to make the transition from his own case to the case of others. When his thinking is freed of the illusion of the priority of his own case, then he is able to look at the familiar facts and to acknowledge that the circumstances, behavior, and utterances of others actually are his *criteria* (not merely his evidence) for the existence of their mental states. Previously this had seemed impossible.

But now he is in danger of flying to the opposite extreme of behaviorism, which errs by believing that through observation of one's own circumstances, behavior, and utterances one can find out that one is thinking or angry. The philosophy of "from one's own case" and behaviorism, though in a sense opposites, make the common assumption that the first-person, present-tense psychological statements are verified by self-observation. According to the "one's own case" philosophy the self-observation cannot be checked by others; according to behaviorism the self-observation would be by means of outward criteria that are available to all. The first position becomes unintelligible; the second is false for at least many kinds of psychological statements. We are forced to conclude that the first-person psychological statements are not (or hardly ever) verified by self-observation. It follows that they have no verification at all; for if they had a verification it would have to be by self-observation.

But if sentences like "My head aches" or "I wonder where she is" do not express observations then what do they do? What is the relation between my declaration that my head aches and the fact that my head aches, if the former is not the report of an observation? The perplexity about the existence of *other* minds has, as the result of criticism, turned into a perplexity about the meaning of one's own psychological sentences about oneself. At our starting point it was the sentence "*His* head aches" that posed a problem; but now it is the sentence "*My* head aches" that puzzles us.

One way in which this problem can be put is by the question, "How does *one know when to say* the words 'My head aches'?" The inclination to ask this question can be made acute by imagining a fantastic but not impossible case of a person who has survived to adult years without ever experiencing pain. He is given various sorts of injections to correct this condition, and on receiving one of these one day, he jumps and exclaims, "Now I feel pain!" One wants to ask, "How did he *recognize* the new sensation as a *pain*?"

Let us note that if the man gives an answer (e.g., "I knew it must be pain because of the way I jumped") then he proves by that very fact that he has not mastered the correct use of the words "I feel pain." They cannot be used to state a *conclusion*. In telling us *how* he did it he will convict himself of a misuse. Therefore the question "How did he recognize his sensation?" requests the impossible. The inclination to ask it is evidence of our inability to grasp the fact that the use of this psychological sentence has nothing to do with recognizing or identifying or observing a state of oneself.

The fact that this imagined case produces an especially strong temptation to ask the "How?" question shows that we have the idea that it must be more difficult to give the right name of one's sensation *the first time*. The implication would be that it is not so difficult *after* the first time. Why should this be? Are we thinking that then the man would have a paradigm of pain with which he could compare his sensations and so be in a position to know right off whether a certain sensation was or was not a pain? But the paradigm would be either something "outer" (behavior) or something "inner" (perhaps a memory impression of the sensation). If the former then he is misusing the first-person sentence. If the latter then the question of whether he compared *correctly* the present sensation with the inner paradigm of pain would be without sense. Thus the idea that the use of the first-person sentences can be governed by paradigms must be abandoned. It is another form of our insistent misconception of the first-person sentence as resting somehow on the identification of a psychological state.

These absurdities prove that we must conceive of the first-person psychological sentences in some entirely different light. Wittgenstein presents us with the suggestion that the first-person sentences are to be thought of as similar to the natural nonverbal, behavioral expressions of psychological states. "My leg hurts," for example, is to be assimilated to crying, limping, holding one's leg. This is a bewildering comparison and one's first thought is that two sorts of things could not be more unlike. By saying the sentence one can make a *statement*; it has a *contradictory*; it is *true* or *false*; in saying it one *lies* or tells the truth; and so on. None of these things, exactly, can be said of crying, limping, holding one's leg. So how can there be any resemblance? But Wittgenstein knew this when he deliberately likened such a sentence to "the primitive, the natural, expressions" of pain, and said that it is "new pain-behavior." This analogy has at least two important merits; first, it breaks the hold on us of the question "How does one *know when to say* 'My leg hurts'?," for in the light of the analogy this will be as nonsensical as the question "How does one know when to cry, limp, or hold one's leg?"; second, it explains how the utterance of a first-person psychological sentence by another person can have *importance* for us, although not as an identification—for in the light of the analogy it will have the same importance as the natural behavior which serves as our preverbal criterion of the psychological states of others.

Suppose we were to answer Malcolm's question, "How does one know when to cry, limp, or hold one's leg?" by interpreting it to mean "when would a person be over-reacting?" (Suppose I scream, roll on the floor, call for an ambulance and cancel my classes for the day because of a paper cut.) The answer to this question certainly depends on where the person is and what the person is expected to be doing *and* how much it really hurts. Thus it is not clear that all references to mental states can be avoided.

NOTE ON SOURCES. The material in this section is from Norman Malcolm, *Knowledge and Certainty* (New York: Cornell University Press, 1963), pp. 130–140.

9 JOHN ECCLES

CONTEMPORARY DUALISM

FROM MALCOLM TO ECCLES.   We began to look into the question "Am I a mind or a body?" in the seventeenth century with René Descartes. Much of the refined argumentation concerning this question can be seen as a response to the Cartesian philosophy. It is all too easy to think that contemporary philosophy and contemporary science have put Descartes to rest. In order to show that dualism and interactionism are still attractive views, we end this section with a selection from the book, *The Self and Its Brain*, which has parts written by Karl Popper and parts by John Eccles. The selection that follows is by Eccles, a well-known neurophysiologist.

BIOGRAPHICAL NOTE.   John Eccles was born in Melbourne, Australia in 1903. He received a D.Phil. degree in physiology from Oxford in 1929. He received the Nobel prize in medicine and physiology in 1963 for his work on neurophysiology, which focused on the mechanism of repolarization of nerve cell membranes. He has taught at Oxford, the Australian National University, SUNY at Buffalo and Johns Hopkins University.

THE ARGUMENT OF THE PASSAGES.   Eccles (and Popper, for that matter) have three sorts of arguments for supporting their form of dualistic-interactionism. The first is that all other answers have been shown to have philosophical, as well as scientific, problems. This is not to say that dualistic-interactionism is free of problems. It is just to say that there is no other clear and correct answer. The second argument stems from their description of what it is like to have certain experiences. They focus on memory. Without a self conscious of itself, without what philosophers call "the self conscious I," we can make no sense of experiences such as trying hard to remember a name. Surely, they say, what is going on is some sort of scanning of brain states by the self. Without the self, there could no such set of experiences. Their third argument rests on their general way of looking at the world. The selection from Eccles begins with a discussion of their world-view; one which sees the world divisible into three parts—a tripartite division. (In Chapter 3 there will be a selection from *The Mind and Its Brain* by Karl Popper, where he will appeal to this Three Worlds View in order to defend the existence of free will.)

> It is desirable to make brief reference to the philosophical basis of my discussion. As illustrated in Figure 2.2, everything in existence and in experience is subsumed in one or other of three worlds: World 1, the world of physical objects and states; World 2, the world of states of consciousness and subjective knowledge of all kinds; World 3, the world of man-made culture, comprising the whole of objective knowledge. Furthermore it is proposed that there is interaction between these worlds. There is reciprocal interaction between Worlds 1 and 2, and between Worlds 2 and 3 generally via the mediation of World 1. When the objective knowledge of World 3 (the man-made world of culture) is encoded on various objects of World 1—books, pictures,

structures, machines—it can be consciously perceived only when projected to the brain by the appropriate receptor organs and afferent pathways. Reciprocally the World 2 of conscious experience can bring about changes in World 1, in the first place in the brain, then in muscular contractions, World 2 in that way being able to act extensively on World 1.

With the three worlds explained, Eccles lists five facts about experience and scientific advances concerning the brain that he believes support the idea of the mind as a separate entity, a scanner of brain states. Here are those facts: (1) Our ability to pay selective attention shows that there is unity to consciousness. We are not just open to all outside stimuli. (2) Events in the brain are necessary for consciousness. (3) Events in the brain and experience are not always the same. He gives the example of how perceived time can differ from actual (real) time. Eccles assumes that real time is registered in the brain in real time, whereas our experience of time can be quite different. (4) We experience the efficacy of our will on our brains as when we rack our brains trying to remember some past event. (5) No one has been able even to come close to explaining how brain events alone can account for the experience of a unified self-consciousness.

It is important now to develop an hypothesis on the mode of interaction between the self-conscious mind and the brain that is much stronger and more definitive than any hypothesis that has hitherto been formulated in relation to what we may term the dualistic postulates. In formulating a strong dualistic hypothesis we build upon the following evidence.

1. There is a *unitary character* about the experiences of the self-conscious mind. There is concentration now on this, now on that, aspect of the cerebral performance at any one instant. This focussing is the phenomenon known as *attention*.
2. We can assume that the experiences of the self-conscious mind have a relationship with neural events in the liaison-brain, there being *a relationship of interaction giving a degree of correspondence, but not an identity*.
3. *There can be a temporal discrepancy between neural events and the experiences of the self-conscious mind*. This is shown particularly clearly with the experiments of Libet, as described above, for example the phenomena of backward masking and of antedating. It also occurs in the slowing down of experienced time in acute emergencies.
4. *There is the continual experience that the self-conscious mind can effectively act on the brain events*. This is most overtly seen in voluntary action but throughout our waking life we are deliberately evoking brain events when we try to recall a memory or to recapture a word or phrase or to express a thought or to establish a new memory.

   A brief initial outline of the hypothesis may be stated as follows. The self-conscious mind is actively engaged in reading out from the multitude of active centers at the highest level of brain activity, namely the liaison areas of the dominant cerebral hemisphere. The self-conscious mind selects from these centers according to attention, and from moment to moment integrates its selection to give unity even to the most transient experiences. Furthermore the self-conscious mind acts upon these neural centers modifying the dynamic spatiotemporal patterns of the neural events. Thus we propose that the self-conscious mind exercises a superior interpretative and controlling role upon the neural events.

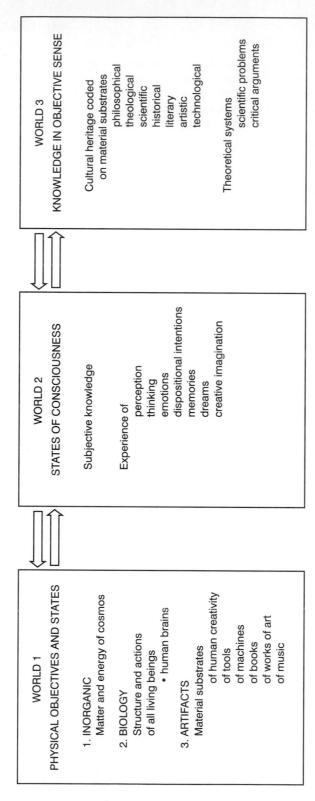

Figure 2.2 *Tabular representation of the three worlds that comprise all existents and all experience as defined by Popper.*

Source: John Eccles and Karl Popper. *The Self and Its Brain.* (London: Springer-Verlag, 1976).

5. *A key component of the hypothesis is that the unity of conscious experience is provided by the self-conscious mind and not by the neural machinery of the liaison areas of the cerebral hemisphere.* Hitherto it has been impossible to develop any neurophysiological theory that explains how a diversity of brain events comes to be synthesized so that there is a unified conscious experience of a global or gestalt character. The brain events remain disparate, being essentially the individual actions of countless neurones that are built into complex circuits and so participate in the spatiotemporal patterns of activity. This is the case even for the most specialized neurones so far detected, the feature detection neurones of the inferotemporal lobe of primates. Our present hypothesis regards the neuronal machinery as a multiplex of radiating and receiving structures: *the experienced unity comes, not from a neurophysiological synthesis, but from the proposed integrating character of the self-conscious mind.* We conjecture that in the first place the self-conscious mind is developed in order to give this unity of the self in all of its conscious experiences and actions. . . .

The self-conscious mind is scanning the modular activities in the liaison areas of the cerebral cortex, as may be appreciated from the very inadequate diagram in Figure 2.3. From moment to moment it is selecting modules according to its interest, the phenomenon of attention, and is itself integrating from all this diversity to give the unified conscious experience. Available for this read-out, if we may call it so, is the whole range of performance of those areas of the dominant hemisphere which have linguistic and ideational performance. Collectively we will call them *liaison areas.*

. . . The self-conscious mind plays through the whole liaison brain in a selective and unifying manner. An analogy is provided by a searchlight in the manner that has

Figure 2.3. *Information flow diagram for brain-mind interaction. The three components of World 2: outer sense, inner sense and the ego or self are diagrammed with their connectivities. Also shown are the lines of communication across the interface between World 1 and World 2, that is from the liaison brain to and from these World 2 components. The liaison brain has the columnar arrangement indicated. It must be imagined that the area of the liaison brain is enormous, with open modules numbering a hundred thousand or more, not just the two score here depicted.*

Source: John Eccles and Karl Popper. *The Self and Its Brain* (London: Springer-Verlag, 1976).

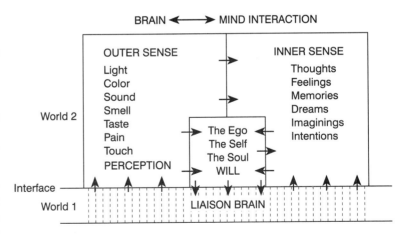

been suggested by Jung [1954] and by Popper [1945]. Perhaps a better analogy would be some multiple scanning and probing device that reads out from and selects from the immense and diverse patterns of activity in the cerebral cortex and integrates these selected components, so organizing them into the unity of conscious experience. . . .

The essential feature of the hypothesis is the active role of the self-conscious mind in its influence on the neural machinery of the liaison brain.

Eccles has clearly done a fine job of redescribing the Cartesian sort of mind in contemporary neurophysiological terminology. But has he really explained the mechanism of interaction? Or has he merely *reasserted* that there is an experienced distinction between the mental and the physical and that there is, at the same time, an experienced relation between the mental and the physical?

NOTE ON SOURCES.   The material in this section is from John Eccles and Karl Popper, *The Self and Its Brain* (London: Springer-Verlag, 1976), pp. 358–365.

Am I Free or Determined?

THE QUESTION POSED

In our quest for self-understanding we have been examining the widespread claim that the human is a part of nature. That claim, which is rather ancient, has received substantial support from the emergence of modern science. Those who make the claim usually intend thereby to deny at least four things about the human being. They intend to say that humans do not have immaterial minds, that humans are not free, that humans do not survive the death of their bodies, and that humans are not creatures of God. We explored the first of those denials in the previous chapter. In the present chapter we will consider the second denial as we examine the question, "Am I free or determined?"

Suppose you have an examination tomorrow and a friend asks you to forgo studying and spend the evening at a party. Your friend does not urge or threaten or coerce you. You consider the alternatives, and after a moment's thought, decide to give up studying for that night, and go to the party. We would ordinarily say that you are responsible for your decision. We think of such cases as actions in which you are free to decide one way or the other. Contrast this to a situation in which a headache leads you to lie down and fall asleep on your bed instead of continuing to study. In this case it would not make sense to say that you are free to decide one way or the other about studying. The dispute between advocates of free will and advocates of determinism is basically a dispute whether incidents like the two so cited, which feel so different, are really radically and essentially different when viewed objectively.

Whereas the advocate of free will would perceive these two sorts of acts as essentially different, the determinist would not. The determinist might argue that although it is quite reasonable for you to believe that your decision to stay home to study for the exam was an expression of free choice, nevertheless closer scrutiny would reveal that your behavior was not really free after all. What you thought was a free choice was really a choice dictated by your desires, which in turn spring from your character, which in its turn is fashioned by the forces of heredity and environment, which are clearly beyond your control. The central affirmation of determinism is that every event has a cause. By an analysis of the causes of any one of your actions, the determinist would cause your so-called freedom to vanish in a chain of causes that stretches back into the remote recesses of your heredity and environment. Nature and nurture, genes and society—those are the facts that made you what you are and cause you to act the way you do. The notion that you are free is really a misapprehension, an illusion.

The battle between libertarians (advocates of free will) and determinists has been joined for centuries. The first of the combatants we have selected for study is the eighteenth-century advocate of determinism, Baron d'Holbach. In a clear and uncompromising fashion he presents the position of determinism. To cross swords with him we have called up Jean-Paul Sartre who depicts the human being as a freedom (*pour soi*) in the midst of a world of determined things (*en soi*). To treat the *pour soi* as an *en soi* as the determinist does, says Sartre, is to destroy the distinctively human. Walter Stace, our third writer, tries to mediate the conflict by blending determinism and freedom in a coherent way. William James argues that the determinist is face to face with a very unpleasant alternative: the determinist must adopt either subjectivism or pessimism—neither of which, we will see, is very attractive. Karl Popper uses science to undercut determinists who claim that science shows that free will is a mere hope, with no basis in fact. Finally, a contemporary look at compatibilism from John Bender has us going through a thought experiment meant to support the compatibilist position that freedom and determinism can coexist.

In due course, when the dust has settled from the conflict of these great warriors, you will have to formulate your own response to the question, "Am I free or determined?" Your response can never be trivial because in it the meaningfulness and seriousness of much of civilization is at stake for you.

1 BARON D'HOLBACH

I AM DETERMINED

You will recall that Descartes, the so-called father of modern philosophy, exploited the method of doubt in order to defeat doubt. The seventeenth century in which Descartes lived was a time when traditional ideas and institutions were challenged. The intellectual fires of the Renaissance and the Reformation had not died out. The skeptic Michel De Montaigne (1533–1592) had cast a cloud of doubt over the reliability of all human knowledge, and Descartes tried to dissipate that cloud. Descartes probably thought he was in step with the new science in that he had discovered by careful scrutiny an indubitable truth rooted in the concrete, empirical data of the thinking self, and in that he had used geometrical-style reasoning to construct his system of truth about reality. Yet, the harmony that Descartes and his followers (the Cartesians) thought they had with the new science was only partial. They seem to have missed the point that the mathematical reasoning of the new science was used to predict the behavior of phenomena, and was accordingly subjected to verification or falsification on the basis of observed data. Without prediction and testing, mathematical reasoning can generate systems of gratuitous fictions. That is precisely the charge that the eighteenth-century French intellectuals of the Enlightenment leveled at the Cartesians. These intellectuals had learned about the new science through the writings of John Locke (1632–1714) and Isaac Newton (1642–1727), for whom empirical data, prediction, and testing were essential. So impressed with the empirical bent of the new science were these French thinkers that they abandoned the dualistic perspective of Cartesian thought and went over to a purely materialistic world view. Perhaps the most radical of this group of French intellectuals was Baron d'Holbach, who affirmed that one's fate is fixed by external causes.

BIOGRAPHICAL NOTE.   Holbach was born in 1723 and died in 1789, aged sixty-six. His name was originally Paul Heinrich Dietrich. He was born in Germany, educated in the natural sciences at the University of Leiden, and came to Paris in 1749. He became a French subject and in 1753 inherited from his uncle the title of Baron d'Holbach and properties that made him financially independent for the rest of his life. He established a circle that included such Frenchmen as Diderot, Helvetius, D'Alembert, Rousseau, Condillac, Turgot, and Condorcet, and such foreigners as Hume, Gibbon, Adam Smith, Priestly, Walpole, Garrick, Sterne, Beccaria, and Franklin. He contributed some four hundred articles to Diderot's *Encyclopedia*. He propagandized and translated on behalf of materialism, atheism, revolution, and republicanism. Perhaps his best-known book, *Le Système de la Nature (The System of Nature)*, appeared in 1770 under the pseudonym of a certain Mirabaud who had been dead for ten years. The book bore the imprint of London as its place of publication, when in truth it had been published in Amsterdam. These fictitious devices were used, no doubt, to protect the author and publisher from reprisals that could result from the radical content of the book. Contrary to the prevailing opinions of the day, d'Holbach claimed that the human is a part of nature, and because there is no free will anywhere in the behavior of matter, there is none in nature and none in humans.

THE ARGUMENT OF THE PASSAGES.   Holbach's claim, called *determinism* or *necessitarianism*, is an answer to this question: "Is anyone ever responsible for *any* of his behavior? He being who *he* is, the circumstances being what *they* are, can he ever do anything other than he does do?" Holbach's answer is a categorical, unqualified no. Your thoughts and actions are the effects of causes over which you have no control. If you think you could have done otherwise, you are mistaken.

The following paragraphs are quoted from Holbach's historically important book *The System of Nature*. Nature, the title says, is a vast interlocked system in which every event is caused, necessitated, determined by all the other events that make up the total system. Many would grant this claim without argument when it is made of physical nature, nature taken as the subject matter of physics; but some demur when this claim is extended to include human nature and human behavior. They hold out for the possibility that some human behavior expresses a will that acts autonomously, is constrained neither by nature nor by events in nature. Holbach wrote these passages to deny any such claim.

Let us begin with several paragraphs in which Holbach reiterates his central claim. Note how the images he selects to depict the human being—"line," "bowl," "machine," "chains"—reinforce his claim that "No human behavior expresses free will." For emphasis, in these paragraphs we have printed the various wordings of that claim in italics.

> *In whatever manner man is considered, he is connected to universal nature, and submitted to the necessary and immutable laws that she imposes on all the beings she contains,* according to their peculiar essences or to the respective properties with which, without consulting them, she endows each particular species. Man's life is a line that nature commands him to describe upon the surface of the earth, without his ever being able to swerve from it, even for an instant. He is born without his own consent; his organization does in nowise depend upon himself; his ideas come to him involuntarily; his habits are in the power of those who cause him to contract them; he is unceasingly modified by causes, whether visible or concealed, over which he has no control, which necessarily regulate his mode of existence, give the hue to his way of thinking, and determine his manner of acting. He is good or bad, happy or miserable, wise or foolish, reasonable or irrational, without his will being for anything in these various states. . . .
>
> The will, as we have elsewhere said, is a modification of the brain, by which it is disposed to action, or prepared to give play to the organs. This will is necessarily determined by the qualities, good or bad, agreeable or painful, of the object or the motive that acts upon his senses, or of which the idea remains with him, and is resuscitated by his memory. In consequence, he acts necessarily, his action is the result of the impulse he receives either from the motive, from the object, or from the idea which has modified his brain, or disposed his will. When he does not act according to this impulse, it is because there comes some new cause, some new motive, some new idea, which modifies his brain in a different manner, gives him a new impulse, determines his will in another way, by which the action of the former impulse is suspended; thus, the sight of an agreeable object, or its idea, determines his will to set him in action to procure it; but if a new object or a new idea more powerfully attracts him, it gives a new direction to his will, annihilates the effect of the former, and prevents the action by which it was to be procured. This is the mode in which reflection, experience, reason, necessarily arrests or suspends the action of man's will; without this he would of necessity have followed the anterior impulse which carried him towards a then-desirable object. In all this *he always acts according to necessary laws from which he has no means of emancipating himself. . . .*
>
> This will, or rather the brain, finds itself in the same situation as a bowl, which, although it has received an impulse that drives it forward in a straight line, is deranged in its course whenever a force superior to the first obliges it to change its direction. The man who drinks the poisoned water appears a madman; but the actions of fools are as necessary as those of the most prudent individuals. The motives

that determine the voluptuary and the debauchee to risk their health, are as powerful, and their actions are as necessary, as those which decide the wise man to manage
his. But, it will be insisted, the debauchee may be prevailed on to change his conduct;
this does not imply that he is a free agent; but that motives may be found sufficiently
powerful to annihilate the effect of those that previously acted upon him; *then these
new motives determine his will to the new mode of conduct he may adopt as necessarily as the
former did to the old mode.* . . .

    Man, then, is not a free agent in any one instant of his life; he is necessarily guided in
each step by those advantages, whether real or fictitious, that he attaches to the
objects by which his passions are roused; these passions themselves are necessary in a
being who unceasingly tends toward his own happiness; their energy is necessary,
since that depends on his temperament; his temperament is necessary, because it
depends on the physical elements which enter into composition; the modification of
his temperament is necessary, as it is the infallible and inevitable consequence of the
impulse he receives from the incessant action of moral and physical beings. . . .

    *There is, in point of fact, no difference between the man that is cast out of the window by
another, and the man who throws himself out of it*, except that the impulse in the first
instance comes immediately from without whilst that which determines the fall in the
second case, springs from within his own peculiar machine, having its more remote
cause also exterior. . . .

    He may be compared to a heavy body that finds itself arrested in its descent by
an obstacle whatever; take away this obstacle, it will gravitate or continue to fall; but
who shall say this dense body is free to fall or not? Is not its descent the necessary
effect of its own specific gravity? The virtuous Socrates submitted to the laws of his
country, although they were unjust; and though the doors of his jail were left open to
him, he would not save himself; but *in this he did not act as a free agent*; the *invisible
chains* of opinion, the secret love of decorum, the inward respect for the laws, even
when they were iniquitous, the fear of tarnishing his glory, *kept him in his prison*; they
were motives sufficiently powerful with this enthusiast for virtue, to induce him to
wait death with tranquility.

Holbach is firmly convinced that human behavior is never expressive of free
will because there is no free will. The human, he might syllogize, is a part of
nature; there is no free will in nature; there is, therefore, no free will in the
human. Not everyone, however, is so convinced as Holbach. Some people believe
they are free; they have the "feeling," the "experience" of acting freely. But such
"experience," says Holbach, is illusory, based upon *ignorance* of the many and
complex causes operating in human life.

    Man believes he acts as a free agent, every time he does not see any thing that
places obstacles to his actions; he does not perceive that the motive which causes him
to will, is always necessary and independent of himself.

    From whence it may be seen, that the same necessity which regulates the physi-
cal, also regulates the moral world, in which every thing is in consequence submitted
to fatality. Man, in running over, frequently without his own knowledge, often in
spite of himself, the route which nature has marked out for him, resembles a swimmer who is obliged to follow the current that carries him along; he believes himself a
free agent, because he sometimes consents, sometimes does not consent, to glide
with the stream, which, not withstanding, always hurries him forward; he believes

himself the master of his condition, because he is obliged to use his arms under the fear of sinking.

It is, then, for want of recurring to the causes that move him; for want of being able to analyze, from not being competent to decompose the complicated motion of his machine, that man believes himself a free agent; it is only upon his own ignorance that he founds the profound yet deceitful notion he has of his free agency; that he builds those opinions which he brings forward as a striking proof of his pretended freedom of action. If, for a short time, each man was willing to examine his own peculiar actions, search out their true motives to discover their concatenation, he would remain convinced that the sentiment he has of his natural free agency, is a chimera that must speedily be destroyed by experience.

It is the great complication of motion in man, it is the variety of his action, it is the multiplicity of causes the move him, whether simultaneously or in continual succession, that persuades him he is a free agent; if all his motions were simple, if the causes that move him did not confound themselves with each other, if they were distinct, if his machine were less complicated, he would perceive that all his actions were necessary, because he would be enabled to recur instantly to the cause that made him act.

The errors of philosophers on the free agency of man, have arisen from their regarding his will as the *primum mobile*, the original motive of his actions; for want of recurring back, they have not perceived the multiplied, the complicated causes which, independently of him, give motion to the will itself; or which dispose and modify his brain, whilst he himself is purely passive in the motion he receives. . . .

To be undeceived on the system of his free agency, man has simply to recur to the motive by which his will is determined; he will always find this motive is out of his own control. It is said: that in consequence of an idea to which the mind gives birth, man acts freely if he encounters no obstacle. But the question is, what gives birth to this idea in his brain? Was he the master either to prevent it from presenting itself, or from renewing itself in his brain? Does not this idea depend either upon objects that strike him exteriorly and in despite of himself, or upon causes, that without his knowledge, act within himself and modify his brain?

Nevertheless it must be acknowledged that the multiplicity and diversity of the causes which continually act upon man, frequently without even his knowledge, render it impossible, or at least extremely difficult for him to recur to the true principles of his own peculiar actions, much less the action of others; they frequently depend upon causes so fugitive, so remote from their effects, and which, superficially examined, appear to have so little analogy, so slender a relation with them, that it requires singular sagacity to bring them into light.

Other people insist that humans are free in order to preserve the meaningfulness of praising or blaming various people for their actions. If people are not free agents how can they possibly merit reward or deserve punishment from either God or society for their actions? Holbach dismisses this argument for freedom as a piece of rationalizing rooted in human vanity that tries to present the human as in some sense "special" when compared with other physical beings in nature.

Nevertheless, in spite of the shackles by which he is bound, it is pretended he is a free agent, or that independent of the causes by which he is moved, he determines his own will, and regulates his own condition.

However slender the foundation of this opinion, of which everything ought to point out to him the error, it is current at this day and passes for an incontestable truth with a great number of people, otherwise extremely enlightened; it is the basis of religion, which, supposing relations between man and the unknown being she has placed above nature, has been incapable of imagining how man could merit reward or deserve punishment from this being, if he was not a free agent. Society has been believed interested in this system; because an idea has gone abroad, that if all actions of man were to be contemplated as necessary, the right of punishing those who injure their associates would no longer exist. At length human vanity accommodated itself to a hypothesis which, unquestionably, appears to distinguish man from all other physical beings, by assigning him the special privilege of a total independence of all other causes, but of which a very little reflection would have shown him the impossibility.

By way of concluding these selections from Holbach's *System of Nature*, let us examine half a dozen paragraphs in which he moves from abstract formulation of his determinism to some concrete applications of it. The passage is clear-cut and vivid. He imagines himself summoning an ambitious man, a miserly man, a voluptuary man, a choleric or bad-tempered man, and a zealous man, and letting each in turn testify to the truth of Holbach's claim:

The *ambitious man* cries out: you will have me resist my passion; but have they not unceasingly repeated to me that rank, honors, power, are the most desirable advantages in life? Have I not seen my fellow citizens envy them, the nobles of my country sacrifice every thing to obtain them? In the society in which I live, am I not obliged to feel, that if I am deprived of these advantages, I must expect to languish in contempt, to cringe under the rod of oppression?

The *miser* says: you forbid me to love money, to seek after the means of acquiring it: alas! does not every thing tell me that, in this world, money is the greatest blessing; that it is amply sufficient to render me happy? In the country I inhabit, do I not see all my fellow citizens covetous of riches? but do I not also witness that they are little scrupulous in the means of obtaining wealth? As soon as they are enriched by the means which you censure, are they not cherished, considered and respected? By what authority, then, do you defend me from amassing treasure? What right have you to prevent my using means, which, although you all them sordid and criminal, I see approved by the sovereign? Will you have me renounce my happiness?

The *voluptuary* argues: you pretend that I should resist my desires; but was I the maker of my own temperament, which unceasingly invites me to pleasure? You call my pleasures disgraceful; but in the country in which I live, do I not witness the most dissipated men enjoying the most distinguished rank? Do I not behold that no one is ashamed of adultery but the husband it has outraged? Do not I see men making trophies of their debaucheries, boasting of their libertinism, rewarded with applause?

The *choleric man* vociferates: you advise me to put a curb on my passions, and to resist the desire of avenging myself; but can I conquer my nature? Can I alter the received opinions of the world? Shall I not be forever disgraced, infallibly dishonored in society, if I do not wash out in the blood of my fellow creatures the injuries I have received?

The *zealous enthusiast* exclaims: you recommend me mildness; you advise me to be tolerant; to be indulgent to the opinions of my fellow men; but is not my temperament violent? Do I not ardently love my God? Do they not assure me, that zeal is pleasing to him; that sanguinary inhuman persecutors have been his friends? As I wish to render myself acceptable in his sight, I therefore adopt the same means.

In short, the actions of man are never free; they are always the necessary consequence of his temperament, of the received ideas, and of the notions, either true or false, which he has formed to himself of happiness; of his opinions strengthened by example, by education, and by daily experience.

If he understood the play of his organs, if he were able to recall to himself all the impulsions they have received, all the modifications they have undergone, all the effects they have produced, he would perceive that all his actions are submitted to that fatality, which regulates his own particular system, as it does the entire system of the universe; no one effect in him, any more than in nature, produces itself by chance; this, as has been before proved, is word void of sense. All that passes in him; all that is done by him; as well as all that happens in nature, or that is attributed to her, is derived from necessary causes, which act according to necessary laws, and which produce necessary effects from whence necessarily flow others.

Fatality, is the eternal, the immutable, the necessary order, established in nature; or the indispensable connexion of causes that act, with the effects they operate.

HISTORICAL POSTSCRIPT TO HOLBACH.   Holbach's *System of Nature* was published in 1770. H. T. Buckle, "who," says Sir Isaiah Berlin, "believed in the science of history more passionately, perhaps, than any man who ever lived," published his *History of Civilization in England* in the years 1857–1861. Buckle offered the *History* as an embodiment of what he understood by history as a science. The natural sciences had nature as their subject matter. Buckle wanted the historians to look upon human history as the subject matter of historical science. In the course of expounding this conception he said:

> The believer in the possibility of a science of history is not called upon to hold either the doctrine of predestined events, or that of freedom of the will; and the only positions which, in this stage of inquiry, I shall expect him to concede are the following: That when we perform an action, we perform it in consequence of some motive or motives; that those motives are the results of some antecedents; and that, therefore, if we are acquainted with the whole of the antecedents, and with all the laws of their movements, we could with unerring certainty predict the whole of their immediate results. This, unless I am greatly mistaken, is the view which must be held by every man whose mind is unbiased by system, and who forms his opinions according to the evidence actually before him. If, for example, I am intimately acquainted with the character of any person, I can frequently tell how he will act under some given circumstances. Should I fail in this prediction, I must ascribe my error not to the arbitrary and capricious freedom of his will, nor to any supernatural prearrangement, for of neither of these things have we the slightest proof; but I must be content to suppose either that I had been misinformed as to some of the circumstances in which he was placed, or else that I had not sufficiently studied the ordinary operations of his mind. If, however, I were capable of correct reasoning, and if, at the same time, I had a complete knowledge both of his disposition and of all the events by which he was surrounded, I should be able to foresee the line of conduct which, in consequence of those events, he would adopt.

A century after Buckle, B. F. Skinner published his *Beyond Freedom and Dignity* in 1971. He calls upon humankind to discard the notion of an "autonomous inner man" or "soul," which is the source of our allegedly free acts. If the science of human behavior, says Skinner, is to make any significant progress, it must adopt the deterministic model and probe the causes of human behavior in the environment and genetic endowment of persons. In abandoning the "autonomous inner man," Skinner removes the legitimacy for praising and blaming people for their actions. After all, how can you justifiably praise or blame someone for doing something that hereditary and environmental factors forced him or her to do? Responsibility is transferred from "autonomous inner man" to heredity and environment, and the human is seen as the manipulated pawn of forces beyond his or her control. Skinner writes:

> In the traditional view, a person is free. He is autonomous in the sense that his behavior is uncaused. He can therefore be held responsible for what he does and justly punished if he offends. That view, together with its associated practices, must be reexamined when a scientific analysis reveals unsuspected controlling relations between behavior and environment . . . Personal exemption from a complete determinism is revoked as a scientific analysis progresses, particularly in accounting for the behavior of the individual.

Like Holbach and Buckle, Skinner negates freedom and affirms determinism. Unabashedly Skinner draws out the implications of his doctrine by inviting us to construe ourselves as complex things that are in fact "beyond freedom and dignity." Jean-Paul Sartre, our next author, refuses to surrender human freedom and dignity.

NOTE ON SOURCES.   The material in this section is quoted from Baron d'Holbach, *The System of Nature*, translated by H. D. Robinson (Boston: J. P. Mendum, 1899), Chapter 11; H. T. Buckle, *History of Civilization in England* (London: Watts, 1930); and B. F. Skinner, *Beyond Freedom and Dignity* (New York: Knopf, 1971).

2   JEAN-PAUL SARTRE

I AM FREE

FROM HOLBACH TO SARTRE.   As determinism marched from the eighteenth century of Holbach through the nineteenth century of Buckle to the twentieth century of Sartre, it assaulted the freedom and dignity that humans had ascribed to themselves for centuries. That assault received monumental support from the brilliant achievements of the physical sciences which operated with a deterministic model of the universe. The impressive work of Darwin and advances in the biological sciences made the assault seem invincible. Must we not view the human as an organism devoid of freedom and driven by forces beyond its control? Voices of protest against this assault were raised in the nineteenth century by several intellectual giants. The Danish philosopher, Sören Kierkegaard (1813–1855), for example, ridiculed philosophers like Hegel (1770–1831) who generated grandiose systems to answer all questions—except one: What does it mean to be an existing individual person? The Russian writer, Fyodor Dostoevsky (1821–1881), poured out his anxieties in mighty novels like *Brothers Karamazov* and *Crime and Punishment* as he declared his belief in human freedom and dignity. The German philosopher and cultural historian, Friedrich Nietzsche (1844–1900), celebrated the freedom of the self-surmounting person who rose above the mediocrity and conformity of the masses in order to create meaning and values to live dangerously and joyfully. The Germany social analyst, Karl Marx (1818–1883), protested vigorously against the reification or "thingification" of persons in bourgeois capitalist society—a society which was stifling the free, conscious activity that distinguishes the human being from the rest of nature.

In the twentieth century the voices of protest have grown in numbers and eloquence. Atheistic philosophers like Martin Heidegger, Christian philosophers like Nicholas Berdyaev, Protestant theologians like Paul Tillich, Roman Catholic thinkers like Gabriel Marcel, Jewish philosophers like Martin Buber—despite their differences—have joined their voices in an affirmation of human freedom and dignity. Perhaps the most intense and famous of these twentieth-century voices of protest is Jean-Paul Sartre, the founder of French existentialism. His published lecture *Existentialism is a Humanism*, from which the material of this section is taken, is an excellent introduction to his protest.

There is much in Sartre that is reminiscent of Descartes; e.g., Sartre's distinction between a *pour soi* and an *en soi* is some sort of descendant of Descartes' distinction between a *res cogitans* and a *res extensa*. Descartes' efforts to track down a not-doubtable as a starting point is detectable in the following passage paraphrased from Sartre's lecture:

> Our point of departure is the subjectivity of the individual (the individual regarded as a *subject* who thinks, not as an *object* thought about). It is because we seek to base our teaching upon the truth. Any doctrine of probabilities which is not attached to a truth will crumble. To define the probable one must possess the true. And there is such a truth. At the point of departure there cannot be any other truth than this: "I think, therefore I am." This theory does not begin by taking man as an object but as a subject. All kinds of materialism treat man as an object, a set of predetermined reactions, no different in this respect from a table or a chair or a stone.

Sartre's insistence on starting with the human as subject, as one who knows and wills and judges, not as some external object that is known and willed and judged, is fundamental to his existentialism. A subject, in contrast to an object, is come at through the activities that it performs, and in performing which it is conscious, aware, of itself as free. Unlike Holbach, Sartre sees no reason to write off this consciousness, this awareness, this experience of freedom as illusory. If freedom is an ineluctable fact about man apprehended as *subject*—as knower, willer, and judger—and if, as Sartre says, "man is condemned to be free," then man makes himself to be whatever he essentially becomes. He does this as he goes along, in the exercise of his freedom. He is the author of his own essential nature. In his case, then, his existence *precedes* his "essence." Whatever he now essentially is, he has made himself to be, and he *existed* before and while he was doing so. This is a step beyond Descartes.

BIOGRAPHICAL NOTE.   Jean-Paul Sartre was born in Paris in 1905. His academic training in philosophy was received in colleges and universities in France and Germany. He taught philosophy in French colleges before and for a few years after World War II. His war experiences included service in the French army, prisoner of war in Germany, and work with the French Resistance movement. He wrote many philosophical monographs, novels, plays, and literary essays. He was a founder and editor of the journal *Modern Times*. He refused the Nobel Prize for literature in 1964 because he believed that the award had become politicized and did not want to become a tool in the cultural struggle between East and West. Of his many publications, we should note *Nausea* (1938), an existentialist novel; *Being and Nothingness* (1943), the major philosophical statement of his existentialism; *No Exit* (1944), his most famous play; and *Existentialism Is a Humanism* (1946), a philosophical conference paper. Sartre died in 1980, unable to complete the huge biography of Gustave Flaubert he had been working on for about two decades.

THE ARGUMENT OF THE PASSAGES.   The passages in this section have been taken from Sartre's lecture *Existentialism Is a Humanism*. The design of his lecture is clear and straightforward: he announced his intention to defend his position against some typical reproaches; formulates his position as clearly as possible; and proceeds to fend off specific attacks on existentialism.

Sartre begins, then, with a brief review of some of the typical reproaches leveled at existentialism: it leads to the quietism of despair; it emphasizes all that is shameful in the human situation; it ignores the solidarity of humankind; and it denies the seriousness of human affairs.

My purpose here is to offer a defence of existentialism against several reproaches that have been laid against it.

First, it has been reproached as an invitation to people to dwell in quietism of despair. For if every way to a solution is barred, one would have to regard any action in this world entirely ineffective, and one would arrive finally at a contemplative philosophy. Moreover, since contemplation is a luxury, this would be only another bourgeois philosophy. This is, especially, the reproach made by the Communists.

From another quarter we are reproached for having underlined all that is ignominious in the human situation, for depicting what is mean, sordid, or base to the neglect of certain things that possess charm and beauty and belong to the brighter side of human nature: for example, according to the Catholic critic, Mlle. Mercier, we forget how an infant smiles. Both from this side and from the other we are also reproached for leaving out of account the solidarity of mankind and considering man in isolation. And this, say the Communists, is because we base our doctrine upon pure subjectivity—upon the Cartesian "I think": which is the moment in which solitary man attains to himself; a position from which it is impossible to regain solidarity with other men who exist outside of the self. The *ego* cannot reach them through the *cogito*.

From the Christian side, we are reproached as people who deny the reality and seriousness of human affairs. For since we ignore the commandments of God and all values prescribed as eternal, nothing remains but what is strictly voluntary. Everyone can do what he likes, and will be incapable, from such a point of view, of condemning either the point of view or the action of anyone else.

It is to these various reproaches that I shall endeavor to reply today; that is why I have entitled this brief exposition "Existentialism Is a Humanism." Many may be surprised at the mention of humanism in this connection, but we shall try to see in what sense we understand it. In any case, we can begin by saying that existentialism, in our sense of the word, is a doctrine that does render human life possible; a doctrine, also, which affirms that every truth and every action imply both an environment and a human subjectivity. The essential charge laid against us is, of course, that of overemphasis upon the evil side of human life. I have lately been told of a lady who, whenever she lets slip a vulgar expression in a moment of nervousness, excuses herself by exclaiming "I believe I am becoming an existentialist." So it appears that ugliness is being identified with existentialism. That is why some people say we are "naturalistic," and if we are, it is strange to see how much we scandalize and horrify them, for no one seems to be much frightened or humiliated nowadays by what is properly called naturalism. Those who can quite well keep down a novel by Zola such as *La Terre* are sickened as soon as they read an existentialist novel. Those who appeal to the wisdom of the people—which is a sad wisdom—find ours sadder still. And yet, what could be more disillusioned than such sayings as "Charity begins at home" or "Promote a rogue and he'll sue you for damage, knock him down and he'll do you homage"? We all know how many common sayings can be quoted to this effect, and they all mean much the same—that you must not oppose the powers-that-be; that you must not fight against superior force, must not meddle in matters that are above your station. Or that any action not in accordance with some tradition is mere romanticism; or that any undertaking which has not the support of proven experience is foredoomed to frustration; and that since experience has shown men to be invariably inclined to evil, there must be firm rules to restrain them, otherwise we shall have anarchy. It is, however, the people who are forever mouthing these dismal proverbs and, whenever they are told of some more or less repulsive action, say "How like human nature!"—it is these very people, always harping upon realism, who complain that existentialism is too gloomy a view of things. Indeed their excessive protests make me suspect that what is annoying them is not so much our pessimism, but, much more likely, our optimism. For at bottom, what is alarming in the doctrine that I am about to try to explain to you is—is it not?—that it confronts man with a possibility of choice. To verify this, let us review the whole question upon the strictly philosophical level. What, then, is this that we call existentialism?

Because many of these reproaches arise from a misunderstanding of what existentialism really is, Sartre proceeds to provide for his audience an authentic picture of existentialism. He acknowledges that his task is complicated at the outset by a division within the ranks of existentialists: some existentialists believe in God and some do not. Furthermore, the atheistic existentialists insist that existentialism's central claim is incompatible with all or most traditional forms of theism. Allowing for this source of ambiguity, Sartre identifies a central claim common to all existentialists: *"existence precedes essence."* With this slogan existentialists intend to affirm human freedom in a radical way. They claim that the human being first of all exists and that through subsequent thinking, willing, choosing, and acting, the human defines himself or herself. Each human creates his or her own essence, his or her own self. Accordingly, the human is *responsible* for what he or she becomes. Furthermore, in choosing to be a certain kind of self, the human is really making a statement of what a self in that situation should be like. Therefore, the human is choosing not simply for himself or herself, but for all humankind. As Sartre observes, "In fashioning myself I fashion man." Consequently, one is responsible not simply for oneself but for all humankind. We can understand now why Sartre titles his lecture "Existentialism Is a Humanism."

> . . . there are two kinds of existentialists. There are, on the one hand, the Christians, amongst whom I shall name Jaspers and Gabriel Marcel, both professed Catholics; and on the other the existential atheists, amongst whom we must place Heidegger as well as the French existentialists and myself. What they have in common is simply the fact that they believe that *existence* comes before *essence*—or, if you will, that we must begin from the subjective. What exactly do we mean by that?
>
> If one considers an article of manufacture—as for example, a book or a paper-knife—one sees that it has been made by an artisan who had a conception of it; and he has paid attention, equally, to the conception of a paper-knife and to the pre-existent technique of production which is a part of that conception and is, at bottom, a formula. Thus the paper-knife is at the same time an article producible in a certain manner and one which, on the other hand, serves a definite purpose, for one cannot suppose that a man would produce a paper-knife without knowing what it was for. Let us say, then, of the paper-knife that its essence—that it to say the sum of the formulae and the qualities which made its production and its definition possible—precedes its existence. The presence of such-and-such a paper-knife or book is thus determined before my eyes. Here, then, we are viewing the world from a technical standpoint, and we can say that production precedes existence.
>
> When we think of God as the creator, we are thinking of him, most of the time, as a supernal artisan. Whatever doctrine we may be considering, whether it be a doctrine like that of Descartes, or of Leibniz himself, we always imply that the will follows, more or less, from the understanding or at least accompanies it, so that when God creates he knows precisely what he is creating. Thus, the conception of man in the mind of God is comparable to that of the paper-knife in the mind of the artisan: God makes man according to a procedure and a conception, exactly as the artisan manufactures a paper-knife, following a definition and a formula. Thus each individual man is the realization of a certain conception which dwells in the divine understanding. In the philosophic atheism of the eighteenth century, the notion of God is suppressed, but not, for all that, the idea that essence is prior to existence; something of that idea we still find everywhere, in Diderot, in Voltaire and even in Kant. Man possesses a human nature; that "human nature," which is the conception of human being, is found in every man; which means that each man is a particular example of a universal conception, the conception of man. In Kant, this universality goes so far that the wild man of the woods, man in the state of nature and the bourgeois are all contained in the same definition and have the same fundamental qualities. Here again, the essence of man precedes that historic existence which we confront in experience.
>
> Atheistic existentialism, of which I am a representative, declares with greater consistency that if God does not exist there is at least one being whose existence comes before its essence, a being which exists before it can be defined by any conception of it. That being is man or, as Heidegger has it, the human reality. What do we mean by saying that existence precedes essence? We mean that man first of all exists, encounters himself, surges up in the world—and defines himself afterwards. If man

as the existentialist sees him is not definable, it is because to begin with he is nothing. He will not be anything until later, and then he will be what he makes of himself. Thus, there is no human nature, because there is no God to have a conception of it. Man simply is. Not that he is simply what he conceives himself to be, but he is what he wills, and as he conceives himself after already existing—as he wills to be after that leap toward existence. Man is nothing else but that which he makes of himself. That is the first principle of existentialism. And this is what people call its "subjectivity," using the word as a reproach against us. But what do we mean to say by this, but that man is of a greater dignity than a stone or a table? For we mean to say that man primarily exists—that man is, before all else, something which propels itself towards a future and is aware that it is doing so. Man is, indeed, a project which possesses a subjective life, instead of being a kind of moss, or a fungus or a cauliflower. Before that projection of the self nothing exists; not even in the heaven of intelligence; man will only attain existence when he is what he purposes to be. Not, however, what he may wish to be. For what we usually understand by wishing or willing is a conscious decision taken—much more often than not—after we have made ourselves what we are. I may wish to join a party, to write a book or to marry—but in such a case what is usually called my will is probably a manifestation of a prior and more spontaneous decision. If, however, it is true that existence is prior to essence, man is responsible for what he is. Thus, the first effect of existentialism is that it puts every man in possession of himself as he is, and places the entire responsibility for his existence squarely upon his own shoulders. And when we say that man is responsible for himself, we do not mean that he is responsible only for his own individuality, but that he is responsible for all men. The word "subjectivism" is to be understood in two senses, and our adversaries play upon only one of them. Subjectivism means, on the one hand, the freedom of the individual subject and, on the other, that man cannot pass beyond human subjectivity. It is the latter which is the deeper meaning of existentialism. When we say that man chooses himself, we do mean that every one of us must choose for all men. For in effect, of all the actions a man may take in order to create himself as he wills to be, there is not one which is not creative, at the same time, of an image of man such as he believes he ought to be. To choose between this or that is at the same time to affirm the value of that which is chosen; for we are unable ever to choose the worse. What we choose is always the better; and nothing can be better for us unless it is better for all. If, moreover, existence precedes essence and we will to exist at the same time as we fashion our image, that image is valid for all and for the entire epoch in which we find ourselves. Our responsibility is thus much greater than we had supposed, for it concerns mankind as a whole. If I am a worker, for instance, I may choose to join a Christian rather than a Communist trade union. And if, by that membership, I choose to signify that resignation is, after all, the attitude that best becomes a man, that a man's kingdom is not upon this earth. I do not commit myself alone to that view. Resignation is my will for everyone, and my action is, in consequence, a commitment on behalf of all mankind. Or if, to take a more personal case, I decide to marry and to have children, even though this decision proceeds simply from my situation, from my passion or my desire, I am thereby committing not only myself, but humanity as a whole, to the practice of monogamy. I am thus responsible for myself and for all men, and I am creating a certain image of man as I would have him to be. In fashioning myself I fashion man.

Suppose you have given a concise exposition of the typical and central claims of some doctrine. You might then go on to single out three or four particular notions consequent upon, diagnostic of, the doctrine you had expounded. Sartre is now at that point. He has provided a concise account of his existentialism. He now selects three notions familiar and important to any Sartrean existentialist, namely, anguish, abandonment, and despair. There are others he might have chosen—bad faith, nausea, absurdity, for example. Given the doctrine that there are two modes of being in the world, *être en soi* and *être pour soi*, being which is not conscious or aware of itself and being which is conscious or aware of itself; call the mode of being that is conscious or aware of itself *existence pour soi*. Sartre's doctrine, existentialism, is about beings whose mode of existence is *pour soi*. You and I are such beings. We are conscious or aware that we exist. Our mode of existence is *pour soi*. A rock or a tree is not such a being. They are not conscious or aware that they exist. Their mode of existence is merely *en soi*. The present question is this: If you are a *pour soi*, why will anguish, abandonment, and despair be important, diagnostic, terms for you?

This may enable us to understand what is meant by such terms—perhaps a little grandiloquent—as anguish, abandonment and despair. As you will soon see, it is very simple. *First*, what do we mean by *anguish*? The existentialist frankly states that man is in anguish. His meaning is as follows—When a man commits himself to anything, fully realizing that he is not only choosing what he will be, but is thereby at the same time a legislator deciding for the whole of mankind—in such a moment a man cannot escape from the sense of complete and profound responsibility. There are many, indeed, who show no such anxiety. But we affirm that they are merely disguising their anguish or are in flight from it. Certainly, many people think that in what they are doing they commit no one but themselves to anything; and if you ask them, "What would happen if everyone did so?" they shrug their shoulders and reply, "Everyone does not do so." But in truth, one ought always to ask oneself what would happen if everyone did as one is doing; nor can one escape from that disturbing thought except by a kind of self-deception. The man who lies in self-excuse, by saying, "Everyone will not do it" must be ill at ease in his conscience, for the act of lying implies the universal value which it denies. By its very disguise his anguish reveals itself. This is the anguish that Kierkegaard called "the anguish of Abraham." You know the story: An angel commanded Abraham to sacrifice his son; and obedience was obligatory, if it really was an angel who had appeared and said, "Thou, Abraham, shalt sacrifice thy son." But anyone in such a case would wonder, first, whether it was indeed an angel and secondly, whether I am really Abraham. Where are the proofs? A certain mad woman who suffered from hallucinations said that people were telephoning her, and giving her orders. The doctor asked "But who is it that speaks to you?" She replied: "He says it is God." And what, indeed, could prove to her that it was God? If an angel appears to me, what is the proof that it is an angel; or, if I hear voices, who can prove that they proceed from heaven and not from hell, or from my own subconsciousness or some pathological condition? Who can prove that they are really addressed to me?

Who, then, can prove that I am the proper person to impose, by my own choice, my conception of man upon mankind? I shall never find any proof whatever; there will be no sign to convince me of it. If a voice speaks to me, it is still myself who must decide whether the voice is or is not that of an angel. If I regard a certain course of action as good, it is only I who choose to say that it is good and not bad. There is nothing to show that I am Abraham; nevertheless I am also obliged at every instant to perform actions which are examples. Everything happens to every man as though the whole human race had its eyes fixed upon what he is doing and regulated its conduct accordingly. So every man ought to say, "Am I a man who has the right to act in such a manner that humanity regulates itself by what I do." If a man does not say that, he is dissembling his anguish. Clearly, the anguish with which we are concerned here is not one that could lead to quietism or inaction. It is anguish pure and simple, of the kind well known to all those who have borne responsibilities. When, for instance, a military leader takes upon himself the responsibility for an attack and sends a number of men to their death, he chooses to do it and at bottom he alone chooses. No doubt he acts under a higher command, but its orders, which are more general, require interpretation by him and upon that interpretation depends the life of ten, fourteen or twenty men. In making the decision, he cannot but feel a certain anguish. All leaders know that anguish. It does not prevent their acting; on the contrary it is the very condition of their action, for the action presupposes that there is a plurality of possibilities, and in choosing one of these, they realize that it has value only because it is chosen. Now it is anguish of that kind which existentialism describes, and moreover, as we shall see, makes explicit through direct responsibility towards other men who are concerned. Far from being a screen which could separate us from action, it is a condition of action itself.

So much for existentialist anguish. Sartre's point has been this: if you are a *pour soi*, conscious or aware of existence, especially of your own existence, in a world containing only others who are also *pour soi*, and objects that are merely *en soi*, and that is all, you will know anguish. Why so? Why is anguish one of the facts of life for a *pour soi*? He moves on now to consider his second notion, *abandonment*. Thus:

And when we speak of "*abandonment*"—a favorite word of Heidegger—we only mean to say that God does not exist, and that it is necessary to draw the consequences of his absence right to the end. The existentialist is strongly opposed to a certain type of secular moralism which seeks to suppress God at the least possible expense. Towards 1880, when the French professors endeavored to formulate a secular morality, they said something like this:—God is a useless and costly hypothesis, so we will do without it. However, if we are to have morality, a society and a law-abiding world, it is essential that certain values should be taken seriously; they must have an *a priori* existence ascribed to them. It must be considered obligatory *a priori* to be honest, not to lie, not to beat one's wife, to bring up children and so forth; so we are going to do a little work on this subject, which will enable us to show that these values exist all the same, inscribed in an intelligent heaven although, of course, there is no God. In other words—and this is, I believe, the purport of all that we in France call radicalism— nothing will be changed if God does not exist; we shall rediscover the same norms of honesty, progress and humanity, and we shall have disposed of God as an out-of-date hypothesis which will die away quietly of itself. The existentialist, on the contrary, finds it extremely embarrassing that God does not exist, for there disappears with Him all possibility of finding values in an intelligible heaven. There can no longer be any good *a priori*, since there is no infinite and perfect consciousness to think it. It is nowhere written that "the good" exists, that one must be honest or must not lie, since we are now upon the plane where there are only men. Dostoevsky once wrote "If God did not exist, everything would be permitted;" and that, for existentialism, is the starting point. Everything is indeed permitted if God does not exist, and man is in consequence forlorn, for he cannot find anything to depend upon either within or outside himself. He discovers forthwith, that he is without excuse. For if indeed existence precedes essence, one will never be able to explain one's action by reference to a given and specific human nature; in other words, there is no determinism—man is free, man *is* freedom. Nor, on the other hand, if God does not exist, are we provided with any values or commands that could legitimize our behavior. Thus we have neither behind us, nor before us in a luminous realm of values, any means of justification or excuse. We are left alone, without excuse. That is what I mean when I say that man is condemned to be free. Condemned, because he did not create himself, yet is nevertheless at liberty, and from the moment that he is thrown into this world he is responsible for everything he does. The existentialist does not believe in the power of passion. He will never regard a grand passion as a destructive torrent upon which a man is swept into certain actions as by fate, and which therefore, is an excuse for them. He thinks that man is responsible for his passion. Neither will an existentialist think that a man can find help through some sign being vouchsafed upon earth for his orientation; for he thinks that the man himself interprets the sign as he chooses. He thinks that every man, without any support or help whatever, is condemned at every instant to invent man. As Ponge has written in a very fine article, "Man is the future of man." That is exactly true. Only, if one took this to mean that the future is laid up in Heaven, that God knows what it is, it would be false, for then it would no longer even be a future. If, however, it means that, whatever man may now appear to be, there is a future to be fashioned, a virgin future that awaits him—then it is a true saying. But in the present one is forsaken.

Thus far, Sartre has claimed that if you are an existentialist you will hold that there are in the world only two modes of existence: existence that is conscious or aware of itself, *être pour soi*, and existence that is not conscious or aware of itself, *être en soi*. He went on to claim that if you are a *pour soi* among others who are *pour soi*, anguish will be one of the facts of life for you. There will be no avoiding that encounter. He has now added the further claim that if you are an atheist *pour soi*, then abandonment, lostness, cosmic aloneness, forlornness will be one of the ineluctable facts of life for you and your kind. There will be no avoiding encounter with the vast "emptiness" of the world. You will realize that you, and all others who are *pour soi*, are abandoned, lost, forlorn, alone. You are not an object of concern to any *en soi*; that would be impossible. And because for Sartre you are also an atheist *pour soi*, an atheist aware that he exists but committed to claiming that there is no super *pour soi*—no God, no Deity, no Creator and Sustainer—you are not an object of concern of any superhuman *pour soi*. There is, for the atheist existentialist, no God, but only other finite *pour soi* and *en soi*. Neither humanity nor nature is any substitute for God at this point. The knowledge that there are others, like yourself, who are *pour soi* will not rid you of this sense of being abandoned in and cast upon the world; *thrown*. The knowledge that every other being who is not a *pour soi* is merely an *en soi*, similar to a rock or a tree, will not rid you of this sense of abandonment, thrownness. He now turns to the existentialist concept of despair.

As for "*despair*," the meaning of this expression is extremely simple. It merely means that we limit ourselves to a reliance upon that which is within our wills, or within the sum of the probabilities, which render our action feasible. Whenever one wills anything, there are always these elements of probability. If I am counting upon a visit from a friend, who may be coming by train or tram, I presuppose that the train will arrive at the appointed time, or that the tram will not be derailed. I remain in the realm of possibilities; but one does not rely upon any possibilities beyond those that are strictly concerned in one's actions. Beyond the point at which the possibilities under consideration cease to affect my action, I ought to disinterest myself. For there is no God and no prevenient design which can adapt the world and all its possibilities to my will. When Descartes said, "Conquer yourself rather than the world," what he meant was, at the bottom, the same—that we should act without hope.

Marxists, to whom I have said this, have answered: "Your action is limited, obviously, by your death; but you can rely upon the help of others. That is, you can count both upon what the others are doing to help you elsewhere, as in China and in Russia, and upon what they will do later, after your death, to take up your action and carry it forward to its final accomplishment which will be the revolution. Moreover you must rely upon this; not to do so is immoral." To this I rejoin, first, that I shall always count upon my comrades-in-arms in the struggle, in so far as they are committed, as I am, to a definite, common cause; and in the unity of a party or a group which I can more or less control—that is, in which I am enrolled as a militant and whose movements are every moment are known to me. In that respect, to rely upon the unity and the will of the party is exactly like my reckoning that the train will run on time or that the tram will not be derailed. But I cannot count upon men whom I do not know, I cannot base my confidence upon human goodness or upon man's interest in the good of society, seeing that man is free and that there is no human nature which I can take as foundational.

Sartre has told us that he will defend his atheist existentialism against certain charges, certain reproaches. He has given us an account of his doctrine and some of its corollaries. He has explained that his doctrine is a form of humanism. In the second half of his lecture he will deal with some of the charges brought against this atheist or humanist existentialism. The first charge ("reproach") is that an existentialism such as his will lead to quietism and pessimism. Thus:

Quietism is the attitude of people who say, "let others do what I cannot do." The doctrine I am presenting before you is precisely the opposite of this, since it declares that there is no reality except in action. It goes further, indeed, and adds, "Man is nothing else but what he purposes, he exists only in so far as he realizes himself, he is therefore nothing else but the sum of his actions, nothing else but what his life is." Hence we can well understand why some people are horrified by our teaching. For many have but one resource to sustain them in their misery, and that is to think, "Circumstances have been against me, I was worthy to be something much better than I have been. I admit I have never had a great love or a great friendship; but that is because I never met a man or a woman who were worthy of it; if I have not written any very good books, it is because I had not the leisure to do so; or, if I have had no children to whom I could devote myself it is because I did not find the man I could have lived with. So there remains within me a wide range of abilities, inclinations and potentialities, unused but perfectly viable, which endow me with a worthiness that could never be inferred from the mere history of my actions." But in reality and for the existentialist, there is no love apart from the deeds of love; no potentiality of love other than that which is manifested in loving; there is no genius other than that which is expressed in works of art. The genius of Proust is the totality of the works of Proust; the genius of Racine is the series of his tragedies, outside of which there is nothing. Why should we attribute to Racine the capacity to write yet another tragedy when that is precisely what he did not write? In life, a man commits himself, draws his own portrait and there is nothing but that portrait. No doubt this thought may seem comfortless to one who has not made a success of his life. On the other hand, it puts everyone in a position to understand that reality alone is reliable; that dreams, expectations and hopes serve to define a man only as deceptive dreams, abortive hopes, expectations unfulfilled; that is to say, they define him negatively, not positively. Nevertheless, when one says: "You are nothing else but what you live," it does not imply that an artist is to be judged solely by his works of art, for a thousand other things contribute no less to his definition as a man. What we mean to say is that a man is no other than a series of undertakings, that he is the sum, the organization, the set of relations that constitute these undertakings.

Sartre's point is this: If, as existentialist, you tell a person that he is a *pour soi*, one who exists and is conscious of, aware of, existing, he may begin by agreeing with you. Why not? Your doctrine rates him above the world of the *en soi*. That is a gratifying, indeed a flattering, perception. However, if you go on to explain to him that his status as a *pour soi* endows him with free will, with perception of alternatives, with power to choose, hence with responsibility, with power to make of himself what he, not external events and forces, decides—if you go on to make this application of your existentialism to his handling of his life and affairs, he will take a dim view of your doctrine. He does not want to think of himself as essentially the architect of his own wrongdoings and of his character as a person. And he does not want your doctrine to constrain him into thinking that way about himself. He prefers to cop out, and your existentialism forbids him to do so. It tells him that he is the author of whatever he is. He has not "become" what he is. That is the way of the *en soi*. He has made of himself what he is, by his own wrong-headed and bad-willed thinking and acting. Hence, your doctrine denies or distorts the image he wants of himself. So what does he do? He contrives to misunderstand, to misinterpret, your doctrine. He will claim that your doctrine ends by inducing those who accept it to become quietists and pessimists. But as Sartre hastens to point out, such a person is only rationalizing his rejection of existentialism by refusing to understand that doctrine correctly. This refusal is an example of what Sartre means by *mauvaise foi*, bad faith. If the person will only snap out of his protective obtuseness, he will see that he is not "refuting" existentialism, not even proposing a relevant criticism, but merely setting up a straw man, and then clobbering it, only spitefully misunderstanding it.

In summary, Sartre has displayed his view of the human being in terms of radical freedom. According to Sartre, I first of all exist, and then by my own activity define my essence. I am free to create myself without having to obey guidelines or requirements established in advance by God or others. I am free to become the kind of person I choose to be. Accordingly, I am responsible for myself, and, Sartre adds, I am also responsible for all humankind. In creating myself, I experience the consequences of this radical freedom: anguish, abandonment, and despair. If instead of acknowledging responsibility for myself and pursuing the task of creating myself in radical freedom, I attempt to shift the responsibility from myself to some other entity (for example, God, others, or the environment), then I am treating myself as if I were an *en soi*, a thing that is manipulated by forces beyond its control. To shift responsibility in this fashion to entities beyond myself would mean that I would be attempting to be what I am not; I would be portraying myself as an *en soi* rather than a *pour soi*. I would be deceiving myself. I would be living a lie. I would be inauthentic. I would be expressing *mauvaise foi*, "bad faith." That is precisely what a determinist such as Holbach would be doing in the eyes of an existentialist like Sartre.

NOTE ON SOURCES.   The material in this section is quoted from Jean-Paul Sartre, translated by P. Mairet in Walter Kaufmann, ed., *Existentialism from Dostoevsky to Sartre* (New York: Meridian Books, 1956), pp. 287–311.

WALTER T. STACE

I AM DETERMINED AND FREE

FROM SARTRE TO STACE.   Holbach and Sartre, as we have seen, are radically opposed to each other. Holbach starts from a materialist posture, which holds that reality is fundamentally material, and proceeds to discuss the human being. Because he can find no freedom in the motions of matter, and because human beings are for the materialist essentially matter in motion, Holbach can find no freedom in human behavior. Those activities in which we think we are free must be written off as illusionary. Sartre, in contrast, begins with the existing, experiencing person and his analysis leads him to affirm two basic aspects of reality. There are things (*en soi*) and no-things (*pour soi*). To reduce reality simply to things would be to ignore the evidence presented to the self that the self is a no-thing, a freedom, a *pour soi*.

Is it possible to reconcile the determinism of Holbach and the libertarianism of Sartre? Can one blend these two radically different views of the human being into a viable, coherent synthesis? Would it be meaningful and harmonious to affirm that the human is both determined and also free? Walter T. Stace offers a resounding Yes! to these questions. The position he takes in the free will/determinism controversy is often called *soft determinism* because his determinism is soft enough, or flexible enough, to make a place for free will. The position of Holbach and like-minded individuals, accordingly, is often called *hard* or *extreme determinism* to sort it out from the mediating position of the soft determinists. In this section we examine the case that Stace makes for soft determinism.

BIOGRAPHICAL NOTE.   Walter Terrence Stace was born in London, England in 1886. He attended Trinity College at Dublin University from which he received his A.B. degree in 1908. From 1910 to 1932 he was enrolled in the British Civil Service in Ceylon serving, among other roles, as judge, secretary to the governor, member of the legislative council of Ceylon, and finally as mayor of Colombo and chairman of the Colombo municipal council. In 1932 he began a distinguished teaching career in philosophy at Princeton University. His ten books on philosophical questions are in general characterized by a clarity that makes them especially attractive and engaging. Of these works, we draw attention to four. *The Philosophy of Hegel* (1924) is a lucid introduction to a philosopher whose writings are notoriously difficult. In *The Concept of Morals* (1937), Stace presents a moral law that is empirically derived and universal. In *The Destiny of Western Man* (1942), he offers a tough-minded defense of the democratic way of life that was being challenged at the time by fascist ideologies. His work, *Religion and the Modern Mind* (1952), from which the following selection is taken, affirms the belief that humans are governed by natural (rather than supernatural) law, but does not deny the validity of religious experience. Stace died at age 81 in 1967.

THE ARGUMENT OF THE PASSAGES.   If people of good will and keen minds have debated a problem, such as free will versus determinism, for centuries without reaching a mutually agreed-upon solution, then it just might be the case that the problem itself has been formulated in an unresolvable way. When the formulation of the problem is carefully scrutinized and restated, then its puzzling nature may vanish and a solution may appear. That is the approach that Walter Stace adopts in the age-old free will/determinism controversy. According to Stace, the key mistake in the formulation of the problem is an inadequate definition of free will adopted by both sides in the controversy. Both sides have assumed, says Stace, that free will means *indeterminism*. That is to say, an act of free will means an *uncaused* act; and that is an incorrect definition. If both sides would embrace a correct definition of free will, then their controversy would be resolved. When a controversy springs from mistaken views about the meaning of words, it is often called a mere verbal dispute or a semantic problem. That is the way Stace views this problem.

> I shall first discuss the problem of free will, for it is certain that if there is no free will there can be no morality. Morality is concerned with what men ought and ought not to do. But if a man has no freedom to choose what he will do, if whatever he does is done under compulsion, then it does not make sense to tell him that he ought not to have done what he did and that he ought to do something different. All moral precepts would in such case be meaningless. Also if he acts always under compulsion, how can he be held morally responsible for his actions? How can he, for example, be punished for what he could not help doing?
>
> It is to be observed that those learned professors of philosophy or psychology who deny the existence of free will do so only in their professional moments and in their studies and lecture rooms. For when it comes to doing anything practical, even of the most trivial kind, they invariably behave as if they and others were free. They inquire from you at dinner whether you will choose this dish or that dish. They will ask a child why he told a lie, and will punish him for not having chosen the way of truthfulness. All of which is inconsistent with a disbelief in free will. This should

cause us to suspect that the problem is not a real one; and this, I believe, is the case. The dispute is merely verbal, and is due to nothing but a confusion about the meanings of words. It is what is now fashionably called a semantic problem.

How does a verbal dispute arise? Let us consider a case which, although it is absurd in the sense that no one would ever make the mistake which is involved in it, yet illustrates the principles which we shall have to use in the solution of the problem. Suppose that someone believed that the word "man" means a certain sort of five-legged animal; in short that "five-legged animal" is the correct *definition* of man. He might then look around the world, and rightly observing that there are no five-legged animals in it, he might proceed to deny the existence of men. This preposterous conclusion would have been reached because he was using an incorrect definition of "man." All you would have to do to show him his mistake would be to give him the correct definition; or at least to show him that his definition was wrong. Both the problem and its solution, would, of course, be entirely verbal. The problem of free will, and its solution, I shall maintain, is verbal in exactly the same way. The problem has been created by the fact that learned men, especially philosophers, have assumed an incorrect definition of free will, and then finding that there is nothing in the world which answers to their definition, have denied its existence. As far as logic is concerned, their conclusion is just as absurd as that of the man who denies the existence of men. The only difference is that the mistake in the latter case is obvious and crude, while the mistake which the deniers of free will have made is rather subtle and difficult to detect.

Throughout the modern period, until quite recently, it was assumed, both by the philosophers who denied free will and by those who defended it, that *determinism is inconsistent with free will*. If a man's actions were wholly determined by chains of causes stretching back into the remote past, so that they could be predicted beforehand by a mind which knew all the causes, it was assumed that they could not in that case be free. This implies that a certain definition of actions done from free will was assumed, namely that they are actions *not* wholly determined by causes or predictable beforehand. Let us shorten this by saying that free will was defined as meaning indeterminism. This is the incorrect definition which has led to the denial of free will. As soon as we see what the true definition is we shall find the question whether the world is deterministic, as Newtonian science implied, or in a measure indeterministic, as current physics teaches, is wholly irrelevant to the problem.

If, as Stace alleges, the definition of free will assumed in the debate is incorrect, how does one know that it is incorrect and how does one formulate the correct one? Stace articulates at this point a very important principle and a rather promising strategy. The principle is that "common usage is the criterion for deciding whether a definition is correct or not." That is to say, if a definition of a word does not square with the meaning people usually associate with the word when they use it, then the definition would be judged incorrect, and vice versa. But how does one discover the meaning people usually associate with a word? Here Stace advances his strategy. He cites a group of acts that people would generally consider to be free, and a group they would generally consider to be unfree. The challenge is to identify the characteristic that the cluster of free acts have in common but that the unfree acts do not possess. In so doing, Stace believes he can isolate the essential meaning of a free act, and hence generate a "new" definition of free will. It will be "new" for the disputants in the controversy, but *not* "new" in the sense that it will simply make explicit the meaning assumed by people in everyday conversation.

Of course there is a sense in which one can define a word arbitrarily in any way one pleases. But a definition may nevertheless be called correct or incorrect. It is correct if it accords with a *common usage* of the word defined. It is incorrect if it does not. And if you give an incorrect definition, absurd and untrue results are likely to follow. For instance, there is nothing to prevent you from arbitrarily defining a man as a five-legged animal, but this is incorrect in the sense that it does not accord with the ordinary meaning of the word. Also it has the absurd result of leading to a denial of the existence of men. This shows that *common usage is the criterion for deciding whether a definition is correct or not*. And this is the principle which I shall apply to free will. I shall show that indeterminism is not what is meant by the phrase "free will" *as it is commonly used*. And I shall attempt to discover the correct definition by inquiring about how the phrase is used in ordinary conversation.

Here are a few examples of how the phrase might be used in ordinary conversation. It will be noticed that they include cases in which the question whether a man acted with free will is asked in order to determine whether he was morally and legally responsible for his acts.

Jones I once went without food for a week.

Smith Did you do that of your own free will?

Jones No. I did it because I was lost in a desert and could find no food.

But suppose that the man who fasted was Mahatma Gandhi. The conversation might then have gone:

Gandhi I once fasted for a week.

Smith Did you do that of your own free will?

Gandhi Yes. I did it because I wanted to compel the British Government to give India its independence.

Take another case. Suppose that I had stolen some bread, but that I was as truthful as George Washington. Then, if I were charged with the crime in court, some exchange of the following sort might take place:

Judge Did you steal the bread of your own free will?

Stace Yes. I stole it because I was hungry.

Or in different circumstances the conversation might run:

Judge Did you steal of your own free will?

Stace No. I stole because my employer threatened to beat me if I did not.

At a recent murder trial in Trenton some of the accused had signed confessions, but afterwards asserted that they had done so under police duress. The following exchange might have occurred:

Judge Did you sign this confession of your own free will?

Prisoner No. I signed it because the police beat me up.

Now suppose that a philosopher had been a member of the jury. We could imagine this conversation taking place in the jury room.

Foreman of the Jury   The prisoner says he signed the confession because he was beaten, and not of his own free will.

Philosopher   This is quite irrelevant to the case. There is no such thing as free will.

Foreman   Do you mean to say that it makes no difference whether he signed because his conscience made him want to tell the truth or because he was beaten?

Philosopher   None at all. Whether he was caused to sign by a beating or by some desire of his own—the desire to tell the truth, for example—in either case his signing was causally determined, and therefore in neither case did he act of his own free will. Since there is no such thing as free will, the question whether he signed of his own free will ought not to be discussed by us.

The foreman and the rest of the jury would rightly conclude that the philosopher must be making some mistake. What sort of a mistake could it be? There is only one possible answer. The philosopher must be using the phrase "free will" in some peculiar way of his own which is not the way in which men usually use it when they wish to determine a question of moral responsibility. That is, he must be using an incorrect definition of it as implying action not determined by causes.

Suppose a man left his office at noon, and were questioned about it. Then we might hear this:

Jones   Did you go out of your own free will?

Smith   Yes. I went out to get my lunch.

But we might hear:

Jones   Did you leave your office of your own free will?

Smith   No. I was forcibly removed by the police.

We have now collected a number of cases of actions which, in the ordinary usage of the English language, would be called cases in which people have acted of their own free will. We should also say in all these cases they *chose* to act as they did. We should also say that they could have acted otherwise, if they had chosen. For instance, Mahatma Gandi was not compelled to fast, he chose to do so. He could have eaten if he had wanted to. When Smith went out to get his lunch, he chose to do so. He could have stayed and done some more work, if he had wanted to. We have also collected a number of cases of the opposite kind. They are cases in which men were not able to exercise their free will. They had no choice. They were compelled to do as they did. The man in the desert did not fast of his own free will. He had no choice in the matter. He was compelled to fast because there was nothing for him to eat. And so with the other cases. It ought to be quite easy, by an inspection of these cases, to tell what we ordinarily mean when we say that a man did or did not exercise free will. We ought therefore to be able to extract from them the proper definition of the term. Let us put the cases in a table:

Free Acts	*Unfree Acts*
Gandhi fasting because he wanted to free India.	The man fasting in the desert because there was no food.

Stealing bread because one is hungry.	Stealing because one's employer threatened to beat one.
Signing a confession because one wanted to tell the truth.	Signing because the police beat one.
Leaving the office because one wanted one's lunch.	Leaving because forcibly removed.

It is obvious that to find the correct definition of free acts we must discover what characteristic is common to all the acts in the left-hand column, and is, at the same time, absent from all the acts in the right-hand column. This characteristic which all free acts have, and which no unfree acts have, will be the defining characteristic of free will.

Stace proceeds to eliminate "uncaused" as the defining characteristic of acts of free will. Instead, he argues that the defining characteristic resides in a special *kind* of causes that are operative in acts of free will.

Is being uncaused, or not being determined by causes, the characteristic of which we are in search? It cannot be, because although it is true that all the acts in the right-hand column have causes, such as the beating by the police or the absence of food in the desert, so also do the acts in the left-hand column. Mr. Gandhi's fasting was caused by the his desire to free India, the man leaving his office by his hunger, and so on. Moreover there is no reason to doubt that these causes of the free acts were in turn caused by prior conditions, and that these were again the result of causes, and so on back indefinitely into the past. Any physiologist can tell us the causes of hunger. What caused Mr. Gandhi's tremendously powerful desire to free India is no doubt more difficult to discover. But it must have had causes. Some of them may have lain in peculiarities of his glands or brain, others in his past experiences, others in his heredity, others in his education. Defenders of free will have usually tended to deny such facts. But to do so is plainly a case of special pleading, which is unsupported by any scrap of evidence. The only reasonable view is that all human actions, both those which are freely done and those which are not, are either wholly determined by causes, or at least as much determined as other events in nature. It may be true, as the physicists tell us, that nature is not as deterministic as was once thought. But what-ever degree of determinism prevails in the world, human actions appear to be as much determined as anything else. And if this is so, it cannot be the case that what distinguishes actions freely chosen from those which are not free is that the latter are determined by causes while the former are not. Therefore, being uncaused or being undetermined by causes must be an incorrect definition of free will.

What, then, is the difference between acts which are freely done and those which are not? What is the characteristic which is present to all the acts in the left-hand column and absent from all those in the right-hand column? Is it not obvious that, although both sets of actions have causes, those in the left-hand column are *of a different kind* from the causes of those in the right-hand column? The free acts are all caused by desires, or motives, or by some sort of internal psychological states of the agent's mind. The unfree acts, on the other hand, are all caused by physical forces or physical conditions, outside the agent. Police arrest means physical force exerted from the outside; the absence of food in the desert is a physical condition of the out-side world. We may therefore frame the following rough definitions. *Acts freely done are those whose immediate causes are psychological states in the agent. Acts not freely done are those who immediate causes are states of affairs external to the agent.*

It is plain that if we define free will in this way, then free will certainly exists, and the philosopher's denial of its existence is seen to be what it is—nonsense. For it is obvious that all those actions of men which we should ordinarily attribute to the exercise of their free will, or of which we should say that they freely chose to do them, are in fact actions which have been caused by their own desires, wishes, thoughts, emotions, impulses, or other psychological states.

An act of free will, then, is not an uncaused act. Rather it is an act whose immediate cause is a psychological state in the agent. Stace now proceeds to discuss three problems that his affirmation of a "deterministic free will" might encounter. First, what about those acts whose immediate cause is a psychological state, but whose penultimate cause is an event in the external environment? That is to say, what if the psychological state is caused by external factors? Is such an act free or unfree?

In applying our definition we shall find that it usually works well, but that there are some puzzling cases which it does not seem exactly to fit. These puzzles can always be solved by paying careful attention to the ways in which words are used, and remembering that they are not always used consistently. I have space for only one example. Suppose that a thug threatens to shoot you unless you give him your wallet, and suppose that you do so. Do you, in giving him your wallet, do so of your own free will or not? If we apply our definition, we find that you acted freely, since the immediate cause of the action was not an actual outside force but the fear of death, which is a psychological cause. Most people, however, would say that you did not act of your own free will but under compulsion. Does this show that our definition is wrong? I do not think so. Aristotle, who gave a solution of the problem of free will substantially the same as ours (though he did not use the term "free will"), admitted that there are what he called "mixed" or borderline cases in which it is difficult to know whether we ought to call the acts free or compelled. In the case under discussion, though no actual force was used, the gun at your forehead so nearly approximated to actual force that we tend to say the case was one of compulsion. It is a borderline case.

Second, determinism facilitates predictability. Does a "deterministic free will," then, mean that acts of free will are predictable? If so, is not the blending of free will and predictability a futile attempt to mix incompatibles?

Here is what may seem like another kind of puzzle. According to our view an action may be free though it could have been predicted beforehand with certainty. But suppose you told a lie, and it was certain beforehand that you would tell it. How could one then say, "You could have told the truth"? The answer is that it is perfectly true that you could have told the truth *if* you had wanted to. In fact you would have done so, for in that case the causes producing your action, namely your desires, would have been different, and would therefore have produced different effects. It is a delusion that predictability and free will are incompatible. This agrees with common sense. For if, knowing your character, I predict that you will act honorably, no one would say when you do act honorably, that this shows you did not do so of your own free will.

Third, free will is widely regarded as a condition of moral responsibility. Is not such responsibility really precluded by the notion of a "deterministic free will"?

Since free will is a condition of moral responsibility, we must be sure that our theory of free will gives a sufficient basis for it. To be held morally responsible for one's actions means that one may be justly punished or rewarded, blamed or praised, for them. But it is not just to punish a man for what he cannot help doing. How can it be just to punish him for an action which it was certain beforehand that he would do? We have not attempted to decide whether, as a matter of fact, all events, including human actions, are completely determined. For that question is irrelevant to the problem of free will. But if we assume for the purposes of argument that complete determinism is true, but that we are nevertheless free, it may then be asked whether such a deterministic free will is compatible with moral responsibility. For it may seem unjust to punish a man for an action which it could have been predicted with certainty beforehand that he would do.

But that determinism is incompatible with moral responsibility is as much a delusion as that it is incompatible with free will. You do not excuse a man for doing a wrong act because, knowing his character, you felt certain beforehand that he would do it. Nor do you deprive a man of a reward or prize because, knowing his goodness or his capabilities, you felt certain beforehand that he would win it.

Volumes have been written on the justification of punishment. But so far as it affects the question of free will, the essential principles involved are quite simple. The punishment of a man for doing a wrong act is justified, either on the ground that it will correct his own character, or that it will deter other people from doing similar acts. The instrument of punishment has been in the past, and no doubt still is, often unwisely used; so that it may often have done more harm than good. But that is not relevant to our present problem. Punishment, if and when it is justified, is justified only on one or both of the grounds just mentioned. The question then is how, if we assume determinism, punishment can correct character or deter people from evil actions.

Suppose that your child develops a habit of telling lies. You give him a mild beating. Why? Because you believe that his personality is such that the usual motives for telling the truth do not cause him to do so. You therefore supply the missing cause, or motive, in the shape of pain and the fear of future pain if he repeats his untruthful behavior. And you hope that a few treatments of this kind will condition him to the habit of truth-telling, so that he will come to tell the truth without the infliction of pain. You assume that his actions are determined by causes, but that the usual causes of truth-telling do not in him produce their usual effects. You therefore supply him with an artificially injected motive, pain and fear, which you think will in the future cause him to speak truthfully.

The principle is exactly the same where you hope, by punishing one man, to deter others from wrong actions. You believe that the fear of punishment will cause those who might otherwise do evil to do well.

We act on the same principle with non-human, and even with inanimate, things, if they do not behave in the way we think they ought to behave. The rose bushes in the garden produce only small and poor blooms, whereas we want large and rich ones. We supply a cause which will produce large blooms, namely fertilizer. Our automobile does not go properly. We supply a cause which will make it go better, namely oil in the works. The punishment for the man, the fertilizer for the plant, and the oil for the car, are all justified by the same principle and in the same way. The only difference is that different kinds of things require different kinds of causes to make them do what they should. Pain may be the appropriate remedy to apply, in certain cases, to human beings, and oil to the machine. It is, of course, of no use to inject motor oil into the boy or to beat the machine.

Thus we see that moral responsibility is not only consistent with determinism, but requires it. The assumption on which punishment is based is that human behavior is causally determined. If pain could not be a cause of truth-telling there would be no justification at all for punishing lies. If human actions and volitions were uncaused, it would be useless either to punish or reward, or indeed to do anything else to correct people's bad behavior. For nothing that you could do would in any way influence them. Thus moral responsibility would entirely disappear. If there were no determinism of human beings at all, their actions would be completely unpredictable and capricious, and therefore irresponsible. And this is in itself a strong argument against the common view of philosophers that free will means being undetermined by causes.

Such, then, is Stace's statement of soft determinism. Is it a satisfactory and viable blend of free will and determinism? Or, does determinism ultimately swallow up free will? Consider again Stace's first of the three problems. If all events have causes, as Stace contends, and if we search for the causes of each and every psychological state, are we not led ultimately to external causes in heredity and environment that are clearly beyond the individual's control? If so, how does Stace's soft determinism really differ from hard determinism? If it doesn't, has not Stace sacrificed free will in favor of determinism?

Consider now the third of his problems: the challenge to affirm and defend the notion that deterministic free wills can be held morally responsible. To build his case Stace focused on the issue of punishment. Presumably we punish people because we hold them morally responsible for their acts. Stace suggests that there are only two grounds for justifying punishment: either on the ground that it will *correct* the punished person's character or on the ground that it will *deter* others from doing similar acts. In both cases, says Stace, determinism is assumed. Is Stace correct, however, in saying that there are only two grounds for justifying punishment? What about the business of *desert*? When justifying punishment do not people ordinarily raise the question of desert or blameworthiness? And if an offender is deemed blameworthy, is it not on the assumption that the person could really have done something other than he or she actually did? Is not that assumption at the heart also of praiseworthiness? And are not blameworthiness and praiseworthiness at the center of moral responsibility, moral accountability? If so, does not the concept of moral responsibility presuppose that people have real alternatives open before them, that they really could have performed deeds other than the ones they did? And does not Stace's determinism in effect preclude *real* alternatives and the possibility that persons could have acted other than they did? Is Stace's attempt, therefore, to show the compatibility of a deterministic free will and moral responsibility, in the final analysis, successful? If it isn't, has Stace attempted the impossible: the blending of free will and determinism? If he hasn't, what adjustments would need to be made in the case for soft determinism to make it successful?

NOTE ON SOURCES.   The material in this section is quoted from Walter T. Stace, *Religion and the Modern Mind* (New York: Harper and Row, 1952), pp. 248–258.

4   WILLIAM JAMES

THE DILEMMA OF DETERMINISM

FROM STACE TO JAMES.   The radically different positions of Holbach and Sartre forcefully represent the dispute between the determinists and the indeterminists (or libertarians) that has been going on for many years. For Holbach, human beings are part of nature, and because there is no free will in nature, there is no free will in humans. To call any human act an "act of free will" is illusionary. For Sartre, reality is made up of *en soi* and *pour soi*: "in itself" and "for itself": "things" and "no-things." To deny human beings freedom is to reduce the *pour soi* to an *en soi*, and thereby to misunderstand what it means to be a human being.

Stace has attempted to resolve the dispute between the determinists and indeterminists by characterizing the dispute as simply "verbal" in the sense that the dispute rests on a confused understanding of what a "free act" is. The solution, according to Stace, is to provide the correct definition of a "free act." In a real sense, Stace's position provides a compromise between the determinists and the libertarians. With a salute to the determinists, Stace declares that all events are caused; and with a nod to the libertarians, he affirms that acts whose immediate causes are psychological states are really "free acts." Libertarians, however, are likely to reply that Stace has really "sold out" to the "hard" determinism of Holbach. After all, has not Stace in fact affirmed the universal causal network of Holbach, and merely selected a certain part of that network (namely, acts whose immediate causes are psychological states) and labeled it the domain of "free acts"? Accordingly, Stace's effort to resolve the dispute, although intriguing, has left the issue still debatable. Another voice worth hearing in that debate is that of William James who, as an indeterminist, focuses on practical consequences to assess the acceptability of determinism.

James graduated from Harvard with his medical degree in 1869, and the following year experienced a profound intellectual, if not spiritual, crisis. As a student of science he had found the doctrine of determinism very compelling. Yet that doctrine seemed to erode his will to live. How could he take seriously the quest to pursue the good, the true, and the beautiful and to avoid the evil, the false, and the ugly, if whatever he did was the only thing he could have done (according to determinism)? James battled with determinism and generated what he considered to be sufficient grounds for rejecting it. His struggle and his solution are recapitulated for us in one of his lectures, published in 1884. That lecture, "The Dilemma of Determinism," is reproduced in this section. It has become a classic document in the free will/determinism controversy, and it certainly merits consideration as one of the finest pieces written by James. His findings reported in this essay contributed significantly to the chapter on will in his famous volume, *The Principles of Psychology*, published in 1890.

BIOGRAPHICAL NOTE.   William James was born in 1842 and died in 1910 at the age of sixty-eight. He was educated at Harvard and in Europe. He was appointed to the teaching staff of Harvard in the department of physiology. From physiology he moved later to psychology, writing his brilliant and epoch-making *Principles of Psychology* and *Varieties of Religious Experience*. From psychology he moved on to philosophy. His best-known and most controversial books were written during his years as professor of philosophy. He gathered about him, at Harvard, what was perhaps the most brilliant group of teachers and writers in philosophy ever assembled at any one time in any university in this country. These philosophical colleagues included Josiah Royce, George Herbert Palmer, George Santayana, and (in psychology) Hugo Münsterberg.

Although James was trained as a physiologist, he had many of the interests of a moralist and theologian. His robust assurance that the good life, in the long run, provides the deepest and most lasting satisfaction; his passionately felt need for a "Friend" sustaining the universe and reaching out to man in his struggle for righteousness and truth, are convictions that pervade many of his writings. His three books, *The Will to Believe and Other Essays, The Varieties of Religious Experience*, and *Pragmatism*, contain popular presentations of these views.

THE ARGUMENT OF THE PASSAGES.   James begins his essay by assuring his readers that the question, "Does any human behavior express free will?" is by no means dead. From the beginning he renounces any attempt to *prove* the truth of his claim that humans have free wills. Instead, James hopes to clarify the issues at stake in the free will controversy, and to induce some of his hearers to assume the truth of his claim and to act as if it were true.

> A common opinion prevails that the juice has ages ago been pressed out of the free-will controversy, and that no new champion can do more than warm up stale arguments which every one has heard. This is a radical mistake. I know of no subject less worn out, or in which inventive genius has a better chance of breaking open new ground,—not, perhaps of forcing a conclusion or of coercing assent, but of deepening our sense of what the issue between the two parties really is, of what the ideas of fate and of free-will imply. . . . My ambition limits itself to just one little point. If I can make two of the necessarily implied corollaries of determinism clearer to you than they have been made before, I shall have made it possible for you to decide for or against that doctrine with a better understanding of what you are about. And if you prefer not to decide at all, but to remain doubters, you will at least see more plainly what the subject of your hesitation is. I thus disclaim openly on the threshold all pretension to prove to you that the freedom of the will is true. The most I hope is to induce some of you to follow my own example in assuming it true, and acting as if it were true. If it be true, it seems to me that this is involved in the strict logic of the case. Its truth ought not to be forced willy-nilly down our indifferent throats. It ought to be freely espoused by men who can equally well turn their backs upon it. In other words, our first act of freedom if we are free, ought in all inward propriety to be to affirm that we are free. This should exclude, it seems to me, from the free-will side of the question all hope of a coercive demonstration,—a demonstration which I, for one, am perfectly contented to go without.

James proceeds to indicate two basic presuppositions that are crucial for his argument. First, philosophizing is pursued to produce "subjective satisfaction."

Second, if there are two rival philosophical views, and if one view seems "more rational" than the other, then the more rational one is likely to be the truer one. Here James is referring to what he called, in an earlier paper, the "sentiment of rationality." If one position produces a greater sentiment of rationality than another, this is a mark in its favor. According to James, one philosophical position can be "more rational" than another, not just in the sense that its claims are presented with more neatly chiseled logic, but additionally in the sense that its claims cohere with, fit in with, more of the features of human experience. Granted our acceptance of his two presuppositions, James (focusing on the practical consequences of accepting each of the doctrines) will be in a position to ask us by the end of his essay, "You have before you two rival philosophical doctrines: free will and determinism. Which of the two supplies the greatest subjective satisfaction? Which of the two is more rational? Which fits in most adequately with your lived experience? Which of the two will you accept?"

> The arguments I am about to urge all proceed on two suppositions: First, when we make theories about the world and discuss them with one another, we do so in order to attain a conception of things which shall give us subjective satisfaction; and, second, if there be two conceptions, and the one seems to us, on the whole, more rational than the other, we are entitled to suppose that the more rational one is the truer of the two. I hope that you are willing to make these suppositions with me; for I am afraid that if there be any of you here who are not, they will find little edification in the rest of what I have to say. I cannot stop to argue the point; but I myself believe that all the magnificent achievements of mathematical and physical science—our doctrines of evolution, of uniformity of law, and the rest—proceed from our indomitable desire to cast the world into a more rational shape in our minds than the shape into which it is thrown here by the crude order of our experience. The world has shown itself, to a great extent, plastic to this demand of ours for rationality. How much farther it will show itself plastic no one can say. Our only means of finding out is to try; and I, for one, feel as free to try conceptions of moral as of mechanical or of logical rationality. If a certain formula for expressing the nature of the world violates my moral demand, I shall feel free to throw it overboard, or at least to doubt it, as if it disappointed my demand for uniformity of sequence, for example; the one demand being, so far as I can see, quite as subjective and emotional as the other is. The principle of causality, for example,—what is it but a postulate, an empty name covering simply a demand that the sequence of events shall some day manifest a deeper kind of belonging of one thing with another than the mere arbitrary juxtaposition which now phenomenally appears? It is as much an altar to an unknown god as the one that Saint Paul found in Athens. All our scientific and philosophic ideals are altars to unknown gods. Uniformity is as much so as is free-will. If this be admitted, we can debate on even terms. But if any one pretends that while freedom and variety are, in the first instance, different, I do not see how we can debate at all.

The question at issue can be worded retrospectively: "You being who you were, the circumstances being what they were, could you ever have done other than you did do?" Faced with this question, the determinist says, "No; you never could have done otherwise"; and the indeterminist, or free-willist, says equally emphatically, "Yes, under some circumstances you could have. It may be that *some* human behavior is determined, necessitated; but not *all* human behavior at all times." When the question is stated like this, in wholly general terms, James's first point is that neither answer can be proved by any single-fact evidence. It is not comparable to yes and no answers to the question "Is Jane older than John?" Or, "Is Chicago farther west from New York than Cleveland is?" The most you are going to be able to do, on behalf of either answer, is "test" it for the amount of "sentiment of rationality" it produces. Doing this, as he began by noting, may lead to an impasse. In that case you pay your money and you take your choice. If some rational animals find no a reasonable answer and some find yes a reasonable answer, that is as far as you may get.

To begin, then, I must suppose you are acquainted with all the usual arguments on the subject. I cannot stop to take up the old proofs from causation, from statistics, from the certainty with which we can foretell one another's conduct, from the fixity of character, and all the rest.

Now, evidence of an external kind to decide between determinism and indeterminism is, as I intimated a while back, strictly impossible to find. Let us look at the difference between them and see for ourselves. What does determinism profess?

It professes that those parts of the universe already laid down absolutely appoint and decree what the other parts shall be. The future has no ambiguous possibility hidden in its womb: the part we call the present is compatible with only one totality. Any other future complement than the one fixed from eternity is impossible. The whole is in each and every part, and welds it with the rest into an absolute unity, an iron block, in which there can be no equivocation or shadow of turning.

> With earth's first clay they did the last man knead,
> And there of the last harvest sowed the seed.
> And the first morning of creation wrote
> What the last dawn of reckoning shall read.

Indeterminism, on the contrary, says that the parts have a certain amount of loose play on one another, so that the laying down of one of them does not necessarily determine what the others shall be. It admits that possibilities may be in excess of actualities, and that things not yet revealed to our knowledge may really in themselves be ambiguous. Of two alternative futures which we conceive, both may now be really possible; and the one becomes impossible only at the very moment when the other excludes it by becoming real itself. Indeterminism thus denies the world to be one unbending unit of fact. It says there is a certain ultimate pluralism in it; and, so saying, it corroborates our ordinary unsophisticated view of things. To that view, actualities seem to float in a wider sea of possibilities from out of which they are chosen; and, somewhere, indeterminism says, such possibilities exist, and form a part of truth.

Determinism, on the contrary, says they exist *nowhere*, and that necessity on the one hand and impossibility on the other are the sole categories of the real. Possibilities that fail to get realized are, for determinism, pure illusions; they never were possibilities at all. There is nothing inchoate, it says, about this universe of ours, all that was or is or shall be actual in it having been from eternity virtually there. The cloud of alternatives our minds escort this mass of actuality withal is a cloud of sheer deceptions, to which "impossibilities" is the only name which rightfully belongs.

The issue, it will be seen, is a perfectly sharp one, which no eulogistic terminology can smear over or wipe out. The truth *must* lie with one side or the other, and its lying with one side make the other false.

The question relates solely to the existence of possibilities, in the strict sense of the term, as things that may, but need not, be. Both sides admit that a volition, for instance, has occurred. The indeterminists say another volition might have occurred in its place: the determinists swear that nothing could possibly have occurred in its place. Now, can science be called in to tell us which of these two point-blank contradictors of each other is right? Science professes to draw no conclusions but such as are based on matters of fact, things that have actually happened; but how can any amount of assurance that something actually happened give us the least grain of information as to whether another thing might or might not have happened in its place?

And the truth is that facts practically have hardly anything to do with making us either determinists or indeterminists. Sure enough, we make a flourish of quoting facts this way or that; and if we are determinists, we talk about the infallibility with which we can predict one another's conduct; while if we are indeterminists, we lay great stress on the fact that it is just because we cannot foretell one another's conduct, either in war or statecraft or in any of the great and small intrigues and businesses of men, that life is so intensely anxious and hazardous a game. But who does not see the wretched insufficiency of this so-called objective testimony on both sides? What fills up the gaps in our minds is something not objective, not external. What divides us into *possibility* men and *anti-possibility* men is different faiths or postulates—postulates of rationality. To this man the world seems more rational with possibilities in it—to that man more rational with possibilities excluded; and talk as we will about having to yield to evidence, what makes us monists or pluralists, determinists or indeterminists, is at bottom always some sentiment like this.

There is a sense in which James might well stop right there. The question is not a scientific one. Neither answer can claim to be a, or the, scientific answer. A few years later he would say that the question was "metaphysical" and that the case for either answer was therefore "pragmatic," therefore an appeal to us to put forth our "will to believe" on behalf of whichever answer produced the greatest amount of the "sentiment of rationality" in us. However, he has a few more points he wishes a hearing for. One of these is that the friends of determinism vote against indeterminism and free will because it says that some events (some human acts) happen "by chance," and they are turned off by the notion that *any* events happen by "chance." If the world is the place that they think it is, it does not contain *any* "chance" events. A chance event would be one that did not happen according to any law. In the scientific, but not in the legislative, sense of *law*, a "chance" event would be a "lawless" event. And they are totally opposed to any such notion. Given what might *appear* to be a chance or lawless event, they would *revise the law* until it included the event as an instance. So far as James is concerned, they need say no more. This shows what outrages their sentiment of rationality. This shows which "metaphysical" party they belong to. If they will recognize that others have an equal right to belong to some incompatible metaphysical party, James has nothing further to say. At this point he is nothing if not tolerant. He may be himself committed to the claim that they have got the world wrong, but he is willing, as between incompatible answers to metaphysical questions, to practice a policy of live and let live.

The stronghold of the deterministic sentiment is the antipathy to the idea of chance. As soon as we begin to talk indeterminism to our friends, we find a number of them shaking their heads. This notion of alternative possibility, they say, this admission that any one of several things may come to pass, is, after all, only a round-about name for chance; and chance is something the notion of which no sane mind can for an instant tolerate in the world. What is it, they ask, but barefaced crazy unreason, the negation of intelligibility and law? And if the slightest particle of it exists anywhere, what is to prevent the whole fabric from falling together, the stars from going out, and chaos from recommencing her topsy-turvy reign? . . .

The sting of the word "chance" seems to lie in the assumption that it means something positive, and that if anything happens by chance, it must needs be something of an intrinsically irrational and preposterous sort. Now chance means nothing of the kind. It is a purely negative and relative term, giving us no information about that of which it is predicated, except that it happens to be disconnected with something else—not controlled, secured, or necessitated by other things in advance of its own actual presence. As this point is the most subtle one of the whole lecture, and at the same time the point on which all the rest hinges, I beg you to pay particular attention to it. What I say is that it tells us nothing about what a thing may be in itself to call it "chance." . . . All that its chance-character asserts about it is that there is something in it really of its own, something that is not the unconditional property of the whole. If the whole wants this property, the whole must wait till it can get it, if it be a matter of chance. That the universe may actually be a sort of joint-stock society of this sort, in which the sharers have both limited liabilities and limited powers, is of course a simple and conceivable notion.

Nevertheless, many persons talk as if the minutest dose of disconnectedness of one part with another, the smallest modicum of independence, the faintest tremor of ambiguity about the future, for example, would ruin everything, and turn this godly universe into a sort of insane sand-heap or nulliverse—no universe at all. Since future human volitions are, as a matter of fact, the only ambiguous things we are tempted to believe in, let us stop for a moment to make ourselves sure whether their independent and accidental character need be fraught with such direful consequences to the universe as these.

What is meant by saying that my choice of which way to walk home after the lecture is ambiguous and matter of chance as far as the present moment is concerned? It means that both Divinity Avenue and Oxford Street are called; but that only one, and that one *either* one, shall be chosen. Now, I ask you seriously to suppose that this ambiguity of my choice is real; and then to make the impossible hypothesis that the choice is made twice over, and each time falls on a different street. In other words, imagine that I first walk through Divinity Avenue, and then imagine that the powers governing the universe annihilate ten minutes of time with all that it contained, and set me back at the door of this hall just as I was before the choice was made. Imagine then that, everything else being the same, I now make a different choice and traverse Oxford Street. You, as passive spectators, look on and see the two alternative universes—one of them with me walking through Divinity Avenue in it, the other with the same me walking through Oxford Street. Now, if you are determinists you believe one of these universes to have been from eternity impossible: you believe it to have been impossible because of the intrinsic irrationality or accidentality somewhere involved in it. But looking outwardly at these universes, can you say which is the impossible and accidental one, and which the rational and necessary one? I doubt if the most iron-clad determinist among you could have the slightest glimmer of light at this point. In other words, either universe *after the fact* and once there, would, to our means of observation and understanding, appear just as rational as the other. There would be absolutely no criterion by which we might judge one necessary and the other matter of chance. Suppose now we relieve the gods of their hypothetical task and assume my choice, once made, to be made forever. I go through Divinity Avenue for good and all. If, as good determinists, you now begin to affirm, what all good determinists punctually do affirm, that in the nature of things I couldn't have gone through Oxford Street—had I done so it would have been chance, irrationality, insanity, a horrid gap in nature—I simply call your attention to this, that your affirmation is what the Germans call a *Machtspruch*, a mere conception fulminated as a dogma and based on no insight into details. Before my choice, either street seemed as natural to you as to me. . . .

The quarrel which determinism has with chance unfortunately has nothing to do with this or that psychological detail. It is a quarrel altogether metaphysical. Determinism denies the ambiguity of future volitions, because it affirms that nothing future can be ambiguous. But we have said enough to meet the issue. Indeterminate future volitions *do* mean chance. Let us not fear to shout it from the house-tops if need be; for we now know that the idea of chance is, at bottom, exactly the same thing as the idea of gift—the one simply being a disparaging, and the other a eulogistic, name for anything on which we have no effective *claim*. . . .

In discussing the word "chance," I may at moments have seemed to be arguing for its real existence, I have not meant to do so yet. We have not yet ascertained whether this be a world of chance or no; at most, we have agreed that it seems so. And I now repeat what I said at the outset, that, from any strict theoretical point of view, the question is insoluble. To deepen our theoretic sense of the *difference* between a world with chances in it and a deterministic world is the most I can hope to do.

Up to this point James has been formulating the question, "Does any human behavior express free will?" To this question determinists and indeterminists propose incompatible answers. James has been fending off one objection that determinists bring against free will—that it implies that some human behavior is a matter of chance. From this point on, he begins to develop the claims and counterclaims implied in the title of his essay, "The Dilemma of Determinism." His aim is to formulate a dilemma that you face if you subscribe to determinism. His first move is to draw attention to the fact that all of us make regret judgments:

I wish first of all to show you just what the notion that this is a deterministic world implies. The implications I call your attention to are all bound up with the fact that it is a world in which we constantly have to make what I shall, with your permission, call judgments of regret. Hardly an hour passes in which we do not wish that something might be otherwise.

Hardly any one can remain *entirely* optimistic after reading the confession of the murderer at Brockton the other day: how to get rid of the wife whose continued existence bored him, he inveigled her into a deserted spot, shot her four times, and then, as she lay on the ground and said to him, "You didn't do it on purpose, did you, dear?" replied, "No, I didn't do it on purpose," as he raised a rock and smashed her skull. Such an occurrence, with the mild sentence and self-satisfaction of the prisoner, is a field for a crop of regrets, which one need not take up in detail. We feel that, although a perfect mechanical fit to the rest of the universe, it is a bad moral fit, and that something else would really have been better in its place.

His next move is to point out that if you are a determinist and if you authorize regret judgments, then you are committed to a pessimism with regard to anything in the world that you do or would find regrettable.

But for the deterministic philosophy the murder, the sentence, and the prisoner's optimism were all necessary from eternity; and nothing else for a moment had a ghost of a chance of being put in their place. To admit such a chance, the determinists tell us, would be to make a suicide of reason; so we must steel our hearts against the thought. And here our plot thickens, for we see the first of those difficult implications of determinism and monism which it is my purpose to make you feel. If this Brockton murder was called for by the rest of the universe, if it had come at its preappointed hour, and if nothing else would have been consistent with the sense of the whole, what are we to think of the universe? Are we stubbornly to stick to our judgment of regret, and say, though it *couldn't* be, yet it *would* have been a better universe with something different from this Brockton murder in it? That, of course, seems the natural and spontaneous thing for us to do; and yet it is nothing short of deliberately espousing a kind of pessimism. The judgment of regret calls the murder bad. Calling a thing bad means, if it means anything at all, that the thing ought not be, that something else ought to be in its stead. Determinism, in denying that anything else can be in its stead, virtually defines the universe as a place in which what ought to be is impossible—in other words, as an organism whose constitution is afflicted with an incurable taint, an irremediable flaw. The pessimism of a Schopenhauer says no more than this—that the murder is a symptom; and that it is a vicious symptom because it belongs to a vicious whole, which can express its nature no otherwise than by bringing forth just such a symptom as that at this particular spot. Regret for the murder must transform itself, if we are determinists and wise, into a larger regret. It is absurd to regret the murder alone. Other things being what they are, *it* could not be different. What we should regret is that whole frame of things of which the murder is one member. I see no escape whatever from this pessimistic conclusion if, being determinists, our judgment of regret is to be allowed to stand at all.

If you make regret judgments, then determinism will commit you to pessimism in regard to all things regrettable: none of them could have been otherwise. Suppose you do not relish this commitment, is there any way out of it or around it? James notes a move you might make:

The only deterministic escape from pessimism is everywhere to abandon the judgment of regret. That this can be done, history shows to be not impossible. The devil, *quoad existentiam*, may be good. That is, although he be a *principle* of evil, yet the universe, with such a principle in it, may practically be a better universe than it could have been without it. On every hand, in a small way, we find that a certain amount of evil is a condition by which a higher form of good is brought. There is nothing to prevent anybody from generalizing this view, and trust that if we could but see things in the largest of all ways, even such matters as this Brockton murder would appear to be paid for by the uses which follow in their train. An optimism *quand même*, a systematic and infatuated optimism like that ridiculed by Voltaire in his *Candide*, is one of the possible ideal ways in which a man may train himself to look upon life. . . .

Thus, our deterministic pessimism may become a deterministic optimism at the price of extinguishing our judgments of regret.

If you are a determinist and you judge anything to be regrettable, then your determinism will commit you to pessimism about all things regrettable. If, to avoid being committed to pessimism, you abandon all regret judgments ("They are wrong-headed," your determinism assures you), then what about these wrong-headed regret judgments? If they are wrong, at least in the sense of being wrong-headed, aren't *they* matter for regret? Would it not have been better if your regret judgments, being wrong-headed, had never been made?

But does not this immediately bring us into a curious logical predicament? Our determinism leads us to call our judgments of regret wrong, because they are pessimistic in implying that what is impossible yet ought to be. But how then about the judgments of regret themselves? If they are wrong, other judgments, judgments of approval presumably, ought to be in their place. But as they are necessitated, nothing else *can* be in their place; and the universe is just what it was before—namely, a place in which what ought to be appears impossible. We have got one foot out of the pessimistic bog, but the other one sinks all the deeper. We have rescued our actions from the bonds of evil, but our judgments are now held fast. When murders and treacheries cease to be sins, regrets are theoretic absurdities and errors. The theoretic and the active life thus play a kind of see-saw with each other on the ground of evil. The rise of either sends the other down. Murder and treachery cannot be good without regret being bad: regret cannot be good without treachery and murder being bad. Both, however, are supposed to have been foredoomed; so something must be fatally unreasonable, absurd, and wrong in the world. It must be a place of which either sin or error forms a necessary part. From this dilemma there seems at first sight no escape. Are we then so soon to fall back into the pessimism from which we thought we had emerged? And is there no possible way by which we may, with good intellectual consciences, call the cruelties and the treacheries, the reluctances and the regrets, *all* good together? . . .

Can the determinist get out of this predicament? James provides an "escape route," which leads straight into a very uncomfortable dilemma for the determinist. The determinist who has the very real experience of regret, and who thinks about that experience in the light of the doctrine of determinism, and who, accordingly, tries to escape the pessimism that seems to be looming on the horizon will eventually come face to face with a troublesome dilemma: a dilemma between pessimism and subjectivism.

The refuge from the quandary lies, as I said, not far off. The necessary acts we erroneously regret may be good, and yet our error in so regretting them may be also good, on one simple condition; and that condition is this: The world must not be regarded as a machine whose final purpose is the making real of any outward good, but rather as a contrivance for deepening the theoretic consciousness of what goodness and evil in their intrinsic nature are. Not the doing either of good or of evil is what nature cares for, but the knowing of them. Life is one long eating of the fruit of the tree of *knowledge*.

We have thus clearly revealed to our view what may be called the dilemma of determinism, so far as determinism pretends to think things out at all. A merely mechanical determinism, it is true, rather rejoices in not thinking them out. It is very sure that the universe must satisfy its postulate of physical continuity and coherence, but it smiles at any one who comes forward with a postulate of moral coherence as well. I may suppose, however, that the number of purely mechanical or hard determinists among you this evening is small. The determinism to whose seductions you are the most exposed is what I have called soft determinism—the determinism which allows considerations of good and bad to mingle with those of cause and effect in deciding what sort of a universe this may rationally be held to be. The dilemma of this determinism is one whose left horn is pessimism and whose right horn is subjectivism. In other words, if determinism is to escape pessimism, it must leave off looking at the goods and ills of life in a simple objective way, and regard them as materials, indifferent in themselves, for the production of consciousness, scientific and ethical, in us.

James's proposition to the determinist is that he or she opt for a combination of determinism and subjectivism. Then, to reassure the determinist, he does what he can to polish up a case for subjectivism when it is to be chosen as an alternative to pessimism. As he says, with something of a flourish:

> So much for the subjectivism! If the dilemma of determinism be to choose between it and pessimism, I see little room for hesitation from the strictly theoretical point of view. Subjectivism seems the more rational scheme. And the world may, possibly, for aught I know, be nothing else. When the healthy love of life is on one, and all its forms and its appetites seem so unutterably real; when the most brutal and the most spiritual things are lit by the same sun, and each is an integral part of the total richness—why, then it seems a grudging and sickly way of meeting so robust a universe to shrink from any of its facts and wish them not be. Rather take the strictly dramatic point of view, and treat the whole thing as a great unending romance which the spirit of the universe, striving to realize its own content, is eternally thinking out and representing to itself.

At this point James starts to back away from subjectivism as a payable price for determinism. If he puts too high a gloss on subjectivism, someone might ask why he did not subscribe to subjectivism and *then* subscribe to determinism. But James neither desires not intends to subscribe to determinism. He must therefore make clear why he, at least, will not subscribe to subjectivism. Thus:

> No one, I hope, will accuse me, after I have said all this, of underrating the reasons in favor of subjectivism. And now that I proceed to say why those reasons, strong as they are, fail to convince my own mind, I trust the presumption may be that my objections are stronger still.
>
> I frankly confess that they are on a practical order. If we practically take up subjectivism in a sincere and radical manner and follow its consequences, we meet with some that make us pause. Let a subjectivism begin in never so severe and intellectual a way, it is forced by the law of its nature to develop another side of itself and end with the corruptest curiosity. Once dismiss the notion that certain duties are good in themselves, and that we are here to do them, no matter how we feel about them; once consecrate the opposite notion that our performances and our violations of duty are for a common purpose, the attainment of subjective knowledge and feeling, and

that the deepening of these is the chief end of our lives—and at what point on the downward slope are we to stop? In theology, subjectivisim develops as its "left wing" antinomianism. In literature, its left wing is romanticism. And in practical life it is either a nerveless sentimentality or a sensualism without bounds.

Everywhere it fosters the fatalistic mood of mind. It makes those who are already too inert more passive still; it renders wholly reckless those whose energy is already in excess. All through history we find how subjectivism, as soon as it has a free career, exhausts itself in every sort of spiritual, oral, and practical license. Its optimism turns to an ethical indifference, which infallibly brings dissolution in its train.

As James makes clear, his grounds for rejecting subjectivism are "practical," not "theoretical." His point is not that if you commit yourself to subjectivism you may find yourself committed to an impossible conception of the world. His point is rather that if you commit yourself to subjectivism you may find yourself committed to a lifestyle that he, for one, rejects. He therefore refuses to subscribe to subjectivism as a way of going on to subscribe to determinism. So he stands committed against determinism and in favor of free willism, indeterminism. This conjures up, all over again, the objections and protests that center on such notions as "chance," "alternative possibilities," "lawless events," and so on. He resumes:

But this brings us right back, after such a long detour, to the question of indeterminism and to the conclusion of all I came here to say tonight. For the only consistent way of representing a pluralism and a world whose parts may affect one another through their conduct being either good or bad is the indeterministic way. What interest, zest, or excitement can there be in achieving the right way, unless we are enabled to feel that the wrong way is also a possible and a natural way—nay, more a menacing and an imminent way? And what sense can there be in condemning ourselves for taking the wrong way, unless we need have done nothing of the sort, unless the right way was open to us as well? I cannot understand the willingness to act, no matter how we feel, without the belief that acts are really good and bad. I cannot understand the belief that an act is bad, without regret at its happening. I cannot understand regret without the admission of real, genuine possibilities in the world. Only *then* is it other than a mockery to feel, after we have failed to do our best, that an irreparable opportunity is gone from the universe, the loss of which it must forever after mourn.

If you insist that this is all superstition, that possibility is in the eye of science and reason impossibility, and that if I act badly it is that the universe was foredoomed to suffer this defect, you fall right back into the dilemma, the labyrinth, of pessimism and subjectivism, from out of whose toils we have just wound our way.

Now, we are of course free to fall back, if we please. For my own part, though, whatever difficulties may beset the philosophy of objective right and wrong, and the indeterminism it seems to imply, determinism, with its alternative of pessimism or romanticism, contains difficulties that are greater still. But you will remember that I expressly repudiated awhile ago the pretension to offer any arguments which could be coercive in a so-called scientific fashion in this matter. And I consequently find myself, at the end of this long talk, obliged to state my conclusions in an altogether personal way. This personal method of appeal seems to be among the very conditions of the problem; and the most any one can do is to confess as candidly as he can the grounds for the faith that is in him, and leave his example to work on others as it may.

What then has he to say for himself? To fend off a commitment to determinism and subjectivism, is he willing to subscribe to a potentially loose and chaotic universe, to stab the entire scientific enterprise in the back, to give aid and comfort to all manner of tender-minded true believers? It may not be quite all that; but the chips are down and James does not hesitate to make clear where he proposes to place his wager:

> Let me, then, without circumlocution say just this. This world is enigmatical enough in all conscience, whatever theory we may take up toward it. The indeterminism I defend, the free-will theory of popular sense based on the judgment of regret, represents that world as vulnerable, and liable to be injured by certain of its parts if they act wrong. And it represents their acting wrong as a matter of possibility or accident, neither inevitable nor yet to be infallibly warded off. In all this, it is a theory devoid either of transparency or of stability. It gives us a pluralistic, restless universe, in which no single point of view can ever take in the whole scene; and to a mind possessed of the love of unity at any cost, it will, no doubt, remain forever inacceptable.

In summary, we have before us two rival philosophical doctrines: free will and determinism. James challenges us, "Which doctrine produces greater subjective satisfaction? Which doctrine exhibits more rationality?" James's whole discussion has attempted to convince us that greater subjective satisfaction and more rationality are to be found on the side of free will. You will recall that his discussion focused on an allegedly regrettable event: the Brockton murder. If the determinist finds such an event regrettable, then the determinist seems committed to pessimism because that event would have been mandated by the universe and to regret it would require regretting the entire universe. But pessimism—regretting the universe day by day, hour by hour—is not a subjectively satisfying perspective. To avoid pessimism, James suggests that the determinist could adopt the view that some evil is necessary in the world to form a beautiful balance of contrasts. In that case, the murder could be celebrated because it would add to the harmony of the whole. Yet the optimism that this move would allow the determinist is short-lived because if the murder is now something to celebrate, then the previous regretting of the murder must have been mistaken and regrettable. If so, then the determinist is committed to regretting the entire universe that caused him or her to be mistaken in the first place. So once again the determinist is thrust back into the unsatisfying posture of pessimism. Finally to avoid pessimism, the determinist could affirm that the universe's goal is the generation of individual theoretical consciousnesses capable of making increasingly subtle distinctions. In that case, the determinist could celebrate all events—including murders and his or her own mistaken ideas—because every event could contribute to his mandated destiny of classifying and analyzing things. So the determinist could now experience the subjective satisfaction of an optimistic perspective, a perspective that allows for the celebration of every event. Yet, says James, take a hard look at what the optimistic determinist has paid for this satisfaction. Has not the determinist at this point fallen into a sea of standardlessness where each individual becomes a law unto him- or herself? After all, my consciousness may not be at the same level of development as yours, and if at my level I happen to value the Holocaust as elegant and good, whereas you evaluate it differently, can you legitimately condemn my view? After all, is it not the only view I could have had? If so, how could you legitimately judge my view as mistaken in some sense? Optimistic determinism, then, seems to slide into subjectivism where each individual is a law unto him- or herself. Is that position, however, really personally satisfying? Furthermore, would not such subjectivism force us to surrender the whole moral experience of humankind where acts like the Holocaust stand condemned as unmitigated evil? Does not determinism, then, fail to cohere with the moral experience of humankind? Does not determinism then reveal itself to be less rational and less satisfying than the doctrine of free will?

NOTE ON SOURCES.   The material in this section is from William James, "The Dilemma of Determinism" in John McDermott, ed., *The Writings of William James* (New York: Random House, 1967), pp. 587–609.

5   KARL POPPER

AN ARGUMENT FOR INDETERMINISM

FROM JAMES TO POPPER.   We have already seen Sartre's attack on determinism. His insistence on free will is based on his characterization of what it is to be human and to act in a world where there is no God to provide meaning and sense. He does not directly challenge what many have seen as the great ally of determinism, science. Moreover, there is some irony in the fact that Sartre's atheism fits well with the atheism (or agnosticism) and determinism that many thinkers have found associated with the assumptions of science. Because Sartre does not challenge determinism as the implication of a scientific world view, Sartre's argument for free will is often found to be less than convincing by those of a scientific temperament.

For an example of a challenge to Sartre, we turn to Karl Popper, a hard-headed philosopher of science; a philosopher well-schooled in mathematics and physics. When such a thinker argues for free will precisely by challenging the so-called implications of science, the result is two-fold. (1) We get an important nonexistentialist look at how philosophers argue. (2) We get an argument that, Popper claims, totally undercuts determinism at its very (scientific) base.

BIOGRAPHICAL NOTE.   Karl Popper was born in Vienna, Austria in 1902. He studied mathematics and physics as well as philosophy at the University of Vienna. Popper was influential in shaping some of the views of Rudolph Carnap, one of the members of the Vienna Circle. (See the section on positivistic philosophy of science and the biographical note on Herbert Feigl.) In 1937, Sir Karl went to teach at Canterbury University College in New Zealand where he stayed until 1945, when he left for a position at the London School of Economics of the University of London. His work on the logic of confirmation, which has come to be termed "falsificationism," is one of the most influential pieces on philosophy of science of the twentieth century. He is also well known for his book on social and political theory, *The Open Society and Its Enemies*, which was published in 1945. For his many contributions to philosophy, he was knighted in 1964.

THE ARGUMENT OF THE PASSAGES.   Popper uses the same tripartite division of the world as Eccles (Chapter 2). Each division is called a world. World 1 is the world of physical entities. World 2 is the world of consciousness, including dispositions to act (Ryle, Chapter 2) and any unconscious states. World 3 is the world of the products of consciousness, especially things like scientific theories, novels, and other works of art.

Popper argues that determinism can be true only if it would be possible to predict all of Worlds 2 and 3 from World 1. This prediction, made in World 3, in turn, would be possible only if the laws governing World 1 and its relation to the other worlds are themselves purely mechanistic. Popper argues that contemporary science, especially quantum mechanics, has shown that this is not so.

Popper's argument is two-fold.

First, he briefly outlines what is called the Heisenberg Uncertainty Principle. It states that electrons (and all subatomic particles) do not have *at any one time*, determinable mass, position, and velocity. Since mass x velocity = momentum, this principle could be restated as "electrons do not have a determinable momentum and position at any one given time." (More accurately, the principle states that, for any chosen degree of accuracy, one can only find a determinate velocity or a determinate momentum, but never both.) It is currently believed that the reason for this is that electrons and other subatomic particles do not have a determinate momentum and position. Electrons and other subatomic particles are inherently indeterministic. Their positions and velocities are random, chance events. (This interpretation of some of the findings of quantum mechanics, called the Copenhagen Interpretation, is different from saying that the indeterminability is due to our not being clever enough to know how to make the appropriate measurements.)

In order to discuss the ideas of indeterminism and determinism, I introduced in 1965 the metaphor of *clouds* and *clocks*. For the ordinary man, a cloud is highly unpredictable and, indeed, indeterminate: the vagaries of the weather are proverbial. By contrast, a clock is highly predictable and, indeed, a perfect clock is a paradigm of a mechanical and determinist material system.

Taking clouds and clocks to start with as paradigms of indeterminist and determinist systems we can formulate the view of a determinist, such as a Democritean atomist, as follows:

All physical systems are, in reality, clocks.

Thus, the whole world is a clockwork of atoms pushing each other along like the cogs of a cogwheel. Even the clouds are parts of the cosmic clockwork; though owing to the complexity and practical unpredictability of the molecular movements in them, they may create in us the illusion that they are not clocks, but undetermined clouds.

Quantum mechanics has had important things to say about this matter. It says, indeed, that the electrons form a *cloud* round the atomic nucleus and that the positions and velocities of the various electrons within this cloud are indeterminate and therefore indeterminable.

. . . .the interpretation of the atomic nucleus as a system of particles in rapid motion and of the surrounding electrons as an electron cloud is sufficient to destroy the old atomistic intuition of a mechanical determinism. The interaction between atoms or between molecules has a *random* aspect, a *chance* aspect; "chance" not only in the Aristotelian sense in which it is opposed to "purpose," but chance in the sense in which it is subject to the objective probabilistic theory of random events, rather than to anything like exact mechanical laws.

Thus the thesis that all physical systems including clouds, are, in reality, clocks, has turned out to be mistaken. According to quantum mechanics we have to replace it by the opposite thesis, as follows:

All physical systems, including clocks, are, in reality, clouds.

The old mechanism turns out to be an illusion, created by the fact that sufficiently heavy systems (systems consisting of a few thousands of atoms, such as the big organic macromolecules, and heavier systems) interact *approximately* according to the clockwork laws of classical mechanics, provided they do not react with each other chemically. Systems of crystals—the solid physical bodies which we handle in ordinary tools like our watches and clocks, and which constitute the main furniture of our environment—do behave approximately (but only approximately) like mechanical deterministic systems. This fact is, indeed, the source of our mechanistic and deterministic illusions.

Each cogwheel of our watches is a structure of crystals, a lattice of molecules held together, like the atoms in the molecules, by electrical forces. It is strange, but it is a fact, that it is electricity which underlies the laws of mechanics. Moreover, each atom and each molecule vibrates, with amplitudes depending on the temperature (or *vice versa*); and if the cogwheel gets hot, the clockwork will stop because the cogs expand. (If it gets hotter still it will melt.)

Second, Popper uses an argument to show how our concept of heat and temperature makes it necessary to conclude that World 1 is not enough to explain Worlds 2 and 3.

The interaction between heat and the watch is very interesting. On the one hand, we can regard the temperature of the watch as defined by the average velocity of its vibrating atoms and molecules. On the other hand, we can heat or cool the watch by putting it in contact with hot or cold surroundings. According to present theory temperature is due to the movement of the individual atoms; at the same time it is something on a level different from that of individual atoms in motion—a holistic or emergent level—since it is defined by the *average* velocity of *all* the atoms.

Heat behaves very much like a fluid ("caloric"), and we can *explain* the laws of this behavior by an appeal to the way in which an increase or decrease in the velocity of an atom—or a group of atoms—spreads to neighboring atoms. This explanation can be described as a "reduction": it reduces the properties of heat to the properties of motion of the atoms or molecules. Yet the reduction is not complete; for new ideas have to be used—the ideas of *molecular disorder* and of *averaging*, and these are indeed, ideas on a new level.

Popper reminds us that in Worlds 2 and 3, we have the concepts of heat and temperature as well as the theory of heat as a fluid. In this theory, temperature measures heat by measuring the average velocity of atoms. World 1 contains only individual atoms in motion. But this is not enough to yield our concept of heat. We add to our concept of atoms in motion the concept of an average and the concept of atoms randomly in motion. Heat is produced when the atoms *on average* begin to increase their velocities. Textbooks usually show heat produced when lots of atoms begin banging against the side of a container. This is a model (see Chapter 2) of heat production. According to Popper, determinists have made a simple error in reasoning. They have assumed that the concepts added in Worlds 2 and 3 must exist in World 1. But this is just an assumption. In *The Open Universe* (Totowa, New Jersey: Rowman and Littlefied, 1956, 1982) Popper points out that determinists have forgotten that it is theories which are simple, not necessarily the world. We create our theories and through our theories come to know the world. In creating the theories, we, therefore, in a sense, create the world. This is a way of saying that there is no way to disentangle the Worlds from each other. There is no independent way of knowing how any one world is independent from the others. Thus, it may well be that the world looks simple, and therefore deterministic, only because our theories are simple and deterministic.

To see this more clearly, suppose I ask you to pick someone up at the airport—someone you have never seen. To make it easier for you, I give you a snapshot of the person. It is a very clear photograph. You understand how cameras work and how pictures are developed. You would never think to ask, "Is this a good likeness?" even though you have never seen the person before. You are making some assumptions. One of those assumptions is that clear photographs properly developed yield accurate likenesses of their subjects.

We can, then, put Popper's critique of determinism another way. Determinists have argued in a circle. They have begged the question by building determinism into the very theories that we use to find out about the world. As if this were not bad enough, determinists have gone on to use what we find out to support the claim that the world is really deterministic.

NOTE ON SOURCES.   The material in this section is from John Eccles and Karl Popper, *The Self and Its Brain* (London: Springer-Verlag, 1976).

JOHN W. BENDER

COMPATIBILISM IS NO QUAGMIRE

FROM POPPER TO BENDER.   Quantum mechanics is a well-established science. One of its implications is that determinism (in the form of strict predictability) cannot be achieved. Quantum mechanics has established that World 1 is, at base, random. The randomness is not a feature of our inability to know the right variables. The randomness is a feature of the microstructure of World 1.

But does quantum mechanics establish a free will? Isn't it possible that quantum mechanics might turn out to be wrong? Isn't it possible that while there is randomness on the subatomic (micro) level, there is determinism on the macro level? One need not have a smooth transition from micro to macro levels. That is, there might be two sets of laws with a discontinuity between the levels. Or, as Bender will point out in his article on compatibilism, the actual affects of the micro world, where there is indeterminism, are negligible on the macro level, which is where human actions take place.

It seems reasonable to ask, "Just how predictable is human behavior?" Certainly, the better we get at predicting human behavior, and the better our psychoactive drugs for controlling and changing behavior, the easier it will be to believe that human behavior is determined. Just as physics seems to make it clear that bodies that obey the laws of physics are determined (in the sense of fully predictable) so it has seemed to many that psychology, especially as put forward by Sigmund Freud, makes it clear that human behavior is just as determined and just as predictable (in principle) as the behavior of pendulums and billiard balls.

It would be a disservice to the free will/determinism issue if we did not examine Freud's theory of human behavior, since many contemporary writers appeal to the strengths and weaknesses of depth psychology in order to support their views on the free will/determinism issue.[1]

FREUD'S DEPTH PSYCHOLOGY AND DETERMINISM

"That pizza tasted so good I couldn't stop."
"It hurt so much I cried; I didn't want to, but I cried."
"I'll just feel terrible unless I do."
"Clean your room or you can't go!"

Those four comments are examples of situations where people are not in total control. Sometimes there is an important aspect of control coming from the inside (the taste of pizza); sometimes it comes from the outside (Clean your room!). There are medical conditions that cause us to look a certain way or to have a certain special physiology. Other medical conditions cause self-destructive behaviors. (For example, Lesch-Nyhan disease causes people literally to bite through and eat their lips. They would continue this self-immolating behavior except that they are restrained.)

Put all of this together with the possibility that

1. Some form of the Identity Theory may be reasonable; and/or;
2. People are very much like computers: a prewritten software being executed by a limited hardware

---

1 A much read article using Freudian ideas to substantiate determinism is "Free Will and Psychoanalysis" by John Hospers. It is reprinted in many anthologies; e.g., Joel Feinberg, ed., *Reason and Responsibility*, 7th ed. (Belmont, CA: Wadsworth Publishing Co., 1989).

and you get the view that people are very limited in the actions that are really open to them. We may *feel* as if we can do just about anything; but this is just a feeling thrown into doubt by science.

DEPTH PSYCHOLOGY AND FREUD

"Don't give me that. I can see right through you."
"Why do I keep falling for the same kind of woman (man)?"

These are everyday examples of our belief that the things we and others do and say have explanations beyond what we see on the surface. The explanations we give are sometimes called deep explanations. Hence the expression, depth psychology. Any psychological theory which focuses on the existence of an unconscious mental life is called a depth psychology.

Sigmund Freud (1856–1939) offered a full-blown depth psychology. In his view, what we see on the surface is a mere glimmer of how our unconscious has been processing our experiences. Something as simple as a dream turns into a complex discovery about a person's deepest anxieties. Something as simple as not remembering a word is revealing. None of this would be possible if we were in total control of our mental lives. Depth psychology, therefore, suggests that some form of determinism is true.

We will focus on one part of Freud's thought, trying to make sense of Freud's claim that all people are determined to seek pleasure; that this is the best explanation for all behavior.

FREUD'S MODEL

According to Freud, all our mental input is transformed into electrical energy. It can be stored as memory or used and discarded (literally discharged). Storing can take at least two forms. It can be put where we can retrieve it, or it can be stored in such a way that we cannot retrieve it. To make it unretrievable requires that the original input be changed. This takes energy that would normally be used for something else. Also, keeping the changed input hidden requires energy that would normally be used to do something else. Thus, every time information is stored in this nonretrievable fashion, our energy equilibrium is thrown off kilter.

On the conscious level, the retrievable energy is what we remember. The nonretrievable energy is what we cannot dredge up from memory. It is in our unconscious. The name for the mechanism for putting it there and keeping it there is "repression." On the mental level, we repress what we find unpleasant.

Combining the physical model and the mental version, we see what Freud meant when he said that repression is always a failure. Our equilibrium is thrown off. The resulting uneasiness will then find its way into consciousness and cause us emotional problems.

For Freud, *pleasure* was a term covering a spectrum from the intense pleasure of sexual activity to the difficult-to-specify feelings that everything's right with the world. In fact, it was this latter sort of pleasure that Freud associated with energetic equilibrium. So Freud's idea that people exhibit a drive to seek pleasure is not strange or demeaning; nor should it seem threatening.

Freud maintained that sexual desires were far more frequent, and occurred earlier, than anyone realized. They were unconscious longings whose existence, Freud felt, provided the best explanation for much of the odd behavior of his patients. The repression of sexual longings often was at the root of psychological problems, according to Freud. At one time, Freud argued that the cause of repression was often trauma; e.g., an incident of incest. But Freud later decided, perhaps incorrectly, that these memories of sexual trauma were really not memories at all. Rather, he came to believe that they were fantasies and that having these forbidden fantasies forced the repression.

FREUD'S EVIDENCE

Freud presented many cases to substantiate his views. There are two significant problems with Freud's use of his cases. First, he developed his theory as he dealt with his patients using a back-and-forth procedure. That is, he used his cases to build his theory as well as to support his theory. Some thinkers who specialize in scientific methodology do not accept this method (a variation of what some call "bootstrapping") as legitimate. Second, to confirm his views, Freud had to interpret his cases as successes; that is, Freud assumed that his patients were cured. There is good reason to think that Freud overestimated his cures.

Freud believed in the principle known as "ontogeny recapitulates phylogeny." This is the principle that the life history of an organism (ontogeny) reflects the total life history of its entire species (phylogeny). Packed into each of us is a history of "nature red in tooth and claw," where desires are acted upon immediately, where the strong take from the weak, and where the primary goal of the individual is to perpetuate the species. Because of the relationship between sex and pleasure, we seek sex, but often this seeking is unconscious.

Thus, according to Freud, our lives are limited by the history of our species, our individual experiences (especially as infants), and our individual biologies. I cannot be (nor could I have become) an Olympic swimmer. This would become clear from an examination of my genes, my biology in general, and my early environment (no pools nearby and parents who were afraid of the water and overprotective). But I did learn how to swim reasonably well and this could have been predicted by a good analyst who knew me well. Of course, just how well I would be able to swim and exactly when, would not be easily predictable. In other words, Freud probably did not believe that each and every particular action we make is fully determined or precisely predictable; but rather, somewhat predictable with enough information. Thus, it would be a mistake to appeal to Freud to underwrite one's belief in strict determinism.

Now let us return to compatibilism, the view that allows causality to coexist with free will. If we know that Fred, a vegetarian, is going to the market, then we can predict that he will not buy beef. Is Fred's act determined? Yes, says Stace—it is determined by Fred's decision not to eat beef, which is a function of Fred's various beliefs about meat-eating. But, Stace points out, determinism in this sense is not incompatible with free will, for it is Fred's deciding that makes him free. This is really how we use the words *free* and *determined*.

Stace may be right about how we use these words, but how we use words may be irrelevant to the question, "Are we free or determined?" Maybe we use these words the way we do because we have made a mistake about our being free. Our dictionaries add entries as scientific advances are made and as the scientific terms become a part of our everyday vocabulary. For example, terms such as *black hole, user-friendly* and *DNA* are now common parts of our vocabulary. If some scientific finding convinced us that we were not free, we might well make some adjustments in the way that we used words.

What role does predictability play in determinism? If we know that our vegetarian friend is allergic to citrus fruits, we can do a pretty good job predicting which fruits he will buy. Our predictions require that there are rough regularities governing human behavior, and that we know certain things. If, for determinism to be true, we had to be able to predict not just that Fred will buy apples but also how many, what kind, how red, and what shape, as well as what Fred was thinking or felt as he looked at the apples, determinism would be just about impossible. "Impossible" meaning that we, as very limited humans, could not make the predictions—but not "impossible" in the sense that there were no regularities. Part of the free will issue, then, is what to count as the appropriate prediction.

What role does the *feeling* of freedom play in deciding the free will/determinism issue? Often we feel that our decisions are constrained by circumstances. For example, we cannot register by computer for a class in college if we lack the prerequisites for it. We use the expression "my arm was twisted" to mean that the constraint was felt as clearly as if we were physically forced to do something. Occasionally, we are physically determined. When a doctor elicits a reflex by using a rubber hammer on our knees, our leg pops up as if it had a life of its own. As we move further and further from cases such as these, our feeling of freedom increases. The determinist does not deny that we feel free when there are no clear constraints. What the determinist does deny is that this *feeling* of freedom shows that we *are* free. Our feeling of freedom may just indicate our inability to sense that we are determined.

Indeed, whether they are free or determined, our feelings are just a mark of how accurately we are able to experience that freedom or determinism. We experience it one way when a gun is held to our heads, another way when we are threatened with being grounded by our parents, another way when we are in the throes of the flu and cannot control our shivering, and still another way when we cannot identify the actual cause of our actions. But in all of these cases, our feeling free or determined is irrelevant to whether we actually are free or determined.

If we are determined, what is the purpose of creating moral theories? After all, whatever is going to happen will happen, no matter what! Here is where inability to predict human behavior may play an important role. Here is where compatibilism has a good point.

Suppose that our being determined is a metaphysical and scientific truth. It still does not follow that we will know and be able to predict exactly how people will act. In this regard, we do the best we can with what we do know. For example, we know that people in general try to avoid pain and seek pleasurable experiences. We have much evidence that the threat of pain can keep people from doing something and the promise of pleasure will act as an incentive. Don't most of us remember being told, "No dessert if you don't eat your vegetables"? Thus, we use pain as punishment and pleasure as rewards to help shape behavior. It makes sense to do this, even if we are convinced that if only we knew more about human behavior, we could ensure accurate predictions. But still, isn't it unfair to punish someone for doing what they are determined to do? The answer is, strictly speaking, "yes." But if our goal is to shape the behavior of individuals and society, then moral theories will do us more good than abstract principles of determinism.

With all these replies and rejoinders concerning predictability, quantum mechanics, the feeling of freedom, and morality, many philosophers have decided that the answer to the free will/determinism issue lies in the analysis of the concept "could have done otherwise." Our next author, John W. Bender, tries to show that analyzing "could have done otherwise" is important and can be done. Once it is done, Bender claims, compatibilism will be seen as a reasonable answer to the free will controversy.

BIOGRAPHICAL NOTE.   John Bender was born in McKeesport, Pennsylvania in 1951. He received a Ph.D. in philosophy from Harvard University in 1978. Before coming to Ohio University in 1985, Bender taught at Dartmouth. He is especially interested in the problems of epistemology and aesthetics, areas in which he has published books and articles.

THE ARGUMENT OF THE PASSAGES.   When reading the article, focus on Bender's examples: the computer and the dam, the golfer, and the prediction room. The finer points of the article, especially the commentary on the philosophers Don Locke, B. Gert, and T. Duggan, are not necessary to make the case for compatibilism that Bender is trying to make. [We have bracketed these passages to make them easier to find.—Eds.]

Bender begins by emphasizing the need for conceptual clarity. By now you should recognize this as a theme in philosophical analysis. Bender then states the thesis of determinism in terms of strict predictability. The determinist considers that the world marches on inexorably and with certainty. Our inability to predict exactly what will happen is just that—our inability. It is because of our ignorance. It is not a feature of the world. Notice how this is similar to the issues raised by the interpretation of quantum mechanics.

Before he analyzes the idea of "ability to do otherwise," Bender dismisses some usual interpretations of determinism. Pay special attention to the example of the dam. A dam can be totally controlled by a computer, which is a totally deterministic system. Bender maintains that it makes sense to say that the computer—not the programmer—is really in control.

This sort of example calls upon you to use your intuitions. What makes sense to you in this case? Many philosophers appeal to these sorts of examples to help defend their positions. It is important to realize that such examples are not arguments. If you do not find them compelling, then all that can be said is that your intuitions do not, in this case, match Bender's intuitions.

I. A FIRST PASS OVER THE REAL QUAGMIRE

Reach for today's paper or any history book and you see clearly how many ways there are to threaten humans' sense of freedom. Lamentably, far too many of us are unfree as a result of force, coercion, and suppression. Others feel a loss of freedom due to drug dependency or psychological disabilities such as compulsions and phobias. Rampant as these political and personal problems are, there may be another, even more widespread, indeed *universal* threat to our freedom—at least if certain philosophical views about the world and our place in it are true. Many philosophers throughout the Western tradition have suggested that if the world is causally deterministic in nature, then the cherished idea that we humans have freedom of the will, and are able to perform actions by freely willing to do so, is nothing more than an illusion we harbor, a kind of romantic and inflated self-image that cannot be squared with the more hard-headed, scientific, and naturalistic view of physical reality. Freedom and determinism just cannot be mixed or blended into one coherent and comforting view; they are, it is argued, *incompatible*.

But if incompatibilism is correct, every scientific advance that uncovers more of the causal workings of our bodies and brains and their interactions with the environment becomes a reason for anxiety and dread, a relentless chipping away at our view of ourselves as free agents. It is a terrible and unenlightened attitude to fear science, but it is even worse to be riddled with doubt about one's freedom of will and moral responsibility for one's actions. It is not surprising, then, that many philosophers have taken up the challenge of arguing that incompatibilism is wrong, that freedom *can* exist in a deterministic world, that the concept of freedom is not, after all, at logical odds with the possibility that our every action may be causally determined.

Arguing effectively for this compatibilism obviously depends on getting clearer than we ordinarily are about the concepts that are central to the philosophical issue, most notably, determinism and acting from one's own free will, but other concepts also have played important roles in the argument, as we will soon see. To be successful and convincing, the compatibilist needs to show that the sense in which a determined action is causally *necessitated* is neither our ordinary nor an important sense in which the agent is not free or able to do some other, different action in the situation.

If this sounds to you like the compatibilist is playing some kind of evasive verbal game rather than doing serious philosophy, it must be conceded that you are not alone, as many fine philosophers, most famously, William James, have charged that compatibilism is a "quagmire of evasion" (1884, p. 40). Remember, however, that no debate can be intelligently stated, let alone carried on and perhaps settled, if the concepts utilized are not carefully analyzed, and their different senses distinguished and evaluated. In the attempt to recover our freedom from the supposed challenge of determinism, vague and unclear concepts offer no shortcut worth taking, and it is precisely such concepts and not compatibilism that produce the quagmire around the problem of freedom of the will. Far from evading the problem, compatibilism *solves* it (or so I will argue) by showing how greater clarity about the concept of freedom also places determinism in a less threatening light. This paper can be viewed as my attempt to *cause* you to believe in the truth of compatibilism; but, being a philosopher and not a brain-washer, I hope that you come to believe it *freely*, and I expect that I have done nothing here that makes you *unable* to disbelieve it.

II. DETERMINISM, FORCE, CONTROL, AND ABILITY TO DO OTHERWISE

There are a number of inferences that are commonly but mistakenly made when assessing the impact determinism would have on our freedom, and these must be avoided if we are to steer clear of the quagmire. First, though, we need to ask what the thesis of determinism actually asserts.

Determinism is a position about the ultimate lawful nature of the events, states, and conditions that constitute the ever-changing physical world. Since I take human actions themselves to be events of various sorts, they are not immune from the deterministic thesis. The thesis is this: that every event and state of affairs that occurs has a complete cause to be found in the antecedent events and conditions occurring in the world. This means that the occurrence of every event or state is in principle deducible from some set of prior occurring conditions and the laws of nature. The thrust of determinism can be restated both in terms of *probability* and *predictability*. The image of the natural world that the deterministic thesis offers is one in which probability plays no essential or ineliminable role. Probabilities enter our actual science, according to the determinist, only because of our partial ignorance of the real causal structure of the world. If we could somehow lift this veil of ignorance and have complete knowledge of the relevant antecedent conditions, as well as precise statements of the laws of nature, rather than our mere approximations, then it would be possible in principle for us, or at least some "super-mind" or super-computer, to predict with *certainty* (not merely high probability) the occurrence and details of any future event of interest.

It may be thought that if *this* is determinism, then determinism is no threat at all to our freedom, since it is just false—our best subatomic physics now tells us that there are *fundamental* indeterminacies or probabilities at the level of quanta. Quantum indeterminacy is at odds with what we may call *universal* determinism, the claim, as I stated it above, that *every* event is causally determined. But it is important to remember that our scientific theorizing goes on at many different levels: micro, macro and astronomical; sociological, psychological, physiological, biochemical, and neurophysical, and the indeterminacies thought to characterize the subatomic level may so cancel each other out that their effects have only the most infinitesimal chance of "percolating up" and violating whatever determinacies may be discovered at higher theoretical levels. As physicist Heinz Pagels notes:

> For a flying tennis ball, the uncertainties due to quantum theory are only one part in about ten million billion billion billion (10^{-34}). Hence, a tennis ball to a high degree of accuracy obeys the deterministic rules of classical physics. Even for a bacterium the effects are only about one part in a billion and it really doesn't experience the quantum world either. (1982,90)

Hence, for all that quantum theory has to say, we could be like the tennis balls; i.e., our actions (or at least the bodily movements that are constitutive of our actions) may be explainable in terms of near-deterministic neurophysical regularities of one sort or another. Anyone worried that determinism undercuts our free will is bound to be equally anxious over this nearly-deterministic scenario in which our actions are, for all intents and purposes, a direct causal function of our neural or physiological states. It is this near-deterministic picture of the world that has some likelihood of being true, I think, but for the sake of the arguments, I am willing to assume that there is some level of physical and neurophysical descriptions of events and states on which our actions can be viewed as their completely deterministic effects.

One inference that appears to many to be correct claims that determinism's truth implies that we are *forced* by natural laws to perform the actions that we in fact perform. But this is a misuse of the concept of force and a misunderstanding of the idea of a physical law. To be forced into an action requires that there is a for*cer* of some sort; if *x* forces *y*, *y* interacts with *x*. But physical events cannot correctly be said to interact with *natural laws*, and true causal laws do not force events to occur; they are merely the regularities that are to be found concerning types of events. Sometimes, we are forced by other people or circumstances to do certain things, and in such cases we often feel unfree. However, deterministic laws don't force us to do anything.

"But even if laws don't force my actions, it is still true that if they are causally determined I am not in *control* of my actions—it is not up to me what actions to perform," it will be replied. Certainly it is true that loss of freedom very often involves loss of control of one sort or another, and none of us wants our actions and lives to be out of our control. But the notion of control is not at odds with determinism, and itself seems to imply that there *is* a strong causal connection between the controlling and controlled events.

Consider a simple example. The flood gates of a dam may be controlled by a computer that receives input about water heights, current rainfall and runoff, water demands downstream, and so on. The computer may output commands to various motors and apparatus that increase or decrease the water flow through the gates. The workings of this system can be viewed as fully deterministic, and yet it is still true that the computer (and not some human gatekeeper, say,) is controlling the water flow. To suggest that the computer is *not* in control, on the grounds that the system is deterministic, would be ludicrous. We, of course, are not as simple as this mechanism, and our control of our actions is infinitely subtler, but complexity does not require or imply indeterminacy.

After establishing a sense for "able to do otherwise," Bender uses an example to clarify the compatibilist position. He asks us to consider a golfer. Bender points out that there is a point in the swing where a hook (as opposed to a straight drive) is just about impossible. But from this it does not follow that before that point, the golfer might have done otherwise—might have hooked his shot. Using this example, Bender concludes that "the ability to do otherwise" is best spelled out in terms of a conditional sense of ability. That is, to be able to have hit a hook and not a straight drive means that *if* the golfer had seen the fairway differently, *if* the golfer had . . . , *if* the golfer had . . . etc., *then* she would have hooked the ball. (The "if . . . then" form is what constitutes the conditional.) These abilities to do otherwise, Bender claims, easily coexist with determinism.

In a third attempt to restate determinism's undermining effect on freedom, it might be retorted: "If I freely will a certain action, then it must be true that I could have done otherwise in the situation; I must have been able to do otherwise if I had so desired, and *this* is what cannot be the case if determinism is true, because given the antecedent conditions of the situation, my action is the only outcome consistent with the relevant physical laws."

Although this response contains what I think is the core of the problem, *viz.*, that acting from a free will requires that the agent be able to do otherwise, the matter is complicated.

Philosophers have long known, for example, that acting from free will does not mean simply that one acts the way one desires or wants to, for if someone cannot control what she desires, her will may not be free when she acts from those desires. So freedom of the will is not just the ability to do what one wants.

Some philosophers have also challenged the main assumption that apparently is being made in this response, namely, that an action is done from the agent's free will only if the agent could have done otherwise, Harry Frankfurt (1969) asks us to consider an imaginary case in which Black is bent on Jones's acting a certain way, so much so that Black has found a way to manipulate the neural processes of Jones's brain to compel the desired action if Jones doesn't decide to perform it of his own accord. As it turns out, Black does not have to use his sinister power because Jones performs the act for reasons of his own. The action in this case seems to be done from Jones's free will even though he could not have done otherwise (since Black would have stepped in).

Even if, as Frankfurt's example may be indicating, freely willing an action does not logically entail that the agent could have done otherwise. I suggest that compatibilists ought to accept as a working principle that freedom in a deterministic world does require that agents be correctly describable as having the *ability to do otherwise* in a strong and ordinary sense of that phrase. This concession should keep us from begging any important questions against the incompatibilist, while allowing us to set aside the difficult and technical matter of the relationship between "could have done otherwise" and "ability to do otherwise." We must turn now to the questions, "Am I or am I not able to do otherwise if my actions are determined?" and "Exactly what sense of 'ability to do otherwise' do we care about when we care about freedom of the will?"

III. ABILITIES WEAK AND STRONG

[As we have already seen, compatibilism has been accused of being evasive, but it is another charge that we're concerned with here: weakness. It is frequently claimed that if our actions are causally necessitated in the way they must be in the determinist's view of the world, then any sense of ability to do otherwise that could be ascribed to the agents in that world is going to be weak, overly qualified, or overly conditional in nature. The "guts" of our notion of freedom will have been lost. Let's look at how one contemporary philosopher has argued in this fashion.

Don Locke (1975, 111–112) has concluded that free action "in any full and important sense" is incompatible with determinism because in a deterministic world we would not have the ability to do otherwise in the "categorical and unqualified" sense he believes free action requires. A categorical and unqualified ability is one true of the agent in the *present* circumstances (not an ability the agent would have if circumstances were different in some way), and it is unconditional in form, i.e., it is not an ability to do something different *if* the agent wants to, or is motivated to; it is an ability the agent presently has *period*, "in the very circumstances," "at the time and on the occasion in question," "then and there," with no "ifs" to it (107–111).

Locke argues that some weaker (conditional) sense of ability *can* be attributed to us in a deterministic world, for example, the ability to act differently *if we had wanted to*. But this is little consolation, since, as I have already suggested, this ability is not enough to guarantee our freedom. If you cannot change your wants because *they* are determined, is your will free in a full enough sense? Locke thinks not:

> [O]nce this distinction [between categorical, unqualified ability and conditional ability] is drawn the question arises whether free action, in any full and important sense, requires only that the agent be able to act differently if he wanted to, or whether it requires rather that he be able to do it categorically and without qualification. Consider finally the case of a man suffering from psychological inhibitions or fixations which render him unable to perform, or alternately refrain from, a certain action precisely because they ensure that nothing can motivate him to any such thing. It may be true of him that he could do it if he wanted, so long as there is nothing which makes it impossible for him to succeed should he be motivated. But nevertheless he is unable to do it, since nothing could ever bring him to do it. Does he act freely? For myself I say not. In this final sense of free action, therefore, free action is after all incompatible with causal determinism. (112)

This passage indicates that Locke conceives the threat of determinism and that of certain psychiatric maladies as sharing the same philosophical explanation: phobias, compulsions and fixations render their victims unable to do otherwise in certain sorts of circumstances, and determinism, if true, would render each of us unable to do otherwise in every action situation.

There is, however, a philosophically important disanalogy between these two cases. It is obviously meaningful to speak, for example, of the ability which most of us have and claustrophobics lack, to spend reasonably long periods in confining spaces. This ability may be called categorical and unqualified, if we like, but only because the conditions which we take to be relevant to having or lacking the ability (size of the space, duration of time, etc.) are clearly far less than a deterministic set of circumstances, and relative to *them* you and I may be said categorically and unconditionally to have the ability to bear certain kinds of confinement. We can ride an elevator twenty-five stories up, any and every day, without much mental preparation, and regardless of our mood-swings or current emotional states. A claustrophobic cannot.

But it cannot similarly be claimed that there *is* an unconditional ability to do otherwise in deterministic circumstances and that each of us lacks that ability. There is *no clear sense* to be made of a categorical and unqualified ability to do otherwise in *deterministic* circumstances; it is *conceptually* impossible for Agent A to have a categorical unqualified ability to do other than x in Circumstance C *and* for C to be so detailed and exhaustive as to *determine* that A does x. Consequently, if Locke were correct in his argument, then the ability that is essential to freedom would be one that is conceptually impossible for anyone to possess in a deterministic world, and incompatibilism would therefore be the only sensible position to hold.

But it simply does not follow from the fact that phobias and compulsions show that there is an inadequacy in the one qualified concept of ability that Locke examines (*viz.*, being able if one wants) nor does it follow from the fact that we can talk sensibly about categorical ability in those cases (because the relevant conditions are not deterministically specified) that our concept of freedom demands an unqualified and categorical ability to do otherwise in the present, *deterministic* circumstances. There may be other notions of ability that, though stronger than the ability to do an act if one wants, are not so strong as to be incompatible with determinism. But aren't we now simply at loggerheads with Locke? He says that one sense of ability is necessary for freedom; I suggest that there may be another sense, compatible with determinism, that is all we need for a will to be free. How can we show that his intuitions about the concepts of ability and freedom are wrong and mine are right?

Well, notice that if Locke is correct, then there is no qualified or conditional concept of ability that will both support our intuition that an agent is free in a "full and important sense" and also be consistent with the action's being determined. So, if Locke is right, we should not be able to construct an example in which an action strikes us as freely done, the agent seems to have the ability to do otherwise in the situation, and yet the whole scenario can be viewed as deterministic. The way to establish that Locke is wrong, then, is to produce such an example, and this is what I will do in the next section.

But it may also help to move us toward this conclusion by observing that a conditional or qualified sense of ability to do otherwise is not necessarily a *weakened* or *hollow* notion of ability, and in our normal discussions of ability, it is almost always what we mean.]

When we ask about our ability to do otherwise "in the circumstances," we mean to be asking about our abilities *given*, or holding constant, the presently obtaining circumstances *that we consider relevant, potentially important, salient, or of interest to us*. We don't mean to be holding constant the overall present conditions *down to the last molecule*! After all, if that is what we meant, we would never be justified in asserting, prior to the action's execution, that a person has the ability to perform that act, since we are wholly ignorant of so many of the physical conditions and variables that compose the "present circumstances" (when they are understood as the prevailing conditions determining the action's occurrence). Yet it is only relative to such a micro-description of the prevailing conditions that an action or any event follows deterministically. No spottier or more general description of the conditions will support the idea that the resulting action is empirically *necessitated* by their occurrence (and the laws of nature). The "present conditions" we are interested in when we ask about our ability to do otherwise are, however, not the complete and never-repeatable necessitating micro-conditions referred to by determinism. They are, at best, a tiny subset of these conditions.[It seems most natural, then, to expect that the notion of ability to do otherwise which is intertwined with our concept of human freedom is not as *categorical* as Locke suggests.] It is not an ability to do otherwise in "the very circumstances" we find ourselves in—down to their last micro-physical detail!

And once we admit that talk of one's ability to do other than x in "the present circumstances" should not be interpreted as referring to some (miracle) ability to do other than x in circumstances that determine that one does x, it will be seen immediately that the sense of ability to do otherwise than we are interested in must also be a *qualified* sense. In the present circumstances, I am able to do *otherwise provided no additional unknown and unforeseen condition interferes; provided my brain and body continue to function regularly; provided I don't suffer some inexplicable decline in my motivation, or alteration of my wants, etc.*

Through example, now, I hope to illustrate these points, and to establish that our concepts of acting from a free will, and being able to do otherwise in the circumstances, are, in fact, compatible with determinism.

IV. GOLFING IN A DETERMINISTIC WORLD

Consider a practiced golfer who can hit intentional hooks (shots that curve right-to-left) whenever the situation requires. Let's imagine that in his present circumstances our golfer considers playing a long hook, but, deciding in favor of a more conservative strategy, he hits a shorter straight shot. Presumably there is a set of facts obtaining at the instant of impact, concerning the momentum of the clubhead, the angle of the clubface, and the trajectory of the swing, that determines (assuming a benign wind, etc.), that the shot played is straight. And there is little doubt that at some instant before impact, our golfer becomes "committed" to the swing: he has started through the swing, intending to bring the clubface to the ball at a right angle; any attempt to hook this late in the swing would wholly botch the shot. At this point, our golfer cannot bring off an intentional hook, we may say; at this late stage it is physically impossible. And given that he has no last-second change of heart, the shot he will hit can be correctly predicted to be straight. But the sense in which the golfer is "unable to hit a hook in the circumstances" is obviously very unattenuated, amounting only to the claim that the mechanics involved in performing one action preclude, at some detailed point in their specification, the occurrence of an alternative action. That our golfer is unable to hook given his state halfway through his swing cannot be much more significant a threat to his freedom than it would be to assert that he is unable to hook the shot after he has played it straight!

Allowing a sense in which our golfer is unable to hook his shot after a certain point in his swing commits us only to a momentary inability, i.e., a temporally severely circumscribed inability. Nothing follows regarding his ability prior to that point. In particular, if we concentrate on the golfer's circumstance as we would describe it from our usual or common sense perspective, the golfer *becomes* unable to hook only at that last moment before impact. Before that point, *he is able to hit a hook, free to hit a hook, hitting a hook is possible for him in this situation,* we naturally would say. His perception of the ball's lie, his strategic reasoning, his estimation of the probability of success for certain shots, his desire to win or fear of losing, his degree of confidence, his state of nervousness or relaxation, his level of concentration, etc.—whatever these facts may be—they do not make hitting a hook a physical impossibility; given them, no physical laws need to be broken if our golfer were to hit a hook.

I hope you agree that it is utterly natural to say that our golfer has the ability to hook in the present circumstances, and altogether unnatural to say that he was unable to hook here, on the grounds that (after deliberating!) he in fact hit a straight shot and was determined to do so. The incompatibilist, however, is likely to have two, related, objections to this example.

First, it might be pointed out that for all the deterministic mechanism that undoubtedly is involved in the golfer's swing, the sense that the golfer is free to hook in the situation derives from our assumption that his choice of shot has been freely arrived at through deliberation. An incompatibilist may not be worried by the fact that certain complex actions are the deterministic results of deliberative choice, as long as the act of choice itself is not causally determined. On this view, in other words, for an action to be freely performed, a gap in the deterministic chain of events is necessary at the point of the choice or decision, while the resultant actions can be admitted to be fully deterministic consequences of that decision and the surrounding conditions.

Although it is true that my example focuses on the mechanics of the golf swing in the attempt to show that the ability to do otherwise is maintained in a deterministic context, I mean the example to be conceived of as deterministic throughout, with no "gaps" even at the point of the golfer's deliberations. In the same way as the swing can be viewed as a free action regardless of its deterministic mechanics, so the deliberations and intentions of the agent can be the expression of the golfer's free will even if we assume a deterministic account of them. I will make this a more obvious feature of my next example.

The incompatibilist's second, and indeed *the* standard, response to cases such as the one before us is to claim that the ability we are ascribing to our golfer is *illusory* precisely because it is based upon our nondeterministic (and consequently inadequate) descriptions of his circumstances. If determinism is true, it is argued, our golfer does not *become* unable to hook after he's begun swinging, rather, he is unable (and hence unfree) *from time immemorial*, because his straight shot is inferrable from laws and any set of complete antecedent conditions obtaining at a given time, even a time before the golfer's birth!

This response seems to me a mistake. To continue with our golfing theme but to change the example, suppose that some complex neurochemical explanation can be given for our golfer's presently being in a very frivolous, "devil-may-care" mood as he stands over the easiest of putts. His overall neurophysical state plus a detailed description of present external stimulation causally determine, let us assume, that he will intentionally miss the putt in order to let his partner win the hole. Do we conclude that in those deterministic circumstances our golfer is *unable* to sink his putt on the grounds that it is causally determined that he *won't* sink it? Or rather, do we ask ourselves how he may have behaved differently if he had been given some reason for trying to sink the putt? If the latter, then attributions of ability or inability may depend upon certain subjunctive or counterfactual matters (what he would have or could have done in relevantly similar circumstances if he'd been given reasons to do so) which are not settled by knowing whether or not the action is causally determined.

V. FREEDOM OF THE WILL AND THE PLASTICITY OF ACTION

In the example given above, whether or not missing the putt is done from the golfer's own free will seemed to have less to do with his actions being determined and more to do with whether the golfer were able to alter his behavior if he were given certain incentives to do so. If an offer of a million dollars or a threat of serious bodily harm would not bring the golfer out of his "who cares" mood and motivate him to sink the putt, we may well start wondering if he *is* in control of his action and begin doubting whether he does what he does freely. He would begin to remind us of the phobic or the compulsive. But if he is able to alter his behavior in ways that we judge reasonable, if his behavior would show the requisite *plasticity* towards various incentives, our judgement would be that he is very likely in control and acting freely.

[This general idea has been further elaborated by two contemporary philosophers, Bernard Gert and Timothy Duggan (1979). The small details of their analysis are not necessary to appreciate their basic idea. On their view, if an agent is free to will to do an act of kind x it is necessary that there be numerous and varied incentives that the agent can believe exist and that are *effective*; i.e., the agent would in most cases bring his behavior into reasonable conformity with those incentives. If an agent, A, has freedom of the will to do an action of type x, it is necessary that A have the following two characteristics:

> (1) he must have the ability to believe that there are coercive and non-coercive incentives both for doing x and for *not* doing x; and (2) his beliefs about these coercive incentives must almost always have the effect that he acts in accordance with them, and his beliefs about these non-coercive incentives must, at least sometimes, have the effect that he acts in accordance with them. The lack of either of these characteristics entails the lack of the ability to will. In a fairly rough sense we might say that those who lack the ability to believe are in that respect like delu-

sional psychotics, and those who believe but are not appropriately affected by those beliefs are in that respect like compulsive and phobic neurotics. (203)

The Gert-Duggan view substantiates the idea that inability to do otherwise implies something different than the fact that some description of antecedent conditions allows the action performed to be viewed as determined. It implies that the disabled agent would fail to alter his behavior in accord with incentives which we rationally expect should lead to behavior-change. Consequently, the analogy, implicit in Locke's view, between the psychiatric examples and the supposed plight of all normal agents if determinism is true, is not to be found here. Regardless of determinism, the actions of agents with freedom of the will *will* exhibit just the plasticity which is absent in the compulsive and company.

Although there are a number of details in the Gert-Duggan analysis which I think demand revision, the proposal is of the correct form for the compatibilist argument I have been presenting here. The plausibility of such an analysis, along with the examples and discussion provided above, count strongly, in my view, against the incompatibilist attitude that freedom is conceptually at odds with determinism.]

My main argument is now concluded. But in the final section of this paper, I wish to offer additional support for the compatibilist position through a colorful and, I think, convincing thought-experiment in which the question of determinism and the question of acting from a free will present themselves as clearly distinct issues, and where the conclusion of the thought experiment expresses the basic idea of this paper, namely, that at least many of our actions are indeed freely willed, even if determinism is true.

VI. THE PREDICTION ROOM

In Section 2, it was noted that one usual way of expressing determinism is in terms of the in-principle-predictability of any event. So let us imagine that Ohio University has in its employ a team of "super-minds" who have been researching the deterministic nature of human behavior, and who now wish to test their belief that they presently have in hand all the laws and all the means of measuring relevant conditions that are necessary for making foolproof predictions of human thoughts and actions. Imagine that, because of my philosophical interest in this research, I have been helping their endeavors by acting as their test subject or guinea pig, and they have now amassed much information about my habits, beliefs, desires, etc., etc., and are ready to test their predictive powers. An experimental situation is designed.

The super-minds equip a room in the Ohio University Inn with many interesting things and diversions: food, books, magazines, television, computer games, stereo, painter's easel, exercise equipment, and so on. The plan is to shut me in this room and allow me to do anything I want, for whatever reason, in whatever order I decide, and for as long as I want.

Sealed in an envelope which they hand to me as they close me in the room is an extremely detailed printout of their predictions of my activities during the day ahead. These predictions will be opened only at day's end, and compared with a timed videotape of my actions. I now go about the business of occupying myself, sometimes doing what I like, sometimes doing things I don't usually do (I want to give the super-minds a run for their money, after all). I let myself freely choose from among the alternatives open to me, and easily fill the time. But can you believe it! When evening comes and the envelope is opened, there on the printout is an exact and detailed record of my day's activities, including the correct report that my first words upon looking at the printout were, "Oh my God, they've done it!"

As our initial excitement ebbs, the super-minds and I begin talking about the ramifications of their success. One of them says, "Well, I guess the idea of free will goes by the boards—another illusion debunked by scientific progress." To this, I respond, "Look, I'm astonished by your feat, but it hasn't shown that I didn't act from my own free will in the Prediction Room. After all, I easily could have done other things than the ones I did and you predicted. If I had *read* your predictions beforehand, I could have decided to falsify them: if you predicted that I would read twenty pages of philosophy from 1:06 to 2:15 p.m., then at 1:06, I could easily have turned on the TV and watched soap operas for the next hour and a half. Unlike, say, a drug addict or a compulsive hand washer who may try but not be able to falsify your prediction that they would take the drugs left on the table or wash their hands a dozen times during the day, my behavior in the Prediction Room was freely willed."

Notice, that if this sounds correct to you, you are accepting the idea that freedom and determinism are compatible. The ability of the super-minds to predict correctly is the analogue in the example to the truth of determinism, while the belief that I am free has to do with my felt ability to have done otherwise. But now, let's introduce a complicating twist to our story to challenge your intuitions further, and to make the case for compatibilism stronger.

Imagine that, next day, I take up the challenge of falsifying the super-minds' predictions. Into the Prediction Room I go, and immediately rip open the envelope containing the printout for the day. I read the prediction for five minutes from now, which says, "Turns on radio to 91.3 FM." So, I form the *intention* to sit down on the couch and read a book, with no radio on, for the next hour.

Now, how might the story continue from this point? I want to mention three possible endings that are of interest. Here is the first.

I sit down and read my book in silence for quite some time, thereby falsifying the prediction that was given to me. Having succeeded, I walk out of the room to confront the super-minds, wondering to myself whether my success shows not only that I acted freely, but also that perhaps determinism is *not* in the end true. But there, at the door, the super-minds stand, with all-knowing smirks on their faces, holding *another* envelope, which they tell me contains their *real* predictions! Feeling duped, I rip open the envelope and read, "Subject looks over our dummy predictions about the radio, and sits down and reads quietly for an hour." Ugh! The super-minds explain their little game in the following way. "We, of course, realize that it is a fact about humans that when given a prediction as a stimulus and challenged to disprove it, they will, under the right conditions, act to falsify that prediction. In fact, in your case, we were able to predict what this falsifying action will be—as you have just read. It is simply another deterministic fact about you that you will act differently when trying to falsify a known prediction than you would if you were unaware of it. Our real prediction takes all of this into account."

I think it is clear that the super-minds could, in fact, do what I have just described. But what is important and perhaps not so easy to see is that this success on their part is no greater threat to our sense of freedom than was their original ability to predict my whole day's actions. They were, after all, super-minds from the start! It is a known psychological fact (and, therefore, obviously knowable by the super-mind) that many humans will try to frustrate attempts to predict their behavior if they know about those attempts. This is just another natural fact about us that any successful deterministic account would have to be sensitive to.

Conversely, the fact that the super-minds apparently cannot announce the correct prediction to a defiant subject and expect it to be self-fulfilling (i.e., true) does *not* show that determinism is *false*. Defiance is perfectly predictable, at least in principle.

So, despite the feeling that the super-minds have conned me and gotten the upper hand in this first ending to our story, the correct philosophical conclusion to draw here is that my actions are free even if they are wholly determined. Freedom in the Prediction Room is measured in this first ending by my ability to falsify the disclosed prediction, and it is in no way compromised by the existence of the undisclosed, correct predictions. Determinism doesn't ruin freedom.

The clearest case of *lack* of freedom in the Prediction Room would be this, and this is the second possible ending to our story:

I sit down and begin reading as planned, but at exactly the time predicted, I am overcome by an uncontrollable impulse to listen to the radio, and I succumb. If every time I attempted to falsify one of the predictions of the super-minds, I found myself in the grip of overwhelming desires that frustrate my intentions, I would be strongly justified in concluding that I am not free in these situations—I am unable to do otherwise.

But notice that we all have very good grounds from our everyday experience for claiming that this is *not* what would occur to me on an average day in a room at the O.U. Inn. Our everyday desires and actions are not as overwhelmingly driven and mysterious as this. This kind of lack of freedom does not, in fact, generally obtain in our world. Notice, also, that the truth of determinism, as expressed in the first scenario by the predictability of my actions, involves no such mysterious compelling forces or loss of control as this second ending presents. Fortunately, as I said, the second ending does not represent the way the world is or is experienced by us. This is because we are generally free to act in our world, even if it is deterministic or nearly deterministic in the relevant ways.

Finally, there is a subtle third possibility to consider. Imagine that the predictions I am trying to falsify are these:

8:14 a.m.: Picks up newspaper
8:16 a.m.: Gets glass of water
8:20 a.m.: Opens window

I plan to falsify these predictions by quietly reading *Oedipus Rex* for the next hour. I light a cigar, sit down on the couch, and open the book. Just then, a fly begins bothering me, so I pick up the newspaper which is next to me and swat the fly. It's 8:14. In disposing of the fly, however, I've knocked an ash off my cigar, which drops between the couch cushions. When I notice them smoldering, I run to the bathroom (8:16 a.m.) for some water to douse the fire, and then settle back to read again. But the burnt-upholstery smell in the room bothers me, so I open the window. It happens to be 8:20.

Realizing, moments later, that I have not falsified the predictions I intended to, I simply read some later entries and make plans to try again. I do not feel bad about my initial failure, because, after all, what could I do? *It was only rational for me* to do what I did. I had *compelling reasons* for momentarily putting aside my desire to falsify the predictions and dealing with the matters at hand.

The question, of course, is this: if the entire day in the Prediction Room turned out to be one urgency after another—not a series of irrational impulses, but of reasonable behaviors in urgent or forced-choice situations, so that none of the known predictions ever got falsified, would my sense of freedom be diminished in such a "world"? *I* would predict a certain amount of disagreement over this third ending; it poses some interesting questions about the relation between having compelling reasons for acting and being compelled to act, questions that we must leave unanswered here. What is important for our purposes, though, is to notice that, luckily, our lives are *not* a continuous series of forced-choice situations. They are easier, and indeed, *freer* than this. Most of us believe that a day in the Prediction Room would end as the first scenario suggests, with us exhibiting our ability to falsify predictions that we are aware of. I hope it has also become clear that this ability, and our sense of freedom, is real—even if the super-minds are standing in the wings, carrying an envelope.

VII. CONCLUSION

We have now seen that compatibilism is not an evasion of the issues surrounding determinism, free will, and the ability to do otherwise. We have rejected the incompatibilist's claim that only a weak and anemic sense of ability to do otherwise—one too weak to support our sense of freedom—can operate in a deterministic world. We have analyzed our ability to do otherwise and have found that there is no reason to be ashamed of discovering that it is a *conditional* ability. In fact, the incompatibilist's concept of a *categorical* ability to do otherwise may well be more deserving of the epithet "quagmire" than compatibilism ever was. Through several examples, the point has been repeated that acting from one's free will does not require that one's actions not be deterministically caused. Our ability to do otherwise is a matter of the plasticity of our actions in light of various incentives for altering our behavior, not a matter of whether a deep, physical understanding of their origins ever shows them ultimately to be determined. Determinism, if it is the correct picture of the physical world (a question, by the way, that the compatibilist need not answer), should not be viewed as the bringer of some sort of global psychiatric disability. Free will and free action, in any full and important sense, may well require that we are unlike the psychologically afflicted, and each of us hopes that we are. This is a genuine concern, but it is not overshadowed by any universal threat to our freedom known as determinism. Quagmire avoided.

REFERENCES AND SUGGESTED READINGS

Dennett, D. C., *Elbow Room*. Cambridge: MIT/Bradford Books, 1984.

Gert, B., and T. Duggan, "Free Will as Ability to Will." *Nous* 13, pp. 179–217.

James, William, "The Dilemma of Determinism," in *Essays in Pragmatism*, A. Castell, ed., Hafner Publishing Co., 1969.

Locke, J., "Three Concepts of Free Action," *Proceedings of the Aristotelian Society*, 1975, pp. 95–112.

Pagels, H., *The Cosmic Code: Quantum Physics as the Language of Nature*. New York: Simon and Schuster, 1982.

Skinner, B. F., *Beyond Freedom and Dignity*. Knopf/Bantam Books, 1971.

Van Inwagen, P., *An Essay on Free Will*. Oxford, England: Oxford University Press, 1983.

Watson, G., ed., *Free Will*. Oxford, England: Oxford University Press, 1982.

Are you convinced by the Prediction Room? If a list of all your actions at the end of a day were handed to you with proof that the list was compiled weeks before, would you still feel confident that you were free? The question is *not* "Would you *feel* free?" because the answer to this question is almost certainly "yes," but "Wouldn't you begin to doubt the accuracy of your feelings of freedom?" And here the answer is also "yes."

We raise these questions not because we think that Bender is wrong. We raise them to remind you that Bender is in fact asking you what you think about the scenarios he has proposed. He sees them as supporting compatibilism. Do not be afraid to challenge his interpretation.

NOTE ON SOURCES.   This article was written for inclusion in this anthology by John W. Bender.

4

Can I Survive Death?

THE QUESTION POSED

You will recall that Socrates, after the death penalty had been pronounced upon him, engaged his judges in a brief philosophical exploration of death. He queried, "Is death going to sleep or is it going on a journey?" If it is the former, then death means the annihilation of the individual self. If it is the latter, then death means the continuation of experience for the individual self, albeit under some rather significantly altered circumstances. Do I perish utterly and entirely at death or can I survive in some sense? Is death the end or is life beyond death possible?

Death can be viewed as a blessing inasmuch as it brings to an end the pain, suffering, and anxiety that characterize so much of human life. Yet death can also be seen as a curse. It menaces our plans and our strivings. It promises sooner or later to tear from our arms the ones we love best. It suggests that our lives are mere puffs of smoke in the winds of eternity: here today and gone tomorrow. Yet, by threatening our very being and meaning, death tempts us to question its finality. Does death really have the last word?

Formulating an acceptable answer to that question is important. Indeed, because death threatens our activities, plans, and loves with termination, and because we do not know exactly when death will cast its shadow over our lives, we can easily fall prey to an anxiety that erodes the joy of living. Socrates was able to conquer the fear of death because he faced up to the question of what lies beyond death and found a satisfying answer. Liberated from that fear, he was able to live his days with remarkable courage and serenity.

To what, then, does death lead? Annihilation or a journey? An end or a transition? Before you formulate an answer to this question, you might wish to recall how you responded to the question examined in Chapter 2. There we considered the issue of whether or not the human is a body and also a mind. The position you take on this issue can certainly influence your view of postdeath survival. If, for example, you affirmed dualism by agreeing with Descartes and Eccles that the human being is both a body and a mind (or soul), then you would have adopted a position that is hospitable to belief in postdeath survival. Clearly if you maintained that the human being is a combination of two quite different substances, one physical and the other mental, then you have set the stage for claiming that when the physical part of the human dies, the mental part need not perish as well. If, however, you adopted one of the anti-dualist materialistic positions (that is, the claim that mental states are impossible without a corresponding physical state), then you would be confronted with an enormous obstacle to belief in postdeath survival. Indeed, if mental states are so inextricably linked to physical states, then the death of the latter seems to preclude the survival of the former.

Now the kind of postdeath survival about which we are talking and with which the philosophers cited in this chapter are concerned is the survival of the personal identity which involves at least such mental states as consciousness, self-awareness, memory, and introspection. We are not concerned with less robust views of survival such as the immortality involved either in one's abiding influence, or in the endless generations of one's descendants, or in the indestructible matter/energy that constitute one's body.

Our first author, Corliss Lamont, opts for annihilation. Calling on the support of modern science, Lamont contends that empirical evidence justifies belief in a materialistic monistic psychology (as opposed to Cartesian dualism) which precludes postdeath survival. Ducasse, our second author, disagrees with Lamont and contends that the evidence against dualism is not as convincing as Lamont claims. Furthermore, says Ducasse, the evidence from paranormal phenomena which could support belief in immortality must not be ignored. Our third author, Robert Almeder, enhances Ducasse's case through his examination of five types of paranormal human experiences that seem to provide evidence in support of the survival hypothesis. Peter Geach rejects the dualism of people like Ducasse and Almeder, but not necessarily postdeath survival. Geach contends that because survival apart from a body is inconceivable, the only plausible survival hypothesis is one involving a postdeath reconstitution of the body such as is claimed in the Hebraic and Christian doctrines of the resurrection of the dead. Finally, Antony Flew provides a hard-hitting rejoinder not only to Ducasse and Almeder but also to Geach.

In brief, the debate in this chapter progresses in this fashion: dualism rejected and annihilation affirmed; dualism affirmed and annihilation rejected; dualism rejected and annihilation rejected; dualism rejected and annihilation affirmed. Each of these positions is a response to the question "Is death the end?" Let us examine the debate and try to identify which position seems most convincing.

CORLISS LAMONT

DEATH IS THE END

BIOGRAPHICAL NOTE.   Corliss Lamont was born in New Jersey in 1902. He received his A.B. degree from Harvard and his Ph.D. from Columbia University. His teaching career included positions at Columbia, the New School for Social Research, Cornell, and Harvard. He was active in the American Civil Liberties Union, the National Council for American–Soviet Friendship, the American Humanist Association, and American Socialist parties. He ran as a Socialist candidate for the U.S. Senate in 1952 and again in 1958. His advocacy of socialism brought him to the attention of Senator Joseph McCarthy who secured an indictment against him for contempt of Congress. The indictment was, however, dismissed by the U.S. Appeals Court in 1956. His many books include *Issues of Immortality* (1932), *The Illusion of Immortality* (rev. ed., 1965), *You Might Like Socialism: A Way of Life for Modern Man* (1939), *The Peoples of the Soviet Union* (1946), *A Humanist Funeral Service* (1947), *The Philosophy of Humanism* (1949), *Soviet Civilization* (1952), *A Humanist Wedding Service* (1970), and *Voice in the Wilderness: Collected Essays of Fifty Years* (1974), and *Yes to Life—Memoirs of Corliss Lamont* (1981).

THE ARGUMENT OF THE PASSAGES.   Lamont begins his discussion with a definition of immortality. That is a good point of departure. By defining his terms at the beginning the philosopher can avoid considerable confusion and misunderstanding.

> Before starting what I consider the fundamental issue involved in the question before us it is necessary to define carefully *immortality*. It should have already become apparent that I mean *personal* immortality, that is, the literal survival of the individual human personality or consciousness for an indefinite period after death, with its memory and awareness of self-identity essentially intact. In other words, one will awaken in the life beyond in very much the same sense as one wakes up here on every new day. And in that other world the awakening, as here, will be to fresh activities and in the midst of friends and family. The memory there will not hold all the particulars of one's past life any more than from day to day or decade to decade on earth, but it will retain enough to provide a definite sense of identity and continuity. This is fundamental, for a personality that had no conscious links with anything that has gone on before would to all intents and purposes be another personality.
>
> All this is not to say that *immortality* has not had other noteworthy meanings, among Christians as well as others. The word has sometimes signified the attainment here and now of a certain eternal quality in life and thought, with "eternal" meaning that which is independent of time and existence. This view has been held by such philosophers as Spinoza and Santayana and is frequently called *ideal* immortality, or, with questionable accuracy, *Platonic* immortality. Often this ideal immortality is combined with the primary meaning of actual personal survival. *Immortality* has likewise designated the survival after death of an impersonal psychic entity which is absorbed into some kind of All or Absolute or God. Akin to this is *material* or *chemical* immortal-

ity through the reabsorption by Nature of the elements of the body. Then there is *historical* immortality through the irreversibility of the past and the permanent place that every life necessarily has in the simple truth and succession of existence; *biological* or *plasmic* immortality through one's children and descendants; and *social* or *influential* immortality through enduring fame or the unending effect of one's life on the minds and acts of succeeding generations.

More foreign to Western minds is the concept of immortality through *reincarnation* on this earth in future human or other living forms. This doctrine is often known as metempsychosis or transmigration, and postulates a pre-existence as well as an after-existence. Influential among ancient peoples such as the Greeks and Egyptians and always the very core of the Buddhist and Hindu religions, the theory today maintains its sway over large sections of the East and has in recent times penetrated to Europe and America through the Theosophists. Perhaps least important and least known of all is the idea of immortality involved in the return of all things over and over again in their precise detail, the *eternal recurrence* theory urged by the Stoics in ancient times and revived in the nineteenth century by the German philosopher Nietzsche.

It is logically possible to believe simultaneously in several of these vicarious forms of immortality. There is no inconsistency, for example, between social, biological and material immortality. No reasonable person would deny the actuality of material immortality, or of social and biological immortality as long as the species man continues to exist. But whether they be true or not, we are not vitally concerned with the eight secondary types of immortality mentioned above. It is immortality as signifying the continuation of the individual personality after death that is the chief and central concern of this book.

He proceeds to identify the key issue in the question of postdeath survival as the relationship between the body and the personality (or soul).

While there are manifold approaches to the question of immortality, the fundamental issue lies, I believe, in the relationship between body or the physical organism on the one hand and personality or soul on the other. Other synonyms or near-synonyms for personality are consciousness, mind, self, spirit, psyche and the ego. In order to avoid controversy and confusion I shall ordinarily use the word *personality* as the definitive term to denote the characteristic mental and emotional activities of a human being.

Referring to the facet of human experience which we called "raw feels" in Chapter 2, Lamont notes an obvious *difference* between body and personality.

Whatever words are used, it is necessary to admit the distinction between body and personality. Death is here the unimpeachable witness. For in death there is still a body—cold, silent, inert—but the personality has completely disappeared. A dead body is indeed very different from a living body. If it were not, there would be no problem of immortality. And also a living sleeping body is quite different from a living waking body. The sleeping body is always active to a certain extent, but what we know as the personality is, except in the case of dreams, quiescent and temporarily in a state of unconscious repose. When a living body is under an anesthetic, the same condition prevails. But men do not have to die or sleep or undergo an operation in order to make plain the distinction between body and personality; they simply need to think and feel. There is surely a difference between the physical state of a bad tooth, on the one hand, and the feeling of pain it causes and the thoughts of a curative it stimulates, on the other. If there were not this difference, there would be no such thing as conscious experience.

Yet there is also a most intimate *connection* between body and personality, as many ordinary experiences testify.

Now however naturally common sense, as well as sage philosophy, differentiates between body and personality, at the same time it links the two together in the most intimate fashion. It is all but impossible to imagine a disembodied personality. When we are thinking of absent persons, whether they be dead or alive, we invariably visualize their natural forms, their bodies through which alone we have known them and been aware of their personalities. Pictures are our favorite and most vivid reminders. that for a time at least we tend towards identifying a dead man with his body. Indeed, we find it very hard to say farewell to the lifeless forms of our loved ones; and we do not like to think of their bodies being mutilated, dissected or resting in a noisy, strange or unbeautiful place. If a person dies away from home or drowns, every effort is usually made to bring back or recover the body. The relatives of thousands of American soldiers killed abroad in the First and Second World Wars insisted that the bodies be shipped back and interred in the United States.

We know from ordinary experience, furthermore, how closely the personality is actually tied up with our body. Bodily changes almost invariably carry with them mental and emotional changes. Coffee stimulates the mind; codeine normally relieves pain; alcohol generally removes inhibitions. A hard knock on the head may result in unconsciousness or even in mental abnormality. The personality is well when the body is well; sick when the body is sick. A walk, a ride, a skate—any sort of exercise— in pure and bracing air can give new zest in short order; sitting in one position too long in a crowded and stuffy room will try the temperament of the most cheerful and dull the mind of the most keen. Conversely, it is well known that, under certain circumstances, one's state of mind can affect one's bodily state, either for better or for worse. The obvious truth of the mind's influence on the body has been stretched by Christian Science beyond all reason and made the basis of a new religion. But we need no religion, either new or old, to tell us that body and personality are interlocking directorates affecting each other in every move they make.

What divides believers in immortality from nonbelievers, says Lamont, are fundamentally different psychological perspectives, by which he means different responses to the mind–body problem. On the one hand, he speaks of the psychological dualists (the advocates of Cartesian dualism) who claim that personality is a different substance from the body, which can accordingly survive the death of the body. On the other hand, he notes the psychological monists (the anti-dualist materialists) who contend that personality is simply a quality or characteristic of the body, which is therefore unable to survive the death of the body.

Those thinkers who have emphasized the distinction between body and personality, and the personality's power over the body, have insisted that the personality is a substance of a different order, an immaterial or non-physical soul that inhabits the body and uses it as its instrument. When the body dies, this soul departs and may go on existing elsewhere; and, according to some, it existed before its earthly body came into being at all. In philosophical and psychological terminology this theory of the personality's independence has been called *dualism* or *Platonism*. It has usually been associated with a far-reaching metaphysical Dualism that divides the whole of existence into the two realms of matter and spirit. But I intend to use *dualism* mainly with a small "d" and in its psychological sense.

Other thinkers, while admitting a distinction between body and personality, have claimed that the personality is the life or function or activity of the body. It is the body acting, the body living; and, to be exact, the body acting and living in certain definite ways closely associated with the brain and the rest of the central nervous system. For purposes of convenience we talk and write about an abstraction, *personality*; but it can in actuality no more be abstracted from the human body than can the activities of breathing and digestion. This personality is, then, a quality of the body, not an independently existing thing, just as redness is an inseparable quality of a red rose. The mind, as part of this personality, has the same kind of relationship to the body; and indeed a wise man has been defined as one who does not know the difference between his mind and his body and cannot tell which is which. Such a personality would have the same difficulty in existing without its body as the flame of a candle would have in burning without its wax base.

This theory of the personality was in ancient times presented most persuasively by Aristotle and Lucretius. It has been variously known as the Aristotelian psychology, the naturalistic psychology, the organistic psychology and the monistic psychology. Most accurate and meaningful, in my opinion, is this last mentioned term, the *monistic** psychology*, signifying that man is an inseparable oneness comprising both body and personality. Psychological monism must not be confused with the philosophical meanings of *Monism* as a great metaphysical or cosmological system.

It now becomes clear what is the basic issue that faces us. Is the relationship between the body and personality which we know in this life so close, deep reaching and fundamental that their indissoluble unity appears to be the most reasonable conclusion? Or is that association so vague, loose and unessential that the personality may be considered as a separable and ultimately independent entity? In a word, is the human self built and nurtured only on the basis of living flesh and blood; or can it somehow, like the captain of a ship that sinks, continue its existence after the dissolution of its life partnership with the bodily organism?

Clearly, Lamont is an advocate of psychological monism. For him there is no spiritual entity or immaterial soul inhabiting the body that can survive the death of the body. For him there is only body, which performs various activities, all of which cease upon the death of the body. To support his claim that humans do not survive the death of their bodies, Lamont adopts two fundamental strategies. First, he tries to show that those activities often associated with a spiritual entity—activities like thinking, remembering, emoting, etc.—are so intimately connected with the body that they cannot survive the death of the body. That is to say, without the body, none of those activities often identified as spiritual can continue; and without those activities, there is no such thing as a person. Second, Lamont urges that there is no need whatever to postulate the existence of a spiri-

---

* From the Greek *monos*, meaning single.

tual entity to account for human activities. Those activities can be explained adequately in terms of the body and physical processes.

Let us examine his first strategy. His first point here is that the history of the human species as well as the development of each individual human show that personality or mind develops only in so far as the body develops, thereby testifying to the intimate relationship between the personality and the body.

> Biology, first of all, has definitely established man—mind and body—as a part of Nature, knit by ties of origin and kinship to the other animals of the earth and evolved like them through countless ages of time.
>
> There is every reason to believe, not only that body was prior in the long evolution which resulted in the species man, but that it is also prior in the long production and growth of every human individual. It is not two particles of mind or consciousness that meet to create a new human being, but two purely material germ cells, the ovum from the mother and the spermatozoon from the father. At the moment of conception there is nothing present that can legitimately be described as personality or mind. And these terms are simply not applicable to the early states of the embryo, if to any stage. . . . the exact point at which it is accurate to say the human organism has mind and personality is not important. The important thing is to observe that the mind and personality develop and expand as the body develops and expands. Any father or mother who carefully watches the growth of a child from birth through adolescence to maturity can make innumerable commonplace observations that convincingly testify to the continuing unity of mind and body. It is an intimately correlated association in which the psychic and physical functions advance together all along the line, in interaction with the economic, social and cultural influences of the environment. And this correlation is on the whole manifest throughout adulthood and old age as well as during childhood and youth.

His second point involves calling upon the science of genetics to show that inherited genetic material determines an individual's inherent physical characteristics and mental abilities. Once again, the close dependence of the personality upon the body is displayed.

> The laws of heredity also point to the close dependence of the personality on the body. The sciences of biology and genetics have shown that it is the multitudinous and extremely minute genes, transmitted through the germ cells of each parent in threadlike group structures known as chromosomes, that largely determine the inherent bodily characteristics and mental capacities of every individual. The genes are the decisive units of inheritance in human beings as in all living things, although there is evidence that other physical factors can affect or supplement them. Some combinations of genes produce imperfect specimens of man—feeble-minded, deformed, monstrous. Dr. Gardner Murphy, Menninger Foundation Director of Research, estimates that deficient heredity accounts for about 90 per cent of all mental defectives, thus pointing conclusively to the decisive effect of the gene patterns on the mind. Most gene combinations, however, give rise to normal and healthy individuals, some decidedly superior to others. But no two combinations are the same (except in the rare cases of identical twins), and that is why all men are different. Of course, when there are identical twins their separate bodies entail distinct and separate selves, even though these selves are very much alike.

No other mixture of genes except that from which my personality sprung could possibly have produced the particular unit of consciousness that I know as *me*. Other mixtures originated by my own parents do not result in *me*, but in brothers or sisters. So if my special synthesis of germ cells had not been made during the adult life of my father and mother, the possibility of my existence would have been cut off forever, no matter how many millions of other syntheses were produced till the end of time.

Among the most important characteristics determined by the genes is that of sex. Sex differentiation originated at an early stage of evolution and gradually developed to the advanced state in which it is found among men and higher animals. It is obvious that some of the fundamental differences between the male and the female personality depend primarily upon different bodily organization and functions. And everyone knows the varying but always powerful and sometimes paramount influence of sex and sexual emotions upon all human beings. It follows naturally that abnormalities closely connected with sex development will drastically alter the personality.

For instance, there are certain pathological conditions of the adrenal glands which may cause a woman to develop a deep voice, a beard, and masculine tastes and instincts in a general. Many examples exist, too, of people born physically malformed in such a way that they are neither truly male or female, but bodily a sort of intersex or hermaphrodite with personality to match. Again we see that the kind of personality one has is conditioned to a substantial degree by the kind of body one has. The pattern of every human personality is so extricably interwoven with sexual characteristics that we are unable to imagine a sexless individual; even the gods have sex.

His third point draws on the testimony of psychology and medicine and their associated sciences. Those disciplines show, says Lamont, that personality is a function of the structure and physiology of bodily organs, especially the brain. Lamont contends that what happens in the brain (i.e., brain states) determines what kind of personality (i.e., mental states) an individual exhibits. To support his claim, Lamont points out the close link between brain disorders (resulting from injury and disease) and mental disorders.

But just as lungs are the specific organ of breathing and legs the specific organs of walking, so in the same sense the brain, and especially that part of it known as the cerebral cortex, is the specific organ of thinking.

The cortex is a thin, outer layer of wrinkled and convoluted gray matter that grows around and over most of the rest of the brain, enfolding it like a cloak or mantle. It comprises approximately half the total weight of the brain; the brainstem and the cerebellum, which take care of less complicated functions, make up the other half. There is no well-developed cerebral cortex in the lowest animals, but with the reptiles it begins to assume a mature form and increases in size and complexity as the higher animal species evolve. In man it attains its culmination, the human cortex being twice as big and more than twice as complicated as that of the nearest animal, the ape.

It is estimated that in the infinitely complex human cerebral cortex there are about 14,000,000,000 nerve cells or neurons; and each of these is enmeshed in a tangle of very fine nerve fibers coming from many different parts of the body. These vast quantities of neurons are related in so intricate a pattern that the total number of ways in which they are and may be linked is staggering and almost beyond comprehension. According to Professor C. Judson Herrick in his *Brains of Rats and Men*, a few minutes of intense thought probably involves interneuronic connections as great in number as the total of atoms—10^{56}—in the entire solar system. If only one million of the billions of neurons in the cortex, he tells us, were combined among themselves in all possible patterns, the total aggregate of such connections would far exceed $10^{2,783,000}$. It is no wonder Professor Herrick concludes that the figure of potential associations among the neurons of the cortex may be regarded for all practical purposes as approaching infinity.

It does not seem astonishing that with such a remarkable and complex instrument at our disposal we should be able to perform with considerable efficiency and success the characteristic human activities of reasoning, willing, imagining, remembering and the like. At the same time it is hard to see how these activities of the personality, bound up as they are from the very start with the cerebral cortex, could possibly get along without it. The proper functioning of memory, for instance, clearly depends in the first place on the associational patterns laid down as enduring structural imprints through means of interneuronic connections. And the functioning of reason itself depends to a large extent upon the facility with which the patterns of memory and past knowledge can be recalled and reactivated in new and useful combinations to fit new situations. However ideas may be defined, it seems certain that awareness of or use of them requires as a condition the cooperation of the neuronic pathways in the cortex. But these pathways, these memory patterns, these records—millions and billions of them—are all imbedded in the gray cortical matter of the brain. And it is difficult beyond measure to understand how they could survive after the dissolution, decay or destruction of the living brain in which they had their original locus. . . . And if a transcendental self or a supernatural soul holds sway behind the empirical curtain, it too must make use of memory; but the logical and apparently only available remembering mechanism for it to work through is the maze-like material organization of the cerebral cortex and associated centers.

This conclusion receives convincing corroboration through the study of various types of mental abnormality and insanity. It is a commonplace that a severe blow on the head may so affect the brain through actual destruction or injury of tissue, that temporary or permanent insanity sets in. Sometimes a fracture or concussion causes complete or partial loss of memory—for days, for months and even for years—of everything that preceded the accident. Even a blow that has no lasting bad effects may make a man totally lose consciousness for a time. On the other hand, a person who is born insane or becomes so through an accident may be completely cured by an operation on the skull to remove the abnormal pressure of bone on the cerebral cortex. But if the brain of a man is too far under the average weight, he will be feeble-minded or worse and no operation can make up for his defect. The pinheaded microcephalics, with their diminutive brains, usually attain at most a mental level comparable to that of a child two or three years old.

Some injuries affect a specific area of the brain and through it specific functions of the man, thus demonstrating that certain activities of the body are definitely associated with certain portions of the brain. For instance, an injury to the frontal lobe of the left cerebral hemisphere disturbs the powers of speech by causing motor aphasia, while one to the temporal lobe affects a person's hearing. Though most of the charts drawn up by phrenologists and their ilk assigning definite functions to definite parts of the brain are false or misleading, it is true that the sciences of psychology and physiology have correlated a number of functions such as seeing, smelling, hearing, limb movements and speech coordination with generally identifiable sections of the cerebral cortex. The center for vision, for example, is in the posterior part of the cortex, while that for hearing is near the middle.

It is to be noted, however, that these cortical centers or fields fade away diffusely into adjacent areas and so cannot be sharply defined anatomically; that they are connected directly or indirectly with all other parts of the cortex through an intricate network of association fibers; and that they are incapable of performing any function independently, but always act together with the cortex as a whole. In some cases of serious damage to a certain area of the cortex other sections may take over the duties formerly allocated to the injured segment. This fact has been cited to show that some kind of supernatural entity is at work, but it rather proves the amazing plasticity and educability of the very sensitive brain tissue.

Diseases have just as distressing an effect on the brain and mental functions as external injuries. The worst brain disease of all is probably paresis, a form of paralysis, which is caused by syphilis germs from other parts of the body invading the cerebrum and destroying the brain cells. It is characterized by progressive mental and physical deterioration eventually leading, unless arrested, to death. The disease usually results in profound changes of the personality. The afflicted individual tends to lose his judgment and self-control; to become reckless, indulgent and morally irresponsible; and to neglect his obligations to family and community. In the final stages his cerebral decay may be so far-reaching that he leads an almost purely vegetative existence, as helpless as a new-born babe. This last condition is also typical of senile dementia, which is caused by deterioration of the brain tissue due to old age in general, to interference with the cerebral circulation from hardening of the arteries and to other such hazards of senescence. Tumors within the brain are also likely to lead to dementia. And if a blood vessel bursts within the cerebrum, the result is apoplexy and often outright death.

Another common trouble is caused by the failure of the thyroid gland in the neck to secrete sufficiently. In a child this results in a stoppage or distortion of growth, and ordinarily in feeble-mindedness or imbecility. This disease is called cretinism. In combating it the administering of thyroid extract from sheep can produce remarkable results and bring physical and mental normality to the child. A similar though less serious ailment in adults is known as myxedema and responds to the same treatment. Here, then, we are able to cure a grave sickness of the mind by giving medicine, as if we were dealing with a bad liver or an upset stomach.

The dependence of mind on body is further illustrated by the importance to mental activity of a proper quantity and quality of blood for the brain. A large proportion of the body's total supply of blood is constantly traversing the brain. If the flow of blood to the brain wholly ceases, certain cells necessary to normal functioning quickly become irreversibly damaged. When the brain becomes tired, its energy diminishes and the flow of blood to it becomes less. So during sleep when the brain, and the mind with it, is resting, there is relatively less blood passing through. The common experience of feeling sleepy after a heavy meal is due to the fact that the digestive processes are making extra demands on the blood supply and are drawing blood away from the brain. It is primarily through the blood stream that drugs and stimulants, poison and starvation, influence in their various ways the mind of man.

Suppose we admit with Lamont that there is a causal link between brain events (which are bodily events) and mental events. Must we not also admit that there is a causal link between mental events and bodily events? Do not our mental states like anxiety, anger, and joy frequently affect our bodily states? And does not that fact suggest that the mind is in some sense independent of the body? And does not that suggestion support dualism? While admitting such interaction between bodily states and mental states, Lamont refuses to affirm dualism. Interaction of bodily and mental states shows interdependence of these states: it does not show the independence of the mind from the body as dualism claims.

This citation of facts showing how physical states affect the personality and its mental life does not in the least imply that mental states do not affect physical. All of us are constantly altering our bodily motions according to the dictates of mental decisions. Everyone is familiar with the far-reaching results that optimism or worry, happiness or sadness, good humor or anger, may have on the condition of the body. Good digestion makes for cheerfulness, but the converse is also true; and scientific research has definitely shown that pleasant emotions favor the secretion of the digestive juices, while unpleasant emotions hinder this process. Anger increases the production of adrenalin by the adrenal glands and this secretion, in greater quantities than usual, sweeps through the blood vessels, raises the pressure and sugar-content of the blood, speeds up the heart beat, delays muscular fatigue and prepares the whole body for strenuous action such as fighting or fleeing. A man during rage may feel no pain from injury until after his wrath has cooled. Intense fear has very much the same effect as anger. And every other emotion has its physiological reverberation, however slight.[1]

Morale is as necessary to the effectiveness of an army as food. Mental depression or irritation can produce many kinds of bodily ills. And if one's state of mind does not actually bring on some organic trouble, it is always of importance in the extent and rate of recovery. A physical process such as the knitting of a broken leg can be prevented or delayed by faulty nutrition resulting from anxiety. Extreme terror may paralyze a man, strike him dumb, or cause palpitation of the heart; after earthquakes men and women are found dead who show no signs of injury. Without accepting all the conclusions of Freud and other psychoanalysts, we can safely say that repressions connected with sex may adversely affect an individual's health. Love-sickness is a real disease which can afflict both men and women. There can be no doubt, either, that what is termed the subconscious plays an important part in the general functioning of the personality.

The remarkable effects sometimes achieved through the acquisition of ordinary self-confidence through auto-suggestion and hypnotism, work, it is thought, primarily through the subconscious. Not long ago in the United States hypnosis saved an eminent citizen from death by putting an end to hiccoughs that were causing grave hemorrhages after a throat operation. Hypnotism can apparently make a receptive mind do almost everything from the trivial and harmless to the serious and violent. The disease of the imagination called hysteria also functions to some extent through the subconscious. The hysterical patient, though organically sound, may suffer paralysis of a limb, lameness, blindness, dumbness and at least the outward symptoms of many other bodily disorders.

It is also appropriate to mention the appearance on the bodies of religious devotees of the stigmata, that is, marks corresponding to the wounds inflicted on Jesus at

---

1 The famous James–Lange theory claims that the physiological reaction is prior and primary. Thus we do not cry because we feel sorry, but we feel sorry because we cry. The acceptance of this extreme theory, however, is by no means necessary for our argument.

the crucifixion. St. Francis of Assisi was the most noted of those who are said to have received this supposed mark of divine favor; but there have been many well authenticated and quite recent cases, mostly of women, in modern times. While in this matter conscious or unconscious impostures are sure to have taken place, a certain residue of cases is probably genuine. In every instance, stigmatization has come about only after prolonged meditation upon the passion and crucifixion of Jesus. Modern psychologists believe that the phenomenon of the stigmata can be explained in entirely naturalistic terms and that it is due to as yet undiscovered mechanisms of the subconscious or unconscious. The attempts, however, to smuggle back the supernatural soul through the subconscious would appear to follow the old and exploded procedure of resorting to the supernatural to explain the relatively unknown.

Such examples as these of the mind's control over the body are often interpreted as conclusively proving that the mind is independent of the body. But they point with at least equal force to a connection between the two so exceedingly intimate that it becomes inconceivable how the one could function properly without the other. Furthermore, it is to be remembered that many of the mental states that exercise an influence on the condition of the body are set up in the first place by phenomena primarily physical. Sex neuroses, for example, follow upon the suppression or thwarting of physical desire and then proceed to react unhappily on the whole being. A bilious attack may make a man mentally depressed, and this psychic condition may then help to bring on insomnia. In short, there is a constant interplay between the mind and body.

Lamont's fourth point elucidates the role of the environment in shaping personality. That role involves the contention that such shaping can occur because the very material processes of the environment impact the very material processes of the body. A supernatural soul or personality does not enter the body at birth from on high. Personality is a bodily quality that is shaped in the confluence of many physical, material forces.

Finally, let us note the extent to which the personality is molded by the human environment. All of us are born into a family and into a society. The kind of family and the kind of society that nurture us make a very great difference in the kind of personalities we develop. Our parents, our teachers, our nationality, our language, our economic condition and many other social factors influence enormously the growth and caliber of our characters and minds. Weighty and dramatic evidence here is the recent well-authenticated discovery of two "wolf-children" in India, as recounted in the scholarly study, *Wolf Child and Human Child*, by Dr. Arnold Gesell of the Yale Medical School. Dr. Gesell's book is based on the diary of the Reverend J. A. L. Singh of Midnapore, who tells how he and his helpers found, in the year 1920, two female human children, one aged about eight and the other about one and a half, in a wolf-den on the edge of the jungle. Several wolves fled at the time of capture, but the mother-wolf stood her ground and was killed. Evidently this mother-wolf had suckled and cared for the two girl children for a considerable time. The natives of the district, having glimpsed them occasionally in the forest, had come to believe that they were "manghosts."

Kamala, the older girl, and Amala, the younger one, had been able to survive by acquiring characteristic wolf habits and adapting themselves as best they could to wolf "culture." Kamala walked and ran on all fours, seized her food by mouth, insisted on nudity, preferred darkness to daylight, and howled at night in a piercing half-animal, half-human wail. She knew no human ways or words. The Reverend Singh put Kamala and Amala into the Orphanage at Midnapore and, with his wife, undertook to train them as normal human beings. Amala, being still a baby, learned more quickly than Kamala, but survived only a year in her new environment. Very slowly the Singhs were able to teach Kamala how to stand upright, how to walk, how to wear clothes, how to talk. In 1924 Kamala had six words in her vocabulary; in 1927, forty-five. Gradually she came to enjoy human association and to lead an essentially human existence, though a retarded one. Unfortunately she died in 1929, at the age of seventeen, nine years after leaving the wolf-cave.

This story cogently illustrates, it seems to me, the point that the personalities of human beings do not enter ready-made into this world, but are the product of culture and circumstances as well as heredity. One of the most striking things about Kamala was that her wolf-life and conditioning prevented her from even learning to walk upright while she was with the wolves. The significance of this fact for the monistic psychology is well brought out by Dr. Gesell in his analysis of the wolf-children. He reminds us that "the basic framework on the action-system of all vertebrates is posture. Even in man the finer and subtler patterns of behavior are grafted on postural sets and postural attitudes. Kamala had basic ways of squatting, reclining, inspecting, sniffing, listening and of locomotion acquired in the wolf era of her developmental career. These motorsets constituted the core of her action system and affected the organization of her personality. . . . Even after several years of sojourn with upright human beings, quadrupedal locomotion was resorted to whenever speed was necessary. On two feet she never learned to run at all; on four feet she ran so fast it was hard to overtake her."

In short, even a normal human body does not automatically produce a characteristic human personality, but only when that body is subject to certain environmental and social influences. The remarkable case of Kamala, in conjunction with a multitude of other scientific data, logically leads to the crucial statement that not only do our individual minds depend upon the accumulated intellectual and cultural heritage of the race, but that mind as we know it is in its very origin a social product. For the human mind matures and attains its distinctive powers of abstract thought only through the symbols of speech and language. Men are born with brains; *they acquire minds*.

It is possible, then, to summarize the entire situation by saying that, in addition to the indissoluble union between body, on the one hand, and mind and personality, on the other, there is the whole man, and the sustaining and conditioning environment, both human and physical.

In brief, Lamont claims that personality is inextricably linked to bodily events because (1) personality develops as the body develops, (2) genetic material determines not only physical but also mental characteristics, (3) brain disorders result in mental disorders, and (4) while humans are born with brains, they acquire minds or personalities through environmental conditioning. Lamont's conclusion: modern science supports a monistic psychology and by implication, denies postdeath survival.

The data I have reviewed unmistakably testify to the fact that man is a unified whole of mind–body or personality–body so closely and completely integrated that dividing him up into two separate and more or less independent parts becomes impermissible and unintelligible. In other words, modern science convincingly sustains the fundamental principle of the monistic psychology. Perhaps no one science alone proclaims this conclusion; but the sciences that deal with man, taken together and as a whole, most certainly do create an overwhelming presumption in its favor. Again and again their findings have inexorably led to the proposition that mind or personality is a function of the body.

Let us now review Lamont's second strategy. Here he makes use of the widely accepted law of parsimony, according to which a scientific explanation ought to use the fewest possible assumptions to generate an adequate account of natural phenomena. Applied to the mind–body problem and from there to the issue of post-death survival, the law of parsimony suggests that if human activity can be explained adequately by recourse only to bodily processes, then it is inadmissible to add an additional layer of explanation relying upon an invented spiritual soul or personality. Lamont contends that resource to a spiritual entity is unnecessary for providing an adequate account of human activity; bodily processes provide sufficient explanatory power.

Another methodological tool of modern science that is of paramount importance for the question at issue is the *law of parsimony* or economy of hypothesis. This law requires that any scientific explanation be based on the fewest possible assumptions necessary for it to account adequately for all the facts involved. The basic principle was first formulated in the fourteenth century by the English philosopher, William of Occam, in the words: "Entities [of explanation] are not to be multiplied beyond need." This fundamental law of parsimony expresses negatively the scientific rule that every hypothesis must meet the requirements of affirmative empirical proof before being accepted. The principle of simplicity of hypothesis does not deny the truth that Nature often operates in a most complex manner; and under no circumstances can it override the observed facts of such complexity, as, for instance, in the organization and functioning of the human body. The law means only that we should not bring in hypotheses unnecessarily to explain a situation, whether it happens to be comparatively simple or comparatively complex.

For example, since Copernicus had no new facts with which to confirm his heliocentric hypothesis, the initial advantage of his theory, that the earth revolved around the sun, over the Ptolemaic theory, that the sun and other heavenly bodies moved around the earth, lay in the reduction of separate assumptions from seventy-nine to thirty-four. This was a sound use of the law of parsimony on the part of Copernicus. Later Newton made an immense improvement over him by accounting for the movements of the earth and heavenly bodies by *one* law of gravitation. Yet even today, with a great many more astronomical facts at our disposal, it would be possible to fit them into Ptolemy's scheme of a motionless earth as the center of the universe, *if* we added a sufficient number of new assumptions.

Another good instance of the meaning of the law of parsimony is provided by a controversy that Galileo had in regard to the mountains which he discovered on the moon. An opponent attempted to refute him by suggesting that the apparent valleys of the moon were filled with an invisible crystalline substance. Galileo answered by saying that if this were so, it was probable that the moon had on it mountains of this same invisible substance at least ten times as high as any he had observed! The reason why Galileo's reply is so effective is that it brings out the point that if we once start disregarding the law of parsimony, as his critic did, then we issue a general invitation to ridiculous hypotheses and impossible vagaries *ad infinitum*.[2]

Now the particular significance of the law of parsimony for the argument between the monistic and dualistic psychologies is that it makes the dualist theory distinctly superfluous. It rules out dualism by making it unnecessary. In conjunction with the monistic alternative it pushes the separate and independent supernatural soul into the limbo of unneeded and unwanted hypotheses. I have previously described in outline form the extraordinary complexity of the human body, its gradual evolution through hundreds of millions of years, and the infinite intricacy of the structure underlying the intellectual and emotional activities of human beings. In view of these facts it is surely not rash to claim that no supernatural soul is required to explain the great and varied achievements, powers and potentialities of man illustrated in every age and clime throughout the vast panorama of history. For the personality, which usually receives the credit for these things, is in truth hardly more remarkable than the body which is its base.

Lamont concludes,

All in all, therefore, the findings of science, coupled with my earlier analysis of various immortality ideas, establish a very powerful case in support of our thesis that immortality is an illusion.

In summary, Lamont claims that scientific evidence supports a monistic psychology according to which human personality is simply a quality or characteristics of the body. To introduce a "spiritual" soul or mind in Cartesian fashion that could survive death is to postulate a totally unnecessary concept that violates the highly respected law of parsimony. In Lamont's discussion, then, dualism is rejected and annihilation of personality at death is affirmed.

NOTE ON SOURCES. The material in this section is quoted from Corliss Lamont, *The Illusion of Immortality* (rev. ed.; Frederick Ungar Publishing Co., 1965), pp. 22–28, 63, 66–71, 74–76, 79–81, 84–86, 88–91, 108, 109–111, 126.

2 CURT JOHN DUCASSE

THE QUESTION IS STILL OPEN

FROM LAMONT TO DUCASSE. Immanuel Kant (1724–1804), one of the most impressive of all modern philosophers, used to say that metaphysics, to the extent that it was colorful and humanly important, shook down to a reflective concern with three questions: God, freedom (meaning free will), and immortality. Can the existence of God be demonstrated and His nature defined? Does any

---

2 For a twentieth-century example of such a hypothesis, let us consider the claim that flowers grow healthily because fairies secretly minister to them during the hours of darkness. This thesis is supported by Sir Arthur Conan Doyle, who became a Spiritualist in his later years. In his book *The Coming of the Fairies* (Hodder, Toronto, 1922), there are submitted alleged photographs of the fairy folk at work. I am of course an admirer of Sir Arthur's stories of Sherlock Holmes, and I believe that his account of the fairies also belongs purely in the realm of the imagination.

human behavior express genuine free will—self-originating, spontaneous auton-omy? Does a human being survive the death of his body? Our present author, the late C. J. Ducasse, thought and wrote on all three of Kant's questions. In the pre-sent section we examine his widely read lecture "Is Life After Death Possible?"

As Ducasse sees it, the position taken and defended by philosophers such as Lamont has been adopted by most people. For them the question of personal immortality has been settled; the answer is in; the question is closed. No person survives the death of the body. For Ducasse, however, the evidence offered by Lamont does not justify the conclusion that belief in immortality is an illusion. For Ducasse, the question of personal immortality is still open; the matter is still debatable. In his lecture Ducasse attempts to convince Lamont and likeminded persons that discussion of the question is worth reopening.

BIOGRAPHICAL NOTE.   Curt John Ducasse was born in France in 1881. He came to the United States in 1900 and became an American citizen ten years later. He received his A.B. degree from the University of Washington and his Ph.D. from Harvard. He spent almost his entire professional philosophical career at Brown University where he chaired the Department of Philosophy for over twenty years. He had a number of prestigious offices in professional societies and filled several distinguished visiting professorships. His many books include *Causation and the Types of Necessity* (1924), *The Philosophy of Art* (1930), *Philosophy as a Science* (1941), *Nature, Mind, and Death* (1951), *A Philosophical Scrutiny of Religion* (1953), *A Critical Examination of the Belief in Life After Death* (1961), and *Knowledge, Truth and Causation* (1969). He died at the age of 88 in 1969.

THE ARGUMENT OF THE PASSAGES.   In the following material selected from his lec-ture, Ducasse proposes to do four things:

1. To explore why people desire, and believe in, some sort of life after death.
2. To state the arguments commonly advanced to prove that such a life after death is impossible.
3. To show that these arguments fail to prove their point.
4. To expose the tacit but arbitrary assumption that makes these arguments against survival appear more convincing than the evidence allows.

Why, then, do people desire and believe in a life after death?

The craving for continued existence is very widespread. Even persons who believe that death means complete extinction of the individual's consciousness often find comfort in various substitute conceptions of survival. They may, for instance, dwell on the continuity of the individual's germ plasm in his descendants. Or they find solace in the thought that, the past being indestructible, their individual life remains eternally an intrinsic part of the history of the world. Also—and more satisfying to one's craving for personal importance—there is the fact that since the acts of one's life have effects, and these in turn further effects, and so on, therefore what one has done goes on for-ever influencing remotely, and sometimes greatly, the course of future events.

Gratifying to one's vanity, too, is the prospect that, if the achievements of one's life have been great or even only conspicuous, or one's benefactions or evil deeds have been notable, one's name may not only be remembered by acquaintances and relatives for a little while, but may live on in recorded history. But evidently survival in any of these senses is but a consolation prize—but a thin substitute for the continuation of conscious individual life, which may not be a fact, but which most men crave nonetheless.

The roots of this craving are certain desires which death appears to frustrate. For some, the chief of these is for reunion with persons dearly loved. For others, whose lives have been wretched, it is the desire for another chance at the happiness they have missed. For others yet, it is desire for further opportunity to grow in ability, knowledge or character. Often, there is also the desire, already mentioned, to go on counting for something in the affairs of men. And again, a future life for oneself and others is often desired in order that the redressing of the many injustices of this life shall be possible. But it goes without saying that, although desires such as these are often sufficient to cause belief in a future life, they constitute no evidence at all that it is a fact.

In this connection, it may be well to point out that, although both the belief in survival and the belief in the existence of a god or gods are found in most religions, nevertheless there is no necessary connection between the two beliefs. No contradiction would be involved in supposing either that there is a God but no life after death or that there is a life after death but no God. The belief that there is a life after death may be tied to a religion, but it is no more intrinsically religious than would be a belief that there is life on the planet Mars. The after-death world, if it exists, is just another region or dimension of the universe.

But although belief in survival of death is natural and easy and has always been held in one form or another by a large majority of mankind, critical reflection quickly brings forth a number of apparently strong reasons to regard that belief as quite illusory.

A belief in postdeath survival comes easily and naturally to many people. That has been Ducasse's first point. It is, however, equally true that critical thinkers like Lamont have come up with apparently strong reasons for regarding such belief as groundless, as an exercise in wishful thinking. So Ducasse proceeds to review those deflationary reasons, the most important of which relate to the mind–body problem. The first reason he examines is the claim that consciousness *depends* on the central nervous system. Ducasse writes,

There are, *first* of all, a number of facts which definitely suggest that both the existence and the nature of consciousness wholly depend on the presence of a functioning nervous system. It is pointed out, for example, that wherever consciousness is observed, it is found associated with a living and functioning body. Further, when the body dies, or the head is struck a heavy blow, or some anesthetic is administered, the familiar outward evidences of consciousness terminate, permanently or temporarily. Again, we know well that drugs of various kinds—alcohol, caffeine, opium, heroin, and many others—cause specific changes at the time in the nature of a person's mental states. Also, by stimulating in appropriate ways the body's sense organs, corresponding states of consciousness—namely, the various kinds of sensations—can be caused at will. On the other hand, cutting a sensory nerve immediately eliminates a whole range of sensations.

Again, the contents of consciousness, the mental powers, or even the personality, are modified in characteristic ways when certain regions of the brain are destroyed by disease or injury or are disconnected from the rest by such an operation as prefrontal lobotomy. And that the nervous system is the indispensable basis of the mind is further suggested by the fact that, in the evolutionary scale, the degree of intelligence of various species of animals keeps pace closely with the degree of development of their brain.

The implication of this close dependence of consciousness on the central nervous system is that when the nervous system dies, consciousness loses its hold on existence. When your bodily nervous system dies, you go out like a light.

The second argument against postdeath survival Ducasse scrutinizes is the claim that consciousness does not merely depend on the nervous system but is *identical with* minute physical or chemical events that take place in the brain. Identity is a much closer relationship than dependence.

That continued existence of mind after death is impossible has been argued also on the basis . . . that what we call states of consciousness—or more particularly, ideas, sensations, volitions, feelings, and the like—are really nothing but the minute physical or chemical events which take place in the tissues of the brain. For, it is urged, it would be absurd to suppose that an idea or volition, if it is not itself a material thing or process, could cause material effects such as contractions of muscles. . . .

Still *another* difficulty confronting the hypothesis of survival becomes evident when one imagines in some detail what survival would have to include in order to satisfy the desires which cause man to crave it. It would, of course, have to include persistence not alone of consciousness, but also of personality; that is, of the individual's character, acquired knowledge, cultural skills and interests, memories, and awareness of personal identity. But even this would not be enough, for what man desires is not bare survival, but to go on living in some objective way. And this means to go on meeting new situations and, by exerting himself to deal with them, to broaden and deepen his experience and develop his latent capacities.

But it is hard to imagine this possible without a body and an environment for it, upon which to act and from which to receive impressions. And, if a body and an environment were supposed, but not material and corruptible ones, then it is paradoxical to think that, under such radically different conditions, a given personality could persist.

To take a crude but telling analogy, it is past belief that, if the body of any one of us were suddenly changed into that of a shark or an octopus, and placed in the ocean, his personality could, for more than a very short time, if at all, survive intact so radical a change of environment and a bodily form.

Thus far Professor Ducasse has asked why so many people find some form of personal survival to be both desirable and credible, and why, nevertheless, other people, more tough-minded perhaps, consider such belief to be lacking sufficient objective evidence. Now he turns to criticism of the position of those tough-minded skeptics: first, their argument from identity; next, their argument from dependence.

Such, in brief, are the chief reasons commonly advanced for holding that survival is impossible. Scrutiny of them, however, will, I think, reveal that they are not as strong as they first seem and far from strong enough to show that there can be no life after death.

Let us consider *first* the assertion that "thought," or "consciousness," is another name for subvocal speech, or for some other form of behavior, or for molecular processes in the tissues of the brain. As Paulsen and others have pointed out, no evidence ever is or can be offered to support that assertion, because it is in fact but a disguised proposal to make the words "thought," "feeling," "sensation," "desire," and so on, denote facts quite different from those which these words are commonly employed to denote. To say that those words are but other names for certain chemical or behavioral events is as grossly arbitrary as it would be to say that "wood" is but another name for glass, or "potato" but another name for cabbage. What thought, desire, sensation, and other mental states are like, each of us can observe directly by introspection; and what introspection reveals is that they do not in the least resemble muscular contraction, or glandular secretion, or any other known bodily events. No tampering with language can alter the observable fact that thinking is one thing and muttering quite another; that the feeling called anger has no resemblance to the bodily behavior which usually goes with it; or that an act of will is not in the least like anything we find when we open the skull and examine the brain. Certain mental events are doubtless connected in some way with certain bodily events, but they are not those bodily events themselves. The connection is not identity.

This being clear, let us *next* consider the arguments offered to show that mental processes, although not identical with bodily processes, nevertheless depend on them. We are told, for instance, that some head injuries, or anesthetics, totally extinguish consciousness for the time being. As already pointed out, however, the strict fact is only that the usual bodily signs of consciousness are then absent. But they are also absent when a person is asleep; and yet, at the same time, dreams, which are states of consciousness, may be occurring.

It is true that when the person concerned awakens, he often remembers his dreams, whereas the person that has been anesthetized or injured has usually no memories relating to the period of apparent blankness. But this could mean that his consciousness was, for the first time, dissociated from its ordinary channels of manifestation, as was reported of the coconscious personalities of some of the patients of Dr. Morton Prince. Moreover, it sometimes occurs that a person who has been in an accident reports lack of memories not only for the period during which his body was unresponsive but also for a period of several hours *before* the accident, during which he had given to his associates all the ordinary external signs of being conscious as usual.

But, more generally, if absence of memories relating to a given period proved unconsciousness for that period, this would force us to conclude that we were unconscious during the first few years of our lives, and indeed have been so most of the time since; for the fact is that we have no memories whatever of most of our days. That we were alive and conscious on any long past specific date is, with only a few exceptions, not something we actually remember, but only something which we infer must be true.

At this point Ducasse launches into an exposition and defense of psychical research because he believes such research provides evidence which must be taken seriously as one addresses the issue of postdeath survival. In examining paranormal phenomena such as apparitions and mediums, the Society for Psychical Research (of which Ducasse was a committed member for many years) has presented evidence that seems (1) to call into question the arguments from identity and dependence, (2) to support dualism, and (3) to provide evidence of postdeath survival.

To assert that [all manifestations of the mind invariably cease at death] is to ignore altogether the considerable amount of evidence to the contrary, gathered over many years and carefully checked by the Society for Psychical Research. This evidence, which is of a variety of kinds, has been reviewed by Professor Gardner Murphy in an article published in the Journal of the Society. He mentions first the numerous well-authenticated cases of apparition of a dead person to others as yet unaware that he had died or even been ill or in danger. The more strongly evidential cases of apparition are those in which the apparition conveys to the person who sees it specific facts until then secret. An example would be that of the apparition of a girl to her brother nine years after her death, with a conspicuous scratch on her cheek. Their mother then revealed to him that she herself had made that scratch accidentally while preparing her daughter's body for burial, but that she had then at once covered it with powder and never mentioned it to anyone. . . .

Other striking instances are those of an apparition seen simultaneously by several persons. It is on record that an apparition of a child was perceived first by a dog, that the animal's rushing at it, loudly barking, interrupted the conversation of the seven persons present in the room, thus drawing their attention to the apparition, and that the latter then moved through the room for some fifteen seconds, followed by the barking dog.

Another type of empirical evidence of survival consists of communications, purporting to come from the dead, made through the persons commonly called sensitives, mediums, or automatists. Some of the most remarkable of these communications were given by the celebrated American medium, Mrs. Piper, who for many years was studied by the Society for Psychical Research, London, with the most elaborate precautions against all possibility of fraud. Twice, particularly, the evidences of identity supplied by the dead persons who purportedly were thus communicating with the living were of the very kinds, and of the same precision and detail which would ordinarily satisfy a living person of the identity of another living person with whom he was not able to communicate directly, but only through an intermediary, or by letter or telephone.

Again, sometimes the same mark of identity of a dead person, or the same message from him, or complementary parts of one message, are obtained independently from two mediums in different parts of the world.

Of course, when facts of these kinds are recounted, as I have just done, only in abstract summary, they make little if any impression upon us. And the very word "medium" at once brings to our minds the innumerable instances of demonstrated fraud perpetuated by charlatans to extract money from the credulous bereaved. But the modes of trickery and sources of error, which immediately suggest themselves to us as easy, natural explanations of the seemingly extraordinary facts, suggest themselves just as quickly to the members of the research committees of the Society for Psychical Research. Usually, these men have had a good deal more experience than the rest of us with the tricks of conjurers and fraudulent mediums, and take against them precautions far more strict and ingenious than would occur to the average sceptic.

But when, instead of stopping at summaries, one takes the trouble to study the detailed, original reports, it then becomes evident that they cannot all be just laughed off; for to accept the hypothesis of fraud or mal-observation would often require more credulity than to accept the facts reported.

To *explain* those facts, however, is quite another thing. Only two hypotheses at all adequate to do so have yet been advanced. One is that the communications really come, as they purport to do, from persons who have died and have survived death. The other is the hypothesis of telepathy—that is, the supposition, itself startling enough, that the medium is able to gather information directly from the minds of others, and that this is the true source of the information communicated. To account for all the facts, however, this hypothesis has to be stretched very far, for some of them require us to suppose that the medium can tap the minds even of persons far away and quite unknown to him, and can tap even the subconscious parts of their minds.

Diverse highly ingenious attempts have been made to devise conditions that would rule out telepathy as a possible explanation of the communications received; but some of the most critical and best-documented investigators still hold that it has not yet been absolutely excluded. Hence, although some of the facts recorded by psychical research constitute, prima facie, strong empirical evidence of survival, they cannot be said to establish it beyond question. But they do show that we need to revise rather radically in some respects our ordinary ideas of what is and is not possible in nature.

If people give fair consideration to the findings of psychical research, and if they scrutinize carefully the arguments against survival, they should, Ducasse thinks, agree with him that those arguments against survival are not nearly so convincing as critics like Lamont lead us to believe. But why do people find these "weak" arguments so convincing? That is a good question to ask. If you have examined a person's arguments on a certain matter, and you find them uniformly weak and unconvincing, it is a good thing to ask why, nevertheless, that person finds them convincing. Ducasse offers the following answer:

> It is, I believe, because these persons approach the question of survival with a certain unconscious metaphysical bias. It derives from a particular initial assumption which they tacitly make. It is that *to be real is to be material*. And to be material, of course, is to be some process or part of the perceptually public world, that is, of the world we all perceive by means of our so-called five senses.
>
> Now the assumption that to be real is to be material is a useful and appropriate one for the purpose of investigating the material world and operating upon it; and this purpose is a legitimate and frequent one. But those persons, and most of us, do not realize that the validity of that assumption is strictly relative to that specific purpose. Hence they, and most of us, continue making the assumption, and it continues to rule judgment, even when, as now, the purpose in view is a different one, for which the assumption is no longer useful or even congruous.
>
> The point is all-important here and therefore worth stressing. Its essence is that the conception of the nature of reality that proposes to define the real as the material is not the expression of an observable fact to which everyone would have to bow, but is the expression only of a certain direction of interest on the part of the persons who so define reality—of interest, namely, which they have chosen to center wholly in the material, perceptually public world. This specialized interest is of course as legitimate as any other; but it automatically ignores all the facts, commonly called facts of mind, which only introspection reveals. And that specialized interest is what alone compels persons in its grip to employ the word "mind" to denote, instead of what it commonly does denote, something else altogether, namely, the public behavior of bodies that have minds.

Only so long as one's judgement is swayed unawares by that special interest do the logically weak arguments against the possibility of survival which we have examined seem strong.

It is possible, however, and just as legitimate, as well as more conducive to a fair view of our question, to center one's interest at the start on the facts of mind as introspectively observable, ranking them as most real in the sense that they are the facts the intrinsic nature of which we most directly experience, the facts which we most certainly know to exist; and moreover, that they are the facts without the experiencing of which we should not know any other facts whatever—such, for instance, as those of the material world.

The sort of perspective one gets from this point of view is what I propose now to sketch briefly. For one thing, the material world is then seen to be but one among other objects of our consciousness. Moreover, one becomes aware of the crucially important fact that it is an object postulated rather than strictly given. What this means may be made clearer by an example. Suppose that, perhaps in a restaurant we visit for the first time, an entire wall is occupied by a large mirror and we look into it without realizing that it is a mirror. We then perceive, in the part of space beyond it, various material objects, notwithstanding that in fact they have no existence there at all. A certain set of the vivid color images which we call visual sensations was all that was strictly given to us, and these we construed, automatically and instantaneously, but nonetheless erroneously, as signs or appearances of the existence of certain material objects at a certain place.

Again, and similarly, we perceive in our dreams various objects which at the time we take as physical but which eventually we come to believe were not so. And this eventual conclusion, let it be noted, is forced upon us not because we then detect that something, called "physical substance," was lacking in those objects, but only because we notice, as we did not at the time, that their behavior was erratic—incoherent with their ordinary one. That is, their appearance was a *mere* appearance, deceptive in the sense that it did not then predict truly, as ordinarily it does, their later appearances. This, it is important to notice, is the *only* way in which we ever discover that an object we perceive was not really physical, or was not the particular sort of physical object we judged it to be.

These two examples illustrate the fact that our perception of physical objects is sometimes erroneous. But the essential point is that, even when it is veridical instead of erroneous, *all* that is literally and directly given to our minds is still only *some set of sensations*. These, on a given occasion, may be only color sensations; but they often include also tactual sensations, sounds, odors, and so on. It is especially interesting, however, to remark here in passing that, with respect to almost all the many thousands of persons and other "physical" objects we have perceived in a life time, *vivid color images* were the only data our perceiving strictly had to go by; that, if the truth should happen to have been that those objects, like ghosts or images in a mirror, were actually intangible—that is, were *only* color images—we should never had discovered that this was the fact. For all we *directly* know, it *may* have been the fact!

To perceive a physical object, then, instead of merely experiencing passively certain sensations (something which perhaps hardly ever occurs), is always to *interpret*, that is to *construe*, given sensations as signs of, and appearances to us of, a postulated something other than themselves, which we believe is causing them in us and is capable of causing in us others of specific kinds. We believe this because we believe that our sensations too must have some cause, and we find none of them among our other mental states.

Such a postulated extramental something we call "a physical object." We say that we observe physical objects, and this is true. But it is important for the present purpose to be clear that we "observe" them never in any more direct or literal manner than is constituted by the process of interpretive postulation just described—never, for example, in the wholly direct and literal manner in which we are able to observe our sensations themselves and our other mental states.

That perception of a physical object is thus always the product of two factors—one, a set of sensations simply given to us, and the other an act of interpretation of these, performed by us—is something which easily escapes notice and has even been denied. This, however, is only because the interpretive act is almost always automatic, instantaneous, and correct—like, for instance, that of thinking of the meaning of any familiar word we hear. But that an interpretive act does occur is forced on our attention when, in a particular case, we discover that we misconstrued the meaning of the sensations. Or again, the interpretive act is noticeable when, because the sensations are too scant and therefore ambiguous, we catch ourselves hesitating between two or more possible interpretations of them and say that we are not sure what object it is we see.

We should recall Ducasse's intentions as expressed in the title that he chose for his lecture. The title was, "Is Life After Death Possible?" His stated intentions do not go beyond that. He is not trying to prove that a person does indeed survive the death of his or her body. Instead, in this lecture he has offered only a defensive skirmish directed against those persons who insist that survival is not possible, and that therefore any belief in it is an impossible belief. Ducasse's defensive strategy is to insist that their arguments are not compelling and that their obliviousness to this may well stem from an unsuspected or unacknowledged metaphysical bias that to be real is to be material. Our next author, Robert Almeder, on the basis of a comprehensive survey of paranormal human experiences, moves somewhat beyond Ducasse to argue that not only is belief in postdeath survival possible, it is indeed rationally warranted.

NOTE ON SOURCES. The material in this section is quoted from Curt John Ducasse, "Is Life After Death Possible?," published in the Forester Lecture Series, Vol. 2 (Berkeley: University of California Press, 1948).

3 ROBERT ALMEDER

DEATH IS NOT THE END

FROM DUCASSE TO ALMEDER. For Lamont the question is closed: postdeath survival is an illusion; death is the end. For Ducasse, however, the question is still open: death may not in fact be the end. Ducasse challenged Lamont's interpretation of the empirical data and invited people like Lamont to consider some additional data: the data harbored by the paranormal experiences of humankind. Robert Almeder has surveyed a multitude of accounts that allegedly portray paranormal experiences, and has winnowed out of these a considerable cluster of accounts that he believes are beyond fraud and hoax. Such "authentic" accounts require an explanation, and the explanation Almeder has reached involves personal postdeath survival. Indeed, Almeder finds the data so convincing that he almost echoes Lamont in saying that the question is *closed* (but closed in a different fashion): death is not the end; persons do survive the death of their bodies. The following case presented by Almeder is taken from his recent book, *Death and Personal Survival: The Evidence for Life After Death*, published in 1992.

BIOGRAPHICAL NOTE.   Robert F. Almeder is Professor of Philosophy at Georgia State University. Almeder received his doctorate in philosophy from the University of Pennsylvania in 1969 and specializes in epistemology, American philosophy and ethics. Among his recent works are *Blind Realism: An Essay on Human Knowledge and Natural Science; Beyond Death: Evidence for Life After Death* (1987); and *Death and Personal Survival: The Evidence for Life After Death* (1992), from which the readings in this section have been taken.

THE ARGUMENT OF THE PASSAGES.   Almeder cites five kinds of human experiences which, he argues, are best explained by the hypothesis of postdeath survival. Given the variety of these experiences and the number of their occurrences, Almeder claims that they provide sufficient evidence for belief in postdeath survival. From the many cases discussed by Almeder we have selected only one or two to illustrate each of the five types.

The first type of experience involves a person remembering that he or she lived an earlier life as a different person. These memories have frequently been so vivid and detailed that people have taken them to be evidence of *reincarnation*. Consider the following case of Mrs. Smith reported by the British psychiatrist, Dr. Arthur Guirdham.

> In his book *The Cathars and Reincarnation*, a British psychiatrist named Dr. Arthur Guirdham describes in detail a particular case that compelled him to accept the belief in reincarnation.[1] The woman in the case, Mrs. Smith, was his patient; and he met her in 1961 when he was chief psychiatrist at Bath Hospital in England. Mrs. Smith's problem was that she had persistent nightmares during which she shrieked so loud that she and her husband feared it would wake the whole neighborhood.
>
> Dr. Guirdham examined her closely for neuroses but found she had none. After a few months, Mrs. Smith told Guirdham that, when she was a girl, she had written her dreams down. She had also written things that came spontaneously to her mind as recollections—things she could not understand that had to do with people, and specific names she had never heard. She gave the papers to the doctor, and he examined them.[2]
>
> Dr. Guirdham was surprised to find that what she had written as a school girl were verses of songs in medieval French and in langue d'oc, the language spoken in southern France in the twelfth and thirteenth centuries. The doctor ascertained that she had never studied these languages in school and that there was no source avail-

[1]   Arthur Guirdham, *The Cathars and Reincarnation* (London: Neville Spearman, 1970).
[2]   Ibid., p. 108.

able for her learning them. He sent a report of her story to Professor René Nelli of Toulouse University, and asked for the professor's opinion on the matter. Nelli responded that her writings gave an accurate account of the Cathars in Toulouse in the thirteenth century. The Cathars were a group of Christian dissidents of the extreme dualist persuasion, whose religious beliefs were close to the Albigensians and centered on the belief in reincarnation. They were persecuted and destroyed during the Inquisition.

Only gradually did Mrs. Smith admit having had an intensive uprush of memory in her early teens[3]—memories of a past life with a Cathar priest named Roger de Grisolles, whom she loved very much, and who taught her Cathar rituals and religious principles.[4] Guirdham states that, apart from her dreams, Mrs. Smith had experienced a number of these spontaneous recollections, and she told him in horrid detail her recollection of the massacre of the Cathars.[5] She also told him that in her dreams and recollections of a previous life she had been kept prisoner in a certain church crypt. Guirdham notes that, at first, experts said this church crypt had never been used for that purpose, but later research showed that so many religious prisoners were taken on one occasion that there was no room for all of them in regular prisons. Some had been kept in that very crypt.

Guirdham visited the south of France in 1967 to investigate the case. He read thirteenth-century manuscripts (available to only a limited number of scholars), and these manuscripts showed that Mrs. Smith's account was accurate. She had given Guirdham names and descriptions of people, places, and events, all of which turned out to be accurate to the last detail. Guirdham claims that there was no normal way in which Mrs. Smith could have known about these things. He even found in the manuscripts four of the songs she wrote as a child. They were correct, word for word.[6]

Guirdham notes that, although his subject claimed never to have read any books on the subject of thirteenth-century life, she made correct drawings of old French coins, jewelry worn at the time, and the layout of buildings—to say nothing of the intricate details of Cathar ritual.

Guirdham attests that Mrs. Smith was able to name and place accurately in their family and social relationships people who do not appear in the textbooks, but who were ultimately traced by going back to the dog–Latin records of the Inquisition. These minor characters are still traceable owing to the antlike industry of the Inquisitors and their clerks. Mrs. Smith remembered members of the Fanjeaux and Mazzarolles families, in particular giving their first names and the roles they played. She recollected treating her friend Roger de Grisolles with sugarloaf as a tonic. However, the experts called this into question: the existence of sugar at this time in Europe was doubted. Further investigation disclosed that sugar in loaf form was derived from Arab medicine and did indeed exist at this period in France.[7]

Even more remarkable was Guirdham's patient's description of her death when she was burned at the stake. This she both dreamed and subsequently claimed to remember. The description, conveyed by Guirdham as part of his case, reads as follows:

---

3   Ibid., p. 10.
4   Ibid., pp. 73–84.
5   Ibid., pp. 107ff.
6   Ibid., pp. 125ff.
7   Ibid., pp. 94–95.

The pain was maddening. You should pray to God when you're dying, if you can pray when you're in agony. In my dream I didn't pray to God. . . . I didn't know when you were burnt to death you'd bleed. I thought the blood would all dry up in the terrible heat. But I was bleeding heavily. The blood was dripping and hissing in the flames. I wished I had enough blood to put the flames out. The worst part was my eyes. I hate the thought of going blind.

. . . . In this dream I was going blind. I tried to close my eyelids but I couldn't. They must have been burnt off, and now those flames were going to pluck my eyes out with their evil fingers. . . .

The flames weren't so cruel after all. They began to feel cold. Icy cold. It occurred to me that I wasn't burning to death but freezing to death. I was numb with the cold and suddenly I started to laugh. I had fooled those people who thought they could burn me. I am a witch. I had magicked the fire and turned it to ice.[8]

Finally, in a lecture entitled "Reincarnation and the Practice of Medicine," Dr. Guirdham reflected on certain crucial details of the case, many of which were also discussed in his book.

Twenty-five years ago, as a student, a school girl at the age of 13, she was insisting that Cathar priests did not always wear black. You will find the statement that they did in any book on the subject written in any language until 1965. Yet she said that her friend in the thirteenth century wore *dark blue*. It now transpires that at one sitting of the Inquisition (the Inquisition of Jacques Fournier, who was Bishop at Palmiers), it came out ten times in one session that Cathar priests sometimes wore dark blue or dark green. But that fact had been lying in the archives in Latin for long enough, and was only accessible to the public in 1965 when Duvernoy edited the record of the said Inquisitors that was published in Toulouse in 1966. But this woman knew this in 1944 as a school girl.

Again she could describe rituals in a house, a kind of convent. . . . Professor Nelli, the greatest living authority on the Troubadors—who definitely are connected with the Cathars—wrote to me and said, "This is almost exactly Cathar ritual, making allowance for local deviation." He also added later that he would tell me where the place was, the Convent of Montreal. By way of future advice, he added that, in case of doubt, one should "go by the patient." Professor Nelli is the most meticulous and skeptical assessor of evidence.

When I first wrote to another specialist, Professor Duvernoy of Toulouse, he said, "Get in touch with me about everything you want. I am astonished at your detailed knowledge of Catharism." I couldn't say, "I've got this by copying down the dreams of a woman of thirty-six or seven which she had when she was a grammar school girl of thirteen." He's found out since, but he's all the more keen to supply me with the evidence. . . .

If the professors at Toulouse are amazed at the accuracy with which an English girl can produce details of Catharism known to few, that is good enough for me. . . . [A]ll I have done in this matter is to listen to the story, act as an ama-

---

8   Ibid., p. 89.

teur historian, and try to verify from many sources the details she had noted. I believe this to be a unique and entirely valid experience.[9]

Almeder observes,

> At this point, then, the argument for reincarnation is very simple. It is this. What would be a better or more plausible explanation for these cases than to assume that human personality (whatever it is) admits of reincarnation? Opponents of reincarnation must provide an equally plausible or better alterative explanation for the data if they are to undermine effectively the claim that the best available explanation for these sorts of cases is reincarnation.

The second type of experience includes *apparitions* of the dead. For many of us, the thought of ghosts engenders ideas of the trickery associated with Halloween and horror movies. Yet there are people who claim that they have in fact encountered apparitions of deceased persons that are neither fraudulent nor hallucinatory, apparitions which have been taken as evidence of postmortem survival. As you assess the following case involving Mrs. Butler, note the measures taken by the Reverend Abraham Cummings to verify the happenings.

> Consider the case noted by C. J. Ducasse in *A Critical Examination of the Belief in Life after Death*—a case that Ducasse thinks provides striking evidence for life after death.[10] The original account was written in 1826 by the Reverend Abraham Cummings, a graduate of Brown University and a Baptist minister in Maine, in a pamphlet entitled *Immortality Proved by Testimony of Sense*.[11]
>
> The apparitions were of the deceased Mrs. George Butler and occurred in a village near Machiasport, Maine. The "specter" of Mrs. Butler appeared *a number of times over a period of several months*. She was seen on different occasions by groups of people numbering as many as 40 persons, and appeared both indoors and outdoors.[12] She presented extended discourses and moved freely among the gathered people. She also accurately predicted both births and deaths, and conveyed intimate and allegedly very private details of the lives of those in the group.[13] For example, she accurately predicted that the new Mrs. Butler would have one child and shortly thereafter die. She also provided one man with the information—unknown to him and everybody else in the group at the time—that his father in a distant town had

9 Arthur Guirdham, "Reincarnation and the Practice of Medicine," lecture delivered at the College of Psychic Science, London, March 1969, unpublished. See also Guirdham, *Cathars*, pp. 92ff.

10 C. J. Ducasse, *A Critical Examination of the Belief in Life after Death* (Springfield, Ill.: Charles C. Thomas, 1961), pp. 21–22.

11 The Reverend Abraham Cummings's *Immortality Proved by Testimony of Sense* was originally published by J. C. Torrey, in Bath, Maine, in 1826. A copy is available in the New York Public Library as well as in the Library of the Division of Personality Studies in the Department of Behavioral Medicine at the University of Virginia School of Medicine in Charlottesville, Virginia. The case has been closely examined by Muriel Roll in her article "A Nineteenth-century Matchmaking Apparition: Comments on Abraham Cummings' 'Immortality Proved by Testimony of the Senses,'" *Journal of the American Society for Psychical Research* 63, no. 4 (October 1969), pp. 396–409.

12 Cummings, *Immortality Proved*, pp. 29ff.

13 Ibid., pp. 32–34.

recently died.[14] Given the time factor involved, Cummings argues that nobody in town could have had normal knowledge of that death. Moreover, Reverend Cummings was astute enough to obtain at the time more than 30 sworn affidavits from some of the 100 or more persons who had heard and/or seen the specter under different circumstances in the company of others.[15] These affidavits are reproduced in the pamphlet.[16] He also examined the testimony very closely and rejected the possibility of fraud or hoax.[17]

Furthermore, on one occasion Captain Butler (Mrs. Butler's living husband) placed his hand "upon" the apparition, and his hand passed through as if its body were made of light. Six or seven persons witnessed this event and made it part of their sworn testimony.[18]

Assuming the absence of fraud or hoax, and assuming that other similar cases exist in which we can equally assume the absence of fraud or hoax (both assumptions we shall establish later), what can be said about this case?

To begin with, the frequency of the apparition, the changing circumstances in which it appeared, and the large and varying numbers of persons involved in testifying to each instance of the apparition suggest that the likelihood of a collective perceptual error on each occasion is remarkably low. Certainly we cannot dismiss this case as readily as we would a report of an apparition by one person or a group of persons on only one occasion. Here, any appeal to delusion or hallucination seems much more difficult to argue, and not very convincing. Certainly the probability of such a mistake on each occasion is remarkably lower than it is in the case of a group sighting on only one occasion. As a matter of fact, the probability of a large group of people being mistaken in their perceptual beliefs about what they have seen when they testify to seeing the same thing repeatedly under different circumstances (both indoors and outdoors) over an extended period of time (many months) in which the membership of the group changes frequently is zero. I know of no case in which a collective mistaken belief of precisely this sort has ever been established.

Also, inasmuch as the specter accurately predicted both births and deaths, and conveyed to the group information (some very private) that nobody in the group could plausibly have known at the time, we cannot easily dismiss as mistaken the information the group obtained in the apparitional experience. If the people in this case were seeing and hearing something other than the postmortem surviving personality of Mrs. Butler (but mistakenly believed that they were seeing as much), what indeed could they have been seeing that is not evidence of personal survival?

It is fashionable to say that they must have been seeing things that were not really there, or seeing things that were really there but not the things they thought they saw. Such a response is predicated on the assumption that they did not see what they say they saw—and what exactly is the evidence that they could not have seen what they say they saw?

You may be inclined to discount the report about Mrs. Butler because it was recorded more than 150 years ago. If so, consider the following case which

14 Ibid., p. 33.
15 Ibid., pp. 70ff.
16 Ibid., pp. 22ff.
17 Ibid., p. 34.
18 Ibid., p. 30.

occurred just a few years ago, the case of "The Ghost of Flight 401." Like the apparition of Mrs. Butler, the Ghost of Flight 401 made specific predictions that accurately foretold future events.

In the dead of night on December 28, 1972, Eastern Airlines Flight 401 plunged into the Florida Everglades, killing 101 passengers and crew. Two months later the alleged ghosts of its pilot and its second officer began to appear on sister ships carrying or using parts salvaged from the original crash. The pilot's name was Captain Robert Loft; the second officer's was Don Repo. According to John Fuller (the principal investigator of the case), testimony regarding the apparition of the two ghosts grew to alarming proportions. Most of the sightings occurred in the galley of Eastern plane 318, which—like a few other L-1011s—was using some of the salvaged parts of the L-1011 that crashed in the Everglades.[19]

One incident occurred on plane 318 as it prepared to depart Newark, New Jersey, for Miami, Florida. The second officer had completed his preflight walk-around check. The captain and the first officer were in the cockpit. The food for in-flight meals had been delivered to the plane, and everything was set for takeoff.

In the first-class section, the senior stewardess was making the usual head count, and her count was off by one passenger too many. An Eastern captain in uniform was in one of the seats. She inferred that he was "deadheading" (going back) to Miami, where the flight originated; he was not on her list, thus accounting for the extra passenger. It was necessary, however, to confirm the count, and she advised the captain that he was not on her list. She asked if he would be riding in the jump seat back to Miami. The captain did not respond, looking straight ahead. She asked him again whether he was a first-class traveler in the jump seat. Still he did not answer and looked straight ahead. Perplexed, she brought the flight supervisor over to ask the same question, and she too received no response. The captain seemed normal in every respect except that he seemed to be in some sort of daze. His unresponsiveness worried the two attendants, and one of them went into the cockpit to tell the flight captain what was transpiring. The flight captain, too, was perplexed. He left the cockpit and went to the first-class compartment.

In reporting this incident, John Fuller notes that half-a-dozen regular first-class passengers were in the immediate vicinity of the silent deadheading captain, and all of them were curious about what was going on.[20] As the flight captain approached the seat, he was puzzled that there was no record of another Eastern captain's being listed as jump-seat occupant, and that this one apparently had no pass for the flight.

With the flight's two stewardesses and their supervisor beside him, the captain leaned down to address the other captain and, just as he did, he froze. "My God, it's Bob Loft," he said. The cabin was totally silent and then, as it is reported, the captain in the seat disappeared before the eyes of all.

The flight captain returned to the operations officer in the cockpit. After a bit of delay, the plane was totally searched. The missing captain could not be found. Plane 318 finally did take off for Miami, its passengers and crew still stunned.

When the three attendants on the flight later sought to examine the flight log (in which, by FAA regulation, every unusual incident had to be recorded), they found the page for that flight missing, even though the entire crew reported the incident.

---

[19] See John Fuller, *The Ghost of Flight 401* (New York: Berkeley Publishing, 1978).
[20] Ibid., p. 138.

All the pages up to and including the incident had been removed, contrary to general practice. The captain's and the crew's comments were completely missing.[21] Thereafter, the plane 318 log book was removed after every flight—a practice not followed in any other planes at Eastern.

Captain Loft was later sighted again on the same plane, in the galley, simultaneously by two stewardesses and the captain. After this incident, however, the flight was cancelled.[22]

Don Repo, Captain Loft's second officer, was seen even more frequently on plane 318. Indeed, whereas Loft's appearances stopped after a short while (seemingly restricted to the one flight that was cancelled), the specter of Don Repo continued to be visible for at least two years after the crash. I shall recount here only a few of the more interesting incidents in which Repo appeared to a number of people. However, in no fewer than two dozen incidents by the end of 1973, various people reported seeing Repo. In general, he appeared in order to do little repairs for the stewardesses or to advise the flight crew of potential mechanical problems. He was a friendly and a helpful specter who was frequently reported to have had discussions with various people on the plane.

Then there was the incident involving a woman passenger in the first-class section of plane 318, scheduled for a New York to Miami flight. The plane was at the ramp, and the head count had not yet been taken by the flight attendant in the first-class section. The woman passenger was seated next to an Eastern flight officer, in the uniform of a flight engineer.

Something about the officer worried the woman. He looked so ghastly pale and ill; and when she said something to him, he would not respond. She asked him if he felt all right and if she should call the stewardess to help him. Still no response came from the sickly looking flight officer. The woman called the stewardess, who agreed that he seemed ill. The stewardess asked him if he needed any help. Other passengers also noticed him. Then, in front of the group—as before—the flight engineer disappeared. The woman became almost hysterical. Later she and the flight attendant picked out a picture of Repo as the officer who had been in the first-class seat.

In 1974 an Eastern captain allegedly told John Fuller that he had once been warned by a flight engineer riding in the jump seat of his L-1011 that there was going to be an electrical failure.[23] The captain ordered a recheck, which revealed a faulty circuit. Later, after a second look, the cockpit crew identified the intruding second officer sitting in the jump seat as Don Repo.

Finally, there is the Mexico City incident. In February 1974, plane 318 was readied for a flight to Mexico City. During the preparations, one of the flight attendants—working in the galley below—looked at the window of one of the ovens and clearly saw the face of Don Repo looking out at her. She ran to the elevator, went up a deck, and grabbed another flight attendant. Together they went down into the galley and approached the oven. The second flight attendant also saw the image. It was not a reflection. They called the flight deck and gave the story to the flight engineer. Immediately he came down. He also recognized Repo's face in the oven window; and as he gazed at Repo, Repo spoke audibly to the engineer and said, "Watch out for fire

---

21 Ibid., p. 141.
22 Ibid., p. 150.
23 Ibid., p. 159.

on this plane." Then he disappeared. Later that day the plane's third engine burst into flame on takeoff, and it returned to the ground on one engine.

Eastern Airlines' official position on the Ghost of Flight 401 (which principally refers to the sightings of Repo) is that it is gossip, and that nobody ever reported seeing any such ghosts. But the log book of plane 318 has never been made available. Sightings of the ghosts finally did stop—after all the salvaged parts were removed from plane 318.

Like the Butler case, this case involved various persons—sometimes in groups—under various circumstances and over a long period of time, who simultaneously had the same apparitional experience. And nobody had anything to gain by reporting such stories.

Almeder offers his summary assessment of the evidence for postdeath survival provided by encounters with apparitions.

In the end, we may not be able to say *how* a disembodied person can be causally effective in producing visual and auditory sensations that are plausibly taken as evidence for its existence. The crucial point, however, is not that we be able to explain *how* all this can happen, or even *why* it happens. We need only show good reasons for thinking *that* it happens. Here again, demonstrating *that* something happens is no substitute for showing *how* or *why* it happens. But failure to show *how* or *why* is quite consistent with showing *that* it happens.

Is the Butler case unique? Well, if it were, this would be sufficient reason to suspect that the case was fabricated—that it was a hoax of some sort, or the product of some sort of a mistake we may not be able now to detect. Fortunately, the fact that there are other cases very similar to the Butler case—such as the Ghost of Flight 401 and the other cases described above—is good reason to think that the Butler case is not a hoax of some sort or the product of some undetectable mistake.

Even so, we must admit that there is a serious problem with the case of the Ghost of Flight 401. The problem is that, unlike in the Butler case, the testimony and evidence is not a matter of public record and carefully recorded testimony. Nor was the matter investigated by more than the one person cited (a journalist) and the data independently verified with careful methodology. This affords good grounds to question the data and raise the question of hoax. And even if it is not a hoax or the product of careless but honest methodology, we cannot at this moment regard it as a well-established case investigated by careful inquirers. In this regard we can only hope that Eastern Airlines will release the log of flights of plane 318, that some of the principals will come forward to be identified, and that the data will be reexamined.

Similarly, there are those who will argue—plausibly—that a close examination of the Butler case as it is depicted in the pamphlet written by Reverend Cummings raises important questions that were not asked at the time. Moreover, the Butler case took place so long ago that the principals cannot be directly examined on the matter. Was Reverend Cummings the right person to investigate and report on the case? Might he have been altogether too careless and naive? For these reasons—while it seems fair to say that nobody has successfully disputed the Butler case, or even the case of the Ghost of Flight 401—the evidence for personal survival based on these cases is certainly not so strong as would be necessary for inducing anything like robustly confirmed belief rather than plausible or likely belief.

The third type of experience examined by Almeder that purportedly provides evidence for postmortem survival is *possession*. "*Possession*," writes Almeder, "is usually defined as the alleged phenomenon in which a clearly established and well-recognized personality is totally replaced, often only temporarily, by another personality occupying the same physical body" (p. 135). Such a concept of possession presupposes a kind of dualism in which one's personality is distinct from and separable from one's physical body. Both of the following cases of possession involve the supplanting of a woman's personality by the personality of a woman who had recently died. The first case we will review is that of Lurancy Vennum/Mary Roff, the so-called "Watseka Wonder," summarized by Almeder.

Any reasonably adequate discussion of the evidence for life after death should include a consideration of the famous Watseka Wonder as a striking instance of possession—an instance that allegedly supports the belief in postmortem personal survival. The case was originally presented and described by Dr. E. W. Stevens in 1887 in a paper entitled "The Watseka Wonder: A Narrative of Startling Phenomena Occurring in the Case of Mary Lurancy Vennum,"[24] and C. J. Ducasse discusses it in detail in his 1961 *Critical Examination of the Belief in Life after Death*.[25] The circumstances took place in Watseka, Illinois, and concern two girls. The first girl, Mary Roff, had died at 18 in 1865. She was said to have suffered from "fits" and was allegedly able to read closed books and the contents of sealed envelopes.

The second girl was Lurancy Vennum, born in April 1864 and over a year old when Mary Roff died. Lurancy seemed quite normal until 1877 when, at age 13, she complained of feeling queer and had a fit, "including a cataleptic state lasting five hours."[26] On later occasions, while in a trance state, she allegedly talked with "angels" or "spirits" of deceased persons. She also seemed to be possessed by various alien spirits, each of whom took turns possessing her. Her sanity was questioned.

The most interesting (according to Ducasse) of Lurancy's "possessions" was that by the mind of Mary Roff. Lurancy claimed to be Mary Roff and gave evidence of being homesick and wanting to see her (Mary's) parents and brothers. After a few days, Lurancy was taken to and permitted to live with the Roff family.

While living with the Roffs, she seemed quite happy and knew everybody that Mary Roff had known in her lifetime 12–25 years earlier. She readily identified by name the persons who had been friends and neighbors of the Roffs during Mary's lifetime. During her stay at the Roffs' residence, she recounted hundreds of incidents that had occurred in Mary's natural life and, unlike any reincarnation case, never had any awareness of her identity as Lurancy; she could not identify or recognize any of the Vennum family members or their friends and neighbors. Her identity as Mary while living with the Roffs lasted more than three and a half months, and she was fully accepted as Mary by the family.

Later, her identity as Lurancy returned and she recognized nothing about the Roffs but had all the memories of Lurancy, including the usual recognitions attending

---

24 E. W. Stevens, "The Watseka Wonder: A Narrative of Startling Phenomena Occurring in the Case of Mary Lurancy Vennum," *Philosophical Journal*, Religio-philosophical Publishing House, Chicago (1887), pp. 286–316.

25 C. J. Ducasse, *A Critical Examination of the Belief in Life after Death* (Springfield, Ill.: Charles C. Thomas, 1961).

26 Ibid., p. 172.

her life with the Vennums. Occasionally later on, when she visited the Roffs, the Mary Roff personality would emerge for a short while, and again she would lose her identity as Lurancy.

Responding to the charge that this is simply a manifestation of alternating personality, or multiple personality—a personality disorder readily characterized in psychiatry—Ducasse notes that the personality that displaced Lurancy's was (by every test that could be applied) not a dissociated part of her own. Rather, it was the personality, including all the memories, of a particular 18-year old girl who had died when Lurancy was 14 months old.[27]

Moreover, Ducasse claims that in no way could Lurancy have obtained by normal means the extensive and detailed knowledge that Mary possessed and that Lurancy manifested. The Vennums were away from Watseka (the town in Illinois where both the Roffs and the Vennums lived) for the first seven years of Lurancy's life. When they returned to Watseka, their acquaintance with the Roffs consisted of only one brief call lasting a few minutes made by Mrs. Roff on Mrs. Vennum, and of a formal speaking acquaintance on the part of the two men, until the time when Mr. Roff brought Dr. Stevens (the principal investigator) to the Vennums because of Lurancy's insane behavior.[28]

Can we explain what transpired in this case without endorsing the explanation that the disembodied postmortem personality of Mary Roff "took possession" of Lurancy Vennum's body? If not, then we have good evidence that human personality in some important way and to some important degree survives biological death. Naturally, we have to assume that the case is not a hoax or a fraud. Perhaps we could justifiably discount it if there never was another case similar to it, or if we had no other documented cases like it. But we have many cases similar to it, some even better examined and more recent.[29]

One of those "better examined and more recent" cases involves the experiences of Sumitra Singh which took place in India in the 1980s. Almeder offers us a summary of the report prepared by a team of on site investigators.

In a 1989 article in the *Journal of Scientific Exploration*, Ian Stevenson, Satwant Pasricha, and Nicholas McClean-Rice describe and discuss what they regard as a rare case of possession with evidence of paranormal knowledge.[30] The case involves two completely unrelated and unacquainted persons whose families lived in widely separated towns and villages, and the relevant testimony justifies believing that they had no contact with each other before the case developed. The following are the main details of the case offered by Stevenson and his associates.

The subject, Sumitra Singh, was a young married woman of about 17 years old when the case developed in 1985. She was living with her husband and their one

---

27 Ibid., p. 173.

28 Ibid.

29 For other cases similar to the Watseka Wonder, see E. Bourguignon, *Possession* (San Francisco: Chandler and Sharp, 1976); I. M. Lewis, *Ecstatic Religion: An Anthropological Study of Spirit Possession and Shamanism* (Harmondsworth, Middlesex, England: Penguin Books, 1971); and E. M. Pattison, J. Kahan, and G. S. Hurd, "Trance and Possession States," in *Handbook of States of Consciousness*, eds. B. B. Wolman and M. Ullman (New York: Van Nostrand Reinhold, 1986).

30 Ian Stevenson, Satwant Pasricha, and Nicholas McClean-Rice, "A Case of the Possession Type in India with Evidence of Paranormal Knowledge," *Journal of Scientific Explanation* 3, no. 1 (1989), pp. 89–101.

child in the husband's family home in the village of Sharifpura, in the Farrukhabad district of the State of Uttar Pradesh, India. Early in 1985 Sumitra began to develop episodes of loss of consciousness along with eye-roll movements and clenching of teeth. Sometimes in these trances she would speak, and in July of that year she predicted she would die three days later. Indeed, three days later—July 19—she seemed to die. All who were around her considered her dead; she had no pulse, was apneic, and her face was totally drained of blood like that of a dead person. They were grieving and preparing for her funeral when suddenly she revived in a confused state.

Thereafter the woman began to behave very much like a different person. She no longer recognized the people around her, saying that her name was Shiva and that she had been murdered by her in-laws at a place called Dibiyapur. She rejected Sumitra's husband and child and asked to be taken to Shiva's two children. She stated many details that were subsequently found to correspond with the life of another young married woman, Shiva Diwedi, who had died violently—whether from murder or suicide is not known—at Dibiyapur on the night of May 18–19, 1985, two months before Sumitra's apparent death and revival. Shiva's parental family were convinced that her in-laws had murdered her and then attempted to simulate suicide by laying her body on the railway tracks nearby. Shiva's father, Ram Siya Tripathi, had filed a complaint and so initiated a judicial inquiry.

Sumitra's in-laws said they knew nothing of a Shiva who had died at a place called Dibiyapur. Initially, they thought that Sumitra had gone mad and only later that she had become possessed by a discarnate spirit. But, importantly enough, they made no attempt whatsoever to verify what she was saying. It was about a month before Ram Siya Tripathi learned about Sumitra's statements. This occurred accidentally when he heard a rumor, while he was visiting Dibiyapur, that his deceased daughter had taken possession of a girl in a distant village. Nearly two more months elapsed before he was able to verify this information by having someone from a neighboring village visit Sumitra and her family. The information gathered in this way prompted Ram Siya, accompanied by a relative, to visit Sumitra. Sumitra recognized him and said that she was his daughter. With Ram Siya, she visited Shiva's village during the following days and recognized at least 13 members of Shiva's family and friends.

Stevenson and his associates note that, in addition to Sumitra's statements about the life of Shiva and her recognitions of persons Shiva had known, she showed a marked change in behavior. Sumitra's family belonged to the Thakur caste and they were villagers with very little education; Sumitra herself had no formal education, although she could read and write a little. The Tripathis, on the other hand, were Brahmins and middle-class urbanites. Ram Siya was a lecturer in a college, and Shiva had been educated up to the level of earning a B.A. degree. After her revival, Sumitra's behavior changed from that of a simple village girl to that of a reasonably well educated woman of higher caste and more urbane manners, who could now read and write Hindi fluently.[31]

Shortly after the first exchanges of visits between the families concerned, the case caught the attention of Ian Stevenson and S. Pasricha who, with others, began to investigate the case promptly in mid-October 1985. The method of investigation consisted basically of interviews with informants, "particularly first-hand witnesses of the

---

[31] Ibid., p. 83.

apparent death of Sumitra and the change in her personality that followed upon her revival."[32] But the investigating team spent almost as much time interviewing the members of Shiva's family. The interviews were conducted simultaneously by various investigators over a two-year period (ending in October 1987), but principally by Stevenson and Pasricha, who spoke with everybody who might in any way be relevant or material to the case. They interviewed 24 members of Shiva's and Sumitra's families, with the most important witnesses among them being interviewed two or more times. Extensive verbatim notes were taken; and during a few special interviews, tape recordings were made either solely or in addition to taking notes. Moreover, the investigators interviewed another 29 persons who were able to furnish background information, especially about communications between the communities involved in the case.

In examining the case, the Stevenson team paid particular attention to the following aspects: the preceding illness, apparent death, and revival of Sumitra; the possibilities for normal communication of information about Shiva's life and death to Sumitra and her family; and the circumstances under which Sumitra after her revival identified Shiva's family in person and in photographs. Informants for Sumitra's side of the case claimed no previous acquaintance with Shiva's family, and members of Shiva's family claimed that they were completely ignorant of Sumitra's family before the case developed. As Stevenson also notes, apart from the long (for India) geographical distances between the families, they were also separated by significant differences of caste, education, and economic condition.[33]

Naturally, from an evidential viewpoint, the informant's denial of prior acquaintance between the two families is important. According to the investigators, strong support for the informants' denial of prior acquaintance derives from the slow and indirect manner in which Shiva's family learned about the personality change in Sumitra. The investigators describe this process in the following way:

> Sumitra's father and her in-laws made no attempt to verify her statements about Shiva. Word about them first reached the neighboring village of Murra, which is 2 km from Sharifpura. From there it traveled to Dibiyapur apparently conveyed by women of Murra who had married and were living there. Ram Siya Tripathi, on a visit to Dibiyapur, heard a rumor that his dead daughter had taken possession of a girl in a distant village called Sharifpura. However, he had never been to Sharifpura and did not even know where it was located. After another two weeks he learned about a man called Ram Prakash Dube, a native of Murra who was living in Etawah, but whom he had not previously known. He asked Ram Prakash Dube to inquire about the truth of the account he had heard in Dibiyapur. The monsoon rains led to further delays. When Ram Prakash Dube next visited Murra, he looked into the story and confirmed its main outlines to Ram Siya Tripathi, who, as we have mentioned, then went to Sharifpura and had his first meeting with Sumitra on Oct. 20, 1985. This was exactly three months after Sumitra's apparent death and revival. We believe that if the families concerned had been previously acquainted or had had any lines of communication through mutual acquaintances, they would have exchanged information about Sumitra's change of personality much sooner than they did. . . .

[32] Ibid., p. 85.
[33] Ibid.

Members of Sumitra's family said that they had heard nothing about Shiva's death before Sumitra's death, revival and personality change. However, in view of the circulation of some newspapers in their area and of some trading between Sharifpura and Etawah, it is best to assume that they might have learned of Shiva's death and perhaps also learned about some of the allegations of suicide and homicide that figured in the newspaper reports. (There was no radio station in the area. Some television had been introduced at Etawah only [Sharifpura had no electricity], but it only relayed programs from Delhi and broadcast no local news.) The newspaper reports included some of the names of Shiva's parental family and in-laws. The important question remaining is, therefore, whether Sumitra, after the change in her personality, demonstrated knowledge and behavior corresponding to Shiva's life that went beyond the information available in the newspapers reporting the death of Shiva and the related judicial inquiry.[34]

The published report of this case offers a detailed statement of the life, last illness, apparent death, and revival of Sumitra. It emphasizes that, prior to her apparent death, she had experienced a number of "possession-type" episodes for which her family sought the help of a healer. The investigators do not claim that Sumitra had in fact died before her revival. Also, the report examines the pertinent details of the life and death of Shiva. Here the investigators concur with the local authorities in saying that Shiva's death was not accidental; she either was murdered by her in-laws who made it look as though Shiva committed suicide, or else did commit suicide by throwing herself before a railway train.

Most importantly, the report shows a large number of detailed and verified claims made by Sumitra about the life and death of Shiva, and concludes that there is no way of explaining Sumitra's knowledge by appeal to the normal sources of knowledge. Also, Sumitra's behavioral traits distinctly replicated the behavioral characteristics of Shiva even though the two had definitely never met. Thus, impersonation cannot be the explanation for the manifestation of those traits. Without seeking to repeat all the facts of the case, let us look a bit more closely at these two factors as described in detail in the case study.

Stevenson and his associates divide Sumitra's statements into three groups. The first group consists of names of persons and places that the newspaper accounts of Shiva's death and her father's lawsuit had published. The investigators think it extremely unlikely that anyone communicated even the fact of Shiva's death—much less the details—to Sumitra's family. Even so, as noted above, the investigators acknowledge that some newspapers were circulated in the general area of Sharifpura, and so it is possible that Sumitra's family might have learned about Shiva's death through normal channels of information. Therefore, none of the facts that Sumitra related were regarded as paranormally derived if they could be found in the various newspaper accounts of Shiva's death and the circumstances attending it. The second group of Sumitra's statements consists of unverified claims. Sumitra's description of Shiva's death, for example, and the role of her in-laws in the death, remains unverified. The third group of statements includes nicknames and other private affairs not published in the newspapers. This group is the most important because it consists of statements that are verified *and* that there is no normal way for Sumitra to have acquired. On this point the report states,

---

[34] Ibid., pp. 85–86 and 87.

We learned of 19 items that we felt justified in placing in this, the important group. These showed that Sumitra had knowledge of: a particular yellow sari that Shiva had owned, a watch that had belonged to Shiva and the box (in the Tripathi home) in which it was kept, the respective order of birth of Shiva's maternal uncles (although one who was younger actually looked older than one of the older uncles), one of Shiva's nicknames familiarly used in the home (Shiv Shanker), the names of two educational institutions where Shiva had studied (Sarvodya College and Sorawal Intermediate College), the pet names of Shiva's two children (Rinku and Tinku), the names of two friends of Shiva who happened to have the same name, and the names of Shiva's two brothers, two of her sisters, two of her maternal uncles, a maternal aunt (by marriage), and a nephew.[35]

Sumitra's uncued recognition of Shiva's various family members and friends is important as evidence of paranormal knowledge, once it had been established that there was no normal way in which Sumitra could plausibly have acquired this information. In talking about how these recognitions were authenticated, the report notes that the method is quite the same as in cases of the reincarnation type. As the researchers note,

> Observers of recognition in cases suggestive of reincarnation—of which the present case may be considered a variant—frequently vitiate them by asking leading questions or by cueing the subject with glances directed toward the person to be recognized.[36] Nevertheless, there remain several circumstances in which recognitions may occur that deserve credit as showing paranormal knowledge on the part of the subject. These are: recognitions that the subject makes spontaneously without anyone's having asked him or her to identify another person; recognitions that occur when the subject is confronted with a person and asked a question like: "Do you know who this person is?" or "Tell me who I am"; and recognitions in which the subject immediately afterward adds a statement about some intimate detail, perhaps a nickname, not known outside a small circle of family and friends. We learned of twelve members of Shiva's family and circle of friends whom Sumitra recognized under conditions that we believed excluded cueing.[37]

The report then describes in detail the circumstances of seven of Sumitra's recognitions, six of which were clearly without any cueing at all. Perhaps the most interesting consisted in her recognizing a friend of Shiva's youth, one Krishna Devi Dube. This recognition occurred at Sikandarpur when Sumitra visited her mother-in-law's family in February 1986. More than eight years earlier, Krishna Devi and Shiva had known each other when Shiva used to visit one of her maternal uncles in the nearby village of Kainjari, Krishna Devi's native place. When Krishna Devi married, she moved to Sikandarpur and had not met Shiva for more than eight years before Shiva's death. As the investigators report, when Shiva saw Krishna Devi, she cried, "Jiji! How come you are here? I died and have come into a Thakur's family and am helpless." Shiva, when alive, had called Krishna Devi "Jiji," the word meaning "sister."[38]

---

[35] Ibid., p. 91.

[36] Citation in original: Ian Stevenson, *Cases of the Reincarnation Type*, vol. 1: *Ten Cases in India* (Charlottesville: University Press of Virginia, 1975), pp. 39–40.

[37] Stevenson, Pasricha, and McClean-Rice, "Case of Possession Type in India," pp. 91–92.

[38] Ibid., p. 92.

Shiva's father, Ram Siya Tripathi, was initially quite skeptical about the alleged possession until he showed Sumitra a family photograph album and she correctly identified (without prompting) 15 of the 17 people shown to her. Later on, Sumitra also correctly identified in person eight members of the family or circle of friends whose photographs she had not seen. Concurrently, Sumitra failed to recognize places, activities, and people that had been very familiar to her, prior to her alleged assumption of the Shiva personality.

Behaviorally, after her revival, Sumitra dressed and in all other ways (including mode of addressing others) acted like a Brahmin—especially toward her new family, which she regarded as inferior because they were Thakurs. She persisted in her belief that she was a Brahmin and acted very much as one would expect a Brahmin to act. Shiva's father also claimed that he recognized in Sumitra certain personality traits very much like the traits of Shiva, namely, a certain boldness and a tendency to joke, which were not traits of Sumitra before her revival.[39]

What conclusions seem warranted by cases like those of Lurancy Vennum/ Mary Roff (the Watseka Wonder) and Sumitra Singh/Shiva Diwedi? Almeder responds:

Even if we can question such past cases as the Watseka Wonder for the reason that the method of examining and reporting the data do not sufficiently exclude the possibilities of misconstrual, fraud, or a purely naturalistic explanation of the data, nevertheless the case seems persuasive as an instance of ostensible possession. Nobody has shown that such stated possibilities in fact obtained. And there is no way of returning to reexamine the alleged facts in the case. By comparison, it seems that the Sumitra case is much stronger because the rich and detailed data collected, as well as the methodology used in examining them, would likely have unearthed fraud, hoax, bias, or a purely naturalistic origin of the circumstances. Certainly, the methods used in the Sumitra case investigation—methods that were clearly not in practice at the time of the Watseka Wonder—show fairly compellingly that the usual objections to the effect that there might be natural ways to explain the data are quite unfounded.

An equally important point is that in nearly all cultures in all of history there are other cases similar to the Sumitra case. We cannot readily return to examine the data in those cases, of course; but as time progresses, the careful documentation of new cases will no doubt produce more compelling evidence for possession if, as we have argued, the two cases examined above are not unique but represent a fairly common phenomenon. If the Sumitra case is typical of what is out there—and many think that it is—we shall look forward to an increasing number of case studies prepared as convincingly as the Stevenson investigation.

The fourth type of experience discussed by Almeder is the *out-of-body experience*. Almeder cites the work of Raymond A. Moody, Jr., who is both a philosopher and a physician, and one of the chief investigators of Near-Death Experiences (NDEs). In his popular book, *The Light Beyond*, Moody presents an overview of his own research and that of others concerning NDEs. While no two NDEs are identical in content, researchers have been able to identify several themes that recur in

---

[39] Ibid., p. 97.

the accounts of people who have had NDEs. NDEers frequently report having experienced such things as travel through a tunnel toward a bright light, feelings of serenity and painlessness, encounter with other beings, and a life review. In addition, just over 25 percent of NDEers claim to have had out-of-body experiences. Moody reviews several of these reports for us.

There are a couple of things that present enormous difficulty to these researchers: How is it that the patients can give such elaborate and detailed accounts of resuscitation, explaining in their entirety what the doctors were doing to bring them back to life? How can so many people explain what was going on in other rooms of a hospital while their bodies were in the operating room being resuscitated?

To me, these are the most difficult points for the NDE researchers to answer. In fact, so far they have been impossible to explain except with one answer: they really occurred.

Before presenting the wide variety of attempted explanations that exist about NDEs, let's look at some examples of these unexplainable events.

A forty-nine-year-old man had a heart attack so severe that after thirty-five minutes of vigorous resuscitation efforts, the doctor gave up and began filling out the death certificate. Then someone noticed a flicker of life, so the doctor continued his work with the paddles and breathing equipment and was able to restart the man's heart.

The next day, when he was more coherent, the patient was able to describe in great detail what went on in the emergency room. This surprised the doctor. But what astonished him even more was the patient's vivid description of the emergency room nurse who hurried into the room to assist the doctor.

He described her perfectly right down to her wedge hairdo and her last name, Hawkes. He said that she rolled this cart down the hall with a machine that had what looked like two Ping-Pong paddles on it (an electroshocker that is basic resuscitation equipment).

When the doctor asked him how he knew the nurse's name and what she had been doing during his heart attack, he said that he had left his body and—while walking down the hall to see his wife—passed right through nurse Hawkes. He read the name tag as he went through her, and remembered it so he could thank her later.

I talked to the doctor at great length about this case. He was quite rattled by it. Being there, he said, was the only way the man could have recounted this with such complete accuracy.

On Long Island, a seventy-year-old woman who had been blind since the age of eighteen was able to describe in vivid detail what was happening around her as doctors resuscitated her after a heart attack.

Not only could she describe what the instruments looked like, but she could even describe their colors.

The most amazing thing about this to me was that most of these instruments weren't even thought of over fifty years ago when she could last see. On top of all this, she was even able to tell the doctor that he was wearing a blue suit when he began the resuscitation.

Another amazing case that says NDEs are more than just tricks of the mind was relayed to me by a doctor in South Dakota.

Driving into the hospital one morning, he had rear-ended a car. It had been very upsetting to him. He was very worried that the people he had hit would claim neck injury and sue him for a large sum of money.

This accident left him distraught and was very much on his mind later that morning when he rushed to the emergency room to resuscitate a person who was having a cardiac arrest.

The next day, the man he had rescued told him a remarkable story: "While you were working on me, I left my body and watched you work."

The doctor began to ask questions about what the man had seen and was amazed at the accuracy of his description. In precise detail, he told the doctor how the instruments looked and even in what order they were used. He described the colors of the equipment, shapes, and even settings of dials on the machines.

But what finally convinced this young cardiologist that the man's experience was genuine was when he said, "Doctor, I could tell that you were worried about that accident. But there isn't any reason to be worried about things like that. You give your time to other people. Nobody is going to hurt you."

Not only had this patient picked up on the physical details of his surroundings, he had also read the doctor's mind.

After a lecture to doctors at the U.S. Army base in Fort Dix, New Jersey, a man approached me and told about his remarkable NDE. I later confirmed it with his attending physicians.

I was terribly ill and near death with heart problems at the same time that my sister was near death in another part of the same hospital with a diabetic coma. I left my body and went into the corner of the room, where I watched them work on me down below.

Suddenly, I found myself in conversation with my sister, who was up there with me. I was very attached to her, and we were having a great conversation about what was going on down there when she began to move away from me.

I tried to go with her but she kept telling me to stay where I was. "It's not your time," she said. "You can't go with me because it's not your time." Then she just began to recede off into the distance through a tunnel while I was left there alone.

When I awoke, I told the doctors that my sister had died. He denied it, but at my insistence, he had a nurse check on it. She had in fact died, just as I knew she did.

These are only a few of the cases that prove to me that NDEs are more than just hallucinations or "bad dreams." There is no logical explanation for the experiences of these people. Although tunnel experiences and beings of light can easily be chalked off as mere "mind play," out-of-body experiences baffle even the most skeptical in the medical profession.

Having examined the findings of Moody and other researchers, Almeder concludes that out-of-body experiences (OBEs) seem to justify belief in (1) some kind of mind–body dualism and (2) some sort of postmortem survival. Yet, Almeder admits that until we have ideal cases of OBEs that are "well documented and repeated frequently under controlled conditions, we cannot claim to have conclusive evidence warranting the dualist's interpretation of the nonhallucinatory OBE." But, Almeder adds, "we can certainly claim that the dualist's interpretation is more rationally warranted than any alternative interpretation presently available" (*Death and Personal Survival*, p. 198).

The fifth type of experience embraces the claims of people who believe that dead persons have been able to communicate with living persons through intermediaries called *mediums*. A medium is a person who usually enters a trance voluntarily, presumably receives information from dead persons, and then communicates that information to living persons who are sitting in the presence of the entranced medium. On some occasions, after a medium has entered a trance his or her personality is apparently supplanted by the personality of a deceased person called the "control." This control allegedly "uses" the body of the medium to communicate to those present at the trance information about deceased persons. When the medium is "taken over" in this fashion by a control, the medium speaks and acts in ways that are uncharacteristic of the medium's own personality but are characteristic of the deceased person who is functioning as the control.

Consider the following case involving Laura Edmonds as a medium and the reactions of her father, Judge John Worth Edmonds of the Supreme Court of New York, as reported by Almeder.

> In 1905 the *Annales des Sciences Psychiques* reported a case in which a medium under trance spoke a language of which, in her normal state, she was entirely ignorant.[40] The medium was a Ms. Laura Edmonds, the daughter of the distinguished Judge John Worth Edmonds, president the New York State Senate and later judge of the Supreme Court of New York. Judge Edmonds was widely regarded as a person of unquestionable integrity and considerable intelligence.
>
> At one time the Judge had undertaken the study of psychical research to demonstrate the worthlessness of the activity and the foolishness of those who took such phenomena seriously. We can image the depth of his concern when his daughter Laura, a fervent Catholic capable of speaking her mother tongue and French only, began to shine as a developing medium.
>
> Anyway, as the case is reported, one evening a Mr. Evangelides, a Greek, visited the Edmondses. At a sitting (a séance) held later that evening, Laura—in trance—was controlled by a friend of Evangelides named Botzaris, who had died earlier in Greece. According to Judge Edmonds, this control (Botzaris) spoke in modern Greek to Evangelides and informed him that his son, whom Evangelides still supposed was well and alive in Greece, had recently died. Evangelides wept at this news and could scarcely believe it. But the fact of his son's death was subsequently confirmed. Judge Edmonds, who submitted an affidavit testifying to the above, made the following observations:
>
>> To deny the fact is impossible, it was too well known; I could as well deny the light of the sun; nor could I think it an illusion, for it is in no way different from any other reality. It took place before ten educated and intelligent persons. We had never seen Mr. Evangelides before; he was introduced by a friend that same evening. How could Laura tell him of his son? How could she understand and speak Greek which she had never previously heard?[41]

Now ponder Almeder's description of the mediumship of Mrs. Willett who, though unsophisticated philosophically, became the intermediary for a highly sophisticated philosophical discussion between two deceased thinkers and a living philosopher.

[40] *Annales des Sciences Psychiqes* 15, no. 317 (1905).
[41] Ibid.

Unlike Mrs. Piper and other mediums, when the English medium Mrs. Willett went into deep trance she did not lose control of her body as if she were asleep or in a swoon. She would sit up and talk in a natural way and in the first-person singular. There was no appearance of her body's being used by the deceased personality that spoke through her. So, while clearly a trance medium, she was not the usual kind of possession medium.

Back in 1885 Mrs. Willett had married a landed proprietor from Neath. Her husband's sister was the wife of F. W. H. Myers, one of the founders of the Society for Psychical Research and the author of *Human Personality and Its Survival of Bodily Death*.[42] Mrs. Willett, a person of notable achievement, was well educated and took a prominent part in public affairs, particularly in South Wales. For example, she served as chairman of the arts and crafts section of the national Eisteddfod in 1918, and later in 1920 was made a justice of the peace for Glamorganshire, being the first woman to occupy that office there. In 1922 she was appointed by the British government as a delegate to the assembly of the League of Nations. In terms of the history of her mediumship, Mrs. Willett became a member of the Society for Psychical Research soon after F. W. H. Myers (whom, by the way, she had never met) died in 1901, and then—for lack of interest—resigned in 1905. However, in 1908 she suffered a death in the family and decided to take up automatic writing—an activity she had dabbled in as a young girl. In 1909 Mrs. Willett's mediumship bloomed, and continued for a number of years.[43] She died in 1956.

What is important about Mrs. Willett's mediumship is that the alleged postmortem persons of F. W. H. Myers and Edmund Gurney—both of them founders of the Society for Psychical Research—seemed to communicate through Mrs. Willett and requested that one of the sitters be their friend G. W. Balfour, a keen psychic researcher and president of the Society for Psychical Research from 1906 to 1907. When alive, Myers and Gurney were avid philosophers, widely read in philosophy, psychology, and theology. Balfour had engaged in numerous philosophical discussions with both Myers and Gurney before they died.

With Balfour and others present on June 4, 1911, Mrs. Willett went into a deep trance. There ensued the first of a series of sittings characterizable as lively philosophical discussions between Balfour, the sitter, and both Myers and Gurney, the communicators.[44] Commenting on the content of these discussions, C. D. Broad noted that all the ostensible communications were "plainly the product of a highly intelligent and cultivated mind or minds, with a keen interest in psychology, psychical research and philosophy, and with a capacity for drawing subtle and significant distinc-

---

[42] F. W. H. Myers, *Human Personality and Its Survival of Bodily Death* (London: Longmans Green, 1903).

[43] The early phase of Mrs. Willett's mediumship was the subject of a long and important paper authored by G. W. Balfour in the *Proceedings of the Society for Psychical Research 43* (1935), pp. 43–318.

[44] As C. D. Broad has noted about the Willett sittings with Balfour, the sittings covered three topics: (1) the conditions under which the communicators were working in communicating through Mrs. Willett; (2) the processes involved in such communication in general, and the special procedures involved in conducting a cross-correspondence (several mediums) experiment; (3) their views on certain philosophical questions about the nature of human personality, its survival of bodily death, and the relation of the human individual to the Absolute. C. D. Broad, *Lectures on Psychical Research* (London: Routledge and Kegan Paul, 1962), p. 296.

tions."[45] Moreover, whatever the source of the utterances, the communicators showed a thorough acquaintance with the views and terminology of Myers's book *Human Personality and Its Survival of Bodily Death*.

It is worth emphasizing that the seances produced a high level of sophisticated philosophizing between the sitter and communicators.[46] Typically, for example, Balfour would examine leisurely the record of a sitting, and then at the next sitting make criticisms or suggestions and ask for explanations. The Gurney communicator would then speak to the issues raised and try to clear up the obscurities. Sometimes the Gurney communicator would accept, and sometimes vigorously reject, Balfour's suggestions and interpretations. Some of the sittings—those held on October 8, 1911, January 21, 1912, and March 5, 1912—were purely philosophical and sound like the transcript of an Ivy League graduate seminar on classical philosophy.[47]

Before determining the strength of these communications as evidence for personal survival, we must keep in mind two crucial considerations. First, Mrs. Willett knew little philosophy and had even less patience for all that kind of talk. When not in trance state, and when subsequently shown a transcript of the sittings, Mrs. Willett could not understand the content. For example, one typical sentence—uttered by the communicator on May 24, 1911—is this: "The Absolute labors to attain self-consciousness through the myriad of self-created sentient beings."[48] When shown this script some time later, Mrs. Willett did not know either the origin or the point of the script. Second, even though Balfour and others were convinced that the Myers and Gurney communicators acted and spoke in ways uniquely characteristic of Myers and Gurney when they were alive, Mrs. Willett had met neither one of them. As we shall see, these two considerations, when combined with the content of the communications, make it impossible to explain the sittings as an instance of the medium's subconsciously impersonating people she had previously met and communicating information obtained through ESP. At any rate, Balfour came to believe that he was indeed in communication with the departed spirits of both Gurney and Myers, and that no other hypothesis could explain the data so well.

Given collective evidence provided by these five types of experiences, Almeder claims that belief in postdeath survival is warranted. He concludes with a reply to three basic skeptical objections to this belief.

First, he summarizes the force of the evidence.

If we had *only* the best available evidence from recent reincarnation studies, or *only* the best evidence on apparitions of the dead and cases of possession, or *only* the best evidence bearing on OBEs, or *only* the best evidence from mediumship, then we might well be inclined to ignore the belief in personal survival of death. After all, extraordinary claims require extraordinary evidence; and even though the evidence seems compelling in each of the above categories of research, we might not find the evidence in each category sufficiently compelling to warrant full-blooded conviction in personal survival.

---

45 Ibid., p. 297.
46 Ibid.
47 Much of the transcripts can be found in ibid., pp. 290ff.
48 Ibid., p. 298.

But the force of the case for personal survival rests on the whole body of evidence viewed collectively as a *set* of arguments. Each argument from each category of research discussed and examined in these past pages is like a thread that, of itself, may well be incapable of carrying the full weight of the belief in some form of personal survival. Bound together, however, they converge and make a strong cord that lifts the belief from the realm of superstition and thoughtless commitment in the absence of sound evidence. We have here support for a confirmed belief based purely on factual evidence. The *multiplicity* of the arguments provides the extraordinary evidence required for conviction. We have reached the point where a critical examination of *all* the evidence available makes such a commitment a good deal easier than it has ever been before. Certainly, we are considerably better off than was Plato in giving his reasons for believing in personal survival and reincarnation.

Next, he replies to the skeptics.

There are three fairly common skeptical objections to the belief in some form of personal survival after death—objections we have not yet considered in detail. Now that we have considered the separate categories of evidence and objections, we are in a position to address these three most fundamental responses of the skeptic. The first objection asserts that personal survival after death is impossible either because we cannot even imagine what a disembodied spirit would be like, or because the very idea of such survival is conceptually incoherent. The second objection is that, even if some form of personal survival were possible, we certainly do not yet have any experimental evidence (and hence no scientific knowledge) of anyone's surviving death. The third objection is related to the second and consists in asserting that the ever-present possibility of fraud or hoax in the evidence offered here for personal survival can only be excluded by insisting on the kind of robust confirmation required in experimental science—and we have nothing like that at present. All three of these objections are fairly common; but, as we shall now see, all rest equally on crucial misconceptions.

THE LOGICAL IMPOSSIBILITY OF PERSONAL SURVIVAL

Skeptics who assert the impossibility of personal survival usually do so on the grounds that the very idea of a human being's personality existing independently of his or her body is just inconceivable or incoherent. In their view, it makes no sense even to talk about personal survival after death either because we cannot imagine what a human personality is if it is not at least partially identifiable with a human body, or else because the very idea of surviving one's death is conceptually incoherent.

Let us consider the first disjunct here: that our very concept of a person is so firmly tied to our understanding of bodily existence and activities that we cannot even imagine what a person is like if it does not possess such characteristics. Just think of it. A disembodied person would need to perceive events clairvoyantly in some way, without any sense organs such as eyes and ears. A disembodied person would need to act upon other things and other persons in some way without using limbs and without the usual feelings of stress and strain that come from the skin, the joints, and the muscles. And a disembodied person would need to communicate with others telepathically without using vocal organs and emitting audible sounds. All this, as C. D. Broad has noted, is *conceivable* as long as we keep it in the abstract; but when we try to think "what it would be like" in concrete detail, we do not seem to have any clear or definite ideas at all.[49]

In urging this objection, however, the skeptic makes a crucial mistake. The mistake consists in thinking that, just because we cannot imagine what a disembodied spirit must be like, there cannot be any. Indeed, an adequate reply to the skeptic is that our inability to imagine fully any particular state of affairs should not be taken as evidence for its nonexistence. We may not be able to imagine an infinite series of numbers, or what it would be like to walk on the moon; still, there are infinite series of numbers, and some people have walked on the moon. In short, the skeptic makes the mistake of inferring the nonexistence of spirits simply because we cannot imagine them as some sort of physical objects. The skeptic might just as well object to belief in the existence of God because we cannot imagine what God looks like. If one believes in the existence of disembodied persons, then one believes in beings who are by definition not understandable in *purely* physical terms. Obviously, our belief or disbelief in such beings should be a function of whether we have sufficient evidence for thinking that some such beings must exist, and not whether we can imagine them as we would a physical object.

What about the second part of the first objections: that the very idea of a person's surviving biological death is incoherent? This argument was offered at one time by Anthony Flew,[50] among others, and seems to have been inspired by the belief that our whole concept of a person is so rooted in the physical that it makes no sense to suggest anybody could survive biological death. There would be nothing to survive. Flew points to numerous instances of ordinary discourse wherein the logic of the usage seems to require that human personality does not survive biological death. We often say, for example, after a shipwreck or a tragedy of some sort, "There were no survivors" or "There was only one survivor." And what does this mean except that, by definition, one does not survive biological death. The ordinary concept of "death" just *means* no survival after biological death. Hence it is simply incoherent to suggest that anybody could possibly survive death.

And how does one answer this sort of argument? The short answer is to say that it is dogmatic. For skepticism of this ilk, it is simply a conceptual truth that human personality—whatever this may be—does not survive physical death. Apart from the question of whether there are such conceptual truths and, if there are, whether they can be derived from the logic of ordinary usage, this particular argument carries with it the unfortunate implication that no matter what happens in the future, no matter what facts ultimately come to light, it is simply not possible that we shall ever get empirical evidence for personal survival. How is such an argument any different from a dogmatic refusal to regard anything as evidence for the thesis? Besides, even on its own terms, this argument is not very persuasive. After all, why can we not mean—when we say, "Nobody survived the accident"—nothing more than that

---

[49] C. D. Broad, *Lectures on Psychical Research* (New York: Humanities Press, 1962), p. 409. For a similar argument, see Anthony Flew's "Can a Man Witness His Own Funeral?" *Hibbert Journal 54* (1956); and William James, "Human Immortality: Two Supposed Objections to the Doctrine," in Gardner Murphy and Robert Ballou, eds., *William James on Psychical Research* (New York: Viking Press, 1960), pp. 279ff.

[50] Flew, "Can a Man Witness?" More recently these same arguments occur in Flew's Gifford Lectures published as *The Logic of Mortality* (Oxford, England: Blackwell, 1987).

everybody suffered biological death? And if so, this only *raises* the question of whether people ever suffer biological death and survive it in some way. It does not settle it. Which raises the further question as to what human personality consists in, and what evidence there may be for the view that human personality is not simply reducible to the physical in such a way as to make the suggestion of surviving biological death incoherent. . . .

THE SCIENTIFIC IMPROBABILITY OF PERSONAL SURVIVAL

As we saw above, the second common skeptical objection to belief in personal survival consists in arguing that even if personal survival is logically and factually possible, still we have no scientific knowledge of anybody's ever surviving biological death, because we have no experimental evidence that will hold up under serious scientific scrutiny. This sort of objection feeds on the belief that all the evidence offered for personal survival (whether it be from reincarnation studies, apparitions of the dead, ostensible possessions, OBEs, or mediumship) is not publicly repeatable in experimental contexts under controlled conditions. We cannot, so the objection goes, generate at will compelling case studies. We cannot, for example, scientifically control disembodied spirits so as to make them appear under empirically desirable conditions. Because the evidence for personal survival lacks this characteristic, the evidence is not, the skeptic asserts, repeatable under the experimental method. For this often-cited reason, some scientists tend to consider the case studies offered in the preceding chapters as "anecdotal" rather than as solid evidence. And some skeptics are downright insistent that, unless a belief is established by the experimental methods of the natural sciences, the belief cannot be an item of human knowledge.

In replying to this objection, we may reflect that although *much* of the evidence for personal survival is not repeatable and accessible in the usual way that, for example, the evidence for the law of gravity is public and repeatable, it is a mistake to think that all knowledge requires experimental evidence that is public and repeatable in the way just suggested. Such repeatability is necessary only when, in the interest of prediction and control, we require causal explanations, or statements of the causes of the nomic phenomena in question. But such causal explanations are not necessary to establish *that* something or other occurs, rather than *why* it occurs. We might, for example, establish *that* dinosaurs existed sometime in the past without having to establish the reasons *why* dinosaurs happened to appear. While there is a kind of repeatability that is necessary for reliability in establishing mere existence or occurrence, it is quite a different kind of repeatability from the experimental repeatability necessary for causal explanations of nomic phenomena. The latter, but not the former, typically require our being able to show at will the conformity of controlled experiment to causal hypothesis, thereby producing at will the data that confirm the hypothesis. However, there is a good deal of legitimate scientific knowledge that does not require the experimentally repeatable kind of evidence. Once again, for example, the evidence for the past existence of dinosaurs is not experimentally repeatable or reproducible at will. The facts that confirm the hypothesis cannot be produced at will and so repeated in the way suggested. What makes the "dinosaur hypothesis" scientifically acceptable is its simplicity, or the fit between the existing data and the hypothesis; also, we know what sensory experiences would refute the hypothesis. The only plausible explanation for the data requires believing in the past existence of dinosaurs.

It is not a necessary condition for empirical knowledge, then, that the evidence be experimentally repeatable at will in the way dictated by laboratory science to provide causal explanations for observed nomic regularities. This type of evidence is necessary for causal explanations of a certain sort, but not necessary for empirically reliable explanations to the effect that something or other has occurred. This basic point has already been well argued and discussed by Stephen Braude in the first chapter of his book *The Limits of Influence*.[51] There is an appropriate sense in which the evidence for belief in the past existence of dinosaurs, say, is repeatable and needs to be repeated, but it is not the same sense in which an experiment is said to be repeated and repeatable in lab science. So much seems fairly obvious.

Also, I know what my father said to me just before he died. The evidence for my knowledge claim—his spoken words—is not experimentally repeatable or publicly accessible. And even if there had been 5,000 people in the room with me when my father spoke his dying words, the evidence would still not be experimentally repeatable in the sense specified by the skeptic. But surely, I (and the 5,000 who may have been with me in the room) know what my father said on that day. His diction was impeccable and his voice loud and clear. In other words, even if all the evidence for personal survival were not experimentally repeatable in the way suggested, it would by no means follow that the belief is not an item of human public knowledge. Do unique historical events need to be repeated in that way in order for us to be justified in believing that they occurred? Or, ceteris paribus, do we accept eyewitness testimony of a sufficiently large number of honorable and generally reliable people?

It is distinctly possible that the methods of the natural sciences, including the requirement of experimental repeatability, make sense only when we seek causal explanations of subject matter understood to be physical and nomic in its behavior. By definition, however, minds or human personalities will not be physical in any usual sense. Thus, not only is the requirement of experimental repeatability not necessary for human or scientific knowledge; it also sometimes seems to argue against the very existence of minds by requiring that they be physical and nomic in the usual sense. Why would anyone assume that the same scientific method, especially when it comes to experimental repeatability, is appropriate for understanding a subject matter so different in fundamental ways? Coherence of the subject matter aside, this is very much like asking the theist for scientifically demonstrable knowledge of the existence of God after she or he has noted that God is not a physical object conforming to nomic regularities.

The third common skeptical objection to belief in personal survival seems to be the most persistent, and this is the assertion that the evidence is persuasive only if the ever-present possibility of fraud can be clearly excluded. This possibility can be excluded, it is argued, only when the thesis is robustly verified in the way specified for experimental theses in the natural sciences. Because we do not yet have that sort of verification for personal survival, the burden of proof is still on the proponent to show that the evidence offered is free from hoax and fraud.

This sort of objection is based on the acceptable principle that extraordinary claims require extraordinary evidence, and extraordinary evidence needs to be fraud-proof—especially in an area of inquiry where extensive fraud and trickery has been richly documented. Given this objection, however, even the best cases for survival cannot be accepted as good evidence, because in each case we cannot exclude the real possibility of fraud in the way that the experimental method excludes such fraud. . . .

[51] Stephen Braude, *The Limits of Influence: Psychokinesis and the Philosophy of Science* (New York: Routledge and Kegan Paul, 1986), pp. 57ff; and also, Stephen Braude, *ESP and Psychokinesis: A Philosophical Examination* (Philadelphia: Temple University Press, 1979), pp. 41ff.

Perhaps the strongest reply to this pointed objection is that we really do not need the experimental method to exclude the possibility of fraud. The same effect can be achieved simply by pointing to the best cases and the fact that the number of cases is not fixed or historically isolated—that such cases are always occurring in different places, and what makes the best cases persuasive (and unlikely to be instances of fraud) is that many logically identical cases occur regularly although not predictably. . . .

Thus the fact that there are many past and current ideal cases of the reincarnation type, in many different lands, offered by many different researchers from differing parts of the world and with strong reasons to avoid fraud or hoax, seems to serve the same purpose as repeatability in experimental science: it excludes any real likelihood of fraud or hoax. Add to this the fact that such cases continue to appear frequently and widely (as we would expect if the hypothesis were true), and we have reason for thinking that we are dealing with a robustly confirmed hypothesis. . . .

So, our reply to the third skeptical objection is, first, that we do not need the experimental method to exclude the real possibility of fraud in the best cases; we only need the continual widespread appearance of cases that have the same logical characteristics as the ideal cases. When enough such cases continue to occur and are examined by many different researchers who are incapable of finding any fraud, the probability of fraud becomes remote just because such cases are repeating themselves in widely differing contexts and in the hands of different researchers. Second, if this reply is not enough, then there is also—for all the reason mentioned above—a very strong case to be made for the claim that not only is belief in reincarnation and personal survival an experimentally viable hypothesis; it is a strongly confirmed one, as well.

How well do you think Almeder has made his case? What would be the skeptic's likely reply? Is there really no connection between our inability to imagine a state of affairs at all and the likelihood that the state of affairs does not exist? Does the fact that the critics Almeder cites do not have a convincing naturalistic explanation for all the paranormal phenomena mean that such an explanation is unavailable?

NOTE ON SOURCES.   The material in this section is quoted from Robert Almeder, *Death and Personal Survival: The Evidence for Life After Death* (Lanham, Maryland: Littlefield Adams, 1992), pp. 8–12, 26, 100–106, 129–130, 136–138, 143–150, 158, 205–206, 217–219, 255–258, 260–265, 267–269 and Raymond Moody, *The Light Beyond* (New York: Bantam Books, 1988), pp. 169–174.

PETER GEACH

DUALISM REJECTED BUT SURVIVAL AFFIRMED

FROM ALMEDER TO GEACH.   Frequently the disputants on the question of post-death survival seem to side with one of two possible positions. Either one is a Cartesian dualist who claims that the human is a combination of a material body and an immaterial mind or soul that can survive the death of the body, or one is an anti-dualist materialist who claims that the human is a unity whose "mind" is so linked with the body that it cannot survive the death of the body. Either one lines up with Ducasse and Almeder or one lines up with Lamont. The debate, however, is more complex than just these two sides. Our present author, Peter Geach, illustrates that complexity. He sides with Lamont in rejecting dualism, but he also sides with Ducasse and Almeder in rejecting annihilation. Geach claims that the only rationally warranted position regarding personal postdeath survival involves bodily resurrection. The case made by Geach comes from his essay "Immortality" that appeared in 1969.

BIOGRAPHICAL NOTE.   Peter Thomas Geach was born in 1916 in Britain. He studied at Balliol College, Oxford and pursued advanced work in philosophy at Cambridge from 1945 to 1951. He taught at the University of Birmingham before becoming Professor of Logic at the University of Leeds. He has held distinguished visiting lectureships at Cambridge University, the University of Uppsala and the University of Notre Dame. His writing includes *Mental Acts* (1957), *Reference and Generality* (1962, third revised edition appearing in 1980), *Three Philosophers* (1961, with G. E. M. Anscombe), *God and the Soul* (1961) in which the essay used in this section originally appeared, *Logic Matters* (1972), *Reason and Argument* (1976); *Providence and Evil* (1977); *The Virtues* (1977); and *Truth, Love and Immortality: An Introduction to McTaggart's Philosophy* (1979). Geach's wife, Gertrude Elizabeth Margaret Anscombe, is also a well-known philosopher and the co-author of *Three Philosophers*.

THE ARGUMENT OF THE PASSAGES.   If one is going to claim that humans survive death, then it is important to ask what postdeath human existence would have to be like in order for one to say, for example, that Peter Geach survived death. Geach examines several different ways of construing postdeath human existence. First, a number of people posit what is frequently called an "astral body," that is, an ordinarily invisible, subtly physical body that is united with, but can survive the death of, the obviously visible, grossly physical body. Second, some people prefer the Platonic notion of an immaterial thing—a mind or soul—that is connected with the material body and is capable of surviving the death of the material body. Third, there are those who, like Almeder, affirm reincarnation. Geach rejects all three of these views as fraught with unresolvable problems. Instead, he presents a fourth way of viewing postdeath human existence: the belief in a bodily resurrection which is found in the Hebraic and Christian traditions. Geach argues that if there is postdeath survival, then it must resemble resurrection of the body. Let us see how convincingly he makes his case.

Geach begins with a distinction between belief in postdeath *survival* and *endless survival* (that is, immortality). His concern is with survival and the character of postdeath human existence.

> Everybody knows that men die, and though most of us have read the advertisement "Millions now living will never die," it is commonly believed that every man born will some day die; yet historically many men have believed that there is a life after death,

and indeed that this after-life will never end. That is: there has been a common belief both in *survival* of bodily death and in *immortality*. Now a philosopher might interest himself specially in immortality, as opposed to survival; conceding survival for the sake of argument, he might raise and examine conceptual difficulties about *endless* survival. But the question of immortality cannot even arise unless men do survive bodily death; and, as we shall see, there are formidable difficulties even about survival. It is these difficulties I shall be discussing, not the special ones about endless survival.

He proceeds now to attack three different views of the character of post-death human existence, beginning with belief in what Flew refers to in the next reading as the "astral body." Geach points out that belief in the existence of this subtle, invisible body encounters very serious evidential problems.

There are various views as to the character of the after-life. One view is that man has a subtle, ordinarily invisible, body which survives the death of the ordinary gross body. This view has a long history, and seems to be quite popular in England at the moment. So far as I can see, the view is open to no philosophical objection, but like-wise wholly devoid of philosophical interest; the mind–body problem must after all be just the same for an ethereal body as for a gross one. There could clearly be no philosophical reasons for belief in such subtle bodies, but only empirical ones; such reasons are in fact alleged, and we are urged to study the evidence.

Philosophy can at this point say something: about what sort of evidence would be required. The existence of subtle bodies is a matter within the purview of physical science; evidence for it should satisfy such criteria of existence as physicists use, and should refer not only to what people say they have seen, heard, and felt, but also to effects produced by subtle bodies on physicists' apparatus. The believer in "subtle bodies" must, I think, accept the physicist's criteria of existence; there would surely be a conceptual muddle in speaking of "bodies" but saying they might be incapable of affecting any physical apparatus. For what distinguishes real physical objects from hal-lucinations, even collective hallucinations, is that physical objects act on one another, and do so in just the same way whether they are being observed or not; this is the point, I think, at which a phenomenalist account of physical objects breaks down. If, therefore, "subtle bodies" produce no physical effects, they are not bodies at all.

How is it, then, that "subtle bodies" have never forced themselves upon the attention of physicists, as X-rays did, by spontaneous interference with physical appa-ratus? There are supposed to be a lot of "subtle bodies" around, and physicists have a lot of delicate apparatus; yet physicists not engaged in psychical research are never bothered by the interference of "subtle bodies." In these circumstances I think it wholly irrational to believe in "subtle bodies." Moreover, when I who am no physicist am invited to study the evidence for "subtle bodies," I find that very fact suspicious. The discoverers of X-rays and electrons did not appeal to the lay public, but to physi-cists, to study the evidence; and so long as physicists (at least in general) refuse to take "subtle bodies" seriously, a study of evidence for them by a layman like myself would be a waste of time.

Geach next turns his attention to Platonic dualism. His initial objection seems to come down to this: the terms we use to describe our private mental states (terms such as seeing, hearing, feeling, thinking, choosing, etc.) are so connected with our *bodily* encounter with the physical world for their meaning that ascribing these private mental states, such as sensations and feelings, to a *disembodied* spirit does not make any sense.

When *philosophers* talk of life after death, what they mostly have in mind is a doctrine that may be called Platonic—it is found in its essentials in the *Phaedo*. It may be briefly stated thus: "Each man's make-up includes a wholly immaterial thing, his mind and soul. It is the mind that sees and hears and feels and thinks and chooses—in a word, is conscious. The mind is the person; the body is extrinsic to the person, like a suit of clothes. Though body and mind affect one another, the mind's existence is quite independent of the body's; and there is thus no reason why the mind should not go on being conscious indefinitely after the death of the body, and even if it never again has with any body that sort of connection which it now has."

This Platonic doctrine has a strong appeal, and there are plausible arguments in its favor. It appears a clearly intelligible supposition that I should go on after death having the same sorts of experience as I now have, even if I then have no body at all. For although these experiences are connected with processes in the body—sight, for example, with processes in the eyes, optic nerves, and brain—nevertheless there is no necessity of thought about the connection—it is easy to conceive of someone who has no eyes having the experience called sight. He would be having the same experience as I who have eyes do, and I know what sort of experience that is because I have the experience.

Let us now examine these arguments. When a word can be used to stand for a private experience, like the words "seeing" or "pain," it is certainly tempting to suppose that giving these words a meaning is itself a private experience—indeed that they get their meaning just from the experiences they stand for. But this is really nonsense: if a sentence I hear or utter contains the word "pain," do I help myself to grasp its sense by giving myself a pain? Might not this be, on the contrary, rather distracting? As Wittgenstein said, to think you get the concept of pain by having a pain is like thinking you get the concept of a minus quantity by running up an overdraft. Our concepts of seeing, hearing, pain, anger, etc., apply in the first instance to human beings; we willingly extend them (say) to cats, dogs, and horses, but we rightly feel uncomfortable about extending them to very alien creatures and speaking of a slug's hearing or an angry ant. Do we know at all what it would be to apply such concepts to an immaterial being? I think not.

One may indeed be tempted to evade difficulties by saying: "An immaterial spirit is angry or in pain if it feels *the same way* as I do when I am angry or in pain." But, as Wittgenstein remarked, this is just like saying: "Of course I know what it is for the time on the Sun to be five o'clock: it's five o'clock on the Sun at the very moment when it's five o'clock here!"—which plainly gets us no forrader. If there is a difficulty in passing from "I am in pain" or "Smith is in pain" to "an immaterial spirit is in pain," there is equally a difficulty in passing from "Smith feels the same way as I do" to "an immaterial spirit feels the same way as I do."

In fact, the question is, whether a private experience does suffice, as is here supposed, to give meaning to a psychological verb like "to see." I am not trying to throw doubt on there being private experiences; of course men have thoughts they do not utter and pains they do not show; of course I may see something without any behaviour to show I see it; not do I mean to emasculate these propositions with neo-behaviourist dialects. But it is not a question of whether seeing is (sometimes) a private experience, but whether one can attach meaning to the verb "to see" by a private uncheckable performance; and this is what I maintain one cannot do to any word at all.

One way to show that a word's being given a meaning cannot be a private uncheckable performance is the following: We can take a man's word for it that a linguistic expression has given him some private experience—e.g., has revived a painful memory, evoked a visual image, or given him a thrill in the pit of the stomach. But we cannot take his word for it that he attached a sense to the expression, even if we accept his *bona fides*; for later events may convince us that in fact he attached no sense to the expression. Attaching sense to an expression is thus not to be identified with any private experience that accompanies the expression; and I have argued this, not by attacking the idea of private experiences, but by contrasting the attaching of sense to an expression with some typical private experiences that may be connected with the expression.

We give words a sense—whether they are psychological words like "seeing" and "pain," or other words—by getting into a way of using them; and though a man can invent for himself a way of using a word, it must be a way that other people *could* follow—otherwise we are back to the idea of conferring meaning by a private uncheckable performance. Well, how do we eventually use such words as "see," "hear," "feel," when we have got into the way of using them? We do not exercise these concepts only so as to pick our cases of seeing and the rest in our separate worlds of sense-experience; on the contrary, these concepts are used in association with a host of other concepts relating, e.g., to the physical characteristics of what is seen and the behaviour of those who do see. In saying this I am not putting forward a theory, but just reminding you of very familiar features in the everyday use of the verb "to see" and related expressions; our ordinary talk about seeing would cease to be intelligible if there were cut out of it such expressions as "I can't see, it's too far off," "I caught his eye," "Don't look round," etc. Do not let the bogy of behaviourism scare you off observing these features; I am not asking you to believe that "to see" is itself a word for a kind of behaviour. But the concept of seeing can be maintained only because it has threads of connexion with these other non-psychological concepts; break enough threads, and the concept of seeing collapses.

If it does not make sense to ascribe sensations and feelings to a disembodied spirit (that is, to the immaterial Platonic soul that purportedly survives the death of the body), and if a lifetime of such sensations and feelings are an essential feature of what makes Peter Geach an individual person, then a disembodied mind whose thought and choices are unaccompanied by Peter Geach's sensations and feelings can hardly be regarded as Peter Geach. If so, could one legitimately claim that any such disembodied spirit was actually Peter Geach in the condition of postdeath survival?

If we conclude that the ascription of sensations and feelings to a disembodied spirit does not make sense, it does not obviously follow, as you might think, that we must deny the possibility of disembodied spirits altogether. Aquinas, for example, was convinced that there are disembodied spirits but ones that cannot see or hear or feel pain or fear or anger; he allowed them no mental operations except those of thought and will. Damned spirits would suffer from frustration of their evil will, but not from aches and pains or foul odors or the like. It would take me too far to discuss whether his reasons for thinking this were good; I want to show what follows from this view. In our human life thinking and choosing are intricately bound up with a play of sensations and mental images and emotions; if after a lifetime of thinking and choosing in this human way there is left only a disembodied mind whose thought is wholly nonsensuous and whose rational choices are unaccompanied by any human feelings—can we still say there remains the same person? Surely not: such a soul is not the person who died but a mere remnant of him. And this is just what Aquinas says (in his commentary on I Corinthians 15): *anima mea non est ego*, my soul is not I; and if only souls are saved, *I* am not saved, nor is any man. If some time after Peter Geach's death there is again a man identifiable as Peter Geach, then Peter Geach again, or still, lives: otherwise not.

Though a surviving mental remnant of a person, preserving some sort of physical continuity with the man you knew, would not be Peter Geach, this does not show that such a measure of survival is not possible; but its possibility does raise serious difficulties, even if such dehumanized thinking and willing are really conceivable at all. For *whose* thinking would this be? Could we tell whether *one* or *many* disembodied spirits thought the thoughts in question? We touch here on the old problem: what constitutes there being two disembodied minds (at the same time, that is)? Well, what constitutes there being two pennies? It may happen that one penny is bent and corroded while another is in mint condition; but such differences cannot be what make the two pennies to be two—the two pennies could not have these varied fortunes if they were not already distinct. In the same way, differences of memories or of aims could not constitute the difference between two disembodied minds, but could only supervene upon a difference already existing. What does constitute the difference between two disembodied human minds? If we could find no ground of differentiation, then not only would that which survived be a mere remnant of a person—there would not even be a surviving individuality.

Could we say that souls are different because in the first instance they were souls of different bodies, and then remain different on that account when they are no longer embodied? I do not think this solution would do at all if differentiation by reference to different bodies were merely retrospective. It might be otherwise if we held, with Aquinas, that the relation to a body was not merely retrospective—that each disembodied human soul permanently retained a capacity for reunion to such a body as would reconstitute a man identifiable with the man who died. This might satisfactorily account for the individuation of disembodied human souls; they would differ by being fitted for reunion to different bodies; but it would entail that the possibility of disembodied human souls stood or fell with the *possibility* of a dead man's living again *as a man*.

Some Scholastics held that just as two pennies or two cats differ by being different bits of matter, so human souls differ by containing different "spiritual matter." Aquinas regarded this ideas as self-contradictory; it is at any rate much too obscure to count as establishing a possibility of distinct disembodied souls. Now this recourse to "spiritual matter" might well strike us merely as the filling of a conceptual lacuna with a nonsensical piece of jargon. But it is not only Scholastic philosophers who assimilate mental processes to physical ones, only thinking of mental processes as taking place in an *immaterial* medium; and many people think it easy to conceive of distinct disembodied souls because they are illegitimately ascribing to souls a sort of differentiation—say, by existing *side by side*—that can be significantly ascribed only to bodies. The same goes for people who talk about souls as being "fused" or "merged" in a Great Soul; they are imagining some such change in the world of souls as occurs to a drop of water falling into a pool or to a small lump of wax that is rubbed into a big one. Now if only people *talked* about "spiritual matter," instead of just thinking in terms of it unawares, their muddle could be more easily detected and treated.

To sum up what I have said so far: The possibility of life after death for Peter Geach appears to stand or fall with the possibility of there being once again a man identifiable as Peter Geach. The existence of a disembodied soul would not be a survival of the person Peter Geach; and even in such a truncated form, individual existence seems to require at least a persistent possibility of the soul's again entering into the make-up of a man who is identifiably Peter Geach.

The third view of postdeath survival that Geach attacks is reincarnation. Simply put, Geach claims that the evidence is insufficient for identifying a living person as, in fact, a deceased person. Furthermore, Geach is highly skeptical of the case for survival made on the basis of mediumship. Geach's essay predates Almeder's discussion. Is Almeder's case strong enough to withstand Geach's objections?

This suggests a form of belief in survival that seems to have become quite popular of late in the West—at any rate as a half-belief—namely, the belief in reincarnation. Could it in fact have a clear sense to say that a baby born in Oxford this year is Hitler living again?

How could it be shown that the Oxford baby was Hitler? Presumably by memories and similarities of character. I maintain that no amount of such evidence would make it reasonable to identify the baby as Hitler. Similarities of character are of themselves obviously insufficient. As regards memories: If on growing up the Oxford baby reveals knowledge of what we should ordinarily say only Hitler can have known, does this establish a presumption that the child is Hitler? Not at all. In normal circumstances we know when to say "only he can have known that"; when queer things start happening, we have no right to stick to our ordinary assumptions as to what can be known. And suppose that for some time the child "is" Hitler by our criteria, and later on "is" Goering? Or might not several children simultaneously satisfy the criteria for "being" Hitler?

These are not merely captious theoretical objections. Spirit-mediums, we are told, will in trance convincingly enact the part of various people: sometimes of fictitious characters, like Martians, or Red Indians ignorant of Red Indian languages, or the departed "spirits" of Johnny Walker and John Jamieson; there are even stories of mediums giving convincing "messages" from people who were alive and normally conscious at the time of the "message." Now a medium giving messages from the dead is not said to be the dead man, but rather to be controlled by his spirit. What then can show whether the Oxford child "is" Hitler or is merely "controlled" by Hitler's spirit? For all these reasons the appearance that there might be good evidence for reincarnation dissolves on a closer view.

Nor do I see, for that matter, how the mental phenomena of mediumship could ever make it reasonable to believe that a human soul survived and communicated. For someone to carry on in a dramatic way quite out of his normal character is a common hysterical symptom; so if a medium does this in a trance, it is no evidence of anything except an abnormal condition of the medium's own mind. As for the medium's telling us things that "only the dead can have known," I repeat that in these queer cases we have no right to stick to our ordinary assumptions about what can be known. Moreover, as I said, there are cases, as well-authenticated as any, in which the medium convincingly enacted the part of X and told things that "Only X could have known" when X was in fact alive and normally conscious, so that his soul was certainly not trying to communicate by way of the medium! Even if we accept all the queer stories of spirit-messages, the result is only to open up a vast field of queer possibilities—not in the least to force us to say that mediums were possessed by such-and-such souls. This was argued by Bradley long ago in his essay "The Evidences of Spiritualism," and he has never been answered.

Geach now builds his case for bodily resurrection as the only reasonably warranted way of construing the character of postdeath survival. For Geach, bodily resurrection alone holds the possibility of personal survival.

How could a living man be rightly identifiable with a man who previously died? Let us first consider our normal criteria of personal identity. When we say an old man is the same person as the baby born seventy years before, we believe that the old man has material continuity with the baby. Of course this is not a criterion in the sense of being what we judge identity by; for the old man will not have been watched for seventy years continuously, even by rota! But something we regarded as disproving the material continuity (e.g., absence of a birthmark, different fingerprints) would disprove personal identity. Further, we believe that material continuity establishes a one-one relation: one baby grows up into one old man, and one old man has grown out of one baby. (Otherwise there would have to be at some stage a drastic change, a fusion or fission, which we should regard as destroying personal identity.) Moreover, the baby-body never coexists with the aged body, but develops into it.

Now, it seems to me that we cannot rightly identify a man living "again" with a man who died until *material* conditions of identity are fulfilled. There must be some one–one relation of material continuity between the old body and the new. I am not saying that the new body need be even in part materially *identical* with the old; this, unlike material continuity, is not required for personal identity, for the old man need not have kept even a grain of matter from the baby of seventy years ago.

We must here notice an important fallacy. I was indicating just now that I favor Aquinas's doctrine that two coexisting souls differ by being related to two different bodies and that two coexistent human bodies, like two pennies or two cats, differ by being different bits of matter. Well, if it is difference of matter that makes two bodies different, it may seem to follow that a body can maintain its identity only if at least some identifiable matter remains in it all the time; otherwise it is no more the same body than the wine in a cask that is continuously emptied and refilled is the same wine. But just this is the fallacy: it does not follow, if difference in a certain respect at a certain time suffices to show non-identity, that sameness in that respect over a period of time is necessary to identity. Thus, Sir John Cutler's famous pair of stockings were the same pair all the time, although they started as silk and by much mending ended as worsted; people have found it hard to see this, because if at a given time there is a silk pair and also a worsted pair then there are two pairs. Again, it is clear that the same man may be in Birmingham at noon and in Oxford at 7 p.m. even though a man in Birmingham and a man in Oxford at a given time must be two different men. Once formulated, the fallacy is obvious, but it might be deceptive if not formulated.

"Why worry even about material continuity? Would not mental continuity be both necessary and sufficient?" Necessary, but not sufficient. Imagine a new "Tichborne" trial. The claimant knows all the things he ought to know, and talks convincingly to the long-lost heir's friends. But medical evidence about scars and old fractures and so on indicates that he cannot be the man; moreover, the long-lost heir's corpse is decisively identified at an exhumation. Such a case would bewilder us, particularly if the claimant's *bona fides* were manifest. (He might, for example, voluntarily take a lie-detecting test.) But we should certainly not allow the evidence of mental connections with the long-lost heir to settle the matter in the claimant's favor: the claimant cannot be the long-lost heir, whose body we know lies buried in Australia, and if he honestly thinks he is then we must try to cure him of a delusion.

"But if I went on being conscious, why should I worry which body I have?" To use the repeated "I" prejudges the issue; a fairer way of putting the point would be: If there is going to be a consciousness that includes ostensible memories of my life, why should I worry about which body this consciousness goes with? When we put it that way, it is quite easy to imagine circumstances in which one would worry—particularly if the ostensible memories of my life were to be produced by processes that can produce entirely spurious memories.

If, however, memory is not enough for personal identity; if a man's living again does involve some bodily as well as mental continuity with the man who lived formerly; then we might fairly call his new bodily life a resurrection. So the upshot of our whole argument is that unless a man comes to life again by resurrection, he does not live again after death. At best some mental remnant of him would survive death; and I should hold that the possibility even of such survival involves at least a permanent *capacity* for renewed human life; if reincarnation is excluded, this means: a capacity for resurrection. It may be hard to believe in the resurrection of the body; but Aquinas argued in his commentary on I Corinthians 15, which I have already cited, that it is much harder to believe in an immortal but permanently disembodied human soul; for that would mean believing that a soul, whose very identity depends on the capacity for reunion with one human body rather than another, will continue to exist forever with this capacity unrealized.

Speaking of the resurrection, St. Paul used the simile of a seed that is planted and grows into an ear of corn, to show the relation between the corpse and the body that rises again from the dead. This simile fits in well enough with our discussion. In this life, the bodily aspect of personal identity requires a one–one relationship and material continuity; one baby body grows into one old man's body by a continuous process. Now similarly there is a one–one relationship between the buried seed and the ear that grows out of it; one seed grows into one ear, one ear comes from one seed; and the ear of corn is materially continuous with the seed but need not have any material identity with it.

There is of course no philosophical reason to expect that from a human corpse there will arise at some future date a new human body, continuous in some way with the corpse; and in some particular cases there appear strong empirical objections. But apart from the *possibility* of resurrection, it seems to me a mere illusion to have any hope for life after death. I am of the mind of Judas Maccabeus: if there is no resurrection, it is superfluous and vain to pray for the dead.

The traditional faith of Christianity, inherited from Judaism, is that at the end of this age Messiah will come and men will rise from their graves to die no more. That faith is not going to be shaken by inquiries about bodies burned to ashes or eaten by beasts; those who might well suffer just such a death in martyrdom were those who were most confident of a glorious reward in the resurrection. One who shares that hope will hardly wish to take out an occultistic or philosophical insurance policy, to guarantee some sort of survival as an annuity, in case God's promise of resurrection should fail.

How convincing is Geach's case? If you agree with him, what sense is to be made of the evidence relating to paranormal human experiences presented by Almeder?

NOTE ON SOURCES. The material in this section is from Peter Geach, "Immortality," *God and the Soul* (London: Kegan Paul, 1969).

 5 ANTONY FLEW

DEATH IS THE END

FROM GEACH TO FLEW. In response to the Socratic question—"Is death going to sleep or is it going on a journey?"—Corliss Lamont argues for "sleep" whereas Ducasse and Almeder favor "journey." In their cases for or against postdeath survival the mind–body problem (which we examined in a previous chapter) appears as a key issue. Corliss Lamont appeals to biological, physiological, and genetic data to support his belief in a monistic psychology which, in turn, seems to support his belief in the finality of death. Ducasse and Almeder appeal to a different set of data, which can be referred to as paranormal human experiences, to support their belief in a dualistic psychology which, in turn, seems to bolster their belief in postdeath survival. Peter Geach, however, affirms survival not on the basis of dualism but on the grounds of a belief in resurrection. Antony Flew lines up on the side of Lamont and makes his case against postdeath survival by attacking Geach's resurrection theory as susceptible to the "Replica Objection," and the dualism of Ducasse and Almeder as seriously flawed because it relies on the basically unintelligible notion of a disembodied mind.

BIOGRAPHICAL NOTE. Antony Garrard Newton Flew was born in 1923 in Britain. He studied at St. John's College, Oxford and taught at several universities including Oxford, Aberdeen, Keele, Calgary, Reading, and York (Canada). From 1986 to 1990 he served as part-time Distinguished Research Fellow in the Social Philosophy and Policy Center of Bowling Green State University, Ohio. He has published a number of major works including *A New Approach to Psychical Research* (1953); *Hume's Philosophy of Belief* (1961); *God and Philosophy* (1966); *Evolutionary Ethics* (1967); *An Introduction to Western Philosophy* (1971); *Crime or Disease?* (1973); *Thinking About Thinking* (1975); *The Presumption of Atheism* (1976) from which the reading is this section is taken; *Sociology, Equality and Education* (1976); *A Rational Animal* (1978); *The Politics of Procrustes* (1981); *Darwinian Evolution* (1984); *Hume, Philosopher of Moral Science* (1986); *The Logic of Mortality* (1987); and *Equality in Liberty and Justice* (1989).

THE ARGUMENT OF THE PASSAGES. Flew begins his case against belief in postdeath survival by noting the universality of death as an enormous obstacle to such belief and by clarifying what he means by "survival."

1. *The enormous initial obstacle*

[The] huge obstacle lying across the path of any doctrine of personal survival or personal immortality is the familiar fact that—with the possible exceptions of the prophet Elijah and Mary the mother of Jesus bar Joseph—all men die and are in more or less short order buried, cremated, or otherwise disposed of. This universal fact of death is what leads us normally to distinguish after a shipwreck or an air crash, exclusively and exhaustively, between the Dead and the Survivors, with no third category of Both or Neither. This is the fact which gave the proposition "All men are mortal" its hallowed status as the first premise of the stock traditional example of a valid syllogism; which proceeds from this and the further premise that "Socrates is (or was) a man)," to the true if unexciting conclusion that "Socrates is (or was) mortal."

2. *Survival and immortality*

Confronted by such an obstacle how is any such doctrine to get started? Before trying to suggest an answer I wish to make a sharp, simplifying move. I propose from now on to speak only of survival, without qualification, rather than of personal survival and personal immortality. I shall thus be taking it for granted, first, that what we are interested in is our personal post-mortem futures, if any. "Survival" through our children and our children's children after we ourselves are irrecoverably dead, "immortality" through the memories of others thanks to our great works, or even our immersion in some universal world-soul—whatever that might mean—may be as much as, or much more than, most of us will in fact be getting. And it may be lamentably self-centered, albeit humanly altogether understandable, that we should be concerned about more than these thin substitutes. But, for better or for worse, what we are discussing now is the possibility of our post-mortem survival as persons identifiable as those we are here and now.

I shall also be taking it for granted, second, that survival is the necessary though of course not the sufficient condition of immortality. We can and shall concentrate on survival because this is pre-eminently a case where it is the first step which counts. Immortality is just more of the same—survival for ever.

Flew proceeds to delineate three ways in which people have tried to reconcile the universal fact that all humans are mortal, that we all die, with the claim that some or all of us will survive that death.

3. *Three ways for survival*

We shall, therefore, have in mind always and only personal survival; and we shall be concentrating on survival rather than on immortality inasmuch as the former is the necessary but not the sufficient first step to the latter. So, now, back to the question of how, granted the undeniable fact that we shall all die, anyone can possibly maintain that some or all of us will nevertheless survive. I distinguish three sorts of way in which attempts can be, and have been, made to overcome this enormous initial obstacle.

(i) The first and most familiar I call the Platonic or Platonic-Cartesian way. This consists in two moves, not one. The first move is to maintain that what is ordinarily thought of as a person in fact consists of two radically disparate elements: the one, the body, earthy, corporeal, and perishable; the other, the soul, incorporeal, invisible, intangible, and perhaps imperishable. The second move in the Platonic or Platonic–Cartesian way consists in the contention that it is the second of these two elements which is the real, essential person. It is obvious that if this way will go, then what I call the enormous initial obstacle is really no obstacle at all: the death of the body is not necessarily the death of the soul, which is the true person; and such an essentially incorporeal entity cannot in principle be touched by the earthy corruptions of the graveyard or the inferno of the crematorium. The case where this soul is stipulated to be not incorporeal but corporeal I classify as a special case of the second way, the way of the astral body.

(ii)   This second suggestion, like the first, consists in two moves, not one. The first move is to claim that inside and, so to speak, shadowing what is ordinarily thought of as the person is another being of the same form. And the second move is, as before, to maintain that this shadow being is the real person. The crucial difference between the Platonic–Cartesian way and the way of the astral body is that, whereas in the former the soul is supposed to be essentially incorporeal, in the latter the astral body is equally essentially in its own way corporeal—albeit, of course, necessarily constituted of a different and somehow more shadowy and ethereal sort of stuff than familiar, workaday matter. Strictly speaking, it could not make sense to ask of a Platonic–Cartesian soul any such everyday and down-to-earth questions as "Where is it?", "How big is it?" "How broad and long is it?." Of the astral body, on the other hand, at least some such questions must be sensibly askable even if not in practice answerable, or what would be the point of talking of an astral body and not simply of a Platonic–Cartesian soul?

Once this crucial distinguishing point is grasped, the best method of increasing one's sympathetic understanding of the way of the astral body is to think of those stock cinematic representations—as long ago in the movie version of Noël Coward's *Blithe Spirit*—in which a shadow person, visible only sometimes and only to some of the characters, detaches itself from a person shown as dead and thereafter continues to participate in the developing action, at one time discernibly and at another time not.

This second way is not, I think, nowadays given the attention which it deserves. Part of the reason for this is that people familiar with the material of psychical research have been persuaded to adopt a different interpretation of those apparitions of the living, the dying, and the dead which have to others seemed to provide the main prop for an astral body view. But partly, I suspect, the way of the astral body is simply ruled out of court as unacceptably crude or intolerably materialist; and this hasty dismissal is made all the easier by the assumption—which I shall soon be challenging—that there are no serious theoretical objections to the Platonic–Cartesian way.

(iii)   The third of the three sorts of way which I want to distinguish and label finds its traditional home in religion rather than in psychical research. This is the one which I call the reconstitutionist way. The nature of this third way cannot be better shown than by quoting an epitaph composed for himself by Benjamin Franklin, Founding Father and Signer of the American Declaration of Independence. This epitaph has been erected not on but near his grave in Christ Church cemetery, Philadelphia, by the Poor Richard Society of that his city: "The body of B. Franklin, Printer, Like the Cover of an old Book, Its Contents torn out, And stript of its Lettering and Gilding, Lies here, Food for Worms. But the work shall not be lost; for it will, as he believ'd, appear once more in a new and more elegant Edition Corrected and improved By the Author."

Flew now launches his attack against all three of these attempts to reconcile the fact of death with the claim of survival. If he is able to show that each attempt is fatally flawed and if there are no other visible attempts stepping forward to take their place, then one could claim that he has dealt a serious blow to rationally warranted belief in postdeath survival. Flew begins with the reconstitutionist way and raises what he calls the "Replica Objection." Does this objection constitute a telling blow to Geach's case for survival?

4. *Difficulties of the reconstitutionist way*

The great, and surely quite decisive, difficulty here may be christened the Replica Objection. Consider a short but most revealing passage from Chapter XVII "The Night Journey" in the *Koran*. As usual it is Allah speaking: "Thus shall they be rewarded: because they disbelieved our revelations and said, 'When we are turned to bones and dust shall we be raised to life?' Do they not see that Allah, who has created the heavens and the earth, has power to create their like? Their fate is preordinated beyond all doubt. Yet the wrongdoers persist in unbelief."

Certainly Allah the omnipotent must have "power to create their like." But in making Allah talk in these precise terms of what He might indeed choose to do, the Prophet was speaking truer than he himself appreciated. For thus to produce even the most indistinguishably similar object after the first one has been totally destroyed and disappeared is to produce not the same object again, but a replica. To punish or to reward a replica, reconstituted on Judgment Day, for the sins or virtues of the old Antony Flew dead and cremated in 1984 is as inept and as unfair as it would be to reward or to punish one identical twin for what was in fact done by the other. Again and similarly, the Creator might very well choose to issue a Second Edition— "Corrected and improved by the Author"—of Benjamin Franklin. But that Second Edition, however welcome, would by the same token not be the original Signer.

Flew next offers a lengthy attack on the Platonic–Cartesian dualism of people like Ducasse. He cites Ducasse's argument for survival based on purported communication with deceased persons via mediums. Flew tries to show that when people like Ducasse (and one could add, Almeder) cite paranormal human experiences in support of postdeath survival, they are assuming (1) that a person is a combination of a corporeal, perishable substance (that is, a body) and an incorporeal, perhaps imperishable substance (that is, a mind or soul), and (2) that the incorporeal mind is the real, essential person. Yet, have dualists like Ducasse shown conclusively that their so-called "paranormal" human experiences are not explicable in terms of "normal" physical processes? More importantly, have the dualists shown convincingly that their concept of an incorporeal personal being, a disembodied soul or mind, is an intelligible and coherent notion? If they haven't, is not the case of Ducasse and other dualists for postdeath survival based on an unjustified belief about the nature of persons?

5. *Difficulties of the Platonic way*

The first thing with which we must try to come to terms here is that the assumptions of the Platonic–Cartesian way, which in some contexts we find it so easy to make, are nevertheless both extraordinary and extraordinarily questionable.

(i)   To appreciate how easy it is in some contexts to make these Platonic–Cartesian assumptions, consider a paper by the late Professor C. J. Ducasse, "What would constitute conclusive evidence of survival after death?." It was published in the *Journal of the Society for Phychical Research* for 1962. Ducasse supposes that our friend John Doe has been on board an aircraft which crashed in the ocean, and no survivors have been found. Our phone rings "and (*a*) a voice we recognize as John Doe's is heard and a conversation with it held which convinces us that the speaker is really John Doe. . . or (*b*) the voice heard is not John Doe's but that of some other person seemingly relaying his words to us and ours to him; and that the conversation so held does convince us that the person with whom we are conversing through that intermediary is John Doe" (p. 401). Ducasse continues: "Obviously, the two imagined situations (*a*) and (*b*) are, in all essentials, analogues of cases where a person is conversing with the purported surviving spirit of a deceased friend who either, in case (*a*), 'possesses' for the time being parts at least of the body of a medium . . . or else who, in case (*b*), employs the medium only as intermediary . . . " (pp. 401–402).

Now certainly this constitutes as clear and vivid a description as could be desired of the model in terms of which mediums and their sitters usually think of the proceedings of the seance room. Yet it is neither obvious nor true that "the two imagined situations . . . are, in all essentials, analogues" of the seance situation. The crucial difference lies in the fact that in the case of the imaginary plane crash we know only "that no survivors have been found," whereas in the seance case we presumably know, beyond any possibility of doubt, that our friend has indeed died, and that his remains have been duly buried, cremated, or in some other way consumed. Now Ducasse, in his own way, appreciated all this perfectly well. The reason why he did not see it as representing any difficulty at all for "the survival hypothesis" is that here he, like almost everyone else when considering what is in psychical research called "the survival evidence," took for granted a Platonic–Cartesian view of man.

These Platonic–Cartesian assumptions are made explicit a little later, when Ducasse continues: "Thus, because the John Doe case and the case of conversation through a medium are complete analogues, the particular kind of content of the conversation that would be adequate to prove or make positively probable that John Doe had survived the crash would likewise be adequate to prove or make positively probable that the mind of our deceased friend has survived the death of his body" (p. 402). This possibly surviving mind of Ducasse's is—as he himself, again in his own fashion, emphasizes—for our purposes nothing else but the Platonic–Cartesian soul: for it is an incorporeal entity which inhabits the body; and it is the real, essential person. Ducasse continues: "When the question of survival is formulated thus in terms not of 'spirits' but of *minds* then the allegation that the survival explanation makes gratuitously . . . four assumptions . . . is seen to be erroneous. For (*a*) that there are minds is not an assumption but a known fact; (*b*) that minds are capable of remembering is likewise not an assumption but known; (*c*) that minds are capable of 'possessing' living human bodies is also a known fact, for 'possession' is but the name of the *normal* relation of a mind to its living body. *Paramount* 'possession' would be possession in the very same sense, but only temporary, and of a living body by a mind other than its own—that other mind either being one which had been that of a body now dead; or being a mind temporarily wandering from its own living body. And (*d*) that telepathic communication between minds is possible is also a known fact" (p. 403: italics and inverted commas original).

(ii) Having shown by reference to Ducasse how easy and natural it is to make Platonic–Cartesian assumptions in the context of what is usually described as the survival evidence, the next thing is to challenge both these assumptions. What I shall now be doing is to develop, in a philosopher's way, a suggestion made many years ago by a leading American psychologist and psychical researcher, Gardner Murphy. Writing on "Difficulties confronting the survival hypothesis" in the *Journal of the American Society for Psychical Research* for 1945 Murphy spoke of the "fact that bodies are the vehicles of personality, and that most people have no conception of personality except in such terms . . .". He challenged "the reader to try for a few minutes to imagine what his personal existence would be like if he were deprived of every device for making contact with his environment, except through the hypothetical use of continuous telepathy to and from other invisible minds" (p. 71).

I think that Murphy understated his case. For, surely, "personality" is a term which has to be defined in terms of persons. My personality is some sort of function of my characteristics and my dispositions; and it could make no more sense to talk of my personality surviving my dissolution—of these characteristics existing without a me for them to be the characteristics of—than it would to talk of the grin of Carroll's Cheshire Cat outlasting the face of which it was one possible configuration. Nor is it just "most people," as Murphy modestly puts it, it is all of us whose conceptions of personality are grounded in the corporeal. For, as I have just said, personality is essentially some sort of function of persons; and persons are—surely equally essentially—corporeal.

Consider, for instance, how you would teach the meaning of any person word to a child. This is done, and I think could only be done, by some sort of direct or indirect pointing at members of that very special class of living physical objects to which we one and all belong. Or again, and slightly more subtly, consider some of the things which we easily and regularly say about people, and think how few, if any, of these things could be intelligibly said about incorporeal entities. We meet people, we shake hands with them, eat with them, see them, hear them; they get up, go to bed, sit down, smile, laugh, cry. All these activities, and many, many more, could only be predicated intelligibly of corporeal creatures.

Now look again at what Ducasse called the "known facts," and what I still want to call his Platonic–Cartesian assumptions. I agree, of course, that there are minds, provided that by this we mean only that such statements as that he has a first-rate mind, or that the child is developing a mind of his own, are often true. But these statements are, in the interpretation in which we know that they are often true, statements about the capacities and dispositions of flesh and blood people. They must not be misconstrued to imply that the people in question already possess, or are in the process of acquiring, important incorporeal components; much less that these—or any—people actually are incorporeal beings.

It is also perfectly true and much to the point to insist that all normal people are capable of a certain amount of remembering. But, to say that minds are the possessors of these capacities is either an oddly artificial and, it appears, highly misleading way of stating a fact about people, or else a speculative suggestion about a possible explanation of that same fact in terms of a hypothetical and, presumably, corporeal entity.

(iii) Suppose we were to grant that ESP is a reality; there is still absolutely no experimental reason to describe it as communication between minds or souls rather than as communication between people. Indeed, I believe that something even stronger and much more interesting might be said—something at which Murphy was perhaps hinting when he spoke a shade disrespectfully of "the hypothetical use of continuous telepathy to and from other invisible minds." For could such bodiless beings, necessarily lacking all conventional sensory equipment, properly be said to communicate with one another by ESP, or even singly to possess any ESP capacity? And, if they could, could they be said to know that they were thus communicating, or that they did possess such a capacity?

These questions arise—although I cannot recall having heard them put before—because the term "ESP" is, whether implicitly or explicitly, defined negatively by reference to the absence or neglect of all ordinary and ultimately perceptual methods of acquiring and communicating information; and because it is only by reference at some stage to the conventional sources that we become able to identify authentic ESP experiences or performances as being truly such; and thus to distinguish these both from acquisitions of information through normal channels and from such autonomous features of our own lives as our spontaneous and not significantly veridical imaginings. We never should forget, what too often is forgotten, that "ESP" is not the name of some directly identifiable means of information transfer. Indeed, despite the close resemblance between the words "telepathy" and "telephony," any performance depending on telephony or any other such known and normal means is for that very reason at once disqualified as a case of telepathy; and the same applies, with appropriate alterations, as regards clairvoyance. Nor can authentic ESP experiences be picked out as such simply by reference to the strong conviction of the subject that this is the real thing. It is, or should be, notorious that subjective conviction is not a sufficient condition of either normal or paranormal knowledge: I may with complete confidence and absolute sincerity claim either to know normally or to have exercised my supposed ESP capacity, and yet in fact be totally mistaken. We must, therefore, distinguish: between (*a*) in fact possessing or exercising some ESP capacity, whether or not you believe or know that you do or are; (*b*) believing that you possess or are exercising an ESP capacity, whether or not you in fact do or are; and (*c*) genuinely knowing—as opposed to believing with however little warrant or however mistakenly—that you do possess or perhaps actually are exercising such a capacity.

Suppose now that in the light of these reminders we try to apply ESP concepts to these putative incorporeal subjects of experiences. Suppose further that it is a fact that there actually is some close correspondence between the mental contents of two such hypothetical bodiless beings, although such a fact would not, surely, be known by any normal means by anyone—whether bodied or bodiless. Now how could either of these bodiless beings have, how indeed could there even be, any reason for saying that this close correspondence must point to some information transfer from one to the other? How could either of these bodiless beings have—indeed how could there even be—any reason for holding that some of its mental contents must have been intruded by, or otherwise correspond with, some of those of another similarly bodiless being; and some particular one, at that? How could either have, indeed how could there be, any good reason for picking out some of its mental contents as—so to speak—messages received, for taking these but not those as the expressions of an exercise not of imagination but of ESP? Fundamentally similar difficulties arise when we attempt to apply ESP concepts to the different cases of information transfer between an ordinary person and a supposed bodiless being, and between material things and such a being (telepathy from the living to a spirit, that is, and clairvoyance by a spirit). The upshot appears to be that the concepts of ESP are essentially parasitical upon everyday and this-worldly notions; that where there could not be the normal, there could not be ESP as the exception to that rule.

It is too often and too easily assumed that ESP capacities could be, or even must be, the attributes of something altogether immaterial and incorporeal; partly for no better reason than that they do indeed seem to be non-physical in the entirely different sense of being outside the range of today's physical theories. Yet the truth appears to be that the very concepts of ESP are just as much involved with the human body as are those of other human capacities. It was this point which Wittgenstein was making, with regard to our normal and known attributes and capacities rather than anything putative or paranormal, when he said gnomically: "The human body is the best picture of the human soul" (L. Wittgenstein, *Philosophical Investigations*, trans. G. E. M. Anscombe. Oxford: Blackwell, 1953, p. 178.)

(iv)   We have no business, therefore, simply to take a Platonic–Cartesian view of man for granted; and to proceed at once to the question of whether the so-called survival evidence is in fact sufficient to establish that we, in our putative essential natures as incorporeal souls, do survive death and the dissolution of our bodies. Before we can possibly become entitled to begin to construe that material as evidence for this conclusion a great deal of work will have to be done to show: (*a*) that there can be a coherent notion of an incorporeal personal being; and (*b*) that a being of this sort could significantly and truly be said to be the same person as he was when he was a creature of flesh and blood.

My own conviction is that no amount of work can turn these two tricks. It is surely significant that Plato himself—an imaginative writer of genius as well as the Founding Father of philosophy—when he came at the end of his *Republic* to describe in the Myth of Er the life of supposedly incorporeal souls, was quite unable to say anything about them which did not presuppose that they must be, after all, in some fashion corporeal. So, against all his wishes and intentions, Plato there lapsed from his own eponymous positions into what was in effect an astral body view.

(v)   But, suppose we take Plato's own failure in the Myth of Er—as, surely, he would have done had it been pointed out to him—as showing only that our vocabulary and our imagination are deplorably limited by our present, but temporary, enmeshment in the body. And suppose we concede—as surely we must—that the person words of our present vocabulary do not refer to incorporeal souls, but to creatures of all too solid flesh. Can we not develop a new and coherent concept of an incorporeal being to whom at least some of the characteristics presently ascribed to people could also significantly be attributed? I do not think that we can. The basic difficulties are, first, to provide a principle of individuation by which one such being could, at least in theory, be distinguished from another such being; and, second, to provide a principle of identity to permit us to say that one such being at a later time is the same as the being at an earlier time.

This is difficult ground, though we can get much help by considering the unsuccessful labors of Descartes and his successors. Since they mistook it that people are incorporeal subjects of experience, our problem appeared to them not as one of developing a coherent new notion, but as that of giving an account of our present notion of a person. But this does not make their efforts any less relevant to us. The first thing which emerges is that such an incorporeal personal being will have to be conceived as consisting of a series of conscious experiences—along, no doubt, with some dispositions, inclinations, and capacities. In the light of what has been argued already in a previous subsection (5 (iii)), we have to add that unless we can solve the theoretical problem of attributing ESP and other putative paranormal capacities to such a being, these dispositions and so on will have to refer exclusively to actual or possible members of the same series of experiences. We now have a choice between two options: either, with Descartes, we attribute these experiences to an incorporeal spiritual substance—the I in Descartes' claim "I am a thinking substance"; or else, with Hume, we say that we can make nothing of the idea of such a substance and then go on to say that such an incorporeal being must simply consist in a series of experiences.

Neither alterative shows promise. Take the second first. Whatever difficulties there may be about the idea of a substance characterized as incorporeal, it should be easy to see why some substance is required. The word "substance" is being used here in its main—not, alas, its only—philosophical sense. In this sense a substance is that which can significantly be said to exist separately and in its own right, so to speak. Any experience requires a substance to the experience of in exactly the same way that a grin requires a face to be the grin of. Since it makes no sense to talk of a pain or a joy or any other sort of awareness without an owner, Hume's suggestion in the *Treatise* (I (iv) 6) that a person might simply and solely consist in a collection of such "loose and separate" experiences must be rated as, strictly, nonsense.

Hume himself never seems to have realised that and why this suggestion cannot do. But he did soon see, and confessed in the Appendix, that there is no available string, no uniting principle, to bind any such collection together and to distinguish it from any other. The obvious candidate might seem to be memory, as Locke has suggested earlier in his *Essay* (II (xxvii)). For, surely, we are inclined to think, the person himself must always be able—if only he would tell us, and would tell us true—to say whether it was in fact he or another who had the thought or did the deed. But this will not work.

Expressed in modern terms, there is no possibility of giving an account of the self-identity and individuation of incorporeal collections of experiences in terms of their memory capacities. Certainly if I truly remember, and do not merely seem to remember, doing the deed, then necessarily I must be the same person as did that deed: true memory thus presupposes true personal identity. But what I remember is that I am the same person as did the deed. That I do so remember is not, and cannot be, itself what it is for me to be the same person as did it.

So what about the Cartesian alternative? Can we accept that an incorporeal person would be the incorporeal substance which enjoyed or suffered certain experiences, and was endowed with certain capacities? The principle of individuation would then be a matter of being, or belonging to, one such substance rather than to another; and the principle of self-identity would be a matter of being, or belonging to, the same such substance.

But now, before we discuss the qualifications of this candidate, can we be told who (or what) he (or it) is? For when we were dealing with regular or conventional (corporeal) persons, there was no difficulty in saying—indeed, in showing—what was the substance to which we were attributing the experiences, the dispositions, etc.: they were the experiences, the dispositions, or whatever, of a flesh and blood person. But what positive characterization can we give to these postulated incorporeal substances? Can we say anything to differentiate such an incorporeal substance from an imaginary, an unreal, a non-existent substance?: "Beyond the wholly empty assurance that it is a metaphysical principle which guarantees continuing identity through time, or the argument that since we know that identity persists some such principle must hold in default of others, no content seems available for the doctrine. Its irrelevance . . . is due to its being merely an alleged identity-guaranteeing condition of which no independent characterization is forthcoming" (T. Penelhum, *Survival and Disembodied Existence*. London: Routledge and Kegan Paul, 1970, p. 76).

The third attempt to reconcile the fact of death with the claim of survival is the hypothesis of an astral body. While Flew finds this way to be preferable to the other two, nevertheless he also rejects it on the grounds that it is neither supported by evidence nor needed as an explanatory hypothesis.

6. *Difficulties in the way of the astral body*

The great, and in my view insuperable, difficulties of the Platonic way, the assumptions of which have so often been taken for granted or even asserted as known facts, should now lead us to look with a new interest and respect at the way of the astral body.

In the context of this more sympathetic approach, it begins to emerge that many of those who have been thought of as—and who probably thought themselves— Platonic–Cartesians have really been believers in astral bodies. There is, for instance, some reason to think that the Latin Father Tertullian, who certainly held the soul to be corporeal, was also inclined to think of it as of human shape; and what is this but an astral body? See Chapter IX of his *de Anima*, in which he cites the visions of the good sister who saw "a soul in bodily shape . . . in form resembling that of a human being in every respect." Tertullian then goes on to argue that such an object must have a color, which could be no other than an "ethereal transparent one."

Since we come to examine this notion of an astral body so soon after deploying the objection to the candidate notion of incorporeal spiritual substance, it will be easy to see what the problem for the protagonist is going to be. It is, obviously, to find some positive characterization for an astral body: such that an astral body really would be a sort of body in a way in which an imaginary body, or a non existent body, or an incorporeal body are not sorts of body; and at the same time such that the hypothesis that we have, or are, astral bodies is not shown to be false by any presently available facts. Confronted by this problem, the danger for the protagonist of an astral body view is that in his concern to avoid immediate falsification by presently known facts he may so qualify the nature of the body which he wants to hypothesize that it becomes in effect not a body, albeit elusive, but instead an incorporeal Platonic–Cartesian soul: "A fine brash hypothesis may thus be killed by inches, the death by a thousand qualifications."

In principle these dangers could, I think, be escaped fairly easily. We should need only to postulate the detectability of astral bodies by an instrument of a kind not yet invented. But such an utterly arbitrary postulation would invite the comment made by Bertrand Russell in another connection: "The method of 'postulating' what we want has many advantages; they are the same as the advantages of theft over honest toil" (B. Russell, *Introduction to Mathematical Philosophy*. London: Allen and Unwin, 1919, p. 21). Such a drastic postulation would be warranted only if we thought—or think—that the survival evidence cannot be interpreted in terms of various ESP ongoings among ordinary corporeal people, and if we also believe—as I have been arguing that we should— that the Platonic–Cartesian way will not go. It would also be much encouraged if evidence for levitating, apporting, and generally rip-roaring physical mediumship were better than it is.

7. *Tentative conclusions on the substantive question*

Certainly I cannot myself recommend the reckless postulation which would be required in order to proceed along the way of the astral body. For I remain persuaded by the sort of considerations deployed so long ago by Professor E. R. Dodds in his "Why I do not believe in survival," in the *Proceedings of the Society for Psychical Research* for 1934. The crux of this landmark paper, which ought to be reprinted in some more accessible and more widely circulating form, is that the so-called survival evidence can be adequately, and therefore better, interpreted in terms of more or less elaborate and unconscious normal and paranormal transactions among the living—without postulating any surviving entities at all. Substantially the same conclusion was reached by Murphy in the paper mentioned in Section 5 (ii). If, however, I were to take the opposite view to that of Dodds and Murphy on this issue, as many do, then I should have to postulate some sort of astral body; and that notwithstanding the rather formidable difficulties indicated in the previous Section 6. For these difficulties, unlike those of the supposed hypothesis of disembodied survival, do not necessarily reduce the proposed postulate to incoherence. My conclusion is, therefore, that if there is to be a case for individual and personal survival, what survives must be some sort of astral body; but that, in the present state of the evidence, we have no need of that hypothesis.

Recall Almeder's reply to the first of three skeptical objections to his case for postdeath survival in which he refers specifically to Flew's charges. Has Almeder defended the notion of a disembodied person as conceivable and coherent? Has he deflected the thrust of Flew's critique?

NOTES ON SOURCES.   The material in this section is from Antony Flew, *The Presumption of Atheism* (New York: Harper & Row, 1976), pp. 103–118.

What Grounds Do I Have for Belief in God?

THE QUESTION POSED

In our pursuit of the examined life we began with the question "Who or what am I?" We observed that one of the responses frequently heard in contemporary society is, "You are a part of nature." And we noted that such a response usually carries with it a fourfold denial: you are not a mind; you are not free; you are not immortal; you are not a creature of God. In the preceding chapters we explored the first three of those denials. In this chapter we direct our attention to the fourth and final denial.

If you are going to claim that you are a creature of God, then a whole series of questions must be faced. What, for example, do you mean by the term *God*? To what does the term refer? Once you have cleared up that issue, you must be prepared to indicate the basis for your belief that such a God does in fact exist. Then you will have to provide a justification of the claim that God in some sense created you. Additional pressing questions would follow these.

People who have believed themselves to be creatures of God have not always faced up to such a series of questions. In biblical times, the Israelites, for example, wrestled with the first question of specifying the nature of God but seldom if ever raised the issue of the grounds for belief in God. It was enormously important for them to specify the nature and identity of their God over and against the many deities of their polytheistic neighbors. But whether or not their God, Yahweh, existed was not really debated. For them, God was an experienced reality who had spoken to their great ancestors Abraham, Isaac, and Jacob, and who continued to speak even to them in many and various ways. These Israelites did not pause to fashion proofs for the existence of God even as you have never paused to prove the existence of your mother or father. No doubt you would consider it mighty strange for someone to require of you a proof for the existence of your parents before you would be allowed to speak about your relationships with them. Similarly, the Israelites would have thought it strange if someone had required of them proofs for God's existence before they would have been allowed to speak of their relationships with Him. They had daily experiences of God. Why did they need to prove His existence? Accordingly, the writer of Genesis, the first book of the Bible, could begin with these words, "In the beginning God created heaven and earth . . .," and not feel the least bit uncomfortable with the fact that he was taking God's existence for granted.

In pursuing the examined life today, however, we cannot escape questioning the existence of God. This situation is due in part to the nature of the God that is being discussed, and in part to modern philosophical trends. Through the religious work and thought of many generations of people of diverse faiths, the term *God* has come to be recognized in the common parlance of Western civilization as referring to an infinite, eternal, uncreated, immaterial Being that transcends the material universe He created. There is no room for such a God, however, in the view of reality depicted by materialism. Materialism, you recall from Chapter 2, is an ancient doctrine that held that matter is the primary feature of reality, whereas spirit or mind either is derived from and dependent upon matter or is not real at all. For centuries materialism was overshadowed by various Greek philosophies and Christian theologies that accorded mind or spirit an important and independent role in reality. Modern science, however, seems to have lent support to the ancient doctrine so that materialism is no longer a pale alternative on the intellectual scene: it has, in fact, garnered the support of many contemporary thinkers. Accordingly, those who believe in God are forced to face up to the question of grounds for belief in God. At the same time, the widespread acceptance of belief in God requires the nonbeliever to examine carefully the case that is made for God's existence. Neither believers nor nonbelievers can rest uncritically and complacently in their beliefs without facing the challenges presented by the opposite side. Both groups must assess carefully the evidence for and against the claim that God exists—if they are going to take seriously the examined life.

As early as the time of Parmenides in the fifth century B.C., philosophers began to construct arguments that could be used to try to prove the existence of God. The proofs that have been generated are basically of two types. On the one hand, there are arguments that start with a premise derived from experience and attempt to infer the existence of God from that premise. These arguments are labeled *a posteriori* because they try to say something about God (i.e., God's existence) on the basis of, after, *posterior to*, saying something about the experienced world. On the other hand, there is the kind of argument that proceeds *a priori*. Such an argument seeks to drive God's existence from grounds that are independent of, or *prior to*, experience.

The major, if not only, *a priori* proof that has been put forward is the ontological argument, first proposed by St. Anselm, the archbishop of Canterbury in the eleventh century A.D. The argument starts from the *concept* of God and attempts, through an analysis of the concept, to demonstrate that there truly exists a being corresponding to this concept. Descartes' argument for the existence of God, which we encountered in Chapter 2, is a version of the ontological argument.

The *a posteriori* arguments are of two basic varieties. They proceed via the laws of causality either from some facet of the experienced world (such as the human eye) to the supreme cause outside the world (that is, God), or they argue from existence in general to the supreme supernatural cause.

Immanuel Kant (1724–1804), an enormously influential German philosopher, some of whose writings we examine in connection with other topics in later chapters, believed that all the proofs for the existence of God that people had offered, or could offer, boiled down to the three types just noted: the "ontological" argument, which proceeds *a priori*, and the two forms of the *a posteriori* arguments, which he labeled "physico–theological" (the type starting from a specific facet of the experienced world) and "cosmological" (the kind proceeding from the experience of existence in general).

Kant mounted a very impressive assessment of these proposed proofs for the existence of God in his *Critique of Pure Reason* (Sec. Div., Bk. II, Chap. III). Having reduced the various arguments to only three types, he argued: (1) that the physico–theological argument is weak and needs the cosmological, (2) that the cosmological is weak and needs the ontological, and (3) that the ontological is fatally flawed. According to Kantian criticism, the physico–theological argument at best can only demonstrate that, for example, the human eye had a "designer" who was perhaps divine but not necessarily the supreme being we call God. To move beyond this "designer" to God, the physico–theological argument needs the cosmological argument, which attempts to show that there is a supreme being that is responsible for the causal network in which things like human eyes are generated. The cosmological argument, however, is also weak inasmuch as the most it can do is bring a person to the alternative that there is either a supreme being responsible for the experienced world with its manifold network of causes, or there is an infinite regress of causes without a supreme being. What the cosmological argument does is lead a person to the idea of a supreme being without demonstrating that there is a referent in reality corresponding to that concept. Thus, the argument needs the ontological argument, which attempts to generate just such a demonstration. The ontological proof, however, is fatally flawed in that no scrutiny of a concept will ever demonstrate that there is, in fact, a referent in reality corresponding to that concept.

Kant himself went on to argue that reason allowed him to postulate the existence of God on the grounds that taking seriously the moral life with its requirement that he perform perfectly his duty without qualification meant that he needed to postulate: (1) a life after death where he would have sufficient opportunity to achieve the moral goal reason set before him, and (2) a supreme being who would insure that those who reach the moral goal are also those that are happy. Kant's so-called moral argument for the existence of God is *not* offered by Kant as a *proof*. A proof would claim that reason *requires* one to believe in the existence of God. Kant rejected all such proofs. Instead, he proposed that reason *allows* one to believe in the existence of God if one takes the moral life seriously.

The writings of the philosophers included in this section all focus primarily on the *a posteriori* proofs that are at the heart of "natural" theology. "Natural" theology attempts to derive knowledge of God (that is, his existence and attributes) from a scrutiny of God's "handiwork" (that is, nature). "Revealed" theology, in contrast, bases knowledge of God on special divine self-disclosure, such as is reported in the Bible.

The first philosopher we consider, Thomas Aquinas, maintains that reason *requires* us to believe in the existence of God. Aquinas offers five different ways in which he believes God's existence can be demonstrated. Blaise Pascal, our second writer, like Kant rejects all proofs for God's existence but believes on other grounds that reason *allows* one to affirm the existence of God. David Hume, our third author, besides claiming that reason does *not require* belief in the existence of God, goes on to question radically whether reason even *allows* belief in an Infinite, Perfect Being. Our next author, John Stuart Mill, taking Hume's challenge seriously, claims that, on the basis of certain evidence in nature, reason does *allow* one to believe in the existence of God, but a God that is *finite*. T. H. Huxley continues the debate and, siding with those who say that reason does *not allow* one to believe in God, claims that belief in God is fundamentally *immoral* because such belief is not supported by compelling evidence. William James, our next writer, defends belief in God against Huxley's attack by showing that both the believer and the nonbeliever adopt their positions ultimately not on the basis of compelling evidence, but on the basis of their passional natures. Our final two authors, who come from the contemporary scene, Antony Flew and John Hick, focus their attention on the question of whether theological assertions like "God exists" are really meaningful statements at all. Flew says they are not; Hick claims they are.

Does reason *require* belief in the existence of God? If not, does reason *allow* belief in the existence of God? If not, is one who believes in God *immoral*? Let us turn to the debate.

THOMAS AQUINAS

BELIEF SUPPORTED BY PROOFS

BIOGRAPHICAL NOTE.   Thomas Aquinas was born in Italy in 1225 and died in 1274 at the age of forty-nine. His father was a nobleman. At the age of five, Thomas was sent for his education to the Benedictine monastery of Monte Cassino, where his uncle ruled as abbot. He studied grammar, poetry, rhetoric, logic, and some elementary philosophy. From the monastery he attended the University of Naples. While there, or shortly after, he formed the design of becoming a monk in the order of St. Dominic. His mother objected, even going so far as to imprison him for two years. However, he escaped and entered the order in 1243. During the next dozen years or so he pursued advanced studies in theology and philosophy at various European universities. In 1256 or 1257 he received the degree of "master of sacred sciences" and began a career of teaching and writing and controversy. His writings are many. Among these the most important was his huge *Summa Theologica* in which he provided his generation with an extraordinarily systematic digest of Christian theology and much ancient philosophy. This great work, which was unfinished at the time of his death, fills many volumes in its English translation. It begins with the question of God's existence, deals then with His attributes, traces the processes of things from God and the return of man to God through Christ by means of the sacraments that Christ instituted. Thomas's thought soon became, and continues to be, the official presentation of Catholic theology and philosophy. At the command of Pope Gregory X, Thomas undertook to be present at an ecclesiastical council to be held in Lyons. On the way he fell sick. He put up at a nearby monastery, but died after a few months' illness. In 1323, almost a half a century after his death, Thomas was canonized by Pope John XXII. A recent translator remarks, "Whatever may be the proper statement of the grounds of his sainthood, his vast intellectual achievements are certainly events out of the natural order and appropriate to a miracle."

THE ARGUMENT OF THE PASSAGES. Thomas's first claim is that the existence of God is not something we can know directly; it is not given as, for example, the color of this page is given; it is not known by intuition; it is not known by direct insights. It is inferred or deduced. In other words, belief in the existence of God rests upon an argument, upon discourse having the form If–then, where the If-part is something directly given and the then-part is something inferred from what is directly given. Such being the case, we are naturally curious about the fact or facts, directly knowable, from which Thomas will infer the existence of God. He proposes five facts. Each gives rise to its proper argument. These are known as the argument from change; the argument from causation; the argument from contingency; the argument from degrees of excellence; and the argument from harmony. In pursuing these arguments, Thomas is engaging in what is often called "natural theology" as distinct from "revealed theology." The latter sets forth in an orderly and rational fashion knowledge of God based on divine revelation; whereas the former presents in a similar fashion the knowledge of God based upon nature without the benefit of divine revelation. In considering Thomas's five arguments, we first offer a rather extensive paraphrase and explanation of the arguments because his manner of stating them can be initially quite elusive and foreign. Then we examine some abridged excerpts from his *Summa Theologica*.

1. THE ARGUMENT FROM CHANGE. Change is an undoubted fact in nature. Wherever we look, things are changing. A-changing-into-B is a phrase that has a very wide application. How are we to explain or account for the fact of change? Any particular instance of change we can refer to some previous change, but this will not help us to account for the presence of change as such. There are three possibilities: (1) we may accept change as the ultimate fact, neither requiring nor permitting any explanation, (2) we may refer every case of change to some prior case, extending our reference backward to infinity, or (3) we may postulate what Saint Thomas calls un Unmoved Mover, or Prime Mover, itself unchanging but the source from which all particular instances of change proceed.

The first two alternatives Thomas rejects. His reasoning is not so clear as one could wish it. He rejects the notion of change as an ultimate fact neither requiring nor permitting any explanation, because such a position would seem to be needless skepticism. Why *should* the fact of change in nature be allowed to fall outside the range of explanation? If there are going to be ultimate mysteries, why should change be among them? Is there any necessity in the claim that change is an ultimate, inexplicable fact? For these and similar reasons Thomas rejects the "skeptical" solution in favor of a more "rationalist" solution; that is, in favor of the claim that there is a reason for the fact of change.

He rejects the notion of explaining changes by referring them to prior changes, and so on back to infinity. His reasoning here seems to be that such an explanation is wrong in principle, and would hence break down and leave one in the first position of accepting change as an ultimate fact. The point here seems to be twofold. First, that referring change to prior change is always to be left with change; whereas to be left with change is precisely the thing we are seeking to avoid. Second, the notion of an infinite regression is itself a highly unsatisfactory one. It involves the mind in many different puzzles and paradoxes that leave matters no better off then the skeptical solution. For these and similar reasons, Saint Thomas rejects the notion of infinite regression as required by the attempt to explain change by referring it to prior change.

If there is no fourth alternative, then he has a strong case for the remaining third explanation. If there are just three possibilities, and you show cause for rejecting two of them, you do not require any further justification for accepting the third. This, at any rate, seems to be Thomas's reasoning in respect to his argument from the fact of change to the existence of an Unmoved Mover, or Prime Mover, or God.

2. THE ARGUMENT FROM CAUSATION.   These arguments in natural theology, as their name suggests, are inferences *from* some fact about nature *to* the existence of God. From the fact of change, Thomas argues to the existence of God. His second argument, known as the argument from causation, is similar in form, but begins with a different fact. This time the fact selected is causation. Like change, causation is a large, obvious, ubiquitous fact. When we examine nature, our minds seem to detect the fact of causation almost everywhere. We have many different words and phrases for expressing this fact. This causes that. This is causally connected with that. The principle of causality is illustrated between this and that.

Granted this fact about nature, Thomas's procedure is the same as in the case of change. How are we to explain or account for the fact of causation? Any particular instance of causation we can refer to some previous instance. Suppose B is the cause of A. We can refer B itself back to C, as its cause, and C itself back to D, as its cause, and so on. The question is not, Does this cause that? It is, Why does this cause that? Why does anything cause anything? Why is there causation in nature? As in the case of change, there are three possibilities: (1) we may accept causation as an ultimate fact, neither requiring nor permitting any explanation, (2) we may refer every instance of causing to some prior instance, extending our reference back to infinity, or (3) we may postulate what Saint Thomas calls a First Cause, itself uncaused.

There is no need to retrace his argument in further detail. He rejects the notion that causation is an ultimate fact neither requiring nor permitting any explanation. He rejects the notion of an infinite regression. He is left with the notion of a First Cause.

3. THE ARGUMENT FROM CONTINGENCY.   We have seen that Thomas's procedure is to select some obvious fact about nature and to argue from the existence of this fact to the existence of God. From the fact of change, he argued to the existence of God as unchanging First Mover. From the fact of causation, he argued to the existence of God as uncaused First Cause. It will be noticed that these arguments begin with one sort of notion and conclude with the "opposite" notion. Thus from change, he argued to an unchanging Being; from causation, he argued to an uncaused Being. This inference from one sort of fact in nature, to God as an "opposite" sort of fact, characterizes Thomas's third argument.

The argument from contingency begins with the fact that in nature many things appear to be contingent, accidental, possible, dependent. A man is walking across a field. He encounters a stray bullet, fired by someone who was ignorant of his presence in that field. Death results. Speaking of this death, we say it was accidental. Among the things we mean when we say this is that it did not *have* to happen. Matters might have been, could have been, otherwise. The man might have been elsewhere when the bullet came by. The shot might have been fired in some other direction. The compresence of the victim and the bullet, at just the same time and place, was not necessary. The man's presence, at just that time and place, did not necessitate the bullet's presence, at just that time and place. There were other possibilities. The way things actually happened did not exhaust all the possibilities. We have many different words and phrases that enable us to describe this sort of thing. We can say that his actual death was possible, but not necessary; that it was contingent or dependent upon the fact that he was there when the bullet came by; that it happened, but did not have to happen; that it was accidental, not necessary.

Like change and causation, contingency is an obvious fact about nature. Many things in nature exhibit this fact of contingency, or what Thomas sometimes calls "dependent being." It may be that *every* object and event in nature exhibits this fact of contingency. The question is, how are we to account for the fact of contingency in nature? The question is not, Was this contingent upon that? It is, Why are there contingent facts in nature? Why is anything contingent? We could put our question about contingency in the same form as our question about change and causation: Why is there change in nature? Why is there causation in nature? Why is there contingency in nature?

Once the *sort* of fact is clear, the rest of the argument is easily grasped. We have again three possibilities: (1) we may accept contingency as an ultimate fact about nature, neither requiring not permitting any explanation, (2) we may refer every instance of contingency to some prior instance, extending our reference back to infinity, or (3) we may postulate what Thomas calls a Necessary Being, itself not contingent upon anything.

There is again no need to retrace his argument in detail. He rejects the notion that contingency is an ultimate fact neither requiring nor permitting any explanation. He rejects also the notion of an infinite regression. He is left with the notion of a Necessary Being.

4. THE ARGUMENT FROM DEGREES OF EXCELLENCE.   Thomas's fourth argument differs slightly from the first three. If we examine the nature of things, we notice the fact of degrees of excellence. This is more excellent than that. These are more excellent than those. What *sort* of excellence is not in question. Saint Thomas seems to suggest that there are kinds or sorts of classes of things, and that particular cases exhibit varying degrees of excellence, each according to its kind. Thus, one horse may be more excellent than another; one tree more excellent than another; one man more excellent than another. Thomas does not seem to suggest that this notion of degrees of excellence cuts across kinds or classes. Thus, his idea is not that a horse is more excellent than a tree, but rather that one horse is more excellent than another. However this may be, nature exhibits degrees of excellence. Degrees of excellence, like change and causation and contingency, is a fact about nature.

Granted this fact, he urges that the notion of degrees of excellence implies the notion of perfection. Unless we have the notion of perfection, we could not say that something was more or less excellent. Imperfect being, of no matter what sort, implies perfect being of that sort. Evaluation of the actual, in terms of degrees of excellence, implies a grasp of the ideal. Now the totality of actuals, exhibiting their degrees of excellence, make up nature: Nature is the whereabouts of degrees of excellence. But what can we say of perfection? Its whereabouts is obviously not nature; nothing in nature is perfect after its kind.

It is easier to state Thomas's problem here than it is to understand exactly what the answer means. What he seems to say is that nature is the realm of imperfect being, and God is the realm of perfect being. In nature, nothing is perfect. In God, all things are perfect. God is the whereabouts of perfect being, just as nature is the whereabouts of imperfect being. And our power to detect imperfect being (degrees of excellence) in nature implies our knowledge of perfect being in God. If knowing imperfect being entails the existence of imperfect being—if it did not exist you could not know it—then knowing perfect being entails the existence of perfect being.

This argument can be given the same formulation as we gave to the others. We can say that the fact in nature this time is degrees of excellence, or imperfect being. We have three possibilities: (1) we may accept this as an ultimate fact, neither requiring nor permitting an explanation, (2) we may refer every instance of a degree of excellence to some other instance of greater excellence, extending our reference to infinity, or (3) we may postulate what Thomas calls Perfect Being, in whom all sorts of perfections live and move and have their being, and through knowledge of whom we are able to recognize the fact of imperfect being, or degrees of excellence, in nature.

5. THE ARGUMENT FROM HARMONY.   Thus far, Saint Thomas has argued from nature as changing being to God as unchanging being; from nature as caused being to God as uncaused being; from nature as contingent being to God as necessary being; from nature as imperfect being to God as perfect being. In each instance we begin with nature as the whereabouts of a certain sort of fact and argue from that to God as the explanatory ground of this fact.

In the fifth and last argument, Thomas selects the fact of what he calls "accord" or "harmony" in nature. We sometimes call it "adaptation." What he refers to is this: Humans require to see, and they have eyes, or humans have eyes and the nature of things is, in great part, visible to such eyes. There is "harmony" or "accord" or "adaptation" here. Polar bears require a covering to withstand arctic rigors, and they have a thick coat of fur, or polar bears have a thick coat of fur, and arctic weather is, in great part, unable to penetrate such fur. There is adaptation here. A list of this sort of "accord" in nature could be extended indefinitely.

We have our fact, then. As in the other instances we have three possibilities: (1) we may accept adaptation as an ultimate fact, neither requiring nor permitting explanation; this is not to say that adaptation is to be "explained" by referring it to "chance," since such reference would either imply the legitimacy of the demand for explanation, or it would be only a covert way of denying the need or possibility of explanation, (2) we may refer each case of adaptation to some prior or some more general instance, extending our reference to infinity, or (3) we may postulate what Saint Thomas calls "design;" that is, we may explain the fact of adaptation as the manifestation of intention or intelligence or foresight or providence.

If we collect the conclusions to these five arguments, we have a general description of the nature of God. He is unchanging. He is uncaused. He is necessary. He is perfect. He is providential. We can add, by implication, that He is omnipresent and omnipotent: if He is present in all things as their cause, it must be the case that in some sense He *is* everywhere and *does* everything.

Let us now examine some of Thomas's own words on these matters.

THE FIRST WAY

The existence of God can be shown in five ways. The first and clearest is taken from the idea of motion. (1) Now it is certain, and our senses corroborate it, that some things in this world are in motion. (2) But everything which is in motion is moved by something else. (3) For nothing is in motion except in so far as it is in potentiality in relation to that towards which it is in motion. (4) Now a thing causes movement in so far as it is in actuality. For to cause movement is nothing else than to bring something from potentiality to actuality; but a thing cannot be brought from potentiality to actuality except by something which exists in actuality, as, for example, that which is hot in actuality, like fire, makes wood, which is only hot in potentiality, to be hot in actuality, and thereby causes movement in it and alters it. (5) But it is not possible that the same thing should be at the same time in actuality and in potentiality in relation the same thing, but only in relation to different things; for what is hot in actuality cannot at the same time be hot in potentiality, though it is at the same time cold in potentiality. (6) It is impossible, therefore, that in relation to the same thing and in the same way anything should both cause movement and be caused, or that it should cause itself to move. (7) Everything therefore that is in motion must be moved by something else. If therefore the thing which causes it to move be in motion, this too must be moved by something else, and so on. (8) But we cannot proceed to infinity in this way, because in that case there would be no first mover, and in consequence, neither would there be any other mover; for secondary movers do not cause movement except they be moved by a first mover, as, for example, a stick cannot cause movement unless it is moved by the hand. Therefore it is necessary to stop at some first mover which is moved by nothing else. And this is what we all understand God to be.

THE SECOND WAY

The Second Way is taken from the idea of the Efficient Cause. (1) For we find that there is among material things a regular order of efficient causes. (2) But we do not find, nor indeed is it possible, that anything is the efficient cause of itself, for in that case it would be prior to itself, which is impossible. (3) Now it is not possible to proceed to infinity in efficient causes. (4) For if we arrange in order all efficient causes, the first is the cause of the intermediate, and the intermediate the cause of the last, whether the intermediate be many or only one. (5) But if we remove a cause the effect is removed; therefore, if there is no *first* among efficient causes, neither will there be a last or an intermediate. (6) But if we proceed to infinity in efficient causes there will be no first efficient cause, and thus there will be no ultimate effect, nor any intermediate efficient causes, which is clearly false. Therefore it is necessary to suppose the existence of some first efficient cause, and this men call God.

THE THIRD WAY

The Third Way rests on the idea of the "contingent" and the "necessary" and is as follows: (1) Now we find that there are certain things in the Universe which are capable of existing and of not existing, for we find that some things are brought into existence and then destroyed, and consequently are capable of being or not being. (2) But it is impossible for all things which exist to be of this kind, because anything which is capable of not existing, at some time or other does not exist. (3) If therefore *all* things are capable of not existing, there was a time when nothing existed in the Universe. (4) But if this is true there would also be nothing in existence now; because anything that does not exist cannot begin to exist except by the agency of something which has existence. If therefore there was once nothing which existed, it would have been impossible for anything to begin to exist, and so nothing would exist now. (5) This is clearly false. Therefore all things are not contingent, and there must be something which is necessary in the Universe. (6) But everything which is necessary either has or has not the cause of its necessity from an outside source. Now it is not possible to proceed to infinity in necessary things which have a cause of their necessity, as has been proved in the case of efficient causes. Therefore it is necessary in itself, not having the cause of its necessity from any outside source, but which is the cause of necessity in others. And this "something" we call God.

THE FOURTH WAY

The Fourth Way is taken from the degrees which are found in things. (1) For among different things we find that one is more or less good or true or noble; and likewise in the case of other things of this kind. (2) But the words "more" or "less" are used of different things in proportion as they approximate in their different ways to something which has the particular quality in the highest degree—e.g., we call a thing hotter when it approximates more nearly to that which is hot in the highest degree. There is therefore something which is true in the highest degree, good in the highest degree and noble in the highest degree; (3) and consequently there must be also something which has being in the highest degree. For things which are true in the highest degree also have being in the highest degree (see Aristotle, *Metaphysics*, 2). (4) But anything which has a certain quality of any kind in the highest degree is also the cause of all the things of that kind, as, for example, fire which is hot in the highest degree is the cause of all hot things (as is said in the same book). (5) Therefore there exists something which is the cause of being, and goodness, and of every perfection in all existing things; and this we call God.

THE FIFTH WAY

The Fifth Way is taken from the way in which nature is governed. (1) For we observe that certain things which lack knowledge, such as natural bodies, work for an End. This is obvious, because they always, or at any rate very frequently, operate in the same way so as to attain the best possible result. (2) Hence, it is clear that they do not arrive at the goal by chance, but by purpose. (3) But those things which have no knowledge do not move towards a goal unless they are guided by someone or something which does possess knowledge and intelligence—e.g., an arrow by an archer. Therefore, there does exist something which possesses intelligence by which all natural things are directed to their goal; and this we call God.

NOTE ON SOURCES.   The material in this section is from Thomas Aquinas, *Summa Theologica*, translated by Laurence Shapcote, Part I, Question 2, Article III.

2   BLAISE PASCAL

BELIEF WITHOUT PROOFS

FROM THOMAS TO PASCAL.   Living in the thirteenth century, Thomas Aquinas wrote in an age of Christian faith. His trust in reason to infer knowledge of God from knowledge of nature was a trust shared by most of his contemporaries and readers. By the time Pascal wrote in the seventeenth century, the Renaissance and Reformation had shaken the accepted beliefs of Thomas's age. In the previous century, Pascal's fellow Frenchman, Michel De Montaigne (1533–1592) penned his *Essais*, which revived the ancient arguments for skepticism, declaring that human reason by itself is unable to attain absolute truth, and rejecting claims of human superiority over the beasts of the field as vain and hollow pretensions. Montaigne encapsulated his skepticism in the motto, "What do I know?" Pascal's seventeenth-century French contemporary, René Descartes (whom we encountered in Chapter 2), was deeply troubled by such skepticism and formulated a philosophical method that would use doubt to conquer doubt. Descartes' method generated for him proofs concerning his own existence as well as the existence of God. Whereas Thomas Aquinas had inferred God's existence from certain facts in nature, Descartes inferred God's existence from certain facts about the self. Pascal found neither approach convincing. For him, reason is unable to prove the existence of God. That does not mean, however, that reason is completely incompetent in the debate the believer has with the nonbeliever. Indeed, Pascal's great ambition was to prepare an intellectual vindication of Christianity that would lead nonbelievers to the threshold of faith. Death prevented Pascal from completing that task. What remains of his effort is a group of several hundred notes and aphorisms gathered together and published after his death under the title *Pensées*, or "Thoughts." The selections in this section come from his *Pensées*.

BIOGRAPHICAL NOTE. Pascal was born in 1623 and died in 1662 at the age of thirty-nine. He was educated at home. His parents, especially his father, were devout Catholics, pious but stern. Blaise early displayed a remarkable precocity in physics and mathematics; at the age of fifteen he was producing monographs on conic sections that were thought important enough to be read by "the most learned and scientific men in Paris." He was considered one of the outstanding physicists and mathematicians of his time. His discoveries were made during the years when most scientists are still mastering the known facts of their field.

The elder Pascal died in 1650, leaving a patrimony to Blaise and his sister Jacqueline. Jacqueline entered a convent; Blaise went off to Paris. During the next four years he lived among scholars, scientists, wits, and the nobility. On November 23, 1654, he had what is termed a mystical experience. That he had this experience, there is no reason to doubt; that it meant what he interpreted it to mean is perhaps open to debate.

That hour, described for posterity in a note found sewn into the coat he was wearing at the time of his death, wrought a change in Pascal's life. Austerity, self-denial, almsgiving, and obedience to his spiritual director replaced his routine of scientist and man-about-town. He threw himself into the defense of the Cistercian abbey of Port Royal des Champs, which was being persecuted by the hierarchy for a number of real or supposed heresies. The case for the Port Royalists was stated by Pascal in his celebrated *Letters to a Provincial*. The closing years of his life were given to planning and sketching in his *Pensées*.

THE ARGUMENT FROM THE PASSAGES. We do not know how Pascal would have marshalled his thoughts into a vindication of Christianity. What he left us is, so to speak, a box of several hundred note cards of his research, which we must try to organize into a coherent whole. Accordingly, the passages we have selected and the order in which we present them involves considerable interpretation on our part. We do not attempt to reconstruct the argument of his entire book. We limit our attention to his discussion as it relates to the question of proving the existence of God.

At the outset Pascal surveys humankind on the issue of belief in God and comes up with three classes of people.

> Before entering the proofs of the Christian religion, I find it necessary to set forth the unfairness of men who are indifferent to the search for truth in a matter which is so

important to them and which touches them so nearly. Among all their errors, this most proves them to be fools and blind.

We know well enough how men of this temper behave. They believe they have made a great effort after their instruction when they have spent a few hours reading some book of Scripture and putting a few questions to some ecclesiastic. Whereupon they boast that they have "in vain consulted books and men." Such carelessness is intolerable.

Among unbelievers I make a vast distinction. I can have nothing but compassion for all who sincerely lament their doubt, who look upon it as the worst of evils, who spare no pains to escape it, who make these matters their chief and most serious occupation. But those who pass their lives without thinking of this ultimate end of existence, who neglect to examine whether these are matters which people receive through credulous simplicity or have a solid and impregnable basis, such persons I regard in a wholly different manner. Their negligence irritates me much more than it excites my pity. It astonishes and overwhelms me; it is for me something monstrous.

There are but three classes of persons: those who have found God and serve Him; those who have not found God, but do diligently seek Him; and those who have not found God, and live without seeking Him. The first are happy and wise. The second are unhappy, but wise. The third are unhappy and fools.

It is a sorry evil to be in doubt. It is an indispensable duty to seek when we are in doubt. Therefore he who doubts and neglects to seek to dispel these doubts, is at once in a sorry plight and guilty of great perversity. If he is calm and contented in his doubt, if he frankly avows it, if he boasts of it, if he makes it the subject of vanity and delight, I can find no terms with which to describe him.

How do men come by these sentiments? What delight is there in such things? What is there to be proud of in beholding ourselves in the midst of impenetrable darkness? How can any rational man reason in this way: "I know not who has put me in the world, nor what the world is, nor what I am myself. I am in terrible ignorance of all these things. I view the awful spaces of the universe that surround me, I find myself fixed to a corner of this vast extent, I see nothing but infinites on every side enclosing me like an atom. All that I know is that I must soon die. Such is my state—full of misery, weakness, obscurity. And from this I conclude that I ought to pass all the days of my life without thinking of what is to happen to me hereafter. It may be that I could find some answers to my doubts; but I am unwilling to take the trouble."

Who would desire to have for a friend a man who discourses in such a fashion? Who would select such a person to be the confidant of his affairs? Who would have resource to such a one in his afflictions? In fine, for what use in life could such a man be destined? It is the glory of religion to have such irrational men for its enemies. Such strange insensibility for the greatest things is something monstrous. It is an incomprehensible delusion.

There must be a strange revulsion in the nature of man, to make him glory in such a state. Most of those who are thus involved are people who have heard that fine worldly manners consist in what they call "throwing off the yoke." This they try to imitate. But, what good does it do us to hear a man say that he has "thrown off the yoke," that he does not believe there is a God, that he is answerable in his conduct to none but himself? Is this a thing to be said gaily? On the contrary, is it not a thing to be said with sadness, as of all things the saddest? It requires all the love of the religion which they despise, not to despise such persons and abandon them in their folly.

Pascal is not prepared to abandon these unbelievers in their folly. Remember his three classes of persons: first, the happy and wise who have sought God and found Him; second, the unhappy and wise who are seeking God but have not found Him; third, the unhappy fools who are not seeking God and have not found Him. Pascal will present arguments to move persons in the third group into the second group; that is, to convert the unhappy fools into being seekers after God who have not yet found him. Then he will offer some suggestions as to how persons in the second group can move into the first group. Let us consider now his strategy for encouraging persons in group three to become members of group two.

First, he declares that the proofs for the existence of God offered by thinkers like Aquinas and Descartes will not dislodge people from their doubts or callous indifference concerning the existence of God.

I wonder at the boldness of those who undertake to speak of God to the irreligious. Their first chapter is to prove the existence of God by reference to the works of nature. I should not be astonished if they addressed their argument to those who already believe; for those who have a lively faith in their heart see at once that all that exists is none other than the handiwork of God. But for those who are destitute of faith—to tell them that they need only look at nature around them in order to see God unveiled, to give them the course of the sun and the moon as the sole proof of this important matter, to imagine with such an argument we have proved anything, is only to give grounds for believing that the proofs of our religion are very feeble. Indeed, I see by reason and experience that nothing is more fitted to excite contempt.

This is what I see, and what troubles me. I look on all sides, and see nothing but obscurity; nature offers me nothing but matter for doubt. If I saw nothing in nature which marked a Divinity, I should decide not to believe in Him. If I saw everywhere the marks of a Creator, I should rest peacefully in faith. But I see too much to deny, and to little to affirm; so my state is pitiful. A hundred times I have wished that God would mark His presence in nature unequivocally, if He upholds nature; or that nature would wholly suppress the signs which she gives of God, if those signs are fallacious; that she would either say all or say nothing, so I might see what part I should take. While in my present state, ignorant of what I am and of what I ought to do, I know neither my condition nor my duty.

The metaphysical proofs of God are so far apart from man's reason, and so complicated, that they are but little striking. If they are of use to any, it is only during the moment that the demonstration is before them. An hour afterwards they fear they have been mistaken. Therefore I do not here undertake to prove by natural reason the existence of God. I do not feel myself strong enough to find in nature proofs to convince hardened atheists. All who seek God in nature find no light to satisfy them. They fall either into atheism or into deism, two things which the Christian religion almost equally abhors.

Second, Pascal uncovers the uneasiness of the human being poised between the infinitely large and the infinitely small. The spatiotemporal universe displays the infinitely large.

Let a man contemplate nature in her full majesty. Let him extend his view beyond the objects which surround him. Let him regard the sun. Let him consider the earth whereon he lives as a point in comparison with the vast orbit described by the sun. Let him learn that his vast orbit is but a point compared with that embraced by the stars which roll in the firmament. Let his imagination pass beyond. All this visible cosmos is but a point in the ample bosom of nature. In vain we extend our conceptions beyond imaginable spaces: We bring forth but atoms in comparison with the reality of things. For the universe is an infinite sphere whose center is everywhere and whose circumference is nowhere.

From the vastness of things, he passes to the other extreme. Compared to the whole of nature, man may be a mere speck. But compared to the infinitely small particles that compose the material world, he is a colossus.

There is another aspect, equally astonishing. Let a man seek things the most minute. Let him consider a mite, in the exceeding smallness of its body; parts incomparably smaller, limbs with joints, veins in those limbs, blood in those veins, humors in this blood, globules in these humors, gases in the globules. Let him divide these globules. Let him exhaust his powers of conception. He will think perhaps that he has arrived at the minutest atoms of nature. I will show him therein a new abyss. I will picture to him the inconceivable immensity of nature in the compass of this abbreviation of an atom. Let him view therein an infinity of worlds, each with its own firmament, its planets, its earth, in the same proportion as the visible world. Let him lose himself in these wonders, as astonishing in their littleness as the others in their magnitude. His body which just before was imperceptible in the universe, is now a colossus in comparison with the infinitely small at which it is possible to arrive.

With this contrast in mind, Pascal pauses to ask: What is man, amid all this? He could have used the words of the Psalmist, "What is man that Thou art mindful of him?" But at this point, that would be begging the question: it is that "Thou" that is in question.

What is man, in the midst of these two infinities? A nothing compared with the infinitely large, all compared with the infinitely small. A mean between all and nothing, infinitely far from comprehending the extremes. Let us, then, know our range. Such is our true state. This is what renders us incapable, alike of absolute knowledge and absolute ignorance.

Nature confounds the skeptics and reason confounds the dogmatists. What will become of you, O man, who would search out your true condition by your natural reason? You can avoid neither skepticism nor dogmatism; but, alas, you can live with neither!

Our intelligence holds the same position as our body, in the vast extent of nature. This middle state between two extremes is common to all our weaknesses: our senses can perceive no extreme; too much noise deafens us, too much light blinds us, too far or too near interferes with our vision, too much brevity or too much prolixity obscures our understanding, too much truth overwhelms us, too much pleasure cloys on us, too many benefits annoy us, we feel neither extreme heat nor extreme cold, too much and too little teaching hinder our minds—in a word, all extremes are for us as though they were not. They escape us or we escape them.

Man is a creature full of natural error. Nothing shows him the truth, everything deceives him. His reason and his senses deceive each other. These senses trick the reason by false appearances; reason in turn avenges herself and deceives the senses.

His emotions trouble his senses and make false impressions on him. Reason, senses, emotions, lie and deceive, outdoing each other.

What a chimera is man! Strange and monstrous! A chaos, a contradiction, a prodigy. Judge of all things, yet a weak earthworm. Depository of truth, yet a cesspool of uncertainty and error; the glory and the scraping of the universe.

Who will unravel such a tangle? Is it beyond the power of dogmatism, of skepticism, of philosophy. Man is incomprehensible by man. We grant that to the skeptics. Truth is not within our reach, nor to our taste; her home is not on earth.

We sail on a vast expanse of being, ever uncertain, ever drifting, ever hurried from one goal to another. If we seek to attach ourselves to any one point, it totters and fails us; if we follow, it eludes our grasp, vanishing forever. Nothing stays for us. This is our natural condition. Yet, it is the condition most contrary to our inclination; for we burn with desire to find a steadfast place and a fixed basis whereupon we may build. But our whole foundation breaks up, and the abysses open before us.

When I consider the short duration of my life, swallowed up in an eternity before and after, the small space I fill engulfed in the infinite immensity of spaces whereof I know nothing and which know nothing of me, I am terrified. The eternal silence of these infinite spaces alarms me. I wonder why I am here, rather than there, now rather than then. Who has set me here? By whose order and design have this place and time been destined for me?

When I see the blindness and misery of man; when I survey the whole dumb universe; when I see man left to himself without a light unto his path, lost in this corner of the cosmos, ignorant of who placed him here, of what he has come here to do, of what will overtake him when he dies, I fall into terror. And my terror is like that of a man who should awake upon a terrible desert island with no means of escape. And I wonder why men do not fall into despair. I see others around me, of like nature. I ask if they are better informed than I am; and they say they are not.

We may not, then, look for certainty or stability. Our reason is always deceived by changing shows. It matters not that man should have a trifle more knowledge of the universe; if he has it, he but begins a littler higher; but he is always infinitely distant from the end. In regard to the infinities, all finites are equal, and I see no reason why we should fix our imagination on one more than on another.

Who would not think, when we declare that man consists of mind and matter, that we really understood this combination? Yet—it is the one thing we least understand. Nothing is more obscure than just this mixture of spirit and clay. Man is, to himself, the most marvelous object in nature, for he cannot conceive what matter is, nor what mind is, nor how a material body should be united to an immaterial mind. This is the crown of all his difficulties, yet it is his very being.

These are some of the causes which render man so totally unable to know nature. For nature has a twofold infinity, while he is finite. Nature is permanent, while he is fleeting and mortal. All things change and fail; he sees them only as they pass. All things have their beginning and their end; he sees neither the one nor the other. Things are simple and homogenous. He is complex and composed of two different elements.

Not from space must I see my dignity. I should have no more if I possessed whole worlds. By space the universe encompasses and swallows me as an atom. Man is but a reed, weakest in nature, but a reed which thinks. A thinking reed. It needs not that the whole universe should arm to crush him. A vapor, a drop of water is enough to kill him. But were the universe to kill him, man would still be more noble than that which has slain him, because he knows that he dies, and that the universe has the better of him. The universe knows nothing of this.

Know then, proud Man, how great a paradox thou art to thyself. Bow down thyself, impotent reason; be silent, thou foolish human nature. Learn that man is altogether incomprehensible by man.

Let man now estimate his value. Let him love himself, because he has a nature capable of good. But let him not love the vileness which exists in that nature. He has in himself the capacity of knowledge and happiness, yet he finds no last truth or satisfaction. I would lead him to desire it; to be freed from passions, to know how his passions obscure his knowledge and his achievement of happiness. I would have him hate in himself the desires which bias his judgment, that they might neither blind him in choosing nor obstruct him when he has chosen.

The net result is that man and woman are ignorant and helpless and alone. The blind forces of nature offer them no haven. The universe at large cares as little for their living as for their dying. Pascal might have let it go at that. Many have; for example, Schopenhauer and Thomas Hardy and Bertrand Russell. Not so Pascal. He presses the discussion further.

The *third* fact of his strategy is to remind the human being who experiences the uneasiness of being confronted by an alien, indifferent, even hostile universe that nothing less than the conquest of true happiness is at stake.

All men seek happiness. To this there is no exception. Our will makes no step, except toward this object. This is the motive of every action of every man. And yet, after so many years no one has arrived, without faith, at the point to which all eyes are turned. All complain, rulers and ruled, nobles and commons, old and young, strong and weak, learned and ignorant, sound and sick, of all countries, all times, all ages, and all conditions.

A trial so long, so constant, so uniform, should have convinced us of our inability to arrive at our complete happiness by our own strength. But example teaches us little. We expect that our efforts will not be foiled on this occasion, as before. Thus while the present never satisfies us, experience never teaches us; and from misfortune to misfortune we are led on to death, the eternal crown of our sorrows.

This desire, and this weakness, cry aloud to us that there is an empty space in man which he seeks vainly to fill from all that surrounds him, seeks vainly to find in things absent the happiness which he finds not in things present.

The *fourth* move made by Pascal is to suggest that the happiness all humans seek but so seldom find is to be found only in God. Pascal's strategy is in fact an autobiographical rehearsal of his own spiritual pilgrimage. He had experienced a great thirst for peace of mind, for happiness of soul. He had tried to find that tranquility and joy through the escapades of high society, the certainties of mathematics, the new insights of the physical sciences, and the inherited wisdom of traditional philosophy. He ended up empty-handed: happiness eluded his grasp. Then came his dark night of the soul when in desperation he cast himself upon God. The mystic experience of God that ensued convinced Pascal that the joy he sought could be found only in God. His thought echoes the confession of Saint Augustine (354–430 A.D.): "Our hearts are restless until they rest in Thee."

Man finds his happiness only in God. Without Him, there is nothing in nature which will take His place; neither the stars, nor heaven, nor earth, nor the elements; not plants, cabbages, animals, insects, calves, serpents, fever, pestilence, war, famine, vices, adultery, incest. Since man has lost track of his true happiness, all things appear equally good to him, even his own destruction, though so contrary to God, to right reason, and to the whole course of nature.

There is no good without knowledge of God. Only as we approach Him are we happy; and our ultimate good is to know Him certainly. We are unhappy, in proportion as we are removed from Him; and the greatest evil would be the certainty of being cut off from Him.

The *fifth* and final feature of his strategy for encouraging people to move out of group three into group two is his famous religious wager. Let us recapitulate his strategy thus far. He has rejected the traditional proofs for the existence of God: Renaissance skepticism, personified in Montaigne, has eroded those. He has displayed the utter loneliness and littleness of the human poised between the two infinites. Must not the most resolute nonbelievers agree with that? He has argued that the happiness we all seek is seldom found through attachment to things of this world. Must not the most resolute nonbeliever in moments of utter honesty also agree with that? But how can Pascal move the nonbeliever who experiences a frustrated quest for happiness to redirect his or her quest toward God? That is the task of his wager.

If there be a God, He is infinitely incomprehensible, since having neither parts nor limits, He has no relation to us. We are, then, incapable of knowing either that He is or what He is.

Let us examine this point: "Either God is, or is not," we can say. But to which side shall we incline? Reason cannot help us. There is an infinite gulf fixed between creature and creator. What will you wager? It is like a game in which heads or tails may turn up. There is no reason for backing either the one possibility or the other. You cannot reasonably argue in favor of either.

If you know nothing either way, it might be urged, the true course is not to wager at all. But you must wager; that does not depend on your will. You are embarked in this business. Which will you choose?

Let us see. Since you must choose, your reason is no more affronted in choosing one way than the other. That point is clear. But what of your happiness? Let us weigh the gain and the loss in wagering that God does exist. If you wager that He does, and He does, you gain all; if you wager that He does, and He does not, you lose nothing. If you win, you take all; if you lose, you lose nothing. This is demonstrable, and if men are capable of any truths, this is one. Wager then, unhesitatingly, that He does exist.

If we ought to do nothing except on a certainty, we ought to do nothing for religion, because it is not a matter of certainty. But it is false to say, "We ought to do nothing except on a certainty." In a voyage at sea, in a battle, we act on uncertainties. If it be the case that we ought to do nothing except on a certainty, then we ought to do nothing at all, for nothing is certain.

Pascal is counting on the prudential calculations of the nonbeliever. There is an infinity of happiness at stake if God exists. Surely it is wiser to wager that He exists, than to wager He doesn't exist. When the nonbeliever takes the gamble of wagering that God exists (with the hoped-for pay-off being an eternal life of happiness in God's presence), has not the nonbeliever moved into group two? But making a wager that God exists is not the same thing as living a life of faith, hope and love in the presence of the Living God. Making a wager is not the same thing as faith. Pascal is too alert to make that mistake, and to let the matter rest with the wager. The issue that now arises is how to move people from group two into group one. Pascal offers a provocative response.

> You may object: "My hands are tied, my mouth is gagged. I am forced to wager, I am not free. But, despite this, I am so made that I cannot believe. What then would you have me do?"
>
> I would have you understand your incapacity to believe. Labor to convince yourself, not by more "proofs" of God's existence, but by disciplining your passions and wayward emotions. You would arrive at faith, but know not the way. You would heal yourself of unbelief, yet know not the remedies. I answer: Learn of those who have been bound as you are. These are they who know the way you would follow, who have been cured of a disease you would be cured of. Follow the way by which they began, by making believe what they believe. Thus you will come to believe.
>
> Now, what will happen to you if you take this side in the religious wager? You will be trustworthy, honorable, humble, grateful, generous, friendly, sincere, and true. You will no longer have those poisoned pleasures, glory and luxury; but you will have other pleasures. I tell you that you will gain this life; at each step you will see so much certainty of gain, so much nothingness in what you stake, that you will know at last that you have wagered on a certainty, an infinity, for which you have risked nothing.
>
> If my words please you, and seem to you cogent, know that they are the words of one who has thrown himself on his knees before and after to pray to that infinite Being to whom he submits all; know too that you also would submit to Him your all for your own good and His glory, and that this strength may be in accord with this weakness.

Is Pascal urging those who are seeking God but cannot find Him to act as if they were already believers? Is he saying that genuine belief would soon appear? Is he suggesting that if you practice the appropriate moral virtues, you will in due course find the God you are seeking, in whose presence abiding happiness is to be found?

Pascal's position, then, on natural theology is clear. According to him, you cannot use what you know about nature to prove the existence of God. Yet you can use what you know about nature and human nature to show a need for God as the solution to the human being's unfulfilled quest for abiding happiness. But, careful thinker that he is, Pascal knows that there is a gap between the fact of our need for God and God's inferred existence to fill that need. Accordingly, he recognizes that the most his arguments can do is to bring a person to the threshold of faith. The wager and what follows it are matters settled in personal decision and action, not in philosophical debate and proof.

NOTE ON SOURCES. The Pascal material in this section is quoted, abridged, or paraphrased from Blaise Pascal, *Thoughts*. That book consists of 923 numbered items. The following items have been used in this chapter: Numbers 194, 195, 205, 206, 229, 233, 347, 348, 434, 437—and a few here and there among the remaining items.

3 DAVID HUME

DOUBTS ABOUT NATURAL THEOLOGY

FROM PASCAL TO HUME. The problem of natural theology continued to command attention. We have seen repudiation by Pascal; a repudiation, however, that left no bitter taste in the devout reader's mouth, since Pascal strove earnestly to restore with one hand what he swept aside with the other. By the middle of the eighteenth century times and tempers had changed. The "Age of Reason" had set in. The French Revolution was drawing nearer. The natural sciences, from their small beginnings with Galileo and Bacon and Harvey in the seventeenth century, had come to exercise considerable dominion over the imaginations of the intellectual classes. It was in this somewhat more chilly climate of opinion that David Hume turned his critical attention to natural theology.

BIOGRAPHICAL NOTE. Hume was born in Scotland in 1711 and died in 1776 at the age of sixty-five. Although he was destined, along with Immanuel Kant, to mark the opening of a chapter in the history of philosophy that is still unclosed, his early life was passed in obscurity, and his fame, among his contemporaries, was based principally upon his writings in the field of political history.

He was intended by his father for the law, and to that end was educated in Edinburgh. However, he abandoned the study of law and tried his hand in a Bristol counting-house. This, too, proved uncongenial. He went to France, where he proceeded to write one of the epoch-making books in modern philosophy, his *Treatise of Human Nature*. The theme of this philosophical masterpiece is simply stated in the form of a question: How much of human knowledge, human emotional preferences and aversions, human mortality, is what it is for no better reason than the fact that human nature is what it is? The suggestion, that once you have taken the "human" out of these things there is nothing left over, was too much for his generation to entertain. It contained too many skeptical implications. The *Treatise* fell, as though stillborn, from the press.

Hume now set about to find employment that would put him in a position of independence. He applied, without success, for the chair of moral philosophy in the University of Edinburgh. For two years he tutored an almost insane Scottish marquis. He accompanied a diplomatic expedition to France. He applied, again without success, for the chair of logic at the University of Glasgow. At last he secured the position of Keeper of the Advocates' Library in Edinburgh. The access to books and original authorities that this gave him suggested the idea of writing a work of history. This he proceeded to do and, between 1754 and 1762, produced his famous *History of England*, which ranked, in that century, with Gibbon's *Decline and Fall of the Roman Empire*.

In the lean years before he became Keeper and turned historian, Hume continued reworking and expanding the ideas of his original philosophical treatise. These were published in a series of short monographs and collections of essays. In this form they gained a gradual acceptance. But it was still the historian who overshadowed the philosopher in the minds of his generation. He retired in 1769, on a combined income and pension of £1,000 a year. He spent the remainder of his days, the recognized head of the intellectual and literary society in Edinburgh, admired by those who read his *History* and his miscellaneous essays, distrusted or misunderstood by those who tried their hand at his philosophy.

THE ARGUMENT OF THE PASSAGES.   The selections that follow provide a skeptical examination of natural theology. They are, for the most part, from Hume's essay "On Miracles" and from *Dialogues Concerning Natural Religion*. They presuppose, as a starting point, that the reader is familiar with the stock arguments for the existence of God.

The position finally occupied by Hume is somewhat complex. We may imagine him saying:

> If we possess, or claim to possess, knowledge of God's existence and nature, then it must rest on some sort of evidence. What is this evidence? It is formulated, usually, in three "arguments." There is the argument from miracles, the argument from design, and the argument from first cause. A skeptical examination of the claims of natural theology will include a skeptical examination of these three arguments. We shall advance two lines of criticism with respect to each: first, that the argument itself is unsound; second, that even if it were accepted without question, it does not prove what it claims to prove.

It is well to remember the limitations of the task that Hume sets himself. He is not attempting to prove that God does not exist; that is, he is not stating the case for atheism. Nor is he seeking to discredit all belief in God. His claim is the more modest one, namely, that such belief, whether true or false, is not susceptible to the traditional argumentative justification; that no "appeal to reason" can be made in support of the claims of natural theology.

Belief in God has, in time past, been supported by what is called the *argument from miracles*. It is to this effect: Miracles, violations of natural laws, occur from time to time. An explanation of such events must therefore refer to something outside or beyond nature. That is, miracles point to a miracle worker, namely, God. Hence Hume's interest in the question of miracles. His approach is indirect. He does not deny that miracles ever happen. He directs attention to the nature of the evidence upon which we believe that miracles happen and claims that the evidence in question is not strong enough to support the belief:

> I flatter myself I have discovered an argument which will be an everlasting check to all kinds of superstitious delusion, all accounts of miracles and prodigies sacred and profane.
>
> A miracle is a violation of the laws of nature. Now, as a firm and unalterable experience has established our belief in those laws, the proof against miracles, from the very nature of the case, is as entire as any argument from experience can possibly be imagined. There must be a uniform experience against any miracle; otherwise it would not be so described. Now, as a uniform experience amounts to a proof, there is here a full proof against the occurrence of any miracle. Nor can such a proof against any miracle be weakened or destroyed, except by an opposite proof which would be superior to it.

The plain consequence is this: No testimony is sufficient to establish a miracle unless the testimony be of such a kind that its falsehood would be as miraculous as, or more miraculous than, the fact which it endeavors to establish. Even in that case there is a mutual destruction of arguments; and the superior only gives us an assurance suitable to that degree of evidential force which remains after deducting the inferior.

A man tells me he saw one dead restored to life. I ask myself: Is it more probable that he should deceive or be deceived, or that the fact which he relates should really have happened? I weigh one miracle against the other, and reject the greater. If the falsehood of his testimony would be more miraculous than the event which he relates, then (but not until then) can he command my belief.

There are two parts to Hume's criticism of the evidence for believing that miracles happen. The first, and most incisive, has been given already: Miracles purport to be violations of the laws of nature. Our evidence for believing in the uniformity of nature is so great that no evidence for doubting it could be strong enough, since it would have to be stronger than the evidence for believing in nature's uniformity and this latter includes practically all our experience. He moves on to a second criticism:

We have supposed in the foregoing that the evidence for a miracle may be so strong that its falsehood would itself be a miracle. But it is easy to show that we have been a great deal too liberal in our concessions, and that no miracle has ever been established on so full an evidence.

First: There is not to be found in all history any miracle attested by a sufficient number of men of such unquestioned good sense, education, and learning, as to secure us against all delusion in themselves; of such undoubted integrity as to place them beyond all suspicion of any design to deceive others; of such credit and reputation as to have a great deal to lose in case of being detected in any falsehood; and, at the same time, attesting facts in such a manner and in so celebrated a place as to render that detection unavoidable.

Second: The many instances of mistaken or fraudulent miracles which have been detected show that mankind have a strong propensity to believe in the extraordinary and marvelous. This fact ought reasonably to beget a suspicion against all narratives concerning such matters.

Third: Reports of miracles abound chiefly among ignorant and barbarous peoples; or if such reports have been admitted by civilized and educated peoples they will be found to have received them from ignorant and barbarous peoples who transmitted them with that sanction and authority which, among such peoples, attends received opinions. This fact constitutes a strong presumption against all accounts of miracles.

Fourth: There is no *a priori* case in favor of the miracles peculiar to any one religion. The miracles of all religions stand on the same footing. If any such should be mutually incompatible, they simply cancel each other out. Nor is there any *a priori* case in favor of religious over secular miracles.

Fifth: The records of miracles in ancient times are not to be placed on an equal level with the records of nonmiraculous events in ancient times. Because some human testimony has the utmost force and authority is some cases, as when it relates to the battle of Philippi or Pharsalia, the assassination of Caesar or the execution of Socrates, it is not therefore reasonable that all kinds of testimony must, in all cases, have equal force and authority.

It appears, then, that no testimony for any kind of miracle has ever amounted to a probability, much less a proof. Experience only gives authority to human testimony, and it is experience which assures us of the laws of nature. When, therefore, these two kinds of experiences are contrary, we can only subtract the one from the other and embrace the opinion with that assurance which arises from the remainder. But, according to the measures of probability above established, this subtraction amounts to entire annihilation. Therefore no human testimony can have such force as to prove a miracle and make it a just foundation for any system of religion.

Mere reason is not sufficient to convince us of the miracles of the Christian religion. Whoever is moved by faith to assent to it, is conscious of a continued miracle in his own person, which subverts all the principles of his understanding and gives him a determination to believe what is most contrary to custom and experience.

The net result thus far: Belief in miracles rests on questionable grounds. Belief in God, therefore, insofar as it rests on belief in miracles, rests on questionable grounds. Hume's case against the argument from miracles ends at that point. He might have rounded out his argument with greater force. This was done by T. H. Huxley, Hume's biographer, in the next century. Huxley's argument proceeded along this line: Suppose the evidence for believing in miracles is left unquestioned. Suppose we admit without argument that miracles do take place. What follows? Belief in the Deity described by orthodox Christian theology? It would seem not. For miracles are an equivocal kind of evidence. They point frequently to a Deity who befriends some people at the expense of others. Consider, for example, the Old Testament miracle of the taking of Jericho. What kind of evidence would this be, in the eyes of a citizen of Jericho? Or consider the miracle of the Gadarene swine recorded in the New Testament. What kind of evidence would this be, in the eyes of the unfortunate individual who owned those swine, or (to stretch a point) in the eyes of the still more unfortunate swine? These, and similar miracles, are equivocal testimony to the Deity's universal benevolence. Moreover, if miracles are evidence of His benevolence, why do they fail to occur in so many cases where benevolence would seem to be in order, for example, when a vessel is sinking in a storm at sea? The point does not need elaboration: miracles, even if not disputed, do not provide us with decisive evidence one way or the other about God. And, when evidence is ambiguous, it is wiser to omit it.

Hume proceeds, in his examination of natural theology, to a statement and refutation of the *argument from design*. This is one of his most famous pieces of destructive criticism. Hume presents the design argument as follows:

> The chief argument for divine existence is derived from the order of nature. Where there appear marks of intelligence and design, you think it extravagant to assign for its cause either chance or the blind unguided force of matter. This is an argument from effects to causes. From the order of the work you infer there must have been project and forethought in the workman.
>
> Look around the world. Contemplate the whole and every part of it. You will find it to be nothing but one great machine, subdivided into an infinite number of lesser machines, which again admit of subdivisions to a degree beyond what human sense can trace and explain.

> All these various machines, and even their most minute parts, are adjusted to each other with an accuracy which ravishes into admiration all men who have ever contemplated them. The curious adapting of means to ends, throughout all nature, resembles exactly, though it much exceeds, the productions of human contrivance, human design, human thought, wisdom, and intelligence.
>
> Anatomize the eye. Survey its structure and contrivance. Does not the idea of contriver immediately flow in upon you with the force like that of a sensation? Behold the male and female of each species, their instincts, their passions, the whole course of their life before and after generation. Millions of such instances present themselves through every part of the universe. Can language convey a more intelligible, more irresistible meaning than the curious adjustment of means to ends in nature?
>
> Since the effects (natural productions and human productions) resemble each other, you are led to infer, by analogy, that the causes also resemble; that the author of nature is somewhat similar to the mind of man, though possessed of larger powers, proportioned to the grandeur of the work He has created.
>
> You compare the universe to productions of human intelligence, to houses, ships, furniture, machines, and so forth. Since both terms of the comparison exhibit adaptation and design, you argue that the cause of the one must resemble the cause of the other.

The argument from design, he says, is an argument from analogy: We examine a watch, a house, or a ship, and we conclude that such things were produced by beings possessing intelligence and controlled by purposes. We can, if we wish, verify this inference by acquainting ourselves with watchmakers, architects, and shipwrights. We examine the universe, or parts of it, and conclude that it too must have been produced by a being possessing intelligence and controlled by purposes. Our reason for drawing this inference is that we find the universe, or parts of it, intelligible and answering to our needs and purposes. That is, we draw the analogy watch–watchmaker and universe–Deity. From the intelligibility and utility of a watch, we infer intelligence and purposiveness in the watchmaker. By analogy, from the intelligibility and utility of nature we infer intelligence and purposiveness in the author of nature. Hume's first line of attack is to question whether the principle of causal analogy is really applicable to the universe.

> When two things (human intelligence and the products of human intelligence) have been observed to be conjoined, you can infer, by custom, from the one to the other. This I call an *argument from experience*. But how this argument can have place in the present case, may be difficult to explain. If you see a house, you can conclude it had an architect or builder because such effects, you have experienced, proceed from such causes.
>
> But does the universe resemble a house so closely that we can with the same certainty infer a similar cause? Is the analogy entire and perfect? Can you pretend here to more than a guess, a conjecture, a presumption, concerning a similar case? To ascertain such reasoning, it were necessary that you have had experience in the origin of the world. Have worlds ever been formed under your eye? Have you experienced the generation of the universe as you have experienced the building of a house?

Suppose we see a column of smoke in the distance. By the principle of causal analogy we would infer that there was some sort of fire in the distance that was the cause of the smoke. We have confidence in the accuracy of such a conclusion because we have seen fires producing smoke in the past. When the principle of causal analogy is applied to a situation, the legitimacy of that application depends on our having experienced similar situations in the past. We can readily argue, for example, that this specific house had an architect or builder because we have encountered houses in the past that have had architects or builders. When it comes to the universe, however, we have no past experience of universes having been designed by an intelligent being on the basis of which we can say, by the principle of causal analogy, that this, our universe, was also designed by an intelligent being. Accordingly, the principle of causal analogy is not really applicable to the universe because we have no past experience of other universes from which we can argue analogically. Suppose, however, that we allow the proponents of the design argument to use the principle of causal analogy (even though its use is unwarranted); the next question Hume would ask is, "Why should one settle on the design–designer analogy? Are not other analogies equally possible?"

You have argued, thus far, on the principle that like effects have like causes. But there is another you might try, based no less on experience: Where several known parts are observed to be similar, the unknown parts will also be found similar. Thus, if you see the limbs of a human body, you conclude that it is attended with a human head, though hid from you. If you see a small part of the sun, through a chink in the wall, you conclude that, were the wall removed, you should see the rest. Within the limits of experience, this method of reasoning is obvious and reliable.

Now I say, if you survey the universe, so far as it falls under your knowledge, it bears a great resemblance to an animal, or organized body, and seems actuated by a like principle of life and motion. A continual circulation of matter produces no disorder. A continual waste in every part is incessantly repaired. Each part, in performing its proper offices, operates both to its own preservation and that of the whole. From all this, why not infer that the world is an organism, an animal, and that Deity is the soul of the world, actuating it and being actuated by it?

If it be legitimate to argue thus by analogy from part to whole, I affirm that other parts of the world bear a greater resemblance to the structure of the world than do matters of human invention; and, therefore, should afford a better conjecture concerning the origin and nature of the whole. These parts are animals and vegetables. The world resembles more an organism than a clock or a knitting loom. Its cause, therefore, more probably resembles the cause of the former, namely generation.

As a tree sheds its seed into neighboring fields, so the great system of the world produces certain seeds which, being scattered into the surrounding chaos, grow into new worlds. A comet, for instance, may be taken as such a seed. After it has been fully ripened, by passing from sun to sun and star to star, it is at last tossed into the unformed elements which surround this universe, and sprouts into a new system.

Or, for variety (for I see no other advantage), suppose this world to be an animal instead of a vegetable. A comet then would be an egg. And, in like manner as an ostrich lays its egg in the sand, which without any further care hatches the egg, so. . . .

You protest: What wild, arbitrary suppositions are these? What data have I for such extraordinary conclusions? Is the slight resemblance of the world to a vegetable or animal sufficient basis for an argument as to further resemblances? You are right. This is what I have been insisting on, all along. We have no data, or insufficient data, for any such speculations. Our experience, from which alone we can argue safely, is so limited in extent and duration as to afford us no probable conjecture concerning the whole of things.

If you agree that our limited experience is an unequal standard by which to judge of the unlimited extent of nature, a too narrow stretch upon which to erect hypotheses concerning so vast a matter, you entirely abandon your case, and must admit of the absolute incomprehensibility of the author of nature.

If one allows the principle of causal analogy to apply to the universe, and if one selects deign–designer as the analogy by which to understand the origin and nature of the universe, then one would have to show why the analogies of an animal or a vegetable are to be rejected. That would be an especially difficult task in view of the fact that the case made for the design–designer analogy (like the animal and vegetable analogies) lacks adequate evidential support and is the product of mere conjecture. Suppose, however, that we allow the proponents of the design argument to reject the other analogies and to use the design–designer analogy (even though its use is unwarranted), the next question Hume would ask is, "Why do proponents of the design argument select only certain qualities of human designers and ascribe those to the divine designer? Why not ascribe to the deity the plurality, mistakes, imperfections, and perversity of human designers?"

> By this argument from analogy, how prove the unity of Deity? Many men join in building a house or ship or city or commonwealth. Why may not several deities have combined in framing a world? This is only so much greater similarity to human affairs, to the operation of human intelligence. By dividing thus the work among several, you would get rid of that extensive power and knowledge which must be supposed in one deity.
>
> Were one deity, who possessed every attribute necessary to the production of the universe, and not many deities, proved by this argument from analogy, it would be needless to suppose any other deity. But while it is still an open question whether all these attributes are united in one deity or dispersed among several independent deities, by what phenomena in nature can you pretend to decide the controversy? On this kind of argument from nature, polytheism and monotheism are on a like footing. Neither has any advantage over the other.
>
> By this method of reasoning from analogy you renounce all claim to perfection in any of the attributes of the Deity. Imperfections in human productions you ascribe to imperfections in human producers. There are many inexplicable difficulties in the work of nature. Are you to ascribe these to the imperfections of the author of nature?
>
> By representing Deity as so intelligible and comprehensible, so similar to a human mind, you make ourselves the model. Is this reasonable? The sentiments of the human mind include gratitude and resentment, love and hate, friendship and enmity, blame and approval, pity and scorn, admiration and envy. Do you propose to transfer such sentiments to a Supreme Being? Or suppose Him actuated by them? Do you propose to ascribe to Him only knowledge and power but no virtues?

Hume has raised some tough-minded objections to the argument from design. The bottom line of his objections is that even if we allow the principle of causal analogy to apply to the universe (which is unwarranted), and even if we allow the design–designer analogy to stand (which is also unwarranted), even then the argument does not establish that the designer of the universe is the single, supreme, intelligent, perfect being that proponents of the argument want. Hume, however, is not finished with this design argument. He has yet another powerful objection to register. The design argument seeks to say something about God on the basis of a scrutiny of his handiwork—nature. What, however, does a scrutiny of nature really reveal about its maker? Do not the suffering and evil in nature call into question the purported omnipotence and/or benevolence of God? Can one seriously maintain that imperfect nature, replete with pain and misery, is the work of a perfect being?

Can any man, by a simple denial, hope to bear down the united testimony of mankind? The whole earth is cursed and polluted. A perpetual war is kindled among all living creatures. Necessity, hunger, want, stimulate the strong and courageous; fear, anxiety, terror, agitate the weak and the infirm. The first entrance into life gives anguish to the newborn infant and to parent. Weakness, impotence, distress, attend each stage of many lives which are finished at last in agony and horror.

Is it not thus in nature? Observe the curious artifices of nature to embitter the life of living beings. The stronger prey upon the weaker, and keep them in perpetual terror and misery. The weaker, too, often prey upon the stronger. Consider those species of insects which are bred on the body of animals, or flying about, infix their stings into them. These insects have others, still more minute, which torment them. On every hand animals are surrounded with enemies which cause their misery and seek their destruction.

Why should man pretend to be exempted from the lot which befalls all other animals? Man is the greatest enemy of man. Oppression, injustice, contempt, slander, violence, sedition, war—by these men torment each other. The external ills of humanity, from the elements, from other animals, from men themselves, form a frightful catalogue of woes; but they are nothing compared with those that arise from conditions within. How many lie under the lingering torment of disease? How many suffer remorse, shame, anguish, rage, disappointment, fear, despair? How many suffer those deep disorders of mind, insanity, idiocy, madness? Who has passed through life without cruel inroads from these tormentors?

Were a stranger to drop into this world, I would show him, as a specimen of its ills, a hospital full of diseases, a prison crowded with malefactors, a battlefield strewn with carcasses, a fleet floundering in the ocean, a nation languishing under tyranny, famine, or pestilence. Labor and poverty are the certain lot of the far greater number, while the few who enjoy riches and ease never reach contentment or true felicity. All the good things of life taken together make a man very wretched indeed.

You ascribe an author to nature, and a purpose to the author of nature. What, I beseech you, is the object fulfilled by these matters to which attention has been drawn? Our sense of music, harmony, beauty, has some purpose. But what of gout, gravels, megrims, toothaches, rheumatisms? How does divine benevolence and purpose display itself here? Why argue for the power and knowledge of the Deity while His moral qualities are in doubt?

You say: But this world is only a point in comparison of the universe; this life is but a moment in comparison of eternity. Present evils are rectified in other regions and future times. And the eyes of men, being then opened to large views of things see the whole connection of general laws, and trace with adoration the benevolence and wisdom of the Deity through all the mazes and intricacies of his providence.

I answer: The only method of supporting divine benevolence is for you to say to me, "Your representations are exaggerated; your melancholy views are mostly fictitious; your inferences are contrary to fact and experience; health is more common than sickness; pleasure, than pain; happiness, than misery; for one vexation we meet, we attain a hundred enjoyments."

I add: Can such apologetics be admitted? Even allowing your claim that human happiness exceeds human misery, yet it proves nothing. For an excess of happiness over misery is not what we expect from infinite power coupled with infinite wisdom and infinite goodness.

The questions asked by Epicurus, of old, are yet unanswered. Is Deity willing to prevent evil, but not able? Then He is not omnipotent. Is He able, but not willing? Then He is malevolent. Is He both able and willing? Then whence cometh evil? Is He neither able nor willing? Then why call Him Deity?

Evil and unhappiness are the rocks upon which all arguments for Deity must finally come to wreck. Why is there any misery and wickedness at all in the world? Not by chance, surely. From some purpose or cause then? Is it from the intention of the Deity? But He is perfectly benevolent. Is it contrary to his intention? But He is almighty. Nothing can shake the solidity of this reasoning, so short, so clear, so decisive; unless we agree that these matters lie beyond human capacity, that our human reason is not applicable to them. This is the counsel of skepticism that I have all along insisted on.

The whole matter is summarized in the two following passages.

In a word, a man who follows this kind of argument from analogy, where one of the terms of the analogy lies beyond his experience, may perhaps be able to conjecture that the universe arose from something like design. But beyond that he cannot go, except by the utmost license of thought.

On this argument for all you know to the contrary, this world may be a very faulty and imperfect copy compared to a superior standard; only the first rude essay of some infant deity who afterwards abandoned it, ashamed of his lame performance; only the work of some dependent, inferior deity, the object of derision to his superiors; only the product of old age and dotage in some superannuated deity, and ever since his death running on at adventures from the first impulse it received from him.

Thus far, we have the argument from the miracles and the argument from design. If these arguments from miracles and from design presented so many difficulties, would one fare better with the argument from the first cause? By this argument could one prove the infinity, the unity, and the perfection, of the author of nature? Hume states this argument as follows:

The argument from first cause is this. Whatever exists must have a cause of its existence. Nothing can produce itself. In mounting up, therefore, from effects to causes, we must go on tracing an infinite regression without any ultimate cause, or must finally have recourse to an ultimate cause. Now, it is insisted, the conception of an infinite regression, or utterly no beginning cause to which all others can be traced, is absurd. We must, therefore, have recourse to a necessarily existent being, the first cause of all things, who carries the reason of His existence in Himself, and whom we cannot suppose not to exist without embracing an absurdity. Such a being is the Deity.

His criticism is brief and to the point:

Wherein do we find the absurdity of an infinite regression? It leads us beyond our powers of conceiving? So also does the conception of an infinite deity.

> Let us admit its absurdity. Let us admit the necessity of a first cause. Shall we then ask for a cause of this cause? If not, then may we not argue a material first cause of this material universe? If not, may we ascribe to the spiritual first cause the origin of evil and misery and waste which we noted in our analysis of the argument from analogy? If not, to what cause then are they to be traced? If so, wherein do we fare better with the argument from the necessity of a first cause than from the probability of an intelligent designer?

His conclusion to the whole business is a plea for skepticism in natural theology:

All religious systems are subject to insuperable difficulties. Each disputant triumphs in his turn, exposing the absurdities, barbarities, and pernicious tenets of his antagonist. But all of them prepare a complete triumph for the skeptic who tells them no system ought ever to be embraced with regard to such questions. A total suspense of judgment is here our only reasonable recourse.

The upshot of Hume's critique of natural theology is skepticism. Its historical importance is along several lines. In the first place, it was a nemesis visited upon the Age of Reason; for what Hume showed was the helplessness of reason to cope with the problems of natural theology. In some minds this work has never been undone. For them, Hume administered a deathblow to the speculations at which he directed his attention. Rational theology in the grand manner has never been completely restored to its former intellectual respectability. In the second place, Hume's handling of these questions led to an interesting attempt, by John Stuart Mill in the following century, to introduce into theology the conception of a finite God; in the twentieth century, to the pragmatic approach to these matters in the writings of the American, William James.

NOTE ON SOURCES. The material in this section is quoted, abridged, or paraphrased from David Hume, "On Miracles," *An Enquiry Concerning Human Understanding* (Oxford: Clarendon Press, 1975) and *Dialogues Concerning Natural Religion* (Indianapolis: Bobbs-Merrill, 1970), Parts 2–10.

4 JOHN STUART MILL

A FINITE GOD

FROM HUME TO MILL. In this chapter we have been examining the grounds for belief in God. In particular, we have been looking at natural theology, which claims that we can use what we know about nature to infer certain knowledge about God. Aquinas, an advocate of natural theology, claimed that from a knowledge of nature he could prove the existence of God in five different ways. Pascal, who was very skeptical about natural theology, maintained that the most argumentation could do was bring people to the threshold of faith; for him, there were no compelling proofs for the existence of God. Hume, like Pascal, was skeptical about the claims of natural theology, but, unlike Pascal, he would not be counted among the believers in God. Hume gave weighty reasons for rejecting any argument from miracles, or design, or causation in nature as the proof of anything like the orthodox Christian beliefs about God. This brings matters close to the end of the eighteenth century. In the century that followed, interesting variations were proposed. Not least among these was John Stuart Mill's celebrated attempt to save natural theology from skepticism by advancing the claim that an appeal to reason, based on what we know about nature, might be made in support of belief in a finite or limited God.

BIOGRAPHICAL NOTE.   John Stuart Mill was born in England in 1806 and died in 1873 at the age of sixty-seven. Lord Morley, in a review of Mill's life and work, referred to him as "the saint of Victorian rationalism." He might well have added "and of Victorian liberalism." For a great portion of Mill's contribution to modern liberalism is summed up in two propositions: that human reason applied to human experience is the only source of human knowledge, and that a maximum of individual liberty of thought and action is the surest means of extending knowledge and increasing happiness. In the elaboration and defense of these claims he wrote books and essays that came, in time, to form the staples of British liberalism in the nineteenth century. That all knowledge comes from experience is the thesis of his *System of Logic*. That the distribution of wealth is the fundamental problem in economics is the thesis of his *Principles of Political Economy*. That freedom of thought and action is the safest guarantee of individual and social well-being is the thesis of his essay *On Liberty*. That an act is right if, and only if, it produces more happiness than any other act possible is the thesis of his *Utilitarianism*. That government by elected representatives is preferable to either constitutional monarchy or an enlightened aristocracy is the thesis of his *Considerations on Representative Government*. That women have as much right to votes and careers as men is the thesis of *The Subjection of Women*. That the evils of a capitalist economy give some point to the doctrines of socialists is the thesis of his *Socialism*. And that only so much as can be grounded in experience should be retained in a living theology is the thesis of *Three Essays on Religion*. For further biographical material, see Chapter 6, Section 3 and Chapter 7, Section 5.

THE ARGUMENT OF THE PASSAGES.   Mill seeks to establish (1) that Deity is a Being of "great but limited power," (2) that He is a Being of "great but perhaps unlimited knowledge and intelligence," (3) that benevolence but not justice is one of His attributes, (4) and that a theology centering in this conception has several things to recommend it over the more traditional views. The selections are from his essay on theism. The argument opens as follows:

> The most important quality of an opinion on any momentous subject is its truth or falsity. It is indispensable that the subject of religion should be reviewed from time to time, and that its questions should be tested by the same methods, and on the same principles as any of the specualtive conclusions drawn by physical science.

From this introductory remark, Mill passes to a consideration of the argument from design. He prefers it because it "is grounded wholly on our experience of the appearances of the universe"; that is, we can see order and harmony and adaptation of some sort by merely observing the nature of things, whereas we have no experience whatever of such things as first causes and unmoved movers.

> Whatever ground there is to believe in an author of nature is derived from the appearances of the universe. The argument from design is grounded wholly on our experience of the appearances of the universe. It is, therefore, a far more important argument for theism than for any other.

Mill's formulation of the argument from design, given in the next six paragraphs, is more elaborate than we have met hitherto. His words bear close attention:

> The order of nature exhibits certain qualities that are found to be characteristic of such things as are made by an intelligent mind for a purpose. We are entitled from this great similarity in the effects to infer similarity in the cause, and to believe that things which it is beyond the power of man to make, but which resemble the works of man in all but power, must also have been made by intelligence armed with a power greater than human.

> The argument from design is not drawn from mere resemblances in nature to the works of human intelligence, but from the special character of those resemblances. The circumstances in which it is alleged that the world resembles the works of man are not circumstances taken at random, but are particular instances of a circumstance which experience shows to have a real connection with an intelligent origin; the fact, namely, of conspiring to an end or purpose.

> To show this, it will be convenient to handle, not the argument from design as a whole, but some one of the most impressive cases of it, such as the structure of the eye or the ear. It is maintained that the structure of the eye proves a designing mind. The argument may be analyzed as follows:

> 1. The parts of which the eye is composed, and the arrangements of these parts, resemble one another in this very remarkable respect, that they all conduce to enabling the animal to see. These parts and their arrangement being as they are, the animal sees. This is the only marked resemblance we can trace among the different parts of the eye; beyond the general likeness in composition which exists among all other parts of the animal.

> 2. Now, the combination of the parts of the eye had a beginning in time and must therefore have been brought together by a cause or causes. The number of instances (of such parts being brought together to enable organisms to see) is immensely greater than is required to exclude the possibility of a random or chance concurrence of independent causes. We are therefore warranted in concluding that what has brought all these parts together was some cause common to them all. And, since the parts agree in the single respect of combining to produce sight, there must be some connection between the cause which brought the parts together, and the fact of sight.

> 3. Now sight, being a fact which follows the putting together of the parts of the eye, can only be connected with the production of the eye as a final cause, to an efficient cause; since all efficient causes precede their effects. But a final cause is a purpose, and at once marks the origin of the eye as proceeding from an intelligent will.

At this point, we should expect Mill to proceed with his evaluation of the design argument. But he proposes, instead, to develop an alternative explanation covering the type of facts that would be explained by the hypothesis of God's existence if that hypothesis were accepted. This alternative to "creative fore-thought," or "intelligent will," is the hypothesis of "natural selection" suggested by Mill's contemporary, Charles Darwin. The important point to notice is the way in which natural selection, if granted as a hypothesis, would account for the type of fact that seems to demand explanation in terms of intelligent will.

Of what value is this argument? Is intelligent will, or creative forethought, the only hypothesis that will account for the facts? I regret to say that it is not. Creative fore-thought is not the only link by which the origin of the mechanism of the eye may be connected with the fact of sight. There is another connection link on which attention has been greatly fixed by recent speculation. This is the principle of natural selection, of "the survival of the fittest."

This principle of the survival of the fittest does not pretend to account for the origin of sensation, or of animal or vegetable life. It assumes the existence of some one or more very low forms of organic life, in which there are no complex adaptations. It next assumes, as experience warrants us in doing, that many small variations from those simple types would be thrown out, which would be transmissible by inheritance, some of which would be advantageous to the creature in its struggle for existence and others disadvantageous. The forms which are advantageous would always tend to survive; and those which are disadvantageous, to perish. Thus there would be a constant, though slow, general improvement of the type as it branched out into many different varieties, until it might attain to the most advanced examples which now exist.

It must be acknowledged that there is something very startling, and *prima facie* improbable in this hypothetical history of nature.

With reference to the eye, for example, it would require us to suppose that the primeval animal could not see, and had almost such slight preparation for seeing as might be constituted by some chemical action of light upon its cellular structure; that an accidental variation (mutation) would produce a variety that could see in some imperfect manner; that this peculiarity would be transmitted by inheritance while other variations continued to take place in other directions; that a number of races would thus be produced who, by the power of even imperfect sight, would have a great advantage over all other races which could not see and would in time extirpate them from all places except perhaps from a few very peculiar situations under-ground. Fresh variations would give rise to races with better and better seeing powers until we might at least reach as extraordinary a combination of structures and functions as are seen in the eye of man and of the more important animals.

Of this theory, when pushed to this extreme point, all that can now be said is that it is not so absurd as it looks; and that the analogies which have been discovered in experience, favorable to its possibility, far exceed what anyone could have supposed beforehand. Whether it will ever be possible to say more than this is at present uncertain.

Leaving this remarkable speculation to whatever fate the progress of discovery may have in store for it, I think it must be allowed that, in the present state of our knowledge, the adaptations in nature afford a large balance of probability in favor of creation by intelligence. It is equally certain that this is not more than a probability.

Having noted these two hypotheses, creative forethought and natural selection, and rejected the latter as less probable, Mill turns to the question of the nature of the being whose creative forethought is under consideration:

> The question of the existence of a Deity standing thus, it is next to be considered what sort of Deity the indications point to. What attributes are we warranted, by the evidence which nature accords of a creative mind, in assigning to that mind?

The first attribute is great but limited power:

> It needs no showing that the power, if not the intelligence, must be so far superior to that of man as to surpass all human estimate. But from this to omnipotence and omniscience there is a wide interval. And the distinction is of immense importance.
>
> For I shall argue that the net result of natural theology, on the question of the divine attributes is this: a Being of great but limited power; how, or by what, limited we cannot even conjecture; of great, perhaps unlimited intelligence; who desires and pays some regard to the happiness of His creatures but who seems to have other motives of action for which He cares more, and who can hardly be supposed to have created the universe for that purpose alone.

Then follow passages in which this claim is supported by a series of ingenious arguments:

> Every indication of design in the cosmos is so much evidence against the omnipotence of the designer. For what is meant by *design*? Contrivance, the adaptation of means to end. But the necessity for contrivance, the need of employing "means" to achieve an "end," is a consequence of the limitation of power.
>
> Who would have recourse to means, to attain his end, if his mere wish or word were enough? The very idea of *means* implies that the means have an efficacy which the direct action of the being who employs them has not. Otherwise, they are not means but an encumbrance.
>
> A man does not use machinery to move his arms; unless he is paralyzed, i.e., has not the power to do so directly by his volition.
>
> But, if the use of contrivance is a sign of limited power, how much more so is the careful and skillful choice of contrivance? Could we speak of "wisdom in the selection of means," if he who selects them could, by his mere will, have achieved the same results without them, or by any other means? Wisdom and contrivance are shown in overcoming difficulties, and there is no room for difficulties, and so no room for wisdom or contrivance, in an omnipotent being.
>
> Any evidences of design in nature, therefore, distinctly imply that the author of nature worked under limitations; that he was obliged to adapt himself to conditions independent of his will and to attain his ends by such arrangements as those conditions admitted of.
>
> On this hypothesis, the Deity had to work out His ends by combining materials of given nature and properties. This required skill and contrivance; and the means by which it is effected are often such as justly excite our wonder and admiration. But, exactly because it requires wisdom, skill, contrivance, it implies limitation of power.
>
> It may be said: An omnipotent Creator, though under no necessity of employing contrivances such as man must use, thought fit to do so in order to leave traces by which man might recognize his Creator's hand.

The answer is: This equally supposes a limit to the Deity's omnipotence, for it is a contrivance to achieve an end. Moreover, if it was His will that man should know that they and the world are His work, He, being omnipotent, had only to will that they should be aware of it.

From the question of God's power, Mill turns to the question of His knowledge and wisdom. The claim here is that there are probably no grounds for ascribing infinite knowledge or intelligence to Deity:

Omnipotence, therefore, cannot be predicated of the Creator on the evidences of design in nature. But what of omniscience? If we suppose limitation of power, must we also suppose limitation of knowledge and wisdom?

To argue that Deity possesses only limited power does not preclude us from ascribing unlimited knowledge and wisdom to Him. But there is nothing to prove it. The knowledge and wisdom necessary to planning and arranging the cosmos are, no doubt, as much in excess of human knowledge as the power implied is in excess of human power. But nothing obliges us to suppose that either the knowledge or the skill is infinite.

We are not even obliged to suppose that the contrivances and arrangements were always the best possible. If we judge them as we judge the work of human artificers, we find abundant defects. The human body, for example, is one of the most striking instances of artful and ingenious contrivance which nature offers. But we may well ask whether so complicated a machine could not have been made to last longer, and not get out of order so easily and frequently.

We may ask why the human race should have been so constituted as to grovel in wretchedness and degradation for countless ages before a small portion of it was enabled to lift itself into the very imperfect state of intelligence, goodness, and happiness which we enjoy.

If, however, Deity, like a human ruler, had to adapt Himself to a set of conditions which He did not make, it is as unphilosophical as it is presumptuous in us to call Him to account for any imperfections in His work; to complain that he left anything in it contrary to what (if indications of design prove anything) He must have intended.

Great but limited power. Great, perhaps unlimited, knowledge and intelligence. What moral attributes? To settle this question Mill suggests a consideration of the probable purposes of the author of nature. The idea here is that one's moral qualities will be embodied in, and therefore inferable from, whatever one devotes time and forethought to making or doing. The only conclusion Mill is able to reach is "some benevolence but no justice." The argument is as follows:

Assuming then, that while we confine ourselves to the evidences of design in nature, there is no ground for ascribing infinite power, and probably no grounds for ascribing infinite knowledge or intelligence to Deity, the question arises as to the same evidence afforded with regard to His moral attributes. What indications does nature give of the purposes of its author?

This question bears a very different aspect to us from what it bears to those who are encumbered with the doctrine of the omnipotence of Deity. We do not have to attempt the impossible problem of reconciling infinite benevolence and justice with infinite power and knowledge in such a world as this. The attempt to do so involves a contradiction, and exhibits to excess the revolting spectacle of a jesuitical defense of enormities.

To what purpose, then, do the expedients and contrivances in the construction of animals and vegetables appear to tend? These are the "adaptations" which most excite our admiration. If they afford evidence of design, of purpose, in nature, we can best hope to be enlightened by examining such parts of nature.

There is no blinking the fact that these animal and vegetable adaptations tend principally to no more exalted object than to make the structure remain in life and in working order for a certain time: the individual for a few years, the species for a longer but still limited period.

The greater part of the design or adaptation in nature, however wonderful its mechanism, is, therefore, no evidence of any moral attributes in the author of nature; because the end to which it is directed is not a moral end: it is not the good of any creature but the qualified permanence, for a limited period of the work itself.

The only inference that can be drawn from most of nature, respecting the character of the author of nature, is that He does not wish His work to perish as soon as created. He wills it to have a certain duration.

In addition to the great number of adaptations which have no apparent object but to keep the organism going, there are a certain number of provisions for giving pleasure and a certain number for giving pain. These, perhaps, should be included among the contrivances for keeping the creature or its species in existence; for both the pleasures and the pains are generally so disposed as to attract to the things which maintain existence and deter from the things which would destroy it.

When these matters are considered, a vast deduction must be made from the facts usually cited as evidence of the benevolence of the Creator; so vast, indeed, that some may doubt whether any remains.

Yet, viewing the matter impartially, it does appear that there is a preponderance of evidence that the Creator desired the pleasure of His creatures. This is indicated by the fact, which cannot itself be denied, that pleasure of one description or another, is afforded by almost all of the powers, mental and physical, possessed by the creature.

The author of these pleasure-giving and pain-preventing adaptations is no doubt accountable for having made the creature susceptible of pain. But this may have been a necessary condition of its susceptibility to pleasure: a supposition which avails nothing on the theory of an omnipotent creator, but is extremely probable in the case of a limited creator.

There is, therefore, much evidence that the creature's pleasure is agreeable to the Creator; while there is very little if any evidence that its pain is so. There is, then, justification for inferring that benevolence is one of the attributes of the Creator.

But to jump from this to the inference that his sole or chief purposes are those of benevolence, and that the single end and aim of creation was the happiness of his creatures, is not only not justified by any evidence but is a conclusion in opposition to such evidence as we have.

If the motive of the Deity for creating sentient beings was the happiness of those beings, His purpose, in our corner of the universe at least, must be pronounced to have been thus far an ignominious failure. If God had no purpose but our happiness, and that of other living creatures, it is incredible that He would have called them into existence with the prospect of being so completely baffled.

If man had not the power, by the exercise of his own energies, to improve himself and his circumstances, to do for himself and other creatures vastly more than God had in the first instance done, then He (God) would deserve something very different from thanks at his (man's) hands.

Of course, it may be said that this very capacity to improve himself was given to man by God, and that the changes which man will be able ultimately to effect will be worth purchasing by the sufferings and wasted lives.

This may be so; but to suppose that God could not have procured these blessings for man at a less frightful cost is to make a very strange supposition concerning the Deity. It is to suppose that God could not, in the first instance, create anything better than a primitive savage, and was yet able to endow this primitive savage with the power of raising himself into a Newton or a Fénelon. We do not know the nature of the barriers which limit the divine omnipotence; but it is a very odd notion of them that they enable the Deity to confer on a primitive savage the power of producing what God Himself had no other means of creating.

Such are the indications respecting the divine benevolence. If we look for any other moral attribute, for example, justice, we find a total blank. There is no evidence whatever in nature of divine justice, whatever standard of justice we may hold. There is no shadow of justice in the general arrangements of nature. Whatever justice exists in human society is the work of man himself, struggling upwards against immense natural difficulties into civilization, and making to himself a second, and far better and more unselfish nature than he was created with.

Looking back, Mill summarizes his findings:

These, then, are the net results of natural theology on the question of the divine attributes. A Being of great but limited power, how or by what limited we cannot even conjecture; of great and perhaps unlimited intelligence; who desires, and pays some regard to the happiness of His creatures, but who seems to have other motives of action which He cares more for, and who can hardly be supposed to have created the universe for that purpose alone.

Such is the Deity whom natural religion points to; and any idea of God more captivating than this comes only from human wishes, or from the teaching of either real or imaginary revelation.

Mill goes on to note that there are several considerations in favor of this hypothesis of a finite Deity. It eliminates the problem of evil and the problem of free will. These problems, it will be recalled, were raised by the claim that Deity combines in Himself the two attributes of omnipotence and complete benevolence. It keeps close to what experience actually tells us about the world we live in. And, by way of conclusion, it gives meaning to the notion of helping or working with God:

This religious idea admits of one elevated feeling, which is not open to those who believe in the omnipotence of the good principle in the universe, the feeling of helping God—of requiting the good He has given by a voluntary cooperation which He, not being omnipotent, really needs, and by which a somewhat nearer approach may be made to the fulfillment of His purposes. This is the most invigorating thought which can inspire a human creature.

A contemporary of Mill had argued "that even if the investigation of the concept of God as the absolute, infinite, all-powerful, all-good Being, leads to self-contradiction, yet we must believe in such a Being, since neither human logic nor human ethics are applicable to such a being." To this Mill replied:

Convince me that the world is ruled by a being whose attributes are infinite, but what they are we cannot learn (except that the highest human morality which we are capable of conceiving does not sanction them) and I will bear my fate as I may. But when I am told that I must believe this, and at the same time call this being names that affirm the highest human morality, I say in plain terms that I will not. Whatever power such a being may have over me, there is one thing which he shall not do; he shall not compel me to worship him. I will call no being good who is not what I mean when I apply that epithet to my fellow creatures; and if such a being can sentence me to hell for not so calling him, to hell I will go.

The notion of a finite or limited deity did not originate with Mill; indeed, it is to be found as far back as Plato's *Republic* in the fourth century B.C.* But Mill did set himself more deliberately to argue the case than any of his predecessors had done. Since his day, it has passed into the writings of William James and has been used by H. G. Wells as the theme of his little book *God the Invisible King*.

When J. S. Mill was still exercising a great influence in England, his work was subjected to considerable critical overhauling by one of his fellow countrymen, F. H. Bradley. In the course of many years' study and writing Bradley declared himself upon most of the major themes in Mill's general philosophy. In *Essays on Truth and Reality* he has a chapter, "On God and the Absolute," which contains some suggestive remarks on the conception of a limited God. It is instructive to watch another philosopher at work on the idea. Moreover, in the concluding sentences, Bradley raises a point that forms, so to speak, a beginning for William James's pragmatic approach to this question. Says Bradley:

> There is a fundamental inconsistency in religion. For, in any but an imperfect religion, God must be perfect. God must be at once the complete satisfaction of all finite aspiration, and yet on the other hand must stand in relation to my will. Religion (at least in my view) is practical, on the other hand in the highest religion its object is supreme goodness and power. We have a perfect real will, and we have my will, and the practical relation of these wills is what we mean by religion. And yet, if perfection is actually realized, what becomes of my will which is set over against the complete good will? While, on the other hand, if there is no such will, what becomes of God? The inconsistency seems irremovable. . . .
>
> An obvious method of escape is to reject the perfection of God. God will remain good, but in a limited sense. He will be reduced to a person who does the best that is in Him with limited knowledge and power. Sufficiently superior to ourselves to be worshipped, God will nevertheless be imperfect, and, with this admitted imperfection, it will be said, our religion is saved. . . .
>
> Now certainly on such terms religion still can persist, for there is practical devotion to an object which is taken to be at a level far above our own. Such a religion even in one sense, with the lowering of the Deity, may be said to have been heightened. To help a God in His struggle, more or less doubtful and blind, with resisting

---

* Plato, *Republic, Book II*: "Then God, if he be good, is not the author of all things, as the many assert, but he is the cause of a few things only, and not of most things that occur to men. For few are the goods of human life, and many are the evils, and the good is to be attributed to God alone; of the evils, the causes are to be sought elsewhere, and not in him."

evil, is no inferior task. And if the issue were taken as uncertain, or if even further the end were known to be God's indubitable defeat and our inevitable disaster, our religion would have risen thereby and would have attained to the extreme of heroism.

But on the other hand, if religion is considered as a whole and not simply from one side, it is not true that with the lowering of God religion tends to grow higher. A principal part of religion is the assured satisfaction of our good will, the joy and peace in the assurance, and the added strength which in the majority of men can come perhaps from no other source. To sacrifice altogether or in part this aspect means on the whole to set religion down to a lower level. And it is an illusion to suppose that imperfection, once admitted into the Deity, can be stopped precisely at that convenient limit which happens to suit our ideas. The assertor of an imperfect God is, whether he knows it or not, face to face with a desperate task or a forlorn alternative. He must try to show (how, I cannot tell) that the entire rest of the universe, outside his limited God, is known to be still weaker and more limited. Or he must appeal to us to follow our Leader blindly and, for all we know, to a common and overwhelming defeat. In either case, the prospect offered entails, I should say, to the religious mind, an unquestionable loss to religion.

And yet it will be urged that we have ourselves agreed that all other ways of escape are closed. For, if God is perfect, we saw that religion must contain inconsistency, and it was by seeking consistency that we were driven to a limited God. But our assumption here, I reply, is precisely that which we should have questioned from the first. Is there any need for our attempt to avoid self-contradiction? Has religion really got to be consistent theoretically? Is ultimate theoretical consistency a thing which is attainable anywhere? And, at all events, is it a thing attainable in life and in practice? That is the fundamental question upon which the whole issue depends. And I need not pause here to ask whether it is quite certain that, when God is limited, the universe becomes theoretically consistent. . . .

Viewed thus, the question as to what may be called religious ideas is seriously changed. To insist upon ultimate theoretical consistency, which in no case can we reach, becomes once for all ridiculous. The main question is as to the real nature and end of religion, and as to the respective importance of those aspects which belong to it. The ideas which best express our highest religious needs and their satisfaction, must certainly be true. Ultimate truth they do not possess, and exactly what in the end it would take to make them perfect we cannot know.

Thus, Bradley questions whether or not the finite God hypothesis of Mill is really beneficial to the believer. To be sure, the problem of evil is eliminated. That problem presented the dilemma: Either God cannot or He will not abolish evil. If he cannot, then He is not all-powerful. If He will not, then He is not all-good. By admitting that God is not all-powerful, Mill simultaneously eliminates this thorny theological puzzle and heightens individual religious seriousness by showing that God really needs individuals to help Him conquer evil and misery in the world because He can't do it alone. Yet, says Bradley, consider the full consequences of believing in a finite God. How can we be sure that our struggles against misery, suffering, and evil have any lasting impact if our God is finite? Is it not possible that evil will triumph in the long run and our struggles will be nothing more than a rhetorical flourish? What does that do to our resolve to continue the struggle against misery, suffering and evil? Perhaps we ought to re-think Mill's "solution."

Perhaps ultimate theoretical consistency in religion is unattainable. Perhaps the important thing about religion is how it functions to enrich human life.

NOTE ON SOURCES. The Mill material in this section is quoted, abridged, or paraphrased from the essay "Theism," in his book *Three Essays on Religion*. That essay is divided into five parts. Part I is itself divided into an introduction and six brief chapters. The present section is based on Part I, especially the Introduction and Chapter 6; and Part II, entitled "Attributes." The concluding ("to hell I will go") paragraph is from Mill's book *An Examination of Sir William Hamilton's Philosophy*. The Bradley material is from *Essays on Truth and Reality*.

5 T. H. HUXLEY

AGNOSTICISM—THE ONLY LEGITIMATE RESPONSE

FROM MILL TO HUXLEY. Two famous books, both published in 1859, enter into discussion of our question. The first is Charles Darwin's *Origin of Species*; the second, John Stuart Mill's *On Liberty*. Our question has been: Can you use what you know about nature to justify what you believe about God? Both books focus on that question.

Darwin's book caused many persons to revise their conception of nature, thus causing them to question their conception of God. The book pictured plants and animals engaged in a ruthless and life-long struggle for existence. In one way or another they must eat or be eaten, kill or be killed. Tennyson's phrase "Nature red in tooth and claw" expressed the point. Under the pressure of this struggle for existence some species were eliminated and some survived. This was "natural selection": nature "selected" the fit and eliminated the unfit. If nature is created and sustained by God, then this natural selection is Divine Selection: God, through the struggle for existence, selects the fit and eliminates the unfit; in so doing, He brings about an evolution from the lowest beginnings of life up the present stage of the higher animals and humans. Suppose this is what we know about nature. Can we use this knowledge to justify what we believe about God? Can we, as one writer asked, proceed "through nature to God"?

Mill's book, especially in its famous second chapter, argued for the right of the individual to think for him- or herself. It provided the classic plea for "the right to pro and con," on all questions, no matter how important or sacred or long established. Darwin's "downgrading" of nature, particularly if you thought about God as the author of nature, produced a crisis in public discussion of these matters. Mill's chapter was a timely warning against obscurantism and intolerance.

That was in 1859. In 1877 William Kingdom Clifford published a paper, *The Ethics of Belief*, in which he argued that ethics as well as logic has something to say on the justification of belief: If you are not logically entitled to hold a particular belief, then you are not morally entitled to hold that belief. Clifford included religious beliefs in this winnowing demand. The result was something of a paradox for many of his readers: they were familiar with the claim that in these matters doubt or disbelief was a sin, and here was Clifford insisting that in the absence of logical justification belief was immoral and sinful.

Thomas Henry Huxley's *Agnosticism*, which repeated and extended Clifford's thesis, became a symbol for the state of mind in which many found themselves. Huxley commanded a wider hearing, spoke with greater authority, and ranged over a wider field. The paper in which he stated and applied his agnosticism provided Victorian England with one of its liveliest controversies. Since Clifford's paper expressed so much of what Huxley meant by agnosticism, we begin by looking at what Clifford had to say:

> A shipowner was about to send to sea an emigrant ship. He knew that she was old, not overwell built, and often had needed repairs. It had been suggested to him that possibly she was not seaworthy. He thought that perhaps he ought to have her overhauled and refitted, even though this should put him to great expense.
>
> Before the ship sailed, however, he said to himself that she had gone safely through so many voyages and weathered so many storms, that it was idle to suppose that she would not come safely home from this trip also. He would put his trust in Providence, which could hardly fail to protect all these unhappy families that were leaving their fatherland to seek for better times elsewhere. He would dismiss ungenerous suspicions about the honesty of builders and contractors. In such ways he acquired a sincere and comfortable conviction that his vessel was safe and seaworthy; he watched her departure with a light heart, and benevolent wishes for the success of the exiles in their new home; and he got his insurance money when she went down in midocean and told no tales.
>
> What shall we say of him? Surely that he was guilty of the death of those men. He sincerely believed in the soundness of his ship; but the sincerity of his conviction can in nowise help him, because he had no *right* to believe on such evidence as was before him. He had acquired his belief not by honestly earning it in patient investigation, but by stifling his doubts.
>
> Let us alter the case a little, and suppose that the ship was not unsound after all; that she made her voyage safely, and many others after it. Will that diminish the guilt of her owner? Not one jot. The man would not have been innocent; he would only have been not found out. The question of right or wrong has to do not with whether his belief turned out to be true or false, but whether he had a *right* to believe on such evidence as was before him.
>
> Although he had sincerely and "conscientiously" believed, yet he had no *right* to believe on such evidence as was before him. His sincere convictions, instead of being honestly earned, were stolen. The question is not whether his belief was true or false, but whether he entertained it on wrong grounds.
>
> If he chose to examine himself *in foro conscientiae*, he would know that he had acquired and nourished a belief, when he had no *right* to believe on such evidence as was before him; and therein he would know that he had done a wrong thing.
>
> No real belief, however trifling and fragmentary it may seem, is ever truly insignificant; it prepares us to receive more of its like, confirms those which resembled it before, and weakens others; and so gradually lays a stealthy train in our inmost thoughts, which may some day explode into overt action, and leave its stamp upon our character forever.

It is wrong to believe on insufficient evidence, or to nourish belief by suppressing doubts and avoiding investigation. Since no belief, however seemingly trivial, and however obscure the believer, is ever actually insignificant or without its effect, we have no choice but to extend our judgment to all cases of belief whatever. Belief, that sacred faculty, which prompts the decisions of our will, and knits into harmonious working all the energies of our being, is ours not for ourselves but for humanity. It is *rightly* used on truths which have been established by long tradition and waiting toil, and which have stood in the fierce light of free and fearless questioning. It is desecrated when given to unproved and unquestioned statements, for the solace and private pleasure of the believer; to add a tinsel splendor to the plain straight road of our life and display a bright mirage beyond it; or even to drown the common sorrows of our kind by a self-deception which allows them not only to cast down, but also to degrade us. Whoso would deserve well of his fellows in this matter will guard the purity of his belief with a very fanaticism of jealous care, lest at any time it should rest on an unworthy object, and catch a stain which can never be wiped away.

It is not only the leader of men, statesman, philosopher, or poet, that has this duty to mankind. Every rustic who delivers in the village alehouse his slow infrequent sentences, may help to kill or keep alive the fatal superstitions which clog his race. No simplicity of mind, no obscurity of station, can escape the universal *duty* of questioning all that we believe.

It is the sense of power attached to a sense of knowledge that makes men desirous of believing, and afraid of doubting. This sense of power is the highest and best of pleasures when the belief on which it is founded has been fairly earned. But if the belief has been accepted on insufficient evidence, the pleasure is a *stolen* one. Not only does it deceive ourselves by giving us a sense of power which we do not really possess, but it is *sinful*, because it is *stolen* in defiance of our *duty*. That *duty* is to guard ourselves from such beliefs as from a pestilence, which may shortly master our own body and then spread to the rest of the town. What would be thought of one who, for the sake of a sweet fruit, should deliberately run the risk of bringing a plague upon his family and his neighbors?

Every time we let ourselves believe for unworthy reasons, we weaken our powers of self-control, of doubting, of judicially and fairly weighing evidence. We all suffer severely enough from the maintenance of false beliefs and the fatally wrong actions which they lead to. The evil born when one such belief is entertained is great and wide. But a greater and wider evil arises when the credulous character is maintained, when a habit of believing for unworthy reasons is fostered and made permanent.

It is *wrong* always, everywhere, and for any one, to believe anything upon insufficient evidence. Habitual want of care about what I believe leads to habitual want of care in others about the truth of what is told to me. The credulous man is father to the liar and the cheat.

If a man, holding a belief which he was taught in childhood or persuaded of afterwards, keeps down doubts which arise about it in his mind, purposely avoids the reading of books and the company of men that call in question or discuss it, and regards as impious those questions which cannot easily be asked without disturbing it; the life of that man is one long *sin* against mankind.

If this judgment seems harsh when applied to those simple souls who have never known better, who have been brought up with a horror of doubt, and taught that their eternal welfare depends of *what* they believe; then it leads to the very serious question, *Who hath made Israel to sin?*

Inquiry into the evidence of a doctrine is not to be made once for all, and then taken as finally settled. It is never lawful to stifle a doubt; for either it can be honestly answered by means of the inquiry already made, or else it proves that the inquiry was not complete.

"But," says one, "I am a busy man; I have no time for the long course of study which would be necessary to make me in any degree a competent judge of certain questions, or even able to understand the nature of the arguments." Then he should have no time to believe.

The beliefs about right and wrong which guide our actions in dealing with men in society, and the beliefs about physical nature which guide our actions in dealing with animate and inanimate bodies, these never suffer from investigation; they can take care of themselves, without being propped up by "acts of faith," the clamor of paid advocates, or the suppression of contrary evidence.

Since it is not enough to say, "It is wrong to believe on unworthy evidence," without saying also what evidence is worthy, we shall now go on to inquire under what circumstances it is lawful to believe on the testimony of others; and more generally when and why we may believe that which goes beyond our own experience, or even beyond the experience of mankind.

BIOGRAPHICAL NOTE.   Thomas Henry Huxley was born near London, England, in 1825, and died in 1895 at the age of seventy. He was a renowned biologist, and one of the most versatile scientists in nineteenth-century England. As a youth he was basically self-educated until the time when he undertook a medical apprenticeship. In 1842 he pursued studies, work, and research at Charing Cross Hospital where he won prizes in chemistry, anatomy, and physiology. For several years, from 1846 to 1850, he served as an assistant surgeon on a British vessel engaged in a surveying operation in Australian waters. Huxley used these voyages to good advantage, gathering data and writing papers that won him respect as a competent biologist. In 1851 he was elected a fellow of the Royal Society. After leaving the navy, he held a number of governmental posts during which time he launched an extended study of paleontology. His erudition, eloquence, clarity of thought, and earnest skepticism soon singled him out as an intellectual leader in Victorian England. For forty years he championed various causes ranging from support of Darwin's theory of evolution to educational reform. Illustrative of his exceedingly diverse interests and writings are his nine volumes of *Collected Essays* and his five volumes of *Scientific Memoirs*.

THE ARGUMENT OF THE PASSAGES.   In reading Huxley on these matters it is well to keep Mill, Darwin, and Clifford in mind. In the following material there are two extended quotations from Huxley. In the *first* he tells how he arrived at the position that he calls agnosticism, and why he coined that word as a name for it. In the *second* he gives a statement of the essential ideas he wants held together by the term *agnosticism*. To put it briefly, agnosticism is the claim that if you cannot use what you know to justify what you believe, then it is immoral to go on believing. Suppose a man asks himself "Am I *morally* entitled to entertain a certain belief of mine?" Agnosticism asks him: "Are you *logically* entitled to entertain the belief to which you refer?" If the answer is no, then agnosticism says to him: "Then you are not *morally* entitled to entertain the belief. You have no *moral* right to a belief you cannot justify logically."

Looking back nearly fifty years, I see myself as a boy, whose education has been interrupted, and who intellectually, was left, for some years, altogether to his own devices. At that time, I was a voracious and omnivorous reader; a dreamer and speculator, endowed with that courage in attacking any and every subject, which is the blessed compensation of youth and inexperience. Among the books and essays, on all sorts of topics from metaphysics to heraldry, which I read at this time, two left indelible impressions on my mind. One was Guizot's "History of Civilization," the other was Sir William Hamilton's essay "On the Philosophy of the Unconditioned." The latter was strange reading for a boy, and I could not possibly have understood a great deal of it; nevertheless, I devoured it with avidity, and it stamped upon my mind the strong conviction that, on even the most solemn and important of questions, men are apt to take cunning phrases for answers; and that the limitation of our faculties, in a great number of cases, renders real answers to such questions, not merely actually impossible, but theoretically inconceivable.

When I reached intellectual maturity and began to ask myself whether I was an atheist, a theist, or a pantheist; a materialist or an idealist; a Christian or a freethinker; I found that the more I learned and reflected, the less ready was the answer; until, at last, I came to the conclusion that I had neither art nor part with any of these denominations, except the last. The one thing in which most of these good people were agreed was the one thing in which I differed from them. They were quite sure they had attained a certain "gnosis,"—had, more or less successfully, solved the problem of existence; while I was quite sure I had not, and had a pretty strong conviction that the problem was insoluble. And, with Hume and Kant on my side, I could not think myself presumptuous in holding fast by that opinion.

This was my situation when I had the good fortune to find a place among the members of that remarkable confraternity of antagonists, long since deceased, but of green and pious memory, the Metaphysical Society. Every variety of philosophical and theological opinion was represented there, and expressed itself with entire openness; most of my colleagues were *-ists* of one sort or another; and, however kind and friendly they might be, I, the man without a rag of label to cover himself with, could not fail to have some of the uneasy feelings which must have beset the historical fox when, after leaving the trap in which his tail remained, he presented himself to his normally elongated companions. So I took thought, and invented what I conceived to be the appropriate title of "agnostic." It came into my head as suggestively antithetic to the "gnostic" of Church history, who professed to know so much about the very things of which I was ignorant; and I took the earliest opportunity of parading it at our Society, to show that I, too, had a tail, like the other foxes. To my great satisfaction, the term took; and when the *Spectator* had stood godfather to it, any suspicion in the minds of respectable people, that a knowledge of its parentage might have awakened was, of course, completely lulled.

This is the history of the origin of the terms "agnostic" and "agnosticism."

Huxley now proceeds to summarize the major contentions of agnosticism:

Agnosticism is properly described as a creed in so far as it expresses absolute faith in the validity of a principle which is as much ethical as intellectual. This principle may be stated in various ways, but they all amount to this: that it is wrong for a man to say that he is certain of the objective truth of any proposition unless he can produce evidence which logically justifies that certainty. This is what agnosticism asserts; and, in my opinion, it is all that is essential to agnosticism.

That which agnostics deny and repudiate as immoral is that there are propositions which men ought to believe, without logically satisfactory evidence; and that reprobation ought to attach to the profession of disbelief in such inadequately supported propositions. The justification of the agnostic principle lies in the success which follows upon its application, in natural or in civil history; and in the fact that, so far as these topics are concerned, no sane man thinks of denying its validity.

Agnosticism is a creed, in so far as its general principle is concerned. The application of that principle results in the denial of, or the suspension of judgment concerning, a number of propositions respecting which contemporary "gnostics" profess entire certainty.

The extent of the region of the uncertain, the number of the problems the investigation of which ends in a verdict of not proven will vary according to the knowledge and the intellectual habits of the individual agnostic. What I am sure about is that there are many topics about which I know nothing, and which, so far as I can see, are out of reach of my faculties. Relatively to myself, I am quite sure that the region of uncertainty is far more extensive than I could wish. Materialism and idealism; theism and atheism; the doctrine of the soul and its mortality or immortality—appear in the history of philosophy like the shades of Scandinavian heroes, eternally slaying one another and eternally coming to life again. It is getting on for twenty-five centuries, at least, since mankind began seriously to give their minds to these topics. Generation after generation, philosophy has been doomed to roll the stone uphill; and, just as all the world swore it was at the top, down it has rolled to the bottom again. All this is written in innumerable books; and he who will toil through them will discover that the stone is just where it was when the work began. Hume saw this; Kant saw it; since their time, more and more eyes have been cleansed of the films which prevented them from seeing it; until now the weight and number has begun to tell in practical life.

Between agnosticism and clericalism, there can be neither peace nor truce. The cleric asserts that it is morally wrong not to believe certain propositions, whatever the results of a strict scientific investigation of the evidence of these propositions. He tells us that "religious error is, in itself, of an immoral nature." He declares that he has prejudged certain conclusions, and looks upon those who show cause for arrest of judgment as emissaries of Satan. It necessarily follows that, for him, the attainment of faith, not the ascertainment of truth, is the highest aim of mental life. And, on analysis, it will be found to be the "power of saying you believe things which are incredible." Now I, and many other agnostics, believe that faith in this sense is an abomination; and we feel that the disagreement between ourselves and those who hold this doctrine is even more moral than intellectual. It is desirable there should be an end of any mistakes on this topic.

Those who appreciate our position will see that when any one declares that we ought to believe this, that, and the other, and are wicked if we don't, it is impossible for us to give any answer but this: We have not the slightest objection to believe anything you like, if you will give us good grounds for belief; but, if you can not, we must respectfully refuse, even if that refusal should wreck morality and insure our own damnation several times over.

Is one able to provide evidence from nature such that belief in the existence of God is *required* by reason? *allowed* by reason? Philosophers like Aquinas say that such belief is required by reason. Others like Pascal claim that belief is not required, but is allowed by reason. Those like Hume argue that belief in a supreme, perfect being is neither required nor allowed by reason. Still others like Mill maintain that the evidence from nature certainly allows belief in a finite deity, and may even require such a belief. For Clifford and Huxley and their agnostic compatriots, belief in a supreme, perfect being is not warranted by the evidence; indeed, such unevidenced belief in the existence of God is to be regarded as immoral. Our next author, William James, continues the debate by arguing that the believer and the agnostic are virtually on the same footing and that if the believer is to be judged to be immoral for embracing a belief in the existence of God, even so the agnostic and atheist are to be considered immoral for holding their positions. If reason allows affirmation of agnosticism, then reason must also allow affirmation of theism.

NOTE ON SOURCES.   The material in this section is quoted or abridged from William K. Clifford, "The Ethics of Belief, and T. H. Huxley, "Agnosticism."

6   WILLIAM JAMES

LEGITIMATE BELIEF IN SPITE OF AGNOSTICISM

FROM HUXLEY TO JAMES.   It will be recalled that Pascal, writing in the seventeenth century, repudiated the possibility of deriving belief in God from beliefs about nature, but he clung to orthodox convictions. John Stuart Mill, writing two centuries later, reversed the procedure. He clung to the idea of deriving belief in God from beliefs about nature, but repudiated the orthodox convictions. The most humans can rationally justify through natural theology, he argued, is the belief in a finite God. William James, writing in America toward the close of the nineteenth and in the opening years of the twentieth centuries, attempted to blend the insights of Pascal and Mill. James was convinced that the appeal to natural theology was bankrupt. No one had ever properly answered Hume on his own grounds. But James found himself believing wholeheartedly in the existence of God. That, he could not shake off. Accordingly, he sought to combine the approaches of Pascal and Mill, respectively: an appeal to what he called "the will to believe" in support of the belief in a finite God.

On the face of it, James's "will to believe," later his pragmatism, is closely related, historically, to Huxley's agnosticism. This is apparent on reading James's essay. Huxley had said that if you couldn't logically justify what you believe, then it was immoral to believe. Such belief would be "stolen." It is this note of moral censure in Huxley's agnosticism that caught James's attention. His argument is that among Huxley's own beliefs are some that he (Huxley) could not justify "logically," "intellectually," but that he (Huxley) nevertheless will not abandon. Such beliefs embody "the will to believe." Beliefs that are *appropriate* objects of the will to believe are not open to the moral criticism proposed by Huxley's agnosticism.

BIOGRAPHICAL NOTE. For biographical information on William James, refer to Chapter 3, Section 4.

THE ARGUMENT OF THE PASSAGES. The passages quoted or abridged hereunder are, for the most part, from James's essay "The Will to Believe." He states somewhere that it might better have been called "The Right to Believe." His aim is to point out that, in certain cases, where the evidence is insufficient to justify belief on "rational" grounds, there may nevertheless be other grounds. In a word, sufficient evidence is not the only thing that justifies belief, is not the only thing that gives us a "right to believe." Agnosticism may not be the last word here. In such cases, upon what does our right to believe rest? Where the evidence is insufficient, is it necessary to say, with agnosticism, that belief is everywhere and always immoral?

That is the central problem of the essay. James begins with a few remarks on hypotheses in general. The purpose of these remarks is to explain what he means by a "genuine option" between rival hypotheses. Where we are faced with a genuine option between rival hypotheses, neither of which is backed by sufficient evidence, upon what principle may we legitimately exercise our will to believe? James then formulates the principle that, he thinks, justifies belief under such circumstances. The question now is: Are there any beliefs that present themselves for acceptance on this principle? James notes that moral judgments are of this nature. If this is so, then the moral judgments proposed by agnosticism, or moral principles embodied in such judgments, would be important exceptions to the rule laid down by agnosticism. However, and more important, the "religious hypothesis" is of this nature. He then states the terms of this hypothesis. In what follows, he deals with two possible lines of criticism that, he knows, will be directed against his position. The first of these is the objection of the agnostic, namely, that where evidence is insufficient to justify belief, we have no right to believe. The second objection is to the effect that once you set up any principle designed to justify belief on insufficient grounds, you have (in principle) obliterated the distinction between intelligent belief and any but the wildest superstition. Finally, in a few passages, we note his acceptance of Mill's limited theism.

James begins:

Let us give the name of *hypothesis* to anything that may be proposed of our belief. And, just as electricians speak of live and dead wires, let us speak of an hypothesis as either live or dead. A live hypothesis is one which appeals as a real possibility to him to whom it is proposed.

Next, let us call the decision between hypotheses an *option*. Options may be of several kinds. They may be living or dead, forced or avoidable, momentous or trivial.

A living option is one in which both hypotheses are live. If I say to you: "Be a theosophist or be a Mohammedan," it is probably a dead option, because for you neither hypothesis is likely to be live. But if I say: "Be an agnostic or be a Christian," it is otherwise. Trained as you are, each hypothesis makes some appeal, however small, to your belief.

A forced option is one which arises when there is no standing outside of the alternative hypothesis. If I say to you: "Choose between going out with your umbrella or without it," I do not offer you a forced option. You can easily avoid it by not going out at all. But if I say: "Either accept this truth or go without it," I put on you a forced option, for there is no third alternative and no standing outside of these two alternatives.

A momentous option is one that is presented when the opportunity is unique, when the stake is significant, or when the decision is irreversible if it later prove unwise. If I were Dr. Nansen and proposed to you to join my North Pole expedition, your option would be momentous; for this would probably be your only opportunity, and your choice now would either exclude you from the North Pole sort of immortality altogether, or put at least the chance of it into your hands. *Per contra*, the option is trivial when the opportunity is not unique, when the stake is insignificant, or when the decision is reversible if it later prove unwise.

An option is genuine when it is of the living, forced, momentous kind.

So much for hypotheses and options. Suppose, now, that a man is confronted by a pair of rival beliefs, neither of which can be said to rest on sufficient evidence to justify belief. What is he to do? Upon what principle can he justify himself in accepting the one or the other? It is the following:

The thesis I defend is this: Our passional (emotional) nature not only lawfully may, but must, decide an option between propositions, whenever it is a genuine option that cannot by its nature be decided on intellectual grounds.

The essence of the matter is contained in this principle. We are curious to know where, among our beliefs, we shall find some that call for acceptance on this principle. One example would be our moral beliefs: that it is better to do this and that, better to be this sort of person than that, and so on.

The question arises: Are there any such forced options in our speculative opinions? Are there some options between opinions in which this passional influence must be regarded both as an inevitable and as a lawful determinant of our choice?

Moral questions immediately present themselves. A moral question is a question not of what exists, but of what is good, or would be good if it did exist.

Science can tell us what exists; but to compare the worths, both of what exists and what does not exist, we must consult not science, but what Pascal calls our "heart," i.e., our passional nature. Science, herself, consults her heart when she lays it down that the infinite ascertainment of fact and correction of false belief are the supreme goods for man. Challenge the statement, and science can only repeat it oracularly, or else prove it by showing that such ascertainment and correction bring man all sorts of other goods which man's heart in turn declares desirable.

Moral beliefs. Is that all? What about religious beliefs. Are they appropriate objects of our sheer "will to believe"?

Let us pass to the question of religious faith. What do we mean by the religious hypothesis? Broadly it is this: Science says things are: morality says some things are better than other things: religion says that the best things are the more eternal things, the things in the universe that throw the last stone, so to speak, and say the final word: and that we are better off, even now, if we believe her first affirmation to be true.

Now let us consider what the logical elements of this situation are in case the religious hypothesis in both its branches be really true. We must admit that possibility at the outset.

We see, first, that religion offers itself as a momentous option. We are supposed to gain, even now, by our belief, and to lose by our nonbelief, a certain vital good.

We see, second, that religion is a forced option so far as that vital good is concerned. We cannot escape the issue by remaining skeptical, because although we do avoid error in that way if religion be untrue, we lose the good, if it be true. Skepticism, then, is not an avoidance of the option.

In these matters, the skeptic's position is this: Better risk the loss of truth than the chance of error. But in this he is actively playing his stake as much as the believer is. He is backing the field against the religious hypothesis, just as the believer is backing the religious hypothesis against the field.

Now, to most of us, religion comes in a still further way. What I mean is this. The more perfect and more eternal aspect of the universe is represented in our religions as having a personal form. The universe is no longer a mere It, but a Thou, if we are religious; and any relation that may be possible from person to person might be possible here. We feel, too, as if the appeal of religion were made to our own active good will, as if evidence for its truth might be forever withheld from us unless we met the hypothesis halfway.

This feeling, forced on us we know not whence, that by obstinately believing that there are gods we are doing the universe the deepest service we can, seems part of the living essence of the religious hypothesis.

God is the natural appellation, for us Christians at least, for the supreme reality, so I will call this higher part of the universe by the name of God. We and God have business with each other; and in opening ourselves to His influence our deepest destiny is fulfilled. The universe, at those parts of it which our personal being constitutes, takes a turn genuinely for the worse or for the better in proportion as each one of us fulfills or evades God's demands.

God's existence is the guarantee of an ideal order that shall be permanently preserved. This world may indeed some day burn up or freeze up; but if it is part of His order, the old ideals are sure to be brought elsewhere to fruition, so that where God is, tragedy is only provisional and partial, and shipwreck and dissolution are not the absolutely final things.

Only when this farther step of faith concerning God is taken, and remote objective consequences are predicted, does religion, as it seems to me, get wholly free from subjective experience, and bring a real hypothesis into play.

What is this but to say that religion, in her fullest exercise of function, is a postulator of new facts? The world interpreted religiously is not the materialistic world over again, with an altered expression. It must have, over and above the altered expression, a natural constitution different at some point from that which a materialistic world would have. It must be such that different events can be expected in it, different conduct must be required.

All this on the supposition that our passional nature may be prophetic and right: and that the religious hypothesis is a live hypothesis which may be true.

We are now in possession of the essentials of James's position. We know what he means by a genuine option between rival hypotheses. We know the principle by which he would justify belief in such circumstances. We know that he considers the religious hypothesis a case in point. We know, finally, what he means by this religious hypothesis. His defense of the whole position is still to be made. He deals first with the skeptic. The point here is this: It may be all very well to talk about the demands of our "passional nature," but, as a matter of fact, why is it not just as legitimate to refuse to believe either hypothesis when neither is backed by sufficient evidence? Why may an agnostic not take the stand, in all conscience, that under the circumstances stipulated by James, the proper attitude is one of suspended judgment? Let us hear, through James, the agnostic's statement of the case:

> It does seem preposterous on the very face of it, to talk of our opinions being modifiable at will. Can our will either help or hinder our intellect in its perceptions of truth? . . . Indeed, the talk of believing by our volition seems from one point of view, simply silly. From another point of view it is worse than silly, it is vile. When one turns to the magnificent edifice of the physical sciences, and sees how it was reared, what thousands of disinterested moral lives of men lie buried in its mere foundations; what patience and postponement, what choking down of preference, what submission to icy laws of outer fact are wrought into its very stones and mortar; how absolutely impersonal it stands in its vast augustness—then how besotted and contemptible seems every little sentimentalist who comes blowing his voluntary smoke wreaths! Can we wonder if those bred in the rugged and manly school of science should feel like spewing such subjectivism out of their mouths? The whole system of loyalties which grow up in the schools of science go dead against its toleration; so that it is only natural that those who have caught the scientific fever should pass over to the opposite extreme and write sometimes as if the incorruptibly truthful intellect ought positively to prefer bitterness and unacceptableness to the heart in its cup.
> Clough sings:

> > It fortifies my soul to know
> > That, though I perish, Truth is so

> while Huxley exclaims: "My only consolation lies in the reflection that, however bad our posterity may become, so far as they hold by the plain rule of not pretending to believe what they have no reason to believe, because it may be to their advantage so to pretend, they will not have reached the lowest depth of immorality."
> And that delicious *enfant terrible*, Clifford, writes: "Belief is desecrated when given to unproved and unquestioned statements for the solace and private pleasure of the believer. Whoso would deserve well of his fellows in this matter will guard the purity of his belief with a very fanaticism of jealous care, lest at any time it should rest on an unworthy object, and cast a stain which can never be wiped away. If a belief has been accepted on insufficient evidence, even though the belief be true, the pleasure is a stolen one. It is sinful because it is stolen in defiance of our duty to mankind. That duty is to guard ourselves from such beliefs as from a pestilence which may shortly master our body and then spread to the rest of the town. It is wrong, always, everywhere, and for everyone, to believe anything upon insufficient evidence."

Now, all of this strikes one as healthy, even when expressed by Clifford with somewhat too much of robustious pathos in the voice. Willing and wishing do seem, in the matter of our beliefs, to be only fifth wheels to the coach.

How shall this indictment be answered? It will be noticed that James has been fair to the agnostic in admitting the genuine possibility here of a moral issue. The agnostic's claim is not, at its best, that we are merely foolish to believe on insufficient evidence. It is the more serious claim that we *ought* not to believe on insufficient evidence; that belief, in such cases, is immoral. That is the point agnosticism adds to skepticism. That is the charge with which James is faced. The first move in his defense is to note that in this unique case of the religious hypothesis doubt is the equivalent of denial; and, the point is, denial is not suspended judgment. (It may be necessary to reread James's wording of the religious hypothesis, especially its *second* part, to follow his argument here.)

> To preach skepticism in these matters is tantamount to telling us, when in the presence of the religious hypothesis, that to yield to our fear of its being false is wiser and better than to yield to our hope that it may be true.

As James points out, this puts a slightly different face on the matter. Why is it "wiser and better" to refrain from belief on all occasions where the evidence is insufficient?

> This is not the case of "intellect" against "passion." It is only intellect, with one passion—the dread or horror of believing what may be false—laying down its law—never to believe what may be false when there is no evidence that it may be true.
>
> And by what, forsooth, is the supreme wisdom of this passion warranted? Dupery for dupery, what proof is there that dupery through hope is so much worse than dupery through fear? I, for one, can see no proof; and I simply refuse to imitate the skeptic's option in a case where my own stake is important enough to give me the right to choose my own form of risk.

And what it comes down to is this:

> We may regard the case for truth as paramount, and the avoidance of error as secondary; or we may treat the avoidance of error as more imperative, and let truth take its chance. Clifford exhorts us to the latter course. Believe nothing, he tells us, keep your mind in suspense forever, rather than, by closing on insufficient evidence, incur the awful risk of believing lies. You, on the other hand, may think that the risk of being in error is a very small matter when compared with the blessings of real knowledge, and be ready to be duped many times rather than postpone indefinitely the chance of guessing true.

This being so, he knows where he stands:

> For my own part, I have also a horror of being duped. But I can believe that worse things than being duped may happen to a man in this world. So Clifford's exhortation has to my ears a thoroughly fantastic sound. Our errors are surely not such awfully solemn things. In a world where we are to sure to incur them, a certain lightness of heart seems healthier than this excessive nervousness on their behalf.

If the religious hypothesis be true, and the evidence for it still insufficient, I do not wish, by putting a skeptical extinguisher upon my nature, to forfeit my sole chance of getting upon the winning side; that chance depending, of course, on my willingness to run the risk of acting as if my passional need of taking the world religiously might be prophetic and right.

When I look at the religious hypothesis, as it really puts itself to men, and when I think of all the possibilities which it involves, then the skeptical command to put a stopper on our heart and wait—acting meanwhile more or less as if religion were not true—wait till doomsday, or till such time as our intellect and senses may have raked in enough evidence—this command, I say, seems to me the queerest idol ever manufactured in the philosophic cave.

If the religious hypothesis were true, then pure intellectualism, with its veto on our willingness to make advances, would be an absurdity; and some participation of our sympathetic nature would be logically required. I, therefore, for one, cannot see my way to accepting the agnostic rules for truth-seeking (never to believe any hypothesis when there is no evidence or insufficient evidence) or to willfully agree to keep my willing nature out of the game.

I cannot do so for this plain reason: A rule of thinking which would prevent me from acknowledging certain kinds of truth if those kinds of truths were really there, would be an irrational rule. That, for me, is the long and short of the logic of the situation.

The great empiricists are only empiricists on reflection; left to their instincts, they dogmatize like infallible popes. When the Cliffords tells us how sinful it is to be Christians on such "insufficient evidence," insufficiency is really the last thing they have in mind. For them the evidence is absolutely sufficient, only it makes the other way. They believe so completely in an anti-Christian order of the universe that there is no living option: Christianity, for them, is a dead hypothesis from the start.

As a kind of Parthian shot, James throws a question at the skeptics themselves:

Our belief in truth itself, for instance, that there is a truth and that our minds and it are made for each other—what is it but a passionate affirmation of desire in which our social system backs us up? We want to have a truth; we want to believe that our experiments and studies and discussions must put us in a continually better and better position toward it; and on this line we agree to fight out our thinking lives.

But if a skeptic asks us how we know all this, can our logic find a reply? It cannot. It is just one volition against another; we are willing to go in for life upon a trust or assumption which he, for his part, does not care to make. As a rule we disbelieve all facts and theories for which we have no use. Clifford's cosmic emotions find no use for Christian feelings. Huxley belabors the bishops because there is no use for sacerdotalism in his scheme of life. But Newman goes over to Romanism, and finds all sorts of reasons good for staying there, because a priestly system is for him an organic need and delight.

So Clifford notwithstanding, our nonintellectual nature evidently does influence our convictions. The state of things is far from simple, and pure insight and pure logic, whatever they may do ideally, are not the only things that really do produce our creeds.

If we had an infallible intellect, with its objective certitudes, we might feel ourselves disloyal to such a perfect organ of knowledge in not trusting to it exclusively, in not waiting for its releasing word. But if we believe that no bell in us tolls to let us know for certain when truth is in our grasp, then it seems a piece of idle fantasticality to preach so solemnly of our duty of waiting for the bell.

James has still to deal with another sort of critic, no less hostile. The charge this time is not that where evidence is lacking it is wiser and better to suspend judgment. It is, rather, this: If you start justifying belief on this basis, where and how are you going to draw the line? The justification is not, by its nature, the peculiar property of the man who desires to believe in God. It would seem to be equally available, as a principle of justification, for other beliefs as well, some of which might be incompatible with those beliefs James used it to defend. A man who advances a principle that would justify incompatible beliefs has some explaining to do. James knew this. Although convinced that his argument was sound, he knew that others would not be. Thus:

> I confess I do not see how this logic can be escaped. But sad experience makes me fear that some of you may still shrink from saying with me that we have the right to believe at our own risk any hypothesis that is live enough to tempt our will.
>
> If this is so, however, I suspect it is because you have got away from the logical point of view altogether, and are thinking of some particular religious hypothesis which for you is dead. The freedom to "believe what you will" you apply to the case of some patent superstition; and the faith you think of is the faith defined by the schoolboy when he said: "Faith is when you believe something that you know ain't true."
>
> I can only repeat that this is a misapprehension of my position. The freedom to "believe what we will," for which I have been arguing, can only cover living options which the intellect by itself cannot resolve; and living options never seem absurd or superstitious to him who has them to consider.
>
> Where there is no such forced option, the dispassionately judicial intellect with no pet hypothesis, saving us, as it does, from dupery, at any rate, ought to be our ideal.

It would appear that James has only restated his difficulty. It is still open to anyone to point out: "Yes, what you have said, you have said. The point is, however, that what you have not said, you have not said. What about the man whose passional nature inclines him to embrace, as true, a proposition that is incompatible with one that your passional nature has inclined you to embrace? As between two passional natures having divergent inclinations, how do you decide?" A glance through the published letters of William James shows that he was bothered by this point. Writing to his brother Henry, the novelist, he protests:

> When I *say* that, *other things being equal*, the view of things that seems more satisfactory morally will legitimately be treated by men as truer than the view that seems less so, *they quote me as saying* that anything morally satisfactory can be treated as true, no matter how unsatisfactory it may be from the point of view of its consistency with what we already know or believe to be true about physical or natural facts, which is rot!!

James has drawn a two-edged sword. To vary the metaphor, his principle may be used to reinforce either theism or atheism, or for the matter of that, some third alternative equally removed from either, say skepticism or polytheism. In the last analysis he merely reinforces the most deeply congenial belief; he does not state which belief is or ought to be the most congenial. However, he is not done protesting. Writing to an English philosopher, he has much the same thing to say:

> Would to God I had never thought of that unhappy title for my essay. What I meant by the title was the state of mind of the man who finds an impulse in him toward a believing attitude, and who resolves not to quench it simply because doubts of its truth are possible. Its opposite would be the maxim: Believe in nothing which you can possibly doubt.
>
> My essay hedged the license to indulge in private overbeliefs with so many restrictions and sign boards of danger that the outlet was narrow enough. It made of tolerance the essence of the situation. It defined the permissible cases. It treated the faith attitude as a necessity for individuals, because the total "evidence" which only the race can draw includes their experiments among its data. It tended to show only that faith cannot be absolutely *vetoed*, as certain champions of "science" had claimed it ought to be.
>
> I cry to heaven to tell me of what insane root my "leading contemporaries" have eaten, that they are so smitten with blindness as to the meaning of printed texts.
>
> In my essay the evil shape was a vision of "Science" in the form of abstraction, priggishness and sawdust, lording it over all. Take the sterilest scientific prig and cad you know, compare him with the richest religious intellect you know, and you would not, any more than I would, give the former the exclusive right of way.

There are two parts to a man's exposition of his ideas concerning God. In the first place, he should make clear why he believes that God exists. In the second, he should make clear what he conceives God's nature to be. So far as God's existence goes, we know where James stands in this essay. "Why do I believe in God? Is it because I have experienced his presence? No; rather because I need that it be true." Before quitting James, it is worth noting that he used his principle to justify his belief in God's finiteness. Like Mill, and other recent and contemporary theologians, James repudiated the celebrated "omni's" of traditional theology.

> I simply refuse to accept the idea of there being no purpose in the objective world. On the other hand, I cannot represent the existence of purpose except as based in a mind. The "not-me," therefore, so far as it contains purpose, must spring from a mind; but not necessarily a *One and Only* mind.
>
> In saying God exists, all I imply is that my purposes are cared for by a mind so powerful as on the whole to control the drift of the universe. That is . . . merely a practical emotional faith.
>
> The only difficulties of theism are the moral difficulties and meanness; and they have always seemed to me to flow from the gratuitous dogma of God being the all-inclusive reality. Once think possible a pluralism of which He may be one member, and piety forthwith ceases to be incompatible with manliness, and religious faith with intellectual rectitude.
>
> In short, the only theism I defend is that of simple unphilosophic mankind. God, in the religious life of ordinary men is the name, not of the whole of things, heaven forbid, but only of the ideal tendency in things. . . . He works in an external environment, has limits, and has enemies. . . . If there be a God, how the devil can we know

what difficulties he may have had to contend with? Possible difficulties! They save everything. But what are they if not limitations to the all-inclusiveness of any single being!

Having an environment, being in time, and working out a history just like ourselves, He escapes from the foreignness from all that is human, of the static, timeless, perfect absolute.

My God, being part of a pluralistic system, is responsible only for such things as He knows enough and has enough power to have accomplished. The "omniscient" and "omnipotent" God of theology I regard as a disease of the philosophy shop.

The line of least resistance, as it seems to me, both in theology and in philosophy, is to accept, along with the Superhuman Consciousness, the notion that It is not all embracing; the notion, in other words, that there is a God, but that He is finite, either in power or in knowledge, or in both at once.

NOTE ON SOURCES.   The material in this section is quoted or abridged from "The Will to Believe." The concluding passages are from the chapters entitled "Conclusion" and "Postscript" in James's book *Varieties of Religious Experience*.

7   ANTONY FLEW AND JOHN HICK

FALSIFICATION AND VERIFICATION

FROM JAMES TO FLEW AND HICK.   With James the debate over the existence of God is brought into the twentieth century where an interesting new dimension is added to the debate through the work of logical positivists and analytic philosophers. Logical positivism as a distinct philosophical viewpoint began in Vienna during the early decades of the twentieth century. At that time, a cluster of prominent intellectuals with a strong interest in science met to discuss the philosophy of science. In due course, they came to be called the "Vienna Circle," and their stated agenda was to propagate the scientific outlook in all fields of human knowledge. Given the very strong empiricist bent of these early positivists, they tended to regard reality as that which is quantifiable—that which can be observed, measured, counted, and reduced to mathematical formulae. If something could not be so quantified, then it was probably not objectively real. Because some of the major traditional concerns of philosophy—such as transcendent deity, aesthetic experience, metaphysics, and ethics—did not lend themselves to such quantification, the positivists concluded that these concerns dealt not with facts and knowledge (as earlier philosophers had assumed), but with sheer speculations or expressions of human emotion. In applying their agenda to philosophy (that is to say, in making philosophy "scientific"), the domain of philosophy for the positivists was purged of its traditional "speculations" and reduced to the role of using philosophy's logical and analytical skills in the service of science.

The positivists achieved this purging of philosophy through their views on verification and meaning. They divided the sentences uttered by people in general and philosophers in particular into two major types: (1) cognitive sentences that were informational, involving claims about the world (e.g., "It is raining outside") or claims about symbols (e.g., "The square root of four is two"), and (2) noncognitive sentences that were noninformational, involving such speech acts as exclamations, imperatives, and interrogatives. Then the positivists claimed that many sentences that people thought were cognitive were really pseudocognitive sentences masquerading as cognitive sentences. To smoke out these fake assertions, the logical positivists used their so-called verification principle according to which a sentence that purports to be cognitive is in fact cognitive only if it is check-up-able in principle. If, for example, you make statements that you think are cognitive, that involve claims about states of affairs, about matters of fact (such as "The Absolute is beyond space and time" or "God exists" or "God is good"), and if those claims are not check-up-able in principle, then the positivists would conclude that your statements were not "factually significant," or to put the matter more candidly, your statements were meaningless, were nonsense.

The logical positivists' challenge to twentieth-century philosophy and theology could be summed up this way: "If you claim to be making cognitive statements, statements about states of affairs, then you had better be prepared to specify how your statements are check-up-able in principle; if you can't, then your statements are really meaningless." This challenge stirred up considerable debate as opponents of positivism argued, among other things, that the positivists' criteria for what counted as meaningful cognitive statements were too narrow.

Although logical positivism as a philosophical movement is now dead, nevertheless it reinforced within the current analytic tradition of philosophy a tendency to associate meaningfulness with some sort of verification. It is within the context of the analytical tradition that the debate between Flew and Hick takes place. Considering the statement "God exists," all our previous authors have been concerned about the evidence to support that claim. As our authors scrutinized the evidence for belief in the existence of God, some of them claimed that reason requires belief; others said reason allows belief; and still others claimed that reason is offended by belief. These authors have been wrestling with the quality of the evidence presented to support belief in the existence of God. Flew and Hick move the debate away from the question of the quality of the evidence to the question of whether the claim that "God exists" is really capable of verification or falsification at all. If the statement is not capable of verification or falsification, then the meaningfulness of the statement is called into radical question. Such a situation would certainly erode the grounds for belief in God.

BIOGRAPHICAL NOTE.   In 1983 Antony G. N. Flew retired from a professorship at the University of Reading, England, and shortly thereafter became Part-time Distinguished Research Fellow at the Social Philosophy and Policy Center of Bowling Green State University in Ohio. Born in 1923, Flew studied at Oxford and went on to hold appointments at a number of major universities including Aberdeen, Keele, Calgary, and Reading. His writings explore a wide range of issues as the following sampling of his book titles indicates: *A New Approach to*

Psychical Research (1961), *Hume's Philosophy of Belief* (1966), *Evolutionary Ethics* (1967), *An Introduction to Western Philosophy* (1971), *Crime or Disease?* (1973), *The Presumption of Atheism* (1976), *Sociology, Equality and Education* (1976), and *Thinking About Social Thinking* (1985). In 1950, during his tenure at the University of Aberdeen, Flew's article, reprinted below, first appeared in a now-defunct journal titled *University*. It was later reprinted in *New Essays in Philosophical Theology*, edited by Flew and Alasdair MacIntyre. Flew's analysis initiated a fresh discussion of the problem of the verifiability of religious statements in general, and of the claim "God exists" in particular.

John H. Hick, one of the important contributors to the discussion opened by Flew, was born in England in 1922. Holding degrees from Edinburgh, Oxford, and Cambridge, Hick has taught philosophy and philosophy of religion at Cornell University, Princeton Theological Seminary, Cambridge University, and Birmingham University in England. In 1979 he became the Danforth Professor of Religion at the Claremont Graduate School. He has delivered several prestigious addresses, including the Arthur Stanley Eddington Memorial Lectureship at Cambridge University (1972), the Ingersoll lectureship at Harvard University (1977), and the Gifford Lectureship at the University of Edinburgh (1986–1987). In 1963–1964 and again in 1985–1986, he was a Fellow of the Guggenheim Foundation. His books, which deal mainly with problems in the philosophy of religion, include *Faith and Knowledge* (1957, 1966), *Philosophy of Religion* (1963, 1973, 1983), *Evil and the God of Love* (1966, 1967), *The Center of Christianity* (1968, 1983), *Arguments for the Existence of God* (1971), *God and the Universe of Faiths* (1973), *Death and Eternal Life* (1976), *God Has Many Names* (1980), *Why Believe in God* (1983), and *Problems of Religious Pluralism* (1985). Hick's response to Flew, which first appeared in the journal *Theology Today* in 1960, takes seriously Flew's own philosophical commitments (i.e, the verification principle) and tries to show how on those grounds the statement "God exists" (whether true or false) is a genuinely factually significant assertion.

THE ARGUMENT OF THE PASSAGES.   Antony Flew constructs an engaging parable to make a point and raise a question. First, his *point*. To make an assertion (such as "God exists") entails denying that such and such is the case. If your assertion entails the denial of nothing, if it is compatible with every and all states of affairs, then we can seriously question if you really made an assertion at all. If it is not clear to us what you are asserting, then you might be able to provide the needed clarity by telling us precisely what your assertion is denying. In so doing, you would be telling us what it would take to falsify your assertion. Clearly, if we discover that what you tell us your assertion is denying is indeed the case, then your assertion would be falsified.

Second, his *question*. Because it is not clear to Flew and others just what statements like "God exists" and "God loves us" mean, and because it is not clear that they are assertions at all, Flew raises the questions: "What do those assertions deny? With what state of affairs are they incompatible?" Clearly, if believers are unable to specify what situation is incompatible with the truth of their assertions, if they are unable to tell us what it would take to falsify their assertions, then we can legitimately question whether they are asserting anything at all with the words "God exists" and "God loves us." Here is how Flew puts it:

> Let us begin with a parable. It is a parable developed from a tale told by John Wisdom in his haunting and revelatory article "Gods."[1] Once upon a time two explorers came upon a clearing in the jungle. In the clearing were growing many flowers and many weeds. One explorers says, "Some gardener must tend this plot." The other disagrees, "There is no gardener." So they pitch their tents and set a watch. No gardener is ever seen. "But perhaps he is an invisible gardener." So they set up a barbed-wire fence. They electrify it. They patrol with bloodhounds. (For they remember how H. G. Wells's *The Invisible Man* could be both smelt and touched though he could not be seen.) But no shrieks ever suggest that some intruder has received a shock. No movements of the wire ever betray an invisible climber. The bloodhounds never give cry. Yet still the Believer is not convinced. "But there is a gardener, invisible, intangible, insensible to electric shocks, a gardener who has no scent and makes no sound, a gardener who comes secretly to look after the garden which he loves." At last the Skeptic despairs, "But what remains of your original assertion? Just how does what you call an invisible, intangible, eternally elusive gardener differ from an imaginary gardener or even from no gardener at all?"
>
> In this parable we can see how what starts as an assertion, that something exists or that there is some analogy between certain complexes of phenomena, may be reduced step by step to an altogether different status, to an expression perhaps of a "picture preference."[2] The Skeptic says there is no gardener. The Believer says there is a gardener (but invisible, etc.). One man talks about sexual behaviour. Another man prefers to talk of Aphrodite (but knows that there is not really a superhuman person additional to, and somehow responsible for, all sexual phenomena).[3] The process of qualification may be checked at any point before the original assertion is completely withdrawn and something of that first assertion will remain (Tautology). Mr. Wells's invisible man could not, admittedly, be seen, but in all other respects he was a man like the rest of us. But though the process of qualification may be, and of course, usually is, checked in time, it is not always judiciously so halted. Someone may dissipate his assertion completely without noticing that he has done so. A fine brash hypothesis may thus be killed by inches, the death by a thousand qualifications.
>
> And in this, it seems to me, lies the peculiar danger, the endemic evil, of theological utterance. Take such utterances as "God has a plan," "God created the world," "God loves us as a father loves his children." They look at first sight very much like assertions, vast cosmological assertions. Of course, this is no sure sign that they either

---

1 *Proceedings of the Aristotelian Society*, 1944–45, reprinted as Ch. X of *Logic and Language*, Vol. 1 (Blackwell, 1951), and in his *Philosophy and Psychoanalysis* (Blackwell, 1953).

2 Cf. J. Wisdom, "Other Minds," *Mind*, 1940; reprinted in his *Other Minds* (Blackwell, 1952).

3 Cf. Lucretius, *De Rerum Natura*, II, 655–60.

> *Hic siquis mare Neptunum Cereremque vocare*
> *Constituet fruges et Bacchi nomine abuti*
> *Mavolat quam laticis proprium proferre vocamen*
> *Concedamus ut hic terrarum dictitet orbem*
> *Esse deum matrem dum vera re tamen ipse*
> *Religione animum turpi contingere parcat.*

are, or are intended to be, assertions. But let us confine ourselves to the cases where those who utter such sentences intend them to express assertions. (Merely remarking parenthetically that those who intend or interpret such utterances as crypto-commands, expressions of wishes, disguised ejaculations, concealed ethics, or as anything else but assertions, are unlikely to succeed in making them either properly orthodox or practically effective).

Now to assert that such and such is the case is necessarily equivalent to denying that such and such is not the case.[4] Suppose then that we are in doubt as to what someone who gives vent to an utterance is asserting, or suppose that, more radically, we are skeptical as to whether he is really asserting anything at all, one way of trying to understand (or perhaps it will be to expose) his utterance is to attempt to find what he would regard as counting against, or as being incompatible with, its truth. For if the utterance is indeed an assertion, it will necessarily be equivalent to a denial of the negation of that assertion. And anything which would count against the assertion, or which would induce the speaker to withdraw it and to admit that it had been mistaken, must be part of (or the whole of) the meaning of the negation of that assertion. And to know the meaning of the negation of an assertion is, as near as makes no matter, to know the meaning of that assertion.[5] And if there is nothing which a putative assertion denies then there is nothing which it asserts either; and so it is not really an assertion. When the Skeptic in the parable asked the Believer, "Just how does what you call an invisible, intangible, eternally elusive gardener differ from an imaginary gardener or even from no gardener at all?" he was suggesting that the Believer's earlier statement had been eroded by qualification that it was no longer an assertion at all.

Now it often seems to people who are not religious as if there was no conceivable event or series of events the occurrence of which would be admitted by sophisticated religious people to be a sufficient reason for conceding "There wasn't a God after all" or "God does not really love us then." Someone tells us that God loves us as a father loves his children. We are reassured. But then we see a child dying of inoperable cancer of the throat. His earthly father is driven frantic in his efforts to help, but his Heavenly Father reveals no obvious sign of concern. Some qualification is made—God's love is "not a merely human love" or it is "an inscrutable love," perhaps—and we realize that such sufferings are quite compatible with the truth of the assertion that "God loves us as a father (but, of course, . . .)." We are reassured again. But then perhaps we ask: what is this assurance of God's (appropriately qualified) love worth, what is this apparent guarantee really a guarantee against? Just what would have to happen not merely (morally and wrongly) to tempt but also (logically and rightly) to entitle us to say "God does not love us" or even "God does not exist"? I therefore put to the succeeding symposiasts the simple central questions, "What would have to occur or to have occurred to constitute for you a disproof of the love of, or of the existence of, God?"

One of the most searching and perceptive responses to Flew offered by a defender of the cognitive status of theological statements like "God exists" and "God loves us" is provided by John Hick. Assuming a posture within a Christian context, Hick provides an explication of the concept of verification and argues that "eschatological verification" fulfills the conditions for legitimate verification,

---

4   For those who prefer symbolism: $p \equiv \sim \sim p$.
5   For by simply negating $\sim p$ we get p: $\sim \sim p \equiv p$.

and accordingly legitimizes certain basic Christian theological statements as genuine cognitive assertions.

In explicating the concept of verification, Hick makes five major points. First, he notes that verification is the exclusion of grounds for rational doubt concerning the truth of some proposition.

> To ask "Is the existence of God verifiable?" is to pose a question which is too imprecise to be capable of being answered.[1] There are many different concepts of God, and it may be that statements employing some of them are open to verification or falsification while statements employing others of them are not. Again, the notion of verifying is itself by no means perfectly clear and fixed; and it may be that on some views of the nature of verification the existence of God is verifiable, whereas on other views it is not.
>
> Instead of seeking to compile a list of the various different concepts of God and the various possible senses of "verify," I wish to argue with regard to one particular concept of deity, namely the Christian concept, that divine existence is in principle verifiable; and as the first stage of this argument I must indicate what I mean by "verifiable."
>
> The central core of the concept of verification, I suggest, is the removal of ignorance or uncertainty concerning the truth of some proposition. That p is verified (whether p embodies a theory, hypothesis, prediction, or straightforward assertion) means that something happens which makes it clear that p is true. A question is settled so that there is no longer room for rational doubt concerning it. The way in which grounds for rational doubt are excluded varies, of course, with the subject matter. But the general feature common to all cases of verification is the ascertaining of truth by the removal of grounds for rational doubt. Where such grounds are removed, we rightly speak of verification having taken place.

Second, the kind of verification that is germane to the debate with Flew is a logico-psychological event that takes place in a particular human consciousness.

> The only sort of verification of theological propositions which is likely to interest us is one in which human beings participate. We may therefore, for our present purpose, treat verification as a logico-psychological rather than as a purely logical concept. . . . "Verification" is thus primarily the name for an event which takes place in human consciousness.[2] It refers to an experience, the experience of ascertaining that a given proposition or set of propositions is true. To this extent verification is a psychological notion. But of course it is also a logical notion. For needless to say, not *any* experience

---

[1]   In this paper I assume that an indicative sentence expresses a factual assertion if and only if the state in which the universe would be if the putative assertion could correctly be said to be true differs in some experienceable way from the state in which the universe would be if the putative assertion could correctly be said to be false, all aspects of the universe other than that referred to in the putative assertion being the same in either case. This criterion acknowledges the important core of truth in the logical positivist verification principle. "Experienceable" in the above formulation means, in the case of alleged subjective or private facts (*e.g.*, pains, dreams, after-images, etc.), "experienceable by the subject in question" and, in the case of alleged objective or public facts, "capable in principle of being experienced by anyone." My contention is going to be that "God exists" asserts a matter of objective fact.

[2]   This suggestion is closely related to Carnap's insistence that, in contrast to "true," "confirmed" is time-dependent. To say that a statement is confirmed, or verified, is to say that it has been confirmed at a particular time—and, I would add, by a particular person. See Rudolf Carnap, "Truth and Confirmation," Feigl and Sellars, *Readings in Philosophical Analysis*. 1949, pp. 119 f.

is rightly called an experience of verifying p. Both logical and psychological conditions must be fulfilled in order for verification to have taken place.

Third, verification is often related to prediction, and such prediction is often conditional (which means that one must go through some specified course of action in order to verify a statement).

Verification is often construed as the verification of a prediction. However, verification, as the exclusion of grounds for rational doubt, does not necessarily consist in the proving correct of a prediction; a verifying experience does not always need to have been predicted in order to have the effect of excluding rational doubt. But when we are interested in the verifiability of propositions as the criterion for their having factual meaning, the notion of prediction becomes central. If a proposition contains or entails predictions which can be verified or falsified, its character as an assertion (though not of course its character as a true assertion) is thereby guaranteed.

Such predictions may be and often are conditional. For example, statements about the features of the dark side of the moon are rendered meaningful by the conditional predictions which they entail to the effect that if an observer comes to be in such a position in space, he will make such-and-such observations. It would in fact be more accurate to say that the prediction is always conditional, but that sometimes the conditions are so obvious and so likely to be fulfilled in any case that they require no special mention, while sometimes they require for their fulfillment some unusual expedition or operation. A prediction, for example, that the sun will rise within twenty-four hours is intended unconditionally, at least as concerns conditions to be fulfilled by the observer; he is not required by the terms of the prediction to perform any special operation. Even in this case, however, there is an implied negative condition that he shall not put himself in a situation (such as immuring himself in the depths of a coal mine) from which a sunrise would not be perceptible. Other predictions, however, are explicitly conditional. In these cases it is true for any particular individual that in order to verify the statement in question he must go through some specified course of action. The prediction is to the effect that if you conduct such an experiment you will obtain such a result; for example, if you go into the next room you will have such-and-such visual experiences, and if you then touch the table which you see you will have such-and-such tactual experiences, and so on. The content of the "if" clause is of course always determined by the particular subject matter. The logic of "table" determines what you must do to verify statements about tables; the logic of "molecule" determines what you must do to verify statements about molecules; and the logic of "God" determines what you must do to verify statements about God.

In those cases in which the individual who is to verify a proposition must himself first perform some operation, it clearly cannot follow from the circumstances that the proposition is true that everybody has in fact verified it, or that everybody will at some future time verify it. For whether or not any particular person performs the requisite operation is a contingent matter.

Fourth, verification and falsification are most often symmetrically related. That is to say, if one is unable to discover the verifying evidence for a statement, then one usually concludes that the one has failed to verify the statement and such failure constitutes falsification of the statement. Yet, under some circumstances verification and falsification may be asymmetrically related. There may be occasions when the failure to verify does not constitute falsification.

What is the relation between verification and falsification? We are all familiar today with the phrase, "theology and falsification." A. G. N. Flew and others,[3] taking their cue from John Wisdom,[4] have raised instead of the question, "What possible experiences would verify 'God exists'?" the matching question, "What possible experiences would falsify 'God exists'? What conceivable state of affairs would be incompatible with the existence of God?" In posing the question in this way, it was apparently assumed that verification and falsification are symmetrically related, and that the latter is apt to be the more accessible of the two.

In the most common cases, certainly, verification and falsification are symmetrically related. The logically simplest case of verification is provided by the crucial instance. Here it is integral to a given hypothesis that if, in specified circumstances, *A* occurs, the hypothesis is thereby shown to be true, whereas if *B* occurs the hypothesis is thereby shown to be false. Verification and falsification are also symmetrically related in the testing of such a proposition as "There is a table in the next room." The verifying experiences in this case are experiences of seeing and touching, predictions of which are entailed by the proposition in question, under the proviso that one goes into the next room; and the absence of such experiences in those circumstances serves to falsify the proposition.

But it would be rash to assume, on this basis, that verification and falsification must always be related in this symmetrical fashion. They do not necessarily stand to one another as do the two sides of a coin, so that once the coin is spun it must fall on one side or the other. There are cases in which verification and falsification each correspond to a side on a different coin, so that one can fail to verify without this failure constituting falsification.

Consider, for example, the proposition that "there are three successive sevens in the decimal determination of π." So far as the value of π has been worked out, it does not contain a series of three sevens, but it will always be true that such a series may occur at a point not yet reached in anyone's calculations. Accordingly, the proposition may one day be verified, if it is true, but can never be falsified, if it is false.

The hypothesis of a continued conscious existence after bodily death provides an instance of a different kind of such asymmetry, and one which has a direct bearing upon the theistic problem. This hypothesis has built into it a prediction that one will after the date of one's bodily death have conscious experiences, including the experience of remembering that death. This is a prediction which will be verified in one's own experience if it is true, but which cannot be falsified if it is false. That is to say, it can be false, but *that* it is false can never be a fact which anyone has experientially verified. But this circumstance does not undermine the meaningfulness of the hypothesis, since it is also such that if it be true, it will be known to be true.

Fifth, Hick points out that verification of a factual proposition is not equivalent to logical certification. The former excludes rational doubt; the latter excludes the logical possibility of error or illusion.

---

3   Antony Flew, editor, *New Essays in Philosophical Theology*, 1955, Chapter VI.
4   "Gods," *Proceedings of the Aristotelian Society*, 1944–45. Reprinted in *Logic and Language*, Antony Flew, editor, First Series, 1951, and in John Wisdom, *Philosophy and Psycho-Analysis*, 1953.

It is important to remember that we do not speak of verifying logically necessary truths, but only propositions concerning matters of fact. Accordingly verification is not to be identified with the concept of logical certification or proof. The exclusion of rational doubt concerning some matter of fact is not equivalent to the exclusion of the logical possibility of error or illusion. For truths concerning fact are not logically necessary. Their contrary is never self-contradictory. But at the same time the bare logical possibility of error does not constitute ground for rational doubt as to the veracity of our experience. If it did, no empirical proposition could ever be verified, and indeed the notion of empirical verification would be without use and therefore without sense. What we rightly seek, when we desire the verification of a factual proposition, is not a demonstration of the logical impossibility of the proposition being false (for this would be a self-contradictory demand), but such weight of evidence as suffices, in the type of case in question, to exclude rational doubt.

Having explicated the concept of verification, Hick now proceeds to apply his explication to the notion of "eschatological verification." In Christian circles, *eschatology* refers to the doctrine of "last things," of things pertaining to the future culmination of individual and corporate histories. Eschatological verification, then, refers to verification that takes place at the future extremity of one's life; it refers to verification that would take place after one dies and presumably confronts divine reality. It is important to note that Hick does not invent the details that describe the situation under which eschatological verification would take place. Those details and that situation are embedded in the traditional Christian biblical perspective. In pursuing his response to Flew's challenge, Hick offers a parable of his own.

I wish now to apply these discriminations to the notion of eschatological verification, which has been briefly employed by Ian Crombie in his contribution to *New Essays in Philosophical Theology*,[5] and by myself in *Faith and Knowledge*.[6] This suggestion has on each occasion been greeted with disapproval by both philosophers and theologians. I am, however, still of the opinion that the notion of eschatological verification is sound; and further, that no viable alternative to it has been offered to establish the factual character of theism.

The strength of the notion of eschatological verification is that it is not an *ad hoc* invention but is based upon an actually operative religious concept of God. In the language of Christian faith, the word "God" stands at the center of a system of terms, such as Spirit, grace, Logos, incarnation, Kingdom of God, and many more; and the distinctly Christian conception of God can only be fully grasped in its connection with these related terms.[7] It belongs to a complex of notions which together constitute a picture of the universe in which we live, of man's place therein, of a comprehensive divine purpose interacting with human purposes, and of the general nature

[5] *Op. cit.*, p. 126.

[6] Cornell University Press, 1957, pp. 150–62.

[7] Its clear recognition of this fact, with regard not only to Christianity but to any religion, is one of the valuable features of Ninian Smart's *Reasons and Faiths* (1958). He remarks, for example, that "the claim that God exists can only be understood by reference to many, if not all, other propositions in the doctrinal scheme from which it is extrapolated" (p. 12).

of the eventual fulfillment of that divine purpose. This Christian picture of the universe, entertaining as it does certain distinctive expectations concerning the future, is a very different picture from any that can be accepted by one who does not believe that the God of the New Testament exists. Further, these differences are such as to show themselves in human experience. The possibility of experiential confirmation is thus built into the Christian concept of God; and the notion of eschatological verification seeks to relate this fact to the logical problem of meaning.

Let me first give a general indication of this suggestion, by repeating a parable which I have related elsewhere,[8] and then try to make it more precise and eligible for discussion. Here, first, is the parable.

Two men are travelling together along a road. One of them believes that it leads to a Celestial City, the other that it leads nowhere; but since this is the only road there is, both must travel it. Neither has been this way before, and therefore neither is able to say what they will find around each next corner. During their journey they meet both with moments of refreshments and delight, and with moments of hardship and danger. All the time one of them thinks of his journey as a pilgrimage to the Celestial City and interprets the pleasant parts as encouragements and the obstacles as trials of his purpose and lessons in endurance, prepared by the king of that city and designed to make of him a worthy citizen of the place when at last he arrives there. The other, however, believes none of this and sees their journey as an unavoidable and aimless ramble. Since he has no choice in the matter, he enjoys the good and endures the bad. But for him there is no Celestial City to be reached, no all-encompassing purpose ordaining their journey; only the road itself and the luck of the road in good weather and in bad.

During the course of the journey the issue between them is not an experimental one. They do not entertain different expectations about the coming details of the road, but only about its ultimate destination. And yet when they do turn the last corner it will be apparent that one of them has been right all the time and the other wrong. Thus although the issue between them has not been experimental, it has nevertheless from the start been a real issue. They have not merely felt differently about the road; for one was feeling appropriately and the other inappropriately in relation to the actual state of affairs. Their opposed interpretations of the road constituted genuinely rival assertions, though assertions whose assertion-status has the peculiar characteristic of being guaranteed retrospectively by a future crux.

This parable has of course (like all parables) strict limitations. It is designed to make only one point: that Christian doctrine postulates an ultimate unambiguous state of existence *in patria* as well as our present ambiguous existence *in via*. There is a state of having arrived as well as a state of journeying, an eternal heavenly life as well as an earthly pilgrimage. The alleged future experience of this state cannot, of course, be appealed to as evidence for theism as a present interpretation of our experience; but it does suffice to render the choice between theism and atheism a real and not a merely empty or verbal choice. And although this does not affect the logic of the situation, it should be added that the alternative interpretations are more than theoretical, for they render different practical plans and policies appropriate now.

The universe as envisaged by the theist, then, differs as a totality from the universe as envisaged by the atheist. This difference does not, however, from our present

8 *Faith and Knowledge*, pp. 150 f.

standpoint within the universe, involve a difference in the objective content of each or even any of its passing moments. The theist and the atheist do not (or need not) expect different events to occur in the successive details of the temporal process. They do not (or need not) entertain divergent expectations of the course of history viewed from within. But the theist does and the atheist does not expect that when history is completed it will be seen to have led to a particular end-state and to have fulfilled a specific purpose, namely that of creating "children of God."

Because Hick recognizes that "the idea of an eschatological verification of theism can make sense . . . only if the logically prior idea of continued personal existence after death is intelligible," he spends considerable time in his paper interpreting and defending the Christian concept of personal "resurrection" life after death as being intelligible and not self-contradictory. According to the Christian perspective discussed by Hick, "the human being is by nature mortal and subject to annihilation by death." But God, in his sovereign power, "either sometimes or always resurrects or (better) reconstitutes" the person—"not, however, as the identical physical organism that he was before death, but as a . . . 'spiritual body' embodying the dispositional characteristics and memory traces of the deceased physical organism" and inhabiting a postdeath environment that makes continuity between the *ante-mortem* and *postmortem* personality possible.

Realizing that postdeath survival *per se* does not constitute the verification of Christian theism, Hick goes on to specify the postdeath conditions that would constitute a religiously unambiguous situation that would provide the desired verification.

> [I have claimed] that this doctrine of the divine creation of bodies, composed of a material other than that of physical matter, which bodies are endowed with sufficient correspondence of characteristics with our present bodies, and sufficient continuity of memory with our present consciousness, for us to speak of the same person being raised up again to life in a new environment, is not self-contradictory. If, then, it cannot be ruled out *ab initio* as meaningless, we may go on to consider whether and how it is related to the possible verification of Christian theism.
>
> So far I have argued that a survival prediction such as is contained in the *corpus* of Christian belief is in principle subject to future verification. But this does not take the argument by any means as far as it must go if it is to succeed. For survival, simply as such, would not serve to verify theism. It would not necessarily be a state of affairs which is manifestly incompatible with the non-existence of God. It might be taken just as a surprising natural fact. The atheist, in his resurrection body, and able to remember his life on earth, might say that the universe has turned out to be more complex, and perhaps more to be approved of, than he had realized. But the mere fact of survival, with a new body in a new environment, would not demonstrate to him that there is a God. It is fully compatible with the notion of survival that the life to come be, so far as the theistic problem is concerned, essentially a continuation of the present life, and religiously no less ambiguous. And in this event, survival after bodily death would not in the least constitute a final verification of theistic faith.
>
> I shall not spend time in trying to draw a picture of a resurrection existence which would merely prolong the religious ambiguity of our present life. The important question, for our purpose, is not whether one can conceive of after-life experi-

ences which would *not* verify theism (and in point of fact one can fairly easily conceive them), but whether one can conceive of after-life experiences which *would* serve to verify theism.

I think that we can. In trying to do so I shall not appeal to the traditional doctrine, which figures especially in Catholic and mystical theology, of the Beatific Vision of God. The difficulty presented by this doctrine is not so much that of deciding whether there are grounds for believing it, as of deciding what it means. I shall not, however, elaborate this difficulty, but pass directly to the investigation of a different and, as it seems to me, more intelligible possibility. This is the possibility not of a direct vision of God, whatever that might mean, but of a *situation* which points unambiguously to the existence of a loving God. This would be a situation which, so far as its religious significance is concerned, contrasts in a certain important respect with our present situation. Our present situation is one which in some ways seems to confirm and in other ways to contradict the truth of theism. Some events around us suggest the presence of an unseen benevolent intelligence and others suggest that no such intelligence is at work. Our situation is religiously ambiguous. But in order for us to be aware of this fact we must already have some idea, however vague, of what it would be for our situation to be not ambiguous, but on the contrary wholly evidential of God. I therefore want to try to make clearer this presupposed concept of a religiously unambiguous situation.

There are, I suggest, two possible developments of our experience such that, if they occurred in conjunction with one another (whether in this life or in another life to come), they would assure us beyond rational doubt of the reality of God, as conceived in the Christian faith. These are, *first*, an experience of the fulfillment of God's purpose for ourselves, as this has been disclosed in the Christian revelation; in conjunction, *second*, with an experience of communication with God as he has revealed himself in the person of Christ.

The divine purpose for human life, as this is depicted in the New Testament documents, is the bringing of the human person, in society with his fellows, to enjoy a certain valuable quality of personal life, the content of which is given in the character of Christ—which quality of life (*i.e.*, life in relationship with God, described in the Fourth Gospel as eternal life) is said to be the proper destiny of human nature and the source of man's final self-fulfillment and happiness. The verification situation with regard to such a fulfillment is asymmetrical. On the one hand, so long as the divine purpose remains unfulfilled, we cannot know that it never will be fulfilled in the future; hence no final falsification is possible of the claim that this fulfillment will occur—unless, of course, the prediction contains a specific time clause which, in Christian teaching, it does not. But on the other hand, if and when the divine purpose *is* fulfilled in our own experience, we must be able to recognize and rejoice in that fulfillment. For the fulfillment would not be for us the promised fulfillment without our own conscious participation in it.

It is important to note that one can say this much without being cognizant in advance of the concrete form which such fulfillment will take. The before-and-after situation is analogous to that of a small child looking forward to adult life and then, having grown to adulthood, looking back upon childhood. The child possesses and can use correctly in various contexts the concept of "being grown-up," although he does not know, concretely, what it is like to be grown-up. But when he reaches adulthood he is nevertheless able to know that he has reached it; he is able to recognize the experience of living a grown-up life even though he did not know in advance just what to expect. For his understanding of adult maturity grows as he himself matures. Something similar may be supposed to happen in the case of the fulfillment of the divine purpose for human life. That fulfillment may be as far removed from our present condition as is mature adulthood from the mind of a little child; nevertheless, we possess already a comparatively vague notion of this final fulfillment, and as we move towards it our concept will itself become more adequate; and if and when we finally reach that fulfillment, the problem of recognizing it will have disappeared in the process.

The other feature that must, I suggest, be present in a state of affairs that would verify theism, is that the fulfillment of God's purpose be apprehended as to the fulfillment of God's purpose and not simply as a natural state of affairs. To this end it must be accompanied by an experience of communication with God as he has made himself known to men in Christ.

The specifically Christian clause, "as he has made himself known to men in Christ," is essential, for it provides a solution to the problem of recognition in the awareness of God. Several writers have pointed out the logical difficulty involved in any claim to have encountered God.[9] How could one know that it was *God* whom one had encountered? God is described in Christian theology in terms of various absolute qualities, such as omnipotence, omnipresence, perfect goodness, infinite love, etc., which cannot as such be observed by us, as can their finite analogues, limited power, local presence, finite goodness, and human love. One can recognize that a being whom one "encounters" has a given finite degree of power, but how does one recognize that he has *un*limited power? How does one observe that an encountered being is *omni*present? How does one perceive that his goodness and love, which one can perhaps see to exceed any human goodness and love, are actually infinite? Such qualities cannot be given in human experience. One might claim, then, to have encountered a Being whom one presumes, or trusts, or hopes to be God; but one cannot claim to have encountered a Being whom one recognized to be the infinite, almighty, eternal Creator.

This difficulty is met in Christianity by the doctrine of the Incarnation—although this was not among the considerations which led to the formulation of that doctrine. The idea of incarnation provides answers to the two related questions: "How do we know that God has certain absolute qualities which, by their very nature, transcend human experience?" and "How can there be an eschatological verification of theism which is based upon a recognition of the presence of God in his Kingdom?"

In Christianity God is known as "the God and Father of our Lord Jesus Christ."[10] God is the Being about whom Jesus taught; the Being in relation to whom Jesus lived, and into a relationship with whom he brought his disciples; the Being whose *agape* toward men was seen on earth in the life of Jesus. In short, God is the transcendent Creator who has revealed himself in Christ. Now Jesus' teaching about the Father is part of that self-disclosure, and it is from this teaching (together with that of the prophets who preceded him) that the Christian knowledge of God's transcendent being is derived. Only God himself knows his own infinite nature; and our human belief about that nature is based upon his self-revelation to men in Christ. As Karl

9 For example, H. W. Hepburn, *Christianity and Paradox*, 1958, pp. 56 f.
10 II Cor. 11:31.

Barth expresses it, "Jesus Christ is the knowability of God." Our beliefs about God's infinite being are not capable of observational verification, being beyond the scope of human experience, but they are susceptible of indirect verification by the removal of rational doubt concerning the authority of Christ. An experience of the reign of the Son in the Kingdom of the Father would confirm that authority, and therewith, indirectly, the validity of Jesus' teaching concerning the character of God in his infinite transcendent nature.

The further question as to how an eschatological experience of the Kingdom of God could be known to be such has already been answered by implication. It is God's union with man in Christ that makes possible man's recognition of the fulfillment of God's purpose for man as being indeed the fulfillment of *God's* purpose for him. The presence of Christ in his Kingdom marks this as being beyond doubt the Kingdom of the God and Father of the Lord Jesus Christ.

It is true that even the experience of the realization of the promised Kingdom of God, with Christ reigning as Lord of the New Aeon, would not constitute a logical certification of his claims nor, accordingly, of the reality of God. But this will not seem remarkable to any philosopher in the empiricist tradition, who knows that it is only a confusion to demand that a factual proposition be an analytic truth. A set of expectations based upon faith in the historic Jesus as the incarnation of God, and in his teaching as being divinely authoritative, could be so fully confirmed in *post-mortem* experience as to leave no grounds for rational doubt as to the validity of that faith.

Through the device of eschatological verification, Hick has attempted to defend certain Christian theological assertions, such as "God exists" and "God is loving," as being genuinely cognitive. Thereby he believes he has responded adequately to the challenge posed by Flew. Has he done so? What would Flew be likely to reply? The debate would, no doubt, continue.

NOTES ON SOURCES.   Flew's discussion forms the inaugural comments for a symposium titled "Theology and Falsification," in which Antony Flew, R. M. Hare, and Basil Mitchell participated. The full symposium is recorded in Antony Flew and Alasdair MacIntyre, eds., *New Essay in Philosophical Theology* (London: SCM Press, 1955). Hick's comments are from John Hick, "Theology and Verification," *Theology Today* 17 (1960).

6

On What Principle Do I Judge Things Right or Wrong?

THE QUESTION POSED

Each of us makes many moral judgments every day. We might declare an act of terrorism to be evil, a tax bill before Congress to be unjust, a parent's discipline of a child to be abusive, and so forth. Seldom, however, do we pause to inquire into the principles and presuppositions that are operative in those moral judgments. Such an inquiry cannot be avoided by those who pursue the examined life. Not to know our principles and presuppositions is to be naive. To get to know them is to achieve sophistication. When we seek such knowledge we are engaging in the branch of philosophy called "ethics."

The term *ethics* is often used to refer to codes of ethics or to relatively well-defined ways of behaving. In the philosophical contexts that follow, we will use *ethics* to mean the careful study of right and wrong human action. Ethical theory and ethics will, in this context, be synonyms. (Some philosophers use the expression *moral theory* for what we are calling ethical theory or ethics. They do this to distinguish the study of right and wrong human action from an articulated code of ethics.)

Ethical theory is usually divided into at least three parts.

A. Normative ethics tells us how we should make our ethical decisions; how we ought to live our lives. It answers the questions: What should I do? What is the good life? What should I strive for? What should I strive to become?

B. Metaethics deals with the meanings of what some philosophers might call the family of ethical terms. Metaethics then deals with words such as *good, bad, evil, right, wrong, justice, fairness, duty, obligation, ought, should, moral, immoral,* etc.

Sometimes philosophers say that metaethics is the study of the logic of these terms; that is, how they interrelate. For example, consider the following moral problem. Suppose I am walking on a country road and I see a sharp nail in the road. I might very well think that I ought to get it out of the road so that a car does not get a flat tire. But am I obligated to remove that nail? Do I violate someone's right if I do not remove it? Am I being immoral if I do not remove the nail from the road? Metaethics would focus on what the words *ought*, *right* and *immoral* mean and how they are related to each other.

C. *Moral psychology* answers the question, "What makes people act the way they do?" Having a theory of human motivation is important if one believes that a moral theory should work to change people's behavior. A moral theory based on a complete misunderstanding of people is very unlikely to work because it is unlikely that any person would want to use it. For example, a moral theory which assumed that people rarely sought or needed pleasure in any form and had a principle which demanded total abstinence from *all* pleasure would not be an inviting moral theory.

Notice that one cannot restrict oneself to normative ethics alone. That is, one cannot answer the question, "What is the good life?" unless one has some idea of what the word *good* means when it is applied to a life. And it would certainly be odd for someone with no sense of what people were like to make an effort to tell them how to live their lives.

Recently, ethics has come to emphasize the problems faced by the professions. Physicians must deal with questions concerning the termination of life, confidentiality, and truth telling. Sometimes their duties as physicians conflict with what they feel is morally appropriate. For example, some doctors feel that helping patients die is sometimes the right thing to do but also believe that they are professionally bound never to do such a thing. Lawyers are often caught in a bind between their professional obligation to help their clients and what they know to be true or feel to be fair in a moral sense. A salesperson may want to tell the truth and say, "That suit looks terrible on you" but that salesperson has obligations to the company and the other employees as well as to her family (to bring home a decent salary). Obligations to stockholders, which are both legal and moral, can conflict with what company owners feel is the moral thing to do with respect to the public. Journalists often feel a conflict between their obligation to inform the public and a particular person's right to privacy. Thus, an ethical theory that could not deal adequately with questions of applied and professional ethics would not be as acceptable as one that could.

It is important to remember that some basic value choices are already made for us by legal and political systems. Our criminal justice system makes it difficult to convict a criminal because it is assumed that it is morally better for a guilty person to go free than for an innocent person to be convicted. Our political and economic system differs from some others by placing relatively greater value on individualism. Totally free enterprise is restrained in regard to child labor and unsafe working conditions, both of which are felt to be morally unacceptable.

This chapter will stress normative ethics, but we will offer three examples of metaethics (A. J. Ayer, C. L. Stevenson, and R. M. Hare).

Given our daily moral judgments and our commitment to the examined life, we must ask such questions as "Upon what principle do we discriminate between right and wrong?" One way for us to launch into this inquiry would be to compile a list of acts or ways of acting that we would judge to be wrong. Then we could ask, "What do these acts or ways of acting have in common by virtue of which we judge them to be wrong?" Is the common ingredient the fact that they are contrary to the will of God? the fact that they are contrary to social custom or convention? the fact that they are contrary to nature, "unnatural"? the fact that they militate against human happiness? Whatever that common ingredient is, let us call it "X." We could then say, "An act is wrong if it is "X" or an "X." In due course, when we would be able to spell out what "X" stands for, we would have formulated the principle that is operative in our moral judgments. We use such a principle when we authorize moral judgments on conduct, on character, on institutions, on laws, on customs. We say, of a given act, that it is right or wrong; of a type of character, that it is the right type or wrong type; of an institution—for example, private property—that it is right or wrong; of a law, say, capital punishment, that it is right or wrong; of a custom, that it is right or wrong. Our present problem is not which particular act or character or institution or law or custom is right or wrong. Our problem is the more general one: On what principle do we judge these things right or wrong?

The authors whose writings are sampled in this chapter present a rich variety of responses to that question. From the eighteenth century we have two moral philosophers who take our questions seriously and provide two very different answers. William Paley argues that *right* means "according to the will of God." Immanuel Kant claims that *right* means "according to reason," or "what reason requires."

From the nineteenth century we also have two very different philosophical viewpoints. John Stuart Mill, a lucid interpreter of Jeremy Bentham's eighteenth-century utilitarianism, contends that *right* means "maximizing the happiness of humankind," or "producing the greatest amount of happiness possible under the circumstances." In contrast to Paley, Kant, and Mill, Friedrich Nietzsche adopts a remarkably different posture in responding to the question we are examining (On what principle do I judge things right or wrong?). That question assumes that the answer to be given is an answer that is appropriate for all human beings. The "I" in the question is not made culturally specific. The "I" stands for each and every person. Accordingly, when Paley, Kant, and Mill provide us with their answers, they are articulating principles that they believe are appropriate for all human beings. Paley, for example, does not say that he is describing what is right *for eighteenth-century Britons* only. Nor does Kant say that he is defining right *for eighteen-century Prussians* only. And Mill does not propose to be formulating an ethic that is appropriate only *for nineteenth-century Londoners*. All of these philosophers assume they are articulating a universal moral norm that is applicable to all persons. Nietzsche, however, from the posture of a cultural historian, perceives the vast diversity in moral beliefs and practices throughout the ages and embraces a relativistic position according to which there is no single universal moral viewpoint common to humankind. Instead there are various moralities that serve the interests of specific groups. Accordingly, Nietzsche would reject the proposals of Paley, Kant, and Mill as being "human, all too human," as being fashioned to promote a specific cultural group's interests. The morality that Nietzsche himself finds most attractive is the one that declares that *right* means "productive of or giving expression to the superman."

From the twentieth century we have included the metaethics of A. J. Ayer (including a critique of his view by Brand Blanshard), as well as two refinements of Ayer's position: one by C. L. Stevenson, the other by R. M. Hare.

Ayer demonstrates affinities with Nietzsche by rejecting the very idea of creating an ethical theory. This clearly sets him apart from Paley, Kant, and Bentham. Blanshard sees through to the ethical subjectivism inherent in Ayer's position and argues that ethical subjectivism is not a position worth holding.

What is ethical subjectivism? It can take a number of forms. The easiest way to explain it is to see it as metaethics. Consider the judgment made by stating "Learning how to do CPR is good." According to ethical subjectivism, "Learing how to do CPR is good" does not refer to, nor is it about, CPR. Rather, it is really a statement about the feelings, emotions, and attitudes of the person who made the statement. (In Ayer's view, it is not even a statement—it *is* the emotion or feeling or attitude.) The judgment might grow out of one's culture, but at bottom, it is only about feelings, emotions or attitudes. Subjectivism does not imply that ethical judgments vary from person to person (that is a different sense of "subjectivism"), but that ethical judgments are subjective because they grow out of feelings and emotions that may derive from a cultural or biological commonality. Indeed, according to Stevenson, ethical judgments are both subjective and objective because it is possible, Stevenson claims, to find out what the feelings, emotions, and attitudes of people are. R. M. Hare continues this balancing of the subjective and objective aspects of moral judgments.

We conclude with a return to normative ethics. Bernard Gert sees morality as a set of rather easily deduced rules, and Dorothy Emmet is a contemporary proponent of virtue theory, a view which had its first systematic expression in the thought of Aristotle.

WILLIAM PALEY

THE WILL OF GOD

One important question we can direct at any human act is this: "Was it right or wrong?" That is, did the agent do as he ought to have done, or as he ought not to have done? Implicit in any answer to this question is a moral principle, a criterion in terms of which we distinguish between right and wrong. As long as humans entertain a lively belief in the existence of God and ascribe to Him an interest in human affairs, many are likely to base their moral judgments upon what they consider to be His will. They are going to say that *right* means "according to the will of God," and *wrong* means "contrary to the will of God." William Paley, a popular moralist in the eighteenth century, was a man of precisely this turn of mind.

If one is going to claim that God's will determines what is good, then one must be prepared to answer at least three crucial questions. First, what grounds do you have for belief in the existence of God? Second, how do you come to know the will of this God in whose existence you believe? Third, what precisely is that will? Responses to the first question were explored by a number of philosophers in Chapter 5. Siding with those who found the teleological or design argument convincing, Paley offered a classic exposition of this proof in which he cited a multitude of apparently designed objects in nature that pointed beyond themselves to their origin in divine purpose. The second and third questions are addressed by Paley in this chapter.

Paley worked out his position concerning the knowledge of God's will in the context of a struggle with deism. The issue at stake was whether God's will was manifested in scripture and/or nature. The deists, impressed by the achievements and development of modern science as it exposed the orderly behavior of natural phenomena, looked to nature as the "sourcebook" for knowledge of the will of God. For them, God created the universe, set it in motion, and then withdrew from it to allow it to function on its own as a complex clockwork, undisturbed by the kind of divine intervention described by the authors of scripture. Clearly such a view called into question the legitimacy of the biblical revelation and the whole religious establishment founded upon it. Paley and other eighteenth-century apologists for the Christian faith took on the deist challenge and argued, among other things, that God's will is made known in two books: the Book of Nature and the Book of Scripture.

BIOGRAPHICAL NOTE. William Paley was born in England in 1743 and died in 1805 at the age of sixty-two. His father was headmaster of the school of Giggleswick in Yorkshire. His early education was obtained under the paternal eye. At the age of fifteen, young Paley went to Cambridge University. That his father had great expectations may be gathered from a remark he made to a friend: "My son is now gone to college. He'll turn out a great man. Very great, indeed. I am certain of it. He has by far the clearest head I ever met in my life." Paley spent four years at Cambridge, obtaining his B.A. in 1762. The following anecdote suggests that he was a normal young man during these years:

> I spent the first two years of my undergraduate life happily, but unprofitably. I was constantly in society, where we were not immoral, but idle and rather expensive. At the commencement of my third year, however, after having left the usual party at a rather late hour in the evening, I was awakened at five in the morning by one of my companions, who stood at my bedside. He said: "Paley, I have been thinking what a fool you are. I could achieve nothing worth while, even were I to try, and anyway I can afford the idle life I lead. You could achieve anything, if you were to try, and you cannot afford to waste your time. I have had no sleep during the whole night on

account of these reflections, and am now come solemnly to inform you that if you persist in your indolence, I must renounce your society." I was so struck with the visit and the visitor that I laid in bed a great part of the day, and formed my plan. I ordered my bedmaker to prepare my fire every evening, in order that it might be lighted by myself the next morning. I rose at five o'clock, read during the whole of the day, except such hours as chapel and lectures required, allotting to each portion of time its peculiar branch of study; and, just before the closing of the gates (9:00 P.M.) I went to a neighboring coffeehouse, where I constantly regaled upon a mutton chop and a dose of milk punch.

After graduating, Paley rose slowly but steadily in the ecclesiastical world. In 1785, he published his *Principles of Moral and Political Philosophy*, from which the following selections have been taken. The book was an immediate success, being adopted as a textbook at Cambridge and passing through fifteen editions. Such was the clarity and cogency of his book that one of his contemporaries remarked: "It may be said to be the only work on moral philosophy fitted to be understood by every class of readers." Other important writings followed. In 1792, his *Reasons for Contentment* appeared in which he warned against revolutionary doctrines. In 1794, his *Evidences of Christianity* firmly established him as one of the premier defenders of the church and state. His last major work, *Natural Theology*, published in 1802, sought to derive knowledge of the existence and nature of God from a scrutiny of nature. After a lengthy illness, Paley died in 1805.

THE ARGUMENT OF THE PASSAGES. Paley's formulation of the fundamental principle of morality is simple and clear: Right is that which agrees with the will of God; wrong is that which does not. Having stated this controlling idea, he sets himself to elaborate it. He provides first a definition of *virtue*, consistent with his basic propositions; he moves on, then, to examine the meaning of moral obligation and the distinction between prudence and duty. These matters settled, he turns to the question: if *right* means "according to the will of God," how are we to tell what is and is not the will of God? His answer here is two-fold: scriptural revelation and the "light of nature." The sense in which God's will may be gathered from Scripture is then explained. But what of the light of nature; what, that is, about the morality of acts where we do not have God's express declaration? Here Paley meets a real problem, and knowing, as he did, that many occasions arise with respect to which Scripture is silent, he could not treat this matter lightly. To solve his problem he assumed that human happiness is God's primary concern. Realizing, as he says, that "this assumption is the foundation of the whole system," he sets himself to "explain the reasons upon which it rests." The explanation in question occupies the remainder of the passages.

Paley begins with a characterization of ethics and proceeds to an explication of the meaning of *right*.

[Ethics is] that science which teaches men their duty and the reasons of it. The use of such a study depends upon this, that without it, the rules of life by which men are ordinarily governed, oftentimes mislead them, through a defect either in the rule or in the application. . . .

Right . . . signifies consistency with the will of God.

Right is a quality of persons or actions.

Of persons; as when we say, such a one has a "right" to this estate; parents have a "right" to reverence from their children. . . .

Of actions; as in such expressions as the following: it is "right" to punish murder with death; his behaviour on that occasion was "right." . . .

In this latter set of expressions, you may substitute the definition of right above given for the term itself, v.g., it is "consistent with the will of God" to punish murder with death—his behaviour on that occasion was "consistent with the will of God." . . .

In the former act, you must vary the phrase a little, when you introduce the definition instead of the term. Such a one has a "right" to this estate, that is, it is "consistent with the will of God" that such a one should have it . . . it is "consistent with the will of God" that children should reverence their parents. . . .

Ethics, says Paley, teaches us what our duty is and the reasons that support it. He has already indicated that our duty is to do what is right, to act in such a way that is consistent with the will of God. Now he presents the reasons that motivate us to do our duty, and at the same time, provides us with definitions of virtue, moral obligation, prudence, and duty.

Virtue is the doing good to mankind, in obedience to the will of God, and for the sake of everlasting happiness. . . .

The four cardinal virtues are prudence, fortitude, temperance, and justice.

But the division of virtue, to which we are now-a-days most accustomed, is into duties; towards God . . . towards other men . . .towards ourselves. . . .

More of these distinctions have been proposed, which it is not worth while to set down. . . .

Why am I obliged to keep my word? . . .

A man is said to be obliged, when he is urged by a violent motive resulting from the command of another.

First, the motive must be violent. If a person, who has done me some little service . . . ask me upon some occasion for my vote, I may possibly give it him, from a motive of gratitude or expectation; but I should hardly say that I was *obliged* to give it him, because the inducement does not rise high enough. Whereas, if a father or a master, or any great benefactor, or one on whom my fortune depends, require my vote, I give it him of course; and my answer to all who ask me why I voted so and so, is, that my father or my master *obliged* me. . . .

Secondly, it must result from the command of another. Offer a man a gratuity for doing anything . . . he is not obliged by your offer to do it; nor would he say he is; though he may be induced, persuaded, prevailed upon, tempted. If a magistrate or the man's immediate superior command it, he considers himself as *obliged* to comply. . . .

Let it be remembered that to be obliged is to be urged by a violent motive, resulting from the command of another.

And then let it be asked, "Why am I obliged to keep my word?" and the answer will be, "because I am urged to do so by a violent motive" (namely, the expectation of being after this life rewarded, if I do, or punished for it, if I do not) "resulting from the command of another" (namely, of God).

This solution goes to the bottom of the subject, as no farther question can reasonably be asked.

Therefore, private happiness is our motive, and the will of God our rule.

There is always understood to be a difference between an act of *prudence* and an act of *duty*. Thus, if I distrusted a man who owed me a sum of money, I should reckon it an act of prudence to get another person bound with him; but I should hardly call it an act of duty. On the other hand, it would be thought a very unusual and a loose kind of language to say that, as I had made such a promise, it was prudent to perform it; or that as my friend, when he went abroad, placed a box of jewels in my hands, it would be prudent in me to preserve it for him till he returned.

Now, in what, you will ask, does the difference consist? ... The difference, and the only difference, is this, that, in the one case, we consider what we shall gain or lose in the present world; in the other case, we consider also what we shall gain or lose in the world to come. [Prudence has regard to the former; duty, to the latter.] Those who would establish a system of morality, independent of a future state, must look out for some different idea of moral obligation.

To us there are two great questions: Will there be, after this life, any distribution of rewards and punishments at all? If there be, what actions will be rewarded and what actions will be punished?

The first question comprises the credibility of the Christian religion, together with the presumptive proofs of a future retribution from the light of nature. The second question composes the province of morality. Both questions are too much for one work. The affirmative therefore of the first, although we confess that it is the foundation upon which the whole fabric rests, must in this treatise be taken for granted.

According to Paley, then, we ought to act in accordance with the will of God because our personal happiness in the life beyond death is at stake. Clearly God has the power to exercise sanctions (rewards and punishments) that will induce us to follow his will. The next question that arises is the precise content of God's will.

As the will of God is our rule, to inquire what is our duty, or what we are obliged to do, in any instance, is, in effect, to inquire what is the will of God in that instance? which consequently becomes the whole business of morality.

Now, there are two methods of coming at the will of God on any point: I. By his express declarations, when they are to be had, and which must be sought for in Scripture. II. By what we can discover of his designs and dispositions from his works, or, as we usually call it, the light of nature.

And here we may observe the absurdity of separating natural and revealed religion from each other. The object of both is the same—to discover the will of God—and, provided we do but discover it, it matters nothing by what means.

An ambassador judging by what he knows of his sovereign's disposition, and arguing from what he has observed of his conduct, or is acquainted with his designs, may take his measures in many cases with safety; and would have him act on most occasions that arise; but if we have his commission and instructions in his pocket, it would be strange not to look into them. He will naturally conduct himself by both rules: when his instructions are clear and positive, there is an end of all farther deliberation (unless indeed he suspects their authenticity): where his instructions are silent or dubious, he will endeavor to supply or explain them, by what he has been able to collect from other quarters of his master's general inclination or intentions. ...

Humankind can know the will of God through his *word* recorded in the scriptures and through his *works* performed in nature. The scriptures provide general rules concerning piety, justice, benevolence, and purity, which are occasionally illustrated. For those matters on which the scriptures are silent we can take advantage of the light of nature: We can derive some very important insight concerning God's will for his creation by scrutinizing the nature of that creation. Paley proceeds to tell us what the light of nature reveals.

The method of coming at the will of God concerning any action, by the light of nature, is to inquire into the tendency of the action to promote or diminish the general happiness. This rule proceeds upon the presumption that God Almighty wills and wishes the happiness of his creatures, and consequently, that those actions which promote that will and wish, must be agreeable to him; and the contrary.

As this presumption is the foundation of our whole system, it becomes necessary to explain the reasons upon which it rests.

When God created the human species, either he wished their happiness or he wished their misery or he was indifferent and unconcerned about both.

If he wished our misery, he might have made sure of his purpose, by forming our senses to be as many sores and pains to us as they are now instruments of gratification and enjoyment. . . . He might have made, for example, everything we tasted bitter; everything we saw loathsome; everything we touched a sting; every smell a stench; and every sound a discord.

If he had been indifferent about our happiness or misery, we must impute to our good fortune . . . both the capacity of our senses to receive pleasure, and the supply of external objects fitted to excite it.

But either of these, and still more both of them, being too much to be attributed to accident, nothing remains but the first supposition, that God, when he created the human species, wished their happiness; and made for them the provision which he has made, with that view, and for that purpose.

The same argument may be proposed in different terms, thus: . . . The world abounds with contrivances; and all the contrivances which we are acquainted with are directed to beneficial purposes. Evil no doubt exists; but is never, that we can perceive, the object of contrivance. Teeth are contrived to eat, not to ache; their aching now and then is incidental to the contrivance, perhaps inseparable from it; or even, if you will, let it be called a defect in the contrivance; but it is not the object of it. This is a distinction which well deserves to be attended to. In describing implements of husbandry, you would hardly say of a sickle, that it is made to cut the reaper's fingers, though from the construction of the instrument, and the manner of using it, this mischief often happens. But if you had occasion to describe instruments of torture or execution, this engine, you would say, is to extend the sinews; this to dislocate the joints; this to break the bones; this to scorch the soles of the feet. Here pain and misery are the very objects of the contrivance. Now nothing of this sort is to be found in the works of nature. We never discover a train of contrivance to bring about an evil purpose. No anatomist ever discovered a system of organization calculated to produce pain and disease; or, in explaining the parts of the human body, ever said, "this is to irritate; this is to inflame; this duct is to convey the gravel to the kidneys; this gland to secrete the humour which forms gout; if by the chance he come at a part of which he knows not the use, the most he can say is that it is useless; no one ever suspects that it is put there to incommode, to annoy, or torment. Since then God hath called forth his consummate wisdom to contrive and provide for our happiness, and the world appears to have been constituted with this design at first, so long as this constitution is upholden by him, we must in reason suppose the same design to continue. . . .

We conclude, therefore, that God wills and wishes the happiness of his creatures. And this conclusion being once established, we are at liberty to go on with the rule built upon it, namely, that the method of coming at the will of God concerning any action, by the light of nature, is to inquire into the tendency of what action to promote or diminish the general happiness.

Stated briefly, what Paley says comes to this: "*Right* means according to God's will. An act is right if it is according to the will of God. This is the principle of morality. God's will is to be found in the Scriptures, or discovered by the light of nature. The light of nature tells us that God intends above all to produce and promote human happiness. Where, therefore, the Scriptures are silent, we determine the rightness of an act by the fact that it produces more happiness than any other act possible at the time," This is both clear and confused. It raises more questions than it settles. For example, does Paley mean that an act is right because it agrees with God's will, or that it agrees with God's will because it is right? These two are not the same. Also, what is the relation between a person's will and God's will? Does Paley believe that God's will causes and governs all things? If so, could a human act ever be contrary to God's will? If it could not, then it would follow that no act is ever wrong. Does Paley want *that*?

Then, of course, there is the problem connected with detecting God's will in the Scriptures. Why the Scriptures? Why not in Plato's dialogues? Or in the Mohammedan *Koran*? In which parts of the Scriptures? In these parts which enjoin an eye for an eye? Or, in those parts which enjoin the golden rule? If in both, what about clashes? If in one, how choose which? Passing to the second half of his argument, has he proved, at all conclusively, that God's will is directed to creating and promoting human happiness? This hypothesis may account for some of the facts. But it does not account for all of them. (See Hume and Schopenhauer on the misery of the human estate.) Going a step further, and admitting his argument, are we justified in arguing that an act is right if it produces more happiness than any other act possible under the circumstances? Is this not to formulate a moral principle that swings clear of the first part of Paley's argument and could stand on its own feet without any aid from Scripture? If so, what about cases where the "appeal to Scripture" and "the appeal to happiness" appear to clash? Finally is it or is it not the case that we are more sure of what is right and wrong than we are of God's very existence? If so, would it not be wiser to begin with what we are more sure of, than to begin with what we are less sure of? These, and other problems that suggest themselves, were engaging the attention of Immanuel Kant during the years in which Paley was writing his *Principles of Moral and Political Philosophy*, published in 1785. Kant had published his *Critique of Pure Reason* in 1781, and was meanwhile engaged on a second *Critique*, directed this time not at the problem of knowledge but at the problem of morality. To a consideration of Kant's views, let us turn our attention.

NOTE ON SOURCES. The materials in this section are quoted from William Paley, *The Principles of Moral and Political Philosophy*. That work is divided into six books. The materials in this section are from Books I and II. Each book is divided into brief chapters. The titles of the chapters in Books I and II will indicate the points at which material has been used for this section.

 IMMANUEL KANT

THE CATEGORICAL IMPERATIVE

FROM PALEY TO KANT. At the same time Paley, in England, was engaged in arguing that morality has its roots in theology, Immanuel Kant, in Prussia, was engaged in showing that such is not the case. For Kant, theology can be a motive for ethics, but it cannot provide the fundamental principle that discriminates right from wrong.

Kant lived in the Age of Reason, the age of Hume and Rousseau and Voltaire and the revolutions in America and France. He was a firm believer in the rationality of humankind. He sought to develop the notion of a rational morality; that is, a morality that resembles rational knowledge by being valid for all persons at all times and in all cases. Just as he could speak of rational science, so he would speak of rational morality. Just as, by *rational science* he would mean knowledge valid and binding for all rational minds, so by *rational morality* he would mean morality valid and binding for all rational minds. To the first kind of rationality he devoted his *Critique of Pure Reason*; to the second, his *Critique of Practical Reason*.

BIOGRAPHICAL NOTE. Kant was born in 1724 in Königsberg, East Prussia, and died there in 1804 at the age of seventy-nine. He studied at the University of Königsberg where he eventually became a Privatdozent, teaching a wide variety of subjects including physics, mathematics, physical geography and philosophy. In 1770 he was appointed to the chair of logic and metaphysics. His personal life was quite uneventful. He scarcely travelled 40 miles beyond his native town of Königsberg, but compensated for this lack of exposure to the world through wide reading. On one occasion he did gain some political notoriety when in 1794, after the publication of his *Religion Within the Limits of Reason Alone*, the Prussian king charged him with misrepresenting and depreciating orthodox Christianity. Under threat of penalties, Kant promised to refrain from further public statements on religion, a vow he kept until the death of the king. Kant's own religious views included beliefs in the immortality of the soul and in the existence of God. In matters of religious experience he concentrated on moral piety rather than prayer, public worship, and mystical communion with the divine. Kant did not publish his *magnum opus*, the *Critique of Pure Reason*, until 1781, when he was fifty-seven years old. Then he entered two decades of unusually productive activity, publishing among other works, *Prolegomena to any Future Metaphysics* (1783), *Fundamental Principles of the Metaphysics of Morals* (1785), *Critique of Practical Reason* (1788), *Critique of Judgment* (1790), *Metaphysics of Morals* (1797). His lifelong regard for Newtonian physics and Rousseauistic piety is often summed up in his acknowledged, profound reverence for "the starry heavens above and the moral law within." (For additional biographical information on Kant, refer to Chapter 10, Section 2.)

THE ARGUMENT OF THE PASSAGES. Kant's handling of the problem of moral principle follows from his conception of what morality is. Without a firm grip on this, one is likely to miss the point of his analysis. For that reason, it is necessary to emphasize his starting point. He begins by assuming that morality, whatever it may be in detail, is something universally binding on all rational minds, comparable, in this respect, to science. Thus, if it is true that two and two make four, then it is binding on all rational creatures to accept this proposition. If this is a truth, it is true for everyone, not merely true for those who care to believe it. If it is true, it is true necessarily and always. It is true, in and of itself, without any reference to why it is true, without any reference to who does nor does not believe it, without any reference to consequences that follow from its being true or from its being believed. It is, to use a favorite phrase of Kant's, true categorically, without any strings or qualifications. To repeat, it is not true because God commands it, nor because it is according to nature, nor because it pays in the long run to believe it, nor because all or most people agree to it, nor for any other reason. It is simply true because it is true. Moreover, it is true of all cases of two's and two's. There are no possible exceptions. It is not something that holds for one period of time and not for another, for one pair of two's and not for another, for one stage of civilization and not for another. In this universality, necessity, objectivity, Kant finds the differential mark of rational knowledge. He has his own word for it. It is, he says, true *a priori*.

This notion of *a priori* he carries over into the field of morality. If there is such a thing as rational science, it is *a priori*. If there is such a thing as rational morality, it is *a priori*. Moreover, just as in the case of *a priori* knowledge he did not undertake to prove that there is such a thing, but assumed its existence as a fact, so in the case of morality he does not undertake to show that there is such a thing, but assumes its existence as a fact. His argument is after this manner: If you admit that there is any rational knowledge, then you must admit that it is *a priori* in character, and if you admit that there is any rational morality, you must admit that it is *a priori* in character. If you admit that there is any rational knowledge, you must recognize that it is binding on all rational beings; so, by analogy, if you admit that there is any rational morality, you must recognize that it is binding on all rational beings. He is content to accept both rational knowledge and rational morality as facts to be recognized, not as hypotheses to be proved.

Once the notion of a rational morality is admitted, Kant is in a position to formulate his problem. It is this: What must be its principle? It will be noticed that he is not seeking to justify morality, any more than one would seek to justify arithmetic; not seeking to explain why right is right and wrong is wrong, any more than one would seek to explain why true is true, or false is false. He is merely saying: The facts of morality are categorical facts, not dependent for their moral quality upon anything beyond themselves. Such being the case, we ask again, what principle must run through all the cases of morality, and be absent from all the cases of immorality?

His answer is simple: an act is moral if and only if the principle that it embodies is capable of universalization without self-contradiction. This notion once stated, Kant proceeds to illustrate his meaning by some examples. His next step is to approach this same notion of categorical rightness from two other angles, namely duty and good will. When these matters have been settled, he turns to consider the problem of human free will. As a moralist, his fundamental problem is, "What ought I to do?" But if, as would appear from the "scientific" view of the world, everything happens "of necessity," what sense is there to claiming that some things "ought" or "ought not" to be done? Here Kant is at once clarifying and baffling. Clarifying because he has the insight and tenacity to hold on to the "ought" as being every bit as much reality as the "is," baffling because he concludes by admitting his inability to solve the paradox involved in their joint acceptance. His treatment of this question would require too much space to be summarized here. From freedom he passes on to God and immortality. It will be necessary to state a few of his claims in the form of a condensed summary. His own language is too involved to permit direct quotation. Wherever possible, however, his own words will be introduced.

Morality, the rightness and wrongness of actions, is categorical (not dependent upon anything) and *a priori* (valid for all persons and all times and all cases). In this it resembles rational knowledge. To quote: "The morality of an action is quite a peculiar thing. When we are considering the goodness of an action, we are concerned with what constitutes the goodness in and of itself."

If morality is of this categorical and *a priori* nature, then we can rule out several misleading attempts to formulate its principle. For example, the morality of an act is said, by some, to reside in the "feeling" that one has about the act. But this could not be for two reasons: (1) If morality is a matter of someone's feelings, then it is not categorical: that is, an act would depend, for its morality, upon the fact (external to the act itself) that it was or was not felt about in some way or other by some person or other. (2) If morality is a matter of feeling, then it is not anything universally binding and valid for all persons; that is, the same act could be both right and wrong provided merely that two persons had opposite feelings about it. But this is to rob morality of its categorical nature, to give as the defining characteristic of morality a quality in virtue of which it would fail to be categorical and *a priori*.

Much the same line of reasoning is adduced by Kant against those who seek to locate the rightness of an act in its agreement with God's will. He says:

> There are those who argue that we must first have God and then morality—a very convenient principle. But ethics and theology are neither of them a principle of the other. We are not discussing, here, the fact that theology is a motive for ethics—which it is—but we are asking whether the principle of ethical discrimination is theological—and it cannot be that.
>
> Were it so, then before a nation could have any conception of duties it would first have to know God. Nations which had no right conception of God would have no duties, and this is not the case. Nations had a right idea of their duties, e.g., were aware that lies were detestable, without having the proper notion of God. Duties must therefore be derived from some other source.

If we do as God commanded, because He has commanded, and because He is so mighty that He can force us to, or punish us if we do not, we act under orders from fear and fright, not appreciating the propriety of our actions and knowing why we should do as God has commanded. Might cannot constitute a *vis obligandi*. Threats do not impose a (moral) obligation; they extort. Such conduct does not make the heart better.

Moral laws can be right without any commander, promulgator, obligator. How do we know the divine will? None of us feels it in his heart. We cannot know the moral law from any revelation, for if we did so, then those who had no revelation would be wholly ignorant of it.

We imagine God as possessing the most holy and most perfect will. But what then is the most perfect will? The moral law shows us what it is. We say the divine will accords with the moral law and is, therefore, holiest and most perfect. Thus we recognize the perfection of the divine will from the moral law. God wills all that is morally good and proper and His will is, therefore, holy and perfect. But what is it that is morally good? Ethics supplies the answer to this question.

These strictures may be summarized. To locate the rightness of an act in its agreement with God's will is to deny its categorical nature; i.e., to make it depend, for its rightness, upon something other than or outside of itself. It is, too, to render morality an impossibility for all who do not know what God's will is, or who have a wrong notion of that will, or (it may be) deny His existence. There is, Kant would say, such a thing as morality apart from God's existence or our knowledge of the same. Finally, the view fails to take into account that when we say, "God is good," we are making goodness prior to and independent of God. He is good because His will or His action corresponds to the good; not vice versa.

There remains for consideration what Kant calls the *pragmatic* view of morality. The pragmatic view of morality is that an act is right because of the nature of its consequences; not right in itself, but because of the results that do or do not follow from it. Kant does not need to concern himself with the question of the nature of the results. He has two objections to doing so: (1) To locate the rightness of an act in the nature of its consequences is to deny the categorical nature of morality. It is to make its morality depend upon something other than the act. (2) To find the morality of an act in its consequences is to deprive morality of its *a priori* nature, because we can never know the consequences of an act until after the act is done, and even then never know them completely. This would reduce morality to a matter of probability; make it, as Kant says, *a posteriori*, instead of *a priori*. At this point, we can get closer to Kant's own words.

Having examined what the principle of morality is not, we must now examine what it is.

What is the one principle of morality, the criterion by which to judge everything and in which lies the distinction between moral goodness and all other goodness? What is the principle upon which we establish morality, and through which we are able to discriminate between what is moral and what immoral?

In this connection we must first notice that there are two points to be considered: the principle upon which we discriminate, and the mainspring or motive of performance. We must distinguish between the measuring rod and the mainspring. The measuring rod is the principle of discriminating; the mainspring is the motive of the performance of our obligation. If we ask, "What is morally good and what is not?" it is the principle or discrimination that is in question; but if we ask, "What is it that leads me to be moral?" it is the motive that is in question. We must guard against confusing the principle of morality with the motive to morality. The first is the norm. The second is the incentive.

The essence of morality is that our actions are motivated by a general rule. If we make it the foundation of our conduct that our actions shall be consistent with a universal rule, valid at all times and for every-one, then our actions exemplify the principle of morality.

In all moral judgments the idea which we frame is this: What is the character of the action taken by itself? If the principle of the action can, without self-contradiction, be universalized, it is moral; if it cannot be so universalized without contradicting itself, it is immoral. That action is immoral whose principle cancels and destroys itself when it is made a universal rule.

From this general statement of the nature of rightness Kant turns to some concrete illustrations. He considers the case of lying and suicide. These, being instances of wrongness, illustrate his notion of rightness only indirectly.

May I, when in distress, make a promise with the intention not to keep it? Considerations of prudence aside, would such an act be moral? The shortest way to answer this question is to ask, "Would I be content that the principle (getting out of difficulties by making false promises) should hold good as a universal law, for myself and all others?"

If I ask, "Can the principle of making deceitful promises to get out of difficulties be universalized?" I realize that it cannot. For with such a law there would be no promises at all. With such a principle made universal, it would be in vain to allege my intentions in regard to future actions. As soon as it were made a universal law, the principle would necessarily destroy itself, necessarily defeat its own end.

A man finds himself forced to borrow money. He knows that he will not be able to repay it, but he sees also that nothing will be lent to him unless he promises to repay it. Would it be right to promise? The principle of his action would be: When in need, borrow and promise to repay knowing that I cannot do so. Could this principle become a universal law? I see at once that it could not. As a universal law, it would contradict itself. For if this principle were a universal law, such promises would become impossible. For no one would consider such promises as binding, and all would ridicule them as vain pretenses.

A man reduced to despair by a series of misfortunes feels wearied of life. Would it be right to take his own life? Could the principle of his action become a universal law of nature? The principle would be: To shorten life when its longer duration is likely to bring more evil than satisfaction. Could this principle become a universal law of nature? Clearly not. A system of nature in which it was a law to destroy life by means of the very feeling whose special office it is to impel to the improvement of life would contradict itself, and therefore could not exist as a system of nature. Hence that principle could not possibly exist as a universal law of nature. Hence it would be wholly inconsistent with the supreme principle of all duty.

If we attend to ourselves on occasion of any transgression of duty, we shall find that we do not will that the principle of our action should become a universal law. On the contrary, we will that the opposite should remain a universal law, only we assume the liberty of making an exception in our own favor—just for this time only, it may be. This cannot be justified to our own impartial judgment, and it provides that we do recognize the validity of the moral principle I have formulated, even while we allow ourselves a few exceptions which we think important and forced upon us.

Thus far Kant has been developing the notion of a rational morality as something categorical and *a priori*. He has used this conception of morality to eliminate certain other theories that are incompatible with it, that is, the theories that morality is a matter of feeling or emotion, that morality is a matter of obeying the will of God, and that morality is a matter of achieving certain consequences. He has disentangled what he takes to be the underlying principle of morality so conceived and advanced a few illustrations of his thesis. He returns again and again throughout his ethical writings to these basic claims.

One example of such a reworking is contained in his distinction between hypothetical and categorical imperatives. The statement of this is given below. But a word first on Kant's use of these terms. The term *imperative*, used as a noun, means "a command." Kant inclines to use it in this sense. We shall come closer to his real meaning if we construe it by the word *ought*. We do, as a matter of everyday usage, employ the term *ought* in precisely the sense Kant would appear to have in mind. We say, for example, "If you wish to be there on time, you *ought* to leave early." Here the force of the *ought* is hypothetical; that is, it depends on whether you do or do not wish to get there on time. But there are occasions, Kant would claim, when we do not so use the term; when, for instance, we are pointing out what we take to be a duty. Thus, "you *ought* to be honest," "you *ought* to respect the rights of others." Here, we might feel, the *ought* is not dependent upon any *if*. It is not a hypothetical *ought*. It is, Kant would say, a categorical *ought*. The same idea could also be expressed in the distinction between a hypothetical obligation and a categorical obligation. Kant says:

> All imperatives command either hypothetically or categorically. The former represent the practical necessity of a possible action as means to something else that is willed or might be willed. The latter would be that which represented an action as obligatory of itself without reference to some other end.
>
> If an action is good only as a means to something else, then the imperative which commands it is hypothetical only; but if it is conceived to be good in itself, that is, without reference to any further end, the imperative which commands it is categorical.
>
> The hypothetical imperative only says that the action is good for some purpose, actual or possible. The categorical imperative declares an action to be binding in itself, without reference to any purpose or end beyond itself.
>
> All sciences have a practical part, consisting of problems connected with ends or purposes possible for us, and of imperatives directing how these may be attained. Here there is no question whether the end is good or rational, but only what one must do in order to attain it. The precepts for the physician to make his patient healthy and for a prisoner to insure his victim's death are of equal value in this respect, namely that each serves to effect its purpose.

There is one imperative which commands certain conduct immediately, without having as its condition any other purpose to be attained by it. This imperative is categorical. It concerns not the matter of the action, not its intended result, but its form and principle. This imperative may be called the imperative of morality.

There is but one categorical imperative, namely, "Act only on that principle which thou canst will should become a universal law."

This imperative of duty may be expressed, by analogy with natural laws, as follows: "Act as if the principle of any action were to become by thy will a universal law of nature."

If there is a supreme practical principle or categorical imperative it must be one which constitutes an objective principle, and can therefore serve as a universal practical law. From this, as a supreme practical law, all laws of the will must be capable of being deduced. Accordingly the categorical imperative may be stated in the third way: "So act as to treat humanity, whether in thine own person or in the person of another, as an end withal, never as a means only."

If all the imperatives of duty can be deduced from this one imperative, from it as their principle, then, although it should remain undecided whether what is called *duty* is not merely a vain notion, yet at least we shall be able to show what we understand by it; be able, that is, to show what the notion means.

To act out of respect for this principle constitutes duty. To this every other motive must give place, because it is the condition of a will being good in itself, good absolutely, good without qualification; and the worth of such a will is above everything.

The direct opposite of acting on the principle of morality is acting on the principle of private happiness. This would ruin morality altogether, were not the voice of reason so clear, so irrepressible, so distinctly audible even to the commonest men. That action should be based on the principle of private happiness can only be maintained by such as are bold enough to shut their ears against that heavenly voice in order to support a theory that costs no trouble.

Two things fill the mind with ever new and increasing admiration and awe, the oftener and more steadily we reflect on them: the starry heavens above and the moral law within. I have not to search for them and conjecture them as though they were veiled in darkness or in a region transcending my horizon. I see them before me and connect them directly with the consciousness of my existence.

Duty! Thou sublime and mighty name! Thou seekest not to move the will by threatening nor by charming. Thou merely holdest forth a law which finds entrance into the mind, a law before which all inclinations and desires are dumb. What origin is worthy of thee? Where is to be found the root of thy noble descent?

I do not, therefore, need any far-reaching penetration to discern what I have to do in order that my will may be morally good. Inexperienced in the course of the world, incapable of being prepared for all its contingencies, I need only ask, "Can I will that the principle of my action should become a universal law?" If not, then it must be rejected.

A second reworking of his fundamental insight, that rational morality is categorical and *a priori*, is contained in his remarks on the intrinsic goodness of a good will. This thought requires a few words of explanation. Kant has spoken thus far of the morality of acts and wherein it resides. He has, also, restated the same notion in terms of *ought* and *ought not*. But, he is quite aware, there is no such thing as an act apart from someone who does the act. We may analyze and define the morality of an act, but we must end by addressing our remarks, not to acts, but to persons who act. There can be right acts only insofar as persons act rightly; hence the need to restate the matter in terms of will or intention. Every moralist, no matter what his principle of morality, is brought around at last to this point; hence Kant's genuine concern over a good will; i.e., a will inspired and controlled by the principle he has defined.

Nothing can be called *good*, without qualifications, except a good will. We now proceed to examine what exactly constitutes that will, simply good in itself, on which moral goodness depends.

Intelligence, wit, judgment, courage, resolution, perseverance, and so on, are no doubt good and desirable in many respects. But these gifts of nature may also be bad and mischievous if the will which is to make use of them is not good.

It is the same with gifts of fortune. Power, riches, honor, even health and happiness, inspire pride and often presumption if there is not a good will to check their influence.

A good will is good, not because of what it performs or accomplishes, not because of its usefulness or fruitfulness, but is simply good in itself. Even if it should happen that, owing to a special disfavor of fortune or the niggardly provision of a stepmotherly nature, a good will should wholly lack power to achieve its purpose, should by its greatest efforts achieve nothing, yet, like a jewel it would shine by its own light as a thing which has its whole value in itself.

We have, then, to develop the notion of a will good in itself and without reference to anything further. This notion already exists in the sound natural understanding, and requires rather to be clarified than taught or proved. In order to define more closely the notion of a good will, we will consider the wider notion of duty which includes the notion of a good will.

To have moral worth an act must be done from a sense of duty alone. We must distinguish between acts which accord with what duty requires, and acts done because duty requires. The latter alone have moral worth. We must distinguish between doing what duty requires, and doing because duty requires. Only the latter possesses moral worth.

If I do a thing because it is commanded, or because it brings advantage, my action is not moral. But if I do a thing because it is absolutely right in itself, my disposition is a moral one. We ought to do a thing, not because God wills it, but because it is righteous and good in itself.

Thus, it is a matter of duty that a dealer should not overcharge an inexperienced customer. Refraining from so doing for any other motive than that duty requires it has no moral worth. It is one's duty to maintain life and happiness. Doing so for any other reason than that duty requires it has no moral worth. It is one's duty to be generous, kind, honest, and so on. Being so for any reason except that duty requires it has no moral worth. An action done from a sense of duty must wholly exclude the influence of inclination. An action, to be wholly moral, must exclude wholly the influence of inclination.

Take for instance a man who pays his debts. He may be swayed by the fear of being punished if he defaults, or he may pay because it is right that he should. In the first case his conduct is legally right, but it is only in the latter case that it is morally right.

It is a very beautiful thing to do good to men out of love for them or to be just from love of order. But this is not the true moral principle suitable to our position among rational beings as men. To pretend it were would be to set ourselves, with fanciful pride, above the thought of duty, like volunteers independent of command; to want to do, of our own pleasure, what we think we need no command to do.

An action done from a sense of duty derives its moral worth, not from the purpose which is to be attained by it, but from the principle upon which it is done. . . . The moral worth of an action does not lie in the results expected from it, but from the principle which it embodies.

What sort of principle, or moral law, can that be, the conception of which must determine the will, without regard to expected consequences, in order that the will may be called *good* absolutely and without qualifications?

It is this: "So act that the principle of your action might become a universal law." Canst though will that the principle of thy action should become a universal law? If not, then it must be rejected.

Kant has now declared himself on one fundamental problem in moral philosophy. Another problem remains. It grows out of his remarks on the nature and importance of a good will. A *good* will may be defined, after Kant, as a will to do what ought to be done. Here the crucial term is *ought*. And it is crucial because it implies that the will in question is a free will. There would be no point to the remark that a man ought to do so-and-so if, as a matter of fact, he cannot; i.e., has no free will. Furthermore, we hold a man responsible for his action, but only if his action expresses his free will in the matter. The moralist in all of us is brought up short by any denial of man's free will. Such a denial would deprive much of our everyday ethical language of meaning.

Without freedom of the will, no moral law and no moral responsibility are possible.

A man commits a theft. By the physical law of causality this deed is a necessary result of the causes preceding it in time; it was impossible that it could not have happened. How then can the moral judgment make any difference, and suppose it could have been omitted? The moral judgment says it ought to have been omitted. How can this be? How can a man be called free, at the same moment and with respect to the same act in which he is subject to an inevitable physical necessity?

Actions which are not free, and do not involve one's personality, do not give rise to obligations. Thus no man can be placed under an obligation to give up swallowing for the very reason that it would not be within his powers. Obligation, therefore, presupposes the use of freedom.

That is the difficulty. No free will, no morality. Deny freedom of will, and you annihilate morality. This is not to say that by denying freedom of will you "discourage" people, so that they will "give up trying to do what is right"; but rather that you make the term *morality* a meaningless term. Kant spent years thinking out a theory of knowledge which would legitimate the notion of free will. In this sense his *Critique of Pure Reason* was thought out with an eye to the *Critique of Practical Reason* that followed it. In the next sentence, we are back in the ideas of the first *Critique*:

If we take things in time as things-in-themselves, as is commonly done, then it is impossible to reconcile the necessity of the causal relation with freedom. They are contradictory. From the former, it follows that every event, even action, is a necessary result of what existed in time preceding. So, since time past is no longer in my power, it would follow that every action I perform is the necessary result of causes which are not in my power. That is, it would follow that at the moment in which I act, I am never free.

Obligation expresses a sort of necessity which occurs nowhere else in nature except in man. It is impossible that anything in nature *ought to be* other than in fact it is. In truth, obligation, if one has before one's eyes only the succession in nature, has simply and solely no meaning. We can as little ask what ought to happen in nature as what attributes a circle ought to have.

If existence in time, that is, existence as phenomena, were the only kind we could ascribe to things-in-themselves, freedom would have to be rejected as a vain and impossible suggestion.

Consequently, if we would save freedom, no other way remains but to consider that the existence of a thing in time and therefore according to the law of physical necessity, is appearance only. Freedom we must attribute to the thing as a reality, as a thing-in-itself. This is inevitable, if we would retain both these contradictory conceptions of necessity and freedom. However, when we try to explain their combination in one and the same action, great difficulties present themselves.

Now, in order to remove the apparent contradiction between freedom and mechanism in one and the same action, we must recall what was said in the *Critique of Pure Reason*, or what follows from what was said there. It was said there that the necessity of nature—which cannot coexist with the freedom of the will—pertains only to things as phenomena. The category of causation, it was argued, extends to phenomena or appearances only. The possibility of freedom was thus left open, although its reality was not thereby proved.

Kant's words are important. He says, "The possibility of freedom was thus left open." That is all the help he claims from his theory of knowledge. It is sufficient, however. As his discourse shows, he proposes to use the undeniable *ought*. That we ought to do some things and ought not to do others is a point upon which all moralists would agree. They might differ as to what we ought or ought not to do. The essential point is that they would all use the notions of "ought-ness" and "ought-notness." Returning to the argument, the only point is to change this "may be free," which Kant's theory of knowledge permits, into an "is free," which his moral practice demands.

The only point is to change this "may be free" into "is free." That is, to show, in an actual case, that certain actions do imply freedom. Now, it is a duty to realize the moral law in our acts. Therefore it must be possible. ("I ought" implies "I can.") Therefore every rational being must assume whatever is implied by this possibility. Freedom of the will, independence of causal necessity, is implied by this possibility. The assumption is as necessary as the moral law, in connection with which it is valid.

Freedom and duty reciprocally imply each other. It is the moral law, of which we become directly conscious, that leads directly to the conception of freedom. It is morality that first discovers to us the notion of freedom. The moral law—"I ought"—which itself does not require any proof, proves the actuality of freedom in those who recognize it as binding on themselves. A man judges he can do, or refrain from doing, a certain act because he is conscious that he ought to. No one would ever have been so rash as to introduce freedom into science had not the moral law forced it upon us.

Morality requires us only to be able to think freedom without self-contradiction, not to understand it. It is enough that our notion of the act as free puts no obstacle in the way of the notion of it as mechanically necessary. Our notion is that the act stands in quite a different relation to freedom from that in which it stands to the mechanism of nature. From the point of view of my *Critique of Pure Reason* this is possible; the doctrine of nature and necessity and the doctrine of morality and freedom may each be true in its own sphere.

How freedom of the will is possible, how we are to conceive it theoretically and positively, how man is a member of two worlds, how man's moral actions must always appear necessitated while they are nonetheless free—all this is not discoverable. Only that there is such a freedom is postulated by the moral law. How freedom is possible no human intelligence will ever fully fathom. That freedom is possible, on the other hand, no sophistry will ever wrest from the conviction of even the commonest man.

It will be said that the solution here proposed to the problem of freedom involves great difficulty. But is any other solution easier and more intelligible?

Thus far Kant gives a clarifying and convincing presentation of what is implied in moral judgment. A transition from moral philosophy to theology comes about in connection with his account of two other "postulates" of morality. One of these postulates we have already seen, namely, free will. But there are two more to come, namely, immortality and God. It is perhaps as well to let Kant tell his own story. First, immortality:

> The immortality of the soul is also a postulate of the moral law. By a *postulate* I mean a theoretical proposition, not demonstrable as such, but which is an inseparable result of an unconditional, *a priori*, practical (i.e., moral) law.
>
> The connection is this. The moral law commands the perfect accordance of the will with it. This must be possible, since it is commanded. But perfect accordance of the will with the moral law is a perfection of which no rational being of the sensible world is capable at any moment of his existence. Since, nevertheless, it is commanded, it can only be realized in an infinite progression toward that perfect accordance. Now, this endless progress is only possible on the supposition of an endless duration of the existence and personality of the same rational being. This is called the *immortality of the soul*. The highest good for man, the perfect accord of his will with the moral law, is only possible on the supposition of the immortality of the soul. Consequently, this immortality, being inseparably connected with the moral law, is a postulate of pure practical reason.
>
> For a rational but finite being, the only thing possible is an endless progress from the lower to higher degrees of perfection. . . . And thus he may hope, not indeed here nor at any imaginable point of his future existence, but only in the endlessness of his duration, to be perfectly adequate in his will.
>
> This principle of the moral destination of our nature, namely, that it is only in an endless progress that we can attain perfect accordance with the moral law, is of the greatest use, not merely for supplementing the impotence of speculative reason, but also with respect to religion.

It is interesting to note that Kant has here reversed the usual order of things, according to which morality is deduced from theology. Kant turns Paley's perspective upside down by inferring theological postulates from morality. Not only does he infer free will and immortality from morality, but he also infers the existence of God, not as a proof, but as a postulate that reason allows him to make. His argument continues:

> The existence of God is also a postulate of the moral law. We proceed to exhibit this connection in a convincing manner.
>
> Happiness is the condition of a rational being in the world with whom everything goes according to his wish and will. It rests, thus, on the harmony of physical nature with his ends and purposes. But the rational being in the world is not the cause of the world and of physical nature. There is, therefore, not the least ground in the moral law for any necessary connection between morality (i.e., virtue) and proportionate happiness.
>
> To repeat: In a being that belongs to the world as part of it, is therefore dependent on it,. and for that reason cannot by his will be a cause of nature nor by his power make it completely harmonize, as far as his happiness is concerned, with his practical (i.e., moral) principles, in such a being there is not the least ground for any connection between morality and proportionate happiness.
>
> Therefore, the *summum bonum*, the union of virtue and happiness, is possible in the world only on the supposition of a Supreme Being having a causality corresponding to moral character.
>
> Accordingly, the existence of a cause of nature, distinct from nature itself, and containing the principle of this connection, this exact harmony of happiness with morality, is postulated.
>
> Now, a being that is capable of acting on the conception of laws is an intelligence, and the causality of such a being according to this conception of laws, is his will. Therefore, the supreme cause of nature, which must be presupposed as a condition of the *summum bonum* (the union of virtue and happiness) is a being who is the cause of nature by intelligence and will, that is, its author; that is, God.
>
> Now, in as much as it is a duty for us to promote the *summum bonum*, it is not merely allowable but a duty to presuppose the possibility of this *summum bonum*. And so, as this is possible only on condition of the existence of God, it is morally necessary, it is a matter of duty, to assume the existence of God.
>
> The postulates of immortality, freedom, and the existence of God, all proceed from the principle of morality which is itself not a postulate but a law, an imperative.... These postulates are not theoretical dogmas, but suppositions practically necessary, i.e., required in the interest of practice. While they do not extend our speculative knowledge, they do give it a right to conceptions the possibility of which it could not otherwise venture to affirm.... Thus respect for the moral law leads, through these postulates, to conceptions which speculation might indeed present as problems but could never solve.

By way of conclusion it might be well to repeat the main turns of Kant's argument. He begins by assuming that a rational morality is the only morality. He shows that this means *categorical* and *a priori*. This enables him to eliminate three misleading conceptions—that it is a matter of feelings, that it is a matter of consequences, that it is a matter of agreeing with God's will, since on these counts it would be neither categorical nor *a priori*. He returns again to the conception of rational morality as categorical and *a priori*, and formulates its principle. This central thesis he then works over in terms of the notion of *ought* or *duty*, and in terms of the *good will*. These considerations raise the problem of free will. He sharpens the point of this problem. He then reaches back to his theory of knowledge for justification of the claim that free will "may be so." He returns, finally, to the conception of morality as necessitating free will as a postulate. There his moral philosophy proper stops, and his theology begins. Kant's moral philosophy, we think, contains some of the soundest and most clarifying analyses to be found anywhere in the history of human thought.

NOTE ON SOURCES. The materials in this section are quoted, abridged, or paraphrased from Immanuel Kant, *Lectures on Ethics*, translated by Louis Infield (New York: Century, 1930); *Fundamental Principles of the Metaphysics of Morals*, translated by Thomas K. Abbott (Indianapolis: Bobbs-Merrill Co., 1949); and *Critique of Practical Reason*, translated by Lewis White Beck (Chicago: University of Chicago Press, 1949).

3 JOHN STUART MILL

THE MAXIMIZATION OF HAPPINESS

FROM KANT TO MILL. Our subject is still the principle of morality. In 1785, Paley published his *Principles of Moral and Political Philosophy* in which he attempted to ground morality in theology, to distinguish between right and wrong by reference to God's will. In that same year, Kant published *Fundamental Principles of the Metaphysics of Morals*, the first in a cluster of works in which he argued that morality is categorical and *a priori*, that it is not grounded in anything, but "stands on its own feet." In Kant we have a complete antithesis to the position represented by Paley. Four years later, in 1789, Jeremy Bentham (1748–1832), the "father of utilitarianism," published his foundational work on utilitarian theory, *Introduction to the Principles of Morals and Legislation*. He criticized the positions represented by Paley and Kant, and argued that the rightness of an act must not be divorced from its consequences, from its tendency to augment or diminish human happiness. In his view, *right* means maximizing the happiness of humankind. One of his disciples was James Mill (1773–1836) whose son, John Stuart Mill (1806–1873), became a renowned interpreter, defender, and reviser of Bentham's utilitarianism. A brief exposure to Bentham's thought can provide a valuable introduction to Mill's discussion.

Bentham's major interest was the reformation of society's laws and institutions so that the wretched conditions of the masses created by the Industrial Revolution and so clearly evident in Bentham's England would be ameliorated. With that goal in mind, he developed his moral philosophy. His starting point was an affirmation of psychological hedonism, which claims that all human beings are so constituted that they in fact always seek to attain pleasure and avoid pain. From this alleged fact about human nature, Bentham derived two major insights. First, the pursuit of pleasure and the avoidance of pain can be regarded as the standard of right and wrong. Accordingly, Bentham formulated the principle of utility as the foundational standard of his moral perspective. "By the principle of utility," he wrote, "is meant that principle which approves or disapproves of every action whatsoever, according to the tendency which it appears to have to augment or diminish the happiness of the party whose interest is in question . . ." Second, pleasures and pains can be used as the stimuli to nudge and entice people to generate a society in which the happiness of humankind is being pursued.

Both of these insights required, for their application, the capacity to assess the quantity of pleasure and/or pain a given action is likely to generate. In order to evaluate acts as right or wrong, one must be able to calculate the amount of net pleasure or net pain those acts are likely to produce. In addition, in order to deploy pleasure-producing acts and pain-producing acts as effective sanctions for the building of a more truly happy society, one must be able to calculate and predict the amount of net pleasure or pain those acts are likely to generate. To accomplish such calculations, Bentham devised his *hedonistic calculus*. Step-by-step this calculus seeks to reduce diverse pleasures and pains to comparable quantities so that various acts can be legitimately compared and rational decisions made. Here is how Bentham described it:

> Pleasures then, and the avoidance of pains, are the *ends* which the legislator has in view: it behooves him therefore to understand their value. Pleasures and pains are the *instruments* he has to work with: it behooves him therefore to understand their force, which is again, in other words, their value.
>
> To a person considered by *himself*, the value of a pleasure or pain considered by *itself*, will be greater or less, according to the four following circumstances.
>
> 1. Its *intensity*.
> 2. Its *duration*.
> 3. Its *certainty* or *uncertainty*.
> 4. Its *propinquity* or *remoteness*.
>
> These are the circumstances which are to be considered in estimating a pleasure or a pain considered each of them by itself. But when the value of any pleasure or pain is considered for the purpose of estimating the tendency of any *act* by which it is produced, there are two other circumstances to be taken into account; these are,
>
> 5. Its *fecundity*, or the chance it has of being followed by sensations of the same kind; that is, pleasures, if it be a pleasure; pains, if it be a pain.
> 6. Its *purity*, or the chance it has of *not* being followed by sensations of the *opposite* kind: that is, pains, if it be a pleasure: pleasures, if it be a pain.
>
> These two last, however, are in strictness scarcely to be deemed properties of the pleasures or the pain itself; they are not, therefore, in strictness to be taken into the account of the value of that pleasure or that pain. They are in strictness to be deemed properties only of the act, or other event by which such pleasure or pain has been produced; and accordingly are only to be taken into the account of the tendency of such act or such event.
>
> To a *number* of persons, with reference to each of whom the value of a pleasure or a pain is considered, it will be greater or less according to seven circumstances: to wit, the six preceding ones . . . and one other: to wit:

7. Its *extent*; that is, the number of persons to whom it extends; or (in other words) who are affected by it.

To take an exact account then of the general tendency of any act, by which the interests of a community are affected, proceed as follows. Begin with any one person of those whose interests seem most immediately to be affected by it; and take an account,

1. Of the value of each distinguishable *pleasure* which appears to be produced by it in the *first* instance.
2. Of the value of each *pain* which appears to be produced by it in the *first* instance.
3. Of the value of each pleasure which appears to be produced by it *after* the first. This constitutes the fecundity of the first *pleasure* and the *impurity* of the first *pain*.
4. Of the value of each *pain* which appears to be produced by it after the first. This constitutes the *fecundity* of the first *pain*, and the *impurity* of the first *pleasure*.
5. Sum up all the values of all the *pleasures* on the one side, and those of all the *pains* on the other. The balance, if it be on the side of pleasure, will give the *good* tendency of the act upon the whole, with respect to the interests of the *individual* person; if on the side of pain, the *bad* tendency of it upon the whole.
6. Take an account of the *number* of persons whose interests appear to be concerned; and repeat the above process with respect to each. *Sum up* the numbers expressive of the degrees of *good* tendency, which the act has, with respect to each individual, in regard to whom the tendency of it is *good* upon the whole; do this again with respect to each individual, in regard to whom the tendency of it is *bad* upon the whole. Take the *balance*; which, if on the side of *pleasure* will give the general *good tendency* of the act, with respect to the total number of community individual concerned; if on the side of pain the general *evil tendency*, with respect to the same community.

By this calculus Bentham believed he was rescuing morality from fickle sentiments and personal preferences, and grounding it in rational considerations. Serious questions, however, were raised about his enterprise. Is the calculus at all practical? Is there sufficient time to apply the calculus to the pressing moral problems of daily life? Can one predict the consequences of any act with precision? Are not some pleasures intrinsically more desirable than others? Furthermore, does not the appeal to happiness rather than an appeal to the will of God make utilitarianism a godless doctrine? Moreover, is it really acceptable to base the rightness of an action on the consequences to the exclusion of the agent's motive? Questions such as these led Mill to interpret, defend, and modify Bentham's position.

BIOGRAPHICAL NOTE. John Stuart Mill grew up in the group that included Jeremy Bentham, James Mill (father of J. S.), T. R. Malthus, David Ricardo, George Grote, and others. These men were interested primarily in political, economic, and social reform. They were the driving force behind the first Reform Bill, the early Factory Acts, and so on. They were known, in their own day, as the Utilitarians and as the Philosophical Radicals. "Utilitarian" refers to the fact that they asked of any law, custom, or institution, "What is its utility? Of what use is it?" If no answer were forthcoming, beyond some vague statement about its prestige or its long standing, they proposed to scrap it. "Philosophical Radical" refers to the fact that they aimed to go to the roots of things, the word *root* being English for the Latin word *radix*. The root to which these men proposed to go was human happiness. That, for them, was the "root question" to be addressed to any law, custom, or institution. For the most part they did not spend time seeking to justify this principle. This task J. S. Mill undertook to do. They applied the principle that *right* means "producing human happiness," or "being maximally productive of human happiness." He undertook to clarify and defend the principle in his book *Utilitarianism*. Most of his other writings are related to his *Utilitarianism*. Thus, in his essay "On Liberty," written a few years before his *Utilitarianism*, but based on the principles subsequently given in the later book, he argued that the greatest happiness of the greatest number is more likely to be achieved by allowing as much freedom of thought and action as possible. In his treatise "Considerations on Representative Government," he argued that government by elected representatives would offer a better guarantee of human happiness than government by monarchs or aristocrats. In his monograph *The Subjection of Women* he argued that the purpose of representative government was, in part, frustrated by refusing votes to women. The range and sincerity of his writings have given him great influence in the past hundred years. (For other biographical notes, see Chapter 5, Section 4 and Chapter 7, Section 5.)

THE ARGUMENT OF THE PASSAGES. Mill's exposition and defense of the appeal to happiness as the basis of morality moves through five turns. He first states the problem: What is the basis or principle of morality? He then explores two "false leads," and shows grounds for rejecting them. He then states his own position at some length. He then asks the question: Is this belief open to any kind of proof or disproof? and answers as best he can. He turns then to a review of objections and misunderstandings that he knows will be brought against his claim. These he seeks to answer. With this accomplished, he is in a position to say, "I have posed an age-long problem. I have criticized two widely held theories. I have advanced my own answer. I have shown what sort of proof it is amenable to. I have stated and removed as many objections as I can think of. My case rests."

His *Utilitarianism* begins as follows:

> There are few circumstances more significant of the backward states of speculation than the little progress which has been made in the controversy respecting the criterion of right and wrong.
>
> From the dawn of philosophy the question concerning the foundation of morality has been accounted the main problem in speculative thought, has occupied the most gifted intellects, and divided them into sects and schools carrying on a vigorous warfare against one another.
>
> After more than two thousand years the same discussions continue. Philosophers are still ranged under the same contending banners. Neither thinkers nor mankind at large seem nearer to agreement than when the youthful Socrates listened to the old Protagoras.

The problem is now before us: What is the foundation of morality? He proposes to examine two familiar answers. The first of these is the observation that this is a matter of personal opinion. Thus one reads the remarks, "There's nothing right or wrong, but thinking makes it so." "Right you are, if you think you are." That is, an act is right if you, or the community, or all mankind, think it is; right and wrong are mere matters of opinion, are merely subjective. There are many different ways of stating this notion. Of all moralists who hold this view Mill says:

> They all, in one phrase or another, place the test of right and wrong in a feeling of approval or disapproval . . . they find certain feelings of approval and disapproval in themselves . . . a great part of all the ethical reasoning in books and in the world is of this sort.

His criticism of this appeal to moral feeling to settle the matter is short and pointed:

> All experience shows that "moral feelings" are eminently artificial and the product of culture; that the most senseless and pernicious "feelings" can be raised to the utmost intensity by inculcation, as hemlock and thistles could be reared to luxuriant growth by sowing them instead of wheat.
>
> Things which have been really believed by all mankind have been proved to be false, as that the sun rises and sets. Can immunity from similar error be claimed for the "moral feelings"?
>
> I do not found the morality of actions upon anybody's opinion or feeling of them. I found it upon facts.

"What facts?" we ask. Let us first glance at another doctrine: the appeal to nature. A thing is right, it will be said, if it is according to nature, if it is natural; wrong, if it is contrary to nature, if it is unnatural.

> We will inquire into the truth of the doctrines which make nature a test of right and wrong, good and evil, or which in any mode or degree attach merit or approval to following, imitating, or obeying nature. A reference to that supposed standard is the predominant ingredient in the vein of thought and feeling which was opened by Rousseau, and which has infiltrated itself most widely into the modern mind.
>
> That any mode of thinking, feeling, or acting is "according to nature" is usually accepted as a strong argument for its goodness. If it can be said, with any plausibility, that "nature enjoins" anything, the propriety of obeying the injunction is considered to be made out. And, conversely, the imputation of being "contrary to nature" is thought to bar the thing so designated from being tolerated or excused. It is thought that nature affords some criterion of what we ought to do.

Mill's handling of the appeal to nature is a good example of condensed refutation. He first points out that the term *nature*, or the phrase *according to nature*, is ambiguous. He states that the two senses in which it might be used. He then shows that, given the first sense, the appeal to nature is meaningless; and, given the second sense, it is irrational and immoral.

> The word *nature* has two principal meanings: it either denotes the entire system of things, with the aggregate of all their properties, or it denotes things as they would be, apart from human intervention.
>
> Such being the two principal senses of the word *nature*, in which of these is it taken when the word and its derivatives are used to convey ideas of commendation, approval, and even moral obligation?

In the first of these senses, the doctrine that man ought to follow nature is unmeaning, since man has no power to do anything else than follow nature; all his actions are done through, and in obedience to, some one or many of nature's physical or mental laws.

In the other sense of the term, the doctrine that man ought to follow nature, or in other words, ought to make the spontaneous course of things the model of his voluntary actions, is equally irrational and immoral.

Irrational, because all human action whatever, consists in altering, and all useful action, in improving the spontaneous course of nature. Immoral, because the course of natural phenomena being replete with everything which when committed by human beings is most worthy of abhorrence, any one who endeavored in his actions to imitate the natural course of things would be universally seen and acknowledged to be the wickedest of men.

The doctrine that the existing order of things is the natural order, and that, being natural, all innovation upon it is criminal, is vicious. Conformity to nature has no connection whatever with right and wrong. The idea can never be fitly introduced into ethical discussions at all. That a thing is unnatural is no argument for it being blamable.

At this point we may give Mill's own position. We have now two alternatives with which to compare it. He says:

All action is for the sake of some end, and rules of action must take their whole character and color from the end to which they are subservient.

The creed which accepts the greatest happiness principle as the foundation of morals holds that actions are right in proportion as they tend to promote happiness, wrong as they tend to produce the reverse of happiness. By happiness is intended pleasure, and the absence of pain; by unhappiness, pain, and the privation of pleasure. This theory I propose to expound and defend.

The standard is not the agent's own greatest happiness, but the greatest amount of happiness altogether. As between his own happiness and that of others, utilitarianism requires him to be as strictly impartial as a disinterested and benevolent spectator.

The test of morality is not the greatest happiness of the agent himself. Utilitarianism does not dream of defining morality to be the self-interest of the agent. The greatest happiness principle is the greatest happiness of mankind and of all sentient creatures.

He who does anything for any other purpose than to increase the amount of happiness in the world is no more deserving of admiration than the ascetic mounted on his pillar. He may be an inspiring proof of what men can do, but assuredly not an example of what they should do.

Pleasure and freedom from pain are the only things desirable as ends, and all desirable things are desirable either for the pleasure inherent in them or as means to the promotion of pleasure and the prevention of pain.

Mill has stated that morality is a matter of consequences. An act is right or wrong, according to its consequences, not because it agrees with someone's opinion, or with universal opinion, or with nature, or (by implication) with God's will. He pauses a moment to elaborate this point:

By "calculating the consequences" is meant, generally, calculating the consequences of classes of actions. There are, as we shall note, exceptions to this, but over all we must look at actions as though multiplied, and in large masses. Take murder for example. There are many persons, to kill whom would be to remove men who are a cause of no good to any human being, who are a cause of cruel physical and moral suffering to several, and whose whole influence tends to increase the mass of unhappiness and vice. Were such a man to be murdered, the balance of traceable consequences would be greatly in favor of the act. But, the counter consideration, still on the principle of utility, is that unless persons were punished for killing, and taught not to kill, nobody's life would be safe.

We say, "generally," not "universally." For the admission of exceptions to rules is a necessity equally felt in all systems of morality. To take an obvious instance: The rule against homicide, the rule against deceiving, the rule against taking advantage of superior strength, are suspended against enemies in the field and partially against malefactors in private life. In each case, the rule is suspended as far as is required by the peculiar nature of the case. That the moralities arising from special circumstances of the action may be so important as to over-rule those arising from the class of acts to which it belongs, is a liability common to all ethical systems.

The existence of exceptions to moral rules is no stumbling block peculiar to the principle of utility. The essential is that the exception should itself be a general rule; so that, being definite, and not left to the partial judgment of the individual, it might not shake the stability of the wider rule in the cases to which the reason of the exception does not extend. This is an ample foundation for "the construction of a scheme of morality."

With respect to the means of inducing people to conform in their actions to the scheme so formed, the utilitarian system depends, like all other schemes of morality, on the external motives supplied by law and opinion and the internal motives produced by education or reason.

The greatest happiness principle is now before us. Is the principle open to any kind of proof? Mill's answer amounts to a denial. The rationale of this denial is as follows:

Of what sort of proof is this principle of the greatest happiness susceptible?

It is evident that it cannot be proof in the ordinary and popular meaning of the term. Questions of ultimate ends are not amenable to direct proof. Whatever can be proved to be good must be shown to be a means to something admitted to be good without proof.

The medical art is proved to be good by its conducing to health. But how is it possible to prove that health is good? The art of music is good, for the reason among others, that it produces pleasures. But what proof is it possible to give that pleasure is good?

No comprehensive formula, including all things good in themselves and not as means to things good in themselves, is a subject of what is commonly meant by *proof*. It may be accepted or rejected, but not proved in the usual sense of that term.

There is a larger meaning of the word *proof* in which this question of ultimate principles is as amenable to proof as any other of the disputed questions of philosophy. The subject is within the cognizance of the rational faculty. Its acceptance or rejection does not depend on blind impulse or arbitrary choice.

The problem has been stated. False solutions have been exposed. His own solution has been given. The meaning of *proof* in these matters has been made clear. He turns to objections that may be raised. A study of these objections and replies will clarify and fix the doctrine in one's mind.

> It may not be superfluous to notice a few of the common misapprehensions of utilitarian ethics, even those which are so obvious and gross that it might appear impossible for any person of candor and intelligence to fall into them.

The first objection is that such a moral philosophy is a godless doctrine:

> Utilitarianism is a godless doctrine. The appeal to happiness, instead of the appeal to the will of God, is a godless, i.e., irreligious, principle of morality.

Mill's answer is to carry the war into the enemy's camp:

> The question [whether the appeal to happiness is a godless doctrine] depends upon what idea we have formed of the moral character of the Deity. If it be a true belief that God desires above all things the happiness of His creatures, and that this was His purpose in their creation, then utilitarianism is not only not a godless doctrine, but more profoundly religious than any other.
>
> Although the existence of God as a wise and just lawgiver is not a necessary part of the feelings of morality, it may still be maintained that those feelings make His existence eminently desirable. No doubt they do, and that is the great reason why we find that good men and women cling to the belief and are pained by its being questioned.
>
> If the objection [that utilitarianism is a godless doctrine] means the utilitarianism does not recognize the revealed will of God as the supreme law of morals, I answer: An utilitarian who believes in the perfect goodness and wisdom of God, necessarily believes that whatever God has thought fit to reveal on the subject of morals must fulfill the requirements of utilitarianism in a supreme degree.

A second objection:

> To suppose that life has no higher end than pleasure, no better and nobler object of desire and pursuit, is utterly mean and groveling; a doctrine worthy only of swine.

Mill's answer:

> This supposes that human beings are capable of no pleasure except those of which swine are capable. If this supposition were true, the charge could not be denied; but it would then be no charge, for if the sources of pleasure were precisely the same for human beings and for swine, then the rule of life which is good enough for the one would be good enough for the other.
>
> The comparison is felt to be degrading precisely because a beast's pleasures do not satisfy a human being's conception of happiness. Human beings have faculties more elevated than the animal appetites, and do not regard anything as happiness which does not include their gratification.

A third objection:

> That utilitarianism [the appeal to the pleasure–pain consequences of action] renders men cold and unsympathizing; that it chills their moral feelings toward individuals; that it makes them regard only the consequences of actions, not taking into account the personal qualities from which those actions emanate.

Mill's answer:

> If this means that utilitarians do not allow their judgment concerning the rightness or wrongness of an act to be influenced by their opinion of the quality of the person who does it, then it is a complaint not against utilitarianism but against having any standard of morality at all. For certainly no known ethical standard decides an action to be good or bad because it is done by a good or bad man; still less because it is done by an amiable, brave, or benevolent man, or the contrary. These considerations are relevant, not to the estimation of actions, but of persons; and there is nothing in utilitarianism inconsistent with the fact that there are other things which interest us in persons besides the rightness or wrongness of their actions.
>
> The stoic moralists, indeed were fond of saying that he who has virtue has everything. But no claim of this description is made for the virtuous man by the utilitarian moralist. There are other desirable possessions and qualities besides virtue. A right action does not necessarily indicate a virtuous character. Actions that are blamable often proceed from qualities entitled to praise. When this is so in any particular case, it modifies one's moral estimation of the agent, but not of the act.

A fourth objection is that the morality of an action depends upon the motive, not upon the consequences. Mill answers:

> As to motive, the utilitarian position is this: Motive has nothing to do with the morality of the action, though much with the worth of the agent. He who saves a fellow creature from drowning does what is morally right, whether his motive be duty or the hope of being paid for his trouble.

A fifth objection:

> A stock argument against utilitarianism consists in saying that an utilitarian will be apt to make his own particular case an exception to moral rules, and when under temptation, will see an utility in the breach of a rule, greater than he will see in its observance.

Mill's answer:

> But is utilitarianism the only creed which is able to furnish us with excuses for evil doing and means of cheating our own conscience? They are afforded in abundance by all doctrines which recognize as a fact in morals the existence of conflicting considerations; which all doctrines do that have been believed by sane persons.
>
> It is not the fault of any creed, but of the complicated nature of human affairs, that rules of conduct cannot be so framed as to require no exceptions, and that hardly any kind of action can safely be laid down as either always obligatory or always condemnable.
>
> There is no ethical creed which does not temper its laws by giving a certain latitude, under the moral responsibility of the agent, for accommodation to peculiarities of circumstances. At the opening thus made, self-deception and dishonest casuistry get in.
>
> There exists no moral system under which cases of conflicting obligation do not arise. These are the real difficulties, the knotty points, both in a theory of ethics and in the conscientious guidance of personal conduct. But is any one less qualified to deal with cases of conflicting obligations by reason of the fact that he possesses an ultimate standard to which such cases can be referred?

A sixth objection:

Utilitarianism is only an appeal to expedience, and an appeal to expedience is not as high morally as an appeal to principle.

Mill's answer:

The objection rests on a loose use of the term *expedience*. Generally, the *expedient* means that which is expedient for the particular interests of the agent himself; as when a minister of state sacrifices the interests of his country to keep himself in place. The expedient in this sense is a branch of the hurtful; and to claim that utilitarianism is an appeal to the expedient, in this sense, is simply to misunderstand or misrepresent its meaning.

Utilitarianism does recognize in human beings the power of sacrificing their own greatest good for the good of others. I must repeat again, what critics seldom have the justice to acknowledge, that the happiness which forms the standard of what is right in conduct, is not the agent's own happiness but the happiness of all concerned.

Utilitarianism does, however, refuse to admit that sacrifice of one's own good is itself a good. A sacrifice which does not increase the sum of happiness is wasted. The only sacrifice which utilitarianism applauds is that which is made in the interests of the happiness either of mankind or of individuals within the limits imposed by the interests of mankind.

A seventh objection:

Happiness cannot be the rational purpose of life, because it is unattainable.

Mill's answer:

This objection, were it well founded, would go to the root of the matter; for if no happiness is to be had at all by human beings, the attainment of it cannot be the end of morality. However, the assertion that it is impossible that human life be happy is an exaggeration.

If by *happiness* be meant a continuity of highly pleasurable excitement, it is evident that this is impossible. A state of exalted pleasure lasts only for a few moments, or in some cases for somewhat longer periods. If this kind of intense rapture be meant by *happiness*, then happiness is unattainable.

But this is not what philosophers have meant by *happiness* when they taught that happiness was the end of life. The happiness which they meant was not a life of rapture, but moments of such in an existence made up of few transitory pains, many and various pleasures, with a decided predominance of the active over the passive, and having as the foundation not to expect more from life than it is capable of bestowing. A life thus composed, to those who have been fortunate enough to obtain it, has always appeared worthy of the name of happiness. And such an existence is even now the lot of many.

An eighth objection:

We cannot calculate all the consequences of any action and thus cannot estimate the degree in which it promotes human happiness.

Mill's answer:

Is there any department of human affairs in which we can do all that is desirable? Because we cannot foresee everything, is there no such thing as foresight? Can no estimate be formed of consequences, which would be any guide for our conduct, unless we can calculate all consequences? Because we cannot predict every effect which may follow from a person's death, are we to say that we cannot know that murder would be destructive to human happiness? Whether morality is or is not a question of consequences, it cannot be denied that prudence is a question of consequences, and if there is such a thing as prudence, it is because the consequences of actions can be calculated.

A ninth objection:

There is not time, previous to action, for calculating and weighing the effects of any line of conduct on the general happiness.

Mill's answer:

This is exactly as if any one were to say that it is impossible to guide our conduct by Christianity, because there is not time, on every occasion on which everything has to be done, to read through the Old and New Testaments.

The answer to the objection is that there has been ample time, namely, the whole past duration of the human species. During all that time mankind have been learning by experience the tendencies of action; on which experience all the prudence, as well as all the morality, of life is dependent.

Nobody argues that the art of navigation is not founded on astronomy, because sailors cannot wait to calculate the nautical almanac. Being rational creatures, they go to sea with it ready calculated, and all rational creatures go out upon the sea of life with their minds made up on the common questions of right and wrong.

There is no difficulty in proving any ethical standard whatever to work ill, if we suppose universal idiocy to be conjoined with it, but on any hypothesis short of that, mankind must by this time have acquired positive beliefs as to the effects of some actions on their happiness. To inform a traveler respecting the place of his ultimate destination is not to forbid the use of landmarks and direction posts on the way.

A tenth objection:

If happiness is made the ultimate standard by which other things are judged to be good or bad, then we are not in a position to distinguish among kinds of happiness with respect to their goodness or badness.

Mill's answer:

It is quite compatible with the principle of utility to recognize the fact that some kinds of pleasure are more desirable and more valuable than others. It would be absurd that while, in estimating all other things, quality is considered as well as quantity, the estimation of pleasures should be supposed to depend on quantity alone.

Of two pleasures, if there be one to which all or almost all who have experience of both give a decided preference, irrespective of any feeling of moral obligation to prefer it, that is the more desirable pleasure.

Now it is an unquestionable fact that those who are equally acquainted with, and equally capable of appreciating the enjoying, both, do give a most marked preference to the manner of existence which employs their higher faculties. It is better to be a human being dissatisfied than a pig satisfied; better to be Socrates dissatisfied than a fool satisfied. And if the fool, or the pig, is of a different opinion, it is because they know only their side of the question. The other party to the comparison knows both sides.

Few human creatures would consent to be changed into any of the lower animals for a promise of the fullest allowance of an animal's pleasures. No intelligent human being would consent to be a fool, no instructed person would consent to be an ignoramus, no person of feeling and conscience would consent to be selfish and base, even though they should be persuaded that the fool, the dunce or the rascal is better satisfied with his lot than they are with theirs.

From this verdict of the only competent judges, I apprehend there can be no appeal. On the question which of two pleasures is the best worth having, which of two modes of existence is the most grateful to the feelings, the judgment of those who are qualified by knowledge of both must be admitted as final. . . . There is no other tribunal to be referred to.

NOTE ON SOURCES. The material in this section is quoted, abridged, or paraphrased from John Stuart Mill's, "Nature" and from Chapters 1, 2, and 4 of his *Utilitarianism* (London: Longmans, Green, & Co., 1901); and Jeremy Bentham, *Principles of Morals and Legislation* (Darien, CT: Hafner Publishing Co., 1970).

4 FRIEDRICH NIETZSCHE

THE RELATIVITY OF MORALITY

FROM MILL TO NIETZSCHE. We have examined three attempts to formulate the principle of morality, to state what makes a right act right. Paley found the rightness of an act to depend upon its agreement with the will of God. Kant denied that the rightness of an act depended upon anything, asserting that an act, if right, is so categorically, without reference to anything outside of itself. Mill found the rightness of an act to depend upon its consequences, those consequences being the amount of happiness that it brought about. Each of these moralists assumed that he was articulating a moral norm that possessed universality, that was applicable to all persons regardless of time and place. Our fourth moralist, Friedrich Nietzsche, challenges that assumption. For him, there are many moralities, and the chief task confronting the moral philosopher is not to generate one universal morality with its basic principle that specifies what makes a right act right, but rather to construct a history of the development of these various moralities and to identify, if possible, the types or kinds of morality that have appeared in the course of human history.

As a cultural historian in the last half of the nineteenth century, Nietzsche wrote at a time when anthropology was being established as a separate discipline. Cultural diversity was receiving careful study. Nietzsche became aware of the kinds of considerations that lead people to adopt a relativistic position in ethics. Ethical relativism claims that there are no universal cross-cultural moral norms; rather, there are only the moral norms that a particular society establishes and those norms vary greatly from society to society. To support their claims, ethical relativists cite a number of factors. First, they note the great diversity in moral beliefs and practices, assuming that if there were universal moral norms, then people would surely be aware of them and a strong measure of moral uniformity would appear throughout human cultures. Since relativists discern no such uniformity, they conclude that cross-cultural universal moral norms do not exist. Second, they note that our moral beliefs and practices are acquired through enculturation, and that our society derived them from its past ancestors who fashion them as useful devices to aid in the struggle for survival and pleasure. Things that promoted survival and pleasure came to be called good or right, and things that detracted from survival and occasioned pain came to be called evil or wrong. Because ancestral environmental struggles varied from society to society, the resulting moral beliefs and practices also differed from culture to culture. Third, relativists often label as ethnocentric (being inordinately proud of one's culture to the disparagement of other cultures) the claims of those who believe they have identified a universal moral norm that is applicable to all people regardless of time and place. Finally, a number of methodological issues are often urged by relativists in support of their doctrine, such as the difficulty in generating universally accepted meanings for such terms as *good* as well as the difficulty in devising a strategy for justifying moral claims that would be acceptable to all cultures.

Nietzsche would regard the efforts of Paley, Kant, and Mill to articulate a universal moral norm as "human, all too human," fatally flawed efforts to philosophize as if one were not a culturally conditioned creature whose ideas invariably bear the mark of a specific society's enculturation. Nietzsche declares the relativity of all moralities and, at the same time, celebrates the values of the "self-transcending person," the "overman," the "superman."

BIOGRAPHICAL NOTE. Friedrich Nietzsche was born in Germany in 1844 and died in 1900 at the age of fifty-six. He was born into a puritanical, religious family and was intended by his parents to enter the church. To this end he was educated privately and at a denominational school. While at the university in Bonn he broke completely with his family in doctrinal matters. He moved on to the university at Leipzig. There he met Wagner, the German composer, and became a fervent Wagnerite. He discovered Schopenhauer's writings in a second-hand bookshop and became a convinced Schopenhauerian. He met Erwin Rhode, the historian of Greek culture, and became engrossed in the problems and perspectives of the cultural history of mankind. He did military service for a year in a war with Austria, returning to the University of Leipzig to complete his studies. The following year he was appointed to the chair of classical philology in the university at Bâle, received his Ph.D., and began work on his important book *The Birth of Tragedy*. The next year, 1870, he was called once more into military service in the Franco–Prussian War, which had just begun. He was head of an ambulance corps, but did only three weeks' service. Diphtheria ended his military career. He returned to the university at Bâle and resumed lectures. For eight years he remained at this work. During this period he was arriving at conclusions that formed the basis of his future writings. He published *The Birth of Tragedy*. It met with a chilly reception. His prestige began to decline. His next book, *Thoughts Out of Season*, continued four essays in which he criticized Strauss, Schopenhauer, German historians, and others. Two years later for reasons of poor health he retired on a small pension from the university.

It should never be forgotten that Nietzsche was, first and last, a cultural historian; that is, he was interested in, and drew his inspiration from, the study of the cultures achieved by various peoples, ancient and modern. He wrote a series of books that develop really one theme. His investigations into humankind's cultural history, understanding by the term *culture* such things as art, religion, science, morality, government, and so on, impressed him with the enormous diversity that has been obtained in these things at different times and places. But that was not all. He was equally impressed with the fact that cultural values are local and transitory affairs. He expressed this in the notion of the relativity of cultural values. By this he meant that cultural values are relative to time and place, relative to the needs peculiar to the peoples among whom they flourish. In other words, there is nothing eternal or absolute or immutable about them, and this, he felt, holds for values of all descriptions: religious, artistic, social, moral, scientific, and so on. On the rebound from his earlier orthodox training, he dismissed them with a great flourish of his pen in his book *Human, All Too Human*. That was his "great discovery." Values, one and all, are "human, all too human." The rest of his work may be described as a series of studies in the natural history of human values. *Human, All Too Human*, was followed by *Dawn of Day*, and it in turn by *Joyful Wisdom*. Clearly, a new note was being struck.

What idea was Nietzsche working out in these books? It was something like this: The cultural history of humankind shows that aristocratic qualities flourish in the early stages of a culture and disappear gradually as that culture becomes old. In Homer's time, the Greeks were "heroes"; by the time of Pericles and the Spartan war, they had become mere "sophists" and "philosophers" and "scientists." In early Roman history there were great kings who founded a race that conquered the ancient world, but centuries later, in the days of imperial decline, this nation of "strong, silent men" had become helpless victims of their own weakening civilization and the new races of barbarians as yet "untouched" by such things. These newcomers swept over Europe, and another page in cultural history was begun, but with the same result. By the nineteenth century these "Germanic" peoples who had made over the civilization of ancient Rome had become democratic, even socialistic; they cultivated "science," "art," "morality" or (in some instances) decadent forms of "immortality," wealth, ease, the "emancipation of women," optimism, pessimism, philosophy, and so on.

There is no quarreling with Nietzsche's likes and dislikes in these matters. The sight of Achilles sulking in his tent was simply something he admired more than the sight of Karl Marx sulking in the library of the British Museum. A Greek athlete or a Roman warrior was simply not in the same degenerate class with J. S. Mill pleading for representative government and the political enfranchisement of women, or Schopenhauer brooding over the misery and folly of human affairs.

Hence, the titles of his books. To "see through" modern degeneration was "the dawn of day," to realize that "real virtues" belong in the context of fresh and vigorous young cultures was the first step in "joyful wisdom." Nietzsche was carried away on the wings of this sort of thing. Lonely, poor, sickly, unpopular, a bachelor *malgré lui*, he nevertheless lived on in the private world of "transvalued values," heaping scorn on "art" and "science" and "morality" and "religion" and "emancipation" and "democracy" and "socialism" and "humanitarianism." He poured his soul into the mold of one beautiful book, *Thus Spake Zarathustra*. This was the fine flower of his genius. Through the mouth of Zarathustra, the prophet of his doctrine, he preached and exhorted and satirized in pages of marvelous beauty and suggestiveness. But the nineteenth century passed Zarathustra by. Only a handful took the trouble to read him, and even these few were puzzled and disturbed. For their enlightenment, Nietzsche wrote two more books, *Beyond Good and Evil* and *The Genealogy of Morals*. They were intended as commentaries on *Zarathustra*. The substance of their argument is given in the passages that follow. The balance of Nietzsche's writings carry further the ideas presented already. The Zarathustra group was followed by *The Twilight of the Idols, Antichrist, The Will to Power* (unfinished), and his own autobiography bearing the significant title *Ecce Homo*.

In 1889, at the age of forty-five, Nietzsche lost the use of his mind. For the next eleven years he was caught in the toils of a steadily increasing insanity. In 1900 he died hopelessly insane.

THE ARGUMENT OF THE PASSAGES. The following passages, chosen principally from Nietzsche's *Beyond Good and Evil* and *The Genealogy of Morals*, exhibit the following turns of thought. He begins by repudiating the whole notion of trying to formulate any principle of morality, in the sense that moralists have traditionally sought to do this. He insists that there is no such thing as morality having one fundamental principle running through it; that, on the contrary, there have been and are many moralities; and that any attempt to think philosophically about morality must begin by recognizing its diversity and the fact of its having had a history like any other phase of human culture. He propounds then a tentative natural history or genealogy of morals. From this he undertakes to draw some far-reaching conclusions. These he calls collectively his *immoralism*, or *transvaluation of values*. One fundamental distinction, arising out of his account of the natural history of morals and forming the foundation of his immoralism, is that between master morality and slave morality. The characteristics of each he then describes at some length. The doctrine is now substantially complete. However, to illustrate it more concretely, he applies it in a critical way to two phenomena of modern morality, namely, the emancipation of woman and the close connection between modern morality and Christianity. He closes with a few reflections on his own significance.

The opening passages are fundamental. In these Nietzsche draws the searching distinction between accepting morality and trying to formulate its principle, and making moralities the subject of descriptive investigation. It is the historian of humanity's manifold cultures and cultural values who speaks:

Hitherto all moralists, with a pedantic and ridiculous seriousness, have wanted to give a "basis" to morality, and each has believed that he has given this "basis" to morality. Morality itself, however, has been regarded as something "given."

That which moralists have called "giving a basis to morality," has proved merely a learned form of good faith in prevailing morality, a new means of expressing prevailing morality, consequently just a phenomenon within one definite morality, a sort of denial that it is lawful for this particular morality to be called in question. In no case has the attempt to "provide a basis for morality" ever involved a testing, analyzing, doubting, and vivisecting of the prevailing moral faith.

The philosophical workers, after the pattern of Kant and Hegel, have to fix and systematize some existing body of valuations, that is to say, creations of value which have become prevalent and are for a time called "the truth." It is for these thinkers to make conspicuous, conceivable, intelligible, manageable what has happened and been esteemed hitherto.

Apart from the value of such assertions as there is a categorical imperative in us, we can always ask: "What does such an assertion indicate about him who makes it?"

Because moralists have known the moral facts imperfectly, in an arbitrary epitome, perhaps the morality of their environment, their position, their church, their *Zeitgeist*, their climate; because they have been badly instructed with regard to nations, eras, and past ages, and were by no means eager to know about these matters; precisely because of this fact, they did not even come in sight of the real problems of morality, problems which disclose themselves only to a comparison of many kinds of morality.

There are systems of morals which are meant to justify their author in the eyes of other people; systems which are meant to tranquilize him and make him self-satisfied; systems which are meant to enable him to crucify and humble himself. By means of one system of morals, he wishes to take revenge; by means of another, to conceal himself; by means of another, to glorify himself and gain superiority and distinction. In short, systems of morals are only sign languages of the emotions.

What is still necessary is the collection of material, the comprehensive survey and classification of sentiments of worth, distinctions of worth, which live, grow, propagate, and perish; and the attempt, perhaps, to give a clear idea of the recurring and more common forms of these living crystallizations. This is necessary as preparation for a theory of types of morality.

So much as a start. The primary problem is not to formulate the principle of morality, but to recognize the existence and study the natural history of many moralities. An acquaintance with these matters, Nietzsche feels, will reveal the fact that genuine moralities arise from the presence in any group of an aristocratic or ruling-class element. He offers a hypothetical reconstruction of the natural history or genealogy of morals.

Every elevation of the type "man" has hitherto been the work of an aristocratic society, and so it will always be; a society believing in a long gradation of rank and differences of worth among human beings, and requiring slavery in some form or other.

Without the pathos of distance, such as grows out of the difference of classes, out of the constant outlooking and downlooking of the ruling class on subordinates and instruments, out of the constant practice of obeying and commanding, out of keeping down and keeping at a distance, without these, that other more mysterious pathos could never have arisen: the longing for the continued self-surmounting of man.

To be sure, one must cherish no humanitarian illusions about the origin of aristocratic societies. The truth is hard. Every higher civilization has originated in barbarism. Men, barbarians in every respect, men of prey, still in possession of unbroken strength of will and desire for power, threw themselves upon weaker, more moral, more peaceful races, upon old mellow civilizations in which the final vital force was flickering out in brilliant fireworks of wit and depravity. In the beginnings, the noble caste was always the barbarian caste.

The essential thing in a good and healthy aristocracy is that it should regard itself not as a function of the king or the people but as the significance and highest justification thereof; that it should accept with a clear conscience the sacrifice of a legion of individuals, who, for its sake, must be suppressed and reduced to imperfect men, to slaves and instruments. Its fundamental belief must be that society is not allowed to exist for its own sake, but only as a foundation and scaffolding by which a select class may be able to elevate themselves to their higher duties; like those climbing, sun-seeking plants in Java which encircle a tree till, high above it but supported by it, they can unfold their tops in the open light and exhibit their happiness.

Consider an aristocratic commonwealth, e.g., an ancient Greek city state, as a voluntary or involuntary contrivance for rearing human beings. There men are beside one another, thrown on their own resources, who want to make their species prevail, chiefly because they must prevail or be in danger of extermination. The favor, the abundance, the protection, are lacking under which variations are fostered. The species needs itself as species; as something which by its hardness, its uniformity, its simplicity of structure, can prevail in the struggle against neighbors or rebellious vassals. Experience teaches it what are the qualities to which it owes its continued existence in spite of gods and men. These qualities it calls *virtues*, and these virtues alone it develops to maturity.

These virtues it develops with severity. Every aristocratic morality is intolerant in the education of its youth, in the control of its women, in the customs which control marriage, in the relations between old and young, in the penal laws (which have an eye only for the degenerating). It counts intolerance itself among the virtues.

Thus is established a type, with few but very marked features. The constant struggle with unfavorable conditions is the cause of the type becoming stable and hard.

Finally, however, a happy state of security results, and the enormous tension is relaxed. Perhaps there are no more enemies among neighboring peoples; perhaps the means of life and enjoyment are present in abundance. With one stroke the bond and constraint of the old discipline snaps. It is no longer regarded as a necessary condition of existence and survival. If it would continue, it can do so only as an archaizing "taste." Variations appear suddenly in the greatest exuberance and splendor. The individual dares to be individual and detach himself.

At this turning point of history there manifest themselves a magnificent manifold growth and an extraordinary decay, owing to the savagely opposed and seemingly exploded egoisms which strive for "light and sun" and can no longer assign any limit or restraint to themselves by the hitherto existing morality. It was this morality itself which piled up the enormous strength, which bent the bow in so threatening a manner, but it is now out of date, or getting out of date.

The dangerous and disquieting point has now been reached. The greater, more manifold, more comprehensive life now coming into existence is lived beyond the old morality. The "individual" stands out and is obliged to have recourse to his own law giving, his own arts and artifices for self-preservation, self-elevation, self-deliverance. Nothing but new "whys"; nothing but new "hows." No longer any common formulae; misunderstanding and disregarded in league together, decay, deterioration, lofty desire, frightfully entangled; the genius of the race overflowing from all the cornucopias of good and bad; new charms and mysteries peculiar to the still inexhausted, still unwearied, corruption.

Danger, the mother of morality, is present once more. This time the danger point has shifted into the individual, the neighbor, the friend; into the street, into their own child, into all the most personal and secret recesses of their desires and volitions.

After the fabric of a society seems established and secure against external dangers, it is the fear of our neighbor which creates new perspectives of moral evaluation.

It is by the loftiest and strongest instincts, when they break out and carry the individual above and beyond the average, above and beyond the low level of the herd conscience, that the self-reliance of the community is destroyed: Its belief in itself breaks. Consequently these instincts will be most branded and most defamed.

Strong and dangerous instincts, e.g., the love of enterprise, foolhardiness, revengefulness, astuteness, rapacity, love of power, which, up till then had to be honored and fostered and cultivated because required in the common dangers against common enemies, are now felt to be themselves dangerous, are gradually branded as immoral and given over to calumny. The opposite instincts and inclinations now attain to moral honor. The herd instinct gradually draws it conclusions.

How much danger to the community or its equality is contained in an opinion, a condition, an emotion, a character, a disposition? That is now the moral perspective. Here again fear is the mother of morals.

The lofty, independent spirit, the will to stand alone, are felt to be dangers. Everything that elevates the individual above the herd, and is a source of fear to the neighbor, is henceforth called evil. The tolerant, unassuming, self-adapting, self-equalizing disposition, the middle-of-the-road desires, attain to moral distinction and honor.

Under peaceful circumstances there is always less opportunity and less need for training the feelings to severity and rigor. Now every form of severity, even severity in justice, begins to disturb the conscience. A lofty and rigorous nobleness and self-responsibility becomes now almost an offense.

The man of an age of dissolution, of an age which mixes the races with one another; who has the inheritance of a diversified descent in his body, contrary instincts and standards of value which struggle among themselves and are seldom at peace; such a man, of late culture and broken lights, will, as a rule, be a weak man.

His fundamental desire is that the war which is in him should come to an end. Happiness appears to him in the character of a soothing medicine and mode of thought; it is above all things the happiness of repose, of undisturbedness, of repetition, of final unity.

All systems of morals which address themselves to "happiness" are only suggestions for behavior adapted to the degree of danger from themselves in which the individuals live. They are thus recipes for their passions, their good and bad propensities, insofar as the individuals would like to play the master. They are all so many small and great expediences, permeated with the musty odor of old family medicines and old wives' wisdom; all grotesque and absurd because they are generalizations where generalization is not justified.

The rank-and-file man assumes an air of being the only kind of man that is allowable. He glorifies, as the peculiarly human virtues, his qualities, such as public spirit, kindness, deference, industry, temperance, modesty, indulgence, sympathy (by virtue of which he is gentle, endurable, and useful to the herd).

In cases where it is believed that a leader cannot be dispensed with, attempt after attempt is made to replace rulers by summing together clever herd-minded men. All representative constitutions, for example, are of this origin.

There arises what I call the moral hypocrisy of the ruling class. They know no other way to protect themselves from bad conscience than to play the role of executors of older and higher orders. (Those "older and higher orders" may be predecessors, the constitution, justice, the law, or God himself.) Or they even justify themselves by maxims drawn from the current opinions of the herd, as, for example, "the first servants of their people," or "instruments of public weal."

The end is quickly approaching; everything decays and produces decay; nothing will endure until the day after tomorrow; nothing, that is, except one species of man, the incurably mediocre. The mediocre alone have a prospect of continuing, of propagating themselves. They will be the men of the future, the sole survivors. "Be like them! Be mediocre!" is now the only morality which has still a significance or obtains a hearing. But it is difficult to preach this morality of mediocrity. It can never avow what it is and what it desires. It has to talk of "moderation" and "dignity," and "duty," and "brotherly love." It will have difficulty in concealing its irony!

But this herding-animal morality is only one kind of morality, beside which, before which, and after which, many other moralities, above all, higher moralities, are or should be possible. Against such a possibility, this herd morality defends itself with all its strength. It says obstinately and inexorably: "I am morality, and nothing else is morality."

The first corollary that follows from Nietzsche's conception of the genealogy of morals is what he calls his *immoralism*, or his proposed *transvaluation of values*. Thus:

What will the moralists who appear at this time have to preach? What shall be the message of these sharp on-lookers, these unhurried ones?

What is essential and invaluable in every system of morals, is that it is a long constraint.

A species originates, a type becomes established and strong in the long struggle with essentially unfavorable conditions. On the other hand, species which receive abundant nourishment, a surplus of protection and care, tend to develop variations, become fertile in prodigies and monstrosities.

The essential thing, to repeat, is that there should be a long obedience in the same direction. Thereby results something which makes life worth living; for instance, virtue, art, music, dancing, reason, spirituality; whatever, in short, is transfiguring, refined, or divine.

One may look at every system or morals in this light. It teaches us to hate the lax, the too-great freedom. It implants the need for limited horizons, for limited duties, for narrow perspectives. "Thou must obey some one, and for a long time; otherwise thou wilt come to grief, and lose all respect for thyself."

The tension of the soul in misfortune, its shuddering in view of rack and ruin, its inventiveness and heroism in enduring and exploiting misfortune, its depth, mystery, greatness; have these not been bestowed through the discipline of great suffering?

Up to now man has been in the worst hands, has been ruled by the misfits, the physiologically botched, the cunning and revengeful, the so-called *saints*—slanderers of the world, traducers of humanity. The morality of decadence, the will to nothingness, passes as morality *par excellence*. Proof of this: Altruism is considered an absolute value, while egoism meets with hostility everywhere. He who disagrees with me on this point I regard as infected.

For a physiologist, such an opposition of altruism and egoism would leave no room for doubt. If the smallest organ in the body neglects its self-preservation, its recuperative powers, its "egoism," the whole organism will degenerate. The physiologist insists that such decayed parts be cut out. He pities them not at all. But the priest wants precisely the degeneration of mankind; hence he strives to preserve the decayed elements in humanity. This is the price of his rule. This is the "harm that good men do."

When one is no longer serious after self-preservation and the increase of bodily energy, when anemia is made an ideal and contempt of the body is construed as "salvation of the soul," what can all this be, if not a recipe for decadence? Loss of ballast, resistance to natural instincts, "selflessness," these have hitherto been called *morality*.

You want, if possible, to do away with suffering. There is not a more foolish "if possible." We would rather have it increased and made worse. Well-being, as you understand it, is certainly not a goal. The discipline of great suffering is the only discipline that has produced all the elevations of humanity hitherto.

To consider distress as something to be destroyed is sheer idiocy. Generally, it is actually harmful in its consequences, a fatal stupidity, almost as mad as the desire to abolish bad weather out of pity for the poor. In the great economy of the universe the terrors of reality, e.g., the passions, the desires, the will to power, are incalculably more essential than that petty happiness, so-called *goodness*.

It is only among decadents that pity is called a virtue. They are too ready to forget modesty, reverence, and that delicacy of feeling which knows how to keep at a distance. They forget that this sentimental emotion stinks of the mob; that pity is only one step removed from bad manners; that pitying hands may be thrust with destructive results into a great destiny, into a wounded isolation. . . . The overcoming of pity I reckon among the noble virtues.

There is nowadays a sickly irritability and sensitiveness to pain, a repulsive complaining, an effeminizing, which, with the aid of religious and philosophical nonsense, seeks to deck itself out as something superior. There is a regular cult of suffering. The unmanliness of what such groups of visionaries call *sympathy* is, I believe, the first thing that strikes the eye. One must resolutely taboo this latest form of bad taste.

There is a point of diseased mellowness and effeminacy in the history of society, at which society itself takes the part of him who injures it, the part of the criminal. To punish now appears to be somehow "unfair." Is it not sufficient, it is asked, if the criminal be rendered harmless? Why should we still punish? Punishment is barbarous! And so on. With these questions, the herd morality, the morality of fear, draws its ultimate conclusion.

On no point is the ordinary mind of Europe more unwilling to be corrected, than on this matter. People rave nowadays, even under the guise of "science," about coming social conditions in which the "exploiting character" of human relations is to be absent. Particularly is this true of socialistic shallowpates and howling anarchistic dogs. Their words sound to me as if they were promising a mode of life which should refrain from all organic functions. "Exploitation" is not the mark of a depraved or primitive society; it belongs to the nature of living, as a primary organic function; it is a consequence of the will to power which is precisely the will to life.

You may note that I do not care to see rudeness undervalued. It is by far the most humane form of contradiction, and amid modern effeminacy, it is one of our first virtues.

To be able to be an enemy, to be an enemy, presupposes a strong nature. Strong natures need resistance, accordingly they seek it. The pathos of aggression belongs to strength as much as feelings of revenge and rancor belong to weakness. The strength of the aggressor is determined by the opposition he needs; every increase of strength betrays itself by a search for a more formidable opponent.

To refrain from mutual injury, from violence, from exploitation, to put one's will on a par with others' may result in a kind of good conduct among individuals; but only when the necessary conditions are given, namely, an equality of the individuals in force and worth, and their correlation within one organization.

To take this principle more generally, however, to use it as the fundamental principle of society, would immediately reveal what it actually amounts to, namely, a principle of dissolution and decay. Here one must think profoundly and resist all sentimentality; life itself is essentially appropriation, injury, exploitation, conquest, suppression, severity, obtrusion, incorporation.

Even the organization within which the members treat each other as equal, must, itself, do that toward other organizations which its members refrain from doing to each other; if, that is, it be a living, growing, and not a dying organization. It will endeavor to grow, to gain ground, to attract to itself, to acquire ascendancy; not owing to any morality or immorality, but simply because it lives, and because life is precisely will to power.

Fortunately, the world is not built merely on those instincts in which the good-natured herd-animal would find his paltry happiness. To demand that everyone become a "good man," a gregarious animal, a blue-eyed benevolent "beautiful soul," or (as Herbert Spencer wished) an altruist, would mean robbing existence of its greatest character, emasculating mankind. And this has been attempted. It is just this that men call *morality*.

The "good" man is the most harmful kind of man. He secures his existence at the cost of truth. He cannot create. He crucifies the man who writeth new values on new tables. He crucifies the whole future of humanity. Whatever harm the slanderers of the world may do, the harm which good men do is the most calamitous of all harm.

Let me say again what I have already said a hundred times. In all our principal moral judgments, that which is sure of itself, that which glorifies itself with praise and blame, that which calls itself good, is the instinct of the herding human animal: the instinct which is coming more and more to the front, coming more and more to dominate other instincts. Morality at present is herding-animal morality.

All questions of politics, of the social order, of education, have been falsified from top to bottom, because the most harmful men have been taken for great men, and because people were taught to despise the fundamentals of life.

Nietzsche's characteristic doctrines have their basis in these conceptions of the genealogy of morals and the transvaluation of values. His distinction between man and superman, between master morality and slave morality, his reiterated criticisms of the softer, more humanitarian virtues and customs, follow reasonably enough. Perhaps the most famous of all Nietzsche's teachings is his distinction between master morality and slave morality. Its point is this:

> Moral systems must be compelled to bow before the gradations of rank. Their presumption must be driven home, until they thoroughly understand that it is immoral to say what "what is right and proper for one is right and proper for another."
>
> In a tour through the many finer and coarser moralities which have hitherto prevailed, or still prevail, on the earth, I have found certain traits recurring regularly together, until finally two primary types revealed themselves to me: there are master morality and slave morality.
>
> Moral valuations have originated, either in a ruling class pleasantly conscious of being different from the ruled, or in a ruled class, among slaves and dependents of all sorts.
>
> In the master morality, when it is the rulers who determine the notion of "goodness," it is the exalted, proud type of character which is regarded as the distinguishing feature, as that which determines the order of rank. The noble man separates from himself the persons in whom these characteristics are absent; them he despises.
>
> They say: "Thus shall it be." They determine the whither and the why of mankind. They grasp at the future with a creative hand. Whatever is and was becomes for them a means, an instrument, a hammer. Their knowing is creating. Their creating is law-giving. Their will to truth is will to power.
>
> In master morality the antithesis is between "noble" and "despicable." The cowardly, the timid, the no-accounts, the narrowly utilitarian, the distrustful, the self-abasing, the doglike who submit to abuse, the mendicant flatterers, and above all the liars, are despised.
>
> A man who says, "I like that, I take it for my own, I mean to guard it and protect it"; a man who can carry out a resolution, keep hold of a woman, punish and overthrow insolence; a man who has his indignation and his sword; a man whom the weak, the suffering, even the animals, willingly submit to and naturally belong to; such a man is a master by nature.
>
> The noble type of man regards himself as the determiner of values; he does not require to be approved of; he passes the judgment; "What is injurious to me is injurious in itself"; he knows that it is he himself only who confers honor on things; he is a creator of values. He honors whatever he recognizes in himself; such morality is self-glorification. In the foreground there is the feeling of plenitude, of power which seeks to overflow, the consciousness of a wealth which would fain give and bestow.
>
> The noble man honors in himself the powerful one, him who has power over himself, who knows how to speak and how to keep silent, who takes pleasure in subjecting himself to severity and hardness and has reverence for all that is severe and hard. "Wotan placed a hard heart in my breast," says an old Scandinavian saga: it is thus rightly expressed from the soul of a proud Viking.
>
> The noble man is furthest removed from the morality which sees the essence of the moral in sympathy, or in "acting for the good of others." Faith in oneself, pride in oneself, a radical irony and enmity toward "self-lessness," belong as definitely to master morality as do scorn and precaution in the presence of sympathy and the "warm heart."
>
> A man of this sort is carved from a single block which is hard, sweet, fragrant. He enjoys only what is good for him. His desire ceases when the limits of what is good for him are overstepped. . . . Whatever does not kill him makes him stronger. He gathers

his material from all he sees, hears, and experiences. He is a selective principle: he rejects much. . . . He reacts slowly to all kinds of stimuli, with that slowness which long caution and pride have bred in him. . . . He is always in his own company, whether mingling with men or books or nature. . . . He honors the thing he chooses.

There is an instinct for rank, which, more than anything else, is the sign of a high rank. The refinement, the goodness, the loftiness of a soul are put to a real test when something of the highest rank passes by but is not yet protected with the awe of authority; something that goes its way like a living touchstone, undistinguished, undiscovered, tentative, perhaps veiled and disguised.

The noble and powerful know how to honor; it is their art, their domain for invention. The profound reverence for age and tradition, the belief and prejudice in favor of ancestors and against newcomers, is typical of master morality. If, contrariwise, men of "modern ideas" believe in "progress" and the "future," and are increasingly lacking in respect for the past, the ignoble origin of these "ideas" is thereby betrayed.

He whose task is to investigate souls will avail himself of many varieties of this very art to determine the ultimate value of a soul, the innate order of rank to which it belongs. He will test it by its instinct for reverence. The vulgarity of many a soul spurs up like dirty water when any holy vessel, any jewel from closed shrines, any book bearing the marks of great destiny, is brought before it. Contrariwise, there is an involuntary silence, a hesitation, a cessation, by which is indicated that a soul frees the nearness of what is worthy of respect.

In the so-called *cultured* classes today, the dealers in "modern ideas," nothing is perhaps so repulsive as their lack of shame, their lack of reverence, the easy insolence of hand and eye with which they touch, finger, and examine everything. It is possible that more tact for reverence exists among the lower classes and peasants than among the newspaper-reading demimonde of "intellect" and "culture."

Much has been achieved when the sentiment of reverence has been finally instilled into the masses, when they realize that they are not allowed to touch everything, that there are some experiences before which they must take off their shoes and restrain their hand.

The master morality is especially foreign and irritating to present-day taste. It is disliked and distrusted for the sternness of its principle that one has duties only to one's equals; that one may act toward persons of a lower rank, toward all that is foreign, just as one pleases; that its values are "beyond good and evil."

It is typical of the master morality to be able and obliged to exercise prolonged gratitude and prolonged revenge, but only within the circle of one's equals; artfulness in retaliation; a need for enemies as outlets for emotions of envy, quarrelsomeness, arrogance. This, of course, is not "modern morality," and is therefore difficult to realize, to discover.

In contrast to the master morality stands the slave morality:

It is otherwise with the second type of morality; what I have named slave morality. If the abused, the oppressed, the suffering, the unemancipated, the weary, the uncertain-of-themselves, should moralize, what will be the common element in their moral evaluations?

The slave has an unfavorable eye for the virtues of the powerful. He has a skepticism and distrust of everything which they honor. He would fain persuade himself that their happiness is not genuine.

On the other hand, those qualities which serve to alleviate the existence of sufferers are brought into prominence and flooded with light. It is here that sympathy, the kind of helping hand, the warm heart, patience, diligence, humility, friendliness, attain to honor. For here these are the most useful equalities, almost the only means of supporting the burden of existence.

Slave morality is essentially the morality of utility. It is oriented around the idea of the "useful." Here is the seat of the origin of the famous antithesis of "good" and "evil," which I have distinguished from the antithesis of "good" and "bad." According to the slave morality, the "evil" man rouses fear. According to master morality, the "good" man rouses fear, and seeks to rouse it, while the "bad" man is regarded as the despicable being.

According to slave morality, the good man must be the "safe" man: he must be good-natured, easily hoodwinked, perhaps a little stupid. Wherever slave morality gains the ascendency, language shows a tendency to approximate the significations of the words *good* and *stupid*.

A last fundamental difference: the desire for freedom, the enthusiasm for "liberty" the instinct of being "happy" belong as inherently to slave morality as artifice in reverence and enthusiasm in devotion belong to master morality. Hence, we can understand, love as a passion, romantic love, with its ardors and endurances and binding ties, is a phenomenon of master morality.

Nietzsche never wearied of criticizing those phases of modern morality that smacked of "degeneration" and "slaves." Among the topics singled out for castigation was the nineteenth-century enthusiasm for the emancipation of women. Says Nietzsche:

To be mistaken in the fundamental problem of "man and woman" is the typical sign of a shallow mind. To deny here the profoundest antagonism, the need for hostile tension; to dream here of "equal rights," equal training, equal claims and obligations; to prove oneself shallow at this dangerous spot, may be regarded as suspicious, nay more, as betrayed. Such an one may probably prove "too short" for all the fundamental issues of life, unable to descend into any of the depths.

In no previous age have women been treated with so much respect by men as at present. This belongs to the tendency and fundamental taste of democracy. Is it any wonder that abuse should be made of this respect? Women want more; they learn to make claims; they become rivals for rights. In a word, they lose their modesty. And, let me add, they also lose their taste.

They unlearn their fear of men. But the woman who "unlearns" her fear of men sacrifices her most womanly instincts. That woman should venture forward when man has ceased to inspire fear, is reasonable enough, and intelligible enough. But what is more difficult to grasp is that precisely thereby woman deteriorates. That is happening these days: let us not deceive ourselves about it.

Wherever the industrial spirit has triumphed over the military and aristocratic spirit, woman strives for the economic and legal independence of a clerk. "Woman as clerk" is inscribed on the portal of that modern society which is in course of formation.

While she thus appropriates new rights, aspires to be master, and inscribes the "progress" of woman on her flags and banners, the very opposite realizes itself with terrible obviousness—woman retrogrades.

There is stupidity in this movement, an almost masculine stupidity, of which a well-bred sensible woman might be heartily ashamed. To lose the ground on which she can most surely achieve victory; to neglect her proper weapons; to let herself go before man where formerly she kept herself in control in artful humility; to neutralize man's faith in a fundamentally different ideal in woman, something eternally feminine; to emphatically and loquaciously dissuade man from the idea that woman must be preserved, protected, and indulged like some delicate, strangely wild and often pleasant domestic animal; what does all this betoken, if not a disintegration of womanly instincts?

There are, to be sure, enough of idiotic friends and corrupters of woman among the learned asses of the male sex, who advise woman to defeminize herself in this manner, and to imitate all the stupidities from which all man suffers, who would like to lower woman to "general culture," indeed, even to newspaper reading and meddling with politics.

In their efforts to rise to the ideal woman, to the higher woman, they have really wished to lower the general level of women, and there are no more certain means to this end than university education, trousers, and the rights of voting like cattle. Fundamentally, the "emancipated" and the "emancipators" (for example, that typical old maid, Henrik Ibsen) are anarchists, misbegotten souls whose most deep-rooted instinct is revenge.

Almost everywhere her nerves are being ruined, and she is daily being made more hysterical and more incapable of fulfilling her first and last function, namely, the rearing of robust children. These "friends of woman" wish to "cultivate" her, to make the weaker sex strong by "culture," as if history did not teach that the "cultivating" of mankind and the weakening of mankind have always kept pace with one another.

That which inspires respect in woman, and often also fear, is her real nature, her genuine, carnivora-like cunning and flexibility, her tiger claws beneath the glove, her naiveté in egoism, her untrainableness, her innate wildness, her incomprehensibleness, the extent and deviation of her virtues.

That which, in spite of fear, excites one's sympathy for the dangerous and beautiful in woman, is that she seems more afflicted, more vulnerable, more needful of love and more condemned to disillusion, than any other creature. Fear and sympathy—it is with these feelings that man hitherto stood in the presence of woman, always with one foot in tragedy which rends while it delights. And all that is now to be at an end? The disenchantment of women is in progress? The tediousness of woman is slowly evolving?

Another object of Nietzsche's criticism was what he describes as "Christian morality." He never tires of railing at it. From among pages and pages, the following passages may be taken as representative:

All the things men have valued heretofore are not even realities. They are mere fantasies; more strictly speaking, they are lies. All the concepts, "God," "soul," "virtue," "sin," "Beyond," "truth," "eternal life," are lies arising from the evil instincts of diseased and harmful natures.

I am the first immoralist. Basically, there are two denials included in this term. First, I deny the type of man who formerly passed as the highest, the "good" man, the "benevolent" man, the "charitable" man. Second, I deny that kind of morality which has become recognized and dominant, namely Christian morality. . . . The second of these denials is the more decisive.

No one before me has felt Christian morality beneath him. To do that one must have height, far vision, depth. Up to now, Christian morality has been the Circe of all thinkers; they stood at her service. What man before me has descended into the caves from which the poisonous fumes of this ideal burst forth? Who before me ever dared to suspect they were caves? What philosopher before me was a real moralist and not a superior swindler, an idealist?

Have you understood me? What defines me is the fact that I unmasked Christian morality. For this reason I needed a word which would contain the idea of a universal challenge: immoralist. Blindness in the face of Christian morality is the essential crime. It is the great uncleanliness.

Christian morality is the most pernicious form of the will to falsehood, the denial of life. It is not error as error which infuriates me here. It is not the age-long lack of "good will," of discipline, of decency, of spiritual courage, which betrays itself in the triumph of Christian morality. It is the ghastly fact that what was unnatural received the highest honors as morality, and remained suspended over man as the law of the categorical imperative. This is the great blundering. To teach contempt of the primal life instincts; to set up a "soul," a spirit, in order to overthrow the body; to teach man to find impurity in sex; to look for the principle of evil in the need for expansion; to see a "higher moral value" in "self-lessness," in "objectivity," in "neighbor love"; these things are the will to nothingness, the denial of life the great nay-saying.

The Jews performed the miracle of the inversion of valuations, by means of which life on earth obtained a new and dangerous charm for a couple of thousand years. Their prophets fused the expressions *rich, godless, wicked, violent, sensual*, into one expression, and for the first time coined the word *world* as a term of reproach. In this inversion of values (which included the use of *poor* as synonymous with *saint* and *friend*) the significance of the Jewish people is to be found. It is with them that slave morality begins.

From the beginning, Christian morality was essentially the surfeit of life which distinguished itself under the belief in "another" and "better" life. The hatred of the world, the condemnation of emotion, the fear of beauty, the distrust of sensuality, all these have always appeared to me as the most dangerous forms of the "will to perish," symptoms of the deepest weariness, exhaustion, anemia.

The teachers and preachers and leaders of mankind, including the theologians, have been decadents. Hence their inversion of values into a hostility to life; hence "morality." Here is a definition of *morality*: the idiosyncrasy of decadents actuated by a desire to avenge themselves successfully upon life. I attach great value to this definition.

Have you understood me? The unmasking of Christian morality is a unique event. It breaks the history of mankind in two. Man lives either before or after that. Everything which was until then called the *truth*, is now recognized as the most harmful, spiteful, and concealed falsehood. The sacred pretext, the "improvement of man," is recognized as a ruse to drain life of its blood. This morality is vampirism.

He who unmasks Christian morality unmasks the worthlessness of the values in which men believe. He sees in them only the most fatal kind of abortions; fatal, because they fascinate. The notion of "God" was invented as the counternotion to life. The notion of a "Beyond" was invented to depreciate the only world that exists.

The notion of an "immortal soul" was invented to despise the body. The notion of "sin" was invented to mislead our instincts. Finally, the notion of a "good man" has come to mean everything that is weak, ill, misshapen, everything which should be obliterated. The law of selection is thwarted. And all this was believed in as morality! *Ecrasez l'infâme!*

We who hold a different view, we who regard Christian morality and democratic politics to be a degenerating form of organization, where have we to fix our hopes?

In new moralists and a new morality. There is no other alternative. In minds strong enough and original enough to initiate a transvaluation of values, to invert "eternal valuations," lies our only hope. In forerunners, in men of the future, who shall fix the constraints and fasten the knots which will compel millenniums to take new paths; make preparations for vast hazardous enterprises and collective attempts in rearing and educating; put an end to the frightful rule of folly and chance which has hitherto gone by the name of *history*; in such do we fix our hopes.

For these purposes a new type of moralist and ruler will some time be needed, at the very idea of which everything that has existed might look pale and dwarfed. The image of such leaders hovers before our eyes.

But their image fills our hearts with anxiety and gloom. How are they to be born? How are they to be bred? How nurtured to that elevation and power which will feel the present needs as their tasks? Of them is demanded a transvaluation of values. In them is needed a new conscience of steel, a new heart of brass, to bear the weight of such responsibility. There is always the danger that they may be lacking or miscarry and degenerate. These are our real anxieties and glooms. These are the heavy thoughts and storms which sweep across our skies.

There are few pains so grievous as to have seen an exceptional man miss his way and deteriorate. But he who has the rare eye to see the danger of mankind itself missing its way and deteriorating; he who has recognized the element of wild chance in human affairs; he who has detected the fate that is hidden under the idiotic unwariness and blind confidence of "modern ideas," and still more of Christian morality and democratic politics; suffers from an anguish beyond comparison.

The universal degeneracy of mankind to the level of the ideals of socialistic fools and humanitarian shallowpates, the dwarfing of man to an absolutely gregarious animal, the brutalizing of man into pygmy with equal "rights" and "claims"—this is undoubtedly possible. He who has foreseen this possibility knows another loathing unknown to the rest of mankind.

From these themes, Nietzsche turns to the question of his own significance for the modern mind. Nietzsche on the genealogy of morals is interesting. Nietzsche on the distinction between master morality and slave morality is suggestive. Nietzsche on woman and Christianity is challenging. But Nietzsche on himself in unique:

Idealism is alien to me. Where you see ideal things I see human things; alas, all too human.

He who would be a creator in good and evil must first be a destroyer, and break values into pieces. I am the most terrible man that has ever existed. But I shall be the most beneficent. I know the joy of annihilation. I am the first immoralist. I am thus the essential destroyer.

I know my destiny. I am not a man. I am a fatality. I am dynamite. Some day my name will be bound up with the recollection of something terrific, a crisis, a profound clash of consciences, a decisive condemnation of all that before me had been believed, required, hallowed.

I am the voice of truth. But my truth is terrible, for hitherto lies have been called truth. "The transvaluation of all values" is my formula for mankind's act of highest self-recognition. I contradict as no one has contradicted before. For when truth engages in a struggle with falsehoods of ages, we must expect shocks, earthquakes, rearrangements of hills and valleys, such as never yet have been dreamt of. All the mighty forms of the old social structure I blow into space, for they rest on falsehoods. Politics on a grand scale will date from me.

My life task is to prepare humanity for a moment of supreme self-consciousness, a great noontide, a transvaluation of all values, an emancipation from all moral values, a yea-saying, a confidence in all that has formerly been forbidden, despised, and damned: when it will gaze both backwards and forwards, emerge from the tyranny of accident and priesthood, and, for the first time, pose the question of the why and wherefore of humanity as a whole.

But with all this there is nothing in me to suggest the founder of a "religion." Religions are the business of the mob. After coming in contact with a religious man, I have always to wash my hands. I want no "believers." I never address myself to the masses. I do not wish to be a saint: I would rather be a clown. Perhaps I am a clown.

Nietzsche's cultural analysis led him to relativize all moralities. For him each morality must be understood in terms of its time and place. There is no such thing as morality having one fundamental principle running through it. There are many moralities with their own distinctive values and principles. This assessment of morality, however, did not lead Nietzsche to say that one morality was no more preferable than any other. Indeed, Nietzsche leaves no room for doubt that he was appalled by the prevailing morality of his day. For Nietzsche, the will to life which all humans share involves the necessity to exploit other life and the will to power to do so. The prevailing morality with its Christian altruism and self-sacrifice violated the fundamental will to life. As such, that morality was a no-saying to life, and with that no-saying came the celebration of equality among humans, suspicion of the person who excels, and a commitment to mediocrity, which means the erosion of civilization. Nietzsche prefers the morality of what he calls the *übermensch* (that is, the self-transcending person, the overman, the super-man): a new egoism, which affirms the basic aggressiveness of the will to life and celebrates the pursuit of individual excellence even at the expense of others. Such a morality would constitute a transvaluation of the prevailing morality: a replacement of the current altruistic no-saying to life with the superman's aggressive yes-saying to life. The superman discerns the current deterioration of civilization, stands apart from the mediocrity of the herd, legislates for himself what is right and wrong, and thereby sets himself beyond the prevailing good and evil. For Nietzsche, then, that which is right is that which is productive of, and expressive of, the *übermensch*.

Clearly Nietzsche presents a challenge to the Paleys, Kants, and Mills of the world. That challenge can be described in terms of the contest between objectivism and subjectivism in ethics. The objectivist claims that moral values and norms are "objective" in the sense that they exist independently of the individual so that certain things are good or evil and certain acts are right or wrong for all persons. The subjectivist claims that moral values and judgments are all ultimately expressions of individual emotions and personal tastes. Although the ethical relativist might say that moral values and norms exist independently of the individual by virtue of the fact that they exist in the corporate beliefs and customs of a society and that moral values and norms are "objective" in this sense, nevertheless the relativist usually admits that those values and norms are rooted in or legitimized by individual tastes and emotions. Accordingly, ethical relativism generally implies a commitment to subjectivism. Paley, Kant, and Mill are on the side of the objectivists; Nietzsche is on the side of subjectivists.

An example might help to clarify the difference in the two positions. Suppose that you said, "Martin Luther King was a good man." From the objectivist's perspective, you would be making a claim that Dr. King possessed a certain quality or characteristic such that it would be true to say that he was "good." From the subjectivist's point of view, you would not be making a factually significant claim about Dr. King at all. Instead, you would be merely expressing a positive emotion that you had toward Dr. King. In the objectivist's world, moral judgments can be assessed as true or false. In the subjectivist's world, moral judgments are expressions of emotion, which seem to be neither true nor false.

What kind of response could a Paley, Kant, or Mill offer to Nietzsche's taunt that their views are "human, all too human"? that morality boils down to individual emotional preferences? It is precisely the issue of objectivism versus subjectivism in ethics that is the focus of the debate between our next two authors from the twentieth century, A. J. Ayer and Brand Blanshard.

NOTE ON SOURCES. The material in this section is quoted, abridged, or paraphrased from many different books, essays, and chapters. The basic argument of the section is derived principally from Friedrich Nietzsche, *Beyond Good and Evil*, translated by Helen Zimmermann (London: T. N. Fouli's 1914), particularly Chapters 1, 5, and 9; and "The Genealogy of Morals," *The Birth of Tragedy and the Genealogy of Morals*, translated by Francis Golfing (Garden City, NY: Doubleday, 1956), Essays 1 and 2. Passages were also taken from Friedrich Nietzsche, "Thus Spoke Zarathustra" in *The Portable Nietzsche*, edited by W. Kaufmann (New York: The Viking Press, 1954); *The Dawning of Day: Thoughts on the Prejudices of Morality*, translated by R. J. Hollingdale (New York: Cambridge University Press, 1982); *Joyful Wisdom*, translated by Thomas Common (New York: F. Ungar Publishing Co., 1960); *Will to Power*, translated by Walter Kaufmann and R. T. Hollingdale, edited by Walter Kaufmann (New York: Random House, 1967); and *Ecce Homo: How One Becomes What One Is*, translated by R. J. Hollingdale (New York: Penguin Books, 1979).

5   A. J. AYER

EMOTIVISM AFFIRMED

FROM NIETZSCHE TO AYER. You begin by being able and willing to authorize moral judgments; e.g., stealing is wrong, truth-telling is right, and so on. You then face a question: What fact, common to all your cases of wrong-doing, is the reason for calling them cases of wrong-doing? Or, what fact, common to all your cases of right-doing, is the reason for calling them cases of right-doing?

Although Nietzsche disallows such questions, much traditional ethical theory centers in those questions. If you get an answer, you are in a position to say, "An act is wrong if and only if. . . . " or "right if and only if. . . ." and supply what is needed to finish the statement. The completed sentence formulates the *principle* that is operative in your moral judgments. Much traditional ethical theory centers on the attempt to formulate the principle of moral judgment.

It will be recalled that Paley, Kant, and Mill each tried to formulate the principle of morality. Paley did so with reference to the will of God; Kant, with reference to the categorical imperative; and Mill, with reference to happiness. Other alternatives would be possible. Let all of them be set down side by side. Then let the question be asked, "To what *logical* type do these statements belong?" This is Professor Ayer's question. His answer empties moral judgments of their traditional content by construing them to be fundamentally expressions of emotion.

BIOGRAPHICAL NOTE. A. J. Ayer was born in London, in 1910. He attended Eton, one of England's best-known public schools, where he excelled in academics and lettered in soccer and rugby. He attended Oxford University, receiving his Bachelor of Arts in 1932. That year he spent several months in Vienna attending meetings of the so-called Vienna Circle—a group of distinguished scholars, including such persons as Hans Hahn, Otto Neurath, Philipp Frank, Herbert Feigl, Moritz Schlick, and Rudolf Carnap, who attempted to propagate the scientific outlook in all fields of human knowledge. When Ayer returned to Oxford to pursue graduate studies, he brought with him the logical positivism of the Vienna Circle and blended it with insights from his contemporaries—Bertrand Russell and Ludwig Wittgenstein—and earlier empiricists such as George Berkeley and David Hume. The product of this synthesis was his book *Language, Truth and Logic* published in 1936, which became one of the most influential philosophical books of the twentieth century. In it Ayer attacks relentlessly the traditional philosophy as it was practiced in Oxford and elsewhere. During the Second World War, Ayer served in several military capacities. Upon his discharge from the army in 1945, he was appointed Dean of Wadham College, Oxford. In 1946, he became Grote Professor of the Philosophy of Mind and Logic at London University, and in 1959 he was named to the distinguished chair of Wykeham Professor of Logic at Oxford University. He died in 1989.

THE ARGUMENT OF THE PASSAGES. Ayer's question for Paley, Kant, Mill, and other traditional moral philosophers is, "To what *logical* type do moral principles and moral judgments belong?" In his hands this question presupposes that there are two possible answers: A statement is either empirical or tautological. He is clear that when you formulate the principle of morality, the resulting proposition is neither empirical nor tautological. His conclusion is that it is not a proposition at all, but a pseudoproposition; that is to say, it looks like a proposition because it is formulated in words and "read" like a sentence expressing a proposition, but it is nevertheless not a proposition because to be a proposition it would have to be either empirical or tautological, and it is neither.

If it is not a proposition, then what is it? To say that it is a pseudoproposition is merely to say that it is not a proposition but looks as though it were. The question remains, "What is it?" Professor Ayer's point could be expressed by saying that it is a symbol, something used to express what is in the mind; and by distinguishing between two kinds of symbols—cognitive and emotive. A cognitive symbol is one that is used to express what you know or could know; an emotive symbol is one that is used to express what you feel or could feel. His claim would then be that when the principle of morality is expressed in words it is an emotive, not a cognitive symbol. In using it you express what you feel or could feel, not what you know or could know. This is the emotive theory about moral concepts and the judgments in which they occur.

Our business is to give an account of "judgments of value" which is both satisfactory in itself and consistent with our general empiricist principles. We shall set ourselves to show that in so far as statements of values are significant, they are ordinary "scientific" statements; and that in so far as they are not scientific, they are not in the literal sense significant, but are simply expressions of emotion which can be neither true nor false. In maintaining this view, we may confine ourselves for the present to the case of ethical statements. What is said about them will be found to apply, *mutatis mutandis*, to the case of aesthetic statements also.

The ordinary system of ethics, as elaborated in the works of ethical philosophers, contains, first of all, propositions which express definitions of ethical terms, or judgments about the legitimacy or possibility of certain definitions. Secondly, there are propositions describing the phenomena of moral experience, and their causes. Thirdly there are exhortations to moral virtue. And, lastly, there are actual ethical judgments.

Only the first of our four classes, namely that which comprises the propositions relating to the definitions of ethical terms, can be said to constitute ethical philosophy. The propositions which describe the phenomena of moral experience, and their causes, must be assigned to the science of psychology, or sociology. The exhortations to moral virtue are not propositions at all, but ejaculations or commands which are designed to provoke the reader to action of a certain sort. Accordingly, they do not belong to any branch of philosophy or science. As for ethical judgments, inasmuch as they are neither definitions nor comments upon definitions, nor quotations, we may say that they do not belong to ethical philosophy. A strictly philosophical treatise on ethics should therefore make no ethical pronouncements. But it should, by giving an analysis of ethical terms, show what is the category to which all such pronouncements belong. And this is what we are now about to do.

A question which is often discussed by ethical philosophers is whether it is possible to find definitions which would reduce all ethical terms to one or two fundamental terms. But this question, though it undeniably belongs to ethical philosophy, is not relevant to our present enquiry. We are not now concerned to discover which term, within the sphere of ethical terms, is to be taken as fundamental: whether, for example, "good" can be defined in terms of "right" or "right" in terms of "good," or both in terms of "value." What we are interested in is the possibility of reducing the whole sphere of ethical terms to non-ethical terms. We are enquiring whether statements of ethical value can be translated into statements of empirical fact.

That they can be so translated is the contention of those ethical philosophers who are commonly called subjectivists, and of those who are known as utilitarians. For the utilitarian defines the rightness of actions, and the goodness of ends, in terms of the pleasure, or happiness, or satisfaction, to which they give rise; the subjectivist, in terms of the feelings of approval which a certain person, or group of people, has towards them. Each of these types of definition makes moral judgments into a sub-class of psychological or sociological judgments; and for this reason they are very attractive to us. For, if either was correct, it would follow that ethical assertions were not generically different from the factual assertions which are ordinarily contrasted with them.

Nevertheless we shall not adopt either a subjectivist or a utilitarian analysis of ethical terms. We reject the subjectivist view that to call an action right, or a thing good, is to say that it is generally approved of, because it is not self-contradictory to assert that some actions which are generally approved of are not right, or that some things which are generally approved of are not good. And we reject the alternative subjectivist view that a man who asserts that a certain action is right, or that a certain thing is good, is saying that he himself approves of it, on the ground that a man who confessed that he sometimes approved of what was bad or wrong would not be contradicting himself. And a similar argument is fatal to utilitarianism. We cannot agree that to call an action right is to say that all of the actions possible in the circumstances it would cause, or be likely to cause, the greatest happiness, or the greatest balance of pleasure over pain, or the greatest balance satisfied over unsatisfied desire, because we find that it is not self-contradictory to say that it is sometimes wrong to perform the action which would actually or probably cause the greatest happiness, or the greatest balance of pleasure over pain, or of satisfied over unsatisfied desire. And since it is not self-contradictory to say that some pleasant things are not good, or that some bad things are desired, it cannot be the case that the sentence "x is good" is equivalent to "x is pleasant," or to "x is desired." And to every other variant of utilitarianism with which I am acquainted the same objection can be made. Therefore the validity of ethical judgments is not determined by the felicific tendencies of actions, any more than by the nature of people's feelings; it must be regarded as "absolute" or "intrinsic," and not empirically calculable.

We are not denying that it is possible to invent a language in which all ethical symbols are definable in non-ethical terms; what we are denying is that the suggested reduction of ethical to non-ethical statements is consistent with the conventions of our actual language. That is, we reject utilitarianism and subjectivisim, not as proposals to replace our existing ethical notions by new ones, but as analyses of our existing ethical notions. Our contention is simply that, in our language, sentences which contain normative ethical symbols are not equivalent to sentences which express psychological propositions, or indeed empirical propositions of any kind.

It is only normative ethical symbols, and not descriptive ethical symbols, that are indefinable in factual terms. There is a danger of confusing these two, because they are commonly constituted by signs of the same sensible form. Thus "x is wrong" may express a moral judgment concerning a certain type of conduct, or it may state that a certain type of conduct is repugnant to the moral sense of a particular society. In the latter case, the symbol "wrong" is a descriptive ethical symbol, and the sentence in which it occurs expresses an ordinary sociological proposition; in the former case, the symbol "wrong" is a normative ethical symbol, and the sentence in which it occurs does not, we maintain, express an empirical proposition at all. It is only with normative ethics that we are at present concerned; so that whenever ethical symbols are used in the course of this argument without qualification, they are to be interpreted as symbols of the normative type.

In admitting that normative ethical concepts are not reducible to empirical concepts, we seem to be leaving the way clear for the view that statements of value are not controlled by observation, as ordinary empirical propositions are, but only by a mysterious "intellectual intuition." This would make statements of value unverifiable. For it is notorious that what seems intuitively certain to one person may seem doubtful, or even false, to another. So that unless it is possible to provide some criterion by which one may decide between conflicting intuitions, a mere appeal to intuition is worthless as a test of a proposition's validity. But in the case of moral judgments, no such criterion can be given. Some moralists claim to settle the matter by saying that they "know" that their own moral judgments are correct. But such an assertion is of purely psychological interest, and has not the slightest tendency to prove the validity of any moral judgment. For dissentient moralists may equally well "know" that their ethical views are correct. And, as far as subjective certainty goes, there will be nothing to choose between them. When such differences of opinion arise in connection with an ordinary empirical proposition, one may attempt to resolve them by referring to, or actually carrying out, some relevant empirical test. But with regard to ethical statements, there is, on the "intuitionist" theory, no relevant empirical test. Therefore on this theory ethical statements are held to be unverifiable. They are, of course, also held to be genuine synthetic propositions.

Considering the use which we have made of the principle that a synthetic proposition is significant only if it is empirically verifiable, it is clear that the acceptance of an "absolutist" theory of ethics would undermine the whole of our main argument. And as we have already rejected the "naturalistic" theories which are commonly supposed to provide the only alternative to "absolutism" in ethics, we seem to have reached a difficult position. We shall meet the difficulty by showing that the correct treatment of ethical statements is afforded by a third theory, which is wholly compatible with our radical empiricism.

We begin by admitting that the fundamental ethical concepts are unanalysable, inasmuch as there is no criterion by which one can test the validity of the judgments in which they occur. So far we are in agreement with the absolutists, But, unlike the absolutists, we are able to give an explanation of this fact about ethical concepts. We say that the reason why they are unanalysable is that they are mere pseudo-concepts. The presence of an ethical symbol in a proposition adds nothing to its factual content. Thus if I say to someone, "You acted wrongly in stealing that money," I am not stating anything more than if I had simply said, "You stole that money." In adding that this action is wrong I am not making any further statement about it. I am simply evincing my moral disapproval of it. It is as if I had said, "You stole that money," in a peculiar tone of horror, or written it with the addition of some special exclamation mark. The tone, or the exclamation mark, adds nothing to the literal meaning of the sentence. It merely serves to show that the expression of it is attended by certain feelings in the speaker.

If now I generalize my previous statement and say, "Stealing money is wrong," I produce a sentence which has no factual meaning—that is, expresses no proposition which can be either true or false. It is as if I had written "Stealing money!!"—where the shape and thickness of the exclamation marks shows, by a suitable convention, that a special sort of moral disapproval is the feeling which is being expressed. It is clear that there is nothing said here which can be true or false. Another man may disagree with me about the wrongness of stealing, in the sense that he may quarrel with me on account of my moral sentiments. But he cannot, strictly speaking, contradict me. For in saying that a certain type of action is right or wrong, I am not making any factual statement, not even a statement about my own state of mind. I am merely expressing certain moral sentiments. And the man who is ostensibly contradicting me is merely expressing his moral sentiments. So that there is plainly no sense in asking which of us is in the right. For neither of us is asserting a genuine proposition.

What we have just been saying about the symbol "Wrong" applies to all normative ethical symbols. Sometimes they occur in sentences which record ordinary empirical facts besides expressing ethical feeling about those facts: sometimes they occur in sentences which simply express ethical feeling about a certain type of action, or situation, without making any statement of fact. But in every case in which one would commonly be said to be making an ethical judgment, the function of the relevant ethical word is purely "emotive." It is used to express feeling about certain objects, but not to make any assertion about them.

It is worth mentioning that ethical terms do not serve only to express feeling. They are calculated to arouse feeling, and so to stimulate action. Indeed some of them are used in such a way as to give the sentences in which they occur the effect of commands. Thus the sentence "It is your duty to tell the truth" may be regarded both as the expression of a certain sort of ethical feeling about truthfulness and as the expression of the command "Tell the truth." The sentence "You ought to tell the truth" also involves the command "Tell the truth," but here the tone of the command is less emphatic. In the sentence "It is good to tell the truth" the command has become little more than a suggestion. And thus the "meaning" of the word "good," in its ethical usage, is differentiated from that of the word "duty" or the word "ought." In fact we may define the meaning of the various ethical words in terms both of the different feelings they are ordinarily taken to express, and also the different responses which they are calculated to provoke.

We can now see why it is impossible to find a criterion for determining the validity of ethical judgments. It is not because they have an "absolute" validity which is mysteriously independent of ordinary sense experience, but because they have no objective validity whatsoever. If a sentence makes no statement at all, there is obviously no sense in asking whether what it says is true or false. And we have seen that sentences which simply express moral judgments do not say anything. They are pure expressions of feeling and as such do not come under the category of truth and falsehood. They are unverifiable for the same reason as a cry of pain or a word of command is unverifiable—because they do not express genuine propositions.

Thus, although our theory of ethics might fairly be said to be radically subjectivist, it differs in a very important respect from the orthodox subjectivist theory. For the orthodox subjectivist does not deny, as we do, that the sentences of a moralizer express genuine propositions. All he denies is that they express propositions of a unique non-empirical character. His own view is that they express propositions about the speaker's feelings. If this were so, ethical judgments clearly would be capable of being true or false. They would be true if the speaker had the relevant feelings, and false if he had not. And this is a matter which is, in principle, empirically verifiable. Furthermore, they could be significantly contradicted. For if I say "Tolerance is a virtue," and someone answers, "You don't approve of it," he would, on the ordinary subjectivist theory, be contradicting me. On our theory, he would not be contradicting me, because, in saying that tolerance was a virtue, I should not be making any statement about my own feelings or about anything else. I should simply be evincing my feelings, which is not at all the same thing as saying that I have them.

The distinction between the expression of feeling and the assertion of feeling is complicated by the fact that the assertion that one has a certain feeling often accompanies the expression of that feeling, and is then, indeed, a factor in the expression of that feeling. Thus I may simultaneously express boredom and say that I am bored, and in that case my utterance of the words, "I am bored," is one of the circumstances which make it true to say that I am expressing or evincing boredom. But I can express boredom without actually saying that I am bored. I can express it by my tone and gestures, while making a statement about something wholly unconnected with it, or by an ejaculation, or without uttering any words at all. So that even if the assertion that one has a certain feeling always involves the expression of that feeling, the expression of a feeling assuredly does not always involve the assertion that one has it. And this is the important point to grasp in considering the distinction between our theory and the ordinary subjectivist theory. For whereas the subjectivist holds that ethical statements actually assert the existence of certain feelings, we hold that ethical statements are expressions and excitants of feeling which do not necessarily involve any assertions.

We have already remarked that the main objection to the ordinary subjectivist theory is that the validity of ethical judgments is not determined by the nature of their author's feelings. And this is an objection which our theory escapes. For it does not imply that the existence of any feelings is a necessary and sufficient condition of the validity of an ethical judgment. It implies, on the contrary, that ethical judgments have no validity.

There is, however, a celebrated argument against subjectivist theories which our theory does not escape. It has been pointed out by Moore that if ethical statements were simply statements about the speaker's feelings, it would be impossible to argue about questions of value. To take a typical example: if a man said that thrift was a virtue, and another replied that it was a vice, they would not, on this theory, be disputing with one another. One would be saying that he approved of thrift, and the other that *he* didn't; and there is no reason why both these statements should be true. Now Moore held it to be obvious that we do dispute about questions of value, and accordingly concluded that the particular form of subjectivism which he was discussing was false.

It is plain that the conclusion that it is impossible to dispute about questions of value follows from our theory also. For as we hold that such sentences as "Thrift is a virtue" and "Thrift is a vice" do not express propositions at all, we clearly cannot hold that they express incompatible propositions. We must therefore admit that if Moore's argument refutes the ordinary subjectivist theory, it also refutes ours. But, in fact, we deny that it does refute even the ordinary subjectivist theory. For we hold that one really never does dispute about questions of value.

This may seem, at first sight, to be a very paradoxical assertion. For we certainly do engage in disputes which are ordinarily regarded as disputes about questions of value. But, in all such cases, we find, if we consider the mater closely, that the dispute is not really about a question of value, but about a question of fact. When someone disagrees with us about the moral value of a certain action or type of action, we do admittedly resort to argument in order to win him over to our way of thinking. But we do not attempt to show by our arguments that he has the "wrong" ethical feelings towards a situation whose nature he has correctly apprehended. What we attempt to show is that he is mistaken about the facts of the case. We argue that he has misconceived the agent's motive: or that he has misjudged the effects of the action, or its probable effects in view of the agent's knowledge; or that he has failed to take into account the special circumstances in which the agent was placed. Or else we employ more general arguments about the effects which actions of a certain type tend to produce, or the qualities which are usually manifested in their performance. We do this in the hope that we have only to get our opponent to agree with us about the nature of the empirical facts for him to adopt the same moral attitude towards them as we do. And as the people with whom we argue have generally received the same moral education as ourselves, and live in the same social order, our expectation is usually justified. But if our opponent happens to have undergone a different process of moral "conditioning" from ourselves, so that, even when he acknowledges all the facts, he still disagrees with us about the moral value of the actions under discussion, then we abandon the attempt to convince him by argument. We say that it is impossible to argue with him because he has a distorted or underdeveloped moral sense; which signifies merely that he employs a different set of values from our own. We feel that our own system of values is superior, and therefore speak in such derogatory terms of his. But we cannot bring forward any arguments to show that our system is superior. For our judgment that it is so is itself a judgment of value, and accordingly outside the scope of argument. It is because argument fails us when we come to deal with pure questions of value, as distinct from questions of fact, that we finally resort to mere abuse.

In short, we find that argument is possible on moral questions only if some system of values is presupposed. If our opponent concurs with us in expressing moral disapproval of all actions of a given type *t*, then we may get him to condemn a particular action *A*, by bringing forward arguments to show that *A* is of type *t*. For the question whether *A* does nor does not belong to that type is a plain question of fact. Given that a man has certain moral principles, we argue that he must, in order to be consistent, react morally to certain things in a certain way. What we do not and cannot argue about is the validity of these moral principles. We merely praise or condemn them in the light of our own feelings.

If anyone doubts the accuracy of this account of moral disputes, let him try to construct even an imaginary argument on a question of value which does not reduce itself to an argument about a question of logic or about an empirical matter of fact. I am confident that he will not succeed in producing a single example. And if that is the case, he must allow that its involving the impossibility of purely ethical arguments is not, as Moore thought, a ground of objection to our theory, but rather a point in favor of it.

Having upheld our theory against the only criticism which appeared to threaten it, we may now use it to define the nature of all ethical enquiries. We find that ethical philosophy consists simply in saying that ethical concepts are pseudo-concepts and therefore unanalyzable. The further task of describing the different feelings that the different ethical terms are used to express, and the different reactions that they customarily provoke, is a task for the psychologist. There cannot be such a thing as ethical science, if by ethical science one means the elaboration of a "true" system of morals. For we have seen that, as ethical judgments are mere expressions of feeling, there can be no way of determining the validity of any ethical system, and, indeed, no sense in asking whether any such system is true. All that one may legitimately enquire in this connection is, What are the moral habits of a given person or group of people, and what causes them to have precisely those habits and feelings? And this enquiry falls wholly within the scope of the existing social sciences.

It appears, then, that ethics as a branch of knowledge, is nothing more than a department of psychology and sociology. And in case anyone thinks that we are overlooking the existence of casuistry, we may remark that casuistry is not a science, but is a purely analytical investigation of the structure of a given moral system. In other words it is an exercise in formal logic.

When one comes to pursue the psychological enquiries which constitute ethical science, one is immediately enabled to account for the Kantian and hedonistic theories of morals. For one finds that one of the chief causes of moral behavior is fear, both conscious and unconscious, of a god's displeasure, and fear of the enmity of society. And this, indeed, is the reason why moral precepts present themselves to some people as "categorical" commands. And one finds, also, that the moral code of a society is partly determined by the beliefs of that society concerning the conditions of its own happiness—or, in other words, that a society tends to encourage or discourage a given type of conduct by the use of moral sanctions according as it appears to promote or detract from the contentment of the society as a whole. And this is the reason why altruism is recommended in most moral codes and egotism condemned. It is from the observation of this connection between morality and happiness that hedonistic or eudaemonistic theories of morals ultimately spring, just as the moral theory of Kant is based on the fact, previously explained, that moral precepts have for some people the force of inexorable commands. As each of these theories ignores the fact which lies at the root of the other, both may be criticized as being one-sided; but this is not the main objection to either of them. Their essential defect is that they treat propositions which refer to the causes and attributes of our ethical feelings as if they were definitions of ethical concepts. And thus they fail to recognize that ethical concepts are pseudo-concepts and consequently indefinable.

As we have already said, our conclusions about the nature of ethics apply to aesthetics also. Aesthetic terms are used in exactly the same way as ethical terms. Such aesthetic words as "beautiful" and "hideous" are employed, as ethical words are employed, not to make statements of fact, but simply to express certain feelings and evoke a certain response. It follows, as in ethics, that there is no sense in attributing objective validity to aesthetic judgments, and no possibility of arguing about questions of value in aesthetics, but only about questions of fact. A scientific treatment of aesthetics would show us what in general were the causes of aesthetic feeling, why various societies produced and admired the works of art they did, why taste varies as it does within a given society, and so forth. And these are ordinary psychological or sociological questions. They have, of course, little or nothing to do with aesthetic criticism as we understand it. But that is because the purpose of aesthetic criticism is not so much to give knowledge as to communicate emotion. The critic, by calling attention to certain features of the work under review, and expressing his own feelings about them, endeavors to make us share his attitude towards the work as a whole. The only relevant propositions that he formulates are propositions describing the nature of the work. And these are plain records of fact. We conclude, therefore, that there is nothing in aesthetics, any more than there is in ethics, to justify the view that it embodies a unique type of knowledge.

It should now be clear that the only information which we can legitimately derive from the study of our aesthetic and moral experiences is information about our own mental and physical make-up. We take note of these experiences as providing data for our psychological and sociological generalizations. And this is the only way in which they serve to increase our knowledge. It follows that any attempt to make our use of ethical and aesthetic concepts the basis of a metaphysical theory concerning the existence of a world of values, as distinct from the world of facts, involves a false analysis of these concepts. Our own analysis has shown that the phenomena of moral experience cannot fairly be used to support any rationalist or metaphysical doctrine whatsoever. In particular, they cannot, as Kant hoped, be used to establish the existence of a transcendent god.

This mention of God brings us to the question of the possibility of religious knowledge. We shall see that this possibility has already been ruled out by our treatment of metaphysics. But, as this is a point of considerable interest, we may be permitted to discuss it at some length.

NOTE ON SOURCES. The passages quoted are from A. J. Ayer "Critique of Ethics and Theology," *Language, Truth, and Logic* (New York: Dover Publications, 1946), Chapter 6.

6 BRAND BLANSHARD

EMOTIVISM CRITIQUED

FROM AYER TO BLANSHARD. In the preceding section we examined A. J. Ayer's exposition and defense of a theory about moral concepts and the moral judgments and moral principles in which they are used. The position is called emotivism. It is the claim that moral concepts (e.g., right, good, duty, together with their negatives, synonyms, and derivatives) do not refer to any facts about any acts or agents, are cognitively meaningless, and serve only to express or arouse emotions, feelings, in those who use them or those to whom they are used. Thus, when you say "Stealing is wrong" or, "You did wrong to steal," the term *wrong*, being a moral concept, does not tell you anything about either stealing or you. What it does is to express an emotion, a feeling, had by the person who made those "moral judgments," or intended to excite some emotion or feeling in the person addressed. An emotive term, or the emotive use of a term, is one that enables you to express an emotion or feeling (e.g., anger, disapproval, contempt, hatred, and so on.) The use of the term therefore tells you, or enables you to infer, something about the person who uses it; namely, that the person has a certain emotion or feeling and that he or she is expressing it, or that the person is endeavoring to excite some feeling in the person whom he or she is addressing. Since expressing or arousing a feeling is *all* that emotive language, or the emotive use of language, accomplishes, it follows that the "moral judgments" or "moral principles" in which they are used are, in the usual sense of the term, meaningless; have no objective reference; are neither true nor false; and so on. The emotive theory of moral "concepts," "judgments," and "principles" was drastically deflationary of all such "concepts," "judgments," and "principles." The deflationary intention was expressed by saying that, according to the emotive theory, these "concepts," "judgments," and "principles" were not concepts, judgments, and principles. They were pseudoconcepts, pseudojudgments, and pseudoprinciples.

Professor Blanshard puts this deflationary theory under attack. His paper, published in 1949, is an interesting example of an essay in counterattack. Emotivism was one road to antiethics. There may be others. The point of the anti-label is that such theories propose to abolish ethics. Professor Blanshard's argument, if successful, would put ethics back in business again, asking questions and making claims about moral concepts, and the judgments and principles in which they are used. The word *emotivism* draws attention to the fact that the theory claims that moral "concepts" do nothing but express or excite emotions or feelings. The word *subjectivism* draws attention to the fact that the theory claims that moral "concepts" tell you nothing about any "objects" (i.e., acts or agents) to which they "apply," but only about the subject, that person, the judger, who uses the pseudoconcept in question. What it tells you about the person, the subject, is that the person has a certain emotion or feeling, and that he or she is using the pseudoconcept to express said emotion or feeling, or to excite it in someone else.

BIOGRAPHICAL NOTE. Brand Blanshard was born in Fredericksburg, Ohio, in 1892. He attended the University of Michigan where he received his A.B. In 1918 he received an M.A. from Columbia University, and after a brief tour of duty in the United States Army, he pursued studies as a Rhodes Scholar at Oxford. Upon receiving his Ph.D. from Harvard in 1921, he returned to the University of Michigan as an assistant professor of philosophy. Several years later he was appointed to a position at Swarthmore College where he remained for two decades until Yale University brought him in as chairman of the philosophy department in 1945. He retired from Yale in 1961 and died in 1987 at the age of ninety-five.

THE ARGUMENT OF THE PASSAGES. Blanshard uses his first four paragraphs to introduce the position that he proposes to attack, and to talk about it with reference to such lead-in questions as, "What does it claim?" "Who are its sponsors?" "What are their interests or specialties or positions or commitments in philosophy?" "What motivated them to develop this antiethical theory?"

> By the new subjectivism in ethics I mean the view that when anyone says "this is right" or "this is good," he is only expressing his own feeling; he is not asserting anything true or false, because he is not asserting or judging at all; he is really making an exclamation that expresses a favorable feeling.
>
> This view has recently come into much favor. With variations of detail, it is being advocated by Russell, Wittgenstein and Ayer in England, and by Carnap, Stevenson, Feigl and others in this country. Why is it that the theory has come into so rapid a

popularity? Is it because moralists of insight have been making a fresh and searching examination of moral experience and its expression? No, I think not. A consideration of the names just mentioned suggests a truer reason. All these names belong, roughly speaking, to a single school of thought in this theory of knowledge. If the new view has become popular in ethics, it is because certain persons who were at work in the theory of knowledge arrived at a new view *there*, and found, on thinking it out, that it required the new view in ethics; the view comes less from ethical analysis than from logical positivism.

As positivists, these writers held that every judgment belongs to one or other of two types. On the one hand, it may be *a priori* or necessary. But then it is always analytic, i.e., it unpacks in its predicate part or all of its subject. Can we safely say that 7 + 5 makes 12? Yes, because 12 is what we mean by "7 + 5." On the other hand, the judgment may be empirical, and then, if we are to verify it, we can no longer look to our meanings only; it refers to sense experience and there we must look for its warrant. Having arrived at this division of judgments, the positivists raised the question where value judgments fall. The judgment that knowledge is good, for example, did not seem to be analytic; the value that knowledge might have did not seem to be part of our concept of knowledge. But neither was the statement empirical, for goodness was not a quality like red or squeaky that could be seen or heard. What were they to do, then, with these awkward judgments of value? To find a place for them in their theory of knowledge would require them to revise the theory radically, and yet that theory was what they regarded as their most important discovery. It appeared that the theory could be saved in one way only. If it could be shown that judgments of good and bad were not judgments at all, that they asserted nothing true or false, but merely expressed emotions like "Hurrah" or "Fiddlesticks," then these wayward judgments would cease from troubling and the weary hands could be at rest. This is the course the positivists took. They explained value judgments by explaining them away.

Now I do not think their view will do. But before discussing it, I should like to record one vote of thanks to them for the clarity with which they have stated their case. It has been said of John Stuart Mill that he wrote so clearly that he could be found out. This theory has been put so clearly and precisely that it deserves criticism of the same kind, and this I will do my best to supply. The theory claims to show by analysis that when we say, "That is good," we do not mean to assert a character of the subject of which we are thinking. I shall argue that we do mean to do just that.

The position is now before us. It is an essay, an exercise, in antiethics, directed against any or all traditional ethics from Socrates to the present day. Is it open to any criticisms, or even to refutation? Blanshard begins by describing a test case: a rabbit that has been caught in a trap, suffered great pain, and died. He then develops five criticisms of the emotivist or subjectivist position in antiethics. The example is this:

Let us work through an example, and the simpler and commoner the better. There is perhaps no value statement on which people would more universally agree than the statement that intense pain is bad. Let us take a set of circumstances in which I happen to be interested on the legislative side and in which I think every one of us might naturally make such a statement. We come upon a rabbit that has been caught in one of the brutal traps in common use. There are signs that it has struggled for days to escape and that in a frenzy of hunger, pain, and fear, it has all but eaten off its own leg. The attempt failed: the animal is now dead. As we think of the long and excruciating pain it must have suffered, we are very likely to say: "It was a bad thing that the little animal should suffer so." The positivist tells us that when we say this we are only expressing our present emotion. I hold on the contrary, that we mean to assert something of the pain itself, namely, that it was bad—bad when and as it occurred.

Blanshard's *first* criticism comes about this way: If you are *not* a committed emotivist or subjectivist, it would be open to you to say, "It was a bad thing that the little animal suffered so," and use the term *bad* to refer to the animal's pain and suffering, especially, I suppose, under those conditions. In your use, the term would have an objective referent, namely, the animal's pain and suffering; and it would have a judgmental force, namely, judging it to be a bad thing that the animal suffered this pain in this way. There would be nothing linguistically incorrect in your judgment. You knew what you were referring to, and you meant what you said. Suppose, however, that you have subscribed to emotivism, or subjectivism, in antiethics. Then what?

Consider what follows from the positivist view. On the view, nothing good or bad happened in the case until I came on the scene and made my remark. For what I express in my remark is something going on in me at the time, and that of course did not exist until I did come on the scene. The pain of the rabbit was not itself bad; nothing evil was happening when that pain was being endured; badness, in the only sense in which it is involved at all, waited for its appearance till I came and looked and felt. Now that this is at odds with our meaning may be shown as follows. Let us put to ourselves the hypothesis that we had not come on the scene and that the rabbit never was discovered. Are we prepared to say that in that case nothing bad occurred in the sense in which we said it did? Clearly not. Indeed we should say, on the contrary, and the accident of our later discovery made no difference whatever to the badness of the animal's pain, that it would have been every whit as bad whether a chance passer-by happened later to discover the body and feel repugnance or not. If so, then it is clear that in saying the suffering was bad we are not expressing our feelings only. We are saying that the pain was bad when and as it occurred and before anyone took an attitude toward it.

The first criticism, then, is that if you subscribe to the theory it will constrain you to say, or refrain from saying, things that, if it were not for the theory, you would not say, or would not refrain from saying. These coercions, constraints, are exercised by the theory, not by your knowledge of and judgment upon the animal's entrapment, suffering, and death. There is nothing to be said for these constraints except that they are required by this antiethical theory.

Blanshard's *second* criticism asks us to suppose that we were mistaken about the facts: the animal was not caught in the trap, did not suffer great pain, and did not die. If you are *not* an emotivist or subjectivist, you will, upon discovering your mistake, retract your judgment on the grounds that the relevant facts were not what you (mistakenly) took them to be. Your judgment, being erroneous as to the facts, lost its point: "There is no point to saying that it was a bad thing for it to suffer if it did not suffer." An error about the objective referent of your judgment requires you to retract your judgment. Suppose, however, that you are an emotivist or subjectivist. In what otherwise odd ways will your theory constrain you?

Let us suppose that the animal did not in fact fall into the trap and did not suffer at all, but that we mistakenly believe it did, and say as before that its suffering was an evil thing. On the positivist theory, everything I sought to express by calling it evil in the first case is still present in the second. In the only sense in which badness is involved at all, whatever was bad in the first case is still present in its entirety, since all that is expressed in either case is a state of feeling, and that feeling is still there. And our question is, is such an implication consistent with what we meant? Clearly, it is not. If anyone asked us, after we made the remark that the suffering was a bad thing, whether we should think it was relevant to what we said to learn that the incident had never occurred and no pain had been suffered at all, we should say that it made all the difference in the world, that what we were asserting to be bad was precisely the suffering we thought had occurred back there, that if this had not occurred, there was nothing left to be bad, and that our assertion was in that case mistaken. The suggestion that in saying something evil had occurred we were after all making no mistake, because we had never meant anyhow to say anything about the past suffering, seems to me merely frivolous. If we did not mean to say this, why should we be so relieved on finding that the suffering had not occurred? On the theory before us, such relief would be groundless, for in that suffering itself there was nothing bad at all, hence in its non-occurrence there would be nothing to be relieved about. The positivist theory would here distort our meaning beyond recognition.

So far as I can see, there is only one way out for the positivist. He holds that goodness and badness lie in feelings of approval or disapproval. And there is a way in which he might hold that badness did in this case precede our own feeling of disapproval without belonging to the pain itself. The pain in itself was neutral; but unfortunately the rabbit, on no grounds at all, took up toward this neutral object an attitude of disapproval, and that made it for the first time, and in the only intelligible sense, bad. This way of escape is theoretically possible, but since it has grave difficulties of its own and has not, so far as I know, been urged by positivists, it is perhaps best not to spend time over it.

Blanshard's *third* criticism asks us to suppose that when we authorized the moral judgment ("It is bad for an animal to suffer such pain and such a death," "It is wrong for people to cause such pain and death," and so on), we did so with considerable feeling, and that this feeling was expressed in our moral judgment. The words we used expressed two things: our moral judgment and our feelings of, say, sympathy and outrage. He further asks us to suppose that sometime later, after our feelings had "died down," we repeated our moral judgment. We might recall our feelings, we might remember that when we originally pronounced the moral judgment we were wrought up, whereas it is now a matter of "emotion recollected in tranquility." Nevertheless we do reiterate our original judgment: "It is bad for an animal to suffer such pain and such a death," "It is wrong for people to cause such pain and death," and so on. If you are *not* an emotivist, what account do you give of your two moral judgments? If you *are* an emotivist, what will your commitment constrain you to say, or to refrain from saying?

I come now to a third argument, which again is very simple. When we come upon the rabbit and make our remark about its suffering being a bad thing, we presumably make it with some feeling; the positivists are plainly right in saying that such remarks do usually express feeling. But suppose that a week later we revert to the incident in thought and make our statement again. And suppose that the circumstances have now so changed that the feeling with which we made the remark in the first place has faded. The pathetic evidence is no longer before us; and we are now so fatigued in body and mind that feeling is, as we say, quite dead. In these circumstances, since what was expressed by the remark when first made is, on the theory before us, simply absent, the remark now expresses nothing. It is as empty as the word "Hurrah" would be when there was no enthusiasm behind it. And this seems to me untrue. When we repeat the remark that such suffering was a bad thing, the feeling with which we made it last week may be at or near the vanishing point, but if we were asked whether we meant to say what we did before, we should certainly answer Yes. We should say that we made our point with feeling the first time and little or no feeling the second time, but that it was the same point we were making. And if we can see that what we meant to say remains the same, while the feeling varies from intensity to near zero, it is not the feeling that we primarily meant to express.

Blanshard's *fourth* criticism of emotivism as a theory about moral concepts and the judgments and principles in which they are used turns on a question about the attitudes that we may take up toward agents or actions and then express in our moral judgments. Suppose someone is needlessly and flagrantly cruel to animals and little children. They are in no position to defend themselves, so that person enjoys causing these helpless ones to squeal and squirm. Suppose our attitude toward such a person is one of disapproval. The question on which Blanshard's fourth criticism turns is whether our attitude of disapproval is fitting, unfitting, or neither. Is it fitting that we should take up an attitude of disapproval, and proceed to express it in a moral judgment? If it is fitting, what does this fittingness depend on? If it is unfitting, why is it unfitting? If you are not an emotivist, you might say that the fittingness of your attitude of disapproval depends on, derives from, the character of the agent or action toward which you have this attitude. It is unlikely that you would say that the fittingness of your attitude depends on the fact that you have this attitude. You might say, "The action [needless and flagrant cruelty to animals and children who cannot protect themselves] is wrong. That is why I disapprove of it. That is the reason for my attitude. In view of the wrongness of the action, my attitude is quite fitting. Indeed, it would be quite *unfitting* for me, or anyone else, to have toward such action an attitude of approval." Here the order is (1) the agent, (2) the agent's action, (3) its wrongness, (4) your attitude of disapproval, (5) the fittingness of your attitude, (6) the expression of the fitting attitude in your moral judgment. You could talk this way so long as you were not an emotivist. But how would emotivism require you to talk? What account would it constrain you to give of the fittingness of your attitude?

I come now to a fourth consideration. We all believe that toward acts or effects of a certain kind one attitude is fitting another not; but on the theory before us such a belief would not make sense. Broad and Ross have lately contended that this fitness is one of the main facts of ethics, and I suspect they are right. But that is not exactly my point. My point is this: whether there is such fitness or not, we all assume that there is, and if we do, we express in moral judgments more than subjectivists say we do. Let me illustrate.

In his novel *The House of the Dead*, Dostoevsky tells of his experiences in a Siberian prison camp. Whatever the unhappy inmates of such camps are like today, Dostoevsky's companions were about as grim a lot as can be imagined. "I have heard stories," he writes, "of the most terrible, the most unnatural actions, of the most monstrous murders, told with the most spontaneous, childishly merry laughter." Most of us would say that in this delight at the killing of others or the causing of suffering there is something very unfitting. If we were asked why we thought so, we should say that these things involve great evil and are wrong, and that to take delight in what is evil or wrong is plainly unfitting. Now on the subjectivist view, this answer is ruled out. For before someone takes up an attitude toward death, suffering, or their infliction, they have no moral quality at all. There is therefore nothing about them to which an attitude of approval or condemnation could be fitting. They are in themselves neutral, and, so far as they get a moral quality, they get it only through being invested with it by the attitude of the onlooker. But if that is true, why is any attitude more fitting than any other? Would applause, for example, be fitting if, apart from the applause, there were nothing good to applaud? Would condemnation be fitting if, independently of the condemnation, there were nothing bad to condemn? In such a case, any attitude would be as fitting or unfitting as any other, which means that the notion of fitness has lost all point.

Indeed we are forced to go much farther. If goodness and badness lie in attitudes only and hence are brought into being by them, those men who greeted death and misery with childishly merry laughter are taking the only sensible line. If there is nothing evil in these things, if they get their moral complexion only from our feeling about them, why shouldn't they be greeted with a cheer? To greet them with repulsion would turn what before was neutral into something bad; it would needlessly bring badness into the world; and even on subjectivist assumptions that does not seem very bright. On the other hand, to greet them with delight would convert what before was neutral into something good; it would bring goodness into the world. If I have murdered a man and wish to remove the stain, the way is clear. It is to cry, "Hurrah for murder."

What is the subjectivist to reply? I can only guess. He may point out that the inflicting of death is *not* really neutral before the onlooker takes his attitude, for the man who inflicted the death no doubt himself took an attitude, and thus the act had a moral quality derived from this. But that makes the case more incredible still, for the man who did the act presumably approved it, and if so it was good in the only sense in which anything is good, and then our conviction that the laughter is unfit is more unaccountable still. It may be replied that the victim, too, had his attitude and that since this was unfavorable, the act was not unqualifiedly good. But the answer is plain. Let the killer be expert at his job; let him despatch his victim instantly before he has time to take an attitude, and then gloat about his perfect crime without ever telling anyone. Then, so far as I can see, his act will be good without any qualification. It would become bad only if someone found out about it and disliked it. And that would be a curiously irrational procedure, since the man's approving of his own killing is in itself as neutral as the killing that it approves. Why then should anyone dislike it?

It may be replied that we can defend our dislike on this ground that, if the approval of killing were to go unchecked and spread, most men should have to live in insecurity and fear, and these things are undesirable. But surely this reply is not open; these things are not, on the theory, undesirable, for nothing is; in themselves they are neutral. Why then should I disapprove men's living in this state? The answer may come that if other men live in insecurity and fear, I shall in time be infected myself. But even in my own insecurity and fear there is, on the theory before us, nothing bad whatever, and therefore, if I disapprove them, it is without a shadow of ground and with no more fitness in my attitude than if I cordially cheered them. The theory thus conflicts with our judgments of fitness all along the line.

Blanshard's *fifth* criticism of emotivism, or subjectivism, turns on the traditional and, as he says, merciful distinction between the act being subjectively right and objectively right. He first explains this distinction, and illustrates its plausibility. He then points out that emotivism, or subjectivism, would abolish this distinction, regardless of how plausible it may be. He then points out, further, that if you abolish the distinction between subjectively right and objectively right you find you have thereby abolished the notion of duty. Your losses pile up; and they are forced upon you by, they are the price you pay for, your commitment to emotivism or subjectivism. At what point does a philosophical commitment price itself out of the market of ideas?

I come now to a fifth and final difficulty with the theory. It makes mistakes about values impossible. There is a whole nest of inter-connected criticisms here, some of which have been made so often that I shall not develop them again, such as that I can never agree or disagree in opinion with anyone else about an ethical matter, and that in these matters I can never be inconsistent with others or with myself. I am not at all content with the sort of analysis which says that the only contradictions in such cases have regard to facts and that contradictions about value are only differences of feeling. I think that if anyone tells me that having a bicuspid out without an anesthetic is not a bad experience and I say it is a very nasty experience indeed, I am differing with him in opinion, and differing about the degree of badness of the experience. But without pressing this further, let me apply the argument in what is perhaps a fresh direction.

There is an old and merciful distinction that moralists have made for many centuries about conduct—the distinction between what is subjectively and what is objectively right. They have said that in any given situation there is some act which, in view of all the circumstances, would be the best act to do; and this is what would be objectively right. The notion of an objectively right act is the ground of our notion of duty; our duty is always to find and do this act if we can. But of course we often don't find it. We often hit upon and do acts that we think are the right ones, but we are mistaken; and then our act is only subjectively right. Between these two acts the disparity may be continual; Professor Prichard suggested that probably few of us in the course of our lives ever succeed in doing *the* right act.

Now so far as I can see, the new subjectivism would abolish this difference at a stroke. Let us take a case. A boy abuses his small brother. We should commonly say, "That is wrong, but perhaps he doesn't know any better. By reason of bad teaching and a feeble imagination, he may see nothing wrong in what he is doing, and may even be proud of it. If so, his act may be subjectively right, though it is miles away from what is objectively right." What concerns me about the new subjectivism is that it prohibits this distinction. If the boy feels this way about his act, then it is right in the only sense in which anything is right. The notion of an objective right lying beyond what he has discovered, and which he ought to seek and do is meaningless. There might, to be sure, be an act that would more generally arouse favorable feelings in others, but that would not make it right for him unless he thought of it and approved it, which he doesn't. Even if he did think of it, it would not be obligatory for him to feel about it in any particular way, since there is nothing in any act, as we have seen, which would make any feeling more suitable than any other.

Now if there is no such thing as an objectively right act, what becomes of the idea of duty? I have suggested that the idea of duty rests on the idea of such an act, since it is always our duty to find that act and do it if we can. But if whatever we feel approval for at the time is right, what is the point of doubting and searching further? Like the little girl in Boston who was asked if she would like to travel, we can answer, "Why should I travel when I'm already there?" If I am reconciled in feeling to my present act, no act I could discover by reflection could be better, and therefore why reflect or seek at all? Such a view seems to me to break the mainspring of duty, to destroy the motive for self-improvement, and to remove the ground for self-criticism. It may be replied that by further reflection I can find an act that would satisfy my feelings more widely than the present one, and that this is the act I should seek. But this reply means either that such general satisfaction is objectively better, which would contradict the theory, or else that, if at the time I don't feel it better, it isn't better, in which case I have no motive for seeking it.

When certain self-righteous persons took an inflexible line with Oliver Cromwell, his very Cromwellian reply was, "Bethink ye, gentlemen, by the bowels of Christ, that ye may be mistaken." It was good advice. I hope nobody will take from me the privilege of finding myself mistaken. I should be sorry to think that the self of thirty years ago was as far along the path as the self of today, merely because he was a smug young jackanapes, or even that the paragon of today has a little room for improvement as would be allowed by his myopic complacency.

Blanshard's criticisms have consisted in pointing out constraints that emotivism imposes upon those who subscribe to it. It requires them to say things they would not otherwise say, or to refrain from saying things they would otherwise say. The constraints are not evidence that emotivism is false considered as a theory of moral concepts together with the judgments and principles in which those concepts are used. They are concessions you make if you are an emotivist, ways in which you are theory-bound if you are an emotivist. As a parting shot, Blanshard draws attention to a less theoretical, more practical, consequence: what emotivism would lead to if it were applied to international law, international politics, international relations.

One final remark. The great problems of the day are international problems. Has the new subjectivism any bearing upon these problems? I think it has, and a somewhat sinister bearing. I would not suggest, of course, that those who hold the theory are one whit less public-spirited than others; surely there are few who could call themselves citizens of the world with more right (if "rights" have meaning any longer) than Mr. Russell. But Mr. Russell has confessed himself discontented with his ethical theory, and in view of his breadth of concern, one cannot wonder. For its general acceptance would, so far as one can see, be an international disaster. The assumption behind the old League and the new United Nations was that there is such a thing as right and wrong in the conduct of a nation, a right and wrong that do not depend on how it happens to feel at the time. It is implied, for example, that when Japan invaded Manchuria in 1931 she might be wrong, and that by discussion and argument she might be shown to be wrong. It was implied that when the Nazis invaded Poland they might be wrong, even though German public sentiment overwhelmingly approved it. On the theory before us, it would be meaningless to call these nations mistaken: if they felt approval for what they did, then it was right with as complete a justification as could be supplied for the disapproval felt by the rest of the world. In the present dispute between Russia and our own country over southeast Europe, it is nonsense to speak of the right or rational course for either of us to take; if with all the facts before the two parties, each feels approval for its own course, both attitudes are equally justified or unjustified; neither is mistaken; there is no common reason to which they can take an appeal; there are no principles by which an international court could pronounce on the matter; nor would there be any obligation to obey the pronouncement if it were made. This cuts the ground from under any attempt to establish one's case as right or anyone else's case as wrong. So if our friends the subjectivists still hold their theory after I have applied my little ruler to their knuckles, which of course they will, I have but one request to make of them: Do keep it from Mr. Molotov and Mr. Vishinsky.

NOTE ON SOURCES. This material is taken from Brand Blanshard, "The New Subjectivism in Ethics," *Philosophy and Phenomenological Research* 9 (1948–1949): 504–511.

7 C. L. STEVENSON

EMOTIVISM REFINED

FROM AYER AND BLANSHARD TO STEVENSON. Stevenson disagrees with Ayer's contention that ethical judgments are nothing more than outbursts of emotion and, therefore, only pseudostatements. Stevenson agrees with Ayer that many ethical disagreements have their root in differing attitudes; that people can agree on the facts and still have moral disputes. For example, management and labor may agree that if wages go up, profits go down. Nonetheless, labor thinks that increases in salary are a good thing and management thinks that increases in salary are a bad thing. Stevenson points out that Ayer has taken this common sense insight about the nature of moral disputes too far. Instead of Ayer's oversimplified emotivism, Stevenson offers a more sophisticated theory of ethical language—one that can account for the role of emotions *and* the role of facts. When Stevenson is finished, "This is good" will be partly factual and partly emotive. Thus, Stevenson is not nearly as open to the charge of being a subjectivist as is Ayer.

BIOGRAPHICAL NOTE. Charles Leslie Stevenson (born in 1908) received his Ph.D. in philosophy from Harvard in 1935 after attending Yale University and Cambridge

University in England. Before coming to the University of Michigan, Stevenson taught at Yale University. He died in 1979.

THE ARGUMENT OF THE PASSAGES. Stevenson begins by distinguishing between two ways we can agree or disagree. There are disagreements in attitude and disagreements in belief. Disagreements in belief are disagreements about the facts of the matter. For example, will profits go down if salaries increase? Isn't it possible that workers, spurred by higher salaries, will produce more and thus increase productivity and profits? Then there are disagreements in attitude. Stevenson wants us to take *attitude* in a broad sense to include our feelings and inclinations toward or about something. In his view, our attitudes are sometimes strongly felt (as is often the case with the abortion issue), and other times, our attitudes are weakly felt (such as whether to eat at one fast food restaurant or another).

Stevenson characterizes the central task of ethics as showing how, in each instance of disagreement, beliefs and attitudes are related.

Our first question, though seemingly peripheral, will prove to be of central importance:

What is the nature of ethical *agreement* and *disagreement*? Is it parallel to that found in the natural sciences, differing only with regard to the relevant subject matter; or is it of some broadly different sort?

If we can answer the question, we shall obtain a general understanding of what constitutes a normative *problem*; and our study of terms and methods, which must explain how this kind of problem becomes articulate and how it is open to argument or inquiry, will be properly oriented. There are certain normative problems, of course, to which the question is not directly relevant—those which arise in personal deliberation, rather than in interpersonal discourse, and which involve not disagreement or agreement but simply uncertainty or growing conviction. But we shall later find that the question is indirectly relevant even to them; and meanwhile there is a convenience in looking chiefly to the interpersonal problems, where the use of terms and methods is most clearly evidenced.

For simplicity let us limit our explicit attention to "disagreement," treating the positive term by implication. And let us begin by distinguishing two broad kinds of disagreement. We can do this in a wholly general way, temporarily suspending any decision about which kind is most typical of normative ethics, and drawing our examples from other fields.

The disagreements that occur in science, history, biography, and their counterparts in everyday life, will require only brief attention. Questions about the nature of light-transmission, the voyages of Leif Ericsson, and the date on which Jones was last in to tea, are all similar in that they may involve an opposition that is primarily of beliefs. (The term "beliefs" must not, at least for the moment, include reference to ethical convictions; for whether or not the latter are "beliefs" in the present sense is largely the point that is to be discussed.) In such cases one man believes that p is the answer, and another that not-p, or some proposition incompatible with p, is the answer; and in the course of discussion each tries to give some manner of proof for his view, or revise it in the light of further information. Let us call this "disagreement in belief."

There are other cases, differing sharply from these, which may yet be called "disagreements" with equal propriety. They involve an opposition, sometimes tentative and gentle, sometimes strong, which is not of beliefs, but rather of attitudes—that is to say, an opposition of purposes, aspirations, wants, preferences, desires, and so on.[1] Since it is tempting to overintellectualize these situations, giving too much attention to beliefs, it will be helpful to examine them with care.

Suppose that two people have decided to dine together. One suggests a restaurant where there is music; another expresses his disinclination to hear music, and suggests some other restaurant. It may then happen, as we commonly put it, that they "cannot easily agree on which restaurant to choose." The disagreement springs more from divergent preferences than from divergent beliefs, and will end when they both *wish* to go to the same place. It will be a mild, temporary disagreement for this simple case—a disagreement in miniature; yet it will be a "disagreement" in a wholly familiar sense.

Further examples are easily found. Mrs. A has social aspirations, and wants to move with the elite. Mr. A is easy-going, and loyal to his old friends. They accordingly disagree about what guests they will invite to their party. The curator of the museum wants to buy pictures by contemporary artists; some of his advisers prefer the purchase of old masters. They disagree. John's mother is concerned about the dangers of playing football, and doesn't want him to play. John, even though he agrees (in belief) about the dangers, wants to play anyhow. Again, they disagree. These examples, like the previous one, involve an opposition of attitudes, and differ only in that the attitudes in question are a little stronger, and are likely to be defended more seriously. Let us refer to disagreement of this sort as "disagreement in attitude."[2] Two men will be said to disagree in attitude when they have opposed attitudes to the same object—one approving of it, for instance, and the other disapproving of it—and when at least one of them has a motive for altering or calling into question the attitude of the other. Let us be careful to observe, however, that when one man is seeking to alter another's attitudes, he may at the same time be preparing to alter his own attitudes in the light of what the other may say. Disagreement in attitude, like disagreement in belief, need not be an occasion for forensic rivalry; it may be an occasion for an interchange of aims, with a reciprocal influence that both parties find to be beneficial.

The two kinds of disagreement differ mainly in this respect: the former is concerned with how matters are truthfully to be described and explained; the latter is concerned with how they are to be favored or disfavored, and hence with how they are to be shaped by human efforts.

Let us apply the distinction to a case that will sharpen it. Suppose Mr. Nearthewind maintains that most voters favor a certain bill, and Mr. Closerstill maintains that most of them are against it. It is clear that the two men disagree, and that their disagreement concerns *attitudes*—namely, the attitudes they believe the voters to have. But are Nearthewind and Closerstill disagreeing in attitude? Clearly not. So far as their above contentions show, they are disagreeing in *belief about* attitudes, and need not be disagreeing *in* attitude at all. Disagreement in belief about attitudes is simply a special sort of disagreement in belief, differing from disagreement in belief

---

1   The term "attitude" is here used in much the same broad sense that R. B. Perry gives to "interest." See his *General Theory of Value* (Longmans, Green, 1926), particularly p. 115.

2   In all of the examples given there may be a *latent* disagreement in belief, in addition to the disagreement in attitude. This is likely to be true of any example that is not painfully artificial; but the present examples are serviceable enough for their introductory purpose.

about head colds only with regard to subject matter. It implies not an opposition of the attitudes of the speakers, but only an opposition of certain of their beliefs that refer to attitudes. Disagreement *in* attitude, however, implies an opposition of the very attitudes of the speakers. Nearthewind and Closerstill may have opposing beliefs about attitudes without having opposing attitudes, just as they may have opposing beliefs about head colds without having opposing head colds. In so far as they are seeking detached descriptions of the state of human attitudes, they are disagreeing in belief; for attitudes enter only as a topic for cognitive study.

A parallel distinction holds for the positive term, "agreement," which may designate either convergent beliefs or convergent attitudes. And agreement in belief must still be distinguished from agreement in attitude, even when the beliefs are about attitudes. It will be convenient to use "agreement," whether in belief or in attitude, as the logical contrary of "disagreement," rather than as its full contradictory. People may neither agree nor disagree—as will happen when they are in a state of mutual indecision or irresolution, or when they simply "differ," having divergent beliefs or attitudes without a sufficient motive for making them alike.

Let us continue to preserve expository economy by giving explicit attention to "disagreement," treating "agreement" mainly by implication. The opposite procedure, which perhaps would seem more natural, has not been adopted for this simple reason: Our distinctions will subsequently be carried over to ethical *methodology*. For this special purpose disagreement requires closer scrutiny than agreement; for although the norms which are generally accepted, and embodied in the mores of any given society, are undoubtedly more numerous than the controversial ones, the latter present instances where methods of reasoning are more overtly employed, and more readily available for illustration and study.

We must now see how the two sorts of disagreement are related, still illustrating our conclusions by examples that are not (or at least not obviously) ethical.

It is by no means the case that every argument represents one sort of disagreement to the exclusion of the other. There is often disagreement of both sorts. This is to say little more than that our beliefs and attitudes must not be compartmentalized. Our attitudes, as many have pointed out, often affect our beliefs, not only by causing us to indulge in wishful thinking, but also by leading us to develop and check such beliefs as point out the means of getting what we want. And conversely, our beliefs often affect our attitudes; for we may alter our form of approval of something when we change our beliefs about its nature. The causal connection between beliefs and attitudes is usually not only intimate but reciprocal. To ask whether beliefs in general direct attitudes in general, or whether the causal connection goes rather in the opposite direction, is simply a misleading question. It is like asking, "Do popular writers influence public taste, or does public taste influence them?" Any implication that the alternatives are mutually exclusive can only be rejected. The influence goes both ways, although at times only one direction of influence may predominate.

There is accordingly a close relationship between the sorts of disagreement that have been distinguished. Indeed, in some cases the existence of one may wholly depend on the existence of the other. Suppose that A and B have convergent attitudes toward the *kind* of thing that X *actually* is, but indicate divergent attitudes to X itself simply because A has erroneous beliefs about it, whereas B has not. Discussion or inquiry, correcting A's errors, may resolve the disagreement in belief; and this in turn may be sufficient to resolve the disagreement in attitude. X was an occasion for the latter sort of disagreement *only* because it was an occasion for the former.

In cases of this sort one might be inclined to reject the expression, "Both kinds of disagreement were initially present, the one depending on the other," and say instead, "Only disagreement in belief was initially present, the disagreement in attitude with regard to X being simply apparent." If X was designated without ambiguity, however, so that the same X could be *recognized* by both parties regardless of their divergent beliefs about it, then the latter idiom would be seriously misleading. One man was definitely striving for X, and the other definitely striving to oppose it; and if this involved ignorance, where one of the men was acting to defeat his broader aims, it remains altogether appropriate to say that the initial divergence in attitude, so far as X was concerned, was genuine. It is convenient to restrict the term "apparent" disagreement to cases which involve ambiguity—to cases where the term that seems to designate X for both parties actually designates Y for one of them.

The relationship between the two sorts of disagreement, whenever it occurs, is always factual, never logical. So far as the logical possibilities are concerned, there may be disagreement in belief without disagreement in attitude; for even if an argument must always be motivated, and to that extent involve attitudes, it does not follow that the attitudes which attend opposed beliefs must themselves be opposed. People may share the ideals and aims which guide their scientific theorizing, for instance, and still reach divergent beliefs. Similarly, there may be disagreement in attitude without disagreement in belief. Perhaps every attitude must be accompanied by some belief about its object; but the beliefs which attend opposed attitudes need not be incompatible. A and B may both believe that X has Q, for instance, and have divergent attitudes to X *on that very account*, A approving of objects that have Q and B disapproving of them. Since it may also happen that both sorts of disagreement occur conjointly, or that neither should occur, the logical possibilities are all open. Hence one must appeal to experience to determine which of the possibilities, in any given case or class or cases, is in fact realized. But experience clearly shows, as we shall later see in detail, that the cases which involve *both* sorts of disagreement (or agreement) are extremely numerous.

We have now seen how the sorts of disagreement can be distinguished, and how (in a very broad way) they are related. There is only one further point, among these preliminary considerations, that deserves mention. Our distinction between the sorts of disagreement has presupposed a more general one—that between beliefs and attitudes. Like so many psychological distinctions, the latter is not easily made clear. Would further analysis serve to undermine it? Does any sharp separation reflect an antiquated school of thought, in which beliefs are so many mental photographs, the product of a special cognitive faculty, whereas attitudes stand apart as the drives or forces of a totally different faculty?

A moment's consideration will show that the distinction can be preserved in a much more legitimate manner. It is possible, for instance, to accept the pragmatic contention that beliefs and attitudes must both be analyzed, partly at least, with reference to dispositions to action. Such a view in no way suggests that beliefs and attitudes are "identical," so long as it is soberly understood. It shows that they are more alike than the older psychologists suspected, but it does not make them alike in every respect. The common genus does not obliterate all differentiae.

If it is difficult to specify just *how* beliefs and attitudes differ, it remains the case that for practical purposes we do and must make such a distinction every day. A chess expert, playing with a novice, uses an opening that appears very weak. An onlooker wonders, "Does he make the move because he *believes* that it is a strong one, or because, out of charity to his opponent, he doesn't *want* to make a strong one?" The distinction here between a belief and a want (attitude) is certainly beyond any practical objection. One can imagine the expert, with constant beliefs about the opening, using it or not in accordance with his changing desires to win; or one can imagine him, with constant desires to win, using it or not in accordance with his changing beliefs. If in imagining this independent variation of the "causal factors" involved one is tempted to hypostatize either "belief" or "attitude," the fault must be corrected not by dispensing with the terms in favor of purely *generic* talk about action, but rather by coming to understand the full complexity of reference that lies behind the convenient simplicity of language. To say that beliefs and attitudes are indistinguishable factors, and that an action which they determine will vary with a variation in either one, is to use a familiar English idiom, which makes good sense so long as it is not pressed into some artificially simple mold. It is parallel to the statement that the selectivity and sensitivity of a radio are distinguishable factors, and that the quality of reception which they determine will vary with a variation in either one. Such a statement need not make "selectivity" and "sensitivity" designate hypostatic "parts" of the radio; nor does the parallel statement about beliefs and attitudes require a hypostatic psychology.

In the example of the chess player, it may be added, there is no lack of empirical criteria by which the onlooker may determine which attitudes and which beliefs determine the expert's play. No matter where the onlooker's inferences may lead him, he must begin by observing the expert's behavior, and can find there all the evidence that a practical decision requires. The behavior that enables him to decide this is endlessly more complicated than the simple move of the pawn. . . .

The present views can now be stated, though at first only in synoptic form.

When ethical issues become controversial, they involve disagreement that is of a *dual* nature. There is almost inevitably disagreement in belief, which requires detailed, sensitive attention; but there is also disagreement in attitude. An analysis which seeks a full picture of ethics, in touch with practice, must be careful to recognize both factors, neither emphasizing the former to the exclusion of the latter, nor the latter to the exclusion of the former. Only by this means can it reveal the varied functions of the ethical terms, and make clear how the methods of ethics compare with those of the natural sciences. Only by this means, indeed, can it envisage its proper task; for the central problem of ethical analysis—one might almost say "the" problem—is one of showing in detail how beliefs and attitudes are related.

If we examine the concrete ethical problems that arise in daily life, we shall easily see that they have much to do with beliefs.

With his foundation set, Stevenson gives us his first approach to the meta-ethical analysis of "This is good." We shall look only at what he terms his first working model. Throughout the book, *Ethics and Language*, Stevenson added refinements to this first model. Yet, it is this model that carries the weight of his view.

Our conclusions about disagreement have prepared the way for a study of the ethical terms, and the characteristic features of ethical methodology. The present chapter will deal with both of these topics, but in a manner that is deliberately oversimplified. In place of a detailed analysis of ethical judgements, it will provide only "working models" for analysis—definitions which approximate to ethical meanings with sufficient accuracy to be of temporary help. Methods of proving or supporting ethical judgments will be considered only to the extent that the working models suggest them. This procedure will serve to introduce the essential features of our study, stress their interdependence, and indicate the points that will later require more careful development.

Let us begin with some remarks about meaning. This much will be directly evident from the preceding chapter: Any definition which seeks to identify the meaning of ethical terms with that of scientific ones, and which does so without further explanation or qualification, is extremely likely to be misleading. It will suggest that the questions of normative ethics, like those of science, give rise to an agreement or disagreement that is exclusively in *belief*. In this way, ignoring disagreement in attitude, it will lead to only a half-picture, at best, or the situations in which the ethical terms are actually used.

This conclusion must not be pressed insensitively, without regard to the ambiguities and flexibilities of language. It may well be that at *some* times *all* of the effective meaning of ethical terms is scientific, and that at *all* times *some* of it is; but there remain multitudes of familiar cases in which the ethical terms are used in a way that is *not exclusively* scientific, and we must recognize a meaning which suits them to their additional function.

What is the nature of this extrascientific meaning? Let us proceed by analogy, comparing ethical sentences with others that are less perplexing but have a similar use.

Interesting analogues can be found in ordinary imperatives. Is there not a ready passage from "You ought to defend your country" to "Defend your country"? Or more prosaically, is not the expression, "You oughtn't to cry," as said to children, roughly interchangeable with "Stop crying"? There are many differences, unquestionably; but there are likewise these similarities: Both imperative and ethical sentences are used more for encouraging, altering, or redirecting people's aims and conduct than for simply describing them. Both differ in this respect from the sentences of science. And in arguments that involve disagreement in attitude, it is obvious that imperatives, like ethical judgments, have an important place. The example about the restaurant, for instance, by which the conception of disagreement in attitude was first introduced, might begin with the use of imperatives exclusively:

A: Meet me at the Glenwood for dinner at 7:00.

B: Don't let's go to a restaurant with music. Meet me at the Ambassador instead.

A: But do make it the Glenwood . . . etc.

So the argument might begin, disagreement in attitude being indicated either by the ordinary second person form of the imperative, or by the first person plural form that begins with "Let's."

On account of this similar function of imperative and ethical sentences, it will be useful to consider some definitions that *in part* identify them. These definitions will not be adequate to the subtleties of common usage; they will be markedly inaccurate. But they will preserve in rough form much that is essential to ethical analysis, and on that account will be instructive approximations. It is they which will constitute the "working models" that have previously been mentioned.

There are many ways in which working models can be devised, but those which follow are perhaps the most serviceable:

(1) "This is wrong" means *I disapprove of this; do so as well.*
(2) "He ought to do this" means *I disapprove of his leaving this undone; do so as well.*
(3) "This is good" means *I approve of this; do so as well.*

It will be noted that the definiens in each case has two parts: first a declarative statement, "I approve" or "I disapprove," which describes the attitudes of the speaker, and secondly an imperative statement, "do so as well," which is addressed to changing or intensifying the attitudes of the hearer. These components, acting together, readily provide for agreement or disagreement in attitude. The following examples will illustrate how this is so:

A: This is good.

B: I fully agree. It is indeed good.

Freely translated in accordance with model (3) above, this becomes,

A: I approve of this; do so as well.

B: I fully concur in approving of it; (continue to) do so as well.

Here the declarative parts of the remarks, testifying to convergent attitudes, are sufficient to imply the agreement. But if taken alone, they hint too much at a bare description of attitudes. They do not evidence the *contagion* of warmly expressed approval— the interaction of attitudes that makes each man's favorable evaluation strengthen and invigorate the other's. This latter effect is highly characteristic of an articulate ethical agreement; and the imperatives in our translated version of the example do something (though in a most imperfect way) to make it evident.

Let us consider an example of disagreement:

A: This is good.

B: No, it is bad.

Translated in accordance with the working models, this becomes,

A: I approve of this, do so as well.

B: No, I disapprove of it; do so as well.

The declarative parts of the remarks show that the men have opposed attitudes, one approving and the other disapproving. The imperative parts show that each man is suggesting that the other redirect his attitudes. Since "disagreement in attitude" has been defined with exclusive reference to an opposition of attitudes and efforts to redirect them or call them into question, it will be clear that a place for this sort of disagreement is retained (though again only in an imperfect way) by the working models that have been suggested.

But if the models are to help us more than they hinder us, they must be used with extreme caution. Although they give a needed emphasis to agreement and disagreement in attitude, they give no emphasis to agreement and disagreement in belief. Hence the *dual* source of ethical problems is not made evident. If traditional theory too often lost sight of attitudes in its concern with beliefs, we must not make the opposite error of losing sight of beliefs in our concern with attitudes. The latter error, which would give ethics the appearance of being cut off from reasoned argument and inquiry, would be even more serious than the former.

It is possible to avoid this error, however, and at the same time to retain the working models as rough approximations. Although it may at first seem that the full nature of ethical issues, and the relative importance of their component factors, should be made evident from the definitions of the ethical terms alone, this require-ment is not an inviolable one. It may be dispensed with provided that the proper weight of emphasis is established elsewhere. The central requirement for a definition, then, is simply that it *prepare the way* for a complete account. Now if the models had accentuated beliefs at the expense of attitudes, the emphasis could not easily have been corrected by subsequent remarks; and for that reason it has been necessary to deviate from definitions of the traditional sort. But when the models accentuate atti-tudes at the expense of beliefs, the correct emphasis can easily be reestablished. We shall later turn to a study of methodology, where in the nature of the case there must be close attention to the cognitive aspects of ethics. If we are careful, in that connec-tion, to restore beliefs to their proper place, recognizing their great complexity and variety, we shall preserve a proper weighting of the factors involved.

Throughout the present chapter, accordingly, and in several of the chapters that follow, the analysis of meanings will emphasize agreement and disagreement in atti-tude, whereas the analysis of methods will emphasize agreement and disagreement in belief. The intimate relationship between the two factors will not be obscured by this procedure, but rather, as we shall see, will be made all the more evident. Yet it is important to realize that the procedure is somewhat arbitrary, and that an alternative to it will be needed to make our analysis complete. In the meanwhile, every care must be taken to prevent the discussion of meaning, whenever it proceeds in temporary isolation from the rest of analysis, from suggesting that beliefs have only an inconse-quential, secondary role in ethics. Such a view is wholly foreign to the present work, and foreign to the most obvious facts of daily experience.

If we avoid this confusion, we shall find that the working models are often instructive. The imperative sentence, which is one of their constituents, has a function that is of no little interest. To understand this, let us compare (3), the working model for "good," with one that is closely parallel to it:

4. "This is good" means *I approve of this and I want you to do so as well.*

This differs from (3) only in that the imperative sentence, "Do so as well," gives place to the declarative sentence, "I want you to do so as well." The change *seems* trivial, for it is often the case that "Do so and so," and "I want you to do so and so" have the same practical use. "I want you to open the window," for instance, has much the same imperative effect, usually, as "Open the window." The imperative function is not confined to the imperative mood. And *if* the declarative sentence which occurs in (4) is taken to have an imperative function, then to belabor the distinction between (3) and (4) is indeed trivial. It remains the case, however, that (4) is likely to be confusing. Although "I want you to do so as well" may be taken to have an imperative function, it also may not. It may be taken as a bare introspective report of the speaker's state of mind, used to describe his wants, to communicate beliefs about them for cognitive purposes, rather than to secure their satisfaction. (If such an interpretation is unlikely to occur in common life, it may easily occur amid the perplexing abstractions of philo-sophical theory.) In particular, (4) may suggest that "This is good" is used primarily, or even exclusively, to express *beliefs about* attitudes. It may accentuate agreement or disagreement in belief to the exclusion of agreement or disagreement in attitude. Definition (3) is preferable to (4) because it is not open to this misinterpretation. Its component imperative, being never used *merely* as an introspective report, renders unambiguously explicit the fact that "good" is used not only in expressing beliefs about attitudes, but in strengthening, altering, and guiding the attitudes themselves.

The misleading character of definition (4) can be shown by a continuation of the second example on page 364. Translated after the manner of (4), rather than (3), this becomes:

A: I approve of this, and want you to do so as well.

B: No. I disapprove of this, and want you to do so as well.

Taken purely as introspective reports, these statements are logically compatible. Each man is describing his state of mind, and since their states of mind may be different, each may be correct. Now remembering that the statements purport to be translations, respectively, of "This is good" and "No, it is bad," one may be inclined to conclude: "Then according to definition (4) people don't really disagree about what is good or bad. They may think that they do, but only because of an elementary confusion in the use of pronouns." G. E. Moore has actually used this as a *reductio ad absurdam* of any definition which makes "good" refer wholly to the speaker's own attitudes;[3] and granted the tacit assumptions on which he works, his point is well taken. [See our discussion of Moore later in this chapter, pp. 374–377—Eds.] But if "I want you to do so as well" is interpreted as having an imperative function, supplementing its descriptive one—or better, if this declarative sentence is replaced by an imperative one, following definition (3)—and if ethical controversy is recognized to involve disagreement in attitude, then the preposterous consequence that "people don't really disagree in ethics" becomes a consequence, it is suggested, not of neglecting Moore's indefinable quality of goodness, but of insisting that ethical controversy centers *entirely* upon beliefs—and indeed, beliefs which are to be found by scrutinizing ethical sentences themselves, isolated from the many other sentences that form a part of their living context. It must be remarked, however, that this refusal to look beyond beliefs (which usually ends, paradoxically enough, by making too little of them rather than too much) is no more characteristic of Moore than of many of his "naturalistic" opponents, and that he is usually more careful than they in pressing a mutual presupposition to its logical conclusions.

The nature of the working models has now been indicated. To the question, "What distinguishes ethical statements from scientific ones?" it has been answered: Ethical statements have a meaning that is approximately, and in part, imperative. This imperative meaning explains why ethical judgements are so intimately related to agreement and disagreement in attitude, and helps to indicate how normative ethics can be distinguished from psychology and the natural sciences.

Having established that ethical statements differ from scientific statements primarily by being, in part, imperatives (our next author, R. M. Hare, develops this insight), Stevenson goes on to discuss the nature of imperatives. He argues that while one cannot prove an imperative, one can argue that some imperatives are more appropriate than others, given certain circumstances. For example, "Shut that window!" makes no sense if the window is already shut. Giving that order makes a good deal of sense if there is a loud party next door and you are

---

3   *Ethics* (Henry Holt, 1911), pp. 100–102; and *Philosophical Studies* (Harcourt Brace, 1922), p. 333. The present writer has made a detailed criticism of this argument, and some parallel ones, in "Some of Moore's Arguments against Ethical Naturalism," in *The Philosophy of G. E. Moore*, edited by P. A. Schilpp (Evanston and Chicago: Northwestern University, 1942).

trying to study. It makes little sense if there is a lot of smoke in the house from burning food. These sorts of examples show that reasons are important in settling ethical disputes, even if what characterizes ethical disputes is their imperative nature. Giving reasons is how we argue for appropriateness. Thus, Stevenson avoids what he takes to be the rather damning charge of subjectivism.

We must now turn to questions about method. When people argue about evaluative matters, by what sort of reasoning can they hope to reach agreement? The answer can as yet be presented only in a schematic form. It will presuppose that the working models can be accepted without further criticism; and since that is manifestly not the case, only rough approximations will be possible.

The model for "This is good" consists of the conjunction of (a) "I approve of this," and (b) "Do so as well." If a proof is possible for (a) and (b) taken separately, then and only then will it be possible for their conjunction. So let us see what can be done with the sentences separately.

Sentence (a) offers no trouble. It makes an assertion about the speaker's state of mind, and like any psychological statement, is open to empirical confirmation or disconfirmation, whether introspective or behavioristic.

Sentence (b), however, raises a question. Since it is an imperative, it is not open to proof at all. What is it like to prove a command? If we told a person to close the door, and received the reply, "Prove it!" should we not, to speak mildly, grow somewhat impatient?

Thus it would seem that ethical judgments are amenable only to a partial proof. So far as "This is good" includes the meaning of (a) a proof is possible, but so far as it includes the meaning of (b) the very request for a proof is nonsensical. We seem forced to a distressingly meager conclusion: If a man says "X is good," and if he can prove that he really approves of X, then he has all the proof that can be demanded of him.

So, indeed, it now *seems*. But it does so only because we have tacitly assumed that a proof in ethics must be exactly like a proof in science. The possibility that ethical judgments may have a *different sort* of proof has not been considered. Or rather, since "proof" may be a misleading term, let us put it this way: It has yet to be considered whether there is some "substitute for a proof" in ethics, some support or reasoned argument which, although different from a proof in science, will be equally serviceable in removing the hesitations that usually prompt people to ask for a proof.

If there is some such analogue to proof, it must unquestionably be considered in the present study of methodology. Otherwise the study will be open to a gross misunderstanding. It may lead people to suppose that the meagerness of proof *in the strict sense* deprives ethics of a "rational foundation" or "intersubjective validity" that is sorely needed; whereas all that is needed may in fact be provided for by the analogue mentioned.

To develop this point, let us return to imperatives, which have presented a methodological perplexity. Although imperatives cannot be "proved," are there not reasons or arguments which may at least "support" them?

The question is by no means difficult. An imperative may be met by the question "Why?" and this "Why?" asks for a *reason*. For instance: If told to close the door, one may ask "Why?" and receive some such reason as "It is too drafty," or "The noise is distracting." Or again, if a person is told to work harder, he may ask "Why?" and receive some such reply as "If you don't you will become an unhappy sort of dilettante." These reasons cannot be called "proofs" in any but a dangerously extended sense, nor are they demonstratively or inductively related to an imperative; but they manifestly do *support* an imperative. They "back it up," or "establish it," or "base it on concrete references to fact." And they are analogous to proofs in that they may remove the doubts or hesitations that prevent the imperative from being accepted.

The *way* in which the reasons support the imperative is simply this: The imperative is used to alter the hearer's attitudes or actions. In asking "Why?" the hearer indicates his hesitancy to comply. He will not do it "just because he is told to." The supporting reason then describes the situation which the imperative seeks to alter, or the new situation which the imperative seeks to bring about; and if these facts disclose that the new situation will satisfy a preponderance of the hearer's desires, he will hesitate to obey no longer. More generally, reasons support imperatives by altering such beliefs as may in turn alter an unwillingness to obey.

But do these remarks require elaboration? A moment's consideration will show that they do not; for they coincide with the remarks about agreement that have been made above. We saw there that since attitudes tend to alter with altered beliefs, agreement in attitude may often be obtained by securing agreement in belief. Here we need only apply this general principle to a special type of case. The connection becomes apparent when the above paragraph is stated in different terminology:

An imperative is used to secure the satisfaction of the speaker's desire. The question "Why?" expressing the hearer's hesitation to comply, indicates an actual or incipient counterdesire. There is accordingly a disagreement in attitude. The reason, supporting the imperative, locates a possible source of disagreement in belief; and if the latter is settled, then, since beliefs and attitudes stand in intimate causal relationship, the disagreement in attitude may be caused to vanish in a way that makes the imperative willingly obeyed.

The "substitute proofs" or "supporting reasons" that we have been seeking can thus be recognized as familiar acquaintances under a new name: they are the expressions of belief that so often play an important, if indirect, role in situations that involve disagreement in attitude. Nor are these supporting reasons peculiar to imperatives. They may be used wherever disagreement in attitude occurs, whether it is indicated by laudatory or derogatory words, rhetorical questions, metaphors, animated inflections of voice, and so on.

With regard to the judgment that here particularly concerns us—"This is good" as schematically analyzed by definition (3), page 363—the relevance of the supporting reasons will be obvious. Although the imperative component of the definiens, "Approve as well," is inadequate to the subtleties of ethics, it is doubly marked for use in disagreement in attitude; the very fact that it is an imperative at all so marks it, and it is marked again by its direct mention of the hearer's approval. Since reasons may support any statement that leads to agreement or disagreement in attitude, they clearly may support this one.

Supporting reasons are particularly important in ethics—far more so than the narrow proof that was mentioned previously.

When a man says "X is good" he is seldom called upon to prove that he now approves of X. He is called upon, rather, to adduce considerations which will make his attitudes acceptable to his opponent, and to show that they are not directed to situations of whose nature he is ignorant. This more important procedure, typical of ethical issues, always requires supporting reasons. We shall find in Chapters 9 and 10, where the working models give place to a descriptively "richer" analysis, that these conclusions must be amended; but the essential features will remain.

The following example, with comments interspersed, will serve to show more concretely how supporting reasons may occur in an argument that is characteristically ethical:

A: *Jones is fundamentally a good man.*
   This judgment (a) asserts that A approves of Jones, and (b) acts (quasi-) imperatively to make B, the hearer, have a similar attitude.
B: *Why do you say that?*
   B indicates his hesitancy or unwillingness to concur in approving of Jones. Disagreement in attitude is thus apparent.
A: *His harsh manner is only a pose. Underneath, he has the kindest of hearts.*
   A reason is now given, describing a characteristic of Jones that B may not know about, and which is likely to elicit B's favor.
B: *That would be interesting, if true. But does he ever express this kind heart of his in actions?*
   The reason is acknowledged to be relevant, but its truth is questioned. Disagreement in belief now comes to play an important part in the argument. It is closely related to the disagreement in attitude previously noted; for if A and B can agree in belief about Jones' kindness, they are likely to agree on whether or not to approve of him.
A: *He does. His old servant told me that Jones never uttered an unkind word to her, and recently provided her with a luxurious pension. And there are many such instances. I was actually present when . . . etc.*
   A here provides an empirical proof—not a direct proof of his initial judgment, but of the reason which supports it.
B: *Well, I confess I do not know him intimately. Perhaps he is a good man.*
   B here complies with the (quasi-) imperative component of A's initial judgment, by indicating his approval. His reluctance has been altered by A's well-proved reason. Agreement in belief has brought about agreement in attitude.

This example shows in miniature how ethical judgments (the working models remaining essentially uncriticized) may be supported by reasons of an important kind, and just how the reasons become relevant. It shows as well how very naturally these reasons serve some of the purposes of a proof. They lead the hearer to accept the judgment willingly, without any feeling that it is "dogmatic" or "arbitrary" or "unfounded."

Before leaving this provisional, introductory account of methods, there is a further question which must receive attention. At the beginning of this section, it will be remembered, ethical proofs were found to be distressingly meager. To supplement them, "substitute proofs" were sought, which might serve the purposes of a proof, even though they were not exactly like scientific proofs. Such substitutes were readily found in the "supporting reason" for the judgments—reasons which may bring about agreement in attitude by securing agreement in belief. But it has yet to be asked whether reasons of this sort are sufficient to provide ethics with an adequate "foundation." That is to say: Theories of ethics which stress attitudes have often been accused of "building morality on shifting sands," providing no check for the caprices and fads to which human attitudes are subject. Or they have been accused of sanctioning a vicious tolerance, tantamount to chaos, by implying that "Anything which a person feels to be good, *is* good, for him." Does the present account of methodology, once support by reasons is acknowledged, become free from such charges? Or is it rather the case that the present account is still too meager, and that some further method must be sought, even though it be sought blindly and despairingly, if ever moral codes are to have their needed authority?

The full answer cannot be developed now; but a provisional, dogmatic answer will helpfully anticipate subsequent chapters. Clearly, the present account of methodology will fail to content the great number of theorists who are embarked on "the quest for certainty." The supporting reasons here mentioned have no sort of *logical* compulsion. Persons who make opposed ethical judgments may (so far as theoretical possibility is concerned) continue to do so in the face of all manner of reasons that their argument includes, even though neither makes any logical or empirical error. Supporting reasons have only to do with beliefs; and in so far as they in turn are proved by demonstrative or empirical methods, only agreement in belief will, in the first instance, be secured. Ethical agreement, however, requires more than agreement in belief; it requires agreement in attitude. Accordingly, unless some further method can be found, a reasoned agreement in ethics is theoretically possible only to the extent that agreement in belief will cause people to agree in attitude.

How serious is this requirement? To what extent *will* agreement in belief cause people to agree in attitude? If the answer is to be grounded not on hopes but on facts, it must inescapably run thus: We usually *do not know*, before the outcome of any argument, whether the requirement holds true for it or not; and although it is often convenient to assume that it does, to prolong enlightening argument and delay purely hortatory efforts to secure ethical agreement, the assumption can be only heuristic, without a proper basis of confirmation. Those who seek an absolutely definitive method for normative ethics, and who want to rule out the possibility of rival moral codes, each equally well supported by reasons, will find that the present account gives them less than they want.

But the serious question concerns not what people now want; for in this connection people want, and have always wanted, what they cannot clearly articulate, and perhaps want an absurdity. The serious question concerns what people *would* want if they thought more clearly. If confusions about ethical methodology were swept away—confusions which are often more serious in ethical theology than in ethical practice—and if the psychological mechanisms which these confusions have fostered were accordingly readjusted, would people *then* feel that some more "objective" conception is required? To this question the present work will answer with a definite negative. But since methodological confusions are deeply rooted, and the psychological mechanisms which they have fostered are very stubborn, the reader must exercise patience in awaiting further explanation.

The working models and the conceptions of method to which they have led are somewhat crude. Let us consider how they must subsequently be altered.

The first inadequacy of the models is simply this: The imperative component, included to preserve the hortatory aspects of ethical judgments, and stressed as useful in indicating agreement or disagreement in attitude, is really too blunt an instrument to perform its expected task. If a person is explicitly commanded to have a certain attitude, he becomes so self-conscious that he cannot obey. Command a man's approval and you will elicit only superficial symptoms of it. But the judgment, "This is good," has no trace of this stultifying effect; so the judgment's force in encouraging approval has been poorly approximated.

A further point, somewhat parallel to this, is more serious. Imperatives are often used to exert a unilateral influence. When a man gives direct orders, he may not take kindly to a dissenting reply. Although this is not the only way in which imperatives are used, it is a familiar one; and when imperatives enter bluntly into a context, as they do in the working models, only this usage may be brought to mind. So the models may give a distorted impression of the purposes for which moral influence is exerted. They may suggest that a moralist is obsessed by a desire to make others over into his own pattern—that he wishes only to propagate his preconceived aims, without reconsidering them.

Now if certain moralists have motives of this sort, there can be no doubt that others do not. One who exerts an influence need not thereby cut himself off from all counterinfluence; he may initiate a discussion in which the attitudes of all parties become progressively modified, and directed to objects whose nature is more fully understood. There are many men whose influence looks beyond their own immediate needs, and takes its welcome place in a cooperative moral enterprise. Proceeding with a desire to see all sides of a question, they have no desire for a debater's conquest, and are anxious to submit their moral judgments to the test of other points of view. Although moral judgments are not always advanced in this spirit, we must remember that there is manifestly such a possibility, which in many cases is actualized. There is no excuse for that hardheadedness which can see no more in human nature than the qualities which human nature is ashamed to recognize.

The working models, then, are likely to misrepresent both the manner in which moral influence is exerted and the motives which attend it. How may their inadequacies be avoided? The answer is suggested by current theories about language and meaning—theories which promise to have marked repercussions on philosophy, and which have been emphasized by several contemporary writers on ethics. The effect of ethical terms in directing attitudes, though not wholly dissimilar to that of imperatives, must be explained with reference to a characteristic and subtle kind of *emotive meaning*. The emotive meaning of a word is the power that the word acquires, on account of its history in emotional situations, to evoke or directly express attitudes, as distinct from describing or designating them. In simple forms it is typical of interjections; in more complicated forms it is a contributing factor to poetry; and it has familiar manifestations in the many terms of ordinary discourse that are laudatory or derogatory. In virtue of this kind of meaning, ethical judgments alter attitudes, not by an appeal to self-conscious efforts (as is the case with imperatives), but by the more flexible mechanism of *suggestion*. Emotive terms present the subject of which they are predicated in a bright or dim light, so to speak, and thereby *lead* people, rather than command them, to alter their attitudes. And they readily permit a mutual influence of this sort, as distinct from a unilateral one. The exact nature of emotive meaning, the way in which it functions, and the way in which it cooperates with beliefs, gestures, tones of voice, and so on, are somewhat involved considerations that must be left until later. It need only be remarked, for the present, that emotive meaning need not be taken as usurping the position that rightfully belongs to descriptive meaning. It has many legitimate functions, in ethics and elsewhere, and becomes objectionable only when it is abused.

It is not sufficient, however, to correct only the imperative component of the working models. A further inadequacy attends their declarative component, which for many contexts is much too simple. In order to accentuate agreement and disagreement in attitude, the models reduce descriptive meaning to a bare minimum, suggest-

ing that ethical judgments express beliefs that are solely about the speaker's own attitudes. Now the most obvious objection to this procedure—that it neglects the many
other beliefs that are relevant to ethics—is one which we have seen to have no foundation. If the beliefs are stressed, as in the preceding section, in connection with
methodology—if they are made evident from the supporting reasons that attend ethical judgments, rather than from the meaning of the judgments themselves—the full
nature of ethical issues is properly recognized. But a more serious difficulty now
arises, revealing an inadequacy of the models that is genuine and not easily sur-
mounted. Ethical terms are noted for their ambiguity; yet of this ambiguity nothing
has been said. So our procedure, though sensitive to the beliefs that enter into ethics,
is by no means sufficiently sensitive to the various forms of language, in which these
beliefs are expressed. If we should suppose, as the working models may easily lead us
to suppose, that important beliefs are *never* expressed by ethical judgments themselves—that they are *always* expressed by the sentences that present supporting reasons for the judgments—we should ignore the flexibility of common language, and
hence obscure the very factor which, throughout the whole body of ethics, is most
urgently in need of attention.

The object of the present study is not to devise, in arbitrary fashion, a sense for
ethical terms that suits them to a limited, technical purpose; it is rather to free the
language of everyday life from confusion. It is essential, for this purpose, to realize
that everyday life presents us not with "1" usage of terms, but with many different
usages. Nor is this a phenomenon which arises from trivial causes, which analysis
can easily offset. Ambiguity will always persist in common discourse; hence the practical task lies not in seeking to eliminate it, but rather in seeking to make its presence
evident, and by a careful study of its origins and functions, to render it no longer a
source of error.[4]

The full complexity of the problem, however, has not as yet been envisaged. In
mentioning the "ambiguity" of ethical terms, the above remarks may call to mind
only clear-cut examples of it, like that of the term "grip," meaning now a grasp of the
hand and now a small suitcase. It suggests that some definite number of senses for
the ethical terms has been sharply if tacitly distinguished in ordinary usage, and that
the separation of one from another requires only a conscious scrutiny of our established verbal habits. In point of fact this is far from the case. Ethical terms are more
than ambiguous; they are *vague*. Although certain factors, at any one time, are definitely included among the designata of the terms, and certain others definitely
excluded, there are many others which are neither included nor excluded. No decision has been made about these, either by the speaker or by the dictionary. The limits
of the undecided region are so subject to fluctuation, with varying contexts and varying purposes, that it becomes arbitrary, so far as common usage is concerned, to specify where one sense of the terms leaves off and another begins.

A simple example of vagueness can be found in the word "red." There is a certain region on the spectrum to which this term definitely refers, and another broader
one to which it definitely does not refer; but between them there are near-orange
hues which (in ordinary usage, as distinct from some technical use in science) people
have neither decided to call "red" nor decided to call "not red." We may, of course,

---

4   See the Bergen Lecture delivered by I. A. Richards at Yale, in 1940, and published in *Furioso*
(Summer issue, 1941). Richards argues, most plausibly, that we should "study . . . ambiguity, not to
fear it but to welcome it as our best opportunity for growth in understanding."

draw an arbitrary line through the undecided region, and say that *this* is where red ends. But if we do so, there will always be many other places where we might have drawn it with equal propriety. Or instead of drawing one line we may draw many, seeking to make explicit the broader and narrower senses of the term by letting each mark represent the boundary of a different sense. But if we do this, the number of lines that we draw, and the places where we draw them, will be no less arbitrary than before. Over the undecided region common usage permits us to do as we please.[5]

The vagueness of ethical terms is of the same sort, but extreme; the undecided referents are more numerous and diverse. An ethical term may accordingly be adapted to a broad range of uses, sometimes for purposes that will easily bear examination, and sometimes not. We all know that a politician who promises "justice" commits himself to very little, unless he defines the term before the election. The term "good" is no less flexible. It may be used to mean such qualities as reliable, charitable, honest, and so on, and may even have such a specific reference as that to going faithfully to church on Sundays. These need not be qualities that a speaker alleges to go along with goodness, contingently, but can be qualities that he wishes to assign to the logical connotation of "good." On the other hand, the term may be denied all this variety of descriptive reference, and thinned out to refer only to the attitudes of the speaker. We have always a choice of making a descriptive meaning rich or poor. And it is of great importance to realize that neither choice will violate the elastic requirement of "natural English usage."

If we now return to the working models, we shall readily see that their inadequacy, so far as descriptive meaning is concerned, is only partial. They provide a meaning which can be *assigned* to the ethical terms, and which is well suited to certain contexts. Yet if they are taken as typical of all contexts, and sufficient in themselves to clarify common usage, they will represent only another contribution to linguistic fiction. They must be supplemented, at least, by a number of alternative definitions. And ultimately, definitions of all sorts must not be conceived as exhausting the possibilities of ethical language, but only of revealing, by example, its enormous flexibility.

Although this chapter has provided only an outline of our study, barely mentioning certain topics, and developing others quite roughly, it has introduced several points that are of central importance. The ethical terms cannot be taken as fully comparable to scientific ones. They have a quasi-imperative function which, poorly preserved by the working models, must be explained with careful attention to emotive meaning; and they have a descriptive function which is attended by ambiguity and vagueness, requiring a particularly detailed study of linguistic flexibility. Both of these aspects of language are intimately related to ethical methodology; and although this relationship has as yet been studied only in a partial, imperfect way, enough has been said to suggest an interesting possibility: The reasons which are given for an ethical judgment, although open to the ordinary tests so far as their own truth or falsity is concerned, may give support *to the judgment* in a way that neither inductive nor deductive logic can exhaustively characterize, and which must therefore become the subject matter of a further type of inquiry.

NOTE ON SOURCES. Charles L. Stevenson, *Ethics and Language* (New Haven: Yale University Press, 1944). Excerpted from Chapters 1 and 2.

---

5 See Bertrand Russell, "Vagueness," *Australasian Journal of Psychology and Philosophy* (1923); and Max Black, "Vagueness," *Philosophy of Science* (1937).

8 R. M. HARE

PRESCRIPTIVISM—REFINEMENTS ON STEVENSON

FROM AYER AND STEVENSON TO HARE. Ayer began by noting that even if "Stealing is wrong" looks in form like "This table is brown," there still is a chasm between the two. The former, an ethical judgment, is not a statement. Statements, according to Ayer, express facts. "This table is brown" is a statement. It states a fact. According to Ayer's theory, "Stealing is wrong" is not about anything. It states nothing—even though it may be voiced noisily. That is why he calls ethical judgments *pseudo*statements. Technically, for Ayer, these pseudostatements are just sounds—they are hisses and boos or hurrahs and yeas. These value judgments look and sound like a real statement—but looks and sounds, in this case, are deceiving. Since ethical statements are just sounds, they cannot be either true or false. In Ayer's view, only factual statements can be true or false. In this regard, Ayer's theory is classified as a noncognitivism, meaning that, in his view, ethical judgments cannot be true or false, since they are not making any claims that could be considered as true or false.

A strength of Emotivist Theory is that it fits well with two insights: one commonsensical, the other more philosophical. The common sense insight was that many ethical disputes seem to go on forever. If we accept Emotivism, we see that ethical disputes are not like factual disputes where a fact can settle a matter in question. Rather, with ethical disputes, all we have is two sides: one side cheering and the other booing. Emotivism fits with a philosophical insight made by David Hume (1711–1776) and developed by G. E. Moore (1876–1958).

Hume noticed that only facts followed logically from facts. To have a valid argument where the conclusion contained a value judgment required a value judgment as a premise. Hume put it this way: that from an *is* one cannot logically deduce an *ought*. (See his *Treatise of Human Nature*, Book III, Section 1, Part 1.) Hume commented that from the fact that the world would pass out of existence unless I wiggled my pinky, it did not follow logically that I *should* wiggle my pinky—unless premises about the goodness of the world and my desire to keep that world in place were added. Hume saw this as a clear dichotomy between facts and values.

To Hume, values arose from human feelings (sentiments). Facts, on the other hand, are presented to us through our senses. The senses as receptors for the outside world are never aware of values, since values come from within. This makes Hume a subjectivist, in the sense that our values are traceable to our sentiments. Hume was not a subjectivist in the sense of believing that moral opinions differ greatly from person to person or that moral disputes could never be settled. Hume believed that, in general, there is enough similarity between people and cultures to guarantee some degree of similarity in morals.

A simple example will illustrate Hume's position on the dichotomy between facts and values. If we are at a scene where someone has just been killed, a list of all the facts might include: the position of the body, the kind of weapon, the shape of the wound, the rigor of the body, etc. But what will not be on the list of facts will be the wrongness of the killing. That is because "being wrong" is not a fact. It is to be expected that, from all the facts, one could deduce only more facts. Hume made "wrongness" not a property of the scene, but a psychological property of the human observers. An example from art may make Hume's point even clearer. Imagine all the facts about the Mona Lisa: its size, the subject, the placement of various colors, etc. Nowhere on this list will be the property "beautiful." It seems clear that, from a list of the facts (which is just a list of the physical characteristics of the painting), it would not follow that the painting was beautiful.

G. E. Moore wanted to keep the fact–value dichotomy (the is–ought distinction). He thought it impossible to derive values from facts alone. Moore also thought that values were objective in the sense of being properties of external things. Thus, Moore was not a subjectivist.

To use Blanshard's rabbit as an example: Hume would have considered the "badness" of the situation to be a property of the observer, while Moore (a forerunner of Blanshard in this regard) considered the "badness" to be a property of the rabbit in the trap.

For Moore, values—as properties—were objective, but not like other objective properties. Remember that Moore could not allow values to be like other objective properties, for if they *were* like other objective properties, then values would be deducible from facts. They would just be facts. Clearly, this would not do.

Instead, Moore claimed that value terms such as "goodness" were "non-natural properties." That is, they were not like the "natural properties" sensed through the five traditional sense modalities—redness, loudness, sourness, smoothness, the smell of rotten eggs. Instead, values were sensed through a moral intuition, through a non-natural sense. To Moore, what Hume had noticed in the is–ought distinction was simply that from natural properties alone one could derive only other natural properties, and that to derive a non-natural property, one needed a non-natural property in the premise.

Moore called the mistaken attempt to derive values from facts alone *the naturalistic fallacy*. The naturalistic fallacy is thinking that *all* properties are natural. If all properties are natural, then any definition of a value term will use natural properties and values could be derived from facts alone. Some interpreters of Moore characterize the naturalistic fallacy as the fallacious claim that a value term can be defined solely in terms of facts. Since the only way to derive a value from facts alone is to smuggle in a factual definition of a value term, these two interpretations of Moore probably come to just about the same point.

For Moore, it was just as much a fallacy to derive a value from a set of facts alone as it was a fallacy to derive "Sitting Bull is vanishing" from "American Indians are vanishing" and "Sitting Bull is an American Indian."

To return for a moment to Blanshard's example, it does not follow from "the rabbit was in the trap" and "the rabbit suffered great pain," that "rabbits should not be trapped" unless one adds a premise containing a non-natural fact such as "Rabbits should not suffer." Strictly speaking, Moore would put it this way.

Situations where rabbits are suffering great pain have the non-natural property of badness.

Now we can reinterpret Ayer's strategy. Ayer was unwilling to accept non-natural properties as the way to explain value judgments. Ayer could no more accept the existence of non-natural properties than he could accept the existence of leprechauns or Santa Claus. To Ayer, claiming that there were non-natural properties was poor philosophy and worse science. Thus, Ayer explained the puzzle of moral judgments (that they seemed to be factual but, unlike other factual statements, were impossible to verify) by pointing out that ethical statements were not really statements. For Ayer, only statements can be the conclusions of other statements. Since value judgments are only pseudostatements, they cannot validly be derived from statements. We can put this a colorful way by asking: How could one logically derive a grunt, groan, or sigh from a set of facts? Of course, one might *feel* a certain way about what was legitimately derived; e.g., that a rabbit was suffering in a trap. And one might give vent to that feeling by making the sounds, "One should not trap rabbits." But the sounds, the feelings, were not derived from the facts. They were *caused* by the facts. So Ayer chose noncognitivism over non-natural properties as a way to explain moral judgments.

To get a bit closer on all this, consider the following argument:

A. Charity is freely giving to the needy.
B. The Red Cross is needful of money.
C. You ought to give some of your money to the Red Cross.

As stated, both A and B are facts. A is a statement defining "charity." B is a statement of fact about the Red Cross. Does C follow from A and B alone? If C is an evaluation, that is, if "ought" is an evaluative term, if it directs you to make an effort to bring about a good (or better) state of affairs, then the answer is that C does not follow. For it to follow, we would need another premise. We would need something like

B'. Charity is good.

We might also need the understanding or even the explicit statement that one ought to do what is good.

Now, what are we to make of "charity is good"? First let us consider philosophers other than Ayer. For them, if it is a factual statement (perhaps it is a descriptive linguistic report of how people actually do use the word "charity"), then the derivation of C from A and B is not made because then we still lack a true value in the premise. If "charity is good" is a value statement, then we do get our derivation of C. But things are different for Ayer.

According to Ayer, if "charity is good" is not given a factual translation into descriptive linguistics, then it is a pseudostatement; nothing more than a sigh of approval. How can a sigh of approval be used to deduce a conclusion? The answer is that, strictly speaking, it cannot. Ayer is committed to the view that logical arguments are impossible when values are involved. This is a steep price to pay for non-cognitivism, a price few philosophers have been willing to pay.

Stevenson, too, wanted to keep the fact–value dichotomy but not at the expense of noncognitivism; thus, his distinction between beliefs and attitudes. Ethical disputes are not always settled by appeal to facts—attitudes play a role in creating and fostering ethical disputes. To Stevenson, "I approve" is not a pseudo-statement. It refers to a feeling of approval. It is a statement that one has a feeling. If one has the feeling, it is true; if one doesn't have the feeling, it is false. To Stevenson, "This is good" is cognitive, since part of the meaning of "This is good" is a statement of fact.

The dichotomy between facts and values and the resulting inability to derive a value from a set of facts alone is not accepted by all philosophers. Those who reject the dichotomy and believe that one *can* derive a value from facts alone are called naturalists. Philosophers who disagree with naturalists say that naturalists commit "the naturalistic fallacy" when they try to deduce a value from facts alone.

Thus, Hume, Moore, Ayer, and Stevenson would deny the legitimacy of naturalism and insist that it was only by committing a logical fallacy that one could (appear to) derive values from facts alone. Of the four, Ayer is the only self-declared noncognitivist. Moore is a cognitivist, since he believed that statements such as "murder is wrong" can be true or false depending upon whether or not there is the non-natural property of goodness. Stevenson is a clear cognitivist. Hume is often interpreted as a noncognitivist, but this may be open to interpretation.

With this background, we can now appreciate the further refinements made on emotivism by R. M. Hare.

BIOGRAPHICAL NOTE. Richard Mervyn Hare was born in England in 1919. He was educated at Oxford (England) and taught at Oxford until 1966 when he became professor of philosophy at the University of Florida in Gainesville, Florida.

THE ARGUMENT OF THE PASSAGES. Hare's view (called *prescriptivism*) is that what creates the dichotomy between facts and values is the commending function of value statements. For Hare, value words and value judgments serve to command. They are, in effect, commands to choose in a certain way. So for Hare, "Stealing is wrong" must be understood as the combination command and commendation: "Do not choose to steal!"

Hare points out that it is part of the "logic" of the word *good* that things are good only with respect to a comparison class. That is, one cannot say merely "This is a good apple." One must specify, good cooking apple, good eating apple, good apple for poisoning Snow White. It is also part of the "logic" of *good* that if something is good because it has certain properties, then all things like it with those properties in the same circumstances must also be judged good. Thus, if my Ferrari is a good racing car because it accelerates to 60 mph in less than 10 seconds and can make hairpin curves, then it would be a contradiction to say that another car had these properties but was not a good racing car.

Continuing with his analysis of *good*, Hare points out that if "This is a good strawberry" means only that the strawberry is red, sweet, and large, it does not serve the prime function of "good," which is to get people to choose in a certain way. That is, the commending function of "good" cannot be derived from facts alone.

Here is an example which should help to make Hare's point. Suppose you are at a restaurant. You have eaten there before, but your friend has not. She asks you, "What's good?" Notice that she might also have said, "What do you recommend?" or "What should I order?" Hare would point out that in this context, these are all just about synonymous. If, in answer to "Should I order the Dover sole?" you say, "Dover sole is a flat fish usually broiled or baked," you would not have been any help to your friend—unless you already knew that your friend was/was not partial to flat, plainly cooked fish. Again, this makes Hare's point that evaluations are commendations and that requests for evaluations could never be satisfied by descriptions (facts) alone.

Here is how Hare puts his views.

> ... The key problem is as follows: there are two sorts of things that we can say, for example, about strawberries; the first sort is usually called *descriptive*, the second sort *evaluative*. Example of the first sort of remark are, "This strawberry is sweet" and "This strawberry is large, red, and juicy." Examples of the second sort of remark are "This is a good strawberry" and "This strawberry is just as strawberries ought to be." The first sort of remark is often given as a reason for making the second sort of remark; but the first sort does not by itself entail the second sort, nor vice versa. Yet there seems to be some close logical connexion between them. Our problem is: "What is this connexion?"; for no light is shed by saying that there is a connexion, unless we can say what it is.
>
> The problem may also be put in this way: if we knew all the descriptive properties which a particular strawberry had (knew, of every descriptive sentence relating to the strawberry, whether it was true or false), and if we knew also the meaning of the word "good," then what else should we require to know, in order to be able to tell whether a strawberry was a good one? Once the question is put in this way, the answer should be apparent. We should require to know, what are the criteria in virtue of which a strawberry is to be called a good one, or what are the characteristics that make a strawberry a good one, or what is the standard of goodness in strawberries. We should require to be given the major premiss. We have already seen that we can know the meaning of "good strawberry" without knowing any of these latter things—though there is also a sense of the sentence "What does it mean to call a strawberry a good one?" in which we should not know the answer to it, unless we also knew the answer to these other questions. It is now time to elucidate and distinguish these two ways in which we can be said to know what it means to call an object a good member of its class. This will help us to see more clearly both the differences and the similarities between "good" and words like "red" and "sweet."
>
> Since we have been dwelling for some time on the differences, it will do no harm now to mention some of the similarities. For this purpose, let us consider the two sentences "M is a red motor-car" and "M is a good motor-car." It will be noticed that "motor-car," unlike "strawberry," is a functional word, as defined in the preceding chapter. Reference to the *Shorter Oxford English Dictionary* shows that a motor-car is a carriage, and a carriage a means of conveyance. Thus, if a motor-car will not convey anything, we know from the definition of motor-car that it is not a good one. But when we know this, we know so little, compared with what is required in order to know the full criteria of a good motor-car, that I propose in what follows to ignore,

for the sake of simplicity, this complicating factor. I shall treat "motor-car" as if it did not have to be defined functionally: that is to say, I shall assume that we could learn the meaning of "motor-car" (as in a sense we can) simply by being shown examples of motor-cars. It is, of course, not always easy to say whether or not a word is a functional word; it depends, like all questions of meaning, on how the word is taken by a particular speaker.

The first similarity between "M is a red motor-car" and "M is a good motor-car" is that both can be, and often are, used for conveying information of a purely factual or descriptive character. If I say to someone "M is a good motor-car," and he himself has not seen, and knows nothing of M, but does on the other hand know what sorts of motor-car we are accustomed to call "good" (knows what is the accepted standard of goodness in motor-cars), he undoubtedly receives information from my remark about what sort of motor-car it is. He will complain that I have misled him, if he subsequently discovers that M will not go over 30 m.p.h., or uses as much oil as petrol, or is covered with rust, or has large holes in the roof. His reason for complaining will be the same as it would have been if I had said that the car was red and he subsequently discovered that it was black. I should have led him to expect the motor-car to be of a certain description when in fact it was of a quite different description.

The second similarity between the two sentences is this. Sometimes we use them, not for actually conveying information, but for putting our hearer into a position subsequently to use the word "good" or "red" for giving or getting information. Suppose, for example, that he is utterly unfamiliar with motor-cars in the same sort of way as most of us are unfamiliar with horses nowadays, and knows no more about motor-cars than is necessary in order to distinguish a motor-car from a hansom cab. In that case, my saying to him "M is a good motor-car" will not give him any information about M, beyond the information that it is a motor-car. But if he is able then or subsequently to examine M, he will have learnt something. He will have learnt that some of the characteristics which M has, are characteristics which make people—or at any rate me—call it a good motor-car. This may not be to learn very much. But suppose that I make judgments of this sort about a great many motor-cars, calling some good and some not good, and he is able to examine all or most of the motor-cars about which I am speaking; he will in the end learn quite a lot, always presuming that I observe a consistent standard in calling them good or not good. He will eventually, if he pays careful attention, get into the position in which he knows, after I have said that a motor-car is a good one, what sort of motor-car he may expect it to be—for example fast, stable on the road, and so on.

Now if we were dealing, not with "good," but with "red," we should call this process "explaining the meaning of the word"—and we might indeed, in a sense, say that what I have been doing is explaining what one means by "a good motor-car." This is a sense of "mean" about which, as we have seen, we must be on our guard. The processes, however, are very similar. I might explain the meaning of "red" by continually saying of various motor-cars "M is a red motor-car," "N is not a red motor-car," and so on. If he were attentive enough, he would soon get into a position in which he was able to use the word "red" for giving or getting information, at any rate about motor-cars. And so, both with "good" and with "red," there is this process, which in the case of "red" we may call "explaining the meaning," but in the case of "good" may only call it so loosely and in a secondary sense; to be clear we must call it something like "explaining or conveying or setting forth the standard of goodness in motor-cars."

The standard of goodness, like the meaning of "red," is normally something which is public and commonly accepted. When I explain to someone the meaning of "red motor-car," he expects, unless I am known to be very eccentric, that he will find other people using it in the same way. And similarly, at any rate with objects like motor-cars where there is a commonly accepted standard, he will expect, having learnt from me what is the standard of goodness in motor-cars, to be able, by using the expression "good motor-car," to give information to other people, and get it from them, without confusion.

A third respect in which "good motor-car" resembles "red motor-car" is the following: both "good" and "red" can vary as regards the exactitude or vagueness of the information which they do or can convey. We normally use the expression "red motor-car" very loosely. Any motor-car that lies somewhere between the unmistakably purple and the unmistakably orange could without abuse of language be called a red motor-car. And similarly, the standard for calling motor-cars good is commonly very loose. There are certain characteristics, such as inability to exceed 30 m.p.h., which to anyone but an eccentric would be sufficient conditions for refusing to call it a good motor-car; but there is no precise set of accepted criteria such that we can say "If a motor-car satisfies these conditions, it is a good one; if not, not." And in both cases we could be precise if we wanted to. We could, for certain purposes, agree not to say that a motor-car was "really red" unless the redness of its paint reached a certain measurable degree of purity and saturation; and similarly, we might adopt a very exact standard of goodness in motor-cars. We might refuse the name "good motor-car" to any car that would not go round a certain race-track without mishap in a certain limited time, that did not conform to certain other rigid specifications as regards accommodation, &c. This sort of thing has not been done for the expression "good motor-car"; but, as Mr. Urmson [a well-known British philosopher—Eds.] has pointed out, it has been done by the Ministry of Agriculture for the expression "super apple."[1]

It is important to notice that the exactness or looseness of their criteria does absolutely nothing to distinguish words like "good" from words like "red." Words in both classes may be descriptively loose or exact, according to how rigidly the criteria have been laid down by custom or convention. It certainly is not true that value-words are distinguished from descriptive words in that the former are looser, descriptively, than the latter. There are loose and rigid examples of both sorts of word. Words like "red" can be extremely loose, without becoming to the least degree evaluative; and expressions like "good sewage effluent" can be the subject of very rigid criteria, without in the least ceasing to be evaluative.

It is important to notice also, how easy it is, in view of these resemblances between "good" and "red," to think that there are no differences—to think that to set forth the standard of goodness in motor-cars is to set forth the meaning, in all senses that there are of that word, of the expression "good motor-car"; to think that "M is a good motor-car" means neither more nor less than "M has certain characteristics of which 'good' is the name."

It is worth noticing here that the functions of the word "good" which are concerned with information could be performed equally well if "good" had no commendatory function at all. This can be made clear by substituting another word, made up for the purpose, which is to be supposed to lack the commendatory force of

---

1 *Mind*, lix (1950), 152 (also in *Logic and Language*, ii, ed. Flew, 166).

"good." Let us use "doog" as this new word. "Doog," like "good," can be used for conveying information only if the criteria for its application are known; but this makes it, unlike "good," altogether meaningless until these criteria are made known. I make the criteria known by pointing out various motor-cars, and saying "M is a doog motor-car," "N is not a doog motor-car," and so on. We must imagine that, although "doog" has no commendatory force, the criteria for doogness in motor-cars which I am employing are the same as those which, in the previous example, I employed for goodness in motor-cars. And so, as in the previous example, the learner, if he is sufficiently attentive, becomes able to use the word "doog" for giving or getting information; when I say to him "Z is a doog motor-car," he knows what characteristics to expect it to have; and if he wants to convey to someone else that a motor-car Y has those same characteristics, he can do so by saying "Y is a doog motor-car."

Thus the word "doog" does (though only in connection with motor-cars) half the jobs that the word "good" does—namely, all those jobs that are concerned with the giving, or learning to give or get, information. It does not do those jobs which are concerned with commendation. Thus we might say that "doog" functions just like a descriptive word. First my learner learns to use it by my giving him examples of its application, and then he uses it by applying it to fresh examples. It would be quite natural to say that what I was doing was teaching my learner the *meaning* of "doog"; and this shows us again how natural it is to say that, when we are learning a similar lesson for the expression "good motor-car" (i.e., learning the criteria of its application), we are learning its meaning. But with the word "good" it is misleading to say this; for the meaning of "good motor-car" (in another sense of "meaning") is something that might be known by someone who did not know the criteria of its application; he would know, if someone said that a motor-car was a good one, that he was commending it; and to know that, would be to know the meaning of the expression. Further, as we saw earlier, someone might know about "good" all the things which my learner learnt about the word "doog" (namely, how to apply the word to the right objects, and use it for giving and getting information) and yet be said not to know its meaning; for he might not know that to call a motor-car good was to commend it.

It may be objected by some readers that to call the descriptive or informative job of "good" its *meaning* in any sense is illegitimate. Such objectors might hold that the meaning of "good" is adequately characterized by saying that it is used for commending, and that any information we get from its use is not a question of meaning at all. When I say "M is a good motor-car," my meaning, on this view, is to commend M; if a hearer gets from my remark, together with his knowledge of the standard habitually used by me in assessing the merits of motor-cars, information about what description of motor-car it is, this is not part of my meaning; all my hearer has done is to make an inductive inference from "Hare has usually in the past commended motor-cars of a certain description" and "Hare has commended M" to "M is of the same description." I suspect that this objection is largely a verbal one, and I have no wish to take sides against it. On the one hand, we must insist that to know the criteria for applying the word "good" to motor-cars is not to know—at any rate in the full or primary sense—the meaning of the expression "good motor-car"; to this extent the objection must be agreed with. On the other hand, the relation of the expression "good motor-car" to the criteria for its application is very like the relation of a descriptive expression to its defining characteristics, and this likeness finds an echo in our language when we ask, "What do you mean, good?", and get the answer "I mean it'll do 80 and never breaks down." In view of this undoubted fact of usage, I deem it best to adopt the term "descriptive meaning." Moreover, it is natural to say that a sentence has descriptive meaning, if the speaker intends it primarily to convey information; and when a newspaper says that X opened the batting on a good wicket, its intention is not primarily to commend the wicket, but to inform its readers what description of wicket it was.

It is time now to justify my calling the descriptive meaning of "good" secondary to the evaluative meaning. My reasons for doing so are two. First, the evaluative meaning is constant for every class of object for which the word is used. When we call a motor-car or a chronometer or a cricket-bat or a picture good, we are commending all of them. But because we are commending all of them for different reasons, the descriptive meaning is different in all cases. We have knowledge of the evaluative meaning of "good" from our earliest years; but we are constantly learning to use it in new descriptive meanings, as the classes of objectives whose virtues we learn to distinguish grow more numerous. Sometimes we learn to use "good" in a new descriptive meaning through being taught it by an expert in a particular field—for example, a horseman might teach me how to recognize a good hunter. Sometimes, on the other hand, we make up a new descriptive meaning for ourselves. This happens when we start having a standard for a class of objects, certain members of which we have started needing to place in order of merit, but for which there has hitherto been no standard, as in the "cactus" example. [Hare contends that we can apply "good" to cactus without knowing what the standards of evaluation actually might be.—Eds.]

The second reason for calling the evaluative meaning primary is, that we can use the evaluating force of the word in order to *change* the descriptive meaning for any class of objects. This is what the moral reformer often does in morals; but the same process occurs outside morals. It may happen that motor-cars will in the near future change considerably in design (e.g., by our seeking economy at the expense of size). It may be that then we shall cease giving the name "a good motor-car" to a car that now would rightly and with the concurrence of all be allowed that name. How, linguistically speaking, would this have happened? At present, we are roughly agreed (though only roughly) on the necessary and sufficient criteria for calling a motor-car a good one. If what I have described takes place, we may begin to say "No cars of the nineteen-fifties were really good; there weren't any good ones till 1960." Now here we cannot be using "good" with the same descriptive meaning as it is now generally used with; for some of the cars of 1950 do indubitably have those characteristics which entitle them to the name "good motor-car" in the 1950 descriptive sense of that word. What is happening is that the evaluative meaning of the word is being used in order to shift the descriptive meaning; we are doing what would be called, if "good" were a purely descriptive word, redefining it. But we cannot call it that, for the evaluative meaning remains constant; we are rather altering the standard. This is similar to the process called by Professor Stevenson "persuasive definition";[2] the process is not necessarily, however, highly coloured with emotion.

We may notice here that there are two chief ways in which a change in standard may be reflected in, and indeed partly effected by, a change in language. The first is the one which I have just illustrated; the evaluative meaning of "good" is retained, and is used in order to alter the descriptive meaning and so establish a new standard. The second does not often occur with the word "good"; for that word is so well-established as a value-word that the procedure would be practically impossible. This pro-

---

2   *Ethics and Language*, ch. ix.

cedure is for the word to be gradually emptied of its evaluative meaning through being used more and more in what I shall call a conventional or "inverted-commas" way; when it has lost all its evaluative meaning it comes to be used as a purely descriptive word for designating certain characteristics of the object, and, when it is required to commend or condemn objects in this class, some quite different value-word is imported for the purpose. The two processes may be illustrated and contrasted by a somewhat over-schematized account of what has happened in the last two centuries to the expression "eligible bachelor." "Eligible" started off as a value-word, meaning "such as should be chosen (*sc.* as a husband for one's daughters)." Then, because the criteria of eligibility came to be fairly rigid, it acquired a descriptive meaning too; a person, if said to be eligible, might, in the eighteenth century, have been expected to have large landed estates and perhaps a title. By the nineteenth century, however, the criteria of eligibility have changed; what makes a bachelor eligible is no longer necessarily landed property or a title; it is substantial wealth of any kind provided that it is well-secured. We might imagine a nineteenth-century mother saying "I know he is not of noble birth; but he's eligible all the same, because he has £3,000 a year in the Funds, and much more besides when his father dies." This would be an example of the first method. On the other hand, in the twentieth century, partly as a reaction from the over-rigid standards of the nineteenth, which resulted in the word "eligible" lapsing into a conventional use, the second method has been adopted. If now someone said "He is an eligible bachelor," we could almost feel the inverted commas round the word, and even the irony; we should feel that if that was all that could be said for him, there must be something wrong with him. For commending bachelors, on the other hand, we now use quite different words; we say "He is likely to make a very *good* husband for Jane," or "She was very *sensible* to say 'yes.'"

The close connexion of standards of values with language is illustrated by the plight of the truly bilingual. A writer equally at home in English and French relates that once, when walking in the park on a rainy day, he met a lady dressed in a way which the English would call sensible, but the French *ridicule*; his mental reaction to this had to be expressed bilingually, because the standards he was applying were of diverse origin; he found himself saying to himself (slipping from English into French) "Pretty adequate armour. How uncomfortable though. Why go for a walk if you feel like this? *Elle es parfaitement ridicule.*" This cleavage of standards is said sometimes to produce neuroses in bilinguals, as might be expected in view of the close bearing of standards of values upon action.[3]

Although with "good" the evaluative meaning is primary, there are other words in which the evaluative meaning is secondary to the descriptive. Such words are "tidy" and "industrious." Both are normally used to commend; but we can say, without any hint of irony, "too tidy" or "too industrious." It is the descriptive meaning of these words that is most firmly attached to them; and therefore, although we must for certain purposes class them as value-words (for if we treat them as purely descriptive, logical errors results), they are so in a less full sense than "good." If the evaluative meaning of a word, which was primary, comes to be secondary, that is a sign that the standard to which the word appeals has become conventional. It is, of course, impossible to say *exactly* when this has happened; it is a process like the coming of winter.

---

3 P. H. J. Lagarde-Quost, "The Bilingual Citizen," *Britain Today*, Dec. 1947, p. 13; Jan. 1948, p. 13.

Although the evaluative meaning of "good" is primary, the secondary descriptive meaning is never wholly absent. Even when we are using the word "good" evaluatively in order to set up a new standard, the word still has a descriptive meaning, not in the sense that it is used to *convey* information, but in the sense that its use in setting up the new standard is an essential preliminary—like definition in the case of a purely descriptive word—to its subsequent use with a new descriptive meaning. It is also to be noticed that the relative prominence of the descriptive and evaluative meanings of "good" varies according to the class of objectives within which commendation is being given. We may illustrate this by taking two extreme examples. If I talk of "a good egg," it is at once known to what description of egg I am referring—namely, one that is not decomposed. Here the descriptive meaning predominates, because we have very fixed standards for assessing the goodness of eggs. On the other hand, if I say that a poem is a good one, very little information is given about what description of poem it is—for there is no accepted standard of goodness in poems. But it must not be thought that "good egg" is exclusively descriptive, or "good poem" exclusively evaluative. If, as the Chinese are alleged to do, we chose to eat eggs that are decomposed, we should call that kind of egg good, just as, because we choose to eat game that is slightly decomposed, we call it "well-hung" (compare also the expression "good Stilton cheese"). And if I said that a poem was good, and was not a very eccentric person, my hearer would be justified in assuming that the poem was not "Happy birthday to you!"

It is now time to inquire into the reasons for the logical features of "good" that we have been describing, and to ask why it is that it has this peculiar combination of evaluative and descriptive meaning. The reason will be found in the purposes for which it, like other value-words, is used in our discourse. The examination of these purposes will reveal the relevance of the matters discussed in the first part of this book to the study of evaluative language.

I have said that the primary function of the word "good" is to commend. We have, therefore, to inquire what commending is. When we commend or condemn anything, it is always in order, at least indirectly, to guide choices, our own or other people's, now or in the future. Suppose that I say "The South Bank Exhibition is very good." In what context should I appropriately say this, and what would be my purpose in so doing? It would be natural for me to say it to someone who was wondering whether to go to London to see the Exhibition, or, if he was in London, whether to pay it a visit. It would, however, be too much to say that the reference to choices is always as direct as this. An American returning from London to New York, and speaking to some people who had no intention of going to London in the near future, might still make the same remark. In order, therefore, to show that critical value-judgments are all ultimately related to choices, and would not be made if they were not so related, we require to ask, for what purpose we have standards.

It has been pointed out by Mr. Urmson that we do not speak generally of "good" wireworms. This is because we never have any occasion for choosing between wireworms, and therefore require no guidance in so doing. We therefore need to have no standards for wireworms. But it is easy to imagine circumstances in which this situation might alter. Suppose that wireworms came into use as a special kind of bait for fishermen. Then we might speak of having dug up a very good wireworm (one, for example, that was exceptionally fat and attractive to fish), just as now, no doubt, sea-fishermen might talk of having dug up a very good lug-worm. We only have standards for a class of objects, we only talk of the virtues of one specimen as against another, we only use value-words about them, when occasions are known to exist, or are conceivable, in which we, or someone else, would have to choose between speci- mens. We should not call pictures good or bad if no one ever had the choice of seeing them or not seeing them (or of studying them or not studying them in the way that art students study pictures, or of buying them or not buying them). Lest, by the way, I should seem to have introduced a certain vagueness by specifying so many alterna- tive kinds of choices, it must be pointed out that the matter can, if desired, be made as precise as we require; for we can specify, when we have called a picture a good one, within what class we have called it good; for example, we can say "I meant a good picture to study, but not to buy."

Some further examples may be given. We should not speak of good sunsets, unless sometimes the decision had to be made, whether to go to the window to look at the sunset; we should not speak of good billiard-cues, unless sometimes we had to choose one billiard-cue in preference to another; we should not speak of good men unless we had the choice, what sort of men to try to become. Leibniz, when he spoke of "the best of all possible worlds," had in mind a creator choosing between the possi- bilities. The choice that is envisaged need not ever occur, nor even be expected ever to occur; it is enough for it to be envisaged as occurring, in order that we should be able to make a value-judgment with reference to it. It must be admitted, however, that the most useful value-judgments are those which have reference to choices that we might very likely have to make.

It should be pointed out that even judgments about past choices do not refer merely to the past. As we shall see, all value-judgments are covertly universal in char- acter, which is the same as to say that they refer to, and express acceptance of, a stan- dard which has an application to other similar instances. If I censure someone for having done something, I envisage the possibility of him, or someone else, or myself, having to make a similar choice again; otherwise there would be no point in censur- ing him. Thus, if I say to a man whom I am teaching to drive "You did that manoeu- vre badly" this is a very typical piece of driving-instruction; and driving-instruction consists in teaching a man to drive not in the past but in the future; to this end we censure or commend past pieces of driving, in order to impart to him the standard which is to guide him in his subsequent conduct.

When we commend an object, our judgment is not solely about that particular object, but is inescapably about objects like it. Thus, if I say that a certain motor-car is a good one, I am not merely saying something about that particular motor-car. To say something about that particular car, merely, would not be to commend. To com- mend, as we have seen, is to guide choices. Now for guiding a particular choice we have a linguistic instrument which is not that of commendation, namely, the singular imperative. If I wish merely to tell someone to choose a particular car, with no thought of the kind of car to which it belongs, I can say "Take that one." If instead of this I say "That is a good one," I am saying something more. I am implying that if any motor-car were just like that one, it would be a good one too; whereas by saying "Take that one," I do not imply that, if my hearer sees another car just like that one, he is to take it too. But further, the implication of the judgment "That is a good motor-car" does not extend merely to motor-cars *exactly* like that one. If this were so, the implication would be for practical purposes useless; for nothing is exactly like anything else. It extends to every motor-car that is like that one in the *relevant* particu- lars; and the relevant particulars are its virtues—those of its characteristics for which I was commending it, or which I was calling good about it. Whenever we commend, we have in mind something about the object commended which is the reason for our commendation. It therefore always makes sense, after someone has said "That is a good motor-car," to ask "What is good about it?" or "Why do you call it good?" or "What features of it are you commending?" It may not always be easy to answer this question precisely, but it is always a legitimate question. If we did not understand why it was always a legitimate question, we should not understand the way in which the word "good" functions.

We may illustrate this point by comparing two dialogues:

1. *X.* Jones' motor-car is a good one.
   Y. What makes you call it good?
   X. Oh, just that it's good.
   Y. But there must be some reason for your calling it good, I mean some property that it has in virtue of which you call it good.
   X. No; the property in virtue of which I call it good is just its goodness and nothing else.
   Y. But do you mean that its shape, speed, weight, manoeuvrability &c., are irrelevant to whether you call it good or not?
   X. Yes, quite irrelevant; the only relevant property is that of goodness; just as, if I called it yellow, the only relevant property would be that of yellowness.
2. The same dialogue, only with "yellow" substituted for "good" and "yellowness" for "goodness" throughout, and the last clause ("just as ... yellowness") omitted.

The reason why X's position in the first dialogue is eccentric is that one may always legitimately be asked when one has called something a good something, "What is good about it?" Now to answer this question is to give the properties in virtue of which we call it good. Thus, if I have said, "That is a good motor-car" and someone asks "Why? What is good about it?" and I reply "Its high speed combined with its stability on the road," I indicate that I call it good in virtue of its having these properties or virtues. Now to do this is *eo ipso* to say something about other motor-cars which have these properties. If any motor-car whatever had these properties, I should have, if I were not to be inconsistent, to agree that it was, *pro tanto*, a good motor-car; though of course it might, although it had these properties in its favor, have other countervailing disadvantages, and so be, taken all in all, not a good motor-car.

This last difficulty can always be got over by specifying in detail why I called the first motor-car a good one. Suppose that a second motor-car were like the first one in speed and stability, but gave its passengers no protection from the rain, and proved difficult to get into and out of. I should not then call it a good motor-car, although it had those characteristics which led me to call the first one good. This shows that I should not have called the first one good either, if it too had had the bad characteristics of the second one; and so in specifying what was good about the first one, I ought to have added " ... and the protection it gives to the passengers and the ease with which one can get into and out of it." This process could be repeated indefinitely until I had given a complete list of the characteristics of the first motor-car which were required to make me allow it to be a good one. This, in itself, would not be saying all that there was to be said about my standards for judging motor-cars—for there might be other motor-cars which, although falling short to a certain extent in these characteristics, had other countervailing good characteristics; for example, soft upholstery, large accommodation, or small consumption of petrol. But it would be at any rate some help to my hearer in building up an idea of my standards in motor-cars; and in this lies the importance of such questions and answers, and the importance of recognizing their relevance, whenever a value-judgment has been made. For one of the purposes of making such judgments is to make known the standard.

When I commend a motor-car I am guiding the choices of my hearer not merely in relation to that particular motor-car but in relation to motor-cars in general. What I have said to him will be of assistance to him whenever in the future he has to choose a motor-car or advise anyone else on the choice of a motor-car or even design a motor-car (choose what sort of motor-car to have made) or write a general treatise on the design of motor-cars (which involves choosing what sort of motor-cars to advise other people to have made). The method whereby I give him this assistance is by making known to him a standard for judging motor-cars.

This process has, as we have noticed, certain features in common with the process of defining (making known the meaning or application of) a descriptive word, though there are important differences. We have now to notice a further resemblance between showing the usage of a word and showing how to choose between motor-cars. In neither case can the instruction be done successfully unless the instructor is consistent in his teaching. If I use "red" for objects of a wide variety of colors, my hearer will never learn from me a consistent usage of the word. Similarly, if I commend motor-cars with widely different or even contrary characteristics, what I say to him will not be of assistance to him in choosing motor-cars subsequently, because I am not teaching him any consistent standard—or any standard at all, for a standard is by definition consistent. He will say, "I don't see by what standards you are judging these motor-cars; please explain to me why you call them all good, although they are so different." Of course, I might be able to give a satisfactory explanation. I might say, "There are different sorts of motor-cars, each good in its way; there are sports cars, whose prime requisites are speed and manoeuvrability; and family cars, which ought rather to be capacious and economical; and taxis, and so on. So when I say a car is good which is fast and manoeuvrable, although it is neither capacious nor economical, you must understand that I am commending it as a sports car, not as a family car." But suppose that I did not recognize the relevance of his question; suppose that I was just doling out the predicate "good" entirely haphazard, as the whim took me. It is clear that in this case I should teach him no standard at all.

We thus have to distinguish two questions that can always be asked in elucidation of a judgment containing the word "good." Suppose that someone says "That is a good one." We can then always ask (1) "Good what—sports car or family car or taxi or example to quote in a logic-book?" Or we can ask (2) "What makes you call it good? To ask the first question is to ask for the class within which evaluative comparisons are being made. Let us call it the class of comparison. To ask the second question is to ask for the virtues or "good-making characteristics." These two questions are, however, not independent; for what distinguishes the class of comparison "sports car" from the class "family car" is the set of virtues which are to be looked for in the respective classes. This is so in all cases where the class of comparison is defined by means of a functional word—for obviously "sports car," "family car," and "taxi" are functional to a very much higher degree than plain "motor-car." Sometimes, however, a class of comparison may be further specified without making it more functional; for example, in explaining the phrase "good wine" we might say "I mean good wine for this district, not good wine compared with all the wines that there are."

"Good," as used in morals, has a descriptive and an evaluative meaning, and the latter is primary. To know the descriptive meaning is to know by what standards the speaker is judging. Let us take a case where the standard is well known. If a parson says of a girl that she is a good girl, we can form a shrewd idea, of what description she is; we may expect her to go to church, for example. It is therefore easy to fall into the error of supposing that by calling her a good girl the parson means simply that she has these descriptive characteristics.

It is quite true that part of what the parson means is that the girl has these characteristics; but it is to be hoped that this is not all he means. He also means to commend her for having them; and this part of his meaning is primary. The reason why we know, when a parson says a girl is good, what sort of girl she is, how she normally behaves, &c., is that parsons are usually consistent in the way they award commendation. It is through being used consistently by parsons for commending certain sorts of behavior in girls that the word comes to have a descriptive force.

To this unkind parody may be added another. If two Indian Army majors of the old school had been talking about a new arrival in the Mess, and one of them had said "He's an awfully good man," we could have guessed that the subaltern referred to played polo, stuck pigs with *élan*, and was not on familiar terms with educated Indians. The remark, therefore, would have conveyed information to one versed in the culture of British India. It would have been informative, because officers of the Indian Army were accustomed to award commendation or the reverse according to consistent standards. But it cannot have been informative in the beginning. The standard must have got established by some pioneer evaluators; when the Indian Army was young there was no established standard for the behavior of subalterns. The standard became established by officers making commendatory judgments which were not statements of fact or informative in the least, to the effect that it was the mark of a good man, for example, to play polo. For these pioneers, the sentence "Plunkett is a good man" did not in any way entail the sentence "Plunkett plays polo" or vice versa. The former was an expression of commendation, the latter a statement of fact. But we may suppose that, after generations of officers had always commended people who played polo, it came to be assumed that, if an officer said that another officer was a good man, he must mean that, among other things, he played polo; and so the word "good," as used by Indian Army officers, came to be, to this extent, descriptive, without in the least losing its primary evaluative meaning.

Of course, the evaluative meaning might get lost, or at least wear thin. It is of the essence of a standard to be stable; but the perpetual danger is that stability may harden to over-rigidity and ossification. It is possible to lay too much stress on the descriptive force and too little on the evaluative; standards only remain current when those who make judgments in accordance with them are quite sure that, whatever else they may be doing, they are evaluating (i.e. really seeking to guide conduct).

That the descriptive meaning of the word "good" is in morals, as elsewhere, secondary to the evaluative, may be seen in the following example. Let us suppose that a missionary, armed with a grammar book, lands on a cannibal island. The vocabulary of his grammar book gives him the equivalent, in the cannibal's language, of the English word "good." Let us suppose, also, that it really is the equivalent—that it is, as the *Oxford English Dictionary* puts it, "the most general adjective of commendation" in their language. If the missionary has mastered his vocabulary, he can, *so long as he uses the word evaluatively and not descriptively*, communicate with them about morals quite happily. They know that when he uses the word he is commending the person or object that he applies it to. The only thing they will find odd is that he applies it to such unexpected people, people who are meek and gentle and do not collect large quantities of scalps; whereas they themselves are accustomed to commend people who are bold and bur'ᵧ and collect more scalps than the average. But they and the missionary are under no misapprehension about the meaning, in the evaluative sense, of the word "good"; it is the word one uses for commending. If they were under such a misapprehension, moral communication between them would be impossible.

We thus have a situation which would appear paradoxical to someone who thought that "good" (either in English or in the cannibals' language) was a quality-word like "red." Even if the qualities in people which the missionary commended had nothing in common with the qualities which the cannibals commended, yet they would both know what the word "good" meant. If "good" were like "red," this would be impossible; for then the cannibals' word and the English word would not be synonymous. If this were so, then when the missionary said that people who collected no scalps were good (English), and the cannibals said that people who collected a lot of scalps were good (cannibal), they would not be disagreeing, because in English (at any rate missionary English), "good" would mean among other things "doing no murder," whereas in the cannibals' language "good" would mean something quite different, among other things "productive of maximum scalps." It is because in its primary evaluative meaning "good" means neither of these things, but is in both languages the most general adjective of commendation, that the missionary can use it to teach the cannibals Christian morals.

Suppose, however, that the missionary's mission is successful. Then, the former cannibals will come to commend the same qualities in people as the missionary, and the words "good man" will come to have a more or less common descriptive meaning. The danger will then be that the cannibals may, after a generation or two, think that this is the only sort of meaning they have. "Good" will in that case mean for them, simply "doing what it says in the Sermon on the Mount"; and they may come to forget that it is a word of commendation; they will not realize that opinions about moral goodness have a bearing on what they themselves are to *do*. Their standards will then be in mortal danger. A Communist, landing on the island to convert people to *his* way of life, may even take advantage of the ossification of their standards. He may say "All these 'good' Christians—missionaries and colonial servants and the rest—are just deceiving you to their own profit." This would be to use the word descriptively with a dash of irony; and he could not do this plausibly unless the standards of the Christians had become considerably ossified.

NOTE ON SOURCES. Richard M. Hare, *The Language of Morals* (New York: Oxford University Press, 1964). These selections were taken from Chapters 7 and 9.

9 BERNARD GERT

MORALITY

FROM HARE TO GERT. The current interest in applied and professional ethics has emphasized normative ethics over metaethics. Indeed, it has served to call attention to what some philosophers believe is the uselessness of theory. Yet for the better part of this century, ethics meant primarily metaethics: researches along the lines of Moore, Ayer, Stevenson, and Hare.

With this selection from Gert, we return to normative ethics. Gert makes an effort to combine the strengths of both utilitarianism and Kantianism. Gert wrote the selection "Moral Theory" as a synopsis of his current views on ethics, which are expressed in great detail in his book, *Morality: A New Justification of the Moral Rules.*

BIOGRAPHICAL NOTE. Bernard Gert was born in Cincinnati, Ohio in 1934. He received his Ph.D. in philosophy from Cornell in 1962 and has taught at Dartmouth College since 1959. Gert's interest in ethics extends beyond moral theory to medical ethics, business ethics, and the ethics of scientific research. He is currently the Eunice and Julian Cohen Professor for the Study of Ethics and Human Values at Dartmouth, as well as adjunct professor of psychiatry at the Dartmouth Medical School.

THE ARGUMENT OF THE PASSAGES. In brief, Gert argues that insights about human nature are an essential feature in the derivation of morality. The most important of these insights involves the close relationship between rationality and avoiding harms or evils. Once this is properly understood, it explains both why the moral ideals encourage preventing the suffering of the evils and why the moral rules, none of which are surprising, turn out to be the following:

> Do not kill.
> Do not cause pain.
> Do not disable.
> Do not deprive of freedom or opportunity.
> Do not deprive of pleasure.
> Do not deceive.
> Keep your promises.
> Do not cheat.
> Obey the law.
> Do your duty (in your job or profession).

Of course, there must be riders on these rules—or else Gert would be just another strict Kantian. Of course, there can't be too many riders—or else Gert would be just another (act) utilitarian, calculating relative costs of e.g., keeping promises. Unlike some authors, Gert does not believe that moral theory can provide clear-cut answers to every moral dispute. Often, he points out, the best a moral theory can do is to provide some limits on reasonable answers.

> It is misleading to discuss any moral problem as if it were an isolated problem whose solution did not have implications for all other moral problems. Morality is a system and the acceptability of the answers that this system gives to any particular problem is affected by the acceptability of the answers that it gives to all other problems. One should not trust a moral system that sometimes provides unacceptable answers. Nor should one use a moral system without understanding it. A moral theory is an attempt to explain and, if possible, justify morality. Therefore, before we discuss the

moral problems involved in medicine, I shall present an account of the moral theory which explains what morality is, and an account of that moral system.

A MORAL THEORY

A moral theory consists of the analysis of the concepts necessary to explain and, if possible, to justify morality, viz., rationality, impartiality, and morality itself, together with an account of how they are related to each other. Rationality is the fundamental normative concept. To justify morality, or anything else, requires showing that it is, at least, compatible with rationality. Since everything else depends on rationality, this means that rationality itself must be such that everyone accepts that no one ever ought to act irrationally. A moral theory must provide an account of rationality that has this feature and show how it is related to morality. Impartiality is universally recognized as an essential feature of morality. A moral theory must provide a clear account of the kind of impartiality that morality requires and also of the way in which this kind of impartiality is related to morality. A moral theory must also identify the essential features of morality, i.e., the actual moral system that, in so far as we are concerned with acting morally, we use to guide our conduct and to make judgments on the conduct of others. A moral theory should explain why morality prohibits some behavior, requires other behavior, and allows or encourages still other behavior.

MORALITY

Morality is a public system for guiding and judging the behavior of all rational persons. A public system is a system (1) that all persons to whom it applies, those whose behavior is to be guided and judged by that system, understand it, i.e., know what behavior the system prohibits, requires, allows and encourages; and (2) that it is not irrational for any of them to accept being guided or judged by. The clearest example of a public system is a game. The rules of the game form a system that is understood by all of the players, i.e., they all know what kind of behavior is prohibited, required, allowed, and encouraged by the rules; and it is not irrational for any player to use the rules to guide his own behavior and to judge the behavior of other players by them. The rules of a game, although they are a public system, apply only to those playing the game. Morality is a public system that applies to all rational persons; a person is subject to morality simply in virtue of being a rational person.

Morality consists of rules which prohibit some kinds of actions, e.g., killing, require others, e.g., keeping promises; and what I call moral ideals, which encourage certain kinds of actions, e.g., preserving life and relieving pain. It also contains a procedure for determining when it is justified to violate a moral rule, e.g., when moral rules conflict or when a moral ideal conflicts with a moral rule. But morality does not provide unique answers to every question, it merely sets the limits to genuine moral disagreement. The content of morality is determined by the content of the rules and ideals that all impartial rational persons would include in a public system that applies to all rational persons. But this content cannot deviate in any significant way from our common conception of morality, for the function of moral philosophy is to clarify, make more precise, and justify, if possible, the common conception of morality, not to put forward some substitute for it.

There are certain kinds of actions that we all regard as being immoral unless one has an adequate justification for doing them. Among these kinds of actions are killing, causing pain, deceiving, and breaking promises. Anyone who kills people, causes them pain, deceives them, or breaks a promise, and does so without an adequate justification, is universally regarded as acting immorally. To say that there is a moral rule prohibiting that kind of act is another way of saying that a certain kind of act is immoral unless it is justified. To say that it is justified to break that moral rule is another way of saying that it is justifiable to act in that way. There are other kinds of actions that we all regard as morally good unless there is a moral rule prohibiting our doing them. Among these kinds of actions are saving lives and relieving pain. Following these moral ideals sometimes even justifies violating a moral rule.

RATIONALITY

My account of rationality, although it accurately describes the way in which we all use the concept, differs radically from that normally provided by philosophers in two important ways. First, it takes irrationality to be more basic than rationality; and second, it defines irrationality by means of a list rather than a formula. The basic definition is as follows: *A person with sufficient knowledge and intelligence to be a moral agent acts irrationally when he acts in a way that he knows, (justifiably believes), or should know, will significantly increase the probability that he will suffer death, pain, disability, loss of freedom or loss of pleasure, and he does not have an adequate reason for so acting.* This list also defines what counts as an evil or harm. *A reason is a conscious belief that one's action will help anyone, not merely oneself, avoid one of these evils, or gain some good, viz., ability, freedom, or pleasure, and this belief is not obviously inconsistent with what one knows.* A reason is adequate if any significant group of rational persons regard the evil avoided or good gained as at least as important as the evil suffered. Any action that is not irrational, is rational.

This account of rationality, and only this account, has the desired result that everyone, who is regarded as sane, always wants himself and his friends to act rationally. Certainly, none of us would ever want ourselves or anyone for whom we are concerned to act irrationally. But if we accept any of the standard philosophical accounts of rationality, e.g., acting rationally is acting so as to maximize the satisfaction of one's desires, it turns out that unless we rule out what I call irrational desires, e.g., desires for anything on the list of evils I have provided, we would not always want those for whom we are concerned to act rationally. If I had a friend who developed an extremely strong desire to kill himself in the most painful possible way, I would not want him to satisfy that desire even if doing so would maximize the satisfaction of his desires; rather I would want him to see a psychiatrist in order to get rid of that desire.

IMPARTIALITY

Impartiality, like simultaneity, is usually taken to be a simpler concept than it really is. Einstein showed that one cannot simply ask whether A and B occurred simultaneously, one must also specify something about C, the point of view of the observer. Similarly, one cannot simply ask if someone is impartial, one must specify the group with regard to which the person must be impartial and also in what respects she is required to be impartial with regard to that group. When discussing morality, the minimal group toward which one must be impartial consists of all moral agents, including oneself, and former moral agents who are still persons; and the respect in which one must be impartial toward this group is in using the moral rules to guide one's behavior and to make moral judgments. This requires that one violate a moral rule, or judge a violation to be justified, only when such a violation can be allowed as part of the public system that applies to all rational persons.

This kind of impartiality can be achieved by using only those beliefs that are shared by all rational persons. These include general beliefs such as: we all know some things about the world, but no one knows everything, i.e., people have limited knowledge; also people are mortal, can suffer pain, etc. Scientific beliefs as well as religious beliefs are excluded, e.g., beliefs about the functions of the brain, heart, etc., are excluded, for rational persons do not share a set of common beliefs about these matters. Included are some personal beliefs, viz., beliefs about oneself that all rational persons have about themselves, e.g., beliefs that one can be killed and suffer pain, etc. Excluded are beliefs about one's race, sex, religion, etc., because these beliefs are not common to all rational persons. Impartiality, however, does not require uniformity, for impartial rational persons may rank the goods and evils differently. Different rankings of the goods and evils, e.g., differences about whether pain of a certain intensity and duration is worse than death, may result in equally informed impartial rational persons disagreeing on how one ought to act.

THE JUSTIFIED MORAL SYSTEM

The moral system that all impartial rational persons would choose as a public system that applies to all rational persons is the justified moral system. This system includes rules prohibiting each of the five evils that all rational persons want to avoid, thus it includes the following five rules.

> Don't kill.
> Don't cause pain.
> Don't disable.
> Don't deprive of freedom.
> Don't deprive of pleasure.

Morality also includes rules prohibiting those kinds of actions which generally cause evil even though not every act of that kind causes an evil. Thus it includes the following five rules.

> Don't deceive.
> Keep your promise. (Don't break your promise.)
> Don't cheat.
> Obey the law. (Don't break the law.)
> Do your duty. (Don't neglect your duty.) I use the term "duty" in its everyday sense to refer to what is required by one's role in society, primarily one's job, not as philosophers customarily use it, simply as a synonym for "what one morally ought to do."

These rules are not absolute, all of them have justified exceptions. The attitude that all impartial rational persons would take toward these rules when considering them as moral rules, i.e., as rules in a public system applying to all rational persons, is the following: *Everyone is always to obey the rule unless an impartial rational person can advocate that violating it be publicly allowed. Anyone who violates the rule when an impartial rational person cannot advocate that such a violation be publicly allowed may be punished.* (The unless clause only means that when an impartial rational person can advocate that such a violation be publicly allowed, impartial rational persons may disagree on whether one should obey the rule, not that they agree one should not obey.)

In deciding whether or not to advocate that a violation of a moral rule be publicly allowed, an impartial rational person can use only morally relevant features. These features are contained in the answers to the following eleven questions.[*]

1. What moral rules are being violated?
2. What evils are being (a) avoided, (b) prevented, (c) caused?
3. What are the relevant desires of the people toward whom the rule is being violated?
4. What are the relevant rational beliefs of the people toward whom the rule is being violated?
5. Does one have a duty to violate moral rules with regard to the person(s), and is one in a unique or almost unique position in this regard?
6. What goods are being promoted?
7. Is an unjustified or weakly justified violation of a moral rule being prevented?
8. Is an unjustified or weakly justified violation of a moral rule being punished?
9. Are there any foreseeable alternative actions that would be preferable?
10. Is the violation being done intentionally or only knowingly?
11. Is it an emergency situation that no person is likely to plan to be in?

When considering the evils being avoided, prevented or caused, and the goods being promoted, one must consider not only their intensity, duration, and probability, one must also consider the kind of good or evil involved. If more than one person is affected, one must consider not only how many people will be affected, but also the distribution of the harms and benefits. If two violations are the same in all of their morally relevant features then they count as the same kind of violation, and any impartial rational person who advocates that one of them be publicly allowed must advocate that the other also be publicly allowed. However, this does not mean that two impartial rational persons, who agree that two actions count as the same kind of violation be publicly allowed, for they may differ in their estimate of the consequences of publicly allowing that kind of violation or they may rank the goods and evils involved differently.

An impartial rational person decides whether or not to advocate that a violation be publicly allowed by estimating what effect this kind of violation, if publicly allowed, would have. If all impartial rational persons would estimate that less evil would be suffered if that kind of violation were publicly allowed, then all impartial rational persons would advocate that that kind of violation be publicly allowed and the violation is strongly justified; if all rational persons would estimate that more evil would be suffered, then no rational person would advocate that that kind of violation be publicly allowed and that the violation is unjustified. However, impartial rational persons, even if equally informed, may disagree in their estimate of whether more or less evil will result from that kind of violation being publicly allowed. When this happens they will disagree on whether or not to advocate that that kind of violation be publicly allowed and such a violation counts as weakly justified.

Disagreements in the estimates of whether a given kind of violation being publicly allowed will result in more or less evil may stem from two distinct sources. The first is a difference in the rankings of the various kinds of evils. (If governments are involved, rankings of goods are also relevant.) If someone ranks a specified amount of pain and suffering as worse than a specified amount of loss of freedom, and some-

---

[*]Questions 9, 10, and 11 were added by Gert after the publication of the original article. Gert retains the copyright to these three questions, and they may not be used without his permission.

one else ranks them in the opposite way, then although they agree that a given action is the same kind of vic' ..on, they may disagree on whether or not to advocate that that kind of violation be publicly allowed. The second is a difference in estimates of how much evil would result from publicly allowing a given kind of violation, even when there seems to be no difference in the rankings of the different kinds of evils. These differences may stem from differences in beliefs about human nature or about the nature of human societies. In so far as these differences cannot be settled by any universally agreed upon empirical method, I call such differences, ideological. However, I suspect that most ideological differences also involve differences in the rankings of different kinds of evils.

For example, one impartial rational person may estimate that if a deception were publicly allowed in order to avoid causing a specified degree of anxiety and other mental suffering, this would result in less overall evil being suffered than if this kind of violation were not publicly allowed, while another person may estimate the opposite. The latter may hold that knowledge that deception of this kind is publicly allowed will actually increase the amount of anxiety suffered, because, e.g., patients will suffer anxiety even when their doctor truthfully tells them that the tests were negative and they have nothing to worry about. She may also hold that deception of this kind may result in loss of freedom, as patients will be deprived of the opportunity to make decisions based upon the facts. The former person may not only claim that publicly allowing the violation will decrease the amount of anxiety, for he does not think that people will be seriously affected by knowing the violation is allowed, he may also not rank the resulting loss of freedom very highly. This disagreement may thus involve either a difference in the rankings of the evils, or ideological differences, or both.

Gert's system is clear. Morality is aimed at guiding and evaluating behavior. Morality must be understandable by those at whom it is aimed. And, morality cannot be irrational to adopt. This is what Gert means by saying that morality is a public system.

Morality, Gert claims, is a set of two kinds of guides. The first kind is the moral rules, which prohibit some actions (e.g., killing) and require others (e.g., keeping promises). The second kind is the moral ideals, which encourage other actions (e.g., relieving pain). An important part of the morality is the method it offers to recognize those times when a moral rule is justifiably broken.

Rationality is a key concept for Gert. He defines it in such a way that irrationality is the more basic concept. Gert concludes that any sane person would want to act rationally and would want those he or she cares about to act rationally, since to act irrationally is always to result in an evil without adequate justification. With rationality defined, Gert points out that impartiality in morality really comes by considering only those beliefs shared by all rational people. To consider, therefore, whether a person has read the novel, *The Red and the Black*, as morally relevant would not, according to Gert, be acting impartially, since not all rational people believe that that particular novel is an important moral document.

The moral rules can be seen as a set of directives for avoiding evils befalling us and those for whom we care. As previously mentioned, the rules do have exceptions (riders). Gert puts it this way: Our attitude toward the moral rules should be one that allows violation if and only if an impartial, rational person can publicly advocate that violation.

CONTRASTS WITH OTHER SYSTEMS FOR GUIDING CONDUCT

In order to clarify the moral system it may be worthwhile to contrast it with systems similar to those proposed by Kant and Mill. On a Kantian system one should never act in any way that one cannot will to be a universal law. If it would be impossible for everyone to do some kind of action, then everyone is prohibited from doing that same kind of action. On the moral system, one is prohibited from doing a kind of action only if no impartial rational person would advocate that that kind of action be publicly allowed. A Kantian system seems to rule out ever making false promises, whereas the moral system allows the making of false promises in some circumstances, e.g., when the evil to be prevented by doing so is sufficiently great that less overall evil would be suffered even if it were publicly allowed.

On a Utilitarian or consequentialist system one not only may, but should, violate any rule if the foreseeable consequences of that particular violation, including the effects on future obedience to the rule, are better than the consequences of not violating the rule. A consequentialist system is concerned only with the foreseeable consequences of the particular violation, not with the foreseeable consequences of that kind of violation being publicly allowed. But on the moral system, it is precisely the foreseeable consequences of that kind of violation being publicly allowed that are decisive in determining whether or not it is morally allowed. The consequences of the particular act are important only in that they help determine the kind of violation under consideration. A consequentialist system favors cheating on an exam if it were extremely unlikely that one would get caught and no harm would result from that particular violation of the rule against cheating. The moral system would not allow this kind of violation of the rule against cheating, for if this kind of violation were publicly allowed, it would eliminate the possibility of even having exams. I am assuming that the exams serve a useful function.

The moral system differs from a Kantian system and resembles a consequentialist system in that it explicitly takes consequences into consideration. It resembles a Kantian system and differs from a consequentialist system in that it takes rules to be an essential feature of morality; it requires impartiality with respect to rules and not merely with respect to consequences. Impartiality with respect to rules is required because of the public nature of morality and the limited knowledge of rational persons. Morality differs from both systems in that it does not require all moral questions to have unique answers, but explicitly allows for disagreements among equally informed impartial rational persons. Morality also includes moral ideals, which cannot possibly be followed by anyone impartially with regard to all other moral agents, and hence need not be followed impartially.

NOTE ON SOURCES. This article was especially written for a presentation Gert made at Ohio University. It is reprinted in *Medical Ethics, A Reader*, eds. A. Zucker, D. Borchert, and D. Stewart (Englewood Cliffs, New Jersey, Prentice Hall, 1992).

10 DOROTHY EMMET

THE MORAL PRISM

FROM GERT TO EMMET. Looking at the moral rules and ideals, one might ask what sort of person would be likely to develop from following them. One might also ask what sort of person would be likely to find these rules and ideals congenial to his or her already established behavior patterns. The answer might be something like this: People with strong senses of restraint, compassion, honesty, and fidelity. These character traits have often been touted as virtues. Gert would see them as virtues because they grow out of the proper attitude toward the moral rules and ideals. Emmet and other virtue theorists have a slightly different slant.

To a virtue theorist, the basic question in morals is *not* how should I act or what are the moral rules, but rather, what kind of a person should I be? Notice that these questions are related. The difference is one of emphasis. The difference is with regard to which one is the more basic. Aristotle (384–322 B.C.) set the tone for virtue ethics with his work, *The Nichomacheaen Ethics*. Emmet is one of many contemporary exponents of virtue theory. Other present-day virtue theorists are G. E. M. Anscombe, Philippa Foot, Alisdair MacIntyre, Iris Murdoch (better known for her novels), and Annette Baier.

Despite some differences, the virtue theorists have in common the idea that a good life is, at the very least, a life that is lived within an ongoing and consistent narrative and that, like all narratives, has an end (goal) that gives consistency to the ongoing flow. Virtue theory sees lives as parts of stories and asserts that these stories should give meaning to life.

According to virtue theory, one should always be vigilant in asking "What sort of a person will doing this make me become?" and, of course, "Do I want to become that sort of person?" Indeed, one could ask, "Would any (rational) person want to become that sort of person?" It should be clear that this approach to ethics is not wholly distinct from that of any of the preceding normative theories.

BIOGRAPHICAL NOTE. Dorothy Emmet was born in England in 1904. She received an M.A. from Oxford in 1930. She taught at the University of Manchester in England from 1932 until 1966. She was named the Sir Samuel Hall Professor of Philosophy in 1946. She became emeritus professor of philosophy in 1966. She has published works on metaphysics and the philosopher A. N. Whitehead (with whom she studied), as well as ethics and virtue theory.

THE ARGUMENT OF THE PASSAGES. Emmet's prism metaphor can be used to better understand her overall view of ethics. Light as we see it under normal circumstances is simple and white, or has no color at all. When we allow light to pass through a prism what is revealed is the complexity and beauty of what had appeared to be simple, white light. The entire spectrum of color is revealed to us. So it is with moral growth. It is all too easy to see the world as a simple place where answers to ethical quandaries are clear and not to be questioned. Growing up morally requires that one see the world of morals for what it really is—through the moral prism. Seen in this way, the ethical disputes become much more complex; the need for careful analysis is obvious and the need for some degree of tolerance of different opinions becomes apparent.

As we grow, we change our beliefs, our goals, and our desires. Emmet sees the possibility for a debilitating form of subjectivism (or egoism) to ally itself to virtue theory. After all, someone could change from the traditional virtues to Nazi or Ku Klux Klan "virtues," claiming all the while that *now* the world is seen in its true beauty and complexity. Emmet tries to defend against this by insisting that justice, fairness, and sympathy are crucial virtues that are the objective mark of a truly moral person.

> . . .there are things which are admirable which we can learn to appreciate, whether or not they further our interests and purposes, and, most importantly. . .there can be growth in appreciation. . . .
>
> To learn to appreciate is not just to register one's desires. It is to educate one's desires; to believe that judgments based on these at any given time can be improved; that one goes on learning, and that there is always likely to be a gap between what one appreciates here and now and what would be full appreciation. This would go for moral judgment as well as other kinds of appreciation such as aesthetic, and for our attempts to narrow the gap between what is subjectively right, as the best judgment one can now make, and what would indeed be the best judgment that could be made. Good, as what could command unqualified approval, is here used as a term with transcendental reference; we have met other such—"Objective Right," "Will of God," "verdict of an Ideal Observer"—and whether or not these have a metaphysical reference they function in affirming a belief that judgments are corrigible and there is indeed a difference between those which are better and those which are worse. "Better and worse" would then not only register preferences, but be grounds for preference.
>
> Grounds for preference can of course, often be specifiable within a recognized purpose, or with references to already existing desires. Since one can normally take for granted that a person does not want to get typhoid, if he is in an unhealthy place he can judge that it is better to boil his water and not just drink it out of the tap. Such cases are easy to defend. One could also easily defend the cases where a person is told that he will very likely enjoy something more, for instance a certain kind of beer, if he takes the trouble to try it on a number of occasions and to acquire the taste. The more difficult cases are where growth in appreciation does not reach this kind of end state. I have suggested that one may educate one's desires as well as one's judgments with reference to an ideal which will not be a particular finite end state at which one stops, and I have called such ideal notions "transcendental." Transcendental notions, if they meant that unless one occupies the transcendental position (which of course one does not) one cannot get going in making judgments, would stultify morality. The reference to them should set a direction; one must be able to get going in making moral judgments from where one is and also be able to say that there are ways of making them which can lead to improvement. Yet this marks out a direction of improvement, not the prospect of an achieved adequacy. The reference to a transcendental notion can have this function of indicating openness to a possibility which cannot be fully satisfied. . . .

To *learn to appreciate* presupposes something to be learnt. This is not to say that we want things which will satisfy us, and had better find out what they are—either what will give most satisfaction or at least, in order to avoid trouble, what will give socially acceptable satisfaction. This was the position of the strict Benthamite Utilitarians, and led to the logical conclusion that, quantity of pleasure being equal, pushpin is as good as poetry. J. S. Mill tried (unsuccessfully on his premises) to maintain that some pleasures were qualitatively superior, on the dubious contention that the superior ones would afford more pleasure. . . .

But the question is not only how to get satisfaction—even more satisfaction— through things of superior quality. It is whether the desire itself may acquire a different character according to the things toward which it is directed—"Where your treasure is, there will your heat be also." "Treasure in heaven" may not stand for the location of what one wants but for a reorientation which can change the character of one's desires. If, instead of thinking of the psyche as a store of energy which can be sent through different pipes, we think of it as a system of active ways of responding and relating, both to one's internal states and to external objects, then a desire to read or write poetry may be not only a different desire, but a different kind of desire from the desire to play pushpin. It was the Utilitarians' way of speaking of pleasure as though it were a thing in itself apart from what it was *pleasure in* that made them think otherwise. . . .

It is the distinction between what one happens to want and what one can come to appreciate—a change in orientation towards learning to appreciate, an orientation guided by the conviction that there is indeed something to be learnt, and that this includes ways of living, the life-styles to which we commit ourselves.

One might say that what is learnt is how better to follow one's chosen life-style, "better" and "worse" having an application within this context. Then if one's life-style is egoistic, promoting one's own interests and manipulating other people to serve one's purposes, one can learn to do this more skillfully and come to appreciate subtler methods. What of saying that there might be a better life-style? Here one must perforce make a first-person recommendation, hoping nevertheless that there are considerations by which it can be supported. I shall here only indicate some features in what might be such a life-style. I should put high any life-style which accepts the complexity of moral issues; the need to think about the worthiness of one's projects; the mutuality of relationships with other people; the need for courage in one's civic roles as well as generosity in one's more personal face-to-face dealings. I should also rank highly the capacity to see how proposed actions could threaten rather than strengthen mutual trust, since I see this trust as a condition for most of the enterprises and relationships which we find rewarding. All this will call on one to enlarge one's imagination in seeing the situations in which one acts; not only seeing single chains of cause and effect, but ramifications and repercussions. It will mean trying to see what one's proposed actions will be likely to do to other people, not only in external help or hurt, but in their effects on internal feelings. A person who sees proposed actions in terms of his own interests can simplify the issues by reducing them to one perspective; he may thereby make his own task of decision easier, but there will be aspects of the situation which he has not opened himself to appreciate. I maintain that a way of living in which such considerations are taken into account is one in which moral judgment is more likely to grow in capacity to face complex issues. It may be said that the considerations I have named are mainly factual, concerned with getting a more adequate grasp of situations. This is so, but I think that the attempt so to see situations is likely to be value-laden. Certain values, notably fairness and sympathy, will be congenial to the effect to detach our view from weighting in favor of our own interests. Even if not natural features of situations fairness and sympathy can be, to use a medieval term, "connatural" to such a way of looking at the facts.

One has, I think, to decide to make the venture of believing that one can come to appreciate situations in greater depth, and this is a venture reinforced through following it rather than one whose correctness can be demonstrated at the start. The start is to change our orientation from preoccupation with our own interests to liberty of spirit to see things disinterestedly. . . .

Morality is not so much an activity in itself as on the back of other activities, concerned with what one does in them, and how and when. The particular feature in morality dominant at any given time will be likely to be that most characteristically associated with whatever activity we are involved in. In acting politically, the feature of purpose will be dominant, in acting in a legal or administrative capacity the emphasis will be on principles to be applied impartially. But other factors within morality may become relevant both to the occasion and manner of what is done; there are times when a purpose in politics may be challenged for a principle, and times when sympathetic discretion will temper judicial impartiality, and times in personal relations when keen-edged criticism is more appropriate than tolerant acceptance. To judge morally calls for one to be alert to this complexity; to see that no activity can rightly be carried on by maintaining a form that can become a stereotype, still less by going by the book. There is also the complexity of what constitutes a "situation." The facts of situations in which one has to act and the likely consequences of one's actions are not just single events leading to other events in a single track; they are networks proliferating into other networks. Moreover, one may judge an action to be right because it fits a new emerging state of affairs, not just the alignment of the situation as it now is. One can never see more than a part of this complexity, but one can try to remove the blinkers which confine one's view. . . .

The most appropriate moral stance [is one] . . . in which one cultivates liberty of spirit in order the better to make moral judgments, in order the better to pursue whatever purposes one thinks worth pursuing, and to know better how to act in one's dealings with other people. . . .

. . . Liberty of spirit is not itself a goal to be sought (like "liberation" in some religious teachings) so much as a disposition to be cultivated in pursuing one's goals; it is to get away from one's preconceptions and from being emotionally preoccupied by chagrin, disappointment, envy, fear, so that one may act with something approaching what Kant called the good will, and with more clarity as to the issues involved.

Emmet discusses three ways to look at social morality. One emphasizes custom (the ethical relativists), another emphasizes reciprocity and the use of reason to see where reciprocity is involved (Kantians), the third is based on what she terms "generosity." By "generosity," she means a humane, outgoing imagination in moral dealings. We need custom in complicated societies. But we also need the other two approaches. Generosity, Emmet points out, differs from reciprocity in that generosity does not lend itself to calculation as reciprocity does. Bentham could not have created a generosity calculus.

Generosity cannot be captured in rules, in large part because it is so personal. Generosity is not a duty, nor do I have a right to expect it. You may decide to be generous even though you have a right to do something else. For example, if someone gave you some candy you would be within your rights to eat it all yourself and not to share any of it with your friends.

With respect to what Emmet calls "institutional morality," she says that we have to know where we stand with respect to each other. We could not be generous all the time. This would lead to anarchy or to an extreme form of morality requiring sainthood of all of us. But to keep institutions humane, an occasional generous act is required. There is no surer road to injustice than an unthoughtful abiding by the rules. Sometimes we have to think in terms of generosity. Loopholes and discretion in rules (all good department chairs know how to find them) are really ways of thinking in terms of generosity.

Emmet, like Gert, tries to find a stable middle ground between the extremes of Kant and utilitarianism. The goal is to find a morality that is not self-centered, not subjective, and not overly restrictive in what it allows as right action.

What would a just action be according to the views of Emmet? The answer is complex. It would be that sort of action that would:

1. Increase our abilities to see complexity,
2. Allow us to see the importance of mutuality over self-interest,
3. Make clear the need for mutual trust,
4. Allow us to enlarge our imagination and thereby develop true sympathy for those in need.

Emmet's morality tries to give us the ability to know when to shift back and forth between custom, reciprocity, and generosity.

Ethics is so important that philosophers will be driven until some clearer answers are obtained. To this hope, Aristotle once commented that there can never be more precision in the theory than there is in the subject matter. Where the subject matter is made of the values and hopes of humankind, ambiguity will always be present to frustrate any attempts at excessive precision. Philosophers, however, will continue their quest for clarity as should be evident from those studied in this chapter.

NOTE ON SOURCES. Dorothy Emmet, *The Moral Prism* (New York: St. Martin's Press, 1979), Chapter 11.

When Should I Conform to the Law?

The Question Posed

As we pursue the examined life, sooner or later we will have to scrutinize one of the truly remarkable creations of humankind: the legislative way of life, the way of life that is productive of those contrived regularities that humans obtain by devising, revising, administering, and enforcing laws. We often use the term *law* in two senses. In sense one we use it to refer to those statements, produced by scientists, in which they formulate or describe regularities that they detect in the order of nature. We are not concerned in this chapter with "law" in this sense. Rather, we focus our attention on "law" in the sense of those demands produced by legislators in which they prescribe regularities they desire to produce. "Do not park by a fire plug" would be a simple and familiar example of a law produced by a legislator, or a legislative body. To the degree that this law is obeyed, a regularity results: it becomes regularly the case that vehicles are not parked within a prescribed distance of fire hydrants. These and other humanly contrived regularities have considerable value. Increasingly, civilized communities are dependent upon laws produced by scientists and laws produced by legislators.

In communities committed to the legislative way of life, laws propose to remove options from the behavior of those who obey them, and to impose penalties upon those who disobey them. As a consequence, sometimes both parties are irked. The person who no longer has the option of parking by a fire hydrant is irked, and the person who is punished for having parked by the fire hydrant is also irked. Under these conditions, the question naturally arises, "When should I conform to the law? And why?" In addition, since a law's demands and threats are backed by very considerable power, the question eventually arises, "Where do those who possess and exercise this power obtain the authority, the right, to do so?" It will not do to say that they get it by law, because that law is itself here in question. So you have the question, "Is there anything not produced by human legislation that is the source from which legislative bodies derive their *authority* to exercise their *powers;* derive, as the Declaration of Independence says, their 'just powers'?"

Our authors direct attention to essential features of the legislative way of life, and to the questions that thereby arise. First of all, Hobbes portrays the conflictual state of nature from which the creation of the legislative way of life rescues humankind, and then provides reasons for obeying as well as disobeying laws. Second, Rousseau, in the *Social Contract,* observes that, typically, humans live under laws; also typically, laws make demands that are backed by threats. He therefore says that humans live under "chains" and asks how this came to pass, and how it can be justified. Third, Edmund Burke, after denying the notion of popular sovereignty, advances the claim that the foundation of the state and law, meaning their principal of justification, is to be sought among the needs of human nature, and specifically in the need to be coerced and restrained in things that are our duties when we might choose to violate these in the name of supposed rights. Fourth, Karl Marx, in the *Communist Manifesto,* declares that laws are demands, backed by threats, for regularities favorable to the interests of the ruling class. The perennial class struggle between the oppressed and the oppressors has become simplified and intensified during the modern bourgeois industrial epoch into a conflict between the proletarian masses and the capitalistic ruling class. In this conflict, legislatures, governmental bureaucrats, and politicians function as agents of the capitalist masters of the economy. Marx summons the oppressed workers of the world to unite and to break the "chains"—the regularities imposed by the bourgeois capitalists—that inhibit their development as human beings. Fifth, Mill, in *On Liberty,* observes that as you democratize a state, a community committed to the legislative way of life, you enable an increasing majority to prescribe for deviant minorities. As majorities increasingly become the source of the powers exercised in their name by legislatures and executives, the chance for individuals and minorities to think and act for themselves is increasingly circumscribed. Finally, Martin Luther King, in his *Letter from Birmingham Jail,* builds a case for civil disobedience based on the distinction between *just* laws (those that are consonant with the moral law and that uplift human personality) and *unjust* laws (those that do not square with the moral law and that degrade human personality). Unjust laws must be broken openly and lovingly, says King, in order to make justice a reality.

THOMAS HOBBES

THE CASE FOR THE LEGISLATIVE LIFE

Thomas Hobbes philosophized in England during the seventeenth century, a time of struggle and achievement for the English. The achievements of the century ranged from the production of classics in English literature, such as the writings of William Shakespeare and John Milton and the King James Bible, to the establishment of the East India Company and (with the exception of Georgia) the founding of the Thirteen Colonies in America. The major struggle was the civil war, which pitted Calvinistic Protestants, called the Puritans, against more moderate Protestants who adhered to the established Church of England. The Puritans advocated the rights of Parliament over the claims of the Crown. Religious differences, however, were often mixed with political, economic, and constitutional issues.

Following the death of Queen Elizabeth I in 1603, the English throne passed to James I, a foreign Scotsman and son of Mary Stuart. A defender of royal absolutism, James wrote a treatise titled *The True Law of Free Monarchy,* in which he defended the notion of a monarchy that was "free" from the control of Parliament, the church, and tradition. He presented the king as one who cared for his realm in a very paternalistic fashion, who derived his authority from God, and who was accordingly responsible to God alone. This doctrine of the divine right of kings did not sit well with members of Parliament. They refused to grant the level of revenue support requested by King James and by his son Charles I, who succeeded him in 1625. In addition, many members of Parliament were Puritans who resented the legal requirement that they belong to the Church of England. Then, too, many members of Parliament were not only lawyers who feared that the common law was in danger of being superseded by kingly "divine" prerogative, but were also landowners who feared that the king might be successful in encroaching on their wealth through new taxes.

In due course, the struggle between Parliament and the crown broke out into open conflict, a conflict that was eventually controlled by Oliver Cromwell, a Puritan, who subdued Parliament and saw to the execution of Charles I in 1649. Under Cromwell, the entire British Isles were declared to be a republic called the "commonwealth" with Cromwell as "lord protector." He ruled with a blend of moral puritanism and political dictatorship. Two years after Cromwell's death in 1658, royalty was restored in the person of Charles II, the son of Charles I. Remembering the fate of his father, Charles II was cautious in his dealings with Parliament; and the members of Parliament, mindful of the "excesses" to which the revolution under Cromwell had led, were inclined to be more loyal to the crown and to the Church of England than they had been in previous years.

Hobbes lived through this English civil war, and the political writings he authored between 1640 and 1651 were intended by him to lend support to the side of the crown. The principles he articulated, however, could be used to support either the monarchy or Parliament in their conflict. Indeed, in the nineteenth century his ideas were incorporated into the views of the Utilitarians where they served the interests of middle-class liberalism, a cause that probably would have garnered very little sympathy from Hobbes.

BIOGRAPHICAL NOTE.   Thomas Hobbes was born in England in 1588 and died at the age of ninety-one in 1679. Educated at Oxford, Hobbes lived through two important revolutions. The first was the English civil war in the light of which his political writings were fashioned. The second was the development of modern science, which provided him with a number of fundamental metaphysical tenets.

Among his acquaintances, Hobbes could number such important scientists as Francis Bacon, Galileo, and William Harvey, and such significant political figures as Charles II (whose tutor he became). Not until he was in his forties did the mathematical logic of Euclid and the astronomical explanations of Galileo have an impact on Hobbes; but when they did, he came to believe that all of reality is ultimately reducible to moving particles that obey simple laws and that careful observation and deductive reasoning from axioms will yield exact knowledge. Hobbes, accordingly, set out to rework the various domains of human thought using this new perspective, and he published such works as *De Cive (The Citizen)* in 1642, *De Corpore (Concerning Body)* in 1655, and *De Homine (Concerning Man)* in 1658. It was his political writings, which proceeded in the same rigorous mathematical fashion and with the same basic metaphysical commitment, that generated his fame. Especially noteworthy is his *Leviathan,* published in 1651, from which the following selections are taken. (For additional biographical information on Hobbes refer to Chapter 9, section 1.)

THE ARGUMENT OF THE PASSAGES.   Hobbes grounds his case for the legislative life in the nature of human beings. Humans, like every other part of the universe, are fundamentally matter in motion. What distinguishes humans from other moving particles is the kind of motion that takes place in them. Hobbes analyzes that motion and discerns two types of animal motion within humans: vital and voluntary. In describing voluntary motion, Hobbes affirms the doctrine of psychological egoism, according to which humans are so constituted that every voluntary act they perform is motivated by self-interest; in other words, every voluntary human act is ultimately selfish. That is the basic proposition about human beings upon which Hobbes's view of the legislative life is constructed.

> There be in animals, two sorts of *motions* peculiar to them: one called *vital;* begun in generation, and continued without interruption through their whole life; such as are the *course* of the *blood,* the *pulse,* the *breathing,* the *concoction, nutrition, excretion,* etc. to which motions there needs no help of imagination: the other is *animal motion,* otherwise called *voluntary motion;* as to *go,* to *speak,* to *move* any of our limbs, in such manner as is first fancied in our minds. That sense is motion in the organs and interior parts of man's body, caused by the action of the things we see, hear, etc.; and that fancy is but the relics of the same motion, remaining after sense, has been already said. . . . And before *going, speaking,* and the like voluntary motions, depend always upon a precedent thought of *whither, which way,* and *what;* it is evident, that the imagination is the first internal beginning of all voluntary motion. And although unstudied men do not conceive any motion at all to be there, where the thing moved is invisible; or the space it is moved in is, for the shortness of it, insensible; yet that doth not hinder, but that such motions are. For let a space be never so little, that which is moved over a greater space, whereof that little one is part, must first be moved over that. These small beginnings of motion, within the body of man, before they appear in walking, speaking, striking, and other visible actions, are commonly called ENDEAVOUR.
>   This endeavour, when it is toward something which causes it, is called APPETITE, or DESIRE; the latter, being the general name; and the other oftentimes restrained to signify the desire of food, namely *hunger* and *thirst.* And when the endeavour is

fromward something, it is generally called AVERSION. These words, *appetite* and *aversion,* we have from the Latins; and they both of them signify the motions, one of approaching, the other of retiring. . . .

That which men desire, they are also said to LOVE: and to HATE those things for which they have aversion. So that desire and love are the same thing; save that by desire, we always signify the absence of the object; by love, most commonly the presence of the same. So also by aversion, we signify the absence; and by hate, the presence of the object.

Of appetites and aversions, some are born with men; as appetite of food . . . The rest, which are appetites of particular things, proceed from experience, and trial of their effects upon themselves or other men. . . .

Those things which we neither desire, nor hate, we are said to *contemn;* CONTEMPT being nothing else but an immobility, or contumacy of the heart, in resisting the action of certain things; and proceeding from that the heart is already moved otherwise, by other more potent objects; or from want of experience of them. . . .

and of the voluntary acts of every man, the object is some *good to himself.*

For Hobbes, things in themselves possess only quantity and motion. In themselves they do not possess intrinsic value; in themselves things are neither good, evil, nor vile. These values we bestow on things in accordance with our personal preferences. My values differ from yours even as my motions differ from yours. Inasmuch as I am constantly in motion, the preferences I express today may change tomorrow with my changing motions. What I deem "good" today, may appear "evil" tomorrow; and what I regard as "evil" today may seem to be "good" or perhaps "vile" tomorrow. "Pleasure" and "displeasure" are also subjective states or "apparences" that vary from person to person and that are associated with the presence of goods and evils.

And because the constitution of a man's body is in continual mutation, it is impossible that all the same things should always cause in him the same appetites, and aversions: much less can all men consent, in the desire of almost any one and the same object.

But whatsoever is the object of any man's appetite or desire, that is it which he for his part calleth *good:* and the object of his hate and aversion, *evil;* and of his contempt, *vile* and *inconsiderable.* For these words of good, evil, and contemptible, are ever used with relation to the person that useth them: there being nothing simply and absolutely so. . . .

As, in sense, that which is really within us, is, as I have said before, only motion, caused by the action of external objects, but in apparence; to the sight, light and colour; to the ear, sound; to the nostril, odour, etc.: so, when the action of the same object is continued from the eyes, ears, and other organs to the heart, the real effect there is nothing but motion, or endeavour; which consisteth in appetite, or aversion, to or from the object moving. But the apparence, or sense of that motion, is that we either call *delight,* or *trouble of mind.* . . .

Pleasure therefore, or *delight,* is the apparence, or sense of good; and *molestation,* or *displeasure,* the apparence, or sense of evil. And consequently all appetite, desire, and love, is accompanied with some delight more or less; and all hatred and aversion, with more or less displeasure and offence. . . .

Hobbes now describes the "state of nature," which is the situation of constant conflict, suffering and fear, which is generated by competing egoistic humans, and from which the legislative life rescues humankind. All humans, Hobbes reminds us, strive for felicity or happiness, which is not a static state of enjoyment and repose, but rather a process of achieving the things one desires from time to time. To achieve those things, and hence happiness, humans need more and more power. Given (1) this universal egoistic thirst for happiness and power, (2) the fact that humans often desire the same things, (3) a condition of scarcity pertaining to those desired things, and (4) the fact that humans are virtually equal in their capacity to kill each other, the outcome is fierce competition, escalating distrust ("diffidence") of each other, and thirst for the glory that results from the subjugation of others. In short, the human condition is characterized by savage and unceasing warfare. In this "state of nature," there is no significant cultural development: after all, why should I work hard and creatively only to have the fruits of my labor stolen stealthily by someone else? Nor is there any legitimate distinction between right and wrong, justice and injustice; there is only a diverse array of competing and equally legitimate claims.

> . . . the felicity of this life, consisteth not in the repose of a mind satisfied. For there is no such *finis ultimus*, utmost aim, nor *summum bonum*, greatest good, as is spoken of in the books of the old moral philosophers. Nor can a man any more live, whose desires are at an end, than he, whose senses and imaginations are at a stand. Felicity is a continual progress of the desire, from one object to another; the attaining of the former, being still but the way to the latter. The cause whereof is, that the object of man's desire, is not to enjoy once only, and for one instant of time; but to assure for ever, the way of his future desire. And therefore the voluntary actions, and inclinations of all men tend, not only to the procuring, but also to the assuring of a contented life; and differ only in the way: which ariseth partly from the diversity of passions, in divers men; and partly from the difference of the knowledge, or opinion each one has of the causes, which produce the effect desired.
>
> So that in the first place, I put for a general inclination of all mankind, a perpetual and restless desire of power after power, that ceaseth only in death. And the cause of this, is not always that a man hopes for a more intensive delight, than he has already attained to; or that he cannot be content with a moderate power: but because he cannot assure the power and means to live well, which he hath present, without the acquisition of more. And from hence it is, that kings, whose power is greatest, turn their endeavours to the assuring it at home by laws, or abroad by wars: and when that is done, there succeedeth a new desire; in some, of fame from new conquest; in others, of ease and sensual pleasure; in others, of admiration, or being flattered for excellence in some art, or other ability of the mind. . . .
>
> NATURE hath made men so equal, in the faculties of the body, and mind; as that though there be found one man sometimes manifestly stronger in body, or of quicker mind than another; yet when all is reckoned together, the difference between man, and man, is not so considerable, as that one man can thereupon claim to himself any benefit, to which another may not pretend, as well as he. For as to the strength of body, the weakest has strength enough to kill the strongest, either by secret machination, or by confederacy with others, that are in the same danger with himself.

And as to the faculties of the mind, setting aside the arts grounded upon words, and especially that skill of proceeding upon general, and infallible rules, called science; which very few have, and but in few things; as being not a native faculty, born with us; nor attained, as prudence, while we look after somewhat else, I find yet a greater equality amongst men, than that of strength. For prudence is but experience; which equal time, equally bestows on all men, in those things they equally apply themselves unto. That which may perhaps make such equality incredible, is but a vain conceit of one's own wisdom, which almost all men think they have in a greater degree, than the vulgar; that is, than all men but themselves, and a few others, whom by fame, or for concurring with themselves, they approve. For such is the nature of men, that howsoever they may acknowledge many others to be more witty, or more eloquent, or more learned; yet they will hardly believe there be many so wise as themselves; for they see their own wit at hand, and other men's at a distance. But this proveth rather that men are in that point equal, than unequal. For there is not ordinarily a greater sign of the equal distribution of any thing, than that every man is contented with his share.

From this equality of ability, ariseth equality of hope in the attaining of our ends. And therefore if any two men desire the same thing, which nevertheless they cannot both enjoy, they become enemies; and in the way to their end, which is principally their own conservation, and sometimes their delectation only, endeavour to destroy, or subdue one another. And from hence it comes to pass, that where an invader hath no more to fear, than another man's single power; if one plant, sow, build, or possess a convenient seat, others may probably be expected to come prepared with forces united, to dispossess, and deprive him, not only of the fruit of his labour, but also of his life, or liberty. And the invader again is in the like danger of another.

And from this diffidence of one another, there is no way for any man to secure himself so reasonable as anticipation; that is, by force, or wiles, to master the persons of all men he can, so long, till he see no other power great enough to endanger him: and this is no more than his own conservation requireth, and is generally allowed. Also because there be some, that taking pleasure in contemplating their own power in the acts of conquest, which they pursue farther than their security requires; if others, that otherwise would be glad to be at ease within modest bounds, should not by invasion increase their power, they would not be able, long time, by standing only on their defence, to subsist. And by consequence, such augmentation of dominion over men being necessary to a man's conservation, it ought to be allowed him.

Again, men have no pleasure, but on the contrary a great deal of grief in keeping company, where there is no power able to over-awe them all. For every man looketh that his companion should value him, at the same rate he sets upon himself; and upon all signs of contempt, or undervaluing, naturally endeavours, as far as he dares, (which amongst them that have no common power to keep them in quiet, is far enough to make them destroy each other), to extort a greater value from his contemners, by damage; and from others, by the example.

So that in the nature of man, we find three principal causes of quarrel. First, competition; secondly, diffidence; thirdly, glory.

The first maketh men invade for gain; the second, for safety; and the third, for reputation. The first use violence, to make themselves masters of other men's persons, wives, children, and cattle; the second, to defend them; the third, for trifles, as a word, a smile, a different opinion, and any other sign of undervalue, either direct in their persons, or by reflection in their kindred, their friends, their nation, their profession, or their name.

Hereby it is manifest, that during the time men live without a common power to keep them all in awe, they are in that condition which is called war; and such a war, as is of every man, against every man. For WAR, consisteth not in battle only, or the act of fighting; but in a tract of time, wherein the will to contend by battle is sufficiently known: and therefore the notion of *time* is to be considered in the nature of war; as it is in the nature of weather. For as the nature of foul weather, lieth not in a shower or two of rain; but in an inclination thereto of many days together; so the nature of war, consisteth not in actual fighting; but in the known disposition thereto, during all the time there is no assurance to the contrary. All other time is PEACE.

Whatsoever therefore is consequent to a time of war, where every man is enemy to every man; the same is consequent to the time, wherein men live without other security, than what their own strength, and their own invention shall furnish them withal. In such condition, there is no place for industry; because the fruit thereof is uncertain: and consequently no culture of the earth; no navigation, nor use of the commodities that may be imported by sea; no commodious building; no instruments of moving, and removing, such things as require much force; no knowledge of the face of the earth; no account of time; no arts; no letters; no society; and which is worse of all, continual fear, and danger of violent death; and the life of man, solitary, poor, nasty, brutish, and short. . . .

To this war of every man, against every man, this also is consequent; that nothing can be unjust. The notions of right and wrong, justice and injustice have there no place. Where there is no common power, there is no law: where no law, no injustice. Force, and fraud, are in war the two cardinal virtues. Justice, and injustice are none of the faculties neither of the body, nor mind. If they were, they might be in a man that were alone in the world, as well as his senses, and passions. They are qualities, that relate to men in society, not in solitude. It is consequent also to the same condition, that there be no propriety, no dominion, no *mine* and *thine* distinct; but only that to be every man's, that he can get; and for so long as he can keep it.

The "solitary, poor, nasty, brutish, and short" life of humankind in the state of nature would have endured had not humans been endowed with passions that drive them toward peace and with reason that enables them to generate the structures of the legislative life, namely, the "articles of peace," the so-called Laws of Nature.

And thus much for the ill condition, which man by mere nature is actually placed in; though with a possibility to come out of it, consisting partly in the passions, partly in his reason.

The passions that incline men to peace, are fear of death; desire of such things as are necessary to commodious living; and a hope by their industry to obtain them. And reason suggesteth convenient articles of peace, upon which men may be drawn to agreement. These articles, are they, which otherwise are called the Laws of Nature. . . .

THE RIGHT OF NATURE, which writers commonly call *jus naturale,* is the liberty each man hath, to use his own power, as he will himself, for the preservation of his own nature; that is to say, of his own life; and consequently, of doing any thing, which in his own judgment, and reason, he shall conceive to be the aptest means thereunto.

By LIBERTY, is understood, according to the proper signification of the word, the absence of external impediments: which impediments, may oft take away part of a man's power to do what he would; but cannot hinder him from using the power left him, according as his judgment, and reason shall dictate to him.

A LAW OF NATURE, *lex naturalis,* is a precept or general rule, found out by reason, by which a man is forbidden to do that which is destructive of his life, or taketh away the means of preserving the same; and to omit that, by which he thinketh it may be best preserved. . . .

And because the condition of man, as hath been declared in the precedent chapter, is a condition of war of every one against every one; in which case every one is governed by his own reason; and there is nothing he can make use of, that may not be a help unto him, in preserving his life against his enemies; it followeth, that in such a condition, every man has a right to every thing; even to one another's body. And therefore, as long as this natural right of every man to every thing endureth, there can be no security to any man, how strong or wise soever he be, of living out the time, which nature ordinarily alloweth men to live. And consequently it is a precept, or general rule of reason, *that every man, ought to endeavour peace, as far as he has hope of obtaining it; and when he cannot obtain it, that he may seek, and use, all helps, and advantages of war.* The first branch of which rule, containeth the first, and fundamental law of nature; which is, *to seek peace, and follow it.* The second, the sum of the right of nature; which is, *by all means we can, to defend ourselves.*

From this fundamental law of nature, by which men are commanded to endeavour peace, is derived this second law; *that a man be willing, when others are so too, as far-forth, as for peace, and defence of himself he shall think it necessary, to lay down this right to all things; and be contented with so much liberty against other men, as he would allow other men against himself.* For as long as every man holdeth this right, of doing any thing he liketh; so long are all men in the condition of war. But if other men will not lay down their right, as well as he; then there is no reason for any one, to divest himself of his: for that were to expose himself to prey, which no man is bound to, rather than to dispose himself to peace. This is that law of the Gospel; *whatsoever you require that others should do to you, that do ye to them.* . . .

The force of words, being, as I have formerly noted, too weak to hold men to the performance of their covenants; there are in man's nature, but two imaginable helps to strengthen it. And those are either a fear of the consequence of breaking their word; or a glory, or pride in appearing not to need to break it. This latter is a generosity too rarely found to be presumed on, especially in the pursuers of wealth, command, or sensual pleasure; which are the greatest part of mankind. The passion to be reckoned upon, is fear; whereof there be two very general objects: one, the power of spirits invisible; the other, the power of those men they shall therein offend. Of these two, though the former be the greater power, yet the fear of the latter is commonly the greater fear. . . .

From that law of nature, by which we are obliged to transfer to another, such rights, as being retained, hinder the peace of mankind, there followeth a third; which is this, *that men perform their covenants made:* without which, covenants are in vain, and but empty words; and the right of all men to all things remaining, we are still in the condition of war.

And in this law of nature, consisteth the fountain and original of JUSTICE. For where no covenant hath preceded, there hath no right been transferred, and every man has right to every thing; and consequently, no action can be unjust. But when a covenant is made, then to break it is *unjust:* and the definition of INJUSTICE, is no other than *the not performance of covenant.* And whatsoever is not unjust, is *just.*

But because covenants of mutual trust, where there is a fear of not performance on either part, as hath been said in the former chapter, are invalid; though the original of justice be the making of covenants; yet injustice actually there can be none, till the cause of such fear be taken away; which while men are in the natural condition of war, cannot be done. Therefore before the names of just, and unjust can have place, there must be some coercive power, to compel men equally to the performance of their covenants, by the terror of some punishment, greater than the benefit they expect by the breach of their covenant; and to make good that propriety, which by mutual contract men acquire, in recompense of the universal right they abandon: and such power there is none before the erection of a commonwealth.

Hobbes goes on to discuss additional Laws of Nature, which need not concern us at this time inasmuch as the train of his thought has become evident. According to Hobbes, humans are matter in motion, selfish particles constantly seeking their own interests. Their selfish quest for happiness, under the conditions of scarcity, distrust, and thirst for glory, results in constant warfare. That same quest for happiness, however, leads them to desire peace and security, and reason suggests the articles of peace under which that happiness can be secured. Yet most humans are not sufficiently enlightened to discern that obedience to these laws will ultimately promote their own selfish interests. Therefore, a sovereign authority is needed to compel humans to conform to these laws. Such, then, is Hobbes's view of the "commonwealth": selfish humans being compelled by absolute authority to do those things that will promote most effectively their own self-interests.

Such a view certainly seems to support the absolute monarchy of the king of England in his conflict with Parliament and Cromwell. Yet, notice that Hobbes's "general rule of reason" from which he derives the first and second laws of nature explicitly articulates a right to revolt that is completely consistent with the fundamental egoistic nature of human beings, as viewed by Hobbes, which the legislative life only constrains and orders but does not fundamentally alter or destroy.

NOTE ON SOURCES.   The material in this section is quoted from Thomas Hobbes, *Leviathan,* Part I, Chapters 6, 11, 13, 14, 15.

2   JEAN JACQUES ROUSSEAU

THE CASE FOR THE COMMON GOOD

FROM HOBBES TO ROUSSEAU.   Hobbes described the situation that gave rise to and justified the legislative life, namely, the "state of nature" where egoistic humans compete aggressively with each other for scarce resources, where life is "solitary, poor, nasty, brutish, and short." To respond to this predicament, humankind generated the "social contract," an agreement that limited the liberties of persons so that peace, security, and prosperity could be achieved, and that established a sovereign power to guarantee the laws set forth in the agreement. Although Hobbes's discussion may be regarded as a fictitious account rather than an historical recapitulation, nevertheless it was a useful fiction. It set forth the problem to which the legislated life seemed to be the solution. Without laws and a sovereign to enforce them, human life would be "solitary, poor, nasty, brutish, and short" as uninhibited egoism would be universally expressed. From this perspective the legislative life is a human creation (indeed, perhaps the most impressive of human creations) intended to insure the survival and advance the interests of humankind. The state of nature might have been a past historical actuality. More importantly, it is a present possibility that might be actualized if the legislative life were to be abandoned. The view that the legislative life functions to suppress the state of nature guides and informs the discussions of most, if not all, of the remaining authors in this chapter.

Rousseau's *Social Contract* possesses a relevance and universality that place it among the great scriptures of the legislated way of life. This little book, from which the following selection has been taken, is among the primary clarifiers of *la condition humaine.*

BIOGRAPHICAL NOTE.   Jean Jacques Rousseau was born in Switzerland in 1712 and died in 1778 at the age of sixty-six. From 1712 to 1748 he was acquiring the elements of a formal education and something more than the elements of a worldly education. These matters are set down in his *Confessions.* As might be expected from the haphazard and undisciplined way in which he conducted himself during these years, Rousseau arrived at a state of some maladjustment. The times looked out of joint. The mores looked cramped and artificial. Civilization looked decadent. Rousseau, had he lived at a later time, might have claimed to be "alienated."

From 1749 to 1762 he formulated his criticisms of the then-modern world in a series of tracts that have given him his place in the scheme of things. The first of these (1749) was addressed to the question, "Have the sciences and arts contributed to purify morals?" Rousseau's answer was no. The second (1755), *On the Origin of Inequality Among Men,* argued that the root of inequality is the institution of property, which permits the strong and wealthy to subject the mass of humankind to toil and poverty. The third (1760), *The New Heloise,* was a protest against the artificialities of marriage and the family. The fourth (1762), *Émile,* was an indictment of education as discipline and restraint. It stated the case for education as expression and development. The fifth (1762), *The Social Contract,* was addressed to the problem: "Man is born free, and is everywhere in chains. How can this be justified?" In these writings, Rousseau touched on important phases of eighteenth-century civilization. His pronouncements were usually in terms of such words as *artificial, unnatural, narrow, selfish, ignoble, crass.* Art, science, society, education, religion, the family, the state—all gave evidence that humankind was paying too great a price for the fruits of "civilized" living.

From 1763 to 1778 he was again a wanderer. The authorities ordered him out of France. He moved to Switzerland. The authorities ordered him out of

Switzerland. He moved, at the invitation of David Hume, to England. This proved no better. He returned to France. During the last years of his life his mind became unbalanced. He died suddenly in 1778, two years after the American Revolution had begun and eleven years before the French Revolution began, for both of which, in *The Social Contract*, he had formulated principles of justification.

THE ARGUMENT OF THE PASSAGES.   The question that Rousseau set himself has been stated already: "Man is born free, and is everywhere in chains. How did this come about? I do not know. What can make it legitimate? That question I think I can answer." It is clear that Rousseau does not propose to account for the fact that humans are everywhere in chains. He is not proposing historical research into origins. Nor is he proposing to remove the chains in question. He is not proposing an argument for anarchism. His question is the more searching one: Granted that humans must live in chains (i.e., under laws) what considerations will justify the fact? He begins by rejecting the notion that the right of this condition is to be found in the might that enforces it. Might does not make right. What does, then? His answer is common need, common confrontation with conditions that no individual could handle if left to himself or herself. This idea is contained in the notion of the social contract. The terms of the contract are noted. The attributes of the sovereignty created and sustained by the contract are noted. The role of lawmaker is noted. The nature of law is noted. The separation of powers within government is argued for. The alternative forms of government (monarchy, aristocracy, democracy) are noted, together with their defining virtues and vices. He notes, finally, "the unavoidable and inherent defect which tends ceaselessly to destroy" any form of political organization in any society. The argument begins as follows:

> Man is born free, and is everywhere in chains. One thinks himself the master of others, and still remains a greater slave than they. How did this come about? I do not know. What can make it legitimate? That question I think I can answer.

The first thing to be clear about is that the restrictions that law imposes cannot be justified by any appeal to the fact of force that lies back of them. Might does not make right. Thus:

> Suppose that "force" creates "right." The result is a mass of nonsense. For if force creates right, then every force that is greater than the first succeeds to its right. As soon as it were possible to disobey with impunity, disobedience would become legitimate; and the strongest being always in the right, the only thing that would matter (so far as concerns "justification") would be to act so as to become the strongest.
>
> But what kind of "right" is it that perishes when force fails? If we "must" obey, there is no question that we "ought" to obey. And, on the principle that force makes right, if we are not forced to obey, we are under no obligation to do so. A brigand surprises me at the edge of a wood. The pistol he holds gives him power. Does it also give him right? Even if I could withhold my purse, am I in conscience bound to give it up? Does his "might" create a "right"?
>
> Force is a physical power, and I fail to see what moral effect it can have. To yield to force is an act of necessity, not of will; at most, an act of prudence. In what sense can it be a duty?

"Obey the powers that be." If this means "yield to force," it is a good precept; but superfluous: I can answer for its never being violated. If it means "Yield, because all power comes from God," the case is no better. All power comes from God, I admit; but so does sickness. Does that mean that we are forbidden to call in a doctor?

Let us admit then that force does not create right, and that we are obligated to obey only legitimate powers. In that case my original question recurs: What is the basis of political obligations?

If might does not make right, if the "chains" are not justified by the fact that we are forced to wear them, what can we say? Rousseau shifts from the force that is admittedly necessary to the existence of law, to the conditions that justify law backed by force. Thus:

> Suppose men to have reached the point at which the obstacles in the way of their preservation in the state of nature are greater than the resources at the disposal of each individual. That primitive condition can then subsist no longer, and the human race would perish unless it changed its manner of existence.
>
> The problem is to find a form of association which will protect the person and goods of each individual with the whole common force of all; and in which each, uniting himself with all, may still obey himself alone and remain as free as before. This is the fundamental problem of which the "social compact" provides the solution.
>
> If we disregard what is not of the essence of the social compact we shall find that it reduces itself to the following terms: "Each of us puts his person and his power in common under the supreme direction of the general will; and, in our corporate capacity, we receive each member as a part of the whole."
>
> At one stroke, in place of the individual personality of each contracting party, this act of association creates a collective body, receiving from this act its unity, its common identity, its life, and its will. This public person, so formed by the union of all other persons, takes the name of *body politic*. It is called *state* when passive, *sovereign* when active, and *power* when compared with others like itself. Those who are associated in it take collectively the name of *people*, are severally called *citizens* as sharing in the sovereign power, and *subjects* as being under the laws of the state.
>
> As soon as this multitude is united in one body politic, it becomes impossible to offend against one of the members without attacking the body politic, and still more to offend against the body politic. Duty and interest, therefore, equally obligate the two contracting parties to give each other help.

The social contract creates the state. It thereby creates the "chains" he had referred to. But it does more than that. The chains are seen to be, in principle, self-imposed restrictions; and they bring with them compensating advantages. Thus:

> In the social compact there is no real "renunciation" on the part of the individuals. The position in which they find themselves, as a result of the compact, is really preferable to that in which they were before. Instead of a "renunciation," they have made an advantageous exchange; instead of an uncertain and precarious way of living, they have got one that is better and more secure; instead of natural independence, they have got liberty; instead of the power to harm others, they have got security for themselves; instead of their strength, which others might overcome, they have got a right which social union makes invincible.

What a man loses by the social compact is his natural liberty, and an unlimited right to everything he tries to get and succeeds in getting. What he gains is civil liberty and the proprietorship of all he possesses. If we are to avoid mistake in weighing one against the other, we must distinguish natural liberty, bounded only by the strength of the individual, from civil liberty, limited by the general will; and we must distinguish possession, the effect of force, from property, founded only on a positive title.

For such physical inequalities as nature may have set up between men, the social compact substitutes an equality that is moral and legitimate: by it, men who may be unequal in strength or intelligence, become every one equal by convention and legal right.

Under bad governments, this equality is only apparent and illusory: it serves only to keep the pauper in his poverty and the rich man in the position he has usurped. In fact, laws are always of use to those who possess, and harmful to those who have nothing: from which it follows that the social state is advantageous to men only when all have something and none have too much.

The general will alone can direct the state according to the object for which it was instituted, i.e., the common good: for, if the clashing of particular interests made the establishing of societies necessary, the agreement of these interests made it possible. The common element in these different interests is what forms the social tie; and, were there no point of agreement between them all, no society could exist. It is solely on the basis of this common interest that every society should be governed.

There is often a great difference between the "will of all" and the "general will." The latter considers only the common interest; the former takes private interest into account, and is no more than a sum of particular wills. But deduct from the sum of particular wills the plusses and minuses that cancel one another, and the general will remains.

Each individual may have a particular will contrary or dissimilar to the general will which he has as a citizen. His particular interest may speak to him quite different from the common interest; may make him look upon what he owes to the common cause of a gratuitous contribution, the loss of which will do less harm to others than the payment of it is burdensome to himself. He may come to regard the moral person which constitutes the state as a *persona ficta,* because not a man; and, as a result, may wish to enjoy the rights of citizenship without being ready to fulfill the duties of a subject. This, continued, would prove the undoing of the body politic.

The social contract creates sovereignty; i.e., a society organized to define and enforce its laws. The sovereignty inheres in the people. Rousseau proceeds to note several of its defining properties:

In order that the social compact may not be an empty formula, it includes the undertaking, that whoever refuses to obey the general will shall be compelled to do so. In this lies the key to the working of the body politic. This alone legitimizes civil undertakings which, without it, would be absurd, tyrannical and liable to the most frightful abuses. The social compact gives the body politic absolute power over all its members. It is this power, under the direction of the general will, which bears the name of *sovereignty.*

The sovereign, being formed wholly of the individuals who compose it, neither has nor can have any interest contrary to theirs. The sovereign, therefore, need give no guarantee to its subjects. Merely by virtue of what it is, the sovereign is always what it should be.

Sovereignty, being nothing less than the exercise of the general will, is inalienable, and the sovereign, who is no less than a collective being, cannot be represented except by himself. The power may be delegated, but not the general will from which it derives. To be "general," the will need not be unanimous, but every vote must count; any exclusion is a breach of generality. For the same reason that it is inalienable, sovereignty is indivisible.

The social compact sets up among the citizens an equality of such a kind that they all bind themselves to observe the same conditions and should therefore all enjoy the same rights. Thus, from the very nature of the compact, every act of sovereignty binds or favors all the citizens equally; so that the sovereign recognizes only the body of the nation and draws no distinctions between those of whom it is made up.

What, then, is an act of sovereignty? It is not a convention between a superior and an inferior, but a convention between the body politic and each of its members. It is legitimate because based on the social contract; equitable, because common to all; useful because it can have no other object than the general good; and stable, because guaranteed by the public force and the supreme power.

The people are sovereign. But what can they do about it? They can delegate their sovereignty to a legislature and an administration. Of themselves the sovereign people cannot draw up good law nor can they administer it.

But how are the people to "regulate the conditions of society?" By a common agreement? By a sudden inspiration? Has the body politic an organ to declare its will? Who can give it the foresight to formulate and announce its acts in advance? How is it to announce them in the hour of need? How can a blind multitude, who often does not know what is good for it and hence what it wills, carry out for itself so great and difficult an enterprise as a system of legislation?

Of itself, the people always wills the good, but of itself it by no means always sees it. The general will is always in the right, but the judgment which guides it is not always enlightened. It must be got to see things as they are, and, sometimes, as they ought to appear to it. It must be shown the good road it is in search of, secured against the seductive influences of individual wills. It must be taught to see times and places, made to weigh the attractions of present and sensible advantages against the dangers of distant and hidden evils.

All stand equally in need of guidance. Individuals must be compelled to bring their wills into conformity with their reason. The public must be taught to know what is the good which it wills. If that is done, there is a union of understanding and will in the social body. The parts work together, and the whole is raised to its highest power. This makes a legislator necessary.

The function of lawmaker needs to be considered. The unique qualifications are noted. The "legislator" is a paradoxical ideal.

To discover the rules of society best suited to nations, a superior intelligence beholding all the passions of men without experiencing any of them, would be needed. This intelligence would have to be wholly unrelated to our nature, while knowing it through and through. Its happiness would have to be independent of our happiness and yet ready to occupy itself with it. It would have to look forward and, working in one century, to be able to enjoy the next. It would take gods to give men laws.

He who dares undertake the making of a people's institutions ought to feel himself capable of changing human nature, of transforming each individual into part of a greater whole, of altering men's constitution for the purpose of strengthening it, of substituting a shared and moral existence for the independent and natural existence which nature has conferred on us all. In a word, he must take away from man his own resources and give him in their stead new ones incapable of being used without the help of other men. The more completely these "natural" resources are annihilated, the greater and more lasting are those which supplant them, and the more stable and perfect are the new institutions.

The office of legislator, which gives form to the state, nowhere enters into its constitution. He who holds command over men (the government), ought not to hold command over the laws. He who holds command over the laws (the legislator) ought not to hold command over men. Else would his laws be the ministers of his passions serving to perpetuate his injustices, and his private aims mar the sanctity of his work.

Thus in the task of legislation we find two things which appear to be incompatible: an enterprise too difficult for human powers, and, for its execution, an authority that is no authority.

The great soul of the legislator is the only miracle that can prove his mission. Any man may engrave on tables, buy an oracle, feign secret connexion with the gods, train a bird to whisper into his ear, or find some other trumpery way to impose on the people. He whose knowledge goes no further may perhaps gather round him a band of fools, but he will never found an empire, and his extravagances will perish with him. Idle tricks form a passing tie; only wisdom can make it lasting.

Provided the miracle of a good law can be performed, what does society have at its disposal? An instrument, essentially, for dealing with general conditions. The particulars must be seen to fall under the law by the wisdom of the executive.

What is law? When the whole people declares for the whole people, this is what I call a *law*.

The matter about which such decree is made is, like the decreeing will, general. When I say that the matter is "general," I mean that law considers subjects *en masse* and actions in the abstract, never a particular person or action. Thus law may declare that there shall be privileges; but it cannot confer them on any one by name. It may set up classes of citizens. It may specify qualifications for membership of these classes. But, as law, it cannot nominate such and such persons as belonging to these classes. Law may, e.g., establish a monarchical form of government and an hereditary succession. It cannot choose a king or nominate a royal family. In a word, no function which has a particular object in view can be a matter of law.

On this view, we see at once that it can no longer be asked whose business it is to make laws, since they are acts of the general will; nor whether "government is above the law," since governors are part of the state; nor whether laws can be unjust, since no one is unjust to himself; nor how we can be both "free" and at the same time subject to laws, since they are but registers of our wills.

The law unites universality of will with universality of object. What any man commands of his own cannot be law. Even what sovereignty commands with regard to some particular matter cannot be law; it is then merely a decree of the government.

Laws are, strictly speaking, the conditions of civil association. The people, being subject to the laws, ought to be their author: the conditions of the society ought to be regulated by those who unite to give it form.

Thus far we have had society, the contract, the sovereign people, the legislator, and laws. We come now to government, what we would call the executive arm of government. It is not to be confused with any of the other terms:

I have argued that the power to make laws belongs to the sovereign people, and can belong to it alone. On the other hand, the power to execute these laws cannot belong to the generality, because such power consists wholly of particular acts which fall outside the competency of lawmaking as such.

The body politic, therefore, needs an agent of its own to bind it together, to set it to work under the direction of the general will, to serve as a means of communication between the (people as) state and the (people as) sovereign. Here we have the basis of government, something which is often confused with the sovereign whose minister it is.

What then, is government? It is an intermediate body, set up between the (people as) subjects and the (people as) sovereign, to secure their mutual correspondence, to execute the laws and to maintain liberty. The members of this body are called governors.

Government is hence simply and solely a commission, in which the governors, mere officials of the sovereign people, exercise in their own name the power which is invested in them by the people. This delegated power the sovereign people can limit, modify, or recover at pleasure.

The government gets from the (people as) sovereign the orders which it gives to the (people as) subjects. For the state to be properly balanced there must be an equality between the power of the government and the power of the citizens, for the latter are, on the one hand, sovereign, and, on the other hand, subject.

None of these three terms—*sovereign, subjects, government*—can be altered without the equality being instantly destroyed. If the sovereign tries to govern, if the government tries to give laws, or if the subjects refuse to obey, disorder replaces order, force and will no longer act together, and the state is dissolved into despotism or anarchy.

Government, then, is distinct from society, sovereignty, legislator, law, and so on. Its function is to administer laws. What form should it have?

There has been at all times much dispute concerning the best form of government. Is it democratic? aristocratic? or monarchical? This question, "What, absolutely, is the best form of government?" is unanswerable and indeterminate. The fact is that each is in some cases the best, and in others the worst.

Let us see. Consider first the notion of democracy:

The sovereign people may commit the charge of the government to the whole people or to a majority of the people. The result would be that more citizens would be actual governors than mere private subjects. This form of government is called *democracy*.

If we take the term in the strict sense, there never has been a real democracy, and there never will be. It is unimaginable that the people should remain continually assembled to devote their time to public affairs.

Besides, how many conditions, difficult to unite, would such a form of government presuppose? First, a very small state, where the people can readily be got together and where each citizen can with ease know all the rest. Second, great simplicity of manners, to prevent business from multiplying and raising thorny problems. Third, a large measure of equality in rank and fortune, without which equality of rights and authority cannot long subsist. Fourth, little or no luxury, for luxury either comes of riches or makes them necessary.

Moreover, it is a certainty that promptitude in execution diminishes as more people are put in charge of it. Where prudence is made too much of, not enough is made of fortune; opportunity is let slip, and deliberation results in the loss of its object.

It may be added that no form of government is so subject to civil wars and intestinal agitations as democracy, because there is none which has so strong and persistent a tendency to change to another form, or which demands more vigilance and courage for its maintenance. Were there a people of gods, their government would be democratic. So perfect a government is not for men.

So, pure democracy is unsuited to the needs of the modern state. Another possibility is an elected aristocracy. It holds more promise:

The sovereign people may restrict the government to a small number, so that there are more private citizens than magistrates. This is named *aristocracy*.

There are three sorts of aristocracy: natural, elective, and hereditary. The first is only for simple peoples; the second is the best, and is aristocracy properly so-called; the third is the worst of all governments.

There is much to be said for an elective aristocracy. It has the advantage of keeping clear the distinction between the two powers, sovereignty and government. Besides this, its members are chosen to be governors, not born to this office, as in the case of a pure democracy or an hereditary aristocracy. By this means uprightness, understanding, experience, and all other claims to preeminence become so many guarantees of wise government.

It is more efficient. Assemblies are more easily held; affairs are better discussed and carried out with more order and diligence; the credit of the state is better sustained abroad.

It is more economical. There is no need to multiply instruments, or get twenty thousand men to do what a hundred picked men can do better.

However, if an elective aristocracy does not demand all the virtues needed by popular government, it demands others which are peculiar to itself; for instance, moderation on the side of the rich, and contentment on the side of the poor. If this form of government carries with it a certain inequality of fortune, this is justifiable on the grounds that the administration of public affairs may be entrusted to those who are most able to give them their whole time.

In Rousseau's day the commonest form of government was hereditary monarchy. It has its good points and its bad points. Thus:

The sovereign people may concentrate the whole government in the hands of a single person from whom all others hold their power. This form of government is the most usual, and is called *monarchy*.

No form of government is more vigorous than this. All answer to a single motive power. All the springs of the machine are in the same hands. The whole moves toward the same end. There are no conflicting movements to cancel one another. In no constitution does a smaller amount of effort produce a greater amount of action. Archimedes seated quietly on the bank of a river, easily drawing a great floating vessel, stands in my mind for a skillful monarch governing vast estates from his study, moving everything while he seems himself unmoved.

For a monarchical state to have a chance of being well governed, its population and extent must be proportionate to the abilities of its governor. It is easier to conquer than to rule. With a lever long enough, the world could be moved with a single finger; to sustain it requires the shoulders of Hercules.

These are some of the virtues to be expected in monarchy. However, Rousseau goes on to note possible defects:

Everything conspires to take away from a man who is set in authority the sense of justice and reason.

Kings desire to be absolute, and men are always crying out to them from afar that the best means is to get themselves loved by their people. This is all very well, and true enough in some respects. Unfortunately, it will always be derided at court. The power that comes of a people's love is no doubt the greatest; but it is precarious and conditional, and princes will never rest content with it. The best of kings desire to be in a position to be wicked, if they so please, without forfeiting thereby their mastery. Political sermonizers may tell them, to their hearts' content, that the people should be prosperous, numerous, and formidable. Kings know this to be untrue. Their personal interest is that the people should be weak, wretched, or unable to resist them.

There is an essential and inevitable defect which will always rank a monarchy below a republic. It is this. In a republic the people hardly ever raises men who are unenlightened and incapable to the highest positions; whereas, under a monarch, those who rise to power are most often petty blunderers, petty swindlers, petty intriguers, men whose petty talents cause them to get into stations of the greatest eminence at court. The people is far less often mistaken in its choice than the monarch. A man of real worth among the king's ministers is almost as rare as a fool at the head of a republic.

Another disadvantage in monarchical government is the lack of any continuous succession. When one king dies, another is needed. In the case of an elective monarchy, dangerous interregnums occur, and are full of storms; unless, that is, the citizens are upright and disinterested to a degree which seldom goes with this kind of government.

What has been done to prevent these evils? Succession has been made hereditary in certain families. That is to say, men have chosen rather to be ruled by children, monstrosities, or imbeciles than to endure disputes over the choice of good kings. Apparent tranquility has been preferred to wise administration.

These difficulties have not escaped our political writers. But they are not troubled by them. The remedy, they say, is to obey without a murmur: God sends bad kings in His wrath, and they are to be borne as the scourges of heaven. Such talk is doubtless edifying, but it would be more in place in a pulpit than in a political book. What are we to say of a doctor whose whole art is to exhort the sufferer to patience?

By way of conclusion we may note the fundamental fact from which political instability continually proceeds:

All forms of government contain within them the seeds of destruction and dissolution. As the particular will acts constantly in opposition to the general will, the government continually exerts itself against the sovereign. The greater this exertion becomes, the more the constitution changes. This is the unavoidable and inherent defect which, from the very birth of the body politic, tends ceaselessly to destroy it, as age and death end by destroying the human body.

Such is the natural and inevitable tendency of the best constituted governments. If Sparta and Rome perished, what state can hope to endure for ever? We desire a long-lived form of government? Let us not dream of making it eternal. If we are to succeed, we must not attempt the impossible; nor must we flatter ourselves that we are endowing the work of man with a stability which human conditions do not permit.

The body politic begins to die as soon as it is born, and carries in itself the causes of its own destruction. The state is a work of art, not of nature. It is for men to prolong its life as much as possible, by giving it the best possible constitution. But even the best will have an end.

The life principle of the body politic lies in the sovereign authority. The legislative power is the heart of the state; the executive power is its brain. The brain may become paralyzed, and the body still live. But as soon as the heart ceases to perform its function, the organism is dead. Wherever the laws grow weak as they become old, there is no longer a legislative power, and the state is dead.

NOTE ON SOURCES. The material in this section is quoted, abridged, or paraphrased from Jean Jacques Rousseau, *The Social Contract*.

3 EDMUND BURKE

THE CASE FOR CONSERVATISM

FROM ROUSSEAU TO BURKE. Rousseau published *The Social Contract* in 1762. The American Revolution began in 1775. It was scarcely over when the French Revolution began, in 1789. This political restlessness in the colonies and in Europe was accompanied by a sharp demand for parliamentary reform in England. The revolutionary Society for Constitutional Information was organized in 1780. Prime Minister Pitt tried three times, each in vain, to persuade the House of Commons to consider the case for parliamentary reform. During these years, Tom Paine was gaining his reputation as spokesman for liberal and revolutionary movements in America and Europe. Jeremy Bentham published in 1789 his epoch-making treatise on liberal social reform, *Principles of Morals and Legislation*, in which he argued that customs, laws, institutions, and constitutions should be evaluated in terms of one standard, namely, the greatest happiness of the greatest number.

Such was the climate of opinion in which Edmund Burke wrote his exposition and defense of political conservatism. On all hands he saw, or thought he saw, signs that the old regimes of monarchies and aristocracies were weakening before popular demand for democratic politics. Wherever he looked, he detected "factions now busy amongst us who endeavor to propagate an opinion that the people, in forming their commonwealth, have by no means parted with their power over it." He set himself to stem this tide. He might as well have bade the sun stand still. These democratizing tendencies swept on and left the memory of his plea stranded amid the welter of wars, revolutions, reforms, and changes. If this were all, there would be little need to include Burke among spokesmen of political philosophy. But there is more to Burke than a neglected warning against democratic politics. In his words may be found a careful account of the principles of political conservatism. It i. an expression of one of man's perennial needs.

BIOGRAPHICAL NOTE.   Edmund Burke was born in Ireland in 1729 and died in England in 1797 at the age of sixty-eight. He received his academic education at Trinity College, Dublin. He spent some time acquiring the rudiments of a legal training in London in the Middle Temple. He entered Parliament in the 1760s and rose there to a position of great prestige. In 1775 he delivered his famous speech, "Conciliation with America." In 1785 he opened his attack on Warren Hastings' India administration with his equally famous speech "The Nabob of Arcot's Debts." In 1790 he published his *Reflections on the French Revolution.* The ideas advanced in this tract were subsequently elaborated in his *Appeal from the New to the Old Whigs,* his *Letter to a Noble Lord,* and his *Letter on a Regicide Peace.* The citations in this chapter are, for the most part, from the *Reflections* and the *Appeal* and the *Letters.*

THE ARGUMENT OF THE PASSAGES.   First of all, Burke sketches the foundation on which government is laid. From this, there results a more austere conception of the state than is held by those who launch and defend revolution in the name of the "rights of man." Does this commit Burke to a repudiation of the notion of the rights of man? "I am far from denying the real rights of man," he protests. The notion of "real" rights, in contrast to spurious rights, is outlined. This involves a clarification of "real" liberties in contrast to spurious liberties. The "real" rights and liberties, which Burke is prepared to ascribe to "the people," presuppose government by a natural aristocracy. This notion is outlined. It is then contrasted with a sham aristocracy of mere lords and dukes.

Burke's fundamental claim is disclosed at this point: He will entertain the notion of rights only in terms of the notion of duties. We have rights because we have duties, and within limits we do not choose our duties. They await us in the society into which we are born and in which we grow up. This idea may involve difficult problems and nice distinctions. In all such cases, it is wiser to keep an eye on duties than on rights. The burden of proof rests with those who violate obligations in the name of their rights. This, however, is not to be taken as a categorical denial of all change and reform, merely an insistence that wisdom ordinarily lies with custom and tradition, and that an individual should address himself or herself to the problem of extracting the wisdom that these contain.

Burke now notes that there are certain "factions now busy amongst us who endeavor to propagate an opinion that 'the people' in forming their commonwealth have by no means parted with their power over it." In other words, the notion of popular sovereignty is being argued for. The substance of such claims is noted by Burke and a general criticism is passed upon them. The concept of "the people," upon which the whole argument turns, is then proposed for analysis. What does one mean by *the people?*

The final point made by Burke is that his conservative political philosophy rests upon a recognition of the fact that wise politics has, in the last analysis, a religious basis. "On religion all our laws and institutions stand." "The awful author of our being has disposed and marshalled us by a divine tactic." The selection from Burke concludes with several eloquent paragraphs setting forth the great wisdom that attends the policy, arising out of these views, of regarding "liberties as an entailed inheritance" to be held as a sacred trust and passed on intact to one's posterity.

> The foundation of government, is laid, not in imaginary rights of men, but in political convenience, and in human nature; either as that nature is universal, or as it is modified by local habits and social aptitudes. The foundation of government is laid in a provision for our wants, and in a conformity to our duties; it is to purvey for the one; it is to enforce the other.
>
> Among men's wants is to be reckoned the want of a sufficient restraint upon their passions. Society requires not only that the passions of individuals should be subjected, but that even in the mass and body, as well as in the individuals, the inclinations of men should frequently be thwarted, their will controlled, and their passions brought into subjection. This can only be done by a power out of themselves; not subject to that will and those passions which it is its office to bridle and subdue.
>
> In this sense the restraints on men, as well as their liberties, are to be reckoned among their rights. But as the liberties and the restrictions vary with times and circumstances, and admit of infinite modifications, they cannot be settled upon any abstract rule; and nothing is so foolish as to discuss them upon that principle.
>
> The state ought to be considered as something better than a partnership agreement in a trade of pepper and coffee, calico or tobacco, to be taken up for a little temporary interest, and to be dissolved by the fancy of the parties. It is to be looked on with reverence, because it is not a partnership in things subservient only to the gross animal existence of a temporary and perishable nature.
>
> The state is a partnership in all science, a partnership in all art, a partnership in every virtue and in all perfection. As the ends of such a partnership cannot be attained in many generations, it becomes a partnership not only between those who are living, but between those who are living, those who are dead, and those who are to be born. People will not look forward to posterity who never look backward to their ancestors.
>
> Each contract of each particular state is but a clause in the great primeval contract of eternal society, linking the lower with the higher natures, connecting the visible and the invisible world according to a fixed compact sanctioned by the inviolable oath which holds all physical and all moral natures each to their appointed places.

The "rights of man" are not the foundation of the state. They are not "prior" to the state. Indeed, they are made possible by the state; and the foundation of anything is not to be sought in that which the things in question makes possible. What then does he think about the "real" rights of men and women that *proceed* from political organization?

> I am far from denying the real rights of men. In denying their false claims of right, I do not mean to injure those which are real, and are such as their pretended rights would totally destroy. If civic society be made for the advantage of man, all the advantages for which it is made become his right.

Men have right to the fruits of their industry, and to the means of making their industry fruitful. They have a right to the acquisitions of their parents; to the nourishment and improvement of their offspring; to instruction in life, and to consolation in death. Whatever each man can separately do, without trespassing upon others, he has a right to do for himself, and he has a right to a fair portion of all which society, with all its combination of skill and force, can do in his favor.

In this partnership all men have equal rights, but not to equal things. He that has but five shillings in the partnership has as good a right to it as he that has five hundred pounds has to his larger proportion. But he has not a right to an equal dividend in the product in the joint stock, and as to the share of power, authority, and direction which each individual ought to have in the management of the state, that I must deny to be amongst the direct original rights of man in civil society; for I have in my contemplation the civil social man, and no other. It is a thing to be settled by convention.

Circumstances (which with some gentlemen pass for nothing) give in reality to every political principle its distinguishing color and discriminating effect. The circumstances are what render every civil and political scheme beneficial or noxious to mankind.

I must be tolerably sure, before I venture publicly to congratulate men upon a blessing, that they have really received one. Flattery corrupts both the receiver and the giver, and adulation is not of more service to people than to kings. I should therefore suspend my congratulations on the acquisition of liberties, until I was informed how it had been combined with government; with public force; with the discipline and obedience of armies; with the collection of an effective and well-distributed revenue; with morality and religion; with solidity and property; with peace and order; with civil and social manners.

All these (in their way) are good things too, and, without them, liberty is not a benefit whilst it lasts, and it is not likely to continue long. The effect of liberty to individuals is that they may do what they please; we ought to see what it will please them to do, before we risk congratulations, which may be soon turned into complaints. Prudence would dictate this in the case of separate, insulated, private men; but liberty, when men act in bodies, is power. Considerate people, before they declare themselves, will observe the use which is made of power, and particularly of so trying a thing as new power in new persons, of whose principles, tempers, and dispositions, they have little or no experience, and in situations where those who appear the most stirring in the scene may possibly not be the real movers.

I flatter myself that I love a manly, moral, regulated liberty as well as any gentleman, be he who he will; and perhaps I have given as good proofs of my attachments to that cause, in the whole course of my public conduct. I think I envy liberty as little as they do, to any other nation. But I cannot stand forward, and give praise or blame to anything which relates to human actions, and human concerns, on a simple view of the object, as it stands stripped of every relation, in all nakedness and solitude of abstraction.

If true rights and liberties presuppose government, and therefore, coercion, the question, as in Rousseau, presents itself: What is the best form of government? Again as in Rousseau, the answer is an aristocracy. But where Rousseau had suggested an elective, Burke suggests a natural aristocracy. Thus:

> Believe me, those who attempt to level never equalize. In all societies, consisting of various descriptions of citizens, some description must be uppermost. The levelers

therefore only change and pervert the natural order of things; they load the edifice of society, by setting up in the air what the solidity of the structure requires to be on the ground. Tailors and carpenters cannot be equal to the situation, into which, by the worst of usurpations, an usurpation on the prerogatives of nature, you attempt to force them.

You will hear it said that all occupations are honorable. If this means only that no honest employment was disgraceful, it does not go beyond the truth. But in asserting that anything is honorable, we imply some distinction in its favor. The occupation of a hairdresser, or of a working tallow chandler, cannot be a matter of honor to any person—to say nothing of a number of other more servile employments. Such men ought not to suffer oppression from the state, but the state suffers oppression, if such as they, either individually or collectively, are permitted to rule. In this you think you are combatting prejudice, but you are at war with nature.

A true natural aristocracy is not a separate interest in the state, or separable from it. It is an essential integrant part of any large body rightly constituted. It is formed out of a class of legitimate presumptions, which, taken as generalities, must be admitted for actual truths. To be bred in a place of estimation; to see nothing low and sordid from one's infancy; to be taught to respect oneself; to be habituated to the censorial inspection of the public eye; to look early to public opinion; to stand upon such elevated ground as to be enabled to take a large view of the widespread and infinitely diversified combinations of men and affairs in a large society; to have leisure to read, to reflect, to converse; to be enabled to draw the court and attention of the wise and learned wherever they are to be found; to be habituated to command and to obey; to be taught to despise danger in the pursuit of honor and duty; to be formed to the greatest degree of vigilance, foresight, and circumspection, in a state of things in which no fault is committed with impunity, and the slightest mistakes draw on the most ruinous consequences; to be led to a guarded and regulated conduct, from a sense that you are considered as an instructor of your fellow citizens in their highest concerns, and that you act as a reconciler between God and man; to be employed as an administrator of law and justice, and to be thereby amongst the first benefactors to mankind; to be a professor of high science, or of liberal and ingenuous art; to be amongst rich traders, who from their success are presumed to have sharp and vigorous understandings, and to possess the virtues of diligence, order, constancy,and regularity, and to have cultivated an habitual regard to commutative justice—these are the circumstances of men that form what I should call a *natural* aristocracy, without which there is no nation.

Men, qualified in the manner I have just described, form in nature, as she operates in the common modification of society, the leading, guiding, and governing part. It is the soul to the body, without which the man does not exist. To give therefore no more importance, in the social order, to such men, than that of so many units, is a horrible usurpation.

When great multitudes act together, under that discipline of nature, I recognize the people, I acknowledge something that perhaps equals, and ought always to guide the sovereignty of convention. In all things the voice of this grand chorus of national harmony ought to have a mighty and decisive influence.

But when you disturb this harmony; when you break up this beautiful order, this array of truth and nature, as well as of habit and prejudice; when you separate the common sort of men from their proper chieftains so as to form them into an adverse army, I no longer know that venerable object called *the people* in such a disbanded race of deserters and vagabonds. For a while they may be terrible indeed, but in such a manner as wild beasts are terrible. The mind owes to them no sort of submission. They are, as they have been reputed, rebels.

Woe to the country which would madly and impiously reject the service of the talents and virtues, civil, military, or religious, that are given to grace and serve it, and would condemn to obscurity everything formed to diffuse luster and glory around a state. Woe to that country too that, passing into the opposite extreme, considers low education, a mean contracted view of things, a sordid, mercenary occupation, as a preferable title to command.

He wishes to be clear about one point. His doctrine of a natural aristocracy does not commit him to a theory of government by lords and dukes. Thus:

> I am accused of being a man of aristocratic principles. If by *aristocracy* they mean the peers, I have no vulgar admiration, nor any vulgar antipathy, toward them; I hold their order in cold and decent respect. I hold them to be of absolute necessity in the constitution, but I think they are only good when kept within their proper bounds.
>
> I am no friend to aristocracy, in the sense at least in which that word is usually understood. If it were not a bad habit to moot cases on the supposed ruin of the constitution, I should be free to declare that, if it must perish, I would rather by far see it resolved in any other form than lost in that austere and insolent domination.
>
> Do not imagine that I wish to confine power, authority, and distinction to blood and names and titles. There is no qualification for government but virtue and wisdom, actual or presumptive. Whenever they are actually found, they have, in whatever state, condition, profession or trade, the passport of Heaven to human place and honor.

From the notion of a natural aristocracy, Burke returns to his earlier theme that government is justified by reason of the fact that men and women have duties they need to have enforced. He desires to point out that "duties" is a basic notion, and that duties are seldom a matter of choice:

> Look though the whole of life, and the whole system of duties. Much the strongest moral obligations are such as were never the result of our option.
>
> I cannot too often recommend it to the serious consideration of all men, who think civil society to be within the province of moral jurisdiction, that if we owe to it any duty, it is not subject to our will. Duties are not voluntary. *Duty* and *will* are even contradictory terms.
>
> Men without their choice derive benefits from association; without their choice they are subjected to duties in consequence of these benefits; and without their choice they enter into a virtual obligation as binding as any that is actual. Look through the whole of life and the whole system of duties. Much the strongest moral obligations are such as were never the result of our option.
>
> When we marry, the choice is voluntary, but the duties are not matter of choice. They are dictated by the nature of the situation. Dark and inscrutable are the ways by which we come into the world. The instincts which give rise to this mysterious process of nature are not of our making. But out of physical causes, unknown to us, perhaps unknowable, arise moral duties, which as we are able perfectly to comprehend, we are bound indispensably to perform.
>
> Parents may not be consenting to their moral relation; but consenting or not, they are bound to a long train of burdensome duties toward those with whom they

have never made a convention of any sort. Children are not consenting to their relation, but their relation, without their actual consent, binds them to its duties, or rather it implies their consent, because the presumed consent of every rational creature is in unison with the predisposed order of things.

Nor are we left without powerful instincts to make this duty as grateful to us, as it is awful and coercive. Our country is not a thing of mere physical locality. It consists, in great measure, in the ancient order into which we are born. We may have the same geographical situation, but another country; as we may have the same country, in another soil. The place that determines our duty to our country is a social civil relation.

Having stated his own position, Burke now turns to a criticism of the notion of popular sovereignty, which was receiving widespread attention and endorsement.

Factions now busy amongst us, in order to divest men of all love for their country, and remove from their minds all duty with regard to the state, endeavor to propagate an opinion that the "people," in forming their commonwealth, have by no means parted with their power over it. Discuss any of their schemes, and their answer is, It is the act of the people and that is sufficient.

These theorists hold, that sovereignty, whether exercised by one or many, did not only originate from the people, but that in the people the same sovereignty constantly and unalienably resides; that the people may lawfully depose kings; not only for misconduct, but without any misconduct at all; that they may set up any new fashion of government for themselves, or continue without any government at their pleasure; that the people are essentially their own rule, and their will the measure of their conduct; that the tenure of rulers is not a proper subject of contracts, because rulers have duties, but no rights; and that if a contract *de facto* is made with them in one age, allowing that it binds at all, it binds only those who are immediately concerned in it, but does not pass to posterity.

They hold that to a majority of the people belongs the right of altering the whole frame of their society, if such should be their pleasure. They may change it, say they, from a monarchy to a republic today and tomorrow back again from a republic to a monarchy, and so backward and forward as often as they like. They are masters of the commonwealth, because in substance they are themselves the commonwealth.

The ceremony of cashiering kings, of which these gentlemen talk so much, can rarely, if ever, be performed without force. It then becomes a case of war, and not of constitution. Laws are commanded to hold their tongues amongst arms, and tribunals fall to the ground with the peace they are no longer able to uphold.

Whilst they are possessed by these notions, it is vain to talk to them of the practice of their ancestors, the fundamental laws of their country, the fixed form of a constitution, whose merits are confirmed by the solid test of long experience, and an increasing public strength and national prosperity. They despise experience as the wisdom of unlettered men, and as for the rest, they have wrought underground a mine that will blow up, at one grand explosion, all examples of antiquity, precedents, charters, and acts of parliament.

There is, it appears, much to be said against this popular doctrine. A few obvious things have already been noted. But nothing fundamental has been offered as yet. Burke moves, accordingly, to the essential point. Everything turns upon the meaning of this phrase, *the people*. So he proceeds:

Believing it a question at least arduous in theory, and in practice very critical, it would become us to ascertain what our incantations are about to call up from darkness and the sleep of ages when the supreme authority of "the people" is in question. Before we attempt to extend or to confine, we ought to fix in our minds, with some degree of distinctness, an idea of what it is we mean when we say, *the people.*

We are so little affected by things which are habitual, that we consider this idea of the decision of a majority as if it were a law or our original nature, but such constructive whole, residing in a part only, is one of the most violent fictions that ever has been or can be made on the principles of artificial incorporation. Out of civil society nature knows nothing of it; nor are men, even when arranged according to civil order, otherwise than by very long training, brought at all to submit to it.

In a state of rude nature there is no such thing as "a people." A number of men in themselves have no collective capacity. The idea of a people is the idea of a corporation. It is wholly artificial, and made like all other legal fictions, by common agreement. What the particular nature of that agreement was, is collected from the form into which the particular society has been cast. Any other is not their covenant.

When men, therefore, break up the agreement which gives it corporate form and capacity to a state, they are no longer a people; they have no longer a corporate existence; they have no longer a legal, coactive force to bind within, nor a claim to be recognized abroad. They are a number of vague, loose individuals and nothing more. With them all is to begin again. Alas! They little know how many a weary step is to be taken before they can form themselves into a mass, which has a true, political personality.

The phrase *the people* cannot be identified with a mere voting majority. Such an idea, namely that a voting majority shall be "the people," is a product of late political experience. Men must have learned much from long trial and error before they can act on that notion. It expresses an agreement or consensus that political experience alone makes possible. If this meaning of the phrase is a product of group experience of state organization, then it cannot be argued to be prior to and more fundamental than state organizations. To overlook or to deny this fact is to court much trouble.

Burke has one last point to make. It is that politics, like morals, is based ultimately on religion. This is the taproot of his conservatism. He begins:

Nothing is more certain than that manners, civilization, and all good things connected with manners and civilization, have, in this European world of ours, depended for ages upon two principles, and were indeed the result of both combined: I mean, the spirit of a gentleman and the spirit of religion.

We know, and what is better, we feel inwardly that religion is the basis of civil society, and the source of all good and all comfort; that on religion, according to our mode, all our laws and institutions stand as upon their base.

The religious sense of mankind, like a wise architect, hath built up the august fabric of states; like a provident proprietor, to preserve the structure from profanation and ruin, as a sacred temple purged from all the impurities of fraud and violence and injustice and tyranny, it hath solemnly and forever consecrated the commonwealth and all that officiate therein.

This consecration is made that all who administer in the government of men should have high and worthy notions of their function and destination; that their hope should be full of immortality; that they should not look to the paltry pelf of the moment, nor to the temporary and transient praise of the vulgar, but to a solid, permanent existence, in the permanent part of their nature, and to a permanent fame and glory, in the example they leave as a rich inheritance to the world.

This principle ought to be impressed, even more strongly, upon the minds of those who compose the collective sovereignty. For the people at large can never become the subject of punishment by any human hand. They ought therefore to be persuaded that they are fully as little entitled and far less qualified, with safety to themselves, to use any arbitrary power whatsoever; that they are not, under a false show of "liberty," tyrannically to exact, from those who officiate in the state, an abject submission to their occasional will.

When the people have emptied themselves of all the lust of selfish will, which without religion it is utterly impossible they ever should; when they are conscious that they exercise a power, which to be legitimate must be according to that eternal and immutable law in which will and reason are the same, they will be more capable how they place power in base and incapable hands.

In their nomination to office they will not appoint to the exercise of authority as to a pitiful job, but as to a holy function; not according to their arbitrary will. They will confer that power, which any man may well tremble to give or to receive, on those only in whom they discern a predominant portion of active virtue and wisdom.

Those who form their opinions on such grounds as they ought to form them, conceive that He who gave our nature to be perfected by our virtue willed also the necessary means to its perfection. He willed therefore the state. He willed its connection with the source and original archetype of all perfection.

Those who believe that God willed the state think some part of the wealth of the country is as usefully employed in maintaining a church and a clergy as in fomenting the luxury of individuals. It is the public ornament. It is the public consolation. It nourishes the public hope. The poorest man finds his own importance and dignity in it. It is for the man in humble life—to raise his nature, to put him in mind of a state in which the privileges of opulence will cease, when he will be equal by nature, and may be more than equal by virtue—that his portion of the general wealth of the country is thus employed and sanctified.

The awful author of our being is the author of our place in the order of existence. Having disposed and marshalled us by a divine tactic, not according to our will, but according to His, He has, in and by that disposition, virtually subjected us to act the part which belongs to the place assigned us. We have obligations to mankind at large, which are not in consequence of any special voluntary pact. They arise from the relation of man to man, and the relation of man to God, which relations are not matters of choice.

An "alliance" between church and state in a Christian commonwealth is, in my opinion an idle and fanciful speculation. An alliance is between two things that are in their nature distinct and independent, such as between two sovereign states. But in a Christian commonwealth, the church and state are one and the same thing, being different integral parts of the same whole.

Religion is so far, in my opinion, from being out of the province or duty of a Christian magistrate that it is, and ought to be, not only his care, but the principal thing in his care; because it is one of the great bonds of human society.

Against infidels [i.e., unbelievers] I would have the laws rise in all their terrors. . . . I would cut up the very root of atheism. The infidels are outlaws of the constitution; not of this country, but of the human race. They are never to be supported, never to be tolerated.

The concluding paragraphs sum up the argument. Rights and liberties are products of the political organization of society. In the political organization of society one is confronted, largely, with matters of tradition—*prescription* is his word—matters of slow growth and gradual change:

> From Magna Charta to the Declaration of Right, it has been the uniform policy of our constitution to claim and assert our liberties as an entailed inheritance from our forefathers and to be transmitted to our posterity; as an estate, specially belonging to the people of this realm without any reference whatever to any other more general or prior right.
>
> By thus regarding our liberties as an entailed inheritance, our constitution preserves a unity in the great multiplicity of its parts. We have an inheritable crown; an inheritable peerage; and a house of commons and a people inheriting privileges, franchises, and liberties, from a long line of ancestors.
>
> This policy appears to me to be the result of profound reflection; or rather, the happy effect of following nature, which is wisdom without reflection, and above it. The idea of inherited liberties, rights, and privileges furnishes a sure principle of conservation and transmission, without at all excluding a principle of improvement. It leaves acquisition free, but it secures what it acquires. Whatever advantages are obtained, are locked fast as in a sort of family settlement, grasped as in a kind of mortmain forever.
>
> We receive, we hold, we transmit our government and our privileges, in the same manner in which we enjoy and transmit our property and our lives. The institutions of policy, the goods of fortune, the gifts of Providence, are handed down to us and from us in the same course and order. Our political system is placed in a just correspondence and symmetry with that mode of existence decreed to a permanent body composed of transitory parts, by the disposition of a stupendous wisdom, molding together the great mysterious incorporation of the human race, the whole at one time, is never old or middle-aged or young, but in a condition of unchangeable constancy moves on through the varied tenor or perpetual decay, fall, renovation, and progression.
>
> By preserving thus the method of nature in the conduct of the state, in what we improve we are never wholly new; in what we retain, we are never wholly obsolete. By adhering in that manner and on those principles to our forefathers, we are guided, not by the superstition of antiquarians but by the spirit of philosophic analogy. In this choice of entailment, inheritance, we have given to our frame of polity the image of a relation in blood; binding up the constitution of our country with our dearest domestic ties; adopting our fundamental laws into the bosom of our family affections; keeping inseparable, and cherishing with the warmth of all their combined and mutually reflected charities, our state, our hearths, our sepulchers, and our altars.
>
> We procure reverence to our civil institutions on the principle upon which nature teaches us to revere individual men, on account of their age, and on account of those from whom they are descended. All your sophisters cannot produce anything better adapted to preserve a rational and manly liberty than the course we have pursued, who have chosen our nature rather than our speculations, our breasts rather than our inventions, for the great conservatories and magazines of our rights and privileges.
>
> A politic caution, a guarded circumspection, a moral timidity, were among the ruling principles of our forefathers in their most decided conduct. They were not illu-

minated with that "light of reason," of which the gentlemen of France tell us they have got so abundant a share. They acted under a strong sense of the ignorance and fallibility of mankind. He that made them thus fallible, rewarded them for having in their conduct attended to their nature. Let us imitate their caution, if we wish to deserve their fortune or retain their bequests. Let us add, if we please; but let us preserve what they have left; let us be satisfied to admire, rather than attempt to follow in their desperate flights the aeronauts of France.

NOTE ON SOURCES.   The materials in this section are quoted, abridged, or paraphrased from three sources: Edmund Burke, *Reflections on the Revolution in France, Appeal from the New to the Old Wings,* and *Letter to a Noble Lord.* The passages from each of these three books do not occur as continuous sequences. Our themes were established, and then passages relevant to each theme were taken from one or other of the books and strung together.

4 KARL MARX

THE CASE FOR REVOLUTION

FROM BURKE TO MARX.   Both Rousseau and Burke did their theorizing in the latter part of the eighteenth century. Marx did his in the nineteenth century, and what emerged from his pen had more kinship to the writings of Rousseau than to those of Burke. In his case for conservatism, Burke claimed that God wills the state, as a mode of living for humankind so that by exercise of their virtues they may perfect their natures. Left to themselves persons would not do this. Hence a state needs a government to enforce the exercise of human virtues. A government should consist of a state's natural aristocracy, those who know the good for humankind and desire that it shall prevail. Marx was unalterably opposed to this position. Burke seemed to claim illegitimately that his natural aristocracy in fact knew and pursued the good for humankind. Burke seemed to ignore the beguiling power of self-interest, which had driven rulers to use the structures of society for their own personal advantage. Burke was pessimistic about the capacity of the masses, unaided by the coercive power of the government, to pursue virtue. Marx, in contrast, was pessimistic about the capacity of the rulers to guide humankind in the pursuit of virtue. Accordingly, Marx's thought had very little compatibility with Burke's. The matter is different, however, with Rousseau's.

In his case for the Common Good, Rousseau claimed that a government was justified in enforcing, indeed was obligated to enforce, laws that expressed the General Will; that is, laws that defined and protected the Common Good or an aspect of the Common Good. Rousseau did not claim that all laws, nor perhaps even most laws, did in fact thus express the General Will for the common Good. His argument therefore was not necessarily supportive of all, nor perhaps even most, governments. His *Social Contract* was, therefore, sometimes read by his contemporaries, and the next generation, as containing if not actually propounding, a doctrine of justifiable revolution. Governments are not justified, let alone obligated, to enforce legislation that does not express the General Will for the Common Good. The inference was that governments would be justified in ignoring, indeed obligated to ignore, laws that were incompatible with, destructive of, the General Will for the Common Good. When governments did not do this, a people was justified in revolution. Such revolution aimed to rid the state of a government that was failing in its duty, and to replace such government by one that would do its duty. So understood, Rousseau influenced revolutionary thinking in America and France.

Marx did not repudiate this revolutionary element in Rousseau's thinking. Instead, he attempted to present a more accurate and detailed account of the conditions that were driving modern societies into the throes of revolution. His most famous tract of revolution, *Manifesto of the Communist Party,* was prepared in 1848 with the assistance of Friedrich Engels, in response to a request from the Communist League for a thorough statement of Communist theory and practice. The basic ideas presented in the Manifesto, Engels openly declared, were the work of Marx. Those ideas can be summarized as follows. Any society consists of two fundamental parts: the economic substructure and the social superstructure. At the core of the economic substructure are the relations of production, that is, the way people associate with each other in order to produce the goods and services of the society. These relations of production have always been conflictual: a small social elite has exploited the majority of those engaged in the productive process. The general form of the relations of production, then, is exploiter versus exploited, oppressor versus oppressed. The exploiting elite is able to pursue the economic exploitation of the others because the social superstructure is developed in such a way that it expresses and guarantees the interests of that exploiting elite. The social superstructure embraces all the social constructs other than the economic ones, ranging from the educational system to the prevailing religions to the current state with its laws. To understand a given society, one must first identify who the economic exploiters are and discern precisely what their interests are. Then it is a rather straightforward matter to expose how the prevailing religion, education, laws, government, etc., serve those interests.

Marx was not content merely to diagram a society in this fashion. He wished to give an account of how one set of relations of production yields to another set, and how the whole social superstructure is therefore reconstituted to express the interest of the new economic exploiters. Such an overhaul of society is called a revolution, and Marx believed that he had discovered the "laws" of social process (that is, the regularities of social development) according to which those revolutions take place. Knowing those "laws," those regularities and patterns of social development, Marx believed he could predict the future to which human society was heading. The basic regularity of social process leading to revolution that he discerned was the conflict between the developing forces of production and the prevailing relations of production. This conflict generated economic crises that triggered crises and unrest in all the segments of the social superstructure. In such unsettled times, a well-organized contending class can wrest the control of the state out of the hands of the ruling class and set themselves up as the new masters of society.

The future to which Marx saw society heading was communism. It was, for Marx, a virtual paradise. He was always deeply troubled by the dehumanization he encountered in bourgeois, capitalistic society. He believed that the essence of humanness is free, conscious activity, which finds expression in the creation of products that vary from symphonies to shoes. Capitalism, in its greed for surplus value, had stifled human creativeness. Humans had been reduced to unthinking appendages of machines. All the facets of the superstructure, especially the laws and government, of capitalistic society were so many chains binding the working class to the wheel of labor. To rid itself of these chains the working class would have to seize control of the state in order to control the forces of social coercion. Then the working class could reconstruct society unhampered by its former rulers. But the working class could only achieve success at the *right* moment in time. That moment would occur when the crises in the economic substructure were so severe and the chaos in the social superstructure was so widespread that it could save itself from the destruction only by means of a radical Communist revolution. Accordingly, Marx spent much of his life analyzing the history of social process to determine more precisely the advent of the revolution and to encourage its coming. His writings offer an extended commentary on the contradictions and inconsistencies in capitalist society that were driving it to destruction.

The new society of the future, communism, will not have an exploiter/exploited relationship at the core of its economic base. Instead, the masses of humankind will have arisen and destroyed their last rulers. Those masses will seize society in the name of and for the sake of humankind. There will be no more exploiter/exploited relationships. There will only be humans working with each other and for each other. The social superstructure will then reflect and guarantee not the interests of one ruling class but the interests of all humankind. In such a situation the state as an instrument of social coercion in the class war will disappear because there will only be one class left—the working, producing, creating mass of humankind. And where there is only one class, there is really no class, and hence no class war and no need for a state as an instrument of class conflict. The state as a bureaucratic machine for organizing society will, however, abide even under communism.

Exploitative, capitalist society, then, according to Marx, is moving inevitably toward a nonexploitative, Communist society. The working class, led by the Communist party, will usher in that new society through a violent revolution. In the *Manifesto,* from which the readings in this section have been taken, Marx provides a theoretical basis and a practical agenda for that party as it pursues its revolutionary goal.

BIOGRAPHICAL NOTE.   Marx was born in 1818 and died in 1883 at the age of sixty-five. He was educated in the universities of Bonn, Berlin, and Jena, beginning with law, but subsequently devoting his entire attention to philosophy. The philosophical perspective that he adopted was so critical of contemporary Prussian society that it prevented him from securing a job teaching philosophy when he graduated with his doctorate. For the next few years, amid a life of newspaper work and radical agitation, he worked out his humanistic/economic interpretation of history in a running battle with the prevailing Hegelian philosophy of his day. It was at this time that he wrote his famous *Economic and Philosophic Manuscripts of 1844*, which were not published until the 1920s. In those *Manuscripts* he presents his ideal view of the human being as a free, conscious creator of products, which stood in glaring contrast to the alienated, dehumanized worker of capitalistic society. In 1848 he collaborated with Engels on the *Manifesto of the Communist Party*, which provides one of the best summaries of his thinking on revolution. Exiled from Prussia, from Belgium, and from the environs of Paris because of his radical views, he settled with his family in London. From there, in 1864, he organized the First International. In 1867 he published volume one of *Capital*. The remainder was edited and published by Engels after Marx's death. In *Capital*, Marx attempts to provide a detailed analysis of the contradictions in capitalist society that are driving it to destruction. Marx and Engels were prolific writers as is evidenced by the thirty-volume anthology of their works published several years ago in East Berlin under the title, *Werke*. In life, judged by ordinary standards, Marx was unhappy, unsuccessful, and largely unknown. In death, he has become, like Darwin, Freud, and Einstein, one of the makers of the modern mind.

THE ARGUMENT OF THE PASSAGES.   The history of all hitherto existing society is the history of class struggles: exploiter versus exploited, oppressor versus oppressed. In early modern times the bourgeoisie triumphed over their feudal masters. They thus became masters of the modern world. Marx provides an account of their multifarious doings. They have, among other things, brought into being a new class, the proletariat. The class struggle is now between the bourgeoisie and the proletarians. When the latter win out, as they are destined to do, the world will see its first classless society. The bourgeois economy will be replaced by the Communist economy. Injustices and dehumanization arising out of bourgeois capitalism will cease to exist. Therefore Marx issues a call to all proletarians to join the Communists in their pursuit of the revolution: they have a new world of human fulfillment to gain, a world of chains to discard. The text:

> A spectre is haunting Europe—the spectre of Communism. All the powers of old Europe have entered into a holy alliance to exorcise this spectre; Pope and Czar, Metternich and Guizot, French Radicals and German police-spies.
>
> Where is the party in opposition that has not been decried as communistic by its opponents in power? Where the Opposition that has not hurled back the branding reproach of Communism, against the more advanced opposition parties, as well as against its reactionary adversaries?
>
> Two things result from this fact.

> I. Communism is already acknowledged by all European Powers to be itself a Power.
> II. It is high time that Communists should openly in the face of the whole world, publish their views, their aims, their tendencies, and meet this nursery tale of the Spectre of Communism with a Manifesto of the party itself.

To this end, Communists of the various nationalities have assembled in London, and sketched the following manifesto, to be published in the English, French, German, Italian, Flemish and Danish languages.

(1)

The history of all hitherto existing society is the history of class struggles.

Freeman and slave, patrician and plebeian, lord and serf, guild-master and journeyman, in a word, oppressor and oppressed, stood in constant opposition to one another, carried on an uninterrupted, now hidden, now open fight, a fight that each time ended either in a revolutionary reconstitution of society at large, or in the common ruin of the contending classes.

In the earlier epochs of history, we find almost everywhere a complicated arrangement of society into various orders, a manifold gradation of social rank. In ancient Rome we have patricians, knights, plebeians, slaves; in the middle ages, feudal lords, vassals, guild-masters, journeymen, apprentices, serfs; in almost all of these classes, again, subordinate gradations.

The modern bourgeois society that has sprouted from the ruins of feudal society, has not done away with class antagonisms. It has but established new classes, new conditions of oppression, new forms of struggle in place of the old ones.

Our epoch, the epoch of the bourgeoisie, possesses, however, this distinctive feature; it has simplified the class antagonisms. Society as a whole is more and more splitting up into two great hostile camps, into two great classes directly facing each other: Bourgeoisie and Proletariat.

From the serfs of the middle ages sprang the chartered burghers of the earliest towns. From these burgesses the first elements of the bourgeoisie were developed.

The discovery of America, the rounding of the Cape, opened up fresh ground for the rising bourgeoisie. The East-Indian and Chinese markets, the colonization of America, trade with the colonies, the increase in the means of exchange and in commodities generally, gave to commerce, to navigation, to industry, an impulse never before known, and thereby, to the revolutionary element in the tottering feudal society, a rapid development.

The feudal system of industry, under which industrial production was monopolized by closed guilds, now no longer sufficed for the growing wants of the new markets. The manufacturing system took its place. The guild-masters were pushed on one side by the manufacturing middle-class; division of labor between the different corporate guilds vanished in the face of division of labor in each single workshop.

Meantime the markets kept ever growing, the demand, ever rising. Even manufacture no longer sufficed. Thereupon, steam and machinery revolutionized industrial production. The place of manufacture was taken by the giant, Modern Industry, the place of the industrial middle-class, by industrial millionaires, the leaders of whole industrial armies, the modern bourgeois.

Modern industry has established the world-market, for which the discovery of America paved the way. This market has given an immense development to commerce, to navigation, to communication by land. This development has, in its turn, reacted on the extension of industry; and in proportion as industry, commerce, navigation, railways extended, in the same proportion the bourgeoisie developed, increased its capital, and pushed into the background every class handed down from the Middle Ages.

We see, therefore, how the modern bourgeoisie is itself the product of a long course of development, of a series of revolutions in the modes of production and exchange.

Each step in the development of the bourgeoisie was accompanied by a corresponding political advance of that class. An oppressed class under the sway of the feudal nobility, an armed and self-governing association in the mediaeval commune, here independent urban republic (as in Italy and Germany), there taxable "third estate" of the monarch (as in France), afterwards, in the period of manufacture proper, serving either the semifeudal or the absolute monarchy as a counterpoise against the nobility, and, in fact, cornerstone of the great monarchies in general, the bourgeoisie has at last, since the establishment of Modern Industry and of the world-market, conquered for itself, in the modern representative State, exclusive political sway. *The executive of the modern State is but a committee for managing the common affairs of the whole bourgeoisie.*

(2)

The bourgeoisie, historically, has played a most revolutionary part.

The bourgeoisie, wherever it has got the upper hand, has put an end to all feudal, patriarchal, idyllic relations. It has pitilessly torn asunder the motley feudal ties that bound man to his "natural superiors," and has left remaining no other nexus between man and man than naked self-interest, callous "cash payment." It has drowned the most heavenly ecstasies of religious fervor, of chivalrous enthusiasm, of philistine sentimentalism, in the icy water of egotistical calculation. It has resolved personal worth into exchange value, and in place of the numberless indefeasible chartered freedoms, has set up that single, unconscionable freedom—Free Trade. In one word, for exploitation, veiled by religious and political illusions, it has substituted naked, shameless, direct, brutal exploitation.

The bourgeoisie has stripped of its halo every occupation hitherto honored and looked up to with reverent awe. It has converted the physician, the lawyer, the priest, the poet, the man of science, into its paid wage-laborers.

The bourgeoisie has torn away from the family its sentimental veil, and has reduced the family relation to a mere money relation.

The bourgeoisie has disclosed how it came to pass that the brutal display of vigor in the Middle Ages, which Reactionists so much admire, found its fitting complement in the most slothful indolence. It has been the first to show what man's activity can bring about. It has accomplished wonders far surpassing Egyptian pyramids, Roman aqueducts, and Gothic cathedrals; it has conducted expeditions that put in the shade all former Exoduses of nations and crusades.

The bourgeoisie cannot exist without constantly revolutionizing the instruments of production, and thereby the relations of production, and with them the whole relations of society. Conservation of the old modes of production in unaltered form, was, on the contrary, the first condition of existence for all earlier industrial classes. Constant revolutionizing of production, uninterrupted disturbance of all social conditions, everlasting uncertainty and agitation distinguish the bourgeois epoch from all earlier ones. All fixed, fast-frozen relations, with their train of ancient and venerable prejudices and opinions, are swept away, all new-formed ones become antiquated before they can ossify. All that is solid melts into air, all that is holy is profaned, and man is at last compelled to face, with sober senses, his real conditions of life, and his relations with his kinds.

The need of a constantly expanding market for its products chases the bourgeoisie over the whole surface of the globe. It must nestle everywhere, settle everywhere, establish connections everywhere.

The bourgeoisie has through its exploitation of the world-market given a cosmopolitan character to production and consumption in every country. To the great chagrin of Reactionists, it has drawn from under the feet of industry the national ground on which it stood. All old-established national industries have been destroyed or are daily being destroyed. They are dislodged by new industries, whose introduction becomes a life and death question for all civilized nations, by industries that no longer work up indigenous raw material, but raw material drawn from the remotest zones, industries whose products are consumed, not only at home, but in every quarter of the globe. In place of the old wants, satisfied by the productions of the country, we find new wants, requiring for their satisfaction the products of distant lands and climes. In place of the old local and national seclusion and self-sufficiency, we have intercourse in every direction, universal inter-dependence of nations. And as in material, so also in intellectual production. The intellectual creations of individual nations become common property. National onesidedness and narrow-mindedness become more and more impossible, and from the numerous national and local literatures there arises a world-literature.

The bourgeoisie, by the rapid improvement of all instruments of production, by the immensely facilitated means of communication, draws all, even the most barbarian, nations into civilization. The cheap prices of its commodities are the heavy artillery with which it batters down all Chinese walls, with which it forces the barbarians' intensely obstinate hatred of foreigners to capitulate. It compels all nations, on pain of extinction, to adopt the bourgeois mode of production; it compels them to introduce what it calls civilization into their midst, i.e., to become bourgeois themselves. In a word, it creates a world after its own image.

The bourgeoisie has subjected the country to the rule of the towns. It has created enormous cities, has greatly increased the urban population as compared with the rural, and has thus rescued a considerable part of the population from the idiocy of rural life. Just as it has made the country dependent on the towns, so it has made barbarian and semibarbarian countries dependent on the civilized ones, nations of peasants on nations of bourgeois, the East on the West.

The bourgeoisie keeps more and more doing away with the scattered state of the population, of the means of production, and of property. It has agglomerated population, centralized means of production, and has concentrated property in a few hands. The necessary consequence of this was political centralization. Independent, or but loosely connected provinces, with separate interests, laws, governments and systems of taxation, became lumped together in one nation, with one government, one code of laws, one national class-interest, one frontier and one customs-tariff.

The bourgeoisie, during its rule of scarce one hundred years, has created more massive and more colossal productive forces than have all preceding generations together. Subjection of Nature's forces to man, machinery, application of chemistry to industry and agriculture, steam-navigation, railways, electric telegraphs, clearing of whole continents for cultivation, canalization of rivers, whole populations conjured out of the ground—what earlier century had even a presentiment that such productive forces slumbered in the lap of social labor?

We see then: the means of production and of exchange on whose foundation the bourgeoisie built itself up, were generated in feudal society. At a certain stage in the development of these means of production and of exchange, the conditions under which feudal society produced and exchanged, the feudal organization of agriculture and manufacturing industry, in one word, the feudal relations of property became no longer compatible with the already developed productive forces; they became so many fetters. They had to burst asunder; they were burst asunder.

Into their places stepped free competition, accompanied by a social and political constitution adapted to it, and by the economical and political sway of the bourgeois class.

A similar movement is going on before our own eyes. *Modern bourgeois* society with its relations of production, of exchange and of property, a society that has conjured up such gigantic means of production and of exchange, *is like the sorcerer, who is no longer able to control the powers of the nether world whom he has called up by his spells.* For many a decade past the history of industry and commerce is but the history of the revolt of modern productive forces against modern conditions of production, against the property relations that are the conditions for the existence of the bourgeoisie and of its rule. It is enough to mention the commercial crises that by their periodical return put on its trial, each time more threateningly, the existence of the entire bourgeois society. In these crises a great part not only of the existing products, but also of the previously created productive forces, are periodically destroyed. In these crises there breaks out an epidemic that, in all earlier epochs, would have seemed an absurdity—the epidemic of overproduction. Society suddenly finds itself put back into a state of momentary barbarism; it appears as if a famine, a universal war of devastation had cut off the supply of every means of subsistence; industry and commerce seem to be destroyed; and why? Because there is too much civilization, too much means of subsistence, too much industry, too much commerce. The productive forces at the disposal of society no longer tend to further the development of the conditions of bourgeois property; on the contrary, they have become too powerful for these conditions, by which they are fettered, and so soon as they overcome these fetters, they bring disorder into the whole of bourgeois society, endanger the existence of bourgeois property. The conditions of bourgeois society are too narrow to comprise the wealth created by them. And how does the bourgeoisie get over these crises? On the one hand by enforced destruction of a mass of productive forces, on the other, by the conquest of new markets, and by the more thorough exploitation of the old ones. That is to say, by paving the way for more extensive and more destructive crises, and by diminishing the means whereby crises are prevented.

(3)

The weapons with which the bourgeoisie felled feudalism to the ground are now turned against the bourgeoisie itself.

But not only has the bourgeoisie forged the weapons that bring death to itself; it has also called into existence the men who are to wield those weapons—the modern working-class—the proletarians.

In proportion as the bourgeoisie, i.e., capital, is developed, in the same proportion is the proletariat, the modern working-class, developed, a class of laborers, who live only so long as they find work, and who find work only so long as their labor increases capital. These laborers, who must sell themselves piecemeal, are a commodity, like every other article of commerce, and are consequently exposed to all the vicissitudes of competition, to all the fluctuations of the market.

Owing to the extensive use of machinery and to division of labor; the work of the proletarians has lost all individual character, and, consequently, all charm for the workman. He becomes an appendage of the machine, and it is only the most simple, most monotonous, and most easily acquired knack that is required of him. Hence, the cost of production of a workman is restricted, almost entirely, to the means of subsistence that he requires for his maintenance, and for the propagation of his race. But the price of a commodity, and also of labor, is equal to its cost of production. In proportion, therefore, as the repulsiveness of the work increases, the wage decreases. Nay more, in proportion as the use of machinery and division of labor increases, in the same proportion the burden of toil also increases, whether by prolongation of the working hours, by increase of the work enacted in a given time, or by increased speed of the machinery, etc.

Modern industry has converted the little workshop of the patriarchal master into the great factory of the industrial capitalist. Masses of laborers, crowded into the factory, are organized like soldiers. As privates of the industrial army they are placed under the command of a perfect hierarchy of officers and sergeants. Not only are they the slaves of the bourgeois class, and the bourgeois State, they are daily and hourly enslaved by the machine, by the over-looker, and, above all, by the individual bourgeois manufacturer himself. The more openly this despotism proclaims gain to be its end and aim, the more petty, the more hateful and the more embittering it is.

The less the skill and exertion of strength implied in manual labor, in other words, the more modern industry becomes developed, the more is the labor of men superseded by that of women. Differences of age and sex have no longer any distinctive social validity for the working class. All are instruments of labor, more or less expensive to use, according to their age and sex.

No sooner is the exploitation of the laborer by the manufacturer, so far at an end, that he receives his wages in cash, than he is set upon by the other portions of the bourgeoisie, the landlord, the shopkeeper, the pawnbroker, etc.

The lower strata of the middle class—the small tradespeople, shopkeepers, and retired tradesmen generally, the handicraftsmen and peasants—all these sink gradually into the proletariat, partly because their diminutive capital does not suffice for the scale on which Modern Industry is carried on, and is swamped in the competition with the large capitalists, partly because their specialized skill is rendered worthless by new methods of production. Thus the proletariat is recruited from all classes of the population.

The proletariat goes through various stages of development. With its birth begins its struggle with the bourgeoisie. At first the contest is carried on by individual laborers, then by the workpeople of a factory, then by the operatives of one trade, in one locality, against the individual bourgeois who directly exploits them. They direct their attacks not against the bourgeois conditions of production, but against the instruments of production themselves; they destroy imported wares that compete with their labor, they smash to pieces machinery, they set factories ablaze, they seek to restore by force the vanished status of the workman of the Middle Ages.

At this stage the laborers still form an incoherent mass scattered over the whole country, and broken up by their mutual competition. If anywhere they unite to form more compact bodies, this is not yet the consequence of their own active union, but of the union of the bourgeoisie, which class, in order to attain its own political ends, is compelled to set the whole proletariat in motion, and is moreover, yet, for a time, able to do so. At this stage, therefore, the proletarians do not fight their enemies, but the enemies of their enemies, the remnants of absolute monarchy, the landowners, the non-industrial bourgeois, the petty bourgeoisie. Thus the whole historical movement is concentrated in the hands of the bourgeoisie; every victory so obtained is a victory for the bourgeoisie.

But with the development of industry the proletariat not only increases in number; it becomes concentrated in greater masses, its strength grows, and it feels that strength more. The various interests and conditions of life within the ranks of the proletariat are more and more equalized, in proportion as machinery obliterates all distinctions of labor, and nearly everywhere reduces wages to the same low level. The growing competition among the bourgeois, and the resulting commercial crises, make the wages of the workers ever more fluctuating. The unceasing improvement of machinery, ever more rapidly developing, makes their livelihood more and more precarious; the collisions between individual workmen and individual bourgeois take more and more the character of collisions between two classes. Thereupon the workers begin to form combinations (Trades' Unions) against the bourgeois; they club together in order to keep up the rate of wages; they found permanent associations in order to make provision beforehand for these occasional revolts. Here and there the contest breaks out into riots.

Now and then the workers are victorious, but only for a time. The real fruit of their battle lies, not in the immediate result, but in the ever expanding union of the workers. This union is helped on by the improved means of communication that are created by modern industry, and that place the workers of different localities in contact with one another. It was just this contact that was needed to centralize the numerous local struggles, all of the same character, into one national struggle between classes. But every class struggle is a political struggle. And that union, to attain which the burghers of the Middle Ages, with their miserable highways, required centuries, the modern proletarians, thanks to railways, achieve in a few years.

This organization of the proletarians into a class, and consequently into a political party, is continually being upset again by the competition between the workers themselves. But it ever rises up again, stronger, firmer, mightier. It compels legislative recognition of particular interest of the workers, by taking advantage of the divisions among the bourgeoisie itself. Thus the ten-hour bill in England was carried.

Altogether collisions between the classes of the old society further, in many ways, the course of development of the proletariat. The bourgeoisie finds itself involved in a constant battle. At first with the aristocracy; later on, with those portions of the bourgeoisie itself, whose interests have become antagonistic to the progress of industry; at all times, with the bourgeoisie of foreign countries. In all these battles it sees itself compelled to appeal to the proletariat, to ask for its help, and thus, to drag it into the political arena. The bourgeoisie itself, therefore, supplies the proletariat with its own elements of political and general education, in other words, it furnishes the proletariat with weapons for fighting the bourgeoisie.

Further, as we have already seen, entire sections of the ruling classes are, by the advance of industry, precipitated into the proletariat, or are at least threatened in their conditions of existence. These also supply the proletariat with fresh elements of enlightenment and progress.

Finally, in times when the class-struggle nears the decisive hour, the process of dissolution going on within the ruling class, in fact, within the whole range of old society, assumes such a violent, glaring character, that a small section of the ruling class cuts itself adrift, and joins the revolutionary class, the class that holds the future in its hands. Just as, therefore, at an earlier period, a section of the nobility went over to the bourgeoisie, so now a portion of the bourgeoisie goes over to the proletariat, and in particular, a portion of the bourgeois ideologists, who have raised themselves to the level of comprehending theoretically the historical movements as a whole.

(4)

Of all the classes that stand face to face with the bourgeoisie today, the proletariat alone is a really revolutionary class. The other classes decay and finally disappear in the face of modern industry; the proletariat is its special and essential product.

The lower middle-class, the small manufacturer, the shopkeeper, the artisan, the peasant, all these fight against the bourgeoisie, to save from extinction their existence as fractions of the middle class. They are, therefore, not revolutionary, but conservative. Nay more, they are reactionary, for they try to roll back the wheel of history. If by chance they are revolutionary, they are so, only in view of their impending transfer into the proletariat, they thus defend not their present, but their future interests, they desert their own standpoint to place themselves at that of the proletariat.

The "dangerous class," the social scum, that passively rotting mass thrown off by the lowest layers of old society, may, here and there, be swept into the movement by a proletarian revolution; its conditions of life, however, prepare it far more for the part of a bribed tool of reactionary intrigue.

In the conditions of the proletariat, those of old society at large are already virtually swamped. The proletarian is without property; his relation to his wife and children has no longer anything in common with the bourgeois family-relations; modern industrial labor, modern subjection to capital, the same in England as in France, in America as in Germany, has stripped him of every trace of national character. Law, morality, religion, are to him so many bourgeois prejudices, behind which lurk in ambush just as many bourgeois interests.

All the preceding classes that got the upper hand, sought to fortify their already acquired status by subjecting society at large to their conditions of appropriation. The proletarians cannot become masters of the productive forces of society, except by abolishing their own previous mode of appropriation, and thereby also every other previous mode of appropriation. They have nothing of their own to secure and to fortify; their mission is to destroy all previous securities for, and insurances of, individual property.

All previous historical movements were movements of minorities, or in the interest of minorities. The proletarian movement is the self-conscious, independent movement of the immense majority, in the interest of the immense majority. The proletariat, the lowest stratum of our present society, cannot stir, cannot raise itself up, without the whole superincumbent strata of official society being sprung into the air.

Though not in substance, yet in form, the struggle of the proletariat with the bourgeoisie is at first a national struggle. The proletariat of each country must, of course, first of all settle matters with its own bourgeoisie.

In depicting the most general phases of the development of the proletariat, we traced the more or less veiled civil war, raging within existing society, up to the point where that war breaks out into open revolution, and where the violent overthrow of the bourgeoisie lays the foundation for the sway of the proletariat.

Hitherto, every form of society has been based, as we have already seen, on the antagonism of oppressing and oppressed classes. But in order to oppress a class, certain conditions must be assured it under which it can, at least, continue its slavish existence. The serf, in the period of serfdom, raised himself to membership in the commune, just as the petty bourgeois, under the yoke of feudal absolutism, managed to develop into a bourgeois. The modern laborer, on the contrary, instead of rising with the progress of industry, sinks deeper and deeper below the conditions of existence of his own class. He becomes a pauper, and pauperism develops more rapidly than population and wealth. And here it becomes evident, that the bourgeoisie is unfit any longer to be the ruling class in society, and to impose its conditions of existence upon society as an over-riding law. It is unfit to rule, because it is incompetent to assure an existence to its slave within his slavery, because it cannot help letting him sink into such a state that it has to feed him, instead of being fed by him. Society can no longer live under the bourgeoisie, in other words, its existence is no longer compatible with society.

The essential condition for the existence, and for the sway of the bourgeois class, is the formation and augmentation of capital; the condition for capital is wage labor. Wage labor rests exclusively on competition between the laborers. The advance of industry, whose involuntary promoter is the bourgeoisie, replaces the isolation of the laborers, due to competition, by their revolutionary combination, due to association. The development of Modern Industry, therefore, cuts from under its feet the very foundation in which the bourgeoisie produces and appropriates products. *What the bourgeoisie therefore produces, above all, are its own grave-diggers.* Its fall and the victory of the proletariat are equally inevitable.

(5)

In what relation do the Communists stand to the proletarians as a whole?

The Communists do not form a separate party opposed to other working-class parties.

They have no interests separate and apart from those of the proletariat as a whole.

They do not set up any sectarian principles of their own, by which to shape and mould the proletarian movement.

The Communists are distinguished from the other working class parties by this only: 1. In the national struggles of the proletarians of the different countries, they point out and bring to the front the common interests of the entire proletariat independently of all nationality. 2. In the various stages of development which the struggle of the working class against the bourgeoisie has to pass through, they always and everywhere represent the interests of the movement as a whole.

The Communists, therefore, are on the one hand, practically, the most advanced and resolute section of the working class parties of every country, that section which pushes forward all others; on the other hand, theoretically, they have over the great mass of the proletariat the advantage of clearly understanding the line of march, the conditions, and the ultimate general results of the proletarian movement.

The immediate aim of the Communists is the same as that of all the other proletarian parties; formation of the proletariat into a class, overthrow of the bourgeois supremacy, conquest of political power by the proletariat.

The theoretical conclusions of the Communists are in no way based on ideas or principles that have been invented, or discovered, by this or that would-be universal reformer.

They merely express, in general terms, actual relations springing from an existing class struggle,from a historical movement going on under our very eyes. The abolition of existing property relations is not at all a distinctive feature of Communism.

All property relations in the past have continually been subject to historical change consequent upon the change in historical conditions.

The French Revolution, for example, abolished feudal property in favor of bourgeois property.

The distinguishing feature of Communism is not the abolition of property generally, but the abolition of bourgeois property. But modern bourgeois private property is the final and most complete expression of the system of producing and appropriating products, that is based on class antagonism, on the exploitation of the many by the few.

In this sense, the theory of the Communists may be summed up in the single sentence: Abolition of private property.

We Communists have been reproached with the desire of abolishing the right of personally acquiring property as the fruit of a man's own labor, which property is alleged to be the ground work of all personal freedom, activity and independence.

Hard-won, self-acquired, self-earned property! Do you mean the property of the petty artisan and of the small peasant, a form of property that preceded the bourgeois form? There is no need to abolish that; the development of industry has to a great extent already destroyed it, and is still destroying it daily.

Or do you mean modern bourgeois private property?

But does wage-labor create any property for the laborer? Not a bit. It creates capital, i.e., that kind of property which exploits wage-labor, and which cannot increase except upon condition of getting a new supply of wage-labor for fresh exploitation. Property, in its present form, is based on the antagonism of capital and wage-labor. Let us examine both sides of this antagonism.

To be a capitalist, is to have not only a purely personal, but a social status in production. Capital is a collective product, and only by the united action of many members, nay, in the last resort, only by the united action of all members of society, can it be set in motion.

Capital is therefore not a personal, it is a social power.

When, therefore, capital is converted into common property, into the property of all members of society, personal property is not thereby transformed into social property. It is only the social character of the property that is changed. It loses its class-character.

Let us now take wage-labor.

The average price of wage-labor is the minimum wage, i.e., that quantum of the means of subsistence, which is absolutely requisite to keep the laborer in bare existence as a laborer. What, therefore, the wage-laborer appropriates by means of his labor, merely suffices to prolong and reproduce a bare existence. We by no means intend to abolish this personal appropriation of the products of labor, an appropriation that is made for the maintenance and reproduction of human life, and that leaves no surplus wherewith to command the labor of others. All that we want to do away with is the miserable character of this appropriation, under which the laborer lives merely to increase capital, and is allowed to live only in so far as the interest of the ruling class requires it.

In bourgeois society, living labor is but a means to increase accumulated labor. In communist society, accumulated labor is but a means to widen, to enrich, to promote the existence of the laborer.

In bourgeois society, therefore, the past dominates the present; in communist society, the present dominates the past. In bourgeois society capital is independent and has individuality, while the living person is dependent and has no individuality.

And the abolition of this state of things is called by the bourgeois, abolition of individuality and freedom! And rightly so. The abolition of bourgeois individuality, bourgeois independence, and bourgeois freedom is undoubtedly aimed at.

By freedom is meant, under the present bourgeois conditions of production, free trade, free selling and buying.

But if selling and buying disappears, free selling and buying disappears also. This talk about free selling and buying, and all the other "brave words" of our bourgeoisie about freedom in general, have a meaning, if any, only in contrast with restricted selling and buying, with the fettered traders of the Middle Ages, but have no meaning when opposed to the Communistic abolition of buying and selling, of the bourgeois conditions of production, and of the bourgeoisie itself.

You are horrified at our intending to do away with private property. But in your existing society, private property is already done away with for nine-tenths of the population; its existence for the few is solely due to non-existence in the hands of those nine-tenths. You reproach us, therefore, with intending to do away with a form of property, the necessary condition for whose existence is, the non-existence of any property for the immense majority of society.

In one word, you reproach us with intending to do away with your property. Precisely so; that is just what we intend.

From the moment when labor can no longer be converted into capital, money, or rent, into a social power capable of being monopolized, i.e., from the moment when individual property can no longer be transformed into bourgeois property, into capital, from that moment, you say, individuality vanishes.

You must, therefore, confess that by "individual" you mean no other person than the bourgeois, than the middle-class owner of property. This person must, indeed, be swept out of the way, and made impossible.

Communism deprives no man of the power to appropriate the products of society; all that it does is to deprive him of the power to subjugate the labor of others by means of such appropriation.

It has been objected, that upon the abolition of private property all work will cease, and universal laziness will overtake us.

According to this, bourgeois society ought long ago to have gone to the dogs through sheer idleness; for those of its members who work, acquire nothing, and those who acquire anything, do not work. The whole of this objection is but another expression of the tautology: that there can no longer be any wage-labor when there is no longer any capital.

All objections urged against the Communistic mode of producing and appropriating material products, have, in the same way, been urged against the Communistic modes of producing and appropriating intellectual products. Just as, to the bourgeois, the disappearance of class property is the disappearance of production itself, so the disappearance of class culture is to him identical with the disappearance of all culture.

That culture, the loss of which he laments, is, for the enormous majority, a mere training to act as a machine.

But don't wrangle with us so long as you apply, to our intended abolition of bourgeois property, the standard of your bourgeois notions of freedom, culture, law, etc. Your very ideas are but the outgrowth of the conditions of your bourgeois production and bourgeois property, just as your jurisprudence is but the will of your class made into a law for all, a will, whose essential character and direction are determined by the economic conditions of existence of your class.

The selfish misconception that induces you to transform into eternal laws of nature and of reason, the social forms springing from your present mode of production and form of property—historical relations that rise and disappear in the progress of production—this misconception you share with every ruling class that has preceded you. What you see clearly in the case of ancient property, what you admit in the case of feudal property, you are of course forbidden to admit in the case of your own bourgeois form of property. . . .

We have seen above that the first step in revolution by the working class is to raise the proletariat to the position of ruling class, to win the battle of democracy.

The proletariat will use its political supremacy, to wrest, by degrees, all capital from the bourgeoisie, to centralize all instruments of production in the hands of the State, i.e., of the proletariat organized as the ruling class; and to increase the total of productive forces as rapidly as possible.

Of course, in the beginning, this cannot be effected except by means of despotic inroads on the rights of property, and on the conditions of bourgeois production; by means of measures, therefore, which appear economically insufficient and untenable, but which, in the course of the movement, outstrip themselves, necessitate further inroads upon the old social order, and are unavoidable as a means of entirely revolutionizing the mode of production.

These measures will of course be different in different countries.

Nevertheless in the most advanced countries the following will be pretty generally applicable:

1. Abolition of property in land and application of all rents of land to public purposes.
2. A heavy progressive or graduated income tax.
3. Abolition of all right of inheritance.
4. Confiscation of the property of all emigrants and rebels.
5. Centralization of credit in the hands of the State, by means of a national bank with State capital and an exclusive monopoly.
6. Centralization of the means of communication and transport in the hands of the State.
7. Extension of factories and instruments of production owned by the State; the bringing into cultivation of waste lands, and the improvement of the soil generally in accordance with a common plan.
8. Equal liability to all labor. Establishment of industrial armies, especially for agriculture.
9. Combination of agriculture with manufacturing industries; gradual abolition of the distinction between town and country, by a more equable distribution of population over the country.
10. Free education for all children in public schools. Abolition of children's factory labor in its present form. Combination of education with industrial production, etc., etc.

When, in the course of development, class distinctions have disappeared, and all production has been concentrated in the hands of a vast association of the whole nation, the public power will lose its political character. Political power, properly so called, is merely the organized power of one class for oppressing another. If the proletariat during its contest with the bourgeoisie is compelled, by the force of circumstances, to organize itself as a class, if, by means of a revolution, it makes itself the ruling class, and, as such, sweeps away by force the old conditions of production, then it will, along with these conditions, have swept away the conditions for the existence of class antagonisms, and of classes generally, and will thereby have abolished its own supremacy as a class.

In place of the old bourgeois society, with its classes and class antagonisms, we shall have an association, in which the free development of each is the condition for the free development of all.

The Communists everywhere support every revolutionary movement against the existing social and political order of things.

In all these movements they bring to the front, as the leading question in each, the property question, no matter what its degree of development at the time.

Finally, they labor everywhere for the union and agreement of the democratic parties of all countries.

The Communists disdain to conceal their views and aims. They openly declare that their ends can be attained only by the forcible overthrow of all existing social conditions. Let the ruling classes tremble at a Communistic revolution. The proletarians have nothing to lose but their chains. They have a world to win.

Working men of all countries, unite!

NOTE ON SOURCES. This material is from Karl Marx and Friedrich Engels, *The Manifesto of the Communist Party,* Sections I, II, and IV.

5 JOHN STUART MILL

THE CASE FOR LIBERTY AND LAW

FROM MARX TO MILL. Thus far we have examined the thinking of Hobbes, Rousseau, Burke, and Marx. Each writes with an eye on the fact that in any community organized as a state, organized to make law possible, force will be brought to bear upon individuals and groups to conform to the law's demands. Hobbes declared that force was needed to compel egoistic humankind to obey the social contract that promotes its survival and best interests. Rousseau claimed that the use of force or coercion to produce conformity to law is justified when, and only when, it is introduced to protect a common good. By implying that some force and some laws may not be in the service of the common good, Rousseau left the door open to revolution. Burke, in contrast, did not. He declared that the natural aristocracy, which headed the government, knew and desired and legislated the good for humankind. Justifiably, then, that aristocracy wielded force to coerce the masses to conform to the laws so legislated. Marx brought the discussion back to revolution and declared not only its legitimacy but also its moral and historical necessity.

Marx pointed out that on the face of it, a community is organized politically to make possible the regulation of some human behavior by laws backed by force. This is the *prima facie* fact. But how is it to be interpreted? Why are communities thus organized? His answer is that "beneath the political face of things," a community is an economic order. That it is organized to make *production* possible is a more basic fact about it than that it is organized to make law possible. Its essential features—such as political community, political society—are to be explained, interpreted, understood, by reference to the more basic fact that it is an economy, an economic order. Unless this were so, it would not be organized as a political order, an order permitting control by laws backed by force. This is the fundamental claim of Marx's *economic* interpretation of politics and political history.

If you look *beneath* the surface of political orders, you discover economic orders. If you look *at* economic orders, you find that they consist of economic classes, and that between these classes there is a relation of class antagonism that can become class war. One of the economic classes, the "dominant" one, organizes the community into a political order so that it may suppress the other class, keep it in line, exploit it, by means of laws backed by force. Marx mentions the "feudal" class as having done this to the "bourgeois" class, and the bourgeois class as staging a "political" revolution enabling them to throw off the feudal class and impose their own modes of "law and order" upon the "proletarian" class. Marx's economic interpretation of politics and political history, law and legal history, thus consists in "class-angling" political organization, domination, revolution, and beginning anew. So long as this recurring cycle marks the political life of a community, there will be class legislation, and the use of force to produce conformity to the laws.

However, Marx foresees an end to these cycles. When the proletarians overthrow the bourgeoisie, they will not in turn be overthrown by a new economic class. Their triumph will mark the end of economic classes within the economic order, and the end of the need for laws backed by force. Thereafter, communities will be *administered,* not coercively governed. There will be no other economic class threatening the proletarian class. Rousseau's "common good" will become the proletarian good. The proletarians will not require to be coerced into acting with reference to *their* common good.

Mill's small book *On Liberty* was published in 1859, ninety-seven years after Rousseau's *Social Contract* and eleven years after Marx's *Manifesto.* It became, and has remained, a classic defense of the right of the individual to think and act for him- or herself. So construed, it is not a defense of the individual's right to think what he or she pleases and do what he or she pleases. It is not a theoretical defense of the idiosyncratic or the anarchical as such. Its claim is along these lines: when a community is organized to make law enforcement possible and has a government backed up by police and an army as its agent, such a community has much more power at its disposal than any dissenting individual. In such a community, whether a democracy or a republic or a constitutional monarchy or an absolute monarchy, a dissenting individual or minority can find itself confronted with virtually irresistible force. Mill's little book is written on behalf of persons so circumstanced. It is addressed to communities and their governments where a monopoly of coercive restraint is exercised in the name of the common good. It is no less applicable to communities and their governments where such restraint is exercised in the name of the proletarian good. Victoria's Britain, Lincoln's America, Lenin's Russia, or Hitler's Germany are, or would be thought of as, answerable to Mill's argument.

BIOGRAPHICAL NOTE.   John Stuart Mill was born in London in 1806 and died in 1873, a few days before his sixty-seventh birthday. He was something of a child prodigy. He tells us in his *Autobiography* that he started to learn Greek at the age of three and that by the time he was twelve years old he was sufficiently adept at Greek, Latin, history, and mathematics to move on to more advanced subjects such as logic. When he was fourteen he stayed for about a year in southern France with Sir Samuel Bentham (the brother of the philosopher Jeremy Bentham), at which time he studied the French language and literature and also pursued courses in chemistry, zoology, logic, and higher mathematics at Montpellier. At the age of seventeen he obtained a clerkship in the East India Company, and in due course became head of the office, drawing a substantial salary. He became deeply committed to Utilitarianism and spent his last teenage years editing Bentham's *Rationale of Evidence* in five volumes. At the age of twenty, he suffered a nervous collapse. During this time he came to appreciate the so-called hedonistic paradox that "happiness to be gotten, must be forgotten." He also concluded that Bentham's view of human nature did not give sufficient consideration to the importance of feelings. Mill published many volumes dealing with economics, philosophy, and political theory. His essay *On Liberty*, from which the material in this section is taken, appeared in 1859. From 1865 until 1868 he served as a Member of the British Parliament. (For additional biographical information, see Chapter 5, Section 4 and Chapter 6, Section 3.)

THE ARGUMENT OF THE PASSAGES.   Suppose you are appointed to a lawmaking group charged with the responsibility of providing legislative definition or redefinition of one of society's major institutions, say, marriage. How would you handle such an assignment? Along what lines would you propose legislative definitions for this institution? What do's and don't's connected with this institution would you make mandatory upon all who would participate in the institution, placing the full weight of the law back of these demands? A reader so circumstanced would be in a position to wield considerable power. As modern communities go, few persons have more power over others than those who devise or revise the laws. To an increasing degree, as legislators decide, the members of a community act or refrain from acting. Such power is not absolute, but it is great. To wield such power is to be responsible for much of what others do or refrain from doing.

A slight familiarity with the history of legislative social control shows that legislative power may be *misused* in either (or both) of two ways:

(1) It may be used to require people to do what is wrong. If a certain way of acting is wrong, and a law is passed requiring people to act in that way, then, to the degree that people are law-abiding, they are being required to do what is wrong. No conscientious legislator would want to be responsible for that state of affairs.

(2) It may be used to require people to do what should be left up to them to do or leave undone. Here the rightness or wrongness of the way of acting is not in question; the point is that it is a way of acting that law should say nothing about. An instance might be found in what is called "breach of promise," in the sense of

promise to marry. If a man engages to marry a woman, he should, as we say, "live up to his promise." But do we want the law to force him to do so? If a woman engages to marry a man, she should live up to her promise. But do we want the law to force her to do so? If we hesitate, or say no at this point, it is not that we regard such promises lightly, nor that we feel that it is right to break them; it is rather that we regard such matters as better left up to individuals to settle for themselves. Parents do right, often, in sending their children to college, but do we want a law requiring them to do so? A man does wrong if he deliberately destroys a masterpiece of painting he has bought and paid for, but do we want a law forbidding him to do so? A woman does wrong to be mean to her friends or miserly or wasteful with her money; but do we want a law forbidding her to be so? There are an indefinite number of ways in which a person of good will would act, but we would not want bad people forced by law to act in these ways. There are matters that we want people "left alone" about, left legally free to do them or not do them, regardless of what good people would do. In some matters we want people left legally free to do what is foolish; in some matters, to do what is wrong. In other words, we don't want the law to force people to do what is wrong; but we also don't want the law to prohibit them in all instances from doing what is wrong nor force them in all instances to do what is right.

These are reflections that might well occur to a person possessing the power to devise and revise a community's laws. In proportion as you possess the power to force people to act or refrain from acting in a certain way, you might well ask whether, in regard to a particular matter, you should use or refrain from using that power.

The selections in this section are taken from John Stuart Mill's *On Liberty*. In this book Mill was concerned to defend the right of the individual to think and act for him- or herself. This right meant a great deal to the author. He believed that societies and governments frequently intrude where they have no right to do so. He wrote his book to point out this fact and to protest against it. His book is Western society's finest handling of the theme. It became the testament of liberalism.

Mill begins by indicating that the problem of liberty throughout most of its history has arisen between individuals and nondemocratic governments, but that, in recent years, since the increase of democratic governments answerable to all or most of the adult population of their states, it is now between individuals and minorities, and democratically elected governments claiming to rule in the name of a political majority. This "majoritarianism," Mill insists, has done little or nothing to solve or dissolve the problem.

> The subject of this Essay is not the so-called Liberty of the Will, so unfortunately opposed to the misnamed doctrine of Philosophical Necessity; but Civil, or Social Liberty: the nature and limits of the power which can be legitimately exercised by society over the individual. A question seldom stated, and hardly ever discussed, in general terms, but which profoundly influences the practical controversies of the age by its latent presence, and is likely soon to make itself recognised as the vital question of the future. It is so far from being new, that, in a certain sense, it has divided mankind, almost from the remotest ages; but in the stage of progress into which the

more civilised portions of the species have now entered, it presents itself under new conditions, and requires a different and more fundamental treatment.

The struggle between Liberty and Authority is the most conspicuous feature in the portions of history with which we are earliest familiar, particularly in that of Greece, Rome, and England. But in old times this contest was between subjects, or some classes of subjects, and the Government. By liberty, was meant protection against the tyranny of the political rulers. The rulers were conceived (except in some of the popular governments of Greece) as in a necessarily antagonistic position to the people whom they ruled. They consisted of a governing One, or a governing tribe or caste, who derived their authority from inheritance or conquest, who, at all events, did not hold it at the pleasure of the governed, and whose supremacy men did not venture, perhaps did not desire, to contest, whatever precautions might be taken against its oppressive exercise. Their power was regarded as necessary, but also as highly dangerous; as a weapon which they would attempt to use against their subjects, no less than against external enemies. To prevent the weaker members of the community from being preyed upon by innumerable vultures, it was needful that there should be an animal of prey stronger than the rest, commissioned to keep them down. But as the king of the vultures would be no less bent upon preying on the flock than any of the minor harpies, it was indispensable to be in a perpetual attitude of defence against his beak and claws. The aim, therefore, of patriots was to set limits to the power which the ruler should be suffered to exercise over the community; and this limitation was what they meant by liberty. It was attempted in two ways. First, by obtaining a recognition of certain immunities, called political liberties or rights, which was to be regarded as a breach of duty in the ruler to infringe, and which if he did infringe, specific resistance, or general rebellion, was held to be justifiable. A second, and generally a later expedient, was the establishment of constitutional checks, by which the consent of the community, or a body of some sort, supposed to represent its interests, was made a necessary condition to some of the more important acts of the governing power. To the first of these modes of limitation, the ruling power, in most European countries, was compelled, more or less, to submit. It was not so with the second; and, to attain this, or when already in some degree possessed, to attain it more completely, became everywhere the principal object of the lovers of liberty. And so long as mankind were content to combat one enemy by another, and to be ruled by a master, on condition of being guaranteed more or less efficaciously against his tyranny, they did not carry their aspirations beyond this point.

A time, however, came, in the progress of human affairs, when men ceased to think it a necessity of nature that their governors should be an independent power, opposed in interest to themselves. It appeared to them much better that the various magistrates of the State should be their tenants or delegates, revocable at their pleasure. In that way alone, it seemed, could they have complete security that the powers of government would never be abused to their disadvantage. By degrees this new demand for elective and temporary rulers became the prominent object of the exertions of the popular party, wherever any such party existed; and superseded, to a considerable extent, the previous efforts to limit the power of rulers. As the struggle proceeded for making the ruling power emanate from the periodical choice of the ruled, some persons began to think that too much importance had been attached to the limitation of the power itself. *That* (it might seem) was a resource against rulers whose interests were habitually opposed to those of the people. What was now wanted was, that the rulers should be identified with the people; that their interest and will should be the interest and will of the nation. The nation did not need to be protected against its own will. There was no fear of its tyrannising over itself. Let the rulers be effectually responsible to it, promptly removable by it, and it could afford to trust them with power of which it could itself dictate the use to be made. Their power was but the nation's own power, concentrated, and in a form convenient for exercise. This mode of thought, or rather perhaps of feeling, was common among the last generation of European liberalism, in the continental section of which it still apparently predominates. Those who admit any limit to what a government may do, except in the case of such governments as they think ought not to exist, stand out as brilliant exceptions among the political thinkers of the continent. A similar tone of sentiment might by this time have been prevalent in our own country, if the circumstances which for a time encouraged it had continued unaltered.

But, in political and philosophical theories, as well as in persons, success discloses faults and infirmities which failure might have concealed from observation. The notion, that the people have no need to limit their power over themselves, might seem axiomatic, when popular government was a thing only dreamed about, or read of as having existed at some distant period of the past. Neither was that notion necessarily disturbed by such temporary aberrations as those of the French Revolution, the worst of which were the work of a usurping few, and which, in any case, belonged not to the permanent working of popular institutions, but to a sudden and convulsive outbreak against monarchical and aristocratic despotism. In time, however, a democratic republic came to occupy a large portion of the earth's surface, and made itself felt as one of the most powerful members of the community of nations; and elective and responsible government became subject to the observations and criticisms which wait upon a great existing fact. It was now perceived that such phrases as "self-government," and "the power of the people over themselves," do not express the true state of the case. The "people" who exercise the power are not always the same people with those over whom it is exercised; and the "self-government" spoken of is not the government of each by himself, but of each by all the rest. The will of the people, moreover, practically means the will of the most numerous or the most active *part* of the people; the majority, or those who succeed in making themselves accepted as the majority; the people, consequently *may* desire to oppress a part of their number; and precautions are as much needed against this as against any other abuse of power. The limitation, therefore, of the power of government over individuals loses none of its importance when the holders of power are regularly accountable to the community, that is, to the strongest party therein. This view of things, recommending itself equally to the intelligence of thinkers and to the inclination of those important classes in European society to whose real or supposed interests democracy is adverse, has had no difficulty in establishing itself; and in political speculations "the tyranny of the majority" is now generally included among the evils against which society requires to be on its guard.

Like other tyrannies, the tyranny of the majority was at first, and is still vulgarly, held in dread, chiefly as operating through the acts of the public authorities. But reflecting persons perceived that when society is itself the tyrant—society collectively over the separate individuals who compose it—its means of tyrannising are not restricted to the acts which it may do by the hands of its political functionaries. Society can and does execute its own mandates: and it issues wrong mandates instead of right, or any mandates at all in things with which it ought not to meddle, it practises a social tyranny more formidable than many kinds of political oppression, since, though not usually upheld by such extreme penalties, it leaves fewer means of escape, penetrating much more deeply into the details of life, and enslaving the soul itself. Protection, therefore, against the tyranny of the magistrate is not enough: there needs protection also against the tyranny of the prevailing opinion and feeling; against the tendency of society to impose, by other means that civil penalties, its own ideas and practices as rules of conduct on those who dissent from them; to fetter the development, and, if possible, prevent the formation of any individuality not in harmony with its ways, and compels all characters to fashion themselves upon the model of its own. There is a limit to the legitimate interference of collective opinion with individual independence: and to find that limit, and maintain it against encroachment, is as indispensable to a good condition of human affairs, as protection against political despotism.

But though this proposition is not likely to be contested in general terms, the practical question, where to place the limit—how to make the fitting adjustment between individual independence and social control—is a subject on which nearly everything remains to be done. All that makes existence valuable to any one, depends on the enforcement of restraints upon the actions of other people. Some rules of conduct, therefore, must be imposed, by law in the first place, and by opinion on many things which are not fit subjects for the operation of law. What these rules should be is the principal question in human affairs; but if we except a few of the most obvious cases, it is one of those which least progress has been made in resolving. No two ages, and scarcely any two countries, have decided it alike; and the decision of one age or country is a wonder to another. Yet the people of any given age and country no more suspect any difficulty in it, than if it were a subject on which mankind had always been agreed. The rules which obtain among themselves appear to them self-evident and self-justifying.

This all but universal illusion is one of the examples of the magical influence of custom, which is not only, as the proverb says, a second nature, but is continually mistaken for the first. The effect of custom, in preventing any misgiving respecting the rules of conduct which mankind impose on one another, is all the more complete because the subject is one on which it is not generally considered necessary that reasons should be given, either by one person to others or by each to himself. People are accustomed to believe, and have been encouraged in the belief by some who aspire to the character of philosophers, that their feelings, on subjects of this nature, are better than reasons, and render reasons unnecessary. The practical principle which guides them to their opinions on the regulation of human conduct, is the feeling in each person's mind that everybody should be required to act as he, and those with whom he sympathises, would like them to act. No one, indeed, acknowledges to himself that his standard of judgment is his own liking; but an opinion on a point of conduct, not supported by reasons, can only count as one person's preference; and if the reasons, when given, are a mere appeal to a similar preference felt by other people, it is still only many people's liking instead of one. To an ordinary man, however, his own preference, thus supported, is not only a perfectly satisfactory reason, but the only one he generally has for any of his notions of morality, taste or propriety, which are not expressly written in his religious creed; and his chief guide in the interpretation even of that. Men's opinions, accordingly, on what is laudable or blamable, are affected by all the multifarious causes which influence their wishes in regard to the conduct of others, and which are as numerous as those which determine their wishes on any other subject. Sometimes their reason—at other times their prejudices or superstitions: often their social affections, not seldom their anti-social ones, their envy or jealousy, their arrogance or contemptuousness: but most commonly their desires or fears for themselves—their legitimate or illegitimate self-interest.

Wherever there is an ascendant class, a large portion of the morality of the country emanates from its class interests, and its feelings of class superiority. The morality between Spartans and Helots, between planters and negroes, between princes and subjects, between nobles and roturiers, between men and women, has been for the most part the creation of these class interests and feelings: and the sentiments thus generated react in turn upon the moral feelings of the members of the ascendant class, in their relations among themselves. Where, on the other hand, a class, formerly ascendant, has lost its ascendancy, or where its ascendance is unpopular, the prevailing moral sentiments frequently bear the impress of an impatient dislike of superiority. Another grand determining principle of the rules of conduct, both in act and forbearance, which have been enforced by law or opinion, has been the servility of mankind towards the supposed preferences or aversions of their temporal masters or of their gods. This servility, though essentially selfish, is not hypocrisy; it gives rise to perfectly genuine sentiments of abhorrence; it made men burn magicians and heretics. Among so many baser influences, the general and obvious interests of society have of course had a share, and a large one, in the direction of the moral sentiments: less, however, as a matter of reason, and on their own account, than as a consequence of the sympathies and antipathies which grew out of them: and sympathies and antipathies which had little or nothing to do with the interests of society, have made themselves felt in the establishment of moralities with quite as great force.

The likings and dislikings of society, or of some powerful portion of it, are thus the main thing which has practically determined the rules laid down for general observance, under the penalties of law or opinion. And in general, those who have been in advance of society in thought and feeling, have left this condition of things unassailed in principle, however they may have come into conflict with it in some of its details. They have occupied themselves rather in inquiring what things society ought to like or dislike, than in questioning whether its likings or dislikings should be a law to individuals. They preferred endeavouring to alter the feelings of mankind on the particular points on which they were themselves heretical, rather than make common cause in defence of freedom, with heretics generally. The only case in which the higher ground has been taken on principle and maintained with consistency, by any but an individual here and there, is that of religious belief: a case instructive in many ways, and not least so as forming a most striking instance of the fallibility of what is called the moral sense: for the *odium theologicum*, in a sincere bigot, is one of the most unequivocal cases of moral feeling. Those who first broke the yoke of what called itself the Universal Church, were in general as little willing to permit difference of religious opinion as that church itself. But when the heat of the conflict was over, without giving a complete victory to any party, and each church or sect was reduced to limit its hopes to retaining possession of the ground it already occupied; minorities, seeing that they had no chance of becoming majorities, were under the necessity of pleading to those whom they could not convert, for permission to differ. It is accordingly on this battle field almost solely, that the rights of the individual against society have been asserted on broad grounds of principle, and the claim of society to exercise authority over dissentients openly controverted. The great writers to whom the world owes what religious liberty it possesses, have mostly asserted freedom of conscience as an indefeasible right, and denied absolutely that a human being is accountable to others for his religious belief. Yet so natural to mankind is intolerance in what-ever they really care about, that religious freedom has hardly anywhere been practi-cally realised, except where religious indifference, which dislikes to have its peace disturbed by theological quarrels, has added its weight to the scale. In the minds of almost all religious persons, even in the most tolerant countries, the duty of toleration is admitted with tacit reserves. One person will bear with dissent in matters of church government, but not of dogma; another can tolerate everybody, short of a Papist or a Unitarian; another every one who believes in revealed religion; a few extend their charity a little further, but stop at the belief in a God and in a future state. Wherever the sentiment of the majority is still genuine and intense, it is found to have abated little of its claim to be obeyed.

In England, from the peculiar circumstances of our political history, though the yoke of opinion is perhaps heavier, that of law is lighter, than in most other countries of Europe; and there is considerable jealousy of direct interference, by the legislative or the executive power, with private conduct; not so much from any just regard for the independence of the individual, as from the still subsisting habit of looking on the government as representing an opposite interest to the public. The majority have not yet learnt to feel the power of the government their power, or its opinions their opin-ions. When they do so, individual liberty will probably be as much exposed to inva-sion from the government, as it already is from public opinion. But, as yet, there is a considerable amount of feeling ready to be called forth against any attempt of the law to control individuals in things in which they have not hitherto been accustomed to be controlled by it; and this with very little discrimination as to whether the matter is, or is not, within the legitimate sphere of legal control; insomuch that the feeling, highly salutary on the whole, is perhaps quite as often misplaced as well grounded in the particular instances of its application. There is, in fact, no recognised principle by which the propriety or impropriety of government interference is customarily tested. People decide according to their personal preferences. Some, whenever they see any good to be done, or evil to be remedied, would willingly instigate the government to undertake the business; while others prefer to bear almost any amount of social evil, rather than add one to the departments of human interests amenable to government control. And men range themselves on one or the other side in any particular case, according to this general direction of their sentiments; or according to the degree of interest which they feel in the particular thing which it is proposed that the govern-ment should do, or according to the belief they entertain that the government would, or would not, do it in the manner they prefer; but very rarely on account of any opin-ion to which they consistently adhere, as to what things are fit to be done by a gov-ernment. And it seems to me that in consequence of this absence of rule or principle, one side is at present as often wrong as the other; the interference of government is, with about equal frequency, improperly invoked and improperly condemned.

Next, Mill examines the issue of what principle should be used by societies and their governments in regulating the behaviors of individuals and minority groups.

The object of this Essay is to assert one very simple principle, as entitled to gov-ern absolutely the dealings of society with the individual in the way of compulsion and control, whether the means used be physical force in the form of legal penalties, or the moral coercion of public opinion. That principle is, that the sole end for which mankind are warranted, individually or collectively, in interfering with the liberty of action of any of their number, is self-protection. That the only purpose for which power can be rightfully exercised over any member of a civilised community, against his will, is to prevent harm to others. His own good, either physical or moral, is not a sufficient warrant. He cannot rightfully be compelled to do or forbear because it will be better for him to do so, because it will make him happier, because, in the opinions of others, to do so would be wise, or even right. These are good reasons for remonstrating with him, or reasoning with him, or persuading him, or entreating him, but not for compelling him, or visiting him with any evil in case he do otherwise. To justify that, the conduct from which it is desired to deter him must be calculated to produce evil to some one else. The only part of the conduct of any one, for which he is amenable to society, is that which concerns others. In the part which merely concerns himself, his independence is, of right, absolute. Over himself, over his own body and mind, the individual is sovereign.

It is, perhaps, hardly necessary to say that this doctrine is meant to apply only to human beings in the maturity of their faculties. We are not speaking of children, or of young persons below the age which the law may fix as that of manhood or womanhood. Those who are still in a state to require being taken care of by others, must be protected against their own actions as well as against external injury. For the same reason, we may leave out of consideration those backward states of society in which the race itself may be considered as in its nonage. The early difficulties in the way of spontaneous progress are so great, that there is seldom any choice of means for overcoming them; and a ruler full of the spirit of improvement is warranted in the use of any expedients that will attain an end, perhaps otherwise unattainable. Despotism is a legitimate mode of government in dealing with barbarians, provided the end be their improvement, and the means justified by actually affecting that end. Liberty, as a principle, has no application to any state of things anterior to the time when mankind have become capable of being improved by free and equal discussion. Until then, there is nothing for them but implicit obedience to an Akbar or a Charlemagne, if they are so fortunate as to find one. But as soon as mankind have attained the capacity of being guided to their own improvement by conviction or persuasion (a period long since reached in all nations with whom we need here concern ourselves), compulsion, either in the direct form or in that of pains and penalties for non-compliance, is no longer admissible as a means to their own good, and justifiable only for the security of others.

It is proper to state that I forego any advantage which could be derived to my argument from the idea of abstract right, as a thing independent of utility. I regard utility as the ultimate appeal on all ethical questions, but it must be utility in the largest sense, grounded on the permanent interests of a man as a progressive being. Those interests, I contend, authorise the subjection of individual spontaneity to external control, only in respect to those actions of each, which concern the interests of other people. If any one does an act hurtful to others, there is a *prima facie* case for punishing him, by law, or, where legal penalties are not safely applicable, by general disapprobation. There are also many positive acts for the benefit of others, which he may rightfully be compelled to perform; such as to give evidence in a court of justice; to bear his fair share in the common defence, or in any other joint work necessary to the interest of the society of which he enjoys the protection; and to perform certain acts of individual beneficence, such as saving a fellow creature's life, or interposing to protect the defenceless against ill-usage, things which whenever it is obviously a man's duty to do so, he may rightfully be made responsible to society for not doing. A person may cause evil to others not only by his actions but by his inaction, and in either case he is justly accountable to them for the injury. The latter case, it is true, requires a much more cautious exercise of compulsion than the former. To make any one answerable for doing evil to others is the rule; to make him answerable for not preventing evil is, comparatively speaking, the exception. Yet there are many cases clear enough and grave enough to justify that exception. In all things which regard the external relations of the individual, he is *de jure* amenable to those whose interests are concerned, and, if need be, to society as their protector. There are often good reasons for not holding him to the responsibility; but these reasons must arise from the special expediencies of the case; either because it is a kind of case in which he is on the whole likely to act better, when left to his own discretion, than when controlled in any way in which society have it in their power to control him; or because the attempt to exercise control would produce other evils, greater than those which it would prevent. When such reasons as these preclude the enforcement of responsibility, the conscience of the agent himself should step into the vacant judgment seat, and protect those interests of others which have no external protection; judging himself all the more rigidly, because the case does not admit of his being made accountable to the judgment of his fellow creatures.

But there is a sphere of action in which society, as distinguished from the individual, has, if any, only an indirect interest; comprehending all that portion of a person's life and conduct which affects only himself, or if it also affects others, only with their free, voluntary, and undeceived consent and participation. When I say only himself, I mean directly, and in the first instance; for whatever affects himself, may affect others through himself; and the objection which may be grounded on this contingency, will receive consideration in the sequel. This, then, is the appropriate region of human liberty. It comprises, first, the inward domain of consciousness; demanding liberty of conscience in the most comprehensive sense; liberty of thought and feeling; absolute freedom of opinion and sentiment on all subjects, practical or speculative, scientific, moral, or theological. The liberty of expressing and publishing opinions may seem to fall under a different principle, since it belongs to that part of the conduct of an individual which concerns other people; but, being almost of as much importance as the liberty of thought itself, and resting in great part on the same reasons, is practically inseparable from it. Secondly, the principle requires liberty of tastes and pursuits; of framing the plan of our life to suit our own character; of doing as we like, subject to such consequences as may follow: without impediment from our fellow creatures, so long as what we do does not harm them, even though they should think our conduct foolish, perverse, or wrong. Thirdly, from this liberty of each individual, follows the liberty, within the same limits, of combination among individuals; freedom to unite, for any purpose not involving harm to others: the persons combining being supposed to be of full age, and not forced or deceived.

No society in which these liberties are not, on the whole, respected, is free, whatever may be its form of government; and none is completely free in which they do not exist absolute and unqualified. The only freedom which deserves the name, is that of pursuing our own good in our own way, so long as we do not attempt to deprive others of theirs, or impede their efforts to obtain it. Each is the proper guardian of his own health, whether bodily, *or* mental and spiritual. Mankind are greater gainers by suffering each other to live as seems good to themselves, than by compelling each to live as seems good to the rest.

Though this doctrine is anything but new, and, to some persons, may have the air of a truism, there is no doctrine which stands more directly opposed to the general tendency of existing opinion and practice. Society has expended fully as much effort in the attempt (according to its lights) to compel people to conform to its notions of personal as of social excellence. The ancient commonwealths thought themselves entitled to practise, and the ancient philosophers countenanced, the regulation of every part of private conduct by public authority, on the ground that the State had a deep interest in the whole bodily and mental discipline of every one of its citizens; a mode of thinking which may have been admissible in small republics surrounded by powerful enemies, in constant peril of being subverted by foreign attack or internal commotion, and to which even a short interval of relaxed energy and self-command might so easily be fatal that they could not afford to wait for the salutary permanent effects of freedom. In the modern world, the greater size of political communities, and, above all, the separation between spiritual and temporal authority (which placed the direction of men's consciences in other hands than those which controlled their worldly affairs), prevented so great an interference by law in the details of private life; but the engines of moral repression have been wielded more strenuously against divergence from the reigning opinion in self-regarding, than even in social matters; religion, the most powerful of the elements which have entered into the formation of moral feeling, having almost always been governed either by the ambition of a hierarchy, seeking control over every department of human conduct, or by the spirit of Puritanism. And some of those modern reformers who have placed themselves in strongest opposition to the religions of the past, have been no-way behind either churches or sects in their assertion of the right of spiritual domination: M. Comte, in particular, whose social system, as unfolded in his *Système de Politique Positive*, aims at establishing (though by moral more than by legal appliances) a despotism of society over the individual, surpassing anything contemplated in the political ideal of the most rigid disciplinarian among the ancient philosophers.

Apart from the peculiar tenets of individual thinkers, there is also in the world at large an increasing inclination to stretch unduly the powers of society over the individual, both by the force of opinion and even by that of legislation; and as the tendency of all the changes taking place in the world is to strengthen society, and diminish the power of the individual, this encroachment is not one of the evils which tend spontaneously to disappear, but, on the contrary, to grow more and more formidable. The disposition of mankind, whether as rulers or as fellow-citizens, to impose their own opinions and inclinations as a rule of conduct on others, is so energetically supported by some of the best and by some of the worst feelings incident to human nature, that it is hardly ever kept under restraint by anything but want of power; and as the power is not declining, but growing, unless a strong barrier of moral conviction can be raised against the mischief, we must expect, in the present circumstances of the world, to see it increase.

It will be convenient for the argument, if, instead of at once entering upon the general thesis, we confine ourselves in the first instance to a single branch of it, on which the principle here stated is, if not fully, yet to a certain point, recognised by the current opinions. This one branch is the Liberty of Thought: from which it is impossible to separate the cognate liberty of speaking and of writing. Although these liberties, to some considerable amount, form part of the political morality of all countries which profess religious toleration and free institutions, the grounds, both philosophical and practical, on which they rest, are perhaps not so familiar to the general mind, nor so thoroughly appreciated by many even of the leaders of opinion, as might have been expected. Those grounds, when rightly understood, are of much wider application than to only one division of the subject, and a thorough consideration of this part of the question will be found the best introduction to the remainder. Those to whom nothing which I am about to say will be new, may therefore, I hope, excuse me, if on a subject which for now three centuries has been so often discussed, I venture on one discussion more.

Mill's overall subject is the right of the individual to think and act for himself or herself. For Mill this does not mean the right to think and act as you please. Mill's individualism was never pushed to anarchism. The appropriate word is *liberalism:* the right to give the best thought of which you are capable to any matter that challenges you to think about it, and then to act as wisely as you can on the conclusion you arrive at, realizing that the right to act for oneself is not an unqualified right inasmuch as society or its government may legitimately intervene coercively. Mill defends the right to think for oneself. His defense here is unqualified. This liberty he regards as an unconditional right. Mill's discussion is one of humanity's great defenses of this right.

The time, it is to be hoped, is gone by, when any defence would be necessary of the "liberty of the press" as one of the securities against corrupt or tyrannical government. No argument, we may suppose, can now be needed, against permitting a legislature or an executive, not identified in interest with the people, to prescribe opinions to them, and determine what doctrines or what arguments they shall be allowed to hear. This aspect of the question, besides, has been so often and so triumphantly enforced by preceding writers, that it needs not be specially insisted on in this place. Though the law of England, on the subject of the press, is as servile to this day as it was in the time of the Tudors, there is little danger of its being actually put in force against political discussion, except during some temporary panic, when fear of insurrection drives ministers and judges from their propriety;[1] and, speaking generally, it is not, in consti-

---

[1]   These words had scarcely been written, when, as if to give them an emphatic contradiction, occurred the Government Press Prosecutions of 1858. That ill-judged interference with the liberty of public discussion has not, however, induced me to alter a single word in the text, nor has it at all weakened my conviction that, moments of panic excepted, the era of pains and penalties for political discussion has, in our own country, passed away. For, in the first place, the prosecutions were not persisted in; and, in the second, they were never, properly speaking, political prosecutions. The offence charged was not that of criticising institutions, or the acts or persons of rulers, but of circulating what was deemed an immoral doctrine, the lawfulness of Tyrannicide.

      If the arguments of the present chapter are of any validity, there ought to exist the fullest liberty of professing and discussing, as a matter of ethical conviction, any doctrine, however immoral it may be considered. It would, therefore, be irrelevant and out of place to examine here whether the doctrine of Tyrannicide deserves that title. I shall content myself with saying that the subject has been at all times one of the open questions of morals; that the act of a private citizen in striking down a criminal, who, by raising himself above the law, has placed himself beyond the reach of legal punishment or control, has been accounted by whole nations, and by some of the best and wisest of men, not a crime, but an act of exalted virtue; and that, right or wrong, it is not of the nature of assassination, but of civil war. As such, I hold that the instigation to it, in a specific case, may be a proper subject of punishment, but only if an overt act has followed, and at least a probable connection can be established between the act and the instigation. Even then, it is not a foreign government, but the very government assailed, which alone, in the exercise of self-defence, can legitimately punish attacks directed against its own existence.

tutional countries, to be apprehended, that the government, whether completely responsible to the people or not, will often attempt to control the expression of opinion, except when in doing so it makes itself the organ of the general intolerance of the public. Let us suppose, therefore, that the government is entirely at one with the people, and never thinks of exerting any power of coercion unless in agreement with what it conceives to be their voice. But I deny the right of the people to exercise such coercion, either by themselves or by their government. The power itself is illegitimate. The best government has no more title to it than the worst. It is as noxious, or more noxious, when exerted in accordance with public opinion, than when in opposition to it. If all mankind minus one were of one opinion, and only one person were of the contrary opinion, mankind would be no more justified in silencing that one person, than he, if he had the power, would be justified in silencing mankind. Were an opinion a personal possession of no value except to the owner; if to be obstructed in the enjoyment of it were simply a private injury, it would make some difference whether the injury was inflicted only on a few persons or on many. But the peculiar evil of silencing the expression of an opinion is, that it is robbing the human race; posterity as well as the existing generation; those who dissent from the opinion, still more than those who hold it. If the opinion is right, they are deprived of the opportunity of exchanging error for truth: if wrong, they lose, what is almost as great a benefit, the clearer perception and livelier impression of truth, produced by its collision with error.

It is necessary to consider separately these two hypotheses, each of which has a distinct branch of the argument corresponding to it. We can never be sure that the opinion we are endeavouring to stifle is a false opinion; and if we were sure, stifling it would be an evil still.

First: the opinion which it is attempted to suppress by authority may possibly be true. Those who desire to suppress it, of course deny its truth; but they are not infallible. They have no authority to decide the question for all mankind, and exclude every other person from the means of judging. To refuse a hearing to an opinion, because they are sure that it is false, is to assume that *their* certainty is the same thing as *absolute* certainty. All silencing of discussion is an assumption of infallibility. Its condemnation may be allowed to rest on this common argument, not the worse for being common. . . .

Mill now moves against those who would refuse to permit free discussion in the case of a false belief. Only two paragraphs are here quoted. Many pages of closely argued test cases are omitted. Thus:

Let us now pass to the *second* division of the argument, and dismissing the supposition that any of the received opinions may be false, let us assume them to be true and examine into the worth of the manner in which they are likely to be held when their truth is not freely and openly canvassed. However unwillingly a person who has a strong opinion may admit the possibility that his opinion may be false, he ought to be moved by the consideration that, however true it may be, if it is not fully, frequently, and fearlessly discussed, it will be held as a dead dogma, not a living truth.

There is a class of persons (happily not quite so numerous as formerly) who think it enough if a person assents undoubtingly to what they think true, though he has no knowledge whatever of the grounds of the opinion and could not make a tenable defense of it against the most superficial objections. Such persons, if they can once get their creed taught from authority, naturally think that no good, and some harm, comes of its being allowed to be questioned. Where their influence prevails, they make it nearly impossible for the received opinion to be rejected wisely and considerately, though it may still be rejected rashly and ignorantly; for to shut out discussion entirely is seldom possible, and when it once gets in, beliefs not grounded on conviction are apt to give way before the slightest semblance of an argument. Waiving, however, this possibility—assuming that the true opinion abides in the mind, but abides as a prejudice, a belief independent of, and proof against, argument—this is not the way in which truth ought to be held by a rational being. This is not knowing the truth. Truth, thus held, is but one superstition the more, accidentally clinging to the words which enunciate a truth. . . .

Next, after a brief resume, he moves against those who would permit free discussion on condition that the manner be temperate and not pass the grounds of fair discussion. Mill rejects their proposed qualification. Thus:

> We have now recognised the necessity to the mental well-being of mankind (on which all their other well-being depends) of freedom of opinion, and freedom of the expression of opinion, on four distinct grounds; which we will now briefly recapitulate.
>
> First, if any opinion is compelled to silence, that opinion may, for aught we can certainly know, be true. To deny this is to assume our own infallibility.
>
> Secondly, though the silenced opinion be an error, it may, and very commonly does, contain a portion of truth; and since the general or prevailing opinion on any subject is rarely or never the whole truth, it is only by the collision of adverse opinions that the remainder of the truth has any chance of being supplied.
>
> Thirdly, even if the received opinion be not only true, but the whole truth; unless it is suffered to be, and actually is, vigorously and earnestly contested, it will, by most of those who receive it, be held in the manner of a prejudice, with little comprehension or feeling of its rational grounds. And not only this, but, fourthly, the meaning of the doctrine itself will be in danger of being lost, or enfeebled, and deprived of its vital effect on the character and conduct: the dogma becoming a mere formal profession, inefficacious for good, but cumbering the ground, and preventing the growth of any real and heartfelt conviction, from reason or personal experience.
>
> Before quitting the subject of freedom of opinion, it is fit to take some notice of those who say that the free expression of all opinions should be permitted, on condition that the manner be temperate, and do not pass the bounds of fair discussion. Much might be said on the impossibility of fixing where these supposed bounds are to be placed; for if the test be offence to those whose opinions are attacked, I think experience testifies that this offence is given whenever the attack is telling and powerful, and that every opponent who pushes them hard, and whom they find it difficult to answer, appears to them, if he shows any strong feeling on the subject, an intemperate opponent.
>
> But this, though an important consideration in a practical point of view, merges in a more fundamental objection. Undoubtedly the manner of asserting an opinion, even though it be a true one, may be very objectionable, and may justly incur severe censure. But the principal offences of the kind are such as it is mostly impossible, unless by accidental self-betrayal, to bring home to conviction. The gravest of them is, to argue sophistically, to suppress facts or arguments, to misstate the elements of the case, or misrepresent the opposite opinion. But all this, even to the most aggravated degree, is so continually done in perfect good faith, by persons who are not considered, and in

many other respects may not deserve to be considered, ignorant or incompetent, that it is rarely possible, on adequate grounds, conscientiously to stamp the misrepresentation as morally culpable; and still less could law presume to interfere with this kind of controversial misconduct. With regard to what is commonly meant by intemperate discussion, namely invective, sarcasm, personality, and the like, the denunciation of these weapons would deserve more sympathy if it were ever proposed to interdict them equally to both sides; but it is only desired to restrain the employment of them against the prevailing opinion: against the unprevailing they may not only be used without general disapproval, but will be likely to obtain him for who uses them the praise of honest zeal and righteous indignation. Yet whatever mischief arises from their use is greatest when they are employed against the comparatively defenceless; and whatever unfair advantage can be derived by any opinion from this mode of asserting it, accrues almost exclusively to received opinions. The worse offence of this kind which can be committed by a polemic is to stigmatise those who hold the contrary opinion as bad and immoral men. To calumny of this sort, those who hold any unpopular opinion are peculiarly exposed, because they are in general few and uninfluential, and nobody but themselves feels much interested in seeing justice done them; but this weapon is, from the nature of the case, denied to those who attack a prevailing opinion; they can neither use it with safety to themselves, nor, if they could, would it do anything but recoil on their own cause. In general, opinions contrary to those commonly received can only obtain a hearing by studied moderation of language, and the most cautious avoidance of unnecessary offence, from which they hardly ever deviate even in a slight degree without losing ground: while unmeasured vituperation employed on the side of the prevailing opinion really does deter people from professing contrary opinions, and from listening to those who profess them.

For the interest, therefore, of truth and justice, it is far more important to restrain this employment of vituperative language than the other; and, for example, if it were necessary to choose, there would be much more need to discourage offensive attacks on infidelity than on religion. It is, however, obvious that law and authority have no business with restraining either, while opinion ought, in every instance, to determine its verdict by the circumstances of the individual case; condemning every one, on whichever side of the argument he places himself, in whose mode of advocacy either want of candour, or malignity, bigotry, or intolerance of feeling manifest themselves; but not inferring these vices from the side which a person takes, though it be the contrary side of the question to our own; and giving merited honour to every one, whatever opinion he may hold, who has calmness to see and honesty to state what his opponents and their opinions really are, exaggerating nothing to their discredit, keeping nothing back which tells, or can be supposed to tell, in their favour. This is the real morality of public discussion: and if often violated, I am happy to think that there are many controversialists who to a great extent observe it, and a still greater number who conscientiously strive towards it.

Mill now develops the argument that liberty is a condition for individuality ("being your own person"), and that individuality is a condition for well-being.

Such being the reasons which make it imperative that human beings should be free to form opinions, and to express their opinions without reserve; and such the baneful consequences to the intellectual, and through that to the moral nature of man, unless this liberty is either conceded, or asserted in spite of prohibition; let us next examine whether the same reasons do not require that men should be free to act upon their opinions—to carry these out in their lives, without hindrance, either physical or moral, from their fellow-men, so long as it is at their own risk and peril.

This last proviso is of course indispensable. No one pretends that actions should be as free as opinions. On the contrary, even opinions lose their immunity when the circumstances in which they are expressed are such as to constitute their expression a positive instigation to some mischievous act. An opinion that corn-dealers are starvers of the poor, or that private property is robbery, ought to be unmolested when simply circulated through the press, but may justly incur punishment when delivered orally to an excited mob assembled before the house of a corndealer, or when handed about among the same mob in the form of a placard. Acts, of whatever kind, which, without justifiable cause, do harm to others, may be, and in the more important cases absolutely require to be, controlled by the unfavourable sentiments, and, when needful, by the active interference of mankind. The liberty of the individual must be thus far limited; he must not make himself a nuisance to other people. But if he refrains from molesting others in what concerns them, and merely acts according to his own inclination and judgment in things which concern himself, the same reasons which show that opinion should be free, prove also that he should be allowed, without molestation, to carry his opinions into practice at his own cost. That mankind are not infallible; that their truths, for the most part, are only half-truths; that unity of opinion, unless resulting from the fullest and freest comparison of opposite opinions, is not desirable, and diversity not an evil, but a good, until mankind are much more capable than at present of recognising all sides of the truth, are principles applicable to men's modes of action, not less than to their opinions. As it is useful that while mankind are imperfect there should be different opinions, so it is that there should be different experiments of living; that free scope should be given to varieties of character, short of injury to others; and that the worth of different modes of life should be proved practically, when any one thinks fit to try them. It is desirable, in short, that in things which do not primarily concern others, individuality should assert itself. Where, not the person's own character, but the traditions or customs of other people are the rule of conduct, there is wanting one of the principal ingredients of human happiness, and quite the chief ingredient of individual and social progress.

In maintaining this principle, the greatest difficulty to be encountered does not lie in the appreciation of means towards an acknowledged end, but in the indifference of persons in general to the end itself. If it were felt that the free development of individuality is one of the leading essentials of well-being; that it is not a co-ordinate element with all that is designated by the terms civilization, instruction, education, culture, but is itself a necessary part and condition of all those things; there would be no danger that liberty should be under-valued, and the adjustment of the boundaries between it and social control would present no extraordinary difficulty. But the evil is, that individual spontaneity is hardly recognized by the common modes of thinking, as having any intrinsic worth, or deserving any regard on its own account. The majority, being satisfied with the ways of mankind as they now are (for it is they who make them what they are), cannot comprehend why those ways should not be good enough for everybody; and what is more, spontaneity forms no part of the ideal of the majority of moral and social reformers, but is rather looked on with jealousy, as a troublesome and perhaps rebellious obstruction to the general acceptance of what these reformers, in their own judgment, think would be best for mankind.

Granted that the thesis of the preceding citation does not entitle an individual to an *unqualified* right to act for himself or herself, without coercive intervention from society or its government; there is still the important question of what is the rightful limit of an individual to act for himself or herself. How is this limit to be defined *in principle?* This turns out to be a large and thorny question.

What, then, is the rightful limit to the sovereignty of the individual over himself? Where does the authority of society begin? How much of human life should be assigned to individuality, and how much to society?

Each will receive its proper share, if each has that which more particularly concerns it. To individuality should belong the part of life in which it is chiefly the individual that is interested; to society, the part which chiefly interests society.

Though society is not founded on a contract, and though no good purpose is answered by inventing a contract in order to deduce social obligations from it, every one who receives the protection of society owes a return for the benefit, and the fact of living in society renders it indispensable that each should be bound to observe a certain line of conduct towards the rest. This conduct consists, first, in not injuring the interests of one another; or rather certain interests, which, either by express legal provision or by tacit understanding, ought to be considered as rights; and secondly, in each person's bearing his share (to be fixed on some equitable principle) of the labours and sacrifices incurred for defending the society or its members from injury and molestation. These conditions society is justified in enforcing, at all costs to those who endeavour to withhold fulfillment. Nor is this all that society may do. The acts of an individual may be hurtful to others, or wanting in due consideration for their welfare, without going to the length of violating any of their constituted rights. The offender may then be justly punished by opinion, though not by law. As soon as any part of a person's conduct affects prejudicially the interests of others, society has jurisdiction over it, and the question whether the general welfare will or will not be promoted by interfering with it, becomes open to discussion. But there is no room for entertaining any such question when a person's conduct affects the interests of no persons besides himself, or needs not affect them unless they like (all the persons concerned being of full age, and the ordinary amount of understanding). In all such cases, there should be perfect freedom, legal and social, to do the action and stand the consequences. . . .

The two maxims which together form the entire doctrine of the Essay . . . are, *first,* that the individual is not accountable to society for his actions, in so far as these concern the interests of no person but himself. Advice, instruction, persuasion, and avoidance by other people if thought necessary by them for their own good, are the only measures by which society can justifiably express its dislike or disapprobation of his conduct. *Secondly,* that for such actions as are prejudicial to the interests of others, the individual is accountable, and may be subjected either to social or to legal punishment, if society is of opinion that the one or the other is requisite for its protection. . . .

The remaining five paragraphs are quoted from near the end of Mill's book. As he says, they introduce something of a new question, or a new qualification of his present question. What about government interference where the liberty principle is not involved?

I have reserved for the last place a large class of questions respecting the limits of government interference, which, though closely connected with the subject of this essay, do not, in strictness, belong to it. These are cases in which the reasons against interference do not turn upon the principle of liberty: the question is not about restraining the actions of individuals, but about helping them; it is asked whether the government should do, or cause to be done, something for their benefit instead of leaving it to be done by themselves, individually or in voluntary combination.

The objections to government interference, when it is not such as to involve infringement of liberty, may be of three kinds:

The first is when the thing to be done is likely to be better done by individuals than by the government. Speaking generally, there is no one so fit to conduct any business, or to determine how or by whom it shall be conducted, as those who are personally interested in it. This principle condemns the interferences, once so common, of the legislature, or the officers of government, with the ordinary process of industry. But this part of the subject has been sufficiently enlarged upon by political economists, and is not particularly related to the principles of this essay.

The second objection is more nearly allied to our subject. In many cases, though individuals may not do the particular thing so well, on the average, as the officers of government, it is nevertheless desirable that it should be done by them, rather than by the government, as a means to their own mental education—a mode of strengthening their active faculties, exercising their judgment, and giving them a familiar knowledge of the subjects with which they are thus left to deal. This is a principal, though not the sole, recommendation of jury trial (in cases not political) of free and popular local and municipal institutions; of the conduct of industrial and philanthropic enterprises by voluntary associations. These are not questions of liberty, and are connected with that subject only by remote tendencies, but they are questions of development. It belongs to a different occasion from the present to dwell on these things as parts of national education, as being, in truth, the peculiar training of a citizen, the practical part of the political education of a free people, taking them out of the narrow circle of personal and family selfishness, and accustoming them to the comprehension of joint interests, the management of joint concerns—habituating them to act from public or semi-public motives, and guide their conduct by aims which unite instead of isolating them from one another. Without these habits and powers, a free constitution can neither be worked nor preserved, as is exemplified by the too-often transitory nature of political freedom in countries where it does not rest upon a sufficient basis of local liberties. The management of purely local business by the localities, and of the great enterprises of industry by the union of those who voluntarily supply the pecuniary means, is further recommended by all the advantages which have been set forth in this essay as belonging to individuality of development and diversity of modes of action. Government operations tend to be everywhere alike. With individuals and voluntary associations, on the contrary, there are varied experiments and endless diversity of experience. What the State can usefully do is to make itself a central depository, and active circulator and diffuser, of the experience resulting from many trials. Its business is to enable each experimentalist to benefit by the experiments of others, instead of tolerating no experiments but its own.

The third and most cogent reason for restricting the interference of government is the great evil of adding unnecessarily to its power. Every function superadded to those already exercised by the government causes its influence over hopes and fears to be more widely diffused, and converts, more and more, the active and ambitious part of the public into hangers-on of the government, or of some party which aims at becoming the government. If the roads, the railways, the banks, the insurance offices, the great joint-stock companies, the universities, and the public charities were all of them branches of the government; if, in addition, the municipal corporations and local boards, with all that now devolves on them, became departments of the central administration; if the employees of all these different enterprises were appointed and paid by the government and looked to the government for every rise in life, not all the freedom of the press and popular constitution of the legislature would make this or any other country free otherwise than in name. And the evil would be greater, the more efficiently and scientifically the administrative machinery was constructed—the more skillful the arrangements for obtaining the best qualified hands and heads with which to work it.

NOTE ON SOURCES.   The material in this section is quoted from John Stuart Mill, *On Liberty*, Chapters I, II, III, IV, and V.

6   MARTIN LUTHER KING

THE CASE FOR CIVIL DISOBEDIENCE

FROM MILL TO KING.   Our last author is Martin Luther King, whose *Letter from Birmingham Jail* was written and published in 1963. King's *Letter* should be read with Hobbes and Mill and Marx and Burke and Rousseau in mind: Hobbes in 1651, Rousseau in 1762, Burke in 1790, Marx in 1848, and Mill in 1859. King's *Letter* was written in response to a public statement directed to him by eight Alabama clergymen, April 12, 1963. That statement reads as follows:

> We clergymen are among those who, in January, issued "An Appeal for Law and Order and Common Sense," in dealing with racial problems in Alabama. We expressed understanding that honest convictions in racial matters could property be pursued in the courts, but urged that decisions of those courts should in the meantime be peacefully obeyed.
>
> Since that time there has been some evidence of increased forbearance and a willingness to face facts. Responsible citizens have undertaken to work on various problems which cause racial friction and unrest. In Birmingham, recent public events have given indication that we all have opportunity for a new constructive and realistic approach to racial problems.
>
> However, we are now confronted by a series of demonstrations by some of our Negro citizens, directed and led in part by outsiders. We recognize the natural impatience of people who feel that their hopes are slow in being realized. But we are convinced that these demonstrations are unwise and untimely.
>
> We agree rather with certain local Negro leadership which has called for honest and open negotiation of racial issues in our area. And we believe this kind of facing of issues can be best accomplished by citizens of our own metropolitan area, white and negro, meeting with the knowledge and experience of the local situation. All of us need to face that responsibility and find proper channels for its accomplishment.
>
> Just as we formerly pointed out that "hatred and violence have no sanction in our religious and political traditions," we also point out that such actions as incite to hatred and violence, however technically peaceful those actions may be, have not contributed to the resolution of our local problems. We do not believe that these days of new hope are days when extreme measures are justified in Birmingham.

We commend the community as a whole, and the local news media and law enforcement officials in particular, on the calm manner in which these demonstrations have been handled. We urge the public to continue to show restraint should the demonstrations continue, and the law enforcement officials to remain calm and continue to protect our city from violence.

We further strongly urge our own Negro community to withdraw support from these demonstrations, and to unite locally in working peacefully for a better Birmingham. When rights are consistently denied, a cause should be pressed in the courts and in negotiations among local leaders, and not in the streets. We appeal to both our white and Negro citizenry to observe the principles of law and order and common sense.

With the eight clergymen's statement in mind, we could turn directly to the text of King's reply, but there is a figure waiting in the wings whom we would do well to remind ourselves of before giving our attention to King's *Letter from Birmingham Jail.* That figure is Henry David Thoreau, who had published an eloquent essay in 1849, "On the Duty of Civil Disobedience." Thoreau was not a Marxist. His 1849 plea for civil disobedience did not rest on premises set forth the year before in Marx's 1848 *Communist Manifesto.* He had refused to pay a state tax as a protest against slavery and against the war going on in Mexico. He had been jailed. It is said that his friend Ralph Waldo Emerson had looked in through the jail window and demanded: "Henry, what are you doing in there?"; and that Thoreau had replied, "The question is, what are you doing out there?" That is the question to which he was led by reflecting on his own refusal to conform to the law. The citizens of Massachusetts, organized into a state under a government, demanded that he pay taxes. He refused on the grounds that his taxes would be used to help support measures and enforce laws that it would be wrong for him to countenance. This was civil disobedience, refusal to obey a law that violates a principle that is *higher* than any man-made law, a principle with reference to which laws themselves were to be judged, and either justified or condemned. His stand here is reminiscent of Antigone in Sophocles's play. The following seventeen paragraphs are quoted, abridged, or paraphrased from the full text of Thoreau's essay on civil disobedience:

I heartily accept the motto,—"That government is best which governs least"; and I should like to see it acted up to more readily and systematically. Carried out, it finally amounts to this, which also I believe,—"That government is best which governs not at all"; and when men are prepared for it, that will be the kind of government which they will have. Government is at best but an expedient; but most governments are usually, and all governments are sometimes, inexpedient. The objections which have been brought against a standing army, and they are many and weighty, and deserve to prevail, may also at last be brought against a standing government. The standing army is only an arm of the standing government. The government itself, which is only the mode which the people have chosen to execute their will, is equally liable to be abused and perverted before the people can act through it. Witness the present Mexican war, the work of comparatively a few individuals using the standing government as their tool; for, in the outset, the people would not have consented to this measure.

But, to speak practically and as a citizen, unlike those who call themselves no-government men, I ask for, not at once no government, but *at once* a better government. Let every man make known what kind of government would command his respect, and that will be one step toward obtaining it.

Must the citizen ever for a moment, or in the least degree, resign his conscience to the legislator? Why has every man a conscience, then? I think that we should be men first, and subjects afterward. It is not desirable to cultivate a respect for the law, so much as for the right. The only obligation which I have a right to assume, is to do at any time what I think right. It is truly enough said, that a corporation has no conscience; but a corporation of conscientious men is a corporation *with* a conscience. Law never made men a whit more just; and, by means of their respect for it, even the well-disposed are daily made the agents of injustice. A common and natural result of an undue respect for law is, that you may see a file of soldiers, colonel, captain, corporal, privates, powder-monkeys and all, marching in admirable order over hill and dale to the wars, against their wills, aye, against their common sense and consciences, which makes it very steep marching indeed, and produces a palpitation of the heart. They have no doubt that it is a damnable business in which they are concerned; they are all peaceably inclined. Now, what are they? Men at all? or small moveable forts and magazines, at the service of some unscrupulous man in power? Visit the Navy Yard, and behold a marine, such a man as an American government can make, or such as it can make a man with its black arts, a mere shadow and reminiscence of humanity, a man laid out alive and standing, and already, as one may say, buried under arms with funeral accompaniments.

The mass of men serve the State thus, not as men mainly, but as machines, with their bodies. They are the standing army, and the militia, jailers, constables, *posse comitatus,* etc. In most cases there is no free exercise whatever of the judgment or the moral sense; but they put themselves on a level with wood and earth and stones; and wooden men can perhaps be manufactured that will serve the purpose as well. Such command no more respect than men of straw, or a lump of dirt. They have the same sort of worth only as horses and dogs. Yet such as these even are commonly esteemed good citizens. Others, as most legislators, politicians, lawyers, ministers, and officeholders, serve the State chiefly with their heads; and, as they rarely make any moral distinctions, they are as likely to serve the devil, without intending it, as God. A very few, as heroes, patriots, martyrs, reformers in the great sense, and *men,* serve the State with their consciences also, and so necessarily resist it for the most part; and they are commonly treated by it as enemies.

How does it become a man to behave toward this American government to-day? I answer that he cannot without disgrace be associated with it. I cannot for an instant recognize that political organization as *my* government which is the *slave's* government also.

All men recognize the right of revolution; that is, the right to refuse allegiance to and to resist the government, when its tyranny or its inefficiency are great and unendurable. When a sixth of the population of a nation which has undertaken to be the refuge of liberty are slaves, and a whole country is unjustly overrun and conquered by a foreign army, and subjected to military law, I think that it is not too soon for honest men to rebel and revolutionize. What makes this duty the more urgent is the fact, that the country so overrun is not our own, but ours is the invading army.

If I have unjustly wrested a plank from a drowning man, I must restore it to him though I drown myself. This, according to Paley, would be inconvenient. But he that would save his life, in such a case, shall lose it. This people must cease to hold slaves, and to make war on Mexico, though it cost them their existence as a people.

Practically speaking, the opponents to a reform in Massachusetts are not a hundred thousand politicians at the South, but a hundred thousand merchants and farmers here, who are more interested in commerce and agriculture than they are in humanity, and are not prepared to do justice to the slave and to Mexico, *cost what it may.* I quarrel not with far-off foes, but with those who, near at home, cooperate with, and do the bidding of those far away, and without whom the latter would be harmless.

There are thousands who are *in opinion* opposed to slavery and to the war, who yet in effect do nothing to put an end to them; who esteeming themselves children of Washington and Franklin, sit down with their hands in their pockets, and say that they know not what to do and do nothing; who even postpone the question of freedom to the question of free-trade, and quietly read the prices-current along with the latest advices from Mexico, after dinner, and, it may be, fall asleep over them both. What is the price-current on an honest man and patriot to-day? They hesitate, and they regret, and sometimes they petition; but they do nothing in earnest and with effect. They will wait, well disposed, for others to remedy the evil, that they may no longer have it to regret.

Unjust laws exist: shall we be content to obey them, or shall we endeavor to amend them, and obey them until we have succeeded or shall we transgress them at once? Men generally, under such a government as this, think that they ought to wait until they have persuaded the majority to alter them. They think that, if they should resist, the remedy would be worse than the evil. But it is the fault of the government itself that the remedy *is* worse than the evil. *It* makes it worse. Why is it not more apt to anticipate and provide for reform? Why does it not cherish its wise minority?

If the injustice is part of the necessary friction of the machine of government, let it go, let it go: perchance it will wear smooth—certainly the machine will wear out. But if it is of such a nature that it requires you to be the agent of injustice to another, then, I say, break the law. Let your life be a counter friction to stop the machine. What I have to do is to see, at any rate, that I do not lend myself to the wrong which I condemn. As for adopting the ways which the State has provided for remedying the evil, I know not of such ways. They take too much time, and a man's life will be gone.

I do not hesitate to say, that those who call themselves abolitionists should at once effectually withdraw their support both in person and property from the government of Massachusetts.

I meet this American government, or its representative directly, and face to face, once a year, no more, in the person of its tax-gatherer; this is the only model in which a man situated as I am necessarily meets it; and it then says distinctly, Recognize me; and the simplest, the most effectual, and in the present posture of affairs, the indispensablest mode of treating with it on this head, of expressing your little satisfaction with and love for it, is to deny it then.

Under a government which imprisons any unjustly, the true place for a just man is also a prison. The proper place to-day, the only place which Massachusetts has provided for her freer and less desponding spirits, is in her prisons, to be put out and locked out of the State by her own act, as they have already put themselves out by their principles. It is there that the fugitive slave, and the Mexican prisoner on parole, and the Indian come to plead the wrongs of his race, should find them; on that separate, but more free and honorable ground, where the State places those who are not *with* her but *against* her—the only house in a slave state in which a free man can abide with honor. A minority is powerless while it conforms to the majority; it is not even a minority then; but it is irresistible when it clogs by its whole weight. If the alternative is to keep all just men in prison, or give up war and slavery, the State will not hesitate which to choose. If a thousand men were not to pay their taxbills this year, that would not be a violent and bloody measure, as it would be to pay them, and enable the State to commit violence and shed innocent blood. This is, in fact, the definition of a peaceable revolution if any such is possible. If the tax-gatherer, or any other public officer, asks me, as one has done, "But what shall I do?" my answer is, "If you really wish to do any thing, resign your office." When the subject has refused allegiance, and the officer has resigned his office, then the revolution is accomplished. But even suppose blood should flow. Is there not a sort of blood shed when the conscience is wounded? Through this wound a man's real manhood and immortality flow out, and he bleeds to an everlasting death, I see this blood flowing now.

I have never declined paying the highway tax, because I am so desirous of being a good neighbor as I am of being a bad subject; and, as for supporting schools, I am doing my part to educate my fellow-countrymen now. It is for no particular item in the taxbill that I refuse to pay it. I simply wish to refuse allegiance to the State, to withdraw and stand aloof from it effectually. I do not care to trace the course of my dollar, if I could, till it buys a man, or a musket to shoot one with—the dollar is innocent—but I am concerned to trace the effects of my allegiance. In fact, I quietly declare war with the State, after my fashion.

I do not wish to quarrel with any man or nation. I do not wish to split hairs, to make fine distinctions, or set myself up as better than my neighbors. I seek rather, I may say, even an excuse for conforming to the laws of the land. I am but too ready to conform to them. Indeed I have reason to suspect myself on this head; and each year, as the tax-gatherer comes round, I find myself disposed to review the acts and position of the general and state governments, and the spirit of the people, to discover a pretext for conformity. Seen from a lower point of view, the Constitution, with all its faults, is very good; the law and the courts are very respectable; even this State and this American government are, in many respects, very admirable and rare things, to be thankful for, such as a great many have described them; but seen from a point of view a little higher, they are what I have described them; seen from a higher still, and the highest who shall say what they are, or that they are worth looking at or thinking of at all?

The authority of government, even such as I am willing to submit to, for I will cheerfully obey those who know and can do better than I, and in many things even those who neither know or can do so well, is still an impure one: to be strictly just, it must have the sanction and consent of the governed. It can have no pure right over my person and property but what I concede to it. The progress from an absolute to a limited monarchy, from a limited monarchy to a democracy, is a progress toward a true respect for the individual. Is a democracy, such as we know it, the last improvement possible in government? Is it not possible to take a step further toward recognizing and organizing the rights of man? There will never be a really free and enlightened State, until the State comes to recognize the individual as a higher and independent power, from which all its own power and authority are derived, and treats him accordingly.

It would be interesting and enlightening to have King's letter of reply to the eight Birmingham clergymen read and commented on by Hobbes, Rousseau, Burke, Marx, Thoreau, and Mill. All six of them would be open to such an experiment. In their own writings they had taken positions that would entitle King to demand that they read his *Letter*, and stand up and be counted. Would they take their stand with the eight clergymen, or with the public authorities who had put King in jail? Or with King himself? Could he appeal to anything they had written, to justify himself in his act of civil disobedience?

BIOGRAPHICAL NOTE.   Martin Luther King, Jr. was born in Atlanta, Georgia, in 1929. He graduated from Morehouse College and pursued advanced studies at Crozier Theological Seminary and Boston University. An ordained Baptist minister, he became pastor of the Dexter Avenue Baptist Church in Montgomery, Alabama, in 1954, and began his civil rights crusade the next year. To coordinate the efforts of various civil rights groups, King helped found the Southern Christian Leadership Conference in 1957. During the 1950s and 1960s his eloquent pleas for racial justice and his commitment to nonviolent resistance won him the support of millions of people, both blacks and whites. He was awarded the Nobel peace prize in 1964. Nonviolent himself, he eventually became the victim of violence. Stabbed in New York City, stoned in Chicago, he was finally cut down by a sniper's bullet in Memphis, Tennessee, in 1968 at the age of forty years. King based his program of nonviolent resistance and civil disobedience on the teachings of Christianity, the social ideas of Henry Thoreau, and the methods of Mohandas K. Gandhi. His thoughts are expressed in five books: *Strike Toward Freedom* (1958), *Strength to Love* (1963), *Why We Can't Wait* (1964), *Where We Go from Here: Chaos or Community?* (1957), and *The Trumpet of Conscience* (1968). The tombstone above his grave in Atlanta, Georgia, bears this inscription from a spiritual: "Free at last, free at last, thank God Almighty, I'm free at last."

THE ARGUMENT OF THE PASSAGES.   The following material, taken from King's *Letter from Birmingham Jail*, begins with an explanation of why King is in Birmingham. He then sets forth his theory of civil disobedience and the conditions that justify it. He reminds his correspondents of some outstanding cases of civil disobedience and expresses regret that the Christian church in the South has not identified itself with civil disobedience on behalf of black groups in this country. After noting some exceptions to his criticism of the church, he expresses a desire and a hope that he and his correspondents will be able to meet as fellow Christians.

April 16, 1963

MY DEAR FELLOW CLERGYMEN:

While confined here in the Birmingham city jail, I came across your recent statement calling my present activities "unwise and untimely." Seldom do I pause to answer criticism of my work and ideas. If I sought to answer all the criticisms that cross my desk, my secretaries would have little time for anything other than such correspondence in the course of the day, and I would have no time for constructive work. But since I feel that you are men of genuine good will and that your criticisms are sincerely set forth, I want to try to answer your statement in what I hope will be patient and reasonable terms.

I think I should indicate why I am here in Birmingham, since you have been influenced by the view which argues against "outsiders coming in." I have the honor of serving as president of the Southern Christian Leadership Conference, an organization operating in every southern state, with headquarters in Atlanta, Georgia. We have some eighty-five affiliated organizations across the South, and one of them is the Alabama Christian Movement for Human Rights. Frequently we share staff, educational, and financial resources with our affiliates. Several months ago the affiliate here in Birmingham asked us to be on call to engage in a nonviolent direct-action program if such were deemed necessary. We readily consented, and when the hour came we lived up to our promise. So I, along with several members of my staff, am here because I was invited here. I am here because I have organizational ties here.

But more basically, I am in Birmingham because injustice is here. Just as the prophets of the eighth century B.C. left their villages and carried their "thus saith the Lord" far beyond the boundaries of their home towns, and just as the Apostle Paul left his village of Tarsus and carried the gospel of Jesus Christ to the far corners of the Greco-Roman world, so am I compelled to carry the gospel of freedom beyond my own home town. Like Paul, I must constantly respond to the Macedonian call for aid.

Moreover, I am cognizant of the interrelatedness of all communities and states. I cannot sit idly by in Atlanta and not be concerned about what happens in Birmingham. Injustice anywhere is a threat to justice everywhere. We are caught in an inescapable network of mutuality, tied in a single garment of destiny. Whatever affects one directly, affects all indirectly. Never again can we afford to live with the narrow, provincial "outside agitator" idea. Anyone who lives inside the United States can never be considered an outsider anywhere within its bounds.

You deplore the demonstrations taking place in Birmingham. But your statement, I am sorry to say, fails to express a similar concern for the conditions that brought about the demonstrations. I am sure that none of you would want to rest content with the superficial kind of social analysis that deals merely with effects and does not grapple with underlying causes. It is unfortunate that demonstrations are taking place in Birmingham, but it is even more unfortunate that the city's white power structure left the Negro community with no alternative. . . .

We know through painful experience that freedom is never voluntarily given by the oppressor; it must be demanded by the oppressed. Frankly, I have yet to engage in a direct-action campaign that was "well timed" in the view of those who have not suffered unduly from the disease of segregation. For years now I have heard the word "Wait!" It rings in the ear of every Negro with piercing familiarity. This "Wait" has almost always meant "Never." We must come to see, with one of our distinguished jurists, that "justice too long delayed is justice denied."

We have waited for more than 340 years for our constitutional and God-given rights. The nations of Asia and Africa are moving with jetlike speed toward gaining political independence, but we still creep at horse-and-buggy pace toward gaining a cup of coffee at a lunch counter. Perhaps it is easy for those who have never felt the stinging darts of segregation to say, "Wait." But when you have seen vicious mobs lynch your mothers and fathers at will and drown your sisters and brothers at whim; when you have seen hate-filled policemen curse, kick and even kill our black brothers and sisters; when you see the vast majority of your twenty million Negro brothers smothering in an airtight cage of poverty in the midst of an affluent society; when you suddenly find your tongue twisted and your speech stammering as you seek to explain to your six-year-old daughter why she can't go to the public amusement park that has just been advertised on television, and see tears welling up in her eyes when she is told that Funtown is closed to colored children, and see ominous clouds of inferiority beginning to form in her little mental sky, and see her beginning to distort her personality by developing an unconscious bitterness toward white people; when you have to concoct an answer for a five-year-old son who is asking: "Daddy, why do white people treat colored people so mean?"; when you take a cross-country drive and find it necessary to sleep night after night in the uncomfortable corners of your automobile because no motel will accept you; when you are humiliated day in and day out by nagging signs reading "white" and "colored"; when your first name becomes "nigger," your middle name becomes "boy" (however old you are) and your last name becomes "John," and your wife and mother are never given the respected title "Mrs."; when you are harried by day and haunted by night by the fact that you are a Negro, living constantly at tiptoe stance, never quite knowing what to expect next, and are plagued with inner fears and outer resentments; when you are forever fighting a degenerating sense of "nobodiness"—then you will understand why we find it difficult to wait. There comes a time when the cup of endurance runs over, and men are no longer willing to be plunged into the abyss of despair. I hope, sirs, you can understand our legitimate and unavoidable impatience.

You express a great deal of anxiety over our willingness to break laws. This is certainly a legitimate concern. Since we so diligently urge people to obey the Supreme Court's decision of 1954 outlawing segregation in the public schools, at first glance it may seem rather paradoxical for us consciously to break laws. One may well ask: "How can you advocate breaking some laws and obeying others?" The answer lies in the fact that there are two types of laws: just and unjust. I would be the first to advocate obeying just laws. One has not only a legal but a moral responsibility to obey just laws. Conversely, one has a moral responsibility to disobey unjust laws. I would agree with St. Augustine that "an unjust law is no law at all."

Now, what is the difference between the two? How does one determine whether a law is just or unjust? A just law is a man-made code that squares with the moral law or the law of God. An unjust law is a code that is out of harmony with the moral law. To put it in the terms of St. Thomas Aquinas: An unjust law is a human law that is not rooted in eternal law and natural law. Any law that uplifts human personality is just. Any law that degrades human personality is unjust. All segregation statutes are unjust because segregation distorts the soul and damages the personality. It gives the segregator a false sense of superiority and the segregated a false sense of inferiority. Segregation, to use the terminology of the Jewish philosopher Martin Buber, substitutes an "I–it" relationship for an "I–thou" relationship and ends up relegating persons to the status of things. Hence segregation is not only politically, economically and sociologically unsound, it is morally wrong and sinful. Paul Tillich has said that sin is separation. Is not segregation an existential expression of man's tragic separation, his awful estrangement, his terrible sinfulness? Thus it is that I can urge men to obey the 1954 decision of the Supreme Court, for it is morally right; and I can urge them to disobey segregation ordinances, for they are morally wrong.

Let us consider a more concrete example of just and unjust laws. An unjust law is a code that a numerical or power majority group compels a minority group to obey but does not make binding on itself. This is *difference* made legal. By the same token, a just law is a code that a majority compels a minority to follow and that it is willing to follow itself. This is *sameness* made legal.

Let me give another explanation. A law is unjust if it is inflicted on a minority that, as a result of being denied the right to vote, had no part in enacting or devising the law. Who can say that the legislature of Alabama which set up that state's segregation laws was democratically elected? Throughout Alabama all sort of devious methods are used to prevent Negroes from becoming registered voters, and there are some counties in which, even though Negroes constitute a majority of the population, not a single Negro is registered. Can any law enacted under such circumstances be considered democratically structured?

Sometimes a law is just on its face and unjust in its application. For instance, I have been arrested on a charge of parading without a permit. Now, there is nothing wrong in having an ordinance which requires a permit for a parade. But such an ordinance becomes unjust when it is used to maintain segregation and to deny citizens the First-Amendment privilege of peaceful assembly and protest.

I hope you are able to see the distinction I am trying to point out. In no sense do I advocate evading or defying the law, as would the rabid segregationist. That would lead to anarchy. One who breaks an unjust law must do so openly, lovingly, and with a willingness to accept the penalty. I submit that an individual who breaks a law that conscience tells him is unjust, and who willingly accepts the penalty of imprisonment in order to arouse the conscience of the community over its injustice, is in reality expressing the highest respect for law.

Of course, there is nothing new about this kind of civil disobedience. It was evidenced sublimely in the refusal of Shadrach, Meshach and Abednego to obey the laws of Nebuchadnezzar, on the ground that a higher moral law was at stake. It was practiced superbly by the early Christians, who were willing to face hungry lions and the excruciating pain of chopping blocks rather than submit to certain unjust laws of the Roman Empire. To a degree, academic freedom is a reality today because Socrates practiced civil disobedience. In our own nation, the Boston Tea Party represented a massive act of civil disobedience.

We should never forget that everything Adolf Hitler did in Germany was "legal" and everything the Hungarian freedom fighters did in Hungary was "illegal." It was "illegal" to aid and comfort a Jew in Hitler's Germany. Even so, I am sure that, had I lived in Germany at the time, I would have aided and comforted my Jewish brothers. If today I lived in a Communist country where certain principles dear to the Christian faith are suppressed, I would openly advocate disobeying that country's antireligious laws. . . .

Oppressed people cannot remain oppressed forever. The yearning for freedom eventually manifests itself, and that is what has happened to the American Negro. Something within has reminded him of his birthright of freedom, and something without has reminded him that it can be gained. Consciously or unconsciously, he has been caught up by the *Zeitgeist*, and with his black brothers of Africa and his brown and yellow brothers of Asia, South America and the Caribbean, the United States Negro is moving with a sense of great urgency toward the promised land of racial justice. If one recognizes this vital urge that has engulfed the Negro community, one should readily understand why public demonstrations are taking place. The Negro has many pent-up resentments and latent frustrations, and he must release them. So let him march; let him make prayer pilgrimages to the city hall; let him go on freedom rides—and try to understand why he must do so. If his repressed emotions are not released in nonviolent ways, they will seek expression through violence; this is not a threat but a fact of history. So I have not said to my people: "Get rid of your discontent." Rather, I have tried to say that this normal and healthy discontent can be channeled into the creative outlet of nonviolent direct action. And now this approach is being termed extremist.

But though I was initially disappointed at being categorized as an extremist, as I continued to think about the matter I gradually gained a measure of satisfaction from the label. Was not Jesus an extremist for love: "Love your enemies, bless them that curse you, do good to them that hate you, and pray for them which despitefully use you, and persecute you." Was not Amos an extremist for justice: "Let justice roll down like waters and righteousness like an ever-flowing stream." Was not Paul an extremist for the Christian gospel: "I bear in my body the marks of the Lord Jesus." Was not Martin Luther an extremist: "Here I stand; I cannot do otherwise, so help me God." And John Bunyan: "I will stay in jail to the end of my days before I make a butchery of my conscience." And Abraham Lincoln: "This nation cannot survive half slave and half free." And Thomas Jefferson: "We hold these truths to be self-evident, that all men are created equal . . ." So the question is not whether we will be extremists, but what kind of extremists we will be. Will we be extremists for hate or for love? Will we be extremists for the preservation of injustice or for the extension of justice? In that dramatic scene on Calvary's hill three men were crucified. We must never forget that all three were crucified for the same crime—the crime of extremism. Two were extremists for immorality, and thus fell below their environment. The other, Jesus Christ, was an extremist for love, truth and goodness, and thereby above his environment. Perhaps the South, the nation and the world are in dire need of creative extremists.

I had hoped that the white moderate would see this need. Perhaps I was too optimistic; perhaps I expected too much. I suppose I should have realized that few members of the oppressor race can understand the deep groans and passionate yearnings of the oppressed race, and still fewer have the vision to see that injustice must be rooted out by strong, persistent and determined action. I am thankful, however, that some of our white brothers in the South have grasped the meaning of this social revolution and committed themselves to it. They are still all too few in quantity, but they are big in quality. Some—such as Ralph McGill, Lillian Smith, Harry Golden, James McBride Dabbs, Ann Braden and Sarah Patton Boyle—have written about our struggle in eloquent and prophetic terms. Others have marched with us down nameless streets of the South. They have languished in filthy, roach-infested jails, suffering the abuse and brutality of policemen who view them as "dirty nigger-lovers." Unlike so many of their moderate brothers and sisters, they have recognized the urgency of the moment and sensed the need for powerful "action" antidotes to combat the disease of segregation. . . .

In spite of my shattered dreams, I came to Birmingham with the hope that the white religious leadership of this community would see the justice of our cause and, with deep moral concern, would serve as the channel through which our just grievances could reach the power structure. I had hoped that each of you would understand. But again I have been disappointed.

I have heard numerous southern religious leaders admonish their worshipers to comply with a desegregation decision because it is the law, but I have longed to hear white ministers declare: "Follow this decree because integration is morally right and because the Negro is your brother." In the midst of blatant injustices inflicted upon the Negro, I have watched white churchmen stand on the sideline and mouth pious irrelevancies and sanctimonious trivialities. In the midst of a mighty struggle to rid our nation of racial and economic injustice, I have heard many ministers say: "Those are social issues, with which the gospel has no real concern." And I have watched many churches commit themselves to a completely otherworldly religion which makes a strange, un-Biblical distinction between body and soul, between the sacred and the secular.

I have traveled the length and breadth of Alabama, Mississippi and all the other southern states. On sweltering summer days and crisp autumn mornings I have looked at the South's beautiful churches with their lofty spires pointing heavenward. I have beheld the impressive outlines of her massive religious-education buildings. Over and over I have found myself asking: "What kind of people worship here? Who is their God? Where were their voices when the lips of Governor Barnett dripped with words of interposition and nullification? Where were they when Governor Wallace gave a clarion call for defiance and hatred? Where were their voices of support when bruised and weary Negro men and women decided to rise from the dark dungeons of complacency to the bright hills of creative protest?"

Yes, these questions were still in my mind. In deep disappointment I have wept over the laxity of the church. But be assured that my tears have been tears of love. There can be no deep disappointment where there is not deep love. Yes, I love the church. How could I do otherwise? I am in the rather unique position of being the son, the grandson and the great-grandson of preachers. Yes, I see the church as the body of Christ. But, oh! How we have blemished and scarred that body through social neglect and through fear of being nonconformists.

There was a time when the church was very powerful—in the time when the early Christians rejoiced at being deemed worthy to suffer for what they believed. In those days the church was not merely a thermometer that recorded the ideas and principles of popular opinion; it was a thermostat that transformed the mores of society. Whenever the early Christians entered a town, the people in power became disturbed and immediately sought to convict the Christians of being "disturbers of the peace" and "outside agitators." But the Christians pressed on, in the conviction that they were "a colony of heaven," called to obey God rather than man. Small in number, they were big in commitment. They were too God-intoxicated to be "astronomically intimidated." By their effort and example they brought an end to such ancient evils as infanticide and gladiatorial contests.

Things are different now. So often the contemporary church is a weak, ineffectual voice with an uncertain sound. So often it is an archdefender of the status quo. Far from being disturbed by the presence of the church, the power structure of the average community is consoled by the church's silent—and often even vocal—sanction of things as they are.

But the judgment of God is upon the church as never before. If today's church does not recapture the sacrificial spirit of the early church, it will lose its authenticity, forfeit the loyalty of millions, and be dismissed as an irrelevant social club with no meaning for the twentieth century. Every day I meet young people whose disappointment with the church has turned into outright disgust.

Perhaps I have once again been too optimistic. Is organized religion too inextricably bound to the status quo to save our nation and the world? Perhaps I must turn my faith to the inner spiritual church, the church within the church, as the true *ekklesia* and the hope of the world. But again I am thankful to God that some noble souls from the ranks of organized religion have broken loose from the paralyzing chains of conformity and joined us as active partners in the struggle for freedom. They have left their secure congregations and walked the streets of Albany, Georgia, with us. They have gone down the highways of the South on tortuous rides for freedom. Yes, they have gone to jail with us. Some have been dismissed from their churches, have lost the support of their bishops and fellow ministers. But they have acted in the faith that right defeated is stronger than evil triumphant. Their witness has been the spiritual salt that has preserved the true meaning of the gospel in these troubled times. They have carved a tunnel of hope through the dark mountain of disappointment.

I hope the church as a whole will meet the challenge of this decisive hour. But even if the church does not come to the aid of justice, I have no despair about the future. I have no fear about the outcome of our struggle in Birmingham, even if our motives are at present misunderstood. We will reach the goal of freedom in Birmingham and all over the nation, because the goal of America is freedom. Abused and scorned though we may be, our destiny is tied up with America's destiny. Before the pilgrims landed at Plymouth, we were here. Before the pen of Jefferson etched the majestic words of the Declaration of Independence across the pages of history, we were here. For more than two centuries our forebears labored in this country without wages; they made cotton king; they built the homes of their masters while suffering gross injustice and shameful humiliation—and yet out of a bottomless vitality they continued to thrive and develop. If the inexpressible cruelties of slavery could not stop us, the opposition we now face will surely fail. We will win our freedom because the sacred heritage of our nation and the eternal will of God are embodied in our echoing demands.

Before closing I feel impelled to mention one other point in your statement that has troubled me profoundly. You warmly commended the Birmingham police force for keeping "order" and "preventing violence." I doubt that you would have so warmly commended the police force if you had seen its dogs sinking their teeth into unarmed, nonviolent Negroes. I doubt that you would so quickly commend the policemen if you were to observe their ugly and inhumane treatment of Negroes here in the city jail; if you were to watch them push and curse old Negro women and young Negro girls; if you were to see them slap and kick old Negro men and young boys; if you were to observe them, as they did on two occasions, refuse to give us food because we wanted to sing our grace together. I cannot join you in your praise of the Birmingham police department.

It is true that the police have exercised a degree of discipline in handling the demonstrators. In this sense they have conducted themselves rather "nonviolently" in public. But for what purpose? To preserve the evil system of segregation. Over the past few years I have consistently preached that nonviolence demands that the means we use must be as pure as the ends we seek. I have tried to make clear that it is wrong to use immoral means to attain moral ends. But now I must affirm that it is just as wrong, or perhaps even more so, to use moral means to preserve immoral ends. Perhaps Mr. Connor and his policemen have been rather nonviolent in public, as was Chief Pritchett in Albany, Georgia, but they have used the moral means of nonviolence to maintain the immoral end of racial injustice. As T. S. Eliot has said: "The last temptation is the greatest treason: To do the right deed for the wrong reason."

I wish you had commended the Negro sit-inners and demonstrators of Birmingham for their sublime courage, their willingness to suffer and their amazing discipline in the midst of great provocation. One day the South will recognize its real heroes. They will be the James Merediths, with the noble sense of purpose that enables them to face jeering and hostile mobs, and with the agonizing loneliness that characterizes the life of the pioneer. They will be old, oppressed, battered Negro women, symbolized in a seventy-two-year-old woman in Montgomery, Alabama, who rose up with a sense of dignity and with her people decided not to ride segregated buses, and who responded with ungrammatical profundity to one who inquired about her weariness: "My feets is tired, but my soul is at rest." They will be the young high school and college students, the young ministers of the gospel and a host of their elders, courageously and nonviolently sitting in at lunch counters and willingly going to jail for conscience' sake. One day the South will know that when these disinherited children of God sat down at lunch counters, they were in reality standing up for what is best in the American dream and for the most sacred values in our Judaeo–Christian heritage, thereby bringing our nation back to those great wells of democracy which were dug deep by the founding fathers in their formulation of the Constitution and the Declaration of Independence.

Never before have I written so long a letter. I'm afraid it is much too long to take your precious time. I can assure you that it would have been much shorter if I had been writing from a comfortable desk, but what else can one do when he is alone in a narrow jail cell, other than write long letters, think long thoughts and pray long prayers?

If I have said anything in this letter that overstates the truth and indicates an unreasonable impatience, I beg you to forgive me. If I have said anything that understates the truth and indicates my having a patience that allows me to settle for anything less than brotherhood, I beg God to forgive me.

I hope this letter finds you strong in the faith. I also hope that circumstances will soon make it possible for me to meet each of you, not as an integrationist or a civil-rights leader but as a fellow clergyman and a Christian brother. Let us all hope that the dark clouds of racial prejudice will soon pass away and the deep fog of misunderstanding will be lifted from our fear-drenched communities, and in some not too distant tomorrow the radiant stars of love and brotherhood will shine over our great nation with all their scintillating beauty.

Yours for the cause of Peace and Brotherhood.

MARTIN LUTHER KING, JR.

NOTE ON SOURCES.   The materials in this section are from Henry David Thoreau, "On the Duty of Civil Disobedience" and Martin Luther King, "Letter from Birmingham Jail—April 16, 1963," *Why We Can't Wait* (New York, Harper & Row, 1964).

8

What Things Shall I Call Art?

THE QUESTION POSED

We sometimes refer to poems, pictures, musical compositions, and statues as works of art, and the activity that produces them as art. Is it possible to define these terms, *art* and *work of art*? What fact about any activity would be our reason for calling it art? What fact about any object would be our reason for calling it a work of art? There would seem to be *some* reason. On some occasions we withhold these terms; on others, we are in doubt. Such behavior on our part would suggest that we at least "know what we are talking about" when we use, or refuse, or are in doubt about using, the terms *art* and *work of art*. If there is *no* detectable reason for using these terms, why do we do so? Why do we refuse to do so? Why do we hesitate to do so?

In any inquiry of this kind, we might begin with judgments that we would be able and willing to authorize. Take, for example, Matthew Arnold's poem "Dover Beach." Is it a work of art? If so, why? If not, why not? Try to settle these questions for yourself. List a dozen items, *any* dozen—poems, pictures, musical compositions, statues—about which you would be prepared to say, "These are works of art. Whatever else they are, they are works of art. Whatever other items are works of art, at least *these* are. Whatever other items are *not* works of art, at least these *are*. And the activity that produced them is art." You might add, "The agent who performs this activity is an artist." How about these three terms: *Work of art, art, artist?* Are they a connected set? Does it matter at which end you begin? If you cannot or will not authorize *any* such judgments, then for you the problem dealt with in this chapter does not arise. But there is no *prima facie* reason to believe that you are thus either unable or unwilling. Why should you be?

Suppose, then, that these aesthetic judgments are forthcoming. "This and this and this are works of art; and the activity that produced them is art." Such judgments are data. Given them, the question arises, "What fact, common and peculiar to these and similar objects, is the reason for calling them *works of art?* And for calling the activity that produced them *art?* And for calling the agent who performed these activities an *artist?*" An answer to this question would define, set limits to, the class "work of art" and "art." Whatever satisfied the definition would fall inside these classes; whatever did not, would fall outside these classes. As these definitions took shape, they would suggest further questions; and as these questions were answered, the answers could be added on to the original definitions. The outcome would constitute a theory of art. The English word *theory* is said to be derived from the Greek word *theoria,* meaning a looking at, a viewing, a beholding. A theory of art is a looking at the particulars that together make up "the world of art." You could start by answering, "What makes these particulars to be works of art?" Your answer would spell out for you the criteria of recognition that are present and operative when you identify a particular as a work of art. It should be noted that the question, "Is this a work of art?" is not the same as the question, "Is this a good work of art?" Your criteria of recognition may not be your criteria of evaluation. Asking what *kind* an identifiable particular is, is not the same as asking whether it is good of its kind.

In the authors brought together in this chapter, you have persons attempting to think about aesthetic judgments, definitions, and theories. They are endeavoring to define and theorize about art. The first author, H. Gene Blocker, discusses what is probably the oldest theory of art: the view advanced by the ancient Greeks that art imitates or represents reality. In the modern period, this ancient Greek view of art has yielded center stage to the view of art as expression of emotion. This modern viewpoint is articulated by our second author, Eugene Véron, who claims that art is an activity in which the agent expresses his or her feelings or emotions, and does this subject to the limitations imposed by some medium, e.g., words, sounds, lines, colors, or stone. The third author, Leo Tolstoy, argues that there must be communication as well as expression if the activity is to be art, and the outcome a work of art. The fourth, R. G. Collingwood, reverts to the position of art as the expression of emotion and offers a more intimate and detailed account of the character of this activity. Criticism of the view of art as expression sets in with the fifth author, Professor John Hospers, who gives reasons for doubting that "expression of emotion" will enable one to formulate a definition of art or work of art. The sixth and final author, Professor Morris Weitz, rejects the entire enterprise of defining the terms art or work of art; he claims that these terms are essentially and in principle impossible to define. His point, to speak in metaphor, is that these terms are "alive" and "growing"; and that therefore any attempt to "contain" them by a definition or a theory is bound to be unsatisfactory.

H. GENE BLOCKER

ART AS REPRESENTATION OF REALITY

A good place to begin a discussion of the nature of art is with what is probably the oldest theory: the view that art imitates reality. But what does it mean to "imitate," and what is the "reality" art is presumably imitating? Is the goal of the artist perfectly achieved by the person who holds up a mirror and presents us with a reflection that is a flawless image or copy of reality? Is such a mirror reflection the "imitation of reality" that the artist seeks? These and other questions are probed by Professor Blocker as he analyzes and assesses this ancient view of art.

BIOGRAPHICAL NOTE.   H. Gene Blocker is professor of philosophy at Ohio University. He pursued his undergraduate studies at the University of Chicago and received his doctorate from the University of California, Berkeley. He has taught at the University of Aberdeen, Scotland, and the Universities of Sierra Leone, Ibadan, and Bendel State in West Africa. In addition to numerous publications in scholarly esthetics periodicals, Dr. Blocker has published several books, including *The Meaning of Meaninglessness* (1974), *Philosophy of Art* (1979) from which the selection below has been taken, *John Rawls' Theory of Social Justice* (1979), *The Metaphysics of Absurdity* (1979), and *Fundamentals of Philosophy* (1982). Professor Blocker is an avid collector of African and Pre-Columbian art and will soon publish a book on this subject, *The Aesthetics of Primitive Art.*

THE ARGUMENT OF THE PASSAGES.   First of all, Blocker clarifies the meaning of "imitation" by distinguishing it from "resemblance." Then he suggests that the goal of artistic imitation is to create the illusion that the copy is not a copy at all but the original. Such a view of art, however, carries a number of liabilities, which, Blocker notes, Plato in Ancient Greece was quick to point out. For example, this view leads to the conclusions that art is inherently false or deceptive, that art does not penetrate to the essence of things but merely deals with appearances, that art always falls short of its goal inasmuch as the imitation is invariably a flawed copy, and that art can have a negative moral effect on the development of human character when it merely copies the sordid side of human life. Problems such as these have led critics who are sympathetic with this tradition of "realism" in art to modify the theory of imitation in the direction of art as "representation" of reality. This modification removes some of the liabilities of the imitation view and allows for a reasonable interpretation of why artistic representation deviates from reality. Blocker provides a lucid account of this theory of art as representation.

> Let's . . . now . . . take a closer look at . . . what the art work represents. This is surely the most recognizable and familiar aspect of art to most people and is associated with the earliest Western theory of art, the Greek view that art is a direct copy or imitation of nature. It is also the most persistent idea in Western art, dominating not only the philosophy of art, but criticism and art itself for over two thousand years. Nor is this theory of art out of the running today. Spokesmen for the most trendy, contemporary art, called appropriately, New Realism, are again proclaiming that the imitative, realistic aspect of art is its most valuable asset. . . .
>
> The ideal art, according to this realist view, is an art inseparable from reality, an art in which the art work transparently reveals but does not interfere with or get in the way of the perceiver's direct grasp of reality. It follows from this view that anything which does get in the way is a distortion, a projection of human biases and wishful thinking. In short the theory implies:
>
> 1. that subject matter is [what is most]. . . important in a work of art;

2. that the work of art is a transparent opening to the subject matter (like looking out of a window at a building outside);
3. that the art work consequently cannot tell us anything *about* the subject matter;
4. that our response to the art work is therefore (ideally) exactly what it is to the subject matter depicted;
5. that there is consequently nothing peculiar to art which differentiates it in any way from reality (except its inherent inaccuracy and phoniness);
6. that art criticism is heteronomously tied to realistic standards outside art (leading to censorship and modern advertising practices);
7. that the artist contributes nothing to the art work (that imitation is the opposite of imagination); and
8. that reality *can* be portrayed just as it is in itself.

Much of this idea is contained in our ordinary notion of imitation and can be extracted . . . by analyzing what the word *imitation* means. The first thing to note about imitation is that it is not the same thing as resemblance. If a stone found on the beach resembles Fidel Castro, it does not follow either that the stone is imitating Fidel or that Fidel is imitating the stone. It is true, on the other hand, that most cases of *successful* imitation involve, or presuppose, some sort of resemblance.

This brings out an important difference between resemblance and imitation. Imitation is something people try to accomplish, something one strives for, succeeds or fails at; whereas resemblance is simply a coincidence. Closely related to the element of failure and success is our attitude of evaluating not only the imitator but also the imitation, according to how much it succeeds in looking like, or resembling the thing which is being imitated. There seems to be the implication that the imitation ought to look like the thing imitated, that it is good to the extent that it does and bad to the extent that it does not. This likeness is the goal, or purpose of the imitator which, in turn, determines our standards of success and failure, both for the imitator and for the imitation. None of this is true in the case of resemblance. Two things may not look alike, but there is no question of failure; nor is there a question of *success* simply because two things look very much alike. And this is because there is, so far, no reason why they *should* look alike.

If we consider one further difference between imitation and resemblance we will have before us the main points to be understood about imitation. If I resemble Fidel Castro, then he resembles me. But if I *imitate* Fidel in some way, he is not thereby imitating me. Resemblance, we may say, goes in *two* directions; imitation, in only one direction. Resemblance, in other words, is a "symmetrical" relation while imitation is "asymmetrical." This last point is probably the most important in our analysis. Imitation aims at one thing: looking exactly like the common sorts of objects we see about us every day—chairs, tables, trees, stones, etc.—and these things, perceived in their ordinary way, become the sole standard by which we judge the accuracy, and hence the worth, of the imitation. This evaluation occurs in two ways; first, insofar as we always match, say, the drawing of a chair with the chair itself to check the accuracy of the imitation, and secondly, in the sense that our everyday estimates of the relative worth of these objects is reflected in our estimate of the corresponding imitations of such objects. Part of our idea of imitation, in other words, is the assumption that if a man is more valuable than an earthworm, then a drawing of a man is more valuable than a drawing of an earthworm, even if both are equally "lifelike." Why? The answer has to do with what was just said about the asymmetrical relation between the imitation and the thing imitated. We tend to think of the copy striving to be as much like the thing copied as possible, the copy becoming a kind of poor substitute for the original. Our only interest in the copy is our interest in the original, and if we could have the original we would not want the copy.

Because of this idea that an imitation should be a replica, substitute, or counterfeit of the original, we have the corresponding idea that the more valuable the original, the more valuable the imitation. In fact almost all the properties of the original are reflected back on the imitation. Advertisers and propagandists make good use of this point. If we respond favorably to South Sea island beaches with immaculate sands, roaring surf, suitably attired girls on a cloudless, sunny day, then we will respond favorably to a picture of this enchanting scene—as well as anything else which may have been included in the picture, such as a can of pineapple. If puppies make us go all soft and mushy, then pictures will make us feel something very similar. In short, whatever may be said, thought, or felt about the original, will be said, thought, and felt about the imitation to the extent . . . that the imitation is *like* the original. That imitations are never in fact just like their originals doesn't mean that this is not their ultimate objective. Indeed, we may say that the *goal* of imitation is an object which is simply interchangeable with the original without being the same thing; in short, to create the illusion that the copy is not a copy at all, but the original. This is certainly the objective in imitation furs, china, leather, and so on.

And this is pretty much what philosophical *theories* of artistic imitation assert. A few examples from the long and illustrious history of realist theories of art are now in order. In *The Republic* Plato said roundly that the artist holds up a mirror to reality.

> Now what name would you give to a craftsman who can produce all the things made by every sort of workman? . . . For besides producing any kind of artificial thing, this same craftsman can create all plants and animals, himself included, and earth and sky and gods and the heavenly bodies and all the things under the earth. . . .
> That sounds like a miraculous fact of virtuosity. . . .
> There is no difficulty; in fact there are several ways in which the thing can be done quickly. The quickest perhaps would be to take a mirror and turn it round in all directions. In a very short time you could produce sun and stars and earth yourself and all the other animals and plants and lifeless objects which we mentioned just now.[1]

That is, the painted object is just like the real object except that it really doesn't exist. It looks so much like the reality depicted that it could actually fool someone. Of course, if we were actually fooled we wouldn't know that it was a copy or representation. The ideal, according to this view, is therefore to be fooled and then *discover* that one has been fooled. Accordingly, the history of art theory from the ancient Greeks to the first motion pictures is full of stories of people and animals mistaking art works for the objects depicted therein. And it is clear from such accounts that those stories were meant as compliments. Indeed, this is obviously the highest form of compliment one could pay to an artist, according to the realist theory; because this is what the theory implies. An art work should appear to be what it is not. For example, according to

---

1 Plato, *The Republic*, F. M. Cornford, trans. (London: Oxford University Press, 1960), pp. 325–26. [Selections in Weitz, and Dickie and Sclafani]

the historian Durius (fourth century B.C.), Appellees painted a horse so lifelike that real horses tried to communicate with the painted horse by neighing. In a contest with Parrhasius, Zeuxis painted grapes so realistically that birds tried to eat them; but when Zeuxis went to pull the curtain from Parrhasius' painting, he discovered the curtain was only painted on the canvas, and so, the prize went to Parrhasius! Plato reports that the statues of Daedalus were thought to be so lifelike that they would walk away if not tied down.

Of course, this also suggests an artistic liability. In *The Republic,* Plato works out the unhappy consequences of the views of his contemporaries that imitation is the essential feature of art. The idea that art is the imitation of reality was not Plato's invention, but a view commonly held at the time by artists, critics, and local teachers. There is a famous passage in the *Iliad,* for example, where this idea is clearly expressed. In describing a pastoral scene embossed in gold on Achilles' shield, Homer writes, "And the field looked black and seemed as though it had been ploughed although it was made of gold, for this was the great marvel of the work."[2] It was just prior to Plato's generation that the wonder of Greek realism and naturalism in painting and sculpture reached its high point, and it was during Plato's lifetime that it caused the greatest stir among intellectuals. . . .

Plato's tough attitude in *The Republic,* censoring and even banishing artists from the state, can be seen as following directly from his unflinching analysis of the imitative character of art. The result is what Bernard Bosanquet in his book *History of Aesthetics* calls an *argumentum ad absurdum* for the theory that art is imitation. Plato's analysis is valuable in showing us that art is either much more limited and worthless than we had supposed, or else that there is something seriously wrong with the idea that art is simply imitation. If Plato's analysis is right we must either accept his harsh conclusion or we must reexamine the application of imitation to art.

Let us look briefly at some of the main consequences of the concept of imitation which Plato develops in *The Republic.* He says that the artist creates the appearance of a bed by painting a picture of a bed. There are several things to note about this. First, Plato's criticism is not just that the painting doesn't *look* sufficiently like a bed; his main objection is that even the most realistic imitation *is* only *like* the thing it imitates. No matter how good the picture of the bed may be, it is still not something you can sleep on. But why should it be? Why should this count for the falseness of art? After all, a book composed of words on paper about the French Revolution may be true, but it is still not the same thing as the French Revolution. How could it be? But the falseness of an imitation, in Plato's view, is that it parades as a thing which it is not; the painter, Plato is suggesting, tries to make us think that colors on a flat board are a bed, something we can really sleep on, which it clearly is not. Plato is not suggesting that works of art typically succeed in creating a complete illusion, which is actually quite rare, but that this is what they set out to do. Thus, for Plato, a picture of a bed is a pseudo-bed. It has no life of its own as a picture, with uniquely aesthetic values and qualities pertinent only to pictures, but is strictly parasitic on the thing it imitates.

Secondly, what can a picture of a bed tell us about the bed, in Plato's view? Nothing about the real nature or structure of a bed. This knowledge is available only to the intellectual who can apprehend clearly the concept of a bed and who is able to

    2   Homer, *The Iliad,* Richmond Lattimore, trans. (Chicago: University of Chicago Press, 1951), xviii, 548–49.

define it correctly. The carpenter, although he can't give a truly rational account of the bed, has at least a practical or working knowledge of such. But the poor artist—all he knows about the bed and all he can possibly convey in a work of art is simply what the bed looks like to the casual observer. The artist can reveal no more about the bed than the lowest common denominator of everyday opinion. This is an indication of the intellectualist bias of Plato, the bias that the only important grasp of the nature of things is through intellectual means, definitions, argumentation, proof, and the like—very similar to the contemporary scientific bias which we'll have more to say about later. Anything less than this is mere common sense opinion about familiar objects. But the artist, by presenting large beds in small paintings and solid beds on flat boards, is not even true to this mundane level of popular opinion.

Plato not only criticized the artist for presenting a pretense, a sham reality which was inherently deceptive in nature, he also criticized artists for mistakes *within* the illusion itself. That is, not only were the painted saddles fake saddles no one could ride, they were also inaccurately done—missing a strap here, a fanciful latch there, and so on. If a painter is going to produce fake saddles, Plato thought, he at least ought to know what saddles actually looked like. Since the artist can imitate anything in the physical world, he cannot possibly know all there is to know about all the things he copies. And this worried Plato—the artist is a jack of all trades, but master of none. The role of the artist is considerably reduced, of course, in this interpretation. He is tied to mundane, commonplace notions of things. This is the ideal upper limit of his achievement. Such objects, understood in their ordinary way, dictate how we understand and evaluate art. But if an artist gives us only copies of what we already know and experience, what good are they? Why not look at the original? The original, according to this view, would always be better than the copy—first because it is real and second because the copy is inevitably inaccurate. The artist adds nothing.

Plato's image of the artist as a man "turning a mirror round and round," thereby creating images, appearances, or illusions, conveys the essentials of the realist view of art. The work of art is simply, at its best, the mirror image of the world. The most it can possibly present is no more than we already see with normal vision. This puts a decided limitation on the usefulness of art. The value of reproductions is generally limited to those circumstances in which the original is inaccessible to us; if I could see my own face in the morning, I would have no use for the mirror on my dresser. When we are separated from our loved ones, we carry around their likenesses, but when we have access to the originals our interest in the pictures declines. Again, we use pictures to give us some idea of what certain things, people or places are like which we have never seen, or to remind us of them if we are no longer in the vicinity. But what use or value to me is a mirror-image likeness of my desk at home which I see every day?

The priority of our ordinary ways of perceiving and understanding the common sorts of objects we daily come in contact with comes out again in Plato's criticism of the artist's attempt to imitate saddles, beds, etc., when he is ignorant of the rudimentary practical information about these things known to the saddlemaker, bedmaker, etc. But why *should* the artist know about such things? The answer is that involved in the idea of imitation is the notion that the competence of the imitator can be judged only in regard to one thing, the object imitated—not as it appears in a picture, but as it exists in real life.

Finally, the only legitimate use Plato can find for art is its value to moral education. Here also lie the greatest dangers of art, in Plato's view, and the main basis for his recommended censorship of the arts. This criticism also follows from the hypothesis that art is imitation, for as we have seen, once the imitation is tied to the original, then our responses, evaluation, and understanding of the imitation are precisely the responses, evaluation, and understanding which we already have, quite independently of art, toward the thing imitated—the bed, nude, or whatever. Hence, whatever is considered to have a bad effect on the development of character and moral sense, such as manifestations of debauchery, violent passion, cowardice, treachery, and the like, are thought to have an equally bad effect on character and moral training when imitated in stories or pictures. And, of course, the reverse holds true for whatever is thought to have an advantageous effect on moral character and training: the *imitation* of such things must also have a good effect on the moral upbringing of young people. Many hold such a view today in thinking seriously about what is suitable for children to see on TV; but we seem to give children considerably more credit than Plato in applying somewhat *different* standards to things as they occur in real life and as they appear in pictures and stories. Children love gory, gruesome stories of things they would be horrified to see in real life. If Plato were merely talking about what should be presented to the very young, our disagreement with him would probably be one of degree. But insofar as his theory is supposed to hold for art generally, and not just bedtime stories for children, his view must strike us as extreme, although it *is* an accurate analysis of the concept of imitation.

After a prolonged eclipse under the religiously motivated art of the middle Ages, realism emerged again prominently during the Renaissance, partly out of a Greek revival and partly out of a new interest in nature and in direct perceptual experience as the key to scientific truth. Artists like Alberti, Leonardo, Brunelleschi, and Dürer developed theories, like that of Plato, that the artist should reproduce the visible aspect of reality as faithfully as possible. Leonardo adopted Plato's analogy of a painting to a mirror image, though he doubted the possibility of ever attaining such a perfect likeness.

> Painters often fall into despair . . . when they see that their paintings lack the roundness and the liveliness which we find in objects seen in a mirror . . . but it is impossible for a painting to look as rounded as a mirror image . . . except if you look at both with one eye only.[3]

As you might expect, the same sorts of stories arose about these Renaissance artists which had been told earlier to flatter Greek and Roman artists. Vasari in his *Lives of the Painters* relates a story about peacocks which pecked at painted strawberries in Bernazzone's fresco and of dogs attacking a dog painted by Francesco Monsignori. Giotto, according to Vasari, graduated from art student to artist when he painted a fly on the nose of a portrait being completed by his teacher, Cimabue, so realistically that Cimabue took it for a real fly and tried to brush it away.

Yet when we examine a representative sampling of this realistically praiseworthy art, we find none of it very persuasive. In the light of the paintings themselves, the typical stories related above seem wildly exaggerated. First, all these art works look highly stylized; second, each is done in a different style. Yet, at the time each was taken to be a paradigm of realism. In fact, the irony can be extended; every age

---

[3] Leonardo, *Treatise*, McMahon, ed., no. 220, in E. H. Gombrich, *Art and Illusion* (Princeton: Princeton University Press, 1969), p. 96.

thinks its art is totally realistic and the art of every other age is completely unrealistic. What can we reasonably conclude from this? The answer has come most forcefully and persuasively from the studies of two prominent psychologists working within aesthetics, Rudolf Arnheim and E. H. Gombrich. Clearly, there is no absolute realism, no "neutral naturalism," according to Arnheim. There is no automatic mechanical duplication of realty. As Gombrich says, we must "translate, not transcribe," "transpose, not copy,"[4] physical objects into lines drawn on paper, or a square mile of landscape into daubs of oil paint on a 3 x 4 canvas in a way that renders the scene comprehensible to the eye. Arnheim puts it this way: "Representation never produces a replica of the object, but its structural equivalent in a given medium."[5] This view led the art historian, Heinrich Wölfflin, to speak of the analogy between artistic style and language. Two styles, he says, "are like two languages, in which everything can be said, although each has its strength in a different direction."[6] Another way to put this is that imitation and imagination are not opposed, as has often been thought. In representing the world the active contributions of the human mind—synthesizing, organizing, selecting, integrating—are at least as important as the passive reception of sense impressions from reality.

Each society has its own interpretation of reality in terms of which it naturally finds its own version of realism realistic and other versions unrealistic. Another way of putting this is that realism is culturally relative. . . . The paintings of a given society look realistic to that society not because they are realistic, but because they conform to the conventions which that society has adopted for depicting realism. As we saw earlier, we are not aware of the concepts we use to interpret the world. If the art of our own society looks realistic to us, it is in part because artists have taught us to see things this way. And this means that all the implications mentioned earlier of the naive realist theory are wrong.

1. It is not subject matter that is important, but the way (style, convention) that subject has been handled in that particular painting;
2. the work of art is not a transparent opening to the world, but a particular human way (among many others) of looking at the world;
3. the artwork does not just *present* the object but says something about it;
4. our response to the art work is not precisely what it is to the object depicted, but has a character of its own depending on how the object is portrayed;
5. the construction of an art object operates on a different plane from that on which the subject matter has been constructed;
6. art criticism is not tied to nonaesthetic, realistic criteria, but has principles of its own, which can sometimes contradict standards found in real life;
7. the artist brings his own individual standpoint to the artwork; and
8. reality *cannot* be portrayed just as it is in itself.

This does not mean that art is unrelated to reality—it just means that that relationship is not one of copying, but of representing or interpreting reality from a given human perspective or set of cultural conventions. We can never see an object just as it

---

4   E. H. Gombrich, *Art and Illusion* (London: Phaidon Press, 1960) [Selections in Rader]

5   Rudolf Arnheim, *Art and Visual Perception* (Berkeley: University of California Press, 1954), pp. 120–25.

6   Heinrich Wölfflin, *Principles of Art History,* M. D. Hottinger, trans. (New York: Dover Publications, 1950), p. 12.

is in itself, but only as it appears to us from our biological and cultural standpoint; similarly, we cannot translate a three-dimensional object onto a two-dimensional surface except in one of many possible conventional, stylized ways.

This point emerges most clearly from considerations of artistic style. All of us, however little we may know about paintings or music, can identify the works of a certain artist, and most of us can place works of art roughly into different groups according to period. That is, most of us would be competent to sort African, Egyptian, Greek, Renaissance, and modern French sculptures and paintings into these five distinct types. Similarly, we would undoubtedly be able without any special musical training to tell which of a group of pieces of music were those of The Beatles, which were those of J. S. Bach, and which were those of Mother Goose. Most of us can distinguish a Van Gogh from a Rembrandt, or a Michelangelo from a Picasso, even if we have seen only a handful of reproductions of each. In short, then, we can fairly easily sort works of art into types corresponding either to individual artists or to some broader grouping such as historical period or geographical location. Each of these groups or types of works of art represents a different style.

It is very difficult, on the other hand, to say just what it is about their music which allows us to distinguish the works of Haydn and Stravinsky, or, if this seems too easy, to formulate in words what it is that enables us to distinguish the works of Haydn from those of Mozart, or the works of Stravinsky from those of Bartók. This is what fascinates art historians, trying to get clear what exactly makes up what we call style, how we are able to detect something so elusive and yet do it so easily. Somehow Rubens paints everything in a certain distinctive way that is different from the way Leonardo da Vinci paints whatever it is he is painting. And similarly, for Mozart, Haydn, Stravinsky, and so on. In the case of artists like Picasso we distinguish several styles over a span of years, and if we were very careful critics or scholars we would be able to tell the earlier paintings of Rembrandt from the later, and so on. Style, then, can be very particular and individual, as the style, say, of Mozart, or, more so, the "blue period" of Picasso, or even the "early blue period," or it can be broad and general, as when we speak of Archaic Greek, or Greek, or African, or even of something as general as Primitive Art or Eastern Art. And, of course, there is every conceivable sort of intermediary case between the two extremes of particularity and generality.

Within any given style there are certain features common to a whole range of works of art, however different among themselves these works may be; these are the abstract elements of style which one tries to articulate in defining a given style. The simplest and clearest example of this can be found in children's art, which has a style all its own. In children's art of a certain developmental stage everything, whether houses, people, trees, or airplanes, is drawn with two basic forms, circles and straight lines. Circles may be used for a person's head, eyes, nose, ears, and perhaps hands and feet, while lines do the job of hair, neck, arms, legs, and torso. Articulating the basic elements of style becomes more difficult when we come to more sophisticated art forms. Wölfflin offers the following examples in his introductory chapter to *Principles of Art History*. Botticelli's "Venus" has "verve, animation, impetuosity," while Credi's "Venus" is "more flaccid"; Botticelli's is conceived in lines, Credi's in volumes; Botticelli's Venus is in motion, Credi's in repose, and so on. Metsu paints satin as weighty, less delicate and elegant than does Terboch; Metsu's rendering is heavy, Terboch's is lighter and finer. Hobbema's canvases are lighter, freer, and more airy than those of Ruysdael. And more generally, Renaissance art expresses or represents containment, rest, repose and well-rounded perfection, while the art of the Baroque period is more restless, expressing a kind of unfulfilled longing and striving.

This notion underlies Wölfflin's analogy of style and language. The analogy suggests that the same thing can be "said" in many different ways, just as the general sense of a statement can be expressed, for example, in English, German, and Japanese. You can transcribe or translate volume into lines on paper, wire sculpture, or ink wash. The analogy also suggests that these artistic techniques are merely translations and not duplications; just as words often do not do complete justice to the experience or the scene we are trying to describe, so lines drawn on paper may not convey the same weight and solidity of the actual object being drawn, but are at best only a picture and not, say, a bed of an inferior grade of reality. And just as certain effects are more readily expressed in one language than another and no translation from one language to another is absolutely equivalent in all shades and grades of meaning, so certain things, like volume, are better expressed or conveyed in oil paint rather than pen and ink or pencil drawing; and the same scene done in oil paint can never express or represent quite the same thing as a water color. Finally, there is the suggestion of a finite vocabulary and a grammar, or syntax, involved in styles of art which, as in a natural language, can be combined and recombined in infinitely many ways, and which, as in the case of languages like English, German, or Japanese, are based on widely accepted conventions which must be learned, and which thereby contain conventional *meanings.*

For example, objects in the real world do not have lines around them as we find in a drawing. A house has its own outline or silhouette or shape, but there is no heavy dark line which traces out this shape—the brick ends and the sky begins at a certain point—that's all. The sharpness of this boundary between red brick and blue sky is *translated* in a drawing into a thin black line separating two white areas representing the picture-house from the picture-sky. And this line is an elementary part of the artist's "vocabulary"; he uses the same convention to indicate all kinds of shapes—the shape of a tree, or a chair, or a person, or of branches. Of course, once the convention is established that lines trace spatial configurations, then we can objectively test the accuracy of a drawing; e.g., an oval is a more accurate drawing of an eye than a star. In drawings of this sort, we have *learned* that lines are supposed to represent shapes and the boundaries between objects, and this is what lines *mean* in such drawings. . . . These notions of style and language suggest that any given artistic style is a cultural achievement, in the same way as a natural language, and not an innate, genetic endowment.

One important *difference* between artistic representation and a natural language is the ease with which we are able to "read" drawings once we understand the basic conventions. Knowing the word *cat* doesn't help me understand what *dog* means, but once I understand a line drawing of a cat, I can immediately, without any additional tutoring, understand a line drawing of a dog, elephant, or horse. In this sense we don't *read* pictures, we *look* at them; there is a visual correlation between pictures and reality which does not exist between words and reality. Language representation is almost entirely conventional, artistic representation is only partially so. But because pictorial representation is partly conventional, there can never be a purely objective artistic representation of the world.

Ludwig Richter relates an experience he had as a young man that reveals still another reason why a purely objective vision is a myth. He and three friends vowed to draw the same view of a river as accurately as possible. The result was four quite different renderings of the scene, reflecting the temperaments of the four young men. One of the four, for example, who happened to be of a rather somber and gloomy disposition, "straightened the exuberant contours and emphasized the blue tinges." We have only to imagine, by way of contrast, how someone of Van Gogh's intense, excitable personality might have rendered the same scene. Each person saw the scene through the eyes of his own personality, and since each personality is different, each representation of that scene was different. Richter concluded that there is no completely objective vision.

Thus far, we have mentioned four main reasons why artistic representation deviates from reality—the artist's personality, the cultural outlook of the time, the art style of the period, and the artistic materials used; each of these can interpose itself between reality and the representation, significantly affecting the outcome. Works of art, we may conclude, do not copy reality but interpret or represent it. But representing an object is representing it in a certain light, interpreting it from a given point of view. The object is always represented, in other words, according to some general idea, or meaning. Apart from portraits, paintings, for example, represent types of people—an old man, a young girl, lovers—and not individual people, such as Mr. Peters or Sally, even though they are *portrayed* concretely. That is, concrete, individual *picture*-people represent types of *real* people. The same is true of fictional characters in stories, plays, and movies, Ahab, Kane, and Macbeth are concrete, individual *characters,* but they represent a much more general dimension of human existence. From our first exposure to children's stories we have been trained to look for the general significance of concrete objects in individualized fictional accounts. Every child, for example, knows that Chicken Little's mistake represents the common but dangerous human foible of leaping to conclusions and spreading unfounded rumors.

Artists and philosophers have long been aware of this generalizing character of artistic representation, and the history of realist theories has shifted back and forth between the two poles of copying the particular actual reality and representing the universal significance of that reality. Aristotle, for example, objected to Plato's view that the artist could produce only deceptive copies of concrete sensible objects, arguing instead that the artist's portrayal of particular objects represented general truths about ideal types. But the general truth about the *kind* of thing in question is not limited, as in the copy theory, to recording the way particular things actually happen, but only to the *kind* of thing that is likely to happen.

In the *Poetics,* Plato's former student Aristotle says that what the poet describes or imitates is *not* the thing as it actually happened, but "a *kind* of thing that *might* happen, i.e., what is possible as being probable or necessary. . . ."[7]

For this reason Aristotle holds that poetry is more philosophical than history; that is, the statements of poetry are universal in that they describe the *kind* of thing a person would *probably* do, in the sense that this is what people *generally* do. The only reason for an artist to imitate what actually happened is that such a thing, being actual, is possible. A tragedy which employs the names of actual people as its characters is convincing because the audience believes that this really happened. Nonetheless, where the actual incidents are in some sense improbable, Aristotle holds

---

[7] Aristotle, *The Poetics,* Ingram Bywater, trans. (London: Oxford University Press, 1920). [Selections in Dickie and Sclafani, and Weitz]

that the playwright must alter them to conform to something more probable. If a poet takes his story from history, he is a poet only insofar as he selects from the historical incidents those which are probable.

Notice how far this account of Aristotle takes us away from the naive view of art as imitation. The artist is no longer limited by the way things actually are, and art is no longer subservient to the character of objects outside of works of art; instead, in Aristotle's view, the artist can alter "truth" and "real life" in a work of art to satisfy internal needs of a work of art, such as consistency, integrity, unity, and plausibility. As he says, a poet or a painter may represent things "either as they were or are, as they are said or thought to be or to have been, or as they ought to be." There are two things to note about this. The first is that such a view disallows practically nothing on the grounds of lack of realism—under the appropriate circumstances the representation of a man with the head of a bull (i.e., things as they were "thought to be"), or an ideal society with no trace of animosity or hostility (i.e., things as they "ought to be"), would find its place in Aristotle's amended notion of imitation. The second thing to note is that imitationist criteria have shifted considerably from heteronomous conformity to the world to the internal and autonomous requirements of a good work of art. What really determines whether something is to be allowed or judged good in a work of art? The answer is still, "that it imitate reality," but this formula has now ceased to function as an external or objective criterion as it did in Plato and has become instead a way of describing internal requirements like consistency. The old slogan remains, though its nonaesthetic teeth have been removed. What really counts now is what is convincing or likely *within the work of art;* the standard has shifted from an ordinary probability to an aesthetic probability. If a story is about Alice in a looking-glass, then there is nothing improbable in Alice shrinking in size when she eats a piece of mushroom; and a description of Hell would be unrealistic if it did not represent demons torturing the souls of the wicked.

True, there is still quite a strong link with reality, even in Aristotle's modified notion of imitation. Our notion of what is probable in a work of art depends on what we believe is likely to happen in real life, and this depends on what actually does happen in a lot of individual cases, and thus reflects *indirectly* the actual course of events in the world. Likewise our notions of what ought to be or what other people believe or would accept as true, depend to a certain extent on what actually happens in the "real world." But this sort of dependence on the "real world" has no legislative force to dictate, in advance from some independent standpoint, what can and cannot appear in a work of art. It doesn't imply that the artist is wrong for deviating from reality; it just means that, like all of us his imagination is not unlimited. The fact that as human beings our imaginary constructions are parasitic on reality imposes no restrictions on the artist to deviate from reality as much as he can and wants.

As Aristotle says, his account of probability and artistic unity is meant to shield the artist from the kind of adverse criticism one finds in *The Republic.* Let's look at an example of this sort of criticism and see how Aristotle's account is meant to deflect it. Suppose a critic says that "Jack and the Beanstalk" is a bad story because it describes a hen laying a golden egg, which is impossible. Now consider the following defense of the story on Aristotelian grounds.

> Ordinarily, a hen laying a golden egg would indeed be strange, but if you look closely at the story you will see that it is entirely convincing and, indeed, this or something like it is necessary to make the story credible. This is a story about *giants,*

and giants live in a very special, magical realm. This is why the author presents the giants as living in the sky. In kingdoms of this kind, as judged by all other accounts, things happen which couldn't happen in our world; and we expect them to happen because this is the difference between their world and ours. So to judge the probability of incidents of this kind, you really must look at what goes on *inside* the story.

Thus on the level of practical criticism—that is, in the business of criticizing works of art or defending them against such criticisms—a perfectly plausible move is made from a damning improbability outside of the work of art to a commendable probability within the work.

But this is a move in the practice of art criticism; it doesn't follow that works of art have nothing to do with "real life" or that "the world" in the work of art is entirely removed from our ordinary world. Look at how much of "Jack and the Beanstalk" is made convincing by the sorts of things we would consider probable outside of that story, that is, in "real life." Why the giant's wife hide Jack? Because she is a woman and women are supposed to be more kind-hearted, and so on. But why, assuming she wishes to save Jack, put him in the woodbox? Because giants, like us, have the sort of vision which cannot penetrate opaque objects like wood boxes. Why is the giant unhappy about Jack's taking the hen? Because he is possessive, just like people. (On the other hand, why do we sympathize with Jack? After all, the hen belongs to the giant who never did anything to Jack and Jack simply stole the thing. Unless we have previously been told something about the wicked nature of giants in general, we would probably not be so sympathetic with Jack. Also, of course, Jack is "one of us" and the giant is not.)

The author of a story can establish within the story something like general laws and regularities which differ from, and even contradict, our own, as in *Gulliver's Travels, Alice in Wonderland,* or *The Hobbit.* Here what counts as probable or likely is determined in a further sense by the internal makeup of the story. But even here there is a certain dependence upon ordinary probability in establishing this extraordinary probability. Swift, for example, constantly relies on our sense of our own political and social institutions in establishing what seem, within the story, to be believable societies. Without this dependency upon our own political and social institutions we would be utterly unable to understand Swift's parody of them. Alice's bizarre encounters depend on our familiarity with the kinds of linguistic expressions of ordinary language which puzzle and delight children: "mad as a hatter," "mock turtle soup," "war of the roses," etc., and, at least for Lewis Carroll's adult readers, traditional philosophical problems arising out of these linguistic puzzles—the smile of the Cheshire cat without the cat. And for all their differences, hobbits are very much like people in their social and psychological makeup.

So, to insist that one must judge the probability of a story by the standards laid down within that story is not to deny that the story is in some sense a representation of incidents, people, or ideas from "real life." The two claims are fully compatible. The artist's concern is not to *duplicate* scenes from real life, but to *represent* certain aspects of life as he sees them from his own special standpoint. Thus, we are gradually led, in Aristotle's analysis, to distinguish the "imitation" of reality from its "representation" in works of art. "Imitation" judges a work of art by comparing it with objects and situations *outside* of works of art. As such, it proves to be an external, heteronomous criterion largely irrelevant to the internal structure of a work of art. "Representation," on the other hand, is the way this reality has been portrayed *within* the work of art and is thus concerned directly with the internal, autonomous requirements of the work of art itself.

"Representation" is thus the more sophisticated offshoot arising from Aristotle's critique of Plato's imitationist theory of the relation of art to the world, and survives the main objection to "imitation," that it is heteronomous and hence aesthetically irrelevant.

In discussing imitation, Aristotle is led first to modify the notion of imitation in art, and then to open up for us new possibilities for representational criteria in aesthetics. Not even Aristotle fully approves of an aesthetic probability which is improbable in the ordinary sense. He says throughout that it is better to make the tragic plot probable in the ordinary as well as in the aesthetic sense. He concedes only that if the artist fails to meet the standard of ordinary probability, he may still be rescued from banishment if he compensates for this by probability within the story. In one passage he advises that tragedians not use improbabilities at all; and secondly, that if they do, they are not to show them on stage; and third, that if they do show them on stage, they are to make them probable (that is, *within* the story).

In another place he remarks: "Any impossibilities there may be in his descriptions of things are faults. But from another point of view they are justifiable, if they serve the end of poetry itself."[8] This statement clearly internalizes the probability requirement. From some nonaesthetic point of view, such as the scientific, educational, or moral, improbabilities in the ordinary sense may be regarded as faults; but from the only point of view that matters to *art,* the point of view that restricts itself to the internal needs and requirements of the work of art, improbabilities are justifiable. . . .

In the history of art theory, opinion has swung back and forth between the heteronomous copy view that the art work directly mirrors the particular, concrete object, and the autonomous representational view that it interprets particular objects in the light of some general significance. But this is only what people *said* about art; is the art itself divisible into these two types—literal copying and a representational art? No, as our previous analysis has already suggested, there is no literal copying, no objective vision, no neutral naturalism. But then why do people believe their own art is objective and neutral? Because . . . people aren't aware of their own conventions—we are ordinarily aware of the conventions of other people, not our own. *Our* conventions seem perfectly objective! In fact they seem realistic in proportion to the degree that we are unconscious of them. Through increased familiarity, social conventions are gradually absorbed into a permanent, unconscious background that is indistinguishable from the objective world. As the great eighteenth-century Scottish philosopher David Hume noted, much of the world as we perceive it is an imaginative construction.

NOTE ON SOURCES. The material in this section is from H. Gene Blocker, *Philosophy of Art* (New York: Charles Scribner's Sons, 1979), Chapter 2.

2 EUGENE VÉRON

ART AS EXPRESSION OF EMOTION

FROM BLOCKER TO VÉRON. The ancient theory of art as imitation of reality suggested that artists in their works were trying to copy reality as perfectly as a mirror reflects an image. In such a view, deviations from reality in the artist's work

---

8 *Ibid.*

would be regarded as flaws in the work of art resulting from deficiencies in the artist's skills. Such an account of art, however, did not do justice to deviations from reality resulting from the artist's perspective, creative imagination, style, materials used, and so forth. Accordingly, the theory of art as representation of reality was developed, which moved the interpretation of art away from a naive "realism" and allowed art to be considered as a blend of the personal distinctive characteristics of the artist and the objective features of reality. But how much liberty should art be allowed in deviating from objective reality? As art moves away from mirroring the objective features of reality, it moves toward expressing the peculiar subjective perspective of the artist. In so doing, art becomes less "cognitive" and more "expressive" of the artist's emotions, feelings, and tastes. This movement away from the "cognitive" toward the "expressive" has received wide acceptance on the modern scene, and the view that art is the expression of emotion has become dominant. It is that view that our next three authors, Véron, Tolstoy, and Collingwood, articulate, modify, and defend.

Eugene Véron (1825–1889) provides a classic statement of the position that art is the expression of emotion. The selections appearing below are taken from Véron's work *Aesthetics,* published in 1878. Translated into English in 1879, his book is now out of print and difficult to come by. This is regrettable because it has the virtues of simplicity and clarity. Whether you agree with Véron or not, at least you know where he stands. If you agree, he leaves you free to develop beyond him if you see the necessity for doing so. If you disagree, he leaves you with a clear picture of that with which you disagree.

THE ARGUMENT OF THE PASSAGES. Véron's proposal is that a work of art is an emotive symbol, something whereby the artist expresses his emotions, his feelings. An emotive symbol can be contrasted with a cognitive symbol, something whereby one expresses what one knows or believes, in contrast to what one feels. It is one thing to have emotions and to express them: this calls for an emotive symbol. It is another to have knowledge or belief, and to express them: this calls for a cognitive symbol. We all need and use both kinds of symbols. But we are not all equally talented at creating either kind. So we put artists and cognizers to work for us. If emotions are to be expressed, a symbol or vehicle must be created enabling them to be expressed. Art is the activity of creating these emotionally expressive symbols. The symbol is the work of art.

Véron distinguishes sharply between this way of conceiving art and the older way, which thought of art as the activity of producing a copy or imitation of some original. According to this imitation theory, an artist looks at a man or a mountain and paints "what he sees." The result would be an imitation or copy or "picture" of some "original." To this way of thinking, the work of art would be something of a cognitive symbol. It would tell you what you would know if you knew the original. You could gauge its excellence by comparing it with the original. To this way of thinking a good camera might produce a better (that is, more accurate) work of art than any painter could do. Compared to an original, a photograph can be more accurate than a painting. Even greater accuracy could be obtained by holding a mirror up to an original. Véron's essential claim would rule out mirror-images, photographs, contrived echoes, tape recordings, and so on as works of art, and the activity of producing them as art. The artist must have a certain feeling or emotion. The work of art must express that feeling or emotion.

This primary claim enables Véron to distinguish between decorative and expressive art. The latter is art proper. It is not to be judged by its power to please, but by its power to express. The claim—art as creation of emotive symbol—enables him also to develop the notions of artistic integrity and artistic style. Integrity demands that one express the emotions one has, whether one is a painter, musician, actor, or some other form of artist. Style is the way in which the person one basically is, determines the way in which one gives expression to the emotions one has.

His theory also enables Véron to distinguish between lyric and dramatic. When art is lyric, the intention is to express feelings, sensations, emotions that the artist has experienced. They may be sharable, but the point is they are the artist's own in the first instance. Had you asked him, Matthew Arnold might have said as much about his "Dover Beach." Is it to be denied that his testimony would count as evidence? When art is dramatic, the intention is to express feelings that belong primarily to someone else. This someone else may be a historical person, as in Plato's Socrates, or an imaginary person, as in Goethe's Faust. These are a few of the good things to be had from a reading of Véron's statement of the emotive theory of art. No matter what awkward questions that theory may give rise to, there is no dismissing it out of hand on the grounds that it does not lead one to think fruitfully about art.

> Art, far from being the blossom and fruit of civilization, is rather its germ. It began to give evidence of its existence so soon as man became self-conscious, and is to be found clearly defined in his very earliest works.
>
> By its psychological origin it is bound up with the constituent principles of humanity. The salient and essential characteristic of man is his incessant cerebral activity, which is propagated and developed by countless acts and works of varied kind. The aim and rule of this activity is the search after *the best*; that is to say, the more and more complete satisfaction of physical and moral wants. This instinct, common to all animals, is seconded in man by an exceptionally well-developed faculty to adapt the means to the end.
>
> The effort to satisfy physical wants has given birth to all the industries that defend, preserve, and smooth the path of life; the effort to satisfy the moral wants—of which one of the most important is gratification of our cerebral activity itself—has created the arts, long before it could give them power sufficient for the conscious elaboration of ideas. The life of sentiment preceded the manifestations of intellectual life by many centuries.
>
> The gratification, *in esse* or *in posse,* of either real or imaginary wants, is the cause of happiness, joy, pleasure, and of all the feelings connected with them; the contrary is marked by grief, sadness, fear, etc.: but in both cases there is emotion to give more or less lively evidence by means of exterior signs. When expressed by gesture and rhythmic movement, such emotion produces the dance; when by rhythmic notes, music; when by rhythmic words, poetry.

As man is essentially sympathetic and his joy or pain is often caused as much by the good or evil fortunes of others as by his own; as, besides, he possesses in a very high degree the faculty of combining series of fictitious facts, and of representing them in colors even more lively than those of reality: it results that the domain of art is of infinite extent for him. For the causes of emotion are multiplied for every man—not only by the number of similar beings who live around him and are attached to him by the more or less closely knit bonds of affection, alliance, similitude of situation or community of ideas and interests; but also, by the never-ending multitude of beings and events that are able to originate or direct the imaginings of poets.

To these elements of emotion and moral enjoyment must be added the combinations of lines, of forms and of colors, the dispositions and opposition of light and shade, etc. The instinctive search after this kind of emotion or pleasure, the special organ of which is the eye, has given birth to what are called the arts of design—sculpture, painting and architecture.

We may say then, by way of general definition, that art is the manifestation of emotion, obtaining external interpretation, now by expressive arrangements of line, form or color, now by a series of gestures, sounds, or words governed by particular rhythmical cadence.

We must conclude, from our definition, that the merit of a work of art can be measured by the power with which it manifests or interprets the emotion that was its determining cause, and that, for a like reason, must constitute its innermost and supreme unity.

Imitation is not the aim of art. The poet arranging his verses, the musician composing his airs and harmonies, are well aware that their real object is not imitation. This distinction is perhaps less clear in matters of painting and sculpture. Some artists, and these not the least capable, are convinced that when they have a model before them, their one duty is to imitate it, copy it. And indeed they do nothing else; and, by virtue of such imitation, they succeed in producing works of incontestable artistic value.

Here we have simply a misunderstanding. If an artist were really able to reduce himself to the condition of a copying machine; if he could so far efface and suppress himself as to confine his work to the servile reproduction of all the details of an object or event, the only value his work would possess would be that of a more or less exact *procès verbal*, and it would perforce remain inferior to reality. Where is the artist who would attempt to depict sunlight without taking refuge in some legerdemain, calling to his aid devices which the true sun would despise? But enough of this. Just because he is endowed with sensibility and imaginative power, the artist, in presence of the facts of nature or the events of history, finds himself, whether he will or not, in a peculiar situation. However thorough a realist he may think himself, he does not leave himself to chance. Now, choice of subject alone is enough to prove that some preference has existed, the result of a more or less predeterminate impression, and of a more or less unconscious agreement between the character of the object and that of the artist. This impression and agreement he sets to work to embody in outward form; it is the real aim of his work, and its possession gives him his claim to the name of artist. Without wishing or even knowing it, he molds the features of nature to his dominant impression and to the idea that caused him to take pencil in hand. His work has an accidental stamp, in addition to that of the permanent genius which constitutes his individuality. Poet, musician, sculptor and architect, all pay more or less strict obedience to the same law. To it, point all those rules of artistic composition which pedantic academicism has subtly multiplied until they contradict each other.

The more of this personal character that a work possesses; the more harmonious its details and their combined expression; the more clearly each part communicates the impression of the artist, whether of grandeur, of melancholy, of joy; in fine, the more the expression of human sensation and will predominates over mere imitation, the better will be its chance of obtaining sooner or later the admiration of the world—always supposing that the sentiment expressed be a generous one, and that the execution be not of such a kind as to repel or baffle connoisseurs. It is not of course impossible that an artist endowed with an ill-regulated or morbid imagination may place himself outside all normal conditions and condemn himself to the eternal misapprehension of the public. Impressions that are too particular, eccentric feelings, fantastic execution or processes, which do nothing to raise the intrinsic value or power of inspiration of a work, may give it so strange and ultra-individual a character that it may become impossible for us to arrive at its real merit. The best qualities, when exaggerated, become faults; and that very personality or individuality which, when added to imitative power, results in a work of art, produces when pushed to extravagance nothing but an enigma.

We see, then, that the beautiful in art springs mainly from the intervention of the genius of man when excited by special emotion.

A work is beautiful when it bears strong marks of the individuality of its author, of the permanent personality of the artist, and of the more or less accidental impression produced upon him by the sight of the object or event rendered.

In a word, it is from the worth of the artist that the worth of his work is derived. It is the manifestation of the faculties and qualities he possesses which attracts and fascinates us. The more sympathetic power and individuality these faculties and qualities display, the easier it is for them to obtain our love and admiration. On the other hand, we, for a similar reason, reject and condemn bold and vulgar works that by their shortcomings demonstrate the moral and intellectual mediocrity of their authors, and prove the latter to have mistaken their vocation.

Consequently, then, beauty in art is a purely human creation. Imitation may be its means, as in sculpture and painting; or, on the other hand, it may have nothing to do with it, as in poetry and music. This beauty is of so peculiar a nature that it may exist even in ugliness itself; inasmuch as the reproduction of an ugly model may be a beautiful work of art, by the ensemble of qualities which the composition of it may prove are possessed by its author

The theory of imitation is but the incomplete and superficial statement of the ideas which we are here advocating. What is it that we admire in imitation? The resemblance? We have that much better in the object itself. But how is it that the similitude of an ugly object can be beautiful? It is obvious that between the object and its counterfeit some new element intervenes. This element is the personality, or, at least, the skill of the artist. This latter, indeed, is what they admire who will have it that beauty consists in imitation. What these applaud, in fact, is the talent of the artist. If we look below the surface and analyze their admiration we shall find that it is so; whether they mean it or not, what they praise in a work is the worker.

This was the opinion of Büger, who says: "In works which interest us the authors in a way substitute themselves for nature. However common or vulgar the latter may be, they have some rare and peculiar way of looking at it. It is Chardin himself whom we admire in his representation of a glass of water. We admire the genius of Rembrandt in the profound and individual character which we imparted to every head that posed before him. Thus did they seem to him, and this explains everything simple or fantastic in his expression and execution."

After all this, we need not stop to refute the theory which would found artistic beauty upon the imitation of "beautiful nature."

The only beauty in a work of art is that placed there by the artist. It is both the result of his efforts and the foundation of his success. As often as he is struck by any vivid impression—whether moral, intellectual, or physical—and expresses that impression by some outward activity, by poetry, music, sculpture, painting or architecture—in such a way as to cause its communication with the soul of spectator or auditor; so often does he produce a work of art the beauty of which will be in exact proportion to the intelligence and depth of the sentiment displayed, and the power shown in giving it outward form.

The union of all these conditions constitutes artistic beauty in its most complete expression. We may define aesthetics as the science of beauty in art. It is the science whose object is the study and elucidation of the manifestations of artistic genius.

There are two distinct kinds of art: decorative and expressive. The main object of decorative art is the gratification of the eye and ear. Its chief means to perfection of form are harmony and grace of contour, diction or sound. Such art rests upon the desire for beauty, and has nothing in view beyond the peculiar delight caused by the sight of beautiful objects. It has produced admirable works in the past, and may produce them again on condition that its inspiration be sought in actual and existing life, and not in the imitation of works sanctified by time.

Modern art has no tendency in this latter decorative direction. Decorative beauty no longer suffices for us in art. Something more has been required. The chief characteristic of modern art is power of expression. Through form this, the second kind of art, traces the moral life, and endeavors to occupy man, body and soul, but with no thought of sacrificing the one to the other.

The moral life is but the general result of the conditions of the physical. The one is bound to the other by necessary connections which cannot be broken without destroying both. The first care of the artist should be to seek out and grasp the methods of manifestation so as to comprehend and master their unity.

Art, thus understood, demands intellectual faculties higher and more robust than if founded solely upon an ideal of beauty. Art founded upon the latter notion would be sufficiently served by one possessing an acute sense of the beautiful—the degree of his sensibility being indicated by the plastic perfection of his work. But expressive art demands a capability of being moved by many sentiments, demands the power to penetrate beneath outward appearances and to seize a hidden thought, the power to grasp either the permanent characteristic or the particular and momentary emotion; in a word, it demands that complete eloquence of representation which art might have dispensed with while it confined itself to the investigation or delineation of a single expression, but which became indispensable the moment the interpretation of the entire man became its object.

We may say, too, that modern art is doubly expressive; because, while the artist is indicating by form and sound the sentiments and ideas of the personages whom he introduces, he is also by the power and manner of such manifestation giving an unerring measure of his own sensibility, imagination, and intelligence.

Expressive art is in no way hostile to beauty; it makes use of it as one element in the subjects which require it, but its domain is not enclosed within the bounds of such a conception. It is not indifferent to the pleasures of sight and hearing, but it sees something beyond them. Its worth must not be measured only by perfection of form, but also and chiefly, by the double power of expression which we have pointed out, and, we must add, by the value of the sentiments and ideas expressed. This latter point is too often and wrongly ignored by artists.

Between two works which give evidence of equal facility to grasp the accents and characteristics of nature, and equal power to bring out both the inner meaning of things and the personality of the artist—we, for our part, would prefer that one of which the *Conception* showed the more vigorous intelligence and elevated feeling. The art critics seem to have made it one of their principles to take no account of choice of subject, but only to look at the technical result. Such a principle is plausible rather than true. The individuality of the author can never be excluded from a work, and choice of subject is frequently one of the points by which this individuality is most clearly indicated.

It is true, of course, that elevation of sentiment can never take the place of art talent. On this point we cannot too strongly condemn the practice of academic juries who, on the one hand, reward mere mechanical labor simply because it has been exercised upon what are called classic subjects; and, on the other, persecute more independent artists to punish their obstinacy in deserting the beaten track. Nothing, then, can be further from our thoughts than to require critics to substitute, in every case, consideration of the subject for that of the work itself; or to condemn *a priori* all artists who remain faithful to the traditions, ideas, and sentiments of the past. In these, indeed, some find their only inspiration. We only wish to affirm our conviction that choice of subject is not so indifferent a matter as some say it is, and that it must be taken into account as of considerable weight in determining an opinion of a work of art.

This is one consequence of the distinction between decorative and expressive art. The former, solely devoted to the gratification of eye and ear, affords no measure of its success beyond the pleasure which it gives. The latter, whose chief object is to express the feelings and ideas, and through them, to manifest the power of conception and expansion possessed by the artist, must obviously be estimated, partly at least, by the moral or other value of the ideas and sentiments in question. And, as the value of a work depends directly upon the capability of its author, and as many artists have been about equal in their technical ability, we must be ready to acknowledge that moral and intellectual superiority is a real superiority, and is naturally marked by the possession of an instinctive and spontaneous power of sympathy.

Style is the man. Get some one who *can* read, to read a page of Demosthenes *and* of Cicero, of Bossuet and of Massillon, of Corneille and of Racine, of Lamartine and of Victor Hugo. You will notice that no two of them sound the same. Apart from the subject or ideas, which may be identical, each one has an air, an accent, which can never be confounded or replaced. In some of them we find elegance, finesse, grace, the most seductive and soothing harmony; in others, a force and *élan* like the sound of a trumpet.

Style only exists by virtue of *the law of separation.* "A being only exists in consequence of his separation from other beings. . . . This law of successive detachment—which alone renders progress possible—may be proved to influence the course of religion, of politics, of literature and of art." It is by style, by the manner of comprehension, of feeling and interpretation, that epochs, races, schools and individuals are separated and distinguished one from the other. In all the arts, analogous differences are to be found; plainly marked, in proportion as a more or less extensive field is offered for the development of artistic personality. Michelangelo and Raphael, Leonardo and Veronese, Titian and Correggio, Rubens and Rembrandt, resembled each other no more and no less than Beethoven resembled Rossini; Weber, Mozart; or

Wagner resembles Verdi. Each has his own style, his peculiar mode of thinking and feeling, and of expressing those feelings and thoughts.

Why have mediocre artists no style? For the same reasons that they are mediocrities. The particular characteristic of mediocrity is commonness or vulgarity of thought and feeling. At each moment in the evolution of a social system, there is a general level which marks, for that moment, the average value of the human psyche and intellect. Such works as rise above this general level imply an amount of talent or genius in proportion to the amount of superior elevation and spontaneity which they display. Mediocrity comes up to the general level, but does not pass it; thus the mediocre artist thinks and feels like the ordinary run of mankind, and has nothing to "separate" him from the crowd. He may have a manner, an ensemble of habits of working, peculiar to himself; but he can have no style in the accurate sense of the word. Facility is not style; for the latter is a product, a reverberation from the soul itself, and can no more be artificially acquired than can the sonorousness of bronze or silver be acquired by lead. . . .

Style, which is a simple reflection of the artist's personality, is naturally found in the work of every artist who possesses any personality. The indescribable quality, the *je ne sais quoi,* is precisely the assemblage of qualities, the condition of being and temperament which caused Rubens to see things differently from Rembrandt. The two extracted, from one and the same object or subject, emotions widely different though congenial to their respective natures; just as a tightened string in a concert room will vibrate in response t the note which it would itself produce if struck. The one thing needful is the power to vibrate, which is too often wanting.

The question of style is important. We might even say that it includes the whole of aesthetics, which is in fact the question of personality in art. . . .

Truth and *personality:* these are the alpha and omega of art formulas; *truth* as to the facts, and the *personality* of the artist. But, if we look more closely, we shall see that these two terms are in reality but one. Truth as to fact, so far as art is concerned, is above all the truth of our own sensations, of our own sentiments. It is truth as we see it, as it appears modified by our own temperaments, preferences, and physical organs. It is, in fact, our personality itself. Reality, as given by the photographer, reality taken from a point of view without connection with us or our impressions, is the negation of art. When this kind of truth predominates in a work of art, we cry, "There is realism for you!" Now, realism partakes of the nature of art, only because the most downright of realists must, whether he will or not, put something of his own individuality into his work. When, on the other hand, the dominant quality is what we call human or personal truth, then we at once exclaim, "Here is an artist!"

And the latter is the right meaning of the word. Art consists essentially in the predominance of subjectivity over objectivity; it is the chief distinction between it and science. The man intended for science is one whose imagination has no modifying influence over the results of his direct observation. The artist on the other hand, is one whose imagination, impressionability—in a word, personality— is so lively and excitable that it spontaneously transforms everything, dyeing them in its own colors, and unconsciously exaggerating them in accordance with its own preferences.

We think ourselves justified, then, in calling art the direct and spontaneous manifestation of human personality. But we must not omit also the fact that personality—individual and particular as it is from some points of view—is nevertheless exposed to many successive and temporary modifications caused by the various kinds of civilization through which it has had to pass.

NOTE ON SOURCES.   The material in this section is from Eugene Véron, *Aesthetics*, published in 1878 and translated in 1879. A few brief passages have been deleted.

 LEO TOLSTOY

ART AS COMMUNICATION OF EMOTION

FROM VÉRON TO TOLSTOY.   Véron published his reflections on art and works of art in 1878. The book was read almost at once by the Russian novelist Leo Tolstoy. By 1878 Tolstoy was himself a well-known European novelist, the author of *War and Peace* and *Anna Karenina*. There was no question but that these were works of art and their author an artist. It is not irrelevant therefore that Véron's thesis made a considerable impression upon Tolstoy. That a man is an artist does not *guarantee* his answer to the question, "What is art?" But it at least makes it difficult to say that, in addressing himself to this question, he "does not know what he is talking about." Tolstoy had read and thought about this question: What, as artist, was he seeking to do when he produced his great novels? In 1896 he published his conclusions in a small but important book, *What is Art?*

BIOGRAPHICAL NOTE.   Leo Tolstoy was born in 1828 and died in 1910, aged eighty-two. He was born into one of the great families of the Russian aristocracy. His three books, *Childhood, Boyhood,* and *Youth,* give a vivid account of the life of a privileged young aristocrat. After completing his university education, he spent time in military service, following it with a period of European travel. He was married in 1863, and for fifteen years led a happy, successful, productive life, earning wealth and world-wide fame as a novelist. To this period belong *War and Peace* and *Anna Karenina.* Beginning in 1878, and lasting until his death in 1910, he became increasingly alienated from modern civilization in most of its "important" phases. Stages in this rejection of modern civilization are set forth in a series of small books, which combine vivid autobiography with social and cultural criticism—e.g., *My Confession, What I Believe, What Then Shall We Do? The Kingdom of God Is Within You,* and *What Is Art?* These essays in criticism and repudiation contain an impressive attempt to formulate a "philosophy of life."

THE ARGUMENT OF THE PASSAGES.   In his book *What Is Art?* Tolstoy admits that Véron's emotive theory of art is correct as far as it goes, but he insists that it does not go far enough. What it says is necessary but not sufficient. If you stop short with Véron's claim that art is the *expression* of emotion, you have told only half the story. You must add that it is the *communication* of emotion; the intentional successful communication to reader or listener or spectator of emotion felt by the artist. He has some refinements on this, but communication of emotion is the essential point. Tolstoy, like Véron, defends this thesis against the older idea of art as imitation. He also defends it, at great length, against the older thesis that art is the creating of beauty. Indeed the book gives the impression that Tolstoy's principal *bête noire* is the notion that there is any necessary connection between art and beauty.

The claim that art is the communication of emotion enables Tolstoy to distinguish between art and nonart; e.g., between a picture of a sunset and a sunset. A picture of a sunset, provided it communicates the emotion that the artist felt about the sunset, is a work of art. But the sunset itself, unless we think of it as the work of a Divine Artist, is not and cannot be a work of art. Once we have a principle that enables us to distinguish between art and nonart, we can raise the further question of the distinction, within art, between good art and bad art; that is, once we have got a criterion of recognition we can ask about a criterion of evaluation. The latter presupposes the former. This question Tolstoy handles by referring to the quality, the character, the nature, of the emotion communicated. If it is one kind of emotion, you have good art; if another kind, bad art. Friends of the emotive theory of art have taken less kindly to Tolstoy's way of distinguishing, within art, between good and bad. Indeed, they have been amused or scandalized by the conclusions he arrived at when he applied this secondary principle to specific works of art; e.g., when he found that his own great novels were art but perhaps neither good nor great.

> In order to define art correctly it is necessary first of all to cease to consider it as a means to pleasure, and to consider it as one of the conditions of human life. Viewing it in this way we see that art is a means of intercourse between man and man.
>
> Every work of art causes the receiver to enter into a certain kind of relationship both with him who produced or is producing the art, and with all those who receive the same artistic impression.
>
> Speech transmitting the thoughts and experiences of men serves as a means of union among them. Art serves a similar purpose. The peculiarity of the latter consists in this, that whereas by words a man transmits his thoughts by art he transmits his feelings.
>
> The activity of art is based on the fact that a man receiving through his sense of hearing or sight another man's expression of feeling, is capable of experiencing the emotion which moved the man who expressed it. To take the simplest example: one man laughs, and another who hears becomes merry, or a man weeps, and another who hears feels sorrow. A man is excited or irritated, and another man seeing him is brought to a similar state of mind. By his movements or by the sounds of his voice a man expresses courage and determination or sadness and calmness, and this state of mind passes on to others. A man suffers, manifesting his sufferings by groans and spasms, and this suffering transmits itself to other people; a man expresses his feelings of admiration, devotion, fear, respect, or love, to certain objects, persons, or phenomena, and others are infected by the same feelings of admiration, devotion, fear, respect, or love, to the same objects, persons, or phenomena.
>
> It is on this capacity of man to receive another man's expression of feeling and to experience those feelings himself, that the activity of art is based.
>
> If a man infects another directly, immediately, by his appearance or by the sounds he gives vent to at the time he experiences the feeling; if he causes another man to yawn when he himself cannot help yawning, or to laugh or cry when he himself is obliged to laugh or cry, or to suffer when he himself is suffering—that does not amount to art.

Art begins when one person with the object of joining another or others to himself in one and the same feeling, expresses that feeling by certain external indications. To take an example: a boy, having experienced fear on encountering a wolf, relates that encounter, and in order to evoke in others the feeling he has experienced, describes himself, his condition before the encounter, the surroundings, the wood, his own lightheartedness, and then the wolf's appearance, its movements, the distance between himself and the wolf, and so forth. All this, if only the boy when telling the story again experiences the feelings he had lived through, and infects the hearers and compels them to feel what he had experienced—is art. Even if the boy had not seen a wolf but had frequently been afraid of one, and if wishing to evoke in others the fear he had felt, he invented an encounter with a wolf and recounted it so as to make his hearers share the feelings he experienced when he feared the wolf, that also would be art. And in the same way it is art if a man, having experienced either the fear of suffering or the attraction of enjoyment (whether in reality or in imagination), expresses these feelings on canvas or in marble so that others are infected by them. And it is also art if a man feels, or imagines to himself, feelings of delight, gladness, sorrow, despair, courage, or despondency, and the transition from one to another of these feelings, and expresses them by sounds so that the hearers are infected by them and experience them as they were experienced by him.

The feelings with which the artist infects others may be very strong or very weak, very important or very insignificant, very bad or very good: feelings of love of one's country, self-devotion and submission to fate or to God expressed in drama, raptures of lovers described in a novel, feelings of voluptuousness expressed in a picture, courage expressed in a triumphal march, merriment evoked by a dance, humor evoked by a funny story, the feeling of quietness transmitted by an evening landscape or by a lullaby, or the feeling of admiration evoked by a beautiful arabesque—it is all art.

If only the spectators or auditors are infected by the feelings which the author has felt, it is art.

To evoke in oneself a feeling one has once experienced and having evoked it in oneself then by means of movements, lines, colors, sounds, or forms expressed in words, so to transmit that feeling that others experience the same feeling—this is the activity of art.

Art is a human activity consisting in this, that one man consciously by means of certain external signs, hands on to others feelings he has lived through, and that others are infected by these feelings and also experience them.

Art is not the manifestation of some mysterious idea of beauty or God; it is not a game in which man lets off his excess of stored-up energy; it is not the expression of man's emotions by external signs; it is not the production of pleasing objects; and, above all, it is not pleasure; but it is a means of union among men joining them together in the same feelings, and indispensable for the life and progress towards well-being of individuals and humanity.

As every man, thanks to man's capacity to express thoughts by words, may know all that has been done for him in the realms of thought by all humanity before his day, and can in the present, thanks to this capacity to understand the thoughts of others, become a sharer in their activity and also himself hand on to his contemporaries and descendants the thoughts he has assimilated from others as well as those that have arisen in himself; so, thanks to man's capacity to be infected with the feelings of others by means of art, all that is being lived through by his contemporaries is accessible to him, as well as the feelings experienced by men thousands of years ago, and he has also the possibility of transmitting his own feelings to others.

If people lacked the capacity to receive the thoughts conceived by men who precede them and to pass on to others their own thoughts, men would be like wild beasts or like Kasper Hauser.*

And if men lacked this other capacity to be infected by art, people might be almost more savage still, and above all more separated from, and more hostile to, one another.

And therefore the activity of art is most important, as important as the activity of speech itself and as generally diffused.

As speech does not act on us only in sermons, orations, or books, but in all those remarks by which we interchange thoughts and experiences with one another, so also art in the wide sense of the word permeates our whole life, but it is only to some of its manifestations that we apply the term in the limited sense of the word.

We are accustomed to understand art to be only what we hear and see in theaters, concerts, and exhibitions; together with buildings, statues, poems, and novels. But all this is only the smallest part of the art by which we communicate with one another in life. All human life is filled with works of art of every kind—from cradlesong, jest, mimicry, the ornamentation of houses, dress, and utensils, to church services, buildings, monuments, and triumphal processions. It is all artistic activity. So that by art, in the limited sense of the word, we do not mean all human activity transmitting feelings but only that part we for some reason select from it and to which we attach special importance.

This special importance has always been given by men to that part of this activity which transmits feelings following from their religious perception, and this small part they have specifically called art, attaching to it the full meaning of the word.

That was how men of old—Socrates, Plato, and Aristotle—looked on art. Thus did the Hebrew prophets and the ancient Christians regard art. Thus it was, and still is, understood by the Mohammedians, and thus it still is understood by religious folk among our own peasantry.

Some teachers of mankind—e.g., Plato in his *Republic,* the primitive Christians, the strict Mohammedians, and the Buddhists—have gone so far as to repudiate all art.

People viewing art in this way (in contradiction to the prevalent view of to-day which regards any art as good if only it affords pleasure) held and hold that art (as contrasted with speech, which need not be listened to) is so highly dangerous in its power to infect people against their wills, that mankind will lose far less by banishing all art than by tolerating each and every art.

Evidently such people were wrong in repudiating all art, for they denied what cannot be denied—one of the indispensable means of communication without which mankind could not exist. But not less wrong are the people of civilized European society of our class and day in favoring any art if it but gives people pleasure.

Formerly people feared lest among works of art there might chance to be some causing corruption, and they prohibited art altogether. Now they only fear lest they should be deprived of any enjoyment art can afford, and they patronize any art. And I think the last error is much grosser than the first and its consequences far more harmful.

Art in our society has become so perverted that not only has bad art come to be considered good, but even the very perception of what art really is has been lost. In

---

* "The foundling of Nuremberg," found in the marketplace of that town on 23rd May 1828, apparently some sixteen years old. He spoke little and was almost totally ignorant even of common objects. He subsequently explained that he had been brought up in confinement underground and visited by only one man, whom he saw but seldom.

order to be able to speak about the art of our society it is therefore, first of all necessary to distinguish art from counterfeit art.

There is one indubitable sign distinguishing real art from its counterfeit—namely, the infectiousness of art. If a man without exercising effort and without altering his standpoint, on reading, hearing, or seeing another man's work experiences a mental condition which unites him with that man and with others who are also affected by that work, then the object evoking that condition is a work of art. And however poetic, realistic, striking, or interesting, a work may be, it is not a work of art if it does not evoke that feeling (quite distinct from all other feelings) of joy and of spiritual union with another (the author) and with others (those who are also infected by it).

It is true that this indication is an *internal* one and that there are people who, having forgotten what the action of real art is, expect something else from art (in our society the great majority are in this state), and that therefore such people may mistake for this aesthetic feeling the feeling of diversion and a certain excitement which they receive from counterfeits of art. But though it is impossible to undeceive these people, just as it may be impossible to convince a man suffering from colourblindness that green is not red, yet for all that, this indication remains perfectly definite to those whose feeling for art is neither perverted nor atrophied, and it clearly distinguishes the feeling produced by art from all other feelings.

The chief peculiarity of this feeling is that the recipient of a truly artistic impression is so united to the artist that he feels as if the work were his own and not some one else's—as if what it expresses were just what he had long been wishing to express. A real work of art destroys in the consciousness of the recipient the separation between himself and the artist, and not that alone, but also between himself and all whose minds receive his work of art. In this freeing of our personality from its separation and isolation, in this uniting of it with others, lies the chief characteristic and the great attractive force of art.

If a man is infected by the author's condition of psyche, if he feels this emotion and this union with others, then the object which has effected this is art; but if there be no such infection, if there be not this union with the author and with others who are moved by the same work—then it is not art. And not only is infection a sure sign of art, but the degree of infectiousness is also the sole measure of excellence in art.

The stronger the infection the better is the art, as art, speaking of it now apart from its subject-matter—that is, not considering the value of the feelings it transmits.

And the degree of the infectiousness of art depends on three conditions: (1) On the degree of individuality of the feeling transmitted; (2) on the degree of clearness with which the feeling is transmitted; (3) on the sincerity of the artist, that is, on the degree of force with which the artist himself feels the emotion he transmits.

The more individual the feeling transmitted the more strongly does it act on the recipient; the more individual the state of psyche into which he is transferred the more pleasure does the recipient obtain and therefore the more rapidly and strongly does he join in it.

Clearness of expression assists infection because the recipient who mingles in consciousness with the author is the better satisfied the more clearly that feeling is transmitted which, as it seems to him, he has long known and felt and for which he has only now found expression.

But most of all is the degree of infectiousness of art increased by the degree of sincerity in the artist. As soon as the spectator, hearer, or reader, feels that the artist is infected by his own production and writes, sings, or plays, for himself, and not merely to act on others, this mental condition of the artist infects the recipient; and, on the contrary, as soon as the spectator, reader, or hearer, feels that the author is not writing, singing, or playing, for his own satisfaction—does not himself feel what he wishes to express, but is doing it for him, the recipient—resistance immediately springs up, and the most individual and the newest feelings and the cleverest technique not only fail to produce any infection but actually repel.

I have mentioned three conditions of contagion in art, but they may all be summed up into one, the last, sincerity; that is, that the artist should be impelled by an inner need to express his feeling. That condition includes the first; for if the artist is sincere he will express the feeling as he experienced it. And as each man is different, his feeling will be individual; and the more individual it is—the more the artist has drawn it from the depths of his nature—the more sympathetic and sincere will it be. And this same sincerity will impel the artist to find clear expression for the feeling which he wishes to transmit.

Therefore, this third condition—sincerity—is the most important of the three. It is also complied with in peasant art, and this explains why such art always acts so powerfully; but it is a condition almost entirely absent from our upper-class art, which is produced by artists actuated by personal aims of covetousness or vanity.

Such are the three conditions which divide art from its counterfeits, and which also decide the quality of every work of art considered apart from its subject-matter.

The absence of any one of these conditions excludes a work from the category of art and relegates it to that of art's counterfeits. If the work does not transmit the artist's peculiarity of feeling and is therefore not individual, if it is unintelligibly expressed, or if it has not proceeded from the author's inner need for expression—it is not a work of art. If all these conditions are present even in the smallest degree, then the work even if a weak one is yet a work of art.

The presence in various degrees of these three conditions: individuality, clearness, and sincerity, decides the merit of a work of art as art, apart from subject-matter. All works of art take order of merit according to the degree in which they fulfill the first, the second, and the third of these conditions. In one the individuality of the feeling transmitted may predominate; in another, clearness of expression; in a third, sincerity; while a fourth may have sincerity and individuality but be deficient in clearness; a fifth, individuality and clearness, but less sincerity; and so forth, in all possible degrees and combinations.

Thus is art divided from what is not art, and thus is the quality of art, as art, decided, independently of its subject-matter, that is to say, apart from whether the feelings it transmits are good or bad.

But how are we to define good and bad art with reference to its content or subject-matter?

A few days ago I was returning home from a walk feeling depressed. On nearing the house I heard the loud singing of a large choir of peasant women. They were welcoming my daughter, celebrating her return home after her marriage. In this singing, with its cries and clanging of scythes, such a definite feeling of joy, cheerfulness, and energy, was expressed, that without noticing how it infected me I continued my way towards the house in a better mood and reached home smiling and in good spirits. That same evening a visitor, an admirable musician, famed for his execution of classical music and particularly of Beethoven, played us Beethoven's sonata, Opus 101. For the benefit of those who might attribute my judgment of that sonata of Beethoven to non-comprehension of it, I should mention that for a long time I used to attune myself to delight in those shapeless improvizations which form the subject-matter of the works of Beethoven's later period. But I had only to consider the question of art seriously, and to compare the impression I received from Beethoven's later works, with those pleasant, clear, and strong, musical impressions which are transmitted, for instance, by the melodies of Bach (his arias), Haydn, Mozart, Chopin (when his melodies are not overloaded with complications and ornamentation), of Beethoven himself in his earlier period, and above all, with the impressions produced by folk-songs,—Italian, Norwegian, or Russian,—by the Hungarian *csárdás,* and other such simple, clear, and powerful music, for the obscure, almost unhealthy, excitement from Beethoven's later pieces, which I had artificially evoked in myself, to be immediately destroyed.

On the completion of the performance (though it was noticeable that every one had become dull) those present warmly praised Beethoven's profound production in the accepted manner, and did not forget to add that formerly they had not been able to understand that last period of his, but that they now saw he was really then at his very best. And when I ventured to compare the impression made on me by the singing of the peasant women—an impression which had been shared by all who heard it—with the effect of this sonata, the admirers of Beethoven only smiled contemptuously, not considering it necessary to reply to such strange remarks.

But for all that, the song of the peasant women was really art transmitting a definite and strong feeling, while the 101st sonata of Beethoven was only an unsuccessful attempt of art containing no definite feeling and therefore not infectious.

For my work on art I have this winter read diligently, though with great effort, the celebrated novels and stories praised by all Europe, written by Zolá, Bourget, Huysmans, and Kipling. At the same time I chanced on a story in a child's magazine, by a quite unknown writer, which told of the Easter preparations in a poor widow's family. The story tells how the mother managed with difficulty to obtain some wheat-flour, which she poured on the table ready to knead. She then went out to procure some yeast, telling the children not to leave the hut and to take care of the flour. When the mother had gone, some other children ran shouting near the window calling those in the hut to come to play. The children forgot their mother's warning, ran into the street, and were soon engrossed in the game. The mother on her return with the yeast finds a hen on the table throwing the last of the flour to her chickens, who were busily picking it out of the dust of the earthen floor. The mother, in despair, scolds the children, who cry bitterly. And the mother begins to feel pity for them— but the white flour has all gone. So to mend matters she decides to make the Easter cake with sifted rye-flour, brushing it over with white of egg and surrounding it with eggs. "Rye-bread we bake is as good as a cake," says the mother, using a rhyming proverb to console the children for not having an Easter cake of white flour, and the children, quickly passing from despair to rapture, repeat the proverb and await the Easter cake more merrily even than before.

Well! the reading of the novels and stories by Zolá, Bourget, Huysmans, Kipling, and others, handling the most harrowing subjects, did not touch me for one moment, and I was provoked with the authors all the while as one is provoked with a man who considers you so naive that he does not even conceal the trick by which he intends to take you in. From the first lines one sees the intention with which the book is written, the details all become superfluous, and one feels dull. Above all, one knows that the author had no other feeling all the time than a desire to write a story or a novel, and so one receives no artistic impression. On the other hand I could not tear myself away from the unknown author's tale of the children and the chickens, because I was at once infected by the feeling the author had evidently experienced, re-evoked in himself, and transmitted.

Beethoven's *Ninth Symphony* is considered a great work of art. To verify its claim to be such I must first ask myself whether this work transmits the highest religious feeling. I reply in the negative, since music in itself cannot transmit those feelings; and therefore I ask myself next: Since this work does not belong to the highest kind of religious art, has it the other characteristic of the good art of our time—the quality of uniting all men in one common feeling—does it rank as Christian universal art? And again I have no option but to reply in the negative; for not only do I not see how the feelings transmitted by this work could unite people not specially trained to submit themselves to its complex hypnotism, but I am unable to imagine to myself a crowd of normal people who could understand anything of this long, confused, and artificial production, except short snatches which are lost in a sea of what is incomprehensible. And therefore, whether I like it or not, I am compelled to conclude that this work belongs to the rank of bad art. It is curious to note in this connection, that attached to the end of this very symphony is a poem of Schiller's which (though somewhat obscurely) expresses this very thought, namely, that feeling (Schiller speaks only of the feeling of gladness) unites people and evokes love in them. But though this poem is sung at the end of the symphony, the music does not unite all men, but unites only a few, dividing them off from the rest of mankind.

NOTE ON SOURCES.   The material in this section is quoted from Leo Tolstoy, *What Is Art?,* translated by Aylmer Maude (1898), Chapters 5, 15, and 16.

4   R. G. COLLINGWOOD

ART AS EXPRESSION OF EMOTION

FROM VÉRON AND TOLSTOY TO COLLINGWOOD.   We began our examination of emotivism with a statement by Eugene Véron: art is the creation of emotive symbols. Tolstoy revised Véron's position slightly by insisting that expression, although necessary, is not sufficient: There must be communication of emotion; the expression must be infectious; and the more infectious, the more art. With Collingwood, the reader is invited to return to Véron and pick up again the aesthetic principle that art is an activity in which an agent expresses, or works at expressing, the emotional charge that marked his or her experience. This retake of the original formulation was worked out in Collingwood's interesting and important book *The Principles of Art,* published in 1937. This book contains one of the twentieth century's most astute and persuasive statements of the emotive theory in aesthetics.

BIOGRAPHICAL NOTE.   R. G. Collingwood was born in England in 1889, and died in 1943 at the age of fifty-four. Professor T. M. Knox concludes his memorial paper for the British Academy with the statement: " . . . his was the most original and constructive mind in English philosophy since Bradley." Collingwood was educated at Eton and Oxford. He became a fellow and tutor of Pembroke College at Oxford in 1912. He served with the Admiralty Intelligence during World War I, and returned to his college when the war was over. In 1934 he was appointed Waynflete Professor of Metaphysical Philosophy to succeed J. A. Smith, and was elected a Fellow of the British Academy. In 1938 he received an Honorary L.L.D. from St. Andrews University in Scotland. He retired in 1941. His most important philosophical books were *Speculum Mentis* (1924), *An Essay on Philosophical Method* (1933), *The Principles of Art* (1937), *An Autobiography* (1939), *An Essay on Metaphysics* (1940), *The New Leviathan* (1942), *The Idea of Nature* (1945), and *The Idea of History* (1946). These books provide ample support for Professor Knox's remark about Collingwood's place in English philosophy.

THE ARGUMENT OF THE PASSAGES.   Much of our experience, perhaps all of it, is marked by a certain "feeling tone," what Collingwood calls its "emotional charge." For example, one lives through a love affair, or an earthquake or a military battle. One is thereby open to the question, "How does it *feel* to be in love, to encounter an earthquake, to engage an enemy in battle? What emotional charge marked the experience?" One may try to answer this question by *describing* the feelings. That would not be art. But one might compose a poem, or a piece of music, or paint a picture, in which one endeavored not to describe the feelings but to express them. That would be tackling the problem by producing or trying to produce a work of art. The author's emphasis here is on *expressing;* an activity that he does not want confused with describing or communicating, or arousing, or betraying, the emotion. These other activities might occur, but their occurrence would not be necessary to making the expressing activity art. It is basic and essential. It is the art activity. Its product or creation is the art object, or work of art.

> Our first question is this. Since the artist proper has something to do with emotion, and what he does with it is not to arouse it, what is it that he does? It will be remembered that the kind of answer we expect to this question is an answer derived from what we all know and all habitually say; nothing original or recondite, but something entirely commonplace.
>
> Nothing could be more entirely commonplace than to say he expresses them. The idea is familiar to every artist, and to every one else who has any acquaintance with the arts. To state it is not to state a philosophical theory or definition of art; it is to state fact or supposed fact about which, when we have sufficiently identified it, we shall have later to theorize philosophically. For the present it does not matter whether the fact that is alleged, when it is said that the artist expresses emotion, is really a fact or only supposed to be one. Whichever it is, we have to identify it, that is, to decide what it is that people are saying when they use the phrase. Later on, we shall have to see whether it will fit into a coherent theory.
>
> They are referring to a situation, real or supposed, of a definite kind. When a man is said to express emotion, what is being said about him comes to this. At first, he is conscious of having an emotion, but not conscious of what this emotion is. All he is conscious of is a perturbation or excitement, which he feels going on within him, but of whose nature he is ignorant. While in this state, all he can say about his emotion is "I feel . . . I don't know what I feel." From this helpless and oppressed condition he

extricates himself by doing something which we call expressing himself. This is an activity which has something to do with the thing we call language: he expresses himself by speaking. It has also something to do with consciousness: the emotion expressed is an emotion of whose nature the person who feels it is no longer unconscious. It has also something to do with the way in which he feels the emotion. As unexpressed, he feels it in what we have called a helpless and oppressed way; as expressed, he feels it in a way from which this sense of oppression has vanished. His mind is somehow lightened and eased.

This lightening of emotions which is somehow connected with the expression of them has a certain resemblance to the "catharsis" by which emotions are earthed through being discharged into a make-believe situation; but the two things are not the same. Suppose the emotion is one of anger. If it is effectively earthed, for example by fancying oneself kicking some one down stairs, it is thereafter no longer present in the mind as anger at all: we have worked it off and are rid of it. If it is expressed, for example by putting it into hot and bitter words, it does not disappear from the mind; we remain angry; but instead of the sense of oppression which accompanies an emotion of anger not yet recognized as such, we have that sense of alleviation which comes when we are conscious of our own emotion as anger, instead of being conscious of it only as an unidentified perturbation. This is what we refer to when we say that it "does us good" to express our emotions.

The expression of an emotion by speech may be addressed to some one; but if so it is not done with the intention of arousing a like emotion in him. If there is any effect which we wish to produce in the hearer, it is only the effect which we call making him understand how we feel. But as we have already seen, this is just the effect which expressing our emotions has on ourselves. It makes us, as well as the people to whom we talk, understand how we feel. A person *arousing* emotion sets out to affect his audience in a way in which he himself is not necessarily affected. He and his audience stand in quite different relations to the act, very much as physician and patient stand in quite different relations towards a drug administered by the one and taken by the other. A person expressing emotion, on the contrary, is treating himself and his audience in the same kind of way: he is making his emotion clear to his audience, and that is what he is doing to himself.

It follows from this that the expression of emotion, simply as expression, is not addressed to any particular audience. It is addressed primarily to the speaker himself, and secondarily to any one who can understand. Here again, the speaker's attitude towards his audience is quite unlike that of a person desiring to arouse in his audience a certain emotion. If that is what he wishes to do, he must know the audience he is addressing. He must know what type of stimulus will produce the desired kind of reaction in people of that particular sort; and he must adapt his language to his audience in the sense of making sure that it contains stimuli appropriate to their peculiarities. If what he wishes to do is to express his emotions intelligibly, he has to express them in such a way as to be intelligible to himself; his audience is then in the position of persons who overhear him doing this. Thus the stimulus-and-reaction terminology has no applicability to the situation.

The means-and-end, or technique, terminology too is inapplicable. Until a man has expressed his emotion, he does not yet know what emotion it is. The act of expressing it is therefore an exploration of his own emotions. He is trying to find out what these emotions are. There is certainly here a directed process: an effort, that is, directed upon a certain end; but the end is not something foreseen and preconceived, to which appropriate means can be thought out in the light of our knowledge of its special character. Expression is an activity of which there can be no technique.

Expressing an emotion is not the same thing as describing it. To say "I am angry" is to describe one's emotion, not to express it. The words in which it is expressed need not contain any reference to anger as such at all. Indeed, so far as they simply and solely express it, they cannot contain any such reference. The curse of Ernulphus, as invoked by Dr. Slop on the unknown person who tied certain knots, is a classical and supreme expression of anger; but it does not contain a single word descriptive of the emotion it expresses.

This is why, as literary critics well know, the use of epithets in poetry, or even in prose where expressiveness is aimed at, is a danger. If you want to express the terror which something causes, you must not give it an epithet like "dreadful." For that describes the emotion instead of expressing it, and your language becomes frigid, that is inexpressive, at once. A genuine poet, in his moments of genuine poetry, never mentions by name the emotions he is expressing.

Some people have thought that a poet who wishes to express a great variety of subtly differentiated emotions might be hampered by the lack of a vocabulary rich in words referring to the distinctions between them; and that psychology, by working out such a vocabulary, might render a valuable service to poetry. This is the opposite of the truth. The poet needs no such words at all; the existence or nonexistence of a scientific terminology describing the emotions he wishes to express is to him a matter of perfect indifference. If such a terminology, where it exists, is allowed to affect his own use of language, it effects it for the worse.

The reason why description, so far from helping expression, actually damages it, is that description generalizes. To describe a thing is to call it a thing of such and such a kind: to bring it under a conception, to classify it. Expression, on the contrary, individualizes. The anger which I feel here and now, with a certain person, for a certain cause, is no doubt an instance of anger, and in describing it as anger one is telling truth about it; but it is much more than mere anger: it is a peculiar anger, not quite like any anger that I ever felt before, and probably not quite like any anger I shall ever feel again. To become fully conscious of it means becoming conscious of it not merely as an instance of anger, but as this quite peculiar anger. Expressing it, we saw, has something to do with becoming conscious of it; therefore, if being fully conscious of it means being conscious of all its peculiarities, fully expressing it means expressing all its peculiarities. The poet, therefore, in proportion as he understands his business, gets as far away as possible from merely labelling his emotions as instances of this or that general kind, and takes enormous pains to individualize them by expressing them in terms which reveal their difference from any other emotion of the same sort.

This is a point in which art proper, as the expression of emotion, differs sharply and obviously from any craft whose aim it is to arouse emotion. The end which a craft sets out to realize is always conceived in general terms, never individualized. However accurately defined it may be, it is always defined as the production of a thing having characteristics that could be shared by other things. A joiner, making a table out of these pieces of wood and no others, makes it to measurements and specifications which, even if actually shared by no other table, might in principle be shared by other tables. A physician treating a patient for a certain complaint is trying to produce in him a condition which might be, and probably has been, often produced in others, namely, the condition of recovering from that complaint. So an "artist" setting out to produce a certain emotion in his audience is setting out to produce not an individual emotion, but an emotion of a certain kind. It follows that the means appropriate to its production will be not individual means but means of a certain kind: that is to say, means which are always in principle replaceable by other similar means. As every good craftsman insists, there is always a "right of way" of performing any operation. A "way" of acting is a general pattern to which various individual actions may conform. In order that the "work of art" should produce its intended psychological effect, therefore, what is necessary is that it should satisfy certain conditions, possess certain characteristics: in other words be, not this work and no other, but a work of this kind and of no other.

This explains the meaning of the generalization which Aristotle and others have ascribed to art. Aristotle's *Poetics* is concerned not with art proper but with representative art, and representative art of one definite kind. He is not analyzing the religious drama of a hundred years before, he is analyzing the amusement literature of the fourth century, and giving rules for its composition. The end being not individual but general (the production of an emotion of a certain kind) the means too are general (the portrayal, not of this individual act, but of an act of this sort; not, as he himself puts it, what Alcibiades did, but what anybody of a certain kind would do). Sir Joshua Reynolds' idea of generalization is in principle the same; he expounds it in connexion with what he calls "the grand style," which means a style intended to produce emotions of a certain type. He is quite right; if you want to produce a typical case of a certain emotion, the way to do it is to put before your audience a representation of the typical features belonging to the kind of thing that produces it; make your kings very royal, your soldiers very soldierly, your women very feminine, your cottages very cottagesque, your oak-trees very oakish, and so on.

Art proper, as expression of emotion, has nothing to do with all this. This artist proper is a person who, grappling with the problem of expressing a certain emotion, says, "I want to get this clear." It is no use to him to get something else clear, however like it this other thing may be. Nothing will serve as a substitute. He does not want a thing of a certain kind, he wants a certain thing. This is why the kind of person who takes his literature as psychology, saying "How admirably this writer depicts the feelings of women, or busdrivers, or homosexuals . . .," necessarily misunderstands every real work of art with which he comes into contact, and takes for good art, with infallible precision, what is not art at all.

Finally, the expression of emotion must not be confused with what may be called the betraying of it, that is, exhibiting symptoms of it. When it is said that the artist in the proper sense of that word is a person who expresses his emotions, this does not mean that if he is afraid he turns pale and stammers; if he is angry he turns red and bellows; and so forth. These things are no doubt called expressions; but just as we distinguish proper and improper sense of the word "art," so we must distinguish proper and improper sense of the word "expression," and in the context of a discussion about art this sense of expression is an improper sense. The characteristic mark of expression proper is lucidity or intelligibility; a person who expresses something thereby becomes conscious of what it is that he is expressing, and enables others to become conscious of it in himself and in them. Turning pale and stammering is a natural accompaniment of fear, but a person who in addition to being afraid also turns pale and stammers does not thereby become conscious of the precise quality of his emotion. About that he is as much in the dark as he would be if (were that possible) he could feel fear without also exhibiting these symptoms of it.

Confusion between these two senses of the word "expression" may easily lead to false critical estimates, and so to false aesthetic theory. It is sometimes thought a merit in an actress that when she is acting a pathetic scene she can work herself up to such an extent as to weep real tears. There may be some ground for that opinion if acting is not an art but a craft, and if the actress's object in that scene is to produce grief in her audience; and even then the conclusion would follow only if it were true that grief cannot be produced in the audience unless symptoms of grief are exhibited by the performer. And no doubt this is how most people think of the actor's work. But if his business is art, the object at which he is aiming is not to produce a preconceived emotional effect on his audience but by means of a system of expressions, or language, composed partly of gesture, to explore his own emotions: to discover emotions in himself of which he was unaware, and by permitting the audience to witness the discovery, enable them to make a similar discovery about themselves. In that case it is not her ability to weep real tears that would mark her out a good actress; it is her ability to make it clear to herself and her audience what the tears are about.

This applies to every kind of art. The artist never rants. A person who writes or paints or the like in order to blow off steam, using the traditional materials of art as means for exhibiting the symptoms of emotion, may deserve praise as an exhibitionist, but loses for the moment all claim to the title of artist. The second category will contain, for example, those young men who, learning in the torment of their own bodies and minds what war is like, have stammered their indignation in verses, and published them in the hope of infecting others and causing them to abolish it. But these verses have nothing to do with poetry.

Thomas Hardy, at the end of a fine and tragic novel in which he has magnificently expressed his sorrow and indignation for the suffering inflicted by callous sentimentalism on trusting innocence, spoils everything by a last paragraph fastening his accusation upon "the president of the immortals." The note rings false, not because it is blasphemous (it offends against no piety worthy of the name) but because it is rant. The case against God, so far as it exists, is complete already. The concluding paragraph adds nothing to it. All it does is to spoil the effect of the indictment by betraying a symptom of the emotion which the whole book has already expressed; as if a prosecuting counsel, at the end of his speech, spat in the prisoner's face.

The same fault is especially common in Beethoven. He was confirmed in it, no doubt, by his deafness; but the cause of it was not his deafness but a temperamental inclination to rant. It shows itself in the way his music screams and mutters instead of speaking, as in the soprano part of the Mass in D, on the layout of the opening pages of the *Hammerklavier* Sonata. He must have known his failing and tried to overcome it, or he would never have spent so many of his ripest years among string quartets, where screaming and muttering are almost, one might say, physically impossible. Yet even there, the old Adam struts out in certain passages of the *Grosse Fuge.*

It does not, of course, follow that a dramatic writer may not rant in character. The tremendous rant at the end of *The Ascent of F6*, like the Shakespearian* ranting on which it is modelled, is done with tongue in cheek. It is not the author who is ranting, but the unbalanced character he depicts; the emotion the author is expressing is the emotion with which he contemplates that character; or rather, the emotion he has towards that secret and disowned part of himself for which the character stands.

---

* Shakespeare's characters rant (1) when they are characters in which he takes no interest at all, but which he simply uses as pegs on which to hang what the public wants, like Henry V; (2) when they are meant to be despicable, like Pistol; or (3) when they have lost their heads, like Hamlet in the graveyard.

NOTE ON SOURCES.   The materials in this section are from R. G. Collingwood, *The Principles of Art* (Oxford: Oxford University Press, 1938), Book I, Chapter 6.

5   JOHN HOSPERS

CRITIQUE OF EXPRESSIONISM

FROM COLLINGWOOD TO HOSPERS.   Any friend of emotivism in aesthetics will find this paper, presented by John Hospers to the Aristotelian Society in 1954, both challenging and valuable. The title of Hosper's paper was "The Concept of Artistic Expression." His purpose was to show that the use of "expression" in the statement of the emotive theory gives rise to difficult questions. This was to be expected. The key notions in any fundamental philosophical theory may be relied on to give trouble. They turn out to be ambiguous and metaphorical. What made Professor Hosper's paper especially challenging was his patience in tracking down bothersome questions that the notion of expression gives rise to.

To see how this comes about, let us retrace our steps to the point where we began, namely by identifying certain activities as art, and the embodiments of these activities as works of art and those who perform those activities as artists. These identifications are primary data. As initially arrived at, they are preanalytical. Once obtained, they must be subjected to conceptual analysis with a view to detecting what they have in common. Hospers emphasizes this point when he says, e.g., "It is, I think, more certain that these men (Bach, Shakespeare, Cézanne, Poe, Eliot, etc.) were artists than that any single theory of art, such as the expression theory, is true"; and again: "If we accept as being artists those men who have created unquestionably great works of art. . . ." The point is worth emphasizing: If you cannot tell chalk from cheese there is no future in asking what marks them as essentially different. If you cannot tell art from nonart, or good art from bad art, you have no *data* about which to ask philosophical questions or propose philosophical theses. This was Hegel's point in speaking of philosophy as a "night owl" that takes flight *after* the heat and battle of the day is over, i.e., after the preanalytical data have been assembled. To put the matter simply: If you don't know *what* you are talking about (e.g., artist, art, work of art), don't propound theories about it.

But suppose you *can* identify examples of artist, art, work of art. Proponents of emotivism, e.g., Véron, Tolstoy, Collingwood, were willing to assume this initial responsibility. Having done so, they then propose the emotive theory about these examples. An artist is one who expresses his or her emotions in the creation of a poem, a picture, a statue, a musical composition, and so on. Art is the activity of doing this. What is thereby created is a work of art. It is clear that the concepts of *express, expressing, expression* are here essential vehicles. Let me suggest an analogy. Suppose you identify certain actions as "moral" and propose the theory that an action is moral if and only if it is done because believed to be right; or, going a step further; that an act is right if and only if it produces more pleasure than pain. There are essential vehicles here; e.g., "done because believed," or "right," or "produces more pleasure than." If you raise difficult questions about these essential vehicles you will embarrass these theories. That is Hosper's strategy. He pitches on the concept of *expression* and proceeds to raise "hard questions" about it. And there is no denying that some, perhaps all, of his questions *are* hard to deal with if you subscribe to emotivism as a theory about artists, art, and works of art. It should be clear that in this strategy Hospers is raising what might be called "second-order" questions; that is, questions about the theory, not about preanalytical data that the theory purports to deal with; and that the questions bear down on the concept of *expression*.

BIOGRAPHICAL NOTE.   John Hospers, born in 1918, has been a member of the department of philosophy in the University of Southern California since 1968. His writings include: *Meaning and Truth in the Arts* (1946), *An Introduction to Philosophical Analysis* (1953), and *Human Conduct: An Introduction to the Problems of Ethics* (1961). He has taught at the University of Minnesota, the University of California (Los Angeles), and elsewhere.

THE ARGUMENT OF THE PASSAGES.   The paper, as reprinted, contained four sections. Sections I and III are given below. In Section I Hospers concentrates on *express* as the name for the activity that the artist performs. In Section II he concentrates on *express* as the name for what the work of art does, and particularly on the notion that its power to evoke something in us is a criterion of expressiveness in it. In Section III he returns to the activity of the artist and concentrates on *express* as meaning *communicate;* e.g., to express a feeling is to communicate it. In Section IV he returns to the work of art, and concentrates on *express* as the name for what it does, regardless of its relation to the artist or to the beholder. At the end of this final section, after pummelling the concept of expression till one wonders how the poor word will ever get back on its feet, Hospers concludes, "in the field of aesthetics, where there are probably more promises and fewer fulfillments than anywhere else in philosophy, I am impelled to be suspicious of the promissory note, especially when the date due is repeatedly postponed, and to be content only with the cold hard cash of fulfillment."

The expression theory of art, in one form or another, has dominated the esthetic scene for the past two centuries as much, perhaps, as the imitation theory had done previously. It is often assumed without question that the distinctive function of the artist is to express emotions; that if the artist does not express in his work, what he does is to that extent less entitled to be called art; and that all art must be expressive of something or other, so much so that a non-expressive work of art is a contradiction in terms. Nor has the predominance of expression been limited to art; it has been extended to all objects of beauty. It is said that all truly beautiful objects are expressive, and some have even asserted their identity: beauty *is* expression.

In all this the terms "express," "expressive," and "expression" are, of course, all-important. It is of the utmost consequence, then, that we know what these terms are being used to mean. What is artistic expression? What does an artist do when he expresses? What is it for a work of art to be expressive? In this paper I shall try to do no more than give a brief critical examination of the principal sense which can be given to the notion of expression as it occurs in the literature of esthetics.

What, then, is expression? One answer seems obvious, though we shall see that it is not the only possible one: expression is an activity of the artist in the process of artistic creation; expressing is something that the artist *does*. What precisely is it that the artist does when he expresses? On this point accounts differ from one another considerably, and I can do no more than mention a few main points to indicate briefly the area in which esthetic philosophers are working when they discuss expression.

Most accounts of the expressive process emphasize the confusion and chaos with which the process begins in the artist's mind; gradually replaced by clarity and order as it approaches completion. Collingwood [in *The Principles of Art*], for example, says:

> When a man is said to express emotion, what is being said about him comes to this. At first, he is conscious of having an emotion, but not conscious of what that emotion is. All he is conscious of is a perturbation or excitement, which he feels going on within him, but of whose nature he is ignorant. While in this state, all he can say about his emotion is: "I feel . . . I don't know what I feel." From this helpless and oppressed condition he extricates himself by doing something which we call expressing himself.

At this point, he writes, he paints, or he carves in stone, and from doing this his emotions become channeled in the exercise of a medium, and his oppressed state is relieved; his inner turbulance ceases, and what was inchoate becomes clear and articulate.

Although Collingwood does not make clear what sense of the phrase "what it is" he is employing when he says that the artist does not know what his emotion is, let us assume that what he is describing is in general clear enough and turn to another aspect of the expressive process which is usually included, namely, its springs in the artist's unconscious life. William James says:

> A man's conscious wit and will are aiming at something only dimly and inaccurately imagined. Yet all the while the forces of organic ripening within him are going on to their own prefigured result, and his conscious strainings are letting loose subconscious allies behind the scenes which in their way work toward rearrangement, and the rearrangement toward which all these deeper forces tend is pretty surely definite, and definitely different from what he consciously conceives and determines. It may consequently be actually interfered with (jammed as it were) by his voluntary efforts slanting toward the true direction. When the new center of energy has been subconsciously incubated so long as to be just ready to burst into flower, "hands off" is the only word for us; it must burst forth unaided.

In all this, the expression of feeling or emotion is to be distinguished sharply from the deliberate *arousing* of it; accounts are fairly unanimous on this point. A writer of fiction, for example, may deliberately attempt to arouse feelings in his readers, which he does not experience himself. In this case he is expressing nothing, but cold-bloodedly adopting what devices he can to arouse feelings in others, remaining himself unmoved. Because the artist, while expressing his feeling, is clarifying it to himself, he cannot before expressing it know or state what he is going to express; therefore he cannot *calculate* in advance what effects he wants to produce and then proceed to produce them. If he could, he would have no need to express, since the emotion would already be clear to him. "Until a man has expressed his emotion," says Collingwood, "he does not yet know what emotion it is. The act of expressing it is therefore an exploration of his own emotions. He is trying to find out what these emotions are." The novelist who tries deliberately and consciously to arouse a certain emotion in his audience cannot, on the expression theory, be an artist; expression is the activity of an artist, while arousal is the activity of a clever craftsman or a trained technician.

In the foregoing characterization of the expressive process, attention has been given primarily to what is going on in the artist; and this, indeed, is the center of emphasis in the Croce-Collingwood school of esthetics. Though they do talk about the artistic medium, and insist that what the artist expresses must be conceived in the medium the artist is going to use—be it words or paints or musical tones—they tend to view the artist's actual manipulation of a physical medium outside himself as an accident or an afterthought. That such a bias, though perhaps affecting most accounts of expression, is no essential part of the expression theory is brought out most clearly by John Dewey in his account of expression in *Art as Experience*. Dewey conceives expression, as (one is tempted to add) he conceives of everything else, as an interaction between the organism and its environment: more specifically, in the case of art, as the recalcitrance of the medium and the artist's attempt to bend the medium to his will. To talk about expression in terms of the artist alone is to omit half the story; no amount of talk about the artist's inner experiences is enough.

> There is no expression without excitement, without turmoil. Yet an inner agitation that is discharged at once in a laugh or a cry, passes away with its utterance. To discharge is to get rid of, to dismiss; to express is to stay by, to carry forward in development, to work out to completion. A gush of tears may bring relief, a spasm of destruction may give outlet to inward rage. But where there is no administration of objective conditions, no shaping of materials in the interest of embodying the excitement, there is no expression. What is sometimes called an act of self-expression might better be termed one of self-exposure; it discloses character—or lack of character—to others. In itself, it is only a spewing forth.

We have already distinguished expressing from arousing; Dewey asks us now to make another distinction, from the opposite direction, between expressing and discharging, getting rid of, or as Dewey puts it, "spewing forth." Esthetic theory, says Dewey, has made the mistake of supposing that the mere giving way to an impulsion, native or habitual, constitutes expression. Such an act is expressive not in itself but only in reflective interpretation on the part of some observer—as the nurse may interpret a sneeze as the sign of an impending cold. As far as the act itself is concerned, it is, if purely impulsive, just a boiling over. While there is no expression, unless there is urge from within outwards, the welling up must be clarified and ordered by taking into itself the values of prior experiences before it can be an act of expression. And these values are not called into play save through objects of the environment that offer resistance to the direct discharge of emotion and impulse. Emotional discharge is a necessary but not a sufficient condition of expression.

There are many questions which one might ask of the above accounts as descriptions of what goes on when artists create. But as a psychological account I shall leave it largely unquestioned. It becomes of interest for the philosopher when it is presented, as it often is, as a theory of art. And as such there are a few questions which should be put to it:

1. Expression theories usually speak of *emotions* as what is being expressed, although sometimes the phrase "expression of *feelings*" is used; but the meaning of

these two terms, and their relation to one another, is not usually made clear. But let that pass: cannot other things be expressed as well, such as ideas? One wants to know more about *what* it is that the artist *qua* artist is expressing, and, if some things are appropriate for artistic expression and not others, why.

2.   But no matter what the artist is said to be expressing, why should one assume that the artist in his distinctively artistic activity is always expressing? Why not say that he is sometimes representing, for example, or just playing around with tones or colors? Many composers do not begin with emotions or feelings at all, but with fragments of melody which they then develop. For them feelings do not particularly enter the picture at all, except possible feelings of frustration at delays and jubilation at having finished the job. Artists have been creating great works of art for many centuries, yet only in the last two centuries or less would it have been customary, or even seemed natural, to say that *the* distinctive activity of the artist was that of expression.

Indeed, if we accept as being artists those who have created unquestionably great works of art—Bach, Shakespeare, Cézanne, and so on—it is by no means clear that the creative processes through which they passed can be adequately labeled under the heading of "expression." In the first place, in the case of most artists we have very little idea of what their creative processes were like, since we have no record of them. And in the second place, even when we have such records, whether by the artist himself or his biographers, they do not always point to the kind of thing set forth by the expression theory. For example, what was Shakespeare doing—was he, necessarily and always, expressing? There are doubtless creative experiences in the life of every artist which could be described by talking about an inner turbulence gradually becoming clarified and ordered, and emotions being released through the manipulation of an artistic medium; but I suspect that, as a general description of artistic activity, this is far too narrow, and is a bit too reminiscent of the mystical concept of genius fostered by the Romantic era. I doubt whether Shakespeare was always expressing feelings; sometimes he probably wrote, although he did not feel like it, to meet a deadline, or to have money coming in for the next month, or because the plot he had borrowed from somewhere else intrigued him and he wondered how he could incorporate it into a five-act drama. The motivation, the ends and aims, as well as the inner springs of artistic activity are, I am sure, a very mixed lot; and to assume that the artist *qua* artist is always expressing seems just as one-sided as the earlier assumption that he is always imitating nature or human action.

The written records left by artists, when we have them, sometimes seem flatly to contradict the expression theory—even though artists as a whole probably tend to glamorize themselves and like to leave the impression that they are solitary geniuses engaged in mysterious acts of self-expression. Thus, Poe gives us an account of cold-blooded calculation in the composition of his poem "The Raven," which is such a far cry from the description of the artistic process given us by the expression theory that it would be difficult to make it fit in at any point. And T. S. Eliot said in *The Sacred Wood* that "poetry is not a turning loose of emotion but an escape from emotion." One may, of course, say that if these men did not go though the process described by the theory, they were therefore not true artists; but this is surely to allow an *a priori* dogma to take precedence over cold facts. It is, I think, more certain that these men were artists than that any single theory of art, such as the expression theory, is true. And if the theory is presented, not as an *a priori* pronouncement but as an actual account of the creative process in artists, it will have to stand the empirical test, namely: in all cases of admitted works of art, was the process of its creation such as the expression theory describes? And I do not see any evidence that it holds true in all cases.

3. If it is true that not all great art was created in the way the theory describes, it is, I think, even more plainly true that not everything created in the way the theory describes is great art. Let us assume that Shakespeare, Virgil, Mozart, Rembrandt, and Hokusai all went through the throes of creation as described by the expression theory; the same can be said of any number of would-be poets, painters, and composers whom one has never heard of for the very good reason that they have never produced anything worth looking at twice. I do not mean, now, the deliberate hacks and quacks, the detective-story writers who spin out half a dozen books a year with an eye on next season's market—these could be accused of trying to arouse emotions in others instead of expressing emotions of their own; I mean the host of deeply earnest would-be artists with delusions of grandeur, so dedicated to Art that they would starve if need be to give proper expression to their genius—but who have neither genius nor, sometimes, even talent. The same turmoil and excitement, the same unpredictability of outcome, the feelings of compulsion and dedication, the surcease from emotion from working in a medium, are experienced not alone by the great creators of art but by their hosts of adoring imitators and camp-followers as well as the supreme individualists who sigh and die alone, ignored and unrecognized but devoted still. This is indeed the most disconcerting fact about the expression theory as a criterion of art: that [according to Harold Osborne in *Aesthetics and Criticism*]

> . . . all the characteristic phenomena of inspiration are described in undistinguishable terms by good and bad artists alike. Nor has the most penetrating psychological investigation succeeded in detecting any general differences between the mental processes which accompany the creation of a masterpiece and the inspirations of a third-rate botcher.

4. In any case, can anything at all relating to the artistic process be validly used as a criterion for evaluating the artistic product? Even if all artists did in fact go through the process described by the expression theory, and even if nobody but artists did this, would it be true to say that the work of art was a good one *because* the artist, in creating it, went through this or that series of experiences in plying his medium? Once the issue is put thus badly, I cannot believe that anyone could easily reply in the affirmative; it seems much too plain that the merits of a work of art must be judged by what we can find in the work of art, quite regardless of the conditions under which the work of art came into being. Its genesis is strictly irrelevant; what we must judge is the work before us, not the process of the artist who created it. And yet much critical writing seems to be beset by the delusion that the artist's creative processes are relevant to judging his product—that a bad work is excused or a great work enhanced by considerations of how hard he tried or whether the conditions of work were unfavorable or whether he was inspired or in a mystical trance, and so on. And, perhaps, such considerations do excuse the *artist*, but they do not change the value of the work of art. It is a moral condemnation of Fitzgerald that he was lazy and indolent, and could have composed many poems like the *Rubaiyat* but failed to do so; but this is no criticism of the *Rubaiyat* itself; and it may be praise of Mozart's genius that every note in a concerto of his popped into his head in one afternoon, but not praise of his work—the concerto would be just as great if it had taken him ten years to complete. Even Collingwood, when he is distinguishing false art from art proper, does so on the basis of the artistic process: the

artist is one who, during creation, expresses emotions formerly unclear to himself, while the false artist is the one who tries to evoke in others emotions which he does not feel. And I cannot emphasize too strongly that, however much this may be a criterion for judging the artist as a man (and I am not saying that it is a good one), it is not a criterion for judging his work. To fudge the distinction between these two is to fall victim to the process–product ambiguity with a vengeance: the word "art" is normally used to name both a process and the product of that process, and because of this fact formulas like "art is expression" can be made to sound true and reasonable; the misfortune here is that this ambiguity, so obvious once it is pointed out, may help to make people think that any considerations about the artistic process can be relevant to judging the merits of the artistic product.

Our conclusion is, then, that when we make a judgment of esthetic value upon a work of art, we are in no way judging the process, including any expressive process, which led to its completion, and therefore the act of expression does not enter into a critical judgment. If we do not know what the process was like, we need not on that account hold our judgment of the work in abeyance; and if we do happen to know what it was like, we should not let this sway our judgment of the work of art. But there *are* times when we *seem* to invoke the process as a criterion of judgment, and these we should now briefly examine. Here is an example from Dewey [in *Art as Experience*]:

> If one examines into the reason why certain works of art offend us, one is likely to find that the cause is that there is no personally felt emotion guiding the selecting and assembling of the materials presented. We derive the impression that the artist . . . is trying to regulate by conscious intent the nature of the emotion aroused.

One example of this occurs, I suppose, when we feel that a novel is "plot-ridden"—for example that the novelist has forced his characters into conformity with the demands of a plot which he had outlined in full before giving much thought to his characters. This feeling, I take it, is familiar enough. But is our criticism here really of the author's creative processes? Are we blaming the novel because he outlined the plot first and then manufactured the characters to fit the plot? I do not think so: we criticize the work because the actions that these characters are made to perform are not such as characters of this kind would do; in other words, they oversimplify and falsify human nature, and it is because of this that we are offended. If the characters strike us as real human beings, we do not care what process the artist went through in creating them: whether he thought of the plot first and the characters afterward, or whatever it may have been.

The same considerations apply in other cases where we seem to make use of the process in criticizing the product. For example, we say, "One must feel that the work of art came out of the artist's own experience, that he himself lived through the things he was describing," or we say, "I don't like this work because I don't feel that the artist was being *sincere* when he wrote it." Now, living through something and being sincere about something are things we say about people; are we not therefore using the process in evaluating the product? Again, I think not. Perhaps we do require that the characters in the drama behave as if the dramatist had personally experienced all their emotions and shared all their fates; but as long as we feel this, must we reverse our judgment if we should subsequently discover that the dramatist had felt none of these things at all, or only a small part of them? Shakespeare could hardly have gone through the experiences of Hamlet, Macbeth, Iago, Cleopatra, Lear, Goneril, Prospero and Coriolanus in one lifetime, but what difference does this make as long as he could present us with a series of vivid, powerful, convincing characterizations? Or suppose we praise a work, say *Uncle Tom's Cabin,* for its sincerity. Does it really change our critical judgment when we know that Mrs. Stowe was weeping tears during many of the hours in which she wrote it, and if we should discover that it was written by a wealthy Southern slaveowner on a wager to prove how well he could present the feelings of "the other side," would it alter our critical judgment of his work? It would alter our judgment about the author, surely; it would change our judgment about the author's sincerity, and it would probably make us attribute to the author much more ingenuity than we now attribute to Mrs. Stowe. But our judgment of the work would not be changed; or, at any rate, I submit, it *should* not—for the novel, after we have made this discovery, would be just the same as before; not a jot or a title of it would be changed by our discovery. And as long as it is the *work* which we are judging, surely our judgment should remain unchanged as long as the work is unchanged.

What difference does it make *what* emotions the artist felt, so long as the work of art is a good one? If the artist was clever enough to compose a work of art without expressing emotion in anything like the manner described by the expression theory, or even if he felt nothing at all, this is no importance so long as we find the work an enduring source of esthetic satisfaction. It may be true as an empirical fact about artists, that *unless* they really feel something, unless they are or have been on fire with emotion, or unless they have deep perturbations which demand resolution, they are not able to create great works of art. This may sometimes be true, though I doubt whether it is true in all cases. But even if it were true in all cases, we need still have no interest in the artist's creative processes as such; knowing facts about the artist's processes would at best be a good indicator of his having created great works of art, which we might then go on to examine, and test the correlation between process and product. To know (supposing it to be true) that a work of art could be produced only when the artist went through this or that kind of creative process would be to know an interesting correlation, but it would not be a means of judging the work of art itself. Even if Bach's Preludes and Fugues had been produced by machinery, would they not be as great as before?—and this in spite of the fact that there were no artist's emotions to be expressed because there was no artist. For appreciating the work of art, the artist's biography is not essential: "by their works shall ye know them."

But we may long since have become impatient with the line of reasoning just pursued. What we have been talking about all through it (it will be said) is evocation—trying to analyze expression in terms of certain effects, of whatever kind, evoked in the listener or reader or observer. And whatever expression is, it is not evocation; no theory of expression is merely a theory about evocation. So we shall have to look elsewhere if we want a sensible meaning for the term "expression," when used to characterize not artistic processes but works of art.

Why is this evocation-talk inadequate, one might ask, to deal with expression? One could imagine the following reply: To say that a work of art expresses something is not to say that the artist underwent certain creative processes, nor to say that the listener had certain experiences. Rather, it is to say that the artist had communicated something *to* the listener by means of his work. Expression is not just something evoked in us, it is something which the artist *did* which he then *communicated* to us. Thus far we have dealt with two aspects—artist and audience—in isolation from each other; but we should have considered them both together; this has been our error. Let us pursue this line of thought a little.

The typical kind of view here is one hallowed by tradition; we might describe it roughly as follows: The artist feels a powerful emotion which he expresses by creating a work of art, in such a way that we, the audience, on reading or seeing or hearing the work of art, feel the same emotion ourselves. Whether the artist did this by intent—i.e., whether in creating he wanted us to feel this emotion, which is what Collingwood denies that a true artist will do—or whether he was working something out within himself without thinking of an audience, does not matter at this point; the important thing is that, whether by intent or not, whether he created with an audience in mind or only to express what he felt, the artist put something into his work which we, the audience, can get out of it; and what we get out is the same thing that he put in. In this way whatever it is that he put in is communicated to us who get it out. Expression is thus a "two-way deal" involving both the artist and his audience.

The language used just now in characterizing the view is deliberately crude, for I do not know how else to describe it with any accuracy. Indeed, this is the very feature of it which makes it, on reflection, extremely difficult to defend. Nor is it easy to remedy it by employing a more sophisticated language in formulating it, for the sophisticated terms usually turn out to be metaphorical. Yet these metaphors seem to be basic to the theory.

For example, it is said that the artist, by means of his work, *transmits* his emotion to us. But what is meant by "transmit" here? When water is transmitted through a pipe, the same water that comes into the pipe at one end comes out at the other; this is perhaps a paradigm case of transmission. When we speak of electricity as being transmitted through a wire, there is not in the same sense something that comes in at one end and out at the other, but at any rate there is a continuous flow of electricity; or if the word "flow" is itself metaphorical, it is perhaps enough to remark that at any point between its two ends the wire will affect instruments and produce shocks. When we transfer this talk about transmission from these contexts to works of art, we may tend to imagine a kind of wire connecting the work of art with the artist at one end and with the audience at the other; or, if we do not actually have such an image, at any rate the term "transmit" takes its meaning from situations such as we have just described; and the question arises, what does it mean in the very different context of art? If it is not like these orthodox cases of transmission, what makes it transmission? What is one committing himself to when he says that in art emotion is transmitted?

A metaphor that may seem to do better justice to the theory is that of deposition. The artist has, as it were, *deposited* his emotion in the work of art, whether we can withdraw it at any time we choose. It is somewhat like the dog burying a bone, which another dog may dig up at his own pleasure. But of course, the artist has not literally buried or deposited emotion in his work; he has, rather, with or without the divine agonies of inspiration, painted in oils or written a complicated set of notes on paper. It is true that on seeing the one or hearing the other performed we may have certain feelings; but in no literal sense has the artist *put* them there in the way that we put money into the bank to withdraw at a later time. Moreover, the bone that is dug up is one and the same bone that was previously buried; whereas the emotion which we feel (I shall not say "extract") when we hear or see the work of art cannot be one and the same numerical emotion as the one which the artist felt (I shall not say "put in").

Let us then substitute the metaphor of *conveying*. Whatever it is that the artist is said to be conveying to his audience, of what does such conveyance consist? One person conveys the ball to another by throwing it; the postman conveys letters from the postoffice to one's door. Is a material continuum necessary for conveyance—the postman between the postoffice and the house, the moving conveyor-belt for trays and machinery? If something mysteriously disappeared at one place and reappeared at another, would it be said to be conveyed? If the emotion ceases in the artist and turns up in the audience when they examine his work, has the artist's emotion been conveyed? Again it is not clear exactly what is involved in the talk about conveying. And even if the emotion ceased in the artist and thereupon occurred in the audience, would it be the same emotion that occurred in the two? In all the cases of conveyance—the ball, the letter, the water through the pipe—it is one and the same thing that is conveyed from the one person or place to the other. This condition is not fulfilled in the case of emotion. One and the same emotion could no more occur in both artist and observer than the same pain can be passed along from one person to another by each person in a row successively pricking his finger with the same pin.

Though the language of the expression theory leaves the impression that it is one and the same emotion which occurs in both artist and observer, on the analogy with the other examples, this is surely not essential to the theory; perhaps it is enough that they be two emotions of the same kind or class. It may be enough that the artist in composing may feel an emotion of kind X, and the observer on seeing it may feel another emotion of kind X. This probably occurs often enough. But suppose it does; is *this* sufficient for saying that X is conveyed from the one to the other? Is this watered-down formulation really what the theory means when it says that art expresses emotion?

Let us, then, speak simply of "communication." The word "communicate" is somewhat more elastic than the previous words—people can communicate in person, by wireless, even telepathically—but it is also more vague and difficult to pin down. We could spend many hours discussing criteria for communication. Since we cannot do this here, let us take an example in which we would probably agree that communication had occurred. A student summarizes the contents of a difficult essay, and the author looks at the summary and says, "That's it exactly!" Similarly, one might say that an emotion had been communicated if the listener to a symphony described a movement as "haunting, tinged with gentle melancholy, becoming by degrees hopeful, ending on a note of triumph" and the composer said, "Exactly so! that's just what I meant to communicate."

I have some doubts about whether even this last example would satisfy us as being a "communication of emotion." At any rate, what the listener did here was intellectual, not emotional—he *recognized* the emotions rather than experiencing them himself; and perhaps this suffices for communication, but it is worth pointing out that in the traditional expression theory the listener does not merely recognize the feeling, he himself *has* the feeling. But, so as not to spend more time tinkering with the highly vulnerable terminology of the expression theory (in the form we are considering in this section), let me state some objections that could be raised to any formulation of it known to me.

1. There are many experiences which the artist undergoes in the process of creation—the divine agonies of inception, the slow working through of ideas to fruition, and the technical details of execution—which the audience need not and probably should not share. This part of the artist's creative activity need in no sense be communicated. For example, much of the creative process may be agonizing or even boring, but the audience on viewing or hearing the work of art should not feel either agonized or bored. At most, then, it is only a selection of the artist's

experiences in creation that should be communicated. One should not speak as if somehow the artist's whole experience in creation were somehow transferred bodily to the observer or listener.

2. Even for the part that the artist wants to communicate to his audience, it is not necessary that he be feeling this at the time of creation, as the theory so often seems to imply. When the artist is under the sway or spell of an emotion, he is all too inclined to be victim and not master of it, and therefore not to be in a good position to create a work of art, which demands a certain detachment and distance as well as considerable lucidity and studied self-discipline. Wordsworth himself said that the emotion should be recollected in tranquility; and others, such as Eliot, have gone further and expunged emotion from the account altogether. Perhaps, then, it might be held essential only that the artist *have had* the emotion at some time or other. But if all that is required is that the artist have some emotion or other of type X, then, since most people of any sensitivity have experienced a considerable part of the gamut of human emotions, including some from type X or any other one chooses to mention, this feature in no way distinguishes the artist from other people, and the theory loses all its punch; it becomes innocuous and like all highly diluted solutions, uninteresting and undistinctive.

3. To say that the audience should feel the same kind of emotion as the artist seems often to be simply not true. Perhaps, in lyric poems and some works of music, the listener may feel an emotion of the same kind as the artist once felt; but in many cases this is not so at all. Even when we do feel emotions in response to works of art (and most of the time what we experience should not, I think be called "emotions" at all, at least if our attitude is esthetic), they are often of a quite different sort: if the author has expressed anger, we feel not anger but (perhaps) horror or repulsion; if he has expressed anguish, we may feel not anguish but pity.

Often it seems quite clear that the audience emotion should be quite different from anything that was or sometimes even could have been in the mind of the artist. We may experience fascination, horror, or sympathy when seeing *Hamlet* because of what we feel is the oedipal conflict unconsciously motivating his inaction; but this response, a result of Freudian psychology, could hardly have been in the mind of Shakespeare. And why indeed should it have been? It is enough that his drama can be consistently interpreted in this way, perhaps even giving it an added coherence; it is enough that he wrote a drama capable of arousing such feelings; it is not necessary that he have experienced them himself.

4. Epistemologically the most ticklish point for the expression theory is simply this: how can we ever know for sure that the feeling in the mind of the artist was anything like the feeling aroused in a listener or observer? Our judgments on this point, in cases where we do have evidence, have notoriously often been mistaken. We might feel absolutely certain that Mozart felt joy when he composed the Haffner Symphony, and be amazed to discover that during this whole period of his life he was quite miserable, full of domestic dissension, poverty, and disease. A happy composition does not imply a happy composer. Strictly speaking the only way we can know how a composer felt is to ask him, and then only if he is not lying. If he is dead, we have to consult his autobiography, if any, or other written records, if any, and hope that they do not misrepresent the facts and that they do not tell us what the composer or biographer wanted us to think rather than what really was the case. And of course [as Harold Osborne said in *Aesthetics and Criticism*] they often do this: "Artists who are dead have rarely left satisfactory psy-

chological records, and the difficulties of appealing to living artists, whose motives and intentions are often mixed and their powers of introspective analysis small, are overwhelming."

This consequence is fatal if the expression theory is made a criterion of good art. For it would follow that if we do not know whether the emotion experienced by a listener is of the same kind as that experienced by the artist, we do not know whether or not this is a good work of art. Therefore in those cases where we have no records or they are of dubious value, we must hold our judgment of the work of art in abeyance. And such a consequence, it would seem, makes the theory in this form pass the bounds of the ridiculous.

"But," it may be said, "we don't have to find out from the artist himself or from written records what emotion the artist felt—we can tell this from seeing or hearing the work of art." But this is precisely what we cannot do. Though in this area conviction is strong and subjective feelings of certainty run high, our inferences from works of art to artists are as likely as not to be mistaken. We cannot tell from just listening to the symphony how Mozart felt, the work simply provides no safe clue to this. The best we can do is guess, after hearing the composition, what he was feeling; and then, if the available evidence should point to the conclusion that he actually was feeling so at the time, our inference would have been correct for at least this instance. But once we do this, we are already checking our inference (made from hearing the work) against the empirical evidence, and it is the evidence that is decisive.

We might, in the light of these objections, wish to revise the theory so as not to require that the audience should feel what the artist felt, but only what the artist wanted or *intended* the audience to feel. But when this is done, difficulties again confront us: (1) The same difficulties that attend our knowing how the artist felt are also present, though sometimes in lesser degree, in knowing what he intended. (2) The artist's whole intention may have misfired; he may have intended us to feel one thing, but if even the most careful and sensitive listeners for generations fail to feel anything like this when they hear his composition, shall we still say that we should feel what the artist intended us to feel? (3) The moment we abandon the stipulation that the audience should feel, not as the artist felt but as the artist intended the audience to feel, we seem to abandon anything that could be called the expression theory. For it is characteristic of the expression theory that the artist must have felt something which he "conveys" through his work and which we on observing the work also feel; if he did not feel it, but only tried to make us feel it or intended us to feel it, this is no longer an expression of feeling on his part but a deliberate attempt to evoke it in others—in other words, not expressing but arousing.

It may seem that in the last few pages we have been flogging a dead horse; yet if one examines much critical writing he must be aware how far from dead this horse is. Critics and laymen alike are dominated, quite unconsciously, by the metaphors of transmission, conveyance, and the like, the emotion in the analogy being usually a kind of liquid that is transmitted bodily from artist to audience. Although when made explicit this kind of formulation would doubtless be rejected, it is precisely these metaphors which are at the very roots (to use another metaphor) of the expression theory in the form we have been considering in this section. And the very strong objections to the theory seem seldom to be realized.

But then, one might say, why should the expression theory be held in any such form as this? What we have been discussing in this section concerns communication between artist and audience; and a theory of communication, one might say, is no more a theory of expression than a theory of evocation is. For an artist to *express* something, however irrelevant this may be to a judgment of its value, is one thing; for him to *communicate* it to an audience is another. For a work to be expressive is one thing; for an audience to feel so-and-so is another. If this is so—if reference to an audience has no place in a theory of expression—it immediately rules out both the evocation forms of the theory which we discussed, and the communication form which we have been discussing.

NOTE ON SOURCES.   The material in this section is from John Hospers, "The Concept of Artistic Expression," *Proceedings of the Aristotelian Society,* Vol. LV, 1954–55 (London: The Aristotelian Society, 1955), pp. 314–344.

6   MORRIS WEITZ

IS AESTHETICS FOUNDED ON A MISTAKE?

FROM HOSPERS TO WEITZ.   Our first four authors—Blocker, Véron, Tolstoy, Collingwood—articula ed the representational and emotive theories about the arts and works of art. Our fifth author, Hospers, selected one of the essential vehicles of the emotive theory—the concept of expression—and subjected it to considerable criticism. Our sixth author, Morris Weitz, is more drastic in his treatment of the question to which the other five addressed themselves. If he is correct, they are in a worse state of confusion than they would seem to recognize. Four of them are stating theories and the fifth is criticizing them. Four of them are addressing themselves to a common question—"What is art" (to use the title of Tolstoy's book)—and proposing an answer. The fifth is criticizing their answer; even, if you will, rejecting their answer. But to criticize or reject an answer is to leave open the possibility that the question makes sense, that it is susceptible of being answered. Weitz proposes a clean sweep. He is convinced that the question itself is wrong-headed, and should not be asked. If this is so, then *no* answer will satisfy. If you are asking the wrong question, or an essentially pointless or meaningless or "impossible" question, then your trouble is more deep-rooted. There is no use in seeking *any* answer; what you must do is abandon the question. Weitz is of the opinion that the question rests on a false or at least indefensible presupposition. If a person asks a man whether he has stopped beating his wife, he may reject the question on the grounds that it presupposes that he has been doing so, whereas he hadn't; or that he has a wife, whereas he hasn't. You would say, "That question does not, because it cannot, arise." Hospers had not proposed any such drastic criticism of the emotive theory. He seemed to allow the question but disallow the answer. He bore down on one particular answer to the question, "What is art?" Weitz would rule out *all* answers to that question because he would rule out the question. As a Spanish proverb has it, these are major words.

BIOGRAPHICAL NOTE.   Morris Weitz was born in 1916. For a number of years he has served as a professor of philosophy at Brandeis University. He is the author of *Philosophy of the Arts* (1950) and the editor of an anthology of readings of aesthetics, *Problems in Aesthetics* (1959). The article repudiating traditional aesthetic theory, "The Role of Theory in Esthetics," was published in *The Journal of Aesthetics and Art Criticism* (1956).

THE ARGUMENT OF THE PASSAGES.   The traditional question, "What is art?" presupposes that works of art have some property or set of properties in common by virtue of which they are works of art. This Weitz denies; works of art do not have *any* such common property or set of properties by virtue of which they are works of art. They are simply works of art, and that is the end of the matter. If you presuppose that there are *any* conditions that are necessary and sufficient to being a work of art, you are mistaken. As long as you entertain this false presupposition you will continue to be misled into posing the question "What makes a work of art to be a work of art?" and, in consequence, misled into proposing answers to your question. If you are convinced by Weitz here, and abandon the presupposition, your question will die on the vine.

Then what will you do? Weitz would have you begin all over again with a radically different question. Don't ask, "What is art?" instead ask, "What kind of concept is your concept of art? How do you conceive of your concept of art?" Two alternatives confront you here: a concept can be either "closed" or "open." A concept, of art or anything else, is closed when you do not entertain the possibility of amending it, extending it, revising it. It is fixed. You "stipulate" that it is not to be altered in any way for any reason. If cases occur that seem as though they ought to be included but don't exactly fit, you close them out. If cases occur that seem as though they ought not to be included yet they do exactly fit, you rule them in. In proceeding thus you are or may be, deliberately arbitrary, not to say high-handed. You operate on the Humpty-Dumpty principle: "*I* stipulate the concept: let the cases fall where they may." Suppose you are a teacher and you stipulate that an *A* student shall be one who has a photographic memory, writes legibly, and never fails to show appreciation of your lectures; and you *hold* to this concept. You keep it closed. Weitz would have you ask whether *this* is the way you conceive of your concept of art. As you conceive of your concept of art, would you say that you hold it thus "closed"? If you do, he would, I think ask you *why* you do; and warn you against the dangers of having a "closed" mind on the question.

In contrast, a concept may be "open." You put it together as you go along. It is "open" to revision, amendment, extension. You "stipulate" nothing in advance. Instead, you "study the field," modifying your concept where you have to, retaining it where you can. Here you don't "stipulate" the concept; you form it and reform it. On these terms you may have no criterion or set of criteria of what constitutes an *A* student held in defiance of what your experience may bring forth. This does not mean that any and every student is an *A* student. It means that your concept of an *A* student is not deliberately and unalterably fixed; you are "open" to what the field may produce. Weitz would have you ask whether *this* is the way you conceive of your concept of art. Would you say that you hold it thus "open"? If you do, he would, I think commend you for having an "open" (*not* a "vacant") mind on the question.

If your concept is "open," and you define it, you will treat your definition as, say, a scientist or a detective treats a hypothesis. If, however, it is "closed," and you define it, you will treat your definition more in the way a geometer treats a concept in geometry.

This is tempting business. The notion of definitions as hypotheses has great charm. On reading Weitz's paper, one might feel a reservation in reference to his sweeping condemnation of his predecessors. It is not clear that they conceived of their conceptions of art as "closed." When great writers with an interest in philosophy turn their minds to questions connected with art, their thought is often characterized by considerable passion; there is such a thing as intellectual passion. And it may be that their manner of expressing themselves expresses both intellect and passion. Where this is so, one does well in reading them to proceed not only cautiously but *con amore*, with a mind held open by a combination of affection and respect.

(1)

Theory has been central in aesthetics and is still the preoccupation of the philosophy of art. Its main concern remains the determination of the nature of art which can be formulated into a definition of it. It construes definition as the statement of the necessary and sufficient properties of what is being defined, where the statement purports to be a true or false claim about the essence of art, what characterizes and distinguishes it from everything else. Each of the great theories of art converges on the attempt to state the defining properties of art. Each claims that it is the true theory because it has formulated correctly into a real definition the nature of art; and that the others are false because they have left out some necessary or sufficient property. Many theorists contend that their enterprise is no mere intellectual exercise but a necessity for any understanding of art and our proper evaluation of it. Unless we know what art is, they say, what are its necessary and sufficient properties, we cannot begin to respond to it adequately or to say why one work is good or better than another. Aesthetic theory, thus, is important not only in itself but for the foundations of both appreciation and criticism. Philosophers, critics, and even artists who have written on art, agree that what is primary in aesthetics is a theory about the nature of art.

Is aesthetic theory, in the sense of a true definition or set of necessary and sufficient properties of art, possible? If nothing else does, the history of aesthetics itself should give one enormous pause here. For, in spite of the many theories, we seem no nearer our goal today than we were in Plato's time. Each age, each art-movement, each philosophy of art, tries over and over again to establish the stated ideal only to be succeeded by a new or revised theory, rooted, at least in part, in the repudiation of preceding ones. Even today, almost everyone interested in aesthetic matters is still deeply wedded to the hope that the correct theory of art is forthcoming. We need only examine the numerous new books on art in which new definitions are proffered;

or, in our country especially, the basic textbooks and anthologies to recognize how strong the priority of a theory of art is.

I want to plead for the rejection of this problem. I want to show that theory—in the requisite classical sense—is *never* forthcoming in aesthetics, and that we would do much better as philosophers to supplant the question, "What is the nature of art?," by other questions, the answers to which will provide us with all the understanding of the arts there can be. I want to show that the inadequacies of the theories are not primarily occasioned by any legitimate difficulty such e.g., as the vast complexity of art, which might be corrected by further probing and research. Their basic inadequacies reside instead in a fundamental misconception of art. Aesthetic theory—all of it—is wrong in principle in thinking that a correct theory is possible because it radically misconstrues the logic of the concept of art. Its main contention—that "art" is amenable to real or any kind of true definition—is false. Its attempt to discover the necessary and sufficient properties of art is logically misbegotten for the simple reason that such a set and, consequently, such a formula about it, is never forthcoming. Art, as the logic of the concept shows, has no set of necessary and sufficient properties, hence a theory of it is logically impossible and not merely factually difficult. Aesthetic theory tries to define what cannot be defined in its requisite sense. But in recommending the repudiation of aesthetic theory I shall not argue from this, as too many others have done, that its logical confusions render it meaningless or worthless. On the contrary, I wish to reassess its role and its contribution primarily in order to show that it is of the greatest importance to our understanding of the arts.

(2)

Let us now survey briefly some of the more famous extant aesthetic theories in order to see if they do incorporate correct and adequate statements about the nature of art. In each of these there is the assumption that it is the true enumeration of the defining properties of art, with the implication that previous theories have stressed wrong definitions. Thus, to begin with, consider a famous version of Formalist theory, that propounded by Bell and Fry. It is true that they speak mostly of painting in their writings but both assert that what they find in that art can be generalized for what is "art" in the others as well. The essence of painting, they maintain, is the plastic elements in relation. Its defining property is significant form, i.e., certain combinations of lines, colors, shapes, volumes—everything on the canvas except the representational elements—which evoke a unique response to such combinations. Painting is definable as plastic organization. The nature of art, what it *really* is, so their theory goes, is a unique combination of certain elements (the specifiable plastic ones) in their relations. Anything which is art is an instance of significant form; and anything which is not art has no such form.

To this the Emotionalist replies that the truly essential property of art has been left out. Tolstoy, Ducasse, or any of the advocates of this theory find that the requisite defining property is not significant form but rather the expression of emotion in some sensuous public medium. Without projection of emotion into some piece of stone or words or sounds, etc., there can be no art. Art is really such embodiment. It is this that uniquely characterizes art, and any true, real definition of it, contained in some adequate theory of art, must so state it.

The Intuitionist disclaims both emotion and form as defining properties. In Croce's version, for example, art is identified not with some physical, public object but with a specific creative, cognitive and spiritual act. Art is really a first stage of knowledge in which certain human beings (artists) bring their images and intuitions into lyrical clarification or expression. As such, it is an awareness, non-conceptual in character, of the unique individuality of things; and since it exists below the level of conceptualization or action, it is without scientific or moral content. Croce singles out as the defining essence of art this first stage of spiritual life and advances its identification with art as a philosophically true theory or definition.

The Organicist says to all of this that art is really a class of organic wholes consisting of distinguishable, albeit inseparable, elements in their causally efficacious relations which are presented in some sensuous medium. What is claimed is that anything which is a work of art is in its nature a unique complex of interrelated parts—in painting, for example, lines, colors, volumes, subjects, etc., all interacting upon one another on a paint surface of some sort. At one time it seemed to me that this organic theory constituted the one true and real definition of art.

My final example is the most interesting of all. This is the theory of Parker. In his writings on art, Parker persistently calls into question the traditional simple-minded definitions of aesthetics. "The assumption underlying every philosophy of art is the existence of some common nature present in all the arts." "All the so popular belief definitions of art—'significant form,' 'expression,' 'intuition,' 'objectified pleasure'—are fallacious, either because, while true of art, they are also true of much that is not art, and hence fail to differentiate art from other things; or else because they neglect some essential aspec of art." But instead of inveighing against the attempt at definition of art itself, Parker insists that what is needed is a complex definition rather than a simple one. "The definition of art must therefore be in terms of a complex of characteristics. Failure to recognize this has been the fault of all the well-known definitions." His own version is the theory that art is essentially three things: embodiment of wishes and desires imaginatively satisfied, language, which characterizes the public medium of art, and harmony, which unifies the language with the layers of imaginative projections. Thus, for Parker, it is a true definition to say of art that it is " . . . the provision of satisfaction through the imagination, social significance, and harmony. I am claiming that nothing except works of art possesses all three of these marks."

Now, all of these sample theories are inadequate in many different ways. Each purports to be a complete statement about the defining features of all works of art and yet each of them leaves out something which the others take to be central. Some are circular, e.g., the Bell–Fry theory of art as significant form which is defined in part in terms of our response to significant form. Some of them, in their search for necessary and sufficient properties, emphasize too few properties, like (again) the Bell–Fry definition which leaves out subject-representation in painting, or the Croce theory which omits inclusion of the very important feature of the public, physical character, say, or architecture. Others are too general and cover objects that are not art as well as works of art. Organicism is surely such a view since it can be applied to *any* causal unity in the natural world as well as to art. Still others rest on dubious principles, e.g., Parker's claim that art embodies imaginative satisfactions, rather than real ones; or Croce's assertion that there is nonconceptual knowledge. Consequently, even if art has one set of necessary and sufficient properties, none of the theories we have noted or, for that matter, no aesthetic theory yet proposed, has enumerated that set to the satisfaction of all concerned.

Then there is a different sort of difficulty. As real definitions, these theories are supposed to be factual reports on art. If they are, may we not ask, Are they empirical

and open to verification or falsification? For example, what would confirm or discon-
firm the theory that art is significant form or embodiment of emotion or creative synthesis of images? There does not even seem to be a hint of the kind of evidence which
might be forthcoming to test these theories; and indeed one wonders if they are perhaps honorific definitions of "art," that is, proposed redefinitions in terms of some
chosen conditions for applying the concept of art, and not true or false reports on the
essential properties of art at all.

(3)

But all these criticisms of traditional aesthetic theories—that they are circular,
incomplete, untestable, pseudo-factual, disguised proposals to change the meaning of
concepts—have been made before. My intention is to go beyond these to make a
much more fundamental criticism, namely, that aesthetic theory is a logically vain
attempt to define what cannot be defined, to state the necessary and sufficient properties of that which has no necessary and sufficient properties, to conceive the concept of art as closed when its very use reveals and demands its openness.

The problem with which we must begin is not "What is art?," but "What sort of
concept is 'art'?" Indeed, the root problem of philosophy itself is to explain the relation
between the employment of certain kinds of concepts and the conditions under which
they can be correctly applied. If I may paraphrase Wittgenstein, we must not ask, What
is the nature of any philosophical "X"?, or even, according to the semanticist, What
does "X" mean?, a transformation that leads to the disastrous interpretation of "art" as a
name for some specifiable class of objects; but rather, What is the use or employment of
"X"? What does "X" do in the language? This, I take it, is the initial question, the begin-
all if not the end-all of any philosophical problem and solution. Thus, in aesthetics, our
first problem is the elucidation of the actual employment of the concept of art, to give a
logical description of the actual functioning of the concept, including a description of
the conditions under which we correctly use it or its correlates.

My model in this type of logical description or philosophy derives from
Wittgenstein. It is also he who, in his refutation of philosophical theorizing in the
sense of constructing definitions of philosophical entities, has furnished contemporary
aesthetics with a starting point for any future progress. In his new work, *Philosophical
Investigations,* Wittgenstein raises as an illustrative question, What is a game? The traditional philosophical, theoretical answer would be in terms of some exhaustive set of
properties common to all games. To this Wittgenstein says, let us consider what we
call "games": "I mean board-games, card-games, ball-games, Olympic games, and so
on. What is common to them all?—Don't say: "There *must* be something common, or
they would not be called "games" but *look and see* whether there is anything common
to all.—For if you look at them you will not see something that is common to *all,* but
similarities, relationships, and a whole series of them at that . . ."

Card games are like board games in some respects but not in others. Not all
games are amusing, nor is there always winning or losing or competition. Some
games resemble others in some respects—that is all. What we find are no necessary
and sufficient properties, only "a complicated network of similarities overlapping and
crisscrossing," such that we can say of games that they form a family with family
resemblances and no common trait. If one asks what a game is, we pick out sample
games, describe these, and add, "This and *similar things* are called 'games.'" This is all
we need to say and indeed all any of us knows about games. Knowing what a game
is is not knowing some real definition or theory but being able to recognize and

explain games and to decide which among imaginary and new examples would or would not be called "games."

The problem of the nature of art is like that of the nature of games, at least in these respects: If we actually look and see what it is that we call "art," we will also find no common properties—only strands of similarities. Knowing what art is is not apprehending some manifest or latent essence but being able to recognize, describe, and explain those things we call "art" in virtue of these similarities.

But the basic resemblance between these concepts is their open texture. In elucidating them, certain (paradigm) cases can be given, about which there can be no question as to their being correctly described as "art" or "game," but no exhaustive set of cases can be given. I can list some cases and some conditions under which I can apply correctly the concept of art but I cannot list all of them, for the all-important reason that unforeseeable or novel conditions are always forthcoming or envisageable.

A concept is open if its conditions of application are emendable and corrigible; i.e., if a situation or case can be imagined or secured which would call for some sort of *decision* on our part to extend the use of the concept to cover this, or to close the concept and invent a new one to deal with the new case and its new property. If necessary and sufficient conditions for the application of a concept can be stated, the concept is a closed one. But this can happen only in logic or mathematics where concepts are constructed and completely defined. It cannot occur with empirically-descriptive and normative concepts unless we arbitrarily close them by stipulating the ranges of their uses.

I can illustrate this open character of "art" best by examples drawn from its subconcepts. Consider questions like "Is Dos Passos' *U.S.A.* a novel?," "Is V. Woolf's *To the Lighthouse* a novel?," "Is Joyce's *Finnegan's Wake* a novel?" On the traditional view these are construed as factual problems to be answered yes or no in accordance with the presence or absence of defining properties. But certainly this is not how any of these questions is answered. Once it arises, as it has many times in the development of the novel from Richardson to Joyce (e.g., "Is Gide's *The School for Wives* a novel or a diary?"), what is at stake is no factual analysis concerning necessary and sufficient properties but a decision as to whether the work under examination is similar in certain respects to other works, already called "novels," and consequently warrants the extension of the concept to cover the new case. The new work is narrative, fictional, contains character delineation and dialogue but (say) it has no regular time-sequence in the plot or is interspersed with actual newspaper reports. It is like recognized novels, A, B, C . . ., in some respects but not like them in others. But then neither were B and C like A in some respects when it was decided to extend the concept applied to A to B and C. Because work N + 1 (the brand new work) is like A, B, C . . . N in certain respects—has strands of similarity to them—the concept is extended and a new phase of the novel engendered. "Is N + 1 a novel?," then, is no factual, but rather a decision problem, where the verdict turns on whether or not we enlarge our set of conditions for applying the concept.

What is true of the novel is, I think, true of every subconcept of art: "tragedy," "comedy," "painting," "opera," etc., of "art" itself. No "Is X a novel, painting, opera, work of art, etc.?" question allows of a definitive answer in the sense of a factual yes or no report. "Is this *collage* a painting or not?" does not rest on any set of necessary and sufficient properties of painting but on whether we decide—as we did!—to extend "painting" to cover this case.

"Art," itself, is an open concept. New conditions (cases) have constantly arisen and will undoubtedly constantly arise; new art forms, new movements will emerge, which will demand decisions on the part of those interested, usually professional critics, as to whether the concept should be extended or not. Aestheticians may lay down similarity conditions but never necessary and sufficient ones for the correct application of the concept. With "art" its conditions of application can never be exhaustively enumerated since new cases can always be envisaged or created by artists, or even nature, which would call for a decision on someone's part to extend or to close the old or to invent a new concept. (e.g., "It's not a sculpture, it's a mobile.")

What I am arguing, then, is that the very expansive, adventurous character of art, its ever-present changes and novel creations, makes it logically impossible to ensure any set of defining properties. We can, of course, choose to close the concept. But to do this with "art" or "tragedy" or "portraiture," etc., is ludicrous since it forecloses on the very conditions of creativity in the arts.

(4)

Of course there are legitimate and serviceable closed concepts in art. But these are always those whose boundaries of conditions have been drawn for a *special* purpose. Consider the difference, for example, between "tragedy" and "(extant) Greek tragedy." The first is open and must remain so to allow for the possibility of new conditions, e.g., a play in which the hero is not noble or fallen or in which there is no hero but other elements that are like those of plays we already call "tragedy." The second is closed. The plays it can be applied to, the conditions under which it can be correctly used are all in, once the boundary, "Greek," is drawn. Here the critic can work out a theory of real definition in which he lists the common properties at least of the extant Greek tragedies. Aristotle's definition, false as it is as a theory of all the plays of Aeschylus, Sophocles, and Euripides, since it does not cover some of them, properly called "tragedies," can be interpreted as a real (albeit incorrect) definition of this closed concept; although it can also be, as it unfortunately has been, conceived as a purported real definition of "tragedy," in which case it suffers from the logical mistake of trying to define what cannot be defined—of trying to squeeze what is an open concept into an honorific formula for a closed concept.

What is supremely important, if the critic is not to become muddled, is to get clear about the way in which he conceives his concepts; otherwise he goes from the problem of trying to define "tragedy," etc., to an arbitrary closing of the concept in terms of certain preferred conditions or characteristics which he sums up in some linguistic recommendation that he mistakenly thinks is a real definition of the open concept. Thus, many critics and aestheticians ask, "What is tragedy?," choose a class of samples for which they may give a true account of its common properties, and then go on to construe this account of the chosen closed class as a true definition or theory of the whole open class of tragedy. This, I think, is the logical mechanism of most of the so-called theories of the subconcepts of art: "tragedy," "comedy," "novel," etc. In effect, this whole procedure, subtly deceptive as it is, amounts to a transformation of correct criteria for *recognizing* members of certain legitimately closed classes, of works of art into recommended criteria for *evaluating* any putative member of the class.

The primary task of aesthetics is not to seek a theory but to elucidate the concept of art. Specifically, it is to describe the conditions under which we employ the concept correctly. Definition, reconstruction, patterns of analysis are out of place here since they distort and add nothing to our understanding of art. What, then, is the logic of "X is a work of art"?

As we actually use the concept, "Art" is both descriptive (like "chair") and evaluative (like "good"); i.e., we sometimes say, "This is a work of art," to describe something and we sometimes say it to evaluate something. Neither use surprises anyone.

What, first, is the logic of "X is a work of art," when it is a descriptive utterance? What are the conditions under which we would be making such an utterance correctly? There are no necessary and sufficient conditions but there are the strands of similarity conditions, i.e., bundles of properties, none of which need be present but most of which are, when we describe things as works of art. I shall call these the "criteria of recognition" of works of art. All of these have served as the defining criteria of the individual traditional theories of art; so we are already familiar with them. Thus, mostly, when we describe something as a work of art, we do so under the conditions of there being present some sort of artifact, made by human skill, ingenuity, and imagination, which embodies in its sensuous, public medium—stone, wood, sounds, words, etc.—certain distinguishable elements and relations. Special theories would add conditions like satisfaction of wishes, objectification or expression of emotion, some act of empathy, and so on; but these latter conditions seem to be quite adventitious, present to some but not to other spectators when things are described as works of art. "X is a work of art and contains *no* emotion, expression, act of empathy, satisfaction, etc.," is perfectly good sense and may frequently be true. "X is a work of art and . . . was made by no one," or . . . "exists only in the mind and not in any publicly observable thing," or . . . "was made by accident when he spilled the paint on the canvas," in each case of which a normal condition is denied, are also sensible and capable of being true in certain circumstances. None of the criteria of recognition is a defining one, either necessary or sufficient, because we can sometimes assert of something that it is a work of art and go on to deny any one of these conditions, even the one which has traditionally been taken to be the basic, namely, that of being an artifact: Consider, "This piece of driftwood is a lovely piece of sculpture." Thus, to say of anything that it is a work of art is to commit oneself to the presence of *some* of these conditions. One would scarcely describe X as a work of art if X were not an artifact, or a collection of elements sensuously presented in a medium, or a product of human skill, and so on. If none of the conditions were present, if there were no criteria present for recognizing something as a work of art, we would not describe it as one. But, even so, no one of these or any collection of them is either necessary or sufficient.

The elucidation of the descriptive use of "Art" creates little difficulty. But the elucidation of the evaluative use does. For many, especially theorists, "This is a work of art" does more than describe; it also praises. Its conditions of utterance, therefore, include certain preferred properties or characteristics of art. I shall call these "criteria of evaluation." Consider a typical example of this evaluative use, the view according to which to say of something that it is a work of art is to imply that it is a *successful* harmonization of elements. Many of the honorific definitions of art and its sub-concepts are of this form. What is at stake here is that "Art" is construed as an evaluative term which is either identified with its criterion or justified in terms of it. "Art" is defined in terms of its evaluative property, e.g., successful harmonization. On such a view, to say "X is a work of art" is (1) to say something which is taken *to mean* "X is successful harmonization" (e.g., "Art *is* significant form") or (2) to say something praiseworthy *on the basis* of its successful harmonization. Theorists are never clear whether it is (1) or (2) which is being put forward. Most of them, concerned as they are with this evaluative use, formulate (2), i.e., that feature of art that *makes* it art in the praise-sense, and then go on to state (1) i.e., the definition of "Art" in terms of its art-making feature. And this is clearly to confuse the conditions under which we say something evaluatively with the meaning of what we say. "This is a work of art," said evaluatively, cannot mean "This is a successful harmonization of elements"—except by stipulation—but at most is said in virtue of the art-making property, which is taken as a (the) criterion of "Art," when "Art" is employed to assess. "This is a work of art," used evaluatively, serves to praise and not to affirm the reason why it is said.

The evaluative use of "Art," although distinct from the conditions of its use, relates in a very intimate way to these conditions. For, in every instance of "This is a work of art" (used to praise), what happens is that the criterion of evaluation (e.g., successful harmonization) for the employment of the concept of art is converted into a criterion of recognition. This is why, on its evaluative use, "This is a work of art" implies "This has P," where "P" is some chosen art-making property. Thus if one chooses to employ "Art" evaluatively, as many do, so that "This is a work of art and not (aesthetically) good" makes no sense, he uses "Art" in such a way that he refuses to *call* anything a work of art unless it embodies his criterion of excellence.

There is nothing wrong with the evaluative use, in fact, there is good reason for using "Art" to praise. But what cannot be maintained is that theories of the evaluative use of "Art" are true and real definitions of the necessary and sufficient properties of art. Instead they are honorific definitions, pure and simple, in which "Art" has been redefined in terms of chosen criteria.

But what makes them—these honorific definitions—so supremely valuable is not their disguised linguistic recommendations; rather it is the *debates* over the reasons for changing the criteria of the concept of art which are built into the definitions. In each of the great theories of art, whether correctly understood as honorific definitions or incorrectly accepted as real definitions, what is of the utmost importance are the reasons proffered in the argument for the respective theory, that is, the reasons given for the chosen or preferred criterion of excellence and evaluation. It is this perennial debate over these criteria of evaluation which makes the history of aesthetic theory the important study it is. The value of each of the theories resides in its attempt to state and to justify certain criteria which are either neglected or distorted by previous theories. Look at the Bell–Fry theory again. Of course, "Art is significant form" cannot be accepted as a true, real definition of art; and most certainly it actually functions in their aesthetics as a redefinition of art in terms of the chosen condition of significant form. But what gives it its aesthetic importance is what lies behind the formula: In an age in which literary and representational elements have become paramount in painting, *return* to the plastic ones since these are indigenous to painting. Thus, the role of the theory is not to define anything but to use the definitional form, almost epigrammatically, to pin-point a crucial recommendation to turn our attention once again to the plastic elements in painting.

Once we, as philosophers, understand this distinction between the formula and what lies behind it, it behooves us to deal generously with the traditional theories of art; because incorporated in every one of them is a debate over and argument for emphasizing or centering upon some particular feature of art which has been neglected or perverted. If we take the aesthetic theories literally, as we have seen, they all fail; but if we reconstrue them, in terms of their function and point, as serious and argued-for recommendations to concentrate on certain criteria of excellence in art, we shall see that aesthetic theory is far from worthless. Indeed, it becomes as central as anything in aesthetics, in our understanding of art, for it teaches us what to look for and how to look at it in art. What is central and must be articulated in all the theories are their debates over the reasons for excellence in art—debates over emotional depth, profound truths, natural beauty, exactitude, freshness of treatment, and so on, as criteria of evaluation—the whole of which converges on the perennial problem of what makes a work of art good. To understand the role of aesthetic theory is not to conceive it as definition, logically doomed to failure, but to read it as summaries of seriously made recommendations to attend in certain ways to certain features of art.

NOTE ON SOURCES.   The material in this section is from Morris Weitz, "The Role of Theory in Esthetics," *The Journal of Aesthetics and Art Criticism,* Vol. XV, No. 1 (September, 1956).

9

What Shall I Say About Ultimate Reality?

THE QUESTION POSED

One of the best-known remarks in the history of philosophy is ascribed to the Greek thinker, Thales. He is said to have held that "all things are made of water." On the face of it, this seems both unimportant and false. Why then its historical importance? Why has Thales been bracketed, along with Copernicus and Darwin, as having initiated a line of thought that marked an epoch in human speculation?

The reason is this. It required, in the first instance, a bold mind to conceive any proposition having the general form "All things are made of . . ."; because if there is one proposition that would appear to be justified by the facts of our everyday experience, it is that all things are not made of any one thing. Multiplicity and variety are the obvious facts about the everyday world. The effort of thought required to break down testimony of the everyday world must have been considerable, as it certainly was subsequently fruitful.

Thales probably had his reasons. Such apparently diverse things as ice, snow, mist, vapor, steam are all "made of" water, if we use the term loosely. Why not other things, too? Whatever his reasons may have been, his remark, once made, continued to re-echo in the minds of generations that came after him. "All things are made of . . ."

In fact, the problem is with us to this day. What are all things made of? What do we intend by the phrase *made of?* If we brush aside Thales's answer, what do we propose in place of it? Speculations on this question constitute part of the philosophical discipline called metaphysics. That is, metaphysics is, in part, an inquiry into the question of what all things are "made of."

Suppose we consider a miscellaneous collection of things, a clay pipe, a bird's egg, a rainbow, a copy of *Hamlet,* an uprising in central China, an act of mercy, a cry in the night, a new planet. What are all these things made of? Varying the words, to what common substance are these all reducible? Of what "underlying reality" are they all manifestations? Is this underlying reality itself further reducible?

The notion that the observed multiplicity and variety of the everyday world are reducible to something common and uniform and *not* given as part of the everyday world is not an unreasonable notion. Few persons would care to deny it in principle, much as they might argue over what that something is to which all things are reducible. Granted the propriety of the notion of an ultimate reality, a "real" world in contrast to the "everyday" world, it is necessary to go one step further. In some sense or other, the everyday world is an appearance or a manifestation of the real world. There is the real world, the world as it really is, and there are its appearances, how it appears.

It is then possible to restate our central problem: What is the nature of that ultimate reality, that real world, of which the everyday world is the appearance? Answers to this question vary. If it is held that there is *an* ultimate reality, we have what is called *monism* in metaphysics, the belief that ultimate reality is one in kind. If it is held that there are at least two ultimate realities, we have what is called *dualism* in metaphysics, the belief that ultimate reality is two in kind. If it is held that there are three or more ultimate realities, we have what is called *pluralism* in metaphysics, the belief that ultimate reality is three or more in kind.

Within these classifications others will occur. You and I might agree that monism is a true belief. Our agreement might extend no further. When we came to the question of the nature of this ultimate reality, we might differ. I might claim that it was matter; you might claim that it was mind; a third person might claim that it was neither, but something more ultimate of which both matter and mind are manifestations.

In this topic we are to be concerned with such inquiries. A metaphysical claim is about the nature of ultimate reality. In considering any such claim, it will be helpful to ask, "Is it a form of monism, or dualism, or pluralism? What reasons are given, or may be given, in support of it? What reasons against it? What consequences follow from it? Do these agree with our experience of the everyday world? Or do they make nonsense of it?" Reflection upon the nature of ultimate reality is not the whole of metaphysics, but it is a large part of it. For a beginner in metaphysics, two things are of primary importance: to demand reasons for accepting any claim, and to note consequences that follow from accepting the hypothesis. If a materialist in metaphysics claims that all and only material things are real things ("If X is real, then X is matter"), we should ask the materialist *why* he or she thinks so; and what follows *from* this metaphysical claim.

The readings and comments that follow help in thinking about this question. There are four sets of them: one from the seventeenth century (Hobbes, materialism) one from the eighteenth century (Berkeley, idealism), and two from the nineteenth century (Schopenhauer, voluntarism, and Comte, positivism). These philosophers have been chosen because they are typical and because, among them, they provide good argument. Each is convinced of his views and eager to spread them among "all rational minds." Each realizes that he must be prepared to argue his case. There is among them no appeal to emotions; at least, not intentionally. They are all, in this respect, "hardheaded rationalists." Here, for the eye that can detect it, is one of humankind's supreme intellectual sports insofar as the human is a "rational" animal. Here are corrosive skepticism, caustic (if obscure) wit, resounding thwacks, closely built arguments, relentless determination to "begin at the beginning" and "think it through," and proud gestures directing attention to "positions established" and "positions overthrown." A taste for metaphysics and a flare for the practice of metaphysics are not widely diffused, but the genuine article, like a love for poetry or painting, is irrepressible once it has become aware of itself.

The readings are in chronological order, but the order exhibits development. Hobbes contributes the claim that all things are made of matter, that matter alone is real; "if X is real, then X is matter." This is monism and materialism, as full-blown as one could wish. The position taken up by Berkeley begins by a deliberate and reasoned-out rejection of Hobbes's materialism. All things, the claim here is, are either mind or objectifications of mind, spirit, *Geist,* and so on. Hobbes's materialism and Berkeley's idealism between them account for much traditional metaphysics. The term *voluntarism,* associated with Schopenhauer, who seems to have been familiar with the claims of both Hobbes and Berkeley, indicates a position somewhat closer to Berkeley than to Hobbes: it covers the claim that neither matter nor mind in the sense of intellect, but *will,* is the ultimate substance of all things. The ultimately real stuff, of which all things are manifestations, to which all things in the world of appearance are "reducible," is will, the power to act, to perform a deed. As Faust says, *Im Anfang war die Tat,* "in the beginning was the deed." Auguste Comte's positivism proposes an abandonment of metaphysics, a doubt that the question asked by metaphysics is a genuine question ("What, and what only, is finally real, and not appearance reducible to a more basic reality?"), susceptible of a meaningful answer. When Comte's repudiation of the reality question is put that way, the argument moves from speculative metaphysics ("What is it to be *real?*") to critical metaphysics. This latter was not initiated by Comte. Indeed, he desired an end of metaphysics, whether speculative (as in Hobbes, Berkeley, or Schopenhauer) or critical, as in Kant or Collingwood. The transition from speculative to critical metaphysics antedated Comte in Hume and Kant.

THOMAS HOBBES

THE CLAIMS OF MATERIALISM

BIOGRAPHICAL NOTE.   Thomas Hobbes was born in England in 1588, the year in which Elizabeth became queen of England, and died in 1679 at the age of ninety-one. The English had their major political revolution between 1641 and 1688. For them this was somewhat comparable to what the Americans had beginning in 1776, the French beginning in 1789, the Russians beginning in 1917, and the Chinese in the years that culminated in 1949. Hobbes was a close student of revolutionary politics and the then recent physical sciences. His life's work was to formulate a conceptual framework, given which a person could assimilate the outcomes of the political and scientific revolutions. He led a long and busy life, interesting in itself and also because of the years through which it was lived. He was educated at Oxford. Thereafter he became tutor and secretary to the Earl of Devonshire. In this capacity he made the acquaintance of Francis Bacon, Ben Johnson, and other literary figures. He published a translation of Thucydides. When his patron died, Hobbes took over the education of his son with whom he made the Grand Tour, making the acquaintance of Galileo, Gassendi, and other scientific luminaries in Europe. He returned to England to study politics. It was the time of England's civil war against Charles I. Hobbes as a Royalist, sided against Cromwell. Circulation of his book, *The Body Politic,* obliged him to leave England and reside in Paris. This time he met Descartes and engaged him in metaphysical controversy. The exiled Prince of Wales, afterward Charles II, was also in Paris. Hobbes became his tutor. He published again on the subject of politics, this time rousing the wrath of some of the Royalists. He returned to England and enjoyed such peace as obtained under Cromwell's regime, making friends with William Harvey, who discovered the circulation of the blood, with the poet Cowley, and others. Upon the restoration of Charles II to the English throne, Hobbes moved once more to a place in the sun and on the pension list. He was one of the most influential men of his day among persons who were open to ideas. He believed that matter is the ultimate reality; that our sense organs are transformers, not revealers; that humans do not have a free will; that all human action is motivated by complete selfishness; that an absolute sovereign is needed, whether in the form of a monarch or a parliament, to insure peace under law; and that religion is a "pill which it is better to swallow without chewing."

THE ARGUMENT OF THE PASSAGES.   The following passages give a simple formulation of metaphysical materialism. From a statement of the essential point, that all is matter moving according to laws, the passages follow Hobbes through the principal turns of his belief. They present a development and, in some cases, a defense of the implications of the fundamental belief. It should be remembered that Hobbes is writing here as a philosopher, not as a scientist. In the strict sense of the word, he was not a scientist, either by temperament or training. He is, where it is relevant, restating or referring to the labors of Copernicus, Kepler, Galileo, Harvey, and the rest. But the point of his writings, in effect, is this: If what such men are finding out, is once accepted without reservation, then over all we are committed to these more comprehensive beliefs.

> Think not, courteous reader, that the philosophy which I am going to set in order is that which makes philosophers' stones. It is the natural reason of man, busily flying up and down among the creatures, and bringing back a true report of their order, causes, and effects. Philosophy is therefore the child of the world and your own mind. Like the world, its father, as it was in the beginning, it is a thing confused. If you will be a philosopher in good earnest, let your reason move upon the deep of

your own cogitations and experience; those things that lie in confusion must be set in order, distinguished, and stamped everyone with its own name.

Philosophy excludes theology, I mean the doctrine of God. It excludes the doctrine of angels and also such things are neither bodies nor properties of bodies. It excludes history, natural as well as political, because such knowledge is but experience or authority and not reason. It excludes astrology and all such divinations. It excludes all such knowledge as is acquired by divine inspiration, or revelation, as not derived to us by reason but by some supernatural sense. Lastly it excludes the doctrine of God's worship as being not to be known by the light of natural reason but the authority of the church.

I am not ignorant how hard a thing it is to weed out of men's minds inveterate opinions that have taken root there, and been confirmed by the authority of eloquent writers; especially since true philosophy rejects the paint and false colors, the ornaments and graces, of language. The first grounds of knowledge are not only beautiful; they are poor and arid, and, in appearance, deformed. Nevertheless, there being some men who are delighted with truth and strength of reason, I thought I might do well to take these pains for the sake of even those few. I proceed therefore and take my beginning from the definition of philosophy.

With these preliminary observations, Hobbes closes in on his theme:

The subject of philosophy is every body [i.e., piece of matter] of which we can conceive any beginning, which we can compare with other bodies, or which is capable of composition and resolution; that is to say, every body of whose beginning or properties we can have any knowledge.

The definition of body may be this: a body is that which, having no dependence upon our thought, is coincident or coextended with some part of space.

The world—I mean the whole mass of things that are—is corporeal, that is to say, body; and that which is not body is no part of the universe. . . . The universe being the aggregate of all bodies, there is no real part thereof that is not also body.

The basic thesis once stated, Hobbes moves on to a series of implications, propositions that follow from the fundamental position. The first of these is that motion is the one thing that "really" takes place; all else is mere appearance, thrown off, so to speak, by matter in motion.

There can be no cause of motion except in a body contiguous and moved.

Mutation, that is, change, can be nothing but motion of the parts of that body which is changed. We say that that which appears to our senses is otherwise than it appeared formerly. Both appearances are effects produced in the sentient creature; and, if they be different, it is necessary that some part of the agent which was formerly at rest is now moved, and so the mutation consists in the motion; or some part which was formerly moved, is now otherwise moved, and so the mutation consists in this new motion; or which, being formerly moved, is now at rest, and so again mutation is motion.

A second corollary is rigid determinism, that is, the belief that everything happens of necessity, or inevitably.

Whatever effect is produced at any time, the same is produced by a necessary cause. For whatsoever is produced had an entire cause, had all those things which, being supposed, it cannot be understood but that the effect follows; that is, it had a necessary cause. In the same manner, whatsoever effects are hereafter to be produced, shall have a necessary cause, so that all the effects that have been or shall be produced have their necessity in things antecedent.

From this determinism it would follow that, given enough knowledge of the past and present, one could predict all future events in the greatest detail. Hobbes is aware of this claim. It has been made off and on ever since his time. Better than a century later the French astronomer, LaPlace, wrote:

> We ought to regard the present state of the universe as the effect of its antecedent state and as the cause of the state that is to follow. An intelligence, who for a given instant should be acquainted with all the forces by which nature is animated, and with the several positions of the beings composing it, if his intellect were vast enough to submit these data to analysis, would include in one and the same formula the movement of the largest bodies in the universe and those of the lightest atom. Nothing would be uncertain for him, the future as well as the past would be present to his eyes.

Hobbes turns to noting further implications of his materialism. All living organisms, it would follow, are just so many complicated machines:

> Seeing that life is but a motion of limbs and organs, why may we not say that all automata (engines that move themselves by springs and wheels as doth a watch) have an artificial life? For what is the heart but a spring, and the nerves but so many strings, and the joints but so many wheels, giving motion to the whole body?

Materialism in metaphysics, he urges, implies sensationism in epistemology; implies, that is, that all knowledge originates in sensations.

> The original of men's thoughts is sense, for there is no conception in a man's mind which hath not, totally or by parts, been begotten upon the organs of sense. The rest are derived from that original.
>
> As I said before, whatsoever we conceive, hath been perceived first by sense, either all at once or by parts. A man can have no thought representing anything, not subject to sense.
>
> Imagination is nothing but decaying sense. From whence it followeth that the longer the time is after the sense, the weaker is the imagination.
>
> Imagination being only of those things which have been formerly perceived by sense, it followeth that imagination and memory are but one thing which for divers considerations have divers names.

Materialism. Determinism. Mechanism. Sensationism. And now the doctrine of representative perception, that is, the belief that sensations represent but do not reveal the real nature of the external world. Hobbes labors this point at great length.

> The cause of sense is the external object which presseth the organ proper to each sense either immediately or mediately. This pressure, by the mediation of the nerves and other strings and membranes, continueth inward and causeth there a reaction or counter-pressure; which endeavor because outward, seemeth to be some matter with-

out. This seeming is that which men call sense; and consisteth as to the eye, in a light or colored figure; to the ear, in a sound; and so on. All which qualities, called sensible qualities, are, in the object that causeth them only so many several motions of the matter by which it presseth our organs diversely. Neither in us that are pressed, are they anything else but divers motions; for motion produceth nothing but motion. For if these sensible qualities (colors, sounds) were in the object which causeth them, they could not be severed from them as by mirrors and echoes they are.

The cause of perception consisteth in this: When the uttermost part of the organ is pressed, it no sooner yields but the next part within it is pressed also. In this manner the pressure or motion is propagated through all the parts of the organ to the innermost. Also, the pressure of the uttermost part proceedeth from the pressure of some more remote body, and so continually till we come to the object. Sense therefore is some internal motion in the sentient organism, generated by some internal motion of the parts of the object, and propagated through all the media to the innermost part of the organ.

I shall endeavor to make plain these points: that the object wherein color is inherent is not the object seen; that there is nothing without us, really, which we call image or color; that color is but the apparition unto us of the motion, agitation, or change which the object worketh in the brain or some internal substance of the head; that as in vision, so also in the other senses, the subject of their inherence is not the object but the sentient creature.

As a color is not inherent in the object, but an effect thereof upon us, caused by motion in the object, so neither is sound in the thing we hear, but in ourselves. The clapper hath no sound in it, but action, and maketh motion in the internal parts of the bell; so the bell hath motion, and not sound, that imparteth motion to the air; and the air hath motion, but no sound, which it imparteth by the ear and nerve unto the brain; and the brain hath motion, but no sound.

From hence it followeth that whatsoever qualities our senses make us think there be in the world, they be not there, but are seeming and apparitions only; the things that really are in the world without us are those motions by which these seemings are caused. And this is the great deception of sense.

Hobbes is stopped by a problem. If the sensation, say the red color of a cherry, is really so much motion of particles in the observer's head, how can we explain the fact that it appears out there in space, located where the cherry is? As Hobbes asks, "Why doth the sensation appear as something situated without the organ?" His answer is:

Why doth the sensation appear as something situated without the organ? It is true: There is in the whole organ, by reason of its own internal natural action some reaction against the motion which is propagated from the object to the innermost part of the organ. In the organ there is an endeavor opposite to the endeavor which proceedeth from the object. That endeavor inwards is the last action in the act of sense. Then from the reaction, an idea hath its being, which by reason that the endeavor is now outward, doth always appear as something situated without the organ.

But though all sense be made by reaction, as I have said, it is not necessary that everything that reacteth should have sense. I know there have been philosophers, and those learned men, who have maintained that all bodies are endued with sense. Nor do I see how they can be refuted if the nature of sense be placed in reaction only.

The argument turns from the subjectivity of sensations to the question of desires. These too must be admitted to be merely so much matter in motion.

> As that which is really within us, in sensation, is only motion caused by the action of external objects, so that which is really within us in appetite or desire is nothing but motion. But the appearance of that motion we call either pleasure or pain.
>
> When appetites and aversions arise alternately concerning the same thing, so that sometimes we have an appetite to it and sometimes an aversion from it, then the whole sum of desires and aversions is what we call *deliberation*.
>
> In deliberation, the last appetite or aversion, immediately adhering to the act or the omission thereof, is what we call *will*.

If this be the whole story of human preferences and desires, Hobbes is in a position to make short shrift of any lofty moral idealism. This he proceeds to do:

> Moral philosophy is nothing else but the science of what is good and evil in the conversation and society of mankind. Good and evil are names that signify our appetites and aversions; which in different tempers, customs, and doctrines of men, are different, and divers men differ not only in their judgment, on the sense of what is pleasant and unpleasant to the taste, smell, hearing, touch, and sight, but also what is comfortable or disagreeable to reason in the actions of common life. Nay the same man, in divers times differeth from himself and at one time praiseth, that is, calleth good what at another time he dispraiseth, that is, calleth evil.
>
> Every man calleth that which pleaseth him, *good;* and that which displeaseth him, *evil*. Since every man differeth from another in constitution, they differ also from one another concerning the common distinction of good and evil. Nor is there any such thing as absolute goodness considered without relation.
>
> Whatsoever is the object of any man's appetite or desire, that it is which he for his part calleth good; and the object of his hate and aversion, evil. For these words *good* and *evil* are ever used with relation to the person that useth them, there being nothing simply and absolutely so, nor any rule of good and evil to be taken from the nature of objects themselves; but from the man, where there is no commonwealth.

To the commitments thus far, Hobbes adds one more: a categorical denial of human free will:

> I conceive that nothing taketh beginning from itself, but from the action of some other immediate agent without itself. Therefore, when a man hath an appetite or will to something, to which before he had no appetite or will, the cause of his will is not the will itself but something else not in his own disposing.
>
> Neither is the freedom of willing or not willing greater in man than in other living creatures. For where there is appetite, the entire cause thereof hath preceded, and, consequently, the appetite could not choose but follow; that is, hath of necessity followed. Therefore such a liberty as is free from necessity is not to be found in the will.
>
> If by *freedom* we understand the power, not of willing but of doing what we will, then certainly that freedom is to be allowed to both men and animals.
>
> The ordinary definition of a *free agent* is that he is one that when all things are present which are needful to produce an effect, can nevertheless not produce it. This implies a contradiction that is nonsense, being as much as to say the cause of anything may be sufficient and yet the effect shall not follow. There is no such thing as an

"agent," which when all things requisite to action are present, can nevertheless forbear to produce it. Or, which is all one, there is no such thing as freedom from necessity.

The essentials of Hobbes's materialism are now before us. The position evokes criticism. With unerring instinct Hobbes places his finger upon the one point which, more than any other perhaps, will be disputed: the denial of human free will. The following passages show Hobbes attempting to defend his determinism against anticipated objections:

> To deny necessity is to destroy the power and foreknowledge of God Almighty. For whatsoever God hath purposed to bring to pass by man, or foreseeth shall come to pass, a man might frustrate and make not come to pass if he hath freedom from necessity. Then would God foreknow such things as never shall be, and decree such things as shall never come to pass.
>
> Liberty and necessity are consistent: as in the water, that hath not only liberty but a necessity to descend by the channel. So likewise in the actions men voluntarily do; which because they proceed from their will are termed *voluntary*. And yet, because every act of man's will and every desire and inclination proceedeth from some cause, and that from some other cause, in a continual chain, it proceedeth from necessity. To him that could see the connection of those causes, the necessity of all men's voluntary actions would appear manifest.
>
> The necessity of an action doth not make the laws that prohibit it unjust. Whatsoever necessary cause precede an action, yet if the action be forbidden, he that doth it willingly may justly be punished. For instance, suppose the law on pain of death prohibit stealing. Suppose there be a man who by the strength of temptation is necessitated to steal, and is thereupon put to death. Doth not this punishment deter others from theft? Is it not a cause that others steal not? Doth it not frame and make their wills to justice? To make the law is thereupon to make a cause of justice, and so to necessitate justice. The intention of the law is not to grieve the delinquent for that which is past and not to be undone; but to make him and others just who might otherwise not be so. It respecteth not the evil act past, but the good to come. But you will say, how is it just to kill one man to amend another, if what were done were necessary? To this I answer: men are justly killed, not because their actions are not necessitated, but because their actions are noxious. We destroy, without being unjust, all that is noxious, both beasts and men.
>
> Repentance is nothing but a glad returning into the right way, after the grief of being out of the way. Even though the cause that made a man go astray were necessary, there is no reason why he should not grieve. So likewise, even though the cause that made a man return into the right way were necessary, there remaineth still the cause of joy. So that I say the necessity of actions taketh away neither of those parts of repentance, neither grief for the error nor joy for the returning.
>
> As for praise and dispraise, they depend not at all on the necessity of the action praised or dispraised. For what is it to praise, but to say a thing is good? Good for me, good for someone else, or good for the commonwealth. What is it to say an act is good, but to say it is as I wish it, or as another wish it, or according to the law of the commonwealth? Can no action please me, or another, or the commonwealth, that should happen of necessity? Doth not praise and dispraise, reward and punishment, make and conform the will to good and evil by example?

Materialism is always with us. It is as old as the record of Western philosophy, having received an elaborate presentation in the fifth century B.C. in the writing—of which we now possess only as a few suggestive fragments—of the Greek materialist Democritus, and several centuries later, in the writings of the Roman materialist Lucretius. Our task is to grasp the meaning of materialism and its implications. To recapitulate: It is the belief that reality is moving particles of matter. Its adherents have usually felt committed to certain further claims, as, for example, all events are rigidly predictable; all organisms are only mechanisms; all knowledge, originating in sensations, is knowledge of appearances only, since sensations are entirely subjective; human conduct is strictly determined by antecedent and concomitant events; human motives are essentially egocentric; and the achievement of happiness, in the sense of the satisfaction of desire, is the only finally good thing. These assorted doctrines are not, of course, as logically interdependent as the materialist would have us believe. But they are temperamentally interdependent. They give expression to a mood or a temperament or a frame of mind which is sufficiently widespread to demand a courteous hearing.

NOTE ON SOURCES.   The material in this section is quoted, abridged, or paraphrased from Thomas Hobbes, *The Elements of Philosophy, Human Nature, Of Liberty and Necessity,* and *Leviathan.* From *The English Works of Thomas Hobbes,* Sir William Molesworth, ed. (London: J. Bohn, 1839).

2   GEORGE BERKELEY

THE CLAIMS OF IDEALISM

FROM HOBBES TO BERKELEY.   It was to be expected that Hobbes's tough-minded materialism would provoke protest and criticism. Throughout the seventeenth and eighteenth centuries, it is not too much to say that materialism was the "specter" that haunted Western metaphysics. Some resorted to the simple expedient of ignoring such views. Some reviled the personal characters of those who held them. Some attacked the premises and disputed the validity of the conclusions that comprised the materialist's position. Among these, in the eighteenth century, was George Berkeley, the founder of modern idealism and one of the shrewdest metaphysicians of modern times.

BIOGRAPHICAL NOTE.   George Berkeley was born in Ireland in 1685 and died in 1753 at the age of sixty-eight. He was educated at the Trinity College, Dublin, where while yet an undergraduate, he conceived the necessity of "refuting atheists and materialists." At the age of twenty-five he published *A Treatise Concerning the Principles of Human Knowledge,* and three years later his *Three Dialogues Between Hylas and Philonous.* These two small volumes, by one of the youngest and brightest philosophical mind of his generation, contain the statement and defense of his case against materialism and his case for idealism. For a while he was laughed at, as readers of Boswell's *Johnson* will remember. But the scattered ranks of those who had been troubled by the fashionable materialism launched by Hobbes and others in the preceding century soon closed in his support. Shortly after publication, Berkeley visited England and was received into the circle of Addison, Pope, and Steele. He traveled on the European continent in various capacities, and on his return was appointed lecturer in divinity and Greek in Trinity College, Dublin. He received a D.D. and was made an ecclesiastical dean. He was promised aid to found a college in Bermuda for training clergymen for the colonies and missionaries for the Indians. He was made, finally, Bishop of Cloyne. He died at Oxford, beloved and respected, if not clearly understood, by all who knew him.

The Argument of the Passages.   Berkeley desires to establish the proposition that reality is spiritual, that a person's mind provides him or her with a better example of the constituent "stuff" of things than is provided by a lump of matter. This is his idealism. The first step is a critique of materialism. This Berkeley proceeds to construct. He starts from premises the materialists themselves admit (any others would be irrelevant) and seeks to show that their conclusions either (1) are incompatible with these premises, or (2) do not follow from these premises. He then approaches materialism from another angle, seeking this time to explain how materialists have come to hold their "misguided" conclusions. Methodologically this procedure is usable. A Communist might apply it to capitalism as the first step in a general statement of the case for communism. A free trader might apply it to protectionism as the first step in a general statement of the case for free trade. A liberal might apply it to conservatism as the first step in a general statement of the case for liberalism. The same remarks are applicable to capitalists, protectionists, and conservatives.

The case against materialism stated, Berkeley moves on to the case for idealism. He formulates a few premises that anyone, he thinks, will admit. From these he seeks to deduce his idealism. He turns then to consider possible objections that might be urged against it before they are made.

The case against materialism stated, the case for idealism stated, the possible objections anticipated, he closes in on what, after all, he considers to be the most important part of the whole business, namely, an elucidation of the implications of his metaphysical idealism, an enumeration of the propositions that are also true if his idealism is true.

The total argument begins as follows:

> It is plain that the notion of what is called *matter* or *corporeal substance* involves a contradiction,* so much so that I should not think it necessary to spend time exposing its absurdity. But belief in the existence of matter seems to have taken so deep a root in the minds of philosophers, and draws after it so many ill consequences, that I choose rather to be thought prolix and tedious than to omit anything that might conduce to the discovery and extirpation of that prejudice.

---

* The "contradiction" would seem to be in saying that all knowledge is from sense-data, and at the same time admitting that matter is not a sense-datum. How then do we know it?

The following distinction between primary and secondary qualities and the claim that primary qualities are alone real, whereas secondary qualities are merely subjective, were familiar notions in Berkeley's day.

> Some there are who make a distinction between primary and secondary qualities. By *primary qualities* they mean extension, figure, motion, rest, solidity, and number. By *secondary qualities* they mean sensible qualities, as colors, sounds, tastes, and so forth.
>
> Our ideas of secondary qualities they acknowledge not to be the resemblances of anything existing without the mind or unperceived. But they will have our ideas of the primary qualities to be patterns or images of things which exist without the mind in an unthinking substance which they call *matter*. By *matter*, therefore, we are to understand an inert, senseless substance in which extension, figure, and motion do actually exist.
>
> Colors, sounds, heat, cold, and such like secondary qualities, they tell us, are sensations existing in the mind alone, depending on and occasioned by the different size, texture and motion of the minute particles of matter. This they take for an undoubted truth, which they can demonstrate beyond all exception.

By *materialism*, then, Berkeley proposes to mean the belief in an inert, senseless substance possessing primary qualities in its own right but not possessing secondary qualities in the same intimate fashion. His first criticism of this belief is as follows:

> But can anyone conceive the extension and motion of a body without any of its secondary qualities? It is not in my power to frame an idea of a body extended and moving but I must withal give it some color or other secondary quality which is acknowledged to exist only in the mind. In short, primary qualities abstracted from secondary qualities are inconceivable. Where therefore the secondary qualities are, to wit, in the mind and nowhere else, there must the primary qualities be also.

His second criticism is this:

> Great and small, swift and slow, degrees of extension and motion, are allowed to exist only in the mind, being entirely relative, and changing as the frame or position of the sense organs varies. The extension therefore that exists independently of the mind is neither great nor small; the action, neither swift nor slow. That is, they are nothing at all.

His third criticism is this:

> Number is entirely a creature of the mind. Even though the other primary qualities be allowed to exist without, it will be evident that the same thing bears a different denomination of number as the mind views it with different respects. Thus the same extension is one, or three, or thirty-six, according as the mind considers it with reference to a yard, a foot, or an inch. Number is so visibly relative and dependent on men's understanding that it is strange anyone should give it an absolute existence without the mind.

His fourth criticism is this:

> One argument whereby modern philosophers would prove that secondary qualities do not exist in matter but in our minds may be turned likewise against primary qualities. Thus, it is said that heat and cold are affections only of the mind and not at

all qualities of real things; for the same body which appears cold to one hand seems warm to another. Thus, too, it is proved that sweetness is not really in the sapid thing; because, the thing remaining unaltered, the sweetness is changed to bitterness, as in the case of a fever or otherwise vitiated palate.

Now, why may we not as well argue that figure and extension are not real qualities existing in matter? To the same eye at different stations, or to eyes of a different texture at the same station, they appear various. By parity of reasoning, therefore, they cannot be ideas of anything settled and determinate without the mind.

In short, those arguments which are thought to prove that secondary qualities (colors, tastes, etc.) exist only in the mind, may with equal force be brought to prove the same thing of primary qualities (extension, figure, motion, etc.).

His fifth criticism is this:

Suppose it were possible that material substances possessing only primary qualities do exist independent of the mind. Yet how is it possible for us to know this? Either we know it by our senses or by our reason. As for our senses, by them we have knowledge only of our sensations: but they do not inform us that things exist independent of the mind or unperceived by the mind, like to those which are perceived. This the materialists themselves acknowledge; nay, insist.

It remains, therefore, that, if we have any knowledge at all of material substances, it must be by our reason inferring their existence from what is immediately perceived by sense. But I do not see what reason can induce us to believe in the existence of bodies independent of the mind, from what we perceive, since the very patrons of matter themselves do not pretend there is any necessary connection betwixt them and our ideas.

His sixth criticism is this:

It may be thought easier to explain the production of our sensations by supporting external bodies, rather than otherwise; and so it might be at least probable that there are such things as bodies that excite ideas in our minds. But neither can this be said. For, though we give the materialists their "external bodies," they by their own confession are no nearer knowing how our ideas are produced, since they own themselves unable to comprehend in what manner body can act upon spirit (or mind) or how it could imprint any idea in the mind.

Hence it is evident that the production of ideas or sensations in our minds can be no reason why we should suppose matter or corporeal substances; since their production is acknowledged to remain equally inexplicable with or without this particular supposition. If therefore it were possible for bodies to exist without the mind, yet to hold that they do so must needs be a very precarious opinion. In short, if there were external bodies, it is impossible we should come to know it; and if there were not, we might have the very same reasons to think there were that we have now. Which consideration were enough to make any reasonable person suspect the strength of whatever arguments he may think himself to have, for the existence of external bodies independent of the mind.

His conclusion is this:

It is on this, therefore, that I insist, to wit, that the absolute existence of unthinking things are words without a meaning, or which include a contradiction. That is what I repeat and inculcate, and earnestly recommend to the attentive thoughts of the reader.

He turns now to an exploration of the reasons that may have led men "to suppose the existence of material substance":

> It is worth while to reflect on the motives which induced men to suppose the existence of material substance; so that having observed the gradual ceasing and expiration of those motives, we may withdraw the assent that was grounded on them.
>
> First it was thought that the sensible qualities did really exist without the mind. And for this reason it seemed needful to suppose that some unthinking substratum or substance wherein they did exist, since they could not be conceived to exist by themselves.
>
> Then, in time, men being convinced that secondary qualities had no existence without the mind, they stripped this substratum or material substance of those qualities, leaving only the primary ones, which they still conceive to exist without the mind and consequently to stand in need of a material support.
>
> But now, it having been shown that none even of these can possibly exist otherwise than in a spirit or mind which perceives them, it follows that we have no longer any reason to suppose the being of "matter," nay, that it is utterly impossible that there should be any such thing so long as that word is taken to mean an unthinking substratum or substance for qualities wherein they exist without mind. It is an extraordinary instance of the force of prejudice that the mind of man retains so great a fondness, against all the evidence of reason, for a stupid, thoughtless Somewhat as a support of the qualities we perceive.

Thus Berkeley on materialism. One is moved to ponder its effect upon Thomas Hobbes. A smile perhaps, a sharpening of his controversial quill as he prepared to do battle with this newcomer. For Berkeley, having "dethroned" matter, sets about to "enthrone" spirit. His first step is to secure one or two propositions that "any rational man" would admit.

> It is evident to anyone who takes a survey of the objects of human knowledge, that they are either ideas imprinted on the senses; or such as are perceived by attending to the passions and operations of the mind; or lastly, ideas formed by help of memory and imagination—compounding, dividing, or merely representing those originally perceived in the aforesaid ways.
>
> As several such ideas are observed to accompany each other, they come to be marked by one name, and so reputed as one thing. Thus a certain color, taste, smell, figure, and consistence having been observed to go together, are accounted one distinct thing, signified by the name *apple*. Other collections of ideas constitute a stone, a tree, a book, and the like.
>
> *Besides the ideas or objects of knowledge, there is something which knows or perceives them, and exercises divers operations as willing, imagining, remembering, about them. This perceiving active being I call "mind," "spirit," "soul," or "myself."*
>
> The existence of an idea consists in its being perceived. Its *esse* is *percipi*. The table I write on I say "exists"; that is, I see and feel it; and if I were out of my study, I should say it "existed"; meaning that if I was in my study, I might perceive it, or that some other spirit actually does perceive it. There was an odor, that is, it was smelt; there was a sound, that is, it was heard; there was a color or figure, that is, it was per-

ceived by sight or touch. That is all I can understand by these and like expressions. Their *esse* is *percipi.* Nor is it possible they should have any existence out of the minds which perceive them.

All our ideas and sensations are visibly inactive. There is nothing of power or agency included in them. One idea or sensation cannot produce or alter another. The very being of an idea implies passiveness and inertness in it; insomuch that it is impossible for an idea to do anything, or be the cause of anything.

We perceive a continual succession of ideas. Some are excited anew, others are changed or totally disappear. There is therefore some cause of these ideas, whereupon they depend, and which produces and changes them.

Having premised the preceding facts, Berkeley proceeds to argue from them:

It is clear, from what hath been said, that this cause cannot itself be any idea or sensation since all such are passive and inert. It must therefore be a substance. But it has been shown that here is no corporeal or material substance. It remains therefore that the cause of our ideas and sensations is an incorporeal active substance, or spirit.

I find I can excite some of my ideas in my mind at pleasure, and vary and shift the scene as oft as I think fit. This making and unmaking of ideas doth very properly denominate the mind active. Thus much is certain and grounded on experience. But when we talk, as do materialists, of unthinking substances producing ideas, we only amuse ourselves with words.

But whatever power I have over some of my ideas, I find that others have not a like dependence on my will. When, for example, I open my eyes in broad daylight, it is not in my power to choose whether I shall see or no, nor to determine what I shall see. It is likewise as to hearing and the other senses. The ideas imprinted on them are not creatures of my will. There is, therefore, some other will or mind or spirit that produces them.

These ideas which I cannot control, these ideas of sense, are more strong, more lively, more distinct than those which I can control. They have, likewise, a steadiness, order, and coherence which belong not to those that are the effects of my will. They speak themselves the products of a mind more powerful and wise than human needs.

Some truths there are so near and obvious to the human mind that a man need only open his eyes to see them. Such I take this important one to be, namely, that all the choir of heaven and furniture of the earth, in a word, all those bodies which compose the mighty frame of the world, have not any subsistence, without a mind; that their being is to be perceived or known; that, consequently, so long as they are not actually perceived by me, or do not exist in my mind or the mind of any other created spirit, they must either have no existence at all or else subsist in the mind of some Eternal Spirit. For it is unintelligible to attribute to any single part of them an existence independent of (perception by a) Spirit.

Until his premises are effectively questioned, or his reasoning from these premises shown to be fallacious, Berkeley may now survey his work with satisfaction. Are there any loopholes? The passages that follow show Berkeley at work on this question.

Before we proceed any farther, it is necessary that we spend some time in answering objections which may probably be made against the principles we have hitherto laid down. In this, if I seem too prolix, I desire I may be excused, since all men do not equally apprehend things of this nature; and I am willing to be understood by every man.

It might be objected:

> By the foregoing principles all that is real and substantial in nature is banished out of the world. All things that exist, it will be said, exist only in the mind, that is, are purely notional. What therefore becomes of the sun, moon, and stars? What must we think of houses, rivers, mountains, trees, stones, nay even of our own bodies? Are all these but so many chimeras and illusions?

To this objection he has an answer:

> We are not deprived of any one thing in nature. Whatever we see, hear, feel, or any wise conceive or understand remains as secure as ever, and is as real as ever. I do not argue against the existence of any one thing that we can apprehend either by sense or reflection. That the things I see with my eyes and touch with my hands do really exist, I make not the least question. The only thing whose existence I deny is that which philosophers call *matter*. There are minds which will or excite ideas in themselves at pleasure. Other ideas, which they do not so excite, speak themselves the effects of a mind more powerful and wise than human spirits. These latter are said to be more real than the former. In this sense the sun I see is the real sun. In this sense, everything in the world is as much a real being by our principles as by any other. If the word *substance* be taken for a combination of sensible qualities, we cannot be accused of denying its existence.
>
> It sounds harsh to say we eat and drink ideas, and are clothed with ideas. But, in common discourse, the word *idea* is not used to signify the several combinations of sensible qualities which are called *things*. But this concerns not the truth of the proposition, which says no more than that we are fed and clothed with those things which we perceive immediately by our senses. The sensory qualities which, combined, constitute the several sorts of victuals and apparel, have been shown to exist only in the mind that perceives them. This is all that is meant by calling them *ideas*. If you agree that we eat and drink and are clad with the immediate object of sense, which cannot exist unperceived, I shall readily grant that it is more conformable to custom that they should be called *things* rather than *ideas*.
>
> "I will still believe my senses and will never suffer any argument, how plausible soever, to prevail over the certainty of them." Be it so. Assert the evidence of your senses. We are willing to do the same. That what I see, hear, feel, etc., doth exist, I no more doubt of than I do of my own being. But, *I do not see how the testimony of sense can be alleged as a proof for the existence of anything which is not perceived by the senses.* We are not for having any man turn skeptic and doubt his senses.

Again, it might be objected:

> From these principles it follows that things are every moment annihilated and created anew. The objects of sense exist only when they are perceived. The trees are in the garden, the chairs in the parlor, only while there is someone there to perceive them. Upon shutting my eyes it is all reduced to nothing, and upon opening them it is again created.

His answer:

> It is thought absurd that, upon closing my eyelids, all the visible objects around me should be reduced to nothing. Yet, is not this what my very critics and opponents commonly acknowledge when they agree on all hands that light and color, which are the immediate objects of sight, are mere sensations, mere "subjective states" which exist no longer than they are perceived?
>
> Indeed we hold the objects of sense to be nothing else but ideas which cannot exist unperceived. Yet we may not hence conclude that they have no existence except only when they are perceived by us; there may be some other spirit that perceives them though we do not. It would not follow, hence, that bodies are annihilated and created every moment, or exist not at all during the intervals between our perception of them.

It might be objected:

> If primary qualities exist only in the mind, it follows that mind is extended, since extension is a primary quality of things.

The answer:

> It no more follows that the mind is extended because extension is in it alone, than that it is red or blue because those qualities exist in it alone and nowhere else. Yet my opponents admit that secondary qualities exist in the mind alone; i.e., are "subjective."

It might be objected:

> There have been a great many things explained by matter and motion. Take these away and you destroy the whole atomic theory, and undermine those principles of mechanics which have been applied with so much success to account for things. In short, whatever advances have been made in the study of nature, do all proceed on the supposition that "matter" doth exist.

To which Berkeley replies:

> To "explain" things is all one has to show why, upon such and such occasions, we are affected with such and such ideas. But, how "matter" operates on mind, or produces any idea in it, is what no philosopher will pretend to explain. Of what use it is, therefore? Besides, things are accounted for by figure, motion and other qualities; not by "matter." Such qualities are no more than ideas, and therefore cannot be the cause of anything, since ideas cannot be the cause of anything.

It might be objected:

> Does it not seem absurd to take away "natural causes" and ascribe everything to the operation of spirit? To say, not that fire heats or water cools, but that a spirit heats or a spirit cools, etc. Would not a man be deservedly laughed at who should talk after this manner?

To which Berkeley rejoins:

> In such things we ought to think with the learned and speak with the vulgar. Those who are convinced of the truth of Copernican astronomy do nevertheless say "the sun rises," and "the sun sets." Yet it doth not. But if such persons affected a contrary style in common talk, it would appear ridiculous. It is the same with our tenets.

It might be objected:

> Is not the universal assent of mankind an invincible argument on behalf of matter? Must we suppose the whole world to be mistaken? If so, what cause can be assigned of so widespread and predominant an error?

To which Berkeley responds:

> It will perhaps not be found that so many do really believe in the existence of "matter." Strictly, to believe that which involves a contradiction, or has no meaning, is impossible. I admit men act as if the cause of their sensations were some senseless, unthinking being. But, that they clearly apprehend any meaning thereby, that they have formed a settled speculative opinion, is what I am not able to conceive.

Adding, too:

> Even though we should grant a notion to be universally and steadfastly held to, yet that is but a weak argument for its truth. A vast number of prejudices and false opinions are everywhere embraced by the unreflecting part of mankind. There was a time when the antipodes and the motion of the earth were looked upon as monstrous absurdities even by men of learning.
>
> It is demanded that we assign a cause of this prejudice that matter exists and is the cause of our sensations. I answer: Men, knowing they perceived several ideas whereof they themselves were not the author, nor depending on their wills, first maintained that those ideas had an existence independent of and external to the mind. But, seeing that the immediate objects of perception do not exist except they are being perceived, they then argued that there are objects, distinct from the colors, etc. immediately perceived by the mind, of which those latter are images or resemblances or effects imprinted on us by those objects. So the notion of an imperceived and unthinking "matter" owes its origin to the consciousness that we are not the author is of our sensations, which must therefore have some cause distinct from our minds upon which they are imprinted.

It might be objected:

> You say: Though the ideas themselves do not exist without the mind, yet there may be things like them whereof they are copies or resemblances, which exist without the mind in an unthinking substance.

To which Berkeley counters:

> It is indeed an opinion strangely prevailing among men that houses, mountains, rivers, in a word, all sensible objects, have an existence distinct from their being perceived by the understanding. But this principle involves a manifest contradiction. For what are the aforementioned objects but the things we perceive by sense? And what do we perceive besides our own ideas or sensations? Could any of these exist unperceived? There was an odor, that is, it was smelt; there was a sound, that is, it was heard; there was a color or figure, that is, it was perceived by sight or touch. That is all I can understand by these and like expressions. Their *esse* is *percipi*. Nor is it possible they should have any existence out of the minds which perceive them.
>
> An idea can be like nothing but an idea; a color can be like nothing but a color. It is impossible for us to conceive a likeness except only between our ideas.

I ask whether the supposed originals or external things, of which our ideas are pictures or representations, be themselves perceivable or no? If they are, then they are ideas, and we have gained our point. If they are not, I appeal to anyone whether it be sense to say a color is like something which is invisible; to say hard or soft is like something intangible and so of the rest.

It might be objected:

Let us admit that the notion of "matter" as the cause or support of the perceived qualities of things, is not needed. Yet there may perhaps be some inert, unperceiving substance, as incomprehensible to us as colors to a man born blind; supporting, it may be, qualities of which we know nothing because we have no senses adapted to them, but which, if we had other senses we should know of.

To which Berkeley replies:

If by *matter* you mean the unknown (and unknowable) cause or support of unknown (and unknowable) qualities, I see no point in affirming or denying its existence. I see no advantage in disputing about something we know not what and we know not why.

And adds:

If we had those other senses, they could only furnish us with new ideas or sensations. In which case we should have the same reason against their existing in an unperceiving substance that has been already offered with relation to such qualities as we do perceive; they would exist only in a mind perceiving them. This is true not only of ideas we are acquainted with at present but likewise of all possible ideas whatsoever.

The case is by now almost completed. He has stated and refuted materialism. He has stated and established idealism. He has anticipated and parried every objection that he can imagine. He proceeds to indicate some implications of his position for a number of traditional issues.

Having posed and met possible objections, we proceed to take a view of our principles with regard to their consequences. After what hath been premised, I think we may lay down the following conclusions.

First: It is plain that men amuse themselves in vain when they inquire for any natural cause distinct from a mind or spirit.

Second: Since the whole creation is the workmanship of a wise and good Agent, it should seem to be in order to employ our thoughts about the final causes, or purposes of things. This not only discovers to us the attributes of the Creator and Sustainer, but may also direct us to the proper uses and applications of things.

Third: The natural immortality of the soul is a necessary consequence of these principles. To assert natural immortality is not to assert that it is incapable of annihilation by the Creator who first gave it being but only that it is not liable to be broken or dissolved by the laws of nature or motion. Bodies are ideas in the mind or soul. The latter is indivisible, incorporeal, unextended, and consequently indissoluble. Changes, decays, dissolutions, which we see in bodies cannot affect a spirit which hath none of their properties. Such a being, a mind or soul or active spirit, is therefore indissoluble by the forces of nature.

Fourth: From what hath been said, it is plain that we cannot know the existence of other minds or spirits otherwise than by their operations or the ideas excited by them in us. I perceive combinations of ideas, and changes thereof, that inform me that there are agents like myself which accompany them and concur in their production. But the knowledge I have of these other spirits or mind is hence indirect; not as is the knowledge of my ideas, but depending on the intervention of ideas by me referred to minds as spirits distinct from myself.

Fifth: Though there be some things (i.e., combinations of sensations) which convince us that human agents are concerned in producing them, yet it is evident that nature, that is, the far greater part of the ideas or sensations perceived by us, is not produced by or dependent on the wills of men. There is therefore some other Spirit that causeth them. But if we consider the regularity, order, and concatenation of natural things, the surprising magnificence, beauty, and perfection of the larger, and the exquisite contrivance of the smaller parts of creation, we shall clearly perceive that the attributes One, Eternal, Infinitely Wise, Good, and Perfect, belong all of them to the aforesaid Spirit, who "works in all" and "by whom all things consist."

Hence it is evident that God is known as certainly and immediately as any other mind or spirit, distinct from ourselves. We may even assert that the existence of God is more evident than the existence of men; because the effects of nature are more numerous and considerable than those ascribed to men. There is not any one mark which denotes a man, or effect produced by him, that does not more strongly evince the being of that Spirit which is the author of nature. A human spirit is not perceived by sense: when we perceive the color, size, etc. of a man, we perceive only sensations or ideas excited in our own minds. These being exhibited to our view in sundry distinct collections, serve to mark out unto us the existence of finite spirits like ourselves. And after the same manner we see God. All the difference is that whereas some one finite and narrow assemblage of ideas denotes a particular human mind, on the other hand wherever we direct our view we perceive manifest tokens of the Divinity, "in whom we live and move and have our being."

It will be objected here that monsters, untimely births, fruits blasted in the blossom, rains falling in desert places, waste, miseries incident to human life, and so on, are evidence that the whole frame of nature is not actuated and superintended by a Spirit of infinite wisdom and goodness. If, that is to say, God is the author of all things, is He not the author of evil and undesirable things? Is this coherent with His infinite wisdom and goodness?

I answer: The very blemishes and defects of nature are not without their use. They make an agreeable variety and augment the beauty of the rest of creation, as shadows in a picture serve to set off the brighter parts.

I add: We do well, before we tax the author of nature with wastefulness, to examine whether such accusation be not the effect of prejudice contracted by our familiarity with impotent and saving mortals. In man, thriftiness with what he cannot easily secure may be wisdom. But, an Omnipotent Spirit can produce everything by a mere fiat. Hence nature's splendid profusion should not be interpreted as wastefulness in the author of nature. Rather it is an evidence of the riches of His power.

I add: As for the pain which is in the world, pursuant to the general laws of nature and the actions of finite imperfect spirits, this is indispensably necessary to our well-being. We consider some one particular pain and account it an evil. But our view is too narrow. If we enlarge our view, so as to comprehend the various ends, connections, and dependencies of things, we shall be forced to acknowledge that those particular things which, considered in themselves, appear to be evil, have the nature of good when considered in connection with the whole system of beings.

From what hath been said, it will be manifest that it is merely for want of attention and comprehensiveness of mind that there are any atheists or Manichaeans. Little and unreflecting souls may indeed burlesque the works of Providence, the beauty and order whereof they have not the capacity or will not be at the pains to comprehend. But those who are masters of any justness and extent of thought can never sufficiently admire the tracks of wisdom and goodness that shine through the economy of nature.

Since it is downright impossible that a soul pierced and illumined with a thorough sense of the omnipresence, holiness, and justice of that Spirit, should persist in a remorseless violation of His laws, we ought therefore earnestly to mediate on those important matters, that so we may attain conviction without scruple.

For, after all, what deserves the first place in our studies, is the consideration of God and duty; which to promote, was the main drift and design of my labors.

What is to be said of this flight of the metaphysical imagination? A generation later it caught the attention of David Hume. He observed, somewhat tartly, "The speculations of the ingenious Dr. Berkeley—they admit of no refutation, but they produce no conviction," and proceeded to deal with idealism as Berkeley had dealt with materialism, rejecting spiritual substance as Berkeley had rejected material substance. But of that, more later. Meanwhile, one does well to know the argument. It has long served as a kind of rallying point for the like-minded in each generation. He provided an apparently coherent case against the "specter" of materialism. He gave articulation to that perennial temperament that dreads and despises and mistrusts the "appeal to matter." For his premises, others have been substituted. To his conclusions, especially his repudiation of materialism, little of importance or variety has been added.

NOTE ON SOURCES. The material in this section has been quoted, abridged, or paraphrased from George Berkeley, *A Treatise Concerning the Principles of Human Knowledge,* Part I in Mary Calkins, ed., *Berkeley Selections* (New York: Charles Scribner's Sons, 1957).

3 ARTHUR SCHOPENHAUER

THE CLAIMS OF VOLUNTARISM

FROM BERKELEY TO SCHOPENHAUER. It is sometimes argued that metaphysics is a question of temperament. There is a half truth in the claim. What it comes to is something like this: Descartes was a somewhat conventional individual, inclined to safe, middle-of-the-road opinions. This is reflected in his orthodox claims about God, human souls, and matter. Hobbes was a hardheaded, realistically minded individual, inclined to discount flights of imagination and to stick to the "facts."

What more natural, then, than his unvarnished materialism? Berkeley was a devout and genial Anglican cleric, inclined to share the pious aspirations enshrined in the institution for which he was a spokesman. Why not an idealism, under these circumstances? Why not the firm conviction that this world is, in the last analysis, but the manifestation of a Supreme Mind? Hume was a canny, skeptically-minded Scot, impressed, above everything else, with humankind's seemingly boundless credulity. What more natural than his carefully reasoned refutation of Descartes, Hobbes, and Berkeley? And so one might continue, seeking to "psychologize" away any claim of metaphysics to rational consideration. There is a flaw in this notion. No explanation in terms of nature and training, of why humans believe anything, has any relevance to the question of whether the beliefs are true or false. It is well to raise this point here for two reasons: (1) One's introduction to a variety of alternative metaphysical hypothesis is usually marked by a sense of confusion and a ready ear to the dissolving suggestion that "after all, it's only a question of temperament." The best reply is that the truth of an opinion has nothing to do with the temperament of the person who holds the opinion. (2) In the case of Arthur Schopenhauer, there is a great tendency to "explain away" his doctrine by reference to his biography. It is known that in life he was bitter, disillusioned, cynical, pessimistic. It is also known that his metaphysical views amount to the claim that the nature of ultimate reality is such as to justify his cynicism and pessimism. The result has sometimes been that persons who reject his metaphysics, with something approaching abhorrence, do so on the ground that "his temperament explains his views." Perhaps it does, but that is not the important point. What one should ask is, "Does the nature of things justify his views?"

BIOGRAPHICAL NOTE. Arthur Schopenhauer was born in Germany in 1788 and died in 1860 at the age of seventy-two. His life was marked by selfishness, suspiciousness, and bitterness. He spent some time in a commercial house before going to the universities at Göttingen, Jena, and Berlin. He left his business career in disgust. He berated most of his fellows and teachers at the universities. Upon the death of his father, his mother moved to Weimar. Schopenhauer followed her, quarreled with her, and took separate lodgings; met Goethe, quarreled with him, and left town to settle a while in Dresden. Here he wrote his great work, *The World as Will and Idea.* As soon as it was published, he left for Italy. There he fumed jealously over the reputation and the gallantries of Lord Byron. He returned to Germany to find his book almost unnoticed. He raged at the obtuseness of his contemporaries and set himself up as a privatdocent at the university in Berlin. Here he was outclassed by the famous Hegel, whom he denounced as a "windbag," and left Berlin for Frankfurt. In Frankfurt, despite squabbles with persons who shared his rooming house, he spent the remaining years of his life writing brilliant essays on various themes in his own philosophy, compiling a scrapbook of all articles and notices dealing with his work, preparing for a second and third edition of his treatise, and watching his doctrines and fame spread slowly over the Western world.

THE ARGUMENT OF THE PASSAGES. Schopenhauer's metaphysics is called *voluntarism*. It may be contrasted with materialism. It is the belief that will, not matter, is the ultimate reality of which all things are manifestations. Reality is *will*, manifested as nature and present in the human. The following passages fall into two groups. The first, given immediately below, without comment, comprises what might be called the *data*. The second sets forth what might be called the *theory*. The first group requires little elucidation. Collectively, they might be inscribed "cynicism and pessimism." They are random reflections on the rottenness of things. It would seem that Schopenhauer would have these disconnected observations on nature and life fall, like so many drops of acid, into the reader's mind, preparing him or her to understand and appreciate the metaphysical theory which is to follow. "See," he seems to say, "see—these are the facts. Think them over. Then, but not until then, I'll give you a theory that will fit them."

> Unless suffering is the direct and immediate object of life, our existence must entirely fail of its aim. It is absurd to look upon the enormous amount of pain that abounds everywhere in the world, originating in needs and necessities inseparable from life itself, as serving no purpose, as being the result of mere chance.
>
> Let us consider the human race. Here life presents itself as a task to be performed. Here we see, in great and in small, universal need, ceaseless wars, compulsory activity, extreme exertion of mind and body. Millions united into nations, striving for a common good, each individual on account of his own. But thousands are sacrificed. Now silly delusions, now intriguing politics, excite them to wars. Then sweat and blood must flow to carry out someone's ideas or expiate someone's folly. In peace time it is industry and trade. Inventions work miracles, seas are navigated, delicacies are brought from the ends of the earth, waves engulf thousands. The tumult passes description. And all to what end? To sustain life through a brief span, and then to reproduce and begin again.
>
> From whence did Dante take the materials for his hell but from our actual world? And a very proper hell he was able to make of it. When, on the other hand, he came to describe heaven and its delights, he was confronted with difficulty, for our world affords no materials for this.
>
> In early youth we are like children in a theater before the curtain is raised, sitting in high spirits and eagerly waiting or the play to begin. It is a blessing we do not know what is actually going to happen . . . the longer you live, the more clearly you feel that life is a disappointment, nay, a cheat.
>
> We are like lambs in a field, disporting under the eye of the butcher who chooses first one and then another. In our good days we are unconscious of the evil which fate may have in store for us—sickness, poverty, mutilation, blindness, insanity, and so on.
>
> It is folly to try to turn this scene of misery into a garden of pleasure. It is folly to aim at joy and pleasure instead of the greatest possible freedom from pain. There is some wisdom in taking a gloomy view of things, in looking upon the world as a kind of hell and in confining one's efforts to securing a little room not too exposed to the fire.
>
> Human life? It is like a drop of water seen through a microscope, teeming with infusoria; or a speck of cheese full of mites invisible to the naked eye. We laugh as they bustle about, and struggle. It is only in the microscope that our life looks so big. It is an almost invisible point, drawn out and magnified by the powerful lenses of time and space.

Unrest is the mark of human existence. We are like a man running down hill who cannot keep on his legs unless he runs on. We are like a pole balanced on the tip of one's finger, or like a planet which would crash into its sun the moment it should cease to hurry on its way.

As far as real physical pleasure is concerned, man is no better off than the brute. The higher possibilities of his brain and nervous system make him sensitive to more and intenser kinds of pleasure, but also to more and intenser kinds of pain. Boredom is a form of suffering unknown to brutes, except perhaps when they are domesticated. Whereas, in man it has become a scourge. Of a truth, need and boredom are the two poles of human life.

In every man there dwells, first and foremost, a colossal egotist who snaps the bands of right and justice with consummate ease. Newspapers show it every day. History shows it on every page. Does not the need of a balance of power in Europe demonstrate it? If it were egotism only, it would be bad enough. But to the egotist in man is joined a fund of hatred, anger, envy, rancor, malice, accumulated like the venom in a serpent's tooth.

I have been reading a book on the condition of the slaves in the southern states. This book constitutes one of the heaviest indictments against the so-called human race. No one can put it down without a feeling of horror. Whatever you may have heard will seem small when you read of how those human devils, those bigoted, church-going, Sabbatarian rascals treated their black brothers whom they had gotten into their clutches.

What is our civilized world but a big masquerade, where you meet knights, priests, soldiers, scholars, lawyers, clergymen, philosophers and so on? But they are not what they pretend to be. They are only masks, and behind the masks, as a rule, you will find moneymakers. It is merchants and moneylenders alone who, in this respect, constitute an honest class.

Formerly faith was the chief support of a throne. Now it is credit. The pope himself is scarcely more concerned over the faithful than over his creditors. In times past it was the guilty debt of the world which was lamented. Now it is the financial debt which arouses dismay. Formerly it was the Last Day which was prophesied. Now it is the great repudiation, the bankruptcy of nations.

Leibniz, you know, argued that this is the best of all possible worlds. Those who agree with him are optimists. If I could conduct a confirmed optimist through hospitals, infirmaries, operating rooms, asylums; through prisons, torture chambers, and slave kennels; over battlefields, places of execution and sudden death; if I were to open to him all the dark abodes where misery hides from cold curiosity—he might come finally to understand the nature of this "best of all possible worlds."

Nature has appointed that the propagation of the species shall be the business of men who are young, strong, and handsome; so that the species may not degenerate. There is no law older or more powerful than this. Woe to the man who sets up claims and interests that conflict with it; they will be unmercifully crushed at the first serious encounter.

If we contemplate life, we behold a turmoil where most are occupied with want and misery, straining to dodge or ward off its multifarious sorrows. In the midst of this tumult, we see the stealthy glance of two lovers, Why so fearful, so secret? Because — unrealized by them, perhaps—these lovers are traitors who seek to perpetuate whole sordid rounds of want and drudgery which would otherwise come to an end.

If children were brought into the world by an act of pure reason, would human life continue to exist? Are not most of us trapped into life? Would not a man rather have so much sympathy with the coming generation that he would spare it the burden of existence?

Kant speaks much of the dignity of man. I have never seen it. It seems to me that the notion of dignity can be applied to man only in an ironical sense. His will is sinful. His intellect is limited. His body is weak and perishable. How shall a man have dignity whose conception is a crime, whose birth is a penalty, whose life is toil, whose death a necessity?

Human life must be some kind of mistake. Else why is man a compound of needs and necessities so hard to satisfy? And why, if perchance they should be satisfied, is he thereby abandoned to boredom? This is direct proof that existence has no real value. For what is boredom but the feeling of the emptiness of life? The fact that this most perfect manifestation of life, the human organism, with the infinite cunning and complex working of its machinery, must oscillate between need and boredom and finally fall to dust and extinction, this fact, I say, is eloquent to him who has the mind to understand it.

Disillusion is the mark of old age. By that time the fictions are gone which gave life its charm and spurred on the mind to activity. By that time the splendors of the world have proved themselves null and vain. Its pomp, grandeur, ideals, and enthusiasms are faded. Not till a man has attained his three score years and ten does he quite understand the first verse of Ecclesiastes.

The world and man is something that had better not have been. This may sound strange. But it is in keeping with the facts. And it reminds us of that which is, after all, the most necessary thing in life—the tolerance, patience, regard, love of neighbor, which everyone needs and which everyone owes to his fellow.

You need only look at the way woman is formed to see that she is not meant to undergo great labor either of mind or body. She pays the debt of life not by what she does but by what she suffers: by the pains of childbearing, by caring for the child, by submission to her husband to whom she should be a patient and cheering companion.

That woman is meant by nature to obey may be seen by the fact that every woman who is placed in the unnatural position of complete independence immediately attaches herself to some man by whom she allows herself to be guided and ruled. If she is young, it will be a lover; if she is old, it will be a priest or a lawyer.

The institution of monogamy, and the marriage laws which it entails, bestow upon women an unnatural position of privilege by considering her as the full equivalent of a man, which is by no means the case. Seeing this, men who are shrewd and prudent often scruple to make so great a sacrifice and to acquiesce in so one-sided an arrangement.

The nobler and more perfect a thing is, the later and slower it is to mature. A man reaches the maturity of his reasoning powers hardly before the age of twenty-eight; a woman at eighteen—and then it is only reason of sort, very niggard in its dimensions.

This weakness of woman's reasoning power explains why she shows more sympathy for the unfortunate than men do; present circumstances have a stronger hold over her, and those concrete things, that lie directly before her eyes, exercise a power which is seldom counteracted to any extent by abstract principles of thought, by fixed rules of conduct, or in general by consideration for the past and the future.

Women are dependent, not upon strength but upon craft. Hence their instinctive capacity for cunning and their inveterate tendency to say what is not true. For as lions are provided with claws and teeth, elephants with boars and tusks, cuttlefish with clouds of inky fluid, so nature has equipped woman with the arts of dissimulation. Therefore a perfectly truthful and straightforward woman is perhaps an impossibility. It may indeed be questioned whether women should be allowed to take an oath in court.

It is only the man whose intellect is clouded by his sexual impulses that could give the name of "fair sex" to the undersized, narrow-shouldered, broad-hipped, short-legged race. For the whole beauty of women is bound up with that impulse.

Nature proceeds with her usual economy. Just as the female ant, after fecundation, loses her wings which are then superfluous, nay, a danger to the business of breeding; so after giving birth to one or two children, a woman generally loses her beauty; probably for similar reasons.

What can you expect of women, when you consider that the most distinguished intellects among them have never produced a single achievement in the fine arts that is really great, genuine, and original? Not even in painting, where mastery of technique is as much within their power as within man's, and where they have diligently cultivated it. The case is not altered by a few partial exceptions. Taken together, women are and remain thorough Philistines and incurable.

There is no proportion between the troubles of life and the gains of life. In the lives of the brute creation, the vanity of life's struggle is easily grasped. The variety and ingenuity of adaptation contrasts sharply with any lasting aim. Only momentary comfort, only fleeting pleasures conditioned and succeeded by want, much suffering, long strife, war of all against all as Hobbes has it, each one a hunter and a hunted, everywhere pressure, need, anxiety, shrieking, howling, and sudden death. And this, *in secula seculorum* or till once again the crust of the planet breaks.

The bulldog ant of Australia affords us a most instructive example. If it is cut in two, a battle begins between the head and the tail. The head seizes the tail with its teeth; the tail defends itself by stinging the head. The battle may last for half an hour, until they die or are dragged off by other ants.

Yunghahn relates that he saw in Java a plain, as far as the eye could reach, entirely covered with skeletons. He took it for a battlefield. They were, however, merely the skeletons of large turtles which come out of the sea to lay their eggs and are then attacked by wild dogs who drag them over onto their backs, strip off the small shell from the stomach, and devour them alive. For this, these turtles are born. Thus life preys upon itself, and in different forms is its own nourishment.

Under the firm crust of the planet dwell powerful forces of nature. Some accident affords them free play. The crust is destroyed, with every living thing on it. The earthquake of Lisbon, the destruction of Pompeii, are only playful hints of what is possible.

The only thing that reconciles me to the Old Testament is the story of the Fall. In my eyes, that is the only metaphysical truth in the book, even though it appears as an allegory. There seems to me no better explanation of our existence than that it is the result of some false step, some sin for which we are paying the penalty.

Vanini, whom his contemporaries burned, finding that easier than refuting him, put the same matter in a very forcible way: "Man is so full of misery that, if it were not contrary to the Christian religion, I should say that evil spirits, if there are any, have passed into human form and are now atoning for their crimes."

Tragedy is the summit of poetical art. The pain and wail of humanity, the triumph of evil, the mastery of chance, the fall of just and innocent, are here presented for us. And in it lies a significant hint of the nature of the world and man: the strife of the will against itself comes here into prominence. It is shown in the sufferings of men due to chance and error, reaching sometimes even the appearance of design. This we are led to see in the noblest works of the tragic muse.

Religious teachers tell us that suicide is cowardice, that only a madman could be guilty of it, and other insipidities of the same kind. Or else they make the nonsensical remark that suicide is wrong, when obviously there is nothing to which every man has a more unassailable title than to his own life and person.

The ancients did not regard the matter in that light. Pliny says "Life is not so desirable as to be protracted at any cost. Whoever you are you are sure to die, even though your life has been full of abomination and crime. The chief remedy for a troubled mind is the feeling that there is no greater blessing than an opportune death; and that every one can avail himself of."

Two Chinamen traveling in Europe paid their first visit to the theater. One of them spent all his time studying the machinery. He succeeded in finding out how it was worked. The other tried to get at the meaning of the piece being presented, in spite of his ignorance of the language. There you have the scientist and the philosopher.

The passages thus far have been expressions of Schopenhauer's pessimism and cynicism. They form a prolegomenon to his metaphysical voluntarism. His general argument is to this effect: Metaphysical voluntarism is the only hypothesis which will account for the many facts upon which I base my cynicism and pessimism. The next four passages set forth his fundamental thesis.

I teach that the inner nature of everything is will.

That which makes itself known to us in the most immediate knowledge as our will is also that which objectifies or manifests itself at different grades in all the phenomena of the world.

If we observe the unceasing impulse with which the waters hurry to the ocean, the persistence with which the magnet turns to the pole, the readiness with which iron flies to the magnet; if we see the crystal take form, the attraction and repulsion of bodies; if we feel how a burden which hampers us by its gravitation toward the earth presses and strains in pursuit of its one tendency—if we note all these things, it requires not great effort of the imagination to recognize in nature what is will in us.

As the magic lantern shows many different pictures made visible by one and the same light, so in all the multifarious phenomena which fill the world, or throng after each other as events, only one will manifests itself, of which everything is the visibility, the objectivity, the manifestation. It is that which is identical in all this variety and change.

To throw his position into bolder relief, Schopenhauer contrasts it with pantheism, the belief that reality is God Himself manifested in everything.

Pantheism is the belief that God is the world—a belief which has always puzzled me. Taking an unprejudiced view of the world as it is, who would regard it as a god? A very ill-advised god, surely, who knows no better than to turn himself into such a world as ours, such a mean, shabby world; there to take the form of countless millions who are fretted and tormented, who live only by preying upon one another. What a pastime for a god!

With the pantheist, I have that One-in-All in common; but my One is not God. I do not go beyond experience, taken in its widest sense; and still less do I fly in the face of the facts which lie before me. The "God" of pantheism, is, and must ever remain, an unknown "X." The will, on the other hand, is the one thing known most immediately in experience and therefore exclusively fitted for the explanation of the rest. What is unknown should always be explained by what is better known, not conversely.

The "God" of pantheism manifests himself to unfold his glory. What glory! Apart from the vanity here attributed to him by pantheism, there is immediately created the obligation to sophisticate away the colossal evil of the world. With me, there is none of this. With me alone, the evil of the world is honestly confessed in its whole magnitude. I alone have no need to have recourse to palliatives and sophistries.

From pantheism, he turns to the more orthodox alternative of theism, the belief, namely, that nature is God's handiwork.

There are two things which make it impossible to believe that this world is the successful work of a wise, good and all-powerful Being. The first is the misery which abounds everywhere. The second is the obvious imperfection of its highest product, man, who is a burlesque of what he should be.

In its explanation of the origin of the world—creation by God—Judaism is inferior to any other form of religious doctrine professed by a civilized people. That Jehovah should have created this world of·misery and woe, because he enjoyed it, and should then have clapped his hands in praise of his own work, declaring everything to be good—that will not do at all!

I shall be told that my philosophy is comfortless—because I speak the truth. People prefer to be assured that everything the Lord has made is good. Go to the priests, then. Or go to your university professors; they are bound to preach optimism; and it is an easy task to upset their theories.

These matters of contrast noted, he resumes the exposition of his own metaphysical thesis:

That which, in us, pursues its ends by the light of knowledge, strives in nature blindly and dumbly in a one-sided and unchangeable manner. Yet in both cases it may be brought under the conception of will: just as the first dim light of dawn must share the name of sunlight with the rays of full midday.

The lowest grades of the objectification of the will are to be found in those most universal forces of nature which partly appear in all matter, as gravity, impenetrability, and so on, which it is the work of physics and chemistry to discover. They are the simplest modes of its objectification.

The conception of "will" has hitherto been subordinated to the conception of "force." I reverse the matter. I desire that every force in nature be understood in terms of will. This is not mere quibbling. For at the basis of the conception of force, as of all conceptions except will, there lies the sense-perceptual knowledge of the objective world, and the conception is constructed out of this. It is hence an abstraction from what is given in sense-perception. We have no direct experience of "forces" in nature, only of connections and sequences. The conception of will, however, is of all conceptions the one which does not have its origin in sense perception, in ideas of things. It comes from within, and proceeds from our immediate consciousness. If therefore, we refer the conception of will to the conception of force we have referred the better known to the less known.

From inanimate nature, Schopenhauer passes to the world of living things. It, too, is only a higher manifestation of the same underlying will:

Every species of animal is a longing of the will-to-live. For instance, the will is seized with a longing to live in trees, to hang from their branches, to devour their leaves. This longing becomes objectified in the sloth. It can hardly walk, being only adapted for climbing. It is helpless on the ground, agile on trees, looks like moss so as to escape its pursuers.

The will is active in nature where no knowledge guides it. This we see in the instincts and mechanical skills of animals. The ends toward which they strive are to them unknown. The bird of a year old has no idea of eggs for which it builds a nest. the young spider has no idea of the prey for which it spins its first web. Ants, marmots, bees, lay in provision for the winter they have never experienced. Insects deposit their eggs where the coming brood find future nourishment. The larva of the stag beetle makes the hole in the wood, in which it is to await its metamorphosis, twice as big if it is going to be a male beetle as it would if it were going to be a female beetle—so that there will be room for the horns which no female beetle possessed. Has it knowledge thus in advance? The point is merely this: Knowledge is not necessary to guide will. It acts instinctively at some levels.

The instincts of plants and animals give us the best illustration of what is meant by teleology in nature. An instinct is an action like that which is guided by a purpose, and is yet entirely without purpose. So all constructions of nature resemble that which is guided by an aim, and yet is entirely without it. What we think to be means and end is, in every case, the manifestation of the unity of the one will.

Everywhere in nature pervading this adaptation we see strife. In this we can recognize that variance with itself which is essential to the will. Every grade of objectification fights for the matter of the others. The permanent matter must continually change its form. This strife may be followed through the whole of nature. It is most visible in the animal kingdom. For animals have the whole of the vegetable kingdom for their food, and within the animal kingdom one order is the prey and food of another. Thus the will everywhere preys upon itself and in different forms is its own nourishment.

From the lower forms of animal life, Schopenhauer turns to consider the higher levels at which instinct and impulse are somewhat modified by the emergence of intellect and knowledge.

From grade to grade, yet still without consciousness, as an obscure striving force, the will rises through matter and the vegetable kingdoms to the point at which the individuals in whom it is manifested can no longer receive food through mere movement following upon stimuli. The chances of the individual that is moved merely by stimuli would be too unfavorable. Its food must be sought out and selected. For this purpose movement following upon motive, and therefore consciousness, becomes necessary.

Consciousness, called in at this stage for the conversation of the individual, appears. It is represented by the brain, just as every other effort of the will is represented by an organ. With this new addition, the "world as idea" comes into existence at a stroke, with all its forms and categories, its subject and object, its time and space and causality and multiplicity. The world now shows its second side.

Till now mere will, it becomes now also idea, object to a knowing conscious subject. Up to this point the will followed its tendency in the dark with unerring certainty. But at this grade it kindles for itself a light as a means to an end, as an instrument needed to deal with the throng and complication of its prior manifestations; a need which would have accrued precisely to its highest manifestation.

The hitherto infallible certainty and regularity with which will worked in unorganized and vegetable matter, rested upon the fact that it alone was active in its original nature as blind impulse, as unconscious will, without interruption from a second and entirely different world, the world of perception. But with consciousness, its infallible certainty comes to an end. Animals are thereby exposed to deception and error. They have, however, only ideas arising out of perception. They have no conceptual powers, no reflective powers, and are therefore bound to the present.

This "knowledge without reason" becomes insufficient. When the will has attained to the highest grade of its objectification, the kind of knowledge which arises out of mere perception confined to what is immediately present to the senses, does not suffice. That complicated and many-sided imaginative being, man, with his many needs, exposed to innumerable dangers, must, if he is to exist, be lighted by a double knowledge. A higher power than mere perception must be given him.

With this new power of reasoning, of framing and using abstract conceptions, there has appeared reflection, surveying the past, anticipating the future, deliberation, care, premeditated action, and finally the full and distinct awareness of one's own deliberate volition as such.

With mere knowledge of perception there arose the possibility of illusion and error, by which the previous infallibility of the blind striving of the will was done away with. With the entrance of reasoning powers that certainty and infallibility are almost entirely lost. Instinct diminishes. Deliberation, supposed to supplant everything from physical causation to instinctive reaction, begets irresolution and uncertainty. Errors become widely possible, and in many cases obstruct the will in action.

Thus knowledge, rational as well as sensuous, proceeds originally from the will itself, belongs to the inner being of the higher grades of objectification as an instrument of selection and adaptation, a means of supporting the individual and the species like any other organ. Destined to forward the aims of the will, it remains almost entirely subject to its service. It is so in all brutes and in almost all men.

In all grades of its manifestations, from the lowest inorganic forms to the highest organic forms, the will is controlled by no final goal or aim. It always strives, for striving is its sole nature which no attaining can put to an end. Therefore it is not capable of any final satisfaction, but only of obstruction. This endless striving, of the will-to-be, the will-to-live, the will-to-conquer, the will-to-reproduce, we see everywhere, and see hindered in many ways. Wherever blocked, we see suffering. So if there be no final aim and no final satisfaction, there are no measure and end of suffering.

We ask: For what purpose does all this torment and agony exist? There is only one consideration that may serve to explain. It is this: The will-to-live, which underlies the whole world of phenomena, must satisfy its cravings by feeding on itself. This it does by forming a graduated scale of phenomena in which one level exists at the expense of another. Note two animals, one of which is engaged in eating the other.

By now the human's place in nature has been indicated. Two passages conclude this somewhat evolutionary account.

In the life of man all this appears with greatest distinctness, illumined by the clearest knowledge. As the manifestation of the will rises higher, the suffering becomes more apparent. In the plant there is no sensibility and therefore no pain. In the lowest forms of animal life, a small degree of suffering may be experienced. As the level rises, sensitivity becomes wider and deeper. It appears in a high degree with the complete nervous system of backboned animals, and increases as intelligence develops. Thus, as knowledge increases, as consciousness attains to greater distinctness, pain also increases, and reaches its highest degree in man. And the more intelligent and finely formed a man is, the more pain he is open to.

Every human being is only another short dream of that endless spirit of nature, the persistent will-to-live; only another fleeting form carelessly sketched on an infinite page, and obliterated to make room for new. And every one of these fleeting forms must be paid for with many deep and long drawn sufferings, and finally with a relentless death. Do you wonder why the sight of a corpse is never funny?

From the vantage point of his metaphysical hypothesis, Schopenhauer feels himself in a position to account for the futility, the restlessness, the unhappiness and boredom which mark human life. If humankind is nothing but an objectification of a blindly striving universal will, what else could be expected?

Man's appetites are insatiable. Every satisfaction he gets lays the seeds of some new desire. There is hence no end to the wishes of any individual will. Why is this? The reason is simple. Will is the lord of all worlds. Everything is but a manifestation of will. Therefore no one single thing can ever give it satisfaction. Only the totality of things—which is endless.

The basis of all willing and striving is need, deficiency, pain. Thus the nature of man is subject to pain originally and in its essence. If, on the other hand, it lacks objects of desire, a terrible void and boredom comes over it. Thus man's life swings like a pendulum, backwards and forwards, between uneasiness and boredom. (Hence, in his speculations, after man had transferred all pains to hell, there remained nothing over for heaven but boredom).

Real boredom is by no means an evil to be lightly esteemed. In the end it depicts on the countenance a real despair. It makes beings who love each other so little as men do, seek each other eagerly. Like its opposite evil, famine in every form, it provokes us to elaborate precautions. People require *panem et circenses*—bread and circuses. As want is the constant scourge of the lower classes, boredom is the lash laid across the back of the fashionable world. In the great middle classes, boredom is represented by Sunday and want by the six weekdays.

Thus, between desiring and attaining, all human life flows on. The wish is, in its nature, uneasiness. The attainment soon begets satiety. The end was only apparent, and possession drives away the charm.

It should be added to this that satisfaction, or what is commonly called *happiness*, is never positive. It is not something original, growing out of itself, so to speak; but must always be the satisfaction of some wish or longing. The wish, the want, the need, the desire, these are the positive things; and these precede, condition, and follow every satisfaction.

The life of every individual, surveyed as a whole, is a tragedy. Here and there in detail, it may have the character of a comedy. The restless irritations of a moment, the needs and vexations of a day, the mishaps and fears of a week, are scenes in a comedy. But the over-aching, never satisfied wishes, the frustrated efforts, the crushed and abandoned hopes, the deep errors of a whole life, with increasing pain or boredom, and death at the close, are always a tragedy. As if the fates would add derision to the miseries to our existence, our life must contain all the ingredients of a tragedy while in detail it will have the foolish look of a comedy.

That happiness is not something positive, that it is merely the satisfaction of some want, to be followed by another or by ennui, finds support in art, that true mirror of the world and life. Every epic and dramatic poem can only represent struggle, effort, fight for happiness; never enduring and complete happiness. It conducts its heroes through a thousand difficulties and dangers to the goal. But, as soon as this is reached, the curtain falls, for now there remains nothing for it to do but show that what lured the hero on as happiness, materialized as disappointment.

Everyone who has awakened from the first dream of youth will realize, if his judgment is not paralyzed, that this world is the kingdom of chance and error, of folly and wickedness. Hence, everything better only struggles through with difficulty. What is noble and wise seldom attains to expression. The absurd and perverse in thought, the dull and tasteless in art, the wicked and deceitful in action, assert a real supremacy broken only by brief interruptions. In vain the sufferer calls on his gods for help. This irremediable evil is only the mirror of the will, of which himself is the objectification.

To me, optimism, when it is not merely the thoughtless verbalizing of those who have nothing but words under their low foreheads is not merely absurd; it is wicked. It is a bitter mockery of the unspeakable misery of mankind. To me, as to the writers of the Gospels, the *world* and *evil* are almost synonymous terms.

Thus far Schopenhauer the metaphysician. Now Schopenhauer the moralist. The latter directs the argument from this point to its despairing conclusion. Thomas Hardy has expressed in poetry what Schopenhauer, up to this point, has been arguing in prose.

Given this view of things, what is Schopenhauer's message for humankind? It is one of pity and self-mortification. His argument turns to these matters, beginning with an explanation of the origin of humanity's pervasive egoism and selfishness, working around gradually to counsels of despair.

What I have been saying comes to this: In the whole of nature, at all the grades of the objectification of the will, there is a necessary and constant conflict, expressing the inner contradiction of the will with itself. This phenomenon exhibits itself with greater distinctness at the highest level of the will's objectification, namely in man. What I propose now is to trace to its source that egoism which is the starting point of all conflict.

The will everywhere manifests itself in separate individuals. But this separateness does not concern the will as it is in itself. The will itself is present, whole and undivided, in every one of these—as the color red is present, whole and undivided, in any red object—and beholds around it the innumerably repeated images of its own nature. Therefore everyone desires everything for himself, and would destroy whatever would oppose it. Every individual feels himself the center of the world, has a primary and inextinguishable regard for his own existence and well-being.

This disposition, which I call *egoism,* is essential to everything in nature. It is by reason of this primary fact that the inner conflict of the will with itself attains such terrible proportions. Yet this egoism has its being and continuance in that opposition of the microcosm and the macrocosm, in the fact that the objectification of the will has individualization as its form, in the act that it manifests itself in the same way in innumerable individuals. In the highest grade of consciousness all this appears in its sharpest form.

We see the consequences of this basic fact everywhere in human life, in small things and great. We see its terrible side in the lives of great tyrants and miscreants, and in world-desolating wars. We see its absurd side in conceit, vanity, and minor selfishness. We see it writ large in history, which is the record of struggles ranging from vast armies to pairs of human alley cats. We see it when any mob of men is set free from law and order and restraint. Then that "war of all against all" which Hobbes has described so admirably, shows itself. This is the highest expression of egoism.

This "primary and ineradicable egoism" is the fact upon which Schopenhauer proceeds to build a moral philosophy, an ethics of pity and despair.

Out of this primary and ineradicable egoism arise both misery and wickedness. Do we desire to know what men so constituted, are worth in moral terms? We have only to consider their fate as a race. This is want, wretchedness, affliction, misery, and death. There is a species of eternal justice in it all. In this sense the world is the judgment of the world. Could we lay the misery of the world in one scale of the balance, and the guilt of the world in the other, the needle would point to the center.

I referred to an eternal justice in the scheme of things. To him who has grasped in all of its ramifications the thought which I have been developing, this will be evident. The world, in all its parts, is the manifestation of one will. The will is free. The will is almighty. The world is its mirror. As the will is, so is the world. It alone bears the responsibility for what comes into being.

However, the world does not stand thus revealed to the knowledge of him whose mind is still bound to the service of his will, as it does to him who has risen to an entirely objective contemplation. The vision of the uncultured individual is clouded. He does not see the reality behind the phenomenon in time and space. He sees not the inner unity and identity of things, but only its separated, individualized, disunited, opposed, manifestations. For him pleasure is one thing and pain another. He sees one manifestation of the will live in abundance and ease, while at his door another dies of want and cold. He asks, "Where is Justice?"

But the vision of eternal justice is beyond him. He sees no inner connection. He sees the wicked flourish and the oppressed suffer. He cannot rise above these individual differences. Hence he does not understand the nature of this world's justice. That man only will grasp and comprehend eternal justice who raises himself above particular things, who sees through the individualizations of the real. He alone sees that the difference between him who inflicts suffering and him who bears it, is phenomenal only and concerns not the will as thing-in-itself. The inflicter of suffering and the sufferer are one. If the eyes of both were opened, the inflicter of suffering would see that he lives in all that suffers pain. The sufferer would see that all the wickedness in the world proceeds from that will which constitutes his own nature.

The comprehension of this eternal justice, of the tie that unites the evil of my crime with the evil of your misery, demands the power to rise above the limits of individuality. Therefore it will always remain unattainable by most men.

What I have been arguing is this: Hatred and wickedness are conditioned by egoism, and egoism rests on the entanglement of knowledge in the principle of individuation, in the fact that the will realizes itself in separate individuals.

If this penetration of the principle of individuation, this direct knowledge of the identity of the will in its diverse manifestations, is present in a high degree of distinctness, it will show an influence upon the will of the individual who has achieved this insight. If the veil is lifted from his eyes so that he no longer makes the egotistical distinction between his self and other selves, then he will regard the infinite suffering of all sufferers as his own.

To such a man no suffering is any longer strange. All the miseries of others work upon his mind like his own. It is no longer the changing joy and sorrow of his own person that he had in view. All lies equally near him. He knows the ultimately real, and finds that it consists in a constant passing away, a vain striving, an inward conflict, a continual suffering. Wherever he looks he sees suffering humanity and a world in passage. But all this now lies as near him as his own person lies to the man who is still in bondage to egoism.

The moralist, backed by the metaphysician, is now in a position to ask pointedly, "Why should man or woman, with this knowledge of ultimate reality, accept life on such terms? Why should man or woman be a yea-sayer? Why not a nay-sayer?"

Why should he, now, with this knowledge of ultimate reality, assert this very life through constant acts of will? Knowledge of the nature of the thing-in-itself becomes a quieter of the individual will. The individual will now turns away from life, now shudders at the pleasures in which it once recognized the assertion of life, now attains to voluntary renunciation, resignation, indifference, will-less-ness.

If we compare life to a course which we must run, a path of red-hot coals with here and there a cool spot, then he who is still entangled in the egoistic delusion is consoled by the cool places and sets out to run the course. But he who sees through individualization to the one will which is identical in all is no longer susceptible to such consolation. He sees himself in all places at once, and withdraws. His will turns around, no longer asserts itself, but denies.

This denial of the will by an individual manifestation of it follows the recognition of the real nature of the thing-in-itself. It is the transition from virtue to asceticism. This is to say, when a man has once seen, it no longer suffices for him to love others as himself. There arises within him a horror of that will of which he is himself a manifestation.

Noting but a manifestation of the will, the individual ceases now to will anything. His body he denies. His health he is indifferent to. His desires he ignores. He desires no gratification of any appetite in any form.

More concretely, what is meant by this exhortation to suppress and deny the will-to-life? Schopenhauer is clear enough about it all. Upon the unhappy human he urges a program of chastity, asceticism, self-chastisement, and ultimate starvation:

Voluntary and complete chastity is the first step in asceticism, the first move in the denial of the will-to-live. It denies the assertion of the will which extends beyond the individual's own life. It gives assurance that the life of this body, the will whose manifestation it is, ceases.

Asceticism shows itself further in voluntary and intentional poverty; not only *per accidens* as when possessions are given away to mitigate the sufferings of others, but directly to serve as a constant mortification of the will, so that the satisfaction of desires, the sweet things of life, shall not rouse the will of which a penetrating self-knowledge has conceived a horror.

Asceticism extends further as humility and patience. He who denies the will as it appears in his own person will not resist if another does wrong to him. Suffering, insult, ignominy, he will receive gladly, as the opportunity to learning that he no longer stands behind his will. Patience and meekness will replace impatience and pride and anger.

Asceticism culminates in self-chastisement, fasting, and starvation. By constant privation and suffering he who has seen the nature and source of the evil of life in the will-to-live is able more and more to break down and destroy that manifestation in himself; to crush in himself that which he recognizes and abhors as the source of his own and humanity's misery and wickedness.

When death comes to such a one, it is almost welcome. Here it is not, as in the case of others, merely the manifestation of the will that ends in death. The inner nature of the will has long been restrained, denied, crushed. The last slight bond is now broken. For him who ends thus, the world also ends.

With a backward glance over the whole argument of his metaphysics and moral philosophy, Schopenhauer concludes:

What I have described here with feeble tongue and only in general terms, is no philosophical fable. It is the moral of the life of saints and ascetics in all ages and all religions. The inner nature of holiness, self-renunciation, mortification, is here expressed, abstractly and free from mythology, as the denial of the will-to-live, appearing after the complete knowledge of its own nature has become a quieter of all volition.

Before us there is certainly only nothingness. We look with deep and painful longing upon the perfect calm of the spirit which has strangled and subdued the will-to-live. Beside it, the misery and evil of life is thrown into clear contrast. Yet, only when we have recognized the incurable suffering and endless wickedness which follows upon the assertion of the will, and have ordered our days to its denial, do we attain any lasting consolation. To those in whom the will has turned against itself, this world of planets, suns, and milky ways is nothing.

NOTE ON SOURCES. The material in this section is quoted, abridged, and paraphrased from Arthur Schopenhauer, *The World as Will and Idea*, translated by R. B. Haldane and J. Kemp (Garden City, NJ: Doubleday & Co., Inc., 1961), especially Book IV and the appendices; *On the Will in Nature;* and two volumes of miscellaneous essays, *Parerga* and *Paralipomena*, e.g., "On Women," "On Suicide," "On Pantheism," and so forth.

4 AUGUSTE COMTE

THE CLAIMS OF POSITIVISM

FROM SCHOPENHAUER TO COMTE. Each century tackles the problem of traditional metaphysics in its own way. The seventeenth century, represented in Hobbes's materialism, differs in method from the eighteenth. The eighteenth, represented by Berkeley's idealism, differs again from the nineteenth century, represented in the writings of Schopenhauer and Auguste Comte. By the 1830s, it seemed unnecessary to reopen the hectic controversies that inspired and followed from earlier attempts to formulate a metaphysics. At least, Comte appears to have felt as much. The picture is altered. Comte approaches philosophy from the point of view of a man who is interested primarily in the range and organization of the various bodies of science. He pins a controversial tag on himself, no doubt: for *positivism*, as will be seen, means "no more metaphysics." But he is inclined to sweep controversy to one side and ask several new leading questions: What common method has the growth of science revealed? What relations, if any, exist among the different sciences? What significance, for general education, may be ascribed to the sciences as a whole? In what fields, if any, may we look for the emergence of new sciences? For these reasons, among others, Comte is perhaps more convincing to one who is either innocent of Hume and Kant or who has lost those peculiar sensibilities that respond to their anxieties and convictions.

BIOGRAPHICAL NOTE.   August Comte was born in France in 1798, and died in 1857 at the age of fifty-nine. He showed an early aptitude for mathematics, which he began to teach in Paris. When he was twenty-eight, he embarked on a series of public lectures designed to offer a synoptic account of the principal sciences. These attracted considerable attention; but after the third lecture, his brain temporarily gave way, and he tried to commit suicide. Two years later he had sufficiently recovered to resume his lectures. In 1830 he began the publication of his great survey of the sciences. It was completed in six large volumes and served through several generations as a storehouse of fact and generalization for students in France and abroad. He continued to maintain himself by teaching mathematics and serving as an examiner in that subject. Unfortunately, however, he became embroiled in controversies that caused him to lose a great part of his means of living. The English philosopher J. S. Mill, who had been impressed by the value of Comte's work, was instrumental in securing a considerable sum of money from Comte's admirers in England. This tided him over his immediate difficulties. When this was used up, Comte faced poverty; however, aid came eventually from admirers in France who banded together to provide the lonely polymath with a small income for the rest of his life.

Comte's interest in metaphysics was not direct. To get this point as clearly and, at the same time, as sympathetically as possible, we need to recall a bit of French history. Comte wrote for the first generation after Napoleon. The old regime, the epoch of the grand monarchy, formed a remote background. It had been swept away by the French Revolution. Liberal hopes had run high, only to be disappointed by the autocratic domination of Napoleon; and now, following the Congress of Vienna, France had been made over once more into a monarchy under Louis XVIII and Charles X. These drastic changes appear to have inspired Comte with the dream of a new era in which they would no longer be possible. This new era was to be built upon science and the application of science to industry. But, as Comte saw it, several obstacles blocked the path of the new age. They were remnants from the past. They were, more particularly, beliefs, or mental sets that still lingered from the Middle Ages, the period of the grand monarchy, the Age of Reason, the French Revolution, and Napoleon. They were beliefs about such matters as God, the soul, ultimate reality, immortality, natural laws, inalienable rights, men of destiny, and so forth. These beliefs, Comte felt, were not only groundless, they were harmful. They had been responsible for continuous tyranny, revolt, suppression, war, and they would continue to be. What the world needed was a riddance of such beliefs, and Comte would supply it under cover of this new term *positivism,* which was to abolish the old loyalties and controversies, to set up the ideal of scientific method and its application to nature in the interests of human welfare.

THE ARGUMENT OF THE PASSAGES.   Comte begins by elaborating what he calls the *law of the three stages.* This enables him to dispose of metaphysics and theology. He turns then to a statement of his theory of the sciences. The passages tell their own story from that point on:

(1)

> In order to understand the true value and character of positivism, we must take a brief general view of the progress of the human mind; for no conception can be understood otherwise than through its history.
>
> From the study of the development of human understanding, in all directions and through all times, the discovery arises of a fundamental law. The law is this: that each of our leading conceptions, each branch of our knowledge, passes through three different theoretical conditions: the theological or fictitious, the metaphysical or abstract, the scientific or positive. This fundamental law should henceforth be, in my opinion, the starting point of all philosophical researches about man and society.
>
> The human mind employs in its progress three methods of philosophizing, the characteristics of which are essentially different and even radically opposed: the theological, the metaphysical, and the scientific. Hence arise three philosophies, or three general systems of thought, each of which excludes the other. The first is the mind's necessary point of departure; the second is merely a state of transition; the third is the mind's fixed and definitive state.

An instance of what Comte means might be the following: In the early stages of human study of the heavens, their motion was accounted for in terms of various deities. Later humans envisaged them as controlled by the force of gravitation. Finally they repudiate explanation in terms of gods and forces and are satisfied to describe the motion in terms of formulae, which enable them to locate and predict:

> Different departments of our knowledge have passed through the three stages at different rates. The rate depends on the nature of the knowledge in question. Any kind of knowledge reaches the positive stage early in proportion to its generality, simplicity, and independence of other branches of knowledge. Thus astronomy, which is above all made up of facts which are general, simple, and independent of other facts, was the first science to attain the positive stage, then physics, then chemistry, and finally physiology.

In the theological stage, the human mind, seeking the essential nature of things, their first and final causes, supposes all things to be produced by the immediate action or supernatural beings. Here imagination predominates over observation.

A natural and irresistible instinct disposes the human race to adopt theological ideas as its earliest principles of explanation. The personal action exerted by man on other things is, at first, the only kind he is able to understand. He is thus led to conceive, in an analogous way, the action of external bodies on himself and on each other. This is animism. Continued observation leads him to convert this primitive hypothesis into another, less enduring one: that of a "dead" inert nature guided by invisible superhuman agents, distinct and independent of one another. This is polytheism. Continued observation and reflection disposes him gradually to reduce the number of these supernatural agencies until he is led from polytheism to monotheism. The theological system arrived at its highest perfection when it substituted the providential action of a single supreme Being for the varied operations of numerous divinities; when, that is, it passed from polytheism to monotheism.

The entire theological system is based on the supposition that the earth is made for man, and the whole universe made for the earth. Remove this supposition, and the system crumbles. Hence the true astronomical theory, proposed by Copernicus and proved by Kepler, Galileo, and Newton, would alone have sufficed to demolish the theological system. In the light of the fact that our planet, one of the smallest, is in no respect different from the others, revolving like them around the sun, the hypothesis that nature is made for mankind alone so shocks good sense and contradicts fact that it must appear absurd and collapse. With it falls the theological edifice.

In the metaphysical stage, which is only a modification of the first, the mind supposes abstract forces, personified abstractions, inherent in all things and capable of producing them, instead of supernatural beings. What is called the *explanation* of anything is, in this stage, a reference of it to its proper force, principle, or abstraction.

To explain sleep, for example, in terms of what used to be called the *dormitive principle* is to explain observed phenomena by reference to what Comte would call a *metaphysical abstraction.* Many such phrases are to be found strewn through the annals of science and philosophy. Thus Hegel's *reason* or *time-spirit,* Schopenhauer's *will,* Bergson's *élan vital,* Freud's *censor,* the erstwhile *vis viva, vis inertia,* and *entelechy* are probably all instances of what Comte would call *metaphysical abstractions.* His objection to them is that they are attempts to explain the known by the unknown, to postulate something that is not revealed in experience to account for what is revealed in experience.

Even today, after all our advance in positive knowledge, if we try to understand how the fact which we name a cause produces the fact which we name its effect, we should be compelled, as Hume points out, to resort to images similar to those which serve as the basis of primitive human theories. (Cause is a metaphysical notion; regularity of succession is the positive notion.)

The metaphysical system arrived at its last stage when men substituted the one great entity—nature—as the cause of everything.

In the scientific or positive stage the mind has given over the vain search after absolute knowledge; abandoned the quest for knowledge of the origin and destination of the universe, of causes and forces; and applies itself solely to the study of laws, to the study of relations of succession and resemblance. Reasoning and observation, duly combined, are the means of this knowledge. What is now called the *explanation* of anything is the establishment of a connection between it and some general laws, the number of which continually diminishes with the progress of science.

Observation of fact is the only solid basis for human knowledge. Taking this principle in its most rigorous sense, we may say that a proposition which does not admit of being reduced to a simple enunciation of fact, particular or general, can have no real or intelligible sense.

The first characteristic of positivism is that it regards all things as subject to invariable laws. Our business—seeing how vain is any search into what are called causes, either first or final—is to pursue an accurate discovery of those laws, with a view to reducing them to the smallest possible number. The best illustration of this is in the case of the law of gravitation. We say things are explained by it, because it connects an immense variety of facts under one head.

The positive system would attain its ultimate perfection if men could represent all particular facts as instances of one general law, e.g., the law of gravitation.

There is no science, which, having attained to the positive stage, does not bear marks of having passed through the two previous stages. At some earlier period it was composed of metaphysical abstractions; and, further back in its evolution, it took its form from theological conceptions. Our most advanced sciences still bear traces of the earlier stages through which they have passed.

(2)

In mentioning just now the four principal categories of phenomena—the astronomical, the physical, the chemical, the physiological—there was an omission. Nothing was said of social phenomena. These demand a distinct classification, by reason of their importance and difficulty. They are the most complicated and the most dependent on others. Their science, therefore, will be the latest to attain positivity.

This branch of science has not hitherto entered the domain of positive knowledge. Theological and metaphysical conceptions and methods, exploded and abandoned in other departments, are still used in the treatment of social subjects, though the best minds are weary of disputes about "divine rights," "sovereignty of the people," and so on. This is the great, the only, gap to be filled to constitute solid and entire the positive philosophy. This is what men have now most need of.

This once done, the philosophical system of the moderns will be complete. There will then be no phenomena which do not enter into one of the five great categories—astronomical, physical, chemical, physiological, and sociological.

So much, then for the law of the three stages. For Comte, its principal virtue seems to reside in the fact that it eliminates, at one fell swoop, a whole army of clamorous hypotheses and controversies that constitute a large portion of modern philosophy.

Comte now turns his attention to the question of the classification of the positive sciences. (It should be noted that, as Comte uses it, the term *physiology* has the broader meaning that we extend today to the term *biology*.)

(3)

We propose to classify the fundamental sciences. They are six, as we shall see. We cannot make them less; and most scientists would make them more. To classify the sciences is not so easy as may appear. It always involves something, if not arbitrary, at least artificial; and in so far, it will always involve imperfection. It is perhaps impossible to exhibit the sciences, quite rigorously, in their natural relations and mutual dependence so as to avoid, in some degree, the danger of overlapping.

What we seek to determine is the dependence of scientific studies. Does physics depend upon physiology? Does sociology depend upon chemistry? Dependence among the sciences can result only from dependence among the corresponding phenomena. For a principle in terms of which to classify the sciences, then, we must look to the different orders of phenomena through which science discovers the laws which are her object.

All phenomena may be included within a very few natural categories, so arranged that the study of each may be grounded on the principal laws of the preceding and serve as the basis of the next ensuing. We have now obtained our rule. We proceed next to our classification.

We are first struck by the clear division of all natural phenomena into two classes: inorganic and organic. Each of these two great halves had subdivisions. Inorganic phenomena may be divided into two classes: celestial and terrestrial. Terrestrial inorganic phenomena may be divided into two classes according as we regard bodies in their mechanical or chemical character. Organic phenomena may be divided into two classes: those which relate to the individual and those which relate to groups.

Thus we have five basic sciences in successive dependence: astronomy, physics, chemistry, physiology, and sociology. The first considers the most general, simple, and remote phenomena known to us, and those which affect all others without being affected by them. The last considers the most particular, complex, and nearest phenomena. Between these two the degrees of speciality and complexity are in regular proportion to the place of the respective sciences in the scale exhibited. This we must regard as the true filiation of the sciences.

It is proposed to consolidate the entire body of positive knowledge into one body of homogeneous doctrine. But it must not be supposed that we are proposing to study this vast variety as proceeding from one single law. There is something so chimerical in attempts at explanations in terms of one single law, that it may be as well to repudiate any such notion. Our intellectual resources are too narrow, and the universe too complex, to justify any hope that it will ever be within our power to carry scientific perfection to this last degree of simplicity.

This notion of all phenomena referable to a single law is by no means necessary to the systematic formation of science. The only necessary unity is that of method. And this is already, in great part, attained: The scientific method of thought is the same for all fields of knowledge, however widely they may vary and however irreducible they may be in content.

Comte's meaning is probably this: In the scientific exploration of any field, the method is the same. Initial data are collected, usually in the light of some tentatively held hypothesis; this hypothesis is then assumed to be true, and its consequences or implications deduced; facts subsequently acquired, by observation or experiment, verify the deductions made from the hypothesis. The hypothesis may be with regard to some particular fact or some general law.

The most interesting point in our hierarchical classification is its effect on education, both general and scientific. This is its direct and unquestionable result. No science can be effectually pursued without a competent knowledge of the anterior sciences upon which it depends.

Your competent physicist must have at least a general knowledge of astronomy. Chemists cannot properly understand chemistry without physics and astronomy. Physiologists require some knowledge of chemistry, physics, and astronomy. Above all, students of social science require a general knowledge of the anterior sciences. As such conditions are rarely fulfilled, there is among us, no genuinely rational scientific education. To this may be attributed, in part, the imperfection of even the most important sciences at this day.

In our enumeration of the basic sciences there is one prodigious omission. We have said nothing of mathematics. The omission was intentional, and the reason was the vast importance and unique status of mathematics. It is, however, less a constituent part of the body of positive knowledge than a basis for the whole of that knowledge. It is the most powerful instrument that the human mind can employ in the investigation of the laws of natural phenomena. It must, therefore, hold the first place in the hierarchy of the sciences and be the point of departure for all education in any of the sciences.

From the question of the classification of the sciences, Comte addresses himself to certain advantages he thinks will arise from the unified view that results. It is interesting to note that these include the elimination of logic and the reduction of psychology to behaviorism.

(4)

We have now considered philosophically the articulation of the positive sciences. The order that results is this: mathematics, astronomy, physics, chemistry, physiology, and sociology. We must glance at the principal advantages to be derived from a study of them. Of these advantages, four may be pointed out.

In the *first* place, the study of the positive sciences affords the only rational means of exhibiting the logical laws of the human mind. Looking at all scientific theories as so many great logical facts, it is only by the observation of these facts that we can arrive at the knowledge of logical laws.

Psychology pretends to discover the laws of the human mind by contemplating the mind itself. Such an (introspective) attempt, made in defiance of the physiological study of our intellectual organs, cannot succeed. The mind may observe all phenomena but its own. There can be nothing like scientific observation of mental phenomena except from without, and by another. The observing and observed organ are here the same. In order to observe its activity, your mind must pause from activity; yet it is this very activity that you want to observe. If you cannot pause, you cannot observe; if you do pause, there is nothing to observe. The results of such a method are in proportion to its absurdity.

After two thousand years of psychology, no one proposition is established to the satisfaction of psychologists. To this day they are divided into a multitude of schools, still disputing about the very elements of their doctrine. The psychologists have done some good in keeping up the activity of our understandings when there was no better work for our minds to do.

What we have said with regard to psychology as a positive science applies yet more strikingly to logic, that is, to the "study" of scientific method. Scientific method can be judged of only in action. It cannot be studied apart from the work on which it is employed. Such a study would be dead, could produce nothing of value in the mind which loses time on it. We may talk forever about scientific method, and state it in terms very wise and learned, without knowing half so much about it as the man who has once put it into practice upon a single piece of research. Thus have logicians, by dint of reading the aphorisms of Bacon and the discourses of Descartes mistaken their own dreams for science. We cannot explain the great logical procedures apart from their applications.

In the *second* place, a study of positive science as here conceived will regenerate education. The best minds are agreed that our European education, still essentially theological, metaphysical, and literary, must be superseded by a scientific education conformable to our time and needs.

Everything yet done to this end is inadequate. What is required is an organic conception of the sciences such as positivism presents. The exclusive specializing tendencies of our sciences spoil our teaching. If any student desires to form a conception of science as a whole, he is compelled to go through each department as it is now taught, as if he were to be only an astronomer or only a chemist. The result, be his intellect what it may, is unsatisfactory when what he requires is a general conception of the entire range of positive knowledge.

It is such a general conception of the entire range of the sciences which must henceforth be the permanent basis of all human combinations. It will constitute the mind of future generations. But to this end it is necessary that the sciences, considered as branches from one trunk should yield us as a whole, their chief methods and results.

In the *third* place, the proposed study of the organically related generalizations of the positive sciences will aid the progress of each separate science. The divisions we establish between the sciences are, though not arbitrary, essentially superficial. The subject of our researches is one; we divide it for convenience, in order to deal more easily with separate problems. But it sometimes happens that we need what we cannot obtain under the present isolation of the sciences, namely a combination of several special points of view. For want of this, important problems wait for their solution.

To go into the past for an example: Descartes' grand conception with regard to analytical geometry, a discovery which has changed the whole face of mathematics, issued from the union of two sciences which had before been separately studied and pursued.

Again, it was undecided whether azote [nitrogen] is a simple or a compound body. Almost all chemists held that azote is a simple body. But the illustrious Berzelius, influenced by the physiological observation that animals which receive no azote in their food have as much of it in their tissue as carnivorous animals, was able to throw new light on the question. Thus must physiology unite with chemistry to inform us whether azote is simple or compound, and to institute a new series of researches upon the relation between the composition of living bodies and their mode of alimentation.

In the *fourth* place, philosophy based on the positive sciences offers the only solid basis for that social reorganization which must succeed the critical condition in which even the most civilized nations are now living.

It cannot be necessary to argue that ideas govern the world or throw it into chaos, that all social mechanism rests upon opinions held by the members of society. The great political and moral crisis that societies are now undergoing proceeds from intellectual anarchy. Stability in fundamental principles is the first condition of genuine social order: We witness an utter disagreement on all such matters. Till a certain number of general ideas can be acknowledged as a rallying point for social doctrine, nations will remain in a revolutionary state whatever palliatives may be advised, and their institutions only provisional and makeshift.

But when necessary agreement on first principles can be obtained, appropriate institutions will issue from them without shock or resistance. It is in this direction that those must look who desire a natural, regular, normal state of society.

Now, the existing disorder is abundantly accounted for by the existence, all at once, of three incompatible philosophies—the theological, the metaphysical, and the positive. Any one of these might alone secure some sort of social order. But while the three coexist, it is impossible for us to understand one another upon any essential point whatever. If this is true, we have only to ascertain which of the philosophies must, in the nature of things, eventually prevail.

Comte's point here might be illustrated by controversies centering in such questions as birth control, sterilization of the subnormal and criminal, and so on. Consider the case of sterilization. A sincere Catholic might oppose the measure as contrary to the will of God; a sincere democrat might oppose it as contrary to the rights of man and woman; a social scientist, disregarding both grounds of opposition, might simply argue that offspring born to such parents are likely to prove a needless burden and menace to a society, which must, in the end, either support them or imprison them.

This problem, once recognized, cannot remain long unsolved; for all considerations point to a philosophy based on the positive sciences as the one destined to prevail. It alone has been advancing during the course of centuries while others have been declining. The fact is incontestable. Some may deplore it, but none deny it or destroy it, nor neglect it save on pain of being betrayed by illusory speculations.

This general revolution of the human mind is nearly accomplished. We have only to complete the hierarchy of the positive sciences by bringing the facts and problems of society within its comprehension. The preference which almost all minds, from the highest to the commonest, accord to positive knowledge over vague and mystical conceptions, is a pledge of what this philosophy will receive when it is once completed by the addition of a positive social science. When this has been accomplished, its supremacy will be automatic and will establish order throughout society.

NOTE ON SOURCES.   The material in this section is quoted, abridged, or paraphrased from Auguste Comte, *The Positive Philosophy*, translated by Harriet Martineau (London: Trubner & Co., 1853), Introduction and Chapters 1 and 2.

10

When Can I Say "I Know"?

THE QUESTION POSED

The question "When can I say I know?" is central to the branch of philosophy called *epistemology*, which is derived from the two Greek words meaning "knowledge" and "the rationale of." It means an inquiry into the nature of knowledge. If the intention were carried out, it would provide us with the knowledge of the nature of knowledge. In the conception of epistemology, knowledge turns in upon itself and seeks to formulate a "theory" of itself. Here knowledge is itself made the object of investigation. How did philosophers find themselves involved in such an inquiry?

From an acquaintance with the questions we have been examining, especially the last two—What things shall I call art? What shall I say about ultimate reality?—one can see in a general way how epistemology came about. Responses to these questions have often been speculative, and there is a cautious turn of mind to which all such speculations seem to be of doubtful value. Such a mind is impressed finally with the futility of such matters and with the confusion that emerges when humans seek to clarify their beliefs about such things. Out of this attitude toward speculation, two widely different things have resulted. There have come, in the first place, the genial and undisciplined doubts of such persons as Montaigne and Anatole France. Here the procedure is largely one of banter and ridicule. But that has not been the doubter's only weapon against the speculator. For in the second place, there has come the demand that flights of speculation be put aside until a preliminary inquiry is made into the nature of knowledge itself and the question faced: Can it be shown, from an analysis of the nature of knowledge itself, whether such speculations are justified, whether they lie within the actual or possible grasp of the mind?

The sections that follow may, therefore, be considered as approaches to a single problem: the condition that needs to be met if speculation is justified at all.

The authors chosen for consideration are David Hume and Immanuel Kant from the eighteenth century, A. J. Ayer and R. G. Collingwood from the early part of the twentieth century, and Alvin Goldman and Keith Lehrer, both examples of contemporary epistemologists.

1 DAVID HUME

AN APPEAL TO EXPERIENCE

For most readers, during the closing years of the seventeenth and most of the eighteenth century, the problem of knowledge meant John Locke's *Essay Concerning Human Understanding*. His general commonsense tone, his homely appeal to experience, his determination not to be led into unverifiable speculations, all combined to secure for him a wide circle of readers and followers. It was only natural, therefore, that the next stage in the development of epistemological theory should take the form of an attempt to "begin where Locke left off." His position briefly was this: All knowledge may be analyzed into ideas. All ideas come to us from experience. All experience is by way of the senses. This *empiricism*, as it is called, was Locke's contribution to epistemological theory. His successor in these matters, David Hume, wrote for a generation that was familiar with the appeal to experience as Locke had formulated it. Hume set himself a simple task: to deduce more rigorously the implications of Locke's position.

BIOGRAPHICAL NOTE.   For a biographical comment on David Hume see Chapter 5, Section 3.

THE ARGUMENT OF THE PASSAGES.   In Chapter 5 we met Hume as a critic of natural theology. His method there was to show what happens in natural theology if one sticks closely to the terms laid down by traditional speculation in these matters. He applies the same method in epistemology. It is proposed to make an appeal to experience, he writes; let the appeal be made, then, and not abandoned because it is found to lead to inconvenient consequences. The argument of his position is simple and direct. All knowledge may be analyzed into impressions and ideas. All ideas are derived from earlier impressions. We use certain "metaphysical" terms, such as "matter," "mind," "causal connection," "free will," "the uniformity of nature." These terms play a large part in human thinking and speculating. In fact, they are the fundamental terms in the modern person's general reflections about the world. What are they worth? From what "impressions" are they derived? What corresponds to them in that actual experience to which Locke proposed to appeal? In each case Hume's answer is "they have no basis in experience." Accordingly, any speculation that incorporates them is a waste of ink and paper. He begins by explaining that an inquiry into the nature of knowledge is directed toward eliminating as mere speculation all abstruse terms that clutter human thinking:

The only method of freeing learning from abstruse questions is to inquire seriously into the nature of human understanding and show, from an exact analysis of its powers and capacity, that it is by no means fitted for such subjects.

The premises of his theory of knowledge are to be the following:

We may divide all perceptions into two classes: impressions and ideas. By impressions I mean all our perceptions when we hear, see, feel, love, hate, desire, etc. Ideas are those less lively perceptions of which we are conscious when we reflect on any of those sensations mentioned above.

All ideas are copies of impressions. . . . Even those ideas which seem most wide of this origin are found, upon a nearer scrutiny to be derived from it. . . . We shall always find that every idea is copied from a similar impression. . . . it is impossible for us to think of anything which we have not antecedently felt by our senses.

The test of all terms is to be "show me the impression":

When we entertain any suspicion of a philosophical term, we need but inquire from what impression is that supposed idea derived. If it be not possible to assign any, this will serve to confirm our suspicion that it is employed without meaning. . . . By this means we can throw light upon ideas and render them precise. Produce the impressions or originals from which the ideas are copied.

The first idea to be tested by the appeal to impressions is the now familiar idea of substance or matter:

Some philosophers found much of their reasonings on the distinction of *substance* and *quality*. I would fain ask them whether the idea of substance be derived from impressions of sensations or impressions of reflection. Does it arise from an impression? Point it out to us, that we may know its nature and qualities. But if you cannot point out any such impression, you may be certain you are mistaken when you imagine you have any such idea.

If the impression from which we derive our idea of substance be conveyed to us by our senses, I ask, by which of them? If by the eyes, it must be a color. If by the ears, it must be a sound. If by the palate, it must be a taste. And so of the other senses. But I believe none will assert that substance is either a color, a sound, or a taste.

Is the idea of substance, then, derived from an impression of reflection [i.e., introspection]? But impressions of reflection resolve themselves into our feelings, passions, and emotions, none of which can possibly resemble a substance. We have, therefore, no idea of substance, apart from that of a collection of qualities.

The idea of substance is nothing but a collection of ideas of qualities, united by the imagination and given a particular name by which we are able to recall that collection. The particular qualities which form a substance are commonly referred to an unknown something in which they are supposed to "inhere." This is a fiction.

We may well ask what causes us to believe in the existence of material substance. 'Tis certain there is no question in philosophy more abstruse. By what argument can it be proved that perceptions must be caused by external objects entirely different from them? By an appeal to experience? But here experience is and must be entirely silent. The mind has never anything present to it but its perceptions and cannot possibly have any experience of their connection with objects. The supposition of such a connection is, therefore, without any foundation in reasoning.

Philosophers distinguish betwixt *perceptions* and *objects*. The perceptions are supposed to be caused by the object, and to be interrupted, perishing and different at different times and for different people. The objects are supposed to cause the perceptions, and to be uninterrupted, continuous, and identical. But, however, this view may be esteemed, I assert that there are no principles, either of the understanding or the fancy which lead us to embrace this opinion of the double existence of perceptions and objects.

This hypothesis of the double existence of perceptions and objects has no primary recommendation to reason. The only existences of which we are certain are perceptions. Being immediately present to us by consciousness, they commend our strongest assent, and must be the foundation of all our reasonings. But, as nothing is ever present to the mind but perceptions, it follows that we can never observe any "object," or any connection, causal or otherwise, between perceptions and objects.

The idea of substance as something underlying a set of qualities is unable to produce its credentials. Away with it, then. As Hume remarks of all such ideas, "Commit it to the flames." From material substance he turns to the idea of mental or spiritual substance:

There are some philosophers (e.g., Berkeley) who imagine we are every moment intimately conscious of what we call our *self*; that we feel its existence and its continuance in existence, and are certain of its identity and simplicity.

Unluckily all these positive assertions are contrary to that very experience which is pleaded for them. Have we any idea of a self? From what impression could it be derived? It must be some impression that gives rise to every idea. But self or person is not any one impression. If any impression gives rise to the idea of one's self, that impression must continue to be the same, since one's self is supposed to continue to be the same. But there is no such continuing, constant impression.

For my part, when I enter most intimately into what I call my *self*, I always stumble on some particular perception or other, of heat or cold, light or shade, love or hatred, pain or pleasure, color or sound, etc. I never catch my self, distinct from some such perception.

If anyone thinks he has a different notion of his self, I must confess I can no longer reason with him. He may perceive something simple and continued which he calls his *self*; though I am certain there is no such principle in me.

Setting aside metaphysicians of this kind, I may venture to affirm of the rest of mankind that they are nothing but a bundle or collection of different perceptions which succeed each other with an inconceivable rapidity and are in a perpetual flux and movement. Our eyes cannot turn in their sockets without varying their perceptions. Our thoughts are still more variable. And all our other senses and powers contribute to this change.

The mind (or self) is a kind of theater where perceptions make their appearance, pass, repass, glide away, and mingle in an infinite variety. But there is no simplicity, no one simple thing present or pervading this multiplicity; no identity pervading this change; whatever natural inclination we may have to imagine that there is. The comparison of the theater must not mislead us: it persists, while the actors come and go. Whereas, only the successive perceptions constitute the mind.

The idea of mind or self or Spirit fails to reveal any basis in immediate impressions. That seals its fate. But the question persists: "Why do we entertain such a notion?" It is one thing to show that an idea is a mere fiction. It is another thing to account for its widespread presence in human thinking.

> Why do we ascribe an identity amid these successive perceptions, and suppose our selves possessed of an invariable and uninterrupted existence through the whole course of our life? The identity which we ascribe to minds and selves is only a fictitious one, but why do we ascribe it?
>
> Suppose we could see clearly into the mind of another, and observe that succession of perceptions which constitutes his mind. Suppose, too, that he always preserves the memory of a considerable part of past perceptions. It is evident that nothing could more readily contribute to bestowing a relation between these successive perceptions. Would not the frequent placing of these remembered perceptions in the chain of thought convey our imagination more easily from one to another? And so make the whole seem like the continuance of one object?
>
> As memory alone acquaints us with the continuance and extent of a succession of perceptions, it is to be considered, on that account chiefly, as the source of personal identity. Had we no memory, we should never have any notion of that succession of perceptions which constitutes our self or person. But having once acquired this notion from the operation of memory, we can extend the same beyond our memory and come to include times which we have entirely forgot. And so arises the fiction of person and personal identity.

Material substance is gone. Mental substance is gone. Hume turns to the notion of causal connection between events. He is here proposing to invade the citadel of eighteenth-century science, a structure that was believed to rest squarely on the notion of causal connection. Hume's handling of this idea should be observed closely. His first question is, "What do people mean by the idea of causal connection?" His answer is that by causal connection they mean necessary connection; they believe that there is a necessary connection between a cause and its effect. His next question is the inevitable one: "What evidence, open to our senses, have we for believing that there is any necessity in causal connection?" His answer is, "None whatever."

> There is no idea in metaphysics more obscure or uncertain than *necessary connection* between cause and effect. We shall try to fix the precise meaning of this term by producing the impression from which it is copied.
>
> When we look at external objects, and consider the operation of causes, we are never able, in a single instance, to discover a necessary connection; any quality which binds the effect to the cause, and renders the one a necessary consequence of the other. We find only that the effect does, in fact, follow the cause. The impact of one billiard ball upon another is followed by the motion of the second. There is here contiguity in space and time, but nothing to suggest necessary connection.
>
> The scenes of the universe are continually shifting, and one object follows another in an uninterrupted succession. But any "force" or necessary connection pervading the whole machine never discovers itself in any of the sensible qualities of the body. We know that heat is a constant attendant of flame. But as to any necessary connection between them, we have no room so much as to conjecture or imagine.
>
> In single instances of causal connection we never, by our utmost scrutiny, discover anything but one event following another. We detect no necessary connection

between the cause and its effect. All events seem loose and separate. One event follows another. But we observe no tie between them, beyond contiguity in space and time. They are contiguous, thus; but never connected. As we can have no idea of anything of which we have had no correspondent impression, the conclusion seems to be that we have no idea of necessary connection, and that these words are absolutely without meaning.

We are apt to imagine that we could discover effects from their causes by the mere operation of our reason, without experience. We fancy that, were we brought on a sudden into this world, we could have inferred that one billiard ball would communicate motion to another upon impact; and that we need not have waited for the event, in order to pronounce with certainty concerning it.

Knowledge of this relation arises entirely from experience. We find that particular objects are constantly conjoined with each other. Knowledge of this relation is not, in any instance, attained by reasonings a priori. Causes and effects are discoverable by experience, not by reason. Every effect is a distinct event from its cause. It could not, therefore, be discovered in the cause (prior to experience of their conjunction). Without the assistance of observation and experience, we should in vain pretend to determine any single event or infer any cause or effect. A man must be very sagacious who could discover by reasoning that ice is the effect of cold, without being previously acquainted with the operation of these qualities.

Hence no philosopher who is rational and modest has even pretended to assign the ultimate cause of any natural operation. Ultimate springs and principles (causes) are totally shut off from human curiosity and enquiry.

As in the case of our idea of mind or self, Hume pauses to inquire why we ascribe to the connection between cause and effect something that is not revealed in experience.

Why do we imagine a necessary connection? From observing many constant conjunctions? But what is there in a number of instances which is absent from a single instance? Only this: After a repetition of similar instances the mind is carried by habit, upon the appearance of the cause, to expect the effect. This connection, which we feel in the mind, this customary and habitual transition of the imagination from a cause to its effect, is the impression from which we form the idea of necessary connection. There is nothing further in the case.

When we say a cause is necessarily connected with its effect, we mean, therefore, that they have acquired a connection in our thought; a conclusion which is somewhat extraordinary, but seems founded on sufficient evidence.

Every idea is copied from some impression. In all single instances of causal connection there is nothing that can suggest any idea of necessity. But when many instances have been experienced, we begin to entertain the idea. We then feel a new impression, to wit, a customary transition in our thoughts or imagination between the cause and its effect. This impression is the original of that idea which we seek for. For, as this idea arises from a number of similar instances, it must arise from the circumstance in which the number of instances differ from each single instance. This customary transition is the only circumstance in which they differ.

His rejection of the idea of cause as necessary connection suggests at once that he may be in a position to say something about the long-standing controversy over free will and determinism. That dispute arises because men and women hold (a) that human acts are caused, and (b) that causes are necessary connections. Hume's claim here is not that he can solve the problem but that he can dissolve it.

The question of man's free will has been long disputed among philosophers. Does man have freedom of will? Or are his acts determined? If motives determine acts, are motives themselves determined? This dispute has been much canvassed on all hands, and has led into such labyrinths of obscure sophistry that a sensible reader inclines to turn a deaf ear to the question, expecting neither instruction nor entertainment. I hope to make it appear that the whole controversy has hitherto turned merely upon words.

We ascribe necessity to matter. The degree and direction of every motion are prescribed with exactness. Do we similarly ascribe necessity to persons? Are the degree and direction of every action prescribed with exactness?

Two circumstances form the whole of the necessity we ascribe to matter: a constant conjunction between cause-events and effect-events, and a consequent inference in our minds from the one to the other. Beyond these two circumstances we have no notion of any necessity in the motion of matter.

Do not these two circumstances take place in the voluntary actions of men? Are not similar motives followed by similar actions? Are there not detectable uniformities in human action? Is it impossible to collect any general observations concerning mankind? Has experience of human affairs, however, accurately digested by reflection, no purpose?

The most irregular and unexpected resolutions of men may be accounted for by those who know every particular circumstance of their character and situation. A genial person, contrary to expectation, may give a peevish answer, but he has a toothache or has not dined. Even when, as sometimes happens, an action cannot be accounted for, do we not put it down to our ignorance of relevant details?

Thus it appears that the conjunction between motive and action is as regular and uniform as between cause and effect in any part of nature. In both cases, constant conjunction and inference from one to the other.

Though constant conjunction and customary transition be all that is discoverable between a cause and an effect in nature, men believe they perceive something like a necessary connection. Then, when they consider the operations of their own wills and feel no such necessary connection between motive and action, they suppose there is a difference between the cause–effect relation and the motive–action relation. And are hence to say that man's will, unlike matter, is free.

But our knowledge of causation, like our knowledge of motivation, is merely of a constant conjunction and a consequent inference in our minds from one to the other. It is the same in both cases. It is different only if it be pretended that the mind can perceive, in the operation of matter, some other connection between cause and effect than has place in the voluntary actions of intelligent beings. It is incumbent on those who pretend thus to make good their assertion. So long as we rashly suppose that we have an idea of some necessity in the operations of external nature, beyond constant conjunction and an habitual inference in our minds; and, at the same time, admit we can find nothing such in the voluntary actions of the mind, we shall continue confusion.

Thus far Hume has examined the ideas of material substance, of mental substance, of causal connection, of free will. Of each in turn he has asked one question: "Upon what impression, received by the senses, does it rest? From each in turn he has received only silence for an answer. One more idea remains, namely, the idea of a uniformity of nature, the unquestioned premise of all our inductions and generalizations from nature. Why do we believe, so unquestioningly, that the "future will resemble the past"? Why do we argue, for instance, that fire will always melt ice, when our only ground for this belief is the fact that it has done so in the past?

All our conclusions from experience proceed on the supposition that the future will resemble the past. To prove that the future will resemble the past, by arguing from experience, is evidently going in a circle, and taking that for granted which is the very point in question.

As to past experience, it can be allowed to give direct and certain information of those precise objects only, and that precise period of time only, which fell under its cognizance. But why this experience should be extended to future times and other objects, is the question on which I would insist. So to extend it is a process of mind or thought of which I would willingly know the foundation.

Not by an argument from experience can we prove this resemblance of the past to the future, for all such arguments are founded on the supposition of that resemblance. Let the course of things be allowed hitherto ever so regular. That alone, without some new inference, does not prove that for the future it will continue so.

My practice, you say, refutes my doubts. But you mistake the purport of my question. In practice I am satisfied. As a philosopher, who has some share of curiosity, I will not say skepticism, I want to learn the foundation of this inference. No reading, no inquiry, has yet been able to remove my difficulty. Upon what grounds can we argue that the future will resemble the past? Upon what grounds expect similar effects from causes which are similar?

Geometry (or any mathematics), when taken into the assistance of science, is unable to remedy this defect. Every part of applied mathematics proceeds on the supposition that certain laws are established by nature in her operations. Mathematical reasonings are employed to assist experiences in the discovery of these laws, or to determine their influence in particular instances. But the discovery of the law itself is owing merely to experience, and all the mathematical reasoning in the world could never lead one step toward the knowledge of it.

In all reasonings from experience, then, there is a step taken by the mind (that the future resembles the past) which is not supported by any argument. Nevertheless, we take this step. There must therefore be some other principle (than rational or demonstrative argument).

Though none but a fool or madman will ever pretend to dispute the authority of experience, it may surely be allowed a philosopher to have so much curiosity as to examine the principle of human nature which gives authority to experience.

This principle is custom, or habit. Wherever repetition produces a propensity to renew the same act, without being impelled by any reasoning, we say this propensity is the effect of custom or habit. That habit or custom is the ultimate principle of all our conclusions from experiences, seems to be the only hypothesis which explains why we draw from many instances an inference which we are not able to draw from one instance that is in no respect different from them.

All inferences from experience are, therefore, effects of habit or custom, not of reasoning. The conclusions which we draw, based on reasoning, from considering one circle, are the same which we would draw from surveying all circles. But no man, having seen only one body impelled by another, could infer that every other similar body would move after a like impulse.

Custom, then, not reason, is the great guide of human life. It is that principle alone which renders our experience useful to us, and makes us expect, for the future, a similar train of events with those which have appeared in the past. Without the influence of custom, we should be entirely ignorant of every matter of fact beyond what is immediately present to the memory or the senses.

What, then, is the conclusion of the whole matter? A simple one, though, it must be confessed, pretty remote from the common theories of philosophy. All belief concerning matters of fact or real existence, is derived merely from some object present to the memory or the senses, and a customary conjunction between that and some other object. Having found, in many instances, that two kinds of objects have been conjoined (say, flame and heat), the mind is carried by custom to expect the same in the future. This is the whole operation of the mind in all our conclusions concerning matters of fact and existence.

Here, then, is a kind of pre-established harmony between the course of nature and formation of our beliefs. Custom or habit is the principle of human nature by which this correspondence, so necessary to the subsistence of our species and the regulation of our conduct, has been effected. Did not the presence of an object excite in us the ideas of other objects commonly conjoined with it, all human knowledge would be limited to the narrow sphere of our memory and senses. Those who delight in the discovery of purposes in nature have here ample subject to employ their wonder and admiration.

As this operation of the mind, whereby we infer like effects from like causes, is so essential to human life, it is not probable that it could be trusted to the fallacious deductions of our reason, which is slow in its operation and extremely liable to error and mistake. It is more comfortable to the ordinary wisdom of nature to secure so necessary an act of the mind by some instinct or mechanical tendency which may be infallible in its operations and independent of all the labored deductions of understanding.

Hume is now at the end of his review:

By way of conclusion to these reflections on diverse questions: When we run over libraries, persuaded of the principles here expounded, what havoc must we make? If we take in hand any volume, of divinity or metaphysics, for instance, let us ask: Does it contain any reasoning concerning quantity or number? No. Does it contain any experimental (probable) reasoning concerning matter of fact? No. Commit it then to the flames: for it can contain nothing but sophistry and illusion.

I am at first affrighted and confounded with that forlorn solitude in which I am placed by my philosophy, and fancy myself some strange uncouth monster, utterly abandoned and disconsolate. Fain would I run into the crowd for shelter and warmth. I call upon others to join me. But no one will hearken to me. Everyone keeps at a distance, and dreads that storm which beats upon me from every side. I have exposed myself to the enmity of all metaphysicians, logicians, mathematicians, and theologians. Can I wonder at the insults I must suffer? I have declared my disapprobation of their systems. Can I be surprised if they should express a hatred of my ideas and my person? When I look about me, I foresee on every hand, dispute, contradiction, anger, calumny, detraction. When I turn my eye inward, I find only doubt and ignorance. Every step I take is with hesitation; every new reflection makes me dread an error and absurdity in my reasoning.

NOTE ON SOURCES.   The material in this section is quoted, abridged, or paraphrased from David Hume, *An Enquiry Concerning Human Understanding* (Oxford: Clarendon Press, 1975), Sections 1, 2, 4, 5, 7, 8, and 12. However, since Hume had already, in an earlier book, *A Treatise of Human Nature*, worked over much of the materials in those sections of the *Enquiry*, we have sometimes drawn on corresponding sections of the *Treatise* to replace or supplement passages in the *Enquiry*.

2   IMMANUEL KANT

A CRITIQUE OF REASON IN EXPERIENCE

FROM HUME TO KANT.   Locke, it will be remembered, was led to pose the problem of knowledge as a measure of caution. His words indicate this:

> If by this inquiry into the nature of the understanding I can discover the powers thereof, how far they reach, to what things they are in any degree proportionate and where they fail us, I suppose it may be of use to prevail with the busy mind of man to be more cautious in meddling with things exceeding its comprehension, to stop when it is at the utmost extent of its tether, and to sit down in a quiet ignorance of things which, upon examination, are found to be beyond the reach of our capacities.

Nothing could be more straightforward. From an insight into the nature of knowledge, Locke recognizes that some things lie beyond its reach. The hypothesis that Locke advanced was this: All knowledge comes from experience and all experience is by way of the senses.

By the middle of the eighteenth century, in Hume's writings, things had undergone a change. Indeed, it would perhaps be more accurate to say that they had come to something of an impasse. What Hume did, in effect, was to take Locke's appeal to experience and push it to its "logical conclusion." This conclusion was that much of the familiar furniture of the human world was dissolved into a series of question marks. The metaphysical notions of material substance, and mental substance were declared to be so much verbiage. No appeal to experience showed any grounds for believing in their existence. The notion of free will went the same way. Only the come-and-go of impressions and ideas remained. The generally accepted notions of cause and uniformity of nature met a like fate; they were mere habits, mere effect of custom. The theological notions of God as first cause and designer were weighed and found wanting. Hume tried, indeed, to undermine the credibility even of mathematics, by arguing, for example, that such geometrical notions as straight line, circle, equal angles, and so on, were "mere notions" to which nothing discoverable in experience could be said to correspond. Hume's own consternation at this reduction of Locke's empiricism was genuine. His words will be recalled:

I am at first affrighted and confounded with that forlorn solitude in which I am placed by my philosophy, and fancy myself some strange uncouth monster, utterly abandoned and disconsolate. Fain would I run into the crowd for shelter and warmth. I call upon others to join me. But no one will hearken to me. Everyone keeps at a distance, and dreads that storm which beats upon me from every side. I have exposed myself to the enmity of all metaphysicians, logicians, mathematicians, and theologians. Can I wonder at the insults I must suffer? I have declared my disapprobation of their systems. Can I be surprised if they should express a hatred of my ideas and my person? When I look about me, I foresee on every hand, dispute, contradiction, anger, calumny, detraction. When I turn my eye inward, I find only doubt and ignorance. Every step I take is with hesitation; every new reflection makes me dread an error and absurdity in my reasoning.

These conclusions, which filled Hume with grave doubts about the whole epistemological enterprise, were meanwhile being reflected upon by the German philosopher, Immanuel Kant. They did not fill his mind with fright and confusion. Their effect was, to quote his well-known words, "to rouse me from my dogmatic slumbers." Where Hume was "affrighted and confounded," Kant was stimulated and enlightened. For he detected an element of irony in the situation. Here was Hume, in the name of a theory of knowledge, denying that there is any knowledge. Knowing that it is the function of a theory to account for that of which it is a theory, not to deny it, Kant was moved to say, in effect, "So much the worse for Hume's theory." If the appeal to experience will not serve as a satisfactory hypothesis, by means of which to account for the fact of knowledge, then so much the worse for the appeal to experience; surely, not so much the worse for knowledge. Hume's conclusions served only to convince Kant that unrelieved empiricism must somehow be mistaken.

That is the first fact to be kept in mind with respect to Kant. There is another fact, equally important. It is this: Kant believed firmly in the existence of God, in the freedom of the will, and the immortality of the soul. But, being also widely read in modern philosophy he knew that his age, the Age of Reason, was unsympathetic with such convictions. The age was willing, in theory, that a man should entertain these convictions as a matter of faith. But it would not in practice let it go at that. It was inclined to challenge, even to ridicule, such faith. It urged an appeal to reason, confident that in such an appeal faith would come off second best. Everything was to be tried at the "bar of reason." Kant's answer to all this was to carry the war into the enemies' country. He determined to put reason itself on trial. To this end he wrote his large and epoch-making treatise *Critique of Pure Reason*.

Kant's handling of the problem of knowledge was motivated, then, by these two considerations. First, a theory of knowledge was required to replace the empiricism of Hume. Second, a theory of knowledge was required to deflate the appeal to reason that was placing obstacles in the way of ventures of faith. What Kant proposed was this: to replace the appeal to experience with the appeal to reason by a critical analysis of the function of reason in experience.

BIOGRAPHICAL NOTE.   Immanuel Kant was born in Germany in 1724 and died in 1804 at the age of seventy-nine. His parents were members of a German sect known as Pietists. This meant that he was associated from infancy with persons of a devout turn of mind. This devotion to the "fundamentalism" of his parents did not outlast his adolescence, but it was succeeded by an equally rigorous adherence to the fundamentals of morality. His early education was intended to direct his thoughts toward the church. University years directed them along secular lines. He graduated in classics, mathematics, science, and philosophy. At the age of thirty-one he became a privatdocent in the University at Königsburg. Here, for fifteen years, he provided coaching in mathematics, physics, physical geography, logic, and metaphysics. During these years he was gradually awakened to the dilemmas of the modern mind. He took his mathematics and his natural sciences with great seriousness; he found, on the one hand, that the kind of world to which they pointed was "incompatible" with his belief in God, free will, immortality, and the supremacy of a high-minded morality; and he found, on the other, that the unquestioned appeal to experience among progressive minds cast doubts on the reliability of mathematics and the sciences. This was not the only respect in which the "modern mind" was at sixes and sevens with itself. In the fields of theology and metaphysics, confusion reigned. In the name of reason there were claims and ounterclaims; theism, atheism, skepticism with respect to Deity; dualism, materialism, idealism, skepticism, with respect to the nature of ultimate reality. All these eddies and cross-currents met in the mind of this young man whose business was to provide instruction in science and philosophy. The thought that gradually took shape in his speculations was this: The modern mind appears to be divided against itself. Used in one field, it has provided us with the beauties and achievements of mathematics and science; used in another field, it has created endless confusion in which unverifiable speculation is met with unverifiable denial. He looked into his own mind and found two unshakable convictions; on the one hand, mathematics and the sciences must be "saved" from the skeptics; on the other, the normal beliefs of a conscientious and God-fearing soul must be "saved" from both the sciences and the skeptics. As these various dilemmas clarified themselves, he saw his task: What was required, apparently, was an examination of the human mind itself. His thoughts began to shape themselves along these lines. He was, at the age of forty-six, appointed to the chair of philosophy in his university. In his inaugural address he communicated to his fellow professors his intention to devote himself to a critical analysis of the mind's power to know. For the next eleven years he did just that, and in 1781, at the age of fifty-seven, published his long-awaited *Critique of Pure Reason*. (For additional biographical information on Kant refer to Chapter 6, Section 2.)

THE ARGUMENT OF THE PASSAGES.   Kant's problem, in its general outlines, was clear enough. The question was where to begin. He found a starting point in the distinction between *a priori* and *a posteriori* knowledge. Both he held to be undoubted facts, but the current appeal to experience would account only for the latter; the former it either ignored or sought to deny. This point gave Kant the opening he required. It is time to let him speak for himself. As the passages begin, he is reflecting upon metaphysics. As his thoughts move around, he hits upon the distinction between *a priori* and *a posteriori* knowledge.

My object is to persuade all those who think metaphysics worth studying, to pause, and, neglecting everything that has been done, to propose the preliminary question: Is metaphysics possible?

How does it come about that metaphysics, unlike other sciences, cannot obtain universal and permanent recognition? It seems almost ridiculous that, while every other science is continually advancing, we should, in metaphysics, move constantly around on the same spot without gaining a single step. We do not find men, confident of their ability to shine in other sciences, venturing their reputation here. And so its followers have melted away.

Time was when metaphysics held a royal place among all the sciences. If the will were taken for the deed, the importance of her subject matter might well have secured her that place of honor. But at present it is the fashion to despise her; and like Hecuba, she languishes forsaken and alone. Time was when her rule was despotic. But intestinal war and anarchy broke out. The skeptics, a kind of nomad tribe, despising all settled cultivation of her lands, broke up all civil society. Fortunately their number was small; they could not prevent the old settlers from returning to till the ground afresh. But the old settlers returning had no fixed plan or agreement. At present there reign in metaphysics weariness and indifference, the mother of chaos and night. Near reforms, ill-applied study have rendered her counsels dark, confused, and useless.

It is vain, however, to assume a kind of artificial intelligence with respect to inquiries to which human nature cannot be indifferent. Nay, even those who pretend indifference, if they think at all, fall back inevitably into those very metaphysical dogmas which they profess to despise.

Nevertheless, this widespread indifference to metaphysics is worth attention and consideration. It is, clearly, not the result of carelessness but of matured judgment. Our age will no longer rest satisfied with the mere appearance of knowledge in these matters. Its patience has run out. This fact constitutes a powerful challenge, a powerful appeal to reason to undertake anew the most difficult of her duties, to institute a court of appeal which, while it will protect her own rights, will dismiss all groundless claims. This court of appeal is no other than a critique of pure reason.

By a *critique of pure reason* I do not mean a criticism of books and systems. I mean a critical analysis of the power of reason itself, touching that whole class of knowledge which it may strive after unassisted by experience. This must decide the questions: Is metaphysics possible or impossible?

Since the origin of metaphysics nothing has ever happened which was more decisive to its fate than the attack made upon it by David Hume. He started from a single, but important concept, namely causal connection. He challenged reason, which pretends to have given birth to this idea, to tell him by what right she thinks anything to be so constituted that it is necessarily connected with something else; for that is the meaning of causal connection. He demonstrated, beyond refutation, that it is impossible for us to see why, in consequence of the existence or occurrence of one thing, another thing must necessarily exist or occur also.

Hence he inferred that reason was deluded with reference to this conception of causal connection; that she erroneously considered it one of her children; that, in reality, it was nothing but a bastard child of imagination impregnated by experience; that a subjective necessity of habit was mistaken for an objective necessity arising from insight. I frankly confess, the suggestion of David Hume was the very thing which, many years ago first interrupted my dogmatic slumber, and gave my investigations in the field of speculative philosophy quite a new direction.

Hume's question was not whether the conception of causal connection was right, useful, even indispensable for our knowledge of nature. This he had never doubted. His question was whether that conception could be thought, by reason, *a priori*; whether it thus possessed an inner truth, independent of all experience. That was Hume's problem. It was, as we see, a question concerning the origin of the conception, not its indispensability.

I tried whether Hume's objection could not be put in a general form, and soon found that the conception of causal connection was by no means the only idea by which the understanding thinks the connection of things *a priori*.

It may be advisable to interrupt the movement of Kant's thought at this point. He has already used this fundamental term *a priori* twice. He is going to explain what it means, give an illustration of its use, and contrast it with *a posteriori*. The entire argument of his position revolves around this idea. It may therefore be well to try to fix its meaning for ourselves. If we say that some fact is known, or can be known, *a priori*, we mean that it is known or can be known in advance of experience of it. Thus, we might say, "I don't know whether there are any triangles on the far side of the moon; but if there are, I can say *a priori* that the sum of their interior angles will equal two right angles." Or we might say, "I don't know whether a slave economy was the cause of the fall of the Roman Empire, but I can say *a priori* that there was a cause." Or we might say, "I don't know whether there are two chairs in the next room, and two in the hall; but if there are, I can say *a priori* that they will add up to four chairs." Or we might say, "I don't know what happened either before or after I ate my dinner, but I can say *a priori* that something happened both before and after." These illustrations could be extended indefinitely. As Kant will indicate, the problem they present is this: How does it happen that we can know certain sorts of facts *a priori*?

It is a question worth investigating, whether there exists any knowledge independent of experience and all sense impressions. Such knowledge is called *a priori* and is distinguished from *a posteriori* knowledge which has its sources in experience. That there is a genuine *a priori* knowledge, that we can advance independent of all experience, is shown by the brilliant example of mathematics.

This term *a priori* requires closer definition. People are wont to say, even with regard to knowledge derived from experience, that we have it or might have it *a priori*. They mean we might derive it from a general rule. Thus, of one who undermines the foundations of his house, they would say he might have known *a priori* that it would tumble down; know it, that is, from the general rule that unsupported bodies fall. But this general rule has itself been derived from experience. Whoever knows this rule had first to learn it from experience. He could not have known this entirely *a priori*. (This Hume has shown.) In what follows, we shall use the term more strictly. We shall understand by *a priori* that which is absolutely independent of all experience, and not of this or that experience only. Opposed to this is *a posteriori* or empirical knowledge, such as is derived from experience.

Experience tells us what is, but not that it must necessarily be as it is. It therefore never gives us any necessary, *a priori*, knowledge. Experience never imparts to its judgments any strict universality, but only relative universality (by means of induction) so that we ought always to say, "so far as we have experienced, there is no exception to this or that rule." Necessity and universality are criteria of the *a priori*. If, therefore, a judgment is thought with strict universality and necessity so that no exception is admitted as possible, it cannot have been derived from experience.

We have here a mystery. We must discover the ground of *a priori* judgments. We must understand the conditions which render them possible. The real problem is contained in the question: How is *a priori* knowledge possible? That metaphysics has hitherto remained in so vacillating a condition of ignorance and contradiction is due entirely to the fact that this problem has been ignored.

David Hume, who among all philosophers approached nearest to this problem, arrived at the conclusion that *a priori* knowledge is impossible. According to his reasoning everything we call metaphysics would turn out to be mere delusion. But if he had grasped clearly the problem of the *a priori* he would never have thought of an assertion which destroys all metaphysics, because he would have seen that, according to such an argument, neither was mathematics possible (since it contains *a priori* judgments). And from such an assertion his good sense would probably have saved him.

It is to be noted that our problem is not: Are *a priori* judgments possible? For there are enough of them to hand, of undoubted certainty, that we need not argue for their possibility. (What is actual must be possible.) We must inquire into the grounds of the possibility of their existence. The proper problem, upon which all depends, when expressed precisely is this: How are *a priori* propositions possible?

It again seems advisable to break in upon Kant's meditations. He is saying things that cut deep. He began by admitting a sort of bankruptcy on all hands in matters philosophical. He added, however, that no philosopher worth his salt would therefore feel justified in crying quits. He realized that Hume had been an important factor, despite his negative conclusions. He wants, above all, a toehold, some fact upon which he can take a stand. His eye catches sight of this apparently neglected distinction between *a priori* knowledge and *a posteriori* knowledge. He fastens on this, realizing that this may have important implications. He sees, also, that the fact of the *a priori* raises a problem. The *a priori* is a fact. The problem is how to account for it.

Although all our knowledge begins *with* experience, it does not follow that it arises entirely *from* experience. For it is quite possible that our empirical knowledge is a compound of that which we receive through impressions and that which our own faculty of knowing (incited by impressions) supplies from itself—a supplement to impressions which we do not distinguish from that raw material (i.e., impressions) until long practice has roused our attention and rendered us capable of separating one from the other.

Hitherto it has been supposed that all our knowledge must conform to the objects, but, under that supposition, all attempts to establish any knowledge about them *a priori* have come to nothing.

The experiment therefore ought to be made, whether we should not succeed better by assuming that objects must conform to our forms of knowledge. For this would agree better with the required possibility of an *a priori* knowledge of objects;

that is, with the possibility of settling something about those objects before they are given us in experience.

We have here the same case as with the first thought of Copernicus. Not being able to explain the movements of the heavenly body so long as he assumed that the stars moved around the spectator, he tried assuming the spectator to be turning around and the stars to be at rest. A similar experiment may be tried in metaphysics, so far as our knowledge of objects is concerned. If our knowledge has to conform to the nature of objects, I do not see how we could know anything *a priori*. But if the object of knowledge has to conform to the constitution of our power of knowing, I can very well conceive the possibilities of such *a priori* knowledge.

If Copernicus had not dared, by an hypothesis which contradicted the senses, to seek the observed movements in the spectator instead of in the heavenly bodies, the laws of planetary motion would have remained for ever undiscovered. I propose my own view, which has so many analogues with the Copernican hypothesis, as, at first, an hypothesis only.

Kant's argument at this point becomes too complicated for reproduction in quotation. For that reason, the next passages are mere descriptions of his argument, not selections or paraphrases from his *Critique*. Thus far, what he has been saying comes to this: Metaphysical speculation is in disrepute. Hume's criticism seems to have put an end to it. His conclusions followed from his dogma that all knowledge comes from experience. Since on this premise, he could not account for *a priori* knowledge, he denied it. But a theory of knowledge that issues in a denial of knowledge is a poor theory. *A priori* knowledge is a fact to be accounted for, not an illusion to be denied. Since the appeal to experience has failed, something else must be tried. A new theory of knowledge is required to account for the fact of *a priori* knowledge. Kant's hypothesis is this: That knowledge is a joint product of mind and external world, arising in experience. This hypothesis raises the following question: If knowledge is a joint product of mind and external world, then what part of the joint product is contributed by the mind? Kant answers by distinguishing between the form and the content of knowledge. The form of knowledge is contributed by the mind. The content is contributed by the external world. In the production of knowledge the mind acts to impose form on content supplied by the external world. This leads to a new problem: If knowledge is a joint product of mind and world, and mind's contribution is the form, can these formal elements in knowledge be isolated and analyzed? What, in other words, is the form that mind contributes?

Kant answers by distinguishing between perceptual, conceptual, and speculative knowledge. To our perceptual knowledge, mind contributes the forms of space and time. These Kant calls *forms of sensibility*. To our conceptual knowledge, mind contributes the forms of quantity, quality, relation, and modality. These, when further analyzed, he calls *categories of understanding*. To our speculative knowledge, mind contributes the forms of self, universe, and God. These he calls *ideas of reason*. We shall refer to them as *forms of speculation*. Space and time are forms of perception, not things perceived. Things are always perceived spread-out and strung-along, are always perceived in a background–foreground and a before-and-after setting. This invariable spatial and temporal character is the form of all perceptual knowledge. On Kant's hypothesis, it is due to the "diffracting" action of mind or consciousness. Except as forms of consciousness, these words have no meaning. They are forms of awareness, not things of which we are aware. In Kant's words, space and time are "empirically real, but transcendentally ideal," that is, real in experience but otherwise only ideal. Quotations are here possible once more:

> Space does not represent any property of things in themselves, nor does it represent them in their relation to one another. . . . Space is nothing but the form of all appearances of outer sense. It is the subjective condition of sensibility under which alone outer perception is possible for us.
>
> Since the capacity to be affected by objects must precede all perceptions of these objects, it can readily be understood how the form of all appearances (i.e., space) can be given prior to all perceptions, and so exist in the mind *a priori*; and how, as a pure intuition, in which all objects must be determined, it can contain, prior to all experiences, principles which determine the relations of these objects. It is, therefore, solely from the human standpoint that we can speak of space, of extended things. If we depart from the subjective, the representation of space stands for nothing whatsoever.
>
> This predicate (i.e., space) can be ascribed to things only insofar as they appear to us; that is, to objects of sensibility. Since, however, we cannot treat the special conditions of sensibility as conditions of the possibility of things, but only of their appearances, we can indeed say that space comprehends all things that appear to us as external, but not all things in themselves. For we cannot judge in regard to the perceptions of other kinds of thinking beings, whether they are bound by the same conditions as limit us.
>
> The proposition that all things are side by side in space is valid under the limitation that these things are viewed as objects of our perception. Our exposition claims the reality, the objective validity, of space in respect of whatever can be presented us; but also, at the same time, the ideality of space in respect of things when they are considered in themselves, that is, without regard to the constitution of our sensibility.
>
> We assert, then, the empirical reality of space, as regards all possible outer experience, and, at the same time, its transcendental ideality, i.e., that it is nothing at all, immediately we withdraw the said condition, namely limitation to possible experience, and look upon it as something that underlies things in themselves.
>
> The transcendental conception of appearances in space is a critical reminder that nothing perceived in space is a thing in itself; that space is not a form inhering in things in themselves as their intrinsic property; that objects in themselves are nothing but mere representations of our sensibility, the form of which is space. The true correlate of sensibility, the thing in itself, is now known, and cannot be known, through these representations; and in experience no question is ever asked in regard to it.

Kant's remarks on the status of time, which parallel, roughly, his remarks on the status of space, may be quoted in part:

> Time is not an empirical conception that has been derived from any experience. For neither coexistence nor succession (the two modes of time) would ever come within our perception, if the representation of time were not presupposed as underlying them *a priori*.
>
> Time is not something which exists of itself or inheres in things. Were it a determination (i.e., property) of things in themselves, it could not be known *a priori*. But

such *a priori* knowledge is quite possible if time is nothing but the subjective condition under which alone perception can take place in us. For, that being so, this form of intuition can be represented prior to the objects and therefore *a priori*.

Time is a purely subjective condition of our human perception, and, in itself, apart from the subject, is nothing. . . . What we are maintaining is the empirical reality of time, its objective validity of all objects which allow of ever being given to our senses. Since our perception is always sensible (i.e., by the senses), no object can ever be given to us in experience which does not conform to the condition of time. On the other hand, we deny to time any claim to absolute reality; that is to say, we deny that it belongs to things absolutely, as their condition or property independently of any reference to the form of our perception. Properties that belong to things in themselves can never be given to us through the senses. This, then, is what constitutes the ideality of time.

What we mean by the *ideality of time* is this: If we abstract from the subjective conditions of sensuous perception, time is nothing, and cannot be ascribed to the objects in themselves apart from their relation to our perception, neither in the way of subsistence nor of inherence.

By *categories* Kant means such forms of understanding things as unity and plurality, substance and quality, cause and effect, and so on. He enumerates twelve. The number is not as important as his recognition that conceptual knowledge has form as well as content, and his hypothesis that the form is the mind's contribution. Thus, to consider one of these categories, causation is a form of understanding, not a reality in its own right. When a drop in temperature causes the water to freeze, there are not three things, namely, dropping temperature, freezing water, and a cause connecting the two. Rather, there are two things understood in terms of a category. Our understanding of anything involves many such categories. Kant's point is the simple, but revolutionary, suggestion that categories of understanding are not objects of knowledge but forms of knowledge; not things known but ways of knowing. Our understanding of things given in experience is conditioned by the categories in terms of which our minds work. These categories are forms of understanding what is given in experience; they are, themselves, not given in experience.

Speculation is the attempt to carry understanding beyond the limits of experience. Since the categories are only forms to which experience gives content, any such attempt is doomed to fail. To use a common expression, it can never be anything more than "mere speculation." Kant notes, and condemns, three forms of speculation, three ways in which the mind perennially seeks to transcend the limits of experience.

The first of these is the attempt to speculate on the nature of the mind itself, to seek to understand the nature of that which contributes form to knowledge. Beyond detecting the forms, we cannot go. The mind itself is outside of experience. It is itself never given in experience. It can never be content for its own forms. The attempt to formulate a rational psychology, that is, to gain an understanding of the mind, soul, self, ego, is on Kant's theory of knowledge, to attempt the impossible. We cannot pierce beyond the stream of consciousness, to a knowledge of the factors that make it to be the kind of thing it is. That there is a mind, beyond the stream of consciousness, Kant is prepared to argue, as against Hume. His reason for refusing to stop short with Hume is simple. The latter, it will be recalled, "reduced" mind to a succession of awareness. To this Kant has a rejoinder. The fact to be accounted for, he points out, is not a succession of aware-nesses, but an awareness of succession. If that which is aware passed with the awareness, there could be no awareness of succession. But there is precisely this, namely, awareness of succession.

The second attempt to extend knowledge beyond experience, is to speculate on the nature of the whole things, beyond what is given piecemeal in experience. The attempt to formulate a rational cosmology, that is, to extend the categories beyond experience is to attempt the impossible. The mind's categories are valid only within experience. As the universe comes within the grasp of experience, it becomes understood in terms of the categories. Beyond that, as in the case of rational psychology, is "mere speculation."

The third attempt to extend knowledge beyond experience is to speculate on the nature of God. Kant believed in the existence of God, but he is prepared to argue that such belief is not to be confused with knowledge. To attempt to formu-late a rational theory, that is, to know God as we know things that fall within our experience, is to attempt the impossible. Kant reiterates and extends Hume's destructive criticism of the grounds for theism. Like rational psychology and rational cosmology, rational theology is "mere speculation." A quotation from Kant is possible here:

> Human reason begins with principles which, in the course of experience it must fol-low. With these again, according to the necessities of its nature, it rises higher and higher to more remote conditions. Thus it becomes involved in darkness and contra-dictions. It may conclude that errors must be lurking somewhere, but it is unable to discover them because the principles which it follows go beyond all limits of experi-ence and so beyond all experimental verification. Metaphysics is the battlefield of these endless controversies.

Kant contrasts the forms of sensibility and the categories of understanding with these three ideas or forms of speculation. The two former are constitutive of knowledge. That is, within the limits of experience, they enter into and contribute to genuine knowledge. The latter, however, is merely regulative. This distinction between constitutive and regulative forms of knowledge is important. The ideas of self, cosmos, and God are regulative goals toward which knowledge moves but never attains.

Kant's distinction between *phenomena* and *noumena*, between things as known and things-in-themselves, follows a corollary from this general theory of knowledge. It arises thus: Knowledge is a joint product of mind and external world arising in experience. There are here two contributing factors: the mind and external world. The latter "appears" through the forms and categories of the former. The word *phenomena* is derived from a Greek word meaning "that which appears." Hence reality as known is appearance, is phenomenal, is to be con-trasted with reality as it is, which is noumenal. As Kant sweepingly remarks, "We only know phenomena."

We are now in a position to return to the one basic fact, that this elaborate theory was invoked to account for, namely, *a priori* knowledge. Our *a priori* knowledge is formal only, and arises out of the dual origin of knowledge. We know *a priori* that things perceived will be perceived as spread-out and strung-along. We know *a priori* that things will be understood as effects of causes. We know *a priori* that things will be understood as qualities inhering in substances. We know *a priori* that things will be understood in terms of part–whole relations. And so on through the categories. But this knowledge is purely formal. We do not know *a priori* what the content of future experiences will be. We know that it will exhibit the various forms referred to, because, by hypothesis, knowledge is a joint product of mind-imposed forms filled with experience-given content. Thus did Kant "answer" Hume. At this point we can resume quoting directly from his writings.

> I must, therefore, even before objects are given me in experience, presuppose the "rules of the understanding," or the "principles of knowledge" as existing within me *a priori*. These rules are expressed in *a priori* concepts to which all objects of experience must necessarily conform and to which they must agree. By thus changing our point of view, the possibility of *a priori* knowledge can well be explained.
>
> After a superficial view of this work, it may seem that its results are negative only, warning us against venturing beyond the limits of experience. Such is no doubt its primary use. But its results are seen to be positive, when we perceive that it leads inevitably to a narrowing, a limiting, of the employment of reason; to the impossibility of going by it beyond the frontier of possible experience.
>
> But thus and thus alone can we cut away the very roof of materialism, idealism, skepticism, fatalism, atheism, fanaticism, and superstition. If governments ever think proper to interfere with the affairs of the learned, it would be consistent with their wise regard for science and society, to favor the freedom of such a criticism as can establish the labors of reason on a firm footing.
>
> To deny that this service, setting limits to the speculative use of reason, is a positive advantage, would be the same as to deny that the police confer any positive advantage on us in preventing that violence which citizens have to fear from citizens. The police protection enables each to pursue his vocation in peace and security. The critique of reason does as much for the powers of the mind.
>
> To illustrate this, let us suppose that the necessary distinction, established in our critique, between things as phenomena and things-in-themselves, had not been made. In that case the principle of causality, and with it the mechanical interpretation of nature, would apply to all things and not to their appearances only. I should then not be able to say of one and the same thing, for instance, the human soul, that it is both free and subject to necessity, without involving myself in a contradiction.
>
> If, however, we may legitimately take an object in two senses, namely, as phenomenon and as thing-in-itself; and if the principle of causality applies to things only as phenomena and not as noumena, then we can, without any contradiction, think one and the same thing when phenomenal as necessarily conforming to the principle of causality and so far not free, and yet, in itself not subject to that principle and therefore free.
>
> Suppose morality necessarily presupposed freedom of the will while speculative reason had proved that such freedom cannot even be thought. In such case freedom, and with it morality, would have to make room for the mechanical interpretation of

nature. But our critique has revealed our inevitable ignorance of things-in-them-selves, has limited our knowledge to mere phenomena. So, as morality requires only that freedom should not entail a contradiction, there is no reason why freedom should be denied to the will, considered as things-in-itself, merely because it must be denied to it as phenomenon. The doctrine of morality may well hold its place, and the doctrine of nature too; which would have been impossible without our theory of the nature and limitations of knowledge.

If I cannot deprive speculative reason of its pretensions to transcendent insight, I cannot even assume freedom of will, not even in the interests of morality. I had, therefore, to remove the possibility of knowledge of what lies beyond experience, in order to make room for faith. This question of free will is but one of many which derive positive advantage from the limitations imposed by my theory of knowledge, on the speculative reach of pure reason beyond experience.

Let any reader who finds these inquiries obscure consider that not every one is bound to study metaphysics; that many minds will succeed very well in the exact sciences more closely allied to practical experience while they cannot succeed in investigations dealing exclusively with abstract conceptions. In such cases men should apply their talents to other subjects.

Thus Kant on the problem of knowledge in his *Critique of Pure Reason*. His ideas here were closely connected with the ideas that he was to put into his second *Critique*. The latter was directed toward a clarification and defense of his convictions in ethics.

NOTE ON SOURCES. The Kant in this section is quoted, abridged, or paraphrased from Immanuel Kant, *Critique of Pure Reason*.

3 A. J. AYER

A CRITIQUE FROM LOGICAL POSITIVISM

FROM KANT TO AYER. Our first author in this chapter, David Hume, proposed *impression* as a catch-all term for present experience. Your present experience is providing you with a direct impression of this, that, and the other "object of experience." From these impressions come your *ideas*. To validate any idea his proposal was "Show me the impression." The outcome of this proposal was a considerable amount of high-level skepticism. Many of our most prestigious "ideas" (for example, the idea of God, of necessary connection, of free will, of immortality, of substance, and so on) appear to lack any such basis in "experience," in the sense of direct impressions. Hume proposed that all such "baseless" ideas be "committed to the flames," thus ridding European learning of "abstruse ideas." In traditional language the outcome was the liquidation of all claims to possess any "metaphysical knowledge."

This collapse of "empiricism" ("show me the impression") into skepticism over the entire range of "metaphysical" claims about knowledge, roused Kant from his dogmatic slumber. He proposed a new task for metaphysics in performing which it would regain a hold on the life of the mind. The task was to arrive at a systematic and orderly knowledge of what he called *synthetic a priori* ideas or principles; to show the role that they played in the derivation of knowledge from experience. Such ideas or principles were "*a ratione priori*"; that is, from reason prior to experience. His usual example was "Every event has a cause." This is not an empirical generalization from experience of events having causes. It is a presupposition laid down in advance of experience enabling us to use experience to support the claim that *A* is the cause of event *B*. It thus makes the appeal to experience possible as a source of empirical knowledge. That these *a priori* principles are not empirically derived by us from experience, but are presupposed by us as a necessary condition for deriving knowledge from experience, he called his "Copernican revolution in philosophy."

In a manner of speaking, this was Kant's "answer" to Hume. It did not restore traditional metaphysics in the sense in which Hume had called that into question. But what it did do was to restore a lively interest in *a priori* ideas, and to give them a kind and degree of importance in the life of the mind that Hume and the Humeans found objectionable indeed. Any "committed" empiricist, any "loyal" follower of Hume, looked for the day when Kant's work on behalf of "synthetic *a priori* principles" would be undone, and his "critical metaphysics" shown to be baseless pretension. This counterattack has been attempted by twentieth-century *positivism*. It will be found supplying dynamic motivation in the philosophical writings of A. J. Ayer, whose *verifiability theory of meaning* has been widely entertained as a possible basis upon which to discredit Kant and restore Hume to his slightly altered but still rightful throne. Hence it has come to pass in our day that "metaphysics" has encountered more than skepticism. It has met with repudiation; and the repudiation has been based, not on the grounds that metaphysics is doubtable or doubtful, but on the grounds that it is meaningless. This is more radical than skepticism. It is one thing to say, "I doubt the truth of your claim. I am skeptical about it"; it is another to say, "The question whether your claim is true or false, probable or improbable, does not arise, because your claim is meaningless." If a person utters what sounds like a meaningful statement, you might say, "I doubt that"; but if you suspect that you were mistaken in thinking that it was a meaningful statement, that, in fact, it was so much meaningless jargon, you would not say, "I doubt that." You would say, "Talk sense if you want me to believe or doubt or deny what you say." This is to go beyond skepticism. The thesis "Metaphysical statements are meaningless" is more radical than the thesis "Metaphysical statements are doubtable, or doubtful, or false." This is not itself metaphysics. It is a thesis about metaphysics. Let us refer to it as antimetaphysics. The antimetaphysician does not have doubts *in* metaphysics. He has doubts *about* metaphysics.

BIOGRAPHICAL NOTE.   Alfred Jules Ayer was born in 1910. He was educated at Eton and Oxford. For fourteen years (1932–1946) he held teaching, research, and administrative positions in Oxford colleges. For thirteen years (1946–1959) he was

Grote Professor of philosophy at the University of London. In 1959 he was appointed Wykeham Professor of philosophy at Oxford University. His best-known book, *Language, Truth and Logic*, proposing an extended critique of metaphysics and related modes of thinking, was published in 1936. Professor Ayer did as much as anyone to secure a wide and sympathetic hearing for antimetaphysics in the English-speaking world. He wrote with clarity and vigor and great personal conviction. This makes him interesting and persuasive. "He that is not with me is against me" sounds through his lively pages. His writings have done more than stimulate; they have challenged. Many persons relish metaphysics. Ayer has given them a bad conscience, or stirred them to indignation. This was all to the good. It made the years between the two world wars memorable. One of the great debates in philosophy was metaphysics versus anti-metaphysics. Ayer's book *Language, Truth and Logic* and Collingwood's book *An Essay on Metaphysics* are excellent handlings, pro and con, of this issue. Ayer died in 1989. (For additional biographical information on Ayer, refer to Chapter 6, Section 5.)

Ayer's Antimetaphysics.   Ayer published several books and a great number of papers. His doubts about metaphysics, his campaign against it, will be found in many of these. But two items in particular let you in on the argument—namely, "Demonstration of the Impossibility of Metaphysics," published in 1934 in the English philosophical journal *Mind*; and "The Elimination of Metaphysics," published in 1936 as Chapter I of his book *Language, Truth and Logic*. These, you might say, are antimetaphysics in the grand manner. As the titles indicate, Professor Ayer does not pull philosophical punches.

His purpose is the same in both papers, namely to evict metaphysics from the mansion of philosophy. The 1934 paper aims to demonstrate that metaphysics is impossible. The 1936 paper aims to eliminate metaphysics. In either case, whether eliminated or shown to be impossible, metaphysics is in for a rough time.

Now, how do you show that discourse is meaningless? Ayer suggests that you need a criterion of meaning, of meaningfulness. This will enable you to settle the question. If discourse satisfies the criterion, then it is meaningful; if not, then not. What then is the criterion of meaning? How do you get at it? Ayer outlines a procedure.

First, you take cases that everyone agrees are meaningful, and cases that everyone agrees are meaningless. These are "given," that is, you do not choose them by having the criterion of meaning and finding that they do or do not satisfy it. You get them first. Then you ask what it is the meaningful statements have in common, by virtue of which they are meaningful; and what it is the meaningless statements lack, by virtue of which they are meaningless. This gives you the criterion of meaning. An analogy might help. Suppose you want the criterion of rightness, satisfying which you judge an act right. You take cases everyone agrees are right, and cases everyone agrees are wrong. These are "given"; that is, you do not choose them by having a criterion of rightness and finding that they do or do not satisfy it. You get them first. Then you ask what it is the right acts have in common, by virtue of which they are right; and what it is the wrong acts lack, by virtue of which they are wrong. This gives you the criterion of rightness. You would proceed similarly if you wanted to get at the criterion for judging whether something is or is not a work of art.

Thus far, then, you have statements whose meaningfulness is not doubtful, statements whose meaninglessness is not doubtful, and the criterion of meaning that the first cases satisfy and the second cases do not. At this point you consider what Ayer calls "doubtful" cases. These would be statements about which you would not be sure, at first glance, whether they were meaningful or meaningless. You apply your criterion to these cases. If they fail to satisfy it, they are meaningless, nonsensical; and out they go. (See *Mind*, p. 345, Vol. 43, 1934.)

So much for procedure. When Ayer followed this procedure, what criterion of meaning did he arrive at? Having ascertained it, he gave it a name: the Verifiability Criterion of Meaning. But we need more than the name. What is the criterion so designated? Here the going is more difficult. Ayer spends many pages in an attempt to find words that will enable him to state the criterion satisfactorily. We will not follow him through the details of this search.

Perhaps this will suffice: He discovers that all unquestionably meaningful statements may be divided into two groups. The first consists of those statements that you would verify or refute by an appeal to experience, an appeal to "observation statements." This verification or refutation would be either direct or indirect. For example, "My neighbor's house is colored green" would be verified directly, by confronting the statement with the experienced fact of the green color of the house. However, "There was a tree there before he cut it down and built his house where the tree stood," or "There are mountains on the far side of the moon," could not be verified directly. The tree is no longer there, and you can't see the other side of the moon. Direct confrontation of statement with experienced fact is not possible. In such cases you show that the statements about the tree and the mountains can be *inferred* from some *other* statements that can be verified directly. In this way the statements about the tree and the mountains are said to be verified indirectly.

To put all this negatively, you would not satisfy yourself of their truth or falsity, probability or improbability, by merely reflecting on their meaning. Their truth or falsity does not stare up at you from their meaning alone. If I say, "There are mountains on the far side of the moon," you do not verify or refute my statement by merely reflecting on its meaning. From a knowledge of its meaning alone you do not get a knowledge of its truth or falsity. Evidence for such statements is not obtained by reflecting on their meaning. This is sometimes expressed in popular speech by saying that they are not their own evidence, are not "self-evident." Ayer calls such statements "empirical." Empirical statements are those that can be verified or refuted either directly or indirectly by an appeal to experience.

The second group stands in sharp contrast. It consists of those statements that you would verify or refute by an appeal to their meaning alone. You would see that they were true or false by reflecting on their meaning. Nothing further would be relevant. To put it negatively, you would not settle their truth or falsity by an appeal, direct or indirect, to any "observation statements." If I say, "All fathers are parents," or "All circles have equal radii," you do not "check" on these statements by investigating examples of fathers or circles. You reflect on the meaning of what is said and that settles it. From a knowledge of their meaning alone you can arrive at a knowledge of their truth or falsity. Here "evidence" is obtained by reflecting on their meaning. This is sometimes expressed in popular speech by saying that they are, or contain, their own evidence, are "self-evident." Ayer calls such statements "tautologies," or "analytic."

His claim is that all unquestionably meaningful statements are either empirical or tautological, empirical or analytic. The basis for this division is the way in which you would go about to verify or refute them. If they are meaningful, they are verifiable or refutable in either of the two ways explained above; and conversely, if they are verifiable or refutable in either of those two ways, they are meaningful. Since Ayer concedes no third way in which any meaningful statement can be verified or refuted, he speaks of their verifiability, or the mode of their verifiability, as the criterion of their meaningfulness. Further, it will be found that no unquestionably meaningless statement can be verified or refuted in either of these two ways; and, conversely, that any statement that cannot be verified or refuted in either of these two ways, is unquestionably meaningless. This is the Verifiability Criterion of Meaning, and its derivation from admittedly meaningful and meaningless statements. As suggested above, it might as a theory in semantics, be compared, *mutatis mutandis*, to a theory in ethics, for example the Utility Criterion of Rightness, and its derivation from admittedly right and wrong acts.

At this point the argument, now possessed of a criterion of meaning, turns from admittedly meaningful and meaningless statements to doubtful cases. Their fate is to be settled by seeing whether they satisfy the Verifiability Criterion of Meaning in either of its modes; that is, by seeing whether they are empirical or tautological. Ayer closes in on metaphysics. Give him any statement from metaphysics and he puts it to the question, "Is it empirical or tautological? Is its claim to be true directly or indirectly supported or supportable by any fact of experience? Is it claimed to be true because self-evident, true by virtue of its meaning alone?" If so, either way, it is meaningful; if not, it is meaningless.

Once the chips are down, Ayer extends no quarter. The stakes are high and he plays for keeps. His purpose is to exhibit the bankruptcy of traditional metaphysics, to remove metaphysics from philosophy. One metaphysical claim after another is audited and declared bankrupt. This is his "demonstration that metaphysics is impossible," his "elimination of metaphysics" from philosophy. If any so-called metaphysical claim satisfies the criterion, that is, makes sense, is found to be meaningful, it is not declared bankrupt but it is ordered out of philosophy on the grounds that it belongs in some empirical science or in mathematics or in formal logic. By the time Professor Ayer is finished he has, by one or the other of these arguments, emptied philosophy of metaphysics. It is thrown out either on the grounds that it is meaningless or on the grounds that it is not philosophy.

Ayer did not stop at metaphysics. He used the same criterion and the same argument to demonstrate the impossibility, the semantic bankruptcy of theology, ethics, aesthetics, and much traditional philosophical psychology. As with metaphysics, their claims were tested, found meaningless, and thrown out of philosophy; or found meaningful, therefore empirical or analytic, and declared part of some inductive or deductive science. Their traditional problems and propositions were written off as pseudo-problems and pseudo-propositions, which hustled them into bankruptcy; or they were unmasked as bonafide scientific problems and propositions masquerading as philosophy. In either case they were eliminated from philosophy. All that was left was semantics and logic. Semantics stayed because the Verifiability Criterion of Meaning was needed to initiate these evictions. Logic stayed because its propositions were found to be analytic and hence meaningful.

It seems that anyone who has the interest of philosophy at heart will feel grateful to Professor Ayer and the "logical positivists." At least they stirred things up. They made a bonfire of much old lumber. They thinned out the traffic in vague, obscure, and pretentious thinking. They forced those interested in philosophy to put up or shut up. And these things were all to the good.

It would be misleading to suggest that Ayer and the friends of "logical positivism" had things all their own way. In these matters it is possible to win the battles and yet lose the war. The attack raised some valuable questions.

1. Consider, for example, the procedure, described by Ayer in his 1934 paper, for arriving at criteria, in his case the criterion of meaning. You start with positive and negative cases agreed to without benefit of the criterion. Everything hinges on that. This places a premium on knowing what you are talking about before beginning to philosophize about it. If there is serious disagreement about the cases, there is no way to derive the criterion. And you cannot use the criterion to enforce agreement about the cases. If there is serious disagreement about the cases, all you can do is establish "party lines." You cannot arrive at a knowledge of the criterion that would enable you to rise above such party lines. What is the status of this knowledge which precedes the derivation of the criterion? Is it "above the battle"?

2. Again, consider the statement of a criterion once it has been arrived at. Let it be the criterion of meaning: "a proposition is meaningful, if and only if. . . " and finish it any way you have to. The completed statement is itself meaningful. No one would want it that a statement of the criterion of meaning was itself meaningless. Therefore the statement itself is either empirical or tautological.[*] If it is empirical, then it does not belong in philosophy, but in some empirical science. If it is a tautology ("all fathers are

---

[*]   The friends of the Verifiability Criterion of Meaning have sought to sidestep this objection by saying that the verbal formulation of the criterion is itself not a statement, not a proposition, therefore neither true nor false. Instead, they say it is a "proposal" or an "imperative." You don't verify or refute proposals or commands; you act on them or refuse to act on them. Therefore they are amendable, not answerable, to the Verifiability Criterion of Meaning. They are not meaningful by virtue of satisfying it. It applies only to statements, propositions. However, proposals, commands, petitions, imperatives and the like *are* meaningful. So, this postpones the agony by leaving unsettled the question of the criterion by which proposals, and so on, are to be declared meaningful or meaningless.

parents," "all circles have equal radii," and so on) then it is "true by definition," to use one of Ayer's expressions. But what is the status of definitions? If they are "arbitrary," you cannot use them to enforce agreement. If
they are not arbitrary, what constrains them?

3. One of Professor Ayer's older contemporaries, Professor G. E. Moore, had
argued in his *Principia Ethica* that the basic concept in ethics, "good," is
indefinable. There is no logically prior concept that you can use to arrive
at a definition of "good." Given "good" as indefinable you can use it to
define other ethical concepts, for example, right. Now you have the
notion of a basic concept and the thesis that it is indefinable. Does this
apply in semantics? If not, why not? If so, is it indefinable? If not, why
not? If so, can you use the criterion of meaning, as Ayer proposes, to
arrive at a definition of meaning? If so, the "structural analogy" between
ethics and semantics does not hold. If not, what is the distinction between
and relation between a criterion and a definition?

4. Ayer's elimination of metaphysics requires that metaphysical statements
can be subject to verification; that the notion of verification should apply to
them; and that if it doesn't, the trouble lies with metaphysical statements
and not with verification. This is to say that every meaningful statement is
either empirical or tautological. Is this true? Are there no meaningful statements that are neither empirical nor tautological? How about the statement
itself? How about such statements as the following: (a) "Every proposition
is either true or false." (b) "No true proposition is inconsistent with any
other true proposition." (c) "Every event has a cause." (d) "Miracles never
happen." (e) "Same cause, same effect." (f) "Matter does not cease to exist."
(g) "No surface is both red all over and green all over." (h) "Change occurs
according to law." (i) "In the last analysis you always do what you want to
do." (j) "Space and time are infinite." (k) "I *ought to* implies I *can*." (l) "If
nothing is necessary, then nothing is probable." (m) "A liar and a thief
ought to change his ways." (n) "If H_1 accounts for more facts than any
other H, then it is probably true."

5. Verifying and refuting are activities. Are there any principles and presuppositions operative in these activities? If not, why not? If so, then their status is crucial. They make these activities possible. Remove them, and the
activities do not get under way. Now, assuming that there are such principles and presuppositions, are they subject to the Verifiability Criterion of
Meaning? Are they either empirical or tautological? If so, there is no problem. But suppose they are neither empirical nor tautological. Then the
Verifiability Criterion does not cover them. Are they, then, meaningless?
Must one say that principles and presuppositions that are operative in
"getting to know," in verifying and refuting, are themselves meaningless?
The alternative would be to say that they are meaningful, but that in their
case some *other* criterion of meaning is involved. Now (a) What is this
other criterion? (b) If there is *this* exception to the Verifiability Criterion,
can we be sure that there are no other exceptions? How?

Consider this second alternative further. It opens up the possibility that there are principles and presuppositions operating in knowing, proving, refuting, which are not themselves candidates for verification. They make verification possible. Therefore the question "Can they themselves be verified?" does not arise. What principles and presuppositions are thus operative in the activities called getting to know, verifying, refuting, and the like? Let the job of metaphysics be to run them down. Call them "ultimate" or "absolute" to indicate the difference between their status and the status of the empirical statements whose discovery or verification or refutation they make possible. They are operative in verifications, but are not themselves verifiable. They enter into the verification. Then you could say that the task of metaphysics is to ascertain the "ultimate" or "absolute" principles and presuppositions of empirical knowledge. And metaphysics would be back in business again.

The following passage is quoted from Ayer's article "Demonstration of the Impossibility of Metaphysics":

> The views expressed in this paper are not original. The work of Wittgenstein inspired it. The arguments which it contains are for the most part such as have been used by writers in *Erkenntnis*, notably by Mortiz Schlick in his *Positivismus und Realismus* and Rudolf Carnap in his *Überwindung der Metaphysik durch logische Analyse der Sprache*. But some may find my presentation of them the clearer. And I hope to convince others by whom the work of Wittgenstein and the Viennese school has so far been ignored or misunderstood.

DEFINITION OF METAPHYSICS

> My purpose is to prove that any attempt to describe the nature or even to assert the existence of something lying beyond the reach of empirical observation must consist in the enunciation of pseudo-propositions, a pseudo-proposition being a series of words that may seem to have the structure of a sentence but is in fact meaningless. I call this a demonstration of the impossibility of metaphysics because I define a metaphysical enquiry as an enquiry into the nature of the reality underlying or transcending the phenomena which the special sciences are content to study. Accordingly if I succeed in showing that even to ask whether there is a reality underlying the world of phenomena is to formulate a bogus question, so that any assertion about the existence or nature of such a reality is a piece of nonsense, I shall have demonstrated the impossibility of metaphysics in the sense in which I am using the term. If anyone considers this an arbitrary definition, let him refer to any work which he would call metaphysical, and consider how it differs from an enquiry in one of the special sciences. He will find, not that the authors are merely using different means to derive from the same empirical premises the same sort of knowledge, but that they are seeking totally different types of knowledge. The metaphysician is concerned with a reality transcending the phenomena about which the scientist makes his generalizations. The metaphysician rejects the methods of the scientist, not because he believes them to be unfruitful in the field in which the scientist operates, but because he believes that by his own metaphysical methods he will be able to obtain knowledge in his own metaphysical field. It will be shown in this paper not that the metaphysician ought to use scientific methods to attain his end, but that the end itself is vain. Whatever form of reasoning he employs, he succeeds in saying nothing.

COMPARISON WITH KANT'S PROCEDURE

That the speculative reason falls into self-contradiction when it ventures out beyond the limits of experience is a proposition maintained by Kant. But by his formulation of the matter he is committed to a view different from that which will here be maintained. For he implies that there is a transcendent reality, but the constitution of our speculative reason is such that we cannot hope to gain knowledge of it: he should therefore find no absurdity in imagining that some other being, say a god, had knowledge of it, even though the existence of such a being could not be proved. Whereas on our view to say that there is or that there is not a transcendent reality is to utter a pseudo-proposition, a word-series empty of logical content; and no supposition about the knowledge of a higher reality possessed by a higher being is for us even a significant hypothesis. The difference between the two views is best expressed by saying that while Kant attempted to show that there were certain problems which the speculative reason was in virtue of its own nature incapable of solving, our aim is to show that these are not genuine problems.

No criticism of Kant's transcendental philosophy will be undertaken in this paper. But the method by which we demonstrate the impossibility of metaphysics, in the sense in which Kant too held it to be impossible, serves also to show that no knowledge is both synthetic and *a priori*. And this is enough to prove the impossibility of metaphysics, in the special sense which Kant reserved for the term, though it in no way discredits the excellent pieces of philosophical analysis which the *Critique of Pure Reason* contains.

FORMULATION OF A CRITERION OF SIGNIFICANCE

The method of achieving these results lies in the provision of a criterion by which the genuineness of all *prima facie* propositions may be tested. Having laid down the conditions which must be fulfilled by whatever is to be a significant proposition, we shall find that the propositions of metaphysics fail to satisfy the conditions and are therefore meaningless.

What is it, then, that we are asking when we ask what is the meaning of a proposition? I say "ask the meaning of a proposition" rather than "ask the meaning of a concept," because questions about the meaning of concepts reduce themselves to questions about the meanings of propositions. To discover the meaning of a concept we form its corresponding primary proposition, i.e., the simplest proposition in which it can significantly occur, and attempt to analyze this. I repeat "what is it that we are asking when we ask what is the meaning of a proposition?" There are various ways in which the correct answer can be formulated. One is to say that we are asking what are the propositions to which the proposition in question is reducible. For instance, if "being an amphisbaena" means "being a serpent with a head at both ends," then the proposition "X is an amphisbaena" is reducible to (or derivable from) the propositions "X is a serpent" and "X has a head at either end of its body." These propositions are in turn reducible to others until we reach the elementary propositions which are not descriptive at all but ostensive. When the analysis reaches its furthest point the meaning of the proposition can no longer be defined in terms of other propositions but only pointed to or shown. It is to this process that those philosophers refer who say that philosophy is an activity and not a doctrine.

Alternatively the procedure of definition may be described by saying that to give the meaning of a proposition is to give the conditions under which it would be true and those under which it would be false. I understand a proposition if I know what observations I must make in order to establish its truth or falsity. This may be more succinctly expressed by saying that I understand a proposition when I know what facts would verify it. To indicate the situation which verifies a proposition is to indicate what the proposition means.

APPLICATION OF THE CRITERION

Let us assume that some one says of my cat that it is corylous. I fail to understand him and enquire what circumstances would make it true to say that the cat was corylous. He replies "its having blue eyes." I conclude that in the sense in which he uses the word corylous "X is corylous" means "X has blue eyes." If he says that, although the fact that my cat has blue eyes and no other fact makes it true to say that it is corylous, nevertheless he means by "corylous" something more than "blue-eyed," we may infer that the use of the word "corylous" has for him a certain emotional value which is absent when he merely says "blue-eyed." But so long as its having blue eyes is all that is necessary to establish the truth of the proposition that something is corylous, and its having eyes of another color all that is necessary to establish its falsehood, then "having blue eyes" is all that "being corylous" means.

In the case when something is called corylous and no description or indication can be given of the situation which verifies the proposition, we must conclude that the assertion is meaningless. If the speaker protests that he does mean something, but nothing that mere observation can establish, we allow that he has certain feelings which are in some way connected with the emission of the sound "corylous": and it may be a matter of interest to us that he should express these feelings. But he does not thereby make any assertion about the world. He utters a succession of words, but they do not form a genuine impression. His sentence may provide good evidence of his feelings. In itself it has no sense.

So in every case where we have a series of words which seems to be a good grammatical sentence, and we wish to discover whether it really makes sense—i.e., whether it expresses a genuine proposition—we must consider what are the circumstances in which the proposition apparently expressed would be called true or false: what difference in the world its truth or falsity would entail. And if those who have uttered it or profess to understand it are unable to describe what in the world would be different, if it were true or false, or in any way to show how it could be verified, then we must conclude that nothing has been asserted. The series of words in question does not express a genuine proposition at all, but is as much a piece of nonsense as "the moon is the square root of three" or "Lenin or coffee how." The difference is merely that in some cases where a very slight transformation of the phrase, say the alteration of a single word, would turn it into a propositional sign, its senselessness is harder to detect.

MEANINGLESSNESS OF EVERY METAPHYSICAL ASSERTION

In this way it can quickly be shown that any metaphysical assertion is nonsensical. It is not necessary to take a list of metaphysical terms such as the Absolute, the Unconditioned, the Ego, and so forth, and prove each of them to be meaningless: for it follows from the task metaphysics sets itself that all its assertions must be nonsense. For it is the aim of metaphysics to describe a reality lying beyond experience, and therefore any proposition which would be verified by empirical observation is *ipso facto* not metaphysical. But what no observation could verify is not a proposition. The fundamental postulate of metaphysics "There is a super (or hinter-) phenomenal reality" is itself not a proposition. For there is no observation or series of observations we could conceivably make by which its truth or falsehood would be determined. It may seem to be a proposition, having the sensible form of a proposition. But nothing is asserted by it.

An example may make this clearer. The old conflict between Idealism and Realism is a fine instance of an illusory problem. Let us assume that a picture is unearthed, and that the finder suggests that it was painted by Goya. There are definite means of settling this question. The critics examine the picture and consider what points of resemblance it has to other works of Goya. They see if there is any contemporary or subsequent reference to the existence of such a work—and so on. Suppose now that two of the experts have also read philosophy and raise a further point of dispute. One says that the picture is a collection of ideas (his own or God's): the other that its colors are objectively real. What possible means have they of settling this question? Can either of them indicate any circumstances in which to the question "are those colors a collection of ideas?" or to the question "are those colors objective sensibilia?" the answer "yes" or "no" could be given? If they cannot then no such questions arise. And plainly they cannot. If it is raining now outside my window my observations are different from what they would be if it were fine. I assert that it rains and my proposition is verifiable. I can indicate the situation by which its truth or falsity is established. But if I ask "is the rain real or ideal?" this is a question which no observations enable me to answer. It is accordingly not a genuine question at all.

It is advisable here to remove a possible source of misunderstanding. I am not maintaining that if we wish to discover whether in a *prima facie* proposition anything is really being asserted, we must consider whether what seems to be asserted is practically verifiable. As Professor Schlick has pointed out, it makes perfectly good sense to say "there is a mountain 10,000 feet high on the other side of the moon," although this is a proposition which through practical disabilities we are not and may never be in a position to verify. But it is in principle verifiable. We know what sort of observations would verify or falsity it. If we got to the other side of the moon we should know how to settle the question. But the assertions of metaphysics are in principle unverifiable. We may take up any position in space and time that our imagination allows us to occupy; no observation that we can make therefrom makes it even probable in the least degree that any answer to a metaphysical question is correct. And therefore we conclude that there are no such questions.

METAPHYSICAL ASSERTIONS NOT HYPOTHESES

So the conclusion is not that metaphysical assertions are uncertain or arbitrary or even false, but that they are nonsensical. They are not hypotheses, in the sense in which general propositions of law are hypotheses. It is true that assertions of such general propositions are not assertions of fact in the way that assertions of singular propositions are assertions of fact. To that extent they are in no better case than metaphysical assertions. But viable hypotheticals (general propositions of law) make sense in a way in which metaphysical assertions do not. For a hypothesis has grounds. A certain sequence of events occurs and a hypothesis is formulated to account for it—i.e., on the strength of the hypothesis, when we make one such observation, we assume that we shall be able to make the others. It is the essence of a hypothesis that it admits of being used. In fact, the meaning of such general propositions is defined by reference to the situations in which they serve as rules for predictions, just as their truth is defined by reference to the accuracy of the predictions to which believing them gives rise. A so-called hypothesis which is not relevant to any situation is not a hypothesis at all. As a general proposition it is senseless. Now there is no situation in which belief in a metaphysical proposition bridges past and potential observations, in the way in which my belief in the poisonousness of arsenic connnects my observation of a man's swallowing it with my expectation that he will shortly die. Therefore metaphysical propositions are not hypotheses. For they account for nothing.

NOTE ON SOURCES.   The material in this section is from A. J. Ayer, "Demonstration of the Impossibility of Metaphysics," *Mind*, Vol. XLIII, No. 171 (July, 1934).

4   R. G. COLLINGWOOD

THE PRESUPPOSITIONS OF KNOWLEDGE

FROM AYER TO COLLINGWOOD.   Ayer's book, *Language, Truth and Logic*, was published in 1936. He aimed to continue the empiricism of Hume, providing it with the benefits of European positivism, especially German and Austrian in the twentieth century. The book became a text, not to say something of a scripture, for much Anglo–American philosophizing during the years before the second World War.

Like Hume in his *Treatise* and *Enquiry*, Ayer argued for the elimination of metaphysics ("commit it to the flames"). It will be recalled that Hume's attack on metaphysics roused Kant from his dogmatic slumber, goading him into writing his *Critique* and *Prolegomena*, in which he argued for a redefinition and reconstitution of metaphysics along lines intended to provide it with a new lease on life. The Kantian "critical metaphysics" was to work out a systematic and orderly account of the role of synthetic *a priori* principles (e.g., "Every event has a cause") in the scientific thinking of rational animals.

Something comparable to Kant's response to Hume is to be found in Collingwood's response to Ayer. Collingwood's book *Essay on Metaphysics* was published in 1940. It proposed a Kant-like alternative to the then lively positivism for which Ayer's book was a symbol. In it he argued for a redefinition and reconstitution of metaphysics along lines intended to provide it with a new lease on life. The Collingwoodian "critical metaphysics" was to work out a systematic and orderly account of absolute presuppositions ("Every event has a cause") in the scientific thinking of rational animals.

BIOGRAPHICAL NOTE.   For biographical information on Collingwood, refer to Chapter 8, Section 4.

THE ARGUMENT OF THE PASSAGES.   The following passages are taken from Collingwood's book *An Essay on Metaphysics*. The thesis of the book is that scientific thinking, thinking productive of science, rests upon presuppositions that are not themselves pieces of scientific knowledge. The title is intended to suggest that the term *metaphysics* be reserved for the name of the activity whereby a knowing mind diagnoses—analyzes out—its science-producing presuppositions. Since the presuppositions cannot be verified or refuted, they are never known to be either true or false. They are never proved or disproved. When presupposed, however, they make proof possible. Collingwood calls them "absolute presuppositions," and his book deals with the role such presuppositions play in the activity called "getting to know." To try to prove an absolute presupposition is to treat it as a hypothesis. This is to mistake its character in relation to knowledge. Ferreting out absolute presuppositions Collingwood calls "metaphysics"; trying to prove them, once they have been tracked down, he calls "pseudo-metaphysics," and warns against it as the besetting mistake of empiricism or positivism when it seeks to promote presuppositions into knowledge, or, seek to abandon them when it finds that such promoting is not possible. His book on these matters is an interesting alternative to Professor Ayer's *Language, Truth and Logic*. It is related to that lively book in something the same way that Kant's *Critique* and *Prolegomena* were related to Hume's *Treatise* and *Inquiry*. Collingwood's absolute presuppositions invite comparison with Kant's synthetic *a priori* propositions.

SCIENTIFIC THINKING

In proportion as a man is thinking scientifically, when he makes a statement, he knows that his statement is the answer to a question and knows what the question is. To ask questions, knowing that you are asking them, is the first stage in high-grade thinking.

HAS PRESUPPOSITIONS

Whenever anybody states a thought there are more thoughts in his mind than are expressed in his statement. Among these, some stand in a peculiar relation to the thought he has stated: they are its presuppositions.

One can make presuppositions without knowing it, and without knowing what presuppositions one is making.

In low-grade or unscientific thinking we hardly know that we are making any presuppositions at all.

Every question involves a presupposition from which it "arises." This presupposition in turn has other presuppositions, which are thus indirectly presupposed by the question. Unless this presupposition were made, the question to which it is logically prior could not be logically asked.

SOME OF THESE ARE "ABSOLUTE"

A presupposition is either relative or absolute. By a relative presupposition I mean one which stands to one question as its presupposition and to another question as its answer.

To question a presupposition, to demand that it be "verified," is to demand that a question be asked to which the affirmative answer would be that presupposition itself. To verify the presupposition that my measuring-tape is accurate is to ask a question admitting of the answer "the tape is accurate." Hence to speak of verifying a presupposition involves supposing that it is a relative presupposition.

An absolute presupposition is one which stands, relatively to all questions to which it is related, as a presupposition, never as an answer. Thus if you asked a pathologist about a certain disease "What is the cause of the event E which sometimes happens in this disease?" he would reply "The cause of E is C. That was established by So-and-so." You might go on to ask: "I suppose before So-and-so found out what the cause of E was, he was quite sure it had a cause? The answer would be "Quite sure, of course." If you now say "Why?" he will probably answer, "Because everything that happens has a cause." If you ask "But how do you know that everything that happens has a cause?" he will probably blow up right in your face, because you have put your finger on one of his absolute presuppositions. But if he keeps his temper and gives you a civil and candid answer, it will be to the following effect: "That is a thing we take for granted in my job. We don't question it. We don't try to verify it. It isn't a thing anybody has discovered, like microbes or the circulation of the blood." He is telling you that it is an absolute presupposition of the science he pursues.

An absolute presupposition is not a "dodge," and people who "start" a new one do not start it because they "like" to start it. People are not ordinarily aware of their absolute presuppositions, and are not, therefore, aware of changes in them; such a change, therefore, cannot be a matter of choice. Nor is there anything superficial or frivolous about it. It is the most radical change a man can undergo, and entails the abandonment of all his most firmly established habits and standards for thought and action.

Why do such changes happen? Briefly, because the absolute presuppositions of any given society, at any given phase of its history, form a structure which is subject to "strains" of greater or less intensity, which are "taken up" in various ways, but never annihilated. If the strains are too great, the structure collapses and is replaced by another, which will be a modification of the old with the destructive strain removed; a modification not consciously devised but created by a process of unconscious thought.

PECULIAR STATUS OF ABSOLUTE PRESUPPOSITIONS

Absolute presuppositions are not verifiable. This does not mean that we should like to verify them but are not able to; it means that the idea of verification is an idea which does not apply to them; because, to speak of verifying a presupposition involves supposing that it is a relative presupposition.

The distinction between truth and falsehood does not apply to absolute presuppositions. Putting the same point differently: absolute presuppositions are never propounded; they are presupposed. To be propounded is not their business; their business is to be presupposed. The scientist's business, as we shall see, is not to propound them but to propound the proposition that this or that one of them is presupposed.

We do not acquire absolute presuppositions by arguing; on the contrary, unless we have them already, arguing is impossible to us. Nor can we change them by arguing; unless they remained constant all our arguments would fall to pieces. We cannot confirm ourselves in them by "proving" them; proof depends on them, not they on proof.

Absolute presuppositions are not "derived from experience," but are catalytic agents which the mind must bring out of its own resources to the manipulation of what is called "experience" and conversion of it into science.

An absolute presupposition cannot be undermined by the verdict of "experience," because it is the yard-stick by which "experience" is judged.

METAPHYSICS IS THE STUDY OF SUCH PRESUPPOSITIONS

There are absolute presuppositions. The analysis which detects them I call metaphysical analysis.

Metaphysics is the science which deals with the presuppositions underlying science.

The business of metaphysics is to reveal the absolute presuppositions that are involved in any given piece of thinking. The general class of study to which metaphysics belongs is thus the study of thought. Metaphysics is one branch of the science of thought.

There are two things you can do with absolute presuppositions. One of them is what the scientist does, and the other what the metaphysician does. You can presuppose them, which is what the scientist does; or you can find out what they are, which is what the metaphysician does. I mean finding out what absolute presuppositions are in fact made.

Metaphysics arises out of the pursuit of knowledge. That pursuit, science, involves disentangling the presuppositions of our thought. This again involves discovering that some of them are relative presuppositions which have to be justified, and that others are absolute presuppositions which neither stand in need of justification nor can in fact be justified. A person who has made this discovery is already a metaphysician.

Science and metaphysics are inextricably united, stand or fall together. The birth of science, the establishment of orderly thinking, is also the birth of metaphysics. As long as either lives the other lives; if either dies the other must die with it.

Metaphysical analysis, the discovery that certain presuppositions are absolute, is an integral part of scientific work. In the interests of science it is necessary that the work of metaphysics should be done.

Physics has become a science by obtaining a firm grasp on its own presuppositions, asking questions that arose from them, and devising experiments by which these should be answered.

It is important for every one who either thinks scientifically, or profits by the fruits of other peoples' scientific thinking, that the work of metaphysics should be done, and well done.

People do not need to analyze their thoughts very deeply in order to find out that there are a good many things they take for granted. Further analysis, however, is needed to settle the question whether the things are taken relatively for granted or absolutely for granted. It might seem that the question should be an easy one to answer, because presupposing is a thing people do in their minds, and the distinction between presupposing relatively and presupposing absolutely is a distinction between two ways of doing it, so that a man need only be ordinarily intelligent and truthful, one might think, to give an accurate answer to the question which of them he is doing.

But it is not quite so simple as that. To begin with, people may have a motive for deceiving themselves and each other. In modern Europe absolute presuppositions are unfashionable. The smart thing is to deny their existence. Even people who regard this as a silly fashion may be so far influenced by it as to weaken at the critical moment when every available ounce of determination is needed in order to decide whether a given presupposition is absolute or relative; and may allow a kind of mass-suggestion to decide them in favour of its being relative.

It is only by analysis that any one can come to know either that he is making absolute presuppositions or what absolute presuppositions he is making. Such analysis may in certain cases proceed in the following manner. If the inquirer can find a person to experiment upon who is well trained in a certain type of scientific work, intelligent and earnest in his devotion to it, and unaccustomed to metaphysics, let him probe into various presuppositions that his "subject" has been taught to make in the course of his scientific education, and invite him to justify each or to abandon it. If the "inquirer" is skillful and the "subject" the right kind of man, these invitations will be contemplated with equanimity, and even with interest, so long as relative presuppositions are concerned. But when an absolute presupposition is touched, the invitation will be rejected, even with a certain degree of violence.

The rejection is a symptom that the "subject," cooperating with the work of analysis, has come to see that the presupposition he is being asked to justify or abandon is an absolute presupposition; and the violence with which it is expressed is a symptom that he feels the importance of this absolute presupposition for the kind of work to which he is devoted. This is what I called being "ticklish in one's absolute presuppositions." This ticklishness is a sign of intellectual health combined with a low degree of analytical skill. A man who is ticklish in that way is a man who knows, "instinctively" as they say, that absolute presuppositions do not need justification.

This is a precarious method, because the qualifications it demands in the "subject" are too delicate. As soon as the "subject" understands what is going on he will lose the ticklishness on which his value depends. The only altogether satisfactory method is for the analyst to experiment on himself; because this is the only case in which familiarity with the experiments will make the subject more valuable, instead of less. But it demands great resolution and the temptation to cheat is stronger than one would expect. The purpose of the experiments is to find out what absolute presuppositions are made. Presuppositions are brought to light, and about each the question is raised and settled whether it is relative or absolute.

It is a mistake to fancy that by investigating the truth of their absolute presuppositions a metaphysician could show that one school of science was fundamentally right and another fundamentally wrong.

Some persons think there are two things you can do with absolute presuppositions: presuppose them, which is what the ordinary scientist does with them; or find out whether they are true or false, which is what the metaphysician does with them. I deny this. The second thing cannot be done. To inquire into the truth of a presupposition is to assume that it is a relative presupposition. Such a phrase as "inquiry into the truth of an absolute presupposition" is nonsense.

I distinguish between metaphysics and pseudo-metaphysics. Pseudo-metaphysics will ask such questions as this, where AP stands for any absolute presupposition: Is AP true? Upon what evidence is AP accepted? How can we demonstrate AP? What right have we to presuppose it if we can't? Answers to questions like these are neither metaphysical truths nor metaphysical errors. They are nonsense: the kind of nonsense which comes of thinking that what is absolutely presupposed must be either true or false. That kind of nonsense I call pseudo-metaphysics. Let the distinction between metaphysics and pseudo-metaphysics be firmly grasped. Let it be understood that the business of metaphysics is to find out what absolute presuppositions have actually been made by various persons at various times in doing various pieces of scientific thinking.

METAPHYSICS IS AN HISTORICAL INVESTIGATION

All metaphysical questions are historical questions, and all metaphysical propositions are historical propositions.

Metaphysics is the attempt to find out what absolute presuppositions have been made by this or that person or group of persons, on this or that occasion or group of occasions, in the course of this or that piece of scientific thinking. Arising out of this, it will consider (for example) whether absolute presuppositions are made singly or in groups, and if the latter, how the groups are organized; whether different absolute presuppositions are made by different individuals or races or nations or classes; or on occasions when different things are being thought about; or whether the same have been made *semper, ubique, ab omnibus*. And so.

The metaphysician is not confined to one single constellation of absolute presuppositions. He has before him an indefinite number of them. He can study the presuppositions of European science at any phase in its history for which he has the evidence. He can study the presuppositions of Arabic science, of Indian science, of Chinese science; again in all their phases, so far as he can find evidence for them. He can study the presuppositions of the science practiced by "primitive" and "prehistoric" peoples. All these are his proper work; not an historical background for his work, but his work itself.

When he has some knowledge about several different constellations of absolute presuppositions, he can compare them. This has its uses. It can convince the metaphysician that there are no "eternal" or "crucial" or "central" problems in metaphysics. It will rid him of the parish-pump idea that the metaphysical problems of his own generation, or, more likely, the one next before his own, are the problems that all metaphysicians have been worrying about. It will give him a hint of the way in which different sets of absolute presuppositions correspond not only with differences in the structure of what is generally called scientific thought but with differences in the entire fabric of civilization.

REFLECTIONS OF POSITIVISM

Positivism is the doctrine that the only valid method of attaining knowledge is the method used in natural sciences, and hence that no knowledge is genuine unless it either is natural science or resembles natural science in method.

Positivists say that scientific thought has no presuppositions.

They never discovered that there were such things as absolute presuppositions. Presuppositions they misunderstood as general propositions about matters of fact, advanced upon credit and awaiting verification. This would do at a pinch as an account of relative presuppositions, in whose case verification is a word that has meaning. As an account of absolute presuppositions, which are neither in need of verification nor susceptible of it, the description of them as generalizations is nonsensical.

The positivist says either of two things about an absolute presupposition. (1) He describes it as a generalization about matters of fact; and consequently maintains that by observing facts one could hope to verify it. Indeed, it must have been arrived at by observing facts; for here it is; and there was no other way in which that could have been arrived at. Heads I win. (2) He says that it was not arrived at by observing facts, for it was not a record of observations; and that, since there was no other way in which it could have been arrived at, it had not been arrived at; consequently, although it looks like a significant statement, it could not be one; it is just a piece of nonsense. Tails you lose.

They take absolute presuppositions and play "heads I win" with them, in order to exhibit them as generalizations from observed facts. Their reason for playing "heads I win" with them, arises from the fact that, having constituted themselves philosophical patrons of natural science, they thought themselves bound to justify any presuppositions which natural science thought fit to make. "Metaphysics," says Bradley, "is the finding of bad reasons for what we believe upon instinct." If I understand this epigram correctly, it is an accurate description of what the positivist does when he attempts to justify some absolute presupposition inductively. What Bradley seems to be saying is this: "Why we believe things of that kind I do not know. Let us give this ignorance a name by saying that we believe them upon instinct; meaning that it is not because we see reason to believe them. Metaphysics is the attempt to find reasons for these beliefs. Experience shows that the reasons thus found are always bad ones."

It is not the business of metaphysics to find reasons for "what we believe upon instinct," to raise the presuppositions of ordinary scientific thinking to the level of ascertained and demonstrated truths.

The positivistic mistake about metaphysics is the mistake of thinking that metaphysics is the attempt to justify by appeal to observed facts the absolute presuppositions of our thought. This attempt is bound to fail because absolute presuppositions cannot stand as the answers to questions, and therefore the question whether they are justifiable, which in effect is identical with the question whether they are true, is a question that cannot logically arise. To ask it is the hall-mark of pseudo-metaphysics.

If metaphysics were an attempt to provide empirical justification for the presuppositions of science, it might prove detrimental to science itself, not by its success but by its failure; for when the discovery was made that no justification of this kind is to be had, the belief that it is nevertheless necessary might lead to the false conclusion that the whole fabric of scientific thought is rotten at the core.

It is a characteristic of modern European civilization that metaphysics is habitually frowned upon and the existence of absolute presuppositions denied. If this denial ever achieves the eradication of metaphysics, the eradication of science and civilization will be accomplished at the same time.

The result of thinking systematically according to any given set of presuppositions is the creation of science. The result of thinking systematically about what presuppositions are actually in use is the creation of metaphysics. The result of simply presupposing our presuppositions, clinging to them by a sheer act of faith, whether or not we know what they are, whether or not we work out their consequences, is the creation of a religion.

NOTE ON SOURCES.   The materials in this section are quoted, with an occasional abridgment or paraphrase, from R. G. Collingwood, *An Essay on Metaphysics* (Oxford: Oxford University Press, 1940). Almost all of the passages are from Parts I and II.

5   ALVIN GOLDMAN

THE ELEMENTS OF EPISTEMOLOGY

FROM COLLINGWOOD TO GOLDMAN.   We have seen the approaches and styles of Hume, Kant, Ayer, and Collingwood. Now we turn to a more contemporary philosopher, Alvin Goldman. Like our following author, Keith Lehrer, but unlike those who preceded him in this chapter, Goldman is not trying to take a position on an epistemological issue. Rather, he (and Lehrer) are making an effort to lay out the issues clearly as the starting point for settling questions. Contemporary philosophy is often characterized as conceptual analysis. If someone were to ask you what that meant, you could point them to the articles by Goldman and Lehrer, for these epitomize contemporary conceptual analysis.

BIOGRAPHICAL NOTE.   Alvin Goldman was born in Brooklyn New York in 1938. He received his Ph.D. in philosophy from Princeton University in 1965. He taught at the University of Michigan and is currently professor of philosophy at the University of Illinois, Chicago Circle. He has published extensively in the field of epistemology.

THE ARGUMENT OF THE PASSAGES.   The selection from Goldman is the introduction to his book *Epistemology and Cognition.* In this introduction, Goldman sets up the topics within epistemology that he finds especially worth pursuing.

Goldman begins by distinguishing between propositions, assertions, and beliefs. This is an example of philosophy calling attention to the common-sensical. Although nonphilosophers might not have words to make these distinctions, we all make them. This is not difficult to demonstrate. We call some things we say "assertions" to distinguish them, e.g., from exclamations and questions. For example, to say, "This dinner is too expensive" is to make a claim about the relative price of some food; whereas, to say (with some vehemence) "Turn down that radio" is not to make a claim, but rather to issue an order or command. Obviously, assertions also differ from questions.

There are many ways to say something or to ask (for) something. "Pass the salt." "Please pass the salt." "May I have the salt?" "This needs salt." Each of the sentences is literally different, but in the right context, each means about the same thing. To indicate that there are different ways to say the same thing, we say that the sentences express the same proposition.

If I say, "This needs salt," it is usually taken to mean that I believe that what I have tasted is too bland for me and that I would like it to taste a bit more salty. While I have expressed this belief in language, it also has a counterpart as a psychological state "in me." This is the sense of "belief" that is distinguished by Goldman.

Now for an example. Suppose I fall while bike-riding. I skin my knee rather badly. I say, "That really stings. I hope it goes away soon." Both sentences are assertions. Both express propositions. But in "That really stings" our assertion is that something is felt in a certain way, whereas in "I hope it goes away soon" our assertion has two parts. First, we are saying that we have (or are "in") the state of hope; and that what we are hoping is that the statement, "It will go away soon" is true. You might be thinking that we could analyze "That really stings" in a similar way. It also could be seen as having two parts. I am in a state of feeling discomfort and the discomfort felt is sting-like. This suggestion is quite sophisticated and if you thought of something like it, then you are doing epistemology!

BELIEFS, ASSERTIONS, AND PROPOSITIONS

Epistemology deals with affairs of the intellect. In common parlance 'intellect' often refers to the remote reaches of the mind. This is not what I mean. I mean the whole range of efforts to know and understand the world, including the unrefined, workaday practices of the layman as well as the refined, specialized methods of the scientist or scholar. It includes the entire canvas of topics the mind can address: the nature of the cosmos, the mathematics of set theory or tensors, the fabric of man-made symbols and culture, and even the simple layout of objects in the immediate environment. The ways that minds do or should deal with these topics, individually or in concert, comprise the province of epistemology.

It is controversial whether different topics call for fundamentally different intellectual approaches or processes. But certain elements are common to virtually all efforts of the intellect; and these form the basic building blocks of epistemology. Deployment of the intellect involves either *mental* acts or states, or *public* utterances, frequently both. Among the mental states, *beliefs* are usually singled out by epistemologists. Among linguistic acts, the ones of central concern are *assertions*. Most intellectual endeavors try to arrive at some belief on a designated topic, or to formulate a statement on the problem at hand. Accordingly, the 'product' of the scientist or scholar is typically a body of assertions—presumably accompanied by a body of beliefs. So epistemology naturally focuses on either beliefs or assertive claims. In this book I will largely abstract from natural language and public speech acts, since there will be enough complexities on our hands without the complexities these topics introduce. I will concentrate on the mental side of epistemology, without implying that this is its only side.

Belief is not the mentalistic concept of choice for all epistemologists. Belief is normally a categorical, or binary, concept, an all-or-nothing affair. You either believe something or you don't. But epistemologists commonly point out that there are degrees of conviction or confidence in a statement. They urge us to do epistemology in terms of degrees of belief, or perhaps subjective probabilities. In describing someone's view of tomorrow's weather, you needn't confine yourself to saying 'He believes it will rain', 'He believes it won't rain', or 'He's undecided'. You can describe him as 'believing-to-degree-.78' that it will rain, or something of this sort.

Whatever the exact concept we select—a categorical or graded notion of belief—some sort of belief-notion seems critical for mentalistic epistemology. Let us now place belief states within a larger map of the mental terrain. This map is implicit in what philosophers call 'folk psychology,' that is, a network of assumptions and views about the mind that is expressed in everyday language. Whether these folk psychological concepts succeed in picking out real mental entities is a controversial question, let us see where folk psychology, as presented by philosophers, places the concept of belief.

Philosophers commonly divide mental states into two sorts: those that have and those that lack propositional content. The former are *propositional attitudes*, and the latter *sensations, qualia,* or the like. Propositional attitudes are recognized by the sentences used to ascribe them, the telltale sign being an embedded 'that'-clause. Typical examples of such sentences are: 'He wishes that the siren would stop', 'She doubts that it will snow this weekend', and 'He fears that war will never end'. Embedded that-clauses apparently pick out contents of the indicated attitudes, contents commonly referred to as 'propositions'. Hence the term 'propositional attitudes'. Propositional attitude types include wanting, hoping, wishing, fearing, doubting, suspecting, and believing. A particular mental state of this type consists in a person having a specific attitude type directed at a specific proposition. In addition to propositional attitudes, the class of mental states includes sensations like pains, itchy feelings, and perceptual experiences, all of which are said to have qualitative character.

However, some theorists hold that even these mental states have propositional content; and a few theorists try to explain away qualitative character in terms of propositional content.

Among propositional attitudes, we distinguish those with a conative or optative attitude toward a proposition—favoring or opposing the proposition's realization—and those with a purely intellectual assessment. The latter involve a stance on the question of whether the proposition is true, quite apart from whether it would be nice if it were true. Such intellectual attitudes include believing, being certain, thinking it likely, doubting, and suspending judgment. These sorts of states are called *doxastic attitudes*, or sometimes *credal attitudes*. They are central to epistemology.

In calling beliefs or other doxastic attitudes *mental* states, philosophers do not imply that beliefs have to occur in consciousness to count as mental. The belief that you reside at 3748 Hillview Road may be held for many years, though you only 'think about' your address intermittently during this period.

Many issues about beliefs and belief ascriptions are controversial. Most of the controversy concerns belief contents. Does a mental state really have a determinate content? If so, what is the source of this content? Is content determined exclusively by what's 'in the head', or by external factors as well? If external factors are relevant, can we really say that belief states (including their contents) are purely mental, that is, inner states of the individual considered in abstraction from his or her environment or causal ancestry?

Another problem concerns the objects of beliefs. The term 'propositional attitude' naturally suggests that the objects in question are propositions. And this is a common way of talking, both among philosophers and psychologists. But propositions are problematic entities. As classically interpreted, they are logical or abstract entities, somewhat akin to Platonic forms. Philosophers widely regard this sort of ontological status with suspicion. There are other theories of propositions, but none is free from criticism. In place of propositions some philosophers posit sentences of an inner language, a *lingua mentis*, as the relata of beliefs. But this sort of posit is also controversial.

These sticky issues about beliefs are relevant to my enterprise. They are relevant, first, because it is hard to do any mentalistic epistemology without using something like the belief construct. Second, they are relevant because of the intended bearing of psychology on mentalistic epistemology. Beliefs may not be a kind of entity with which psychology is capable of dealing. Or, being a construct of folk psychology, scientific psychology may choose to replace the belief construct entirely and work with different theoretical resources. . . .

For convenience, I will proceed on the assumption that the objects, or relata, of beliefs are propositions. The utility of proposition-talk is that it nicely unifies the treatment of mental attitudes, overt speech, and truth-value ascriptions. Suppose Alex says 'The moon is round', and Kurt says 'Der Mond is rund'. It is natural to say not merely that both asserted a truth, but that they asserted the *same* truth, namely, that the moon is round. But this single truth cannot be their two sentences, since these were different. The suggestion is that the two sentences expressed one proposition, which is the truth in question. Suppose further that Oscar utters no such sentence, but has a belief he could express as 'The moon is round'. Then it is tempting to say that he *believes* the *same truth* that Alex and Kurt *assert*. How can this be explained? Again, proposition-talk can do the job. If Oscar's belief content is a proposition—the same one expressed by Alex's and Kurt's sentences—then it is easy to identify the single truth with this very proposition. Thus, by letting propositions be

(1) the contents of verbal assertions, (2) the contents of beliefs, and (3) the bearers of truth, we nicely unify a whole range of discourse. . . .

I regard propositions as a temporary theoretical posit from which we should ultimately ascend to a better theory. Since such a theory may be quite complex, and its details probably would not seriously affect my project, it is an issue to which I will devote little attention.

The bearing of psychology on the belief construct, however, is more central to my concerns. So let me briefly anticipate a fuller discussion of this matter in later chapters. What stance should cognitive science adopt toward beliefs? At least four approaches are possible: reduction, replacement, neutrality, and refinement.

A reductionist says that beliefs are perfectly fine entities for a serious cognitive science, only they need to be reduced to, or explained in terms of, scientifically respectable elements. Since propositions, for example, are dubiously respectable, beliefs need to be understood as relations to syntactic entities, such as sentences in a language of thought.

An advocate of replacement holds that beliefs are not scientifically tenable posits. As part of a radically false theory, a degenerating research program, they will ultimately be discredited and abandoned. . . .

An advocate of neutrality holds that cognitive science can remain neutral about beliefs. It can proceed perfectly well without them, but this does not imply their overthrow or illegitimacy. Cognitive science may not be in a position to ascribe (propositional) content, or to say how such content should be ascribed. But it may allow that a suitable theory of interpretation—a good 'psychosemantics'—*can* ascribe content, or show how content is standardly ascribed.

The refinement position I have in mind is not an *alternative* to the preceding approaches, mainly because it does not address the problem of content. Content is not the only dimension of interest in the belief construct. Psychology should also be interested in the range of contentful states. Cognitive science could endorse the notion of content but stress the need for acknowledging a richer array of distinct content-bearing states. Many different states, it may hold, are all lumped under the folk-psychological label of 'belief,' and these need to be sorted out for the purposes of an adequate science of the mind.

I favor a combination of the neutrality and refinement approaches. I do not expect cognitive science to force the total abandonment of content states. But I do expect it to foster a more fine-grained set of descriptive resources. This richer set of resources should help epistemology; not by making it easier, but by making it (psychologically) more realistic.

Goldman raises the question of how to interpret the truth. The realist position he favors says that a proposition is true if what it says matches the world and is false otherwise. To use an old philosophical example, "The cat is on the mat" is true when (and only when) the cat is in fact on the mat. "The cat is on the mat" is false (when and only when) the cat is not on the mat. Notice that we may have to decide what counts as "being on the mat." Suppose only the cat's tail is on the mat . . . is the cat on the mat or not? Naturally, after deciding what counts as "on the mat," we have to look (or feel) to decide if the cat is on the mat or not.

Suppose that we could only photograph the cat. Then the photograph (and what we know about taking photographs) would count as evidence for the claim that the cat was (or wasn't) on the mat. But how we come to know whether it is true (or not) that the cat is on the mat and what makes it true (or not) are two separate things. What makes it true is how the world is. This distinction is crucial to the realist view that Goldman will try to defend as his book unfolds. To bolster his view, Goldman criticizes philosopher Richard Rorty, who holds an anti-realist view of truth. (We will read Rorty's anti-realism later in Chapter 11.)

TRUTH-VALUES AND KNOWLEDGE

Beliefs are commonly said to be true or false, and so are assertions. But, strictly, it is not *acts* of assertion, or *states* of belief, that are true and false. It is the *contents* of these acts or states. Since we are taking propositions to be the contents of beliefs and assertions, they have the role of bearers of truth or falsity. What is primarily true or false is a proposition. A belief qualifies as true only derivatively: when its content is a true proposition.

Ignoring assertions, then, there are three basic categories that need to be distinguished. First, there are psychological, or mental, states. Second, there are propositions, which are the contents of (certain of) these states. Third, there are truth-values, such as true, false, and perhaps indeterminate. (The possible need for a third truth-value arises because some propositions may be neither true nor false, for example, propositions with vacuous referring terms, like the one expressed by 'The present king of France is bald'.)

It is essential to distinguish carefully between these categories. In general, the mere fact that someone believes a proposition does not make it true, or false. The proposition's truth-value is not determined by its being the content of some belief state. (Of course, there are exceptions. If the proposition is 'There are beliefs,' then the mere fact that someone believes it guarantees its truth.) Moreover, there are true propositions that nobody believes. Presumably there is a true proposition saying precisely how many people will have a toothache in 1993. But nobody believes that proposition now, and probably nobody will ever believe it.

What makes a proposition have the truth-value it has? The natural answer is: the way the world is. I believe this natural answer is right, and philosophically defensible. Philosophers of this persuasion are often called realists, so I am a realist (of sorts).

In discussing truth one must distinguish firmly between the question of what *makes* a proposition have a certain truth-value and the question of how people can *determine* its truth-value. The former question concerns the nature of truth. The latter concerns the *evidence* for a proposition's truth-value, or the methodology of trying to figure out a proposition's truth-value. This distinction is elementary, but it still needs emphasis. Some philosophers hold, to be sure, that a proposition's meaning (or truth-conditions) is a function of the evidence that would count for or against it. Still, at a minimum, one must distinguish between a proposition's *being true* and people *having evidence* in its favor. Surely there are plenty of cases of true propositions for which nobody now (or perhaps ever) has good evidence. The example of the 1993 toothache sufferers is a case in point.

Since many people, including philosophers, insist on conflating truth with other notions—mostly related to evidence, justification, or the like—it is worth dilating on this point at this early juncture. To take a recent example, consider Richard Rorty's claim that there is a sense of 'true' in which it means (roughly) "what you can defend against all comers." The idea of "what can be defended against all comers" is some sort of social justification notion. According to Rorty, there is a sense of 'true' in which it is necessary and sufficient for a proposition's truth that somebody can defend it, presumably successfully, against all who argue against it.

There is no such sense of 'true'. To appreciate what's wrong with this definition, suppose you are an unfortunate victim of circumstance and misidentification. A horrible crime has been committed of which you stand accused. You are totally innocent—such is the truth. But you are a lookalike of the dastardly criminal, and numerous witnesses come forward to identify you as the doer of the deed. Sadly, you have no alibis. You were out for a walk at the time of the act, and nobody can vouch for your whereabouts. Meanwhile, the real criminal has died in an accident. Given these facts, the real truth cannot be successfully defended against all comers. You cannot defend it successfully, for there are too many eyewitnesses to make your case believable. (Furthermore, we may suppose, you actually did have a motive for the act, though it did not motivate you enough to do it.) Nor is there anyone else who could successfully defend your innocence against all comers. Nonetheless, the truth is: you are innocent. The only correct sense of 'true' makes truth independent of how well it can be defended. Its defensibility is a separate matter, which may depend on a variety of extraneous circumstances. Any innocent person accused of a crime surely wants the *real* truth to emerge; and the real truth is all that is normally meant by 'true.'

The innocent defendant case shows that "what can be defended against all comers" is not a necessary condition of truth. But neither is it sufficient. A totalitarian regime may arrange a successful defense of certain false propositions against all comers (at least all comers in that society); but this cannot make the false true. . . . Let me pause here to make a few remarks about the concept of knowledge. There is a loose and a strict sense of 'knowledge'. In a loose sense a person knows something (a proposition) if he believes it and it is true. If he believes the truth, he is not ignorant of it. He is cognizant of the fact, and so, in a loose sense, knows it. Many writers, especially in the behavioral and social sciences, use 'knowledge' in an ultra-loose sense, to mean simply belief, or representation of the world. This is probably a misuse, though one so common that perhaps it has achieved legitimacy. In more proper usage, to which I shall cleave, no proposition can be known unless it is true.

To repeat: in the loose sense of 'know' someone knows proposition p if and only if he believes p, and p is true. This suffices to show that knowledge is not equivalent to truth: truth does not require belief, but knowledge does. There is also, however, a strict sense of 'know', which has much occupied epistemologists. In this strict sense knowledge requires more than belief and truth. It requires satisfaction of some third, and perhaps fourth, condition beyond belief and truth. Since epistemology has often been regarded as 'the theory of knowledge', many epistemologists have devoted great energy to analyzing this strict sense of 'know'.

A principal reason for resisting a realist construal of truth is an alleged threat to knowledge. Many philosophers fear that if truth is definitionally prized off from evidence, or justification, it will be impossible for anyone to know the truth. Truth(s) will be epistemically inaccessible, or unknowable. But this dire consequence is not at all indicated, at least not without lengthy argumentation. The mere fact that extramental reality is what makes a proposition true (or false), as realists maintain, does not imply that no truths can be known. The mere fact that truth does not (definitionally) require knowledge, or justification, does not mean that it *precludes* knowledge, or justification. (These comments do not convey the most serious historical or contemporary arguments against realism. I mention them only in an introductory fashion, to forestall very simple confusions that may befall those unfamiliar with *epistemology*.)

NOTE ON SOURCES.   Alvin Goldman, *The Elements of Epistemology* (Cambridge: Harvard University Press, 1986), Chapter 1.

6   KEITH LEHRER

THE ANALYSIS OF KNOWLEDGE

FROM GOLDMAN TO LEHRER.   The selection from Goldman ends with a brief discussion of the word, "know." We continue this discussion as we turn to the thoughts of Keith Lehrer.

BIOGRAPHICAL NOTE.   Keith Lehrer was born in Minneapolis, Minnesota in 1936. He received his Ph.D. in philosophy from Brown University in 1960. He has taught at the University of Rochester and is currently professor of philosophy at the University of Arizona. He has published extensively in the area of epistemology.

THE ARGUMENT OF THE PASSAGES.   Lehrer offers four versions of what it means to have knowledge, each one a bit more refined than the last. Each succeeding definition is the result of changes made because of weaknesses in the preceding definition. Since this reading from Lehrer's book, *Theory of Knowledge*, is meant only to set the stage for in-depth analysis later in his book, Lehrer's accounts are only suggestive. The first three versions of what it means to have knowledge are:

1. if *x* is knowledge, then *x* is true.
2. If *x* is known, then *x* is accepted. Put another way, If *x* is known, then *x* is believed, in the sense of believed because one is trying to get knowledge.
3. If *x* is known, then the acceptance of *x* is completely justified.

What is it to be justified? Lehrer gives three traditional answers.

A. *Foundationalism*. This is the view that some beliefs are self-evidently true. All other knowledge claims must be able to be related to one or some of these basic beliefs. Lehrer mentions one kind of foundationalism, which says the foundation of knowledge is in our perceptions. This should remind you of Hume. Descartes offered another foundation for knowledge: clear and distinct ideas such as the *cogito*.
B. *Coherence theory*. This view sees justification in the way claims are related to each other. There need not be a foundational support according to coherentists. All we need is a careful interlocking of claims.
C. *Externalism*. This is a view that finds knowledge produced by the proper relation between belief and reality. An example of an externalist position would be: My belief that the cat is on the mat is knowledge when and

only when it is caused by the cat's being on the mat. Obviously, externalism requires a detailed analysis of causality.

The first condition of knowledge is that of *truth*. If I know that the next person to be elected President of the United States will have assets of at least one million dollars, then it must be true that the next President will have assets of at least one million dollars. Moreover, if the next person to be elected President will, in fact, not have assets of at least a million dollars, then I do not know the next President will have assets of at least a million dollars. If I claim to know, my knowledge claim is incorrect. I did not know what I said I did.

The second condition of knowledge is *acceptance*. If I deceitfully claim to know that Jan and Jay married on 31 December 1969, when I do not accept it, then I do not know Jan and Jay married on that date even if they were married then. If I do not accept that p, then I do not know that p. . . .

Accepting something that is true does not suffice for knowledge. If I accept something without evidence or justification, that my wife has exactly fourteen dollars in her purse, for example, and, as luck would have it, this turns out to be right, I fall short of *knowing* that what I have accepted is true. Thus, we require a third condition affirming the need for *justification*. While we allowed that a person need not be completely certain of p in order to know that p, we shall insist that he be justified, indeed, completely justified in his acceptance of p in order to be said to know that p.

The reason for requiring that a person be *completely* justified rather than simply justified is to indicate that slight justification is not enough. I may be justified in accepting that my secretary is in her office now because she is ordinarily there at this time. Not being there myself, however, I do not know that she is there, for, though justified, I am not completely justified in accepting that she is there. I am unable to exclude the possibility that she is out of the office on an errand, for example, and, in that way, my justification is incomplete.

Lehrer offers two counterexamples to the view that knowledge is completely justified true acceptance. (One, the Gettier example, is a classic in contemporary philosophy.) In both examples, it is clear that someone is completely justified in making a claim which is true, and yet we are not at all convinced that it is correct to say that the person *knows* what they are completely justified in asserting.

Edmund Gettier has presented us with a counterexample to the claim that knowledge is completely justified true acceptance which runs as follows. Suppose a teacher wonders whether any member of her class owns a Ferrari and, moreover, suppose that she has very strong evidence that one student, a Mr. Nogot, owns a Ferrari. Mr. Nogot says he does, drives one, has papers stating he does, and so forth. The teacher has no other evidence that anyone else in her class owns a Ferrari. From the premise that Mr. Nogot owns a Ferrari, she draws the conclusion that at least one person in her class owns a Ferrari. The woman might thus be completely justified in accepting that Mr. Nogot owns a Ferrari.

Now imagine that, in fact, Mr. Nogot, evidence to the contrary notwithstanding, simply does not own the Ferrari. He was out to deceive his teacher and friends to improve his social status. However, another student in the class, a Mr. Havit, does own a Ferrari, though the teacher has no evidence or inkling of this. In that case, the teacher would be quite correct in her belief that at least one person in her class owns a Ferrari, only it would not be Mr. Nogot who she thinks owns one, but Mr. Havit instead. In this case, the teacher would have a completely justified true belief when she accepts that at least one person in her class owns a Ferrari, but she could not be said to know that this is true because it is more due to good fortune than good justification that she is correct.

To put the argument schematically, Gettier argues that a person might be completely justified in accepting that F by her evidence, where F is some false statement, and deduce T from F, where T is some true statement. Having deduced T from F, which she was completely justified in accepting, the person would then be completely justified in accepting that T. Assuming that she accepts that T, it would follow from the analysis that she knows that T. In such a case, the belief that T will be true, but the only reason the person has for accepting T to be true is the inference of T from F. Since F is false, it is a matter of luck that she is correct in her belief that T.

One might be inclined to reply that inference from a false statement can never yield complete justification, but similar examples may be found that do not seem to involve any inference. An example taken from R. M. Chisholm illustrates this. Suppose a man looks into a field and spots what he takes to be a sheep. The object is not too distant and the man knows a sheep when he sees one. In such a case, it would be natural to regard the man as being completely justified in accepting that he sees a sheep in the field without any reasoning at all. Now imagine that the object he takes to be a sheep is not a sheep but a dog. Thus, he does not know that he sees a sheep. Imagine, further, that an object in the deeper distance which he also sees but does not think is a sheep, happens in fact to be a sheep. So it is true that the man sees a sheep and, moreover, accepts and is completely justified in accepting that he sees a sheep. Of course, he still does not know that he sees a sheep because what he takes to be a sheep is not, and the sheep that he sees he does not take to be a sheep.

Lehrer suggests that the counterexamples depend on false statements. Thus he settles on a fourth version of what it is to have knowledge.

4. x is known if and only if the acceptance of x is completely justified without any appeal to a false statement. (The expression "if and only if" can be taken to mean "is equivalent to.")

In the two cases we have described, a person has justified true acceptance but lacks knowledge and in one case does not infer what he thus accepts from any false statement. There is some merit, however, in the idea that falsity of some statement accounts for the lack of knowledge. Somehow, it is the falsity of the two statements (that Mr. Nogot owns a Ferrari and that what the man takes to be a sheep really is one) which accounts for the problem. It is false that Mr. Nogot owns a Ferrari, and it is also false that what the man takes to be a sheep is really a sheep (because it is a dog). We may say that in the first case the teacher's justification for her belief that at least one person in her class owns a Ferrari depends on the false statement that Mr. Nogot owns a Ferrari, and in the second case that the man's justification for his belief that there is a sheep in the field depends on the false statement that what he takes to be a sheep is really a sheep.

We shall explore the kind of dependence involved subsequently, but here we may notice that the teacher would be unable to justify completely her acceptance that there is a Ferrari owner among her students were she to concede the falsity of the statement that Mr. Nogot owns a Ferrari. Similarly, the man would be unable to justify completely his acceptance that there is a sheep in the field were he to concede the falsity of the statement that what he takes to be a sheep really is a sheep.

To render our analysis impervious to such counterexamples, we must add the condition that the complete justification that a person has for what she accepts must not depend on any false statement—whether or not it is a premise in inference. We may thus add the following condition to our analysis:

> If S knows that p, then S is completely justified in accepting that p in some way that does not depend on any false statement.

A FINAL ANALYSIS OF KNOWLEDGE

The preceding condition enables us to complete our preliminary analysis of knowledge as follows:

> S knows that p if and only if (i) it is true that p, (ii) S accepts that p, (iii) S is completely justified in accepting that p, and (iv) S is completely justified in accepting p in some way that does not depend on any false statement.

Our next task is to examine each of these conditions of knowledge in order to formulate a theory of knowledge explaining how and why claims to knowledge are justified. We begin in the next chapter with an account of truth and acceptance and then proceed to consider theories of justification. The discussion of such theories will lead us to an account that brings central features of the various theories under the umbrella of a coherence theory. The correct theory of knowledge must provide the correct blend of subjective acceptance and truth in what is accepted, the right match between mind and reality. A match between mind and world sufficient to yield knowledge rests on coherence with a system of things we accept, our acceptance system, which must include an account, undefeated by error, about how we may succeed in our quest for truth. When we have such a theory before us, we shall return, at the end, to the speculations of skeptical and metaphysical epistemologists supplied with the scale of knowledge to weigh their claims.

Let us go through this reasoning in a more everyday sense. Suppose I ask you if the local department store is still running its unannounced sale on jeans. You were just at the store and bought a pair of jeans at the reduced sale price. So you say "Yes." You would probably not say "I know that sale is still on." Nor is it likely that you would even say, "Yes, I know that the sale is still on." But it is reasonable to think that that is what your "Yes" reply means. I might ask you after your "Yes," "Are you sure?" Perhaps I have to take the bus to the store, which I dislike doing, so I want to make sure that I am not going out of my way for nothing. If you said "Yes" to this question, then it is pretty clear that we can say that you are making a claim to have knowledge.

Why are you so sure? You actually experienced the sale (and you remember it correctly). This is an appeal to foundationalism. There is no easy way to deny your having had this experience. But, why does it follow that because the sale was still running when you were there at 11 A.M., it will still be running at 3 P.M.? It follows because of everything else that we know about stores and sales and store managers, etc. This is an appeal to a sort of coherence approach to understanding knowledge.

The externalist would point out that what makes the answer "Yes the sale is still running" knowledge is not your experience. (You might have been the last person allowed to buy at the sale price.) Nor is it the link between "The sale is still running" and other statements. (This may have been a one-hour sale.) Rather, your statement is knowledge because your belief was caused in some special way by the facts at the store. That is, if your belief that the sale is still going on is the result of, and only the result of (caused by, and caused only by) the sign stating "UNANNOUNCED JEAN SALE—1/3 OFF: SALE RUNS UNTIL MIDNITE" on display in the store, then you have knowledge. The "right" fact caused your belief. What makes your answer knowledge is not a foundational belief or coherence with other beliefs. The thing that makes your answer knowledge is external to your belief. It is a sign.

Remember, Descartes proposed in his hyperbolic skepticism that we might be deceived when we see things like trees and houses. There might be an Evil Demon who gives us the experiences of trees and houses when we are in fact not experiencing anything. Descartes uses this kind of example to show that what we are sure is knowledge may not be knowledge. The externalist agrees with this Cartesian point. If what we claim to know was caused in us by an Evil Demon, then we do not have knowledge because this is not the appropriate way to get knowledge.

Consider another, just as fanciful, example. If you hear the wind rustling through the leaves, saying "the second derivative of distance with respect to time is acceleration," and you have never had calculus or physics, then what you heard is not knowledge because, in general, believing what the wind seems to be saying is not the route to knowledge.

"When can I say 'I know'?" has turned out to be a troublesome and complex question. Answers in terms of experience or reason seem to be too general. Specific answers in terms of how beliefs are formed and which are more valid than others take us into the realms of cognitive psychology (for empirical research into how we actually come to our beliefs), philosophy of mind (for discussions of the sorts of mental states we call beliefs) and philosophy of language (for an analysis of truth). Another way to answer "When can I say 'I know'?" is to look at clear examples of knowledge. Those examples, according to some philosophers, are to be found in the well-established sciences. So it is, that in our next chapter we discuss science from a philosophical standpoint in order to see if the claim that science constitutes a clearly defined body of knowledge is trustworthy.

NOTE ON SOURCES.   The material in this section is from Keith Lehrer, *Theory of Knowledge* (Boulder: Westview Press, 1990), Chapter 1.

What is Science? Positivism to Postmodernism

THE QUESTION POSED

Epistemology asks "When can I say I know?" In Chapter 10, we saw some traditional philosophical answers to this question: from Hume, who was a skeptic, through Kant and Collingwood, who tried to articulate the necessary conditions for knowledge. We also looked at the contemporary analytic views of Goldman and Lehrer.

The question "When can I say I know?" is a very general question. It is not about this claim or that claim but about all and any claims to knowledge. In this regard, it is different from asking "But do I really know that the moon is not made of green cheese?"

Yet for all our philosophical perplexities about epistemology, we really do not question the well-established findings of science. This is an indication that if we want an answer to "When can I say I know?" perhaps we should be looking at science to see what there is about it that makes us so sure it is trustworthy. To help us in answering the question of epistemology, we turn next to philosophy of science, that branch of philosophy that aims at understanding science.

 HERBERT FEIGL

THE POSITIVIST VIEW OF SCIENCE

Feigl was a member of the Vienna Circle, a group of young intellectuals from diverse disciplines (especially physics and mathematics) who gathered at the

University of Vienna in the 1920s. They looked at philosophy and science, and something became very clear to them: Philosophy was still raising the same issues it had at the time of Plato and Aristotle. Worse, it was still giving the same answers and using very similar arguments in support of each conflicting position. Now this may be intellectually stimulating to some but to these men, it just showed a stagnating discipline.

Science seemed quite different. If one dates the beginning of modern science with Galileo, then it is very easy to say that science has been successful. Science has raised questions and answered them. Mistakes in science are recognized and not made over and over again. One does not see the same rejected theories in science being brought forward time and time again. Science is more than just intellectually stimulating, it is making progress.

The reason was fairly clear to the Vienna Circle. Science deals with facts. Even when science makes theories, it is still held down to earth by appeal to facts. That is, theories are accepted or rejected by how well they fit or do not fit the facts. Put another way, scientific statements are either clearly verifiable or not verifiable. One can point to facts which make them true or make them false. This is where philosophy has gone astray.

Philosophers ask "What is a mind?" or "What is the good life?" or "What exists?" But most often, the answers proposed to these questions cannot be verified by appeal to facts. For example, it is unclear that any fact (or facts) would verify the view, "Everything is really mental." But a claim such as "Blood circulates through the body" is much more readily verifiable.

In general, it seemed that philosophical claims were immune to the verification process that worked so well for science. Thus it was that the Vienna Circle proposed that if philosophy were to be saved, it had to reject as meaningless those questions whose answers clearly had no factual content. Philosophy should restrict itself, they held, to questions whose answers could be verified (or shown to be false) by appeal to fact. This view was called by the Circle, logical positivism. (Later, in a slightly different form, it was sometimes referred to as logical empiricism).

If you have read the contributions by Ayer in Chapter 6 or Chapter 10, the views of the Vienna Circle should sound familiar. Ayer was a proponent of the views of the Vienna Circle. Indeed, he was a popularizer of logical positivism.

BIOGRAPHICAL NOTE.   Herbert Feigl was born in what was then Austria–Hungary in 1902. He studied physics, mathematics, and philosophy at the University of Vienna. It was there, in 1924, that he and Friedrich Waismann began a Thursday evening discussion group that came to be the Vienna Circle. After receiving his doctoral degree in philosophy in 1927, Feigl taught astronomy and philosophy of science in Vienna. Feigl came to the United States in 1930 on a Rockefeller Fellowship in order to work with physicist Percy Bridgman on the foundations of physics. Feigl went on to teach at the University of Iowa from 1931 to 1940. In 1940 he took a position at the University of Minnesota, where he became head of the Minnesota Center for Philosophy of Science. He came to focus his attention on the mind–body problem and was one of the most ardent supporters of the Identity Thesis. Feigl died in 1988.

THE ARGUMENT OF THE PASSAGES.   To Feigl, science is the premier source of knowledge, because it is objective in a very important sense. A scientific truth requires verifiability by many scientists. There has to be an agreed-upon method all scientists can use to determine whether or not some claim has been verified. The method cannot be a function of any one person's particular beliefs. The method has to "transcend" particular psychologies and deal with the real, objective features of the world.

That there is a real and objective world, a world that exists over and above our attempts to find its features, is a position called realism. Postmodernists (such as Richard Rorty) as well as some contemporary philosophers of science (e.g., Kuhn and W. V. O. Quine) challenge the legitimacy of realism. We will read selections from Kuhn and Rorty as well as an essay on postmodernism.

Feigl draws a distinction between discovery and justification; between the psychological, economic, and sociological factors that affect science and the logic of science itself. To insure objectivity, the logic must be free of the psychological, economic, and sociological factors. Indeed, the very success of science is proof that there is this sharp distinction. Sometimes the distinction is put this way: The logic of verification or justification, which is objective, is internal to science; the other factors are external.

Thus Feigl's main point can be made in the following way. The sociology of science, the economics of science, and the psychology of science are all very interesting and worth studying. But they will not reveal the logic of scientific methodology that sets science apart from other, more flawed, ways of finding out what is true. Feigl's point is that how anyone comes to believe a particular hypothesis in science makes no difference. What does make a difference is whether that hypothesis is verified or not and how it is verified. To take a famous example, the structure of the chemical benzene came to August Kekulé in a dream. For Feigl, this is very interesting but irrelevant to understanding science. What counts, for Feigl, is how Kekulé verified in the laboratory that what he dreamt was true.

> What . . . are the basic characteristics of the scientific method? The often alleged difficulties of an adequate definition of science seem to me mainly a matter of terminology. We must first distinguish between pure mathematics as an exclusively formal-conceptual discipline, and the factual (or empirical, that is, the natural and the social-cultural) sciences. The certainty, complete exactitude, and necessity of pure mathematics depends precisely on its detachment from empirical fact. Mathematics as applied in the factual sciences merely lends its forms and deductive structures to the contents furnished by experience. But no matter how predominant mathematics may be in the formulations and derivations of empirical facts, factual knowledge cannot attain either the absolute precision or necessity of pure mathematics. The knowledge claimed in the natural and the social sciences is a matter of successive approximations and of increasing degrees of confirmation. Warranted assertibility or probability is all that we can conceivably secure in the sciences that deal with the facts

of experience. It is empirical science, thus conceived as an unending quest (its truth-claims to be held only "until further notice"), which is under consideration here. Science in this sense differs only in degree from the knowledge accumulated throughout the ages by sound and common sense.

The aims of science are description, explanation, and prediction. The first aim is basic and indispensable, the second and third (closely related to each other) arise as the most desirable fruits of scientific labors whenever inquiry rises beyond the mere fact-gathering stage. History, often and nowadays quite fashionably declared an art, is scientific to the extent that it ascertains its facts concerning past events by a meticulous scrutiny of present evidence. Causal interpretation of these facts (in history, but similarly also in psychology, sociology, cultural anthropology, and economics) is usually much more difficult than, but in principle not logically different from, causal interpretation (that is, explanation) in the natural sciences. The aims of the pure (empirical) sciences are then essentially the same throughout the whole field. What the scientists are seeking are descriptions, explanations, and predictions which are as adequate and accurate as possible in the given context of research.

The quest for scientific knowledge is therefore regulated by certain standards or criteria which may best be formulated in the form of ideals to be approximated, but perhaps never fully attained. The most important of these regulative ideals are:

1. *Intersubjective Testability*. This is only a more adequate formulation of what is generally meant by the "objectivity" of science. What is here involved is not only the freedom from personal or cultural bias or partiality, but—even more fundamentally—the requirement that the knowledge claims of science be in principle capable of test (confirmation or disconfirmation, at the least indirectly and to some degree) on the part of any person properly equipped with intelligence and the technical devices of observation or experimentation. The term *intersubjective* stresses the social nature of the scientific enterprise. If there be any "truths" that are accessible only to privileged individuals, such as mystics or visionaries—that is, knowledge-claims which by their very nature cannot independently be checked by anyone else—then such "truths" are not the kind that we seek in the sciences. The criterion of intersubjective testability thus delimits the scientific from the nonscientific activities of man.

Religious ecstasy, the elations of love, the inspiration of the artist, yes, even the flash of insight on the part of a scientific genius are not in themselves scientific activities. All these processes may eventually become subject matter for scientific study. But in themselves they do not validate knowledge-claims. They may, as in the case of the scientific intuition (or empathy in the psychological-cultural field) be instrumental in the generation of knowledge claims. But it is these knowledge-claims which have to be, first, formulated in an intersubjectively intelligible (or communicable) manner, and, second, subjected to the appropriate kind of tests in order to ascertain their validity. Beliefs transcending all possible tests by observation, self-observation, experiment, measurement, or statistical analysis are recognized as theological or metaphysical and therefore devoid of the type of meaning that we all associate with the knowledge-claims of common sense or factual science. From the point of view of the scientific outlook in philosophy it may be suggested that the sort of significance with which the in-principle-unconfirmable assertions of transcendent theology and metaphysics impress so many people is largely emotive. The pictorial, emotional, and motivational appeals of language, no matter how indispensable or valuable in the contexts of practical life, art, education, persuasion, and propaganda, must, however, not be confused with the cognitive meanings (purely formal- and/or factual-empirical) that are of the essence of science. Each type of significance has its function, and in most uses of language both are combined or even fused. The only point stressed here is that they must not be *con*fused, that is, mistaken for one another, if we wish to be clear as to what we are about.

2. *Reliability, or a Sufficient Degree of Confirmation.* This second criterion of scientific knowledge enables us to distinguish what is generally called "mere opinion" (or worse still, "superstition") from knowledge (well-substantiated belief). It may be considered as the delimitation of the scientific from the unscientific knowledge-claims. Clearly, in contrast to the first criterion, we face here a distinction of degree. There is no sharp line of demarcation between the well-confirmed laws, theories, or hypotheses of science, and the only poorly substantiated hunches and ideas-on-trial which may ultimately either be included in the corpus of scientific knowledge or else rejected as unconfirmed. Truth-claims which we repudiate as "superstition," and, quite generally, as judgments based upon hasty generalization or weak analogy (if they fulfill the criterion of testability), differ from what we accept as "scientific truth" in the extremely low degree of probability to which they are supported by the available evidence. Astrology or alchemy, for example, are not factually meaningless, but they are considered false to fact in that all available evidence speaks overwhelmingly against them. Modern techniques of experimentation and of statistical analysis are the most powerful tools we have in the discernment between chance and law and hence the best means of enhancing the reliability of knowledge.

3. *Definiteness and Precision.* This obvious standard of scientific method requires that the concepts used in the formulation of scientific knowledge-claims be as definitely delimited as possible. On the level of the qualitative-classificatory sciences this amounts to the attempt to reduce all border-zone vagueness to a minimum. On the level of quantitative science the exactitude of the concepts is enormously enhanced through the application of the techniques of measurement. The mensurational devices usually also increase the degree of objectivity. This is especially clear when they are contrasted with purely impressionistic ways of estimating magnitudes. Of course, there is no point in sharpening precision to a higher degree than the problem in hand requires. (You need no razor to cut butter.)

4. *Coherence or Systematic Structure.* This is what T. H. Huxley had in mind when he defined science as "organized common-sense." Not a mere collection of miscellaneous items of information, but a well-connected account of the facts is what we seek in science. On the descriptive level this results, for example, in systems of classification or division, in diagrams, statistical charts, and the like. On the explanatory levels of science sets of laws, or theoretical assumptions, are utilized. Explanation in science consists in the hypothetico-deductive procedure. The laws, theories, or hypotheses form the premises from which we derive logically, or logico-mathematically, the observed or observable facts. These facts, often belonging to heterogeneous domains, thus become integrated into a coherent, unifying structure. (Theological and metaphysical systems have, frequently enough, ambitiously tried to imitate this feature of science; but even if they succeeded in proceeding *more geometrico*, the important difference from science remains: they either lack testability or else reliability in the senses specified in our previous points.)

5. *Comprehensiveness or Scope of Knowledge.* This final point in our enumeration of criteria of science also characterizes scientific knowledge as different in degree (often enormously) from common-sense knowledge. Not only through bold and sweeping hypotheses, but especially through the ingenious devices by means of which they are

tested, science acquires a reach far beyond the limits of our unaided senses. With telescopes, microscopes, spectroscopes, Geiger Counters, lie detectors, and the thousands of other contrivances of modern science we manage to amplify our senses and thus open up avenues of at least indirect access to the worlds of the very distant, the very large, the extremely small, or the disguised and concealed. The resulting increase in the completeness of our knowledge is, of course, popularly the most impressive feature of science. It must be kept in mind, however, that the scope thus achieved is a product of hard labor, and not to be confused with the sham completeness metaphysicians procure for their world pictures by verbal magic. Instead of presenting a finished account of the world, the genuine scientist keeps his unifying hypotheses open to revision and is always ready to modify or abandon them if evidence should render them doubtful. This self-corrective aspect of science has rightly been stressed as its most important characteristic and must always be kept in mind when we refer to the comprehensiveness or the unification achieved by the scientific account of the universe. It is a sign of one's maturity to be able to live with an unfinished world view.

The foregoing outline of the criteria of science has been set down in a somewhat dogmatic tone. But this was done only for the sake of brevity.[1] The spirit behind it is that of a humble account of what, I think, an impartial and elaborate study of the history of thought from magic to science would reveal. In any case, these criteria seem unquestionably the guiding ideals of present-day empirical science. They may therefore be used in a definition of science as we understand this term today. It seems rather useless to speculate about just what this term, by a change of meaning, might come to connote in the future.

It should be remembered that the criteria listed characterize the *pure* factual (empirical) sciences. The aims of the *applied* sciences—the technologies, medicine, social and economic planning, and others—are practical control, production, guidance, therapy, reform, and so forth. Responsible activity in the application of science clearly presupposes information which is fairly well substantiated by the methods of the pure sciences. (These remarks intend to draw merely a logically important distinction. The obvious practical interpenetration and important mutual fertilization of the pure and the applied disciplines is of course not denied here.)

CRITIQUE OF MISCONCEPTIONS

Having indicated at least in broad outline the nature of scientific method we may now turn to the critique of some of the misconceptions to which it is all too commonly exposed. In what follows, a dozen typical charges against science are stated and answered consecutively.[2]

Science arises exclusively out of practical and social needs and has its only value in serving them in turn. (Dialectical Materialism and Vocationalism)

---

[1]   A thorough discussion of the logical, epistemological, methodological, and historical issues connected with the criteria would require a whole book, not just another essay.

[2]   These charges are not straw men. In more than twenty years of reading, listening, teaching, and argument I have encountered them again and again in Europe and just as frequently in this country. If space permitted and time were less valuable, I could quote many well-known writers in connection with each charge.

While this is important it does not tell the whole story. Science has always also been the pursuit of knowledge, the satisfaction of a deep-rooted curiosity. It should be recognized as one of the cultural values along with art, literature, and music. Better teaching of the sciences and their history can redress the balance. Fuller utilization of results and suggestions from the history and the philosophy of science would give the student a deeper appreciation of the evolution of scientific knowledge and of the scientific point of view. Through proper instruction, the student could be led to rediscover some of the important results of science. The intellectual gratification that comes with a grasp of the order of nature, with the understanding of its processes by means of laws and theories, is one of the most powerful incentives in the pursuit of pure knowledge.

Science cannot furnish a secure basis for human affairs since it is unstable. It changes its views continually. (Traditionalism)

While there is constant evolution, and occasionally a revolution, in the scientific outlook, the charge is a superficial (usually journalistic) exaggeration. The typical progress of science reveals that later views often contain much of the earlier views (to the extent that these have stood the test of repeated examination). The more radical or revolutionary changes usually amount to a revision of the conceptual frame of a scientific discipline. The criticism often also presupposes other sources of certainty which will simply not bear critical scrutiny. The quest for absolute certainty is an immature, if not infantile, trait of thinking. The best knowledge we have can be established only by the method of trial and error. It is of the essence of science to make such knowledge as reliable as is humanly and technically possible.

Science rests on uncritical or uncriticized presuppositions. It validates its outlook by its own standards. It therefore begs the question as regards alternative approaches for settling problems of knowledge and action.

Science has been clarifying and revising its basic assumptions throughout its development. Particularly since the beginning of the modern age and still more intensively since the beginning of our century, an increasing awareness of, and critical attitude toward, the fundamental presuppositions has been most fruitfully applied in the repudiation of dogmatic prejudices and in the articulation of the conceptual frame of scientific method. It can be shown (through logical analysis) that the procedure of science is the only one we are *certain* will yield the results (reliable knowledge, that is, valid explanation and predictions) *if* such results can at all be achieved. Any alleged rival method—theology, metaphysics, mysticism, intuition, dialectics—if it made any contributions at all could not be examined and appraised on any basis other than the usual inductive criteria of science. Generally, it seems that these alleged alternatives do not even aim primarily at knowledge but, like the arts, at the enrichment of experience. They may therefore more properly be said to be *non*-scientific, rather than *un*scientific.

Science distorts the facts of reality. In its Procrustean manner it introduces discontinuities where there is continuity (and vice versa). The abstractions and idealizations used in science can never do justice to the richness and complexities of experience.

Since the task of science is to discover reliable and precise knowledge of what happens under what conditions, it always tries to approximate the facts as closely as the problem on hand requires and permits. Both continuity and discontinuity can be formulated mathematically and be given an adequate formulation only with the help of modern mathematics.

Science can deal only with the measurable and therefore tends to "explain away" that which it cannot measure.

While measurement is eminently desirable in order to enhance the precision and objectivity of knowledge, it is not indispensable in many branches of science or, at least, on their more qualitative levels of analysis. Science does not explain away the qualities of experience. It aims at, and often succeeds in, making these qualities more predictable.

Science never explains, it merely describes the phenomena of experience. The reality beyond the appearances is also beyond the reach of science.

This is partly a terminological issue and partly a result of the (traditional but most misleading and useless) metaphysical distinction between appearance and reality. In the sense in which the word *explaining* is used in common life, science *does* explain facts—it deduces them from laws or theoretical assumptions. Questions which are in principle incapable of being answered by the scientific method turn out, on closer analysis, not to be questions of knowledge. They are expressions of emotional tensions or of the wish for soothing (or exciting) experience.

Science and the scientific attitude are incompatible with religion and the religious attitude.

If by religion one refers to an explanation of the universe and a derivation of moral norms from theological premises, then indeed there is logical incompatibility with the results, methods, and general outlook of science. But if religion means an attitude of sincere devotion to human values, such as justice, peace, relief from suffering, there is not only no conflict between religion and science but rather a need for mutual supplementation.

Science is responsible for the evils and maladjustments of our civilization. It is creating ever more powerful weapons of destruction. The employment of scientific techniques in the machine age has contributed to the misery, physical and mental, of the multitudes. Moreover, the biological facts of evolution imply the negation of all morality: the law of the jungle.

These are particularly superficial charges. It is the social-political-economic structure of a society that is responsible for these various evils. Scientific knowledge itself is socially and morally neutral. But the manner in which it is applied, whether for the benefit or to the detriment of humanity, depends entirely on ourselves. Scientists are becoming increasingly aware that they, even more than the average citizen, have to work for enlightenment toward the proper use of knowledge. The facts and theories of evolution have ben construed in many ways as regards their implications for ethics. Julian Huxley reads them very differently from the way his grandfather Thomas Henry did.[3] It should be easy to see that the forces active on the level of human civilization and intelligent communal life are not completely reducible to those involved in the ruthless struggle for survival.

The ethical neutrality of scientific truth and the ivory tower situation of the pure researcher is apt to generate an attitude of indifference toward the pressing problems of humanity.

---

[3] Compare Julian Huxley, *Touchstone for Ethics* (Harper, 1947); but see also C. D. Broad, "Review of Julian S. Huxley's Evolutionary Ethics" (*Mind*, 53, 1944), reprinted in H. Feigl and W. Sellars, *Readings in Philosophical Analysis* (Appleton-Century-Crofts, 1949).

Only maladjusted individuals are unable to combine the detachment necessary for the pursuit of truth with an ardent interest in the improvement of the condition of humanity.

Scientific method, while eminently successful in the explanation, prediction, and control of physical phenomena, is distinctly less successful in regard to the facts of organic life and almost altogether hopeless in the mental and social realm. The methods of the physical sciences are essentially mechanistic (if not materialistic) and therefore reductionistic; they cannot do justice to the complex organismic, teleological, and emergent features of life and mind.

"Scientism" as a slogan of criticism and reproach is very fashionable these days. It is true that some sciences and especially some of the popularizers of science have indulged in reductive fallacies of various sorts. But the true scientific spirit as exemplified in some of the foremost researchers is free from that impatience and simplemindedness that tries to finish the unfinished business of science by hasty speculation. Admittedly, there are tremendous problems yet to be solved. On the other hand what method is there but the method of science to solve them? Explanations of the mechanistic type (in *one* sense of the term) have been abandoned even in physics. But mechanistic explanation in the wider sense of a search for law (deterministic or statistical) is still the indispensable procedure for all sciences that have gone beyond the purely classificatory level. Organic wholeness, teleology, and emergence can be understood, if at all, only by causal analysis on the usual empirical basis. Purposiveness and freedom of choice, far from being incompatible with causality, presuppose causal order.

The methods of science can never replace the intuitive insight or empathic understanding of the practical psychologist, psychiatrist, cultural anthropologist, or historian. This claim is made particularly wherever the object of knowledge is the individual, the unique and unrepeatable.

It is only through the scientific method that the validity and reliability of the intuitive approach can be gauged. There is, on this ground, some doubt as to its more exaggerated claims. However, there is nothing in the principles of scientific method that would deny the occasional, or even frequent, efficacy of intuitive judgments based, as they must be, on a rich (but often not articulated) background of experience in the given field. Aside from the mere artistic contemplation of the unique and individual, knowledge, in the proper sense of the word, always means the subsumption of the specific case under general concepts of laws. This holds in the social sciences just as much in the natural sciences.

Science cannot determine values. Since scientific knowledge can (at best) find out only what is the case, it can, by its very nature, never tell what ought to be.

This final challenge often comes from theology or metaphysics. It usually maintains that questions of aims, goals, and ideals cannot be settled by the methods of science but rather require recourse either to divine revelation, the voice of conscience, or some metaphysical *a priori* truths. The answer to this in a scientific age would seem to be that a mature mankind should be able to determine its own value standards on the basis of its needs, wants, and the facts of the social condition of man. But it is true that science cannot dictate value standards. It can, as in social psychology, ascertain the actual evaluations of groups and individuals, study their compatibilities and incompatibilities, and recommend (that is *applied* science!) ways and meanings of harmonizing conflicting evaluations. True enough, in many of the urgent issues that confront us, we do not possess enough scientific knowledge to warrant a course of action. This means that we have to act, as so often in life, on the highest probabilities available even if these probabilities be low in themselves. But such estimates of probabilities will still be made most reliable by the scientific method. Common life experience and wisdom, when freed from its adherence to prescientific thought patterns, is not fundamentally different from scientific knowledge. In both we find the procedure of self-correction, so essentially needed if knowledge is to be a guide for action. There is an important common element in mature thinking (as we find it in science) and mature social action (as we find it in democracy): progress arises out of the peaceful competition of ideas as they are put to intersubjective test. Cooperative planning on the basis of the best and fullest knowledge available is the only path left to an awakened humanity that has embarked on the adventure of science and civilization.

The scientific view of the world that we have characterized and defended against criticisms from various quarters may with historical and terminological justice be called Naturalism.[4] It differs from mechanistic materialism (too often a mere straw man put up by theologians or idealistic metaphysicians) in that it steers clear of reductive fallacies. If uninformed persons insist on viewing science as essentially materialistic and the humanities as essentially idealistic (not to say spiritualistic) the hopes of fruitful collaboration of both fields in education are slim indeed. But science, properly interpreted, is not dependent on any sort of metaphysics. It merely attempts to cover a maximum of facts by a minimum of laws. On the other side, a mature humanism requires no longer a theological or metaphysical frame either. Human nature and human history become progressively understood in the light of advancing science. It is therefore no longer justifiable to speak of science *versus* the humanities. Naturalism *and* humanism should be our maxim in philosophy and in education. A Scientific Humanism emerges as a philosophy holding considerable promise for mankind—*if* mankind will at all succeed in growing up.

Note on Sources.   Herbert Feigl, "The Scientific Outlook: Naturalism and Humanism," *American Quarterly*, Vol. 1, No. 1 (Spring, 1949).

2   THOMAS KUHN

PROBLEMS WITH THE POSITIVISTIC INTERPRETATIONS OF SCIENCE

From Feigl to Kuhn.   Feigl's view was accepted by many philosophers until the early 1960s, when Thomas Kuhn published *The Structure of Scientific Revolution*. Notice that Feigl had, in 1949, anticipated many of the challenges which were to be made by Kuhn and others.

To get a sense of Kuhn's argument, go back to Feigl's article. There he lists a dozen claims made against science and against his characterization of science. The third criticism Feigl discusses is: "Science rests on uncritical or uncriticized presuppositions. . . . It therefore begs the question as regards alternative

---

4   It should scarcely need mentioning that this meaning of naturalism has only a distant and tenuous relation to the other meaning in which it is applied to a certain type of literature.

approaches for settling problems of knowledge and action." Kuhn develops this criticism in a very sophisticated way by appealing to the history of science.

Kuhn points out that the views of the positivists about science are derived from what he terms "finished scientific achievements." That is, philosophy of science was paying no attention to the history of science. Indeed, it was thought to be an error to do so. History was interesting but could never lead to the discovery of the logic of the scientific method. The view of science that one gets by looking at completed episodes of science is the one put forward by philosophers like Feigl. They see science as slowly but surely approaching the truth. The scientific method works in increments, piling truth upon truth.

Kuhn points out that if one allows the history of science to do more than just list who did what when, it becomes clear that much more is going on in the development of science and that philosophers like Feigl have oversimplified the nature of science by insisting that philosophy of science be done in an ahistorical manner.

What did Kuhn find in his researches? First, he highlights what he calls the arbitrary element. By this he means that at any given era in the development of a science, there is a general consensus (often unstated) among scientists about which problems are worth studying, how to study them, and what an acceptable range of answers might be. This arbitrary element, the unstated consensus, Kuhn refers to as a paradigm. The science that is done under a paradigm is called normal science.

Sometimes, normal science is clearly insufficient to answer certain questions. These questions arise because of things that do not fit the consensus-picture of the world. Kuhn calls such discoveries "anomalies." At first anomalies are suppressed in some way because they are so threatening. But real anomalies do not go away—even if they are ignored. Finally, it becomes clear that the only way to deal with the anomalies is to overthrow the accepted paradigm and give up the normal science until a new paradigm has been accepted. When, as a result of the above process, a new paradigm has been accepted, we say that there has been a scientific revolution.

The implications of Kuhn's work are these. Science does not change by increments, but by wholesale revolution. Because the paradigms are so controlling and because they are so different, one cannot really compare paradigms. Thus, Kuhn is actually saying that the idea of scientific progress, as someone like Feigl would define it, makes no sense. Finally, because paradigms require consensus, and because getting consensus is never just a logical procedure, the sociological, psychological, and economic factors dismissed by Feigl and the positivist philosophers play an important role in science.

We can now restate the third criticism mentioned by Feigl using Kuhn's terminology. "The uncriticized presuppositions that science rests on are paradigms. Anytime science pats itself on the back for being a sure source of knowledge it is begging the question, for its decision that something is knowledge is actually determined by the paradigm in use. Thus, in this sense, normal science always begs the question, 'Is there a better but very different approach?'" Kuhn sees this as a fact he has discovered about science (and knowledge in general) and not as a weakness of his view.

BIOGRAPHICAL NOTE.   Thomas Kuhn was born in Cincinnati, Ohio in 1922. He received a Ph.D. in physics from Harvard in 1949. He has taught at Harvard, the University of California at Berkeley, and Princeton, and is currently at MIT in the Department of Philosophy and Linguistics.

THE ARGUMENT OF THE PASSAGES.   Kuhn rejects the picture of science that we get in textbooks. It is a picture which is developed by limiting historical questions to only two sorts. (1) Who made a particular discovery and when? (2) What accounts for the error which has held up the incremental development of science? Kuhn says that these questions are wrongheaded. The more historians search, the more they find that they cannot give clear answers to these questions.

Many historians of science have given up the search for simple priorities (e.g., who discovered something first). They have also given up the incremental view of science. These historians find much evidence to support the view that science develops as a result of large-scale shifts in thinking. Science makes its major changes through revolutions. A famous example of such a revolution is the shift from an Earth-centered to a sun-centered astronomy.

Kuhn, like Feigl, anticipates a criticism. Has not he merely confused the distinction between the internal and the external factors of science? Has he not confused the logic of discovery and the logic of justification? To this, Kuhn answers that the distinction between internal and external factors of science is itself part of a theory about the nature of science. If the distinction is to be kept, it must be shown that it helps us to understand actual episodes in science. But, Kuhn claims, the distinction is not much help at all and, therefore, should be questioned.

In this essay, 'normal science' means research firmly based upon one or more past scientific achievements, achievements that some particular scientific community acknowledges for a time as supplying the foundation for its further practice. Today such achievements are recounted, though seldom in their original form, by science textbooks, elementary and advanced. These textbooks expound the body of accepted theory, illustrate many or all of its successful applications, and compare these applications with exemplary observations and experiments. Before such books became popular early in the nineteenth century (and until even more recently in the newly matured sciences), many of the famous classics of science fulfilled a similar function. Aristotle's *Physica*, Ptolemy's *Almagest*, Newton's *Principia* and *Opticks*, Franklin's *Electricity*, Lavoisier's *Chemistry*, and Lyell's *Geology*—these and many other works served for a time implicitly to define the legitimate problems and methods of a research field for succeeding generations of practitioners. They were able to do so because they shared two essential characteristics. Their achievement was sufficiently unprecedented to attract an enduring group of adherents away from competing modes of scientific activity. Simultaneously, it was sufficiently open-ended to leave all sorts of problems for the redefined group of practitioners to resolve.

Achievements that share these two characteristics I shall henceforth refer to as 'paradigms,' a term that relates closely to 'normal science.' By choosing it, I mean to suggest that some accepted examples of actual scientific practice—examples which include law, theory, application, and instrumentation together—provide models from which spring particular coherent traditions of scientific research. These are the traditions which the historian describes under such rubrics as 'Ptolemaic astronomy' (or 'Copernican'), 'Aristotelian dynamics' (or 'Newtonian'), 'corpuscular optics' (or 'wave optics'), and so on. The study of paradigms, including many that are far more specialized than those named illustratively above, is what mainly prepares the student for membership in the particular scientific community with which he will later practice. Because he there joins men who learned the bases of their field from the same concrete models, his subsequent practice will seldom evoke overt disagreement over fundamentals. Men whose research is based on shared paradigms are committed to the same rules and standards for scientific practice. That commitment and the apparent consensus it produces are prerequisites for normal science, i.e., for the genesis and continuation of a particular research tradition.

Because in this essay the concept of a paradigm will often substitute for a variety of familiar notions, more will need to be said about the reasons for its introduction. Why is the concrete scientific achievement, as a locus of professional commitment, prior to the various concepts, laws, theories, and points of view that may be abstracted from it? In what sense is the shared paradigm a fundamental unit for the student of scientific development, a unit that cannot be fully reduced to logically atomic components which might function in its stead? . . . answers to these questions and to others like them will prove basic to an understanding both of normal science and of the associated concept of paradigms. That more abstract discussion will depend, however, upon a previous exposure to examples of normal science or of paradigms in operation. In particular, both these related concepts will be clarified by noting that there can be a sort of scientific research without paradigms, or at least without any so unequivocal and so binding as the ones named above. Acquisition of a paradigm and of the more esoteric type of research it permits is a sign of maturity in the development of any given scientific field.

If the historian traces the scientific knowledge of any selected group of related phenomena backward in time, he is likely to encounter some minor variant of a pattern here illustrated from the history of physical optics. Today's physics textbooks tell the student that light is photons, i.e., quantum-mechanical entities that exhibit some characteristics of waves and some of particles. Research proceeds accordingly, or rather according to the more elaborate and mathematical characterization from which this usual verbalization is derived. That characterization of light is, however, scarcely half a century old. Before it was developed by Planck, Einstein, and others early in this century, physics texts taught that light was transverse wave motion, a conception rooted in a paradigm that derived ultimately from the optical writings of Young and Fresnel in the early nineteenth century. Nor was the wave theory the first to be embraced by almost all practitioners of optical science. During the eighteenth century the paradigm for this field was provided by Newton's *Opticks*, which taught that light was material corpuscles. At that time physicists sought evidence, as the early wave theorists had not, of the pressure exerted by light particles impinging on solid bodies.[1]

These transformations of the paradigms of physical optics are scientific revolutions, and the successive transition from one paradigm to another via revolution is the

---

1   Joseph Priestley, *The History and Present State of Discoveries Relating to Vision, Light, and Colors* (London, 1772), pp. 385–90.

usual developmental pattern of mature science. It is not, however, the pattern characteristic of the period before Newton's work, and that is the contrast that concerns us here. No period between remote antiquity and the end of the seventeenth century exhibited a single generally accepted view about the nature of light. Instead there were a number of competing schools and sub-schools, most of them espousing one variant or another of Epicurean, Aristotelian, or Platonic theory. One group took light to be particles emanating from material bodies; for another it was a modification of the medium that intervened between the body and the eye; still another explained light in terms of an interaction of the medium with an emanation from the eye; and there were other combinations and modifications besides. Each of the corresponding schools derived strength from its relation to some particular metaphysic, and each emphasized, as paradigmatic observations, the particular cluster of optical phenomena that its own theory could do most to explain. Other observations were dealt with by *ad hoc* elaborations, or they remained as outstanding problems for further research.[2]

At various times all these schools made significant contributions to the body of concepts, phenomena, and techniques from which Newton drew the first nearly uniformly accepted paradigm for physical optics. Any definition of the scientist that excludes at least the more creative members of these various schools will exclude their modern successors as well. Those men were scientists. Yet anyone examining a survey of physical optics before Newton may well conclude that, though the field's practitioners were scientists, the net result of their activity was something less than science. Being able to take no common body of belief for granted, each writer on physical optics felt forced to build his field anew from its foundations. In doing so, his choice of supporting observation and experiment was relatively free, for there was no standard set of methods or of phenomena that every optical writer felt forced to employ and explain. Under these circumstances, the dialogue of the resulting books was often directed as much to the members of other schools as it was to nature. That pattern is not unfamiliar in a number of creative fields today, nor is it incompatible with significant discovery and invention. It is not, however, the pattern of development that physical optics acquired after Newton and that other natural sciences make familiar today. . . .

History, if viewed as a repository for more than anecdote or chronology, could produce a decisive transformation in the image of science by which we are now possessed. That image has previously been drawn, even by scientists themselves, mainly from the study of finished scientific achievements as these are recorded in the classics and, more recently, in the textbooks from which each new scientific generation learns to practice its trade. Inevitably, however, the aim of such books is persuasive and pedagogic; a concept of science drawn from them is no more likely to fit the enterprise that produced them than an image of a national culture drawn from a tourist brochure or a language text. This essay attempts to show that we have been misled by them in fundamental ways. Its aim is a sketch of the quite different concept of science that can emerge from the historical record of the research activity itself.

Even from history, however, that new concept will not be forthcoming if historical data continue to be sought and scrutinized mainly to answer questions posed by the unhistorical stereotype drawn from science texts. Those texts have, for example, often seemed to imply that the content of science is uniquely exemplified by the observations, laws, and theories described in their pages. Almost as regularly, the

---

2 Vasco Ronchi, *Histoire de la lumière*, trans. Jean Taton (Paris, 1956), chaps. i–iv.

same books have been read as saying that scientific methods are simply the ones illustrated by the manipulative techniques used in gathering textbook data, together with the logical operations employed when relating those data to the textbook's theoretical generalizations. The result has been a concept of science with profound implications about its nature and development.

If science is the constellation of facts, theories, and methods collected in current texts, then scientists are men who, successfully or not, have striven to contribute one or another element to that particular constellation. Scientific development becomes the piecemeal process by which these items have been added, singly and in combination, to the ever growing stockpile that constitutes scientific technique and knowledge. And history of science becomes the discipline that chronicles both these successive increments and the obstacles that have inhibited their accumulation. Concerned with scientific development, the historian then appears to have two main tasks. On the one hand, he must determine by what man and at what point in time each contemporary scientific fact, law, and theory was discovered or invented. On the other, he must describe and explain the congeries of error, myth, and superstition that have inhibited the more rapid accumulation of the constituents of the modern science text. Much research has been directed to these ends, and some still is.

In recent years, however, a few historians of science have been finding it more and more difficult to fulfill the functions that the concept of development-by-accumulation assigns to them. As chroniclers of an incremental process, they discover that additional research makes it harder, not easier, to answer questions like: When was oxygen discovered? Who first conceived of energy conservation? Increasingly, a few of them suspect that these are simply the wrong sorts of questions to ask. Perhaps science does not develop by the accumulation of individual discoveries and inventions. Simultaneously, these same historians confront growing difficulties in distinguishing the "scientific" component of past observation and belief from what their predecessors had readily labeled "error" and "superstition." The more carefully they study, say, Aristotelian dynamics, phlogistic chemistry, or caloric thermodynamics, the more certain they feel that those once current views of nature were, as a whole, neither less scientific nor more the product of human idiosyncrasy than those current today. If these out-of-date beliefs are to be called myths, then myths can be produced by the same sorts of methods and held for the same sorts of reasons that now lead to scientific knowledge. If, on the other hand, they are to be called science, then science has included bodies of belief quite incompatible with the ones we hold today. Given these alternatives, the historian must choose the latter. Out-of-date theories are not in principle unscientific because they have been discarded. That choice, however, makes it difficult to see scientific development as a process of accretion. The same historical research that displays the difficulties in isolating individual interventions and discoveries gives ground for profound doubts about the cumulative process through which these individual contributions to science were thought to have been compounded.

The result of all these doubts and difficulties is a historio-graphic revolution in the study of science, though one that is still in its early stages. Gradually, and often without entirely realizing they are doing so, historians of science have begun to ask new sorts of questions and to trace different, and often less than cumulative, developmental lines for the sciences. Rather than seeking the permanent contributions of an older science to our present vantage, they attempt to display the historical integrity of that science in its own time. They ask, for example, not about the relation of Galileo's views to those of modern science, but rather about the relationship between his views and those of his group, i.e., his teachers, contemporaries, and immediate successors in the sciences. Furthermore, they insist upon studying the opinions of that group and other similar ones from the viewpoint—usually very different from that of modern science—that gives those opinions the maximum internal coherence and the closest possible fit to nature. Seen through the works that result, works perhaps best exemplified in the writings of Alexandre Koyré, science does not seem altogether the same enterprise as the one discussed by writers in the older historio-graphic tradition. By implication, at least, these historical studies suggest the possibility of a new image of science. This essay aims to delineate that image by making explicit some of the new historiography's implications.

What aspects of science will emerge to prominence in the course of this effort? First, at least in order of presentation, is the insufficiency of methodological directives, by themselves, to dictate a unique substantive conclusion to many sorts of scientific questions. Instructed to examine electrical or chemical phenomena, the man who is ignorant of these fields but who knows what it is to be scientific may legitimately reach any one of a number of incompatible conclusions. Among those legitimate possibilities, the particular conclusions he does arrive at are probably determined by his prior experience in other fields, by the accidents of his investigation, and by his own individual makeup. What beliefs about the stars, for example, does he bring to the study of chemistry or electricity? Which of the many conceivable experiments relevant to the new field does he elect to perform first? And has aspects of the complex phenomenon that then results strike him as particularly relevant to an elucidation of the nature of chemical change or of electrical affinity? For the individual, at least, and sometimes for the scientific community as well, answers to questions like these are often essential determinants of scientific development. We shall note, for example, in Section II that the early developmental stages of most sciences have been characterized by continual competition between a number of distinct views of nature, each partially derived from, and all roughly compatible with, the dictates of scientific observation and method. What differentiated these various schools was not one or another failure of method—they were all "scientific"—but what we shall come to call their incommensurable ways of seeing the world and of practicing science in it. Observation and experience can and must drastically restrict the range of admissible scientific belief, else there would be no science. But they cannot alone determine a particular body of such belief. An apparently arbitrary element, compounded of personal and historical accident, is always a formative ingredient of the beliefs espoused by a given scientific community at a given time.

That element of arbitrariness does not, however, indicate that any scientific group could practice its trade without some set of received beliefs. Nor does it make less consequential the particular constellation to which the group, at a given time, is in fact committed. Effective research scarcely begins before a scientific community thinks it has acquired firm answers to questions like the following: What are the fundamental entities of which the universe is composed? How do these interact with each other and with the senses? What questions may legitimately be asked about such entities and what techniques employed in seeking solutions? At least in the mature sciences, answers (or full substitutes for answers) to questions like these are firmly embedded in the educational initiation that prepares and licenses the student for professional practice. Because that education is both rigorous and rigid, these answers come to exert a deep hold on the scientific mind. That they can do so does much to account both for the peculiar efficiency of the normal research activity and for the direction in which it proceeds at any given time. When examining normal science in Sections III, IV, and V, we shall want finally to describe that research as a strenuous and devoted attempt to force nature into the conceptual boxes supplied by professional education. Simultaneously, we shall wonder whether research could proceed without such boxes, whatever the element of arbitrariness in their historic origins and, occasionally, in their subsequent development.

Yet that element of arbitrariness is present, and it too has an important effect on scientific development, one which will be examined in detail in Sections VI, VII, and VIII. Normal science, the activity in which most scientists inevitably spend almost all their time, is predicated on the assumption that the scientific community knows what the world is like. Much of the success of the enterprise derives from the community's willingness to defend that assumption, if necessary at considerable cost. Normal science, for example, often suppresses fundamental novelties because they are necessarily subversive of its basic commitments. Nevertheless, so long as those commitments retain an element of the arbitrary, the very nature of normal research ensures that novelty shall not be suppressed for very long. Sometimes a normal problem, one that ought to be solvable by known rules and procedures, resists the reiterated onslaught of the ablest members of the group within whose competence it falls. On other occasions a piece of equipment designed and constructed for the purpose of normal research fails to perform in the anticipated manner, revealing an anomaly that cannot, despite repeated effort, be aligned with professional expectation. In these and other ways besides, normal science repeatedly goes astray. And when it does—when, that is, the profession can no longer evade anomalies that subvert the existing tradition of scientific practice—then begin the extraordinary investigations that lead the profession at last to a new set of commitments, a new basis for the practice of science. The extraordinary episodes in which that shift of professional commitments occurs are the ones known in this essay as scientific revolutions. They are the tradition-shattering complements to the tradition-bound activity of normal science.

The most obvious examples of scientific revolutions are those famous episodes in scientific development that have often been labeled revolutions before. Therefore, in Sections IX and X, where the nature of scientific revolutions is first directly scrutinized, we shall deal repeatedly with the major turning points in scientific development associated with the names of Copernicus, Newton, Lavoisier, and Einstein. More clearly than most other episodes in the history of at least the physical sciences, these display what all scientific revolutions are about. Each of them necessitated the community's rejection of one time-honored scientific theory in favor of another incompatible with it. Each produced a consequent shift in the problems available for scientific scrutiny and in the standards by which the profession determined what should count as an admissible problem or as a legitimate problem-solution. And each transformed the scientific imagination in ways that we shall ultimately need to describe as a transformation of the world within which scientific work was done. Such changes, together with the controversies that almost always accompany them, are the defining characteristics of scientific revolutions.

These characteristics emerge with particular clarity from a study of, say, the Newtonian or the chemical revolution. It is, however, a fundamental thesis of this essay that they can also be retrieved from the study of many other episodes that were not so obviously revolutionary. For the far smaller professional group affected by them, Maxwell's equations were as revolutionary as Einstein's, and they were resisted accordingly. The invention of other new theories regularly, and appropriately, evokes the same response from some of the specialists on whose area of special competence they impinge. For these men the new theory implies a change in the rules governing the prior practice of normal science. Inevitably, therefore, it reflects upon much scientific work they have already successfully completed. That is why a new theory, however special its range of application, is seldom or never just an increment to what is already known. Its assimilation requires the reconstruction of prior theory and the re-evaluation of prior fact, an intrinsically revolutionary process that is seldom completed by a single man and never overnight. No wonder historians have had difficulty in dating precisely this extended process that their vocabulary impels them to view as an isolated event.

Nor are new inventions of theory the only scientific events that have revolutionary impact upon the specialists in whose domain they occur. The commitments that govern normal science specify not only what sorts of entities the universe does contain, but also, by implication, those that it does not. It follows, though the point will require extended discussion, that a discovery like that of oxygen or X-rays does not simply add one more item to the population of the scientist's world. Ultimately it has that effect, but not until the professional community has re-evaluated traditional experimental procedures, altered its conception of entities with which it has long been familiar, and, in the process, shifted the network of theory through which it deals with the world. Scientific fact and theory are not categorically separable, except perhaps within a single tradition of normal-scientific practice. That is why the unexpected discovery is not simply factual in its import and why the scientist's world is qualitatively transformed as well as quantitatively enriched by fundamental novelties of either fact or theory.

This extended conception of the nature of scientific revolutions is the one delineated in the pages that follow. Admittedly the extension strains customary usage. Nevertheless, I shall continue to speak even of discoveries as revolutionary, because it is just the possibility of relating their structure to that of, say, the Copernican revolution that makes the extended conception seem to me so important. The preceding discussion indicates how the complementary notions of normal science and of scientific revolutions will be developed in the nine sections immediately to follow. The rest of the essay attempts to dispose of three remaining central questions. Section XI, by discussing the textbook tradition, considers why scientific revolutions have previously been so difficult to see. Section XII describes the revolutionary competition between the proponents of the old normal-scientific tradition and the adherents of the new one. It thus considers the process that should somehow, in a theory of scientific inquiry, replace the confirmation or falsification procedures made familiar by our usual image of science. Competition between segments of the scientific community is the only historical process that ever actually results in the rejection of one previously accepted theory or in the adoption of another. Finally, Section XIII will ask how development through revolutions can be compatible with the apparently unique character of scientific progress. For that question, however, this essay will provide no more than the main outlines of an answer, one which depends upon characteristics of the scientific community that require much additional exploration and study.

Undoubtedly, some readers will already have wondered whether historical study can possibly effect the sort of conceptual transformation aimed at here. An entire arsenal of dichotomies is available to suggest that it cannot properly do so. History, we too often say, is a purely descriptive discipline. The theses suggested above are, however, often interpretive and sometimes normative. Again, many of my generalizations are about the sociology or social psychology of scientists; yet at least a few of my conclusions belong traditionally to logic or epistemology. In the preceding paragraph I may even seem to have violated the very influential contemporary distinction between "the context of discovery" and "the context of justification." Can anything more than profound confusion be indicated by this admixture of diverse fields and concerns?

Having been weaned intellectually on these distinctions and others like them, I could scarcely be more aware of their import and force. For many years I took them to be about the nature of knowledge, and I still suppose that, appropriately recast, they have something important to tell us. Yet my attempts to apply them, even *grosso modo*, to the actual situations in which knowledge is gained, accepted, and assimilated have made them seem extraordinarily problematic. Rather than being elementary logical or methodological distinctions, which would thus be prior to the analysis of scientific knowledge, they now seem integral parts of a traditional set of substantive answers to the very questions upon which they have been deployed. That circularity does not at all invalidate them. But it does make them parts of a theory and, by doing so, subjects them to the same scrutiny regularly applied to theories in other fields. If they are to have more than pure abstraction as their content, then that content must be discovered by observing them in application to the data they are meant to elucidate. How could history of science fail to be a source of phenomena to which theories about knowledge may legitimately be asked to apply?

NOTE ON SOURCES.   Thomas Kuhn, *The Structure of Scientific Revolutions* (Chicago: University of Chicago Press, 1970). Our pages 642–644 are Kuhn's pages 10–13; our pages 644–649 are Kuhn's pages 1–9. Note that Kuhn's original order of presentation has changed.

3   PAUL FEYERABEND

RELATIVISM, EVEN IN SCIENCE, IS THE ONLY CONCLUSION

FROM KUHN TO FEYERABEND.   Paul Feyerabend argues that science is not a privileged source of knowledge—it is just one way among many to find out about the world. In Kuhnian language, science uses one group of related paradigms, but there are other, competing, paradigms that stand behind other methods. For example, Western, so-called scientific, medicine is one way to look at health problems, but there are other ways. Some of these other ways (herbal medicine, homeopathy, Ayurvedic, Christian science)* do not even recognize the same problems. Some use very different sorts of cures. Each way to deal with health problems may have its own standards for judging success. These standards are found in the paradigms of each method. Thus it would be a mistake to insist that all types of alternative medicines be subject to the evaluative criteria of Western medicine.

---

* See the Glossary for definitions of these alternative styles of practicing medicine.

BIOGRAPHICAL NOTE.   Paul Feyerabend was born in Vienna, Austria in 1924. He received a Ph.D. in philosophy and physics from the University of Vienna in 1951. He has taught at Yale University, University College London, Free University Berlin, the University of California at Berkeley, and the Federal Institute of Technology in Zurich. Prof. Feyerabend is now retired. He has published technical papers and broader appeals for political control of science which, he argues, is only one of the many ways of gaining knowledge.

THE ARGUMENT OF THE PASSAGES.   To understand the success of science one must realize that there is no single procedure which, if followed, guarantees success. Rather, what works at one time for one science may not work at another time for another science. Feyerabend believes that this is a lesson taught by the history of science. Like Kuhn, he demystifies what is often referred to as "*the* scientific method." There can be different sciences. Each science is a function of how people live and what they value. One important implication of Feyerabend's view is that there is no single way to judge science as good or bad. Feyerabend concludes by pointing out that, "The stories told and the activities they (people all over the world) engaged in enriched their lives, protected them and gave them meaning." So to Feyerabend, Western science should be seen as one story among many. One story among equals. (In the Epilogue, we use the concept of story to help answer the question, "How can I make sense out of life?") Total objectivity, the claim that truth is held by one story and one story alone, is an impossibility. (Feyerabend notes that the seeds for this sort of relativism were sown by Sextus Empiricus, a skeptic philosopher of the second century A.D., long before Kuhn ever wrote.)

Kuhn's position leads to relativism regarding what counts as knowledge, and Feyerabend has been quick to point this out. Kuhn stresses the importance of social and political factors in science. Kuhn notes the role of paradigms in the historical development of science. At any given time, Kuhn maintains, a science can be judged only relative to its paradigm. Feyerabend makes it plain that on these grounds, knowledge itself is relative to cultural standards. His example of the Cuahuila Indians is very vivid in this regard. Feyerabend wants us to realize that without modern science, these Indians were able to flourish in a way that modern Americans cannot.

This book proposes a thesis and draws consequences from it. The thesis is: *the events, procedures and results that constitute the sciences have no common structure*; there are no elements that occur in every scientific investigation but are missing elsewhere. Concrete developments (such as the overthrow of steady state cosmologies and the discovery of the structure of DNA) have distinct features and we can often explain why and how these features led to success. But not every discovery can be accounted for in the same manner, and procedures that paid off in the past may create havoc when imposed on the future. Successful research does not obey general standards; it relies now on one trick, now on another; the moves that advance it and the standards that define what counts as an advance are not always known to the movers. Far-reaching changes of outlook, such as the so-called 'Copernican Revolution' or the 'Darwinian Revolution,' affect different areas of research in different ways and receive different impulses from them. A theory of science that devises standards and structural elements for *all* scientific activities and authorizes them by reference to 'Reason' or 'Rationality' may impress outsiders—but it is much too crude an instrument for the people on the spot, that is, for scientists facing some concrete research problem.

In this book I try to support the thesis by historical examples. Such support does not *establish* it; it makes it *plausible* and the way in which it is reached indicates how future statements about 'the nature of science' may be undermined; given any rule, or any general statement about the sciences, there always exist developments which are praised by those who support the rule but which show that the rule does more damage than good.

One consequence of the thesis is that *scientific successes cannot be explained in a simple way*. We cannot say: 'the structure of the atomic nucleus was found because people did A, B, C . . . ' where A, B and C are procedures which can be understood independently of their use in nuclear physics. All we can do is to give a historical account of the details, including social circumstances, accidents and personal idiosyncrasies.

Another consequence is that *the success of 'science' cannot be used as an argument for treating as yet unsolved problems in a standardized way*. That could be done only if there are procedures that can be detached from particular research situations and whose presence guarantees success. The thesis says that there are no such procedures. Referring to the success of 'science' in order to justify, say, quantifying human behavior is therefore an argument without substance. Quantification works in some cases, fails in others; for example, it ran into difficulties in one of the apparently most quantitative of all sciences, celestial mechanics (special region: stability of the planetary system) and was replaced by qualitative (topological) considerations.

It also follows that *'non-scientific' procedures cannot be pushed aside by argument*. To say: 'the procedure you used is non-scientific, therefore we cannot trust your results and cannot give you money for research' assumes that 'science' is successful and that it is successful because it uses uniform procedures. The first part of the assertion ('science is always successful') is not true, if by 'science' we mean things done by scientists—there are lots of failures also. The second part—that successes are due to uniform procedures—is not true because there are no such procedures. Scientists are like architects who build buildings of different sizes and different shapes and who can be judged only *after* the event, i.e., only after they have finished their structure. It may stand up, it may fall down—nobody knows.

But if scientific achievements can be judged only after the event and if there is no abstract way of ensuring success beforehand, then there exists no special way of weighing scientific promises either—scientists are no better off than anybody else in these matters, they only know more details. This means that *the public can participate in the discussion without disturbing existing roads to success* (there are no such roads). In cases where the scientists' work affects the public it even *should* participate: first, because it is a concerned party (many scientific decisions affect public life); secondly, because such participation is the best scientific education the public can get—a full democratization of science (which includes the protection of minorities such as scientists) is not in conflict with science. It is in conflict with a philosophy, often called 'Rationalism,' that uses a frozen image of science to terrorize people unfamiliar with its practice.

A consequence I did not develop in my book but which is closely connected with its basic thesis is that *there can be many different kinds of science*. People starting from different social backgrounds will approach the world in different ways and learn different things about it. People survived millennia before Western science arose; to do this they had to know their surroundings up to and including elements of astronomy. 'Several thousand Cuahuila Indians never exhausted the natural resources of a desert region in South California, in which today only a handful of white families manage to subsist. They lived in a land of plenty, for in this apparently completely barren territory, they were familiar with no less than sixty kinds of edible plants and twenty-eight others of narcotic, stimulant or medical properties' (C. Levi-Strauss, *The Savage Mind*, Chicago, 1966, pp. 4f). The knowledge that preserves the lifestyles of nomads was acquired and is preserved in a non-scientific way ('science' now being modern natural science). Chinese technology for a long time lacked any Western-scientific underpinning and yet it was far ahead of contemporary Western technology. It is true that Western science now reigns supreme all over the globe; however, the reason was not insight in its 'inherent rationality' but power play (the colonizing nations imposed their ways of living) and the need for weapons: Western science so far has created the most efficient instruments of death. The remark that without Western science many 'Third World nations' would be starving is correct but one should add that the troubles were created, not alleviated by earlier forms of 'development.' It is also true that Western medicine helped eradicate parasites and some infectious diseases but this does not show that Western science is the only tradition that has good things to offer and that other forms of inquiry are without any merit whatsoever. *First-world science is one science among many*; by claiming to be more it ceases to be an instrument of research and turns into a (political) pressure group. More on these matters can be found in my book *Farewell to Reason*, London, 1987.

My main motive in writing the book was humanitarian, not intellectual. I wanted to support people, not to 'advance knowledge.' People all over the world have developed ways of surviving in partly dangerous, partly agreeable surroundings. The stories they told and the activities they engaged in enriched their lives, protected them and gave them meaning. The 'progress of knowledge and civilization'— as the process of pushing Western ways and values into all corners of the globe is being called—destroyed these wonderful products of human ingenuity and compassion without a single glance in their direction. 'Progress of knowledge' in many places meant killing of minds. Today old traditions are being revived and people try again to adapt their lives to the ideas of their ancestors. I have tried to show, by an analysis of the apparently hardest parts of science, the natural sciences, that science, properly understood has no argument against such a procedure. There are many scientists who act accordingly. Physicians, anthropologists and environmentalists are starting to adapt their procedures to the values of the people they are supposed to advise. I am not against a science so understood. Such a science is one of the most wonderful inventions of the human mind. But I am against ideologies that use the name of science for cultural murder.

NOTE ON SOURCES.   The material in this section comes from the introduction of Paul Feyerabend's book, *Against Method*, rev. ed. (London: Routledge Chapman & Hall, 1988), pp. 1–4.

4 LARRY LAUDAN

KUHN HAS MISREAD SCIENCE AND ITS HISTORY

FROM FEYERABEND TO LAUDAN.   Kuhn's new approach to science and its history fomented a revolution of its own, but many philosophers were skeptical. They were skeptical because (1) their intuitions told them that Western-style science did reveal the real way the world was; and, (2) because they just could not accept the extreme relativism about knowledge which seemed to follow from Kuhn's central theses. These philosophers aimed their analytic skills at Kuhn and found much to question. Focusing on his concept of paradigm, Kuhn's critics often pointed out that Kuhn was never clear on exactly what he meant. Another way of attacking Kuhn was to claim that he had misread history and thereby had drawn the wrong philosophical conclusions.

Our next author, Larry Laudan, pursues this line of attack. Laudan tries to show how Kuhn may have been misled by the history of science.

BIOGRAPHICAL NOTE.   Larry Laudan was born in Austin, Texas in 1941. He received his Ph.D. in philosophy from Princeton University in 1965. He has taught at the University of Pittsburgh, where he was chairperson of the Department of History and Philosophy of Science. He is currently professor of philosophy at the University of Hawaii. Laudan has published extensively in the area of philosophy and history of science. His most recent book, *Science and Relativism* (Chicago: University of Chicago Press, 1990), is an attack (in dialogue form) on the sort of relativism outlined by Feyerabend and Rorty.

THE ARGUMENT OF THE PASSAGES.   If Kuhn is right, then all methodological orthodoxies (especially positivism) are wrong. But Kuhn has made some crucial errors. First, according to Laudan, paradigms can exist at three levels:

1. conceptual framework–ontological claims,
2. rules that specify methods and techniques,
3. cognitive goals or ideals.

KUHN ON THE UNITS OF SCIENTIFIC CHANGE

It is notorious that the key Kuhnian concept of a paradigm is multiply ambiguous. Among its most central meanings are the following three: First and foremost, a paradigm offers a conceptual framework for classifying and explaining natural objects. That is, it specifies in a generic way the sorts of entities which are thought to populate a certain domain of experience and it sketches out how those entities generally interact. In short, every paradigm will make certain claims about what populates the world. Such ontological claims mark that paradigm off from others, since each paradigm is thought to postulate entities and modes of interaction which differentiate it from other paradigms. Second, a paradigm will specify the appropriate methods, techniques, and tools of inquiry for studying the objects in the relevant domain of application. Just as different paradigms have different ontologies, so they involve substantially different methodologies. (Consider, for instance, the very different methods of research and theory evaluation associated with behaviorism and cognitive psychology respectively.) These methodological commitments are persistent ones, and they characterize the paradigm throughout its history. Finally, the proponents of different paradigms will, according to Kuhn, espouse different sets of cognitive goals or ideals. Although the partisans of two paradigms may (and usually do) share some aims in common, Kuhn insists that the goals are not fully overlapping between followers of rival paradigms. Indeed, to accept a paradigm is, for Kuhn, to subscribe to a complex of cognitive values which the proponents of no other paradigm accept fully.

Paradigm change, on this account, clearly represents a break of great magnitude. To trade in one paradigm for another is to involve oneself in changes at each of the three levels defined . . . above. We give up one ontology for another, one methodology for another, and one set of cognitive goals for another. Moreover, according to Kuhn, this change is *simultaneous* rather than *sequential*. It is worth observing in passing that, for all Kuhn's vitriol about the impoverishment of older models of scientific rationality, there are several quite striking similarities between the classical version of the hierarchical model and Kuhn's alternative to it. Both lay central stress on the justificatory interactions between claims at the factual, methodological, and axiological levels. Both emphasize the centrality of values and standards as providing criteria of choice between rival views lower in the hierarchy. Where Kuhn breaks, and breaks radically, with the tradition is in his insistence that rationality must be relativized to choices within a paradigm rather than choices between paradigms. Whereas the older account of the hierarchical model had generally supposed that core axiological and methodological commitments would typically be common property across the sciences of an epoch, Kuhn asserts that there are methodological and axiological discrepancies between any two paradigms. Indeed (as we shall see below), one of the core failings of Kuhn's position is that it so fully internalizes the classical hierarchical approach that, whenever the latter breaks down (as it certainly does in grappling with interparadigmatic debate, or any other sort of disagreement involving conflicting goals), Kuhn's approach has nothing more to offer concerning the possibility of rational choices.[1]

For now, however, the immediate point to stress is that Kuhn portrays paradigm changes in ways that make them seem to be abrupt and global ruptures in the life of a scientific community. So great is this supposed transition that several of Kuhn's critics have charged that, despite Kuhn's proclaimed intentions to the contrary, his analysis inevitably turns scientific change into a nonrational or irrational process. In part, but only in part, it is Kuhn's infelicitous terminology that produces this impression. Notoriously, he speaks of the acceptance of a new paradigm as a "conversion experience,"[2] conjuring up a picture of the scientific revolutionary as a born-again

---

[1]   It has been insufficiently noted just how partial Kuhn's break with positivism is, so far as cognitive goals and values are concerned. As I show in detail below, most of his problems about the alleged incomparability of theories arise because Kuhn accepts without argument the positivist claim that cognitive values or standards at the top of the hierarchy are fundamentally immune to rational negotiation.

[2]   Kuhn, 1962.

Christian, long on zeal and short on argument. At other times he likens paradigm change to an "irreversible Gestalt-shift."[3] Less metaphorically, he claims that there is never a point at which it is "unreasonable" to hold onto an old paradigm rather than to accept a new one.[4] Such language does not encourage one to imagine that paradigm change is exactly the result of a careful and deliberate weighing-up of the respective strengths of rival contenders. But impressions based on some of Kuhn's more lurid language can probably be rectified by cleaning up some of the vocabulary of *The Structure of Scientific Revolutions*, a task on which Kuhn has been embarked more or less since the book first appeared.[5] No changes of terminology, however, will alter the fact that some central features of Kuhn's model of science raise serious roadblocks to a rational analysis of scientific change. The bulk of this chapter is devoted to examining some of those impedimenta. Before we turn to that examination, however, I want to stress early on that my complaint with Kuhn is not merely that he has failed to give any normatively robust or rational account of theory change, serious as that failing is. As I show below, he has failed even at the descriptive or narrative task of offering an accurate story about the manner in which large-scale changes of scientific allegiance occur.

But there is yet more fundamental respect in which Kuhn's approach presents obstacles to an understanding of the dynamics of theory change. Specifically, by insisting that individual paradigms have an integral and static character—that changes take place only between, rather than within, paradigms—Kuhn has missed the single feature of science which promises to mediate and rationalize the transition from one world view or paradigm to another. Kuhn's various writings on this subject leave the reader in no doubt that he thinks the parts of a paradigm go together as an inseparable package. As he puts it in *The Structure of Scientific Revolutions*, "In learning a paradigm the scientist acquires theory, methods, and standards together, usually in an *inextricable* mix."[6] This theme, of the inextricable and inseparable ingredients of a paradigm, is a persistent one in Kuhn's work. One key aim of this chapter is to show how drastically we need to alter Kuhn's views about how tightly the pieces of a paradigm's puzzle fit together before we can expect to understand how paradigmlike change occurs.

Loosening up the fit.—Without too heavy an element of caricature, we can describe world-view models such as Kuhn's along the following lines: one group or faction in the scientific community accepts a particular "big picture." That requires acquiescence in a certain ontology of nature, acceptance of a specific set of rules about how to investigate nature, and adherence to a set of cognitive values about the teleology of natural inquiry (i.e., about the goals that science seeks). On this analysis, large-scale scientific change involves the replacement of one such world view by another, a process that entails the simultaneous repudiation of the key elements of the old picture and the adoption of corresponding (but of course different) elements of the new. In short, scientific change looks something like Figure 3.

---

3   Ibid.
4   Ibid., p. 159.
5   As Kuhn himself remarks, he has been attempting "to eliminate misunderstandings for which my own past rhetoric is doubtless partially responsible" (1970, pp. 259–260).
6   Kuhn, 1962, p. 108; my italics.

WV1 (ontology 1, methodology 1, values 1)

↓

WV2 (ontology 2, methodology 2, values 2)

Figure 3.   *Kuhn's Picture of Theory Change*

When scientific change is construed so globally, it is no small challenge to see how it could be other than a conversion experience. If different scientists not only espouse different theories but also subscribe to different standards of appraisal and ground those standards in different and conflicting systems of cognitive goals, then it is difficult indeed to imagine that scientific change could be other than a whimsical change of style or taste. There could apparently never be compelling grounds for saying that one paradigm is better than another, for one has to ask: Better relative to which standards and whose goals? To make matters worse—much worse—Kuhn often suggested that each paradigm is more or less automatically guaranteed to satisfy its own standards and to fail the standards of rival paradigms, thus producing a kind of self-reinforcing solipsism in science. As he once put it, "To the extent, as significant as it is incomplete, that two scientific schools disagree about what is a problem and what is a solution, they will inevitably talk through each other when debating the merits of their respective paradigms. In the partially circular arguments that regularly result, *each* paradigm will be shown to satisfy more or less the criteria that it dictates for itself and to fall short of those dictated by its opponent."[7] Anyone who writes prose of this sort must think that scientific decision making is fundamentally capricious. Or at least so many of us thought in the mid- and late 1960s, as philosophers began to digest Kuhn's ideas. In fact, if one looks at several discussions of Kuhn's work dating from that period, one sees this theme repeatedly. Paradigm change, it was said, could not possibly be a reasoned or rational process, Kuhn, we thought, has made science into an irrational "monster."

Next, Laudan claims that we rarely shift ontological claims, methodological rules, and cognitive goals all at once, as Kuhn implies. Too, rationality is not so paradigm-relative as Kuhn believes. Kuhn makes these mistakes because he doesn't present an accurate reflection of history and because ontological claims, methodological rules, and cognitive goals are logically separate, not all to be lumped together by Kuhn's term, *paradigm.* Moreover, external considerations are not always the deciding factors as paradigms shift. For example, Kuhn claimed that Lavoisier won out over Priestley because the followers of Priestley died out, but many historians have disputed Kuhn's reading of this episode.

The clear implication of Kuhn's writings is that interparadigmatic debate is necessarily inconclusive and thus can never be brought to rational closure. When closure does occur, it must therefore be imposed on the situation by such external factors as the demise of some of the participants or the manipulation of the levers of power and reward within the institutional structure of the scientific community. Philosophers of science, almost without exception, have found such implications troubling, for they

---

7   Ibid., pp. 108–109.

directly confute what philosophers have been at pains for two millennia to establish: to wit, that scientific disputes, and more generally all disagreements about matters of fact, are in principle open to rational clarification and resolution. It is on the strength of passages such as those I have mentioned that Kuhn has been charged with relativism, subjectivism, irrationalism, and a host of other sins high on the philosopher's hit list.

There is some justice in these criticisms of Kuhn's work, for (as I suggested in Chap. 1) Kuhn has failed over the past twenty years to elaborate any coherent account of consensus formation, that is, of the manner in which scientists could ever agree to support one world view rather than another. But that flaw, serious though it is, can probably be remedied, for I want to suggest that the problem of consensus formation can be solved if we make two fundamental amendments in Kuhn's position. First (as argued in Chap. 3), we must replace the hierarchical view of justification with the reticulated picture, thereby making cognitive values "negotiable." Second, we must simply drop Kuhn's insistence on the integral character of world views or paradigms. More specifically, we solve the problems of consensus once we realize that *the various components of a world view are individually negotiable and individually replaceable in a piecemeal fashion* (that is, in such a manner that replacement of one element need not require wholesale repudiation of all the other components), Kuhn himself grants, of course, that some components of a world view can be revised; that is what "paradigm articulation" is all about. But for Kuhn, as for such other world view theorists as Lakatos and Foucault, the central commitments of a world view, its "hard core" (to use Lakatos's marvelous phrase), are not revisable—short of rejecting the entire world view. The core ontology of a world view or paradigm, along with its methodology and axiology, comes on a take-it-or-leave-it basis. Where these levels of commitment are concerned, Kuhn (along with such critics of him as Lakatos) is an uncompromising holist. Consider, for instance, his remark: "Just because it is a transition between incommensurables, the transition between competing paradigms cannot be made a step at a time . . . like the Gestalt-switch, it must occur all at once or not at all."[8] Kuhn could hardly be less ambiguous on this point.

But paradigms or research programs need not be so rigidly conceived, and typically they are not so conceived by scientists; nor, if we reflect on it a moment, should they be so conceived. As I show in earlier chapters, there are complex justifactory interconnections among a scientist's ontology, his methodology, and his axiology. If a scientist's methodology fails to justify his ontology; if his methodology fails to promote his cognitive aims; if his cognitive aims prove to be utopian—in all these cases the scientist will have compelling reasons for replacing one component or other of his world view with an element that does the job better. You need not modify everything else.

To be more precise, the choice confronting a scientist whose world view is under strain in this manner need be nothing like as stark as the choice sketched in figure 3 (where it is a matter of sticking with what he knows best unchanged or throwing that over for something completely different), but rather a choice where the modification of one core element—while retaining the others—may bring a decided improvement. . . .

But, once we begin to play around with the transformations permitted by the reticulational model, we see that the transition from one paradigm or world view to another can itself be a step-wise process, requiring none of the wholesale shifts in

8   Ibid., p. 149.

allegiance at every level required by Kuhn's analysis. . . . As William Whewell showed more than a century ago, precisely some such series of shifts occurred in the gradual capitulation of Cartesian physicists to the natural philosophy of Newton.[9]

In effect, I am claiming that the solution of the problem of consensus formation in the multiparadigm situation to be nothing more than a special or degenerate instance of unitraditional change. It follows that, if we can show that the unitraditional fairy tale has something going for it, then we will solve both forms of the consensus-formation problem simultaneously. The core question is whether the gradualist myth, which I have just sketched out, is better supported by the historical record than the holistic picture associated with Kuhn.

As an alternative to the Kuhnian view, Laudan suggests what he calls the "reticulated view." On this view, the three parts of a paradigm can be negotiated. One part can be kept, another changed. The point is that it is not necessary (nor is it likely) that all three must change at once. According to Laudan, history is on his side.

Kuhn says that there can be no change in values unless there is a revolution. Laudan offers counterexamples.

One striking way of formulating the contrast between the piecemeal and the holistic models, and thus designing a test to choose between them, is to ask a fairly straightforward question about the historical record: Is it true that the major historical shifts in the methodological rules of science and in the cognitive values of scientists have invariably been contemporaneous with one another *and* with shifts in substantive theories and ontologies? The holistic account is clearly committed to an affirmative answer to the question. Indeed, it is a straightforward corollary of Kuhn's analysis that changes in rules or values, when they occur, will occur only when a scientific revolution takes place, that is, only when there is a concomitant shift in theories, methods, and values. A change in values without an associated change in basic ontology is not a permissible variation countenanced in the Kuhnian scheme.[10] Nor is a change in methods possible for Kuhn without a paradigm change. Kuhn's analysis flatly denies that the values and norms of a "mature" science can shift in the absence of a revolution. Yet there are plenty of examples one may cite to justify the assertion made here that changes at the three levels do not always go together. I shall mention two such examples.

---

[9]   See Whewell's remarkably insightful essay of 1851, where he remarks, apropos the transition from one global theory to another: "the change . . . is effected by a transformation, or series of transformations, of the earlier hypothesis, by means of which it is brought nearer and nearer to the second [i.e., later]" (1851, p. 139).

[10]   Some amplification of this point is required. Kuhn evidently believes that there are some values that transcend specific paradigms. He mentions such examples as the demand for accuracy, consistency, and simplicity. The fortunes of these values are not linked to specific paradigms. Thus, if they were to change, such change would presumably be independent of shifts in paradigms. In Kuhn's view, however, these values have persisted unchanged since the seventeenth century. Or, rather, scientists have invoked these values persistently since that time; strictly speaking, on Kuhn's analysis, these values are changing constantly, since each scientist interprets them slightly differently. For a detailed discussion of Kuhn's handling of these quasi-shared values, see the final selection of this chapter.

Consider, first, a well-known shift at the level of methodological rules. From the time of Bacon until the early nineteenth century most scientists subscribed to variants of the rules of inductive inference associated with Bacon, Hume, and Newton. The methods of agreement, difference, and concomitant variations were a standard part of the repertoire of most working scientists for two hundred years. These rules, at least as then understood, foreclosed the postulation of any theoretical or hypothetical entities, since observable bodies were the only sort of objects and properties to which one could apply traditional inductive methods. More generally (as shown in Chap. 3), thinkers of the Enlightenment believed it important to develop rules of inquiry which would exclude unobservable entities and bring to heel the tendency of scientists to indulge their *l'esprit de système*. Newton's famous third rule of reasoning in philosophy, the notorious "hypotheses non fingo," was but a particularly succinct and influential formulation of this trenchant empiricism.

It is now common knowledge that by the late nineteenth century this methodological orientation had largely vanished from the writings of major scientists and methodologists. Whewell, Peirce, Helmholtz, Mach, Darwin, Hertz, and a host of other luminaries had, by the 1860s and 1870s, come to believe that it was quite legitimate for science to postulate unobservable entities, and that most of the traditional rules of inductive reasoning had been superseded by the logic of hypothetico-deduction. Elsewhere I have described this shift in detail. What is important for our purposes is both that it occurred and when it occurred. That it took place would be denied, I think, by no one who studies the record; determining precisely when it occurred is more problematic, although probably no scholar would quarrel with the claim that it comes in the period from 1800 to 1860. And a dating as fuzzy as that is sufficient to make out my argument.

For here we have a shift in the history of the explicit methodology of the scientific community as significant as one can imagine—from methods of enumerative and eliminative induction to the method of hypothesis—occurring across the spectrum of the theoretical sciences, from celestial mechanics to chemistry and biology. Yet where is the larger and more global scientific revolution of which this methodological shift was the concomitant? There were of course revolutions, and important ones, in this period. Yet this change in methodology cannot be specifically linked to any of the familiar revolutions of the period. The method of hypothesis did not become the orthodoxy in science of the late nineteenth century because it rode on the coattails of any specific change in ontology or scientific values. So far as I can see, this methodological revolution was independent of any particular program of research in any one of the sciences, which is not to say that it did not reflect some very general tendencies appearing across the board in scientific research. The holistic model, which would have us believe that changes in methodological orientation are invariably linked to changes in values and ontology, is patently mistaken here. Nor, if one reflects on the nature of methodological discussion, should we have expected otherwise. As noted in Chapter 2, methodological rules can reasonably be criticized and altered if one discovers that they fail optimally to promote our cognitive aims. If our aims shift, as they would in a Kuhnian paradigm shift, we would of course expect a reappraisal of our methods of inquiry in light of their suitability for promoting the new goals. But, even when our goals shift not at all, we sometimes discover arguments and evidence which indicate that the methods we have been using all along are not really suitable for our purposes. Such readjustments of methodological orientation, in the absence of a paradigm shift, are a direct corollary of the reticulational model as I described it earlier; yet they pose a serious anomaly for Kuhn's analysis.

What about changes in aims, as opposed to rules? Is it not perhaps more plausible to imagine, with Kuhn, that changes of cognitive values are always part of broader shifts of paradigm or world view? Here again, the historical record speaks out convincingly against this account. Consider, very briefly, one example: the abandonment of "infallible knowledge" as an epistemic aim for science. As before, my historical account will have to be "potted" for purposes of brevity; but there is ample serious scholarship to back up the claims I shall be making.

That scholarship has established quite convincingly that, during the course of the nineteenth century, the view of science as aiming at certainty gave way among most scientists to a more modest program of producing theories that were plausible, probable, or well tested. As Peirce and Dewey have argued, this shift represents one of the great watersheds in the history of scientific philosophy: the abandonment of the quest for certainty. More or less from the time of Aristotle onward, scientists had sought theories that were demonstrable and apodictically certain. Although empiricists and rationalists disagreed about precisely how to certify knowledge as certain and incorrigible, all agreed that science was aiming exclusively at the production of such knowledge. This same view of science largely prevailed at the beginning of the nineteenth century. But by the end of that century this demonstrative and infallibilist ideal was well and truly dead. Scientists of almost every persuasion were insistent that science could, at most, aspire to the status of highly probable knowledge. Certainty, incorrigibility, and indefeasibility ceased to figure among the central aims of most twentieth-century scientists.

The full story surrounding the replacement of the quest for certainty by a thoroughgoing fallibilism is long and complicated: I have attempted to sketch out parts of that story elsewhere. What matters for our purposes here is not so much the details of this epistemic revolution, but the fact that this profound transformation was not specifically associated with the emergence of any new scientific paradigms or research programs. The question of timing is crucial, for it is important to see that this deep shift in axiological sensibilities was independent of any specific change in scientific world view or paradigm. No new scientific tradition or paradigm in the nineteenth century was associated with a specifically fallibilist axiology. Quite the reverse, fallibilism came to be associated with virtually every major program of scientific research by the mid- to late nineteenth century. Atomists and antiatomists, wave theorists and particle theorists, Darwinians and Lamarckians, uniformitarians and catastrophists—all subscribed to the new consensus about the corrigibility and indemonstrability of scientific theories. A similar story could be told about other cognitive values which have gone the way of all flesh. The abandonment of intelligibility, of the requirement of picturable or mechanically constructible models of natural processes, of the insistence on "complete" descriptions of nature—all reveal a similar pattern. The abandonment of each of these cognitive ideals was largely independent of shifts in basic theories about nature.

Once again, the holistic approach leads to expectations that are confounded by the historical record. Changes in values and changes in substantive ontologies or methodologies show no neat isomorphism. Change certainly occurs at all levels, and sometimes changes are concurrent, but there is no striking covariance between the timing of changes at one level and the timing of those at any other. I conclude from such examples that scientific change is substantially more piecemeal than the holistic model would suggest. Value changes do not always accompany, nor are they accompanied by, changes in scientific paradigm. Shifts in methodological rules may, but need not, be associated with shifts in either values or ontologies. The three levels, although unquestionably interrelated, do not come as an inseparable package on a take-it-or-leave-it basis.

This result is of absolutely decisive importance for understanding the processes of scientific change. Because these changes are not always concomitant, we are often in a position to hold one or two of the three levels fixed while we decide whether to make modifications at the disputed level. The existence of these (temporarily) fixed and thus shared points of perspective provides a crucial form of triangulation. Since theories, methodologies, and axiologies stand together in a kind of justificatory triad, we can use those doctrines about which there is agreement to resolve the remaining areas where we disagree. The uncontested levels will not always resolve the controversy, for underdetermination is an ever-present possibility. But the fact that the levels of agreement are sometimes insufficient to terminate the controversy provides no comfort for Kuhn's subjectivist thesis that those levels of agreement are never sufficient to resolve the debate. As logicians say, we need to be very careful about our quantifiers here. Some writers have not always exercised the care they should. Kuhn, for instance, confusedly slides from (*a*) the correct claim that the shared values of scientists are, in certain situations, incapable of yielding unambiguously a preference between two rival theories to (*b*) the surely mistaken claim that the shared values of scientists are never sufficient to warrant a preference between rival paradigms. Manifestly in some instances, the shared rules and standards of methodology are unavailing. But neither Kuhn nor anyone else has established that the rules, evaluative criteria, and values to which scientists subscribe are generally so ambiguous in application that virtually any theory or paradigm can be shown to satisfy them. And we must constantly bear in mind the point that, even when theories are underdetermined by a set of rules or standards, many theories will typically be ruled out by the relevant rules; and if one party to a scientific debate happens to be pushing for a theory that can be shown to violate those rules, then the rule will eliminate that theory from contention.

The rules of inductive inference shifted without a revolution. By the mid-nineteenth century, theorizing was considered *de rigeur*, replacing the demand for experiment. This was a shift in methodology across many different disciplines. But no single revolution accompanied this methodological shift. So Kuhn is wrong.

Giving up the idea of certain knowledge and replacing it with probability is a shift in values. But this very shift did occur with no scientific revolution. Again, Kuhn is wrong.

Laudan concludes that there may have been some Kuhnian revolutions, but scientific change in general is gradual. There is no good reason to suppose that what we all take to be rationality cannot be used to decide between rival scientific outlooks. To claim that it is just as rational to believe in medicine based on witches as it is to believe in medicine based on present-day biochemistry and physiology just makes no real sense.

> . . . It is my impression that the overwhelming majority of theory transitions in the history of science (including shifts as profound as that from creationist biology to evolution, from energeticist to atomistic views on the nature of matter, from catastrophism to uniformitarianism in geology, from particle to wave theories of light)

have not taken place by means of Gestalt-like shifts at all levels concurrently. Often, change occurs on a single level only (e.g., the Darwinian revolution of the triumph of atomism, where it was chiefly theory or ontology that changed); sometimes it occurs on two levels simultaneously; rarely do we find an abrupt and wholesale shift of doctrines at all three levels.

This fact about scientific change has a range of important implications for our understanding of scientific debate and scientific controversy. Leaving aside the atypical case of simultaneous shifts at all three levels (discussed in Chap. 3), it means that most instances of scientific change—including most of the events we call scientific revolutions—occur amid a significant degree of consensus at a variety of levels among the contending parties. Scientists may, for instance, disagree about specific theories yet agree about the appropriate rules for theory appraisal. They may even disagree about both theories and rules but accept the same cognitive values. Alternatively, they may accept the same theories and rules yet disagree about the cognitive values they espouse. In all these cases there is no reason to speak (with Kuhn) of "incommensurable choices" or "conversion experiences," or (with Foucault) about abrupt "ruptures of thought," for there is in each instance the possibility of bringing the disagreement to rational closure. Of course, it may happen in specific cases that the mechanisms of rational adjudication are of no avail, for the parties may be contending about matters that are underdetermined by the beliefs and standards the contending parties share in common. But, even here, we can still say that there are rational rules governing the game being played, and that the moves being made (i.e., the beliefs being debated and the arguments being arrayed for and against them) are in full compliance with the rules of the game.

Above all, we must bear in mind that it has never been established that such instances of holistic change constitute more than a tiny fraction of scientific disagreements. Because such cases are arguably so atypical, it follows that sociologists and philosophers of science who predicate their theories of scientific change and cognition on the presumed ubiquity of irresolvable standoffs between monolithic world views (of the sort that Kuhn describes in *Structure of Scientific Revolutions*) run the clear risk of failing to recognize the complex ways in which rival theories typically share important background assumptions in common. To put it differently, global claims about the immunity of interparadigmatic disputes to rational adjudication (and such claims are central in the work of both Kuhn and Lakatos) depend for their plausibility on systematically ignoring the piecemeal character of most forms of scientific change and on a gross exaggeration of the impotence of rational considerations to bring such disagreements to closure. Beyond that, I have argued that, even if interparadigmatic clashes had the character Kuhn says they do (namely, of involving little or no overlap at any of the three levels), it still would not follow that there are no rational grounds for a critical and comparative assessment of the rival paradigms. In sum, no adequate support has been provided for the claim that clashes between rival scientific camps can never, or rarely ever, be resolved in an objective fashion. The problem of consensus formation, which I earlier suggested was the great Kuhnian enigma, can be resolved, but only if we realize that science has adjudicatory mechanisms whose existence has gone unnoticed by Kuhn and the other holists.

Note on Sources.   Larry Laudan, *Science and Values* (Berkeley: University of California Press, 1984), Chapter 4.

5   ALISON JAGGAR

SCIENCE IS NEITHER OBJECTIVE NOR UNEMOTIONAL

FROM LAUDAN TO JAGGAR.   Laudan represents a current reaction to the view of Feyerabend, and those who agree with him, that our feeling that science is objective represents nothing more than a bias. Laudan is trying to find something of worth in the traditional view of science as objective. Alison Jaggar takes what appears to be an extremist view on the nature of science. Looking at science as a feminist, she sees science as a male-dominated institution. She concludes that science has never been, and could not be, free of emotion.

BIOGRAPHICAL NOTE.   Alison Jaggar was born in England. She received a M.Litt. degree from the University of Edinburgh in 1967 and a Ph.D. in philosophy from the State University of New York at Buffalo in 1970. She has taught at Miami University (of Ohio) and the University of Cincinnati. She is currently at the University of Colorado. Her publications cover many of the traditional areas of philosophy.

THE ARGUMENT OF THE PASSAGES.   Jaggar points out that once the positivist distinction between the logic of discovery and the logic of justification is denied, then emotion can become a part of science. She maintains that emotion has always been a part of science—but only men have decided which emotions are allowable. Jaggar calls emotions not allowed by men "outlaw emotions." She mentions Nobel prize-winning geneticist Barbara McClintock as one scientist who had outlaw emotions. McClintock often described herself as having a feeling for the organism she researched, corn. It was this feeling—a kind of empathy with the corn—that allowed her insights beyond those of her colleagues. Thus it was that she discovered the fact that genes "jump," or move on the chromosome. Previously, scientists had believed genes were positionally stable. Her views were at first rejected, but she turned out to be correct.

Jaggar uses this sort of example to support her contention that emotions can direct our attention to new investigations and thence to new pictures of the world.

> . . . Western epistemology has tended to view emotion with suspicion and even hostility. This derogatory western attitude towards emotion, like the earlier western contempt for sensory observation, fails to recognize that emotion, like sensory perception, is necessary to human survival. Emotions prompt us to act appropriately, to approach some people and situations and to avoid others, to caress or cuddle, fight or flee. Without emotion, human life would be unthinkable. Moreover, emotions have an intrinsic as well as an instrumental value. Although not all emotions are enjoyable or even justifiable, as we shall see, life without any emotion would be life without any meaning.
>
> Within the context of western culture, however, people often have been encouraged to control or even suppress their emotions. Consequently, it is not unusual for people to be unaware of their emotional state or to deny it to themselves and others.

This lack of awareness, especially combined with a neopositivist understanding of emotion that construes it just as a feeling of which one is aware, lends plausibility to the myth of dispassionate investigation. But lack of awareness of emotions certainly does not mean that emotions are not present subconsciously or unconsciously, or that subterranean emotions do not exert a continuing influence on people's articulated values and observations, thoughts and actions.

Within the positivist tradition, the influence of emotion usually is seen only as distorting or impeding observation or knowledge. Certainly it is true that contempt, disgust, shame, revulsion, or fear may inhibit investigation of certain situations of phenomena. Furiously angry or extremely sad people often seem quite unaware of their surroundings or even their own conditions; they may fail to hear or may systematically misinterpret what other people say. People in love are notoriously oblivious to many aspects of the situation around them.

In spite of these examples, however, positivist epistemology recognizes that the role of emotion in the construction of knowledge is not invariably deleterious and that emotions may make a valuable contribution to knowledge. But the positivist tradition will allow emotion to play only the role of suggesting hypotheses for emotion. Emotions are allowed this because the so-called logic of discovery sets no limits on the idiosyncratic methods that investigators may use for generating hypotheses.

When hypotheses are to be tested, however, positivist epistemology imposes the much stricter logic of justification. The core of this logic is replicability, a criterion believed capable of eliminating or cancelling out what are conceptualized as emotional as well as evaluative biases on the part of individual investigators. The conclusions of western science thus are presumed "objective," precisely in the sense that they are uncontaminated by the supposedly "subjective" values and emotions that might bias individual investigators.

But if, as has been argued, the positivist distinction between discovery and justification is not viable, then such a distinction is incapable of filtering out values in science. For example, although such a split, when built into the western scientific method, generally is successful in neutralizing the idiosyncratic or unconventional values of individual investigators, it has been argued that it does not, indeed cannot, eliminate generally accepted social values. These values are implicit in the identification of the problems that are considered worthy of investigation, in the selection of the hypotheses that are considered worthy of testing, and in the solutions to the problems that are considered worthy of acceptance. The science of past centuries provides ample evidence of the influence of prevailing social values, whether seventeenth century atomic physics . . . or nineteenth century competitive interpretations of natural selection.

Of course, only hindsight allows us to identify clearly the values that shaped the science of the past and thus to reveal the formative influence on science of pervasive emotional attitudes, attitudes that typically went unremarked at the time because they were shared so generally. For instance, it is now glaringly evident that contempt for (and perhaps fear of) people of color is implicit in nineteenth century anthropology's interpretations and even constructions of anthropological facts. Because we are closer to them, however, it is harder for us to see how certain emotions, such as sexual possessiveness or the need to dominate others, currently are accepted as guiding principles in twentieth century sociobiology or even defined as part of reason within political theory and economics.

Values and emotions enter into the science of the past and the present not only on the level of scientific practice but also on the metascientific level, as answers to various questions: What is science? How should it be practiced? And what is the status of scientific investigation versus nonscientific modes of enquiry? For instance, it is claimed with increasing frequency that the modern western conception of science, which identifies knowledge with power and views it as a weapon for dominating nature, reflects the imperialism, racism and misogyny of the societies that created it. Several feminist theorists have argued that modern epistemology itself may be viewed as an expression of certain emotions alleged to be especially characteristic of males in certain periods, such as separation anxiety and paranoia, . . . or an obsession with control and fear of contamination.

Positivism views values and emotions as alien invaders that must be repelled by a stricter application of the scientific method. If the forgoing claims are correct, however, the scientific method and even its positivist construals themselves incorporate values and emotions. Moreover, such an incorporation seems a necessary feature of all knowledge and conceptions of knowledge. Therefore, rather than repressing emotion in epistemology it is necessary to rethink the relation between knowledge and emotion and construct a conceptual model that demonstrates the mutually constitutive rather than oppositional relation between reason and emotion. Far from precluding the possibility of reliable knowledge, emotion as well as value must be shown as necessary to such knowledge. Despite its classical antecedents and like the ideal of disinterested enquiry, the ideal of dispassionate enquiry is an impossible dream, but a dream nonetheless, or perhaps a myth that has exerted enormous influence on western epistemology. Like all myths, it is a form of ideology that fulfills certain social and political functions.

THE IDEOLOGICAL FUNCTION OF THE MYTH

So far, I have spoken very generally of people and their emotions, as though everyone experienced similar emotions and dealt with them in similar ways. It is an axiom of feminist theory, however, that all generalizations about "people" are suspect. The divisions in our society are so deep, particularly the divisions of race, class, and gender, that many feminist theorists would claim that talk about people in general is ideologically dangerous because such talk obscures the fact that no one is simply a person but instead is constituted fundamentally by race, class and gender. Race, class, and gender shape every aspect of our lives, and our emotional constitution is not excluded. Recognizing this helps us to see more clearly the political functions of the myth of the dispassionate investigator.

Feminist theorists have pointed out that western tradition has not seen everyone as equally emotional. Instead, reason has been associated with members of dominant political, social, and cultural groups and emotion with members of subordinate groups. Prominent among those subordinate groups in our society are people of color, except for supposedly "inscrutable orientals," and women.

Although the emotionality of women is a familiar cultural stereotype, its grounding is quite shaky. Women appear to be more emotional than men because they, along with some groups of people of color, are permitted and even required to express emotion more openly. In contemporary western culture, emotionally inexpressive women are suspect as not being real women, whereas men who express their emotions freely are suspected of being homosexual or in some other way deviant from the masculine ideal. Modern western men, in contrast with Shakespeare's heroes, for instance, are required to present a facade of coolness, lack of excitement, even boredom, to express emotion only rarely and then for relatively trivial events, such as sporting occasions, where the emotions expressed are acknowledged to be dramatized and so are not taken entirely seriously. Thus, women in our society form the main group allowed or even expected to feel emotion. A woman may cry in the face of disaster, and a man of color may gesticulate, but a white man merely sets his jaw.

White men's control of their emotional expression may go to the extremes of repressing their emotions, failing to develop emotionally, or even losing the capacity to experience many emotions. Not uncommonly, these men are unable to identify what they are feeling, and even they may be surprised, on occasion, by their own apparent lack of emotional response to a situation, such as a death, where emotional reaction is perceived appropriate. In some married couples, the wife implicitly is assigned the job of feeling emotion for both of them. White, college-educated men increasingly enter therapy in order to learn how to "get in touch with" their emotions, a project other men may ridicule as weakness. In therapeutic situations, men may learn that they are just as emotional as women but less adept at identifying their own or others' emotions. In consequence, their emotional development may be relatively rudimentary; this may lead to moral rigidity or insensitivity. Paradoxically, men's lacking awareness of their own emotional responses frequently results in their being more influenced by emotion rather than less.

Although there is no reason to suppose that the thoughts and actions of women are any more influenced by emotion than the thoughts and actions of men, the stereotypes of cool men and emotional women continue to flourish because they are confirmed by an uncritical daily experience. In these circumstances, where there is a differential assignment of reason and emotion, it is easy to see the ideological function of the myth of the dispassionate investigator. It functions, obviously, to bolster the epistemic authority of the currently dominant groups, composed largely of white men, and to discredit the observations and claims of the currently subordinate groups including, of course, the observations and claims of many people of color and women. The more forcefully and vehemently the latter groups express their observations and claims, the more emotional they appear and so the more easily they are discredited. The alleged epistemic authority of the dominant groups then justifies their political authority.

The previous section of this paper argued that dispassionate inquiry was a myth. This section has shown that the myth promotes a conception of epistemological justification vindicating the silencing of those, especially women, who are defined culturally as the bearers of emotion and so are perceived as more "subjective," biased, and irrational. In our present social context, therefore, the ideal of the dispassionate investigator is a classist, racist, and especially masculinist myth.

EMOTIONAL HEGEMONY AND EMOTIONAL SUBVERSION

As we have seen already, mature human emotions are neither instinctive nor biologically determined, although they may have developed out of presocial, instinctive responses. Like everything else that is human, emotions in part are socially constructed; like all social constructs, they are historical products, bearing the marks of the society that constructed them. Within the very language of emotion, in our basic definitions and explanations of what it is to feel pride or embarrassment, resentment or contempt, cultural norms and expectations are embedded. Simply describing ourselves as angry, for instance, presupposes that we view ourselves as having been wronged, victimized by the violation of some social norm. Thus, we absorb the standards and values of our society in the very process of learning the language of emotion, and those standards and values are built into the foundation of our emotional constitution.

Within a hierarchical society, the norms and values that predominate tend to serve the interest of the dominant groups. Within a capitalist, white supremacist, and male-dominant society, the predominant values will tend to be those that serve the interests of the rich white men. Consequently, we are all likely to develop an emotional constitution that is quite inappropriate for feminism. Whatever our color, we are likely to feel what Irving Thalberg has called "visceral racism"; whatever our sexual orientation, we are likely to be homophobic; whatever our class, we are likely to be at least somewhat ambitious and competitive; whatever our sex, we are likely to feel contempt for women. The emotional responses may be rooted in us so deeply that they are relatively impervious to intellectual argument and may recur even when we pay lip service to changed intellectual convictions.

By forming our emotional constitution in particular ways, our society helps to ensure its own perpetuation. The dominant values are implicit in responses taken to be precultural or acultural, our so-called gut responses. Not only do these conservative responses hamper and disrupt our attempts to live in or prefigure alternative social forms but also, and insofar as we take them to be natural responses, they limit our vision theoretically. For instance, they limit our capacity for outrage, they either prevent us from despising or encourage us to despise; they lend plausibility to the belief that greed and domination are inevitable human motivations; in sum, they blind us to the possibility of alternative ways of thinking.

This picture may seem at first to support the positivist claim that the intrusion of emotion only disrupts the process of seeking knowledge and distorts the results of that process. The picture, however, is not complete; it ignores the fact that people do not always experience the conventionally acceptable emotions. They may feel satisfaction rather than embarrassment when their leaders make fools of themselves. They may feel resentment rather than gratitude for welfare payments and hand-me-downs. They may be attracted to forbidden modes of sexual expression. They may feel revulsion for socially sanctioned ways of treating children or animals. In other words, the hegemony that our society exercises over people's emotional constitution is not total.

People who experience conventionally unacceptable, or what I call "outlaw," emotions often are subordinated individuals who pay a disproportionately high price for maintaining the status quo. The social situation of such people makes them unable to experience the conventionally prescribed emotions: for instance, people of color are more likely to experience anger than amusement when a racist joke is recounted, and women subjected to male sexual banter are less likely to be flattered than uncomfortable or even afraid.

When unconventional emotional responses are experienced by isolated individuals, those concerned may be confused, unable to name their experience; they may even doubt their own sanity. Women may come to believe that they are "emotionally disturbed" and that the embarrassment or fear aroused in them by male sexual innuendo is prudery or paranoia. When certain emotions are shared or validated by others, however, the basis exists for forming a subculture defined by perceptions, norms, and values that systematically oppose the prevailing perceptions, norms, and values. By constituting the basis for such a subculture, outlaw emotions may be politically (because epistemologically) subversive.

Outlaw emotions are distinguished by their incompatibility with the dominant perceptions and values, and some, though certainty not all, of these outlaw emotions are potentially or actually feminist emotions. Emotions become feminist when they incorporate feminist perceptions and values, just as emotions are sexist or racist when they incorporate sexist or racist perceptions and values. For example, anger becomes feminist anger when it involves the perception that the persistent importuning endured by one woman is a single instance of a widespread pattern of sexual harassment, and pride becomes feminist pride when it is evoked by realizing that a certain person's achievement was possible only because that individual overcame specifically gendered obstacles to success.

Outlaw emotions stand in a dialectical relation to critical social theory: at least some are necessary to developing a critical perspective on the world, but they also presuppose at least the beginnings of such a perspective. Feminists need to be aware of how we can draw on some of our outlaw emotions in constructing feminist theory and also of how the increasing sophistication of feminist theory can contribute to the reeducation, refinement, and eventual reconstruction of our emotional constitution.

OUTLAW EMOTIONS AND FEMINIST THEORY

The most obvious way in which feminist and other outlaw emotions can help in developing alternatives to prevailing conceptions of reality is by motivating new investigations. This is possible because, as we saw earlier, emotions may be long-term as well as momentary; it makes sense to say that someone continues to be shocked or saddened by a situation, even if she is at the moment laughing heartily. As we have seen already, theoretical investigation is always purposeful, and observation is always selective. Feminist emotions provide a political motivation for investigation and so help to determine the selection of problems as well as the method by which they are investigated. Susan Griffin makes the same point when she characterizes feminist theory as following "a direction determined by pain, and trauma, and compassion, and outrage."

As well as motivating critical research, outlaw emotions may also enable us to perceive the world differently than we would from its portrayal in conventional descriptions. They may provide the first indications that something is wrong with the way alleged facts have been constructed, with accepted understandings of how things are. Conventionally unexpected or inappropriate emotions may precede our conscious recognition that accepted descriptions and justifications often conceal as much as reveal the prevailing state of affairs. Only when we reflect on our initially puzzling irritability, revulsion, anger, or fear, may we bring to consciousness our "gut-level" awareness that we are in a situation of coercion, cruelty, injustice, or danger. Thus, conventionally inexplicable emotions, particularly, though not exclusively, those experienced by women, may lead us to make subversive observations that challenge dominant conceptions of the status quo. They may help us to realize that what are taken generally to be facts have been constructed in a way that obscures the reality of subordinated people, especially women's reality.

But why should we trust the emotional responses of women and other subordinated groups? How can we determine which outlaw emotions we should endorse or encourage and which reject? In what sense can we say that some emotional responses are more appropriate than others? What reason is there for supposing that certain alternative perceptions of the world, perceptions informed by outlaw emotions, are to be preferred to perceptions informed by conventional emotions? Here I can indicate only the general direction of an answer, whose full elaboration must await another occasion.

I suggest that emotions are appropriate if they are characteristic of a society in which all humans (and perhaps some nonhuman life too) thrive, or if they are conducive to establishing such a society. For instance, it is appropriate to feel joy when we are developing or exercising our creative powers, and it is appropriate to feel anger and perhaps disgust in those situations where humans are denied their full creativity or freedom. Similarly, it is appropriate to feel fear if those capacities are threatened in us.

This suggestion obviously is extremely vague and may even verge on the tautological. How can we apply it in situations where there is disagreement over what is or is not disgusting or exhilarating or unjust? Here I appeal to a claim for which I have argued elsewhere: the perspective on reality that is available from the standpoint of the oppressed, which in part at least is the standpoint of women, is a perspective that offers a less partial and distorted and therefore more reliable view.... Oppressed people have a kind of epistemological privilege insofar as they have easier access to this standpoint and therefore a better chance of ascertaining the possible beginnings of a society in which all could thrive. For this reason, I would claim that the emotional responses of oppressed people in general, and often of women in particular, are more likely to be appropriate than the emotional responses of the dominant class. That is, they are more likely to incorporate reliable appraisals of situations.

Even in contemporary science, where the ideology of dispassionate inquiry is almost overwhelming, it is possible to discover a few examples that seem to support the claim that certain emotions are more appropriate than others in both a moral and epistemological sense. For instance, Hilary Rose claims that women's practice of caring, even though warped by its containment in the alienated context of a coercive sexual division of labor, nevertheless has generated more accurate and less oppressive understandings of women's bodily functions, such as menstruation.... Certain emotions may be both morally appropriate and epistemologically advantageous in approaching the nonhuman and even the inanimate world. Jane Goodall's scientific contribution to our understanding of chimpanzee behavior seems to have been made possible only by her amazing empathy with or even love for these animals.... In her study of Barbara McClintock, Evelyn Fox Keller describes McClintock's relation to the objects of her research—grains of maize and their genetic properties—as a relation of affection, empathy and "the highest form of love: love that allows for intimacy without the annihilation of difference." She notes that McClintock's "vocabulary is consistently a vocabulary of affection, of kinship, of empathy." ... Examples like these prompt Hilary Rose to assert that a feminist science of nature needs to draw on heart as well as hand and brain.

SOME IMPLICATIONS OF RECOGNIZING THE EPISTEMIC POTENTIAL OF EMOTION

Accepting that appropriate emotions are indispensable to reliable knowledge does not mean, of course, that uncritical feeling may be substituted for supposedly dispassionate investigation. Nor does it mean that the emotional responses of women and other members of the underclass are to be trusted without question. Although our emotions are epistemologically indispensable, they are not epistemologically indisputable. Like all our faculties, they may be misleading, and their data, like all data, are always subject to reinterpretation and revision. Because emotions are not presocial, physiological responses to unequivocal situations, they are open to challenge on various grounds. They may be dishonest or self-deceptive, they may incorporate inaccurate or partial perceptions, or they may be constituted by oppressive values. Accepting the indispensability of appropriate emotions should be attended to seriously and respectfully rather than condemned, ignored, discounted, or suppressed.

Just as appropriate emotions may contribute to the development of knowledge so the growth of knowledge may contribute to the development of appropriate emotions. For instance, the powerful insights of feminist theory often stimulate new emotional responses to past and present situations. Inevitably, our emotions are affected by the knowledge that the women on our faculty are paid systematically less than the men, that one girl in four is subjected to sexual abuse from heterosexual men in her own family, and that few women reach orgasm in heterosexual intercourse. We are likely to feel different emotions towards older women or people of color as we reevaluate our standards of sexual attractiveness or acknowledge that Black is beautiful. The new emotions evoked by feminist insights are likely in turn to stimulate further feminist observations and insights, and these may generate new directions in both theory and political practice. There is a continuous feedback loop between our emotional constitution and our theorizing such that each continually modifies the other and is in principle inseparable from it.

The ease and speed with which we reeducate our emotions unfortunately is not great. Emotions are only partially within our control as individuals. Although affected by new information, they are habitual responses not quickly unlearned. Even when we come to believe consciously that our fear or shame or revulsion is unwarranted, we may still continue to experience emotions inconsistent with our conscious politics. We may still continue to be anxious for male approval, competitive with our comrades and sisters and possessive with our lovers. These unwelcome, because apparently inappropriate, emotions should not be suppressed or denied; instead, they should be acknowledged and subjected to critical scrutiny. The persistence of such recalcitrant emotions probably demonstrates how fundamentally we have been constituted by the dominant world view, but it may also indicate superficiality or other inadequacy in our emerging theory and politics. We can only start from where we are—beings who have been created in a cruelly racist, capitalist, and male-dominated society that has shaped our bodies and our minds, our perceptions, our values and our emotions, our language and our systems of knowledge.

The alternative epistemological model that I suggest displays the continuous interaction between how we understand the world and who we are as people. It shows how our emotional responses to the world change as we conceptualize it differently and how our changing emotional responses then stimulate us to new insights. The model demonstrates the need for theory to be self-reflexive, to focus not only on the outer world but also on ourselves and our relation to that world, to examine critically our social location, our actions, our values, our perceptions and our emotions. The model also shows how feminist and other critical social theories are indispensable psychotherapeutic tools because they provide some insights necessary to a full understanding of our emotional constitution. Thus, the model explains how the reconstruction of knowledge is inseparable from the reconstruction of ourselves.

A corollary of the reflexivity of feminist and other critical theory is that it requires a much broader construal than positivism accepts of the process of theoretical investigation. In particular, it requires acknowledging that a necessary part of theoretical process is critical self-examination. Time spent in analyzing emotions and uncovering their sources should be viewed, therefore, neither as irrelevant to theoretical investigation nor even as a prerequisite for it; it is not a kind of clearing of the emotional decks, "dealing with" our emotions so that they will not influence our thinking. Instead, we must recognize that our efforts to reinterpret and refine our emotions are necessary to our theoretical investigation, just as our efforts to reeducate our emotions are necessary to our political activity. Critical reflection on emotion is not a self-indulgent substitute for political analysis and political action. It is itself a kind of political theory and political practice, indispensable for an adequate social theory and social transformation.

Finally, the recognition that emotions play a vital part in developing knowledge enlarges our understanding of women's claimed epistemic advantage. We can now see that women's subversive insights owe much to women's outlaw emotions, themselves appropriate responses to the situations of women's subordination. In addition to their propensity to experience outlaw emotions, at least on some level, women are relatively adept at identifying such emotions, in themselves and others, in part because of their social responsibility for caretaking, including emotional nurturance. It is true that women (like all subordinated peoples, especially those who must live in close proximity with their masters) often engage in emotional deception and even self-deception as the price of their survival. Even so, women may be less likely than other subordinated groups to engage in denial or suppression of outlaw emotions. Women's work of emotional nurturance has required them to develop a special acuity in recognizing hidden emotions and in understanding the genesis of those emotions. This emotional acumen can now be recognized as a skill in political analysts and validated as giving women a special advantage both in understanding the mechanisms of domination and in envisioning freer ways to live.

CONCLUSION

The claim that emotion is vital to systematic knowledge is only the most obvious contrast between the conception of theoretical investigation that I have sketched here and the conception provided by positivism. For instance, the alternative approach emphasizes that what we identify as emotion is a conceptual abstraction from a complex process of human activity that also involves acting, sensing, and evaluating. This proposed account of theoretical construction demonstrates the simultaneous necessity for and interdependence of faculties that our culture has abstracted and separated from each other: emotion and reason, evaluation and perception, observation and action. The model of knowing suggested here is nonhierarchical and antifoundationalist; instead, it is appropriately symbolized by the radical feminist metaphor of the upward spiral. Emotions are neither more basic than observation, reason, or action in building theory, nor secondary to them. Each of these human faculties reflects an aspect of human knowing inseparable from the other aspects. Thus, to borrow a famous phrase from a Marxian context, the development of each of these faculties is a necessary condition for the development of all.

In conclusion, it is interesting to note that acknowledging the importance of emotion for knowledge is not an entirely novel suggestion within the western epistemological tradition. The archrationalist, Plato himself, came to accept in the end that knowledge required a (very purified form of) love. It may be no accident that in the *Symposium* Socrates learns this lesson from Diotima, the wise woman!

NOTE ON SOURCES.   Alison Jaggar, "Love and Knowledge: Emotion in Feminist Epistemology," in *Women, Knowledge and Reality*, Ann Garry and Marilyn Pearsall, eds. (Boston: Unwin and Hyman, 1989).

6   RICHARD RORTY

RELATIVISM MEANS THE END OF PHILOSOPHY

FROM LAUDAN AND JAGGAR TO RORTY AND POSTMODERNISM.   The final reading in this section is an overview of a contemporary movement in philosophy known as postmodernism. Very briefly, it is a view which can be characterized (some would say caricatured) as rejecting all possibility of finding objective knowledge of anything. Thus postmodernism is not just about philosophy or science. Its claims extend to all areas. It is especially important in art, where it would force-fully deny that there can be a best meaning of, for example, *Hamlet*, the *Mona Lisa*, or *Catch-22*. Indeed, the entire notion of meaning is subjected to scrutiny in a way that ensures that meaning will always be subjective.

But before we get to postmodernism, we will look at the arguments of Richard Rorty. Rorty, like Feyerabend, takes the insights of Kuhn (and some other philosophers) just about as far as they can possibly be taken. Rorty pro-pounds more than just relativism. He actually finds grounds for rejecting philoso-phy as it has been practiced by most philosophers since Socrates.

Traditional philosophy has been based on the assumptions that Kuhn seem-ingly undercut. Objective truth, objective reality, and the distinction between the logic of justification and the logic of discovery (psychology) are the bedrock of philosophy. Once they are rejected—as Kuhn demands—then so must philoso-phy itself be rejected. Rorty suggests replacing traditional philosophy with what he terms "edifying conversation." Instead of debate based on the assumptions of traditional philosophy and proceeding according to the fixed rules of logic, Rorty suggests urbane discussion: discussion about anything, meandering discussion, until everyone is satisfied, or everyone leaves.

BIOGRAPHICAL NOTE.   Richard Rorty was born in New York City in 1931. He received his Ph.D. in philosophy from Yale University in 1956. He taught at Yale and at Wellesley College before coming to Princeton, where he taught from 1961 to 1982. Rorty took his turn away from philosophy quite seriously, becoming University Professor of Humanities at the University of Virginia, where he has been since leav-ing Princeton in 1982. In a way, Rorty has had two careers: one based on traditional, analytic philosophy; the other based on spreading the word of postmodernism.

THE ARGUMENT OF THE PASSAGES.   The basic mistake of philosophy has been to assume that the world is one particular way independent from us and that phi-losophy (and science) can find that way. Using the terminology of "objective" and "subjective," the world has no objective existence. There are only our subjective interpretations. To assume otherwise, and then to build a discipline on this assumption must lead to error.

Our present notions of what it is to be a philosopher are so tied up with Kant . . . that it is difficult to imagine what philosophy without epistemology could be. More gener-ally, it is difficult to imagine that any activity would be entitled to bear the name "philosophy" if it had nothing to do with knowledge—if it were not in some sense a theory of knowledge, or a method for getting knowledge, or at least a hint as to where some supremely important kind of knowledge might be found. The difficulty stems from a notion shared by Kantians, and positivists: that . . . our chief task is to mirror accurately . . . the universe around us. . . .

This classic picture . . . must be set aside before epistemologically centered philosophy can be set aside. "Hermeneutics," as a polemical term in contemporary philosophy, is a name for the attempt to do so.

Rorty uses Sartre to point out that another mistake has been to make a distinction between epistemology and ethics. Insisting that the world is independent from us (totally objective) is a way of not taking responsibility for the way that the world is. We do make the world and we have to take responsibility for it. To existentialists like Sartre, objectivity takes on a different meaning. To be objective is just to be a part of the consensus; part of what one's culture believes. At this point, you should be reminded of how similar this sounds to Kuhn's arguing that science cannot be objective except in the sense that normal science is in accord with a paradigm.

Rorty realizes that Sartre's point sounds like nothing more than a refusal to recognize the fact-value distinction (discussed in Chapter 6). Isn't Sartre saying only that everything is partially a value? And isn't this fairly easy to deny? Rorty's reply is this: The only way to insist, as positivists do, on the fact–value distinction is to assume that there is a neutral, value-free vocabulary in which all problems, scientific and philosophical, can be stated. Put another way, positivists have assumed the existence of a totally objective world. But even to assume the existence of this vocabulary (of a totally objective world) is to assume a value-laden attitude toward ourselves and the world. Thus, the fact–value distinction represents nothing more than the hopes and dreams of some philosophers.

Sartre . . . sees the attempt to gain an objective knowledge of the world, and thus of oneself, as an attempt to avoid the responsibility for choosing one's project. For Sartre, to say this is not to say that the desire for objective knowledge of nature, history, or anything else is bound to be unsuccessful, or even bound to be self-deceptive. It is merely to say that it presents a temptation to self-deception insofar as we think that, by knowing which descriptions within a given set of normal disclosures apply to us, we thereby know ourselves. For . . . Sartre, . . . objective inquiry is perfectly possible and frequently actual—the only thing to be said against it is that it provides only some, among many, ways of describing ourselves, and that some of these can hinder the process of edification.

To sum up this "existentialist" view of objectivity, then: objectivity should be seen as conformity to the norms of justification (for assertions and for actions) we find about us. Such conformity becomes dubious and self-deceptive only when seen as something more than this—namely, as a way of obtaining access to something which "grounds" current practices of justification in something else. Such a "ground" is thought to need no justification, because it has become so clearly and distinctly perceived as to count as a "philosophical foundation." This is self-deceptive not simply because of the general absurdity of ultimate justification's reposing upon the unjustifiable, but because of the more concrete absurdity of thinking that the vocabulary used by present science, morality, or whatever has some privileged attachment to reality which makes it *more* than just a further set of descriptions.

This "existentialist" attempt to place objectivity, rationality, and normal inquiry within the larger picture of our need to be educated and edified is often countered by the "positivist" attempt to distinguish learning facts from acquiring values. From the positivist point of view, [this existentialist point] may seem little more than reiteration of the commonplace that even when we know all the objectively true descriptions of ourselves, we still may not know what to do with ourselves. From this point of view . . . the demands for justification offered by normal inquiry would still leave us free to draw our own morals from the assertions so justified. But from the viewpoint of . . . Sartre, the trouble with the fact–value distinction is that it is contrived precisely to blur the fact that alternative descriptions are possible in addition to those offered by the results of normal inquiries. It suggests that once "all the facts are in" nothing remains except "noncognitive" adoption of an attitude—a choice which is not rationally discussable. It disguises the fact that to use one set of true sentences to describe ourselves is already to choose an attitude toward ourselves, whereas to use another set of true sentences is to adopt a contrary attitude. Only if we assume that there is a value-free vocabulary . . . can the positivist distinction between facts and values, beliefs, and attitudes, look plausible. But the philosophical fiction that such a vocabulary is on the tips of our tongues is, from an educational point of view, disastrous. It forces us to pretend that we can split ourselves up into knowers of true sentences on the one hand and choosers of lies or actions or works of art on the other.

Finally, Rorty opts for total relativism. There is no one way to be rational (a point made by Feyerabend). Thus arguments cannot be settled by appeal to facts, values, or anything for that matter. Arguments, in an edifying conversation, are just ways of giving one side of an issue. Argument becomes merely a translation of one point of view into another. The search for a neutral middle ground is baseless.

There is no "normal" philosophical discourse which provides common . . . ground for those who see science [and only science as] "rational" and . . . those who see the quest for objectivity as one possibility among others. . . . If there is no such common ground, all we can do is to show how the other side looks from our own point of view. That is, all we can do is be hermeneutic about the opposition—trying to show how the odd or paradoxical or offensive things they say hang together with the rest of what they want to say, and how what they say looks when put in our own alternative idiom.

NOTE ON SOURCES.   Richard Rorty, *Philosophy and the Mirror of Nature* (Princeton: Princeton University Press, 1979), Chapter 8.

7   H. GENE BLOCKER

AN EXPLANATION OF POSTMODERNISM

FROM RORTY TO BLOCKER.   Now that we have traced relativism from its beginnings as a reaction against positivist history of science to its culmination in the rejection of philosophy itself, it is time for an overall look at this movement in philosophy. For this, we turn to H. Gene Blocker's essay, "The Challenge of Postmodernism."

BIOGRAPHICAL NOTE.   See Chapter 8.

THE ARGUMENT OF THE PASSAGES.   Modernism is the view represented by traditional philosophy. In this text, all selections except those by Feyerabend and Rorty would be considered modernist. (The works of Kuhn can be given a postmodernist interpretation, but he would not consider himself a postmodernist.) Postmodernism is a position which extols the skepticism of many traditional philosophers of the past. But whereas skepticism is seen by traditional philosophy as a fringe position, postmodernism makes it central to all understanding.

To a postmodernist, the inextricable link between finding out what the world is really like and the fact that we are limited in what we can say about the world by language is proof that there is no such thing as an objective reality. Showing how language actually affects our interpretation of the world is called "deconstruction."

By using the methods of deconstruction, postmodernists are convinced that they have also shown that objectivity in knowledge is impossible. Blocker tries to show that there is a way to accept the insights of postmodernism without giving up all senses of the word *objective*.

Blocker suggests that the distinctions and dichotomies that the postmodernists apparently destroyed (real/apparent, knowledge/belief, science/non-science, etc.) are still sensible distinctions to make on pragmatic grounds. That is, they are useful for getting along in the world. Blocker shows this by examining the objective–subjective distinction and the reality–appearance distinction. His general point is this: Just because these distinctions are made relative to some accepted set of beliefs does not make the distinctions useless. Only if, relative to the same set of beliefs, something turned out to be both real and apparent, both objective and subjective, both fact and non-fact, would we have to give up entirely on using these distinctions.

Let us use a different example to make the same sort of point. It can be argued that there is no sharp line that can be drawn between people who sometimes have minor emotional problems, people who are always emotionally troubled but not seriously, and people whose emotional problems are continuous and serious, whose actions are a threat to themselves and to others. But it does not follow from this assertion that we cannot recognize clear cases of each in practice. Nor does it follow that we should not treat the clear cases of each differently.

Blocker concludes that the main difference between postmodernism and traditional philosophy is the attitude they take toward the discovery that there are no absolutes. The postmodernists react to this by taking the extreme position that "anything goes." The more traditional philosopher is willing to accept some form of relativism but only if it stops short of being an "anything goes" type of relativism. In terms of the earlier discussion of philosophy of science, Laudan's attempt to save some objectivity for science represents what Blocker would call a modernist philosophical view. Feyerabend would represent the postmodernist position.

The question currently being debated in philosophy is this: Can one consistently be only a partial relativist? Once one admits to relativism in any degree, isn't one also committed to the "anything goes" of the postmodernists?

What *is* "Post-Modernism?" It is a term which is more and more frequently mentioned, but which is seldom explicitly defined, defended or discussed. It is often mentioned as a highly controversial "theory" which has displaced or is about to displace many long-standing traditions in the modern tradition of philosophy, and especially, aesthetics and art and literary criticism, and yet it is still not very well understood. This is due in part to the fact that the theoretical underpinning of Post-Modernism has not arisen from within familiar AngloAmerican traditions, but from a variety of very different Continental European traditions with which American and British philosophers are not very familiar. Just to mention the main elements in the pedigree of Post-Modernism—French semiotics, e.g., Saussure; French structuralists, e.g., Levi-Strauss; German phenomenologists, especially Heidegger; French deconstruction, e.g., Derrida; the American followers of Derrida (the Yale group), de Man, J. Hillis Miller, Bloom; Hermeneutics, especially Gadamer and Habermas; Foucault and his followers; neoMarxists, like Althusser; neoFreudians, like Lacan. Much of this tradition is very alien to American and British traditions. To understand de Man, for instance, one would have to know something of Derrida and Heidegger; but in order to appreciate the work of these writers, one would have to know something of Husserl and phenomenology (in the case of Heidegger) and the Structuralist tradition of Saussure and Levi-Strauss (in the case of Derrida). Without such a background and preparation, virtually every sentence of de Man, for example, is incomprehensible. Naturally, there has been great resistance to this "invasion" of alien ideas by those working in the mainstreams of the AngloAmerican philosophical tradition—not only are the Post-Modernist ideas themselves highly controversial; they are also written in an alien and incomprehensible *style*.

Without going into a detailed analysis of these difficult and complex theories, let us simply try to explain how all this is being transmitted to the AngloAmerican "modernist" philosophical tradition. Whatever its historical origins in French and German traditions, it is penetrating the domain of AngloAmerican philosophy as a series of extremely radical challenges to most of the assumptions, indeed the very foundations of traditional, "modernist" philosophical thinking. Especially in Derrida's "deconstruction," Post-Modernism challenges what is probably the most fundamental assumption of modern philosophy and science—the possibility of discovering the "truth" about anything.

This is not, of course, an entirely new idea. Philosophers have always been aware of the gap between theory and reality, and skeptics and idealists in different ways have despaired of ever getting a correct correspondence of thought to some external reality. Since the way we describe the world affects the way we experience the world, it is hard to see how we can ever get outside the language to see if our language correctly matches the reality we think it describes. Carried to its logical conclusion such thoroughgoing skepticism about the possibility of objective knowledge leads to radical subjectivism and relativism—the position that any opinion is as good as any other. The challenge to "truth" also undermines, as we will see shortly, the traditional philosophical idea of an independent reality which theories and interpretations seek to describe.

Nonetheless, despite a long philosophical tradition of skepticism, idealism, subjectivism and relativism, the main tradition of philosophy has always rejected such a complete skepticism and has always sought ways of overcoming or at least modifying it. In the history of philosophy these positions almost always appear as *challenges* to be answered; they seldom represent major philosophical traditions. The position adopted by Post-Modernism is far more radical and controversial in the sense that it rejects completely the attempt of mainstream Western intellectual tradition to overcome complete subjectivity and relativity and all that that would logically entail. If a theory cannot be normatively judged by its faithful correspondence to reality, then no statement can be any more true or false than any other, and therefore no one can be any more correct or incorrect in their descriptions than anyone else—everyone's opinion is as good as anyone else's. The main criterion, therefore, becomes how you, as an individual, feel about it. Traditionally, most philosophers have found such a consequence unacceptable and have sought ways round it. Post-Modernism is radical and controversial in that it joyfully embraces such radical skeptical subjectivism and relativism and tries to help the rest of us come to terms with this "brave new world." Whether Post-Modernism represents a major turning point in philosophy or simply one more in a long series of periodical skeptical, "critical" phases in the history of philosophy remains to be seen.

Let us look for a moment at just what this radical claim means for traditional philosophical assumptions. The only reason it makes sense to speak of *one* real object or event about which there have been many *different* theories or interpretations over the years is the assumption, which Post-Modernism denies, that these interpretations are "about," that is, more or less true or accurate descriptions of that real object or event. It is because of this modernist assumption that we imagine we are comparing an interpretation to the reality, to see how accurate or inaccurate it is. Since, on this traditional, modern philosophical assumption, there are many more or less accurate interpretations describing the same object, we assume that there is a single reality which all these interpretations are interpretations of and at which they all aim. Imagine many people shooting at the same target; to speak of some shots as "close" and others as "way off" presupposes they are all directed at a single bulls-eye. But if language fails completely to describe an external reality, then there is really no longer any point in talking about an object apart from particular interpretations, or "readings" of it. In the target analogy, if shots going up, down, north, south, east and west were all said to be equally accurate, we would begin to wonder whether there was a target at all.

The myth of an independent external reality is one which Post-Modernism tries to expose by "deconstructing" language, that is, by showing first the gap between word and object, language and reality, and then by showing that the so-called reality is simply created by the language itself. De-construction shows how language has constructed what we call "reality"; it then deconstructs these linguistic constructions. What this basically accomplishes, where successful, is to expose as myths linguistic descriptions which masquerade as reality—the myth of truth as the correspondence of idea to reality, the myth of universal cross-cultural objectivity and rationality, the myth of neutral, value-free scientific investigation, and so on. As the Zen Buddhists say (borrowing from much earlier Taoist philosophers), "When you point to the moon, don't mistake the finger for the moon." The things we refer to are not real, objective parts of reality; they are just ways of speaking which have caught on, become popular and then "internalized" so that we wrongly assume they accurately describe and reveal an independent reality.

As Derrida, and other decontructionalists put it, what is deconstructed are traditional Western value-laden dichotomies ("binaries")—presence/absence; nature/culture; male/female, central/marginal, in which, in each case, the first of the pair is preferred and ranks above the second. Such value-laden, hierarchical binaries, according to decontructionists, provide the foundations for our Western intellectual tradition. In order to settle disputes, for example, we must have standards which we all agree on for distinguishing true from false, correct from incorrect, real from illusory, and in order to do that we must be able, in the final analysis, to appeal to something which is beyond dispute. This is what dichotomous "binaries" provide. Without such binaries, there can be no foundation.

For Derrida, "presence" (and its binary opposite, "absence") is the root idea in Western culture that knowledge begins by just *seeing* the object "right in front of us", and then comparing "representations" (i.e., interpretations) of the object to the object actually "present" to us. If I say it's green and you say it's red, we simply look at the object and see that it is in fact red—so, you are right and I am wrong. Without presence, there can be no representation, and without representation there can be no stability of meaning, that is, no way to decide on the one correct meaning, or interpretation, and therefore no way to determine intersubjectively the final and complete truth about anything, once and for all.

Of course, there are many visible aspects of an object, so we must also distinguish those which are "central" (color, shape, for example) from those which are of only "marginal" importance (aesthetic properties, perhaps). And without priority or preference for "centrality," what has traditionally been considered marginal is just as important as what had traditionally been considered central—since there really is no difference between what is "central" and what is "marginal," where previously the evaluatively laden binaries constrained and limited thought and language to a supposed presence (that is, objective truth to which thought and language had to conform), the rejection of presence frees thought and language to "play," as Derrida calls it, with the "reading" or interpretation of the "text," that is, to freely interpret the object or event without being restricted by considerations or correctness or truth.

But if no one theory or interpretation is any better than any other, how is it that in fact some theories and interpretations have succeeded historically where others have failed? Post-Modernism interprets this politically. There are no truer or better interpretations, only "stronger" interpretations, that is, those which are more persuasive at a particular time and for a particular audience. But what is persuasive is rhetorically powerful for one particular social group at the expense of another. The traditional creation of an official list of accepted theories is therefore just an advertising "selling job" to elevate one social group into power (aristocratic white European males), and to hold other social groups (lower class, women, nonEuropean) down. But once we realize that this is the case, then there is a revolutionary side to Post-Modernism which encourage all the left-out, "marginalized" groups to demand their full share of center-stage. Distinctions of scientific and popular, major and minor, good and bad, established and alternative—all are swept away.

For many philosophers today, Post-Modernism is therefore both disturbing and also attractive. On the one hand, it means cutting ourselves adrift from solid and stable boundary markers of what is right and wrong, good and bad, correct and incorrect, true and false, real and illusory and sailing off into the unknown without benefit of map or compass. But it also means an emphasis on the legitimacy of the individual's "reading," or interpretation of an object or event, however it may deviate from the opinion of the "experts," and to the "liberation" of the marginalized thought of women, minorities, and disenfranchised groups, such as Native Americans, African Americans, Hispanics, and homeless street people.

Most philosophers probably find themselves somewhere in the middle of these extremes. The problem for most philosophers, therefore, is not whether to accept or reject Post-Modernism, but how to find the right blend or balance between modernism and Post-Modernism. As often happens when new movements challenge older, established positions, confrontational battle lines are drawn up in which differences between the established tradition and the new challenger are exaggerated and each is pictured to the other as an extreme, simplistic caricature. Each side ceases to really listen to the other, but only to ridicule its straw-man caricature. It is also true in any intense intellectual debate, like this one, that there are those who embrace extreme positions as the best way of differentiating *their* position from "the opposition" as sharply as possible, and this, too, contributes to a sense of an irreconcilable gulf between the two positions, resulting in an uncomfortable either/or dichotomy.

But in fact differences between modernism and Post-Modernism are *not* irreconcilable. When we look closely at the "moderns" we can see many anticipations of "Post-Modern" thought, and when we look closely at the work of the Post-Moderns we can see that much of their work continues to follow, in a modified form, certain traditional elements of modern philosophical analysis. Indeed, in many ways, the very labels, "modern," "Post-Modern" are exaggerated and pretentious. As with all historical labels there is no sharp dividing line when modernism comes to a complete halt and is suddenly replaced by Post-Modernism. These are journalistic labels; the reality is one of gradual change—Kierkegaard, who lived in the early and middle nineteenth century, and Nietzsche, who died around the turn of the century, are often cited as Post-Moderns, while many university philosophy departments remain today predominantly modernist in emphasis.

Thus we can distinguish a radical version of Post-Modernism which is deeply antithetical to modern philosophy from a more modest, less extreme version of Post-Modernism which is not absolutely incompatible with modernist assumptions and toward which a modern philosophy has been evolving in light of Post-Modernist criticisms. And between the less extreme versions of modernism and Post-Modernism the possibility of reconciliation surely exists.

How so? We can deny with Post-Modernism any *absolutely* privileged foundation (in fact or in reality) without abandoning the *relative* use of such concepts as a heuristic device. For example, we ordinarily distinguish between facts" and "interpretations" of those facts. Suppose someone of a Post-Modern bent convinces us that anything which we can point to as a fact is also an interpretation. But even if we agree with that, it would not mean that we could not continue to speak, in *one* context, about "facts" which are given various "interpretations," knowing full well that in *another* context, those same "facts" might be "interpretations," and vice versa. At first the "fact" is that Jones committed suicide by jumping out a 15th story window and we look for an "interpretation" of that fact (why did he do it?); but later that "fact" may be called into question by new evidence which suggests that Jones was actually murdered, and now Jones's suicide is no longer a "fact" but an "interpretation" (which may later be rejected entirely). So, in our "relative" use of the term, a "fact" might simply be what is relatively undisputed by a certain group of people at a particular time; if Jones's suicide is undisputed, then it is a "fact," if it is disputed it is an "interpretation"—but it can't be both in the same context.

Or, suppose we agreed that it is impossible for any human being to be completely, absolutely objective; it would not necessarily follow that there was no longer any useful distinction between being objective and being biased (the distinction, for example, between history and propaganda). There could still be a *relative* distinction between what is considered biased and objective in a given society at a given time in a specific context. In discussions of history, we can distinguish and try to eliminate those biases we are aware of at a particular time (for example, today we may recognize male bias, and Eurocentric bias), and nonetheless recognize that we are probably still victims of biases which we are not currently aware of. Later, if and when we become aware of *these* biases we work to eliminate them, and so on, step by step—at any given stage, defining objectivity as eliminating those biases which we are aware of, allowing the possibility of other biases we are not aware of at that time. At any given stage (and we only live in one stage at a time) some things can be meaningfully said to be "objective" relative to others which are seen to be "biased." Propaganda would therefore differ from history, not in the sense that the one is subjectively biased while the other is completely "objective," but that propaganda is *deliberately* biased while history tries and *intends* to be objective though it cannot avoid some unconscious biases.

Or, suppose we agreed that human beings could never know reality as it is in itself, that all so-called knowledge of reality involves a subjective point of view. That does not destroy the utility of the reality/appearance distinction, which, again, can be useful in marking a recognized distinction between what is relatively more stable and agreed upon among this group of people at this time and context and what is more open to question and debate. Suppose you and I disagree who that person is standing over there in the corner. I say it is Mary and you say it Taiwo. Once we go over to speak to her we discover that you were right and I was wrong. At least relative to this particular situation, we can distinguish reality from appearance; truth from falsity—though not absolutely in a way which makes us immune from error, or removes entirely the subjective human situation we all find ourselves in all of the time. Later, it may turn out, for example, that it really wasn't Taiwo, either, but her twin sister, Tanya, whom we both wrongly assumed was Taiwo. But now in this new context we can still distinguish reality from appearance, truth from falsity. So long as the same thing cannot be both true and false, real and apparent *in the same context*, we can distinguish the true from the false, the real from the apparent in any given context.

Thus, we could continue to talk sensibly about the same object or event existing over time, about which interpretations have varied over the centuries, even though we recognize that we have no knowledge of that object or event over and above these interpretations of it. Despite the facts of conventionality and subjectivity, it is very useful as a heuristic device to be able to refer different interpretations to a single, autonomous object. And once we become more sophisticated about what we are doing, there is no longer the danger which Post-Modernists are concerned about.

In this relative sense the assumptions of modernism are not incompatible with Post-Modernism. There is a relative sense in which we can speak of foundations, objectivity, truth, rationality, and so on, though in modified form. While it is probably true that there are no morally or politically neutral judgments or assertions, nonetheless we can and should distinguish judgments which are primarily, overtly moral or political and those which are only marginally, unconsciously, or peripherally so. While it is true that the standards by which art and behavior are judged are conventional and can therefore change, it is also true that until that change occurs art works and behavior can be judged by those standards. And while it is true that the standards by which art and behavior are judged are conventional and therefore socially relative, it is also true that within a given culture or society certain standards do operate and can be used to communicate relatively objective judgments within a community of shared values.

More generally, the fact that standards are conventional does not negate but reinforces the objectivity of criteria of correctness. It is purely conventional that in

English we distinguish between trees and shrubs, but once we have accepted that convention and so long as it remains in force (and such things do not typically change very quickly), then it is objectively true (for all those who speak English) that an oak is a tree and false to say that it is a shrub. Similarly with colors. It is completely arbitrary and therefore conventional how we divide the color spectrum into distinct segments and which color labels ("red," "orange," and so on) we assign to each segment, but once that is agreed upon then it is correct to call indigo "blue" and false to call it "red."

Thus, our response to Post-Modernism is, first, to try to understand it, and not to run away from it, pretend it doesn't exist, claim it is incomprehensible, or dismiss it as outrageous madness. Secondly, we should try to distinguish the more radical claims, some of which *are* outrageous, from its more sensible claims. Then, while we may argue against the more extreme claims with which we disagree, we can begin the task of reconciling the more moderate claims with the more sophisticated and progressive elements of the modernist tradition. This will mean modifying modernism in light of Post-Modernist criticism, but not throwing it out entirely. In general, we must modify modernism by acknowledging a larger measure of subjectivity, conventionality, and politics in our attitudes and judgments about things. But that is not a rejection of modern philosophy, but a sophistication of it.

When we finally work through all this to make an assessment of Post-Modernism, we therefore see some major points of similarity with the mainstream tradition of modern philosophy and some major points of difference.

The major points of similarity lie in the Post-Modernist rejection of "absolutes"—the alleged discovery that it is a fundamental illusion, deeply embedded in our Western intellectual outlook, to think that there are, or that we can ever discover, an absolutely secure and certain foundation for knowledge, reality (the thing in itself as it is in itself), objective truth (free of all human bias), brute fact, a presuppositionless beginning, an objective standard of assessment (whether in epistemology, ethics, or aesthetics). But this is also an important part of the modern philosophical tradition (though not universally accepted by all)—from Locke's rejection of innate ideas to Kant's rejection of knowledge of the thing itself, to the rejection by many 20th century philosophers of an absolute empiricist foundation for knowledge in an indubitable given (sense-data), to Wittgenstein's rejection of essential meaning, to recent epistemological rejections of "foundationalism," and so on.

The major points of difference between Post-Modernism and the tradition of modern philosophy have mainly to do with difference in the *responses* we make to this rejection of absolutes. The Post-Modern response is to go from one extreme position to the opposite extreme. The attitude of Post-Modernism seems to be that "if God is dead, everything is possible." Much of the language of Post-Modernism is a language of extremes. If there are no absolutes then in place of knowledge and the rational search for intersubjective, objective truth, we are now free to "play," or, in Derrida's expression, to "trope." There are no external standards nor even internal standards of personal or cultural consistency and coherence to restrict us. We are therefore free to go with what seems at the moment compelling to us and we are guided in our articulations only by the desire to persuade, to gain a receptive following.

Within the modern philosophic tradition, by contrast, there has been the attempt to "recover" regulative, relative, pragmatic standards which take the place of (and more or less do the job of) the old absolutes. Even if there's no knowledge of the thing in itself as it is in itself, we can learn more and more about things as they appear to us; even if our knowledge is biased by our interests, we can still learn what an object is like relative to our interests (interests which we more or less share with others for a longer or shorter period of time); even if our knowledge, beliefs and meanings are based on changing social conventions, these conventions change slowly enough to allow establishing acceptable and workable rules operating within a given time span; even if there is no indubitable empirical given (sense-data), we can still continue to assess our theories in the light of our experience of the world; even if there's no certainty there can be higher and higher probabilities; even if "analytic" statements are true relative to social conventions, there can still be at any given time a very high degree of social agreement on conventions over a long period of time; even if there are no essences, there are family resemblances; even if there are not brute facts, there are relatively more socially acceptable beliefs in any given situation which function as and can be regarded as the "facts" relative to that context; and even if we can't know reality (the thing in itself), we can know aspects of reality and we can continue to meaningfully talk about the regulative ideal of improving our understanding so as to approximate an unattainable "reality."

NOTE ON SOURCES.   This essay "The Challenge of Post-Modernism" was especially written by H. Gene Blocker for inclusion in this anthology.

This chapter, like all the rest, began with a crucial question for understanding ourselves and our place in the world. Like the other chapters, it offered a number of answers—where only rarely is one answer clearly better than any other. To philosophers such as Rorty, this signals a fatal flaw in philosophy. Is there no hope for finding an answer to the questions of knowledge? How else to respond to philosophy's impotence when faced with really important questions?

Blocker's suggestion that we take a pragmatic approach is echoed by Laudan. In other writings, Laudan (and others) argue that commonsense and the need for getting on in the world demand that some answers and some general approaches be rejected. Laudan would call for us to turn from extreme relativism if only because it leads to chaos in everyday life and would make what we all identify as science impossible. Rorty can live his life untroubled, Laudan would point out, only because Rorty does not actually live according to the rules that postmodernism would beget.

Notice, however, that the philosophical injunction, "If it works, do it" needs much modification before it can be embraced. What is it to "work"? Is the concept of "works" relative? Are there things that "work" that should not be done? This is a reminder that even the most practical approach to getting through life requires philosophical examination.

Epilogue

Making Sense Out of Life

THE QUESTION POSED

In pursuing the examined life, we have explored a number of questions ranging from the mind–body problem and the issue of postdeath survival to the basis for making value judgments and the grounds for claiming that one possesses knowledge. Our final chapter ended with the challenge of postmodernism, whose radical advocates would deconstruct all perspectives, leaving us adrift in a sea of relativism and subjectivism.

At first glance, the student of philosophy might discern the practical implication of postmodernism to be welcome indeed: *tolerance* for diverse perspectives resulting from the realization that none of us has a privileged perspective from which to adjudicate the claims of others.

At second glance, however, the student of philosophy might become aware of another practical consequence of postmodernism that seems to be far less welcome: the threat of *nihilism* that appears to follow from the disprivileging of any single philosophical posture. Does not this disprivileging suggest that the meaning I think life holds is nothing more than what *I* think *at this moment*? Indeed, is not my *present* philosophical posture disprivileged not only vis-à-vis other persons but even vis-à-vis myself *at a later moment*? Must I not, therefore, live with the burden of having to create and recreate day by day, hour by hour, and moment by moment, the meaning I think life holds? If so, then the meaning I think life possesses for me is extremely mutable. If that be the case, would I not find myself in a position similar to that of Cratylus, the disciple of Heracleitus, the ancient Greek philosopher of change? Cratylus concluded that, because the world is changing so rapidly, he was unable to give things names, because once named the thing changed and was no longer the thing named. The upshot for Cratylus was to give up language entirely and to become a silent philosopher.

Analogously, would I perhaps have to give up attempting to make sense out of life if the sense I created in this moment is so disprivileged that I must recreate it or reconstruct it in the next moment?

We are confronting here a major philosophical issue, with theoretical as well as practical implications. To accept nihilism would be to admit that life has no meaning. But what then would become of purposeful, goal-directed action over time? What would become of the moral life? Indeed, and more importantly, what would become of me? In response to this last question, Viktor Frankl, the first author we examine in this epilogue, would say that I would atrophy and probably perish.

There are at least two alternatives to caving in to nihilism that I could adopt. On the one hand, I could follow the advice of Sartre (see Chapter 3) and courageously create my human meaning, boldly defining and redefining myself moment by moment, with full acceptance of the despair that goes hand in hand with the disprivileging of all philosophical positions and with a celebration of my freedom unconstrained by the prescriptions declared by others. This Sartrean strategy might work for me, but if I take it seriously, it might force on me an unbearable burden of a constant recreation of my meaning that paralyzes short-term and long-range planning. In brief, such a strategy could compromise seriously my ability to act.

On the other hand, I could follow the pragmatic approach of James (Chapter 3) and Blocker (Chapter 11) by adopting a position that enables me to get on with the practical business of daily acting and living. Such a position might occupy the middle ground between the imperialistic arrogance of privileging only one view as the truth and the relativistic humility of disprivileging all views. Such a position might involve living and acting "as if" I had grasped a sense of meaning in my life, but allowing for modifications and enhancement of that sense of meaning as I encounter new data and develop fresh insight.

Acting "as if" I had grasped a sense of meaning is a provisional strategy also seen in the stories human beings create in their attempt to articulate the meaning of life. Unlike the ideal philosophical treatise that is a model of precision and clarity, these stories frequently harbor ambiguities and unresolved questions that imply their provisional nature. Furthermore, these stories are set within specific cultural contexts that relativize them, but that does not preclude them from sharing a measure of commonality.

We encounter the issue of meaning and human life almost on a daily basis. For example, when newspapers and television reports portray the suffering of little children ravaged by war, disease, or hunger, we often protest that it is not fair for young ones to suffer so, that such events should not happen, or that some other events would have been far more fitting. These protests reflect our affirmation of a norm or ideal state of affairs that is being violated by this suffering. Moreover, our protests seem to expose a deep-seated belief that human life should be moving in a certain direction, and that it would be a better place if it unfolded without the suffering of these little children. Things like the unmerited suffering of children frustrate and defeat the direction we believe life *should* be taking. Life moving in a desired direction is life that is goal-oriented, purposeful, meaningful. (Recall that life moving toward a goal is a central notion of virtue ethics.)

This movement of events toward a purpose is very much at the heart of the stories we construct about ourselves, and these stories harbor a great deal of the meaning we think life holds for us. Some of the stories we construct are quite short, such as an account of a trip to the supermarket which embraces the movement and connectedness of probably only a few events during part of one day. Other stories are very long, such as autobiographies that attempt to connect all the major events of our lived experience. Still other stories try to set our lives within the context of the story of our nation, our civilization, our world, and indeed our universe, as if our nation, world, and universe exhibit story lines that connect events to each other to produce meaningful overall stories.

Why are humans storytellers? Why do we find ourselves constructing these kinds of stories? The first author in this epilogue, Viktor Frankl, has developed the theory of logotherapy according to which humans have three fundamental drives: the will to power, the will to pleasure, and the will to meaning. Frankl focuses on the will to meaning and claims that unless people satisfy their basic drive for meaning, they cannot survive, cannot endure the suffering that humans encounter day after day.

It is noteworthy that Frankl associates human meaning and the problem of suffering. As we have already suggested, the apparent surplus of suffering in the world, like the unmerited suffering of children, calls into question the story line that we frequently think the world should be following. In the material that follows Frankl's discussion, we have selected stories from disparate cultures that illustrate human beings reaching out in different ways for the same thing: an answer to the question, "How does one make sense out of life, especially in the light of suffering?" We have selected material from the biblical, Buddhist, and African traditions to illustrate the diversity of stories humans construct in order to invest their lives with meaning.

The stories we have selected from these three traditions all seem to assume a religious context, a belief in some sort of divine or transcendent realm that plays an important role in the human quest for meaning. But suppose one does not find the religious context of human meaning desirable or necessary. Suppose one accepts the Marxian opiate theory that religion is a human creation which expresses and guarantees the interests of the ruling class by sanctifying the status quo and providing postdeath compensation for current privation. Suppose one jettisons religious beliefs and practices. Does one therefore surrender meaning in life? Albert Camus, the final author in this epilogue, rejects the religious perspective and in so doing suggests that the question "What is the meaning of life?" needs to be rephrased. For Camus, there is no cosmic story line waiting to be discovered. Yet he does not think that human life is without meaning. For him, the question to be answered is not "What is the meaning of life?," but rather, "What gives meaning to life?" He provides an engaging response to that question in his novel *The Plague*, from which we have excerpted several sections.

Before proceeding to the readings in this section another point needs to be emphasized. In general, people do not find themselves reflecting on the meaning of life unless they come face-to-face with trouble of one sort or another—the death of a child, parent, friend, or lover. The examined life, which we have pursued in this book, attempts to think philosophically (that is, rigorously, clearly, and coherently) about questions that relate to my understanding who I am, what I can know, and what I ought to do. Clearly, the question of the meaning my life does or can possess is germane to this self-understanding that philosophy seeks. Recall the advice carved in stone at the entrance to the Oracle of Apollo at Delphi to which we referred in Chapter 1: *gnothi seauton*, know thyself. Is it not preferable to think about these issues in the quiet and cool moments of life rather than to raise them perhaps for the first time, when life tumbles in upon us? Let us turn, then, to a consideration of the human as a seeker of meaning and a teller of stories.

VIKTOR E. FRANKL

THE WILL TO MEANING

BIOGRAPHICAL NOTE. Viktor Frankl was born in Vienna, Austria in 1905. Upon receiving his M.D. from the University of Vienna in 1930, he pursued a career in neurology and psychiatry. In 1940 he became the head of the neurology department at the Rothschild Hospital in Vienna. In 1942, he was imprisoned in a concentration camp by the Nazis because of his Jewish origins. When the Third Reich collapsed in 1945 and the war in Europe came to a halt, Frankl was released. On the basis of his concentration camp experiences he generated a new view of psychiatry called logotherapy which has received world-wide attention. Frankl has served as a visiting professor in the United States at Stanford, Harvard, and Southern Methodist University and has been a guest lecturer in Argentina, Australia, Sri Lanka, China, India, Israel, Japan, Mexico, Costa Rica, and South Africa. Frankl is the author of numerous books including *The Doctor and the Soul: From Psychotherapy to Logotherapy*, 1955; *Man's Search for Meaning: An Introduction to Logotherapy*, 1962; *Psychotherapy and Existentialism*, 1967; *The Will to Meaning: Foundations and Applications of Logotherapy*, 1969; and *The Unconscious God: Psychotherapy and Theology, 1976.*

THE ARGUMENT OF THE PASSAGES. Dr. Frankl was imprisoned in a Nazi concentration camp for no other reason than that he was a Jew. For three grim years he was subjected to unspeakably dehumanizing conditions. Upon entering the camp he was stripped of all outward signs of individuality: all his body hair was shaved and a number was inscribed on his flesh. He was starved, insulted, and beaten without apparent reason. His fellow prisoners received similar treatment—or worse. In the midst of this human agony, Frankl developed a new vision of the human condition, a vision which represented a radical departure from the psychiatric perspective with which he had entered the camp. He distinguishes three different schools of psychotherapy: (1) Freudian psychoanalysis which focuses on the will to pleasure; (2) Alderian psychology which stresses the will to power; and (3) his own new perspective which he calls logotherapy or existential analysis. It emphasizes the will to meaning. Frankl offers a clear and engaging presentation of his views in his book *Man's Search for Meaning: An Introduction to Logotherapy*, from which the following selections have been taken. Part 1 of the book is devoted to an autobiographical summary of his experiences in the concentration camp, and Part 2 is dedicated to an outline of the major tenets of logotherapy.

As he reflected on his experiences in the camp, Frankl came to the conclusion that the most basic human motivating principle is the will to meaning, the need to engage in goal-oriented, purposeful activity. The prerequisite for such activity is what Frankl calls "spiritual freedom," which not even the brutal constraints of a concentration camp could completely destroy in all of the inmates. Frankl writes,

> I may give the impression that the human being is completely and unavoidably influenced by his surroundings. (In this case the surroundings being the unique structure of camp life, which forced the prisoner to conform his conduct to a certain set pattern.) But what about human liberty? Is there no spiritual freedom in regard to behavior and reaction to any given surroundings? Is that theory true which would have us believe that man is no more than a product of many conditional and environmental factors—be they of a biological, psychological or sociological nature? Is man but an accidental product of these? Most important, do the prisoners' reactions to the singular world of the concentration camp prove that man cannot escape the influences of his surroundings? Does man have no choice of action in the face of such circumstances?
>
> We can answer these questions from experience as well as on principle. The experiences of camp life show that man does have a choice of action. There were enough examples, often of a heroic nature, which proved that apathy could be overcome, irritability suppressed. Man *can* preserve a vestige of spiritual freedom, of independence of mind, even in such terrible conditions of psychic and physical stress.
>
> We who lived in concentration camps can remember the men who walked through the huts comforting others, giving away their last piece of bread. They may have been few in number, but they offer sufficient proof that everything can be taken from a man but one thing: the last of the human freedoms—to choose one's attitude in any given set of circumstances, to choose one's own way.
>
> And there were always choices to make. Every day, every hour, offered the opportunity to make a decision, a decision which determined whether you would or would not submit to those powers which threatened to rob you of your very self, your inner freedom; which determined whether or not you would become the plaything of circumstance, renouncing freedom and dignity to become molded into the form of the typical inmate.
>
> Seen from this point of view, the mental reactions of the inmates of a concentration camp must seem more to us than the mere expression of certain physical and sociological conditions. Even though conditions such as lack of sleep, insufficient food and various mental stresses may suggest that the inmates were bound to react in certain ways, in the final analysis it becomes clear that the sort of person the prisoner

became was the result of an inner decision, and not the result of camp influences alone. Fundamentally, therefore, any man can, even under such circumstances, decide what shall become of him—mentally and spiritually. He may retain his human dignity even in a concentration camp. Dostoevski said once, "There is only one thing that I dread: not to be worthy of my sufferings." These words frequently came to my mind after I became acquainted with those martyrs whose behavior in camp, whose suffering and death, bore witness to the fact that the last inner freedom cannot be lost. It can be said that they were worthy of their sufferings; the way they bore their suffering was a genuine inner achievement. It is this spiritual freedom—which cannot be taken away—that makes life meaningful and purposeful.

An active life serves the purpose of giving man the opportunity to realize values in creative work, while a passive life of enjoyment affords him the opportunity to obtain fulfillment in experiencing beauty, art, or nature. But there is also purpose in that life which is almost barren of both creation and enjoyment and which admits of but one possibility of high moral behavior: namely, in man's attitude to his existence, an existence restricted by external forces. A creative life and a life of enjoyment are banned to him. But not only creativeness and enjoyment are meaningful. If there is a meaning in life at all, then there must be a meaning in suffering. Suffering is an ineradicable part of life, even as fate and death. Without suffering and death human life cannot be complete.

The way in which a man accepts his fate and all the suffering it entails, the way in which he takes up his cross, gives him ample opportunity—even under the most difficult circumstances—to add a deeper meaning to his life. It may remain brave, dignified and unselfish. Or in the bitter fight for self-preservation he may forget his human dignity and become no more than an animal. Here lies the chance for a man either to make use of or to forgo the opportunities of attaining the moral values that a difficult situation may afford him. And this decides whether he is worthy of his sufferings or not.

When a prisoner would "lose faith in the future," that is to say, give up on fulfilling the will to meaning, he would atrophy and die. Consider the following incident.

The prisoner who had lost faith in the future—his future—was doomed. With his loss of belief in the future, he also lost his spiritual hold; he let himself decline and became subject to mental and physical decay. Usually this happened quite suddenly, in the form of a crisis, the symptoms of which were familiar to the experienced camp inmate. We all feared this moment—not for ourselves, which would have been pointless, but for our friends. Usually it began with the prisoner refusing one morning to get dressed and wash or to go out on the parade grounds. No entreaties, no blows, no threats had any effect. He just lay there, hardly moving. If this crisis was brought about by an illness, he refused to be taken to the sick-bay or to do anything to help himself. He simply gave up. There he remained, lying in his own excreta, and nothing bothered him any more.

I once had a dramatic demonstration of the close link between the loss of faith in the future and this dangerous giving up. F___, my senior block warden, a fairly well-known composer and librettist, confided in me one day: "I would like to tell you something, Doctor. I have had a strange dream. A voice told me that I could wish for something, that I should only say what I wanted to know, and all my questions would be answered. What do you think I asked? That I would like to know when the war would be over for me. You know what I mean, Doctor—for me! I wanted to know when we, when our camp, would be liberated and our sufferings come to an end."

"And when did you have this dream?" I asked.

"In February, 1945," he answered. It was then the beginning of March.

"What did your dream voice answer?"

Furtively he whispered to me, "March thirtieth."

When F___ told me about his dream, he was still full of hope and convinced that the voice of his dream would be right. But as the promised day drew nearer, the war news which reached our camp made it appear very unlikely that we would be free on the promised date. On March twenty-ninth, F___ suddenly became ill and ran a high temperature. On March thirtieth, the day his prophecy had told him that the war and suffering would be over for him, he became delirious and lost consciousness. On March thirty-first, he was dead. To all outward appearances, he had died of typhus.

Those who know how close the connection is between the state of mind of a man—his courage and hope, or lack of them—and the state of immunity of his body will understand that the sudden loss of hope and courage can have a deadly effect. The ultimate cause of my friend's death was that the expected liberation did not come and he was severely disappointed. This suddenly lowered his body's resistance against the latent typhus infection. His faith in the future and his will to live had become paralyzed and his body fell victim to illness—and thus the voice of his dream was right after all.

The observations of this one case and the conclusion drawn from them are in accordance with something that was drawn to my attention by the chief doctor of our concentration camp. The death rate in the week between Christmas, 1944, and New Year's 1945, increased in camp beyond all previous experience. In his opinion, the explanation for this increase did not lie in the harder working conditions or the deterioration of our food supplies or a change of weather or new epidemics. It was simply that the majority of the prisoners had lived in the naive hope that they would be home again by Christmas. As the time drew near and there was no encouraging news, the prisoners lost courage and disappointment overcame them. This had a dangerous influence on their powers of resistance and a great number of them died.

As we said before, any attempt to restore a man's inner strength in the camp had first to succeed in showing him some future goal. Nietzsche's words, "He who has a *why* to live for can bear with almost any *how*," could be the guiding motto for all psychotherapeutic and psychohygienic efforts regarding prisoners. Whenever there was an opportunity for it, one had to give them a why—an aim—for their lives, in order to strengthen them to bear the terrible *how* of their existence. Woe to him who saw no more sense in his life, no aim, no purpose, and therefore no point in carrying on. He was soon lost. The typical reply with which such a man rejected all encouraging arguments was, "I have nothing to expect from life any more."

The preceding selections from Frankl's book are taken from Part 1, where Frankl offers a reflective autobiographical account of his experiences in the concentration camps. The following selections, which describe some of the key concepts of logotherapy, come from Part 2.

The Will to Meaning.   For Frankl, the will to meaning involves the self's discovering the meaning that life seems to harbor for that self, as opposed to the self's simply inventing meaning for itself. The meaning, the values and ideals, that life holds out to me at this moment beckon me, pull me; they do not push me. To pull me suggests a future possibility open to me which is at the heart of freedom. To push me suggests a past force that drives me and is at the core of determinism. He writes:

> Man's search for meaning is a primary force in his life and not a "secondary rationaliza-tion" of instinctual drives. This meaning is unique and specific in that it must and can be fulfilled by him alone; only then does it achieve a significance that will satisfy his own will to meaning. There are some authors who contend that meanings and values are "nothing but defense mechanisms, reaction formations and sublimations." But as for myself, I would not be willing to live merely for the sake of my "defense mecha-nisms," nor would I be ready to die merely for the sake of my "reaction formations." Man, however, is able to live and even to die for the sake of his ideals and values! . . .
>
> We have to beware of the tendency to deal with values in terms of the mere self-expression of man himself. For *logos*, or "meaning," is not only an emergence from existence itself but rather something confronting existence. If the meaning that is waiting to be fulfilled by man were really nothing but a mere expression of self, or no more than a projection of his wishful thinking, it would immediately lose its demand-ing and challenging character; it could no longer call man forth or summon him. This holds true not only for the so-called sublimation of instinctual drives but for what C. G. Jung called the "*archetypes*" of the "collective unconscious" as well, inasmuch as the latter would also be self-expressions, namely, of mankind as a whole. This holds true as well for the contention of some existentialist thinkers who see in man's ideals noth-ing but his own inventions. According to Jean-Paul Sartre, man invents himself, he designs his own "essence"; that is to say, what he essentially is, including what he should be, or ought to become. However, I think the meaning of our existence is not invented by ourselves, but rather detected.
>
> Psychodynamic research in the field of values is legitimate; the question is whether it is always appropriate. Above all, we must keep in mind that any exclusively psychodynamic investigation can, in principle, only reveal what is a driving force in man. Values, however, do not drive a man; they do not *push* him, but rather *pull* him . . . Now, if I say man is *pulled* by values, what is implicitly referred to is the fact that there is always freedom involved: the freedom of man to make his choice between accepting or rejecting an offer, i.e., to fulfill a meaning potentiality or else to forfeit it.
>
> However, it should be made quite clear that there cannot exist in man any such thing as a *moral drive*, or even a *religious drive*, in the same manner as we speak of man's being determined by basic instincts. Man is never driven to moral behavior; in each instance he decides to behave morally.

Existential Frustration and Noögenic Neurosis.   When the will to meaning, the striving to find concrete meaning in one's personal existence, is stymied, the con-dition is referred to as "existential frustration." It can result in a type of neurosis called "noögenic," at whose core is a conflict in values. Frankl cites the case of an American diplomat who was dissatisfied with his career. Does not Frankl's inter-pretation of the case suggest that five years of psychoanalytic therapy were wasted? Would not a depth psychiatrist differ with Frankl and claim that Frankl's "solution" only touched the surface of the diplomat's problem?

> Existential frustration can result in neurosis. For this type of neurosis, logotherapy has coined the term "noögenic neurosis" in contrast to neurosis in the usual sense of the word, i.e., psychogenic neurosis. Noögenic neuroses have their origin not in the

psychological but rather in the "noölogical" (from the Greek "noos" meaning mind) dimension of the human existence. This is another logotherapeutic term which denotes anything pertaining to the "spiritual" core of man's personality. It must be kept in mind, however, that within the frame of reference of logotherapy, "spiritual" does not have a primarily religious connotation but refers to the specifically human dimension.

Noögenic neuroses do not emerge from conflicts between drives and instincts but rather from conflicts between various values; in other words, from moral conflicts or, to speak in a more general way, from spiritual problems. Among such problems, existential frustration often plays a large role.

It is obvious that in noögenic cases the appropriate and adequate therapy is not psychotherapy in general but rather logotherapy; a therapy, that is, that dares to enter the spiritual dimension of human existence. In fact, *logos* in Greek means not only "meaning" but also "spirit." Spiritual issues such as man's aspiration for a meaningful existence, as well as the frustration of this aspiration, are dealt with by logotherapy in *spiritual* terms. They are taken sincerely and earnestly instead of being traced back to unconscious roots and sources, thus being dealt with merely in *instinctual* terms.

Whenever a doctor fails to distinguish between the spiritual dimension as against the instinctual, a dangerous confusion may arise. Let me quote the following instance: A high-ranking American diplomat came to my office in Vienna in order to continue psychoanalytic treatment that he had begun five years previously with an analyst in New York. At the outset I asked him why he thought he should be analyzed, why his analysis had been started in the first place. It turned out that the patient was discontented with his career and found it most difficult to comply with American foreign policy. His analyst, however, had told him again and again that he should try to reconcile himself with his father because the government of the U.S. as well as his superiors were "nothing but" father images and, consequently, his dissatisfaction with his job was due to the hatred he unconsciously harbored toward his father. Through an analysis lasting five years, the patient had been prompted more and more to accept his analyst's interpretations until he finally was unable to see the forest of reality for the trees of symbols and images. After a few interviews, it was clear that his will to meaning was frustrated by his vocation, and he actually longed to be engaged in some other kind of work. As there was no reason for not giving up his profession and embarking on a different one, he did so, with most gratifying results. He has remained contented in this new occupation for over five years, as he recently reported. I doubt that, in this case, I was dealing with a neurotic condition at all, and that is why I thought that he did not need any psychotherapy, nor even logotherapy, for the simple reason that he was not actually a patient. Not every conflict is necessarily neurotic; some amount of conflict is normal and healthy. In a similar sense suffering is not always a pathological phenomenon; rather than being a symptom of neurosis, suffering may well be a human achievement, especially if the suffering grows out of existential frustration. I would strictly deny that one's search for a meaning to his existence, or even his doubt of it, in every case is derived from, or results in, any disease. Existential frustration is in itself neither pathological nor pathogenic. A man's concern, even his despair, over the worthwhileness of life is a *spiritual distress* but by no means a *mental disease*. It may well be that interpreting the first in terms of the latter motivates a doctor to bury his patient's existential despair under a heap of tranquilizing drugs. It is his task, rather, to pilot the patient through his existential crisis of growth and development.

Logotherapy regards its assignment as that of assisting the patient to find meaning in his life. Inasmuch as logotherapy makes him aware of the hidden *logos* of his existence, it is an analytical process. To this extent, logotherapy resembles psychoanalysis. However, in logotherapy's attempt to make something conscious again it does not restrict its activity to *instinctual* facts within the individual's unconscious, but also cares for *spiritual* realities such as the potential meaning of his existence to be fulfilled, as well as his *will* to meaning. Any analysis, however, even when it refrains from including the noölogical or spiritual dimension in its therapeutic process, tries to make the patient aware of what he actually longs for in the depth of his being. Logotherapy deviates from psychoanalysis insofar as it considers man as a being whose main concern consists in fulfilling a meaning and in actualizing values, rather than in the mere gratification and satisfaction of drives and instincts, the mere reconciliation of the conflicting claims of id, ego and superego, or mere adaptation and adjustment to the society and environment.

Noö-Dynamics.   Ideally, the human being exists in a condition of "noö-dynamics" rather than equilibrium. Noö-dynamics refers to the tension between what I am and what I ought to be, between what I have already achieved and what I still ought to accomplish. This tension is inherent in the human being and is indispensable to mental well-being. Frankl observes,

> To be sure, man's search for meaning and values may arouse inner tension rather than inner equilibrium. However, precisely this tension is an indispensable prerequisite of mental health. There is nothing in the world, I venture to say, that would so effectively help one to survive even the worst conditions, as the knowledge that there is a meaning in one's life. There is much wisdom in the words of Nietzsche: "He who has a *why* to live for can bear almost any *how*." I can see in these words a motto that holds true for any psychotherapy. In the Nazi concentration camps, one could have witnessed (and this was later confirmed by American psychiatrists both in Japan and Korea) that those who knew that there was a task waiting for them to fulfill were most apt to survive.
>
> As for myself, when I was taken to the concentration camp of Auschwitz, a manuscript of mine ready for publication was confiscated. Certainly, my deep concern to write this manuscript anew helped me to survive the rigors of the camp. For instance, when I fell ill with typhus fever I jotted down on little scraps of paper many notes intended to enable me to rewrite the manuscript, should I live to the day of liberation. I am sure that this reconstruction of my lost manuscript in the dark barracks of a Bavarian concentration camp assisted me in overcoming the danger of collapse.
>
> Thus it can be seen that mental health is based on a certain degree of tension, the tension between what one has already achieved and what one still ought to accomplish, or the gap between what one is and what one should become. Such a tension is inherent in the human being and therefore is indispensable to mental well-being. We should not, then, be hesitant about challenging man with a potential meaning for him to fulfill. It is only thus that we evoke his will to meaning from its state of latency. I consider it a dangerous misconception of mental hygiene to assume that what man needs in the first place is equilibrium or, as it is called in biology, "homeostasis," i.e., a tensionless state. What man actually needs is not a tensionless state but rather the striving and struggling for some goal worthy of him. What he needs is not the discharge of tension at any cost, but the call of a potential meaning waiting to be fulfilled

by him. What man needs is not a homeostasis but what I call "noö-dynamics," i.e., the spiritual dynamics in a polar field of tension where one pole is represented by a meaning to be fulfilled and the other pole by the man who must fulfill it. And one should not think that this holds true only for normal conditions; in neurotic individuals, it is even more valid. If architects want to strengthen a decrepit arch, they *increase* the load that is laid upon it, for thereby the parts are joined more firmly together. So, if therapists wish to foster their patients' mental health, they should not be afraid to increase that load through a reorientation toward the meaning of one's life.

The Existential Vacuum.   When persons feel that their lives are ultimately meaningless, when they lack awareness of something worth living for, when they experience an inner emptiness, they are in the midst of what Frankl calls the "existential vacuum." The liberation of humans from certain animal instincts and cultural traditions has set them adrift and made them susceptible to the existential vacuum. This vacuum may find expression in a state of boredom, the pursuit of power, or the pursuit of pleasure.

The existential vacuum is a widespread phenomenon of the twentieth century. This is understandable; it may be due to a twofold loss that man had to undergo since he became a truly human being. At the beginning of human history man lost some of the basic animal instincts in which an animal's behavior is embedded and by which it is secured. Such security, like Paradise, is closed to man forever; man has to make choices. In addition to this, however, man has suffered another loss in his more recent development: the traditions that had buttressed his behavior are now rapidly diminishing. No instinct tells him what he has to do, and no tradition tells him what he ought to do; soon he will not know what he wants to do. More and more he will be governed by what others want him to do, thus increasingly falling prey to conformism.

A cross-sectional, statistical survey of the patients and the nursing staff was conducted by my staff in the neurological department at the Vienna Poliklinik Hospital. It revealed that 55% of the persons questioned showed a more or less marked degree of existential vacuum. In other words, more than half of them had experienced a loss of the feeling that life is meaningful.

This existential vacuum manifests itself mainly in a state of boredom. Now we can understand Schopenhauer when he said that mankind was apparently doomed to vacillate eternally between the two extremes of distress and boredom. In actual fact, boredom is now causing, and certainly bringing to psychiatrists, more problems to solve than is distress. And these problems are growing increasingly crucial, for progressive automation will probably lead to an enormous increase in the leisure hours of average workers. The pity of it is that many of them will not know what to do with all their newly acquired free time.

Let us think, for instance, of "Sunday neurosis," that kind of depression which afflicts people who become aware of the lack of content in their lives when the rush of the busy week is over and the void within themselves becomes manifest. Not a few cases of suicide can be traced back to this existential vacuum. Such widespread phenomena as alcoholism and juvenile delinquency are not understandable unless we recognize the existential vacuum underlying them. This is also true of the crises of pensioners and aging people.

Moreover, there are various masks and guises under which the existential vacuum appears. Sometimes the frustrated will to meaning is vicariously compensated for by a will to power, including the most primitive form of the will to power, the will to money. In other cases, the place of frustrated will to meaning is taken by the will to pleasure. That is why existential frustration often eventuates in sexual compensation. We can observe, in such cases, that the sexual libido becomes rampant in the existential vacuum.

An analogous event occurs in neurotic cases. There are certain types of feedback mechanisms and vicious-circle formations that I will touch upon later. One can observe again and again, however, that this symptomatology has invaded an existential vacuum wherein it continues to flourish. In such patients, what we have to deal with is not a noögenic neurosis. However, we will never succeed in having the patient overcome his condition if we do not supplement the psychotherapeutic treatment with logotherapy. For by filling the existential vacuum, the patient will be prevented from further relapses. Therefore, logotherapy is indicated not only in noögenic cases, as pointed out above, but also in psychogenic cases, and in particular in what I have termed the "somatogenic (pseudo-) neuroses." Viewed in this light, a statement once made by Magda B. Arnold[1] is justified: "Every therapy must in some way, no matter how restricted, also be logotherapy."

The Meaning of Life. What, then, *is* the meaning of life that fills the existential vacuum? In Frankl's reply, which follows, note that Frankl suggests that the meaning of one's life fluctuates from day to day, from hour to hour. Is Frankl adopting the Sartrean perspective that we are called upon to define and redefine ourselves day by day, moment by moment? Is he suggesting, again in Sartrean fashion, that humans invent their meanings moment by moment rather than discover them? Or is Frankl simply saying that the meanings or purposes life holds for each of us must be discovered in specific settings and that there is no overall general meaning to life? What is the difference between inventing meaning and discovering it? Is this an important distinction?

I doubt whether a doctor can answer this question in general terms. For the meaning of life differs from man to man, from day to day and from hour to hour. What matters, therefore, is not the meaning of life in general but rather the specific meaning of a person's life at a given moment. To put the question in general terms would be comparable to the question posed to a chess champion, "Tell me, Master, what is the best move in the world?" There simply is no such thing as the best or even a good move apart from a particular situation in a game and the particular personality of one's opponent. The same holds for human existence. One should not search for an abstract meaning of life. Everyone has his own specific vocation or mission in life; everyone must carry out a concrete assignment that demands fulfillment. Therein he cannot be replaced, nor can his life be repeated. Thus, everyone's task is as unique as is his specific opportunity to implement it.

As each situation in life represents a challenge to man and presents a problem for him to solve, the question of the meaning of life may actually be reversed.

---

1 Magda B. Arnold and John A. Gasson, *The Human Person* (New York: The Ronald Press Company, 1954), p. 618.

Ultimately, man should not ask what the meaning of life is, but rather must recognize that it is *he* who is asked. In a word, each man is questioned by life; and he can only answer to life by *answering for* his own life; to life he can only respond by being responsible. Thus, logotherapy sees in responsibleness the very essence of human existence. . . .

Thus far we have shown that the meaning of life always changes, but that it never ceases to be. According to logotherapy, we can discover this meaning in life in three different ways: (1) by doing a deed; (2) by experiencing a value; and (3) by suffering. The first, the way of achievement or accomplishment, is quite obvious. The second and third need further elaboration.

The second way of finding a meaning in life is by experiencing something, such as a work of nature or culture; and also by experiencing someone, i.e., by love.

Love is the only way to grasp another human being in the innermost core of his personality. No one can become fully aware of the very essence of another human being unless he loves him. By the spiritual act of love he is enabled to see the essential traits and features in the beloved person; and even more, he sees that which is potential in him, that which is not yet actualized but yet ought to be actualized. Furthermore, by his love, the loving person enables the beloved person to actualize these potentialities. By making him aware of what can be and of what he should become, he makes these potentialities come true.

In logotherapy, love is not interpreted as a mere epiphenomenon of sexual drives and instincts in the sense of a so-called sublimation. Love is as primary a phenomenon as sex. Normally, sex is a mode of expression for love. Sex is justified, even sanctified, as soon as, but only as long as, it is a vehicle of love. Thus love is not understood as a mere side effect of sex but sex as a way of expressing the experience of that ultimate togetherness that is called love.

A third way to find a meaning in life is by suffering.

Whenever one is confronted with an inescapable, unavoidable situation, whenever one has to face a fate that cannot be changed, e.g., an incurable disease, such as an inoperable cancer, just then is one give a last chance to actualize the highest value, to fulfill the deepest meaning, the meaning of suffering. For what matters above all is the attitude we take toward suffering, the attitude in which we take our suffering upon ourselves.

Let me cite a clear-cut example: Once, an elderly general practitioner consulted me because of his severe depression. He could not overcome the loss of his wife who had died two years before and whom he had loved above all else. Now how could I help him? What should I tell him? Well, I refrained from telling him anything, but instead confronted him with the question, "What would have happened, Doctor, if you had died first, and your wife would have had to survive you?" "Oh," he said, "for her this would have been terrible; how she would have suffered!" Whereupon I replied, "You see, Doctor, such a suffering has been spared her, and it is you who have spared her this suffering; but now, you have to pay for it by surviving and mourning her." He said no word but shook my hand and calmly left my office. Suffering ceases to be suffering in some way at the moment it finds a meaning, such as the meaning of a sacrifice.

Of course, this was no therapy in the proper sense since, first, his despair was no disease; and second, I could not change his fate, I could not revive his wife. But in that moment I did succeed in changing his *attitude* toward his unalterable fate inasmuch as from that time on he could at least see a meaning in his suffering. It is one of the basic tenets of logotherapy that man's main concern is not to gain pleasure or to avoid pain, but rather to see a meaning in his life. That is why man is even ready to suffer, on the condition, to be sure, that his suffering has a meaning.

It goes without saying that suffering would not have a meaning unless it were absolutely necessary; e.g., a cancer that can be cured by surgery must not be shouldered by the patient as though it were his cross. This would be masochism rather than heroism. But if a doctor can neither heal the disease nor bring relief to the patient by easing his pain, he should enlist the patient's capacity to fulfill the meaning of his suffering. Traditional psychotherapy has aimed at restoring one's capacity to work and to enjoy life; logotherapy includes these, yet goes further by having the patient regain his capacity to suffer, if need be, thereby finding meaning even in suffering.

In this context Edith Weisskopf-Joelson, professor of psychology at Purdue University, contends, in her article on logotherapy,[2] that "our current mental-hygiene philosophy stresses the idea that people ought to be happy, that unhappiness is a symptom of maladjustment. Such a value system might be responsible for the fact that the burden of unavoidable unhappiness is increased by unhappiness about being unhappy." And in another paper,[3] she expresses the hope that logotherapy "may help counteract certain unhealthy trends in the present-day culture of the United States, where the incurable sufferer is given very little opportunity to be proud of his suffering and to consider it ennobling rather than degrading" so that "he is not only unhappy, but also ashamed of being unhappy."

There are situations in which one is cut off from the opportunity to do one's work or to enjoy one's life; but what never can be ruled out is the unavoidability of suffering. In accepting this challenge to suffer bravely, life has a meaning up to the last moment, and it retains this meaning literally to the end. In other words, life's meaning is an unconditional one, for it even includes the potential meaning of suffering.

Let me recall that which was perhaps the deepest experience I had in the concentration camp. The odds of surviving the camp were no more than one to twenty, as can easily be verified by exact statistics. It did not even seem possible, let alone probable, that the manuscript of my first book, which I had hidden in my coat when I arrived at Auschwitz, would ever be rescued. Thus, I had to undergo and to overcome the loss of my spiritual child. And now it seemed as if nothing and no one would survive me; neither a physical nor a spiritual child of my own! So I found myself confronted with the question of whether under such circumstances my life was ultimately void of any meaning.

Not yet did I notice that an answer to this question with which I was wrestling so passionately was already in store for me, and that soon thereafter this answer would be given to me. This was the case when I had to surrender my clothes and in turn inherited the worn-out rags of an inmate who had been sent to the gas chamber immediately after his arrival at the Auschwitz railway station. Instead of the many pages of my manuscript, I found in a pocket of the newly acquired coat a single page torn out of a Hebrew prayer book, which contained the main Jewish prayer, *Shema Yisrael*. How should I have interpreted such a "coincidence" other than as a challenge to *live* my thoughts instead of merely putting them on paper?

[2]   Edith Weisskopf-Joelson, "Some Comments on a Viennese School of Psychiatry," *The Journal of Abnormal and Social Psychology*, Vol. 51, pp. 701–3 (1955).

[3]   Edith Weisskopf-Joelson, "Logotherapy and Existential Analysis," *Acta psychotherap.*, Vol. 6, pp. 193–204 (1958).

A bit later, I remember, it seemed to me that I would die in the near future. In this critical situation, however, my concern was different from that of most of my comrades. Their question was, "Will we survive the camp? For, if not, all this suffering has no meaning." The question which beset me was, "Has all this suffering, this dying around us, a meaning? For, if not, then ultimately there is no meaning to survival; for a life whose meaning depends upon such a happenstance—whether one escapes or not—ultimately would not be worth living at all."

Modern Collective Neurosis: Nihilism. Frankl claims that much of modern psychotherapy is informed by what he calls "pan-determinism," the view that the human is *fully* conditioned by hereditary and environmental factors. This view, says Frankl, breeds both fatalism (the claim that there is not much one can do to alter the predetermined course of his or her life) and also nihilism (the claim that life has no meaning). Indeed, if I accept the contention that I am a pawn of forces beyond my control, that I cannot alter the inexorable playing out of those forces, am I not induced to think of myself as merely a puff of smoke in the capricious winds of primal forces, an ephemeral thing devoid of meaning, a thing whose existence is like a tale told by an idiot—full of sound and fury but signifying nothing? For Frankl, nihilism is the disease of modern humankind, and Frankl offers some strong words in response.

> Every age has its own collective neurosis, and every age needs its own psychotherapy to cope with it. The existential vacuum that is the mass neurosis of the present time, can be described as a private and personal form of nihilism; for nihilism can be defined as the contention that being has no meaning. As for psychotherapy, however, it will never be able to cope with this state of affairs on a mass scale if it does not keep itself free from the impact and influence of the contemporary trends of a nihilistic philosophy; otherwise it represents a symptom of the mass neurosis rather than its possible cure. Psychotherapy would not only reflect a nihilistic philosophy but also, even though unwillingly and unwittingly, transmit to the patient what is actually a caricature rather than a true picture of man.
>
> First of all, there is a danger inherent in the teaching of man's "nothingbutness," the theory that man is nothing but the result of biological, psychological and sociological conditions, or the product of heredity and environment. Such a view of man makes him into a robot, not a human being. This neurotic fatalism is fostered and strengthened by a psychotherapy that denies that man is free.
>
> To be sure, a human being is a finite being, and his freedom is restricted. It is not freedom from conditions, but freedom to take a stand toward the conditions. For example, I am certainly not responsible for the fact that I have gray hair; however, I am responsible for the fact that I did not go to the hairdresser to have him tint my hair—as a number of ladies might have done. So there is a certain amount of freedom left to everyone, even if only the choice of the color of one's hair.
>
> Psychoanalysis has often been blamed for its so-called pan-sexualism. I, for one, doubt whether this approach has ever been legitimate. However, there is something that seems to me to be an even more erroneous and dangerous assumption, namely, that which I call "pan-determinism." By that I mean the view of man that disregards his capacity to take a stand toward any conditions whatsoever. Man is *not* fully conditioned and determined; he determines himself whether to give in to conditions or stand up to

them. In other words, man is ultimately self-determining. Man does not simply exist, but always decides what his existence will be, what he will become in the next moment.

By the same token, every human being has the freedom to change at an instant. Therefore, we can predict his future only within the large frame of a statistical survey referring to a whole group; the individual personality, however, remains essentially unpredictable. The basis for any predictions would be represented by biological, psychological or sociological conditions. Yet one of the main features of human existence is the capacity to rise above such conditions and transcend them. In the same manner, man ultimately transcends himself; a human being is self-transcending being.

Let me cite the case of Dr. J___. He was the only man I ever encountered in my whole life whom I would dare to call a Mephistophelean being, a satanic figure. At that time he was generally called "the mass murderer of Steinhof," the name of the large mental hospital in Vienna. When the Nazis started their euthanasia program, he held all the strings in his hands and was so fanatic in the job assigned to him that he tried not to let one single psychotic individual escape the gas chamber. After the war, when I came back to Vienna I asked what had happened to Dr. J___. "He has been imprisoned by the Russians in one of the isolation cells of Steinhof," they told me. "On the next day, however, the door of his cell stood open and Dr. J___ was never seen again." Later I was convinced that, like others, he had by the help of his comrades made his way to South America. More recently, however, I was consulted by a former Austrian diplomat who had been imprisoned behind the Iron Curtain for many years, first in Siberia and then in the famous Ljubljanka prison in Moscow. While I was examining him neurologically, he suddenly asked me whether I happened to know Dr. J___. After my affirmative reply he continued: "I made his acquaintance in Ljubljanka. There he died, at about forty, from cancer of the urinary bladder. Before he died, however, he showed himself to be the best comrade you can imagine! He gave consolation to everybody. He lived up to the highest conceivable moral standard. He was the best friend I ever met during my long years in prison!"

This is the story of Dr. J___, "the mass murderer of Steinhof." How can you dare to predict the behavior of man! You may predict the movements of a machine, of an automaton; more than this, you may even try to predict the mechanisms or "dynamisms" of the human *psyche* as well: but man is more than *psyche*. . . .

For too long a time, for half a century in fact, psychiatry tried to interpret the human mind merely as a mechanism, and consequently the therapy of mental disease merely as a technique. I believe this dream has been dreamt out. What now begin to loom on the horizon are not the sketches of a psychologized medicine, but those of a humanized psychiatry.

A doctor, however, who would still interpret his own role mainly as that of a technician, would confess that he sees in his patient nothing more than a machine, instead of seeing the human being behind the disease!

A human being is not one thing among others; *things* determine each other, but *man* is ultimately self-determining. What he becomes—within the limits of endowment and environment—he has made out of himself. In the concentration camps, for example, in this living laboratory and on this testing ground, we watched and witnessed some of our comrades behave like swine while others behaved like saints. Man has both potentialities within himself; which one is actualized depends on decisions but not on conditions.

Our generation is realistic, for we have come to know man as he really is. After all, man is that being who has invented the gas chambers of Auschwitz; however, he is also that being who has entered those gas chambers upright, with the Lord's Prayer or the *Shema Yisrael* on his lips.

In reflecting upon Frankl's argument several questions are worth noting. What if the Nazis, who ran the concentration camps where Frankl and his fellow prisoners suffered, claimed that they were simply fulfilling the meaning that life harbored for them at that time? Are all meanings equally warranted because all are disprivileged? Would not Frankl find repugnant the goal or purpose of some Nazis (namely, building a master race through racial, ethnic, and genetic cleansing), a goal which invested their lives with meaning and enabled them to survive? But by what criteria would Frankl reject this Nazi sense of meaning? By what criteria would he adjudicate diverse human projects? Is not this same problem encountered by the virtue ethicists (see Chapter 6) when they challenge us to ask "What kind of a person will I become if I do this act, and is that the kind of person I wish to become?" Are we perhaps driven to affirm Bernard Gert's five moral rules as reflecting five fundamental human evils (death, pain, disability, loss of freedom, loss of pleasure) that must be recognized and avoided, if possible, for humans to survive and flourish?

Note on Sources.   The material in this section is quoted from Viktor Frankl *Man's Search for Meaning: An Introduction to Logotherapy* (New York: Pocket Books, 1963), pp. 103–107, 117–122, 154–173, 176–183, 204–209, 212–214.

2   THE BIBLICAL TRADITION

THE STORY OF THE GOD WHO ACTS

From Frankl to the Biblical Tradition.   According to Frankl, life presents each person with an *open* and *distinctive* future. My future is open because there are real possible future alternatives presented to me from which I can, must, and do choose. I am free. I have tasks to perform, and/or values to be experienced, and/or inescapable sufferings to endure that are uniquely mine. The specific meaning or purpose that I am called upon to fulfill each day is uniquely mine, no one else's. Frankl declares that "the meaning of life differs from man to man, from day to day and from hour to hour. . . . One should not search for an abstract meaning of life. Everyone has his own specific vocation or mission in life . . ." (*Man's Search for Meaning*, pp. 171–172).

If, as Frankl says, my meaning for today is uniquely mine and yours is uniquely yours, does that mean that the general or cosmic question which embraces all of us (What is the meaning of life?) and which is frequently answered by the world's religious traditions is an inappropriate question? Not necessarily. As a logotherapist, Frankl focuses on the individual's specific, personal story, not on humankind's story in general. Yet he neither criticizes nor ignores the cosmic stories that his patients bring with them. Indeed, on occasion he draws on a patient's cosmic story to help the patient exit the existential vacuum. Clearly, Frankl is not an enemy of the cosmic story. One could even argue that his view of the will to meaning being fulfilled through a task performed, a value experienced, or an inescapable suffering endured is itself a cosmic story that describes the form that human meaning takes, a form that all humans share and a form that each individual is called upon to fill with content through personal, specific choices. Furthermore, a case could be made that the cosmic stories of the great religious traditions focus on Frankl's three categories: work, love, and suffering. Let us proceed, then, to examine the cosmic stories offered by several representative religious traditions beginning with the biblical view, bearing in mind of course that not all cosmic stories are religious.

HISTORICAL NOTE.   The Bible, from which the excerpts in this section have been taken, is not just one book. It is, rather, a mini-library of more than sixty volumes. It was written over the course of more than ten centuries by scores of contributing writers. Some of these writers are known; others unknown. Indeed, one of the finest theological treatises in the collection was written by an anonymous person called "Second Isaiah" by scholars because his or her treatise was simply attached to the end of the book written by Isaiah. Diverse literary forms are present in the Bible, including poetry, parables, letters, myths, historical narratives, and regulations for secular and sacred activities.

As the biblical narrative unfolds, we encounter Abraham leaving Mesopotamia, around 1750 B.C., in search of a land where he can raise his family and serve his God. He settled in the land of Canaan where his son Isaac, grandson Jacob (also referred to as "Israel"), and their descendants lived until a famine drove Jacob and his family to Egypt for food. In Egypt they flourished until the Egyptians forced them into servitude. Around 1290 B.C. Moses masterminded the Exodus of the children of Israel from Egypt and their journey back to Canaan. In Canaan, after a protracted struggle, they subdued their rivals for the land and established a kingdom around 1020 B.C., first ruled by Saul and then by David. The rising and falling fortunes of this kingdom are chronicled in page after page of the Bible.

Infused into this political story is the theme that the children of Israel, in all their actions, are either cooperating with their God or frustrating his revealed plans for them. Indeed, it would be safe to say that the Bible, in spite of its being a multivolume work, contains a single unifying perspective of a God who acts purposefully. The Bible presents us with the picture of a God who has a purpose, who is involved in events to promote that purpose, and who reveals himself to humans to invite them to participate with him in accomplishing that purpose. The goal of divine action in the Bible seems to be the creation of a "people of God," a human community that is holy, just, and righteous, a community that eventually would bring spiritual enlightenment to humankind. The story that unfolds in the Bible is, accordingly, a drama of the vacillating responses of the children of Israel to the divine summons to be a people of God.

ARGUMENT OF THE PASSAGES.   The first passage we have selected comes from Deuteronomy, the fifth book of the Bible. It was probably written no earlier than the late seventh century B.C., but it represents a more ancient oral tradition that in all likelihood stems from Moses. This passage prescribes the prayer a faithful Israelite is to offer when bringing the firstfruits of the harvest to the priest as an expression of thankfulness to God. "Homeless Aramaean" in verse 5 refers to Jacob.

26 WHEN YOU COME INTO THE LAND WHICH the LORD your God is giving you to occupy as your patrimony and settle in

2 it, you shall take the firstfruits of all the produce of the soil, which you gather in from the land which the LORD your God is giving you, and put them in a basket. Then you shall go to the place which the LORD your God will choose

3 as a dwelling for his Name and come to the priest, whoever he shall be in those days. You shall say to him, 'I declare this day to the LORD your God that I have entered the land which the LORD swore to our forefathers to give us.'

4 The priest shall take the basket from your hand and set it down before the

5 altar of the LORD your God. Then you shall solemnly recite before the LORD your God: 'My father was a homeless Aramaean who went down to Egypt with a small company and lived there until they became a great, powerful, and numerous nation. But the Egyptians ill-treated us, humiliated us and imposed **6** cruel slavery upon us. Then we cried to **7** the LORD the God of our fathers for help, and he listened to us and saw our humiliation, our hardship and distress; and so the LORD brought us out of **8** Egypt with a strong hand and out-stretched arm, with terrifying deeds, and with signs and portents. He **9** brought us to this place and gave us this land, a land flowing with milk and honey. And now I have brought the **10** firstfruits of the soil which thou, O LORD, hast given me.' You shall then set the basket before the LORD your God and bow down in worship before him. You shall all rejoice, you and the **11** Levites and the aliens living among you, for all the good things which the LORD your God has given to you and to your family.

Some scholars regard this prayer to be a very ancient tradition that exposes the heart of the Israelites' faith. Notice that the prayer is historically oriented and that it celebrates the Exodus as divine liberation. Clearly, Israelite faith sets human action within the context of divine action, from which the human action derives its ultimate significance.

The next passage summarizes the vacillating commitment of the Israelites to the God of their liberation from bondage in Egypt. Moses, you will recall, led the Israelites in their Exodus from Egypt. He did not, however, guide them into Canaan, their "promised land." That task was left to his successor, Joshua, an able military leader who led the Israelites successfully in their attempt to establish settlements among the inhabitants of Canaan. The Israelites were unable, however, to destroy the indigenous Canaanites. They remained as a constant military threat to the Israelite newcomers, and their polytheistic religion, with its emphasis on fertility and the cycles of nature, represented a powerful alternative to the Israelite faith centered in the God of the Exodus. The following passage suggests that in times of prosperity the Israelites tended to forget the God of the Exodus with His ethical demands and instead embraced the Baal of the Canaanites with his sexually sensuous religious rites. In times of adversity, however, the Israelites would return to the worship of the God of deliverance, the one who brought them out of bondage in Egypt.

6 JOSHUA DISMISSED THE PEOPLE, AND THE Israelites went off to occupy the country,
7 each man to his allotted portion. As long as Joshua was alive and the elders who survived him—everyone, that is, who had witnessed the whole great work which the LORD had done for Israel—the people worshipped the
8 LORD. At the age of a hundred and ten Joshua son of Nun, the servant of the
9 LORD, died, and they buried him within the border of his own property in Timnath-heres north of Mount Gaash
10 in the hill-country of Ephraim. Of that whole generation, all were gathered to their forefathers, and another generation followed who did not acknowledge the LORD and did not know what he
11 had done for Israel. Then the Israelites did what was wrong in the eyes of the LORD, and worshipped the Baalim.
12 They forsook the LORD, their fathers' God who had brought them out of Egypt, and went after other gods, gods of the races among whom they lived; they bowed before them and provoked
13 the LORD to anger; they forsook the LORD and worshipped the Baal and
14 the Ashtaroth. The LORD in his anger made them the prey of bands of raiders and plunderers; he sold them to their enemies all around them, and they
15 could no longer make a stand. Every time they went out to battle the LORD brought disaster upon them, as he had said when he gave them his solemn warning, and they were in dire straits.

The LORD set judges over them, who 16 rescued them from the marauding bands. Yet they did not listen even to 17 these judges, but turned wantonly to worship other gods and bowed down before them; all too soon they abandoned the path of obedience to the LORD's commands which their forefathers had followed. They did not obey the LORD. Whenever the LORD set up 18 a judge over them, he was with that judge, and kept them safe from their enemies so long as he lived. The LORD would relent as often as he heard them groaning under oppression and illtreatment. But as soon as the judge 19 was dead, they would relapse into deeper corruption than their forefathers and give their allegiance to other gods, worshipping them and bowing down before them. They gave up none of their evil practices and their wilful ways. And the LORD was angry with 20 Israel and said, 'This nation has broken the covenant which I laid upon their forefathers and has not obeyed me, and now, of all the nations which 21 Joshua left at his death, I will not drive out to make room for them one single 22 man. By their means I will test Israel, to see whether or not they will keep strictly to the way of the LORD as 23 their forefathers did.' So the LORD left those nations alone and made no haste to drive them out or give them into Joshua's hands.

This view of the Israelite struggle with Canaanite culture, with the implicit claim that fidelity to God and His purposes leads to peace and prosperity, while rejection of God and His plans leads to strife and adversity, is at the core of an enormously influential stream of thought called the Deuteronomic theology of history. Indeed, does it not seem fitting that the righteous should be happy and that the unrighteous should be miserable? Accordingly, adversity and suffering in the life of a nation (or individual) would be interpreted as evidence that the will of God was being violated.

The Deuteronomic moral law of cause and effect (that is, the claim that as you sow, so shall you reap) seemed to explain quite well the adversities that befell people and offered the Israelites a cosmic story whose power to interpret events endured for centuries.

In 586 B.C. Nebuchadrezzar, King of Babylon, destroyed Jerusalem and carried the leading citizens of the nation into exile in Babylon. For years, prophets had warned of a coming doom that would be a fitting punishment for Israel's neglect of righteousness and disregard for social justice. The destruction of Jerusalem seemed to be not only that prophesied punishment for Israel's sins, but also a devastation of the nation itself, and even an incentive to abandon faith in the cosmic story that God was working with the "chosen people," the children of Israel to create a holy and just human community. One might think that the cosmic story beginning with God's summons to Abraham would be discredited beyond recovery. No doubt there was some loss of faith; but the destruction of Jerusalem and the exile in Babylon inspired a fresh outpouring of religious seriousness. Great prophetic voices like those of Ezekiel and Second Isaiah helped to keep faith alive. Indeed, Second Isaiah went so far as to internationalize Israel's cosmic story. Second Isaiah discerned the purposes of God to be more inclusive than merely creating a nation of Israelites who pursued righteousness and justice. For Second Isaiah, the community of God's concern embraced all peoples. In one of the famous "Servant of God" passages, Second Isaiah envisions an international mission for the Servant. Some scholars think that the "Servant" refers to an individual, while others believe the reference is to the Israelite community. No matter who "Servant" refers to, Israel's cosmic story here takes on a global dimension.

42 Here is my servant, whom I uphold,
my chosen one in whom I delight,
I have bestowed my spirit upon
him,
and he will make justice shine on
the nations.
2 He will not call out or lift his voice
high,
or make himself heard in the open
street.
3 He will not break a bruised reed,
or snuff out a smoldering wick;
he will make justice shine on every
race,
4 never faltering, never breaking
down,
he will plant justice on earth,
while coasts and islands wait for
his teaching.

5 Thus speaks the LORD who is God,
he who created the skies and
stretched them out,
who fashioned the earth and all
that grows in it,

who gave breath to its people,
the breath of life to all who walk
upon it:
I, the LORD, have called you with 6
righteous purpose
and taken you by the hand;
I have formed you, and
appointed you
to be a light to all peoples,
a beacon for the nations,
to open eyes that are blind, 7
to bring captives out of prison,
out of the dungeons where they
lie in darkness.

I am the LORD; the LORD is my 8
name;
I will not give my glory to another
god,
nor my praise to any idol.
See how the first prophecies have 9
come to pass,
and now I declare new things;
before they break from the bud I
announce them to you.

Almost fifty years after the destruction of Jerusalem, Cyrus the Great of Persia conquered Babylon and allowed the exiled Israelites to return to Palestine to rebuild their nation. To many of the exiles it must have seemed as if the Deuteronomic moral law was being vindicated. Israel had paid heavily for her centuries of sins, but her renewed commitment to God was now being rewarded. With understandable zeal, the repatriates attempted to establish a holy community in Palestine that would remain faithful to God come what may. Scrupulously, they tried to obey the laws of Moses.

According to Deuteronomic theory, this building of a holy community should have produced peace and prosperity, but it did not. Strife and adversity plagued the Israelites in their rebuilding. The Deuteronomic cosmic story was seriously challenged. Pious Israelites began to ask, "Why do the righteous suffer? Why do bad things happen to good people?" Those are the questions with which the Book of Job wrestled in the post-exilic period. In the Book of Job, one of humankind's poetic masterpieces, we encounter Job, a righteous, thinking man whose suffering calls into question the established Deuteronomic doctrine that whatsoever one sows that will one also reap.

Job had lived a righteous life and had tasted the sweet fruits of prosperity. As the poem begins, Job is deluged by a tidal wave of adversity. Three friends come to comfort him. By his side they sit in silence for seven days. Job breaks the silence with a cry of dereliction, wishing that he had never been born. Wondering why he has been called upon to suffer when he has tried so diligently to live uprightly, feeling betrayed by God and scoffed at by miscreants, Job cries out for healing words. Does he receive such healing from his friends? Hardly. An extended debate ensues, in which they affirm over and over the orthodox doctrine of divine retribution and try to convince Job that his afflictions are punishments for sins. They challenge Job to search his past, to acknowledge his misdeeds, and to seek forgiveness. Job, a thinking and honest man, cannot discern anything in his past conduct that merits such affliction. Indeed, his experience stands as evidence that seems to falsify the Deuteronomic cosmic story championed by his three compatriots. But Job's quarrel is not just with those three friends. Because Job believed that God was ultimately responsible for all events, his complaint, in the final analysis, is directed against God Himself. Indeed, Job declares that if he could just find God, he would challenge Him to his face on the issue of the unjust suffering of the righteous. The poem reaches its climax and conclusion when God Himself enters the debate and asks questions that reveal how puny is the wisdom of Job that has called into question the wisdom of God. God's interrogation of Job reduces him to submission and silence. Here are but a few verses from this grand poem that calls into question the Deuteronomic story.

We begin with the arrival of Job's three friends, who have come to console him on the loss of his material wealth, the death of his sons and daughters, and the savage affliction of his body with disease.

11 When Job's three friends, Eliphaz of Teman, Bildad of Shuah, and Zophar of Naamah, heard of all these calamities which had overtaken him, they left their homes and arranged to come and con-

12 dole with him and comfort him. But when they first saw him from a distance, they did not recognize him; and they wept aloud, rent their cloaks and tossed

13 dust into the air over their heads. For seven days and seven nights they sat beside him on the ground, and none of them said a word to him; for they saw that his suffering was very great.

3 1–2 After this Job broke silence and cursed the day of his birth:

3 Perish the day when I was born
and the night which said, 'A man is
conceived'! . . .

11 Why was I not still-born,
why did I not die when I came out
of the womb?

12 Why was I ever laid on my mother's
knees

or put to suck at her breasts?
Why was I not hidden like an
untimely birth,   16
like an infant that has not lived to
see the light?
For then I should be lying in the
quiet grave,   13
asleep in death, at rest,
with kings and their ministers
who built themselves palaces,   14
with princes rich in gold
who filled their houses with silver.   15
There the wicked man chafes no
more,   17
there the tired labourer rests;
the captive too finds peace there
and hears no taskmaster's voice;   18
high and low are there,
even the slave, free from his master.   19

Why should the sufferer be born to   20
see the light?
Why is life given to men who find it
so bitter?

One of his friends replies to Job's cry with an affirmation of the Deuteronomic moral order: as one sows, so one reaps.

4 Then Eliphaz the Temanite began:

2 If one ventures to speak with you,
will you lose patience?
For who could hold his tongue any
longer?

3 Think how once you encouraged
those who faltered,
how you braced feeble arms,

4 how a word from you upheld the
stumblers
and put strength into weak knees.

5 But now that adversity comes upon
you, you lose patience;

it touches you, and you are unmanned.   6
Is your religion no comfort to you?
Does your blameless life give you no
hope?
For consider, what innocent man has   7
ever perished?
Where have you seen the upright
destroyed?
This I know, that those who plough   8
mischief and sow trouble
reap as they have sown;
they perish at the blast of God   9
and are shrivelled by the breath of
his nostrils.

Job responds, demanding that he be made aware of his misdeeds.

6 Then Job answered:

2 O that the grounds for my resentment
might be weighed,

and my misfortunes set with them on
the scales!
For they would outweigh the sands   3
of the sea:

what wonder if my words are wild?

4 The arrows of the Almighty find their
    mark in me,
and their poison soaks into my spirit;
God's onslaughts wear me away.

5 Does the wild ass bray when he has
    grass
or the ox low when he has fodder?

6 Can a man eat tasteless food
    unseasoned with salt,
or find any flavor in the juice of
    mallows?

7 Food that should nourish me sticks
    in my throat,
and my bowels rumble with an
    echoing sound.

8 O that I might have my request,
that God would grant what I hope
    for:

that he would be pleased to crush me, 9
to snatch me away with his hand and
    cut me off!

For that would bring me relief, 10
and in the face of unsparing anguish
    I would leap for joy.

Have I the strength to wait? 11
What end have I to expect, that I
    should be patient?

Is my strength the strength of stone, 12
or is my flesh bronze?

Oh how shall I find help within 13
    myself?
The power to aid myself is put out
    of my reach. . . .

Tell me plainly, and I will listen in 24
    silence;
show me where I have erred.

Another of his friends reiterates the Deuteronomic doctrine, in response to which Job protests that he is blameless and claims that God destroys the innocent and the wicked alike.

8 Then Bildad the Shuhite began:

2 How long will you say such things,
the long-winded ramblings of an old
    man?

3 Does God pervert judgment?
Does the Almighty pervert justice?

4 Your sons sinned against him,
so he left them to be victims of their
    own iniquity.

5 If only you will seek God betimes
and plead for the favor of the
    Almighty,

6 if you are innocent and upright,
then indeed will he watch over you
and see your just intent fulfilled.

7 Then, though your beginnings were
    humble,
your end will be great. . . .

9 Then Job answered:

2 Indeed this I know for the truth,
that no man can win his case against
    God.

3 If a man chooses to argue with him,
God will not answer one question
    in a thousand.

He is wise, he is powerful; 4
what man has stubbornly resisted him
    and survived? . . .

Though I am right, I get no answer, 15
though I plead with my accuser for
    mercy.
If I summoned him to court and he
    responded,
I do not believe that he would listen 16
    to my plea—
for he bears hard upon me for a
    trifle 17
and rains blows on me without cause;
he leaves me no respite to recover 18
    my breath
but fills me with bitter thoughts.
If the appeal is to force, see how 19
    strong he is;
if to justice, who can compel him to
    give me a hearing?
Though I am right, he condemns me 20
    out of my own mouth;
though I am blameless, he twists my
    words.
Blameless, I say; of myself 21
I reck nothing, I hold my life cheap.
But it is all one; therefore I say, 22

'He destroys blameless and wicked
    alike' . . .

10 I am sickened of life;
    I will give free rein to my griefs,

I will speak out in bitterness of soul.
I will say to God, 'Do not condemn
    me,   2
but tell me the ground of thy
    complaint against me.

Job reminds his friends that, like them, he has a lifetime of experience, and that he does understand what they are saying. Unlike them, however, he is prepared to argue with God Himself about unmerited suffering.

13 All this I have seen with my own eyes,
    with my own ears I have heard it, and
        understood it.
2   What you know, I also know;
    in nothing do I fall short of you.
3   But for my part I would speak with
        the Almighty
    and am ready to argue with God,
4   while you like fools are smearing
            truth with your falsehoods,
    stitching a patchwork of lies, one and
        all.
5   Ah, if you would only be silent
    and let silence be your wisdom!
6   Now listen to my arguments
    and attend while I put my case.
7   Is it on God's behalf that you speak
        so wickedly,
    or in his defence that you allege what
        is false?
8   Must you take God's part,
    or put his case for him?
9   Will all be well when he examines
        you?
    Will you quibble with him as you
        quibble with a man?
10 He will most surely expose you

if you take his part by falsely accusing
    me.
Will not God's majesty strike you   11
    with dread,
and terror of him overwhelm you?
Your pompous talk is dust and ashes,   12
your defenses will crumble like clay.
Be silent, leave me to speak my mind,   13
and let what may come upon me!
I will put my neck in the noose   14
and take my life in my hands.
If he would slay me, I should not   15
        hesitate;
I should still argue my cause to his
        face.
This at least assures my success,   16
that no godless man may appear
        before him.
Listen then, listen to my words,   17
and give a hearing to my exposition.
Be sure of this: once I have stated my   18
        case
I know that I shall be acquitted.
Who is there that can argue so   19
        forcibly with me
that he could reduce me straightway
        to silence and death?

Intransigently, Job's friends cling to the Deuteronomic doctrine and repeatedly challenge Job to repent of his sins so that God will cease to afflict him.

22 Then Eliphaz the Temanite answered:

2   Can man be any benefit to God?
    Can even a wise man benefit him?
3   Is it an asset to the Almighty if you
        are righteous?
    Does he gain if your conduct is
        perfect?
4   Do not think that he reproves you
        because you are pious,

that on this count he brings you to
    trial.

No: it is because you are a very   5
    wicked man,
and your depravity passes all
    bounds. . . .

Come to terms with God and you   21
    will prosper;

that is the way to mend your fortune.
22 Take instruction from his mouth
and store his words in your heart.
23 If you come back to the Almighty in
true sincerity,
if you banish wrongdoing from your
home,
24 if you treat your precious metal as dust
and the gold of Ophir as stones from
the river-bed,
25 then the Almighty himself will be
your precious metal;
he will be your silver in double measure.
26 Then, with sure trust in the
Almighty,

you will raise your face to God;
you will pray to him, and he will hear   27
    you,
and you will have cause to fulfill your
    vows.
In all your designs you will   28
    succeed,
and light will shine on your path;
but God brings down the pride of   29
    the haughty
and keeps safe the man of modest
    looks.
He will deliver the innocent,   30
and you will be delivered, because
    your hands are clean.

Job really wants to argue with God, not with these purveyors of conventional wisdom. Job's desire is realized. God addresses him from the midst of a storm.

38 Then the LORD answered Job out of
the tempest:

2 Who is this whose ignorant words
cloud my design in darkness?
3 Brace yourself and stand up like a
man;
I will ask questions, and you shall
answer.
4 Where were you when I laid the
earth's foundations?
Tell me, if you know and understand.
5 Who settled its dimensions? Surely
you should know.
Who stretched his measuring-line over
it?
6 On what do its supporting pillars
rest?
Who set its corner-stone in place,
7 when the morning stars sang
together
and all the sons of God shouted
aloud?
8 Who watched over the birth of the
sea,
when it burst in flood from the
womb?—
9 when I wrapped it in a blanket of
cloud
and cradled it in fog,
10 when I established its bounds,

fixing its doors and bars in place,
and said, 'Thus far shall you come   11
    and no farther,
and here your surging waves shall
    halt.'
In all your life have you ever called   12
    up the dawn
or shown the morning its place? . . .

Have you descended to the springs of   16
    the sea
or walked in the unfathomable deep?
Have the gates of death been revealed   17
    to you?
Have you ever seen the door-keepers
    of the place of darkness?
Have you comprehended the vast   18
    expanse of the world?
Come, tell me all this, if you know.
Which is the way to the home of   19
    light
and where does darkness dwell?
And can you then take each to its   20
    appointed bound
and escort it on its homeward path?
Doubtless you know all this; for you   21
    were born already,
so long is the span of your life!

Have you visited the storehouse of   22
    the snow

or seen the arsenal where hail is
    stored,
which I have kept ready for the day
23   of calamity,
for war and for the hour of battle? . . .

40   Then the LORD said to Job:

2   Is it for a man who disputes with the
      Almighty to be stubborn?
    Should he that argues with God
      answer back?

3   And Job answered the LORD:

4   What reply can I give thee, I who
      carry no weight?
    I put my finger to my lips.
5   I have spoken once and now will
      not answer again;
    twice I have spoken, and I will do so
      no more.

6   Then the LORD answered Job out of
    the tempest:

7   Brace yourself and stand up like a man;
    I will ask questions, and you shall
      answer.
8   Dare you deny that I am just
    or put me in the wrong that you may
      be right?

Have you an arm like God's arm,   9
can you thunder with a voice like
    his?
Deck yourself out, if you can, in   10
    pride and dignity,
array yourself in pomp and splendour;
unleash the fury of your wrath,   11
look upon the proud man and
    humble him;
look upon every proud man and   12
    bring him low,
throw down the wicked where they
    stand;
hide them in the dust together,   13
and shroud them in an unknown
    grave.
Then I in my turn will acknowledge   14
that your own right hand can save you. . . .

Then Job answered the LORD: **42**

I know that thou canst do all things   2
and that no purpose is beyond thee.
But I have spoken of great things   3
    which I have not understood,
things too wonderful for me to
    know.
I knew of thee then only by report   5
but now I see thee with my own eyes.
Therefore I melt away;   6
I repent in dust and ashes.

So Job's question "Why do bad things happen to good people?" remains unanswered; his outspoken challenge to the Deuteronomic story is silenced. Does that silence suggest that the Deuteronomic view is validated? Or does the silence suggest that the suffering of the righteous person is a riddle that does not fit neatly into the story as structured by conventional wisdom? If so, does that silence suggest that the Deuteronomic cosmic story needs revision? If so, in what way?

There are several ways in which that cosmic story could be revised. One approach would be to claim, along with John Stuart Mill (see Chapter 5), that God is finite. In that case, God could be viewed as willing but unable to ensure that bad things will not happen to good people. God would be seen as genuinely needing human beings to promote his purposes. To be needed by God is no insignificant task for a human. Would not such a revision of the cosmic theory provide a solution to Job's puzzle, and invest human life with abiding purpose and meaning? Or would regarding God as finite remove the assurance that God's purposes would ultimately prevail, and thereby divest this cosmic story of its power to satisfy the human quest for meaning? Would affirming a finite God only make matters worse as Bradley claims in his response to Mill? (See Chapter 5, again.)

Another approach would be to build on Bradley's suggestion that "mysteries" are to be expected in religious thinking. One might claim, for example, that God acts, through events, to promote his purposes; that God does reward righteousness and punish evil; and that righteous people do frequently experience unmerited suffering. But one could add the further claim that suffering is a mystery that currently transcends human intelligence. Would that addendum to the cosmic story really satisfy the questions of the innocent who suffer?

Still another approach would be to extend the concept of human life to include postdeath survival (the issue addressed in Chapter 4). One could then claim that unmerited suffering would in due course receive appropriate compensation, if not on this side of death, then surely on the other. The notion of postdeath compensation for current privation became an increasingly appealing addition to the cosmic story during the post-exilic period when thinking about life after death gained increased attention. This approach became especially attractive to Christians in light of their belief in the resurrection of Jesus as the Christ. But what kind of postdeath situation would be, indeed could be, adequate compensation for the painful death of a little child or for the innocent victims of war?

Since Job, the biblical cosmic story has been questioned, rethought, and refined. It will, no doubt, continue to be pondered and revised because it brings together three important human realities: the will to meaning; the sense of the divine; and the experience of unmerited suffering.

As you reflect on the selections in this section, remember that space limitations have allowed us to include only a very few passages from an extensive and diverse literary tradition. We invite you to enhance the discussion of this section by examining on your own the rich variety of that tradition.

The biblical story of a God who acts to accomplish his purposes invests the lives of some people, but not all, with meaning. Other people look to other cosmic stories for meaning. We turn next to an ancient story that has been widely received by diverse peoples: the Buddhist story.

NOTE ON SOURCES. The material in this section is quoted from *The New English Bible with the Apocrypha* (New York: Oxford University Press, 1976). Passages are from Deuteronomy 26:1–11; Judges 2:6–23; Isaiah 42:1–9; and Job 2:11–3:3; 3:11–20; 4:1–9; 6:1–13, 24; 8:1–7; 9:1–4, 15–22; 10:1–2; 13:1–19; 22:1–5, 21–30; 38:1–12, 16–23; 40:1–14; 42:1–6.

3 THE BUDDHIST TRADITION

THE STORY OF TRANSCENDING SUFFERING

FROM THE BIBLICAL TO THE BUDDHIST TRADITION. In this chapter we examine the stories people tell about themselves to try to connect human events with each other so that life appears to be moving in a certain direction, toward an intelligible goal. The biblical story portrayed the patriarchs (Abraham, Isaac, and Jacob) and their descendants responding to the summons from God to become a holy, righteous, and just community that would eventually bring spiritual enlightenment to humankind. Running through this story is the Deuteronomic theme that God rewards the righteous with peace and prosperity but punishes the wicked with strife and adversity. Apparently, this story was able to invest the lives of believers with a sense of meaning and purpose for centuries. Presumably the suffering of innocent individuals could be explained as divine punishment for the sins of their ancestors. But when the children of Israel seemed to have paid fully for their past sins, through the destruction of Jerusalem and the subsequent exile in Babylon, the suffering of innocent persons became a serious challenge to the biblical story. That challenge was articulated powerfully by the Book of Job some time after the return of the exiles to Palestine in the middle of the sixth century B.C. In the twentieth century the questions asked by Job have again been raised, because of the carnage of two World Wars, the horrors of the Holocaust, the destruction of Hiroshima and Nagasaki, and the killing fields of Southeast Asia. As in Job's time, completely satisfying answers are not easy to find.

At the same time Job was raising his questions in the Near East, during the sixth century, a different religious tradition in another part of the world was also seriously challenged. The place was India. The conventional wisdom under consideration was enshrined in the *Upanishads*, part of the sacred writings of the early Indian tradition. The challenger was a young prince named Siddhartha of the Gautama family. The outcome was Buddhism.

HISTORICAL NOTE.   Two doctrines were articulated in the *Upanishads* (probably for the first time in Indian literature) that are important for our discussion: the doctrines of *samsara* and the *Law of Karma. Samsara* involves the belief in reincarnation. It is claimed that the soul of a human being who dies is, with one exception, reborn in another state of existence. That new state of existence (which may be in a heaven or a hell; as a vegetable, animal, or human; and for a long or short time) is determined by the *Law of Karma*, according to which good deeds result in a more favorable future existence while evil deeds lead to a less favorable future existence. The consequences of one's deeds are inescapable. If one has an elevated social status and wealth at the present time, it is because of good deeds in previous existences. Similarly, low social status, poverty, and affliction are indicators of evil deeds in previous existences. The doctrines of *karma/samsara* are blended in the following passage from the oldest and best known of the *Upanishads*: "those who are of pleasant conduct here—the prospect is, indeed, that they will enter a pleasant womb, either the womb of a *brahmin* [i.e., a priest], or the womb of a *ksatriya* [i.e., a noble], or the womb of a *vaisya* [i.e., a peasant or artisan]. But those who are of stinking conduct here—the prospect is, indeed, that they will enter a stinking womb, either the womb of a dog, or the womb of a swine, or the womb of an outcast" (*Chandogya Upanishad* V.x.7). The one exception to the cycle of rebirths mandated for humankind involves the person who achieves *moksha*, that is, deliverance or release from that cycle. *Moksha* comes to the person who is enlightened, who has no negative karma remaining for which redress must be made in another existence.

Siddhartha Gautama challenged this doctrine of *karma/samsara* not by rejecting it as false, but by discovering a strategy for overcoming it, a method for achieving release from the relentless cycle of rebirths, a technique presumably available to any person.

The story of how Siddhartha actually reached Enlightenment and what he actually taught his followers is difficult, and probably impossible, to reconstruct. The story of his life as well as his teachings were handed down orally from one generation to another for many years before the oral tradition began to be committed to writing. By then, pious imagination and theological reflection had embellished and enriched the original story beyond recognition. Many different stories circulated about Gautama's life and about his previous lives as a Bodhisattva (a term applied to the Buddha prior to his achieving Enlightenment). A recovery of the historical Gautama, however, is not essential for our discussion. It is sufficient for us to summarize a few of those stories which have been told and retold by Buddhists through the centuries in order to gain some insight about what they consider to be the essence of Gautama's message—a message that invests their lives with purpose and meaning.

THE ARGUMENT OF THE PASSAGES.   Siddhartha was born about 560 B.C. in northern India. According to tradition, his father was a ruler with considerable wealth. Although Siddhartha was surrounded by material possessions, and although he married a beautiful and devoted woman who bore him a son, he renounced these pleasures and became a homeless, wandering ascetic in search of spiritual enlightenment. Legend has it that Siddhartha's father had a premonition that his son might renounce the kingly life in order to search for an answer to the question of human suffering. Accordingly, the father tried to shield the young prince from all sights of suffering that might awaken in him the urge to solve the problem of suffering. The gods, however, intervened during several of the young prince's excursions to a park outside the family's palace, and caused the young prince to encounter the three great bearers of human suffering: old age, disease, and death. Here is the story as told in the *Jataka*.

> Now on a certain day the Future Buddha wished to go to the park, and told his charioteer to make ready the chariot. Accordingly the man brought out a sumptuous and elegant chariot, and adorning it richly, he harnessed to it four state-horses of the Sindhava breed, as white as the petals of the white lotus, and announced to the Future Buddha that everything was ready. And the Future Buddha mounted the chariot, which was like to a palace of the gods, and proceeded towards the park.
>
> "The time for the enlightenment of prince Siddhartha draweth nigh," thought the gods; "we must show him a sign:" and they changed one of their number into a decrepit old man, broken-toothed, gray-haired, crooked and bent of body, leaning on a staff, and trembling, and showed him to the Future Buddha, but so that only he and the charioteer saw him.
>
> Then said the Future Buddha to the charioteer, in the manner related in the Mahapadana,—
>
> "Friend, pray, who is this man? Even his hair is not like that of other men." And when he heard the answer, he said, "Shame on birth, since to every one that is born

old age must come." And agitated in heart, he thereupon returned and ascended his palace.

"Why has my son returned so quickly?" asked the king.

"Sire, he has seen an old man," was the reply; "and because he has seen an old man, he is about to retire from the world."

"Do you want to kill me, that you say such things? Quickly get ready some plays to be performed before my son. If we can but get him to enjoying pleasure, he will cease to think of retiring from the world." Then the king extended the guard to half a league in each direction.

Again, on a certain day, as the Future Buddha was going to the park, he saw a diseased man whom the gods had fashioned; and having again made inquiry, he returned, agitated in heart, and ascended his palace.

And the king made the same inquiry and gave the same orders as before; and again extending the guard, placed them for three quarters of a league around.

And again on a certain day, as the Future Buddha was going to the park, he saw a dead man whom the gods had fashioned; and having again made inquiry, he returned, agitated in heart, and ascended his palace.

And the king made the same inquiry and gave the same orders as before; and again extending the guard, placed them for a league around.

Finally, the gods presented to the young prince a model he could follow in seeking to understand and deal with the suffering he had come to know: a monk who had retired from the world.

And again on a certain day, as the Future Buddha was going to the park, he saw a monk, carefully and decently clad, whom the gods had fashioned; and he asked his charioteer, "Pray, who is this man?"

Now although there was no Buddha in the world, and the charioteer had no knowledge of either monks or their good qualities, yet by the power of the gods he was inspired to say, "Sire, this is one who has retired from the world;" and he thereupon proceeded to sound the praises of retirement from the world. The thought of retiring from the world was a pleasing one to the Future Buddha. . . .

Nothing could deter the young Siddhartha, the Future Buddha, from renouncing his princely life: neither the beauty of women, nor affection for his son Rahula, nor the pleasures of kingly rule.

But the Future Buddha in his splendid chariot entered the city with a pomp and magnificence of glory that enraptured all minds. At the same moment Kisa Gotami, a virgin of the warrior caste, ascended to the roof of her palace, and beheld the beauty and majesty of the Future Buddha, as he circumambulated the city; and in her pleasure and satisfaction at the sight, she burst forth into this song of joy:—

> "Full happy now that mother is,
> Full happy now that father is,
> Full happy now that woman is,
> Who owns this lord so glorious!"

On hearing this, the Future Buddha thought, "In beholding a handsome figure the heart of a mother attains Nirvana, the heart of a father attains Nirvana, the heart of a wife attains Nirvana. This is what she says. But wherein does Nirvana consist?"

And to him, whose mind was already averse to passion, the answer came: "When the fire of lust is extinct, that is Nirvana; when the fires of hatred and infatuation are extinct, that is Nirvana; when pride, false belief, and all other passions and torments are extinct, that is Nirvana. She has taught me a good lesson. Certainly, Nirvana is what I am looking for. It behooves me this very day to quit the household life, and to retire from the world in quest of Nirvana. I will send this lady a teacher's fee." And loosening from his neck a pearl necklace worth a hundred thousand pieces of money, he sent it to Kisa Gotami. And great was her satisfaction at this, for she thought, "Prince Siddhartha has fallen in love with me, and has sent me a present. . . ." "It behooves me to go forth on the Great Retirement this very day," said he; and he arose from his couch, and coming near the door, called out,—

"Who's there?"

"Master, it is I, Channa," replied the courtier who had been sleeping with his head on the threshold.

"I wish to go forth on the Great Retirement to-day. Saddle a horse for me."

"Yes, sire." And taking saddle and bridle with him, the courtier started for the stable. There, by the light of lamps fed with sweet-smelling oils, he perceived the mighty steed Kanthaka in his pleasant quarters, under a canopy of cloth beautified with a pattern of jasmine flowers. "This is the one for me to saddle to-day," thought he; and he saddled Kanthaka. . . .

Now the Future Buddha, after he had sent Channa on his errand, thought to himself, "I will take just one look at my son;" and, rising from the couch on which he was sitting, he went to the suite of apartments occupied by the mother of Rahula, and opened the door of her chamber. Within the chamber was burning a lamp fed with sweet-smelling oil, and the mother of Rahula lay sleeping on a couch strewn deep with jasmine and other flowers, her hand resting on the head of her son. When the Future Buddha reached the threshold, he paused, and gazed at the two from where he stood.

"If I were to raise my wife's hand from off the child's head, and take him up, she would awake, and thus prevent my departure. I will first become a Buddha, and then come back and see my son." So saying, he descended from the palace. . . .

Thus the Future Buddha, casting away with indifference a universal sovereignty already in his grasp,—spewing it out as if were but phlegm,—departed from the city in great splendor on the full-moon day of the month Asalhi, when the moon was in Libra. And when he had gone out from the city, he became desirous of looking back at it; but no sooner had the thought arisen in his mind, than the broad earth, seeming to fear lest the Great Being might neglect to perform the act of looking back, split and turned round like a potter's wheel. When the Future Buddha had stood a while facing the city and gazing upon it, and had indicated in that place the spot for the "Shrine of the Turning Back of Kanthaka," he turned Kanthaka in the direction in which he meant to go, and proceeded on his way in great honor and exceeding glory.

Donning a coarse yellow robe and shaving his hair and beard, Siddhartha set off on a six-year struggle for enlightenment. Legend tells us that he tested the two most widely accepted paths to salvation in ancient India. First he tried the path of philosophic meditation advocated by Brahmanism but found it too ethereal for his pragmatic disposition. Second, he tried the path of bodily asceticism championed by such sects as Jainism but discovered that years of severe self-mortification and self-starvation failed to lead to enlightenment. Accordingly,

Siddhartha took nourishment and sat down under the Tree of Wisdom at Gaya (also known as the Bodhi-tree or Bo-tree). There he meditated; and there he received the answer for which he had been searching. He discerned that the cause of human misery is "desire" or "craving," and he discovered a strategy for eliminating that craving. Having gained enlightenment, he went to Varanasi, the ancient name for Benares. There, in the deer park outside the city, he encountered five ascetics, former friends who had disassociated themselves from him when he abandoned the way of asceticism. The Buddha, the Enlightened One, explained his newly discovered insight to these five monks in his famous "Sermon in the Deer Park in Benares." In the Sermon, the Buddha outlines three of the most important concepts of Buddhism: the Four Noble Truths, the Noble Eightfold Path, and the Middle Way.

THE FIRST SERMON[1]

These two extremes, O monks, are not to be practiced by one who has gone forth from the world. What are the two? That conjoined with the passions, low, vulgar, common, ignoble, and useless. Avoiding these two extremes the Tathagata[2] has gained the knowledge of the Middle Way, which gives sight and knowledge, and tends to calm, to insight, enlightenment, *nirvana*.

What, O monks, is the Middle Way, which gives sight. . . . ? It is the noble Eightfold Path, namely, right views, right intention, right speech, right action, right livelihood, right effort, right mindfulness, right concentration. This, O monks, is the Middle Way. . . .

(1) Now this, O monks, is the noble truth of pain: birth is painful, old age is painful, sickness is painful, death is painful, sorrow, lamentation, dejection, and despair are painful. Contact with unpleasant things is painful, not getting what one wishes is painful. In short the five *khandhas* of grasping are painful.[3]

(2) Now this, O monks, is the noble truth of the cause of pain: that craving which leads to rebirth, combined with pleasure and lust, finding pleasure here and there, namely, the craving for passion, the craving for existence, the craving for non-existence.

(3) Now this, O monks, is the noble truth of the cessation of pain: the cessation without a remainder of that craving, abandonment, forsaking, release, non-attachment.

(4) Now this, O monks, is the noble truth of the way that leads to the cessation of pain: this is the noble Eightfold Path, namely, right views, right intention, right speech, right action, right livelihood, right effort, right mindfulness, right concentration. . . .

As long as in these noble truths my threefold knowledge and insight duly with its twelve divisions was not well purified, even so long, O monks, in the world with

---

1   *Samyutta-nikāya* v. 420; in Edward J. Thomas, *The Life of Buddha as Legend and History* (New York: Alfred A. Knopf, 1927), pp. 87–8.

2   "Tathagata" is a name for the Buddha. Literally it means one who has "thus come."

3   The five *khandhas* (groups or aggregates) are form, feeling (or sensation), perception (volitional disposition), predispositions (or impressions), and consciousness.

its gods, Mara,[4] Brahma,[5] with ascetics, *brahmins*, gods, and men, I had not attained the highest complete enlightenment. Thus I knew.

But when in these noble truths my threefold knowledge and insight duly with its twelve divisions was well purified, then, O monks, in the world . . . I had attained the highest complete enlightenment. Thus I knew. Knowledge arose in me; insight arose that the release of my mind is unshakable; this is my last existence; now there is no rebirth.

The five ascetics were converted by the Buddha's sermon, and became the founding members of the Sangha, the Buddhist monastic order. The Sangha grew. Eventually, a thousand priests gathered around the Buddha to pursue his path of enlightenment. To this congregation of priests, the Buddha delivered "The Fire-Sermon," a famous message that focuses on the need to develop an aversion for those features of human existence that burn with the passion of craving, a craving that attaches humans to their individual lives and to the cycle of rebirths, a craving that must be extinguished if one is to experience the coolness of liberation, nirvana.

THE FIRE-SERMON
Translated from the Maha-Vagga (i.21.1)

Then The Blessed One, having dwelt in Uruvela as long as he wished, proceeded on his wanderings in the direction of Gaya Head, accompanied by a great congregation of priests, a thousand in number, who had all of them aforetime been monks with matted hair. And there in Gaya, on Gaya Head, The Blessed One dwelt, together with the thousand priests.

And there The Blessed One addressed the priests:—

"All things, O priest, are on fire. And what, O priests, are all these things which are on fire?

"The eye, O priests, is on fire; forms are on fire, eye-consciousness is on fire; impressions received by the eye are on fire; and whatever sensation, pleasant, unpleasant, or indifferent, originates in dependence on impressions received by the eye, that also is on fire.

"And with what are these on fire?

"With the fire of passion, say I, with the fire of hatred, with the fire of infatuation; with birth, old age, death, sorrow, lamentation, misery, grief, and despair are they on fire.

"The ear is on fire; sounds are on fire; . . . the nose is on fire; odors are on fire; . . . the tongue is on fire; tastes are on fire; . . . the body is on fire; things tangible are on fire; . . . the mind is on fire; ideas are on fire; . . . mind-consciousness is on fire; impressions received by the mind are on fire; and whatever sensation, pleasant, unpleasant, or indifferent, originates in dependence on impressions received by the mind, that also is on fire.

"And with what are these on fire?

"With the fire of passion, say I, with the fire of hatred, with the fire of infatuation; with birth, old age, death, sorrow, lamentation, misery, grief, and despair are they on fire.

---

4 The goddess of temptation.
5 God in the role of creator.

"Perceiving this, O priests, the learned and noble disciple conceives an aversion for the eye, conceives an aversion for forms, conceives an aversion for eye-consciousness, conceives an aversion for the impressions received by the eye; and whatever sensation, pleasant, unpleasant, or indifferent, originates in dependence on impressions received by the eye, for that also he conceives an aversion. Conceives an aversion for the ear, conceives an aversion for sounds, . . . conceives an aversion for the nose, conceives an aversion for odors, . . . conceives an aversion for the tongue, conceives an aversion for tastes, . . . conceives an aversion for the body, conceives an aversion for mind-consciousness, conceives an aversion for the impressions received by the mind; and whatever sensation, pleasant, unpleasant, or indifferent, originates in dependence on impressions received by the mind, for this also he conceives an aversion. And in conceiving this aversion, he becomes divested of passion, and by the absence of passion he becomes free, and when he is free he becomes aware that he is free; and he knows that rebirth is exhausted, that he has lived the holy life, that he has done what it behooved him to do, and that he is no more for this world."

Now while this exposition was being delivered, the minds of the thousand priests became free from attachment and delivered from the depravities.

Here Endeth the Fire-Sermon

At the heart of the Buddha's story about dealing with suffering is the Dharma, "the Doctrine and the Path." The simplest statement of the Dharma is the *Four Noble Truths* cited above: all life is full of suffering; the cause of suffering is human craving, desire; cessation of suffering (nirvana) is attainable through the cessation of craving; the cessation of craving can be achieved by the Noble Eightfold Path, involving a program of disciplined moral conduct that culminates in a life of contemplation. When craving is eradicated, *The Fire Sermon* declares, the individual is freed from suffering, from the cycle of rebirths, and achieves Nirvana. Thus, the Dharma offers both theory and practice: an explanation of suffering and a strategy for liberation.

As Buddhism spread it developed two major traditions: a northern branch known as Mahayana Buddhism (prevalent today in Nepal, Tibet, China, Korea, and Japan) and a southern branch known as Theravada Buddhism (prevalent today in Sri Lanka, Burma, and Thailand). Theravada Buddhism cherished the ideal of the saint, an *arhat*, who, in accordance with the mandates of *The Fire Sermon*, extinguishes craving, loses individual personality, and becomes absorbed in an impersonal bliss that foreshadows nirvana. Mahayana Buddhism, in contrast, cherishes the ideal of the *bodhisattva*, who, out of compassion for other humans, refrains from entering fully into the impersonal bliss of nirvana in order to help others find the path to nirvana. Although the ideal of the Theravadans seems to be fixed on the specific individual's achievement of nirvana while the Mahayanists' ideal is more other-affirming, both traditions emphasize the development of certain human virtues that bring the cessation of sorrow and suffering. The strong emphasis on the elimination of human craving in both traditions seems to have committed Buddhism to the elimination of selfishness and the facilitation of benevolence. It is not surprising, therefore, that Buddhism came to be regarded as "the religion of infinite compassion."

In due course, Buddhists came to speak of "taking refuge" in the Buddha, the Dharma, and the Sangha. In one sense, taking refuge means following the example of the Buddha by practicing the Dharma within the monastic community of the Sangha. In another sense, taking refuge means accessing the power of the Buddha, the Dharma, and the Sangha through religious rites. Indeed, the Buddha came to be regarded not only as the great teacher and example, but also as a source of power available to succor the faithful in time of need. And multitudes did, in fact, take refuge in the Buddha, the Dharma, and the Sangha. To be sure, Buddhism's refuge attracted the patronage of powerful monarchs and elicited the devotion of millions of common folk, thereby demonstrating the relevance and capacity of the Buddha's story for responding to the human quest for meaning.

As you reflect on these selections from Buddhist sources, bear in mind that we have chosen to display only two or three jewels from a very large and very rich literary tradition. We invite you to explore that tradition on your own in greater detail.

NOTE ON SOURCES. The material in this section has been taken from the introduction to the *Jakata* (i.58.81) and the *Maha-Vagga* (i.21.1) in Henry Clarke Warren, *Buddhism in Translations* (New York: Atheneum, 1987), pp. 56ff., 351ff. and from S. Radhakrishnan and C. A. Moore, eds., *A Source Book in Indian Philosophy* (Princeton: Princeton University Press, 1957), pp. 274–275.

4 THE AFRICAN TRADITION

THE STORY OF PURSUING THE MORAL IDEAL

FROM THE BUDDHIST TO THE AFRICAN TRADITION. When studying several cultures and their traditions simultaneously, as we are doing in this chapter, there are two ways to approach the study. One could adopt an absolutist stance, in which one claimed to have transcultural standards with which to analyze and assess all cultures. Or one could assume a relativistic posture, according to which there are no legitimate cross-cultural standards and every culture must be understood on its own terms. The absolutist approach tries to grasp certain commonalities among human beings, but ends up running roughshod over important cultural diversities. The relativist approach tries to respect cultural differences but ends up denying a common ground for humankind. We have adopted a middle ground between these two approaches, a mean between the extremes that acknowledges both diversity and commonality. To take cultural diversity seriously is to acknowledge the remarkable richness of human imagination and creativeness. To take human commonality seriously is to recognize that cross-cultural communication does take place, albeit sometimes imperfectly. Without some common ground of shared concepts and themes, language translation would be impossible and cross-cultural communication hopeless.

We were working from this middle ground when we discussed the biblical and Buddhist traditions. We recognize both the rich diversity of belief and practice and the commonality within those traditions. There is, however, the ever-present danger of misrepresenting or overstating the commonality. That danger is particularly acute when we approach the African tradition. Here we encounter centuries of religious and philosophical experiences so diverse that even the term "African tradition" may be inappropriate. The scholarly study of African cultures is expanding so rapidly that fresh insights and interpretations appear almost daily. Under these circumstances, we must be unusually cautious both about the material we select and the generalizations we make.

What is the meaning of life? That is one of the questions that all major religious traditions have tried to answer through the cosmic stories they construct. Those stories suggest that life is, or should be, moving in a certain direction. And it is that movement toward a certain goal that constitutes the meaning of life. In the biblical tradition, human destiny is declared to be the creation of a people of God, a holy, righteous, and just community. In the Buddhist tradition human destiny is proclaimed to be the achievement of nirvana.

Does the African tradition offer such a claim concerning the destiny of humankind? Perhaps. We have selected material from the wisdom traditions of ancient Egypt, the Swahili-speaking peoples of east central Africa, and the Ewe tribe of west Africa. Each of these selections holds up a moral ideal to the hearer or reader. The ideal is presented within a religious context; that is, within an overarching belief that the deity rewards those who pursue the ideal. At least in these three samples of wisdom literature, it seems that African voices are declaring that human destiny involves actualizing a certain moral ideal sanctioned by deity.

If we are correct in ascribing such an ideal to these African traditions, then we could legitimately make the further observation that these African ideals have counterparts in the Buddhist tradition. Recall that at the heart of the Buddhist strategy for transcending suffering is the portrayal of Gautama, idealized either as the Theravadan *arhat* (the saint absorbed in impersonal bliss) or as the Mahayanist *bodhisattva* (the compassionate Buddha-to-be who postpones attainment of personal nirvana to help others along the Middle Path to nirvana). Would it be safe to say that many humans (perhaps, most humans) relate the meaning of life to human destiny and the pursuit of a moral ideal? Recall how important the pursuit of such an ideal was for the contemporary virtue ethicists in Chapter 6.

HISTORICAL NOTE. While the readings in this section lack the connected narrative that we frequently associate with stories, they do tell stories that provide pictures of the moral ideals cherished by the people who passed these stories on from one generation to another.

The first sample of wisdom literature comes from North Africa, from ancient Egypt, where this genre seems to have flourished. In the twenty-fifth century B.C., over a thousand years before Moses masterminded the Exodus from Egypt and almost two thousand years before the Buddha achieved enlightenment, a high-ranking government official in Egypt composed the *Wisdom of Ptahhotpe*, complete ancient copies of which are extant.

The second sample of African wisdom literature comes from east central Africa where Swahili is spoken. These Swahili proverbs probably represent many years of an oral wisdom tradition that was common to a multitude of ethnic groups for whom Swahili was a shared language. Proverbs generally represent conventional wisdom and may at times seem contradictory, such as these two from Anglo-American culture: "Haste makes waste" and "He who hesitates is lost." But the contradiction is troublesome only if one tries to apply the proverbs simultaneously in the same situation. Proverbs are frequently situational: they must be applied in the appropriate context.

One third and final sample of African wisdom literature is a cluster of proverbs and their explanations from the Ewe tribe in west Africa, in Ghana, Togo, and Benin. The proverbs were collected, translated, and interpreted by Professor N. K. Dzobo, himself a member of the Ewe tribe in Ghana.

THE ARGUMENT OF THE PASSAGES.   The *Wisdom of Ptahhotpe* begins with the aged Vizier Ptahhotpe complaining about the miseries of old age, after which he offers advice to his son on a number of matters.

First, he offers his wisdom relating to speech.

1. Do not be arrogant because of your knowledge, but confer with the ignorant man as with the learned, for the limit of skill has not been attained, and there is no craftsman who has (fully) acquired his mastery. Good speech is more hidden than malachite, yet it is found in the possession of women slaves at the millstones.

2. If you find a disputant arguing, one having authority and superior to you, bend down your arms and bow your back; if you disagree with him, he will not side with you. You should make little of the evil speaking by not opposing him in his argument; it means that he will be dubbed an ignoramus when your self-control has matched his prolixity.

3. If you find a disputant arguing, your equal who is on your own level, let your virtue be manifest against him in silence when he is speaking ill; great will be the talk on the part of the hearers, and your name will be fair in the opinion of the magistrates.

4. If you find a disputant arguing, a humble man who is not your equal, do not be aggressive against him in proportion as he is humble; let him alone, that he may confute himself. Do not question him in order to relieve your feelings, do not vent yourself against your opponent, for wretched is he who would destroy him who is poor of understanding; men will do what you wish, and you will defeat him by the disapproval of the magistrates.

Next, he gives advice on leadership and on the use of terror or cruel scheming.

5. If you are a leader, controlling the destiny of the masses, seek out every good thing, until there is no fault in your governance. Truth is great and <its> effectiveness endures; it has not been confounded since the time of Osiris. Men punish him who transgresses the laws, and it is a transgression (even) in the eyes of the rapacious; it is baseness which takes away wealth, and wrongdoing has never brought its

venture safe to port. He says, "I acquire for myself," and does not say, "I acquire because of my occupation," but when the end comes, rightdoing endures. That is what a man learns from his father.

6. Do not inspire terror in men, for God also is repelled. A man expects to live by it and (consequently) is lacking bread to eat. A man expects to become wealthy <through it> and says, "I will acquire for myself what I perceive"; a man says, "I will plunder someone else," and he ends by giving it to someone whom he does not know. No terror of man has ever been effective; it is (only) the ordinance of God which is effective. Plan to live in peace, and what men give will come of its own accord.

Next an admonition against boasting about prosperity, and advice to respect wealth. Is not the principle guiding his advice the notion that prosperity and wealth are God-given? If God-given, is prosperity for Ptahhotpe a gift or a reward? If a reward, is he affirming the karmic moral law: what one sows, that one also reaps?

9. If you cultivate and there is growth in the field, and God puts it into your hand in quantity, do not sate your mouth in the presence of your kindred, for great respect is given to the quiet man. . . .

10. If you are lowly and serve a wealthy man, let all your conduct be good before God. When <his> former poverty is known to you, do not be arrogant against him because of what you know about his former state; respect him in proportion to what has accrued to him, for property does not come of itself: such is its law for whoever desires it. If <it> becomes superabundant, men respect him on his own account, for it is God who made him wealthy, and he defends him when he is asleep. . . .

12. If you are a wealthy man, beget a son who will make God well-disposed. If he is straightforward and reverts to your character and takes care of your property in good order, do for him everything good, for he is your son who belongs to what your spirit begot. Do not separate your heart from him, for ill-will makes quarreling. If he errs and disobeys your counsel and defies all that is said and babbles evil words, punish him for all his speeches, show displeasure at them; /it will mean that an impediment is implanted in the body for him. Their [i.e., the gods] guidance cannot err, and those whom they make boatless cannot cross (the river). . . .

30. If you have become great after your poverty and have achieved property after former need in the city which you know, do not boast of what has accrued to you in the past, do not trust in your riches, which have accrued to you by the gift of God; you will not be subordinate to anyone else to whom the like has happened.

Ptahhotpe, who is purportedly 110 years old, offers a wide variety of advice to his son. The following samples of advice address the issues of lust, greed, loving one's wife, propitiation or generosity toward friends, theft, and (perhaps) homosexuality.

18. If you desire to preserve friendship in a home into which you enter, whether as lord or as brother or as friend, at any place into which you enter, beware of approaching the women, for no good comes to a place where this is done, nor is it clever to reveal them; a thousand men are turned aside from what is good for them. A little moment, the semblance of a dream, and death reaches you because of know-

ing them. As for him who fails by reason of lusting after them no plan at all will succeed in his hand.

19. If you desire your conduct to be good, refrain yourself from all kinds of evil. Beware of an act of avarice; it is a bad and incurable disease. Intimacy is made impossible by it; it alienates fathers and mothers and maternal brothers, it drives wife and husband apart, it is a gathering of all that is evil and a bag of all that is hateful. The man who is exact in right-doing and who walks according to its procedure will long endure; he will achieve a testament thereby, but there is no tomb for the rapacious man. . . .

21. If you are well-to-do and can maintain your household, love your wife in your home <according to good> custom. Fill her belly, clothe her back; oil is the panacea for her body. Make her happy while you are alive, for she is land profitable to her lord. . . . Soothe her heart with what has accrued to you; it means that she will continue to dwell in your house. If you repulse her, it means tears. A vagina is what she gives for her condition; what she asks about is who will make a canal for her.

22. Propitiate your friends with what has accrued to you, that being possible to one whom God favors; as for one who fails to propitiate his friends, men will say that he is a selfish character. No one knows what may happen when he perceives tomorrow, and the straightforward character who is content with it is a (real) character. If occasions of favor arise, it is friends who say "Welcome!" If one cannot bring peace to an abode, one has recourse to friends when there is trouble. . . .

Do not rob the house of neighbors, do not steal the goods of one who is near you, lest he should make a complaint against you until you hear about it; it is a fault of a recalcitrant heart. If he knows it, he will litigate, and wretched is he who is in opposition against his environment.

32. Do not copulate with a woman-boy, for you know that what is (generally) opposed will be a necessity to his heart, and that which is in his body will not be calmed. Let him not spend the night doing what is opposed in order that he may be calm after he has quenched his desire.

The Egyptian vizier concludes with praise for the son who follows his advice. Indeed, such a son will be loved by God and honored in the memories of generations to come.

How good it is that a son should accept what his father says! Old age comes about for him by means of it; he who hears is one whom God loves, but one who does not hear is one whom God detests. It is the heart which educates its owner in hearing or in not hearing, for the life, prosperity, and health of a man depend on his heart; it is the hearer who hears what is said, and he who acts according to what is said is one who loves hearing. How good it is that a son should obey his father, and how joyful is he to whom this is said! A son is pleasing to a lord of hearing, (even) one who hears whoever says it to him, that he may be efficient in his body, one honored by his father, and he will be remembered in the mouths of the living who survive on earth or who are yet to be.

Turning now to our Swahili selection, a number of virtues in the following proverbs seem to be affirmed repeatedly which, taken together, may provide a composite picture of the ideal a person should seek to actualize. Notice that the karmic moral law seems to be affirmed in several of the proverbs.

CHARACTER

> Living is the intention.
> [What makes life worthwhile is having a purpose, an aim.]
> A person becomes what he wants to become.
> What one cultivates is what one harvests.
> When you serve, serve well. . . .

KINDNESS AND VIOLENCE

> One who throws mud gets himself soiled as well.
> By continual piercing one pierces oneself.
> Peace comes not save by the point of the sword.
> Peace is a way to love and understanding. . . .
> Know-how, not force.
> He who does good to people does it also to himself.
> The man who does good to others, God requites him with good things too.
> To him who does kind things, kind things will be done.
> Do not render evil for good.
> Goodness and kindness are stronger than harshness.
> A person who has no enemies is not a human being.

WISDOM

> Wisdom creates well-being.
> The ignorant praises his own ignorance.
> He who says, "I didn't understand" is not stupid.
> The most precious qualities of a person are two: intelligence and modesty. . . .
> When you have gained some experience in life, it [life] is over.
> Experience is the mother of knowledge.

AMBITION

> The good luck of your colleague should not keep you out of sleep. . . .
> Whether you have little or much, be content. . . .
> The bird does not think that his own nest is shabby.

ACHIEVEMENT

> Aiming is not the same as hitting.
> A bridge is not a dwelling place.
> A beginning is a beginning, there is no beginning which is bad. . . .
> Good beginnings make good endings. . . .

CAUTION

> Careful, careful, is better than medicines.
> Don't play with the young of a leopard. . . .

PATIENCE

> What is in the sea, go and wait for it on the beach.
> To stand up for justice needs patience.
> Begin with patience, end with pleasure.
> Today is yours, tomorrow is not. . . .

WORK

He who gets blisters from the hoe handle will not die of hunger.
Only he who goes into the forest comes back with firewood.
A little, but earned. . . .

COURAGE

Fear is also a shield.
Courage proves itself in difficulties.
Courage is not the same as fighting someone stronger than you.
Are you a leopard, show your claws.

SELF-CONTROL

Anger is loss. . . .
To lose one's temper is to go astray.

HUMILITY

First humility, then perfection.
He who does not see his own vices should not take notice of the faults of his
      companions.
He who does not listen to the advice of an elder will see bad things.

ANCESTRY

He who leaves his ancestry is bold.
One who leaves his ancestry is never a hero.
He who leaves his own people is a liar.

HONESTY

Speaking the truth is no disgrace.
An unpleasant truth is better than a pleasant falsehood.

FAIRNESS

The judge has no personal preferences.
A man's excellence is not determined by his color.

RESPECT

He who laughs at a scar has not received a wound.
He who ridicules the good will be overtaken by evil.
A man may be regarded as a thing, but he is not [only] a thing.
Kiss the hand you cannot cut. [Respect those who have authority over you, or
      they will destroy you.]
A fool is a person too, don't say he is a cow.
A man's greatness and respect come from himself.

RECIPROCITY

He who does not know how to forgive, let him not expect to be forgiven.
He who does not trust others cannot be trusted.
It is useless for me to recognize him who does not recognize me.
Help him who helps you. . . .
He who supports a worthless person has trouble for nothing.

Respect for a stupid person is stupidity. . . .
He who does not harm you, do no harm to him.
Hatred for hatred, light for light.
Love your enemy.
Do harm to him who harms you.
When your enemy falls, lift him up. . . .
He who does not wrong is not done wrong.

COOPERATION

It is better to build bridges than walls.
He who does not help me putting down my load, must not expect [help] when
he has his own [load].

CONFLICT AND LIMITATIONS

You cannot cross the ocean by swimming.
If you can't build a hut, build a shack.
You do not have the strength to defeat an elephant.
If you bake fish, you cannot pluck a chicken.
If you want to build you must be willing to destroy.
There is no rainy season without mosquitoes. . . .
Do not carry what you cannot master.
He who wants everything loses everything.
He who chooses is never satisfied.
Whatever is superior is found at great price.
He wrecked the ship for the sake of a pancake.
He says "No! No!" and nevertheless his heart is there.

GOD AND THE WORLD

A person saved by God is not crooked.
He who pays heed to Satan makes himself deserve divine anger.
Payment on earth is the reckoning of the hereafter. . . .
The world is nothing, depend not on it.
The delusions of this world, one usually knows them in hell.
The world is a mixture of good and evil.

Finally, let us consider the Ewe selection. Once again, a number of virtues
are commended: accepting one's limitations, adapting oneself to changing circumstances, persistence in the pursuit of goals, humility, industriousness, modesty, patience, patriotism and cooperation. Can you discern in the following
description of these virtues an Ewe affirmation of the karmic moral law?

"The child who breaks a snail's shell cannot break a tortoise's shell. . . ."
"A dog can catch some animals but cannot catch a lion. . . ."
"A kitten can catch only a baby mouse. . . ."

The proverbs discussed above stress the evil of excessive ambition, especially in
children, and the importance of accepting one's powers as they are and acting within
their limits. It is believed that if children behave according to the teachings of these
proverbs they will be spared the pains of unfulfilled and unrealisable aspirations. . . .

"Suffering and happiness are twins."

Moral Teaching: Life is a mixture of joy and suffering and so we must learn to accept both, and the acceptance of both is a sign of maturity. . . .

"You change your steps according to the change in the rhythm of the drum."

Explanation: During the course of drumming and dancing the rhythm of the leading drum causes the steps of the dancers to change.

Moral Teaching: Adapt yourself and your conduct to changing circumstances and do not be unreasonably rigid in your thinking and behavior.

"Tasty soup (meal) draws seats (people) to itself."

Explanation: Ewes like tasty and good smelling and spicy soup and so when a tasty meal is prepared it becomes inviting to people.

Moral Teaching: Good behaviour does not have to be advertised, because it is good for its own sake. Good behaviour is never denied a due social recognition and so it pays to be good. . . .

"The person who steals mushrooms hears the evening announcement."

Explanation: In the villages people who have found their crops or any personal belongings stolen cause an announcement to be made in the evening about the stolen crops or articles. In the announcement they ask the thieves to return the stolen goods or else they will be handed over to the gods for punishment. Usually they mention the name of a powerful god who is believed to invariably kill all evildoers. Thieves therefore listen carefully to the evening announcement and they also dread it. It may happen that someone has stolen some crops and his guilty conscience will cause him to behave as if he had heard an announcement about the crops he has stolen, even though there is no announcement. In other words, his conscience will be accusing him of his wrong deed.

Moral Teaching: Guilty conscience is a form of punishment for wrong-doing which any normal wrong-doer cannot escape and so it is better to stop doing wrong and do good.

"The person who has gone into a patch of giant-grass does not complain of skin irritation."

Explanation: This proverb comes from a farming experience and especially from farmers who work on the grassland. Sometimes they have to walk through the giant-grass to go to their farms and this produces a lot of skin irritation.

Moral Teaching: The skin irritation caused by the giant-grass may be compared to minor distractions in the pursuance of one's objectives. The moral lesson of this proverb and of similar ones that will follow is that you must expect minor distractions in any effort that you put forth to realize certain objectives but do not let these minor

distractions deter you from achieving your goals. You should not vacillate but be resolute and persistent in the pursuance of your goals. . . .

"If a whiteman wants to give you a hat, look at the one he is wearing before you
accept it."

Moral Teaching: This proverb is used to warn people against the tendency to be
gullible and credulous. Always weigh carefully what others tell you and evaluate it by
their social consequences. . . .

"There is no rain whose flood can submerge all mountains" i.e. there is an end to
every fall of rain.

Moral Teaching: There is an end to everything and people are supposed to use this
knowledge to guide their behaviour or to comfort themselves in their sufferings.

"Even the longest life ends in a grave, it does not prolong its longevity beyond
the grave."

Moral Teaching: This proverb also teaches that there is an end to everything especially to wealth and life. This warning, however, is not supposed to lead to a preparation for another life, or for a life that has no end. The purpose is rather to warn people
to live *circumspectively* and to avoid living without any thought of the end. . . .

"You do not become a chief simply by sitting on a big stool."

Explanation: Chiefs' stools and sandals and cloths are specially made to enhance
their status and so a chief's stool is normally larger than ordinary stools.

Moral Teaching: You cannot arrogate greatness to yourself, it has to be conferred on
you by others who think you deserve it. True greatness is the result of the judgment
of history. . . .

"A lazy man's farm is a breeding ground for snakes."

Explanation: A lazy farmer does not keep his farm clear of weeds and so snakes can
easily live there and he may be bitten by them, and this will be regarded as a punishment for his laziness.

Moral Teaching: Laziness has its own appropriate punishment and so people must
learn to be hard-working so as to avoid the inevitable punishment for laziness. . . .

"The person who comes round to lick the soup pot will never be filled."

Moral Teaching: You are never well fed by living on the crumbs from the tables of
others, or by depending on charity. It is only through hard work that you can be comfortably and satisfactorily fed, because the reward of hard work is having what you
want in abundance and so work hard and you will eat the fruits of your own
labour. . . .

"The antelope doesn't wear the shoes of an elephant."

Moral Teaching: Accept your humble status and do not aspire after greatness that is beyond your reach. This proverb offers a lesson also in the importance of self-acceptance and warns again unrealistic and inordinate aspirations.

"The stone cannot tell the ground to push away so that it will sit down."

Explanation: The Ewe expression *te da*, meaning "push away" is an insolent expression and if the stone says this to the ground, the it is being rude to the ground. However, the relationship between the stone and the ground is such that the stone is unconditionally dependent on the ground. The stone is insolubly attached to the ground by the force of gravity and it cannot exist without the ground. It must therefore humble itself to accept its dependent status.

Moral Teaching: There are some dependent human relationships that are absolutely necessary, e.g. teacher-student relationship; such relationships must be accepted with humility.

"The salt does not praise itself." (It is others who say that salt is good.)

Moral Teaching: Do not brag about your goodness but be modest about it. This proverb therefore teaches people to have a humble estimate about their merits. . . .

"When you are carrying beef on your head you do not use your feet to catch grasshoppers."

Explanation: Beef is a better meat than grasshopper and so if you have beef you do not go after a grasshopper.

Moral Teaching: Be able to tell the relative value of things you have and do not spend your energy on less valuable things. This proverb teaches the importance of the right judgment of the relative value of things. . . .

"The mother of twins does not lie on one side while she is in bed with the twin children."

Explanation: The common practice is for a mother of twins to lie in between them in bed so that she can equally mind them.

Moral Teaching: The main lesson of this proverb is this, as a head of a family or a leader you must treat all to whom you are responsible fairly. This proverb can therefore be used to warn people against discriminatory practices.

"Knowledge is like a baobab tree (monkey-bread tree) and no one person can embrace it with both arms."

Explanation: The baobab tree usually has a very huge base stem and cannot be embraced by the two arms of any human being.

Moral Teaching: Knowledge and truth are like the unbounded ocean and so no one individual can claim to have a corner on them. Individuals must therefore be humble in their claims to knowledge and in such a humble frame of mind they can always acquire more knowledge since there is no limit to what any man can know.

"One head does not go into a consultation."

Explanation: In the traditional society judgments in disputes are usually given by the elders after they have consulted separately among themselves. This practice is based on the belief that a correct judgment is more likely to come from the deliberations of more than one person.

Moral Teaching: This proverb shows the belief of our fathers in the value of consultation in arriving at sound decisions. It is also a warning to individuals who are over-confident in their own judgments. . . .

"Love is like an egg, it breaks easily" (and so it should be handled carefully).

Moral Teaching: The loving relationship is very vulnerable and so must be carefully handled otherwise it will turn into hate or indifference.

"The world is like the skin of a chameleon" (i.e. it changes fast).

Moral Teaching: Since times change and our fortunes are changed in them we must always behave modestly and not arrogantly.

"If you are patient enough you can cook a stone and it will become soft."

Moral Teaching: With patience you can achieve seemingly impossible tasks.

"If you are cooking a stone you do not become impatient or complain of using too much firewood."

Explanation: There are two proverbs here and they all emphasize the value of patience, but the second one advises against the practice of complaining under difficult tasks.

Moral Teaching: To achieve success in the performance of difficult tasks you need patience and you must be ready to pay the necessary price for the success you want.

"The chicken is never ashamed of its coop."

Moral Teaching: Be proud of your own home/village/country, however humble and lowly it may be, never be ashamed of it, but love it. . . .

"A stump that stays in a river for a hundred years does not become a crocodile."

Moral Teaching: The Ewe on the whole are very patriotic and they teach their children to love their places of birth. This proverb . . . warns people who go to live in foreign lands that they will never become real citizens of those lands. Even if they stay abroad for a long time they will be regarded as "strangers" and because of this they must learn to love and honor their homelands. . . .

"The goat places its white spot anywhere it likes on its body." (Sometimes the white spot will be on one leg, or on the head or on the chest.)

Moral Teaching: This proverb is used to confirm the right of every individual to self-determination and to counsel against unnecessary interference in other people's affairs.

"When it is threatening to rain you look in the direction of your farm" (i.e. you make sure that it is raining on your farm.)

Moral Teaching: This is one of the rare proverbs which is used to justify a concern for one's own interests. In plain words the proverb means, look after your own interests. If you know how to love yourself then you can love others.

"The new is woven on to the old."

Moral Teaching: In this proverb "the old" stands for the "traditions of the past," and it is maintained that the traditions of the past form the foundation of the present and so traditions should be respected. The proverb is meant to develop a positive attitude to and respect for traditional practices. . . .

"One hand cannot hold a bull's horns."

Explanation: The "bull's horn" represents any difficult task which cannot be done by one man alone but as he teams up with others they could do it.

Moral Teaching: This proverb stresses the need for a united effort in solving difficult problems, and it also advises individuals who trust too much in their own strengths to learn to cooperate with others in solving difficult tasks. The two virtues commended by the two preceding proverbs are *unity* and *cooperation.*

"One pole cannot build a house, i.e. carry a roof."

Moral Teaching: Unity is strength.

The three samples of African wisdom literature we have examined commend virtues that, taken together, form a composite picture of ideal human conduct. Are not some of those virtues, such as humility, modesty, and fairness, recommended by all three traditions? Also, do not all three seem to affirm the karmic moral law: as you sow, so shall you reap? And, do not all three traditions seem to indicate that the way people conduct their lives influences the way deity regards and reacts to them?

NOTE ON SOURCES. Selections from the *Wisdom of Ptahhotpe* have been taken from William Kelly Simpson, ed., *The Literature of Ancient Egypt* (New Haven: Yale University Press, 1972), pp. 161–164, 166–168, 170–171, 173–174. The Swahili proverbs come from Albert Scheven, ed., *Swahili Proverbs* (Lanham, Maryland: University Press of America, 1981), and the Ewe proverbs are taken from N. K. Dzobo, *African Proverbs: Guide to Conduct* (Ghana: Department of Education, University of Cape Coast, 1973), Vol. I, Chapter 2.

5 ALBERT CAMUS

THE STORY OF COMBATTING SUFFERING

FROM THE AFRICAN TRADITION TO CAMUS.   The Buddhist ideals of human conduct, exemplified either in the Theravadan *arhat* (the saint absorbed in impersonal bliss) or the Mahayanist *bodhisattva* (the compassionate Buddha-to-be who postpones attainment of personal nirvana to help others along the path to nirvana), are set within a religious context. The ideals of human conduct portrayed in the African wisdom literature we have examined are also presented within a religious context, as is evident from references to divine sanctioning of the ideal. Recall that Ptahhotpe declares that the son who hears and follows his father's advice is God-loved, while the one who rejects his father's advice is God-detested. The Swahili proverbs conclude that "Payment on earth is the reckoning of the hereafter" which means, as one scholar observes, that "God returns one's good or evil deed often while one is still on earth." (S. A. Mohamed, *Vito vya hekima, simo na maneno ya mshangao*. Nairobi: Longman, Kenya, 1967.) Professor Dzobo's explanation of the Ewe proverb, "The person who steals mushrooms hears the evening announcement," refers to the retribution of a powerful God who destroys evil-doers.

Suppose, however, that we were to strip away the religious context of wisdom literature. Suppose that we were left only with ideals composed of clusters of virtues. Would we still be able to ask legitimately about human meaning? Within a religious context, we could legitimately ask "What is the meaning of life?" because we would be assuming the existence of some sort of divine reality that could be the source of the meaning we were seeking to discover. But if we divest our lives of divine reality, do we not thereby remove from them the source of a preestablished goal or direction or meaning that our lives have, and which we are seeking to discover?

Jean-Paul Sartre, the famous existentialist we encountered in Chapter 3, would say that removing God from life *does* divest life of any preestablished meaning that we could discover. But Sartre adds that the removal of God is to be celebrated, because we are thereby made free indeed. With the nonexistence of God, we are not required to live up to some divinely established ideal; we are not forced into a Procrustean mold of meaning; we are free to create our own goals, our own ideals, our own meanings. For Sartre, God, if he existed, would be an enemy of our freedom. Within the Sartrean perspective we could no longer legitimately ask, "What is the meaning of life?" Instead, we would ask, "What gives meaning to my life? How shall I make my life meaningful?" The burden of meaning is upon each free individual person: I am now responsible for selecting and pursuing the goals and ideals with which I will invest my life with meaning. Instead of discovering a meaning embedded in the world and placed there by some other being, I create meaning by myself for myself.

Our final author, Albert Camus, a twentieth-century north African writer, moves beyond the samples of the African tradition we have examined and, in

Sartrean fashion, divests life of its religious context leaving only self-selected virtues to pursue.

BIOGRAPHICAL NOTE. Albert Camus was born in Mondovi, Algeria in 1913, and educated at the University of Algiers. During the 1930s he wrote and produced plays in Algiers. In 1940 he moved to Paris and became involved in the resistance movement during the German occupation of France. There, in 1942, he published *The Myth of Sisyphus* (a philosophical essay) and *The Stranger* (a novel), works that brought him to the attention of intellectual circles world-wide. Following the end of World War II, his name became associated with the political activity of Jean-Paul Sartre. In 1947, he published his second major novel, *The Plague*, from which the passages below have been selected. Four years later he published an essay on the idea of revolt, *The Rebel*, that precipitated a feud between himself and Sartre and eventually ended their friendship. His last major work was a novel, *The Fall*, appearing in 1956. In 1957 he was awarded the Nobel Prize for literature. On January 4, 1960, he was killed in an automobile accident.

THE ARGUMENT OF THE PASSAGES. In his novel *The Plague*, Camus portrays how he thinks a person who has rejected the religious context for human meaning can still pursue a meaningful life. The setting is the walled town of Oran, a large, French port on the Algerian coast. The time is the 1940s. The key event is the outbreak of a deadly plague transferred from rats to humans. As the disease spreads and fatalities rise, the only option for combatting the raging epidemic is quarantine. The gates of the walled city are closed and Oran is transformed into a virtual prison. Isolated from the rest of the world, the focus of attention, which had been on the accumulation of wealth, is directed toward coping with monumental human suffering and massive death.

Father Paneloux, the priest-spokesperson for Christian orthodoxy, tries to interpret the sudden devastation theologically. In a sermon delivered in the town's cathedral, he identifies the plague as the just punishment for the sins of the townsfolk.

> The air inside the Cathedral was heavy with fumes of incense and the smell of wet clothes when Father Paneloux stepped into the pulpit.
>
> He was a stockily built man, of medium height. When he leaned on the edge of the pulpit, grasping the woodwork with his big hands, all one saw was a black, massive torso and, above it, two rosy cheeks overhung by steel-rimmed spectacles. He had a powerful, rather emotional delivery, which carried to a great distance, and when he launched at the congregation his opening phrase in clear, emphatic tones: "Calamity has come on you, my brethren, and, my brethren, you deserved it. . . . The first time this scourge appears in history, it was wielded to strike down the enemies of God. Pharaoh set himself up against the divine will, and the plague beat him to his knees. Thus from the dawn of recorded history the scourge of God has humbled the proud of heart and laid low those who hardened themselves against Him. Ponder this well, my friends, and fall on your knees. . . .
>
> "If today the plague is in your midst, that is because the hour has struck for taking thought. The just man need have no fear, but the evildoer has good cause to

tremble. For plague is the flail of God and the world His threshing-floor, and implacably He will thresh out His harvest until the wheat is separated from the chaff. There will be more chaff than wheat, few chosen of the many called. Yet this calamity was not willed by God. Too long this world of ours has connived at evil, too long has it counted on the divine mercy, on God's forgiveness. Repentance was enough, men thought; nothing was forbidden. Everyone felt comfortably assured; when the day came, he would surely turn from his sins and repent. Pending that day, the easiest course was to surrender all along the line; divine compassion would do the rest. For a long while God gazed down on this town with eyes of compassion; but He grew weary of waiting, His eternal hope was too long deferred, and now He has turned His face away from us. And so, God's light withdrawn, we walk in darkness, in the thick darkness of this plague. . . .

"My brothers," he cried, "that fatal hunt is up, and harrying our streets today. See him there, that angel of the pestilence, comely as Lucifer, shining like Evil's very self! He is hovering above your roofs with his great spear in his right hand, poised to strike, while his left hand is stretched toward one or other of your houses. Maybe at this very moment his finger is pointing to your door, the red spear crashing on its panels, and even now the plague is entering your home and settling down in your bedroom to await your return. Patient and watchful, ineluctable as the order of the scheme of things, it bides its time. No earthly power, nay, not even—mark me well— the vaunted might of human science can avail you to avert that hand once it is stretched toward you. And winnowed like corn on the blood-stained threshing-floor of suffering, you will be cast away with the chaff. . . .

"Yes, the hour has come for serious thought. You fondly imagined it was enough to visit God on Sundays, and thus you could make free of your weekdays. You believed some brief formalities, some bendings of the knee, would recompense Him well enough for your criminal indifference. But God is not mocked. These brief encounters could not sate the fierce hunger of His love. He wished to see you longer and more often; that is His manner of loving and, indeed, it is the only manner of loving. And this is why, wearied of waiting for you to come to Him, He loosed on you this visitation; as He has visited all the cities that offended against Him since the dawn of history. Now you are learning your lesson, the lesson that was learned by Cain and his offspring, by the people of Sodom and Gomorrah, by Job and Pharaoh, by all that hardened their hearts against Him. And like them you have been beholding mankind and all creation with new eyes, since the gates of this city closed on you and on the pestilence. Now, at last, you know the hour has struck to bend your thoughts to first and last things."

Paneloux ends his sermon by asserting that the evil of the plague may be transformed into goodness if it becomes the means whereby the townsfolk are brought closer to God.

Later, Paneloux softens his claim that the plague is the punishment the townsfolk merit, especially after witnessing the long, agonizing death of a little child. Rather than punishment, Paneloux now views the plague as an inexplicable part of God's ultimately good plan for humankind.

Juxtaposed to this religious view of human suffering is the atheistic view of Dr. Bernard Rieux, the respected surgeon who spearheads the battle against the plague. Shortly after Father Paneloux's first sermon, Jean Tarrou, a traveller who becomes "imprisoned" in the besieged city, approaches Dr. Rieux and offers to help organize a group of volunteer citizens to help fight the plague. The ensuing conversation between the two men reveals Rieux's (and Camus's) interpretation of the meaning of human life, burdened as it is with suffering and death.

" . . . I've drawn up a plan for voluntary groups of helpers. Get me empowered to try out my plan, and then let's sidetrack officialdom. In any case the authorities have their hands more than full already. I have friends in many walks of life; they'll form a nucleus to start from. And, of course, I'll take part in it myself."

"I need hardly tell you," Rieux replied, "that I accept your suggestion most gladly. One can't have too many helpers, especially in a job like mine under present conditions. I undertake to get your plan approved by the authorities. Anyhow, they've no choice. But—" Rieux pondered. "But I take it you know that work of this kind may prove fatal to the worker. And I feel I should ask you this; have you weighed the dangers?"

Tarrou's gray eyes met the doctor's gaze serenely.

"What did you think of Paneloux's sermon, Doctor?"

The question was asked in a quite ordinary tone, and Rieux answered in the same tone.

"I've seen too much of hospitals to relish any idea of collective punishment. But, as you know, Christians sometimes say that sort of thing without really thinking it. They're better than they seem."

"However, you think, like Paneloux, that the plague has its good side; it opens men's eyes and forces them to take thought?"

The doctor tossed his head impatiently.

"So does every ill that flesh is heir to. What's true of all the evils in the world is true of plague as well. It helps men to rise above themselves. All the same, when you see the misery it brings, you'd need to be a madman, or a coward, or stone blind, to give in tamely to the plague."

Rieux had hardly raised his voice at all; but Tarrou made a slight gesture as if to calm him. He was smiling.

"Yes." Rieux shrugged his shoulders. "But you haven't answered my question yet. Have you weighed the consequences?"

Tarrou squared his shoulders against the back of the chair, then moved his head forward into the light.

"Do you believe in God, Doctor?"

Again the question was put in an ordinary tone. But this time Rieux took longer to find his answer.

"No—but what does that really mean? I'm fumbling in the dark, struggling to make something out. But I've long ceased finding that original."

"Isn't that it—the gulf between Paneloux and you?"

"I doubt it. Paneloux is a man of learning, a scholar. He hasn't come in contact with death; that's why he can speak with such assurance of the truth—with a capital T. But every country priest who visits his parishioners and has heard a man gasping for breath on his deathbed thinks as I do. He'd try to relieve human suffering before trying to point out its excellence." Rieux stood up; his face was now in shadow. "Let's drop the subject," he said, "as you won't answer."

Tarrou remained seated in his chair; he was smiling again.

"Suppose I answer with a question."

The doctor now smiled, too.

"You like being mysterious, don't you? Yes, fire away."

"My question's this," said Tarrou. "Why do you yourself show such devotion, considering you don't believe in God? I suspect your answer may help me to mine."

His face still in shadow, Rieux said that he'd already answered: that if he believed in an all-powerful God he would cease curing the sick and leave that to Him. But no one in the world believed in a God of that sort; no, not even Paneloux, who believed that he believed in such a God. And this was proved by the fact that no one ever threw himself on Providence completely. Anyhow, in this respect Rieux believed himself to be on the right road—in fighting against creation as he found it.

"Ah," Tarrou remarked. "So that's the idea you have of your profession?"

"More or less." The doctor came back into the light.

Tarrou made a faint whistling noise with his lips, and the doctor gazed at him.

"Yes, you're thinking it calls for pride to feel that way. But I assure you I've no more than the pride that's needed to keep me going. I have no idea what's awaiting me, or what will happen when all this ends. For the moment I know this; there are sick people and they need curing. Later on, perhaps, they'll think things over; and so shall I. But what's wanted now is to make them well. I defend them as best I can, that's all."

"Against whom?"

Rieux turned to the window. A shadow-line on the horizon told of the presence of the sea. He was conscious only of his exhaustion, and at the same time was struggling against a sudden, irrational impulse to unburden himself a little more to his companion; an eccentric, perhaps, but who, he guessed, was one of his own kind.

"I haven't a notion, Tarrou; I assure you I haven't a notion. When I entered this profession, I did it 'abstractedly,' so to speak; because I had a desire for it, because it meant a career like another, one that young men often aspire to. Perhaps, too, because it was particularly difficult for a workman's son, like myself. And then I had to see people die. Do you know that there are some who *refuse* to die? Have you ever heard a woman scream 'Never!' with her last gasp? Well, I have. And then I saw that I could never get hardened to it. I was young then, and I was outraged by the whole scheme of things, or so I thought. Subsequently I grew more modest. Only, I've never managed to get used to seeing people die. That's all I know. Yet after all—"

Rieux fell silent and sat down. He felt his mouth dry,

"After all—?" Tarrou prompted softly.

"After all," the doctor repeated, then hesitated again, fixing his eyes on Tarrou, "it's something that a man of your sort can understand most likely, but, since the order of the world is shaped by death, mightn't it be better for God if we refuse to believe in Him and struggle with all our might against death, without raising our eyes toward the heaven where He sits in silence?"

Tarrou nodded.

"Yes. But your victories will never be lasting; that's all."

Rieux's face darkened.

"Yes, I know that. But it's no reason for giving up the struggle."

"No reason, I agree. Only, I now can picture what this plague must mean for you."

"Yes. A never ending defeat."

Tarrou stared at the doctor for a moment, then turned and tramped heavily toward the door. Rieux followed him and was almost at his side when Tarrou, who was staring at the floor, suddenly said:

"Who taught you all this, Doctor?"
The reply came promptly:
"Suffering."

The plague rages on. Before subsiding it claims scores of lives, including that of Father Paneloux. Tarrou becomes its final victim. Rieux survives and becomes the chronicler who tells the story of the plague in Oran.

Dr. Rieux resolved to compile this chronicle, so that he should not be one of those who hold their peace but should bear witness in favor of those plague-stricken people; so that some memorial of the injustice and outrage done them might endure; and to state quite simply what we learn in time of pestilence: that there are more things to admire in man than to despise.

Nonetheless, he knew that the tale he had to tell could not be one of a final victory. It could be only the record of what had had to be done, and what assuredly would have to be done again in the never ending fight against terror and its relentless onslaughts, despite their personal afflictions, by all who, while unable to be saints but refusing to bow down to pestilences, strive their utmost to be healers.

And, indeed, as he listened to the cries of joy rising from the town, Rieux remembered that such joy is always imperiled. He knew what those jubilant crowds did not know but could have learned from books: that the plague bacillus never dies or disappears for good; that it can lie dormant for years and years in furniture and linen-chests; that it bides its time in bedrooms, cellars, trunks, and bookshelves; and that perhaps the day would come when, for the bane and the enlightening of men, it would rouse up its rats again and send them forth to die in a happy city.

For Rieux, and for Camus, suffering is the great teacher. Presumably it teaches us the shallowness of theodicies, like Paneloux's, that interpret human suffering as punishment for individual as well as communal sins. Presumably it teaches us the inadequacy of believing in an all-powerful and all-good God. And presumably it teaches us the absurdity of the meaning we create. What gives meaning to Rieux's life (and to Tarrou's as well) is the freely chosen goal of combatting suffering, of fighting the plague. What makes his meaning absurd, self-contradictory, is his knowledge that he cannot win the battle against suffering and the plague, but he must live and act *as if* he can win. To believe that victory is assured is possible only for those who still hold onto belief in an all-powerful, all-good God who will see to it that human happiness will triumph, in due course, over misery and suffering. For Rieux to surrender that "*as if*" would be to surrender to the hopelessness of a nihilism that could erode his motivation to combat suffering.

In effect, Camus leaves the reader of *The Plague* with a choice among "as ifs" in the pursuit of human meaning. One can choose the religious "as if": leading one's life "as if" human suffering will ultimately be resolved by divine action. Or one can choose the nonreligious "as if": leading one's life "as if" the battle against human suffering can be won, but knowing that it can't. Or one can choose the agnostic "as if": leading one's life "as if" the ultimate outcome of the struggle against human suffering is uncertain. This third "as if" could be pursued in either a religious or a nonreligious context. Camus leaves no doubt in the reader's mind, however, that he favors the second "as if."

What then shall we conclude about the business of making sense out of life? If Frankl is correct in claiming that humans have a will to meaning which must be satisfied if they are to survive and flourish, and if we desire such survival and flourishing, then it seems that we must become story tellers. In this epilogue we have examined diverse stories of disparate cultures that represent human attempts to grasp meaning. Is such meaning discovered or invented? Is such meaning to be grasped within a religious or nonreligious context? Regardless of how we answer these questions, is it not the case that we all encounter unmerited suffering that requires us to reconstruct and revise our stories again and again, and yet to live "as if" our stories had grasped some measure of abiding meaning?

NOTE ON SOURCES.   The material in this section is taken from Albert Camus, *The Plague*, translated by Stuart Gilbert (New York: Vintage Books, 1972), pp. 89–92, 118–121, 286–287.

Glossary

Absolutism: In the theory of value (ethics and aesthetics), the view that standards of value are objective rather than relative. In theory of knowledge, the view that objective, absolute (not merely relative) truth is possible. (Compare with **Objectivism** and contrast with **Subjectivism**.)

Ad hoc: From the Latin, "to this." The defense of a thesis against an objection by a claim that serves only to answer that particular objection. *Ad hoc* defenses are considered weak.

Aesthetics: The branch of philosophy that analyzes the human experience of beauty. Questions such as—What features make objects beautiful? Are there standards of beauty? What is the relation of works of art to nature?—are explored. The philosophy of art has a narrower focus than aesthetics because the former examines the experience of works of art and usually excludes the experience of beauty in nature.

After image: After having started at a light for a few seconds, a person with normal vision will still see a faint glow after the light source is removed. That faint glow is called an after image.

Agnosticism: A term coined by T. H. Huxley (1825–1895) to describe his philosophical position: "It is morally wrong for a person to affirm that a proposition is true without evidence which logically justifies that affirmation." Following Huxley, people have called themselves "agnostics" to indicate that they believe that certain kinds of knowledge—especially knowledge of God—lack sufficient supporting evidence, and these are highly suspect.

Alienation: A term Marx borrowed from Hegel to describe the condition of the human producer who creates all the artifacts and institutions of culture and then becomes separated or divorced from those products which, in turn, are perceived as something foreign and alien to the human creator rather than as expressions of the human being's own creative energies. Such alien products appear to dominate and rule the human producer. Such is the human condition, according to Marx, in capitalistic society.

Anarchism: The doctrine which claims that all forms of government are evil and should be abolished.

Animism: A primitive belief that objects are infused by spirits or souls.

Antinomianism: The view which advocates freedom from law and the external regulation of human life.

A posteriori: A term used by Kant and others to characterize knowledge derived from sense experience.

Apparition: A ghost.

A priori: A term used by Kant and others to characterize knowledge derived by reason independent of sense experience. Such knowledge, says Kant, is true universally and necessarily; that is, true for everyone, and true in and of itself without reference to who believes or does not believe it, without reference to the consequences that follow from its being true or from its being believed.

Arguing in a circle: A fallacious form of argument in which one begins with some assertion, argues using that assertion, and then concludes with that very same assertion—as if the original claim had been proved.

Atheism: The assertion that, given what most people *mean* by the term *God*, there is no God.

Autonomous inner man: B. F. Skinner's term for the mind or soul which has autonomy or independence from the body and its physical processes to the extent that human freedom is a reality. Skinner entirely rejects this notion of the inner man and freedom, and instead embraces a form of determinism.

Axiology: Theory of value.

Ayurvedic: An ancient Tibetan form of medicine. It stresses close attention to the pulse for diagnosis and the use of heavy metals such as gold in treatment. It is now also practiced widely in India.

Begging the question: A fallacious form of argument in which what is supposed to be proved is assumed. It differs from arguing in a circle in that, when begging the question, it is often not clear that the assertion meant to be proved has actually been assumed.

Behaviorism: The contemporary school of psychology associated with J. B. Watson and B. F. Skinner, which abandons the concepts of mind and consciousness, and restricts its analysis to the study of human and animal behavior. This approach usually denies the existence of human freedom and generally advocates a form of materialism.

Bona fides: A Latin phrase meaning "good faith." Also, one's credentials.

Bourgeoisie: In Marx's theory, the capitalist class, which controls the means of production and whose interests are expressed in and guaranteed by the social superstructure.

Cartesianism: The philosophy of René Descartes.

Casuistry: A method of determining right or wrong in matters of conscience and conduct by fastidiously applying general principles to particular concrete cases.

Catastrophists: Those who assume that differences in species are best explained by catastrophes, such as great floods. Catastrophists are opposed to Darwin's theory of evolution. This view conflicts with Uniformitarianism.

Categorical imperative: According to Kant, the supreme, absolute moral law which is understood by any rational creature to be one's duty without any qualifications or exceptions. Such duty involves acting on those principles which one could universalize (that is, make a universal law).

Categories of understanding: According to Kant, the forms of knowledge as distinguished from the content of knowledge. The mind brings to any knowing situation certain categories or forms through which it grasps the objects of knowledge. These categories such as unity and plurality, cause and effect, are not things known but are ways of knowing.

Category-mistake: According to Ryle, the error made when one assumes incorrectly that two different things exist in the same sort of way. To affirm that minds and bodies exist in the same sort of way is, says Ryle, to commit this mistake.

Cause: Something that is responsible for change, motion or action in another thing. Hume questions the necessary connection that is often assumed to be present between two causally related events. According to Hume, the evidence of our senses may indicate that when event A happens, event B follows; but the evidence of our senses does not indicate that event A is responsible for event B.

Central state identity theory: Also called identity theory. The name calls attention to the fact that the mental is identical to states of the central nervous system and not to states of the entire nervous system.

Cerebral cortex of the brain: The grey matter on the outside of the mammalian brain.

Ceteris paribus: A Latin phrase meaning literally "with other things equal," or more smoothly "with other factors being the same."

Christian Science: A religion based on an interpretation of the Bible first given by Mary Baker Eddy in the mid-nineteenth century. In her view, disease is purely subjective, i.e., a defect of spirit, and can be overcome by prayer and improvement in character. There are Christian Science practitioners who help with the appropriate prayers.

Cogito, ergo sum: "I think, therefore I am." This statement is Descartes' *indubitandum*, the not doubtable and self-evident principle on which he attempts to construct a body of knowledge that is beyond the power of skeptics to destroy.

Cognition: From the Latin *cognoscere*, "to know," cognition refers, in the broadest sense, to knowledge or the act of knowing.

Cognitive symbol: A symbol, such as a word or group of words, used to indicate what you know or could know. Such symbols are usually assessed as true or false. Contrast with **Emotive symbol**.

Communism: The society of the future to which Marx and Engels believed historical process was irresistibly moving. In that society, exploitation of the masses by the ruling elite would no longer exist because the economic productive process would be owned and controlled by humankind at large for the benefit of all persons.

Contingency: A state of affairs or a being is said to be contingent when it may or also may not be. A contingent being depends on other beings and states of affairs for its existence: when those conditions are removed, the contingent being ceases to exist. (See **Empirical possibility**.)

Copernican Revolution: Sixteenth-century astronomer Nicolaus Copernicus reversed the traditional account of the solar system by substituting a helio-centric view for the prevailing geocentric view derived from second-century Greek astronomer Ptolemy. In epistemology, Kant considered his views to be something of a Copernican revolution in that he reversed the prevailing view by emphasizing the active role played by the mind in generating knowledge as opposed to the passive role of the mind emphasized by empiricists such as Locke and Hume. In the speculative philosophy of history, Spengler considered his position also to be a Copernican revolution in that he reversed the prevailing view which subdivided history into an ancient-medieval-modern scheme. In its place, Spengler presented the model of a process in which cultures mature and decline into civilizations.

Cybernetics: The comparative study of the human nervous system and complex electronic systems.

Cynicism: (1) The personal attitude which scorns and mocks the motives and virtues of others. (2) The doctrines of the Cynics, a school of Greek Philosophy founded by Antisthenes, a friend of Socrates. The Cynics claimed that a person's true happiness is to be achieved through a virtuous life which involves independence from events and facts external to the self. To achieve such independence, the Cynics attempted to master their desires and wants. In extreme cases, Cynics reduced their desires to a bare minimum and attempted to live an unencumbered, natural life in the midst of civilized society. No doubt, they appeared to be scorning civilization and perhaps thereby facilitated the development of the broader meaning of cynicism when it refers to an attitude rather than to a school of philosophy.

Darwinian: Any of a number of theories of evolution stressing natural selection as opposed to miracles or goal-oriented evolution. Darwinian evolution conflicts with a teleological approach to evolution. (See **Teleology**.)

Deconstructionism: A twentieth-century movement with roots in Marxism and certain strands of contemporary European philosophy (especially French philosopher Jacques Derrida) that seeks to expose (deconstruct) the cultural influences that inescapably condition every language and the interpretation of any text and thereby relativize or disprivilege any particular interpretation. This perspective can lead to radical relativism and subjectivism. (See **Postmodernism, Relativism**, and **Subjectivism**.)

Deduction: A method of reasoning in which a conclusion is claimed to follow necessarily from one or more premises. (Compare with **Induction**.)

Deism: The view that after God created the world, he allowed it to function on its own without divine intervention. Deists depreciate supernatural revelation and confine religion to the realm of that which is accessible to human reason.

Democritean atomist: Democritus (460–370 B.C.) was a Greek philosopher who stressed the idea that everything is made of indivisible, small units which he called atoms.

Determinism: The doctrine that every event has a cause. Such a doctrine seems to preclude human freedom by explaining all human behavior in terms of chains of causes that stretch back into the dim recesses of one's heredity and environment.

Dialectic: The critical thinking process in which an idea is set forth, criticized, reformulated, and in its revised form set forth to be criticized and reformulated again. The process continues almost without end. Such dialectical thinking is as ancient as Socrates' question-and-answer method of philosophizing. In the dialectical process Hegel perceived what he considered to be the pattern of historical development: thesis, antithesis and synthesis (which becomes a new thesis, etc.)

Dialectical materialism: The view developed by some of Marx's disciples that reality is material and that matter develops according to the Hegelian pattern of thesis, antithesis, synthesis. In the realm of human history the dialectical movement of matter appears as the class struggle which is driving to its final synthesis in a Communist society.

Digital computer: A computer in which data is represented by discrete units— usually either the flow or lack of flow of an electric current.

Dilemma: An argument in which a choice between two or more alternatives (each being unsatisfactory if not fatal) is presented to an opponent.

Dualism: A theory which holds that in any given domain there are two independent and irreducible substances. For example, Descartes' view that the human being consists of *res cogitans* (a thinking thing or mind) and *res extensa* (an extended thing or body) is a metaphysical dualism. Other forms of dualism affirm pair of substances such as the intelligible world of ideas and the material world of things, the forces of good and the forces of evil, the realm of light and the realm of darkness.

Economic substructure: Marx's term for the economic dimension of society which consists of all the raw materials, technology and interpersonal relations involved in producing and distributing the goods and services of a society. The key factor in the substructure is the relations of production which in all pre-Communist societies have been characterized by the struggle between the exploiting elite and the exploited masses.

Egoism: As a moral doctrine, ethical egoism declares that one ought to pursue his or her own interests exclusively. As a theory of motivation, psychological egoism declares that each person always acts in the pursuit of self-interest and can do no other.

Electron: A small negatively charged particle that orbits the nucleus of an atom. Electrons are not really particles and they do not really orbit the nuclei in the way that planets orbit the sun. (See **Quantum mechanics**.)

Elephant Man Syndrome: Also known as Von Recklinghausen's Syndrome. A genetic condition whose symptoms are many fibrous tumors on the body, often, but not always, on the face.

Emergent properties: The usual example is self-consciousness. From the physiology of the human brain, it could not have been predicted that humans would have self-consciousness. The properties of the chemicals that make up the brain do not themselves have self-consciousness. It is as if something is added when all the properties come together in a certain way. Emergent properties are more than just the sum of their parts. (See **Holism**.) Emergent properties are not reducible to their parts. (See **Reductionism**.)

Emotive symbol: A symbol used to express what you feel or could feel. Such symbols are usually assessed as fitting or unfitting, authentic or inauthentic, rather than as true or false. Contrast with **Cognitive Symbol**.

Emotivism: In ethics, emotivism claims that ethical sentences *express* the feelings of the speaker and seek to *evoke* similar feelings in the hearers. As such, ethical sentences do not make claims about the world that are either true or false. Some radical emotivists claim that ethical sentences merely *evince* emotions, which means that certain emotions are put on display by the speaker, without the claim being made that the speaker possesses those emotions. In aesthetics, emotivism maintains that a work of art is an emotive symbol with which the artist expresses his or her feelings. In contrast, a cognitive symbol expresses what one knows or believes rather than what one feels.

Empirical possibility: Factually possible; even if highly unlikely. (See **Contingent**.)

Empiricism: The theory that claims that all human knowledge is derived from the senses, which implies that humans neither possess inborn knowledge nor are able to generate knowledge by the use of reason alone.

En soi: Sartre's term for existence that is not conscious of itself. Such existence is "in itself." It does not project itself into the future and attempt to achieve that future self for itself.

Epiphenomenalism: The theory of the mind-body relation which holds that consciousness or mind is simply a by-product of the bodily neurological processes that underlie it, and that while mental events are caused by brain events, mental events never cause brain events.

Epistemology: An inquiry into the nature, origin and validity of knowledge.

Eschatological verification: A term used by John Hick to refer to a future possible post-death situation in which the claims of Christian theism (such as "God exists" and "God is good") could be verified.

ESP: Extra-Sensory Perception.

Esse est percipi: "To be is to be perceived." A slogan adopted by George Berkeley to convey one of his fundamental tenets that reality depends upon mind and is, accordingly, basically "spiritual." Berkeley developed this idealist position over-against the materialism of Thomas Hobbes.

Essence: The basic characteristic or function of a thing by virtue of which it is a distinct or unique entity.

Essence precedes existence: Sartre's term for describing the technological and theological viewpoints in which the idea of a thing appears first of all in the mind of a creator who then manipulates matter to make the thing appear in existence. Although Sartre accepts the technological view concerning things humans fashion, he rejects the claim that essence precedes existence in the case of the creation of humans. Each human creates himself or herself unencumbered by a prior essence which must be actualized. A prior essence would violate the fullness of human freedom which Sartre affirms.

Ethics: An investigation of the principles by which we distinguish goodness from badness and assess actions as right or wrong.

Existence precedes essence: Sartre's slogan with which he declares that the human being first exists and then defines himself or herself through his or her actions. The human creates his or her own existence rather than attempting to achieve a pre-established essence fixed by God. A pre-established essence would be incompatible with human freedom.

Existentialism: A philosophical movement rooted in nineteenth century philosophers such as Kierkegaard and Nietzsche who emphasized the importance of exploring meaning for the concrete existing individual as opposed to grandiose philosophical systems, such as Hegel's, which provide extensive explanations of reality without raising the question of what it means to be an existing, struggling, choosing individual. The movement flourished especially after the Second World War through the writings of such thinkers as Jean-Paul Sartre, Gabriel Marcel, Jacques Maritain, Nikolai Berdyayev, and Martin Heidegger.

Expressionism: The theory of art which holds that the distinctive function of the artist is to express emotions. A form of emotivism.

Fallibilism: The view that any knowledge claim may turn out to be false.

Fatalism: Occasionally used as a synonym for determinism. (See also **Determinism**.)

"Fido"—fido theory of meaning: The playful name give to the view that statements mean what they refer to just as the name "Fido" refers to Fido, the dog.

Folk psychology: Any common sense account of human behavior. Folk psychology is opposed to "scientific" psychologies such as Freudian, Jungian, physiological, behaviorist, etc.

Formalism: The theory of art which holds that only intrinsic features in a work of art are relevant to the interpretation and criticism of the art.

Foucault: Michel Foucault (1926–1984), a contemporary French philosopher who championed the postmodernist cause.

Galileo: Galileo Galilei (1564–1642) was a physicist and astronomer. He studied the motion of objects to discover the laws of motion and showed that Copernicus was correct in asserting that the sun, and not the Earth, is the center of the solar system. For this, Galileo was condemned for heresy by the Church. Most important, according to many scholars, was Galileo's insistence that science deal with those properties that could be expressed mathematically.

Gedankenexperiment: A thought experiment. A conceptual experiment. The tool of philosophers and theoretical scientists, such as Einstein and Hawking.

Einstein once asked himself, "What would a light wave look like if I could run alongside it?" This is a thought experiment.

Genuine option: According to William James, an option that is living (both hypotheses are live or realistic alternatives), forced (one cannot walk away from the option without choosing one of the alternatives), momentous (the opportunity is unique, the stake significant, and the decision irreversible).

Gestalt shift: A total shift in the way one views something; first by focusing on foreground and then by focusing on background. The shift need not be intentional. Sometimes, one just sees differently. For example, the duck-rabbit:

Gnosticism: The name given by historians of religion to a cluster of religious movements widespread in the Graeco-Roman world, in which it was held that salvation involved release of the spirit from bondage to the flesh by means of secret knowledge (gnosis).

God: A being that transcends nature, is *more* than nature, and is often regarded as the creator, producer, and sustainer of nature.

Hedonistic paradox: The notion that "happiness to be gotten, must be forgotten." That is to say, one achieves happiness not as the goal of one's actions, but as the unintentional by-product of other intended goals.

Herbal medicine: Medicine based on the use of herbs as treatment for disease.

Heuristic: Helpful in teaching or learning.

Holistic: Systems are said to be holistic if their parts are so interrelated that the system cannot be understood except by appeal to the interconnectedness. Holistic systems are said to be more than the sums of their parts. Holistic systems cannot be properly understood by means of reductionism. (See **Reductionism**.)

Homeopathy: A medical theory based on the idea that disease should be treated with minute amounts of whatever caused the disease.

Homunculus: A scale model of a person. Originally it was thought that in the tip of sperm was an exact—but tiny—replica of a person.

Humanism: Any view in which concern for human beings, their achievements and welfare, is central.

Hydra: A small, tentacled coelenterate (jellyfish-like creature).

Hypothesis: Any statement proposed for one's belief. (William James)

Idealism: The view that mind (or soul, or spirit) is the ultimate reality and that matter is dependent upon mind, in contrast to materialism which regards reality as fundamentally material.

Imitation: The theory of art which suggests that the goal of the artist is to create the illusion that the copy is not a copy at all, but the original.

Incommensurability: Unable to be measured together against the same standard.

Indeterminism: The view that human decisions are in some sense independent of prior causes; the affirmation of free will.

Indubitandum: That which is not doubtable. (See also **Cogito, ergo sum.**)

Induction: A method of reasoning whereby one proceeds from a number of observed particular facts to a generalization about all such facts. Such generalizations can be supported by the particular facts, but the truth of those generalizations cannot be completely demonstrated by those facts. (Contrast with **Deduction**.)

Inductive inference: Usually contrasted to deductive inference. A statement is said to be inferred inductively when it might be false even if the beliefs (or statements, or facts) on which it is based are true. For example, "the water must be boiling because the water has been heating for 20 minutes" is an inductive inference; an inference inductively made. A statement is said to be made deductively when there is no way the statement inferred can be false if the supporting beliefs (statements, purported facts) are true.

Inferotemporal lobe of the brain: The lobe of the brain below (inferior to) the temporal lobe of primates, which is the lobe at the "side" of the brain; at the temples. Or, the lower part of the temporal lobe. The precise function of the temporal lobe is unknown. The term *inferotemporal* is unknown to contemporary American neuroanatomists. It is probably a British anatomical term that has long since ceased to be used.

Innate ideas: Ideas with which, according to Descartes and others, one is born. Such ideas are considered to be *a priori* and possessed by all rational humans.

Intentionality: Mental states such as beliefs have a content. Beliefs are always beliefs about something. Mental states that have content in this fashion are said to be intentional. Pain is a mental state that is not intentional.

Intrinsic good: That which is desirable for its own sake as distinct from an instrumental good which is desirable for the sake of something else.

Introspection: The act of turning one's attention inward so that it is focused on one's inner mental life. In doing this, one might notice slight aches previously gone unnoticed. One might also be able to concentrate on one's thoughts and feelings.

Intuition: The direct and immediate apprehension by the self of certain knowledge about the self and the world without the need for deductive or inductive reasoning as the basis for affirming the truth of certain propositions.

Jung: Carl Jung (1875–1961) was an early member of the Vienna Psychoanalytic Circle, a group studying psychological theories of, and with, Freud. He later broke with Freud and Freudian approaches. Jung is best known for his theory of archetypes, an attempt to explain personality characters by appeal to general patterns. Because Jung felt that these patterns were not culturally specific, he came to believe in the idea of a collective (human) consciousness.

Lakatos: Hungarian historian and philosopher of science and mathematics (1922–1974). Known for his critique of Karl Popper's views of falsification and Kuhn's ideas on paradigms.

Lamarckian: A follower of Lamarck; a view similar to Lamarck's. Lamarck held that evolution was a fact of nature and that its mechanism was a combination of inner desire on the part of organisms and the inheritance of acquired characteristics.

Lavoisier/Priestly/Phlogiston: In the late seventeenth century, phlogiston was the name for the principle that allowed for combustion. It is a substance since shown not to exist, although at the time there was good reason to believe that it might exist. Antoine Lavoisier (1743–1794) often gets credit for having discovered oxygen. Joseph Priestley (1733–1804) also isolated oxygen, but he thought it was dephlogisticated air; i.e., air which totally lacked phlogiston. The chemical reactions we explain by oxygen being taken up were explained by Priestley in terms of phlogiston being given off.

Law of parsimony: The widely accepted view that scientific explanation ought to use the fewest possible assumptions to generate an adequate account of natural phenomena.

Law of the three stages: Comte's theory that each branch of human knowledge passes through three stages of development: the theological or fictitious; the metaphysical or abstract; and the scientific or positive.

Laws of science: Universal generalizations such as the ideal gas law, $PV=nRT$, or Newton's law of gravitational attraction, $\bar{F}=Gm_1m_2/r^2$. Finding such laws is sometimes said to be the goal of science.

Lesch-Nyhan Syndrome: First described in 1964 by Lesch and Nyhan, this is a condition characterized by severe mental retardation and a compulsion to gnaw the lips and fingers. The conditions is controlled by a gene on the X chromosome; sometimes referred to as the self-immolator gene.

Libertarianism: The view which affirms freedom of the will.

Lingua mentis: Latin for "language of the mind."

Linguistics: The scientific study of language.

Logically follow: When an inference is deductive, it is said to follow logically from its premises. See the discussion of "deductive inference" in the entry for **Inductive inference**.

Logical positivism: A movement originating in Vienna in the early twentieth century, which tried to propagate "the scientific outlook" in all fields of human knowledge. A fundamental tenet of the movement was that statements are meaningful only if they can be verified or falsified either directly or indirectly through the data of experience. Applied to philosophy, this view eliminated as nonsense much of traditional philosophy which pursued knowledge in the non-empirical realms of theology, metaphysics, and ethics. (Note A. J. Ayer.)

Materialism: The doctrine which claims that matter is the primary feature of reality and relegates mind (or spirit) either to a secondary, dependent status or to no status at all.

Master morality: Nietzche's term for the type of morality which originated in the ruling class and which values the exalted, proud noble who decides and decrees what is to be regarded as good and evil, right and wrong. (Contrast with **Slave morality**.)

Mauvaise foi: Sartre's term meaning "bad faith," a condition exhibited by the person who tries to avoid accepting responsibility for what he or she is, but instead tries to shift that responsibility to such factors as heredity and environment which are beyond the person's control. Such a person treats himself or herself as an *en soi* (or thing) instead of as a *pour soi* (a freedom, a person).

Metaphysics: The branch of philosophy which examines the nature of ultimate reality.

Micro/Macro: *Micro* refers to very small entities. *Macro* refers to large entities. Obviously, these are relative terms. Roughly, anything readily visible with the naked eye could be considered macro. Anything requiring a microscope should be considered micro.

Miracle: A violation of the laws of nature. (Hume) An interference with nature by a supernatural power. (Lewis)

Monism: The view which holds that in any given domain there is but one fundamental substance. For example, Smart attacks any mind-body dualism and affirms body (or matter) as the fundamental human substance.

More goemetrico: Latin for "in the manner of geometry." That is, in the style of geometrical proofs.

Naturalism: The doctrine that nature is the whole of reality, and that nature is a self-existent and self-operating interlocking system in which no part can claim the slightest independence from the total event. As such, naturalism precludes free will. (Contrast with **Supernaturalism**.)

Natural theology: Knowledge, or beliefs, about God based on knowledge, or beliefs, about nature. Contrast with *revealed* theology in which knowledge about God is derived from divine revelation.

NDE: Near death experience.

Necessary condition: A condition, C, is said to be necessary for an event, E, when (and only when) E cannot occur without the presence of the condition, C. For example, the presence of oxygen is a necessary condition for combustion. But notice that the presence of oxygen is not enough to insure combustion. Thus the presence of oxygen is a necessary, but not sufficient, condition for combustion.

Neuron(e)**:** A nerve cell.

Neurophysiology: The study of the physiology of the nervous system.

Neurosis: A functional disorder of the mind or emotions without obvious organic injury or change that results in anxiety, phobia, or other abnormal behavioral symptoms. Frankl refers to this kind of neurosis as psychogenic neurosis (arising from conflicts between drives and instincts) in order to distinguish it from what he calls noögenic neurosis which emerges from moral conflicts or spiritual problems.

Newtonian mechanics: The branch of physics that studies the motion of objects on the macro scale. The laws governing the motion of such objects originally discovered by Newton. For example, $F = ma$.

Nihilism: Based on the Latin word for "nothing" (*nihil*), this term has been used to describe people who say that there are no rationally justified moral norms or standards, and perhaps more frequently on the current scene to characterize people who claim that life has no meaning.

Nomic: Law-like, from the Greek word for "law" (*nomos*).

No-saying: Nietzsche's term for describing those moralities which advocate selflessness in one form or another. Selflessness is a no-saying to life, a negation of the self and of life which is, at its core, the will to survive.

Noumena: According to Kant, things-in-themselves or reality as it is. Knowledge is a joint product of the mind and the external world. The external world "appears" through the forms and categories of the mind. Accordingly, we only know "phenomena" or "appearances." We never really know noumena or things-in-themselves apart from the forms and categories our minds impose on them in the knowing situation.

OBE: Out-of-body experience.

Objectivism: In ethics, the view that moral values and principles exist objectively, that is to say, independent of a particular person's views and tastes. Such objective values and principles provide norms by which ethical statements can be judged as true or false. (Contrast with **Subjectivism**.)

Official doctrine: Gilbert Ryle's term for mind-body dualism which is derived chiefly from Descartes. (See also **Dualism**.)

Optimism: The personal attitude of hopefulness about human destiny and a positive evaluation of the world.

Option: The decision between two hypotheses. (William James)

Pantheism: The doctrine which identifies God (*theos*) with all things (*pan*). All things are appearances or manifestations of God.

Paranormal: Beyond the range of normal experience.

Pessimism: The personal attitude of despondency, hopelessness, and gloom toward the self and the world. The most famous philosophical justification of this attitude is that presented by Schopenhauer.

Phenomena: Derived from the Greek word meaning "that which appears," *phenomena* refers to reality as it appears to us, as contrasted with *noumena* which is reality without the structures of knowledge we impose on things in order to know them. Kant made much of this distinction.

Phenomenalism: The doctrine that percepts and concepts in the mind (that is, phenomena) are the sole object of knowledge or the only form of reality.

Phlogiston: See **Lavoisier/Priestley/Phlogiston**.

Phylogenetic scale: A continuum of organisms or species based on closeness of evolutionary relationships.

Platonic Forms: Abstract entities postulated to exist by Plato. They were perfectly real and, therefore, unchanging. Earthly objects were just copies—mere shadows—of the Forms.

Pluralism: The doctrine that there are many ultimate substances, as opposed to monism (which affirms only one) and dualism (which affirms two).

Positivism: A term first associated with Auguste Comte's doctrine that the highest form of knowledge is the scientific or positive. (Note his law of the three stages.)

Postmodernism: A point of view that has become prominent during the second half of the twentieth century which insists that it is impossible to achieve any sort of cognitive reliability. Humans can achieve only various interpretations, none of which can claim to be *the* truth. No point of view is privileged. All points of view are "decentered." (See also **Deconstructionism.**)

Postulates of morality: Three fundamental features of reality—freedom, immortality, and God—which one is justified in postulating or assuming if one is to be able to take seriously and interpret meaningfully the moral experience of humankind. (Kant)

Pour soi: Sartre's term for existence that is conscious of itself. Such existence is "for itself." It selects various possible future selves and tries to actualize those possibilities for itself. The "for itself" is the locus of freedom.

Pragmatism: A philosophical position, associated with such thinkers as C. S. Peirce and William James, which interprets the meaning of a statement or ideas generally in terms of its practical consequences. Also, pragmatists often assess propositions as true or false on the basis of their practical consequences.

Predestination: The theological doctrine which is often taken to hold that before the creation of the world, God foreordained all that would come to pass. More accurately, the doctrine refers to the notion that before creation (or perhaps shortly after the Fall) God decreed the eternal destiny of every individual intelligent creature.

Presupposition: A postulate or assumption which must be taken for granted if a desired result is to be achieved. R. G. Collingwood argues that scientific thinking rests upon "absolute" presuppositions which are themselves not pieces of scientific thinking, and which are incapable of proof or disproof.

Priestley: See **Lavoisier/Priestley/Phlogiston**.

Primary qualities: The qualities or characteristics believed to be inherent in bodies, such as extension, figure, motion, rest, solidity and number. Such qualities are seen as constant within objects and inseparable from them, in contrast to secondary qualities, such as color, which are variable and thought not to exist in objects in the same way. (John Locke)

Pro tanto: Latin for "to that extent" or "so far."

Procrustean: A method whereby something is made to fit a decided-upon scheme, whether it really fits or not. From the mythological giant, Procrustes, who had a bed which he would make his victims fit either by cutting off their legs or stretching their legs.

Proletarians: In Marx's theory, the working class, the wage-laborers, who are exploited by the capitalist class, and who are destined to revolt and to abolish forever the exploitation of the masses by a ruling elite.

Providence: The theological doctrine that embraces the idea that God preserves and guides his creation to ensure that his purposes will be accomplished.

Pushpin: A game, something like tic-tac-toe, played with pins and a pin-cushion.

Putnam-Kripke account of the semantics of thought: Hilary Putnam and Saul Kripke are two well-known contemporary American philosophers. Their account of thought referred to in the text (by Ned Block) allows for our commonsense idea of what thinking is to be reconstructed out of symbol manipulations without any intentionality. (See **Intentionality**.)

Quantum mechanics: The branch of physics that deals with the properties of entities that are so small (subatomic) that they do not have the properties of the objects dealt with in Newtonian mechanics. In Newtonian mechanics, entities are either waves or particles but never both. In quantum mechanics, this clear duality does not seem to hold.

Quietism: A view which advocates passive contemplation and restraint of the passions.

Rationalism: The philosophical view which appeals to reason rather than to sense impressions as the source of knowledge. Descartes's philosophy, built on his *cogito, ergo sum*, is a fine example of rationalism.

Realism: In medieval thought, realism stood for the doctrine that universals (ideas or essences of things) have a real, objective existence. In modern times, realism stands for the view that material objects exist externally and independently of our sense experience. Often realism is now used to refer to views that emphasize literalism and pragmatism. (See **Pragmatism**.)

Reductio ad absurdam: Literally, from the Latin, a reduction to absurdity. A style of argument. The idea is to take a statement and show that from it follows a conclusion that is absurd; suggesting that the original statement itself must be absurd.

Reductionism: A method which assumes that entities with parts are best studied by studying their component parts. A variation insists that the only proper way to learn about anything is to use the reductionistic method. Thus to study why people enjoy sweet food one would study the physiology of the taste buds along with the neurophysiology of certain parts of the brain. The comment, "It just tastes good" would not be an acceptable reductionistic answer. This view conflicts with a teleological approach and with a holistic approach.

Reincarnation: The belief that when the body dies the soul returns to earth, reborn or reincarnated in another body or physical form.

Relations of production: Marx's term for the way people relate to each other in order to produce the goods and services of society. In all pre-Communist societies (with the possible exception of an early primitive Communism) the relations of production have been conflictual: exploiting elite versus the exploited masses. In the future Communist society, Marx maintained that exploitation would be replaced by cooperation and mutual good will.

Relativism: The view that there is no absolute truth because what is regarded as true varies from person to person and from age to age. Truth, accordingly, is seen as relative to a person's time, place and circumstances.

Representation: The theory of art which holds that art neither imitates nor copies an object outside the work of art, but rather is a symbol which stands for or represents the object.

Res cogitans: A thinking thing; the mind. (Descartes)

Res extensa: An extended thing; the body. (Descartes)

Revolution: In Marx's thought, the transformation of a society that occurs when the prevailing relations of production are supplanted by a new set and the social superstructure is reconstituted to reflect the interests of the new ruling class. In a communist revolution, non-exploitative socialistic relations of production replace the exploitative capitalistic relations and the social superstructure is altered to reflect the interests of all humankind.

Scholastics: Disciples or adherents of scholasticism, the dominant system of theological and philosophical teachings in the Middle Ages, based on the authority of the Latin church fathers and Aristotle and his commentators. A term sometimes applied to persons who are dogmatic or pedantic.

Secondary qualities: Those sensible qualities, such as colors, sounds, tastes, smells, which do not exist *in objects* but are generated *in us* through the impact of the primary qualities (which do exist in objects) on our sense organs. (John Locke)

Semantic: Referring to the truth or meaning of statements. Contrasted to syntax, which refers to the form of a statement. Thus, "The girl hit the ball" and "The ball was hit by the girl" are identical in semantics (they mean the same and if one is true/false, then so must be the other) but they differ in syntax, or form (one is in the active voice and the other is in the passive voice).

Skepticism: Proponents of this view doubt that the knowledge we have achieved thus far is absolute and advocate a continued search for more carefully refined truth. Some skeptics doubt whether perfect certainty about some or all forms of knowledge is ever attainable.

Slave morality: Nietzsche's term for the type of morality which originated among the slaves in their need for comfort and mutual support, and which highly valued benevolence, submissiveness, selflessness, patience, etc. (Contrast with **Master morality.**)

Social contract: The original agreement by which individual persons united to form a state and consented to be governed. Although the idea of a social contract is ancient, it is likely that no such ancient agreement ever existed. The idea has, however, served as a criterion against which to judge whether governmental acts actually possessed the consent of the governed.

Social superstructure: Marx's term for all the prevailing social constructs other than the economic ones, ranging from the educational system to religion, state and law. All these constructs, says Marx, are generated by the economic exploiting class to express and guarantee its interests.

Soft determinism: The view which seeks to affirm both determinism and human free will by regarding free will as one of the causes in the causal network responsible for human behavior.

Solipsism: The view that only I exist. Not you—me!

Sophists: Itinerant Greek scholars of the fifth century B.C. who popularized knowledge and offered lessons in rhetoric, especially to the politically ambitious youth.

Spiritualism: The belief that spirits or souls can survive bodily death and can and do communicate wiht the living, especially through people called mediums who, in a trance, temporarily become the mouthpieces for those departed spirits.

State of nature: The hypothetical condition of humankind prior to the social contract and the birth of the state. Some thinkers emphasize the individual rights and liberty which existed in the state of nature, and which have been curtailed through the social contract. Others emphasize the chaotic struggle of each against all in the state of nature, and celebrate the social contract which has brought a measure of peace, security, and progress to humankind.

Stoicism: A school of Greek philosophy founded by Zeno (about 308 B.C.), which holds up the model of the virtuous person who achieves happiness through knowledge. The virtuous person has mastered self and passions so that the self's happiness is internal and independent of the changing conditions of the external world.

Subjectivism: A view which emphasizes the individual self or subject as the creator of meaning, truth, or values. In ethics, subjectivism involves the claim that moral values and principles represent the individual's subjective feelings and reactions which, in the absence of objective moral norms, cannot be assessed as true or false. (Contrast with **Objectivism**.)

Substance: (1) The essence of a thing; that which makes a thing what it is rather than something else. (2) Also, that which underlies the things of the experienced world; matter. Substance in this second sense is severely criticized by Hume.

Sufficient condition: See **Necessary condition**.

Summum bonum: The highest or supreme good. The ultimate intrinsically worthy goal of human conduct. (See also **Intrinsic good**.)

Supernaturalism: The doctrine that nature is not the whole of reality and that part of reality transcends, or is beyond, nature. That part which transcends nature possesses an independence from nature that allows for the existence of such things as free will and rational thought. (Contrast with **Naturalism**.)

Syllogism: A form of deductive reasoning consisting of a major premise, a minor premise, and a conclusion. For example, "All men are mortal." (major premise); "Socrates is a man." (minor premise); "Therefore, Socrates is mortal." (conclusion).

Synchronicity: A view put forward by psychologist Carl Jung. He claimed that there are instances of coincidences that are so meaningful and appropriate that they cannot be true coincidences; somehow they are caused not by the usual causal chain, but by what he termed an "acausal connecting principle." A standard example is thinking of a friend you haven't heard from in a long time, then the phone rings and it is your friend calling. She says, "I don't know, I just felt like calling you." (See **Jung**.)

Syntactic: See **Semantic**.

Teleological: A term derived from two Greek words: *telos* meaning "Purpose or goal" and *logos* meaning "principle or reason." Hence, teleological is "reasoning related to goals." The teleological argument for God's existence proceeds from alleged purposes in nature to a Divine Designer. A teleological ethic assesses an act as right or wrong on the basis of the goals or consequences it produces.

Teleology: The view that everything has a design or purpose and that this is the best way to understand anything. This view conflicts with a reductionistic approach.

Theism: A religion or philosophy that involves belief in the existence of a god or gods.

Theodicy: The attempt to reconcile God's attributes (divine goodness, omnipotence, justice) with the existence of evil and suffering in the world.

Theoretical entity: An entity postulated in order to fill out an explanation. The entity itself is not observed. In Freud's depth psychology, the *id* is a theoretical entity. When Newton first put forward his three laws, gravity was a theoretical entity.

Transvaluation of values: Nietzsche's term for the inversion of good and evil affected by the aristocracy when it declared aggressive egoism to be evil (when initially it had been regarded as good) and selfless altruism to be good (when initially it had been regarded as evil). Nietzsche calls for a new transvaluation of values which will celebrate aggressive egoism as good and regard selflessness as evil.

Übermensch: Nietzsche's term for the superman (the overman or self-transcending person) who discerns the current deterioration of civilization, stands apart from the mediocrity of the masses, legislates for himself what is right and wrong, and thereby sets himself beyond the prevailing good and evil.

Uniformitarianism: In geology, the view that the laws acting now have always acted. Thus, there is uniformity in the earth's history.

Utilitarianism: The ethical theory which recommends that we ought to do that act which, more than any other act open to us on a particular occasion, is likely to maximize the happiness (or pleasure) of humankind; that is, is likely to generate the greatest happiness for the greatest number of people. (Jeremy Bentham and John Stuart Mill)

Verification: The procedure of checking up on a statement to determine if it is true or false.

Verification principle: A tenet of the logical positivists according to which a sentence that purports to be cognitive is, in fact, cognitive only if it is able to be confirmed in principle.

Voluntarism: In metaphysics, the doctrine that blindly striving universal will is the ultimate reality of which all things are manifestations. (Schopenhauer)

Whewell: William Whewell (1794–1866) was a British scientist. He studied geology, physics, and astronomy. Whewell is considered one of the first philosophers of science. His name is pronounced Hūăl.

Wicket: A term from the game cricket.

Will to believe: According to William James, when one confronts two opposing hypotheses in a genuine option (e.g. to believe in God vs. not to believe in God), and when the available evidence is insufficient to demonstrate the truth or falsity of either hypothesis, then one is justified in exercising one's will to believe—that is, assenting to the hypothesis which one hopes is true because its rejection as false would generate very undesirable practical consequences.

Wittgenstein: Ludwig Wittgenstein (1889–1951) was a philosopher best known for his thoughts on the workings of language and philosophy itself.

Yes-saying: Nietzsche's term for assessing those moralities which advocate aggressive egoism. Because life involves the will to survive, the will to power, aggressive egoism is an affirmation of, a yes-saying to, life.

Index

ISBN 0-02-320092-8

90000>

9 780023 200922